WINDOWS 98

Professional Reference

Bruce A. Hallberg and
Joe Casad

201 W. 103rd Street
Indianapolis, IN 46290

Windows 98 Professional Reference

Copyright © 1998 by New Riders

All rights reserved. No part of this book shall be reproduced, stored in a retrieval system, or transmitted by any means, electronic, mechanical, photocopying, recording, or otherwise, without written permission from the publisher. No patent liability is assumed with respect to the use of the information contained herein. Although every precaution has been taken in the preparation of this book, the publisher and author assume no responsibility for errors or omissions. Neither is any liability assumed for damages resulting from the use of the information contained herein.

International Standard Book Number: 0-56205-786-3

Library of Congress Catalog Card Number: 97-69120

Printed in the United States of America

First Printing: June 1998

00 99 98   4 3 2 1

Trademarks

All terms mentioned in this book that are known to be trademarks or service marks have been appropriately capitalized. New Riders cannot attest to the accuracy of this information. Use of a term in this book should not be regarded as affecting the validity of any trademark or service mark.

Executive Editor
Jeff Koch

Development Editor
Joe Casad

Acquisitions Editors
Sean Angus
Jack Belbot
Jane K. Brownlow

Managing Editor
Sarah Kearns

Project Editor
Tom Lamoureux

Copy Editor
Daryl Kessler

Indexer
Craig Small

Technical Editors
Walter Glenn
Brad Lindaas
Bill Bruns

Software Development Specialists
Todd Pfeffer
Jack Belbot

Production
Elizabeth Deeter
Rebekah Stutzman

About the Authors

Bruce A. Hallberg (lead author) has been in the computer industry since 1980. He has consulted nationally on accounting, distribution, and manufacturing system implementations for small, medium, and large (Fortune 1000) companies. He is presently Director of IS and Corporate Services for a public biotechnology company headquartered in the Silicon Valley area of California.

Since 1992, he has been actively authoring and co-authoring over 15 books on a variety of computing topics, best-sellers on subjects like Microsoft Office, Excel, and Windows NT.

Joe Casad (Development Editor and author) Joe Casad is an engineer and finite element analyst who has written widely on PC networking and system administration. He has worked with Windows NT, UNIX, and VMS systems. Mr. Casad is an author of *The MCSE Windows NT Server and Workstation Study Guide*, *MCSE Networking Essentials Training Guide*, and the *Windows NT Server 4.0 Professional Reference*. He is the former managing editor of Network Administrator magazine.

Christa Anderson is a contributing editor to *Windows NT* magazine and contributor to and coauthor of several books on networking and network operating systems, including the best-selling *Mastering Windows NT Server* (Sybex). Formerly of a DC-area consulting firm, in 1995 she moved her consulting and writing business to Charlottesville, VA to take advantage of the city's better parking and more numerous bookstores. You can contact her at candersn@adelphia.net.

Scott Downie spent too many of his formative years in the classroom. Degrees in electrical engineering, music theory, and the history of science left him with deep mental scars and an abiding wanderlust. When not a ward of the state (i.e. enrolled as a student), he has analyzed Sidewinder air-to-air missile data, pumped up the volume as a sound engineer, tuned pianos and harpsichords, taught classes in electronics technology, played keyboards and bassoon in various ensembles, taught classes in the history of science, functioned as the senior music editor and technical director for a player-piano company, designed sounds for a PC sound card, created printed manuals and online help for Windows and Macintosh software, and worked to maintain the high quality and reliability of Intel products. He is always on the lookout for more MIPS, higher bandwidth, and a bigger monitor.

David Egan is a Microsoft Certified Trainer and a recognized applications programming and systems administration expert in UNIX, Windows NT, VMS, Novell, and DOS environments. David has developed UNIX courses and UNIX & NT Integration courses for American Research Group, a subsidary of Global Knowledge Network. With an excess of 18 years of information technology and training experience, David has consulted internationally for a diverse client base ranging from financial and sales organizations to manufacturing, government, and engineering institutions. Having firsthand knowledge of needs analysis, network design, installation, security, performance tuning and systems management, David has conducted public and in-house seminars for numerous Fortune 1000 companies. His project management background, diverse educational experience, and command of the leading network operating systems make David Egan one of the industry's most respected instructors and course developers.

Kevin Frank is an MCSE and is currently Senior Project Leader at Penguin Putnam Inc. He is managing several projects including the implementation of Microsoft Exchange Server 5.5 with a rollout of MS Outlook to over 1,000 workstations. Prior to this, Kevin served different Fortune 500 companies as a member of project teams that installed, supported, and customized document imaging systems on the NT platform. He is fluent in Visual Basic as well as versed in two proprietary 4GL Lisp derivatives. He has written extensively for several business re-engineering projects. He can be reached at kfrank@putnam.com.

Christopher Gagnon is a Network Analyst and Consultant with an Atlanta-based software development firm. He has worked with Digital Equipment Corporation, IBM, and several practice management firms in the healthcare industry. He has served as Network Administrator on several occasions and knows only too well the politics and technical nuances of this unique environment. While he's not reading trade magazines and technical manuals, he enjoys playing his didgeridoo, chasing his cat, and reading about theoretical physics. He currently resides in the Atlanta suburb of Roswell, Georgia with his wife Keshly and their daughter Paige.

Grant King is a software developer, author, and attorney who lives in Atlanta with his wife Nancy and daughter Elizabeth. He has been either the lead author or a contributing author on several books and articles relating to 32-bit Windows operating systems and software development. He also maintains *The Windows Mill*, a Web site devoted to news about Windows 95, Windows 98, and Windows NT. Grant received his B.A. from The University of the South and his J.D. from Georgia State University College of Law where he graduated *magna cum laude*. His email address is ggking3@mindspring.com.

James M. Spann is a Microsoft Certified Professional who has spent the last six years working as a trainer and lecturer in the computer industry. James received his Bachelor of Science degree in 1984 and immediately started working as a computer and networking troubleshooter. From there, James advanced to the Director of Information Systems for a large investment corporation headquartered in Orlando, Florida. In 1992, James went out on his own and began working with Spann & Associates, Inc. to provide training and consulting services to Fortune 500 companies and government clients. Since then, Mr. Spann has logged more than 5,000 hours teaching classes in both the United States and Europe. Most recently, James has started another new company in Lake Mary, Florida. This new company, Surf Solutions, Inc., is dedicated to providing networking and Internet solutions to small businesses in the Orlando metropolitan area. James can be reached at jay@surfsol.com.

Robert Ward is best known as the founder of the *C/C++ Users Journal*, *Windows Developers Journal* and *System Administrator*. In addition to writing numerous technical articles for these and other magazines he has also authored *Debugging C (Que)* and coauthored *Windows Custom Controls*. He has worked as a consulting digital engineer and was named Professor of the Year while teaching computer science at McPherson College.

Bob Willsey MCSE, MCSD, MCT has 19 years of experience in the computer field, including 15 years with Burroughs / Unisys Corporations and four years teaching Microsoft courses. Mr. Willsey is a Microsoft Certified Trainer; currently, he teaches and consults for QuickStart Technologies, Inc. His experience includes Windows NT, Windows 95, TCP/IP, SMS, and Visual Basic, and he has experience supporting Novell and proprietary mainframe systems.

Serdar Yegulalp has been writing both as a freelancer and staffer for a number of computer publications, including *Computer Buyer's Guide and Handbook* and *Computer Retail Week*, and has contributed to other MCP books in the past, including the *Platinum Edition Using NT 4.0* and *Windows 98 Installation and Configuration Handbook*. He is currently Associate Technology Editor for *WINDOWS* magazine, where he writes and researches on Windows 98, Windows NT 4.0 and Windows NT 5.0. Email him at syegul@winmag.com.

Dedication

For Christy and Calliope.
– Bruce A. Hallberg

To the makers of the shape-note hymns.
– Joe Casad

Acknowledgments

The biggest debt of gratitude owed for this book is to Joe Casad, who originally proposed it to Macmillan Computer Publishing sometime prior to August of 1997, which is when I first heard about the project. Joe is the Lead Editor on the book, and he played a far greater role in doing this job than is normally seen. Not only did he initially propose the project, but he also worked up the initial outline, and kept it in front of various people at MCP during the long gestation period before we actually began writing (since Windows 98 was originally going to be known as Windows 97, we thought we were going to finish the book and have it on the shelves in 1997!). Not only did Joe act as Development Editor, but he also wrote several chapters of the book. His job as Lead Editor meant that he had to coordinate the work of all the authors and technical editors, review all the text, adding in his ideas and comments as we went along. Having worked with more than 20 Development Editors over the years on various projects, I can state with certainty that Joe is the cream of the crop. His comments and suggestions were invariably helpful, and reflected a profound knowledge of the Windows family of operating systems. Most of the quality of this book can be attributed to Joe's efforts. And besides his skills, he was a delight to work with!

Also playing key roles were the book's Technical Editors, who check every screen shot, statement, tip, and sentence for technical accuracy. We were greatly aided by the capable reviews of Brad Lindaas, Walter Glenn, and Bill Bruns. They performed quick and technically accurate work, and caught mistakes that crept into the original manuscript.

Because this book had a long incubation period, there were several Acquisitions Editors who worked on the project, although foremost is Jane Brownlow, who took over just as we began serious work on the project (and so bore the brunt of the work). Jane's job is a tough one; she's chiefly responsible not only for finding the qualified team of authors who worked on the project and negotiating the contracts involved, but also had to shepherd all of us so that we were able to meet the deadline for the book. During the months I worked with Jane, she proved to be efficient, organized, helpful, and pleasant. She was also unfailingly polite, even when cracking the whip! Also taking some earlier responsibility for performing the AE duties on the book were Sean Angus, Jack Belbot, and Jeff Koch.

Special thanks go to the copy editor, Daryl Kessler who worked behind the scenes to edit the book for grammatical accuracy. Project Editor Tom Lamoureux had the challenging task of coordinating with editors and the Production department to ensure all the text and figures were in the correct places and the book got shipped on time. He deserves kudos for his outstanding work.

For the people in the Production department (whom I unfortunately never get to meet) who lay out the pages, fix up the graphics, do the line art, and generally make everything look spiffy and readable, thank you very much for your tireless and excellent work. Seeing the final product that you produce is what makes writing these books worth the months of slavery!

Finally, I'd like to thank Don Fowley of MCP for his support and guidance over the years.

-Bruce A. Hallberg

I wish to thank all who played a part in creating the *Windows 98 Professional Reference*. My personal acknowledgments must begin with Jack Belbot, who first approached me about working on this book, and Sean Angus, who was largely responsible for defining my role. Thanks also to Jeff Koch, who supervised the outline process and supplied leadership throughout the project, and to the others at Macmillan who helped this book along: Tom Lamoureux, Daryl Kessler, and Craig Small.

Each of the authors brought something unique to this book; I will always consider myself as having been part of a very formidable team: thanks to Christa Anderson, Grant King, Jay Spann, Dave Egan, Bob Willsey, Scott Downie, Serdar Yegulalp, and Robert Ward, and to the book's technical editors, Brad Lindaas, Bill Bruns, and Walter Glenn. Special thanks to Robert Ward, my computer-writing mentor, without whom I would not now be leading a different life. If we were a team, the star of our team was certainly lead author Bruce Hallberg. Bruce's knowledge of the networking business, and his talent as a writer, are at the core of this book's vision. I don't think I've ever seen anyone write with such freshness, energy, and precision about the practical affairs of network administration, and all under circumstances that a lesser voice would have considered desperate. I felt privileged to have had the opportunity to work with him, and I would jump at the chance to work with him again.

I would also jump at the chance to work again with Ms. Jane Brownlow, who deserves a special note of gratitude for investing her considerable talent and energy into this book. Jane is a master of her craft. I don't know how to describe her contribution other than to say that, when she showed up, things suddenly started to happen and we all suddenly knew what we were doing. She knew when to call and when not to call, when to worry and when not to worry. I honestly believe this book wouldn't have happened without her, and if there is ever an Acquisition Editor's Professional Reference, I think she should write it.

Thanks to my family for their support and love throughout the tumultuous completion of this project, especially to my wife Barbara Dinneen, who underwent the knife of Julius as the year (and the operating system) turned '97 to '98, but who still managed to carry on with a job, a house, three children, and new diapers while her helpmate writhed before five computers and a deadline.

-Joe Casad

Contents at a Glance

Introduction 1

Part I: Introducing Windows 98
  1 Deploying Windows 98 9
  2 Installing Windows 98 37
  3 Network Installation 79
  4 Windows 98 and Total Cost of Ownership 95

Part II: Configuring Windows 98
  5 Understanding Windows 98 Configuration 105
  6 Control Panel 115
  7 System Policies 153
  8 User Profiles 181
  9 Hardware Profiles 191
  10 Mastering the Windows 98 Registry 199

Part III: Windows 98 Operations
  11 Windows 98 Architecture and Application Support 231
  12 Supporting Devices 261
  13 Printing 283
  14 Multimedia 305
  15 OLE, COM, DCOM, and ActiveX 353
  16 Windows 98 ODBC Connectivity 379
  17 File Systems: File and Disk Resources 403
  18 Viruses in Windows 98 431
  19 Windows 98 for Portables 441
  20 Backup and Restore 453

Part IV: Networking Windows 98
  21 Understanding Windows 98 Networking 469
  22 Peer-to-Peer Networking 503
  23 Windows 98 in Windows NT Domains 517
  24 Windows 98 with NetWare/InternetWare Networks 529

25	Windows 98 with TCP/IP	539
26	Windows 98 and Remote Communication	563

Part V: Windows 98 and the Internet

27	Internet Browsers in Windows 98	595
28	Setting Up Windows 98 for the Internet	651
29	Windows 98 as an Internet/Intranet Server	667
30	Internet Security	689
31	Mail Management in Windows 98	709

Part VI: Customizing Windows 98

32	Windows 98 Configuration Files	729
33	Windows Scripting with Windows 98 Scripting Host	741
34	Automating Tasks	777

Part VII: Troubleshooting and Optimizing Windows 98

35	Tools and Strategies for Optimizing Windows 98	791
36	The Windows 98 Boot Process and Emergency Recovery	819
37	Tools and Strategies for Troubleshooting Windows 98	835

Part VIII: Appendixes

A	Windows 98 Accessories	861
B	Windows 95/98 Device Manager Error Codes	865
C	Command-Line Reference	873
D	Installation Script	905

Index 921

Table of Contents

Introduction   1

How This Book Is Organized 2
   Part I: Introducing Windows 98 2
   Part II: Configuring Windows 98 2
   Part III: Windows 98 Operations 3
   Part IV: Networking Windows 98 4
   Part V: Windows 98 and the Internet 5
   Part VI: Customizing Windows 98 5
   Part VII: Troubleshooting and Optimizing Windows 98 5

Part I: Introducing Windows 98

1   Deploying Windows 98   9

When You Should Use Windows 98 11
The Windows 98 Network Environment 14
Deciding on Network Components 16
Planning the Windows 98 User Environment 17
   Choosing Components 19
   Defining the Desktop 21
   Launching Programs at Startup 32
Active Desktop 32
   Active Channels 34
Preparing for Installation 35
Conclusion 36

2   Installing Windows 98   37

Preparing to Install Windows 98 38
   Check System Requirements 39
   Make Sure That Hardware Is Supported 39
   Disable TSRs and Timeout Features 40
   Close Applications—Especially Virus Checkers 40
   Scan and Defragment Disks 41
   Back Up Key System Files 42
   Check Network Configuration 42
Understanding the Installation Process 43
Using the Setup Command 45

Upgrading to Windows 98 from Windows 95 or Windows 3.x 47
    Installing Windows 98 on DOS, Windows 3.0, and Windows NT
        Systems 51
Dual-Booting Windows 98 with Windows 3.x and DOS 56
Using Windows 98 with Windows NT Systems 57
Creating a CD-ROM-Aware BootFloppy Disk 58
Customizing Windows 98 Setup with Installation Scripts 59
    Using Installation Script Templates 61
    Creating Installation Scripts with Batch98 62
Uninstalling Windows 98 71
Troubleshooting Setup 73
    Using Setup's Built-In Recovery Features 73
    Inspecting the Logs 74
Troubleshooting Tips 75
    ScanDisk 76
    Compressed Drives 76
    Conventional Memory 76
    MS-DOS Boot Partition 77
    Incorrect Configuration of Legacy Hardware 77
    Default User Policy Settings 77
Conclusion 77

3 Network Installation   79

Understanding Network Installation 80
Network Installation in Windows NT Domains 81
Network Installations on NetWare Networks 83
Specifying Installation Scripts for Network Installations 84
Push Techniques 85
    Logon Script Installation Commands for MS-DOS, Windows 3.x,
        and Windows 95 86
    Push Installations for Windows for Workgroups 86
Other Methods for Initiating Setup 87
Creating a Network Boot Disk 88
    Using Windows NT's Network Client Administrator to Create a
        Network Boot Disk 88
    Using Windows for Workgroups to Create a Network Boot Disk 91
Troubleshooting Network Installation 93
Conclusion 94

4 Windows 98 and Total Cost of Ownership   95

Simplifying Management with
Windows 98 System Tools 97
    Updating Windows 98

Limiting the Windows 98 User Interface 98
    Creating a Limited Operating Mode Using System
    Policies 99
Conclusion 102

Part II: Configuring Windows 98

5 Understanding Windows 98 Configuration — 105

Understanding the Registry 106
    Registry Structure 107
    Registry Management Features 109
Understanding User Profiles 110
Understanding System Policies 111
Understanding Hardware Profiles 112
Conclusion 113

6 Control Panel — 115

Understanding the Control Panel 116
    Control Panel Files 116
    Control Panel and System Registry 118
    Sending Control Panel Settings to Users 119
    Control Panel Tricks 121
Control Panel Quick Reference and Tour 123
    32-bit ODBC 126
    Accessibility Options 128
    Add New Hardware 130
    Add/Remove Programs 130
    Date/Time 131
    Display 132
    Fonts 136
    Game Controllers 137
    Internet 137
    Keyboard 137
    Mail 139
    Modems 139
    Mouse 141
    Multimedia 141
    Network 143
    Passwords 143
    Power Management 145
    Printers 145
    Regional Settings 145

	Sounds	147
	System	147
	Telephony	151
	Users	151
	Conclusion	152

7 System Policies   153

	Understanding System Policies	154
	Implementing System Policies	155
	Enabling User Profiles	156
	Enabling Group System Policies	156
	Creating the System Policy File	157
	Installing the System Policy Editor	158
	Applying the Policy File to the Network	160
	Using the System Policy Editor	162
	Creating Specific User and Computer Policies	165
	Creating Group Policies	167
	Understanding and Creating Policy Templates	168
	Base Policies in WINDOWS.ADM	176

8 User Profiles   181

	System Policies or Mandatory User Profiles?	183
	Understanding User Profile Files	183
	Enabling User Profiles	185
	Managing Roving User Profiles	185
	Creating Mandatory User Profiles	187
	Common Problems and Solutions	187
	Conclusion	189

9 Hardware Profiles   191

	Hardware Profile Boot Process	192
	Creating New Hardware Profiles	192
	Setting Up Hardware Profiles: An Example	194
	Understanding Hardware Profiles and the Registry	196
	Common Problems and Solutions	197
	Backing Up the Original Hardware Profile	197
	Unknown Monitor Errors	197
	Conclusion	198

10 Mastering the Windows 98 Registry   199

	Understanding the Registry	200
	Understanding the Main Registry Branches	203

Using Registry Editor 208
   Searching the Registry 209
   Editing a Value's Data 210
   Adding Keys and Values 211
   Renaming Keys and Values 212
   Deleting Keys and Values 212
   Importing and Exporting Registry Keys 212
   Registry Editor Command-line Parameters 214
Backing Up and Restoring the Registry 215
   Using Batch Files to Back Up the Registry 215
   Using CFGBACK to Back Up the Registry 216
Remotely Administering the Registry 216
Specific Registry Tips and Tricks 217
   Managing File Associations 217
   Add Actions to Pop-up Menus 221
   Adding New Sound Events 222
   Changing Desktop Icons 223
   Changing Windows Folder Locations 224
   Expanding the Icon Cache 225
   Changing the Menu Delay 225
   Removing Inbox from the Desktop 226
   Viewing Bitmap Contents as Icons 226
   Change How Short Filenames are Generated 226
   Assigning a Viewer to Unknown File Types 227
   Setting Double-Click Hot Zones 227
   Disabling Window Animation 228
   Changing User Information 228
Conclusion 228

Part III: Windows 98 Operations

11 Windows 98 Architecture and Application Support   231

Understanding the Architecture of Windows 98 232
   Multitasking and Scheduling 232
   Understanding Processes and Threads 235
   Understanding Semaphores, Waits, and Critical Sections 238
   Understanding the Windows 98 Memory Model 239
   Understanding Windows 98 Components 242

The Core Components 246
   Summarizing the Windows 98 Architecture 247
   Understanding Application Support 247
   APIs 247
   OLE Support 248
   MS-DOS Support 249
   Performing a Local Reboot 259
   Conclusion 259

12 Supporting Devices 261

   About Windows 98 Device Support 262
   Understanding IRQs, DMAs, Memory, and I/O Settings 264
   Configuring IRQ Addresses 266
   Understanding Plug and Play 269
   Understanding Real-Mode versus Protected-Mode Drivers 270
   Managing Devices 271
   Installing New Devices 271
   Updating and Removing Device Drivers 275
   Recovering from Windows 3.x Driver Installations 275
   Understanding Specific Devices 276
   System Devices 276
   Display Adapters 278
   Multiple Monitor Support 280
   Serial Ports 281
   Conclusion 281

13 Printing 283

   Windows 98 Printing Subsystem 284
   Local versus Network Printers 285
   Using the Printers Folder 286
   Default Printer 288
   Configuring Printers 288
   Printing from MS-DOS Applications 291
   Installing a Local Printer 292
   Setting Up a Network Printer 295
   Point and Print 297
   Printing from Applications 297
   Managing Print Jobs 298
   Special Printing Considerations 299
   Drag-and-Drop Printing 299
   Printing Files from Disk 300
   Printing Frames in Internet Explorer 300

Printing in Color 300
Offline Printing 301
Removing Printers 301
Working with Fonts 302
Troubleshooting Printer Problems 303
Your Printer Does Not Print 303
You Receive a Message about an Error for Insufficient Memory or
Disk Space 304
Your Print Spooler Might Not Be Functioning Properly, Causing an
Error When You Try to Print 304
Conclusion 304

14 Multimedia   305

The PC 98 Specification 306
Installing Multimedia 307
Understanding Bus Standards 309
USB 309
IEEE 1394 (FireWire) 310
SCSI 311
Understanding Software Standards 312
DirectX 312
Codecs 314
Understanding Video Requirements 318
Video Card Memory 318
Video Card Speed 319
General Video/TV Tuner/MPEG Decoder Card Installation Tips 320
DVD (Digital Versatile Disc or Digital Video Disc) 320
TV Tuners 324
Video Capture 325
Cameras and Scanners 326
Media Player 327
ActiveMovie Control 328
WordPad and Cardfile 330
Understanding Sound Requirements 331
Installing a Sound Card 331
Microphones 332
Speakers 332
3D and "Surround" Sound 333
MIDI Capabilities 333
CD Player 336
Volume Control 337
Sound Recorder 338
Understanding Touch (Input/Output) Hardware 342

A Simple Example 343
Troubleshooting 345
   Dodging the Bullet 345
   Biting the Bullet 347
Conclusion 352

15 OLE, COM, DCOM, and ActiveX — 353

Understanding Client/Server Application Concepts 354
   What is a Client/Server Application? 354
   What Benefits Does Client/Server Provide? 355
   What Are 3-Tier and N-Tier Applications? 355
   What are OLE, COM, DCOM, and ActiveX? 357
   What Are Objects, Classes, and Instances? 359
   What are GUIDs and CLSIDs? 360
   Understanding HKEY_CLASSES_ROOT 361
   How Windows 98 Creates an Instance of an Object 361
   What Are Compound Documents? 362
   What Is Structured Storage? 363
Sample Files Included on the CD 363
Using OLE 364
   Building Compound Documents 364
   Creating Embedded Documents 364
   Using In-place Editing 366
   Creating Linked Documents 366
   Editing Linked Documents 367
   Drag-and-Drop Linking 367
Using the DCOMCNFG Utility 368
   DCOM on Windows 98 369
   Client/Server Program Included on the CD-ROM 369
   Changing Windows 98 to User-level Security 370
   Select a Location in Which to Run the Server 372
   Use Appropriate Security Settings 374
   Establish Default DCOM Settings 376
Conclusion 377

16 Windows 98 ODBC Connectivity — 379

Client/Server Database Concepts 380
An Overview of ODBC 382
   ODBC Drivers 382
   The ODBC Manager 383
   Connecting to the Database 383
The ODBC Connect String 384
Creating a DSN 386
   Steps to Create a DSN 386

Table of Contents

Installing or Upgrading ODBC 396
Troubleshooting ODBC Connection Problems 398
    Correcting Network Connectivity Problems 398
    Correcting Security Problems 398
    Correcting Basic ODBC Parameter Problems 399
    Correcting Advanced ODBC Parameter Problems 399
    Correcting Functionality Problems 400
Advanced ODBC Tuning Options 401
Conclusion 402

17   File Systems: File and Disk Resources   403

Exploring Hard Disk Drives 404
    Understanding Partitions 404
    Understanding FAT 406
    Understanding FAT32 410
    Understanding Long Filenames on FAT 411
    Understanding NTFS 412
    Understanding DriveSpace 414
    Comparing File Systems 415
Understanding Storage Hardware 415
Configuring Disk Subsystems 417
Understanding Windows 98 Disk Operations 418
    Partitioning Hard Disks 418
    Formatting Disks 419
    Defragmenting Hard Disks 420
    Testing Hard Disk Drives 422
    Using DriveSpace 424
    Maintaining a Compressed Drive 426
    Disk Compression Notes 428
Conclusion 429

18   Viruses in Windows 98   431

Understanding Malicious Programs 432
    Understanding Virus Types 434
    Understanding How Viruses Infect Files 436
    Understanding Virus Creation 436
    Understanding Viral Transmission 436
    Recognizing Viruses 437
Preventing Viruses 437
Conclusion 439

19 Windows 98 for Portables — 441
PC Card Devices 442
Hardware Profiles 443
Power Management 444
Direct Cable Networking 447
Infrared Monitor 447
Mastering the Briefcase 448
Conclusion 452

20 Backup and Restore — 453
Evaluating Backup Requirements 454
Choosing Backup Hardware 456
Choosing Backup Software 457
Choosing a Backup Rotation Strategy 458
Using Microsoft Backup 462
Conclusion 465

Part IV: Networking Windows 98

21 Understanding Windows 98 Networking — 469
Network Adapters 473
Network Services 478
Network Protocols 479
Network Clients 482
Cabling 485
Configuring Identification Properties 489
Windows 98 Security 490
Share-level Security 491
User-level Security 493
Windows 98 Logon 495
Finding Network Resources 498
Mapping Network Shares 502
Conclusion 502

22 Peer-to-Peer Networking — 503
Understanding Windows 98 Peer Networking Capabilities 504
    Choosing Microsoft or NetWare Peer Services and Protocols 506
    Choosing Hardware for a Small Peer Network 506

Table of Contents

Setting Up Windows 98 for Peer Networks 508
   Direct Cable Peer Networking 510
   Understanding Workgroups and Identification 513
Troubleshooting Peer Networking Problems 515
Conclusion 516

23 Windows 98 in Windows NT Domains 517

What You Get with Windows NT Server 518
Configuring Windows 98 as a Domain Client 519
Windows 98 in Windows NT Domains 522
   Home Directories 522
   User Profiles 523
   Group Memberships 524
   Logon Hours 525
   Logon Workstations 525
Managing Windows 98 from the Domain 526
Managing the Domain from Windows 98 527
Conclusion 528

24 Windows 98 with NetWare/InternetWare Networks 529

Understanding NetWare 530
Understanding NetWare Support in Windows 98 530
   Microsoft Client for NetWare Networks 532
   Installing Microsoft Client for NetWare Networks 532
   Long Filename Support on NetWare Volumes 535
Common Problems and Solutions 536
   The Windows Logon Appears Instead of the NetWare Logon 536
   Logon to NetWare Servers Is Rejected 537
   Logon Script Does Not Run 537
Conclusion 538

25 Windows 98 with TCP/IP 539

TCP/IP Concepts 540
Configuring TCP/IP 543
   Dynamic IP Address Assignment with DHCP 544
   Automatic IP Address Assignment with APIPA 545
Name Resolution 546
   Setting Up Windows 98 for a DNS Server 547
Setting Up Windows 98 for a HOSTS File 548
   HOSTS Files 548
   Setting Up Windows 98 for a WINS Server 549
   Setting Up Windows 98 for an LMHOSTS File 549

TCP/IP Tools 550
    WINIPCFG 550
    Telnet 550
    FTP 551
    PING 552
    ROUTE 552
    TRACERT 553
    Other Utilities 553
Understanding IP Addressing 554
    The IP Address Format 554
    Network and Host IDs 554
    Address Classes 555
    Subnets 556
    Subnet Masking 556
    Developing Your Network 557
SNMP and Windows 98 558
Accessing UNIX Hosts with Windows 98 558
    Personal Web Server Service 559
Common Problems and Solutions 560
Conclusion 562

26   Windows 98 and Remote Communication   563

Understanding Dial-Up Networking Capabilities 564
    Internet Connectivity 565
    VPN (Virtual Private Network) Connectivity 565
    Direct-Dial Connectivity 566
Protocols Used in Remote Communications 566
    TCP/IP 566
    IPX/SPX 567
    NetBEUI 567
    PPTP 567
Servers Used in Remote Communications 567
    UNIX or Generic Internet 568
    Windows NT 4.0 or Higher 568
    Windows NT 3.5/3.1 and Windows 3.x 568
    Windows 98/95 568
Installing Dial-Up Networking 568
    Installing Dial-Up Networking Manually 569
    Installing Commonly Needed Network Protocols 570
Configuring Hardware for Dial-Up Networking 572
    On-Board Hardware Settings 572
    Software and Hardware Compression Settings 573

Table of Contents

    Hardware Buffering 574
    Other Settings and Configurations 575
Configuring Dial-Up Properties 575
    The Make New Connection Wizard 576
    Connection Properties 577
Dial-Up Scripting 583
Multilink 584
Using Dial-Up Networking 585
    Dialing Out and Logging In 586
    Configuring PPTP 587
    Troubleshooting Dial-Up Connections 588
Dial-Up Server 589
    Installing Dial-Up Server 589
    Configuring Dial-Up Server 590
    Dial-Up Server in Operation 591
Conclusion 592

Part V: Windows 98 and the Internet

27 Internet Browsers in Windows 98 — 595

Overview of Browsing in Windows 98 596
    How Windows 98 Integrates Browsing with the Desktop 596
    The Role of the Default Browser 601
Configuring and Using Browsers 601
Internet Explorer 4 602
    Setting Up IE4 602
    Fine-Tuning Internet Explorer 4 615
    Using Internet Explorer 4 617
Netscape Communicator 627
    Setting Up Netscape 628
    Configuring Other Options 636
    Using Communicator 637
    Using Netcaster 647
IE4 Versus Netscape: Which Is Better? 648
Conclusion 650

28 Setting Up Windows 98 for the Internet — 651

The Connection Tab 652
    Setting Up an Internet Connection 652
Internet Service Providers 656
    Basic Internet Access 656
    ISDN 657

Cable Modems 658
ISP Tips 658
Using Internet Proxies 659
Understanding Java and ActiveX 660
Implications for Browsing 661
Implications for Internet Security 661
Problems and Solutions 663
Cannot Connect to ISP 663
Cannot Connect to Email or Web 664
HTML Documents Are Not Opening with Desired Browser 664
Conclusion 666

29 Windows 98 as an Internet/Intranet Server — 667

Some Initial Considerations 668
What's Included with Personal Web Server 669
Installing Personal Web Server 670
Configuring Personal Web Server 671
Planning Your Web Site 671
Security Issues 672
Using Personal Web Manager 673
Creating Content for Your Site 677
General Considerations 678
Using the Home Page Wizard 681
Using FrontPage Express 682
Using the Publishing Wizard 684
Developing with New Content Types 684
Conclusion 687

30 Internet Security — 689

The Problem of Internet Security 690
Possible Threats (Ways to Break In) 691
File and Printer Sharing 691
ActiveX Controls 692
Java Applets 693
Active Scripting 693
Other Threats 694
Setting Up Internet Security 695
Configuring File and Printer Sharing 695
Protocol Isolation 698
Security Zones 698
Types of Security Zones 698
Adding Sites to Security Zones 699

Table of Contents

Customizing Security Zones 700
Customizing Java Settings 703
Authenticode 703
Certificate Management 704
128-Bit Encryption 704
Other Security Features in Internet Explorer 705
Secure Transactions 706
Encryption 706
Microsoft Wallet 707
Conclusion 707

31 Mail Management in Windows 98   709

Email and How it Works 710
The Simple Mail Transfer Protocol (SMTP) 710
Elements of an Email Message 711
Attachments 711
Encoding Formats 711
BinHex 712
UUencode 713
MIME 713
Configuring an Email Client 715
POP (Post Office Protocol) Server 716
SMTP (Simple Mail Transfer Protocol) Server 716
LDAP (Lightweight Directory Access Protocol) Server 717
Working with Specific Email Clients 719
Anatomy of an Emailer 719
Email Functionality 720
Conclusion 726

Part VI: Customizing Windows 98

32 Windows 98 Configuration Files   729

IO.SYS and MSDOS.SYS 730
CONFIG.SYS 732
AUTOEXEC.BAT 735
WIN.INI and SYSTEM.INI 736
Conclusion 739

33 Windows Scripting with Windows 98 Scripting Host   741

Background 742
The WSH Object Model 746

The Execution Environment 751
Writing Scripts 752
　Basic I/O 752
　Enumerating the Environment 754
　Using the Network Object 756
　Sequencing Jobs 761
　An Extended Example 763
Using the Script Debugger 771
　Starting a Session 771
An Open Architecture 773
Scripting Resources 774
Conclusion 775

34 Automating Tasks 777

Understanding Task Scheduler 778
　Automating Tasks with the Task Scheduler 779
　Using the Scheduled Task Wizard 779
　Deleting and Modifying Tasks 782
　Task Scheduler Advanced Options 782
　Task Scheduler Limitations 784
Scheduling Tune-Ups with the Maintenance Wizard 784
　Maintenance Wizard and Improved System Performance 786
The Windows Scripting Host 786
Conclusion 787

Part VII: Troubleshooting and Optimizing Windows 98

35 Tools and Strategies for Optimizing Windows 98 791

Understanding Performance Problems and Bottlenecks 792
　Understanding TOTE Methodology 792
General Performance Improvements for Windows 98 793
　Memory Optimization 794
　Virtual Memory Optimization 795
　File System Optimization 797
　Hard Disk Optimization 798
　Graphics Optimization 798
　Optimizing Printing 799
　Network Optimization 803
　Optimizing Application Performance 804
Using Windows 98 Performance Tools 806
　Windows Tune-Up 806
　Resource Meter 806

  System Monitor 807
  Other Performance Tools 815
 Windows 98 Configuration Recommendations 815
 Conclusion 816

36   The Windows 98 Boot Process and Emergency Recovery   819

 Understanding the Windows 98 Boot Process 820
  Windows 98 Startup Files 821
 Understanding Startup Problems 822
  Resolving Hard Disk Problems 823
  Resolving Other Hardware Problems 825
  Resolving System File Problems 826
  Troubleshooting Startup Problems with System
   Configuration Utility 827
 Understanding the Windows Startup Menu 830
 Understanding, Preparing, and Using an Emergency Boot Disk 831
  Preparing the EBD 832
  Understanding the EBD 833
  Using the EBD 833
 Conclusion 834

37   Tools and Strategies for Troubleshooting Windows 98   835

 Troubleshooting Overview 836
  Communicating with Users 836
  Identifying Problems 838
  Solving Problems Systematically 839
  Knowing the Top Causes for System Problems 839
 Windows 98 Troubleshooting Tools 840
  Microsoft System Information 841
  Signature Verification Tool 845
  Windows Report Tool 845
  Version Conflict Manager 846
  System File Checker 847
  Registry Checker 850
  Automatic Skip Driver Agent 850
  Dr. Watson 851
  ScanDisk 852
  FileWise 852
 Troubleshooting Specific Problems 854
  Application Crashes Regularly 855
  System Crashes Regularly 856

Hard Disk Trouble 857
Modem/Serial Port Trouble 857
Conclusion 858

Part VIII: Appendixes

A Windows 98 Accessories — 861

B Windows 95/98 Device Manager Error Codes — 865

Summary 866
More Information 866
   Code 1 866
   Code 2 867
   Code 3 867
   Code 4 867
   Code 5 867
   Code 6 867
   Code 7 868
   Code 8 868
   Code 9 868
   Code 10 868
   Code 11 868
   Code 12 869
   Code 13 869
   Code 14 869
   Code 15 869
   Code 16 869
   Code 17 870
   Code 18 870
   Code 19 870
   Code 20 870
   Code 21 870
   Code 22 870
   Code 23 871
   Code 24 871
   Code 25 871
   Code 26 871
   Code 27 872
   Code 28 872
   Code 29 872
   Code 30 872

C	**Command-Line Reference**	**873**
	Command-Line Structure	874
	Internal Commands	874
	BREAK	874
	CD (CHDIR)	874
	CHCP	874
	CLS	875
	COPY	875
	CTTY	875
	DATE	875
	DEL (ERASE)	875
	DIR	875
	EXIT	875
	LH	875
	MD (MKDIR)	875
	PATH	875
	PROMPT	876
	RD (RMDIR)	876
	REN (RENAME)	876
	SET	876
	TIME	876
	TYPE	876
	VER	876
	VERIFY	876
	VOL	876
	System Commands	876
	ACCWIZ	877
	DEBUG	877
	DOSKEY	877
	EDIT	878
	KEYB	879
	MEM	880
	MORE	880
	NLSFUNC	881
	PROGMAN	881
	REGEDIT	881
	SETVER	881
	START	882
	WINFILE	883
	WINVER	883
	Disk and File Commands	883
	ATTRIB	883
	CHKDSK	884

DELTREE	884
DISKCOPY	885
EXTRACT	886
FC	886
FDISK	887
FIND	887
FORMAT	888
LABEL	889
MOVE	889
SORT	890
SUBST	890
XCOPY	891
Network Commands	893
ARP	893
FTP	894
IPCONFIG	897
NBTSTAT	898
NET	899
NETSTAT	901
PING	902
ROUTE	902
TRACERT	903

D Installation Script — 905

Automated Installation	907
Regional Settings	910
Network Settings	911
Optional Components	915
Printers	916
Setup's MRU List	916
Installing New Files, Changing Configuration Files, and Modifying the Registry	917

Index — 921

INTRODUCTION

Windows 98 Professional Reference is a book for administrators of large and small networks—those who toil to keep systems running and users content. You'll find detailed advice on configuring, troubleshooting, and networking Windows 98. The goal of this book is to provide a well-written description of Windows 98 and to deliver the best available coverage of topics such as configuration, networking, ODBC, optimization, and Windows scripting.

How This Book Is Organized

Windows 98 Professional Reference is divided into seven parts, each covering an aspect of Windows 98 operations. Within the parts, each chapter focuses on a pertinent Windows 98 topic.

Part I: Introducing Windows 98

Chapter 1, "Deploying Windows 98," describes the new features of Windows 98 and discusses configuration options. This chapter also looks at networking scenarios and explores desktop configuration options.

Chapter 2, "Installing Windows 98," describes the steps you'll need to take before you install Windows 98 and discusses the installation process in detail. You'll learn about dual-booting Windows 98 and you'll learn how to create a CD-ROM-enabled boot floppy. This chapter also shows how to customize Windows 98 Setup using installation scripts.

Chapter 3, "Network Installation," shows how to install Windows 98 across the network. This chapter describes the network installation process and looks at special issues concerning network installations from Windows 3.x and NetWare. You'll also learn how to create a network boot disk using Windows for Workgroups or NT Server's Network Client Administrator.

Chapter 4, "Windows 98 and Total Cost of Ownership," describes Microsoft's Zero Administration initiative and discusses some of Zero Admin features in Windows 98.

Part II: Configuring Windows 98

Chapter 5, "Understanding Windows 98 Configuration," provides an overview of Windows 98 configuration components that will be discussed in great detail in later chapters: the Registry, User Profiles, System Policies, and Hardware Profiles.

Chapter 6, "Control Panel," describes the applets of the Control Panel. Control Panel is often the first stop for Windows 98 configuration. This chapter describes how to use each of the common Control Panel applications.

Chapter 7, "System Policies," describes the purpose of System Policies and explains how to configure System Policies in Windows 98. You'll learn about user and group policies and about using Windows 98's System Policy Editor.

Chapter 8, "User Profiles," describes how you can customize the user environment with user profiles, and how you can set up network-based roving and mandatory user profiles that follow the user to other network workstations.

Introduction

Chapter 9, "Hardware Profiles," shows how Windows 98 uses hardware profiles. A hardware profile is a predefined description of system hardware. You can use hardware profiles with a portable computer to adapt quickly to a change in docking state.

Chapter 10, "Mastering the Windows 98 Registry," is a guide to the Registry, the center for Windows 98 configuration information. This chapter describes the structure of the Registry and shows how to navigate the Registry using Windows 98's Registry Editor. This chapter also shows how to back up and restore the Registry and describes some Registry tips and tricks.

Part III: Windows 98 Operations

Chapter 11, "Windows 98 Architecture and Application Support," describes Windows 98 System architecture. The chapter describes scheduling and multitasking, time-slicing, and other concepts. The chapter also describes the Windows 98 memory model and discusses Windows 98's support for Win32, Win16, and MS-DOS applications.

Chapter 12, "Supporting Devices," describes what you'll need to know to support devices in Windows 98. The chapter discusses IRQ, DMA, and I/O Port settings. This chapter also describes Windows 98 Plug and Play and discusses how to install and troubleshoot system devices.

Chapter 13, "Printing," discusses Windows 98 printing components and shows how to install and manage printers in Windows 98.

Chapter 14, "Multimedia," provides a thorough discussion of multimedia support in Windows 98. This chapter describes how to install multimedia devices and also provides some background on Universal Serial Bus (USB) and Digital Versatile Disk (DVD). This chapter also discusses Copecs, TV tuners, and video and sound support. You'll also find a section on multimedia troubleshooting.

Chapter 15, "OLE, COM, DCOM, and ActiveX," discusses Windows 98's COM architecture. This chapter also describes both the theory and the procedures behind embedding and linking OLE objects. The chapter also includes a discussion of DCOM and Windows 98's DCOMCNFG utility.

Chapter 16, "Windows 98 ODBC Connectivity," describes client/server data database concepts and shows how to implement ODBC in Windows 98.

Chapter 17, "File Systems: File and Disk Resources," describes how to manage disks, files, and file systems in Windows 98. This chapter provides some background on hard disks and partitions, and discusses Windows 98's FAT and FAT32 file systems. This chapter also describes how Windows 98 handles long filenames and discusses system hardware and disk operations. And, the chapter also describes how to format, compress, and degragment disks in Windows 98.

Chapter 18, "Viruses in Windows 98," discusses strategies for virus protection in Windows 98.

Chapter 19, "Windows 98 for Portables," describes Windows 98 features designed to support portables. The chapter discusses PC Card devices and features such as power management, infrared monitor, and briefcase.

Chapter 20, "Backup and Restore," discusses tools and strategies for performing backups in Windows 98.

Part IV: Networking Windows 98

Chapter 21, "Understanding Windows 98 Networking," describes Windows 98 network architecture and discusses some basic networking concepts. This chapter describes how to install and configure network components: adapters, services, protocols, and clients. This chapter also discusses some common LAN cabling schemes and shows how to implement user-level and share-level security. The chapter also includes a discussion of Windows 98 logon options and a section on finding resources in Windows 98. And, this chapter includes a look at Windows 98 peer-to-peer networking concepts.

Chapter 22, "Peer-to-Peer Networking," takes a look at Windows 98 in the workgroup environment.

Chapter 23, "Windows 98 in Windows NT Domains," provides a brief look at some of the networking features available to Windows 98 clients on a Windows NT domain. This chapter also shows how to implement remote administration of a Windows 98 machine and how to install Windows NT Server tools, which allow you to administer an NT network from a Windows 98 computer.

Chapter 24, "Windows 98 with NetWare/InternetWare Networks," describes Windows 98's support for NetWare networks. You'll learn how to install NetWare clients and how to operate on a NetWare network from Windows 98.

Chapter 25, "Windows 98 with TCP/IP," describes the TCP/IP network protocols and shows how to install and configure TCP/IP in Windows 98. This chapter also discusses IP address assignment options, including Windows 98's new Automatic Private IP Addressing (APIPA), and describes Windows 98 name resolution features. This chapter also describes Windows 98's TCP/IP tools and provides a complete discussion of IP addressing.

Chapter 26, "Windows 98 and Remote Communication," discusses Windows 98's Dial-Up Networking features and shows how to implement Dial-Up Networking. This chapter also discusses Dial-Up Server and shows how to implement a virtual private network using Windows 98's new Point-to-Point Tunneling Protocol (PPTP).

Part V: Windows 98 and the Internet

Chapter 27, "Internet Browsers in Windows 98," discusses Windows 98's Active Desktop and provides detailed instructions for configuring and using the two most common Internet browsers: Internet Explorer and Netscape Communicator.

Chapter 28, "Setting Up Windows 98 for the Internet," describes how to set up a Windows 98 computer to access the Internet.

Chapter 29, "Windows 98 as an Internet/Intranet Server," describes Windows 98's Personal Web Server and shows how to administer a Web site using Personal Web Manager. This chapter also describes Windows 98's two Web content tools: Home Page Wizard and FrontPage Express.

Chapter 30, "Internet Security," describes Windows 98's Internet security features and provides advice on how to protect yourself from threats from the Internet.

Chapter 31, "Mail Management in Windows 98," shows how Internet email works. This chapter also discusses common encoding formats, describes the structure of an email message, and shows how to configure a typical email client.

Part VI: Customizing Windows 98

Chapter 32, "Windows 98 Configuration Files," describes Windows 98 startup configuration files msdos.sys, io.sys, config.sys, autoexec.bat, win.ini, and system.ini.

Chapter 33, "Windows Scripting with Windows 98 Scripting Host," is a complete tutorial on VBScript and Windows 98's new Windows Scripting Host. You can use Windows Scripting Host to run custom scripts that perform complex tasks on your network.

Chapter 34, "Automating Tasks," shows how to schedule tasks to run automatically in Windows 98 using Windows 98's Task Scheduler and Scheduled Tasks Wizard.

Part VII: Troubleshooting and Optimizing Windows 98

Chapter 35, "Tools and Strategies for Optimizing Windows 98," provides methodologies for optimizing performance in Windows 98. The chapter looks specifically at optimizing virtual memory, file systems, hard disks, graphics, printing, network operations, and applications. The chapter also discusses Windows 98 performance tools, such as Windows Tune-Up Wizard, Resource Meter, and System Monitor.

Chapter 36, "The Windows 98 Boot Process and Emergency Recovery," describes the Windows 98 boot process and provides techniques for solving boot problems. The chapter discusses how to troubleshoot boot problems using Windows 98's System Configuration Utility.

Chapter 37, "Tools and Strategies for Troubleshooting Windows 98," discusses Windows 98 troubleshooting strategies. This chapter also shows how to use Windows 98's troubleshooting tools, such as Microsoft System Information, Version Conflict Manager, Registry Checker, Dr. Watson, and System File Checker.

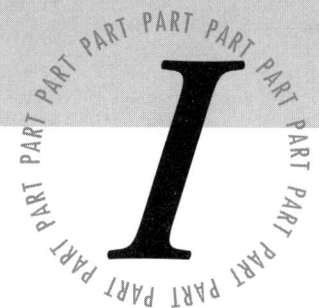

Introducing Windows 98

1 Deploying Windows 98 9

2 Installing Windows 98 37

3 Network Installation 79

4 Windows 98 and Total Cost of Ownership 95

Deploying Windows 98

Windows 98 succeeds Windows 95 as Microsoft's everyday, mass-market operating system. Windows 98 will ship with millions of new PCs in the next few years, and millions of existing systems will be upgraded to Windows 98 from Windows 95 or Windows 3.1. Windows 98 will undoubtedly be the system of choice for home users with Intel or equivalent systems, but you can expect Windows 98 to also carry a sizable portion of the corporate market because of its low price, its (relative) simplicity, and its similarity to the vastly popular Windows 95.

Windows 98 is very much descended from Windows 95; the two operating systems are so similar that you could easily work all day and honestly not remember if you're using Windows 95 or Windows 98. Nevertheless,

Windows 98 adds some significant new features, both on and below the surface, that make it more configurable, more adaptable, and more automated than its predecessor. Table 1.1 lists some of Windows 98's new features. Later chapters of this book describe these features in detail.

Table 1.1
Windows 98 New Features

Feature	Description
System	Win32 Driver Model FAT32 Support for advanced MMX features Windows Scripting Host
Hardware Support	New Power Management Features Multiple Monitor support Universal Serial Bus (USB) Accelerated Graphics Port (AGP) Digital Video Disk (DVD) Infrared Monitor PCMCIA Enhancements
Networking	Multilink PPTP Remote Access Server IP Autoconfiguration NDS Client Support DCOM 32-bit DLC
Management and Troubleshooting	System Update Tune-up Wizard Disk Defragmenter Optimization System File Checker System Information Utility Dr. Watson Scheduled Tasks Improved Backup Automatic Skip Driver Agent Registry Checker Version Conflict Manager

As Microsoft developed and refined Windows 98, they concentrated on the following areas:

- *Management tools.* Windows 98 includes several new tools that make it easier to configure, manage, and troubleshoot than earlier versions of Windows.

- *Support for new hardware and hardware standards.* Microsoft invested considerable effort in keeping pace with new developments in computer hardware. You'll find support for DVD and USB, as well as the new FAT32 file system (which actually debuted in the latter-day Windows 95 era) designed to increase efficiency on newer, larger hard drives.

- *Tighter Internet integration.* Windows 98 brings Microsoft closer to its goal of fully integrating the Internet with the desktop. You can browse your own desktop and even use an Internet web page as your wallpaper.

- *Scripting.* Windows 98 supports Windows scripting, allowing users and site administrators to quickly and easily write custom scripts for specific tasks.

Although some have speculated that Microsoft is positioning Windows 98 for the home environment and Windows NT Workstation for corporate workstations, the fact is that Windows 98 includes some very useful and powerful features that seem to target the corporate user and the professional site administrator. You will learn about these features in later chapters of this book.

This chapter discusses some of the reasons for deploying Windows 98 and reviews some of the choices you'll face when configuring and customizing Windows 98 for your environment. If you're familiar with the Windows 95/98 environment and you're not inclined to study any deployment and desktop configuration details at this time, you might want to proceed to Chapter 2, "Installing Windows 98," and save these details for when you need them.

When You Should Use Windows 98

Windows 98 is in direct competition with its cousin Windows NT Workstation 4.0/5.0 in the market for desktop operating systems. Both systems are easily networkable, and both provide the familiar Explorer/Start Menu user interface. Both make use of recent innovations such as DCOM, PPTP, and DirectX.

Windows 98 has the following advantages over Windows NT Workstation:

- *Price.* As of this writing, Windows 98 is still considerably less expensive than Windows NT Workstation.

- *Plug and Play support.* Windows 98 has better support for Plug and Play, a feature that lets the system automatically detect and configure new devices. Adding new hardware to a Windows 98 machine therefore requires less time and expertise.

- *Legacy software support.* Both Windows 98 and Windows NT Workstation support MS-DOS, Win16, and Win32 applications, but NT's support for MS-DOS applications is limited. NT does not support DOS apps that directly access the hardware and may have more trouble with apps that use undocumented, obsolete features of DOS. Windows 98 supports a fuller range of DOS applications.

- *Hardware support.* Windows 98 supports an extremely large number of hardware devices on the market today. Support for Windows NT is growing, but Windows 98 still has the edge for hardware support.

- *Internet integration.* Windows 98 represents an attempt by Microsoft to seamlessly integrate Windows 98 with the Internet. It is almost as if the difference between browsing the Internet and browsing one's own computer has begun to disappear in Windows 98. Windows 98 also includes other Internet integration features. For instance, local applications and even the operating system itself can be automatically updated from the Internet. NT 5.0 includes some of these integration features, but the greater security of NT makes it doubtful that NT will ever achieve Windows 98's level of Internet integration.

Windows NT, in turn, offers the following advantages over Windows 98:

- *Better security.* Basic security is achievable through Windows 98, but Windows NT's security subsystem is more versatile and sophisticated.

- *Better stability.* Applications run in separate memory space, improving stability.

- *Tools.* Windows NT Workstation provides some management tools you won't find in Windows 98, such as Event Viewer and Performance Monitor.

- *Domain client functionality.* Windows NT Workstation provides a somewhat higher level of integration with domain-based security and management features.

Microsoft used to say that Windows 95 could run on slimmer hardware than Windows NT, but with Windows 98, Microsoft has upgraded the hardware requirements so that the minimums for Windows NT Workstation and Windows 98 look about the same. In reality, though, it is likely that Windows 98 will perform better on a low-end system.

There is no reason why NT Workstations and Windows 98 workstations can't coexist on the same network: File and print services are fully compatible, and both can receive user-level network logon security from a Windows NT Domain system or a Novell NetWare networking environment. Ultimately, the choice of a desktop operating system will depend on the requirements of your network.

> **Note** There are, of course, other competitors in the market for desktop operating systems, including the Macintosh OS (if you have Macintosh hardware) and the UNIX-like Linux operating system.

> The next few years will mark the arrival of the much-heralded thin-client operating systems, which should shake up the market a bit and provide more choices for corporate consumers.

If you're considering whether to upgrade from Windows 95 to Windows 98, the question you'll need to answer is whether the new features of Windows 98 (shown in Table 1.1) are a worthwhile addition to your environment. Some of the more significant benefits of upgrading to Windows 98 are as follows:

- *PPTP.* PPTP brings virtual private network technology to Windows 98. PPTP provides LAN-like privacy over Internet connections.

- *Power management.* Windows 98's power-management features conserve power. A computer can automatically go on standby when not in use, and it will spring back to full power when activated by a user. Power management also makes it more economical to leave a computer running between sessions, thus eliminating the inconvenience of the log reboot process.

- *Multiple screen support.* Windows 98 lets you use multiple monitors with one PC.

- *FAT32.* The FAT32 file system allows larger partitions and offers better performance on large partitions. (FAT16 partitions were limited to 2GB.) FAT32 debuted with Windows 95 OSR 2, so it may be present on some Windows 95 systems.

- *New hardware.* Windows 98 provides support for DVD and Universal Serial Bus (USB) devices.

- *Management tools.* Windows 98 comes with a System Configuration utility, System file Checker, Microsoft System Information Manager, Version Conflict Manager, and more.

If you're running Windows 3.1 on a system that can support Windows 98 and you're considering an upgrade to Windows 98, just do it. Windows 98 represents years of work from hundreds of programmers, improving and perfecting Windows technology; it is far superior to Windows 3.1.

> **Note** For a Typical Windows 98 installation, you'll need the following:
>
> Processor—Intel 486DX 66MHz or better (or equivalent), Pentium recommended
>
> RAM—16MB (minimum), 24MB recommended
>
> 200MB free disk space (45MB of which is temporary disk space required by the Setup program)
>
> See Chapter 2 for more information about Windows 98 system requirements.

The Windows 98 Network Environment

As you develop a plan for deploying Windows 98, you'll need to make some choices about the type of system you want and the way you want users to interact with it. In essence, this entire book is about those choices. But it helps to have those choices in mind before you start the installation.

The first decision you'll need to make is whether your Windows 98 system will be part of a network. Windows 98 is designed to operate in any one of the following three scenarios:

- *No network.* Windows 98 is fully functional as a standalone operating system.
- *Peer-to-peer network.* In a peer-to-peer network, all computers are more or less equal. All can share files and printers, and each is responsible for its own security (see Figure 1.1).
- *Server-based network.* Windows 98 can act as a client in a server-based networking system, such as a Novell NetWare network or a Windows NT domain (see Figure 1.2).

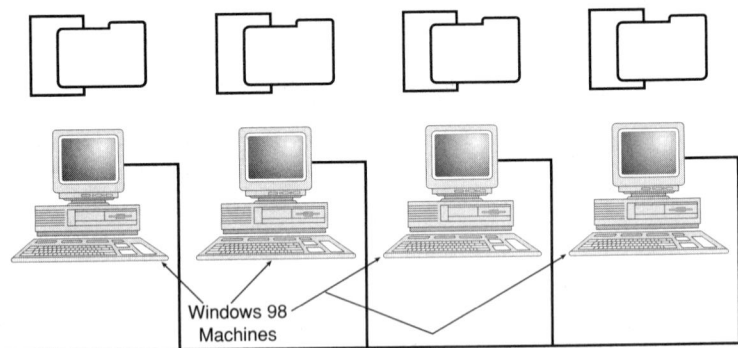

Figure 1.1
In a peer-to-peer network, all computers are equal: Each is a server and a client.

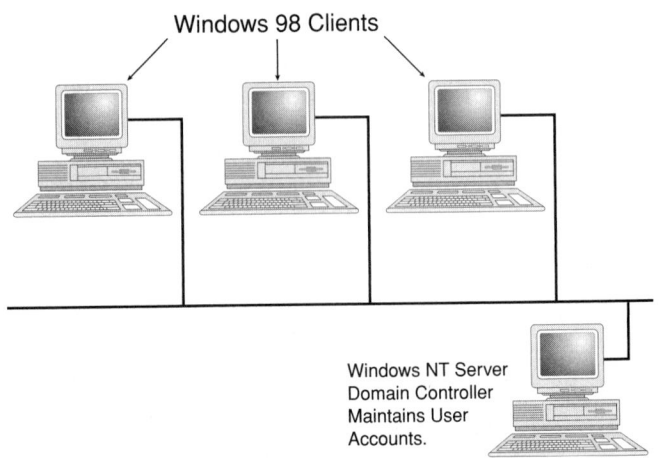

Figure 1.2
A Windows NT domain is a server-based networking system.

Chapter 1: Deploying Windows 98

The recent rise of the Internet has somewhat complicated these network archetypes. A computer can serve as a peer or a client in a local network (or it can be a standalone, for that matter) and also connect to the big network (the Internet) through a cable or dial-up connection. The Internet is a vast treasure of information, but it also poses dangers that, in many cases, must be met with prudent security.

A standalone system is all that an individual user really needs, and there is no reason to consider a network if you only have and only need one computer. (However, if you are connected to the Internet, you must remember that you are in fact on a network and, depending on your type of Internet connection, you may wish to apply some basic security measures. See Chapter 30, "Internet Security," for more information about Internet security.)

If you work with a large network that already exists, there is no need to reinvent your network in order to employ Windows 98. Windows 98 can serve all the same client functions Windows 95 served; in fact, Windows 98 has some enhanced network client features, most notably its support for NetWare Directory Services (NDS). If you're starting from scratch and purchasing several computers, however, you'll need to decide whether or how you'd like to network your Windows 98 machines.

Windows 98 is amazingly easy to network. If you have 2 to 10 computers on your site, you'll find that networking them in a peer-to-peer configuration requires very little effort or expertise. You will need some basic hardware: network adapter cards for each PC ($50–$150 each) and network cabling and connectors. A peer-to-peer network offers the advantages of a network, such a file and printer sharing, with minimal complexity and confusion. The computers basically act independently unless the user needs to access a network resource, in which case the user can achieve that access through a convenient extension of the local user interface. Each computer in a peer-to-peer network acts (or can act) as both a server and a client. A peer to peer network can include a dedicated *file server* (that is, a computer that serves the role of providing file resources for other computers). What distinguishes a peer-to-peer network from a server-based network is that the security systems for the computers on a peer-to-peer network all act independently—each computer is responsible for the security of its own resources. See Chapter 22, "Peer-to-Peer Networking," for more information about Windows 98 peer-to-peer networks.

Maintaining password synchronization and multiple password lists for the multiple computers in a peer-to-peer configuration is impossible on large networks and is often difficult even on small networks. A server-based system such as a Windows NT domain provides centralized, user-level security for network resources. This adds some complexity to the configuration, but it makes for simpler, more uniform, more effective security. The user's logon is authenticated by a Windows NT Server domain controller, and the user's access to network resources is thereafter controlled by user and group permissions applied to the user's account.

The server-based model lends itself to a scenario in which files are stored on a central, continuously operating server system. A user can then log on from anywhere on the network and access the files. If the user's desktop PC goes down, a different PC can provide access to the files. The user can even log on from a remote location over a dial-up connection to reach the centrally stored and managed files. Windows 98's User Profile feature (see Chapter 8, "User Profiles") allows the user's personal desktop environment (shortcuts, wallpaper, and other personal settings) to follow the user to other computers on the domain. Centralized storage of the files also simplifies the task of providing backups and fault tolerance for file resources. In the case of a Windows NT domain, the NT domain controller that authenticates logons does not have to be the central file storage system; however, on small networks, it often is. In a simple Windows NT Server domain like the one shown in Figure 1.2, the Windows NT Server machine could provide file service for the Windows 98 clients and also provide dial-up access using NT's RAS service for Windows 98 clients dialing in from remote locations.

A Windows NT Server domain is one of many server-based network systems that Windows 98 supports. Windows 98 can also act as a client on Novell NetWare networks or UNIX networks (among others).

> **Note** A peer-to-peer network is conceptually simple—it is not much more complicated than individual users working on standalone systems.
>
> A Windows NT domain or NetWare server-based network offers better and more uniform security but requires more expertise to manage. A well-managed system can offer a simpler and more versatile work environment for users.

Deciding on Network Components

Your decisions about a network configuration will precipitate further decisions about the network components you'll want to include with Windows 98. See Chapters 21 through 26 (in Part IV, "Networking Windows 98") for a full discussion of networking components in Windows 98. You do not have to face all the networking issues prior to installation unless you want to. Windows 98 Setup will migrate networking components from a preexisting Windows 95 or Windows 3.1 system, or, if you are installing on a new system or a system that wasn't previously networked, Setup will provide a default network configuration if it detects networking hardware.

If you plan to install Windows 98 on multiple systems, you might want to create an installation script that automatically configures networking components. See Chapter 2 for more information about Windows 98 installation scripts.

To summarize networking component choices, the following lists Windows 98 built-in network client systems:

- Banyan DOS/Windows 3.1 client
- FTP Software NFS client (InterDrive 95)

- Client for Microsoft Networks
- Client for NetWare Networks
- Microsoft Family Logon
- Novell NetWare Workstation Shell 3.X (NETX)
- Novell NetWare Workstation Shell 4.0 and above

You can also install a different client software system.

If your Windows 98 machine is to be part of a Windows 98 domain, you'll want to use Client for Microsoft Networks. If your machine will be part of a NetWare network, you'll use Client for NetWare networks, one of the Workstation shells, or equivalent client software supplied with your NetWare server system.

You'll also need to choose one or more networking protocols for your network. Your choice will most likely be one of the following:

- *NetBEUI.* A non-routable network protocol used on small Microsoft networks.
- *IPX/SPX-compatible protocol.* A protocol system for NetWare networks.
- *TCP/IP.* A routable protocol system that is starting to emerge as the universal networking protocol. The Internet uses TCP/IP, and most large non-NetWare networks use TCP/IP.

After you settle on a protocol system, you'll need to decide on additional networking features. For instance, an IPX/SPX computer needs a network number. A TCP/IP computer needs an IP address and a subnet mask. All of these protocols are discussed in detail later in the book.

Planning the Windows 98 User Environment

Windows 98 offers choices that enable you to build a custom environment for the users on your network; you can create the environment that best suits the needs of your organization. The Windows 98 features help you shape the user environment in the following ways:

- You can create User Profiles for the users on your system. A *User Profile* is a bundle of configuration settings that let the user develop a personal desktop configuration. You can make those settings specific to a single computer (local User Profile) or you can set up a roaming User Profile that will follow the user to other workstations on the network. See Chapter 8, "User Profiles," for more information about Windows 98 User Profiles.

- You can create Hardware Profiles that will enable you to efficiently switch between two or more hardware operating environments (for instance, a portable PC can boot to either a docked or an undocked state). See Chapter 9, "Hardware Profiles," for more information about Hardware Profiles in Windows 98.

- You can create System Policies that define the user desktop and restrict user activities. *System Policies* are powerful tools for controlling the user environment. A System Policy can restrict the user's access to configuration tools or provide the user with a specially designed desktop. You can hide Start menu items, remove the Run command, or disable the MS-DOS prompt by using System Policies. See Chapter 7, "System Policies," for more information about System Policies in Windows 98. See Chapter 4, "Windows 98 and Total Cost of Ownership," for a discussion of how you can use System Policies to create a limited user interface in the spirit of Microsoft's Zero Administration Kit.

- You can restrict access through a network logon and shape the user environment using logon scripts. You can use logon security with either peer-to-peer networks, domain-based networks, or NetWare networks. See Chapter 21, "Understanding Windows 98 Networking," for more information about Microsoft network logons.

- You can define which directories you'd like to share on the network and restrict access to those directories using passwords. You can specify whether the password will provide read-only access or full access. See Chapter 21 for more information about sharing files on Microsoft networks.

- Windows 98 lets you choose which of its components you'll use for your configuration. You can customize your Windows 98 configuration by choosing whether to include dozens of Optional Components. Windows 98 Optional Components are discussed later in this chapter.

- You can customize desktop items such as the Start menu and the Taskbar, and place shortcuts to commonly used documents or applications directly on the desktop so that they're never more than a mouse-click away. You can configure Windows 98 to start certain applications automatically by placing the applications in the Startup folder. Desktop customization has become even more exotic under Windows 98. You can use a web page (with active links) as your wallpaper or automatically download a screen saver with active content, such as a display of current stock market information. You'll learn more about desktop customization later in this chapter.

- *Windows Scripting Host*, a new feature included with Windows 98, is quite possibly the most powerful tool yet for customizing the Windows environment. You can write custom scripts that access applications, invoke Windows interface features, and automate complex tasks. See Chapter 33, "Windows Scripting with Windows 98 Scripting Host," for more information about the powerful Windows Scripting Host.

Choosing Components

During one heated salvo in the browser wars of early 1998, a Microsoft official stated that Internet Explorer could not be removed from the Windows 98 desktop because only Microsoft can define what is part of Windows 98. The fact is, however, that the user has the freedom to pick and choose from dozens of Windows components when defining a system configuration.

Windows 98 has four Setup options, each with a predefined collection of optional components. When you install Windows 98, Setup asks you to choose one of the Setup options in the following list. The components provided with each of the Setup options are outlined in Table 1.2. The Custom option allows you to choose any components in addition to the defaults.

- *Typical.* A general purpose, typical desktop configuration
- *Compact.* For PCs with a shortage of disk space—offers comparatively fewer components
- *Portable.* Components commonly required for a portable PC
- *Custom.* Lets you define your own configuration by which components you'd like to include

If you upgrade from Windows 95, Setup will retain the Setup option (and the active component list) from the previous installation. You won't be asked to specify a Setup option.

Most home users simply choose the Setup options that suit their configuration and install additional components later if necessary through the Add/Remove Programs Control Panel. Many corporate networks follow this philosophy as well, although in a business setting, there are often advantages in keeping the configuration as simple as possible to narrow the range of support services (see Chapter 4).

If you're using an installation script (see Chapter 2), you can specify a Setup option and optional components within the script.

Table 1.2
Windows 98 Optional Components for Various Setup options;
Y=Yes (included) N=No (not included)

Group	Component	Typical	Portable	Compact	Default	Custom
Accessibility	Accessibility Options	N	N	N	N	
	Enhanced Accessibility	N	N	N	N	
Accessories	Briefcase	N	Y	N	N	
	Calculator	Y	N	N	Y	
	Desktop Wallpaper	N	N	N	N	

continues

Table 1.2, Continued
Windows 98 Optional Components for Various Setup options;
Y=Yes (included) N=No (not included)

Group	Component	Typical	Portable	Compact	Default	Custom
	Document Templates	Y	N	N	Y	
	Games	N	N	N	N	
	Imaging	Y	N	N	Y	
	Mouse Pointers	N	N	N	N	
	Paint	Y	N	N	Y	
	QuickView	N	N	N	N	
	Screen Savers	Y	N	N	Y	
	Windows Scripting Host	Y	Y	N	Y	
	WordPad	Y	Y	N	Y	
Communications	Dial-Up Networking	Y	Y	Y	Y	
	Dial-Up Server	N	N	N	N	
	Direct Cable Connection	N	Y	N	N	
	HyperTerminal	N	Y	N	N	
	Infrared	N	N	N	N	
	Microsoft Chat	N	N	N	N	
	Microsoft NetMeeting	Y	N	N	Y	
	Phone Dialer	Y	Y	N	Y	
	Virtual Private Networking	N	Y	N	N	
Desktop Themes		N	N	N	N	
Internet Tools	FrontPage Express	Y	Y	N	Y	
	VRML 2.0 Viewer	Y	Y	N	Y	
	Microsoft Wallet	N	N	N	N	
	Personal Web Server	Y	Y	N	Y	
	Web Publishing Wizard	N	N	N	N	
	Web-based Enterprise Management	N	N	N	N	
Outlook Express		Y	Y	N	Y	
Multi-language Support	Baltic	N	N	N	N	
	Central European	N	N	N	N	
	Cyrillic	N	N	N	N	
	Greek	N	N	N	N	
	Turkish	N	N	N	N	

Group	Component	Typical	Portable	Compact	Default Custom
Multimedia	Audio Compression	Y	Y	N	Y
	CD Player	Y	Y	Y	Y
	DVD Player	N	N	N	N
	Macromedia Shockwave Director	Y	N	N	Y
	Macromedia Shockwave Flash	Y	N	N	Y
	Media Player	Y	Y	N	Y
	Microsoft NetShow Player	N	N	N	N
	Multimedia Sound Schemes	N	N	N	N
	Sample Sounds	N	N	N	N
	Sound Recorder	Y	Y	N	Y
	Volume Control	Y	Y	N	Y
Online Services	AOL	Y	Y	Y	Y
	AT&T WorldNet Service	Y	Y	Y	Y
	CompuServe	Y	Y	Y	Y
	Prodigy Internet	Y	Y	Y	Y
	The Microsoft Network	Y	Y	Y	Y
System Tools	Backup	N	N	N	N
	Character Map	N	N	N	N
	Clipboard Viewer	N	N	N	N
	Disk Compression Tools	N	Y	N	N
	Drive Converter (FAT32)	Y	Y	N	Y
	Group Policies	N	N	N	N
	Net Watcher	N	N	N	N
	System Monitor	N	N	N	N
	System Resource Meter	N	N	N	N
TV Viewer	Broadcast Data Services	N	N	N	N
	TV Viewer (43.9 MB)	N	N	N	N

Defining the Desktop

The Windows 98 desktop will look familiar to anyone accustomed to the Windows 95 or Windows NT 4.0 desktop, but the Windows 98 desktop is even more customizable than its already-customizable precursors. The basic desktop appears in Figure 1.3. Some of Windows 98's desktop features are as follows:

- Start menu
- Explorer
- Taskbar
- My Computer
- Network Neighborhood
- Briefcase
- Shortcuts
- Recycling Bin

The following sections briefly describe these features and provide tips on how you can customize your desktop to increase the efficiency of your workstation.

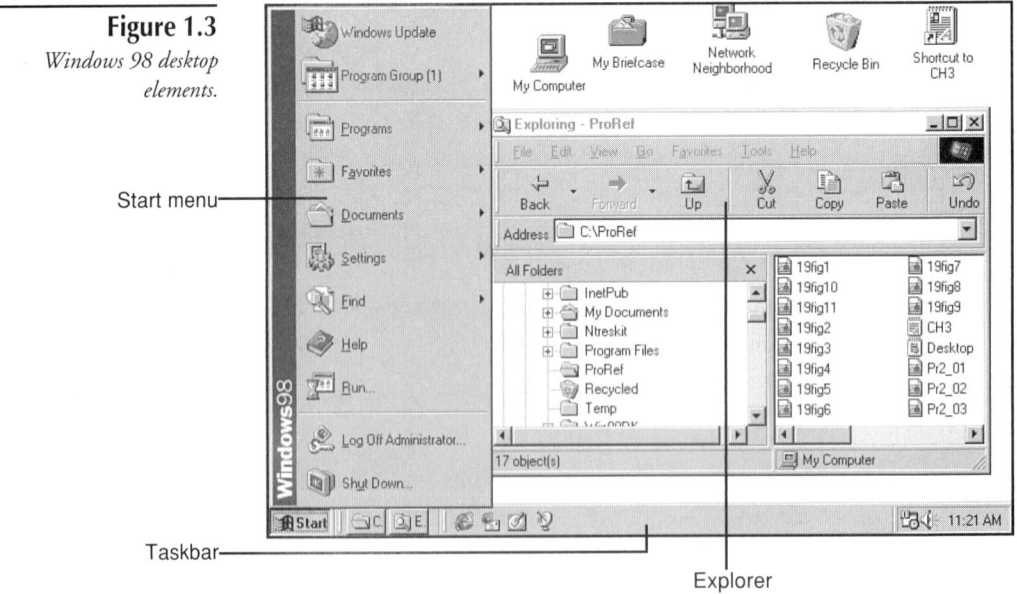

Figure 1.3
Windows 98 desktop elements.

Start Menu

The Start menu (refer to Figure 1.3) is the place to "Start" for almost anything in Windows 98. The first-level options, many of which are self-explanatory, appear in Figure 1.3. Brief descriptions of the first-level Start Menu options are given in Table 1.3.

Table 1.3
First-level Start Menu Options

Option	Description
Windows Update	Launches the Windows Update Wizard, which updates Windows 98 over the Internet.
Programs	A menu of programs and program groups on your system.
Favorites	Favorite Internet links from the Internet Explorer Favorites list. Windows 98 automatically attempts to connect to a link if you click on it.
Documents	Recently accessed text and document files on your system. By using this feature, you can open a file directly without starting the application or hunting for the file in Explorer or My Computer.
Settings	A menu of configuration components. You can move directly to Control Panel (see Chapter 6, "Control Panel"), the Printers folder (see Chapter 13, "Printing"), the Taskbar and Start Menu dialog box (discussed later in this chapter), the Folder Options dialog box (which lets you define file type associations and Explorer View properties), and Active Desktop options (discussed later in this chapter).
Find	You can locate files, folders, or computers on your network by using Explorer's Find option. You can invoke an Internet search by using Internet Explorer, or you can search for a person by using the Outlook Express Address book's Find People dialog box.
Help	Opens Windows 98 Help. (Tip: If you can't find what you're looking for in Help, try the Getting Started book, which appears in the list of Help topics. The Getting Started book is an online version of a Windows 98 manual available through Microsoft).
Run	Lets you enter and execute a command line. You can run an application, open a file, or access an Internet link.
Log Off *user_name*	Logs off the current user without shutting down Windows.
Shut Down	Invokes the Shut Down Windows dialog box, which shuts down your system or lets you enter MS-DOS mode (see Chapter 11, "Windows 98 Architecture and Application Support"). Microsoft strongly recommends that you perform an orderly shutdown by using the Shut Down option rather than just switching your computer off. Windows 98 performs several cleanup operations as it shuts down, and you ignore these operations at your peril.

The Start Menu Programs options are generated from a Start Menu folder in the Windows directory. The Start Menu folder contains a Programs subfolder, which contains additional subfolders defining the various program groups that appear in the Programs menu. The program entries are all shortcuts to program items elsewhere on your system. If you upgraded from Windows 3.1, the program groups and program items correspond to the program groups in items in Windows 3.1 Program Manager. You can change the Programs folder directly by using standard Explorer options (cutting, deleting, pasting, copying, adding shortcuts, and so on) and those changes will be reflected in the Start menu; however, it is easier to change the Start menu by using the Taskbar Properties dialog box, discussed in the numbered steps that follow.

If User Profiles are enabled on your system, the Favorites and Documents Start menu entries come (respectively) from the Favorites and Recent subfolders of the User Profile directory.

To customize the Start menu, follow these steps:

1. Right-click on an empty area of the Taskbar and choose Properties.

2. Click on the Start Menu Programs tab.

3. In the Start Menu Programs tab (see Figure 1.4), click on the Add button to add a new program or command line to the Start menu. Enter a command line or browse for a file or program item. Windows 98 then enables you to select where in the Start menu you want the new item to appear. If you click on the New Folder button, Windows 98 creates a new first-level option for the new item.

Figure 1.4
The Start Menu Programs tab.

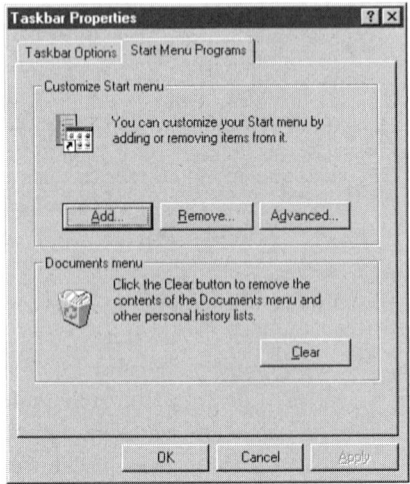

Click on the Remove button in the Start Menu Programs tab to remove a Start Menu item.

The Advanced button invokes the Explorer application, so that you can customize to the Start Menu folders as you would through Explorer.

The Clear button lets you delete user-specific items from the Start Menu's Documents and Favorites options.

Explorer

The Explorer application (EXPLORER.EXE in the Windows directory) is the all-purpose file and folder manipulation window in Windows 98. For those familiar with Windows 95, Explorer requires no introduction. For those familiar with Windows 3.1, Explorer is your "File Manager."

On some OEM versions of Windows 98, Explorer may appear as a desktop icon. If not, you can invoke Explorer by right-clicking on the Start menu and choosing Explore. If Explorer does not appear on your desktop but you want it to, you can create a desktop shortcut to the Explorer (see "Shortcuts," later in this chapter).

Explorer displays the directory structure of all system drives in a hierarchical format. You can select an item and cut, paste, or copy it by using the options in the Edit menu or the Toolbar. Or, you can simply drag a file or folder to another location.

> **Note** If you drag a file or folder to another location on the same drive, Explorer will *move* the file (removing it from its original location). If you drag a file or folder to a location on a different drive, Explorer will *copy* the file (retaining it at its original location).
>
> If you drag an executable file to another location, such as the desktop, Explorer will place a shortcut at the new location instead of moving or copying the executable file.

Each item in Explorer has a Properties dialog box. A Properties dialog box is a source of information and configuration options for the item. The tabs and entries of the Properties dialog box depend on what the item is (whether it is a drive, folder, application, or shortcut); specific properties options are discussed later in this book. You can use the Properties dialog box to share a folder, set file attributes (such as read-only, system, hidden, or archive), or check for the file size or MS-DOS name. If you need more information on a file, check the Properties dialog box. You can invoke the Properties dialog box in any of the following ways:

- Right-click on an item and choose Properties.

- Select an item and click on Properties in the Explorer toolbar.
- Select an item and choose Properties from the File menu.

The Context menu (invoked with a right-click) is a fast track to several useful Explorer options, such as Properties, Sharing, Find, Cut, Copy, Delete, and Create Shortcut.

The best way to learn about Explorer is to explore, as most readers of this book probably already have. A few features worth noting are as follows:

- *Find.* The Find command in the Tools menu lets you search for a file, folder, or computer on your network. Windows 98 also adds options for a web search (through Internet Explorer) or a search for Address Book entries in the Outlook Express Address book. The Find Files or Folders command is very useful for locating resources on your PC. The Find function supports wild card searches. You can search for a filename or a text string. You can search by date or limit the search to a certain file size or file type. The Find Computer option is useful for finding computers that are on your network but, for whatever reason, do not appear in the Network Neighborhood browse list.

- *Map Network Drive.* The Map Network Drive command in the Tools menu lets you associate a drive letter with a shared directory on another computer. The drive letter will then provide seamless access to the network share as if it were another drive on the local system. (See Chapter 21, "Understanding Windows 98 Networking," for more information about drive-letter mapping.)

- *Folder Options.* The Folder Options command in the View menu lets you define Explorer display settings. In the View tab, you can select what types of file and folder entries will appear and what information will accompany those entries. The File Types tab (see Figure 1.5) lets you create and manage file associations. A file association maps a filename extension (such as .doc) to a particular application (such as Word). Windows 98 uses file associations to determine what application to use to open a file when you double-click on it. A large number of file associations are preconfigured into Windows 98. You can add more associations or edit or remove an association using the Folder Options File Types tab.

A Network Neighborhood icon appears near the bottom of the Explorer directory tree. Double-click on this icon for a view of computers currently sharing folders and files on the network. Shares appear below the computer that shares them. Double-click on a share to reveal folders and files within that share. The Explorer interface thus provides access not only to local resources but also to shared resources on the network.

Taskbar

Taskbar, like Explorer, requires no introduction for Windows 95 users. The intent of the Windows 95 taskbar was to display easily clickable labels for any minimized tasks. You could click on the task and immediately bring the task to the foreground. Windows 98's taskbar serves this function, but also provides some additional features. For instance, the Windows 98 taskbar can include icons that launch shortcuts to commonly used files, folders, or applications.

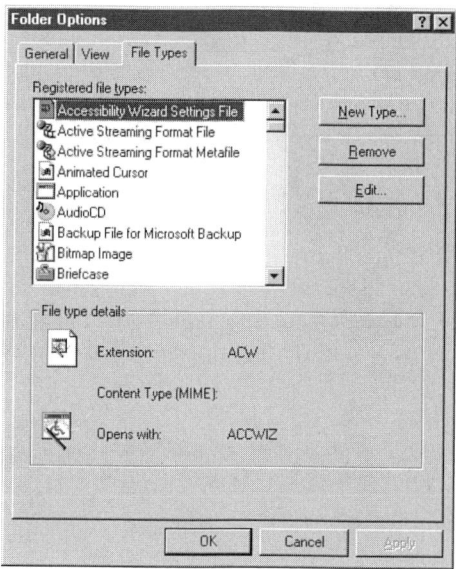

Figure 1.5
The Folder Options File Types tab.

The Windows 98 taskbar, in addition to displaying minimized applications, can include built-in toolbars that provide quick access to various functions. To add or remove a taskbar toolbar, right-click on an empty portion of the taskbar and choose Toolbars. You can check or uncheck a toolbar from the toolbar list, or you can add a new toolbar. The built-in toolbar options are as follows:

- *Address.* The Address toolbar lets you enter an URL directly on the taskbar. Window 98 attempts to locate an offline copy of the specified resource or launches a browser to find an online copy.

- *Links.* The Links toolbar displays Internet links from the Windows Favorites folder. The Links list is a list of Internet links in Internet Explorer's Favorites menu.

- *Desktop.* The Desktop toolbar displays the icons presently available on the desktop in the taskbar. This allows you to avoid minimizing a foreground application to hunt for a desktop shortcut.

- *Quick Launch.* The Quick Launch toolbar provides quick access to commonly used applications. By default, the Quick Launch toolbar appears just to the right of the Start menu. You can add an item to the Quick Launch toolbar simply by dragging the item to the toolbar. To remove an item from the toolbar, right-click on the item and choose Delete.

28   Part I: Introducing Windows 98

You can also create a new toolbar by using the Toolbars command of the Taskbar context menu.

You will quickly discover that turning on all (or even some) of the taskbar toolbars will make your taskbar so crowded that the simplicity of the taskbar concept is completely lost. If all the bars and icons won't fit on the taskbar, a scroll arrow appears to reveal additional choices. Your taskbar configuration will depend on your needs, but one prudent option would be to configure an appropriate Quick Launch toolbar and leave the other toolbars turned off. You can reach the Links or enter an URL from the Start menu, and you can already access desktop icons from the desktop.

The Taskbar Properties dialog box (see Figure 1.6) offers a few additional taskbar configuration options. To invoke the Taskbar Properties dialog box, right-click on an empty portion of the taskbar and choose Properties. The *Autohide* function makes the taskbar disappear when a foreground application is open until you move the cursor in the vicinity of the taskbar area, at which time the taskbar will reappear.

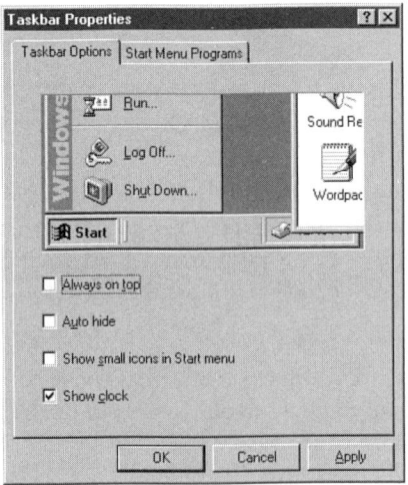

Figure 1.6
The Taskbar Properties dialog box.

> **Note** By default, the taskbar appears at the bottom of the screen. To move the taskbar to the top or the left or right edge of the screen, just drag the taskbar to the new location.

My Computer

The My Computer icon offers a view of local resources. You can browse a drive or access Control Panel, the Printers folder, the Dial-Up Networking folder, or the Scheduled task application (see Figure 1.7).

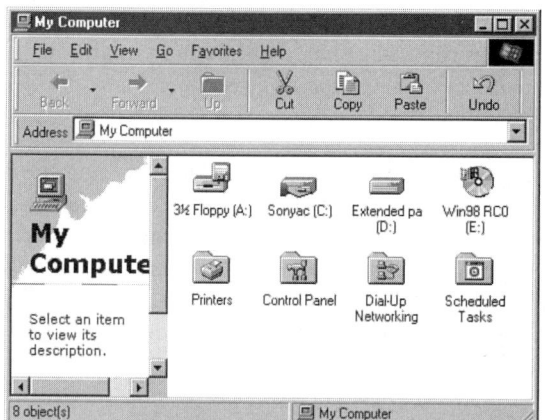

Figure 1.7
Inside My Computer.

Right-click on the My Computer icon and choose Properties to access the System Control Panel (see Chapter 6, "Control Panel").

Network Neighborhood

Network Neighborhood offers a view of network resources—it's kind of like My Computer for the network. You can browse through a list of network PCs, and access any shares located on each of the PCs. See Chapter 21 for more information about Network Neighborhood.

As mentioned earlier in this chapter, Network Neighborhood also appears as an icon in Explorer.

Right-click on the Network Neighborhood icon and choose Properties to access the Network Control Panel (see Chapter 6).

Briefcase

Briefcase is a useful version-control application commonly used with portable PCs. See Chapter 19, "Windows 98 for Portables," for more information about the Briefcase application.

Shortcuts

Shortcuts are another feature inherited from the Windows 95 interface. A *shortcut* is an object that provides a link to another object.

You can move shortcuts to your desktop to link automatically to a given application, or place shortcuts anywhere else they might be useful, such as in the Start Menu Programs folder or in an application folder.

To create a shortcut, right-click on an object and choose Create Shortcut. You can then drag, cut, copy, paste, or delete the shortcut as you wish. Alternatively, you can right-drag an object (drag it with the right mouse button down) to a new location, and Windows 98 will ask if you want to create a shortcut.

Right-clicking on a shortcut (and choosing Properties) reveals the Shortcut Document Properties dialog box (see Figure 1.8). The Shortcut Document Properties dialog box lists some basic information about the shortcut, such as the name of the target (the object to which the shortcut provides access). Click the Find Target button in the Shortcut tab to go directly to the target in My Computer. (The Find Target button is useful because, often, when users access the Properties dialog box of the shortcut they're really looking for the Properties dialog box of the target.)

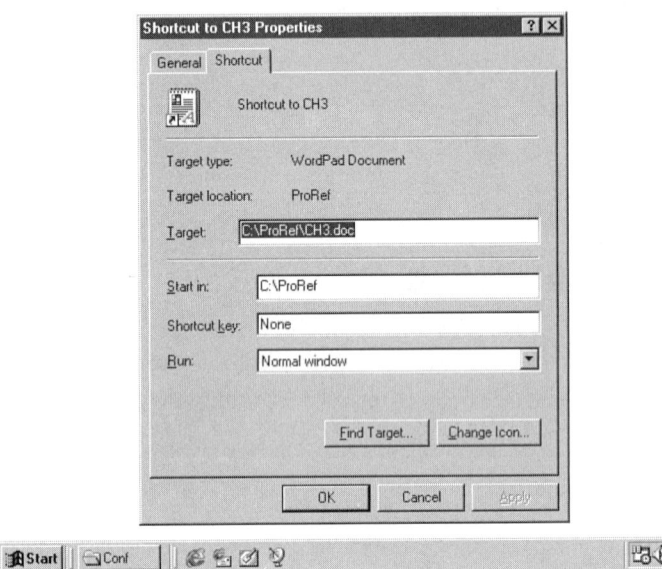

Figure 1.8
The Shortcut Document Properties dialog box.

If you are moving so fast that you don't even have time to look for a shortcut and click on it, you can associate the shortcut with a keyboard combination. Typing the keyboard combination will then automatically invoke the shortcut. The keyboard shortcut must begin with the Ctrl+Alt characters. To define a shortcut key, click on the Shortcut Key box in the Shortcut tab of the Shortcut Properties dialog box (refer to Figure 1.8) and type a key. If you type 3, the entry will appear as Ctrl+Alt+3.

If the object to which a shortcut points moves, Windows 98 attempts to automatically update the link to the shortcut target; however, it isn't always successful. If the shortcut object moves and the link isn't updated, the shortcut can become *orphaned*—it won't point to anything. If a shortcut suddenly becomes inoperable, check the Target entry in the Shortcuts tab and update the link if necessary.

Chapter 1: Deploying Windows 98

The General tab (see Figure 1.9) lists additional information about the shortcut and lets you set file attributes. Note that the shortcut object has its own MS-DOS name with an .lnk extension.

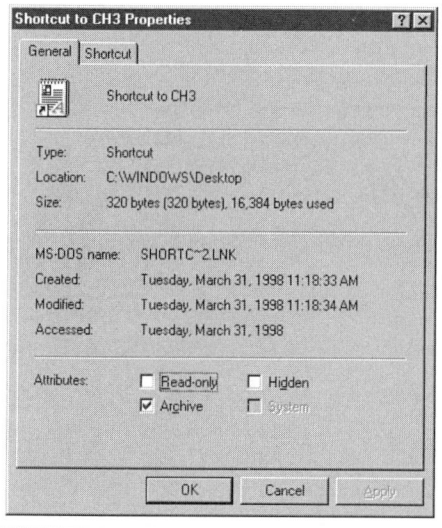

Figure 1.9
The Shortcut Properties General tab.

Recycling Bin

Recycling Bin is another feature from Windows 95 that requires little introduction. The idea behind Recycling Bin is that, when you delete a file, the file disappears to a retrievable location instead of disappearing from your disk completely. When you delete a file, you don't really delete it—you move it to the Recycling Bin.

The Recycling Bin has its own Properties dialog box with its own configurable features. Right-click on Recycling Bin and choose Properties to configure Recycling Bin.

The Recycle Bin Properties Global tab (see Figure 1.10) lets you define a maximum size for the Recycling Bin. The option buttons at the top of the dialog box let you specify whether the dialog boxes will be configured independently, or whether the global settings will apply to all drives. The default maximum size is 10% of the total drive space. Uncheck the box labeled Display Delete Confirmation Dialog Box if you don't want Windows 98 to issue a warning before deleting.

If you select the Configure Drives Independently option button (refer to Figure 1.10), you can set a maximum Recycling Bin size for each drive on your system. The Drive Configuration tabs offer another option: You can elect to bypass the Recycling Bin and remove files immediately when they are deleted.

Figure 1.10
The Recycle Bin Properties Global tab.

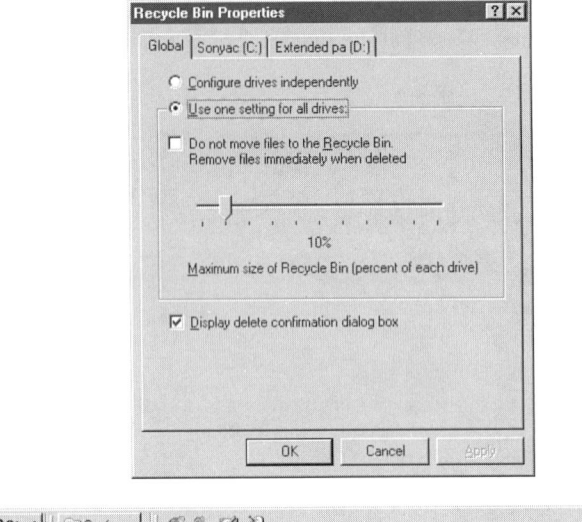

Launching Programs at Startup

You can configure Windows 98 to start an application automatically when you log on. To start an application automatically, place a shortcut to that application in the StartUp subfolder of the Start Menu\Programs folder. If your system is configured for user profiles (see Chapter 8), and if the active user profile is configured to include the Start Menu (see the discussion of the Users Control Panel in Chapter 6), the Start Menu\Programs\StartUp directory will be in the user's Profile directory (Windows\Profiles\username). Otherwise, Windows 98 will check the default Windows\Start Menu\Programs\StartUp directory for startup information.

Active Desktop

Active is the word for Windows 98 as Microsoft attempts to build a bridge from the DOS kingdom to the world of web-based technologies. Windows 98's Active Desktop consists of both new and newly-named features designed to enhance the user's desktop experience.

Some Active Desktop features are not really recent developments—file type associations are now considered an Active Desktop item. Other features are new enough but hardly seem profound—for example, you can add a background image to your document folders. But behind it all, Microsoft's attempt to integrate HTML with the desktop could yield some interesting results if users take an interest in it.

Windows 98's Active Desktop consists of two layers. A transparent foreground layer contains traditional Windows shortcuts and icons. A background HTML layer brings the power of active HTML to your desktop. A few of the Active Desktop's tricks are as follows:

Chapter 1: Deploying Windows 98

- You can display a Web page as wallpaper, complete with links to other HTML-based documents.

- You can add special Active Desktop items to your display—updatable floating components such as a stock market ticker or a clock. Microsoft provides an online library of Active Desktop items called the Active Desktop Gallery (described later in this chapter).

- You can customize folders to appear more like web pages.

Potentially, the single most significant aspect of the Active Desktop may be its relationship to another of Microsoft's initiatives and another important feature of Windows 98: Active Channels. You'll learn more about Active Channels in the next section.

To activate Web-based desktop features, follow these steps:

1. Right-click on an empty part of the desktop and click on Properties.
2. Select the Web tab. Check View my Active Desktop as a Web Page.

To add HTML wallpaper to your desktop, follow these steps:

1. Right-click on an empty part of the desktop and click on Properties.
2. Select the Web tab. Check View my Active Desktop as a Web Page.
3. Select the Background tab. Click on Browse. Browse for an HTML page you'd like to use as wallpaper.

An Active Desktop item can be a graphics file, an HTML document, a ready-made item from the Microsoft Active Desktop Gallery, or an Active Channel (see the next section).

To add an Active Desktop item, follow these steps:

1. Right-click on an empty part of the desktop and click on Properties.
2. Select the Web tab. Check View my Active Desktop as a Web Page.
3. Click on New.
4. Windows 98 asks if you'd like to choose an item from the Microsoft Active Desktop Gallery. Click on Yes to choose an item. Windows 98 automatically connects to the Active Desktop Gallery Web site. If you want to choose a graphics file, an HTML file, or an Active Channel, click No, then enter the path to the item.

If you are receiving the Active Desktop item through an Active Channel, you can configure how and when you'll receive updates for the item. The content will be updated automatically through an Active Channel subscription.

To configure the subscription for an Active Channel desktop item, follow these steps:

1. Right-click on an empty part of the desktop and choose Properties.

2. Select the Web tab. Choose the Active Desktop item for which you'd like to configure a subscription and click on Properties.

3. Configure subscription options.

To customize the appearance of a folder, follow these steps:

1. Select a folder in Explorer or My Computer.

2. From the View menu, choose Customize this Folder.

3. In the Customize this Folder Wizard, choose whether you'd like to create an HTML document, add a background picture, or cancel the current customization.

Active Channels

The Active Channel feature is an extension of the automation and update themes that are central to Windows 98. An *Active Channel* is a channel into the computer from an Internet or intranet web server. When you open an Active Channel, you create a pathway through which the server can automatically deliver updated HTML content to the Windows 98 machine. An example of this might be an Active Desktop item such as Microsoft's Stock Ticker (described earlier in this chapter). You can place the stock ticker on your desktop and configure the Active Channel subscription (see the preceding section) to automatically update the stock market information periodically. A corporate intranet can use Active Channels to distribute work schedules, calendars, sales figures, and dynamic information to Windows 98 workstations.

To subscribe to an Active Channel, follow these steps:

1. Browse the Active Channel site. (Microsoft recommends using Internet Explorer.)

2. At the Active Channel web site, click on the button labeled Add to Channels.

3. Provide the necessary subscription information in the Subscribe Channel dialog box.

Active Channel web sites appear in the channel bar (see Figure 1.11). During Setup, you can choose a predefined set of Internet channels for the channel bar based on your home country (see Chapter 2). When you subscribe to a new Active Channel, the channel appears in the channel bar. To delete a site from the channel bar, right-click on the site and choose Delete.

Chapter 1: Deploying Windows 98   **35**

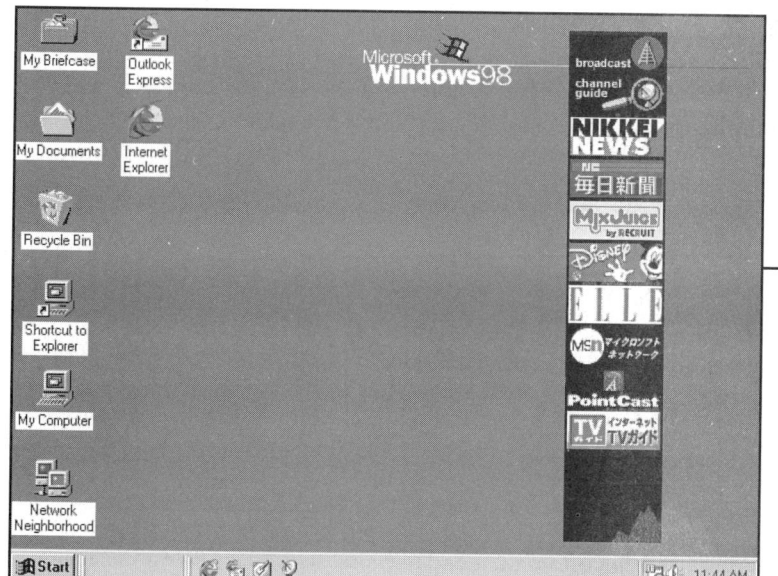

Figure 1.11
The Windows 98 channel bar.

Preparing for Installation

A large-scale deployment of a new desktop operating system is a major event for most organizations. The deployment and configuration options discussed in this chapter (and in later chapters) will help you decide whether, how, and when you'll upgrade to Windows 98. But part of the planning process is planning the installation itself.

A large-scale rollout is a management challenge as well as a technical challenge. All recommendations for the rollout process are necessarily general because the real procedures depend so much on the features of particular situations and corporate cultures. Microsoft and others recommend a deployment process that falls roughly along these lines:

1. Develop a detailed vision of the role you want Windows 98 to serve. Determine how you'll deploy the features described in this chapter. This could require detailed input from users, managers, and technical staff.

2. Develop a configuration for your network based on user needs and sound design principles. Determine where to put servers, routers, printers, and so forth.

3. Develop an overall deployment plan for the Windows 98 installation process. If you are installing over the network, determine where you'll place the Windows 98 installation files and how you'll initiate Setup on the client machines (see Chapter 2). Devise installation scripts that meet your deployment and configuration requirements.

4. Test the installation procedures you plan to employ. (This is very important!) Microsoft recommends that you set up a complete testing lab to model and troubleshoot all aspects of the deployment process. It is important to accurately test the installation techniques you plan to deploy on representative hardware and software platforms. Identify any glitches in advance.

5. Provide training for technical personnel who will be assisting with the installation or upgrade.

6. Provide Windows 98 training for users, so they'll be ready for productive work when the new systems are in place. Get feedback from users on the trial configuration for any necessary adjustments to the proposed configurations.

7. Notify users in advance of the deployment schedule. Make sure critical deployment steps don't conflict with other critical events within your organization.

8. Conduct a pilot rollout, a small-scale simulation of the complete installation process.

9. Get feedback on the pilot rollout from users and technical staff. Make final adjustments to the process.

10. Gather all necessary tools and make final assessments of cost and time requirements. Create file templates that technical staff will use for tracking and documenting the installation process.

11. Roll out Windows 98.

For more on the Windows 98 Setup process, see Chapters 2 and 3.

Conclusion

This chapter examined some of the choices you'll need to make when deciding how to deploy Windows 98 in your environment. You'll continue to make choices throughout the life of your Windows 98 installation. For a more in-depth look at how to configure and customize Windows 98 for your environment, read on.

Chapter 2

Installing Windows 98

Windows 98 includes new features that make it easier than previous versions to upgrade, install, or uninstall. Windows 98 Setup can take either of two approaches to installing Windows 98 on your system:

- **Upgrade:** If your computer currently uses Windows 3.1 or Windows 95, you can upgrade your existing operating system to Windows 98. If you perform an upgrade, Setup retains your existing network and system settings.

- **New Installation:** If your current system uses MS-DOS, Windows 3.0, or Windows NT, or if you're installing to a freshly formatted hard disk, Setup runs under MS-DOS and does not automatically upgrade your present configuration.

Chapter 1 described planning and configuration choices you have to make when preparing to install Windows 98. This chapter describes the actual installation process:

- Preparing to install Windows 98
- Understanding the installation process
- Using the Setup command
- Upgrading to Windows 98 from Windows 3.x or Windows 95
- Installing Windows 98 on MS-DOS, Windows 3.0, or Windows NT systems
- Dual-booting Windows 98 with Windows 3.x and DOS
- Using Windows 98 with Windows NT systems
- Creating a CD-ROM-enabled boot floppy disk
- Customizing Windows 98 with installation scripts
- Uninstalling Windows 98

You can install Windows 98 either locally or over the network. This chapter discusses the principles of Windows 98 installation. For a detailed discussion of network installation techniques, see Chapter 3, "Network Installation."

Preparing to Install Windows 98

Microsoft recommends that you undertake some preliminary tasks before you install a new version of Windows. Specifically, those tasks are as follows:

- Check system requirements
- Make sure that hardware is supported
- Disable TSRs and timeout features
- Close virus checkers (and other applications)
- Disable third-party display utilities and video drivers
- Scan and defragment disks
- Back up key system files
- Check network configuration

The following sections discuss these preliminary installation tasks.

> **Note** Of course, part of preparation is deciding what you want from your new system. Refer to Chapter 1 for more information about planning and deployment of Windows 98.

Check System Requirements

Take a moment to ensure that the PC on which you're installing Windows 98 meets the following system requirements:

Processor: Intel 486DX 66 MHz or better (or equivalent). Pentium recommended.

RAM: 16 M minimum; 24 M recommended.

Disk space: *For Typical installation:* 200 M free disk space (of which 45 M is temporary disk space required by the Setup program).

For Compact installation: 21 M.

For Custom installation: As much as 250 M.

If you plan to save existing operating system files (see "Uninstalling Windows 98," later in this chapter), you need an additional 50 M of disk space. You must install Windows 98 onto a FAT partition. You can't use a Windows NT NTFS partition or an OS/2 HPFS partition.

Monitor: VGA 256 color; SuperVGA 16-bit or 24-bit color recommended.

Installation Source: CD-ROM drive (for local installation using the Windows 98 CD-ROM) or a network connection to a server that holds the Windows 98 installation files. See Chapter 3 for more on network installations.

Make Sure That Hardware Is Supported

Windows 98 is fairly efficient at detecting and installing hardware automatically, but if you want to ensure a flawless setup, you may want to verify that your hardware is supported. If your system is now working under Windows 95 and you're planning to upgrade to Windows 98, you shouldn't have a problem with hardware compatibility in most cases. If you're upgrading from another operating system, or if you're installing Windows 98 on a new system, there are several ways to check whether your hardware is supported. The easiest way may be to check the vendor documentation.

If you have Windows 98 running somewhere in your organization, a good way to check for built-in hardware support is through the Control Panel Add New Hardware Wizard:

1. In the Control Panel, double-click Add New Hardware.

2. Click Next twice to pass the first two screens. When the wizard asks whether you want Windows to search for new hardware, select No, I Want to Select the Hardware from a List, and click Next.

3. From the list of component types that appears, select the relevant component type (floppy disk controller, display adapter, CD-ROM controller, and so on) and click Next.

4. Choose a manufacturer and scan through the list of models with built-in Windows 98 support.

If your hardware device is not present in the Add New Hardware Wizard list, you still may be able to use it in Windows 98, but you may have to supply a driver for it during or after installation. Setup attempts to select a generic driver if it doesn't recognize the device. If the generic driver doesn't work, or if Setup fails to find a suitable generic driver, be ready to install a Windows 95 or Windows 98 driver directly from the manufacturer's floppy disk that accompanied the device. (See Chapter 12, "Supporting Devices," for more about installing new hardware.)

The Add New Hardware Wizard lists only the devices included on the Windows 98 CD-ROM. Microsoft provides a document called the Windows 98 Hardware Compatibility list that contains a regularly updated list of devices that have been tested for Windows 98 compatibility. You can obtain the Windows 98 Hardware Compatibility list from the Microsoft web site at `http://www.microsoft.com`. You can also check the `HARDWARE.TXT` file in the `README` directory of the Windows 98 installation CD-ROM for more information about specific hardware issues.

Disable TSRs and Timeout Features

Microsoft recommends that you disable all TSRs and device drivers in `AUTOEXEC.BAT` and `CONFIG.SYS` except those necessary for essential features such as hard disk control, network access, CD-ROM access, and so forth.

Some portable PCs include a timeout feature that shuts down the system after a predefined timeout period. Timeout mechanisms should be disabled before you start Setup.

Close Applications—Especially Virus Checkers

It is best to close all applications before you start Setup. Setup attempts to detect Windows applications and prompts you to close them, but the safest approach is to close all applications before you begin.

For upgrades from Windows 3.1 (or earlier), it is especially important to disable any antivirus software and to make sure that antivirus software doesn't start automatically when the system boots. Windows 3.1 (or earlier) antivirus software is *not* compatible with Windows 98 (principally because of Windows 95/98's mechanism for handling long filenames; refer to Chapter 17, "File Systems: File and Disk Resources"). Running earlier antivirus programs under Windows 95/98 can cause loss of data and other unpredictable consequences. If you're upgrading from a pre-Windows 95 OS, make sure that your antivirus software doesn't start automatically. You may be able to shut off automatic startup from within the application, or you may have to manually remove the program from AUTOEXEC.BAT, WIN.INI, or the Startup program group.

> **Note** If you are converting to the FAT32 file system, make sure that your antivirus software and disk software is compatible with FAT32. The FAT32 Drive Converter Wizard searches out incompatible disk utilities and antivirus programs and describes the nature of the incompatibility, so watch for warnings when you convert to FAT32. To be on the safe side, check vendor documentation or check directly with the software vendor.

Even if your antivirus software is compatible with Windows 98, it is better to disable automatic startup of antivirus software if you're upgrading from Windows 95. Microsoft advises you to disable your antivirus software because it is an outside application and also because the changes Setup makes to your system (for example, changes to the master boot record) will appear suspicious to your antivirus program. The program may offer to "restore" the original configuration (which essentially makes the new Windows 98 system unusable); one false mouse-click could bring you hours of regret.

If the antivirus program prompts you to restore the original configuration, be prepared to click Cancel. If you're using Windows 3.x antivirus software, close the antivirus program immediately and upgrade to a Windows 95/98-compatible equivalent. If you're using compatible antivirus software and you plan to keep using it, you will eventually have to inoculate your system by registering the new configuration with the antivirus program. Consult the antivirus program documentation.

Scan and Defragment Disks

It is a good idea to defragment your hard drive before upgrading to Windows 98.

Setup automatically invokes the ScanDisk utility to scan for disk errors before beginning an installation or upgrade. However, if you use a third-party disk compression utility, you should use the accompanying disk checking utility to scan and defragment the disk before you begin. Microsoft recommends that you defragment all compressed drives because Windows 98 overestimates available disk space on highly fragmented, compressed drives.

Back Up Key System Files

It is a good idea to back up important system files for your existing operating system before you install Windows 98. Windows 98 Setup includes an option for automatically backing up system files (see the section entitled "Upgrading to Windows 98," later in this chapter). Microsoft recommends that you use this system file backup option.

If, for some reason, you choose not to use Setup's system file backup option (for example, if you want to save the required 50 M of disk space), you can back up key files by using a tape drive or floppy disks, or you can copy those files to a temporary location across the network.

Microsoft recommends that you back up the following files if you're upgrading from Windows 3.1 (or earlier):

- From the Windows directory: `.INI` files, `.DAT` files, `.PWL` files (password files), `.GRP` files (Program Manager group files)

- `CONFIG.SYS`, `AUTOEXEC.BAT`, and any real-mode drivers specified in `CONFIG.SYS` or `AUTOEXEC.BAT`

- Network configuration files (`NET.CFG`)

- Logon scripts and important batch files

If you're upgrading from Windows 95, make sure that you have a working Windows 95 emergency boot disk (and create a Windows 98 emergency boot disk when Setup asks you to do so; remember that Windows 95 and Windows 98 boot disks aren't compatible). Make backup copies of the Registry files `SYSTEM.DAT` and `USER.DAT`, logon scripts, proprietary configuration files, and any important real-mode drivers. See Chapter 36, "The Windows 98 Boot Process and Emergency Recovery," for more about emergency recovery.

Check Network Configuration

For upgrades from Windows 3.1 or Windows 95, Windows 98 Setup automatically creates a network configuration that matches the previous network settings. If your network configuration is working properly before you use Setup, Setup does most (or all) of the work of converting your configuration to Windows 98. If you wait until after you install Windows 98 to configure your network settings, you'll be doing the configuration on an unfamiliar system, and you'll have more unknowns if you're faced with a troubleshooting situation. It is generally a good idea to check your network configuration before you begin.

If your system isn't currently part of a network but you want it to be (for example, if you're upgrading to Windows 98 *because you want* an operating system you can network easily), it isn't necessary to install and configure network client software on the old OS just so that you can perform the upgrade. You can install Windows 98 and configure your network settings afterwards. (Refer to Chapters 20 through 25 for more about networking Windows 98.) If you're installing multiple systems, you can use an installation script with Setup to install Windows 98 with customized network settings. You learn more about Windows 98 installation scripts later in this chapter.

Understanding the Installation Process

Before you start to install Windows 98, it is wise to be aware of exactly what Setup is doing. The procedures and prompts that appear during installation may vary depending on your configuration and on your Setup settings. Schematically, Microsoft divides the Windows 98 Setup process into five phases:

- *Preparing to run Windows 98 Setup:* Setup scans your disk, checks for existing copies of Windows, prepares the Setup Wizard, and asks you to accept the license agreement.

- *Collecting information about your computer:* Setup analyzes your system and collects the data it needs to carry out the installation. Setup also prepares the new directory, asks whether you want to save an existing DOS or Windows installation, and lets you create an emergency repair disk. In some cases, Setup may also ask for additional input: Windows directory, installation type (Typical, Custom, Compact, Portable), user name and company, computer name, workgroup or domain, computer description, optional components, and so forth.

- *Copying Windows 98 files to your computer:* Setup copies the necessary files from the source medium to the target PC. (If you're installing interactively, your screen will display a slide show describing Windows 98's new features while Setup copies files.)

- *Restarting your computer:* Setup shuts down your computer and attempts to boot Windows 98.

- *Setting up hardware and finalizing settings:* Setup sets up local hardware, restarts, finishes hardware configuration, and attends to final configuration items (such as time zone, Control Panel, Start menu programs, Windows Help, MS-DOS program settings, and system configuration options).

The name of the active Setup phase appears in the bar on the left side of the screen as you progress through installation.

While the relatively few screen prompts pass across the user interface, Setup undertakes hundreds of checking, detecting, polling, and configuration tasks behind the scenes. Much of the hidden complexity within the Setup process results from the need for thorough and reliable hardware detection.

Setup can detect and configure a vast range of system hardware. Setup automatically detects not only Plug and Play devices, it also detects legacy hardware. The methods Setup uses to detect hardware are similar to the methods Windows 98 uses to detect new devices at startup. See Chapter 12, "Supporting Devices," for Plug and Play in Windows 98.

After the first boot in the Setup process (following the file-copy phase), Setup begins a systematic search for system hardware. First, Setup detects all Plug and Play devices using Plug and Play detection. Setup then employs an elaborate process for finding legacy (non-Plug and Play) components. It reads configuration files such as `CONFIG.SYS` and scans `INF` files, searching for device information. Setup scans device drivers and ROM strings, fishing for hints about system devices.

Setup uses a basic form of detection for components that can be detected and configured more reliably (for example, processors and COM ports) and uses a more robust scheme (that Microsoft has dubbed *safe detection*) to find devices that are more likely to cause configuration problems.

Setup uses safe detection to detect the following classes of devices:

- Network adapters
- SCSI controllers
- Proprietary CD-ROM adapters
- Sound cards

If Setup finds hints of any of the preceding device classes, it looks directly to I/O ports (except in the case of sound cards, as noted later in this section). If Setup doesn't find any evidence of one of these device classes, it stops detecting for that class rather than risking hanging the system with a search for a nonexistent component.

For Windows 3.1 upgrades, the preliminary search for network adapters begins with a search for and a scan of the `LSL.COM`, `IPX.COM`, and `PROTOCOL.INI` files. The search for SCSI controllers and proprietary CD-ROM adapters begins with `CONFIG.SYS`. Setup searches internal ROM strings for the presence of SCSI hard drives. Setup checks `CONFIG.SYS` and `SYSTEM.INI` for information about sound cards. If it finds evidence of a sound card, however, Setup does not scan the I/O ports to locate the device (as it does with the other safe-detect device classes). Instead, Setup performs only the specific detection routines defined in the information file `MSDET.INF`.

> **Note** `MSDET.INF` is an `INF` file in the Windows/INF directory that defines the specific devices for which Setup searches. A manufacturer's `INF` can add a device to `MSDET.INF`, causing Windows 98 to search for that device at startup.

Windows 98 includes a Setup recovery feature. If the installation fails for some reason, and you have to start over, Setup picks up where it left off. Setup can accomplish this smart recovery because it keeps a log of installation events. When you run Setup, Setup checks for the Setup log and resumes the installation after the last successful step. See the section titled "Troubleshooting Windows 98 Setup," later in this chapter, for more about Setup recovery and the Setup log.

Windows 98 creates a log of the hardware detection process called DETLOG.TXT. If detection fails or the computer hangs, Windows 98 creates a file called DETCRASH.LOG. You learn more about DETLOG.TXT and DETCRASH.LOG later in this chapter.

Registering Windows 98

Like most software vendors, Microsoft encourages users to register their software. When you register Windows 98, you add your name to Microsoft's user database, and you provide Microsoft with a description of your Windows 98 implementation (hardware resources, system settings, and so on). If you register, you're entitled to certain benefits. Microsoft will notify you of upgrades and new products, and you may be eligible for special upgrade prices. Some third-party vendors use the Microsoft's registration database to notify users of their own products. When you register, you'll have the option of choosing whether you want to receive third-party materials.

The traditional way to register is to fill out the registration card included with the software and mail it in. Windows 98 includes a registration card, but it also provides another option: the Windows 98 Registration Wizard. The Registration Wizard prompts you for registration-related input, searches out the necessary system information, and then automatically registers your Windows 98 implementation with Microsoft over the Internet.

You can access the Registration Wizard through the Welcome to Windows 98 application. Welcome to Windows 98 typically opens automatically when you start Windows 98 for the first time (although this may depend on your OEM implementation). Otherwise, you'll find Welcome to Windows 98 in the System Tools Accessories (click Start, Programs, Accessories, System Tools, Welcome to Windows).

In the Welcome to Windows main screen, click Register Now to launch the Registration Wizard.

Using the Setup Command

The Windows 98 Setup program (SETUP.EXE) initiates and implements basic setup operations. You can use Setup to upgrade Windows 95 or Windows 3.1 systems or to perform a full installation under MS-DOS, Windows 3.0, or Windows NT systems.

> **Note** The Windows 98 Setup program can run from within MS-DOS, OS/2, Windows 3.1, Windows for Workgroups, or Windows 95. Microsoft recommends that you run Windows 98 Setup from within Windows, if possible. If you are installing Windows 98 on a system with an early version of Windows (Windows 3.0 or earlier), you must exit Windows and run Setup from DOS.

The Setup command can include a reference to an INF installation script that contains custom setup information. For more about using installation scripts with Setup, refer to "Customizing Installation," later in this chapter.

In addition to an optional installation script, the Setup command can contain one or more optional switches. Setup switches are listed in Table 2.1. Consider the following example:

```
setup msbatch1.inf /id /im
```

In this example, Setup uses configuration information located in the installation script msbatch1.inf. The /id switch tells Setup to skip the disk space check; the /im switch tells Setup to skip the memory test.

Table 2.1
Setup Command Switches

Switch	Description
/T:tmpdir	Specifies a temporary directory where Setup will copy its files. Replace tmpdir with the directory name. Any files already in the directory will be deleted. Setup creates the directory if it doesn't exist.
/c	Does not load the SmartDrive disk cache.
/d	Does not use existing Windows version for Setup.
/domain domain_name	Specifies a domain name used by the client for Microsoft networks for logon verification during Setup.
/id	Skips the disk-space check.
/ie	Does not create emergency boot disk.
/ih	Skips the Registry check.
/im	Skips the memory check.
/in	Skips the setup of networking components.
/iq	Skips the check for cross-linked files.
/is	Skips ScanDisk and routine system check.

Switch	Description
/iv	Skips the display of billboards during Setup.
/ix	Skips the character-set check.
/iw	Skips the display of the End User License Agreement.

Upgrading to Windows 98 from Windows 95 or Windows 3.x

One of the first things Setup does is to search your system for existing versions of Windows. If Setup finds Windows 95, it automatically upgrades the Windows 95 system to Windows 98 and preserves system settings from the old configuration.

If Setup finds Windows 3.x, Setup asks whether you want to install Windows 98 to a new directory or to the existing Windows directory. If you install to the existing Windows directory, Setup replaces system files and upgrades the existing system. If you install to a different directory, Setup automatically configures the PC to dual-boot between the previous OS and Windows 98. You learn more about dual-boot options later in this chapter.

Setup gives you the option of preserving the existing system files so that you can uninstall Windows 98 if necessary. (Note that this is for the upgrade option—installing Windows 98 to the existing Windows directory. If you install to a different directory, the existing OS remains unchanged and you aren't asked whether you want to preserve it.) If you elect to preserve the existing OS, Setup will save the existing system files in a file called WINUNDO.DAT, located in the root directory of the hard drive. (If the hard drive contains multiple logical drives, Setup asks you to specify a logical drive.) Setup also creates the file WINUNDO.INI, which contains information about the original location of the system files. If you save the existing system files, Uninstall Windows 98 becomes an uninstall option in the Install/Uninstall tab of Control Panel's Add/Remove Programs application. Setup warns you that backing up the existing system files requires approximately 50 M of disk space.

Note If you install Windows 98 to a different directory, you will probably have to reinstall any existing applications to run them in Windows 98. In many cases, you can get Windows 98 to run an existing application by specifying the path to the required DLLs using the `path` command, but Microsoft does not support or recommend this solution.

If you compress the drive with DriveSpace or convert to FAT32 after you have saved the system files, you cannot restore the system files.

The interactive Setup process described in the following sections is designed for speed and simplicity and does not provide a full range of configuration options. Use an installation script if you want to customize the Setup process. Installation scripts are described later in this chapter.

The Windows 95/98 upgrade requires little user input. Be prepared to supply Setup with the following information:

- Whether or not you want to save your Windows 95 system files so that you can uninstall Windows 98. (You need an additional 50 M of disk space to save the system files.)

- Your Windows 98 Product ID number.

- An Internet channel set (see Chapter 1; typically, you can just choose your country from the list).

- Whether or not you want to create an emergency startup disk.

In most cases, Setup can obtain the other necessary settings from defaults or from the existing configuration; in some situations, however, you may be asked to supply additional information.

If you're upgrading from Windows 3.x to Windows 98, you may also be asked to supply the following information:

- *A Windows directory name.* If you install to the existing Windows directory, you cannot access the old operating system. (You can, however, save the system files so that you can later uninstall Windows 98 and return to the old OS; refer to the following procedure.) If you install to a new directory, you can dual boot to the old operating system, but you'll probably have to reinstall any existing applications.

- *A Setup option.* Choose Typical (for most users), Custom (for users who want the maximum flexibility in defining their configuration), Compact (for systems with limited hard drive resources), or Portable (for portable computers). Refer to the discussion of Setup options in Chapter 1. Choose the Custom option if you want to select any of the following options:

    - A keyboard layout for a particular country or language (the default is USA 101).

    - Language support for Baltic, Central European, Cyrillic, Greek, or Turkish languages (the default is to enable English and Western European language support).

    - Regional settings such as languages and dialects (the default is English/USA).

    - To configure Windows 98 to use the optional Windows 3.1 user interface (Program Manager, File Manager, and so on). The default is (no surprise) to install Windows 98 with the Windows 98 interface.

Chapter 2: Installing Windows 98

- To specify Windows components. The Setup option you select defines a set of default Windows components. Setup asks whether you want to add or remove any components from the default settings.

If your present operating system isn't configured for Microsoft networking (but you have networking hardware installed on your system), you are also asked to supply networking parameters such as computer name, workgroup name, and computer description (if your computer was not previously configured for the network, as described in the following procedure).

To upgrade from Windows 95 to Windows 98, follow these steps:

1. Place the Windows 98 CD in the CD-ROM drive and double-click Setup in the top-level directory of the CD. (Alternatively, connect to the Windows 98 installation files over the network; network installation options are discussed in Chapter 3.)

> **Note** Some versions of Windows 95 can auto-detect a newer version of Windows on the CD-ROM and ask whether you want to install it before you ever click the Setup program.

2. You see an announcement that says, "Welcome to Windows 98 Setup." Additional announcements follow, proclaiming that Setup is checking your system and preparing the Setup Wizard.

3. The Windows 98 license agreement appears. You must either accept the agreement or cancel Setup. Setup then continues to check your system and prepares an installation directory.

4. Setup asks whether you want to save the existing DOS or Windows system files so that you can uninstall Windows 98 if necessary. (The uninstall option was discussed earlier in this chapter, in "Upgrading Windows 98.") Click Yes or No. Preserving the System files requires approximately 50 M of disk space.

5. Setup asks you to enter the Windows 98 Product ID number supplied by Microsoft.

6. Setup asks you to select a channel set for Internet channels. Internet channels were introduced in Chapter 1, "Deploying Windows 98." The channel sets are organized by geographical region. The default is the United States. Select a channel set.

7. Setup asks whether you want to create an emergency startup disk. An *emergency startup disk* lets you reboot your system and recover certain key system files in the event of a system failure (see Chapter 36, "The Windows 98 Boot Process and Emergency Recovery"). It is a very good idea to create an emergency startup disk, label it, and store it where you can find it. Note that, because of changes to the file system, Windows 95 emergency startup

disks typically do not work under Windows 98. You should create a Windows 98 emergency startup disk when you upgrade to Windows 98. If you elect to create an emergency startup disk, Setup prompts you to insert a disk in the floppy drive and warns that any files on the disk will be deleted. When the necessary files are copied to the emergency startup disk, Setup tells you to remove the disk.

8. The file-copy phase of Setup begins. Setup starts copying files to the local hard drive. This takes several minutes. In the meantime, Setup describes Windows 98's new features and displays some misty photos of users reacting to those features with gratitude.

9. When the file-copy phase is complete, Setup announces that it will restart the computer in 15 seconds. (You can preempt the progress bar by clicking Restart Now.)

10. When the computer restarts, you'll see the Windows 98 splash screen. Setup then attempts to configure your hardware.

> **Note** If you're installing over the network, Setup has to reconnect to the installation share after the system restarts. This may require that you log on to the network by using the appropriate user-level authentication method (for example, domain, Windows NT system, NetWare server). Make sure that you have the correct credentials to access the installation share and that the appropriate Primary Network Logon is active. Otherwise, the files will be inaccessible and the installation will fail.

11. The system shuts down and restarts again. Hardware setup continues. Setup announces that it is attending to the final configuration items:

    - Control Panel
    - Programs in Start menu
    - Windows Help
    - MS-DOS program settings
    - Tuning up application Start menu
    - System configuration

12. After these final items are configured, the upgrade is complete. The system restarts with Windows 98.

To upgrade from Windows 3.x or Windows for Workgroups to Windows 98, follow these steps:

Don't forget to disable all Windows 3.x antivirus software and to disable any auto-start capability for virus checking before upgrading to Windows 98.

1. Click the **F**ile menu in Program Manager, select **R**un, and enter the Setup command with the necessary path and switches. (If you're installing over the network, refer to Chapter 3, "Network Installation," for more information about initiating a network installation.)

2. Setup announces that it is checking your system. Setup launches the ScanDisk utility, which looks for disk errors. You'll see a message that says Setup is preparing the Setup Wizard.

3. Setup displays the licensing agreement. You must accept the agreement or cancel Setup.

4. Setup asks you to provide a name for the Windows directory. The default option is `C:\Windows`. Alternatively, you can click Other Directory and enter a directory name. If you provide a different directory name, Microsoft displays a warning that only advanced users use a different directory name. If you want the old operating system to remain accessible in a multiboot configuration, select Other Directory and enter a different directory name.

    If you choose to install Windows 98 into the directory that contains the existing operating system, Setup asks if you want to save the system files of the previous operating system. Saving the system files enables you uninstall Windows 98. See "Uninstalling Windows 98," later in this chapter, for more information.

5. The remaining installation steps are similar to the steps for DOS-based installation, described in the following section.

Installing Windows 98 on DOS, Windows 3.0, and Windows NT Systems

You can install Windows 98 on a system running MS-DOS, Windows 3.0, or Windows NT.

With each passing year, the number of DOS machines diminishes—and the number of DOS-only machines capable of supporting a Windows 98 upgrade is small to begin with (see "System Requirements," earlier in this chapter). For what it's worth, however, you can run Setup on any computer with MS-DOS 5.0 or later.

You can upgrade Novell's DR-DOS to Windows 98 in the same way that you upgrade MS-DOS, except that you cannot configure a dual-boot with DR-DOS.

You can configure Windows 98 to dual-boot with OS/2, but you can't run Setup from OS/2—you must configure an MS-DOS/OS/2 dual-boot and then upgrade MS-DOS to Windows 98. Remember that Windows 98 cannot read HPFS partitions.

If you're installing on a Windows 3.0 system (or earlier) or a Windows NT system, you have to run Setup from MS-DOS—you can't install from Windows.

If you perform a new installation to a reformatted or a newly formatted hard disk, you will need a CD-ROM-enabled boot disk to access the Windows 98 CD-ROM. The steps for creating a CD-ROM-enabled boot disk are described later in this chapter. If your PC's BIOS supports CD-ROM boot, you can boot directly to the Windows 98 CD.

For installations from MS-DOS, Setup does not migrate settings from the previous operating system. You can, however, define a specific configuration using an installation script. (Windows 98 installation scripts are described later in this chapter.)

For network installations, Setup must be able to reconnect to the installation share under Windows 98 if it is to complete the installation process. If real-mode network drivers are running when you start the Windows 98 installation from MS-DOS (as they would have to be if you're installing over the network), Setup installs the required network client. You can specify additional networking information by using an installation.

If you're running MS-DOS-based Setup on an MS-DOS, Windows 3.0, or Windows NT machine, you have to supply the following information:

- A Windows directory name.

- A decision about whether or not you want to save your system files so that you can uninstall Windows 98. (You need an additional 50 M of disk space to save the system files.)

- Your Windows 98 Product ID number.

- A Setup option. Choose Typical (for most users), Custom (for users who want the maximum flexibility in defining their configuration), Compact (for systems with limited hard drive resources), or Portable (for portable computers). See the discussion of Setup Options in Chapter 1. Choose the Custom option if you want to select any of the following options (other Setup options use default values):

    - A keyboard layout for a particular country or language (the default is USA 101).

    - Language support for Baltic, Central European, Cyrillic, Greek, or Turkish languages (the default is to enable English and Western European language support).

    - Regional settings such as languages and dialects (the default is English/USA).

    - To set up Windows 98 to use the optional Windows 3.1 user interface (Program Manager, File Manager, and so on). The default is (no surprise) to install Windows 98 with the Windows 98 interface.

Chapter 2: Installing Windows 98

- User information. Your name and your company's name.

- Windows components. The Setup option you select defines a set of default Windows components. Setup asks whether you want to add or remove any components from the default settings.

- Computer name, workgroup name, and computer description (if your computer was not previously configured for the network, as described in the following procedure). A computer name is a unique name identifying your computer on the network. A computer name consists of 15 or fewer characters; characters can include 0 through 9, A through Z, and these characters: ! @ # $ % ^ & ( ) - _ ' { } . ~

- Internet channels. Refer to Chapter 1 for more information about choosing an Internet channel.

- A decision about whether or not you want to create an emergency startup disk. (Do it! Choose Yes.)

Additional choices may appear depending on what Setup finds on your system.

Follow these steps to install Windows 98 on MS-DOS, Windows 3.0 systems or to perform a new installation:

1. Start Setup from the MS-DOS prompt. If you are performing a local installation to a reformatted hard disk, boot your PC using a CD-ROM-aware boot floppy disk (see "Creating a CD-ROM-Aware Boot Floppy Disk," later in this chapter). The Setup command should include the required path and switches and the path and name of an installation script if you are using one.

2. Setup announces that it is checking your system. It may launch the ScanDisk utility, which looks for disk errors. (See Chapter 17, "File Systems: File and Disk Resources," for more information about ScanDisk.)

3. Setup displays the licensing agreement. You must accept the agreement or cancel Setup.

4. Setup asks you to provide a name for the Windows directory. The default option is C:\Windows. Alternatively, you can click Other Directory and enter a directory name. If you provide an alternative directory name, Microsoft displays a warning that only advanced users use a different directory name.

5. Setup asks whether you want to save the existing DOS or Windows system files so that you can uninstall Windows 98 if necessary. (The uninstall option was discussed earlier in this chapter, in "Upgrading Windows 98.") Click Yes or No. Preserving the System files requires approximately 50 M of disk space.

6. Setup asks you to enter the Windows 98 Product ID number supplied by Microsoft.

7. Setup announces that it is preparing files and then prompts you to select a Setup option (Typical, Portable, Compact, or Custom). Windows 98 Setup options were discussed in detail earlier in this chapter and in Chapter 1. Choose a Setup option.

8. Setup asks you to enter user information. Enter an (optional) name and a company name. Note that the name you enter is not related to a user name or to the computer name. The name and company name are part of the licensing information. The name and company name you enter appear in the General tab of the Control Panel System application.

9. A dialog box asks if you want to select optional Windows components. (See Chapter 1 for a detailed discussion of Windows optional components.) The Setup option you chose in step 7 (Typical, Compact, Custom, or Portable) defines a set of default components that appear in this dialog box. You can add or remove components from the set. Choose Install the Most Common Components if you are satisfied with the default set. Select Show Me the List if you want to select additional components. Remember that you can add a component at any time, even if you don't choose it during Setup, by using the Control Panel Add/Remove Programs application (described in Chapter 6, "Control Panel"). If you chose the Custom option in step 7, you are automatically given the chance to select Windows components.

10. Setup asks for a computer name, a workgroup name, and a computer description. These parameters appear in the Identification tab of Control Panel's Network application. The computer name identifies the computer on the network. The computer name must be 15 characters or fewer; each character can be an alphanumeric character or one of the following characters: ! @ # $ % ^ & ( ) - _ ' { } ~ .

    The workgroup name describes the group of computers to which the PC belongs. The group can be a workgroup, and Windows NT Server domain, or a NetWare server network.

    The computer description appears along with the computer name in network resource lists (such as Network Neighborhood, if you select Details from the Network Neighborhood View menu).

11. Setup asks you to select a channel set for Internet channels. Internet channels were introduced in Chapter 1, "Deploying Windows 98." The channel sets are organized by geographical region. The default is the United States. Select a channel set.

12. Setup asks if you want to create an emergency startup disk. An emergency startup disk lets you reboot your system, regain access to your hard drive, and replace or recover certain key system files in the event of a system failure (see Chapter 36, "The Windows 98 Boot Process and Emergency Recovery"). It is a very good idea to create an emergency startup disk, label it, and store it where you can find it. Note that, because of changes to the file

Chapter 2: Installing Windows 98

system, Windows 95 emergency startup disks typically do not work under Windows 98. You should create a Windows 98 emergency startup disk when you upgrade to Windows 98. If you elect to create an emergency startup disk, Setup prompts you to insert a disk in the floppy drive and warns you that any files on the disk will be deleted. When the necessary files are copied to the emergency startup disk, Setup tells you to remove the disk.

13. The file-copy phase of Setup begins. Setup starts copying files to the local hard drive. This takes several minutes. In the meantime, Setup describes Windows 98's new features.

14. When the file-copy phase is complete, Setup announces that it will restart the computer in 15 seconds. (You can preempt the progress bar by clicking Restart Now.)

15. When the computer restarts, you see the Windows 98 splash screen. Setup then attempts to configure your hardware.

Note If you're installing over the network, Setup has to reconnect to the installation share after the system restarts. This may require that you log on to the network by using the appropriate user-level authentication method (such as domain, Windows NT system, NetWare server). Make sure that you have the correct credentials to access the installation share and that your new Windows 98 configuration will give you access to the appropriate logon. Otherwise, the files will be inaccessible and the installation will fail. See the discussion earlier in this section.

16. The system shuts down and restarts again. Hardware setup continues. Setup announces that it is attending to these final configuration items:

    - Time zone
    - Control Panel
    - Windows Help
    - MS-DOS program settings
    - Tuning up the application Start menu
    - System configuration

    Setup asks you to enter the correct time zone and to set or verify the system time.

17. After these final items are configured, the upgrade is complete. The system restarts with Windows 98.

Dual-Booting Windows 98 with Windows 3.x and DOS

When you run Windows 98 Setup from a Windows 3.x machine, Setup prompts you to name the Windows 98 directory. If you install Windows 98 in the existing Windows directory, Setup converts your existing Windows 3.x installation into a Windows 98 installation—you won't be able to boot to Windows 3.x (although you can still boot to DOS, as described later in this section).

If you install Windows 98 to a directory that is different from the existing Windows 3.x directory, Setup automatically configures your PC to dual-boot with MS-DOS. To start MS-DOS on a dual-boot-enabled Windows 98 system, do either of the following:

- Press F4 as the system starts to boot to the previous operating system.

- Press F8 or press the left Control key as the system starts to invoke the Windows 98 Startup menu and choose Previous Version of MS-DOS from the Startup menu.

From the DOS prompt, you can start Windows 3.x by typing the WIN command.

If you originally installed Windows 98 to the Windows 3.x directory, you cannot start Windows 3.x, but you can still configure your PC to boot to MS-DOS. To enable your Windows 98 PC to dual-boot to DOS, perform the following steps (your system must have MS-DOS 5.0 or later):

1. Turn off the hidden and read-only attributes for the file MSDOS.SYS in the top-level directory of the boot drive (usually drive C) by using the following command:

   attrib -h -s -r msdos.sys

2. Edit MSDOS.SYS. Change the value of the BootMulti parameter in the [Options] section of MSDOS.SYS to BootMulti=1. This change enables the multiboot feature for your PC.

3. Insert a DOS 5.0 (or later) system disk. Turn off the hidden and read-only attributes for the files IO.SYS and MSDOS.SYS (as described in step 1).

4. Copy the files IO.SYS, MSDOS.SYS, and COMMAND.COM from the MS-DOS system disk to the boot drive, giving the new files a .DOS extension:

   copy a:\MSDOS.SYS c:\MSDOS.DOS
   copy a:\IO.SYS c:\IO.DOS
   copy a:\COMMAND.COM C:\COMMAND.DOS

5. Create files called AUTOEXEC.DOS and CONFIG.DOS in the top-level directory of the boot drive. Your multiboot MS-DOS system will use these files in place of AUTOEXEC.BAT and CONFIG.SYS. Add any commands to these files that you want to include in AUTOEXEC.BAT and CONFIG.SYS files. (If you copy these files from a DOS floppy disk, edit the path

references as necessary—watch out for references to drive A and make sure that all referenced files are accessible.)

After you complete these steps, reboot your system and start MS-DOS by pressing F4, F8, or the left Control key at system startup.

> **Note** If you're using disk compression software, Microsoft warns that you should also copy `IO.DOS`, `MSDOS.DOS`, `COMMAND.DOS`, `CONFIG.DOS`, and `AUTOEXEC.BAT` to your host drive. See Chapter 17, "File Systems: File and Disk Resources," for a discussion of file compression and host drives in Windows 98.

Booting to DOS can be useful in certain situations, but it is worth noting that there are also several options for redefining and customizing the MS-DOS operating environment from within Windows 98. If you're having trouble getting an MS-DOS application to work under Windows 98, try configuring the DOS properties for the application within Windows 98 before you resign yourself to booting DOS. See Chapter 11, "Windows 98 Architecture and Application Support," for more information about using MS-DOS applications in Windows 98.

Using Windows 98 with Windows NT Systems

Setup cannot perform a true *upgrade*—converting Registry and system settings, replacing the old OS, and so on—from Windows NT to Windows 98.

If you're considering converting a Windows NT computer to Windows 98, or if you're planning a Windows 98/Windows NT dual-boot configuration, be aware that Windows 98 can't read a Windows NT NTFS partition and that Windows NT 4.0 or earlier can't read a Windows 98 FAT32 partition. (Microsoft says that Windows NT 5.0 will support FAT32 partitions.) See Chapter 1, "Deploying Windows 98," and Chapter 17 for more about file system choices. Any directories used by both Windows NT and Windows 98 must reside on a FAT16 partition.

> **Note** Many people would say that converting a Windows NT machine to Windows 98 would actually be more of a *downgrade*, given Windows NT's superior security and stability. There are, of course, always exceptions for particular users in special situations. If you are running Windows NT 3.5 (or earlier) and you prefer the Windows 95/98 user interface, consider upgrading to Windows 4.0 rather than Windows 98. Windows 4.0 uses the Windows 95 user interface and includes many of the advanced features provided by Windows 98.

The Windows 98 Setup program won't run under Windows NT. If you want to convert a Windows NT system to Windows 98, first make sure that you have a working Windows NT emergency repair disk. Then boot to MS-DOS or Windows 95 from a CD-ROM-enabled floppy disk and run Setup. Do not install Windows 98 to the same directory that contains Windows NT. When Setup is complete, your system will boot to Windows 98—you cannot start Windows NT. If you want to restore the Windows NT boot capability, boot to your Windows NT emergency repair disk and choose the repair option to repair the Windows NT boot files.

If your system is presently dual-booting Windows NT with another operating system (DOS, Windows 95, or an earlier version of Windows), you can upgrade the other operating system to Windows 98. You will still be able to boot to DOS from the Windows 98 startup menu, as described in the section "Dual-Booting Windows 98 with Windows 3.x and DOS."

If your system currently isn't using either Windows 98 or Windows NT, the easiest way to configure a Windows 98/Windows NT dual boot is to install Windows 98 first and then install Windows NT to a different directory. Windows NT's Setup program takes care of configuring the dual boot, and both operating systems will appear in Windows NT's boot menu.

Creating a CD-ROM-Aware Boot Floppy Disk

If you're performing a full installation on a newly formatted hard drive, you'll need a floppy boot disk that provides access to the Windows 98 installation files. You may also need to use a CD-ROM-enabled boot floppy if the Windows 98 installation fails in a way that requires you to boot from a floppy to restart the installation. The Windows 98 CD is a bootable CD, so you can boot to it directly if your PC's BIOS supports CD-ROM boot.

The Windows 98 emergency startup disk includes a generic real-mode ATAPI CD-ROM driver. Once you have installed Windows 98 on your system, you can boot from the Windows 98 emergency startup disk and then access your CD-ROM by entering the drive letter at the command prompt (assuming that the generic driver works with your CD-ROM drive; it is a good idea to test as soon as possible to ensure that the startup disk can reach your CD). Windows 98 startup disks, however, are not always compatible with Windows 95 PCs because of the changes to the kernel necessary for supporting FAT32. If you're upgrading to Windows 98 from Windows 95 or an earlier version of Windows, you need a boot floppy that loads the necessary CD-ROM drivers. Some vendors may supply a CD-ROM-enabled boot floppy along with the Windows system software. If you don't have a CD-ROM-enabled boot floppy, you must create one.

To enable the CD-ROM drive from a boot floppy, you must *load real-mode CD-ROM drivers*. The exact procedure for how to do this depends on your hardware and on your configuration. The general procedure is as follows:

1. Specify the filename of your real-mode CD-ROM driver in CONFIG.SYS by using the DEVICE or DEVICEHIGH command, as shown here:

   DEVICE=CDROMDRV.SYS /D:mscd001

   In this syntax, the following parameters are used:

CDROMDRV.SYS	The real-mode driver for the CD-ROM drive. Make sure that the driver is present in the directory or provide a complete path to the driver.
D:	The drive letter designation for the CD-ROM.
mscd001	The field name. Whatever you use for this name in CONFIG.SYS must match the corresponding value in AUTOEXEC.BAT. The values MSCD001, MSCD002, MSCD003, MSCD004, and so on are often used. If you use a name that matches an actual filename, the file with that filename will be inaccessible while the driver is active on the system.

2. Load the MSCDEX driver (MSCDEX.EXE) in AUTOEXEC.BAT and reference it to the CD-ROM driver designation defined in CONFIG.SYS (see step 1), as shown here:

   MSCDEX.EXE /D:MSCD001

   In this syntax, /D:MSCD001 matches the parameter provided with the DEVICE command in CONFIG.SYS (see step 1).

Make sure that the file MSCDEX.EXE is present in the directory or provide a complete path. Look for MSCDEX.EXE on your OEM Windows 98 CD or on the CD-ROM manufacturer's driver disk. You can also find MSCDEX.EXE in the Windows\COMMAND directory of a Windows 98 PC.

Consult your CD-ROM manufacturer for additional instructions.

Customizing Windows 98 Setup with Installation Scripts

A Windows 98 *installation script* is a file that describes a complete Windows 98 configuration. The Windows 98 Setup program can install Windows 98 according to the specifications defined in an installation script. The installation script provides automatic answers for installation screen prompts, and it also specifies aspects of the configuration that otherwise could not be defined through Setup, such as the default gateway and the LMHOSTS file.

An installation script is basically a text file that uses the INF format (a format used for installing devices and applications on Microsoft systems). Although it is possible to create an installation script from scratch, more typically, network administrators create installation scripts in the following ways:

- By using the Batch98 utility (tools\reskit\batch\batch.exe on the Windows 98 CD), described later in this chapter. Batch98 enables you to create custom installation scripts through a convenient user interface.

- By adapting an installation script template. Microsoft provides several sample installation scripts with the Windows 95 Resource Kit that show how to implement installation scripts in various situations. You may be able to adapt one of these scripts for your situation. The Windows 95 Resource Kit is available for download at www.microsoft.com/windows95/info/w95reskit.htm. At this writing, it isn't clear whether Microsoft will continue to provide the sample Setup scripts with the Windows 98 Resource Kit. The INF file structure for Windows 98 installation scripts is largely unchanged from Windows 95, so you may be able to use Windows 95 installation scripts for Windows 98 (possibly with some adjustments—make sure you perform adequate testing before undertaking a rollout). If Microsoft does not include the sample scripts with Windows 98 or the Windows 98 Resource Kit, they will probably not officially support using Windows 95 scripts for Windows 98 installations. You're on your own. But studying the Windows 95 Resource Kit's sample scripts is still a good way to learn how installation scripts work.

You can modify an installation script using a text editor application such as Windows 98's Notepad accessory. Appendix D provides a detailed description of installation script structure.

To run Setup using an installation script, provide the path and name of the script along with the Setup command. For example, if your installation script is named FREDINF.INF, and if it is located in the C:\ directory, you would initiate Setup using the following command:

```
setup c:\Fredinf.inf
```

The one-line Setup command is the easy part. The tricky part is creating the right installation script so that you get exactly the installation you want. Installation scripts are especially useful for network installations in which you may have to install several identical or nearly identical systems and you don't want to take the time to answer all the screen prompts. But you can also use installation scripts for local installations. You can save yourself some steps and free yourself from interactive Setup's baby-sitting duties if you use an installation script.

Here are some of the uses for an installation script:

- You can automate all or part of the Setup process so that you don't have to answer screen prompts.

- You can configure a custom configuration (including network settings, optional components, and user and company information).

Chapter 2: Installing Windows 98

- You can set up local or network printers automatically.

- You can automatically configure your PC for System Policies and specify a System Policy file.

- You can specify a Registry export file that Setup will use to configure your PC. This powerful option lets you define a complete configuration on one PC and use Setup to *copy* that configuration to other computers on the network.

The following sections introduce the installation script template files and describe how to create installation scripts using the Batch98 utility.

Using Installation Script Templates

Microsoft provides several sample installation scripts you can adapt for your own situations. These sample scripts are part of the Windows 98 Resource Kit. You can obtain the Windows 95 Resource Kit online at www.microsoft.com/windows95/info/w95reskit.htm. At this writing, it appears that the sample scripts won't be available with the Windows 98 Resource Kit.

The sample scripts are well commented and are a useful tool for learning how installation scripts work. The best way to learn to use the sample installation script files is to open them with a text editor and study them. You can use some of the scripts as is; some scripts require additional editing. (The comments tell you what to do.) Modify and merge the scripts to suit your purposes. (For more information about the structure of installation scripts, refer to Appendix D, "Installation Script.")

> **Note** The sample scripts are a valuable resource for learning about installation scripts, but if you want a quick and simple way to create a script for a specific situation, consider the Batch98 utility (described in the next section) before you bury yourself too deeply in the sample scripts. You may find it useful to generate a script using Batch98 and then check that script by comparing it to an appropriate sample script.

The sample installation scripts available with the Windows 95 Resource Kit are as follows:

Script Name	Description
AUTOMATE.INF	Shows how to implement an automated installation.
DEFAULT.INF	Shows how to implement an interactive (non-automated) setup, but with different default settings.
INIPREP.INF	Shows how to modify and remove settings in INF files.

continues

Script Name	Description
MINBATCH.INF	Shows the minimum script required for automated upgrade.
MSNET.INF	Shows how to configure Microsoft networking components.
MWNET.INF	Shows how to configure Microsoft Client for NetWare Networks and other NetWare-related items using an installation script.
REGIONAL.INF	Shows how to configure regional settings such as keyboard layout, language preferences, locale.
USERPROF.INF	Shows how to configure user profiles, group policies, and remote administration of the Registry.

For more information about configuring and troubleshooting installation scripts, see Appendix D.

Creating Installation Scripts with Batch98

Microsoft's Batch98 utility (tools\reskit\batch\batch.exe on the Windows 98 CD) enables you to create Windows 98 installation scripts for automated installations. Batch 98 is also part of theWindows 98 Resource Kit which you can purchase in book form, or you can electronically through Microsoft: www.microsoft.com.Batch98 (shown in Figure 2.1), which provides an interface for entering configuration information that will become part of the installation script. Batch98 offers significantly more customization than you get if you interactively step through the Setup process, but it still offers only a subset of possible Windows 98 configuration settings.

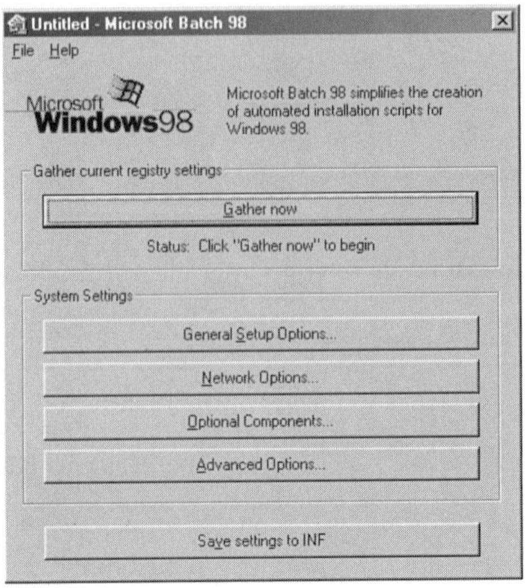

Figure 2.1
The Batch98 dialog box.

Chapter 2: Installing Windows 98

You can use a Batch98-generated installation script to automatically configure the following elements:

- Desktop icons
- Printers
- Network protocols, services, and clients
- Display settings
- User profile settings
- Location of the System Policy file

Batch98 also enables you to preconfigure responses to Setup prompts. You can tell Setup to auto-accept the user license agreement or to answer No to all version-conflict messages.

You can also use Batch 98 to specify an exported Registry file (that is, a .REG file; see Chapter 10, "Mastering the Windows 98 Registry") that will accompany the automated installation. In this way, you can extend the scope of Batch98 to include features that aren't referenced directly in the Batch98 user interface.

Using Batch98

To use Batch98, install and launch the Batch98 application (refer to Figure 2.1). Enter or modify the settings that Batch98 will use when generating the installation script by clicking one of the four System Settings buttons described in the following chart. The System Settings dialog boxes are discussed in greater detail later in this chapter.

Button	Description
General Setup Options	Setup prompts, user information, computer name, desktop icons, printers, and other configuration options.
Network Options	Network protocol, client, and service information. You can also define access control settings (share-level or user-level).
Optional Components	Optional Windows 98 components. These are the optional components available (after Setup is complete) through the Windows Setup tab of the Control Panel Add/Remove Programs application. The defaults do not precisely coincide with any of the basic installation types (Custom, Typical, Portable, Compact). If you're going to use the defaults, you may want to scan through the list to make sure that you know what you're getting. Note that if you use the Gather Now button (described in the next paragraph) to gather the current Registry settings, Batch98 selects the components currently installed on the system as optional components.
Advanced Options	Designate a Registry file and/or a System Policy file.

You can use the Gather Now button in the Batch98 dialog box to automatically assign values for the system settings parameters that coincide with the present configuration of the machine you're using. Gather Now scans the Registry for all settings applicable to Batch98.

When you have finished configuring system settings for the Windows 98 installation script, click Save Settings to INF to save the installation script. The default name for the script is MSBATCH.INF. Make sure that the reference to the installation script in the Setup command (as described in the preceding section, "Customizing Windows 98 Setup with Installation Scripts") includes a complete path to the directory in which you save the script.

After an installation script is created, you can review or revise the settings by opening the file using the Open command in the Batch98 File menu. You can then make your modifications and click Save in the File menu to save any changes.

The following sections detail the Batch98 System Settings dialog boxes and describe a few advanced features, as follows:

- Generating multiple installation scripts
- Installing Registry files
- Installing a System Policy file
- Installing other important files

Batch98 General Setup Options

Click the General Setup button in the Batch98 dialog box to invoke the General Setup Options dialog box. The General Setup Options dialog box contains several tabs defining various aspects of the installation process and the general configuration. The tabs and settings of the General Setup Options dialog box are described in Table 2.2.

Table 2.2
Batch98 General Setup Options

Tab	Setting	Comment
Install Info	Product ID	Optional Windows 98 Product ID number.
	Installation Directory	Destination directory for Windows 98 files.
	Do Not Show Installation Directory Warning	Disables Setup warning that appears when a previous version of Windows is in a directory other than the installation directory.
	Uninstall Options	Radio buttons let you choose whether or not to create uninstall information during Setup.

Tab	Setting	Comment

	User Info	Responses to computer- and user-info prompts that normally appear during Setup:
		    User Name
		    Company Name
		    Computer Name
		    Workgroup
		    Description

	Setup Prompts	Items cause Setup to skip or auto-respond to certain prompts that appear during the Setup process (for a fully automated installation, select all the boxes):
		    Auto-Accept End-User License Agreement
		    Do Not Prompt for Emergency Startup Disk
		    Auto-Answer "No to All" to Version Conflict Dialogs
		    Automatically Reboot PCI and PnP Machines During Setup
		    Do Not Search Source Folder for New Devices
		    Skip the PC Card Microsoft warns (PCMIA) Wizard that this option enables protected-mode socket services, which may cause problems. If you don't have a PC card, you normally don't have to check this box for unattended installation.

	Regional Settings	Region-specific settings such as time zone, language, and keyboard layout:
		    Time Zone
		    Keyboard Layout
		    Language and dialect settings

	Desktop	Lets you decide whether to include the standard icons and miscellaneous accouterments on the desktop:
		    My Documents
		    Internet Explorer
		    Network Neighborhood
		    Outlook Express
		    Recycle Bin
		    Setup the Microsoft Network
		    Delete Online Service from the Desktop After Setup
		    Do Not Show Windows 98 Welcome Screen
		    Do Not Show the Windows 98 Registration Wizard

	Printers	Lets you add one or more printers automatically during Setup (see Figure 2.3). Use this dialog box to install either a local or a network printer.

continues

Table 2.2, Continued
Batch98 General Setup Options

Tab	Setting	Comment
	Printer Name	
	Printer Type	Printer model (must be the exact name of printer driver; see the printer model designations listed in the Add Printer Wizard).
	Printer Port	Printer port for a local printer; share name and path for a network printer.
MRU Locations		Most Recently Used (MRU) lists are the lists of recent paths or names that appear throughout Windows 98 when you click the down arrow to the right of a text box. Use the MRU Locations tab to enter paths that will appear in the MRU list during Setup. Enter an item and click Add MRU.
Display Settings		Display settings for color depth and resolution. These settings appear in the Settings tab of the Control Panel Display application.
User Profiles		Lets you choose whether or not the system will use User Profiles. If you choose to enable User Profiles, you can opt to include desktop icons and Network Neighborhood contents and/or Start Menu and program groups in the profile settings.

The Setup Prompts tab (shown in Figure 2.2) lists the auto responses you need to accomplish an unattended installation. By default, all items in the Setup prompt are enabled except Skip the PC Card (PCMIA) Wizard option. Microsoft warns that enabling the Skip the PC Card option can cause problems because so doing enables protected mode socket services. If you don't have a PC card, you can leave the Skip the PC Card option deselected and, most likely, you won't get a prompt from Setup.

Network Options

The Network Options button in the Batch98 dialog box invokes the Network Options dialog box (see Figure 2.3). The Network Options dialog box lets you configure network protocols, services, and clients; it also lets you choose share-level or user-level access. The Network Option settings are roughly similar to the values configured in the Control Panel Network application (as described in Chapter 5). The tabs of the Network Options dialog box are described in Table 2.3.

Chapter 2: Installing Windows 98

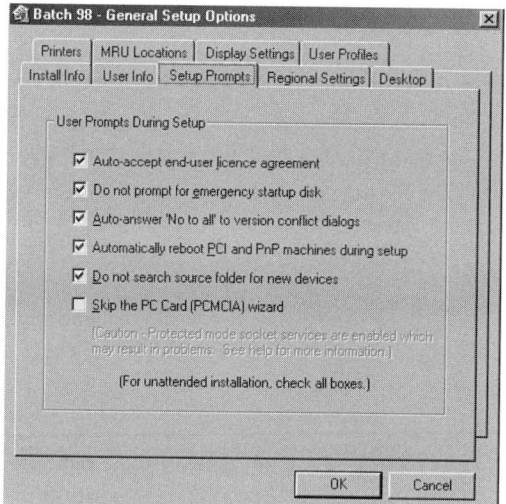

Figure 2.2
Batch98's Setup Prompts tab.

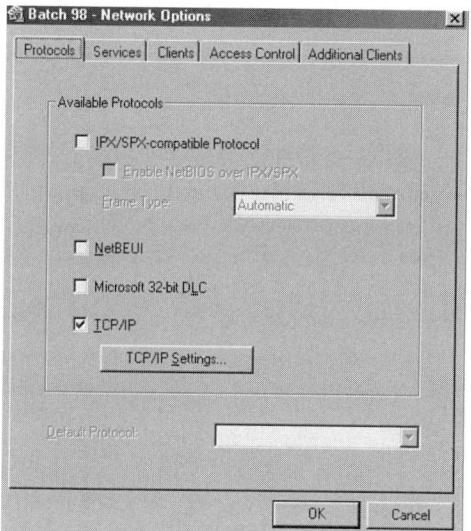

Figure 2.3
Batch98's Network Options dialog box.

Table 2.3
Batch98 Network Options

Tab	Comment
Protocols	Choose IPX/SPX-Compatible, NetBEUI, Microsoft 32-Bit DLC, or TCP/IP. Click the TCP/IP Settings button to configure TCP/IP settings. If you select more than one protocol, you can choose one as the default.

continues

Table 2.3, Continued
Batch98 Network Options

Tab	Comment
Services	You can choose No File and Print Sharing, File and Printer Sharing for Microsoft Networks, or File and Print Sharing for NetWare Networks. (You must choose one of the three options.) Each of the network service options offers a number of configuration settings.
Clients	Choose Client for Microsoft Networks, Client for NetWare 3.x/4.x Networks, and/or NetWare Directory Service. Then set logon options.
Access Control	Identical to the Access Control tab in the Control Panel Network application. Choose share-level or user-level access; designate a source for user and group information—a Windows NT domain, a Windows NT Server or Workstation (v3.51 or v4.0), or a NetWare Server.
Additional Clients	Choose Banyan DOS/Windows 3.1 Client or Novell NetWare 3.x or 4.x Workstation Shell. You can also add other clients by entering the appropriate strings for protocol, client, and services.

Batch98's network options provide a quick and efficient way of fine-tuning the network configuration during Setup, but they have one major limitation (at least, at this writing). Batch98's network options do not provide the capability to enter a separate network configuration for each network adapter. The settings you enter in the Network Options dialog box apply to *all adapters* present on the system at the time of setup. This applies not only to systems (with two or more adapter cards) but also to systems that include both a network card (such as an Ethernet card) and also the dial-up adapter provided automatically when you install dial-up networking.

The configuration for the dial-up adapter is often different from the configuration for the network adapter card. For example, you may want to obtain an IP address automatically through DHCP for your dial-up Internet account, and you may have a static IP address on your local LAN. (Microsoft actually recommends that you not even configure TCP/IP properties for the dial-up binding but instead configure TCP/IP properties through individual dial-up networking connections.) If you plan to use more than one adapter on the new system, you may have to modify the settings for one of the adapters in the Network application after Setup. Another consequence of the two-adapter problem is that, if you configure the installation script to enable file and print sharing for the local network, Setup may configure file and print sharing on the dial-up adapter. (Sharing files with the Internet from a Windows 98 machine presents some serious security issues—this should never happen by accident.)

Batch98's inability to recognize multiple adapters also applies to the Registry Scan feature invoked through the Gather Now button (described earlier in this chapter). If you have multiple adapters, Batch98 simply uses one of the adapters to formulate the network configuration settings. Make sure that the settings you use to generate the installation script coincide with the settings you need to connect to the installation share and to log on at the conclusion of Setup.

Optional Components

The Optional Components button invokes the Optional Components dialog box, which lets you choose Windows 98 components (accessories, system tools, multimedia and communications components, and so forth). This list is similar to the list of components you'll encounter if you choose Select Components during installation or if you choose Windows Setup in the Control Panel Add/Remove Programs application. For some reason, Batch98's default components do not correspond to any of the standard installation types (Custom, Typical, Compact, or Portable). Choose the components you want to install on the new system. If you use the Batch98's Gather Now button to collect existing Registry settings, the components now on the system are enabled for the installation script.

Advanced Options

The Advanced Options button invokes the Advanced Options dialog box (see Figure 2.4). You can used the Advanced Options dialog box to designate either of the following items:

- A Registry file that will provide a complete Registry for the new system.
- A System Policy file for the new system.

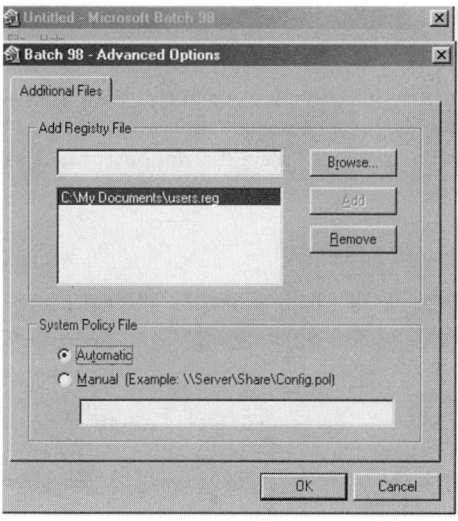

Figure 2.4
Batch98's Advanced Options dialog box.

Windows 98's Registry editor (described in Chapter 10) lets you export the partial or complete copy of the Registry to a text file. That Registry text file (which, by default, has a `.REG` extension) provides a complete description of the Registry or a branch of the Registry. Batch98's Advanced Options dialog box lets you add an exported Registry file to the installation script.

Enter the Registry filename in the uppermost text box in the Advanced Options dialog box. You can also browse for a Registry file by clicking the Browse button. You must click the Add button to add the file to the current Registry file list.

Generating Multiple Installation Scripts with Batch98

On Microsoft networks, each computer must have a unique computer name. Even if all other settings on all computers are identical, each computer requires a unique computer name if it is to coexist with other computers on the network. If your network is a TCP/IP network with manually configured IP addresses, each computer also needs a unique IP address. Batch98 includes a Multiple Machine-Name Save feature that uses a collection of installation script settings (as defined in Batch98) to generate a series of installation scripts—with each script bearing a unique computer name and (optionally) a unique IP address.

The Multiple Machine-Name Save feature works a little like a list processor. The script settings are "merged" with a file that contains a list of computer names and IP addresses. The format for the list file (called the *machine name file*) is as follows:

```
computer1
computer2, 155.121.131.45
Zoro
BrueghelElder, 162.134.14.66
```

Each line starts with a computer name (in this example, `computer1`, `computer2`, `Zoro`, or `BrueghelElder`); each computer name appears on a separate line. If you want to configure an IP address for the computer, separate the IP address from the computer name with a comma. Note that you don't need an IP address for every entry.

A blank line marks the end of the file.

Batch98 does not check for errors in the list file (such as illegal computer names, duplicate IP addresses, and so forth). It is a good idea to check each line of the file carefully to make sure that the information is correct.

When you perform a multiple machine-name save, Batch98 asks you for the name of the machine name file and the name of the directory in which you want to save the set of installation scripts. The filenames for the scripts are `BSTP0001.INF`, `BSTP0002.INF`, `BSTP003.INF` and so on (up to `BSTP9999.INF`).

Chapter 2: Installing Windows 98

To use Batch98's Multiple Machine-Name Save feature, follow these steps:

1. Create a machine name file of computer names and IP addresses, as described earlier in this section.

2. Use Batch98 to create an installation script specification.

3. In the main Batch98 dialog box (refer to Figure 2.1), pull down the **F**ile menu and select Multiple Machine-Name Save.

4. In the Multiple Machine-Name Save dialog box, click the Machine Name File button and select the machine name file you want to use. Click the Destination of Save button to choose a directory for the installation scripts.

5. Click the Save Files button to generate and save the installation scripts.

Uninstalling Windows 98

As this chapter has described, if you're performing an upgrade, you can configure your system so that you can uninstall Windows 98 at a later date and revert to your previous operating system.

To set up Windows 98 so that you can automatically uninstall it, follow these steps:

1. Install Windows 98 to the previous Windows directory.

2. When Setup asks if you want to save system files, click Yes.

If you have to uninstall Windows 98, go to the Control Panel and double-click the Add/Remove Programs application. In the Install/Uninstall tab, select Windows 98 and click Add/Remove.

If you didn't set up Windows 98 for the uninstall option, use the following procedure to uninstall Windows 98. You'll need a bootable floppy to complete this procedure—see step 10:

1. Boot Windows 98 in command-line mode by pressing F8 or the left Control key at startup and selecting Command Prompt Only; alternatively, boot to another operating system using the F8 startup menu (if you're configured to dual boot) or boot to a startup disk. Microsoft recommends that you copy the `SCANDISK.EXE`, `SCANDISK.INI`, and `DELTREE.EXE` files from the `\Windows\commands` directory to the root directory.

2. Run ScanDisk to delete any long filenames on your system (if you're reverting to DOS or Windows 3.x/3.1.x). Edit the file `SCANDISK.INI` to set the following parameters:

    `labelcheck=on`   Checks for invalid characters in volume labels

    `spacecheck=on`   Checks for invalid spaces in filenames

3. Run ScanDisk on your boot drive:

   `scandisk c:`

4. Delete the Windows directory (and all subdirectories) using `deltree` command:

   `deltree windows`   If your Windows directory is called `windows`

5. Delete `IO.SYS`, `MSDOS.SYS`, `CONFIG.SYS`, and `AUTOEXEC.BAT` from the root directory of your boot drive.

6. Delete the `winboot` directory (if it exists):

   `deltree winboot.*`

7. Delete the following log files from the root directory:

   ```
   setuplog.*
   bootlog.*
   detlog.*
   ```

8. Delete the `DBLSPACE.BIN` and `DRVSPACE.BIN` compression drivers from the root directory of the boot drive or host drive (if the drive is compressed).

9. Delete `COMMAND.COM` from the root directory.

10. Boot to a bootable DOS floppy. If you are removing Windows 98 in a dual-boot situation and you want to be able to boot to another operating system that is currently present on your system, the system files on the boot disk (for example, `autoexec.bat`, `config.sys`) should contain the commands necessary to boot the other operating system. Or, the `autoexec.bat` and `config.sys` files from the other operating system may be stored in your root directory under the names `AUTOEXEC.DOS` and `CONFIG.DOS`, in which case you can simply rename these files (after you perform the `SYS` command—see step 13). Be ready to copy a version of `COMMAND.COM` that is compatible with the new operating system to the root directory (see Step 12). You may want to include `COMMAND.COM` on the boot floppy. Also, be sure the floppy boot configuration supports the `SYS` command (contains the file `SYS.COM`). Restore the system files using the `SYS` command:

    `sys C:`

    In this syntax, `C:` is the boot drive (or host drive if the drive is compressed).

11. If you have a compressed drive, make sure that the file `DBLSPACE.BIN` is in the root directory of the boot drive. If it isn't, place a copy of `DBLSPACE.BIN` in the root directory.

12. Make sure that `COMMAND.COM` is in the root directory of the boot drive. If it isn't, place a copy of `COMMAND.COM` in the root directory.

13. In the root directory, change the name of CONFIG.DOS to CONFIG.SYS. Change the name of AUTOEXEC.DOS to AUTOEXEC.BAT. (This action restores the CONFIG.SYS and AUTOEXEC.BAT files from the previous operating system.)

Troubleshooting Setup

Any process as internally complicated as Windows 98 Setup offers untold opportunities for errors and failures. The state of the computer after a failure—and therefore the procedure for recovery—depends on where in the process Setup failed.

If your system stops unexpectedly during Setup, follow these steps (in this order):

1. Press F3 or click the button labeled Exit.

2. Press Ctrl+Alt+Del.

3. Turn off your computer, wait 15 seconds, and then restart.

Windows 98 includes built-in mechanisms for troubleshooting Setup. Setup logs each step of the installation process and can later use the logged information to circumvent many types of failures.

Setup stores information on the installation in the following log files:

SETUPLOG.TXT   A log of installation events.

DETCRASH.LOG   A record of the hardware detection process, created if Setup fails during hardware detection. Setup also creates a text file equivalent to DETCRASH.LOG called DETLOG.TXT.

When you restart your computer after a crash, Setup attempts to use the logged information to retrace its steps and resume the installation.

Using Setup's Built-In Recovery Features

If Setup fails during the early phase of an installation (before hardware detection), when you restart, Setup asks whether you want to use Safe Recovery to resume the installation process. If you elect to use Safe Recovery, Setup reads the log file SETUPLOG.TXT and uses the information to determine the point at which the installation failed.

> **Note**   If you choose not to use Safe Recovery, Setup starts over with the installation.

Setup records the start and completion of each installation step in SETUPLOG.TXT. When you attempt to recover after a crash, Setup reads SETUPLOG.TXT to learn which steps began but did not finish—those unfinished steps are the most likely to have caused the failure. Setup then skips any steps that might have caused the failure and proceeds from that point with the installation. If Setup fails again because of another installation step, Setup again recovers (after rebooting), skips the step that caused the failure, and resumes the installation.

If Setup fails during hardware detection, Setup places the hidden file DETCRASH.LOG in the root directory of the drive on which you're performing the installation. (Windows 98's elaborate detection routines for non-Plug and Play hardware are a common cause of installation failures.) DETCRASH.LOG includes a record of memory and I/O port information at the moment of the crash. After the computer restarts, if Setup finds DETCRASH.LOG, it immediately switches the operating system to Safe Mode, checks the devices currently in the Registry, skips the failed component, and proceeds with the installation.

Windows 98's built-in Safe Recovery can successfully circumvent many types of installation failures. However, Safe Recovery does not always solve the problem. In some cases, Setup cannot recover the installation. Also, because Safe Recovery finishes the installation by *skipping* failed components, the resultant system may include hidden instabilities. Note, however, that the Do Not Use Safe Recovery option does not really solve the problem, either, because you will most likely be executing an instant replay of the failed installation. Microsoft recommends the Safe Recovery option when restarting after an installation failure.

Inspecting the Logs

If Setup fails and you want to determine why, you can do what the Safe Recovery feature does: Read the setup log files and look for suspicious entries. Look for components that started to install and never finished. Look for error messages or other unusual entries. The logged entries are sequential: Start at the end of the file for the last events.

SETUPLOG.TXT is an ASCII text file you can read with a text editor such as Notepad. DETCRASH.LOG is a binary file only Setup can access directly, but when DETCRASH.LOG is created, an equivalent ASCII file called DETLOG.TXT is also created (as a hidden file) in the root directory of the drive on which you're performing the installation.

You may also want to examine the following files:

    NETLOG.TXT   A log of the detection and installation of networking components.

    BOOTLOG.TXT   A log file created during the system startup process. BOOTLOG.TXT is a tool for troubleshooting all types of Windows 98 startup problems. A BOOTLOG.TXT file is created automatically when Windows 98 boots for the first time during Setup.

Table 2.4 shows Windows 98 Setup log files and some entries to watch for in each of the files.

Table 2.4
Setup Log Files and Some Critical Troubleshooting Entries

Setup Log File	Contents	Entries to Watch
SETUPLOG.TXT	Log of Setup process	error (system error) failed (installation failure) [not Configured] (items that were not configured) COMPLETE (indicates that a section completed successfully)
DETLOG.TXT	Log of hardware detection process (the ASCII equivalent of DETCRASH.LOG)	error (system error) detected (devices detected) devices verified (devices with settings in Registry) AvoidMem (UMB address ranges Setup avoided)
NETLOG.TXT	Log of network component detection	NDiCreate (*object_name*) (Setup successfully created an internal object, where *object_name* is the name of the protocol, adapter, service, and so on) ClassInstall (used to define binding) Validating (adds object to the Registry and creates binding)

Troubleshooting Tips

Some of the most common causes of Setup failures are listed here:

- *Hardware detection failures.* If your computer stops unexpectedly during hardware detection, restart your system. Setup will attempt to resume the installation (as described in the preceding section).

- *Antivirus software.* Some antivirus programs stop Setup from executing. Make sure that antivirus programs are disabled and that automatic startup is disabled for antivirus software, then reboot and resume the installation. Some computers may have CMOS-enabled antivirus protection that doesn't appear as an application. If you see a message telling you to disable antivirus programs but it doesn't appear that you have any antivirus programs running, contact your hardware vendor.

- *Network connection failures (for network installations).* Make sure that the network is working properly. Make sure that Setup is configuring the correct network logon and the correct network client. Make sure that your logon information is correct (user name, password, domain).

Some of the preparatory steps described earlier in this chapter are important for avoiding trouble, and these steps are important remedies if trouble is found. For example, you should disable TSRs and timeout features, check the system requirements, and disable display utilities and video drivers. It is also good idea to scan your hard disk for viruses before you start Setup.

Some other common Setup problems are described in the following sections.

ScanDisk

If ScanDisk displays a message that says you don't have enough memory, try freeing some conventional or upper memory. See Chapter 11, "Windows 98 Architecture and Application Support," or Chapter 32, "Windows 98 Configuration Files."

If you're running Setup from MS-DOS, Setup may report errors from long filenames. Setup proceeds in spite of these errors.

If you can't get ScanDisk to work in Setup, you can always disable Setup's ScanDisk check using Setup's /is switch.

Compressed Drives

If you are installing Windows 98 to a compressed drive, you may see an error message warning you that there is not enough space on the host partition. See Chapter 17 for a discussion of host drives and compression software in Windows 98. If you have an uncompressed drive available, try installing Windows on the uncompressed drive instead. If that isn't possible, delete files on the host partition. Alternatively, free up space on the host drive (refer to the documentation for your compression software). For Windows 3.1 systems, if you have a permanent swap file, try making the swap file smaller: click Virtual Memory in the 386 Enhanced Control Panel.

Conventional Memory

Windows 98 Setup needs 432 K of conventional memory. The purpose of removing unnecessary TSRs is to free up conventional memory. Microsoft recommends the following CONFIG.SYS settings for making the best use of available memory:

MS-DOS 5.0 or later:

```
device=himem.sys
device=emm386.exe noems
dos=high,umb
```

Also try using the MS-DOS MEMMAKER utility to optimize memory (if it is available on your system).

MS-DOS Boot Partition

Windows 98 can't install unless your system has an MS-DOS boot partition. If you see a message that says Setup can't find a valid boot partition, you may have a hard disk problem. However, Microsoft points out that this error may also result from a hidden compression host drive or a network drive mapping over the boot drive. Verify the viability of the boot partition using Fdisk. Check all drive mappings and host drive assignments.

Incorrect Configuration of Legacy Hardware

Some hardware detection problems are caused by hardware that was configured incorrectly under the previous operating system. If Setup's Safe Detection and Safe Recovery features can't circumvent the problem, try disabling the ISA enumerator in the SYSTEM.INI file:

```
device=ISAPNP.386
```

Default User Policy Settings

Default User Policy settings can cause a failure when Setup attempts to launch Windows.

Conclusion

This chapter described the Windows 98 Setup process and discussed some preliminary tasks you must attend to before installing Windows 98. The chapter also outlined procedures for upgrading to Windows 98 and performing a full installation from a newly formatted disk. You also learned about automating the installation process using Windows 98 installation scripts, and you learned how to uninstall Windows 98.

Chapter 3 discusses network installation techniques.

Network Installation

Network installation is an installation method in which the source files for the installation reside on a network server. The client machines (on which the product is being installed) can connect to the server and execute the Setup program through a network connection. This method saves the time and effort a network administrator would have to spend visiting each PC with the installation CD and executing every installation locally.

In recent years, network installation has become an essential technique for large networks, and it is becoming increasingly viable for mid-sized and even smaller deployments. This trend continues with Windows 98. Microsoft actively promotes network installation as an effective and efficient means of installing Windows 98 on multiple machines.

Almost any deployment in which you install Windows 98 in a networking environment is a candidate for a network installation. The network installation options discussed in this chapter are easily adaptable to specific situations, and the automation and customization features provided by Windows 98 installation files, although (theoretically) available for local installations, are specifically designed to support fast and efficient network installations.

Understanding Network Installation

In its most basic form, a network installation is identical to a local installation except that the installation files reside on a network share (either a hard drive or a shared CD-ROM drive) rather than on the workstation's local CD-ROM drive. The basic steps for a network installation are as follows:

1. Create a network share that contains the contents of the Windows 98 installation CD—either share a CD-ROM drive or copy the contents of the installation CD to a shared hard drive.

> **Note** See Chapter 21, "Understanding Windows 98 Networking," for more information about sharing files and directories on Microsoft networks.

2. Make a connection from the PC on which you want to install Windows 98 to the network share.

3. Locate the Windows 98 Setup program (setup.exe) in the installation share and run it from the client PC.

Running Setup over the network is, of course, of little benefit if a network administrator has to sit in front of the local workstation and answer screen prompts. In practice, a network install is almost always implemented by using a Windows 98 installation script. (Refer to Chapter 2, "Installing Windows 98," for more information about the Windows 98 Setup program and Windows 98 installation scripts.)

Some administrators find it advantageous to shave still more time from the installation process by placing the Setup command in a logon script that executes on the workstation or by creating a batch file that includes the Setup command and placing an icon for the batch file on each user's desktop. The following sections discuss some of these so-called *push* installation techniques and provide a description of network installation methods.

Network Installation in Windows NT Domains

To install Windows 98 across the network on a Windows NT domain, share the installation files on the network, then enter the following command from the workstation on which you want to install Windows 98:

`\\server\share_name\setup W98_scrpt.inf`

In this command, *server* is the name of the server on which the installation files reside, *share_name* is the name of the installation file share you created on the Windows NT machine, and *W98scrt.inf* is the name of the Windows 98 installation script that contains settings for the installation. The installation script name can also include a path.

> **Note** Remember that you must obtain a valid license for every copy of Windows 98 you install. If you put the installation files on the server, take precautions to ensure that no one can perform an unauthorized (and unlicensed) installation.

As noted previously, an installation script is optional for network installations, but an installation script almost always accompanies a network installation because the primary purpose of a network installation is usually to reduce the need for user intervention. Refer to Chapter 2 for a discussion of Windows 98 installation scripts and the Batch98 tool for creating installation scripts. (For further information about installation scripts, see Appendix D, "Installation Script.") If you *don't* specify an installation script with a network installation, Setup will display all the same screen prompts on the client machine that it typically displays for local scriptless installations.

To perform a network installation on an NT domain, follow these steps:

1. Share the Windows 98 installation files on the network, either by placing the installation CD in a shared CD-ROM drive or by copying the files to a network hard drive and sharing the installation files. Using a hard drive is faster—especially if you're going to be installing several systems at once, but directly sharing the CD saves the step of copying all the files to the server hard drive.

> **Note** Windows 98 remembers the location of its installation files. If you add a driver or an applet at some later date, Windows 98 will automatically check for the required files along the original installation path. If you place the installation files at some permanent storage location such as a hard drive, you won't have to reinsert the Windows 98 CD whenever you make a change to your configuration.

2. Set share, directory, and file permissions so that any user who performs the installation will have read and execute access to the installation files. Your security arrangements will depend on your network configuration and your deployment strategy.

3. Create a Windows 98 installation script with configuration settings for the installation (optional). Review Chapter 2 and Appendix D for more information about Windows 98 installation scripts. Settings that produce an automated installation are particularly useful when installing across the network. Also, pay particular attention to the Workgroup, PrimaryLogon, Security, and PassThroughAgent settings in the [Network] section of the installation script. During the last phase of installation, the computer restarts, and the user must log on under the new configuration to complete the installation. If the new network settings do not provide access to the installation share, you won't be able to resume the installation. The following [Network] section settings represent familiar parameters you'll find in the Control Panel Network application for Windows 95 and Windows 98 machines:

   - *Workgroup.* Workgroup or domain name (appears in the Identification tab of the Control Panel Network application)

   - *PrimaryLogon.* Should be set to VREDIR (for Client for Microsoft Networks) if you're logging on to a domain (appears in the Configuration tab of the Control Panel Network application)

   - *Security.* Should be set to DOMAIN (for user-level security on an NT domain)

   - *PassThroughAgent.* Should be the domain name for a domain logon (appears in the Access Control tab of the Control Panel Network application)

   You do not have to provide values for these settings in the installation script. If you're upgrading an existing network-enabled Windows 3.1 or Windows 95 system, Setup will preserve settings from the old operating system.

   Note If you're using Batch98's Gather Now option to scan the Registry for installation script settings on a computer with more than one adapter, Batch98 sometimes doesn't base the script settings on the adapter that supports the local network logon. Refer to Chapter 2 for further information.

4. Log on from the client that is to receive Windows 98. If the client does not presently support network communications (for example, it is a new machine or a machine with a reformatted hard drive), you can boot the client and make the connection to the installation share using a network-enabled boot disk. Network-enabled boot disks are discussed later in this chapter.

5. From the prospective Windows 98 client, execute the Setup utility in the top-level directory of the installation share, as follows:

```
\\server\share_name\setup W98_scrpt.inf
```

In this command, *server* is the name of the server on which the installation files reside, *share_name* is the name of the installation file share on the Windows NT machine, and *W98scrt.inf* is the name of the Windows 98 installation script that contains settings for the installation. The installation script name can also include a path.

Network Installations on NetWare Networks

You can also perform a network installation from a NetWare server on a NetWare network. Conceptually, the procedure is similar to the network-installation procedure on an Windows NT network, as follows:

1. Mount the installation CD as a NetWare volume (or place the installation files on a NetWare volume).

2. From a NetWare-enabled client, log on to the server.

3. Map a drive letter to the installation directory.

4. Run Setup.

The details of this procedure may depend upon your network and your deployment strategy. You can designate an installation script and any Setup command-line switches for a NetWare-based installation just as you would for any network installation. You can also employ *push* installation techniques by placing the Windows 98 Setup commands in a NetWare logon script.

A NetWare-based installation is like other network installations in that, for the installation to succeed, the client machine on which you're installing Windows 98 must be capable of accessing the installation files for the final phase of the installation. Make sure the new Windows 98 machine will support the protocol, network client, and logon information necessary to make the connection. Perform a test installation to make sure the procedure is working properly before you begin the entire network upgrade.

Specifying Installation Scripts for Network Installations

If you're performing several network installations, your deployment strategy should include some consideration of how to manage the necessary installation scripts. Some possible approaches are as follows:

- Use a minimal script for automated upgrade of Windows 3.1 and Windows 95 machines that suppresses screen prompts and does not impose other settings. Allow other settings, such as network settings, to migrate from the preexisting Windows 95 configuration.

- Create unique installation script for each PC, specifying unique settings (such as computer name, IP address, and other computer-specific configuration items) within the script. This option is often preferable if you are installing new PCs or if you are changing your network configuration along with the upgrade.

Your situation may, of course, require you to draw from some combination of the preceding options in order to successfully migrate to Windows 98. The installation script template automate.inf (described in Chapter 2 in the section "Using Installation Script Templates") provides minimal settings for automated Setup. You can use automate.inf to specify automated Setup without imposing other settings. Automate.inf contains comments describing each of the settings and providing instructions for preparing the script. Open automate.inf with a text editor and make modifications as necessary.

If you want to define computer-specific settings in the installation script, you'll need computer-specific installation scripts. Every computer on a Microsoft network, for instance, must have a unique computer name. If you are using the installation script to define a computer name (as would be the case if you were automating installation for a new machine without a preexisting configuration), you do not have the option of using a generic script for all installations. The Batch98 utility includes a Multiple Machine-Name Save feature that will automatically generates predefined installation scripts with unique computer names and (optional) IP addresses. (See Chapter 2 for information about on Batch98's Multiple Machine-Name Save feature.) You can use Batch98 to list-process a group of installation scripts that are identical except for unique computer names and IP addresses. After you've created the scripts, you may want to devise a scheme for naming and managing the files so that the correct file runs on the correct PC. (Batch98 provides the illuminating monikers BSTP001.INF, BSTP002.INF, and so on, for scripts created using the Multiple-Machine Name Save feature.) One solution is to give each script a name that refers to the computer name it creates. If you choose the machine-generated names, make sure you have a list that associates script names with computer names.

If you decide to use descriptive names for the installation scripts, you may find it easier to simply use Batch98's File Save feature rather than using the script generator, as follows:

Chapter 3: Network Installation

1. Configure Batch98 settings as described in Chapter 2. Save the settings to an INF file. Specify a descriptive name for the file.

2. Make any necessary changes to the Batch98 settings.

3. Choose Save As from the File menu and specify a descriptive name for a second installation script.

4. Change the settings and save additional scripts as required.

Push Techniques

Microsoft uses the term *push* to describe an installation in which the commands that execute the installation are imposed on the installing PC. The PC is thus forced into performing an installation. The most common method for push installation is to create a logon script that connects to the network share and then executes Setup.

The commands necessary for connecting to the server and beginning Setup require only a few lines in the logon script. The following sections discuss the logon-script commands for push installations on the following PCs:

- MS-DOS, Windows 3.x and Windows 95 computers

- Windows for Workgroups computers

If you tie the installation logon script to a user account and the user logs on more than once, Setup performs more than one installation. Also, tying the installation logon script to a user's regular account forces the upgrade at the next logon—the user won't have a chance to plan an ideal time for the upgrade. For these reasons, one common method for push installation (and a method Microsoft recommends) is to create a user account called *Upgrade* and configure it to run the installation logon script. You can then tell users to log on to the Upgrade account to begin the upgrade.

Consult a Windows NT reference for a complete discussion of how to add new user accounts with User Manager for Domains. Microsoft recommends that you use the following password settings for the Upgrade account:

- Users Cannot Change Password

- Password Never Expires

Place the script in the Windows NT Domain Controller's winnt\system32\repl\export\scripts directory. To add a logon script to a user account by using Windows NT's User Manager for Domains, click on the Profiles button in the User Properties dialog box or the New User dialog box and, in the User Environment Profile dialog box, enter the script name in the box labeled Logon Script Name.

> **Note** The Upgrade account method causes all PCs to use a common installation script. This method therefore presupposes that you won't need to set computer-specific values (such as computer name and IP address) through the installation script. In an upgrade situation in which the clients are already configured to access a Windows NT domain, a common script with automation settings is typically all that is required.

Logon Script Installation Commands for MS-DOS, Windows 3.x, and Windows 95

The logon script for a push installation on a MS-DOS, Windows 3.x, or Windows 95 machine should map a drive to the installation share and then run Setup using a path with the network drive letter, as follows:

```
net use driveID \\server_name\install_share
driveID:\setup driveID:W98scrpt.inf
```

```
where driveID is a drive letter for the network drive (e.g., X or Y or Z)
```

```
server_name is the name of the server that contains the installation files
```

```
install_share is the name of the share with the installation files
```

```
w98scrpt.inf is the name of the installation script.
```

Note that in the preceding example, the installation script is located in the same directory as the Setup utility. (Both are in the top-level driveID directory.)

If the MS-DOS, Windows 3.x, or Windows 95 machine is using a real-mode client, precede these commands with the net start full command, as follows:

```
net start full
net use driveID \\server_name\install_share
driveID:\setup driveID:W98scrpt.inf
```

Push Installations for Windows for Workgroups

When a Windows for Workgroups computer logs on to a Windows NT network using a protected-mode client, the logon script runs in a virtual machine. Because Windows 98 Setup cannot run in a virtual machine, you cannot place the Setup command in the logon script when logging on from a Windows for Workgroups protected-mode client. Fortunately, Microsoft suggests a workaround for this problem. The idea is to create a Startup program group and then place a command-line program item within the Startup group that executes the Setup command, as these steps describe:

1. Using File, New in Word for Windows Program Manager, create a new Startup program group (startup.grp) that contains the following command line program item:

   ```
   driveID:setup
   ```

2. Copy the Startup.grp file you created in step 1 to the directory that contains the domain logon script.

3. Add the following lines to the logon script. These commands preserve the existing Startup group and copy the Startup group you created in step 1 to the WfW machine.

   ```
   Net use driveID: \\server\install_share
   rename C:\Windows\Startup.grp *.sav
   copy  \\Servername\netlogon\startup.grp C:\Windows\startup.grp
   ```

4. The following installation script entries restore the original startup group:

   ```
   [install]
   renfiles=replace.startup.grp
   [replace.startup.grp]
   startup.grp startup.sav
   [destinationdirs]
   replace.startup.grp=10
   ```

See the Windows 98 Resource Kit for more information about this method. For more about Windows 98 installation scripts, see Appendix D.

Other Methods for Initiating Setup

Some other options for delivering Setup commands and initiating the Setup process are as follows:

- *Batch file.* You can deliver a batch file to the user that, when executed, will start the Setup process.

- *System management system such as Microsoft's Systems Management Server.* Systems Management Server (SMS) and other third-party system management packages can facilitate large-scale distribution and setup of client Windows 98 systems.

Creating a Network Boot Disk

For new installations over the network, you can save yourself considerable trouble by creating a network boot disk. A *network boot disk* is a bootable system disk that is capable of connecting to a network share and initiating a network installation. A network boot disk is useful for situations in which you want the speed and ease of unattended network installation, but the machines on which you're installing Windows 98 are not network enabled (for instance, new computers or computers with newly reformatted hard drives).

You can generate a network boot disk by using Windows NT Server's Network Client Administrator tool. If you don't have a Windows NT Server system, Microsoft provides a method (described on the TechNet CD) for creating a network boot disk using Windows for Workgroups. The following sections discuss these methods for creating a network boot disk.

Using Windows NT's Network Client Administrator to Create a Network Boot Disk

Windows NT Server's Network Client Administrator utility lets you create a network-enabled boot disk that you can use to connect to an installation share. Network Client Administrator's boot disk feature is designed to provide access to the client installation files included with the Windows NT Server CD-ROM, but with some minor alterations, you can use a Network Client Administrator boot disk to connect to another directory or share name with the required Windows 98 installation files.

The following instructions refer to Windows NT Server 4.0 Network Client Administrator. The instructions for Windows NT Server 3.5 are similar. Microsoft will most likely include a method for installing Windows 98 along with the Windows NT Server 5.0, but details of that method are not available at this writing.

To create a network boot disk using Network Client Administrator, follow these steps:

1. Create an MS-DOS system disk (place a newly formatted floppy in the A: drive and type `C:\sys A:` from the DOS prompt).

    It is helpful to also copy the file EDIT.COM (the DOS text editor) to the system disk. EDIT.COM is not necessary for the system disk to function, but a text editor will prove useful if you're installing more than one PC and you need to make computer-specific changes to the disk.

2. On a Windows NT Server system, select Network Client Administrator from the Administrative Tools group (Start/Programs/Administrative Tools/Network Client Administrator). In the Network Client Administrator dialog box, choose the Make Network Installation Startup Disk option button and click on Continue.

Chapter 3: Network Installation 89

3. The Share Network Client Installation Files dialog box appears (see Figure 3.1). Insert the Windows NT Server installation disk in the CD-ROM drive. In the box labeled Path, select the \CLIENTS directory on the Windows NT installation CD-ROM. You must set up the installation disk using the Windows NT \CLIENTS and then modify the path later to access the Windows 98 CD-ROM.

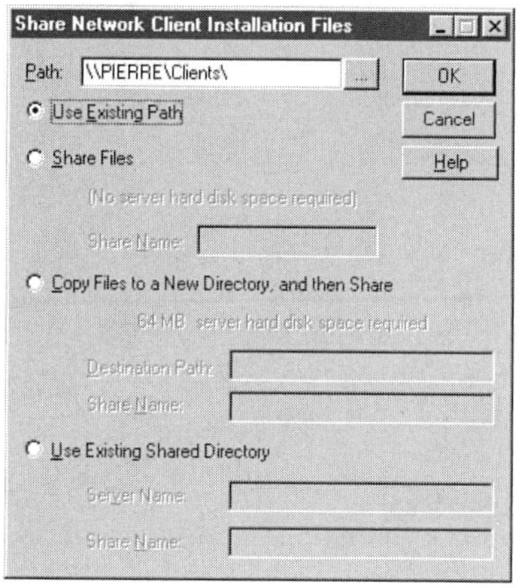

Figure 3.1
The Share Network Client Installation Files dialog box in Windows NT's Network Client Administrator.

Note Network Client Administrator is designed to install client files that are present on the Windows NT Server CD-ROM. This example modifies the network boot floppy so that you can use it to install directly from the Windows 98 CD-ROM. The purpose of the Network Client Administrator network startup disk is to simplify the installation process—not to circumvent any licensing requirements. You still need a valid license for every workstation whether you use the Windows NT Server CD-ROM or the Windows 98 CD-ROM as a source for network installations. Network Client Administrator warns you that the "license accompanying Windows NT Server does NOT contain a license to install and use Windows 95"—the same warning applies to Windows 98.

4. Select the Share Files option button and enter a share name. (The share name can be anything because you won't really be accessing the Windows NT \CLIENTS directory. Just enter a name so Network Client Administrator will let you proceed.) Click on OK.

5. In the Target Workstation Configuration dialog box (see Figure 3.2), select the option button describing the floppy disk size (3.5" or 5.25"). Choose Windows 95 in the network client list. Click on the arrow to the right of the box labeled Network Adapter Card and select the new workstation's network adapter card from the drop-down list. If you can't find the correct network adapter in the list, choose the default (for now) and see the discussion at the end of this procedure.

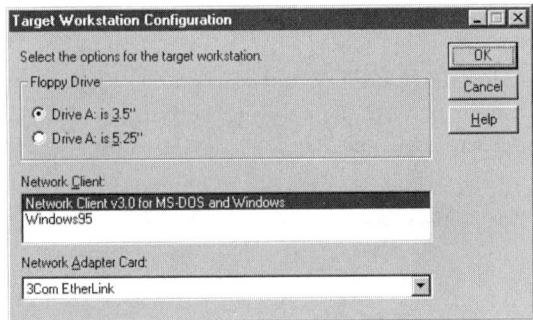

Figure 3.2
The Target Workstation Configuration dialog box in Windows NT's Network Client Administrator.

6. A warning appears, notifying you that you'll need a valid client license to install Windows 95. This warning also applies to Windows 98—all licensing requirements are independent of installation method. Read the warning and click on OK.

7. In the Network Startup Disk Configuration dialog box (see Figure 3.3), enter a computer name for the new workstation. Verify the User Name and the Domain name that floppy-boot client will use to connect to the installation share, and select a network protocol from the drop-down list. (Your network configuration must, of course, be capable of supporting the protocol you choose from the list.) If you choose TCP/IP, enter TCP/IP settings in the boxes provided. To enter an IP address and subnet mask, you must clear the DHCP configuration checkbox. The Destination Path box specifies the location of the floppy disk drive for the NT Server system that is creating the boot floppy. Click OK to create the network-enabled boot disk.

8. After you've created the network-enabled boot disk, open the autoexec.bat file on the boot disk by using NotePad or another text editor. Note that the final three lines of the autoexec.bat file map a network drive to the client installation files, display the message `Running Setup....`, and execute the Setup program on the installation share. You need to modify these lines so that they map a drive to the Windows 98 installation share and execute the Windows 98 setup program, as follows:

```
net use z: \\computer_name\share_name
echo Running Setup...
z:\setup.exe z:\W98_script.inf
```

In this example, *computer_name* and *share_name* are the computer name and share name specifying the location of the Windows 98 installation files.

See Chapter 2 for a discussion of the Setup command. In most cases, you will want to specify an installation script file when performing a network installation. You can specify an installation script and any of the optional setup-command switches, along with the setup command in the autoexec.bat file.

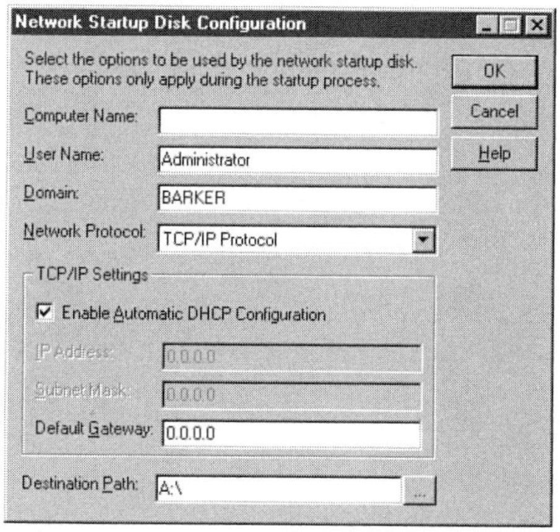

Figure 3.3
The Network Startup Disk Configuration dialog box in Windows NT's Network Client Administrator.

If the network adapter for the workstation on which you're installing Windows 98 doesn't appear in the Network Adapter list (see step 5 of the preceding procedure), you must manually configure the network boot disk to access your adapter. You must find the disk that accompanied the network adapter card in order to make the necessary adjustments to the network installation disk. Specifically, you'll need to accomplish the following tasks:

1. Copy the appropriate NDIS-compatible .dos driver from the manufacturer's disk to the \net directory of the network boot floppy.

2. Look for a sample protocol.ini file on the network card manufacturer's disk. Change the value of the drivername parameter in the net\protocol.ini file of the boot disk to match the drivername value in the sample protocol.ini file of the manufacturer's disk. If you can't find a sample protocol.ini file, consult other documentation on the manufacturer's disk. If you have to guess a drivername, try the name of the .dos driver (refer to step 1) without the extension and followed by $. For instance, the drivername line for the NDIS-compatible driver pcind.dos is drivername=PCIND$.

3. In the net\system.ini file on the boot disk, change the value of the *netcard* setting (in the network drivers section) to the name of the NDIS-compatible driver (refer to step 1).

Using Windows for Workgroups to Create a Network Boot Disk

Microsoft provides an interesting alternative method for creating a network boot floppy. This alternative uses Windows for Workgroups. The basic idea is to run a shared network installation to a directory on a hard drive (using Windows for Workgroups Setup with the /n switch), and then delete nonessential Windows for Workgroups files from the directory until the contents of the directory is small enough to fit on a floppy disk. You must create autoexec.bat and config.sys for the boot disk and make some minor changes to system.ini. Although

Microsoft describes this method, they make it clear that they do not officially support it. You should test this method first and experiment with it until it works for your network.

To create a network boot disk using Windows for Workgroups:

1. Create a bootable DOS disk. (You can delete DBLSPACE.BIN from the boot floppy if you're not using DoubleSpace.)

2. Create a new directory on the hard drive and run Windows for Workgroups Setup with the /n switch; create a shared network installation in the new directory.

3. Delete all of the following from the directory you created in step 2:

   ```
   BOOTLOG.TXT
           EMM386.EXE
           MOUSE.INI
           MSCDEX.EXE
           NCDINFO.INI
           SPART.PAR
   *.CLN
           *.WIN
   ```

4. Copy the contents of the new directory to the boot disk you created in step 1.

5. Create an autoexec.bat file in the root directory of the boot floppy. Autoexec.bat should contain these lines:

   ```
   a:\SMARTDRV A+
   path=a:\;z:
   a:\NET LOGON user_name user_password
   a:\NET USE z: \\computer_name\share_name /p:No
   ```

6. Create a config.sys file on the boot floppy. Config.sys should contain the following lines:

   ```
   Files=30
   Buffers=20
   Lastdrive=z
   Device=A:\HIMEM.SYS
   Device=A:\IFSHLP.SYS
   Also include any 3rd party device information that may be appropriate for
   ↪your network.
   ```

7. In the boot disk's system.ini file, set DEVDIR (in the [Network Drivers]) to A:\. Delete AutoStart=FULL from the [Network] section of system.ini.

8. Use the boot floppy to boot a workstation that is connected to the network. Be prepared to enter the username and password you specified in autoexec.bat.

9. In step 5, you mapped the Z: drive to the installation share. Enter Z: at the command prompt to see whether you can connect. To start Setup, enter the following:

   ```
   z:\setup z:\W98_install.inf
   ```

Note that the preceding method requires that the network card and network settings for the new workstation match the network card and network settings for the machine on which you created the shared installation (refer to step 2). If the network settings for the new machine are different, you'll need to edit the protocol.ini and system.ini settings on the floppy disk accordingly. Consult a Windows for Workgroup reference for more information about configuring network adapters and network settings.

Troubleshooting Network Installation

A network installation is similar to a local installation, and the troubleshooting strategies for network installations and local installations are similar. See Chapter 2 for a discussion of Windows 98 installation troubleshooting.

The unique aspect of a network installation is the network connection. Needless to say, you must have already made a network connection before you even begin a network installation. If you can't make the initial connection to the installation share, your problem is not an installation problem but a networking problem. (See Chapters 21–25 in Part IV, "Networking Windows 98," for details about network connections and network troubleshooting.)

After the final reboot in the installation process, your computer starts for the first time under Windows 98. The installation, however, is not yet complete, and your system still must reconnect to the installation share. If Windows 98 changes your network configuration for some reason, you may not be able to reconnect to the installation share. For instance, if the installation files are located on a Windows NT domain and Setup configures Windows 98 to use the Windows logon instead on the Client for Microsoft Networks domain logon, you won't be able to finish the installation. If Setup senses that you can't complete the network connection, Setup may ask if you want to change your network configuration. If you choose YES, Setup displays a dialog box similar to the Network Control Panel, and you'll have a chance to change your network settings. Changing the settings at this point, however, doesn't always solve the problem.

The best way to avoid the reconnect problem described in the preceding paragraph is to not let it happen. Make extra certain that Setup will deliver the network configuration you're expecting. Keep the following facts in mind:

- If you install under Windows, Setup will retain the existing network settings. If you install under DOS, Setup will configure a network client for the network drivers that are currently loaded; use an installation script to specify additional settings.

- Batch98's Gather Now feature (described in Chapter 2), doesn't always choose the correct network adapter when creating an installation script for a computer with more than one adapter. If you create an installation script using Batch98's Gather Now feature, ensure that the script configures the network settings necessary to connect to the installation share.

- By default, Setup enables DHCP for TCP/IP networking. If you don't have a DHCP server and Setup is installing the default configuration, you won't be able to connect to other machines.

If you're going to perform multiple installations, it is best to test your network installation process in a controlled setting before unleashing it on the network.

Conclusion

Network installation is a popular method for installing Windows systems in corporate environments. Network installation is fast and it minimizes the need for human intervention. This chapter described how to perform a network installation. This chapter is a continuation of the material presented in Chapter 2. Refer to Chapter 2 for more information about installation scripts, the installation process, or installation troubleshooting.

Windows 98 and Total Cost of Ownership

By 1997, Microsoft had subdued all competition and stood alone atop a lucrative market with its versatile PC-based operating systems. By then, though, the company was facing a new and unexpected opponent. The so-called thin client solution, once denigrated as a throwback to the era of the obsolete mainframe, was gaining new attention because of advances in PC networking and Internet technology and because of new attention to the cost of supporting full-featured clients in the field.

Managers had come to realize that the labor cost for administration and technical support of a corporate workstation figured significantly in the overall cost of implementing the workstation. A simpler and less-versatile PC, they reasoned, would have the following advantages:

- Reduced capital cost (for a cheaper PC)
- Reduced labor cost (for technical support—because fewer things could go wrong)

Microsoft, having invested millions over the years to give Windows more power and flexibility, initially downplayed the idea that the public would actually want less power and less flexibility. Behind the scenes, however, they put their legion of large brains to work on addressing how they might position themselves to accommodate this new thin-client paradigm.

Over the years, Microsoft had been collecting data on work habits and accompanying costs associated with PC operations. They were also aware of the work of other groups, such as the Garter Group, which showed that the single largest line item associated with the cost of operating a PC was so-called end-user operations—unproductive labor costs generated by a workstation user interacting directly with features of the operating system and with non-work–related applications (as opposed to interacting with application(s) required for the user's work assignment). The Garter Group cost model is shown in Table 4.1.

Table 4.1
Total Cost of Operating a Corporate Workstation

Operation	Percentage of Total Cost
Nonbillable End-user Operations	46
Technical Support	21
Capital Cost	21
Administrative Cost	13

Furthermore, although the capital, technical, and administrative costs are easily discernible from a corporate spreadsheet, the ellusive end-user operation cost is invisible, hidden in the overall labor cost, providing a permanent lag in user productivity.

It soon became as clear to Microsoft as it was to Microsoft's competitors that a maintenance-free PC with a more-limited, less-flexible user interface could provide a far lower total cost of ownership in many corporate environments. Microsoft's first act was to declare victory—Windows, they argued, already has the features necessary to create a limited-use environment that will reduce the cost of end-user operations. They then set to work developing additional tools designed to reduce administrative and technical costs. Their goal was to provide a system that offered not only the power and flexibility of a modern PC operating system (if you wanted it) but also the limited, low-cost operating mode of a thin client (if you wanted it). This virtual thin-client approach, according to Microsoft, is better than the permanent limitations of cheap, thin-client hardware. Total cost of ownership, they said, would not depend on a new kind of hardware but rather on new software and on a new approach to system management.

Chapter 4: Windows 98 and Total Cost of Ownership

> **Note** Microsoft nevertheless set to work adapting Windows for the approaching arrival of network PCs and other thin-client hardware units. A new generation of network-based Windows products, such as the new NT Hydra system (named for the many-headed serpent of antiquity) will support clients in a variety of thicknesses.

With much fanfare, Microsoft launched their Zero Administration Windows (ZAW) campaign. *Zero Administration* is a set of existing methodologies and a promise to develop new methodologies to help reduce the total cost of operating a Windows system. Zero Administration features fall into two basic groups:

- Tools that simplify administration and technical support of Windows systems
- Tools that limit or standardize the user interface to limit the cost of end-user operations

Many of these Zero Administration features are built directly into Windows 98. (Other, more-advanced features will appear in NT 5.0 and future Windows releases.)

Simplifying Management with Windows 98 System Tools

The natural development of the Windows operating system has simplified some of the tasks associated with system administration. Windows 98 is certainly the most hands-off operating system Microsoft has developed. Some of the Zero Administration tools provided with Windows 98 include the following:

- **Windows Tune-up Wizard**: a tool that automatically tunes up your system (see Chapter 35, "Tools and Strategies for Optimizing Windows 98")
- **Windows Update Wizard**: a utility that automatically updates drivers and file system files via the Internet (described later in this chapter)
- **System File Checker:** a tool that looks for corrupted or modified Windows 98 system files (see Chapter 37, "Tools and Strategies for Troubleshooting Windows 98")
- **System Information Tool**: a utility that provides a central source for information on hardware and software system components (see Chapter 37)
- **The Scheduled Task Utility**: a tool that lets you schedule routine events so that they'll happen automatically (see Chapter 34)

- **Windows Scripting Host**: a feature that lets you write your own custom scripts for automating complex tasks (see Chapter 33, "Windows Scripting with Windows 98 Scripting Host")

These labor-saving features are discussed throughout the book. Refer to specific chapters for additional information. I mention these features here so that you can view them as a natural consequence of Microsoft's initiative to reduce total cost of ownership.

Updating Windows

Research has shown that one of the biggest time sinks in system administration is the need to update system software in order to maintain compatibility with new hardware and new versions of applications. Windows 98 includes a tool called Windows Update. Windows Update logs onto the Internet and consults a large, online database to see whether any drivers or system files on your computer need updating. Any out-of-date files are then updated from the Web site.

To access the Windows Update Wizard:

1. From the Start Menu, choose Windows Update.

2. Windows 98 will attempt to connect you to the Internet to access the Windows Update Web page (www.microsoft.com/windowsupdate/x86/en/download/default.htm).

3. When you reach the Update Web page, follow the instructions. If this is the first time you've accessed the Windows Update Web page, you may need to provide registration information.

Limiting the Windows 98 User Interface

The Windows 95 Zero Administration Kit was Microsoft's first effort to market the potential of Windows for supporting a terminal-like, dedicated workstation environment. The Windows 95 Zero Administration Kit was a ready-made implementation that used several existing Microsoft Networking features (most notably, the System Policies feature). The Windows 95 Zero Administration Kit also helped you set up a Windows 95 installation share on a server for easy network client installation and, optionally, configured the client to access Office 97 running on the server.

One important aspect of the Windows 95 Zero Administration Kit was that it classified Windows corporate workstations and client workstations according to two operating modes:

- TaskStation mode, in which the workstation is devoted to a single task, such as database entry.

- AppStation mode, in which a user may need to work with a few specific applications, possibly applications running on the server, such as those included in Office 97.

In both cases, the user's access to local file system and local operating system features is limited, so as to limit the cost of end-user operations.

> **Note** At this writing, Microsoft has not announced whether they will release Windows 98 Zero Administration Kit. (Check the Microsoft web site at www.microsoft.com for the latest information on Zero Admin in Windows 98.)

Microsoft implemented the TaskStation and AppStation operating modes through a system policy file with predefined policies for TaskUser and AppUser global groups. You don't need a special Zero Administration Kit to create a similar environment in Windows 95 or Windows 98. You just need a severe and systematic approach to System Policies, as you'll learn later in this chapter.

Creating a Limited Operating Mode Using System Policies

You can create an operating mode similar to the TaskStation or AppStation mode by using Windows 98 System Policies. Chapter 7, "System Policies," describes how to configure System Policies in Windows 98; see that chapter for information on System Policies and Windows 98's System Policy Editor.

Follow these steps to create a limited operating mode for Windows 98 users:

1. Make sure the workstation you're using is configured for Group Policies (see Chapter 7).

2. Create a global group called LimOp (or whatever), using User Manager for Domains on a Windows NT domain controller. (Remove any users or groups that may appear as part of the global group.)

3. Use Windows 98's System Policy Editor to create a system policy for the new group, using the Add Group command on the System Policy Editor's Edit menu (described in Chapter 7). The policy should be included in the config.pol file that is accessed by domain user accounts at logon. The policy for the new group should severely limit the user's access to system features and resources. The system policy settings for the AppUser group in the Windows 95 Zero Administration Kit are shown in Table 4.2 as they appear in Windows 98 System Policy Editor. This table is offered for purposes of illustration only. (Note that the Windows 95 and Windows 98 policies differ slightly, so some settings may vary.)

4. Create domain user accounts for the users who will work within the new limited operating mode (using Windows NT's User Manager for Domains). Add the users to the new global group you created in step 2. You may want to specify a path to a logon script in User Manager for Domains by clicking on the Profiles button in the Add New User dialog box. The logon script can map a drive to the path that contains Desktop and Start Menu folders (more about this shortly, after these steps and the table).

5. Log on using the user account you created in step 4. The Windows 98 user interface should reflect the system policy settings for the new limited operation mode. If you don't see the new restricted interface, verify that your PC is configured for group policies and that your domain controller is accessing the system policy file at logon. (For additional information, see Chapter 7.)

Table 4.2
System Policy Settings for Windows 95 Zero Administration Kit AppUser Group

Tree	Subtree	Setting
Windows 98 Network	Sharing	Disable file-sharing controls
		Disable print-sharing controls
Windows 98 System	Shell (Custom Folders)	Path to Programs items: O:\Start Menu\Programs
		Path to Desktop items: O:\Desktop
		Hide Start Menu subfolders (no setting; check if you use custom folder or desktop icons)
		Path to Startup folder items: O:\StartMenu\Programs\Startup
		Path to Network Neighborhood items: (no setting; enter a path to create a custom Network Neighborhood)
		Path to Start Menu: O:\Start Menu
	Shell (Restrictions)	Remove "Run" command
		Remove folders from "Settings" on Start Menu
		Remove Taskbar from "Settings" on Start Menu
		Remove "Find" command
		Hide drives in My Computer
		Hide Network Neighborhood (no setting; check to hide)
		No "Entire Contents" in Network Neighborhood (no setting; check to hide)
		No workgroup contents in Network Neighborhood
		Hide all items on desktop
		Disable "Shut Down" command (no setting; check to disable; usually not a good idea to disable shutdown: leave unchecked)
		Don't save settings at Exit

Chapter 4: Windows 98 and Total Cost of Ownership   **101**

Tree	Subtree	Setting
	Control Panel (Display)	Disable Display Control Panel Hide background page Hide screen-saver page Hide appearance page Hide settings page
	Control Panel (Network)	Disable Network Control Panel Hide Identification page Hide Access Control page
	Control Panel (Passwords)	Disable Passwords Control Panel Hide Change Passwords page Hide Remote Administration page Hide User Profiles page
	Control Panel (Printer Settings)	Hide General and Details pages Disable deletion of printers Disable addition of printers
	Control Pane (System)	Hide Device Manager page Hide Hardware Profiles page Hide File System button Hide Virtual Memory button
	Desktop Display	Wallpaper (no setting) Color Scheme (no setting)
	Restrictions	Disable Registry Editing Tools Only run allowed Windows applications; no setting (Note: useful for limiting and defining the user's environment) Disable MS-DOS prompt Disable single-mode MS-DOS applications

The Shell Custom Folders settings (refer to Table 4.2) provide an additional opportunity for customization and control. Note that, in Table 4.2, custom folder settings refer to the mapped drive O:. The Windows 95 Zero Administration Kit uses the mapped O: drive to define the location of the custom Desktop and Start Menu folders. A logon script assigned to each user account maps the O: drive to the location of the custom folders that this user account will access.

The Only Run Allowed Windows Applications setting, under Windows 98 System/Restrictions, is another useful setting that helps limit the user's choices. You can specify a list of Windows applications that the user can run; all others will be inaccessible.

Conclusion

This chapter discussed Microsoft's Total Cost of Ownership initiative and described some of the features of Windows 98 that help reduce the cost of operating a PC in a corporate environment.

User profiles are another useful feature that can help you limit the user's access to the system. See Chapter 8, "User Profiles," for a discussion of how to limit and customize the desktop environment through mandatory user-profile settings.

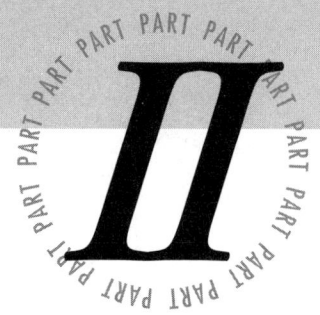

Configuring Windows 98

5	Understanding Windows 98 Configuration	105
6	Control Panel	115
7	System Policies	153
8	User Profiles	181
9	Hardware Profiles	191
10	Mastering the Windows 98 Registry	199

Understanding Windows 98 Configuration

If you've been working with computers for a while, you'll no doubt remember the difficulties involved in supporting DOS and Windows 3.x on a network. Although you could configure the systems to operate reasonably well, it was essentially an unmanaged (and unmanageable) system in a networked environment.

Initially, with the advent of Windows NT 3.1, followed by Windows 95, Microsoft brought a powerful system configuration design to bear on the problem of configuring and managing computers on a network. The requirements were incredibly broad:

- Support stand-alone computers
- Support multiple users on stand-alone computers

- Support stand-alone computers that occasionally connect to a network, either over a modem or through a network connection

- Support peer-to-peer services (in which you must have both server and client capabilities, albeit in a limited fashion)

- Support networked clients connected to Novell, LAN Manager, or Windows NT networks

- Support computers with regularly changing configurations, such as dockable portable computers

- Support resource sharing (printers, folders, and, to a limited extent, modems) in any of the networked configurations

When you consider that all of these requirements were met with Windows 95—and, in extension Windows 98—you'll realize that it's really quite commendable what was accomplished. Most importantly, all of these capabilities exist, and are both powerful and relatively easy to manage and use. Best of all, the features that you don't need don't get in your way and make you deal with them; they remain available should you want to use them, but otherwise are transparent to systems that don't need or use them.

In this chapter, you learn about the overall concepts involved in Windows 98 configuration and how the different parts of the whole work together to provide a manageable desktop environment. In succeeding chapters in this section, you learn about the details involved in managing and troubleshooting the different configuration aspects of Windows 98.

Understanding the Registry

Understanding Windows 98 configuration really begins with understanding the Registry. If you recall the "bad old days" of DOS and Windows 3.x, you'll remember the miasma of configuration .INI files, object registration databases, CONFIG.SYS and AUTOEXEC.BAT files, and so forth. Trying to manage all of these repositories of system management information was often like trying to keep a hundred plates spinning in the air—no mean feat.

> **Note** This section introduces the Registry and discusses how it fits into Windows 98 systems management. Detailed Registry information is discussed in Chapter 10, "Mastering the Windows 98 Registry."

Starting in Windows NT 3.1 and then in Windows 95, Microsoft introduced the concept of a system "registry" in which all configuration information about a system and about user preferences was kept. Known more informally simply as the *Registry*, in it you find all of the configuration information that used to be spread out among many different files. In the Windows 95 and 98 architecture, the operating system—as well as all applications and support software—are supposed to store their configuration information in the Registry. However, the old methods are still supported in Windows 98; an application can still use .INI files, the CONFIG.SYS file, or the AUTOEXEC.BAT file if required (usually just when an application hasn't yet been updated for Windows 95 or 98).

The Registry is a database used by the system to store all of the system configuration information. It is made up of two files: USER.DAT contains user-specific configuration data (such as desktop preferences) and SYSTEM.DAT contains computer-specific information (such as hardware configurations). Collectively, these two files make up the Registry. In fact, the Registry Editor tool in Windows 98 (REGEDIT.EXE) transparently loads from both files and presents a unified set of Registry folders in which you can make changes.

Within the Registry exist various other configuration tools: Hardware Profiles and User Profiles are stored and activated through the Registry, while System Policies are Registry settings that are forced onto the system when it logs on to a network on which System Policies are implemented.

> **Note** Not a mandatory part of Windows 98 installations, the file that contains System Policies (POLICY.POL) is also considered a Registry file.

Registry Structure

When you access the Registry in Windows 98, you won't see any real changes from Windows 95; it operates in the same fashion and uses the same categories of settings. However, Microsoft has optimized the Registry handling code significantly in Windows 98 so that the Registry operates much more quickly on the system. In fact, this is one of the things that gives Windows 98 a performance edge over Windows 95.

The Registry is organized into two main branches of Registry settings, as follows:

- **HKEY_LOCAL_MACHINE** stores the local computer's hardware settings.
- **HKEY_USERS** stores user-specific settings for all users who access the local computer.

In addition to the two main branches, there are four alias branches that appear as main branches, but are really reflections of lower-level settings in one of the main branches. One of these alias branches consists entirely of dynamic data stored in RAM. These four alias branches are as follows:

- **HKEY_CLASSES_ROOT** stores object registration information, such as file types and object types. This key maps to **HKEY_LOCAL_MACHINE\Software\Classes**.

- **HKEY_CURRENT_CONFIG** is a shortcut to the current configuration of the computer (which is actually stored within HKEY_LOCAL_MACHINE). For instance, on a dockable notebook computer, there are different settings in HKEY_LOCAL_MACHINE depending on whether the computer is in its docked or undocked state; whichever state is active is found in HKEY_CURRENT_CONFIG.

- **HKEY_CURRENT_USER** is a shortcut to the current user's settings on the computer (which is actually stored within HKEY_USERS). Each user has his preferences stored in HKEY_USERS under his logon name, and HKEY_CURRENT_USER provides a convenient shortcut to the settings within HKEY_USERS.

- **HKEY_DYN_DATA** stores dynamic data used by applications as they execute and process information; the data is not stored within either of the two Registry files (SYSTEM.DAT and USER.DAT) and is destroyed when Windows closes down.

So, when you view the complete Registry with Registry Editor, you see six branches, even though only two of them hold "real" data. Figure 5.1 shows Registry Editor open with these six branches visible.

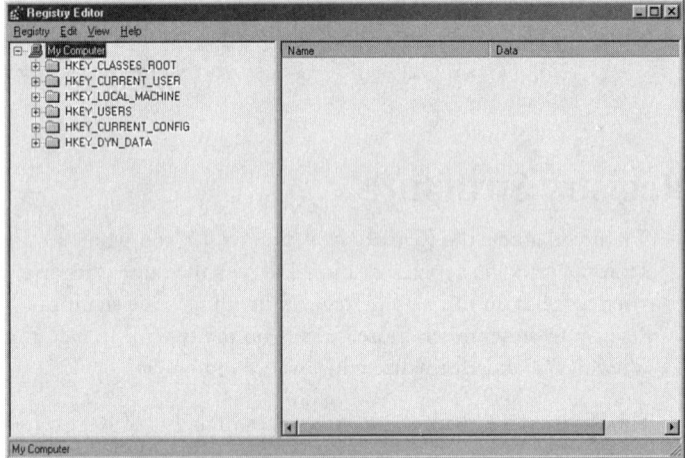

Figure 5.1
The two main branches and the four alias branches in Registry Editor.

> **Note** You can make changes in either the alias branches or the "real" branches; the data is stored properly regardless.

Within each branch is a number of keys. A *key* is simply a Registry folder that contains settings, also called *values*. For example, look at Figure 5.2. Each folder within a branch, no matter its level, is a key. Sometimes, lower-level keys are referred to as *subkeys*, although really they're all keys. When you select a key, the right pane of Registry Editor shows the values within the key. In Figure 5.2, Config, 0001, Display, and Settings are all keys.

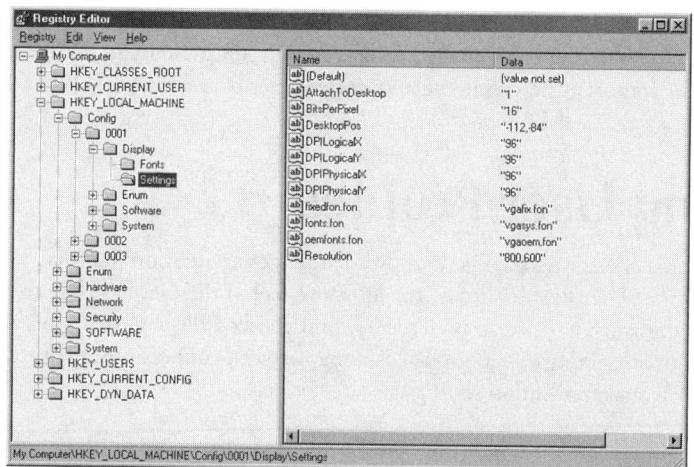

Figure 5.2
Keys and values within the HKEY_LOCAL_MACHINE branch.

AttachToDesktop, BitsPerPixel, and DesktopPos are all values within the Settings key.

When a key is specified, it always uses its complete path, so the Settings key highlighted in Figure 5.2 is actually known as **HKEY_LOCAL_MACHINE\Config\0001\Display\Settings**. (You can see the full key in the status line at the bottom of Registry Editor's window.)

Values can contain different types of data. Some values, such as fixedfon.fon in Figure 5.2, contain string, or text, data. Other keys might contain numeric values. Under Windows 98, keys can contain three different value types: String, Binary, and DWORD (a double word, or a 32-bit numeric value).

Registry Management Features

Depending on your system management needs, you can locate a computer's Registry files (USER.DAT and SYSTEM.DAT) in different locations. For example, you can store a computer's USER.DAT on a network share so that it's available for a user no matter where she logs on to the network. SYSTEM.DAT can also be located on a network, which can be useful for diskless workstations (also known as Remote Initial Program Load—RIPL—workstations).

The Registry supports *Remote Procedure Calls*, such that you can connect to another computer's Registry and make changes over the network.

Note Installing and using the Remote Registry Service are covered in Chapter 10.

By using System Policies, you can apply forced Registry changes to a system every time it boots up. As an example, if your company has a policy of only displaying an approved company logo on its computer desktops as wallpaper, you can force the Registry setting that uses that wallpaper each time a user logs on to the computer. Combined with System Policies, you can also configure the system so that a user can't change certain settings on the system. (While this may sound trivial, it can be important in certain customer-service applications.)

Understanding User Profiles

A User Profile is a collection of Registry settings and user-specific configuration files that pertains to an individual user. User Profiles define the look and feel of the user interface for a given user, specifying settings such as desktop preferences, font choices, display resolution and color depth, shortcuts, network settings (workgroup, existing network connections, preferred servers, and so on), and personal application settings.

You can turn User Profiles on and off through the User Profiles tab of the Passwords Control Panel, as shown in Figure 5.3. The Passwords Control Panel lets you choose whether you want Windows 98 to maintain separate User Profiles for each user, or whether you want all users to use the same preferences and desktop settings Actually, what happens "behind the scenes" when you enable User Profiles in the Passwords Control Panel is the following:

- A directory called \Windows\Profiles is created. Under that directory, users will have stored their own Start menus, Desktop settings, Internet shortcuts, and the like, using subdirectories specified by their logon name. So, for example, if a computer with User Profiles enabled had two users: Bruce and Christy, you would find \Windows\Profiles\Bruce and \Windows\Profiles\Christy. Each of those directories would be a "home profile" directory.

- Users will have their own copies of USER.DAT, stored in their home profile directories. When they log on to Windows 98, their own copies of USER.DAT are copied to the \Windows directory and made active for that session.

The example shown in Figure 5.3 shows User Profiles enabled.

Figure 5.3
Enable User Profiles using the Passwords Control Panel.

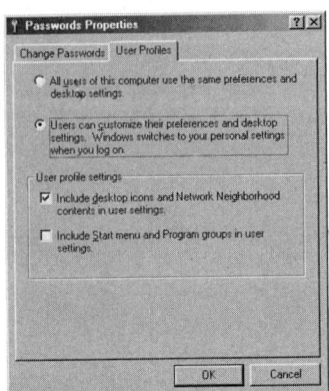

Learn about User Profiles in depth, including using them with networks and managing them in detail, in Chapter 8, "User Profiles."

Understanding System Policies

At times you may need to impose certain configuration choices on users. For example, perhaps you need to deny your users the ability to change certain configuration settings within Windows 98, either to prevent problems if they do so, or to maintain a coherent, consistent user environment at all times to reduce support costs. This is where System Policies come into play. *System Policies* can be thought of as *imposed*, or forced, Registry settings. A System Policy is a Registry setting that overrides any default or user-selected configuration changes. Some System Policies, for example, also deny access to configuration areas within Windows 98, such as access to the Run command on the Start menu, to prevent people from making changes that will cause eventual problems.

System Policies are kept in a file called CONFIG.POL, and are usually stored on a network server; all users process the file automatically when they log on to the network. You edit this file with a tool called the *Policy Editor* (POLEDIT.EXE). Within the Policy Editor, you can establish policies for the computer, for users, and for groups. Figure 5.4 shows the Policy Editor open with some examples of a computer, users, and groups.

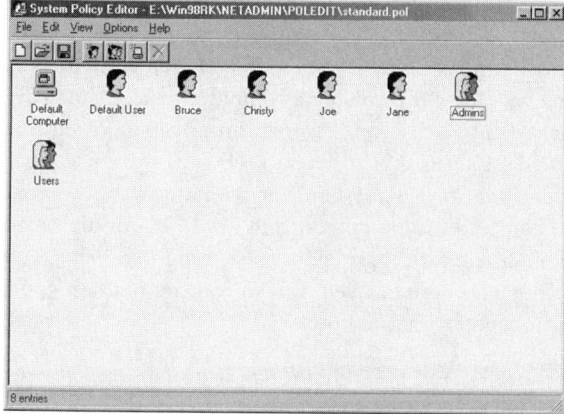

Figure 5.4
Policy Editor.

When you open a computer, user, or group, you are shown a hierarchical list of policies that you can set through the Policy Editor, somewhat similar to Registry Editor's arrangement of keys. Figure 5.5 shows a sample User Policy. When the user with the specified logon name logs on to the computer, the policy settings shown are imposed onto his Registry automatically.

Figure 5.5
Sample User Policy.

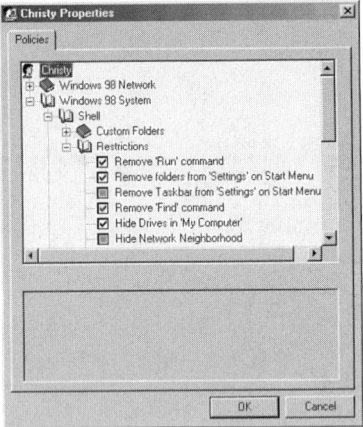

You can find more detailed information about System Policies, how they work, and how you can implement and manage them in Chapter 7, "System Policies."

Understanding Hardware Profiles

As you already know, the Registry stores configuration information for the computer, such as what devices are installed, how they are configured, and so forth. However, there are times when computers go through regular and radical changes to their configurations, exactly as would happen with a notebook computer when it is used with and then without a docking station. A typical docking station will allow the notebook computer to access many resources not available to it when it is not docked, such as an Ethernet card, a more powerful video display adapter, SCSI devices such as CD-ROMs, different keyboards and mice, and so forth. Certainly, every time you dock or undock such a system, you wouldn't want to have to reconfigure all of those choices (Plug and Play or no Plug and Play!). Hardware Profiles come to the rescue by letting you define different configurations for a computer. When you boot a system on which Hardware Profiles have been enabled, you see a menu that lets you choose which Hardware Profile should be used for that session.

The configuration information for different Hardware Profiles is stored in the Registry under HKEY_LOCAL_MACHINE. When you choose a particular Hardware Profile during system boot, the selected settings are copied from within HKEY_LOCAL_MACHINE into HKEY_CURRENT_CONFIG (more accurately, a pointer is created in HKEY_CURRENT_CONFIG that points to the correct hardware configuration in HKEY_LOCAL_MACHINE).

Therefore, through the magic of Hardware Profiles, you can have multiple, regularly used hardware configurations for a particular machine that are easy to select and switch between without repeatedly having to reconfigure the computer's hardware.

You should understand that Hardware Profiles don't relate to User Profiles in any way, or to System Policies. Rather, Hardware Profiles are separate and perform only the function discussed here. The only real similarity that Hardware Profiles have to the other configuration components that you've learned about is that they, too, are stored in and make use of the Registry.

You can learn much more about Hardware Profiles in Chapter 9, "Hardware Profiles."

Conclusion

In this chapter, you learned first about the Windows 98 Registry, the central repository of configuration information for Windows 98, and the foundation on which the other system management features operate. You then learned about User Profiles, which allow multiple users to maintain their personal settings on a single computer, or even across a network when they log on to another computer elsewhere on the same network. The third item discussed was System Policies, which allow you to force certain settings onto the Windows 98 Registry, overriding any user settings that conflict with your systems management agenda. Finally, you learned about Hardware Profiles, which let you manage changing hardware in an elegant fashion.

In the remaining chapters of this section, you learn the details behind all of this technical wizardry, and you learn how to implement these features, how to maintain and manage them, and how to use them to make system management of Windows 98 desktops as easy as possible.

Control Panel

The Windows 98 Control Panel is a folder that contains a number of Control Panel objects, each one modifying the behavior of a different part of Windows 98. For example, there is a Network object to change network settings, a Display object to change display settings, and so forth. The Control Panel, encompassing all of these objects, provides users and administrators with a convenient single point with which to change Windows 98 settings.

Understanding the Control Panel

The Control Panel, which you can see in Figure 6.1, includes different objects for each distinct area that can be customized under Windows 98. Each icon represents a Control Panel properties page (dialog box), typically using more than one tabbed page within the dialog box.

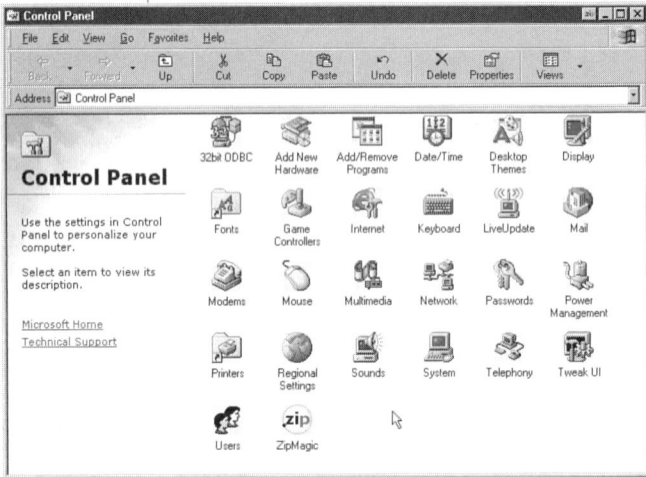

Figure 6.1
The Control Panel folder.

Double-clicking on any of the Control Panel objects opens its dialog box, such as the Display Properties dialog box shown in Figure 6.2.

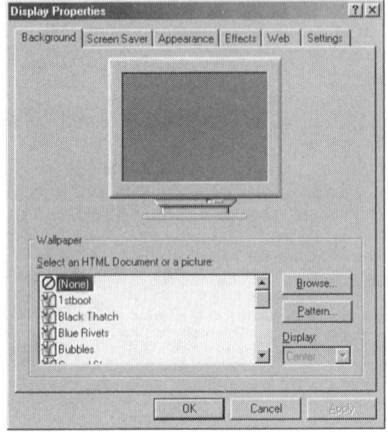

Figure 6.2
A sample Control Panel—Display Properties.

Control Panel Files

Each Control Panel dialog box is contained in a file ending with a .CPL extension and stored in the \Windows\System folder. These Control Panel files can be ones that were included as

Chapter 6: Control Panel

part of Windows 98, or that have been provided by third parties as adjunct controls for their hardware, applications, or utilities. Figure 6.3 shows a standard list of these Control Panel .CPL files.

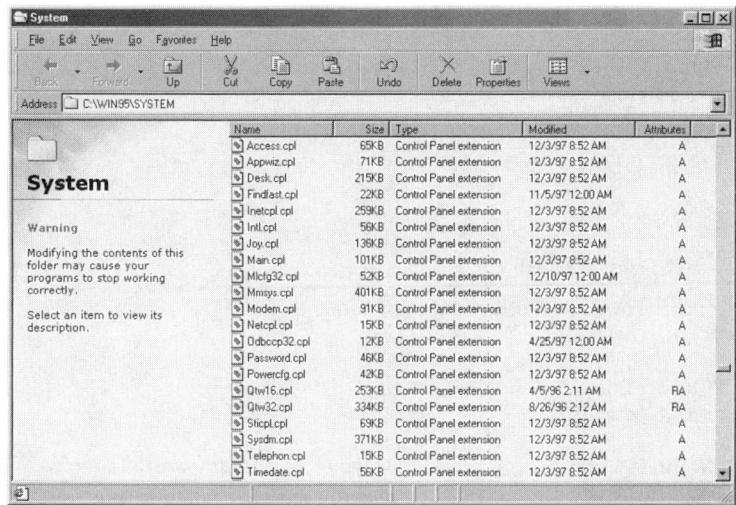

Figure 6.3
Control Panels are kept in .CPL files in the \Windows\System.

Generally, you can identify which .CPL file corresponds to which Control Panel object simply by looking at its name. However, some of the names aren't completely obvious, so Table 6.1 lists each of the default .CPL files along with their corresponding Control Panel objects.

Table 6.1
Control Panel .CPL Files

Filename	Control Panel Object	Notes
ACCESS.CPL	Accessibility	
APPWIZ.CPL	Add/Remove Programs	
DESK.CPL	Display	
FINDFAST.CPL	FindFast	From MS Office
INETCPL.CPL	Internet	Internet Explorer Settings
INTL.CPL	Regional Settings	
JOY.CPL	Game Controllers	
MAIN.CPL	Mouse	
MLCFG32.CPL	Mail	Inbox, Exchange Client, or Outlook

continues

Table 6.1, Continued
Control Panel .CPL Files

Filename	Control Panel Object	Notes
MMSYS.CPL	Multimedia	
MODEM.CPL	Modems	
NETCPL.CPL	Network	
ODBCCP32.CPL	32 Bit ODBC	
PASSWORD.CPL	Passwords	
POWERCFG.CPL	Power Management	
QTW16.CPL	QuickTime for Windows 16-bit	
QTW32.CPL	QuickTime for Windows 32-bit	
STICPL.CPL	Scanners and Cameras	May not appear in Control Panel depending on installation choices
SYSDM.CPL	System	
TELEPHON.CPL	Telephony	
TIMEDATE.CPL	Date/Time	

Control Panel and System Registry

Control Panel objects generally store their settings in the Registry. However, not all settings are stored in the Registry; it is up to the programmer of each Control Panel object to determine where their settings are stored. For example, a third-party Control Panel object may store its settings in an application-specific file that is not within the Registry. The common practice, however, is to store Control Panel settings in the Registry because Registry-based settings enable better management of computers in a corporate environment.

User-specific Control Panel settings can be found in the Registry under the following key:

HKEY_CURRENT_USER\Control Panel

This key stores the Registry settings for the current user. The current user's settings are determined by the System Profile active at any given time, and are usually controlled by the user. You can also see all the different users' Control Panel settings in the following Registry key (where *username* is each person's Windows logon name):

HKEY_USERS*username*\Control Panel

Chapter 6: Control Panel

Within the Control Panel Registry folder, you can see a number of subfolders, each one containing different user-specific Control Panel settings. Figure 6.4 shows the Registry Editor with the current user Control Panel settings open.

Computer-based Control Panel settings are stored in HKEY_LOCAL_MACHINE\System\CurrentControlSet.

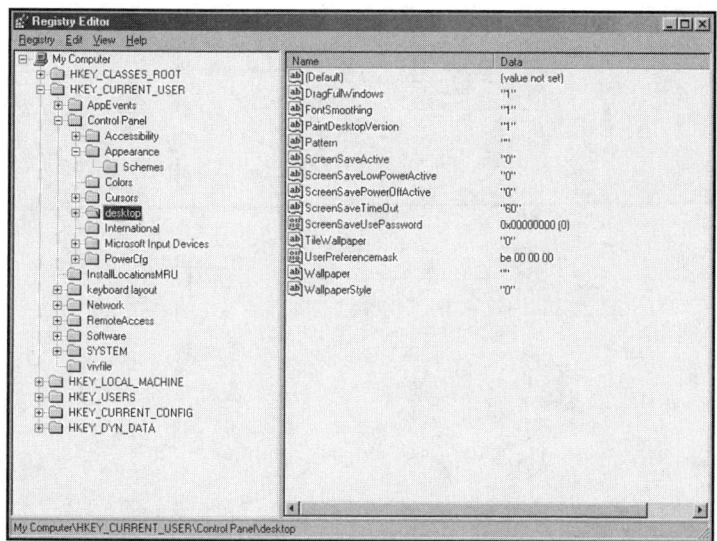

Figure 6.4
Example Control Panel settings in the Registry Editor.

Sending Control Panel Settings to Users

Although you should never need to change your Control Panel settings by changing them with the Registry Editor, it is a good idea to familiarize yourself with the Registry's Control Panel settings. You can solve some common support problems by sending users certain Registry Control Panel setting changes via an exported Registry fragment.

For example, say a user calls and complains that she was making changes in the Accessibility Control Panel, and doesn't like the changes, but doesn't know how to return all of the settings to their defaults. You can solve this problem by exporting the Registry key from a profile that contains default Accessibility settings and emailing the exported file to the user in question. She can then double-click on the .REG file that she receives from you to instantly apply all of the appropriate settings to return to the default. To send a Registry fragment for use in Control Panel setting changes, follow these steps:

1. Start the Registry Editor on a machine that is using a default User Profile.

2. Select the Registry key that contains the default settings. In this example, you would choose HKEY_CURRENT_USER\Control Panel\Accessibility. Note that you would use this Registry key rather than HKEY_USERS*username*\Control Panel, so you won't have

to worry about matching a username with the one on the source machine. The HKEY_CURRENT_USER key is correct after the user has logged on, and changes made there are saved back to that user's HKEY_USERS folder anyway.

3. Open the **R**egistry menu and choose **E**xport Registry File. You see the dialog box shown in Figure 6.5.

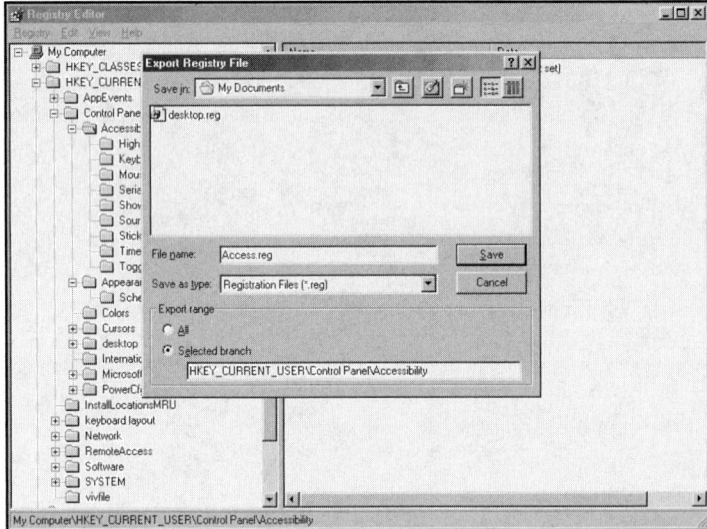

Figure 6.5
Exporting a Registry key for a Control Panel.

4. Ensure that the Selected Branch option button is selected, and that the indicated Registry key is correct.

> **Warning** It is *very important* that you do not export the entire Registry and send it to a remote user to apply. This would apply *all* Registry settings from one machine to another, which is something that you would never want to do to a computer that has been in use for any amount of time.

5. Assign a name for the exported Registry file. Make sure you choose a .REG extension.

6. Click OK to save the exported file. Send the exported file to the user on a disk, over email, or through some other mechanism.

7. Have the user double-click on the .REG file. She will be asked if she wants to update her Registry with the information in the file (this confirmation message is new to Windows 98). Have her acknowledge the warning and the changes will be instantly applied. She will need to shut down properly to save the new settings completely, although she can do so at a later time.

Chapter 6: Control Panel

> **Note** Exported Registry files (.REG files) contain text information that you can manually edit prior to importing them into a system's Registry. For example, Figure 6.6 shows the previous example's exported Registry file open in Notepad.

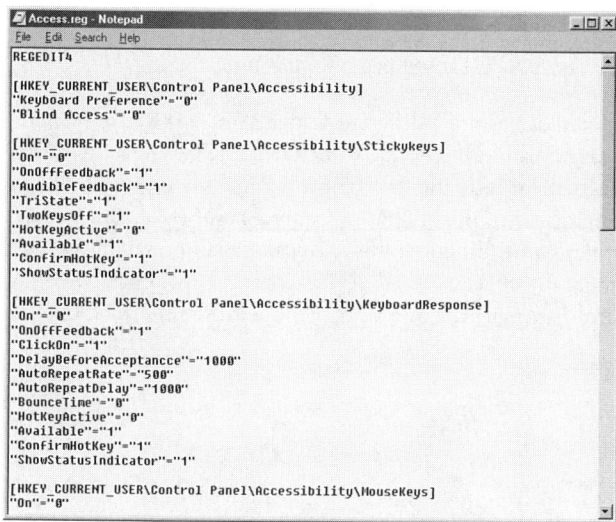

Figure 6.6
A sample .REG file open in Notepad.

Control Panel Tricks

There are several tricks you can perform with the Control Panel and its .CPL files that may fill a customization or administrative need of yours at some point.

The first of these tricks involves launching a Control Panel object directly. If you double-click on any .CPL file, its associated Control Panel will be activated on the desktop. This might prove useful if you ever need speedy access to a particular Control Panel through a link on the desktop. You can simply create a shortcut to one of the .CPL files anywhere you want it.

You can also launch Control Panels from the command line, or from the Start menu's Run command. But you can't simply use the .CPL filename to launch a Control Panel in this way (as you might expect because double-clicking works), but instead must use the following command syntax:

rundll32.exe shell32.dll,Control_RunDLL *control_panel.CPL*

Substitute *control_panel.CPL* for the actual .CPL file you want to activate. For example, to launch the Game Controller Control Panel (JOY.CPL) from a command prompt or the Run dialog box, you must type the following:

rundll32.exe shell32.dll,Control_RunDLL JOY.CPL

Another trick involves opening the Control Panel window by using a little stub application called CONTROL.EXE. Simply use the Run command in the Start menu (or a command prompt) and type CONTROL to open the Control Panel.

You can create a copy of the Control Panel folder wherever you want on your system. To do this, create a new folder and assign it the following name (the values in the brackets *must* be typed exactly):

Control Panel.{21EC2020-3AEA-1069-A2DD-08002B30309D}

In the preceding object name, you can assign a different folder name in place of "Control Panel," so long as the period and the bracketed value is included after whatever name you use. It is the bracketed value that actually creates the new Control Panel folder, not the name "Control Panel." One nice application of this trick is to create a new Start menu folder, and type this name for the new folder name. By doing this, you can get a normal Start menu cascading folder that allows more direct access to all of the Control Panel objects. For example, Figure 6.7 shows a new Control Panel created in a Start menu with the cascaded Control Panel objects open.

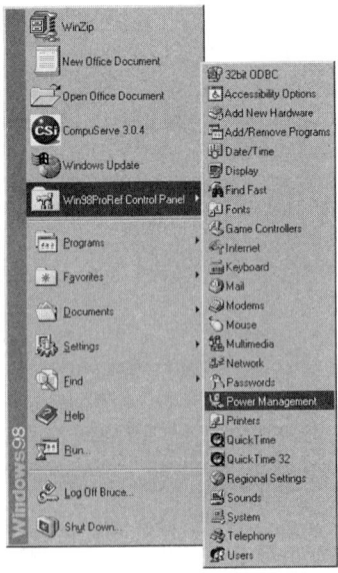

Figure 6.7
A cascading Control Panel in the Start menu.

To do this yourself, follow these steps:

1. Right-click on the Start menu and choose Open.

2. Right-click in the resulting window's background and choose New, Folder.

3. Type the Control Panel object name for the new folder's name. The example shown in Figure 6.7 used this name:

   Win98ProRef Control Panel.{21EC2020-3AEA-1069-A2DD-08002B30309D}

4. Press Enter to save the folder name. The bracketed value will vanish, leaving just the folder name preceding the period as the name of the folder.

Control Panel Quick Reference and Tour

Each Control Panel object controls settings affecting very different areas of Windows 98's functioning. You will find detailed information about how to use some of these settings in the appropriate chapters in this book. For example, you will find detailed information about using the Network Control Panel in the Networking chapters (Table 6.3 provides a quick reference for finding the appropriate chapters for many of these Control Panels). You can use the information in the following table, however, to quickly locate settings within the Control Panel structure. Table 6.2 shows important Control Panel settings or classes of settings along with the actual Control Panel object and tab where you would go to change those settings. You can use this information as a quick reference to find these settings. Following Tables 6.2 and 6.3 are examples of each of the Control Panel objects, all of their pages, and descriptions of what each setting controls.

Table 6.2
Finding Common Control Panel Settings

To change…	…look here
CD music settings	Multimedia, CD Music tab
CD-ROM caching	System, Performance tab
Computer identification	Network, Identification tab
Create a startup disk	Add/Remove Programs
Current date and time	Date/Time
Date and time display formats	Regional Settings
Date and time entry methods	Regional Settings
Desktop wallpaper	Display
Device DMA settings	System, Device Manager tab
Device I/O addresses	System, Device Manager tab
Device IRQ settings	System, Device Manager tab

continues

Table 6.2, Continued
Finding Common Control Panel Settings

To change...	...look here
Device memory addresses	System, Device Manager tab
Dialing properties	Telephony
Display options: disabilities	Accessibility Options
Docking station hardware profiles	System, Hardware Profiles tab
Email profile settings	Mail
Embedded desktop web objects	Display, Web tab
Existing hardware devices	System, Device Manager tab; Multimedia; Display, Options tab; Game Controllers; Keyboard; Mouse; Network; Printers
Existing printers	Printers
Hard disk performance	System, Performance tab
Installed applications	Add/Remove Programs
Installed fonts	Fonts
Installed memory (view)	System
Internet browser settings	Internet
Joystick settings	Game Controllers
Keyboard language	Keyboard
Keyboard options	Keyboard
Keyboard options: disabilities	Accessibility Options
MIDI instrument settings	Multimedia
Modem settings	Modems
Monitor refresh rate	Display, Settings tab, Advanced button
Mouse acceleration	Mouse, Motion tab
Mouse options	Mouse
Mouse options: disabilities	Accessibility Options
Mouse pointer trails	Mouse

Chapter 6: Control Panel

To change...	...look here
Mouse pointers	Mouse, pointers tab
Movie display formats	Multimedia
Network cards	Network
Network clients	Network
Network protocols	Network
New hardware devices	Add New Hardware
New printers	Printers
ODBC driver settings	32-bit ODBC
Password tracking for users	Passwords, User Profiles tab
Power saving	Power Management
Remove installed device	System, Device Manager tab
Screen color depth	Display
Screen height and width	Display
Screen savers	Display
Sound card devices	Multimedia
Sound options: disabilities	Accessibility Options
Sounds: system events	Sounds
Special effects: display	Display, Effects tab
Time zone	Date/Time
User accounts	Users
User profiles: activating	Passwords, User Profiles tab
Video acceleration	System, Performance tab
Virtual memory	System, Performance tab
Windows 98 installed options	Add/Remove Software, Windows Options tab
Windows build number (view)	System
Windows colors	Display
Your passwords	Passwords, Change Passwords tab

Table 6.3
Chapter Cross-Reference for Control Panels

Control Panel	Chapter #	Chapter Title
32-Bit ODBC	16	"Windows 98 ODBC Connectivity"
Add New Hardware	12	"Supporting Devices"
Add/Remove Programs	11	"Windows 98 Architecture and Application Support"
Fonts	13	"Printing"
Game Controllers	14	"Multimedia"
Internet	27	"Internet Browsers in Windows 98"
Mail	31	"Mail Management in Windows 98"
Modems	12	"Supporting Devices"
Multimedia	14	"Multimedia"
Network	21–26	Part IV, "Networking Windows 98"
Passwords	21–22	"Understanding Windows 98 Networking"; "Peer-to-Peer Networking"
Power Management	19	"Windows 98 for Portables"
Printers	13	"Printing"
Sounds	14	"Multimedia"

32-bit ODBC

The 32-bit ODBC Control Panel has been revised significantly since Windows 95 and now contains considerable additional functionality. It is also easier to use. You use the 32-bit ODBC Control Panel to set up and maintain Data Source Names (DSNs) for ODBC functionality. ODBC is used by many database access programs, including Crystal Reports, Excel, and Access. ODBC data sources provide a standard interface for a data access program to communicate with an underlying database of some sort. Figure 6.8 shows the first tab of the 32-bit ODBC Control Panel.

The User DSN and System DSN tabs are very similar. Each one is used to maintain DSNs that are unique to the logged-on user or the system, respectively. You use these tabs to add, remove, or maintain these DSN settings. The File DSN tab, on the other hand, maintains locally connected data sources that are usable by any user of the system, provided they have the equivalent DSN defined in either the User or System DSN tabs. The File DSN tab is shown in Figure 6.9.

Chapter 6: Control Panel

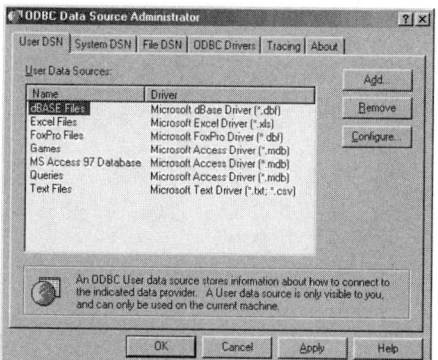

Figure 6.8
32-bit ODBC Control Panel: User DSN tab.

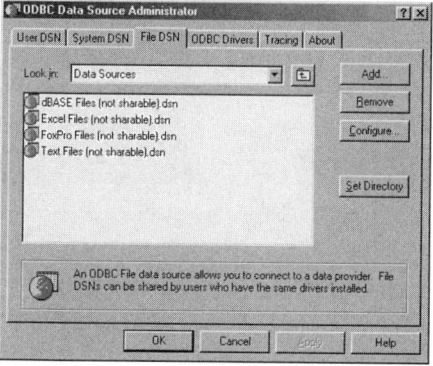

Figure 6.9
32-bit ODBC Control Panel: File DSN tab.

The ODBC Drivers tab (see Figure 6.10) displays version information for all of the installed ODBC drivers, whereas the About tab (see Figure 6.11) shows version information for the ODBC core components.

Finally, the last tab shown, Tracing, offers new capabilities to trace an ODBC dialogue between a requester and a data source in order to debug problems. You can see the Tracing tab in Figure 6.12.

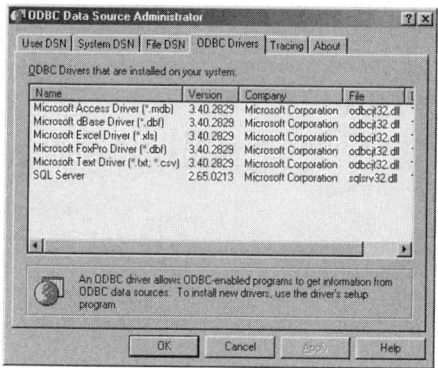

Figure 6.10
32-bit ODBC Control Panel: ODBC Drivers tab.

Figure 6.11
32-bit ODBC Control Panel: About tab.

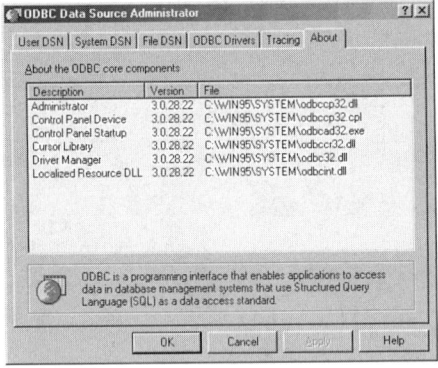

Figure 6.12
32-bit ODBC Control Panel: Tracing tab.

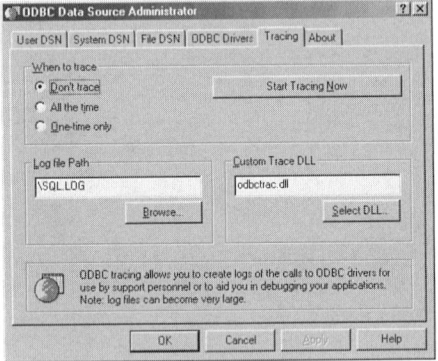

Accessibility Options

The Accessibility Options Control Panel controls how Windows meets the needs of people with special requirements for interacting with the computer. For example, a person with reduced hearing or manipulation abilities can use the settings in Accessibility to make Windows more usable (or even simply usable). There are quite a few new settings and features in Windows 98 that dramatically improve this vital function. Figure 6.13 shows the first tab of the Accessibility Options Control Panel, while Table 6.4 overviews the main setting categories available.

Table 6.4
Accessibility Options Control Panel Main Settings

Tab	Setting	Description
Keyboard	Use StickyKeys	Allows a single press of a "chorded" key (i.e., Shift, Alt, or Ctrl) to keep it depressed
	Use FilterKeys	Filters out unwanted keystrokes, such as quickly typed keys or double keystrokes

Chapter 6: Control Panel

Tab	Setting	Description
	Use **T**oggleKeys	Sounds audible tones when Shift, Alt, or Ctrl is activated
Sound	Use **S**oundSentry	Provides visual cues for system sounds
	Use S**h**owSounds	Provides captions for speech or system sounds (if application is enabled)
Display	**U**se HighContrast	Sets the screen colors to use the highest possible contrast, possibly making it easier for people with visual impairments to read
Mouse	Use **M**ouseKeys	Allows the numeric keypad, rather than a mouse or other pointing device, to control the pointer
General	**T**urn Off Accessibility Features After Idle For	Lets you set a number of minutes after which all accessibility features will automatically be turned off (useful for setting Accessibility options on a shared computer)
	Give a Warning Message when Turning a Feature On	Displays a warning message box when an accessibility feature is activated
	Make a **S**ound when Turning a Feature On or Off	Causes a system sound to occur whenever a feature is turned on or off
	S**u**pport SerialKey Devices	Allows Windows 98 to easily use devices that connect through a serial port

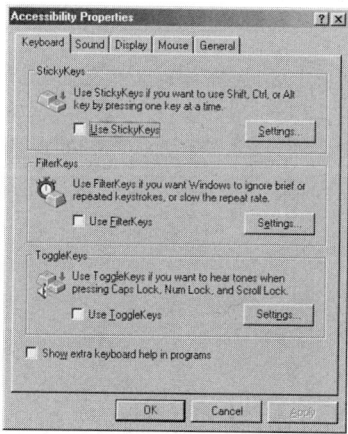

Figure 6.13
Accessibility Properties Control Panel: Keyboard tab.

Add New Hardware

The Add New Hardware Control Panel is not actually a Control Panel, but rather invokes the Add New Hardware Wizard, which guides you through the addition of new hardware device support to Windows 98. You can see the opening dialog box of the Add New Hardware Wizard in Figure 6.14.

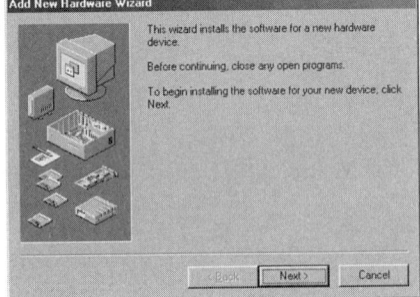

Figure 6.14
Add New Hardware Control Panel: Wizard.

The Add New Hardware Wizard will first search the system for any new detectable devices. If it finds none, the wizard offers you the chance to specify a hardware installation file that it uses to set up the new hardware.

Add/Remove Programs

The Add/Remove Programs Control Panel lets you perform three main tasks: add or remove Windows 98-compliant applications, add or remove Windows 98's components, and create a system startup disk that can be used in case you have trouble booting the system. Figure 6.15 shows the Install/Uninstall tab, which lets you add and remove applications, Figure 6.16 shows the Windows Setup tab that lets you change which features of Windows 98 are installed on the system, and Figure 6.17 shows the Startup Disk tab.

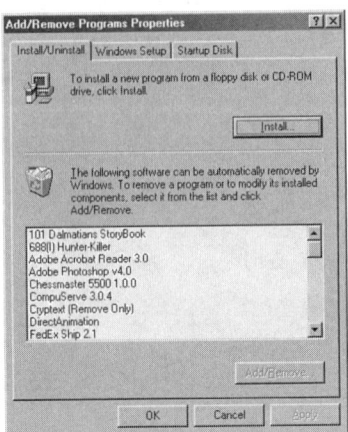

Figure 6.15
Add/Remove Programs Control Panel: Install/Uninstall tab.

Chapter 6: Control Panel   **131**

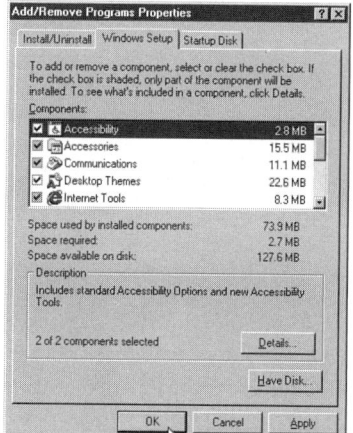

Figure 6.16
Add/Remove Programs Control Panel: Windows Setup tab.

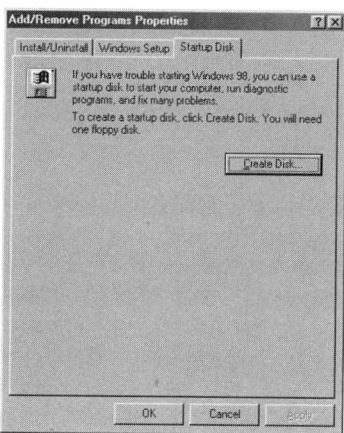

Figure 6.17
Add/Remove Programs Control Panel: Startup Disk tab.

Date/Time

Use the Date/Time Control Panel to set the system's date and time (see Figure 6.18) and to set the system's time zone (see Figure 6.19).

> **Note** Some application programs make use of the Time Zone tab to coordinate time-sensitive information across a network or across the Internet. For example, Microsoft Outlook sends the system's time zone along with meeting requests to other Outlook or Schedule+ users, so that the recipient's computer can automatically adjust the requested meeting time across different time zones. (In other words, if you generate a meeting request for 11a.m. from a computer set to
>
> *continues*

> *continued*
>
> Pacific time and send it to someone in New York with their time zone set to Eastern time, it will show on their system automatically as 2 p.m.). If a user changes this setting incorrectly (as they might do if they're trying to find out the time in another part of the world), then some applications, such as group scheduling or project management programs, will produce erroneous results.

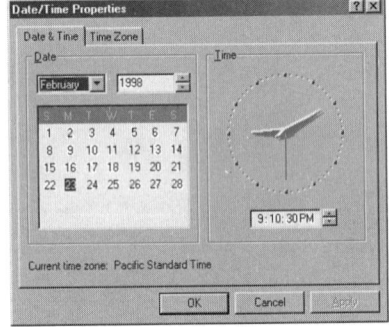

Figure 6.18
Date/Time Control Panel: Date & Time tab.

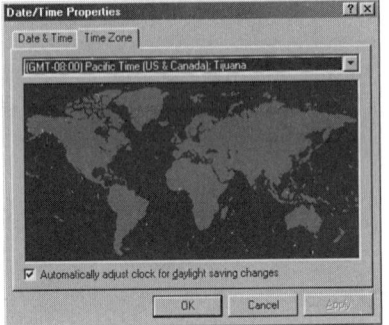

Figure 6.19
Date/Time Control Panel: Time Zone tab.

Display

The Display Control Panel allows a myriad of different choices that affect how Windows 98 displays information. It can be used to set background wallpapers, change the display geometry and color depth, change the colors the system uses, and so forth. This Control Panel will probably be the one most often used by your users, since people love to customize their computer's settings in these ways. Of more importance to support personnel, you can solve many problems with the Display Control Panel's Settings tab, which enables you to control screen geometry and color depth, install new or updated video drivers, and set the monitor type that is connected to the computer.

Chapter 6: Control Panel

The Background tab (see Figure 6.20) lets you choose desktop wallpaper or a pattern to apply to the desktop. The Screen Saver tab, seen in Figure 6.21, lets you choose a screen saver, its settings, and also the power-saving settings for a connected Energy Star monitor. The Appearance tab (see Figure 6.22) lets you choose a Windows color scheme, or lets you select the exact color desired for different Windows 98 display elements. These three tabs are basically unchanged from Windows 95, while the tabs discussed next offer new functionality as part of Windows 98.

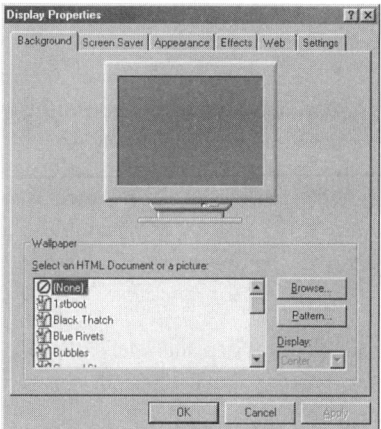

Figure 6.20

Display Control Panel: Background tab.

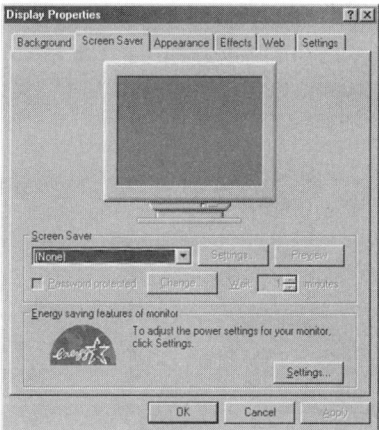

Figure 6.21

Display Control Panel: Screen Saver tab.

The Effects tab (see Figure 6.23) of the Display Control Panel includes some settings available previously only if the Microsoft Plus! Pack was installed on top of Windows 95. With it, you can change some of the default system icons, and can select a number of other options detailed in the following table.

Part II: Configuring Windows 98

Setting	Description
Hide Icons When the Desktop is Viewed as a Web Page	Deactivates *all* desktop icons when the desktop is set to display as a web page; in this model, web page links (or the Start menu) would have to activate all typical desktop icon objects.
Use **L**arge Icons	Uses a different version of each icon that is approximately twice the size of the default icons.
Show **I**cons Using All Possible Colors	When more than 256 colors are available, uses full-color versions of the desktop icons, if such versions are available on the system; most Windows 98 icons have high-color versions that display automatically when this is set.
Use **M**enu Animations	Causes menus to open in an animated fashion instead of simply displaying as quickly as possible. This setting can make using the computer more understandable for very novice users, or more attractive to some users.
Smooth Edges of Screen Fonts	When a high-color depth is selected (more than 256 colors), the system can use anti-aliasing techniques to make some screen text appear more like printed type.
Show **W**indow Contents While Dragging	Instead of dragging a window outline, the window and its contents are displayed during the entire drag process. You should turn this off for systems with very slow video subsystems or that are easily taxed, such as low-RAM 80486-based computers with ISA video systems.

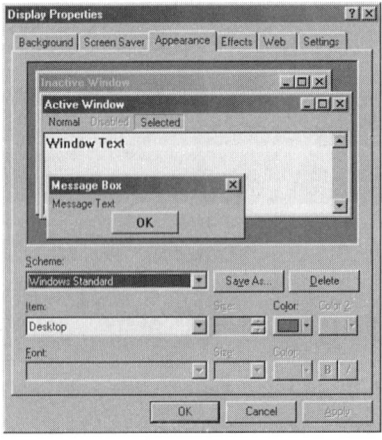

Figure 6.22
Display Control Panel: Appearance tab.

Chapter 6: Control Panel   **135**

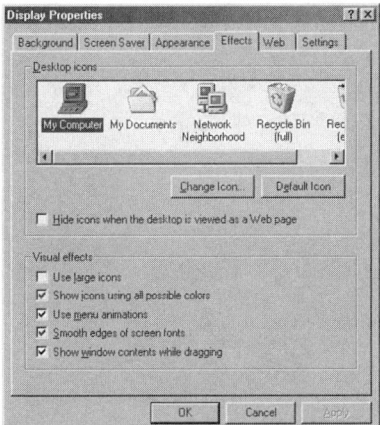

Figure 6.23
Display Control Panel: Effects tab.

The Web tab is new to Windows 98 and Internet Explorer 4. It lets you customize the desktop when the desktop is displayed as a web page. You can, for instance, embed certain web objects onto the desktop without consuming a window. In the example shown in Figure 6.24, a few web objects were downloaded that can be used with these functions. You will generally only want to activate such objects when using a computer that has a full-time connection to the Internet.

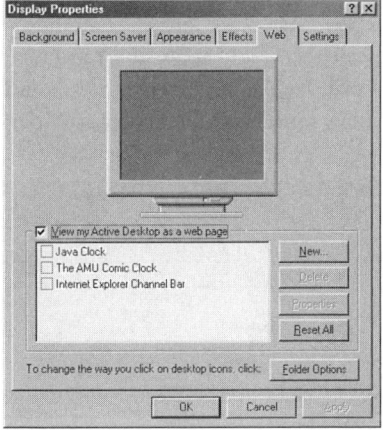

Figure 6.24
Display Control Panel: Web tab.

The final tab, Settings, enables you to change the resolution and color depth of the display. You can also use the **A**dvanced button to access other features for the installed display adapter, such as color matching. The Settings tab is shown in Figure 6.25.

Figure 6.25
Display Control Panel: Settings tab.

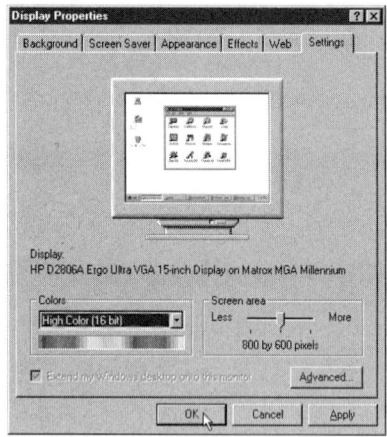

Fonts

The Fonts Control Panel lets you view all of the installed fonts in the system. You can also add new fonts by dragging the appropriate files into this folder, and you can move fonts to another system by copying these files onto a disk or network share and then dragging them into a destination system's fonts folder.

Opening the Fonts Control Panel opens the folder \Windows\Fonts just as if you had opened it through My Computer. However, although this folder looks like all other folders, there is a key difference that you may not immediately see. If you access the View menu (shown along with the Fonts folder in Figure 6.26) you will see the font-specific view commands, such as List Fonts by **S**imilarity and **H**ide Variations. Otherwise, the folder acts like any other.

Figure 6.26
Fonts Control Panel: Fonts folder.

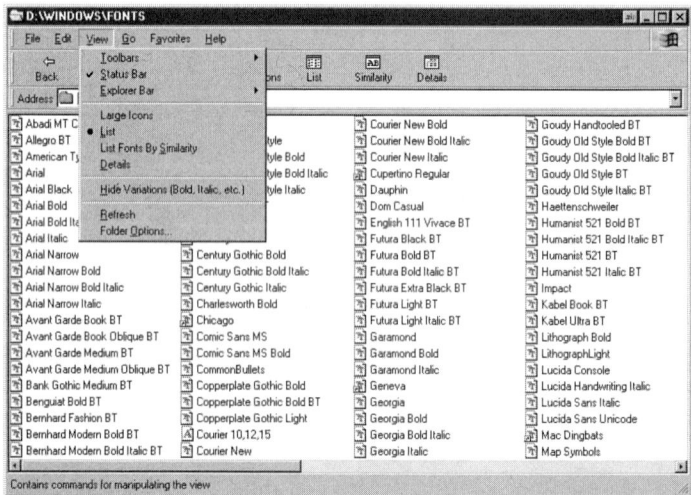

Game Controllers

Use the Game Controllers Control Panel to control any game devices connected to the system, such as joysticks, steering wheels, pedals, and so forth. The General tab (shown in Figure 6.27) lists all attached game controllers and enables you to add or remove game controllers and change their individual property settings. The Advanced tab lets you set which interface each controller is connected to.

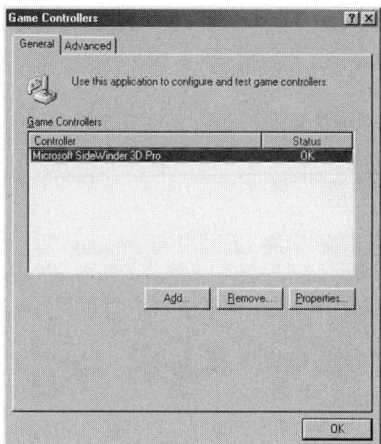

Figure 6.27
Game Controllers Control Panel: General tab.

Internet

The Internet Control Panel, seen in Figure 6.28, lets you control how Microsoft Internet Explorer behaves on the system. This Control Panel can also be accessed in two other ways: You can right-click on the Internet Explorer icon on the desktop and choose Properties from the pop-up menu, or you can choose Internet Options from Internet Explorer's View menu. The settings for the Internet Control Panel are detailed in Chapter 27, "Internet Browsers in Windows 98."

Keyboard

Use the Keyboard Control Panel to change the characteristics of the keyboard. There are two tabs: Speed and Language. The Speed tab (see Figure 6.29) lets you change how quickly keys repeat when held down, and how long you must wait before a held-down key automatically repeats. You also set the cursor blink rate on the Speed tab. The Language tab, shown in Figure 6.30, lets you define different keyboard types that can be used with Windows 98, such as international keyboards or keyboards utilizing an alternative key placement format (such as the DVORAK layout).

Figure 6.28
Internet Control Panel:
General tab.

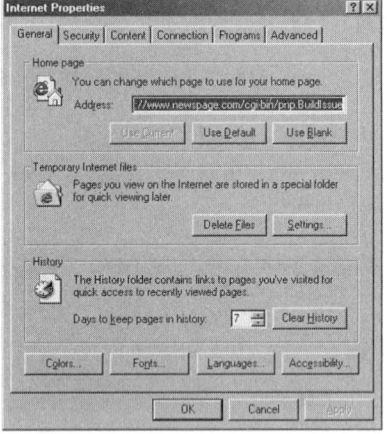

Figure 6.29
Keyboard Control Panel:
Speed tab.

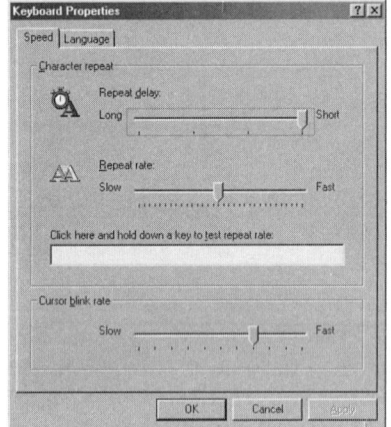

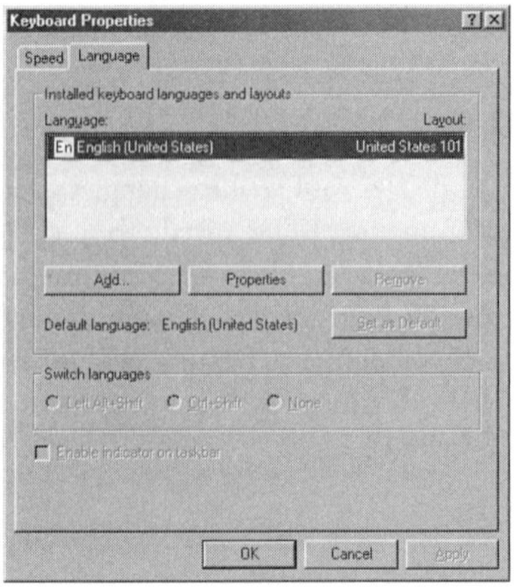

Figure 6.30
Keyboard Control Panel:
Language tab.

Tip

For you multilingual typers: You can set a hotkey on the Language tab of the Keyboard Control Panel to toggle between languages when you have an alternative language defined for the system. You could then, for instance, simply press the selected hotkey combination to switch languages.

Mail

In the Mail Control Panel you can change how an installed email program operates. Choosing this Control Panel is the same as choosing the Properties pop-up command for the default system Inbox, Exchange Client, or Microsoft Outlook, as appropriate. The example shown in Figure 6.31 is for a system that Microsoft Outlook installed as the default email client application. You can find detailed information on the settings in this Control Panel in the documentation for the email client you have installed.

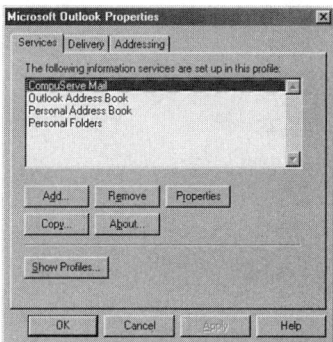

Figure 6.31

Mail Control Panel: Microsoft Outlook's Services tab.

Modems

All modems installed in a system should be managed through the Modems Control Panel. Use the General tab, shown in Figure 6.32, to add or remove modems, or to change their properties (each modem can display a different Properties dialog box). You can also set characteristics for how the system dials through the modem by clicking the Dialing Properties button, which then displays the Dialing Properties dialog box shown in Figure 6.33.

The Diagnostics tab of the Modems Control Panel (see Figure 6.34) can be used to sort out some modem problems, primarily by letting you quickly interrogate the modem to see if it's working properly (click the **M**ore Info button), and by letting you launch the Modems troubleshooter (click the **H**elp button), a new web page-based troubleshooting tool in Windows 98.

Part II: Configuring Windows 98

Figure 6.32
Modems Control Panel: General tab.

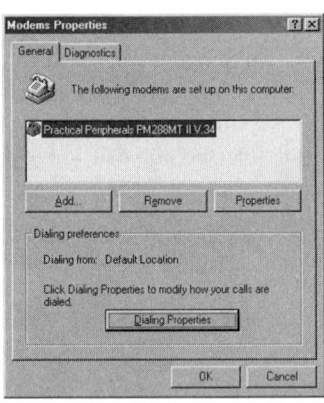

Figure 6.33
Modems Control Panel: General tab's Dialing Properties dialog box.

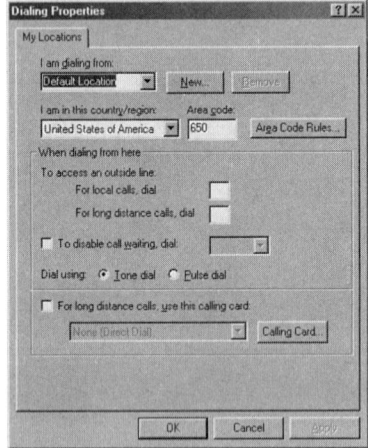

Figure 6.34
Modems Control Panel: Diagnostics tab.

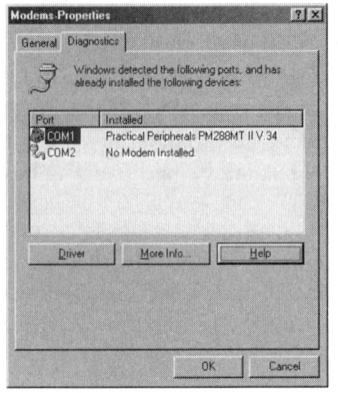

Mouse

The Mouse Control Panel is an easily used set of tabs that lets you control how the mouse (or a trackball) behaves under Windows 98. Figure 6.35 shows the Buttons tab of the Mouse Control Panel. All of the tabs in this Control Panel are basically unchanged from Windows 95. Refer to the following table for a listing of the available settings.

Tab	Setting	Description
Buttons	**R**ight-Handed/ **L**eft-Handed	Quickly reverses the mouse button's functions.
	Double-click Speed	Lets you set how quickly double-clicks must be accomplished in order for them to be accepted by Windows 98 as a double-click instead of two single-clicks.
Pointers	**S**cheme	Lets you quickly select from the installed mouse pointer schemes in Windows 98; each different scheme changes the displayed mouse pointers' appearances. Double-clicking on any of the individual mouse pointers shown lets you browse for a different pointer file for that type of pointer only.
Motion	Pointer **S**peed	Adjusts the pointer acceleration that occurs when you quickly move the pointing device. For instance, if you move a mouse one inch slowly, it will travel less distance on the screen than if you move it quickly with this setting.
	Pointer **T**rail	Lets you enable pointer trails, which leave a trail of mouse pointers whenever you move the mouse. You can also adjust the length of the trails with the available slider control. Pointer trails can make it easier to locate a mouse pointer on a dim notebook computer's display.

Multimedia

The Multimedia Control Panel configures all of the installed multimedia devices on the system. The settings in this Control Panel are detailed in Chapter 14, "Multimedia." Figure 6.36 shows the Audio tab of the Multimedia Control Panel, and the following table summarizes the settings you can control through the entire Control Panel.

Part II: Configuring Windows 98

Figure 6.35
Mouse Control Panel: Buttons tab.

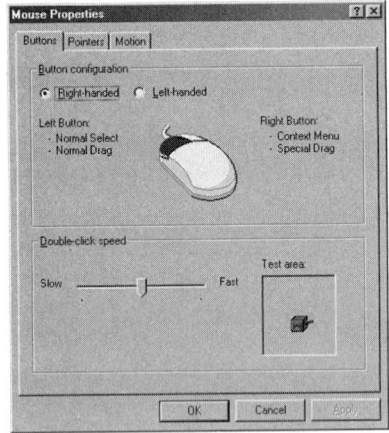

Figure 6.36
Multimedia Control Panel: Audio tab.

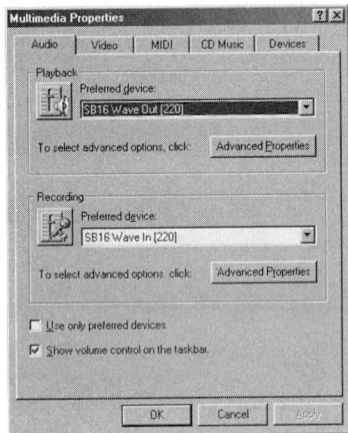

Tab	Description
Audio	Controls the devices used for audio playback and recording; clicking on the Advanced Properties buttons enables control of the quality of audio sound that is played back or recorded, and can control audio performance on the system.
Video	Sets the default playback size for played movie files (such as .AVI or .MPEG).
MIDI	Controls connected MIDI devices, such as an attached piano keyboard or other MIDI instruments.
CD Music	Controls the playback of music CDs.

Chapter 6: Control Panel

Tab	Description
Devices	Shows all connected multimedia devices, including motherboard-based support devices. A Properties button lets you adjust the settings for any selected device in the list.

Network

The Network Control Panel is one of the most complicated in Windows 98. There are many different valid configurations, depending on the network to which Windows 98 is connected. Even when using a machine not connected to a physical network, all networking protocols and client software are controlled through the Network Control Panel, and you use this Control Panel to manage, for instance, TCP/IP settings used to connect to an ISP over a dial-up modem connection, or other network settings for remote modem access to a network server. The settings available in the Network Control Panel are detailed in Chapter 21, "Understanding Windows 98 Networking." You can see the Configuration tab in Figure 6.37, which you would use to control installed network adapters, protocols, and network client software. The Identification tab lets you set the ID information for the computer, which is used to identify the computer to a connected network. The Access Control tab lets you toggle between Share-level access control and User-level access control. (Share-level control lets you assign a password to each resource shared from the current machine, while User-level control lets you create and maintain a list of users, to whom you can then grant access to resources shared from the current machine.)

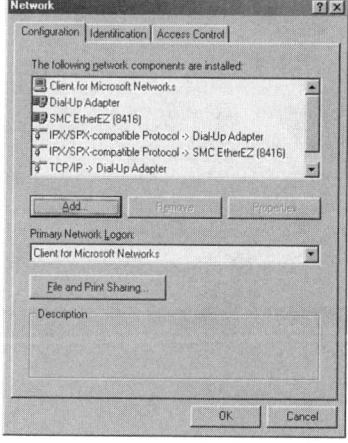

Figure 6.37
Network Control Panel: Configuration tab.

Passwords

The Passwords Control Panel is used for two things. First, you can change your password both for the local Windows computer and for any networks to which you are connected (such as a Windows NT domain or Novell network). On the Change Passwords tab (see Figure 6.38), click Change **W**indows Password to change the local logon password to the machine, and click Change **O**ther Passwords to change any other network passwords.

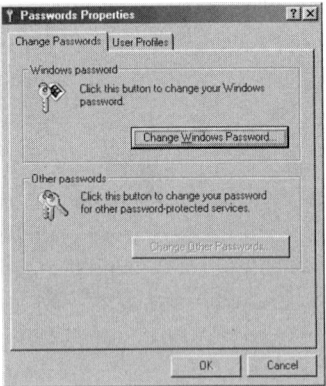

Figure 6.38
Passwords Control Panel: Change Passwords tab.

Second, you can use the Passwords Control Panel to change whether the local computer keeps track of individual desktop settings based on the account name and password used to log on to Windows. As you can see in Figure 6.39, you can change the settings on the User Profiles tab to tell Windows to track individual user settings for the desktop and Start menu based on the account name used.

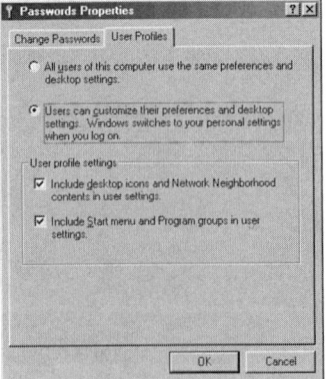

Figure 6.39
Passwords Control Panel: User Profiles tab.

> **Note** If Remote Administration has been installed (the Remote Registry Service), you will also see a Remote Administration tab on the Passwords Control Panel. Remote Administration is discussed in Chapter 10, "Mastering the Windows 98 Registry."

Power Management

A relatively simple Control Panel, Power Management lets you choose how the computer conserves power when not in use, and how long it waits before powering down different aspects of the system to a stand-by mode. Use the Power Schemes tab (see Figure 6.40) to choose from preprogrammed power-saving modes, and if you want to, you can then customize the amount of time that the system waits before powering down the display and hard disk.

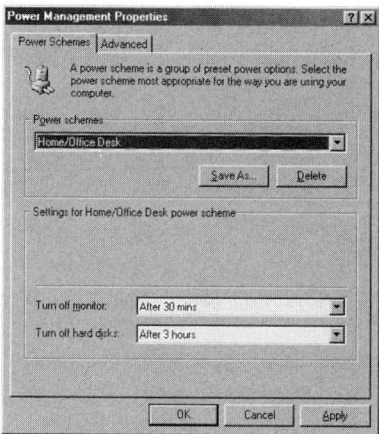

Figure 6.40
Power Management Control Panel: Power Schemes tab.

Note The Power Management dialog box you see may differ significantly from the example shown here, depending on the power-saving features available on your specific computer.

The second tab in Power Management, Advanced, simply lets you choose whether Windows displays a power status indicator on the Task Bar. For a battery-powered computer, you would typically display the power meter; for an AC-powered desktop, you would not.

Printers

The Printers Control Panel opens up the Printers folder, just as if you had opened the Printers folder from within My Computer. You use this folder to add and manage any connected printers. Details for performing these tasks can be found in Chapter 13, "Printing." Figure 6.41 shows a sample Printers folder opened through the Control Panel.

Regional Settings

Use the Regional Settings Control Panel to "localize" Windows 98's behavior for the particular country's standards that you want to use. You can control what currency symbol is used, how

Part II: Configuring Windows 98

numbers are represented, and how times and dates are displayed by the system. (Generally, application programs get these settings from the Registry and then use them for their own displays and inputs). There are a number of tabs and settings, summarized in the following table. Figure 6.42 shows the Regional Settings tab, which lets you choose from a number of predefined regional settings. (All the settings in the rest of the tabs are adjusted based on the country you choose in the Regional Settings tab; you can then make any small adjustments to those settings using the remaining tabs.)

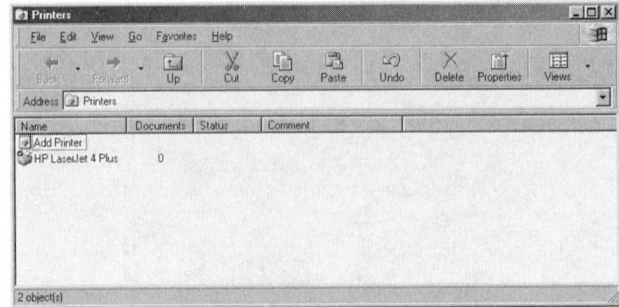

Figure 6.41
Printers Control Panel: Printers folder.

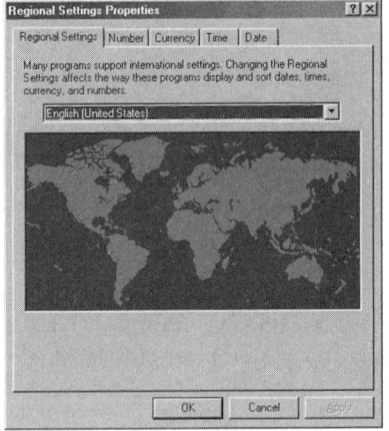

Figure 6.42
Regional Settings Control Panel: Regional Settings tab.

Tab	Description
Regional Settings	Quickly selects from a pre-defined set of settings for the other tabs
Number	Changes how numbers are entered and displayed
Currency	Changes how currencies are entered and displayed
Time	Changes how time is entered and displayed
Date	Changes how dates are entered and displayed

Sounds

Windows 98 lets you assign different sound files to different system events. You can choose from a number of sounds that are included with Windows 98 for this purpose, or reference sound files that are downloaded from the Internet or came with other application programs. All system sounds must be in the .WAV file format in order to assign them to system events. Figure 6.43 shows the Sounds tab (the only tab in this Control Panel) in which you can choose the sounds to be played for all possible system events. If any sound schemes are installed on the system, you can also choose from among them to quickly set many system event sounds.

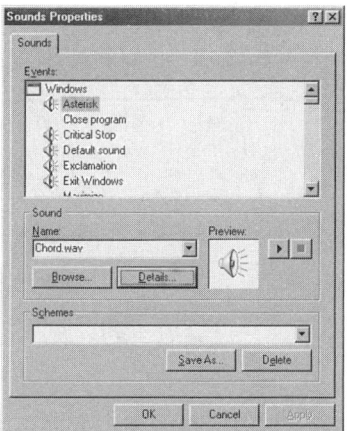

Figure 6.43

Sounds Control Panel: Sounds tab.

Tip	To install sound schemes included with Windows 98, use the Windows Setup tab in the Add/Remove Programs Control Panel and ensure that the Multimedia Sound Schemes option is installed (you find this option in the Multimedia installation set).

System

The System Control Panel is one of the most important for support personnel to master. With it, you can control most of the underlying hardware drivers and some very critical system settings for Windows 98.

Figure 6.44 shows the General tab of the System Control Panel. Use this tab to quickly find out which build of Windows 98 is installed onto a system, and also to find out what the product ID code is for the installation (which you will need if you call Microsoft Support).

The Device Manager tab (see Figure 6.45) is used to manage all system devices. A tree is displayed with all of the major device categories, from which you can open up any of the branches to see the installed devices. Select a device and click the Properties button to see the hardware settings for the device. There are a few tricks you can use in the Device Manager tab. First, if you select Computer at the top of the tree and then click Properties, a window displays summaries of all system IRQs, I/O addresses, DMA settings, and memory addresses (this can be crucial in resolving conflicts). Second, if you select Computer and press the asterisk key *on the numeric keypad*, all branches of the tree will open automatically.

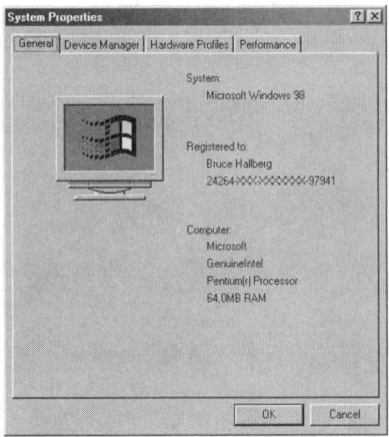

Figure 6.44
System Control Panel: General tab.

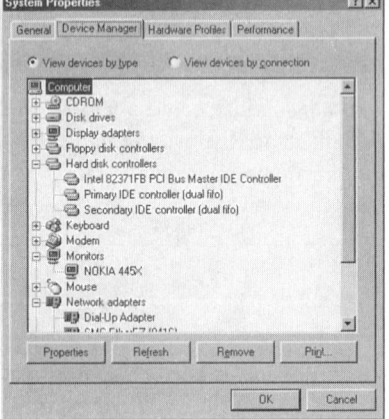

Figure 6.45
System Control Panel: Device Manager tab.

Tip | The Print button on the Device Manager tab can generate useful reports to keep on file in your MIS support office for each system for which you are responsible. You might consider printing one of these reports each time you install a new computer, and then filing it where it's readily available for support calls.

Chapter 6: Control Panel

The Hardware Profiles tab (see Figure 6.46) is generally only used with docking notebook computers. By using this tab, you can create different Hardware Profiles for when the unit is docked and undocked. See Chapter 19, "Windows 98 for Portables," for more information about how this is done.

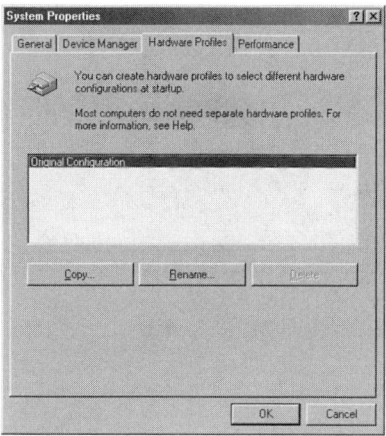

Figure 6.46
System Control Panel: Hardware Profiles tab.

The last tab of the System Control Panel is one of the most important. On the Performance tab (see Figure 6.47) you can control many key settings affecting Windows 98's performance on a particular system.

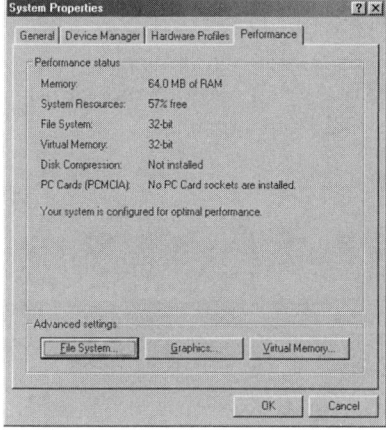

Figure 6.47
System Control Panel: Performance tab.

The Performance tab displays summary performance setting information about the system and offers three buttons that can control more detailed settings. Click the File System button to open the File System Properties dialog box, shown in Figure 6.48. In this dialog box, you can control file system performance for CD-ROM drives, hard disks, floppy disk drives, and removable disks. You can also activate a number of different troubleshooting settings that might be needed for Windows 98 compatibility on some systems.

Figure 6.48
System Control Panel: Performance Tab, File System dialog box.

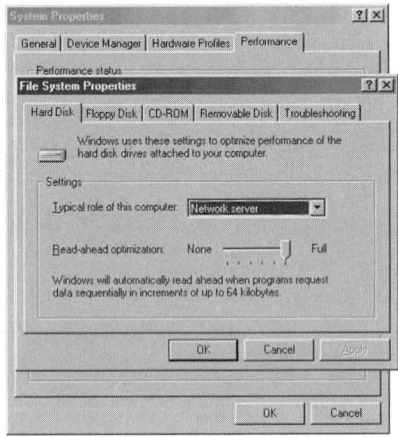

The Graphics button on the Performance tab opens an Advanced Graphics Settings dialog box in which you can "dial-in" the amount of graphics performance available from the installed video card. Generally, this setting is always set at the highest level, although you can decrease it if the video display exhibits occasional problems.

The Virtual Memory button of the Performance tab opens the Virtual Memory dialog box shown in Figure 6.49. Here, you can choose to let Windows manage the virtual memory settings for the computer or you can choose your own. As a rule, letting Windows manage the virtual memory is almost always the best choice, although you might want to use this dialog box to relocate the virtual memory swap file or set a large minimum virtual memory file size so that the system doesn't have to spend time increasing its size.

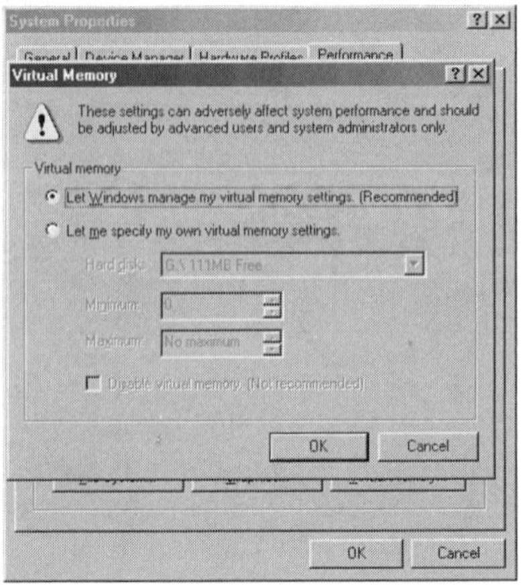

Figure 6.49
System Control Panel: Performance tab, Virtual Memory dialog box.

Warning Using the Virtual Memory dialog box to disable virtual memory on the system can cause the system to be unable to boot, or to behave erratically. You should experiment with disabling virtual memory only on systems that have *at least* 64–128MB of RAM installed, and even then this experimentation is fairly risky if many applications are loaded and used.

Telephony

The Telephony Control Panel lets you control the dialing parameters for the locations from which you make modem calls with the system. You can define as many dialing locations as you want, each one using different area codes or dialing strings. For instance, you might have locations set for home, the office, and for a few hotels. You can then create different Dial Up Networking connections that utilize these different dialing rules automatically.

The other tab on the Telephony Control Panel, Telephony Drivers, lets you control the installed telephony drivers on the system, such as the Unimodem driver, or any required TAPI (Telephony API) drivers.

Users

With the Users Control Panel (see Figure 6.50) you can create and maintain accounts for people who use the system. You can easily create a new user account by clicking the **N**ew User button, which leads you through the process of creating the new account, deciding which of the user's current settings will be copied to the new user account, and assigning a password for the new user to use. You can also select a listed user and click the **S**et Password or **C**hange Settings buttons to affect those aspects of each user account on the local computer.

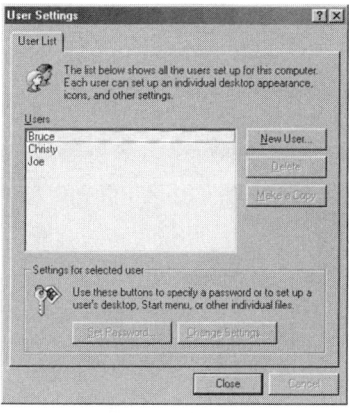

Figure 6.50
Users Control Panel: User List tab.

Conclusion

In this chapter you learned all about Windows 98's Control Panel, how to manage it, how the various Control Panels are stored on the system, and how you can access them in a variety of ways. Also, each different core Windows 98 Control Panel was shown and summarized for quick reference, with pointers to other chapters, as appropriate, for more detailed discussion.

The next chapter, "System Policies," discusses user management of Windows 98 desktop computers in much more detail, focusing on how System Policies and User Profiles are maintained and used in a networked environment. Mastering System Policies and Profiles is key to being able to support Windows 98 effectively in the corporate environment.

CHAPTER 7

System Policies

In any business computing environment, you must have certain policies that help you manage the overall system. Information Systems (IS) policies are designed to do many things, including the following:

- *Ensure the security of data*
- *Ensure the safety (against loss) of data*
- *Minimize the cost to support IS systems*
- *Minimize training requirements for users*
- *Minimize hardware and software costs*
- *Maximize IS efficiency (and, it is hoped, overall company efficiency)*

Some of the policies that accomplish these objectives rely on users conscientiously following policies that have been communicated to them, whereas others can be enforced at various points, such as at network servers, through occasional audits, and by controlling each user's desktop operating system and applications.

This chapter shows you how to use Windows 98's built-in capabilities to create, deploy, and enforce certain IS policies that relate to the desktop operating system. You'll learn how to do the following:

- Use the System Policy Editor tool (Policy Editor) to set Windows 98 policies for your users.

- Set up each system so that policies are automatically applied at logon.

- Set up and maintain Group Policies on a network.

- Create your own policies.

By learning and applying the information in this chapter, you can significantly ease the administrative burden of supporting many Windows 98 clients on a network.

Understanding System Policies

In Chapter 5, "Understanding Windows 98 Configuration," you learned a bit about how the Windows 98 Registry works and what it does (more detailed information is found in Chapter 10, "Mastering the Windows 98 Registry"). In order to understand System Policies in Windows 98, you first need to understand how the Registry works, so review the material related to the Registry in Chapter 5 before proceeding with this chapter.

System Policies are actually just *forced Registry settings*. When a user logs on to a Windows 98 computer, he automatically selects his User Profile during logon, which causes his own personal Registry settings to load. After his User Profile is selected and loaded, any System Policies are then applied on top of their personal Registry settings. In this way, System Policies override any settings that they changed during his last session. With the System Policies that come with Windows 98, you can accomplish many things, including the following:

- Hide the Run command from the Start menu.

- Hide the local hard disk drives.

- Hide the Find command on the Start menu.

- Disable File or Printer Sharing.

- Force certain desktop settings, like wallpaper.

- Enable user-level access control.

- Disable password caching.

- Set minimum Windows password lengths, and require alphanumeric Windows passwords.

- Control various network-specific settings, such as supporting long filenames in different ways on Novell networks.

- Hide various Control Panel objects.

> **Note** System Policies can only be used when User Profiles are active.

It is possible for a user to "countermand" any System Policy changes to their Registry after he logs on to Windows 98. However, you can solve this problem by using certain System Policies that deny access to various features in the Control Panel, effectively shutting the user out from making Registry-level changes to his own system. For example, you can remove the Run command from the Start menu, force the user to use a customized (and limited) Start menu, hide his local drive, and so forth, so that he cannot "get into trouble" with his system. Obviously, you must consider user needs and the culture of the company before setting draconian System Policies like these.

System Policies can be set in several ways:

- Default settings made for every computer and user
- User-specific System Policies
- System-specific System Policies
- Network group-based policies

Using these different types of System Policies, you have considerable flexibility in what capabilities you enable or disable for different computers, users, and groups of users.

When you use the System Policy Editor for Windows 98, you can choose from a number of standard policy settings. You can also create your own. Custom System Policies let you apply any Registry setting you want as part of the System Policies. You can use this feature to cause Registry-based application settings to remain a particular way, for example.

Implementing System Policies

There are several things you must do in order to begin using System Policies:

- Enable User Profiles for Windows 98 at the desktop (usually done during the initial setup of the system).

- If Group Policies are needed, install Windows 98 support for them.
- Create the CONFIG.POL file with the Policy Editor.
- Locate the CONFIG.POL file in the appropriate directory of the network logon server.

The following sections describe these actions.

Enabling User Profiles

System Policies can be used only when User Profiles are enabled on a given machine. User Profiles are, broadly speaking, user-specific settings on a Windows 98 computer, often retrieved from a network server at logon, but otherwise stored in special subdirectories in the \Windows directory. Not only are User Profiles required for System Policies to work at all, but they also enable you to create user-specific System Policy settings.

To enable User Profiles, open the Passwords Control Panel object and move to the User Profiles tab, shown in Figure 7.1. Make sure that the option button indicated in Figure 7.1 is selected, which enables User Profiles. You will then need to shut down and restart Windows 98.

Figure 7.1
Enable User Profiles before using System Policies.

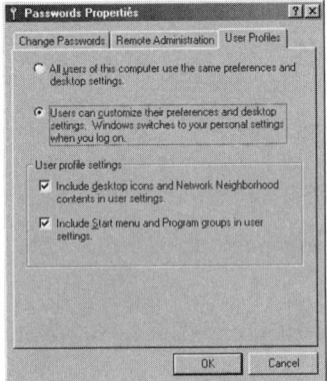

Note You can learn about User Profiles in detail in Chapter 8, "User Profiles."

Enabling Group System Policies

In order to use network group-specific policies, you must install that feature of Windows 98 if it is not already installed. To enable Group Policies, follow these steps:

1. Open the Add/Remove Programs Control Panel object.

Chapter 7: System Policies 157

2. Move to the Windows Setup tab.

3. Select the System Tools installation topic and click the Details button.

4. Select the Group Policies installation choice, as shown in Figure 7.2.

5. Click OK to close all the Add/Remove Programs dialog boxes. You may be prompted for a Windows 98 CD-ROM as part of this process.

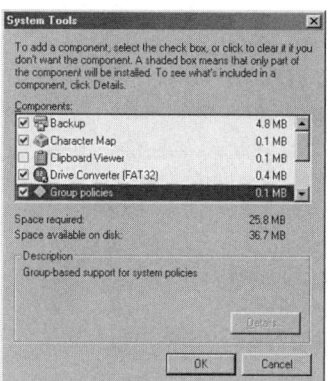

Figure 7.2
Selecting group-based System Policy capabilities.

Tip | You should always install support for Group Policies when setting up new Windows 98 systems. Even if you never use the capability, at least you won't have to visit each desktop to make this change if you do decide to start using Group Policies. See Chapter 23, "Windows 98 in Windows NT Domains," for more information about group security in NT domains. Windows 98 also supports Group Policies in NetWare networks.

Creating the System Policy File

You use a tool called the System Policy Editor (POLEDIT.EXE) to create and maintain your System Policies. In the Policy Editor, you define users, computers, and groups, and then select the policies to apply to each of those categories. After doing this, you save the policy file to a particular directory on the user's logon server, from which location the policy file is automatically downloaded and applied when a user logs on.

In the Policy Editor, you first choose *policy templates*, which are collections of possible policies that you can use. You can choose to use only a few templates, or to use all of the templates included with Windows 98. Applications might also supply template files that you can use to enforce application-specific policies. You can also create your own policy templates.

> **Warning** Keep in mind that System Policies directly modify the Registry of any user that logs on to the network. Creating your own policies should be done with great care, and you should implement them cautiously to avoid problems.

Installing the System Policy Editor

To install the System Policy Editor, locate the \Tools\Admin\Poledit directory on the Windows 98 CD-ROM. Copy the entire contents to a location from where you want to run the Policy Editor. It's a good idea to locate this destination directory on a network server where only Administrator-level accounts can access it.

After selecting which policy templates to use, you then create a new policy file and choose the default policies for users and computers. After doing this, you can create specific users, computers, and groups and assign them policies that are unique from the defaults. Finally, you save the CONFIG.POL file from the System Policy Editor.

Use the following steps to create a sample policy file using the Policy Editor:

1. Open the Policy Editor by running the POLEDIT.EXE program (double-click on it or start it in any other fashion).

2. Choose at least one policy template. Pull down the Options menu and choose Policy Template. You see the dialog box shown in Figure 7.3.

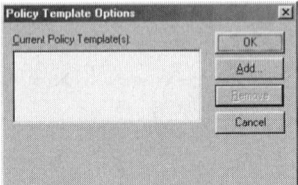

Figure 7.3
Selecting policy templates with the Policy Template Options dialog box.

3. Click the Add button. You see a standard file selection dialog box. Choose the file WINDOWS.ADM from the directory where you copied all of the Policy Editor files. Click OK to close the dialog boxes you opened and return to the Policy Editor.

4. Access the File menu and choose New Policy. A standard policy is then created based on the installed policy templates, with a default user and default computer initialized, as shown in Figure 7.4.

5. Double-click on the Default Computer icon, which shows you the Default Computer Properties dialog box (see Figure 7.5), which somewhat resembles the Windows 98

Registry Editor. Using the plus signs and subfolders, you select each policy in turn and set it as needed. Perform the same actions with the Default User Properties. (Computers and users have different possible policies from which you can choose).

Figure 7.4
Creating a New Policy file starts with a default user and computer.

> **Note** You learn details of using the System Policy Editor in a succeeding section of this chapter called "Using the System Policy Editor."

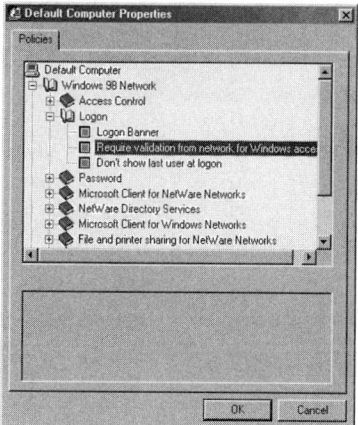

Figure 7.5
The Default Computer Properties dialog box with a sample policy selected.

After setting all of the policies in the Policy Editor, use its File, Save As command to save a file called CONFIG.POL. This is the policy file, which you apply to the network in the following section.

Applying the Policy File to the Network

The network clients included with Windows 98 for NetWare and Windows NT networks support automatic downloading of the CONFIG.POL file from the user's logon server. For NetWare servers, place the CONFIG.POL file in the SYS:PUBLIC directory of each user's preferred server (to which all users should already have read and file scan rights necessary for them to read the policy file). Also, NetWare 4.x servers must have Bindery Emulation Support turned on. For Windows NT networks, place the file in the \NETLOGON\ directory of the Primary Domain Controller.

Before doing this, however, there are a number of things you will need to consider and test:

- As soon as you place the CONFIG.POL file in the necessary directory, any Default User or Default Computer Policies will automatically be applied to any user who logs on afterwards. You should first test your desired System Policies with a few computers and users. Consider deleting the Default User and Default Computer policy settings and instead creating some sample policies for a few specific users and specific computers. This will enable you to test how well your policies are working before deploying them widely.

- You may want to test the CONFIG.POL file on the network after hours, when most users aren't present, using some test accounts to ensure that they are working correctly.

> **Tip** You should create a User account in the System Policy Editor with a username that matches your administrative logon name (such as Admin, Administrator, or Supervisor) that has no System Policy restrictions placed on it. This provides you with a "back door" in case you create System Policies that are too restrictive; your administrative account won't then be restricted.

- On Windows NT networks the CONFIG.POL file is automatically downloaded only from the Primary Domain Controller (PDC). If you have a large network, the reading of this file can create logon bottlenecks. You can solve this by enabling a System Policy called Load Balancing. After enabling Load Balancing, you must manually copy the CONFIG.POL file to all of your Backup Domain Controllers (BDCs), and users will then get their CONFIG.POL from any controller they use to log on to the network. This does mean that you must manually keep all of the CONFIG.POL files on the PDC and BDCs in sync, so keep this in mind.

To turn on Load Balancing, make sure that WINDOWS.ADM is one of the selected policy templates. Open a computer policy, and then select the policy path \Windows 98 Network\Update\Remote Update. In the policy that appears, click the Load-Balance checkbox.

Chapter 7: System Policies   **161**

- On NetWare networks, you must set the Preferred Server setting in the Network Client's properties (right-click on Network Neighborhood and choose Properties, then open the client's settings and set this). The CONFIG.POL file must be stored in each server's SYS:PUBLIC directory that a user has defined as a preferred server. (In other words, if you have three servers that different groups use as their preferred servers, you'll need to make sure that CONFIG.POL is in the SYS:PUBLIC directory for each of those three servers, and that you keep all copies in sync.)

- Most important, you'll want to carefully evaluate the impact that your proposed policy settings have on a set of test users, and make sure that you haven't adversely affected their productivity with the policies you've set.

You can also configure System Policies to download from a manual location (a directory that you specify). You might need to do this, for instance, if you are using network client software that doesn't support automatic policy downloading at logon, such as computers using NetWare VLM drivers, or some other type of network client. Unfortunately, you must make this setting manually on each computer that will use System Policies in this scenario. To cause System Policies to be downloaded from a manual location, follow these steps:

1. Start the System Policy Editor on the computer that you want to set to a manual download location.

2. Ensure that the WINDOWS.ADM template is selected in Options, Policy Template.

3. From the File menu, choose Open Registry. This opens the local computer's Registry.

4. Open the Default Computer icon, and then open the /Windows 98 Network/Update/ Remote Update/ policy. You'll see the policy setting shown in Figure 7.6.

5. Use the drop-down list to choose the Manual option, and then type the path where you will locate the system policy file (CONFIG.POL).

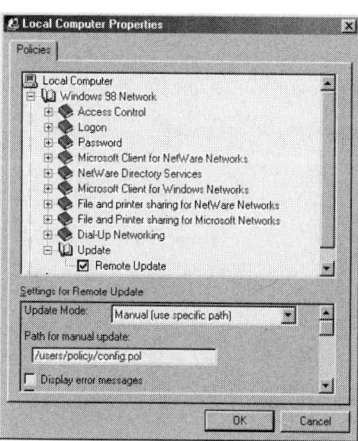

Figure 7.6
Setting a Manual Download Location.

6. Close the Default Computer properties dialog box and then choose Save from the Policy Editor's File menu. This saves your setting to the local Registry.

After completing the preceding steps on a particular computer, restart the system. The CONFIG.POL file will be read from the location you specified after the system has logged on using the network client it's set up to use.

> **Note** When using a manual download location, make sure to set the same manual download location in the CONFIG.POL file that each user accesses when he actually logs on, to continue to enforce this particular policy.

Using the System Policy Editor

You use the System Policy Editor (POLEDIT.EXE) to create and maintain System Policies. The Policy Editor can work with policies in a variety of ways, enabling you to create new policy (*.POL) files, open existing policy files, open the local computer's Registry for direct policy-based Registry modification, or even open a remote computer's Registry for direct modification.

Before using the Policy Editor, you first have to choose which policy templates you want to use. This is true no matter how you want to use the Policy Editor; policy templates "teach" the Policy Editor which policies to display and edit. *Policy templates* are files that define the possible choices you can make with the Policy Editor—in other words, the policies from which you can choose. The Policy Editor comes with a number of different template files (*.ADM files) that define policies in different areas, and you can also create your own. Policy template files are ASCII text files that describe each policy, the choices available, and the associated Registry settings that must be applied to enable the policy.

> **Tip** Applications designed to run in a corporate environment on Windows 9x or Windows NT often include their own policy template files that you can use to customize their behavior. Simply apply their .ADM files to the Policy Editor in the same way as with the templates that come with the Policy Editor.

To choose policy template files in the System Policy Editor, access the Policy Template command from the Editor's Options menu. Using the resulting dialog box, click the Add button to add new templates to the Policy Editor.

In the same directory that contains the Policy Editor you will find a number of policy template files from which you can choose:

- **CHAT.ADM** offers policies that control Microsoft Chat (formerly Comic Chat), one of the tools that comes with Internet Explorer 4 and that is used for IRC chat sessions over the Internet.

- **COMMON.ADM** is a blank policy template file that you can modify to contain your own policies.

- **CONF.ADM** contains policies for Microsoft NetMeeting, an Internet-based group collaboration application.

- **INETRES.ADM** holds policies that can restrict changes to Internet Explorer's settings through the Internet Control Panel.

- **INETSET.ADM** holds policies that can restrict other (non-Control Panel) settings for Internet Explorer.

- **OE.ADM** contains policies for Outlook Express.

- **PWS.ADM** contains policies that can enable or disable running Personal Web Server under Windows 98.

- **SHELL.ADM** has policies that control access to the Windows 98 shell, known as Explorer.

- **SUBS.ADM** has policies that control Internet subscriptions through Internet Explorer 4.

- **WINDOWS.ADM** contains the largest number of possible policies, and controls many fundamental aspects of how Windows 98 operates for users and which features they can access.

When you choose templates for the Policy Editor, you should choose only the templates that apply for your organization. For example, if you never install Microsoft NetMeeting on user desktops, there is no need to apply the CONF.ADM policy template file. While including all of the templates is possible (and in some cases necessary), remember that the CONFIG.POL file that you create will have all of the policies in it that are part of the chosen templates. Including templates that you don't need will slow the processing of the CONFIG.POL file unnecessarily.

> **Tip** By using the information in the later section "Understanding and Creating Policy Templates," you can remove individual policies from the policy template files that you don't want or need, which further speeds the processing of the CONFIG.POL file for your users.

There are four ways that you can use Policy Editor after you have selected the appropriate template files:

- Create an entirely new set of policies, which results in a saved .POL file (typically CONFIG.POL).

- Open an existing .POL file for editing.

- Open the local computer's Registry, retrieving the current settings that correspond to the defined policies.

- Open a remote computer's Registry to make direct changes to the settings that correspond to its defined policies.

To create a new set of policies, choose New Policy from the File menu. To open an existing set of policies, choose Open Policy from the File menu. To retrieve the current computer's Registry, choose Open Registry from the File menu.

If you want to open a remote computer's Registry, use the Connect command in Policy Editor's File menu. Any remote computer that you want to work with in this fashion must have Remote Registry Services installed and running, as does the computer from which you want to make the changes. You can acquire the Remote Registry Services as part of the Windows 98 Resource Kit utilities.

Figure 7.7 shows the Policy Editor open after choosing to create a new set of policies. (Policy Editor works the same way, using any of the four policy modification methods.) As you can see, a Default User and Default Computer are automatically created.

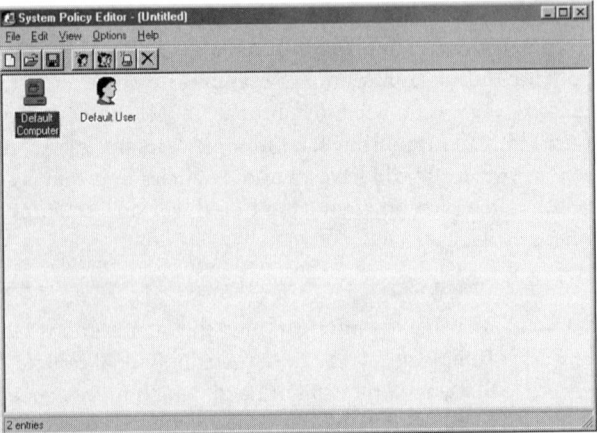

Figure 7.7
Creating new policies in Policy Editor.

Different policies exist for both users and computers. Open either the Default User or Default Computer icon to view the policies possible. Figure 7.8 shows the Default User open, along with a policy selected.

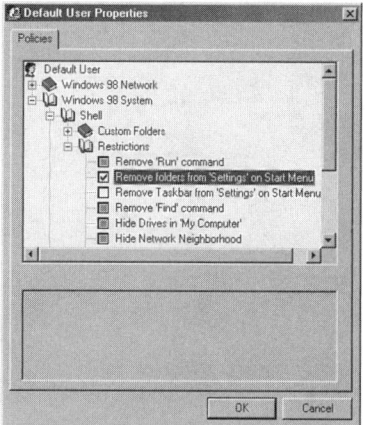

Figure 7.8
The Default User Properties enables you to modify user-based System Policies.

There are three possible states for each policy:

- A checked box means that the policy will be applied as being true (such as the Remove Folders from 'Settings' on Start Menu Policy in Figure 7.8).

- A grayed box means that the policy will be ignored; any user-chosen settings will not be changed when the policy is applied during logon (see the Remove 'Run' Command Policy in Figure 7.8).

- A clear box means that the policy will be cleared; if the user has set it himself, the policy will be unselected when he next logs on and the policy file is applied (see the Remove Taskbar from 'Settings' on Start Menu Policy in Figure 7.8).

Some policies require only that you select one of the three possible states, while others require additional information. For example, Figure 7.9 shows the Restrict Display Control Panel policy with a number of checkboxes that also must be chosen in the Settings window. Some other policies—for instance ones that cause a particular BMP to load as desktop wallpaper—might require other information, such as a path and filename.

Creating Specific User and Computer Policies

You can create policies for specific users and computers with the Policy Editor. When a policy file is processed during logon, Windows 98 first checks to see if there is a policy for the user logging on; if so, that policy is applied. If there is no specific policy for the user, then the Default User Policy is applied.

To create a specific user policy, open the Edit menu and choose Add User. You see the Add User dialog box shown in Figure 7.10. Type the name of the user that he uses as his logon name (it must match exactly, but is not case-sensitive) and click OK to create the user. You can then open the user's policy settings by double-clicking on the User icon in Policy Editor and set the individual policies as needed.

Figure 7.9
Some policies require additional settings.

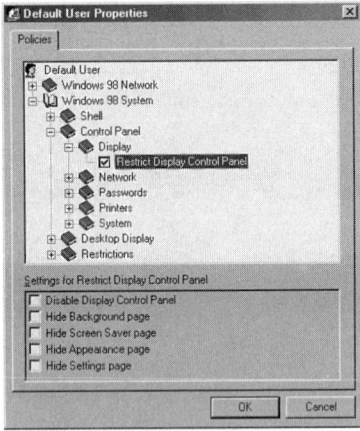

Figure 7.10
Using the Add User dialog box in Policy Editor.

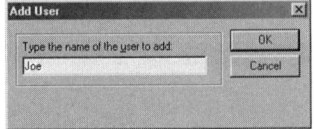

You can also create policies for specific computers on the network. Similar to how users are processed, when a Windows 98 computer logs on to the network and processes the policy file, it checks to see if there is a policy defined for the specific computer; if not, the Default Computer Policy is applied. Windows 98 uses the computer name specified in Network Neighborhood's properties dialog box for this purpose. To set a computer's name (or see what it is set to), right-click on Network Neighborhood and choose Properties from the pop-up menu. Then move to the Identification tab as shown in Figure 7.11.

Figure 7.11
The Computer Name field on the Identification tab must match the computer name in Policy Editor.

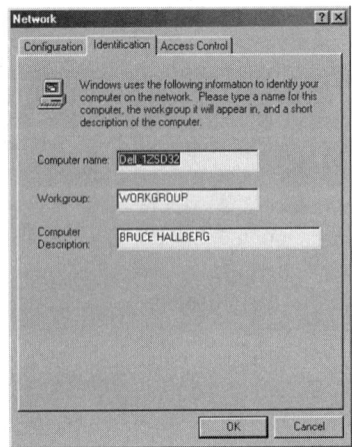

Chapter 7: System Policies

To create a specific computer policy in Policy Editor, access the Edit menu and choose Add Computer. You see the Add Computer dialog box. Type the name of the computer as it appears on the Identification tab in Network Neighborhood's properties, or click the Browse button to choose from the computers logged on to the network (see Figure 7.12).

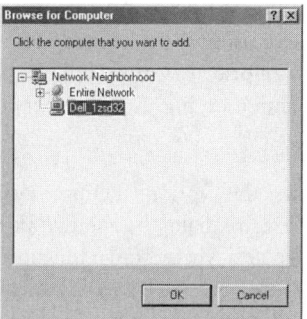

Figure 7.12
Use Add Computer to type a computer's name, or use the Browse dialog box to locate it on the network.

| Tip | Here's a timesaver: If specific computers and users contain slight modifications of the policies in Default Computer and Default User, set the policies for Default Computer and Default User first. The policies contained in Default Computer and Default User are copied to new specific Computer and User Policies that you create. |

Creating Group Policies

If you want to set different policies for different groups of users, and want to avoid having to maintain separate policies for individual users, you can use Group Policies. Group Policies let you set policies for network groups (either Windows NT or NetWare groups can be used). When you have installed support for Group Policies in Windows 98 (see the earlier section "Enabling Group System Policies"), then the processing of the policy file works like this at logon time:

- Is there a user-specific policy defined? If so, it is processed and no other user- or group-type policies are processed.

- Are there Group Policies defined for groups to which this user belongs? If so, all Group Policies that apply to the user are processed, in an order that you specify, and no other user- or group-type policies are processed.

- If there is no user-specific policy and no Group Policies that apply for the user, then the Default User Policy is processed.

The first thing you do to use Group Policies is to create the groups in Policy Editor. From the Edit menu, choose Add Group. In the resulting Add Group dialog box, type the exact name of the group as it exists on the network. After creating all of the groups you want to use, you can then set the policies for each group, and then define their priority in Policy Editor.

You assign a processing priority to groups in Policy Editor. When a user logs on, the policies in each group to which they belong are processed, using the processing priority that you set. Higher-priority Group Policies overwrite lower-priority Group Policies, so the processing priorities that you set are vital to making sure that each group member ends up with the appropriate set of policies.

To set Group Policy processing priority, access the Options menu in Policy Editor and then choose Group Priority. You see the Group Priority dialog box shown in Figure 7.13. Select each group in turn and then use the Move Up and Move Down buttons to position the group relative to the others. Higher-priority groups are processed after lower-priority groups. Generally, less restrictive policy groups should be set to a higher priority than more restrictive policy groups. For example, you would set the policy group for Administrators to be higher than Users. Otherwise the Users Group Policy settings will override the Administrators settings when members of the Administrators group log on.

Figure 7.13
Use the Group Priority dialog box to set the processing priority for Group Policies.

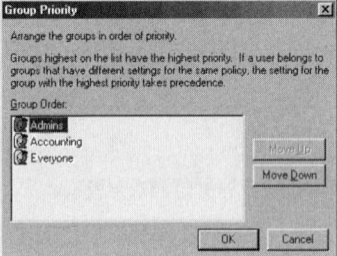

Understanding and Creating Policy Templates

Windows 98 comes with a number of policy templates that you can use. Often, however, you will need to create your own policies. You do this when you want to apply one or more Registry changes to users or computers as they log on to the network. For example, perhaps there is a particular application that you use on your network, and you want to prevent a particular configuration choice that often causes problems. Since the configuration choice is stored in the Registry, you must create a policy that forces the proper choice each time a user logs on. To do this, follow these steps:

1. Determine the Registry settings that are needed.

2. Create a new policy template that contains the proper Registry settings.

Chapter 7: System Policies

3. Apply the new policy template to the CONFIG.POL file with the Policy Template command.

4. Set the policy for each user, computer, or group that needs it.

Policy template files are in plain ASCII text and are easy to create and modify after you understand how they work (they're a bit like a Registry programming language). You can look at existing policy templates (.ADM files) in the Policy Editor directory for examples of how they work. Figure 7.14 shows a sample policy template file open in Notepad.

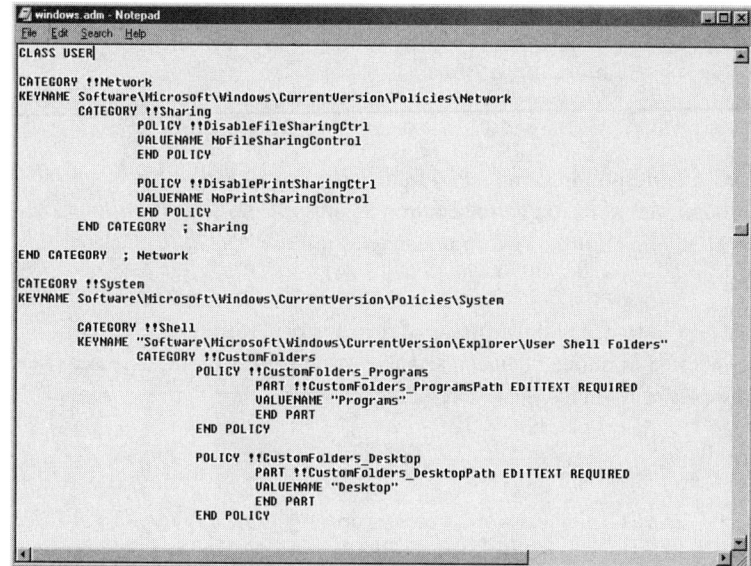

Figure 7.14
The WINDOWS.ADM file open in Notepad illustrates how policy templates work.

Policies defined in a template follow this structure:

```
CLASS class_type
   CATEGORY category_name
   KEYNAME Registry_key
      POLICY policy_name
         KEYNAME Registry_key
         PART part_name part_type
            KEYNAME key_name
            VALUENAME value_name
         END PART
      END POLICY
   END CATEGORY
```

The following sections detail each of these keywords and show you how they work.

CLASS

You precede all policies with the class type. There are two possible classes in a policy template: USER and MACHINE. The USER class automatically applies all policies following the keyword to HKEY_CURRENT_USER and contains user- and group-type policies. The MACHINE class applies all policies following the keyword to HKEY_LOCAL_MACHINE and contains Computer Policies. There are only two forms of the CLASS keyword, as follows:

```
CLASS USER

CLASS MACHINE
```

Simply place the CLASS keyword above all policies for that class. No class-ending keyword is used.

CATEGORY

The CATEGORY keyword corresponds to the initial folders you see when you open a set of policies in Policy Editor. This keyword lets you break down your policies so that they're easier to locate and use within the Policy Editor. You do not have to use the CATEGORY keyword to break down policies, but doing so helps keep them organized.

You follow the CATEGORY keyword with the name of the category. If the name contains spaces, then it must be enclosed in quotes. You can also use string substitution (discussed later) for category names. Examples of CATEGORY statements follow:

```
CATEGORY CorpNetSettings
CATEGORY "Corporate Network Settings"
```

Immediately following the CATEGORY keyword, you can optionally specify the KEYNAME keyword. All policies that follow use the Registry key named in the KEYNAME statement. (KEYNAME is discussed in more detail later).

You can nest CATEGORY statements to create lower-level folders.

The CATEGORY keyword requires a corresponding END CATEGORY statement.

POLICY

The POLICY keyword specifies an actual policy. It is immediately followed by the policy name, which must be surrounded with quotes if it contains spaces. Within each POLICY, you can optionally specify any PARTS (which gather additional information about the policy). POLICY statements cannot be nested, although they can exist at any CATEGORY level.

Within each POLICY (and PART, if needed) you can specify KEYNAME and VALUENAME settings. Each KEYNAME corresponds to a Registry key, while each VALUENAME corresponds to a value setting within the preceding key. For example, here is a simple POLICY statement in pseudocode:

```
POLICY "My Policy"
    KEYNAME Registry_key_path
    VALUENAME Setting_name
VALUEON NUMERIC 1
VALUEOFF NUMERIC 0
END POLICY
```

Each POLICY statement must have a corresponding END POLICY statement. Also, note that you can have multiple KEYNAME and VALUENAME statements for each policy (in other words, a single policy can modify as many Registry settings as needed).

PART

PART statements exist within POLICY statements. A PART is an extra choice or setting for the POLICY. For example, if you have a policy that requires a network pathname as an additional parameter if the policy is enabled, you would gather this additional information through the PART statement. Here is a pseudocode example:

```
POLICY "My Policy"
    PART "Path Name" EDITTEXT
        VALUENAME Setting_name
        MAXLEN 255
        DEFAULT "F:\PUBLIC\filename.ext"
    END PART
END POLICY
```

In the preceding example, *Setting_name* is the Registry value that will be filled with whatever is typed into the edit box of the Policy Editor for this policy. The following two statements, MAXLEN and DEFAULT modify the EDITTEXT control for the PART statement.

Each PART statement has a name and a type. The name can be anything you wish, and is used to describe the control. The type is the type of control that you can use. Possible part controls are as follows:

- CHECKBOX
- NUMERIC
- EDITTEXT
- COMBOBOX
- TEXT
- DROPDOWNLIST
- LISTBOX

Each different part control type can have additional settings that you can use with it. Table 7.1 shows all of these modifiers.

Table 7.1
Part Control Modifiers

Part Type	Modifier	Description
CHECKBOX	DEFCHECKED	The checkbox is selected (on) by default.
	VALUEON	Overrides the default behavior when the checkbox is selected.
	VALUEOFF	Overrides the default behavior when the checkbox is unselected.
	ACTIONLISTON	Contains a list of actions (Registry changes) if the checkbox is selected.
	ACTIONLISTOFF	Contains a list of actions if the checkbox is unselected.
NUMERIC	DEFAULT *x*	Sets the default value.
	MIN *x*	Sets a minimum acceptable value.
	MAX *x*	Sets a maximum acceptable value.
	SPIN *x*	Creates a spin control for the numeric value, where *x* is the increment for each click of the spin control.
	REQUIRED	Causes Policy Editor to require a value.
	TXTCONVERT	Writes the entered or selected numeric value as a string instead of a number (for example, "101" instead of 101).
EDITTEXT	DEFAULT *x*	Sets the default string.
	MAXLEN *x*	Sets the maximum length of the entered string.
	REQUIRED	Causes Policy Editor to require a string value.
COMBOBOX	SUGGESTIONS	In addition to accepting all the modifiers of EDITTEXT, you can use the SUGGESTIONS keyword, which lets you build a list for the ComboBox. End the list of suggestions with an END SUGGESTIONS keyword. Also, any suggestions that contain spaces must be surrounded with quotes.
DROP-DOWNLIST	REQUIRED	Causes Policy Editor to require a selection.
	ITEMLIST	Builds a list of selections for the DropDownList box. Each item is specified with a NAME keyword

Chapter 7: System Policies

Part Type	Modifier	Description
		and a VALUE keyword, which correspond to the visible name in the DropDownList box and to the value that will be chosen for each name. Optionally, you can specify an ACTIONLIST after each NAME/VALUE combination. End the list with the END ITEMLIST keyword.
LISTBOX	VALUEPREFIX *x*	Sets a prefix that will be prepended to each entered value.
	EXPLICITVALUE	Creates a two-column list box into which the user of Policy Editor enters both a value name and corresponding value.
	ADDITIVE	Values entered into the list box will be added to the values already present in the Registry.

Strings and Comments

You can define string substitution in a policy template file to make it easier to read and maintain the file. You define these substitutions by creating a section at the bottom of the file with the keyword [strings]. Within that section, each string is defined as StringName=Actual string value. For instance, the following defines two strings:

```
[strings]
NW4="Netware 4.x"
WNT="Windows NT Server"
```

After defining the string substitutions, you access them with the !! operator (two exclamation points) in front of a string name to automatically replace the string name with one defined at the bottom of the policy file. For example, you could use this statement:

```
CATEGORY !!NW4
```

In this example, the category will actually display as "NetWare 4.x" in the Policy Editor instead of NW4.

You can (and should) include comments in your policy template files. Simply precede a line with a semicolon (;) and that line will be ignored, such as in the following example:

```
; This line is a comment and will not be processed
```

Example Policy Template File

Using the information in the foregoing sections, examine the following policy template file, which is the OE.ADM file that comes with the Windows 98 Policy Editor and contains policies for Outlook Express. It illustrates most of the possible controls, and shows you how a complete policy template file should look after it is complete.

```
; oe.adm
;
;;;;;;;;;;;;;;;;;;;;;;;;
CLASS USER ;;;;;;;;;;;;;;
;;;;;;;;;;;;;;;;;;;;;;;;

CATEGORY !!OutlookExpress
    KEYNAME "Software\Microsoft\Outlook Express"
    POLICY !!Zones
        PART !!RestSite CHECKBOX
        VALUENAME "Security Zone"
        VALUEON NUMERIC 4
        VALUEOFF NUMERIC 3
        END PART
    END POLICY

    POLICY !!HTMLMail
        PART !!DisableHTMLinMail CHECKBOX
        KEYNAME "Software\Microsoft\Outlook Express\Mail"
        VALUENAME "Message Send HTML"
        VALUEON NUMERIC 0
        VALUEOFF NUMERIC 1
        END PART

        PART !!DisablePlaininNews CHECKBOX
          KEYNAME "Software\Microsoft\Outlook Express\News"
        VALUENAME "Message Send HTML"
        VALUEON NUMERIC 1
        VALUEOFF NUMERIC 0
        END PART
    END POLICY
END CATEGORY

CATEGORY !!OENav
    KEYNAME "Software\Microsoft\Outlook Express\"
    POLICY !!Navigation
        PART !!OutlookBar CHECKBOX
        VALUENAME "OutBar"
        VALUEON NUMERIC 1
        VALUEOFF NUMERIC 0
        END PART

        PART !!FolderView CHECKBOX
        VALUENAME "Tree"
        VALUEON NUMERIC 0
        VALUEOFF NUMERIC 1
        END PART
```

```
            PART !!FolderBar CHECKBOX
                VALUENAME "FolderBar"
                VALUEON NUMERIC 1
                VALUEOFF NUMERIC 0
            END PART

            PART !!TipofDay CHECKBOX
                VALUENAME "Tip of the Day"
                VALUEON NUMERIC 0
                VALUEOFF NUMERIC 1
            END PART
        END POLICY
END CATEGORY

[strings]
OutlookExpress="General Settings"
OENav="View Customization"
ServerSettings="Mail, news, and directory server settings"
Zones="Mail and news security zones"
RestSite="Put mail and news in the Restricted Sites zone (instead of the Internet
➥zone)"
HTMLMail="HTML mail and news composition settings"
DisableHTMLinMail="Mail: Make plain text message composition the default for mail
➥messages (instead of HTML mail)"
DisablePlaininNews="News: Make HTML message composition the default for news posts
➥(instead of plain text)"
Navigation="Folder and Message Navigational Elements"
OutlookBar="Turn on Outlook Bar"
FolderView="Turn off Folder List (tree view of folders)"
FolderBar="Turn on Folder Bar (horizontal line that displays the selected folder's
➥name)"
TipofDay="Turn off the Tip of the Day"

IEAK_Title=Outlook Express
IEAK_DescriptionTitle=Outlook Express Policy Settings and Restrictions
IEAK_Description1=Outlook Express provides system policies designed to reduce mail
➥and news support costs.
IEAK_Description2=Outlook Express uses Internet Explorer 4.0's security zones.
➥Normally, all user mail is placed in the Internet zone, where users are prompted
➥before potentially dangerous active content is run. However, you can place Outlook
➥Express mail and news in the Restricted Sites zone. The default settings for the
➥Restricted Sites zone prohibit running almost all active content (the user will be
➥protected from the content without any prompts).
IEAK_Description3=By default, Outlook Express composes mail messages in HTML and
➥news messages in plain text. You are strongly encouraged to retain these settings.
IEAK_Description4=Outlook Express allows you to customize your default view for
➥consistency with the configuration of other programs familiar to your users.

[IEAK]
Lock=1
Roles=011
NumOfDescLines=4
```

Base Policies in WINDOWS.ADM

Windows comes with a policy template called WINDOWS.ADM that contains most of the policies that you would ever want to use. Tables 7.2 and 7.3 list all of the policies available with WINDOWS.ADM for your review as you plan the policies you want to implement.

Table 7.2
WINDOWS.ADM Computer Policies

Policy	Description
Windows 98 Network/Access Control	
User-level Access Control	Enables user-level access control
Windows 98 Network/Logon	
Logon Banner	Displays a custom logon banner
Require Validation from Network for User Access	Requires that the network server validate the user to access the local Windows 98 computer
Don't Show Last User at Logon	Doesn't display the last username in the Logon dialog box
Windows 98 Network/Password	
Hide Share Passwords with Asterisks	Hides shared file and printer passwords with asterisks
Disable Password Caching	Turns off password caching; passwords must be typed for each network resource accessed
Minimum Windows Password Length	Requires Windows passwords of a certain length
Preferred Server	Sets preferred server for NetWare networks
Windows 98 Network/Microsoft Client for NetWare Networks	
Support Long Filenames	Specifies long filename support for NetWare networks
Disable Automatic NetWare Login	Disables default passwords for NetWare networks
Preferred Tree	Sets preferred NDS tree for NetWare networks

Chapter 7: System Policies

Windows 98 Network/NetWare Directory Service

Default Name Context	Sets default name context for NetWare networks
Load NetWare DLLs at Startup	Loads NetWare-specific DLLs at startup
Disable Automatic Tree Login	Disables automatic NDS tree logon
Enable Login Confirmation	Causes NDS logons to be confirmed
Don't Show Advanced Login Button	Takes away the ability to choose different NetWare logon types, such as a bindery logon
Default Type of NetWare Login	Sets NetWare logon type to NDS or bindery
Don't Show Servers that aren't NDS Objects	Hides bindery-only servers
Don't Show Peer Workgroups	Hides any peer workgroup servers
Don't Show Server Objects	Hides servers
Don't Show Container Objects	Hides NDS containers
Don't Show Print Queue Objects	Hides print queues
Don't Show Volume Objects	Hides volumes

Windows 98 Network/Microsoft Client for Microsoft Networks

Log On to Windows NT	Forces a logon domain; also can disable password caching
Workgroup	Forces a Workgroup name
Alternate Workgroup	Forces an alternate Workgroup name

Windows 98 Network/File and Printer Sharing for NetWare Networks

Disable SAP Advertising	Disables advertising file and printer sharing from workstations

Windows 98 Network/File and Printer Sharing for Microsoft Networks

Disable File Sharing	Disables file sharing
Disable Print Sharing	Disables printer sharing

Windows 98 Network/Dial-Up Networking

Disable Dial-In	Disables dial-in to clients

continues

Table 7.2, Continued
WINDOWS.ADM Computer Policies

Policy	Description
Windows 98 Network/Update	
Remote Update	Controls how System Policies are updated for the client computer
Windows 98 System/User Profiles	
Enable User Profiles	Activates User Profiles
Windows 98 System/Network Paths	
Network Path for Windows Setup	Path for the Windows 98 setup files
Network Path for Windows Tour	Path for the Windows 98 Tour files
Windows 98 System/SNMP	
Communities	Defines SNMP communities to which the client belongs
Permitted Managers	Defines permitted SNMP managers by IP or IPX address
Traps for 'Public' Community	Sets target addresses to which traps will be reported
Internet MIB	Specifies the contact name and location for the Internet SNMP MIB
Windows 98 System/Programs to Run	
Run	Defines programs that will be run when the user logs on
Run Once	Lets you define a temporary program to run; you must change this policy after the program is run by the logged-on user
Run Services	Defines programs that will be run when the system starts
Windows 98 System/Install Device Drivers	
Digital Signature Check	Forces a signature check of drivers being installed; you can choose to permit all drivers or only Microsoft drivers, or to warn when non-Microsoft drivers are installed

Table 7.3
WINDOWS.ADM User and Group Policies

Policy	Description
Windows 98 Network/Sharing	
Disable File Sharing Controls	Prevents access to file-sharing controls
Disable Print Sharing Controls	Prevents access to printer-sharing controls
Windows 98 System/Shell/Custom Folders	
Custom Program Folder	Defines a custom folder for the Programs folder in the Start menu
Custom Desktop Icons	Defines a path from which desktop icons will be loaded
Hide Start Menu Subfolders	Checked when a custom program folder is loaded, hides other Program subfolders that otherwise will appear
Custom Startup Folder	Defines a custom Startup folder
Custom Network Neighborhood	Defines a custom Network Neighborhood folder
Custom Start Menu	Defines a custom Start menu folder
Windows 98 System/Shell/Restrictions	
Remove Run Command	Removes the Start menu's Run command
Remove Folders from Settings on Start Menu	Removes Settings subfolders
Remove Taskbar from Settings on Start Menu	Removes the Taskbar settings from the Settings folder
Remove Find Command	Removes the Find command from the Start menu
Hide Drives in My Computer	Hides all My Computer drives
Hide Network Neighborhood	Hides the Network Neighborhood object on the desktop
No Entire Network in Network Neighborhood	Hides the Entire Network entry in Network Neighborhood
No Workgroup Contents in Network Neighborhood	Hides any Workgroup-type entries in Network Neighborhood
Hide All Items on Desktop	Hides all desktop items
Disable Shutdown Command	Removes the Shutdown command from the Start menu
Don't Save Settings at Exit	Prevents any changed settings from being saved

continues

Table 7.3, Continued
WINDOWS.ADM User and Group Policies

Policy	Description
Windows 98 System/Control Panel/Display	
Restrict Display Control Panel	Prevents opening of the Control Panel
Windows 98 System/Control Panel/Network	
Restrict Network Control Panel	Disables various features of the Network Control Panel (selectable within the policy)
Windows 98 System/Control Panel/Passwords	
Restrict Passwords Control Panel	Disables various features of the Passwords Control Panel (selectable within the policy)
Windows 98 System/Control Panel/Printers	
Restrict Printer Settings	Disables various features of workstation printer management (selectable within the policy)
Windows 98 System/Control Panel/System	
Restrict System Control Panel	Disables various features of the System Control Panel (selectable within the policy)
Windows 98 System/Desktop Display	
Wallpaper	Defines a specific wallpaper file
Color Scheme	Defines a specific color scheme
Windows 98 System/Restrictions	
Disable Registry Editing Tools	Disables Registry Editor and Policy Editor from being run
Only Run Allowed Windows Applications	Defines allowed applications within the policy
Disable MS-DOS Prompt	Prevents access to the MS-DOS prompt
Disable Single-Mode MS-DOS Applications	Prevents MS-DOS mode

User Profiles

User Profiles in Windows 98 let users retain their personal settings when they share a computer with others or when they use other computers on the same network. User Profiles store the following user-specific information:

- *Control Panel settings*
- *User-specific Registry settings*
- *Start menu's Programs folder*
- *Start menu's Recent folder*
- *Desktop configuration, including files and shortcuts*
- *Persistent network connections*

At the simplest level, you can enable User Profiles on a stand-alone computer so that multiple users can log on and receive their own settings from one session to the next. A home computer, for instance, can store User Profiles for each family member. (This can avert a lot of family squabbling on a shared computer!)

With certain networks (Windows NT and NetWare), a copy of each person's User Profile information can also be stored on the network server. When you enable this capability, each person receives his own personal settings when he logs on to any computer on the network. When he logs off, any changes he made are automatically saved back to the server to be used at the next computer at which they log on. These network-based profiles are called *Roving User Profiles*.

> **Note** Microsoft interchangeably uses the terms "Roving User Profiles" and "Roaming User Profiles." They both refer to the same thing.

Finally, you can create a class of User Profiles called *Mandatory User Profiles*. When you do this, each person that you define to use them has a complete set of User Profile settings applied to any computer from which he logs on. Although the user can make changes once logged on (assuming any System Policy setting allows him the ability to do so), those changes are not saved and the system reverts to the Mandatory User Profile settings the next time he logs on from any computer.

The following list gives you specific advice for when to implement these different types of profiles:

- **Local Profiles**—Use Local Profiles when you are setting up a computer that more than one person will use, and where you care only about keeping any Windows 98 settings made by the users local to that machine. You can use local profiles on both stand-alone and networked desktop computers.

- **Roving User Profiles**—Use Roving User Profiles when you want a user's personal Windows 98 settings to follow her around the network. Implementing Roving User Profiles does mean that you must set up each computer that will allow the use of Roving User Profiles. One way to think about Roving User Profiles is like this: They're simply local User Profiles (kept on every computer that a user logs on to) that save a copy of their settings on a network server, where they are available should a user log on to another participating Windows 98 computer on the network.

- **Mandatory User Profiles**—If you're in a situation where a number of users must all have the same Windows 98 settings, all the time, every time, then use Mandatory User Profiles to keep each user's desktop environment consistent.

> ### System Policies or Mandatory User Profiles?
>
> There is no need to use both Mandatory User Profiles *and* System Policies. Either one of these tools provides you with the same abilities to restrict or force user-specific settings, although System Policies additionally enable you to affect system settings.
>
> You use Mandatory User Profiles when you want each user (you can choose which users) that logs on to a network to always receive exactly the same settings. This might be appropriate, for instance, for a customer service department where each user has exactly the same needs as the other users. Mandatory User Profiles can ease the training and support burdens in such an environment. Mandatory User Profiles affect settings only in the USER.DAT component of the Registry, and not SYSTEM.DAT. You use System Policies when you want users to be able to make *some* personal settings that can be accessed elsewhere on the network (or between sessions on the same computer). You also use System Policies when you need to enforce computer settings stored in SYSTEM.DAT, like various network policies you can implement. System Policies are applied on top of User Profile settings and can override them. System Policies are more powerful than Mandatory User Profiles because they can affect settings in the complete Registry: both USER.DAT and SYSTEM.DAT.
>
> Both approaches are appropriate in different circumstances. Mandatory User Profiles are much easier to set up and maintain, as long as you can realistically apply a single set of user settings for each user. System Policies, however, give you more flexibility at the cost of greater complexity.

Understanding User Profile Files

When User Profiles are enabled, a set of directories and files is created for each user that logs on to the computer. These user-specific directories and files are stored in the \Windows\Profiles directory, and each user has a subdirectory that corresponds to his logon name. For instance, Figure 8.1 shows a computer's \Windows\Profiles directory with four User Profiles defined: Bruce, Christy, Deborah, and Joe. The profile directory for user Bruce has been expanded so you can see its contents.

| Tip | You can see what profiles have been created on a particular machine in two ways: by looking in the \Windows\Profiles directory or by checking the contents of the **HKEY_LOCAL_MACHINE\Software\Microsoft\Windows\Current Version\ProfileList** Registry key. |

Figure 8.1

An example of a \Windows\Profiles directory structure.

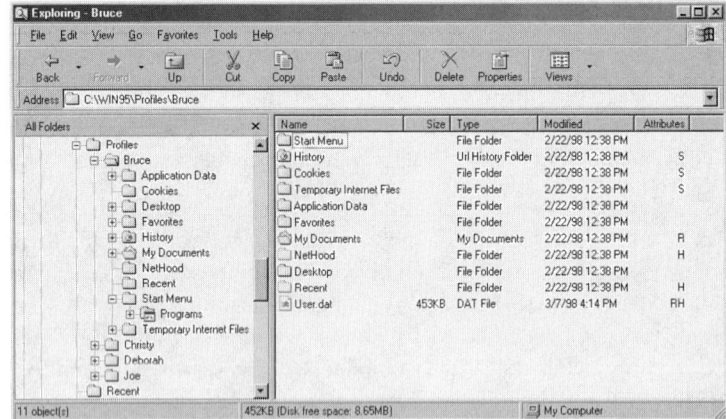

Each user's profile directory contains (at most) the following:

- The user's own personal USER.DAT (which contains the user-based Registry settings)

- A \Desktop subdirectory that holds the configuration of the user's desktop

- An \Application Data subdirectory (if needed by any installed applications) that contains the user's own personal application settings

- A \Cookies subdirectory that holds the user's own personal Web cookies

- A \Favorites subdirectory that holds the user's personal Internet Explorer favorite places

- A \History subdirectory that holds a list of Web sites that the user has visited

- A \My Documents subdirectory, holding the contents of the user's My Documents folder that appears on the desktop

- A \NetHood subdirectory, which contains any special contents of the user's Network Neighborhood folder

- A \Recent subdirectory, containing shortcuts to the user's 10 most recently opened files

- A \Start menu subdirectory holding the contents of the user's Start menu, and possibly a subdirectory with the user's Programs folder contents

- A \Temporary Internet Files subdirectory, holding the user's cached Internet Explorer files

The preceding files and directories, in total, make up a single User Profile.

Enabling User Profiles

You enable User Profiles by using the Passwords Control Panel object. After opening Passwords, move to the User Profiles tab, shown in Figure 8.2.

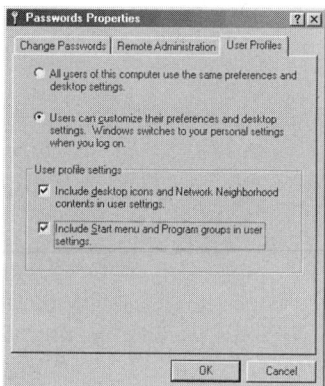

Figure 8.2
You enable User Profiles through the Passwords Control Panel.

Select Users Can **C**ustomize Their Preferences and Desktop Settings. Windows switches to your personal settings when you log on to enable User Profiles. You can then choose with the appropriate checkboxes whether desktop shortcuts and Network Neighborhood contents, or the Start menu and Program groups are stored along with the User Profiles. Selecting these other options creates the matching folders and contents in each user's \Windows\Profiles directory.

Managing Roving User Profiles

Roving User Profiles are automatically enabled in the following circumstances:

- User Profiles are enabled on the client computer.

- The Windows 98 computer uses a 32-bit networking client for NetWare or Windows NT networks (such as the ones included with Windows 98).

- Every Windows 98 computer that accesses Roving User Profiles has Windows 98 installed on the same drive and directory (such as C:\Windows).

- One of those valid network clients is selected as the Primary Network Logon client. (Open the Network Control Panel and choose the client in the Primary Network **L**ogon drop-box.)

- Under Windows NT, the user has a valid home directory defined.

- Under NetWare, the user has a valid MAIL directory (it should be created automatically when the user account is created). If the user has the Novell NDS service installed in addition to the client, her profile files are stored in her home directory instead.

When all of the preceding circumstances are true, each user's User Profile directories and files are copied to either her Windows NT home directory or her NetWare MAIL directory when she logs off the network. When the user logs on from another computer, the profile information is accessed from the network location.

> **Note** When a user logs off after using a Roving User Profile, both the local copy in \Windows\Profiles and her network copy is updated with any changes she made during that session.

You can have User Profiles and yet not have them be Roaming Policies. Using Registry Editor, select the Registry key **HKEY_LOCAL\MACHINE\Network\Logon** and add a DWORD value named **UseHomeDirectory**.

> **Note** Roving User Profiles are not shared between Windows 98 and Windows NT clients.

What if you want to use Roving User Profiles, but aren't using a networking client that supports them? You can still set up Roving Profiles in this scenario by following these steps:

1. Create a read-only network directory to which all users have access.

2. Create a read-only file in the directory called PROFILES.TXT.

3. In the PROFILES.TXT file, place the following information:

    - A **[Profiles]** heading

    - A list of all users with profiles, in which each user's logon name is listed, followed by an equal sign (=), followed by her home directory specified by a Universal Naming Convention name. An example would be **Christy=\\SERVER\HOMEDIRS\Christy**.

4. On each computer, use Registry Editor to locate the key **HKEY_LOCAL_MACHINE\Network\Logon**.

5. Create a string value named **SharedProfileList** and set the string value to be the full pathname of the PROFILES.TXT file you created in step 2—for example, **\\SERVER\EVERYONE\PROFILES.TXT**.

After following the preceding steps, Roving User Profiles will work for each user defined in the PROFILES.TXT file (provided each computer has the necessary settings).

Creating Mandatory User Profiles

Mandatory User Profiles can be used when you want to force a particular set of User Profile settings on a user or group of users (or all users, for that matter) over a network. Mandatory User Profiles let you create a complete User Profile, and then force those settings on select users.

Creating Mandatory User Profiles is quite easy; just follow these steps:

1. On a Windows 98 computer that has User Profiles enabled, log on to the network using a new user name. This creates the new User Profile files in the \Windows\Profiles directory. For this example, say you create a user called NEWUSER.

2. Modify the user settings as needed, so that the Windows 98 environment is exactly as you want it to be for everyone that will use the Mandatory User Profile. This could include adding or removing Start menu items, changing Control Panel settings, mapping persistent network shares, changing the Registry directly, and so forth. Make sure to test all aspects of the environment you create!

3. Log off the computer using the Log Off command in the Start menu. This saves the changes you made in step 2 to the \Windows\Profiles\Newuser directory.

4. Log back on as Administrator.

5. Copy the entire contents of \Windows\Profiles\Newuser to the network profile location for a target user. Under Windows NT, this is her home directory. Under NetWare, this is her MAIL directory, or her home directory if she is using the NDS service.

6. In the target user's profile directory, rename the USER.DAT file to USER.MAN.

After following these steps, try logging on as the target user (or work with the target user to test these updates). After you're happy with how the Mandatory User Profile is working, you can copy the files to other user home directories as needed.

Common Problems and Solutions

When you use User Profiles, there are a few common complaints you might receive from your users:

- "I went to another computer to use it, and I added a program shortcut there (or made some other change), but when I logged back on to my own computer the next morning the shortcut had vanished! And it's also missing from the computer where I added it!"

This is common when you have shared computers with resources (like scanners) that users may use from time to time in addition to their main desktop computer. What's happening here is the following:

1. User logs on to his main computer, Computer #1

2. While logged on to Computer #1, the user logs on to Computer #2. As you would expect, he gets all of his Roving User Profiles from the network when he logs on.

3. The user makes some change to his configuration on Computer #2, such as adding a program shortcut or changing their wallpaper.

4. The user logs off from Computer #2. His User Profile changes are stored on the network.

5. Later that day, when the user logs off from Computer #1, his User Profile settings on Computer #1 *replace* the ones stored by Computer #2.

6. The next morning, the user gets his Roving User Profile settings that were saved from Computer #1, and wonders what happened to the change he made on Computer #2. And of course, this happens no matter which computer he logs on to.

In this scenario, you simply explain to the user how their settings are stored on the network, and how using two computers simultaneously can cause this behavior. Nothing is actually amiss in this scenario. The user can solve it this problem himself by logging off their main computer before using other computers.

- "I installed a program on a computer for everyone to use, but no other users can see it when they log on."

One of the settings on the User Profiles tab of the Passwords Control Panel is responsible for this. If the checkbox called Include **S**tart Menu and Program Groups in User Settings is enabled, each user has his own private Start menu. Any changes he makes to his Start menu, such as the shortcuts added when an application is installed, are private to that user.

There are a few solutions to this complaint. First, you can turn off the Include **S**tart Menu setting, which means that all users of that computer share a common Start menu. Second, you can show the other users how to create shortcuts to the main program file for their own desktops. (This second alternative may not work properly if the application also depends on user-specific settings in the Registry).

Conclusion

In this chapter you learned how User Profiles work in Windows 98 and how to enable them. You also learned about Roving User Profiles and Mandatory User Profiles, what each is for, and how to work with them.

Chapter 9, "Hardware Profiles," shows you how Windows 98 can accommodate shifting configurations on a single computer, such as what happens to a portable computer with a docking station, or a desktop computer that only periodically connects to a device like a scanner.

CHAPTER 9

Hardware Profiles

*U*nder Windows 3.x there was no easy way to handle computers that had their hardware configurations changed regularly. These configuration changes might occur with notebook computers that dock and undock or desktop computers that have frequent device changes (such as if you frequently connect and disconnect a parallel port-based CD-ROM device). The only way to handle these situations was to have alternate sets of *.INI, CONFIG.SYS, and AUTOEXEC.BAT files, and then use batch files to swap the versions of these configuration files around before you switched to the new hardware configuration and restarted. Certainly, this was an ugly and inefficient way to manage this requirement!

To solve this problem, Windows 95 added support for Hardware Profiles, which let you store frequently used hardware settings in different profiles. You then select from a list of possible Hardware Profiles when the system is started. For example, you might have two profiles for a notebook computer, one for when it is undocked, and another for when it is docked. At boot time, you can select which of these profiles to use for the session.

> **Note** A *Hardware Profile* is simply a collection of settings defining what hardware is installed in the computer, and how that hardware is configured.

You should note that Hardware Profiles typically do not need to be used with computers that are fully Plug and Play-compliant, as long as the devices being activated and deactivated are also Plug and Play-compliant, because the Plug and Play (PnP) software will automatically manage shifting hardware in the system in this case. However, because there are still many hardware devices in use that are not PnP-compliant and computers that poorly implement PnP, familiarity with Hardware Profiles is required, even with newer computers and Windows 98.

Hardware Profile Boot Process

When a Windows 98 computer is started, the operating system scans the computer for new or changed devices that it can detect. If it can determine exactly which hardware profile is needed, it automatically uses it. If it can match up the computer configuration with a defined hardware profile, it automatically uses the matching profile. If it finds more than one hardware profile that suits the hardware it senses installed in the computer, it automatically prompts you during boot to determine which of those profiles it should use.

Creating New Hardware Profiles

You cannot create a new hardware profile "from scratch." Rather, you copy the initial hardware profile for the system, after which you can modify the new copy. To do this, follow these conceptual steps:

1. Copy the Original Configuration hardware profile to a new profile.

2. Boot the computer, selecting the new profile during the boot.

3. Make changes in Device Manager to modify the new hardware profile's settings.

To modify a hardware profile, first boot the system using that profile. You can then make changes by deleting devices in Device Manager, by disabling devices through a checkbox on the device's Properties dialog box, or by adding or changing the configuration of device drivers as necessary.

Chapter 9: Hardware Profiles

To copy and activate a new profile, follow these steps:

1. Open the System control panel object from within the Control Panel.

> **Tip** A quick way to open the System control panel is to right-click on My Computer, and then choose Properties.

2. Move to the Hardware Profiles tab, shown in Figure 9.1.

3. Select the hardware profile that you want to copy. Typically, you will see only the Original Configuration profile if you've not yet modified the Hardware Profiles on a particular machine.

4. Click the *C*opy button, which displays the Copy Profile dialog box shown in Figure 9.2.

5. Type a name for the new profile and click OK.

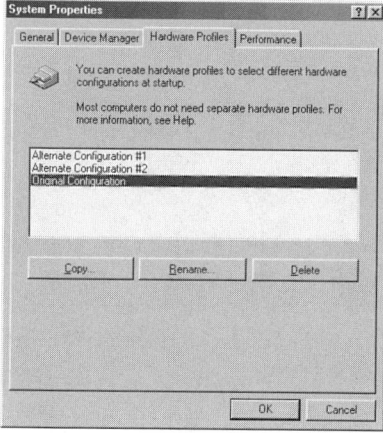

Figure 9.1
The Hardware Profiles tab of the System Properties control panel.

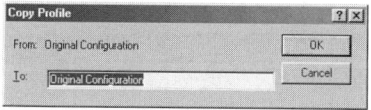

Figure 9.2
The Copy Profile dialog box.

After copying the base hardware profile, you must activate it so that you can modify it. Restart the system to do this. When the system boots, it will automatically prompt you (in a text message before the Windows 98 desktop appears) to choose which profile you want to use. Select the new profile and let the system finish booting.

After the system starts with the new hardware profile, you can make changes to the Windows 98 hardware configuration settings, typically using the Device Manager tab of the System Properties control panel. Any changes you make are automatically stored with no special action required on your part.

> **Note** How do you know which hardware profile is the active one at any given time?
>
> To learn which profile is activated, open the System Properties dialog box and move to the Hardware Profiles tab. The active profile is the one that's selected when you open the tab. You can also find out which one is active another way: Select each of the listed Hardware Profiles in turn. The active hardware profile is the one that does not let you choose the **D**elete button. The other Hardware Profiles offer you the choice of clicking **D**elete (it isn't grayed when these profiles are selected), so you know that they aren't active.

Setting Up Hardware Profiles: An Example

Say you have a dockable portable computer that you want to set up to use Hardware Profiles for when it is docked and undocked. When docked, the system has a CD-ROM drive, an Ethernet card, a normal keyboard and mouse, and a different display connected to it. When undocked, it has no CD-ROM drive or Ethernet card and uses the notebook's built-in keyboard, pointing device and display. To set up the Hardware Profiles for this example, follow these steps:

1. With the computer docked, start Windows 98 and copy the Original Configuration profile to a new profile. Call the new profile Undocked.

2. Restart the computer (still docked) and choose the Undocked profile when prompted during boot.

3. Open the System Properties control panel, move to the Device Manager tab, and open the device drivers for devices that are available only when the computer is docked, such as the CD-ROM drive and the Ethernet card. On the Properties page for each device, click the checkbox **D**isable in This Hardware Profile. Also, change the drivers for the mouse, keyboard, and display. The goal is to change the settings in Device Manager to match the configuration of the system when it's undocked.

   When you remove a device in Device Manager and you have multiple Hardware Profiles available, you are prompted for the profile from which you should remove the device. When you choose a device and click the R**e**move button, you will see the Confirm Device Removal dialog box shown in Figure 9.3. Make sure that the correct profile is selected in this dialog box before confirming the removal.

Chapter 9: Hardware Profiles **195**

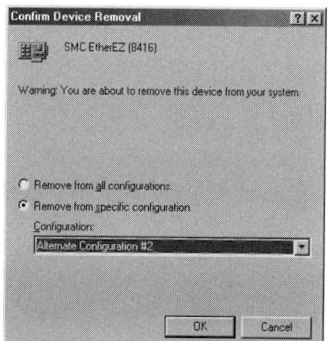

Figure 9.3
The Confirm Device Removal dialog box.

> **Note** Changing the settings in Device Manager won't affect the current session with Windows 98. For instance, deleting the driver for a CD-ROM player while in Device Manager won't make the CD-ROM suddenly stop working. Settings in Device Manager are applied only when the system starts using the selected hardware profile.

4. Shut down the system and undock it. Then restart the system and choose the Undocked profile again during startup.

5. As a wise practice, after the system boots with the new profile and the new hardware configuration (undocked), you should run Add/Remove Hardware from the Control Panel to ensure that Windows 98 has detected all available hardware devices in the alternate configuration.

Assuming that all of your changes in Device Manager truly match the configuration of the notebook computer in its undocked state, you've completed setting up its Hardware Profiles. The user can now simply boot the system and Windows 98 should properly detect and automatically choose the correct hardware profile. If for some reason it doesn't do so, the user can still simply choose from the hardware profile menu when booting the system.

> **Note** If you make mistakes in Device Manager such that the system won't boot with that profile whether it's docked or undocked, don't panic! Simply restart the system (docked) with the Original Configuration hardware profile, delete the bad profile, copy a new one from Original Configuration, and start over again.

Understanding Hardware Profiles and the Registry

The settings for each hardware profile are stored in the Windows 98 Registry. While you should never have to make Registry settings that affect Hardware Profiles, you should understand where in the Registry this information is kept. As a Windows 98 support professional, you must understand the structure of the Registry.

You can find the settings for the active profile in the key HKEY_CURRENT_CONFIG, where all of the subfolders represent different categories of settings for the current hardware profile. The settings in the HKEY_CURRENT_CONFIG key are copied from the complete set of hardware profile Registry settings when a profile is selected during boot.

You can find the settings for all of the Hardware Profiles, including the current profile, in the key HKEY_LOCAL_MACHINE\Config*hardware_profile_number*. The *hardware_profile_number* corresponds to the order in which the Hardware Profiles were created.

You may not remember (or know) the order in which the Hardware Profiles were created, so you need a way to determine which Hardware Profiles the *hardware_profile_key* numbers correspond to. The "master key" in the Registry that shows you this information (the number and name of each hardware profile, as well as which one is currently active) is found in the following key (also shown in Figure 9.4):

```
HKEY_LOCAL_MACHINE\System\CurrentControlSet\control\IDConfigDB
```

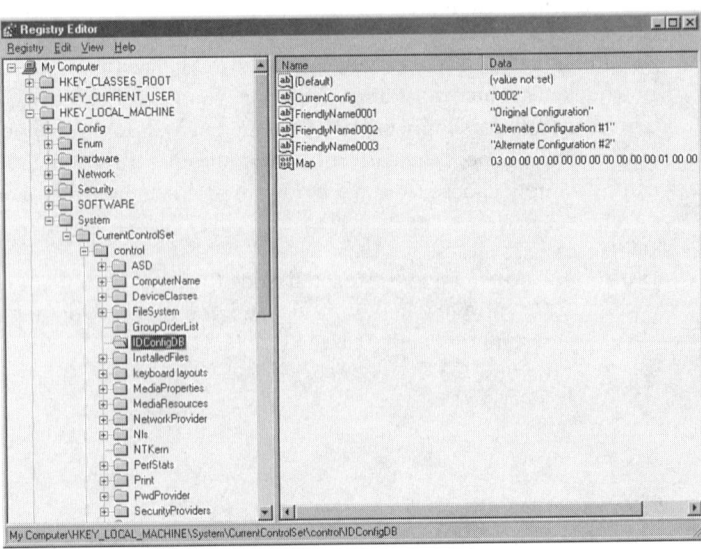

Figure 9.4
The Registry key that shows you the names and numbers of all available Hardware Profiles.

Common Problems and Solutions

Managing Hardware Profiles is not really a very difficult task after you understand how profiles work and how to work with them. Most problems associated with Hardware Profiles result from configuration changes in Device Manager. These problems are actually hardware configuration problems; they are not necessarily problems with Hardware Profiles. For more information about hardware configuration in Windows 98, see Chapter 12, "Supporting Devices."

You should remember to avoid any modification of the Original Configuration hardware profile, and instead make changes to alternate Hardware Profiles as needed. That way, you can always return to the Original Configuration hardware profile if something goes awry. You can also often boot a particular hardware profile in Safe Mode and correct any Device Manager settings that are incorrect before trying to re-create the alternate hardware profile from scratch.

Backing Up the Original Hardware Profile

There are no tools for backing up and restoring Hardware Profiles in Windows 98, but you can use the Registry Editor for this job. To back up the Original Configuration hardware profile, follow these steps:

1. Open the Registry Editor (from the Start menu, choose Run and then type REGEDIT and click OK).

2. Select the key **HKEY_LOCAL_MACHINE\Config\001**. The 001 profile is always the Original Configuration hardware profile.

3. Access the **R**egistry menu and choose **E**xport Registry File. In the Export Registry File dialog box that appears, choose a name for the exported Registry fragment (possibly a filename on a disk), and make sure that the **S**elected Branch button is selected, showing the key name listed in step 2. Click OK to save the selected Registry fragment.

If something should happen to the Original Configuration Registry settings, you can use the **I**mport Registry File command in the Registry Editor to reload the Registry fragment, restoring the settings to the Original Configuration hardware profile in the process. Obviously, it is important that the installed hardware on the computer exactly match the configuration when you initially created the Registry fragment by using this method.

Unknown Monitor Errors

When you boot a Windows 98 system for the first time by using a new hardware profile, you see a message during system boot telling you that new hardware (a display) has been detected and that the drivers are being loaded for the new hardware. This message is not a cause for concern. When you copy a hardware profile, the monitor settings are not copied along with all of the other hardware configuration choices, and so Windows 98 must determine the connected monitor type the first time you use a new hardware profile.

Conclusion

In this chapter you learned how Hardware Profiles work, where they are stored, and how to use them to manage frequently changing hardware configurations on a Windows 98-based computer. By using this knowledge, you can support and solve problems relating to the use of Hardware Profiles.

Chapter 10, "Mastering the Windows 98 Registry," concludes this section about configuring Windows 98 and provides a thorough look at the Windows 98 Registry, the "mother lode" of configuration databases for Windows 98. While managing the Registry can be tricky at times and often looks very complex, you will learn in the next chapter that it really isn't as difficult as it might appear. Mastering the Registry in Windows 98 enables you to really understand and master the configuration of Windows 98.

Mastering the Windows 98 Registry

As a computer professional working with Windows 98, you really need to master the Windows 98 Registry to earn your wings. In a sense, the Windows 98 Registry is the foundation on which Windows 98—and its applications—run. Becoming proficient with the Registry is one of the things that set support professionals above their peers.

You'll undoubtedly recall with no amount of fondness the miasma of configuration files in Windows 3.x: CONFIG.SYS, AUTOEXEC.BAT, WIN.INI, SYSTEM.INI, and so on. On a system with many applications and drivers installed, these files could grow quite large, were relatively difficult to work with, and weren't very fast for the operating system to access.

Starting with Windows NT 3.1 and followed by Windows 95, Microsoft did away with these files (they're still present, but only for backward compatibility) and replaced them with a single point in which all the configuration information about the system could be stored: the Registry.

There are a number of benefits that the Registry brings to the Windows family of operating systems, including the following:

- Single point of storage for configuration information for the operating system, the hardware, and all applications

- Easily searchable

- Can be remotely administered across a network

- Stores all its information in two files: USER.DAT and SYSTEM.DAT

- Is automatically backed up every time the system boots

- Does not need to be edited manually in order to configure the system; it's there if you need to get "behind the scenes" but otherwise is maintained through various tools, such as Control Panel objects

- Can easily contain different types of data: binary strings, text strings, and numeric values

- Allows long, easy-to-read and easy-to-understand descriptions of each entry

In this chapter you learn about the Registry, how it works, how to edit it directly with the Registry Editor, and how to back it up and restore it. You also learn some of the important Registry keys that you might need to modify from time to time. You'll even learn about some hot "hacks" that you can do in the Registry!

Understanding the Registry

The Windows 98 Registry contains all of the configuration information about a Windows 98 system and its applications (at least those applications that are Windows 9x-compliant). All the information for the Registry is stored in two main files, SYSTEM.DAT and USER.DAT, and one optional file (if you are configured to use System Policies), CONFIG.POL or POLICY.POL.

SYSTEM.DAT and USER.DAT both reside in your \WINDOWS directory unless User Profiles are enabled, in which case there will be multiple copies of USER.DAT, one for each user that has a profile on the system. The user-specific copies of USER.DAT are stored in \WINDOWS\Profiles*username* where *username* is the logon name used to log on to Windows and access individual User Profiles. If User Profiles are being stored on a network server, then

USER.DAT resides in the user's home directory or in some other server directory that you've configured for this purpose.

> ### Is it Safe to Modify the Registry Directly?
>
> In just about any book that makes reference to making changes to the Registry, you will find dire warnings about the terrible things that can happen if you make a mistake. Those warnings are all true: Inappropriate changes to the Registry can make Windows 98 unstable or unable to boot, or cause other negative impacts.
>
> However, modifying the Registry isn't really very difficult, and as long as you're careful with the changes you make, you will find that there are a lot of profitable things you can do with the Registry, and will rarely have problems. While you should treat the Registry with respect, you don't have to be paranoid about working with it.

The SYSTEM.DAT file contains all of the configuration information for the computer on which it is located. USER.DAT contains all user-specific information, such as desktop settings, application preferences, and user-specific Control Panel settings.

When you open the Registry Editor (REGEDIT.EXE), you see two main branches (called *root keys*) and four "shadow" (or alias) branches (see Figure 10.1). The two root keys are described here:

- **HKEY_LOCAL_MACHINE** stores the local computer's hardware settings.

- **HKEY_USERS** stores user-specific settings for all users who access the local computer.

In addition to these two main branches, there are four alias branches that appear as main branches, but are really reflections of lower-level Registry keys in one of the two main branches:

- **HKEY_CLASSES_ROOT** stores object registration information, such as file associations and object types. This key maps to HKEY_LOCAL_MACHINE\Software\Classes.

- **HKEY_DYN_DATA** stores dynamic data used by applications as they execute and process information. This branch is not really an alias, but represents dynamic data that is created as Windows 98 runs, and is not stored in USER.DAT or SYSTEM.DAT.

- **HKEY_CURRENT_CONFIG** is a shortcut to the current configuration of the computer (which is actually stored within HKEY_LOCAL_MACHINE). For instance, on a dockable notebook computer, there will be different settings in HKEY_LOCAL_MACHINE for the computer in its docked and undocked state; the active state is found in HKEY_CURRENT_CONFIG.

- **HKEY_CURRENT_USER** is a shortcut to the current user's settings on the computer (which is actually stored within HKEY_USERS). Each user has preferences stored in HKEY_USERS under his logon name, and HKEY_CURRENT_USER provides a convenient shortcut to the settings within HKEY_USERS.

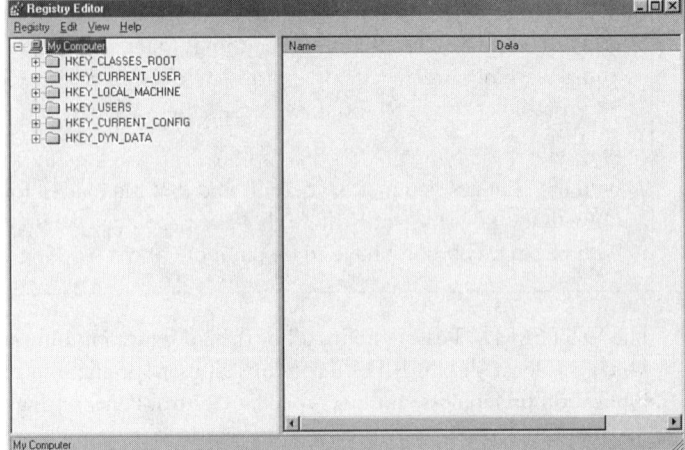

Figure 10.1
Opening the Registry Editor reveals the main branches of the Registry.

> **Note** Alias branches exist in the Registry to make it easier to locate specific information within the main branches. For instance, if an application wants to store user-specific data, it doesn't have to figure out which User Profile is active, and how it is stored in HKEY_USERS. Instead, it can store its data in HKEY_CURRENT_USER and Windows 98 automatically takes care of placing the data in the correct user-specific subkey of HKEY_USERS. The same goes for HKEY_LOCAL_MACHINE and HKEY_CURRENT_CONFIG; applications don't have to determine which Hardware Profile is active—for that matter, neither do you when you use the Registry Editor!

If you use the Registry Editor to navigate down a few levels in one of the branches, you will eventually select a folder where the right pane displays data. The left pane displays the Registry *keys*, which are specific locations within the Registry. The right pane displays *values*, which are different values stored in a key. A single Registry key can contain many values. Figure 10.2 illustrates this.

Keys are specified using their complete path, with backslashes to denote different key levels. For example, in Figure 10.2 the key HKEY_LOCAL_MACHINE\Config\001\Display\Settings is selected. In the right pane you can see a number of values, such as BitsPerPixel and DesktopPos.

Chapter 10: Mastering the Windows 98 Registry

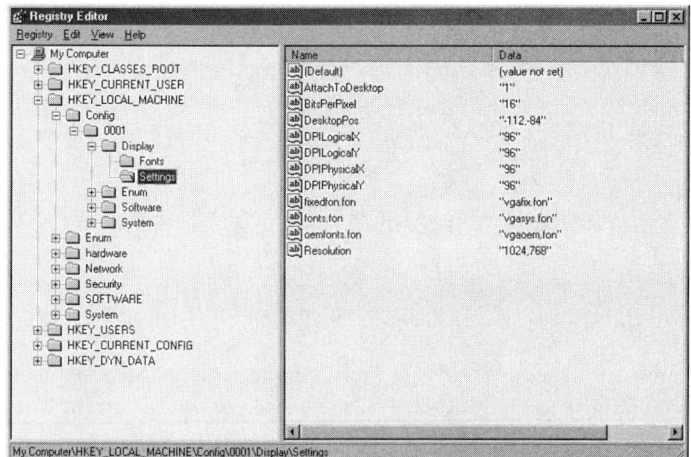

Figure 10.2
Navigating the Registry reveals keys and values.

When values are created, they are created as a certain *type*. Under Windows 98, values can contain three types of data:

- **String**—These values store strings of text or numbers (or both), such as "My Computer" or "1024x800." Strings are always enclosed in quotes, and can be any length.

- **Binary**—Binary values are strings of binary data using hexadecimal notation. Binary values can be any size. You could, for instance, store an icon as a binary value in the Registry.

- **DWORD**—Also known as a double-word, these values store 32-bit numbers in hexadecimal notation. You can enter DWORD values using either hexadecimal numbers (base16) or decimal numbers (base10).

> **Note** Each key contains one value called the *default value*. It usually doesn't store any data, and its presence is for compatibility with the old Windows 3.1 Registry (there was a rudimentary Registry in Windows 3.1, believe it or not). The default value (called simply [Default]), if it contains data, contains string data.

Understanding the Main Registry Branches

As you've already seen, there are two main branches of keys in the Registry, and four alias branches that are actually mirrors of data in one of the two main branches. In this section, you'll learn, broadly, what each of the two main branches contains.

HKEY_LOCAL_MACHINE

The HKEY_LOCAL_MACHINE root key stores settings for the local computer itself. Examples include hardware devices, device drivers installed, current hardware configuration data, and uninstall information. HKEY_LOCAL_MACHINE does not store user-specific data.

There are seven main keys in the HKEY_LOCAL_MACHINE root key, described in the following sections.

Config

The Config key contains information about Hardware Profiles on the system (See Chapter 9, "Hardware Profiles" for more information). For each available Hardware Profile on the system, there is a subkey named with a number (such as 0001, 0002, and so forth). Within each of the numbered profiles is a subkey called Enum, which contains all of the entries for hardware devices that are active when that profile is being used by the computer.

You can decode what each numbered Hardware Profile is named by examining the key HKEY_LOCAL_MACHINE\System\CurrentControlSet\control\IDConfigDB. Here you will find values that show the names and numbers of each Hardware Profile on the system.

Enum

The Enum subkey under HKEY_LOCAL_MACHINE holds all of the device driver information for the computer. The information in this key is not dependent on which Hardware Profile is active; every possible device ever installed on the system will be listed in this subkey.

Within Enum are a number of subkeys, each one corresponding to a different type of hardware device. Figure 10.3 illustrates these subkeys.

Figure 10.3
Subkeys of HKEY_LOCAL_MACHINE\ Enum correspond to different device types.

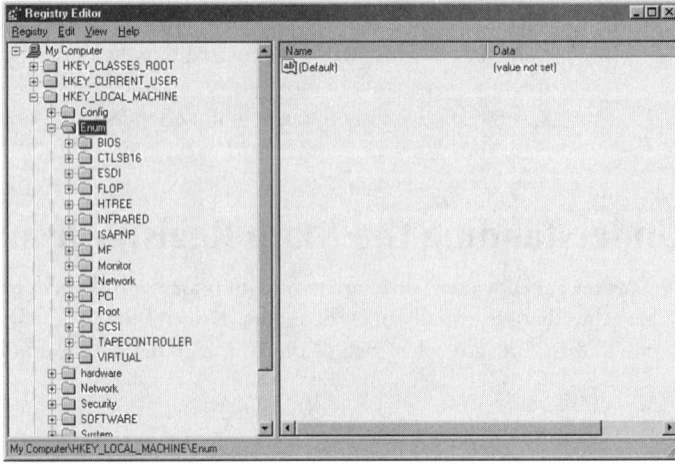

The main types of information stored within Enum will depend on the configuration of the computer. For instance, a system with an EISA bus will have an EISA subkey. On a standard ISA/PCI system, the following are standard subkeys within Enum:

- **BIOS** stores information on the Basic Input/Output system of the computer. Plug and Play information is here, with subkeys for each main category of PnP device.
- **ESDI** holds information about all of the IDE disk controllers and their connected devices.
- **FLOP** holds information about the disk drives on the system.
- **INFRARED** holds information on any attached Infrared communications devices.
- **ISAPNP** holds information on ISA-based devices that are Plug and Play-compliant.
- **Monitor** contains information about any attached monitors.
- **Network** stores information about the bindings for all network clients, protocols, and services.
- **PCI** has information about the PCI bus.
- **Root** holds information about older devices.
- **SCSI** has information about SCSI interface cards and devices.
- **TAPECONTROLLER** holds information about any installed tape controllers, including the floppy disk drive controller (which some tape devices use).

Hardware

Contrary to what you would expect, the Hardware subkey doesn't hold much information, mostly just descriptions of the processor and COM port mappings.

Network

Within the Network subkey is a single key called Logon. This key's values are updated each time a user logs on to the computer, and contains user-specific logon information. You will find values here for the username, network provider, and System Policy handler.

Security

The Security key holds information for any security providers being used by the computer. You can also find information about any users that are logged on to the Windows 98 system using a peer-to-peer network connection, as well as information about shared devices that are accessible through a network connection.

Software

One of the more interesting keys in HKEY_LOCAL_MACHINE, the Software key holds data stored by software installed on the computer. The subkeys present depend on which applications are installed, and what they choose to store here. Figure 10.4 shows a sample Software key.

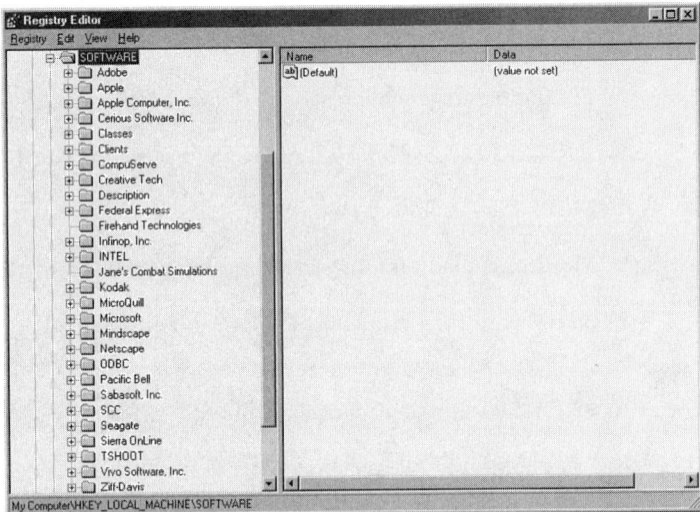

Figure 10.4
A sample HKEY_LOCAL_MACHINE\Software key.

As you can see in Figure 10.4, most keys correspond to a software manufacturer. Within a particular manufacturer's key are subkeys, usually one for each of the installed applications. In addition to the company-specific keys, you will also find some other keys of interest:

- **Classes** holds information on object class registrations and file type associations.

- **Microsoft**, while obviously one of the software manufacturers, is also notable because it contains information on Windows 98 itself (in HKEY_LOCAL_MACHINE\Software\Microsoft\Windows\CurrentVersion).

- **ODBC** holds information on Open Database Connectivity drivers installed on the machine.

System

Under the HKEY_LOCAL_MACHINE\System key you will find a CurrentControlSet key, which is the complete set of information that Windows 98 needs to boot. The two main subkeys of CurrentControlSet, Control and System, are described in the following list:.

- **Control** contains boot information for the system, such as the computer name, file system configuration information, keyboard layouts, network providers, print devices and drivers, time zone information, and so forth.

- **Services** holds information about device drivers and services that are automatically loaded when Windows 98 starts.

HKEY_USERS

Under HKEY_USERS you will find one key for each user of the computer, plus one other key called .Default, which is a default user. User-based subkeys are named for the logon name that the user uses. Within each user key, you find a number of subkeys, detailed in the following subsections.

AppEvents

AppEvents defines the possible events to which sounds can be associated, within Windows itself and for any applications that can also make use of sound events (such as Microsoft Office). There are two main subkeys: EventLabels and Schemes. EventLabels holds a description of each possible event, while Schemes holds scheme information for the sounds chosen, as well as references to the actual .WAV files that are played for each event. Within each event listed in Schemes\Apps are two keys: .Default and .Current, which define the sounds played for the default scheme and the currently selected scheme.

Control Panel

User-specific Control Panel settings are stored in this key. Within Control Panel, you'll find one key for each different Control Panel that holds user-specific information, as follows:

- **Accessibility** holds settings for accessibility settings (such as StickyKeys or ShowSounds).

- **Appearance** contains the color schemes defined in the Display Control Panel.

- **Colors** holds the current Windows color settings.

- **Cursors** holds a subkey called Schemes, which defines all of the available cursor schemes for Windows 98.

- **Desktop** holds screen-saver information, desktop wallpaper settings, and font codes for desktop fonts.

- **International** holds the currently selected locale, used for various system settings.

- **PowerCfg** holds information about the different power-saving schemes available on the system.

InstallLocationsMRU

This key holds the most recently used (MRU) installation locations for Windows 98. There are several values, lettered starting from A. There is a also a value called MRUList that holds the order in which those different installation locations should be tried when adding a driver or installing other Windows 98 software.

Keyboard Layout

This set of keys defines the keyboard layout for Windows 98.

Network

This key holds the Windows 98 persistent (and current) network connections, most notably mapped network drives. Each persistent mapped drive is stored in HKEY_USER\Network\Persistent, and there are several subkeys: Provider Name for the network client used to access the network resources, RemotePath for the UNC of the mapped resource, and UserName for the username used to attach to the remote resource. Located in HKEY_USER\Network\Recent are similar subkeys for accessed (but not mapped) network drives.

RemoteAccess

In HKEY_USERS\RemoteAccess you will find definition information for any dial-up networking settings stored for the users, including their provider names, any IP settings, and their user names. These entries correspond to the entries found in the Dial Up Networking folder.

Software

The Software key in HKEY_USERS holds user-specific information for the software on the system. Its structure is similar to HKEY_LOCAL_MACHINE\Software, in that there is a key for each software manufacturer, with subkeys for their applications.

Using Registry Editor

The Registry Editor is installed on every Windows 98 system in the \Windows directory, and is named REGEDIT.EXE. By default, there is no program shortcut created in the Start menu for the Registry Editor, so most people start it by using the Run command in the Start menu and then typing REGEDIT.

The Registry Editor's display is divided into two panes. The left pane shows the organization of the Registry. If you are running Registry Editor on a local computer, you see My Computer at the top of the organization. If you're administering a remote computer, you see that computer's network name at the top. Within My Computer are the six main root keys of the

Registry: the two main root keys and the four alias root keys, as described previously. As is probably obvious, you click on the plus symbols next to keys to open them and on any minus symbols to close them.

The right pane shows any values attached to the key selected in the left pane. Each value has both a value name and value data.

Most people navigate Registry Editor using the pointing device. However, there are also some keyboard shortcuts that will save you time if you frequently use Registry Editor, as detailed in the following table:

Key	Action
Keypad +	Expands the selected key
Keypad -	Collapses the selected key
Keypad *	Expands the selected key, and all expandable keys within it
Up arrow	Moves up one key
Down arrow	Moves down one key
Right arrow	Expands the current key if it's collapsed, otherwise moves to its first subkey
Left arrow	Collapses the current key if it's expanded, otherwise moves to its parent key
Home	Moves to the top key (usually My Computer)
End	Moves to the last expanded key (does not expand any keys)
Page Up	Moves up one screen
Page Down	Moves down one screen
Tab	Switches between the right and left panes

In the right pane, each value appears with one of two icons: one, with the letters AB on it, indicates a string value is being stored, and one, with a set of 1s and 0s, indicates that binary or DWORD data is stored there.

Searching the Registry

You can search through the entire Registry using Registry Editor, looking for keys, value names, or string value data that match your search criteria. Use the **E**dit, **F**ind command to access the Find dialog box shown in Figure 10.5.

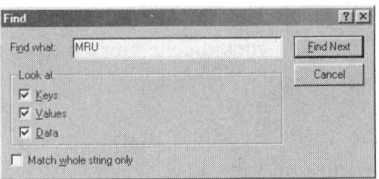

Figure 10.5
The Find dialog box lets you rapidly search the entire Registry for information.

After typing your search text, use the **K**eys, **V**alues, and **D**ata checkboxes to determine what will be searched. You can also select Match **W**hole String Only to avoid searching for partial matches.

After finding the first key or value that matches your search criteria, use the **E**dit, Find **N**ext command to find the next match, or press the F3 key to also continue the search.

There is an abbreviated way to find keys quickly, assuming they are already expanded and don't contain spaces: With the left pane active in Registry Editor, simply start typing the name of the key. You will continue jumping to matching keys as you type more of the key name that you want.

> **Note** Searching for keys can sometimes take a while. Also, remember that four of the main root keys are aliases, so you might get multiple hits for a particular search phrase, each hit possibly representing the same actual data in the Registry.

Editing a Value's Data

After finding the key you're searching for and selecting one of the values in the right pane, you can edit the value data. There are three ways to edit a value's data: Double-click on the value's name, select a value and choose Modify from the **E**dit menu, or right-click on a value and choose Modify from the pop-up menu. Depending on the type of data being stored in that value, you then see one of three different dialog boxes, presenting string, DWORD, or binary data, as shown in Figures 10.6, 10.7, and 10.8, respectively.

> **Note** You cannot change the type of data stored by a value. Instead, you must remove the value and then re-create it (using the same name) for the type of data you want it to contain.

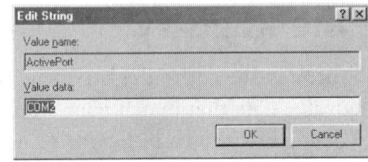

Figure 10.6
*To edit string data, simply type the new data in the **V**alue Data field.*

Chapter 10: Mastering the Windows 98 Registry   **211**

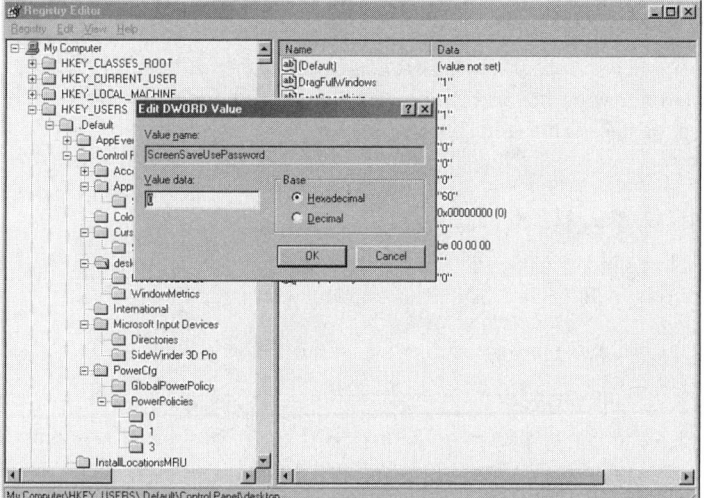

Figure 10.7
*To edit DWORD data, enter the data in the field and choose **H**exadecimal or **D**ecimal, depending on how you entered the value.*

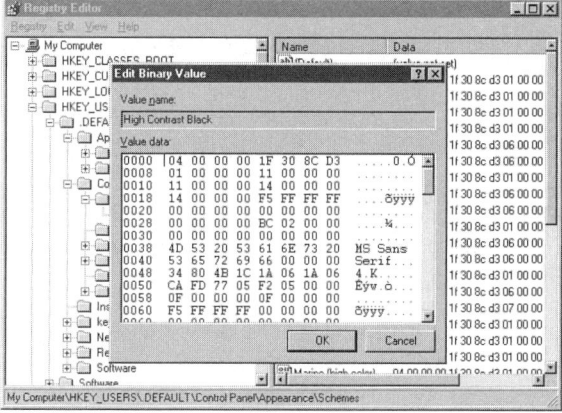

Figure 10.8
*To edit binary data, start typing the hexadecimal values for each byte in the **V**alue Data area.*

Adding Keys and Values

To create a new key in Registry Editor, first select the key that will contain the new key. Then, choose **E**dit, **N**ew, **K**ey to create the new key. A new key is created with the name New Key #1; you can start typing immediately to assign a different name to the key.

To create a new value, first select the key that will hold the value. Then use one of the three other commands you see when you open the **E**dit, **N**ew menu: **S**tring Value, **B**inary Value, or **D**WORD Value. Select the appropriate command based on the type of data the value will hold. The value is created with an editable name; start typing immediately to assign the value its new name. You then modify the contents of the new value just as you would do for an existing value (double-click on the value entry, for instance).

Renaming Keys and Values

The easiest way to rename a key is to right-click on it and choose **R**ename from the pop-up menu. You can then type the new name for the key. You can do the same for values: Simply right-click on them and choose **R**ename from their pop-up menus.

Deleting Keys and Values

To delete a key, simply select the key and press the Delete key. That key, *as well as all keys and values within that key*, are then deleted after you acknowledge a warning message box.

Similarly, you can select a value and press the Delete key to quickly delete that value.

> **Warning** Deleting keys and values should be done only if you're absolutely sure that you want to remove the key or the value. Deleting keys can be particularly dangerous because all of its subkeys are also deleted. When in doubt, don't do it!

Importing and Exporting Registry Keys

Registry Editor provides the ability to export and import Registry keys—and even the entire Registry—to ASCII text files. This can be useful when you want to send a Registry key and its values to another user and import the Registry information into their Registry. You can also export Registry information so that you can examine it or analyze it in different ways, or even make a backup copy of the Registry information. You can also export the Registry to perform Search and Replace operations on the data: Use a text editor to perform the Search and Replace, and then import the modified Registry data from the text file.

Exported Registry keys are stored in .REG files, which can be viewed and edited with any text editor (such as WordPad or Notepad). Figure 10.8 shows an exported Registry fragment in WordPad.

To export a Registry key, first select the key you want to export and then access the **E**xport Registry File command from the **R**egistry menu. This brings up the Export Registry File dialog box seen in Figure 10.9.

In the Export Registry File dialog box, assign a name for the exported Registry file, and then choose whether you want to export only the current key and its subkeys (S**e**lected Branch) or the entire Registry (**A**ll).

There are two easy ways to import an exported Registry file. The most obvious way is to start Registry Editor and then choose **I**mport Registry File from its **R**egistry menu. Occasionally, it is easier to simply double-click on a .REG file. Windows 98 has a file association for .REG files that corresponds with the Registry Editor, and so .REG files are automatically imported when you double-click on them. Under Windows 98 you (or the user) are warned before the key is imported, whereas in Windows 95 the key was immediately imported.

Chapter 10: Mastering the Windows 98 Registry

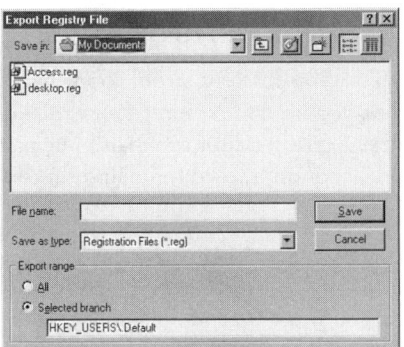

Figure 10.9

The Export Registry File dialog box.

Tip	You can import .REG files using various command-line options for REGEDIT. See the next section, "Registry Editor Command-line Parameters," for details.

The layout of the .REG files is straightforward. Each key is listed, with its full Registry pathname, in square brackets. Following each key are all of the values that the key contains, in this format:

`"Valuename"=data`

Data can be any of the three value types. String data is specified with surrounding quotation marks. DWORD data is specified with the format dword:00000000, with the 0s replaced with whatever value is appropriate, in hexadecimal format. Binary values are given in the form hex:00,00,00,00..., with each byte specified in hexadecimal, separated by commas. If binary data exceeds a single line in the text editor, use a backslash to continue the series of values. For instance, the following is a valid .REG entry for a large binary value:

```
[HKEY_USERS\.Default\Software\Microsoft\Windows\CurrentVersion\Applets\Regedit]
"View"=hex:2c,00,00,00,00,00,00,00,01,00,00,00,ff,ff,ff,ff,ff,ff,ff,ff,ff,ff,\
  ff,ff,ff,ff,ff,ff,20,00,00,00,06,00,00,00,fa,02,00,00,2f,02,00,00,63,01,00,\
  00,dd,00,00,00,20,01,00,00,01,00,00,00
```

Warning	When sending an exported .REG file to others for them to import, make sure that you only send them the keys that they need. For example, you wouldn't generally want to send them any keys that configure their hardware, unless you know exactly what you're doing and you intend to do that. If you're sending them more than a single key, it's a good idea to double-check the .REG file with a text editor to make sure that they're only going to get the keys that you want them to get. Importing inappropriate keys can have disastrous consequences for the recipient of a .REG file!

Registry Editor Command-line Parameters

You can start Registry Editor with one of several different sets of command-line parameters. These can be useful in batch files or when you need to perform a set of actions with Registry Editor and need to automate them. These Registry Editor command-line parameters also work if you start the system in MS-DOS mode, and can be used for maintenance activities in that mode.

The first method imports .REG files into the Registry. The syntax is as follows:

```
REGEDIT [/L:location_of_system.dat] [/R:location_of_user.dat] importfile1.reg importfile2.reg ...
```

All methods for starting Registry Editor from the command line can use the optional /L and /R parameters to locate the SYSTEM.DAT and USER.DAT files. By default, Registry Editor finds them in the \Windows directory. After specifying those parameters, if needed, you can simply list all of the .REG files that you want to import into the Registry, each one separated by a space.

Just as you can import Registry keys from the command line, so too can you export keys from the command line. Use this syntax for exporting .REG files:

```
REGEDIT [/L:location_of_system.dat] [/R:location_of_user.dat] /e filename.REG Registry_Key_Name_To_Export
```

The final command replaces the complete contents of the Registry with the contents of a specified .REG file. Use great care with this command. The syntax is as follows:

```
REGEDIT [/L:location_of_system.dat] [/R:location_of_user.dat] /c filename.REG
```

> **How Can I Completely Rebuild my Registry Files? (And Why Would I Want To?)**
>
> When you add and remove keys from the Registry, Windows doesn't compact the SYSTEM.DAT and USER.DAT files—it just marks the deleted data space as being deleted. If you're using a system that has had a lot of software added and removed from it, the Registry file can become quite large, much of it actually consisting of deleted data (you can't see the deleted data in REGEDIT, but it's probably there.) To compact the Registry in this case, start the system in MS-DOS mode (hold down the left Ctrl key while Windows 98 boots and choose Command Prompt Only from the Windows Startup menu). Then, use the following command:
>
> ```
> REGEDIT /L:C:\WINDOWS\SYSTEM.DAT /R:\WINDOWS\USER.DAT /e C:\FULLREG.REG \
> ```
>
> (If you are using User Profiles, make sure to use the appropriate User Profile path for the /R parameter).

> After exporting the Registry in this fashion, clear the attributes on the USER.DAT and SYSTEM.DAT files with ATTRIB filename.DAT -r -h -s. Then, copy USER.DAT and SYSTEM.DAT to a backup location and erase the originals in \WINDOWS. Use the following command to rebuild the Registry using the export file you just created:
>
> ```
> REGEDIT /L:C:\WINDOWS\SYSTEM.DAT /R:\WINDOWS\USER.DAT /c C:\FULLREG.REG
> ```
>
> To keep things nice and tidy, remember to reset the attributes on the Registry's .DAT files with the command ATTRIB filename.DAT +r +h +s.

Backing Up and Restoring the Registry

Because the Registry is made up of two normal files, SYSTEM.DAT and USER.DAT, it is easy to back up the Registry. One way to do this is to create a batch file that runs as part of your Startup folder. In the batch file, you can use XCOPY to backup the Registry files to a new location. Keep in mind that SYSTEM.DAT and USER.DAT are normally flagged as hidden, read-only when you do this, however.

Using Batch Files to Back Up the Registry

If you really want to get fancy and make multiple backup copies, you can store them in several locations, and the batch file can move the files from location to location. Here's an example of a set of commands that will keep the three most current Registry sets in three directories, called \RegBack1, \RegBack2, and \RegBack3 (you must create the directories before running this batch file):

```
REM Begin Registry Backup Batch File
ERASE C:\REGBACK3\*.DAT
MOVE C:\REGBACK2\*.* C:\REGBACK3
MOVE C:\REGBACK1\*.* C:\REGBACK2
ATTRIB C:\WINDOWS\USER.DAT -r -h
ATTRIB C:\WINDOWS\SYSTEM.DAT -r -h
XCOPY C:\WINDOWS\USER.DAT C:\REGBACK1
XCOPY C:\WINDOWS\SYSTEM.DAT C:\REGBACK1
ATTRIB C:\WINDOWS\USER.DAT +r +h
ATTRIB C:\WINDOWS\SYSTEM.DAT +r +h
```

To restore the Registry from a backup, simply copy SYSTEM.DAT and USER.DAT back to their appropriate places (C:\Windows and C:\Windows\Profiles*username* if User Profiles are active) from whatever backup copy you have. Remember to clear the hidden and read-only file attribute bits on the real ones before you do this, and then restart the system immediately.

Using CFGBACK to Back Up the Registry

A more elegant way to back up the Registry is to use a Windows 98 Resource Kit utility called CFGBACK. The CFGBACK utility can store up to nine versions of your Registry files, letting you restore any of the nine at any time.

To run CFGBACK, you'll simply need to copy the CFGBACK.EXE file to your \Windows directory. If you want to, you can place a shortcut for the program on your Start menu or desktop.

When you run CFGBACK, you see the screen shown in Figure 10.10. Simply type a name for the backup in the Selected Backup Name field and click the **B**ackup button. CFGBACK takes a few minutes to back up the Registry on most systems.

Figure 10.10
CFGBACK makes quick work of backing up and restoring the Registry.

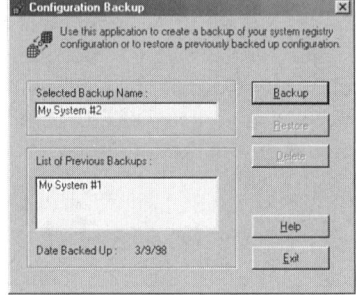

To restore a previous version of your Registry, select the one you want to restore in the List of Previous Backups list and click the **R**estore button. It doesn't get much easier than this!

CFGBACK stores its backups of the Registry in the \Windows directory, with the names being REGBACK1.RBK, REGBACK2.RBK, and so forth. One nice benefit of CFGBACK is that it compresses its backups, so each backup file doesn't take up nearly as much disk space as the USER.DAT and SYSTEM.DAT files.

Note CFGBACK is installed from the Resource Kit CD-ROM as one of the Resource Kit's Registry Tools.

Remotely Administering the Registry

The Windows 9x Registry can be remotely administered across a network. A program that comes with Windows 98, called Microsoft Remote Registry, enables this feature.

In order to remotely administer a computer's Registry, you must perform the following steps on both the computer to be administered, and the computer from where you will be administering the remote Registry:

1. Enable User-level access control. Open the Network Control Panel's properties and move to the Access Control tab. Select the **U**ser-Level Access Control option button.

2. Using the Configuration tab of the Network Control Panel, click the **A**dd button. You see the Network Configuration Type dialog box.

3. Click on Service in the Network Configuration Type dialog box and click the **A**dd button.

4. Click the **H**ave Disk button.

5. Use the Browse dialog box to select the file REGSRV.INF. It should be located in the \TOOLS\RESKIT\NETADMIN\REMOTEREG directory on the Windows 98 CD-ROM.

6. Complete the addition of the new service, and restart the computer when prompted.

After completing the preceding steps on both computers, you can then edit the remote computer's Registry using the Registry Editor, provided both computers share a common network protocol. Open the **R**egistry menu and choose **C**onnect Network Registry, and then type the remote computer's name in the dialog box that appears.

Tip | If you want to store the Remote Registry Service files on a network server for easy installation on client computers, you'll need to have these three files: REGSRV.EXE, REGSRV.INF, and WINREG.DLL.

Specific Registry Tips and Tricks

Because you've read the preceding information in this chapter, you now understand what the Registry is, what it does, how it works, and how to manage it. In the remaining sections of this chapter, you learn about specific things you can do to the Registry in different circumstances. Each heading lists the action you can perform, so you can rapidly find it by searching this book's Table of Contents.

Managing File Associations

File association information is stored in the HKEY_CLASSES_ROOT root key, shown open in Figure 10.11. Every file extension registered on the system can be found in one of its subkeys.

Part II: Configuring Windows 98

Figure 10.11
File associations are maintained in HKEY_CLASSES_ROOT.

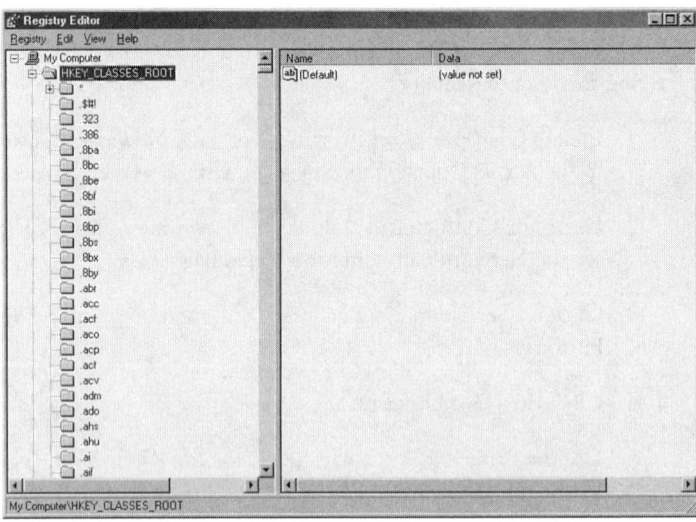

> **Note** HKEY_CLASSES_ROOT is an alias of HKEY_LOCAL_MACHINE\Software\Classes. You can make changes to either location, whichever is more convenient for you.

The HKEY_CLASSES_ROOT root key holds a listing of file association keys (all beginning with a period, and showing the actual file association) as well as keys that tell Windows how to behave with files of that extension. For example, examine the entries for .BAT files. Figure 10.12 shows the value settings for files of .BAT type.

Figure 10.12
A .BAT file simply holds a [Default] value with the name of the file type.

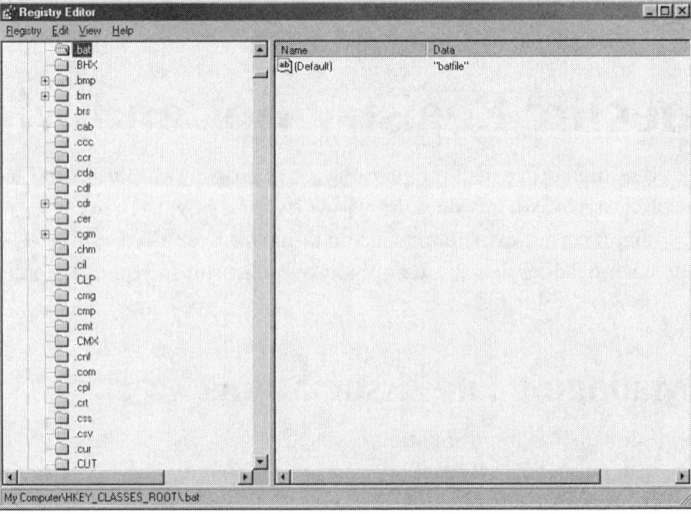

Chapter 10: Mastering the Windows 98 Registry

As you can see in Figure 10.12, .BAT files just have a [Default] value with the string "batfile" as its data. Alone, this information isn't useful and doesn't tell you what Windows will do with this file when manipulated from Explorer. However, if you scroll further down the HKEY_CLASSES_ROOT key, you will find another key called HKEY_CLASSES_ROOT\batfile. It is in this key that you can find the information for how Windows 98 works with .BAT files, as shown in Figure 10.13.

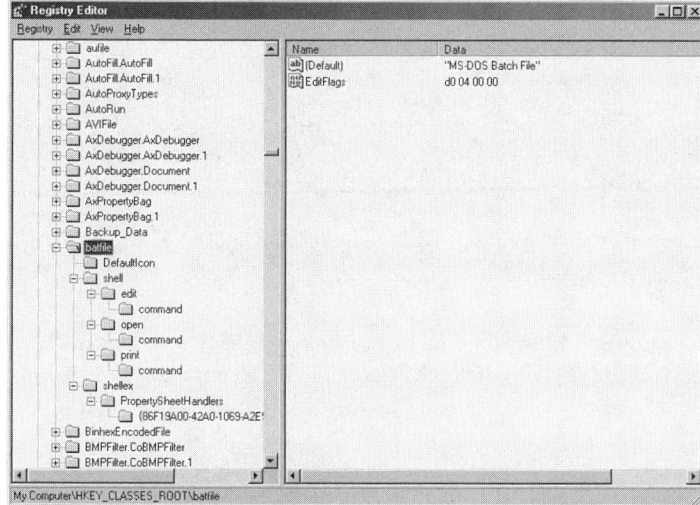

Figure 10.13

The Class Definition Subkey for batfile.

The HKEY_CLASSES_ROOT\batfile key is known as a *class definition subkey*. It defines the Explorer behavior for files of that type. As you can see in Figure 10.13, there are several types of subkeys for the class definition subkey.

The [Default] entry contains the description for the file type. This name shows on the Properties dialog box for files of this type. The DefaultIcon subkey defines the location for the default icon for files of this type.

The *shell* subkey holds information for how Windows 98 should perform certain user actions on the file. There is one subkey for each possible action, with this batfile example showing commands for Edit, Print, and Open. In each command there is another subkey called *command*. This command subkey contains the command that will be executed in its [Default] value. For instance, examine Figure 10.14, which shows the Edit command's command subkey.

As you can see, if you choose Edit from the pop-up menu for a .BAT file, you are actually executing the command NOTEPAD followed by the %1 parameter (which is the name of the file).

Figure 10.14
A batfile's Edit command in Explorer.

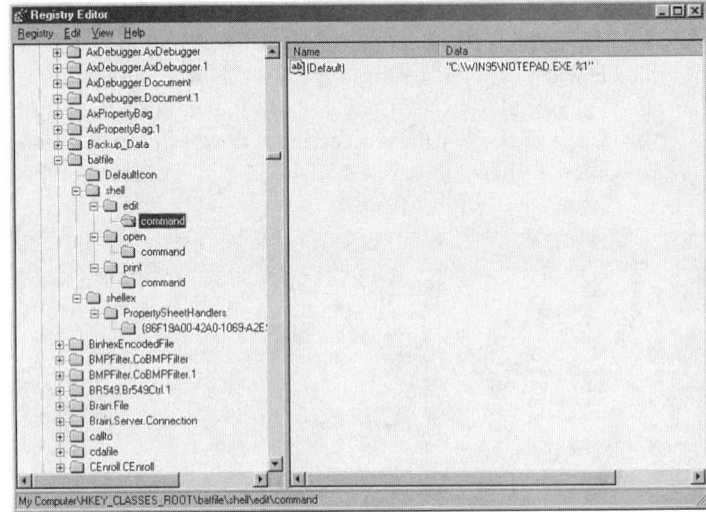

Any file extension or class definition key that contains a ShellNew subkey will appear when you right-click in a folder in Windows Explorer and choose the New submenu, as shown in Figure 10.15.

Figure 10.15
The ShellNew subkeys are responsible for a file type appearing when you open the New menu in Explorer.

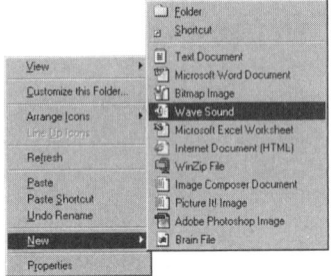

Why Class Definition Subkeys?

Class definition subkeys are used to make the Registry storage of different files more efficient. For example, you can have many different file extensions for a single type of file (.HTM and .HTML are both valid file types for HTML files). By storing only a class definition subkey name within each file extension, and then placing all of the information for how to handle that type of file within the class definition subkey itself, a single set of information can be made to work with multiple file extensions.

Changing File Type Icons

To change the icon displayed for a file using the Registry, open the key HKEY_CLASSES_ROOT, and then find the extension that the file uses (for example, .WAV). Select that key, and look at the data for the [Default] value. It will specify the class definition subkey name that handles the file. (For .WAV files it is SoundRec.)

Then, locate the class definition key (SoundRec in this example) within HKEY_CLASSES_ROOT and open it. You should see a subkey called DefaultIcon. The DefaultIcon subkey only has a [Default] value, which contains a pointer to an icon file. Change the value of [Default] so that it instead points to a file that contains icons, such as a .ICO file. You can also indicate a .DLL file that contains icons. The two syntaxes for the [Default] value are as follows:

```
[Default]="pathname\filename.ico,0"
```

```
[Default]="pathname\dllfile.dll,-xx"
```

Note that *xx* is the resource identifier for the icon within the .DLL file.

Add Actions to Pop-up Menus

You can easily add new actions to Explorer's pop-up menus for different file types. One reason for doing this would be to open a particular type of file with more than one program from Explorer. For example, you might want to open some .TXT files with Windows Notepad, and others with a programmer's text editor, like Brief or SlickEdit. Follow these steps (substituting your own chosen extension and programs as needed) to see how this works:

1. Open the Registry Editor and locate the .TXT file type in HKEY_CLASSES_ROOT.

2. Find the class definition subkey name (in this case, txtfile) and then locate that entry in HKEY_CLASSES_ROOT.

3. Open the subkey txtfile\shell.

4. Add a new subkey to txtfile\shell. This new subkey will be the command that appears when you right-click on any .TXT files. In this example, use the key name Open with SlickEdit.

5. To that new subkey, add another subkey called command. In this case, you would create the key txtfile\shell\Open with SlickEdit\command.

6. Set the [Default] value of the command key to be a string value, containing the program name followed by %1 to denote the actual filename. In this case, e:\util\slickdos\s.exe %1 is specified.

You should close the Registry Editor after making these changes, although it is not necessary; the changes are effective as soon as you complete step 6 in the preceding instructions. Figure 10.16 shows the new pop-up menu command.

Figure 10.16
The added command on the pop-up menu for a .TXT file.

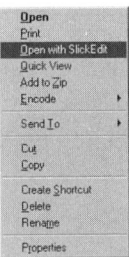

Tip
> In Figure 10.16 you can see that both the **O**pen command and the **O**pen with SlickEdit command share the same hotkey. You can define alternate hotkeys for pop-up menu commands. Select the key that contains the actual command (in this example, the key \txtfile\shell\Open with SlickEdit) and set its [Default] value to equal the command name, but insert an ampersand in front of the letter that you want to act as the hotkey. For example, to use the *w* in *with* as the hotkey, you would specify the string Open & with SlickEdit as the [Default] string value.

Adding New Sound Events

You use the Sounds Control Panel to control what sounds happen with which application events. You can use the Registry Editor to create new sound events, too. For example, say you want to assign special sounds for when Registry Editor itself is opened and closed. Follow these steps to do this:

1. Using Registry Editor, navigate to the HKEY_CURRENT_USER\AppEvents\Schemes\Apps key.

2. Add a new subkey with the name of the program. In this case, create a subkey called regedit.

3. Within the regedit key, create a key for the common application events such as Open and Close.

4. Set the [Default] value of the regedit key to be a friendly name, such as Registry Editor.

5. Open the Sounds Control Panel. If you scroll down to the bottom, you'll now see Registry Editor listed, along with the Open and Close events (if those are the events you defined in step 3).

6. Assign .WAV sound files to the two events.

After doing this, try opening and closing Registry Editor. If everything was done correctly, you'll hear the sounds you selected when you open and close it.

Chapter 10: Mastering the Windows 98 Registry

You can use the following Windows event names for each application:

Event Name	Description
Open	An application starts
Close	An application closes normally
Maximize	An application's window is maximized
Minimize	An application's window is minimized
MenuCommand	A menu command is chosen in the application
MenuPopup	A pop-up menu command is chosen in the application
SystemAsterisk	An "asterisk" system message is generated from the application
SystemExclamation	An "exclamation" system message is generated from the application
SystemQuestion	A "question mark" system message is generated from the application

Changing Desktop Icons

Some of the objects on the Windows 98 desktop don't make it easy for you to change their icons. With the Registry, however, you can change just about anything, including the names and icons for any of the standard desktop objects. To do so, follow these steps:

1. Using Registry Editor, open the key \HKEY_CLASSES_ROOT\CLSID.
2. Find the numeric subkey corresponding to the object you want to change (see Table 10.1)
3. Open the key you located in step 2, and you will find a DefaultIcon subkey.
4. Change the DefaultIcon subkey's [Default] entry to point to a different .ICO file.

Table 10.1
Standard Desktop Icon CLSIDs

Name	CLSID
Briefcase	{85BBD920-42A0-1069-A2E4-08002B30309D}
Control Panel	{21EC2020-3AEA-1069-A2DD-08002B30309D}

continues

Table 10.1, Continued
Standard Desktop Icon CLSIDs

Name	CLSID
Dial-Up Networking	{992CFFA0-F557-101A-88EC-00DD010CCC48} folder
Inbox	{00020D75-0000-0000-C000-000000000046}
My Computer	{20D04F#0-3AEA-1069-A2D8-08002B30309D}
Network Neighborhood	{208D2C60-3AEA-1069-A2D7-08002B30309D}
Printers	{2227A280-3AEA-1069-A2DE-08002B30309D}
Recycle Bin	{645FF040-5081-101B-9F08-00AA002F954E}
Internet	{FBF23B42-E3F0-101B-8488-00AA003E56F8}

> **Tip** You can usually locate CLSID numbers yourself by searching the Registry for the name of the object. For instance, searching the Registry for My Documents helps you locate the CLSID of {450D8FBA-AD25-11D0-98A8-0800361B1103}.

Changing Windows Folder Locations

Windows maintains a number of default folder locations that you can't easily move. For example, you cannot relocate the \Windows\Recent folder or the \Windows\Fonts folder without making use of the Registry Editor.

To change the locations for Windows 98 folders, locate the key HKEY_CURRENT_USER\ Software\Microsoft\Windows\CurrentVersion\Explorer\ShellFolders. The values in this key define where Windows 98 looks for different types of information, and depends on whether or not User Profiles are being used. For example, Figure 10.17 shows this key for user Bruce when User Profiles are being used.

The value names (such as Startup, Fonts, Start Menu) are self-explanatory and map to the folder functions. Before changing one of these values, however, you should make sure that the new destination folder is in place and that it contains the necessary files that Windows will expect for that type of folder.

> **Note** You must restart Windows in order for the new folder locations to take effect.

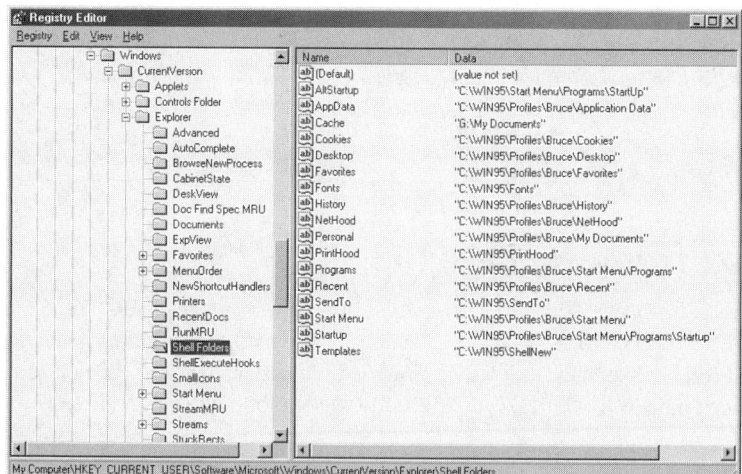

Figure 10.17
You can use this key to move Windows default folder locations.

Expanding the Icon Cache

Windows Explorer caches displayed icons in a file named C:\Windows\ShellIconCache. The file has no extension and is hidden by default. Windows 98 stores up to 512 icons in the cache, which it uses to more quickly display icons on the desktop or in Windows Explorer. When the cache fills, it is re-created from scratch, using the icons stored in the actual source files. You can expand the number of icons stored in this file, possibly eliminating the need for Windows to re-create it when it fills.

Using Registry Editor, navigate to the key \HKEY_LOCAL_MACHINE\Software\Microsoft\Windows\CurrentVersion\Explorer, and add a new value named Max Cached Icons holding a string value. The string value should be set to a number representing how many icons will be stored, such as 2000.

Changing the Menu Delay

When you move your mouse to a submenu, such as the Programs menu inside the Start menu, there is a pause before the submenu opens. The pause makes it easier for novices to work with Windows 98, but more advanced users often find the delay annoying. You can change the duration of the delay with a simple Registry change.

Using Registry Editor, navigate to the key HKEY_CURRENT_USER\Control Panel\Desktop. In that key, look for a value called MenuShowDelay. If it is not present, add it as a string value. The default string value (even if the value isn't present) is 400. You can reduce this to a much smaller number, even all the way to 0 if you like. Note that Windows must be restarted for this change to take effect.

Tip	You'll find that setting the MenuShowDelay setting too low makes Windows menus frustrating to use, even for experienced people. You'll want to experiment with the value, but you'll probably find that a delay of 200–300 is best overall.

Removing Inbox from the Desktop

You can remove the Inbox from the Windows desktop. Locate the key HKEY_LOCAL_MACHINE\Software\Microsoft\Windows\CurrentVersion\Explorer\Desktop\NameSpace. In this key you will find several subkeys, each of which is named with the CSLID of the desktop objects. Locate the subkey named {00020D75-0000-0000-C000-000000000046} and remove the key.

Viewing Bitmap Contents as Icons

If you maintain a lot of .BMP files on your system, you can set Windows 98 to display the contents of the .BMP files as their icons. To do this, find the key HKEY_CLASSES_ROOT\Paint.Picture\DefaultIcon and set its [Default] value to "%1". After restarting Windows, the bitmap file contents are displayed as their icons, as shown in Figure 10.18.

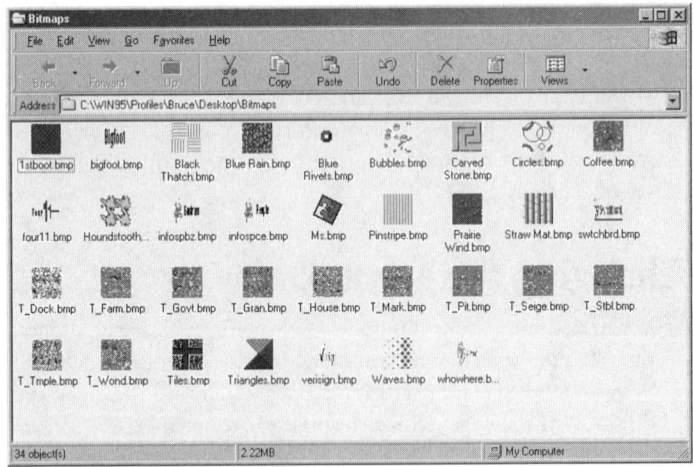

Figure 10.18
With the proper Registry change, you can view BMP contents as icons.

Change How Short Filenames are Generated

Windows 98 lets you use names for your files that are up to 254 characters long. As you probably know, however, Windows always stores a short version of the long filename for compatibility with DOS and older Windows programs. These short versions follow the 8.3

naming convention. When Windows generates a short filename for this purpose, it adds a tilde (~) in the seventh position of the eight-character filename, and then adds a number as the eighth character. For example, two files called "My Letter to Mom.DOC" and "My Letter to Dad.DOC" will have their short names set to "MYLETT~1.DOC" and "MYLETT~2.DOC". Windows adds the tilde and the number whether or not there are any conflicts within that directory.

As an experienced user or support person, you've probably noticed how annoying it is to type the tilde character when working with short filenames at a command prompt. Fortunately, with a simple Registry change, you can alter this behavior somewhat. Locate the key HKEY_LOCAL_MACHINE\System\CurrentControlSet\Control\FileSystem and create a new binary value called NameNumericTail. Set the data of the new value to 0.

After you make this change, the tilde will be eliminated from the short version of filenames. However, if you create new files in the same directory that would conflict with an existing short filename, the tilde, along with a number, will return for those conflicting files.

Assigning a Viewer to Unknown File Types

As a computer professional you often have to view the contents of files that don't have a registered file association. Perhaps you want to view the contents of a binary file in a text editor for some reason, or you want to view a text file that uses a non-standard extension. Unfortunately, Windows doesn't offer an Open command for files that don't have a registered file type.

You can use the Registry to make it easier to open files with an unknown type with whatever program you want to use, such as Notepad or your favorite programmer's editor. To do this, locate the key HKEY_CLASSES_ROOT\Unknown\Shell. Add a new subkey, whose name is the command you want to appear on the pop-up menu for unknown files. For this example, say you want to use SlickEdit to view such files, so create a subkey called Slick Edit. In the new subkey, set the data for the [Default] string value to be the command line that needs to be executed. In this example, you would set [Default] to be "C:\SlickEdit\S.EXE %1". Voilà! After making this change, you can right-click on any unknown file types and you'll see the command you created, letting you quickly view or edit such files.

Setting Double-Click Hot Zones

If you've observed beginning users with Windows, you've probably seen them make a frequent mistake: They let the mouse pointer move ever so slightly while performing a double-click. Because the pointer was moving, Windows interprets their action as a really small move instead of a double-click. You can change the sensitivity for this interpretation.

Locate the key HKEY_CURRENT_USER\Control Panel\Desktop. Create two new string values called DoubleClickHeight and DoubleClickWidth. Set the data for the values to string numbers, where the numbers you enter are given in pixels. You'll want to experiment with these settings, but start with setting each one to 5 or 10. Restart Windows to check the setting.

Disabling Window Animation

Windows animates the openings and closings of windows, making it easier for novices to see what their computer is doing. This animation takes a little bit of time, however, and can slow down more advanced users. You can make Windows seem livelier if you disable these animations.

Locate the key HKEY_CURRENT_USER\Control Panel\Desktop\WindowMetrics. Create a new string value called MinAnimate, and set its value to 0 (a 1 means to enable animations). Minimize and maximize a window to remember what it looks like, and then restart Windows and do the same thing again. You'll notice that windows open and close faster with the animations off.

Changing User Information

An individual's name and company are provided during a Windows installation. You can see this information if you open the System Control Panel and look at the first tab. Using the Registry Editor, you can easily change these values if needed, such as when a new person is hired at your company and inherits a computer used by another person.

Locate the key HKEY_LOCAL_MACHINE\SOFTWARE\Microsoft\Windows\CurrentVersion. In this key, you will see two values: RegisteredOrganization and RegisteredOwner. Simply change the data for those two values to whatever information you want to use.

Conclusion

In this chapter you learned about the Windows Registry—what it is, how it's structured, how it works, and how to manipulate it. You learned how to use Registry Editor, the main tool for working with the Registry. You also learned about backing up and restoring the Registry, and about doing remote administration with the Registry.

This chapter concludes the section on Configuring Windows 98. In this section, you learned everything you should need to know about the Registry, the Control Panel, User Profiles, Hardware Profiles, System Policies, and how these different features work together to let you configure and manage Windows 98 systems.

Part III of this book, "Windows 98 Operations," details Windows 98's architecture, followed by a number of chapters about working with and supporting Windows 98.

Windows 98 Operations

11	Windows 98 Architecture and Application Support	231
12	Supporting Devices	261
13	Printing	283
14	Multimedia	305
15	OLE, COM, DCOM, and ActiveX	353
16	Windows 98 ODBC Connectivity	379
17	File Systems: File and Disk Resources	403
18	Viruses in Windows 98	431
19	Windows 98 for Portables	441
20	Backup and Restore	453

Windows 98 Architecture and Application Support

If a surgeon knew all the best surgical techniques, all the different procedures, and all the proper practices for surgery but didn't understand the underlying reasons for all those things, you probably wouldn't want that surgeon operating on you, would you? On a different but related note, a musician who knows and can play a large number of songs can't really improvise unless he or she understands the underlying musical theory.

To be a top-notch Windows 98 professional, you have to understand the fundamental design and architecture of the operating system. Understanding its capabilities, limitations, and design can help you solve problems that arise in different situations. In this chapter, you learn about the fundamentals of Windows 98: its architecture, how it multitasks, what programming models it supports, how it uses memory, how it handles its drivers, and so forth.

Understanding the Architecture of Windows 98

Before exploring the architecture of an operating system such as Windows 98, you must first ask what an operating system needs to do. Broadly speaking, today's operating systems are expected to do the following:

- Manage the hardware resources of a computer. The operating system is the only entity that directly addresses the computer's hardware.

- Provide interfaces to the hardware for the end-user, the administrator, and the applications.

- Coordinate the activities of multiple applications, all running simultaneously.

- Ease application developers' burdens by providing system services such as font rendering, window and menu management, printer rasterizing or bitmapping, and support for storage systems.

- Provide a user interface with which the end user can interact with the computer and his or her applications.

All these tasks are designed to make the user of the system as productive as possible. In the following sections, you learn how Windows 98 does these things. The sections are arranged according to the different areas, which together provide the operating system's management of the system.

Multitasking and Scheduling

Even in the days of DOS, people wanted to be able to run multiple applications at the same time. When a computer using a single-tasking operating system (such as DOS) is busy downloading a file for several hours or printing a large report, for example, it can't be used for any other purpose. Various attempts were made to try to mimic multitasking behavior under DOS—such as the various Terminate-and-Stay-Resident (TSR) programs that performed some work in the background or products such as DesqView or TopView—but all these solutions were essentially unsatisfying.

Note Throughout this discussion, you will see references to *applications*, *tasks*, or *processes* when we talk about software programs. In this context, all these terms

> refer to the same thing: discrete software programs running on the computer. These software programs include actual applications software, device drivers, operating system processes, and so on.

Computers with a single processor never really do more than one thing at a time, but they're fast enough that they can be made to appear to do many things at once. *Multitasking* is basically: the ability to run multiple programs—or tasks—"at the same time." When you think about it, building this illusion and making it seamless to the user is quite complicated. Consider that the microprocessor and the memory in the system must be constantly doing small pieces of work for all the running applications, each with its own set of data, hardware requirements, and so forth. Coordinating these activities reliably is immensely complicated.

All multitasking operating systems divide the processor's time into units called time slices. A *time slice* is the smallest unit of time that can be allocated to a program. Under Windows 98, a time slice lasts only about twenty milliseconds (depending on the processor speed and its architecture). Depending on the needs of the applications and the system, an application may be allocated one time slice or many time slices before another task gets to use the processor. Determining which tasks get which time slices, and how they arrange their activity, is called *scheduling*.

Note In Windows 98, a time slice is sometimes called a *quantum*.

Cooperative Versus Preemptive Multitasking

There are two main ways of building a multitasking system: cooperative multitasking and preemptive multitasking. A *cooperative multitasking system* relies on all the tasks running on the system to cooperate in sharing the processor. The system trusts each application to use the processor and then give it up voluntarily when the application has completed some atomic process. Then the next application does the same thing. All the running applications continue to do this in a *round-robin* fashion: Imagine all the applications in a circle, each one passing the ball (that is, the processor) to the next application, around and around.

In most cooperative multitasking schemes, there are both explicit and implicit yields. A *yield* is the process through which an application signals to the operating system that it's okay for the next application to commence work. An *explicit yield* is when an application literally sends a signal to the operating system saying, "I'm through for a moment, so you can give the next program a turn." Programmers of software running under a cooperative multitasking system issue explicit yield commands in their programs to do this.

An *implicit yield* is when the application performs some operation that implies that the operating system is free to let another application do some work while the first application's operation completes. An example of an implicit yield under Windows 3.1 is when an application makes a request of the operating system to retrieve some data from a hard disk. The operating system receives the request and sends the request to the hard disk interface card to process. While the hard disk controller and the disk itself are busy retrieving the data (this may take several seconds), the operating system can let other applications do some work on the processor until the hard disk interface signals that it's ready to provide the requested data through a signal on one of the processor's interrupt request lines (IRQs). The requesting application doesn't have to explicitly signal a yield in this case; the yield is assumed with certain operations.

Cooperative multitasking operating systems are the easiest kind to build (although they are still much more complicated than single-tasking operating systems). However, there are many problems with cooperative multitasking systems. The chief problem is that most software programs have a tendency to "hog" the system and aren't well written in terms of being truly cooperative. (In other words, they don't play well together). In addition, if an application crashes while it owns the processor, there may not be any way for the operating system to detect that occurrence and terminate the offending application gracefully—resulting in a hung computer. If you are running many applications, all presumably having important data, failures like this can cost much more in productivity than the multitasking features added to begin with. In addition to the risk of crashing the system, many programs running under a cooperative scheme are almost guaranteed to *not* cooperate consistently, so you almost always end up with "jerky" behavior from the system.

A *preemptive multitasking system* is very different in concept from a cooperative system. A preemptive system keeps control of the processor and can preempt a program that's using the processor at any time (thus the name). In a preemptive scheme, programs don't have to worry about yielding the processor to other programs; the operating system takes care of all those details and can more fairly and reliably apportion the finite resources of the system to all the programs using the system. In a preemptive scheme, a single program cannot "hog" the system, whether it wants to or not, or whether it's well written or badly written. Although a badly written application can make excessive demands of the system, the operating system ensures that all running programs get a fair chance to use the system resources. The user is left with the impression of a much more smoothly multitasking system, and is generally more productive using such a system.

Time Slicing Versus Managed Scheduling

Different programs have different needs. For example, software that provides network services generally expects the operating system to let it do its work whenever required, without waiting around for other, less time-sensitive programs to do their work. For example, if you're running Personal Web Server services under Windows 98, you don't want the Web services to stop responding to requests just because your system is busy printing a document. The way an operating system determines the priorities of different running programs and apportions system time to them is known as *scheduling*.

Cooperative systems have relatively unsophisticated scheduling mechanisms—if they have any at all. Many operate in a true round-robin fashion, in which every program has the same priority as any other program. Some cooperative schemes have rudimentary scheduling, with which the user of the system can assign different "weights" to different programs (DesqView did this, for example). For example, all else being equal, you may want your email program to be given fewer time slices on the system than your word processing program. Windows 3.1 had a very basic scheduling scheme with which you could weight the foreground and background priority, but it wasn't application specific. All these scheduling schemes are called *time-slicing* scheduling mechanisms.

A system that uses managed scheduling, on the other hand, lets each program signal its priority needs when it starts. The operating system takes care of doling out the processor's time based on the priorities claimed by the programs. A program can also signal that it temporarily requires a higher priority for some task; it is the application's responsibility to lower its own priority after it finishes the critical task. The priority of a program can be elevated (also called *boosting*) under certain circumstances. Generally, priority boosts occur in the following situations:

- A program signals that it temporarily needs a higher priority.

- The priority of a program running in the foreground is typically boosted above background programs to make the system more responsive to the user.

- The operating system can boost the priority of a program to avoid locking some resource of the system (more on this later in this chapter).

- A user can signal that he or she wants an application to run at a higher priority. (In the world of Windows, this is possible only with Windows NT, where you can choose to manually boost a process's priority.)

Before discussing program priorities in more detail, you must first have a better understanding of another topic: processes and threads.

Understanding Processes and Threads

Until now, we've discussed only generic programs, meaning any software running on the system. To continue the overall discussion of Windows 98's architecture, you must understand how programs are structured in the system, which means that you have to understand processes and threads.

Under single-tasking operating systems and some multitasking operating systems, a *process* is a program—a series of machine code instructions—along with all the resources of the program.

These resources include memory addresses allocated to the program, hardware devices the program has reserved for its exclusive use, memory variables, and so forth.

Process-based multitasking operating systems have a big inherent weakness: If an application program has to do simultaneous work (such as printing a document while it also paginates), it does so by starting up an entirely new process to do that alternate work. The problem is that each process is a complete entity and must have its own memory space and other resources. Two processes being operated by a single application program have to pass a lot of data back and forth through a process called *interprocess communication*. Starting processes to do relatively simple tasks (such as spell-checking the last word the user entered in a word processor) is very expensive in terms of overhead requirements. It's almost as if the program has to create a complete clone of itself to do additional simultaneous work—and then the clones have to spend a lot of time talking to one another so that they can get their jobs done in sync.

To answer this need, a concept called *threading* was introduced many years ago. The idea is this: In a multitasking, multithreaded operating system, each process is still a complete program, with program code, memory addresses, and so forth, but it doesn't do *any* work. Instead, each process has at least one *thread of execution* (called Thread 0) which actually performs the work. A process must have at least one thread, but it can also have as many threads as it needs. Here's the neat thing: All the threads within a process share the resources of the process. A program can create new threads without having to copy a lot of data for the threads to use; all the threads use the same resources. Programs that use multithreading techniques can appear to do many things at once, and little overhead is required to accomplish this.

Programs written using the Win32 Application Programming Interface (API) can be multithreaded. It's entirely up to the needs (and abilities) of the programmer.

How Windows 98 Schedules Threads

Windows 98 allows both processes and threads to have their own priority levels, and it apportions the processor's time based on those priority levels. When a process is created in the system, it specifies its own *base priority class*. The threads within the process, unless otherwise specified, share that base priority class.

There are four different priority classes for Win32 programs under Windows 98:

- **Idle Priority Class.** Threads running at the idle priority class are allocated processor time only when no other higher-priority threads on the system have work to do. Programs that should be set at the idle priority class are those that should work only when there is nothing else to do on the system (for example, screen savers or background spell checkers).

- **Normal Priority Class.** Most programs running on the system run at the normal priority class. This class is for standard applications (and their threads) such as word processors, spreadsheets, database programs, and so forth.

- **High Priority Class.** This class is the highest class generally used. Threads at a high priority class are those that must respond to time-sensitive events. An example is a process that validates users logging in to the system or that provides database services to other network users. When a thread has to do its work regardless of other programs running at the normal priority class, that thread should be assigned high priority class.

- **Real-Time Priority Class.** This class is the highest priority class in the system. Threads at this level can actually preempt system functions such as updating the mouse pointer or responding to keyboard input. Only threads that do very short intervals of work but that require all the resources of the system during these brief intervals should be set to this priority class.

Within each priority class are 32 different levels, from 0 (the lowest priority within the class) to 31 (the highest priority within the class). When you combine the 4 classes with the 32 levels, you see that there are 128 distinct priority levels within Windows 98.

For programming ease, the 32 priority levels within each class are divided into seven requested levels. When a thread is created within a priority class, the programmer can easily set its priority using one of these levels. From lowest priority to highest, the levels are IDLE, LOWEST, BELOW NORMAL, NORMAL, ABOVE NORMAL, HIGHEST, and TIME CRITICAL. Often, the thread of a program that processes the program's user interface is set to ABOVE NORMAL or HIGHEST so that the application is responsive; other threads are set to NORMAL or BELOW NORMAL, depending on the work they do.

When a thread is created, it has a *base priority level*. It also has a *dynamic priority level*, which is adjusted by the operating system's scheduler. At certain times, a thread's dynamic priority level may be boosted by the scheduler. Threads with a priority level of 0 through 15 can receive dynamic boosts; threads with a priority level of 16 through 31 cannot. Here are the three main circumstances in which a thread's priority can be boosted by the scheduler:

- When a process is moved from the background to the foreground by a user, the scheduler boosts that process's priority (and therefore the priorities of its threads) to ensure that the priorities of the process and its threads are higher than those of background programs running at the same class (for example, those at normal priority class). When the user moves the process back into the background, the priorities of the process and all its threads are returned to their original base settings.

- Threads can get a priority boost when they receive a message from a device, so that they have a better chance of processing that new message in a timely fashion. Any threads associated with a window that receives messages from a device are boosted.

- Sometimes, a thread can be *blocked* (that is, it must wait for some event to complete before it can do more work). For example, a thread may request data from a hard disk and then it is blocked (the scheduler won't give it any processor time) pending the satisfaction of that request. (It makes sense that the thread is blocked because it doesn't have any work to do until it gets its requested data.) When the request is satisfied, the scheduler in Windows 98 boosts the thread's priority level so that it can process the results it just received.

There is one other case in which a thread's priority is boosted: *priority inversion*. When a high priority thread depends on the results of a low priority thread, the low priority thread is temporarily boosted up to the level of the high priority thread for as long as the dependency exists. In a sense, the system recognizes that the low priority thread in this case is really an extension of the high priority thread, and so raises its priority. If priority inversion did not occur, situations could arise in which the high-low thread dependency could become stuck by a thread running at an intermediate level.

When threads are boosted by a dynamic priority boost from the scheduler, the scheduler reduces the priority of the threads by one level for each time slice they complete until they return to their base level. A thread is never forced to run at a priority level lower than its base priority level.

When multiple threads are set to the same level, and all are "ready to run" (in other words, are unblocked), the scheduler apportions processor time to each of the threads in a round-robin fashion.

Understanding Semaphores, Waits, and Critical Sections

Consider a process with many threads. Each of the threads can access the memory objects within the process. It is possible that while one thread is writing new data to a memory object, another thread may be reading that same data. In another case, two threads may try to write new data at the same time to the same memory location. Either of these situations could cause catastrophe and unpredictable results. As you can see, programmers need a way to coordinate access to the resources within the process so that threads aren't constantly "stepping on each others' toes."

Several mechanisms are available to let programmers perform this coordination. The first of these mechanisms are semaphores. Named for the flags used to signal trains (and keep them from accidentally colliding), a *semaphore* is also sometimes referred to as a *flag*. When a program creates a memory object that may be used by different threads, it attaches a semaphore to that memory object. The semaphore is then checked by each thread before that thread tries to access the memory object. If the semaphore signals that another thread is using the object, the intruding thread waits until the semaphore indicates that the object is available; the thread then sets the semaphore to indicate that it now owns the memory object temporarily. Semaphores can be created for other resources the process uses or accesses, or for any other purpose of the programmer for which this mechanism is helpful. Semaphores can be created to allow more than one thread to access the resource; for example, you can specify that a certain number of threads at once are allowed access to the resource.

Chapter 11: Windows 98 Architecture and Application Support

Another coordination mechanism is a *mutex object*, which is a different breed of semaphore. A mutex ensures mutually exclusive access to a resource (thus the name).

Win32 threads under Windows 98 can also use *wait functions*, or *waits*, that can set specific criteria. When the criteria are met, the scheduler lets the threads continue. The wait criteria can be for a single object to become free, for multiple objects to become free, or for an object to become free and for something else to happen that the thread has to process (called an *alertable wait*).

Semaphores and wait functions can be used when a thread has to wait to use an object owned by any process in the system. When a thread is waiting for an object within its own process, it can use a mechanism called a *critical section* to coordinate access between itself and other threads within the same process. Because critical sections work within a single process, they carry less overhead than the other mechanisms.

Understanding the Windows 98 Memory Model

The early versions of the Intel family of processors used a segmented memory architecture to allow programs to access up to 1M of memory space. Early programs were limited to only 16 bits of memory addresses, yielding only 64K of addressable memory space. With the 8088 Intel processor, Intel crafted an additional 4 bits of memory addressing onto the chip (20 bits total), but to maintain compatibility with the 16-bit programs already in existence, Intel broke the memory into 16-bit (64K) chunks, called *segments*. Programs that wanted to access more than 64K of memory space had to access the memory by specifying two addresses: a segment and an offset. (Offsets were the actual address within the 64K segment.) Notice that the 20-bit addressing scheme yields 1M of addressable memory. Because the original PC set aside 384K of that 1M for the hardware devices in the computer, you can see where the original 640K memory limit came from—it was a function of both DOS's 16/20-bit design and the hardware design for which DOS was originally built.

Beginning with the 80386 chip, Intel packaged 32 bits of memory addressing onto the processor chips. (32 bits lets you access up to 4G of memory.) Although this allowed for full 32-bit addresses (a *flat memory model* without segment and offset addresses), earlier DOS and Windows operating systems couldn't take advantage of it.

Windows 98 uses the flat memory model. Each memory address on the system is specified using 32 bits, giving each program the capability to address up to 4G of memory. However, this brings up some interesting questions: If each program can address up to 4G of memory, and if you can have multiple programs, does that mean that you can have more than 4G of memory in the system? How is that possible when there are only 32 bits' worth of addressing on the processor itself? And when you think about it, any Windows 98 system addresses a lot more physical memory than actually exists on the system (which is certainly less than 4G). These questions lead to the next discussion: *virtual memory*, a key component of Windows 98 and virtually all modern operating systems.

Virtual Memory

The current Intel family of processors has a feature called *paging*. When paging is disabled on the processor, there is a 1:1 correlation between a memory address and a location in a physical memory chip (RAM, generally). When paging is disabled, the processor can address up to 4G of physical memory, and programs can access all that memory. But all that memory must be actual RAM when the paging feature is disabled.

However, virtually all modern operating systems, including Windows 98, operate with the paging feature of the processor enabled. When paging is enabled, there is no longer a 1:1 correlation between a memory address used by a program and a physical memory location. Instead, the operating system and processor maintain tables that let them locate a specific physical memory address for each *logical memory address* used.

The system divides up all memory in the system into 4K *pages* (this is where the name *paging* comes from). A 32-bit address used by an application is translated into a physical address using a table. The first 20 bits of a 32-bit memory address locate a specific page of memory. Thus, the system can manage a little more than 1 million 4K pages at a time. The remaining 12 bits specify an actual address within the selected page.

Why does the system maintain complicated tables to resolve a memory address? Wouldn't it be easier to simply map a memory address directly to a physical memory location, where address 11245 meant physical memory address 11245, for example? The reason is that the system must implement *virtual memory*, where both physical RAM in the system and emulated memory in a disk file both serve as addressable memory. Because the system must be free to move memory data between RAM and the virtual memory file, the system must keep track of where all the memory is at any given time. Managing this on a byte-by-byte basis would bog the system down unnecessarily, making it figure out whether each memory address was in virtual memory or real RAM. Instead, the system manages 4K pages of memory. Entire 4K pages of memory—not individual bytes—are moved back and forth between the virtual memory file on the disk and real RAM. Using this scheme, the overall system is more efficient.

As far as the applications on the system are concerned, each 32-bit address is simply that: a 32-bit address indicating a specific memory location. The operating system, however, needs a way to figure out whether the memory is in RAM or in the paging file, and so this scheme of memory indirection is used.

Windows 98 implements a memory page management system called *demand paging*. In this system, memory pages are preferentially kept in real RAM based on how recently they have been used (how much they are in demand). Memory pages that are least recently used (LRU) are moved to the paging file on a hard disk. The system constantly examines the pages of memory and their usage history to determine which pages can most likely be moved to the paging file. When an application requests a memory address for a page of data that has been moved to the paging file, the operating system transparently moves the page back into physical RAM before letting the application continue working with the page. The thread requesting the page is blocked automatically until the transfer occurs (it's typically a fairly fast operation).

Paging schemes such as the one used by Windows 98 are a great boon to users—and are virtually required with a multitasking operating system in which many software components and memory objects are in use at one time. When you're using a word processor, its memory pages (or at least the memory pages relating to the features you're using at that time) are kept in RAM; programs and memory objects that are loaded but not doing anything are paged to the paging file, ready to be called back at a moment's notice. Virtual memory lets the system accomplish much more work than it could otherwise and lets the system process much larger programs (and many more of them) than would be possible without paging.

The danger with virtual memory systems (from a performance standpoint) is a condition called *thrashing*. Thrashing occurs when multiple programs are running, all of which combined require more memory pages than can fit in the physical RAM of the system. The system *thrashes* as it constantly moves memory pages back and forth from the paging file, trying to satisfy all the running applications at once. When this happens, you have only two courses of action: You can reduce the program load by running fewer programs (or by reducing the amount of data with which they have to work) or you can add more physical RAM to the system.

Tip | Because of the way virtual memory works, you can sometimes accomplish more work with a system by doing your work in sequence rather than in parallel (simultaneously). If you have enough RAM for all the programs, running them simultaneously accomplishes the work about as fast as running the programs sequentially. If you overburden RAM by opening all your programs at once, however, you can get better results by running the programs sequentially because you avoid the severe performance penalty that thrashing entails.

Under Windows 98, you can manage the virtual memory settings for the system using the System Control Panel. Chapter 35, "Tools and Strategies for Optimizing Windows 98," contains details about these settings.

Memory Protection

Windows 98 is essentially a 32-bit protected-memory operating system. It's called *protected* because the system ensures that programs don't improperly access the memory of other programs. Each process owns its own memory pages; if another program inadvertently tries to access a memory page that it doesn't own, it is denied access. This protection scheme helps prevent bugs in one program from corrupting the memory of other programs.

The Intel architecture supports a concept called *privilege rings*. A privilege ring is really just a way of sorting all the memory of the system in a useful way. Intel processors allow up to four different privilege rings (Rings 0 through 3), but only two are implemented by Windows 98 and Windows NT: Ring 0 and Ring 3.

Different programs run at different privilege rings. The operating system and processor know at which ring each program runs and restrict its access to memory based on that ring. Programs running at Ring 0 have unrestricted access to all the memory of the system; programs running at Ring 3 have restricted access to memory. A program running at Ring 0 can access any memory, including memory "owned" by any processes at any other rings. Programs running at Ring 3 can access only their own memory. This scheme is enforced by the processor hardware of the computer and is supported by the operating system.

It is desirable to restrict the software running at Ring 0 to only the most trusted areas of the operating system, which require Ring 0 access to do their work. Everything else—including application programs and parts of the operating system that don't require Ring 0 access—should run at Ring 3. The Windows 98 kernel (the core of the operating system) runs at Ring 0, as do various performance-sensitive components such as video drivers. Programs running at Ring 0 operate much more quickly than those running at Ring 3 because there is no memory protection mechanism slowing down their ability to access system memory.

Windows 98 divides memory in a way that supports privilege rings. Within the total 4G memory address space, applications and their data are restricted to occupying the first 2G of memory addresses (although real-mode device drivers exist in the first 640K). The next 1G of memory addresses are occupied by core operating system components and DLLs. The final 1G of memory addresses are restricted to Ring 0 software (the fundamental core software of Windows 98). Figure 11.1 shows you this layout. (Tip: This information may be on the MCSE test.)

Figure 11.1
The Windows 98 memory address space.

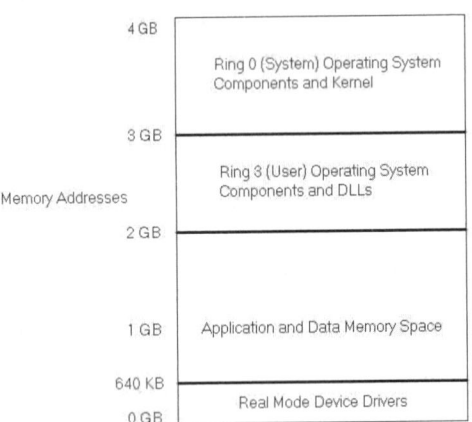

Understanding Windows 98 Components

A number of different components make up the architecture of Windows 98. The following sections discuss each component and how it fits into the overall scheme. Figure 11.2 shows the overall arrangement of these components.

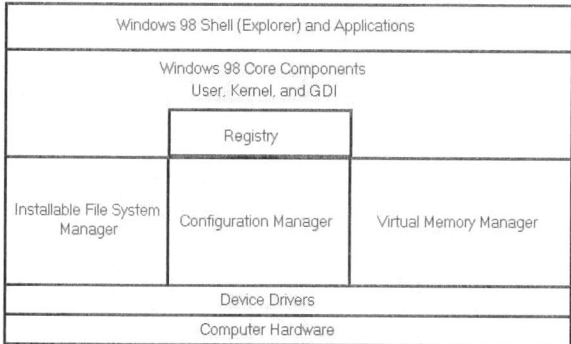

Figure 11.2
Overall arrangement of Windows 98 components.

Device Drivers

Interacting directly with the computer's hardware, device drivers are software entities customized to work with each different possible hardware device. Device drivers exist for different video cards, different hard disk subsystems, different communication and printer ports, different modems and printers, and so forth. Device drivers are customized for the hardware components with which they interact. For example, a device driver that knows how to talk to a SCSI hard disk is different from a driver that knows how to talk to an EIDE-based hard disk.

Because device drivers interact directly with the hardware with which they communicate and serve as the ultimate interface between the hardware and the rest of the system, they are thought to be at the lowest possible level of the system's architecture.

Windows 98 makes use of a universal driver/minidriver design that makes individual device drivers simpler and more robust. For example, there is a universal modem driver (called UNIMODEM.DRV) that knows how to talk to all modems that use an AT command set. Working in concert with the universal driver is a minidriver that knows how a particular model of modem behaves. This duality reduces the complexity of developing individual modem minidrivers because the universal driver already has most of the logic required for devices of that general type.

New to Windows 98 is a Unified Device Driver model; in this model, drivers for Windows NT and Windows 98 can be the same. By adding certain simulated Windows NT kernel services to a DLL running in Windows 98, vendors can now develop single drivers for both operating system targets.

What Is a DLL?

Dynamic Link Libraries (DLLs) are files containing executable program code that can be shared by different components of a single application—or even other applications on the system. In fact, some core components of Windows itself are implemented as

continues

> *continued*
>
> DLLs, partly so that applications can make use of the routines included in those DLL files.
>
> When an application links to a DLL, it can then call routines within the DLL file to do work for the application. DLLs allow applications to be much smaller than they would be otherwise because they keep common code in a single location instead of forcing each separate `.EXE` file to contain all the functions it has to call.

Many device drivers in the system are called *virtual device drivers* (VxDs), which are each assigned to a particular piece of hardware in the system. The *x* in VxD refers to the actual type of device driver: A printer driver is a VPD, a display driver is a VDD, and so forth. The actual virtual device driver files in Windows 98 all have a `.VXD` extension.

Configuration Manager

Above device drivers in the architecture of Windows 98 components are three system components: Configuration Manager, Virtual Machine Manager, and the Installable File System Manager. Configuration Manager is the system component that handles Plug and Play devices (and functionality) on the system. Configuration Manager is responsible for coordinating all the IRQs, DMA ports, I/O port addresses, and other system resources for all the installed devices. Configuration Manager ensures that no device uses the resources needed by other devices; when there is a conflict, Configuration Manager has the power to change the settings for a device to avoid conflict.

The Configuration Manager uses *bus enumerators* to build a tree of all the hardware in a Windows 98 system. A bus enumerator is a driver that can enumerate (list) all the devices connected to a particular bus, such as EISA or PCI buses. The hardware tree is a hierarchical listing of devices on the system, starting at the root of the tree, expanding into different buses, and including the devices on each bus. You can view the hardware tree for a given system by opening Registry Editor and navigating to the key `HKEY_LOCAL_MACHINE/Enum`.

When Configuration Manager detects a conflict in the resource requirements for different hardware devices, it invokes a *resource arbitrator* to resolve the difficulty automatically.

As the system boots and any device configuration problems are resolved, Configuration Manager notifies the supporting device drivers of the exact configuration of each device in the system.

Virtual Machine Manager

The second operating system component above device drivers (that is, the second component that can talk directly to device drivers), the Virtual Machine Manager is responsible for virtualizing access to all the devices in the computer. *Virtual machines* are emulated, complete computers that exist in memory. For different purposes, different virtual machines are created as needed.

All of Windows 98 itself and any Windows-based applications run within one virtual machine, called the System Virtual Machine. Each MS-DOS application running on the system gets its own private virtual machine. Separate virtual machines are required for MS-DOS applications because most MS-DOS applications—being written for a single-tasking operating system—are written as if they own the complete computer. They make direct hardware calls, manipulate hardware directly, and so forth. Because this behavior can't be tolerated in a multitasking operating system in which other applications have to run, each MS-DOS application gets its own virtual machine, which emulates the hardware devices in the computer and prevents the MS-DOS application from monopolizing those devices. (The DOS programs just *think* they're monopolizing the devices!)

The Virtual Machine Manager (VMM) is also responsible for process scheduling, virtual memory management, and of course MS-DOS support. The VMM is an essential part of the system and plays a crucial role in the operation of Windows 98.

Through the efforts of the VMM, Windows 98 supports both preemptive and cooperative multitasking. All Win32 applications are preemptively multitasked with respect to one another and to the system itself. All MS-DOS applications are also preemptively multitasked with respect to one another and to the system itself. Win16 applications developed for Windows 3.1, however, are all cooperatively multitasked with respect to each other (because Windows 3.1 only supported cooperative multitasking for Windows applications developed for Windows 3.1—known as Win16 applications).

Another service provided by the VMM is virtual memory management. Under Windows 98, each process can access up to 2G of logical memory addresses. The upper 2G of logical memory addresses (within the total 4G limit) is reserved for shared code and for the operating system itself.

Installable File System Manager

The Installable File System Manager (IFSM) manages the installable file systems in Windows 98. An *Installable File System* (IFS) is a sort of driver that provides file system services to the operating system. Different IFSs provide access to FAT16, FAT32, CD-ROM, and network file systems. Because the Windows 98 system uses file systems that are installable, support for other file systems is possible: The file system support must merely be developed, and then it can be easily installed into Windows 98 to add support for that file system. For example, when the FAT32 file system was developed and deployed for Windows 95 OSR2, the operating system didn't have to be changed; support for the new file system was added using the Installable File System Manager.

Installable File Systems insulate applications from dealing with the peculiarities of each different file system. An application (as well as the OS itself) doesn't have to worry about how files are stored on a CD-ROM, FAT16, FAT32, or network file system. Instead, the file system driver handles the interaction with the file system itself and interprets the results for the operating system and applications.

Installable File Systems run at Ring 0 privilege level, giving them greater speed. They also use full 32-bit paths for moving data between the operating system and the file system, also adding to their performance.

The Core Components

Above the device drivers and the three next-level components sit the Windows 98 core components. The so-called *core components* include the User, Kernel, and GDI components.

The User component handles all input from the user and outputs messages to the system's user interface; it also handles the sound drivers and communication ports. The User component manages the messages within the system. A *message* is an event that occurs when a user minimizes or closes a window, presses a key on the keyboard, or moves or uses the mouse. Messages are routed by the User component to the appropriate input queue for the window from which they were sent. Input queues accumulate messages for their applications until the applications process the messages and remove them from the queues.

Each Win32 application in the system can have its own message queue; Win16 applications share a single message queue. Handling message queue logic is integral to the design of applications; because Windows 3.1 supported only a single message queue, the system must provide only a single message queue for Win16 applications to be able to run. Win32-based applications are more sophisticated and can handle their own, private message queues.

The Kernel core component handles the most basic operating system functions such as loading and unloading programs, handling exceptions, and allocating virtual memory.

The final core component is the Graphical Device Interface, called the GDI. The GDI is responsible for all display output, drawing of bitmaps and graphic primitives, and interacting with the display device drivers on the system. The GDI component also provides support to the printing subsystem, which handles printed output from the system.

The Shell

The final Windows 98 architecture component you learn about in this chapter is the shell, a 32-bit application that handles the Windows 98 desktop and Explorer. The shell runs in its own thread, which can be restarted in the event of an error in the shell. Although it runs at the same level as applications in the system, the shell also provides services to those other applications. For example, the shell provides the various Windows 98 user-interface components the applications may use, such as button support, drop-down list boxes, checkboxes, File Open dialog boxes, and so on.

Summarizing the Windows 98 Architecture

As you have seen, Windows 98 is made up of a number of different components, all of which operate in concert to make Windows 98 work and to give it so many capabilities. People used to sneer at the architecture of Windows 3.1; it was a very weak operating system. Windows 98, however, brings all the benefits of a modern multitasking, multithreaded, graphical, protected-mode operating system to common desktop computers. Although Windows 98 does not possess the same "industrial-strength" architecture of Windows NT, it also does not have Windows NT's resource requirements. Moreover, Windows 98 had to make certain architectural sacrifices to continue running Win16 and MS-DOS applications as well as it does. Because there still persist, even today, many applications developed for these older platforms, and because running those applications is a requirement for many users, the sacrifices made in Windows 98 are a fair tradeoff.

Understanding Application Support

An operating system is nothing without applications that can run on it. Any operating system must provide rich support for the widest possible range of applications, which are the actual tools people use to accomplish work with their computers. The design requirements for the Windows 95 and 98 family were stringent and difficult to meet: Windows 95 and 98 must support legacy MS-DOS and Win16 applications and also provide a foundation for a new class of more powerful 32-bit applications that use the Win32 Applications Programming Interface. The following sections explain how Windows 98 supports these different application types.

APIs

Windows 98 supports three different application types: Win32, Win16, and MS-DOS. This section discusses Win32 and Win16 support under Windows 98; a later section discusses MS-DOS support.

When Windows NT 3.1 was developed, a new Applications Programming Interface (API) called Win32 was introduced. The Win32 API is a full 32-bit API that supports modern application features and takes advantage of advanced operating system services. Initially, Win32 was limited to Windows NT. Microsoft later introduced a limited API called Win32s, which was designed for 32-bit application support under Windows 3.1 (with the appropriate services installed), and ultimately for Windows 95 and 98. Maintaining the two APIs was confusing, however. Eventually, a single Win32 API came to be supported, with comments when certain functions in the API required Windows NT or Windows 95 or 98. For example, certain Win32 API functions that involve Windows NT's advanced security do not work under Windows 98. Application developers can write Win32 applications that use only broad functions supported in both families of Windows products, or they can make use of operating system-specific features in the Win32 API that restrict the application to running under only one of the two platforms. (Generally, any Windows 95 or 98 application runs under the latest version of Windows NT; the Win32 API calls supported by Windows 95 and 98 are generally a subset of those supported by Windows NT.)

Win32 applications are the native type of application supported by Windows 98. An application written for Windows 98 using Win32 also takes advantage of all the features of Windows 98, is fully preemptive, can use multiple threads, and so forth. Win32 applications are therefore much more powerful than their Win16 predecessors.

Each Win32 application under Windows 98 runs in its own private, protected memory space, in which its memory is protected from other applications running on the system. Win32 applications can take advantage of long filenames and threads and receive other advantages from the operating system. Generally, Win32 applications are also faster than Win16 applications, all else being equal.

Support for Win16 applications (those originally developed for Windows 3.x) is built into Windows 98. These applications typically run without modification under Windows 98, although a very few restrictions exist. The promise of Windows 95 and 98 was that all Win16 applications would run as well as or better than they did under Windows 3.x. Most often, this goal was met. Because some of the underlying system services of Windows 95 and 98 are much faster than those in Windows 3.x, Win16 applications are faster in the Windows 95 and 98 environment than they were in their original native environment.

All Win16 applications running under Windows 98 share a single virtual machine, in which they cooperatively multitask with respect to one another. The virtual machine they share, however, is preemptively multitasked with respect to the rest of the system. Although you cannot say that Win16 applications are preemptively multitasked because their virtual machine is, you can say that they are "sort of preemptive" when there is only a single Win16 application running at one time. The sharing of a single virtual machine means, however, that if one Win16 application crashes, chances are that all the other Win16 applications will also crash. The good news is that the crashes are restricted to the VM in which they run and should not affect the rest of the system.

OLE Support

Integral to Win32 and Win16 applications is their support for a system service called Object Linking and Embedding (OLE, pronounced like the *Olé!* of a bullfighter). OLE is a technology that lets Windows applications share their data with one another, managed by the user. The biggest reason to support OLE within an application is so that entities called *compound documents* can be created and used by the application. A compound document is one that incorporates document objects from other applications installed on the system. For example, Word can incorporate Excel objects (such as cell ranges, charts, or entire worksheets) into a Word document and can also incorporate PowerPoint objects (such as individual slides or drawing objects). OLE allows you to build documents that incorporate the features of all the OLE applications installed on a system, seamlessly and easily.

OLE is covered in detail in Chapter 15, "OLE, COM, DCOM, and ActiveX."

MS-DOS Support

Even today, literally thousands of MS-DOS applications are still useful and are still required by users. Windows 95 and 98 had to support those DOS applications, or people would not have been able to make full use of Windows 95 and 98 and would have had to wait for all those applications to be ported to one of the Win*XX* APIs to use them. Unfortunately, MS-DOS applications are not designed to run in a multitasking operating system. Because they were developed for a single-tasking operating system that allowed them complete access to system memory and the computer hardware, they often make use of programming techniques that are anathema in a multitasking environment. Supporting MS-DOS applications is therefore a complex undertaking for the operating system.

Each MS-DOS application under Windows 98 runs in its own private virtual machine. The virtual machine *virtualizes* all the hardware devices in the system, insulating the MS-DOS application from the actual hardware. The MS-DOS application thinks it is running on a standalone PC running only MS-DOS. The MS-DOS application is free to directly manipulate its hardware. Although this is how it appears to the MS-DOS application, the reality is that the application only manipulates the virtual hardware within the virtual machine. The virtual device drivers then take care of doing the actual hardware interface and of letting other applications in the system share the actual hardware through their interfaces.

MS-DOS applications are not designed for multitasking of any kind whatsoever. They don't support cooperative or preemptive multitasking. Their virtual machine, however, *is* preemptive within the system, and therefore each MS-DOS application behaves as if it is preemptively multitasked. It cannot, however, signal priority requirements to the operating system, although the operating system can sense what it is doing and can take appropriate scheduling actions based on the application's requirements.

Working with MS-DOS applications under Windows 98 is a bit different from working with other types of applications. For one thing, MS-DOS applications must be installed and removed using their native installation and removal procedures rather than using the Windows 98 Add/Remove Programs dialog box. For another thing, each MS-DOS application has many specific settings that can be activated to change how the system supports the application, and these settings are unique to MS-DOS applications.

Installing and Removing MS-DOS Applications

Installing and removing MS-DOS applications is easy. You simply open a command prompt and then follow the application's installation procedures (which usually involves running a program called `SETUP.EXE` or `INSTALL.EXE`). MS-DOS applications do not appear in the Add/Remove Programs dialog box under Windows 98 and so cannot share in the unified program installation management that Win32-based applications make use of. To remove MS-DOS applications, follow the instructions that come with the program.

Installing an MS-DOS application is only half the battle. Afterwards, you'll want to create an entry in the Start menu (or on the desktop) for launching the application. You may also have to customize the Windows 98 settings for MS-DOS applications to enable the application to run as well as possible.

Setting MS-DOS Program Properties

Creating program shortcuts is covered in many other areas, and you probably need no guidance in this area if you're reading this book. Setting an MS-DOS program's properties, however, is a slightly different matter. In this section, you learn about the possible settings and what they do.

To access the settings for a DOS application, right-click the actual program file and choose Properties, or right-click any shortcuts pointing to the program file and choose Properties. You see the program's Properties dialog box, shown in Figure 11.3.

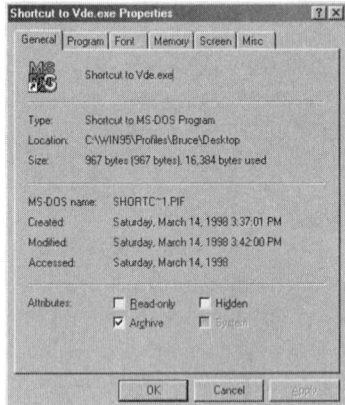

Figure 11.3
A DOS program's Properties dialog box.

When you create a shortcut to a DOS program, you are actually creating a Program Information File (PIF) for the program. The PIF file stores the settings for the program, which are used when the shortcut is used to open the program. If needed, you can have multiple shortcuts to a single program file, each of which has different settings.

| Tip | When you start a DOS program from a command prompt, its PIF settings are not used. |

The following sections discuss each tab of the program's Properties dialog box.

General Page

The General page of a DOS program's Properties dialog box is primarily informational (see Figure 11.3). You see the actual name of the program (or its shortcut name), its 8.3 MS-DOS

Chapter 11: Windows 98 Architecture and Application Support

name, its size and location, and date and time information about the file. There are also four checkboxes that let you control the file attributes of the program file itself (or its PIF, if that's what you're editing). You can choose to set or clear the following attributes:

- **R**ead-Only specifies that the file cannot be erased and cannot be written to or modified.

- **A**rchive means that the file has been modified since the last system backup (either full or incremental) and will be backed up the next time an incremental backup is performed.

- Hi**d**den means that the file cannot be seen in a DIR listing at the DOS prompt (except by certain commands, such as ATTRIB).

- **S**ystem indicates that the program is a system file that is crucial to the proper functioning of the operating system. For some files, the System checkbox may be grayed out and cannot be modified.

Program Page

The Program page (see Figure 11.4) of a DOS program's Properties dialog box contains many important settings that control how the program starts and runs. Table 11.1 details the fields on this page.

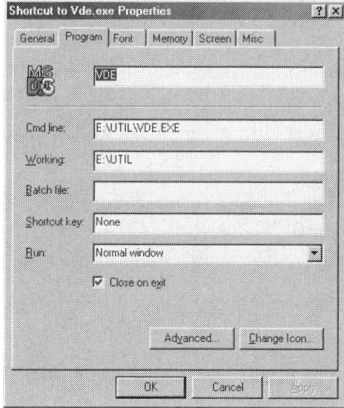

Figure 11.4
The Program page of a DOS program's Properties dialog box.

Table 11.1
Program Page Fields

Field Name	Description
Top field	The top field, which does not have a name, controls the name of the program that appears in the title bar when it is running in a window on your desktop.

continues

Table 11.1, Continued
Program Page Fields

Field Name	Description
Cmd **L**ine	The Cmd **L**ine field specifies the exact filename (or path and filename if the file is not in the defined search path) used to run the program. If the program requires any command-line parameters, add them to this line just as you would if you were typing the command and parameters at a DOS prompt.
Working	Use the **W**orking field to control the working directory the program uses when it starts. When this field is blank, the directory in which the program is stored is used as the working directory. In most cases, this setting should be left unchanged, or the DOS program may not run properly.
Batch File	This field lets you specify a batch file to run whenever the program is started.
Shortcut Key	Use this field to define a key combination that will instantly invoke the program from your Windows 98 desktop. Click in the field and then press the key combination you want to assign. You must include the Ctrl or Alt key (or both keys). If the key combination you choose conflicts with a Windows shortcut key, the combination you define will not work.
Run	Use this field to choose what type of window is used to run the program. Your choices are Normal, Maximized, and Minimized. The program starts using whatever window choice you select.
Close on E**x**it	If this box is checked, the virtual machine that is started to run the program automatically closes when the program terminates.

The Program page also lets you choose a customized CONFIG.SYS and AUTOEXEC.BAT file to be used with the program. To access this feature, click the Ad**v**anced button to display the dialog box shown in Figure 11.5.

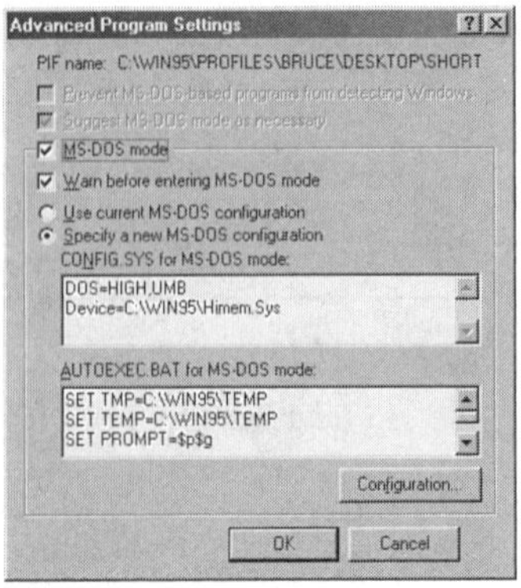

Figure 11.5
A program's Advanced Settings dialog box.

Chapter 11: Windows 98 Architecture and Application Support

You can control how a program starts with the Advanced Settings dialog box. Choose from the following options:

- **P**revent MS-DOS-based Programs From Detecting Windows. Certain DOS programs can detect that they're running under Windows and may refuse to run. Select this checkbox to cause Windows 98 to ignore such queries from DOS programs.

- **S**uggest MS-DOS Mode as Necessary. Some DOS programs run better when Windows 98 is not running. Windows 98 can go into a special MS-DOS mode to support such programs, where only MS-DOS is running on the computer. Choosing this checkbox causes a warning to appear for the user, suggesting this alternate mode when the user runs the program.

- **M**S-DOS Mode. Selecting this checkbox causes MS-DOS mode to be used when the program is started. You can additionally select the **W**arn Before Entering MS-DOS Mode checkbox to alert the user that MS-DOS mode is about to be entered, and offering the user the choice of canceling the application before it begins.

MS-DOS mode removes Windows 98 from memory and starts the system with only MS-DOS running, along with any real-mode drivers that are loaded through the `CONFIG.SYS` or `AUTOEXEC.BAT` files. You use MS-DOS mode to run legacy MS-DOS programs that run poorly under Windows 98, or when MS-DOS application performance is paramount (as is true of MS-DOS–based games). If you are using an MS-DOS program that has problems under Windows 98, MS-DOS mode may allow the program to run without error.

> **Tip** You can enter MS-DOS mode manually by choosing the Shut Down command and then choosing the Restart in **M**S-DOS Mode option.

In the Advanced Settings dialog box, you can define custom `AUTOEXEC.BAT` and `CONFIG.SYS` files for the program by typing the commands you want to use for each. This is useful when you need to load TSR programs or real-mode device drivers to support the MS-DOS program, or when you want to set application-specific environment variables for a particular MS-DOS program. By default, `AUTOEXEC.BAT` and `CONFIG.SYS` are used from the root of the drive from which you booted Windows 98.

When setting a custom `AUTOEXEC.BAT` or `CONFIG.SYS` file for a particular program, you can also choose which system services will be provided to the MS-DOS session by clicking the Con**f**iguration button at the bottom of the dialog box. Doing so displays a new dialog box from which you can choose whether or not Windows 98 will provide EMS memory, disk cache services, DOSKEY services, or direct disk access services to the MS-DOS program.

Finally, the General page lets you choose a new icon for the DOS program. Click the **C**hange Icon button to display the Change Icon dialog box shown in Figure 11.6. Simply select a new icon from the list and click OK to apply the change. You can also click the Bro**w**se button to choose a new `.ICO` file from a folder.

Part III: Windows 98 Operations

Figure 11.6
Use the Change Icon dialog box to choose a new desktop icon for the program.

Font Page

You use the Font page of the program's Properties dialog box to choose the font to be used when the program runs in a window on your desktop. You can also use the Font page to choose the types of fonts available for the program. The Font page is shown in Figure 11.7.

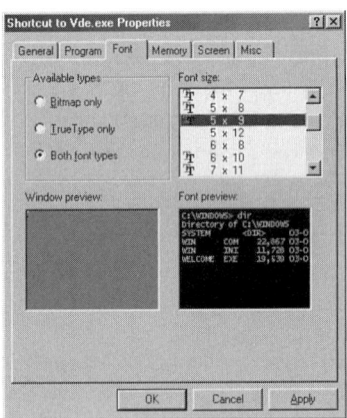

Figure 11.7
The Font page of a DOS program's Properties dialog box.

From the Available Types area of the dialog box, you can choose bitmap fonts, TrueType fonts, or both types of fonts. Generally, choose Both **F**ont Types to have the most choices available.

Tip | On some systems, bitmap fonts may display more quickly than TrueType fonts.

Use the Font Si**z**e window to choose the exact font size you want to use for the DOS program. Sizes are listed in terms of the number of pixels taken up horizontally and vertically. The font size bears a direct relationship to the size of the DOS window, which you can see in the Window Preview box as you select different fonts. You can also preview how the font will appear on your desktop in the Font Preview box. Depending on the type of program you're running, you may want to use a small font that takes up a minimum of screen space; alternatively, you may want to use a large font so that you can clearly see what you are working with.

Memory Page

The Memory page contains a number of settings that control how much memory the program "sees" when it runs. You want to control these settings, because some programs require minimum values if they are to work properly. However, many DOS programs—because they were written for an operating system in which they could take control of the machine—grab all the memory they are aware of and attempt to use it. For example, a spreadsheet program may try to use a full 16M of EMS or XMS memory, even when it's not really needed by the program. Using the Memory page of the Properties dialog box, you can place limits on what the program can use. You see the Memory page in Figure 11.8; Table 11.2 describes its settings.

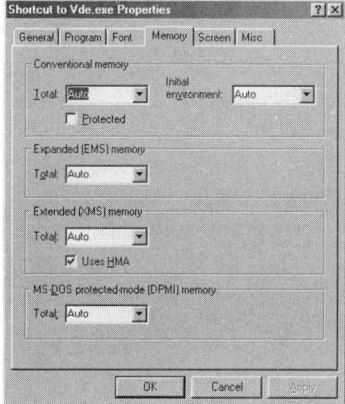

Figure 11.8
The Memory page of a DOS program's Properties dialog box.

Table 11.2
Memory Page Settings

Setting	Description
Conventional Memory	The settings in this section control the amount of conventional memory (memory from 0 to 640K) that the program has available.
Initial En**v**ironment	DOS programs make use of environment variables, and you can control the size of the initial environment provided with this setting.
Protected	Specifies that the program will be run in a more protected mode. Selecting this option may slow the program somewhat, but will help protect certain critical memory structures in Windows 98 itself from the DOS program.

continues

Table 11.2, Continued
Memory Page Settings

Setting	Description
Expanded (EMS) Memory	This setting controls the amount of LIM (Lotus-Intel-Microsoft) expanded memory available to your program. Up to 16M can be allocated.
Extended (XMS) Memory	Controls the amount of XMS memory available to your program. Up to 16M can be allocated.
Uses **H**MA	If your program makes use of the High Memory Area available to XMS-aware programs, select this checkbox.
MS-**D**OS Protected-Mode (DPMI) Memory	Controls the amount of DOS Protected Mode Interface (DPMI) memory available to the program, up to 16M.

Screen Page

The Screen page controls various video-related settings for DOS programs. You see this page in Figure 11.9; Table 11.3 lists the settings available.

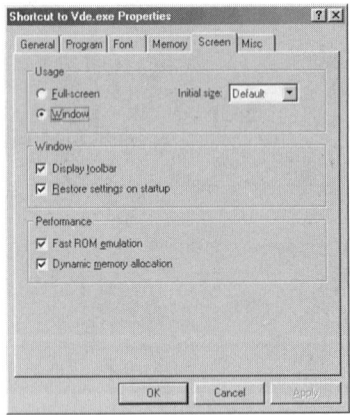

Figure 11.9
The Screen page of a DOS program's Properties dialog box.

Table 11.3
Screen Page Settings

Setting	Description
Full-Screen	Causes the program to start in full-screen mode.
Window	Causes the program to start in windowed mode on your desktop (the settings on the Font page control how the window appears).

Setting	Description
Initial Si**z**e	Some DOS programs can use a larger screen size than the traditional 80 characters wide by 25 characters tall. If you are using such a program, use this setting to control the size of the DOS window.
Display **T**oolbar	Displays an MS-DOS toolbar when the program is run in a window.
Restore Settings on Startup	Restores any settings for the program window when you restart it (window position, size, font selection, and so on). This setting has no effect when you run the program in full-screen mode.
Fast ROM **E**mulation	Selecting this option causes most DOS programs to display more quickly than they otherwise would. However, some DOS programs require access to special features in the ROM on a video card and must have this setting turned off if they are to function.
Dynamic **M**emory Allocation	Some DOS programs switch between graphics mode and text mode. Graphics mode requires more RAM in your system to display properly. If you select this checkbox and switch from a graphics mode to a text mode in your DOS program, the extra memory is released back to the system until you switch back to graphics mode. There is some system overhead in managing this extra memory, so this option should be selected only if your system does not have ample RAM installed.

Misc Page

The final tab in a DOS program's Properties dialog box is the Misc page, which controls a variety of functions. You can see this page in Figure 11.10; Table 11.4 details its options.

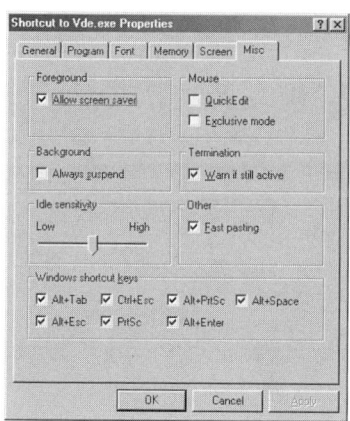

Figure 11.10

The Misc page of a DOS program's Properties dialog box.

Table 11.4
Misc Page Settings

Setting	Description
Allow Screen Saver	When this is selected, your Windows 98 screen saver will run, even when the DOS program is in the foreground. There is a very slight system overhead when this option is selected.
Quick Edit	This option lets you simply drag across a DOS window to select text within it for use with the Clipboard.
Exclusive Mode	This option causes the mouse pointer to work only with the DOS program until the program is exited, even when the program runs in a window.
Always Suspend	Some DOS programs do no useful work when you are not actually using them. For such programs, you can speed up the rest of the system by making them inactive when they are minimized or otherwise placed in the background by selecting this option.
Warn If Still Active	If you select this option, you are warned if you try to terminate this program from Windows NT Workstation while it is still running.
Idle Sensitivity	DOS programs typically poll the keyboard for input; this polling consumes processor cycles. Setting Idle Sensitivity to High causes Windows 98 to assume that the program is merely polling for input sooner, at which point it reduces the amount of processor time allocated to the program to avoid wasting processor resources. Low sensitivity causes Windows 98 to be more lenient in assuming that the program is truly idle.
Fast Pasting	You can copy text from the Windows 98 Clipboard into DOS programs. Two methods accomplish this: When Fast Pasting is selected, the quicker method is used. Some DOS programs cannot accept input in this way, however; in such cases, you should turn this option off.
Windows Shortcut Keys	The selected key combinations are intercepted from being sent to the DOS program and are instead sent to Windows 98 (they are Windows 98 shortcut keys). In some cases, you want your DOS program to accept some of these key combinations. When this is true, clear the checkbox for the key combination you want your DOS program to accept.

Performing a Local Reboot

Any application can freeze up from time to time and become unresponsive to the user and to the operating system. Windows 98 allows you to perform what is called a *local reboot* of such applications, closing them gracefully without affecting other running applications. This feature is enhanced in Windows 98 and works better than it did under Windows 95.

To perform a local reboot, press Ctrl+Alt+Delete to display the Close Program dialog box. Select the offending program (it often displays the Not Responding message next to its name in the list) and click the **E**nd Task button. Windows 98 then attempts to close the program and free up its memory resources. In some cases, after about 20 seconds, you may be prompted that the program is not responding to the Terminate command from Windows 98, and asking whether it's okay to force the application to close.

Conclusion

This chapter covered quite a lot of ground. You learned a great deal about Windows 98 architecture—how it is built and what fundamental capabilities it possesses. You also learned about how it supports the three types of applications you can use with it: Win32, Win16, and MS-DOS applications. For MS-DOS applications, you learned details about how they are configured for the Windows 98 environment.

The next chapter discusses Windows 98 device support in much greater detail. You learn about how Plug and Play works and how various hardware resources in the system are handled (such as IRQs, I/O port addresses, DMAs, and so forth).

Supporting Devices

Devices, devices, devices! Back when PCs were new, there was a straightforward list of devices you could install and use, and the choices from different manufacturers all worked pretty much the same. You had Winchester-type hard disks, floppy disk drives, maybe a serial port or two, a parallel port, a display adapter, and a monitor. Oh, and maybe you had a modem hooked up to one of those serial ports, and a printer connected to a parallel port. The most difficult decision was whether you wanted to use a color graphics adapter or a monochrome display adapter. And all this was accomplished on a single bus type, the Industry Standard Architecture (ISA) bus.

Well, progress being what it is, it was obvious that new devices would have to be invented to take advantage of new techniques that offer better performance and greater capabilities in PCs. Unfortunately, all the old device types still have to be supported, too! (Well, within limits, anyway. For instance, we don't think you can even *get* a driver for a Hercules monochrome graphics adapter card for Windows 98!)

Of course, operating systems in those days were rudimentary beasts, at best. But as device sophistication grew in PCs, operating systems had to improve dramatically to keep up with things—and so that you wouldn't have to hold a PhD in computer science to manage the myriad devices available today and make them all work together.

Windows 95 introduced the idea of Plug and Play (PnP) support in the operating system. Furthermore, Microsoft worked with hardware designers to come up with the hardware portion of PnP, so that with today's computers, setting up devices is generally a snap. Although unique problems can occur, PnP has made support for different devices much easier than in years past.

Note Although it's *de rigueur* to pretend that the PC world is the one, true, personal-computing arena, it's not really true that Windows 95 introduced the idea of Plug and Play support in operating systems. Using no name at all (and, of course, using different specifications), Macintosh computers have long supported the concept of "plug and play." We're not apologists for the many shortcomings of the Macintosh OS, but you have to give Apple credit for making some things much easier than the state of the art at the time, which in the early PC world meant dip switches, jumper blocks, and figuring out IRQs, DMAs, and I/O port addresses on your own.

In this chapter you learn about device support under Windows 98. You'll learn about the technology of device support, about the capabilities Windows 98 includes to support different devices, and how to manage devices.

About Windows 98 Device Support

Windows 98 includes the following key features that enable you (and it) to manage multiple devices in computer systems:

- **Plug and Play device resource mediation**. This technology enables the operating system to mediate resource requests from multiple devices automatically, and communicate appropriate setting information back to Plug and Play devices. Although some people delight in calling this feature "Plug and Pray," the reality is that it works surprisingly well in most systems manufactured since 1996, and even more smoothly in current hardware running Windows 98.

- **Automatic hardware detection.** Using a combination of PnP features and good old bus-scanning and device-querying technology, Windows 98 detects just about any device connected to modern computer systems, including many devices you don't even notice, such as different motherboard resources, different possible bus types, and so forth.

- **Hardware configuration wizards.** Certain devices can be complex to configure, no matter how well PnP works, so Windows 98 provides several hardware configuration wizards that walk less-experienced users through necessary choices to configure certain devices.

- **Control panels.** All devices installed in a Windows 98 system support control panel objects that allow easy access to necessary device configuration choices.

- **Minidriver/Universal driver architecture.** Many devices share certain underlying characteristics. For instance, most modems work with slight variations on the AT modem command set. In cases like this, a universal driver takes care of the most common chores of communicating with and configuring these devices. Specific device manufacturers only have to write minidrivers that modify (usually slightly) the behavior of the universal driver. This model of device driver support makes the system more reliable because writing minidrivers is much easier than writing monolithic device drivers for a particular device, and the universal device driver can be much more thoroughly tested.

- **Hardware device tree.** Windows 98 uses a single tree that includes all installed hardware devices. This tree is stored in the Registry, and can also be viewed by using the Device Manager tab of the System control panel.

- **Registry-based hardware management.** The Windows Registry provides a single location in which to store all configuration information about all the installed devices in a Windows 98 system. Using a single storage location for this information imposes a common structure on all device settings and makes it easier for the system to manage multiple devices.

- **Virtual device drivers.** Because Windows 98 must continue to provide MS-DOS compatibility, it implements 32-bit protected-mode virtual device drivers that enable an MS-DOS application to "think" it is working directly with a device, while still making the actual device usable by other applications on the system, including other MS-DOS applications as well as Win16 and Win32 applications.

- **Hot-pluggable devices.** Windows 98 supports *hot-pluggable* (also called *hot docking*) devices. One of these devices can be inserted or removed from a running system, and the operating system can adequately compensate for the insertion or removal.

Understanding IRQs, DMAs, Memory, and I/O Settings

The nice thing about Windows 98 is that you really don't need to understand IRQs, DMAs, and I/O port addresses, even though they still exist and are vital ways for devices to communicate with the computer system itself. There are times, however, when you will need to know this information—mostly to support legacy hardware devices or to resolve some sort of conflict that Windows 98 can't resolve for itself. To prepare for those times, review the information in the following sections.

About Interrupt Requests (IRQs)

IRQ is short for *Interrupt Request*. Connected to the processor are a number of Interrupt Request lines, which are used by devices to signal the processor that they have data to send to the processor or require some sort of attention by the processor. In the standard PC architecture, there are 16 IRQ lines, divided into two groups of 8 lines. Each hardware device that communicates with the processor over one of the system busses (ISA, EISA, or PCI) uses an IRQ to signal its needs to the processor. On ISA and PCI busses, IRQs are said to be *edge sensitive,* meaning that they can simply signal on and off states by using a single signal level. On the EISA bus, IRQs can be *level sensitive,* with multiple levels of signals, each one supporting a different device, on a single IRQ. The idea on EISA was that devices could share the scarce IRQ lines on the system, but the unfortunate reality is that this doesn't work very well; you should dedicate a single IRQ to a single device that requires one, even on EISA systems. Technically, even on ISA busses, IRQs can be shared among devices, although in such cases two devices cannot use the IRQ at the same time; if there is any chance of this happening, then the IRQ should not be shared. Generally, always try to avoid sharing IRQs. Figure 12.1 shows a standard set of IRQ assignments seen with the System Information utility built into Windows 98.

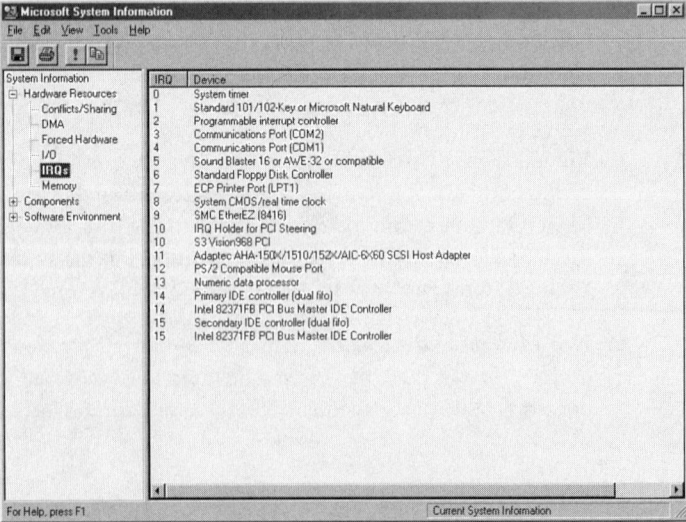

Figure 12.1
IRQ assignments in a standard system.

Chapter 12: Supporting Devices

Note   IRQs are also called *hardware interrupts*. They are completely distinct from *software interrupts*. A software interrupt (Int) is a signal from an application to the operating system, telling the operating system to carry out some function for the program. For instance, you may see references at times to different DOS function interrupts such as Int 27h, or Int 10h, which is used for BIOS calls (and there are many others). The point is, software interrupts shouldn't be confused with hardware interrupts.

Direct Memory Access (DMA)

At times, a device needs to transfer large amounts of data directly into a system's memory, and doesn't require the processor to examine all that transferred memory as it is transmitted. For example, hard disks often transfer a great deal of data into and out of memory at one time, and can use DMA techniques to accelerate this transfer. (Although modern EIDE drives do not use DMA, SCSI hard disks often do.) Other examples include some network interface cards and many sound cards. Such devices can realize significant performance advantages by setting up a Direct Memory Access transfer, in which the system lets them transfer data directly into memory, using certain rules. Generally, DMAs allow data to be transferred into or out of memory without involving the processor, which is free to carry out other tasks while the DMA operation is running. Eight DMA channels (0–7) are available on most PCs. DMA channels cannot be shared between devices. Figure 12.2 shows a typical set of DMA assignments.

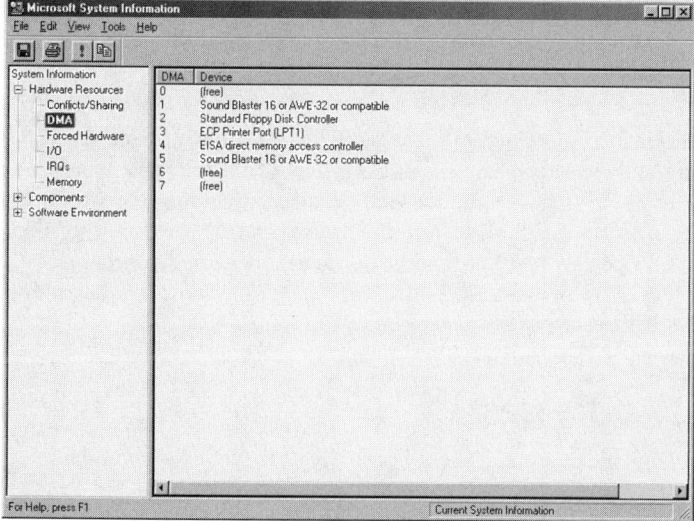

Figure 12.2
Typical DMA assignments.

Memory Assignments

Memory assignments refer to the requirement of some hardware devices that they have some of the system's memory addresses designated to them, usually because the device contains some memory that an application or driver needs to access. An example of this is a display adapter, which has its own memory that contains all the information shown on the screen. These memory assignments cannot overlap real RAM installed in the system, and clearly cannot be shared between devices. Figure 12.3 shows a typical set of memory address assignments.

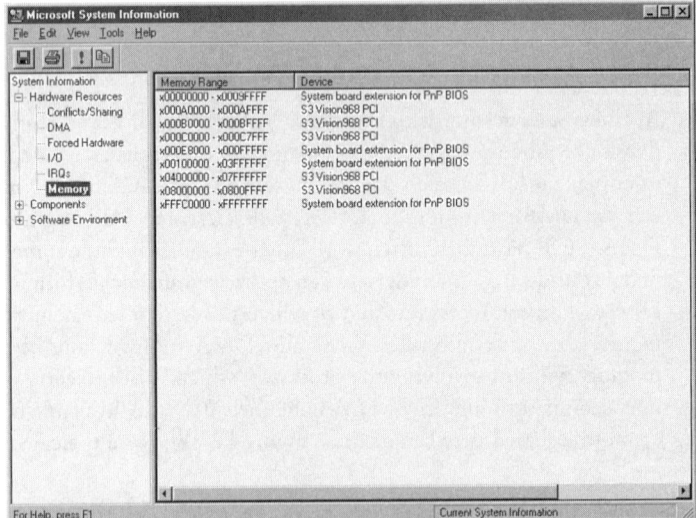

Figure 12.3
Typical memory assignments.

I/O Port Addresses

I/O port addresses identify small areas of system memory (RAM) that are set aside so that information can be transferred between a program on the system (such as a driver) and an installed device (such as a mouse). Programs cannot send data directly to most devices; instead, they place the data in a set of I/O port addresses, and the device can take the data from that small chunk of memory, and vice versa. I/O port addresses cannot be shared; even more important, there can be no overlaps between the addresses. Figure 12.4 shows the beginning of a list of typical I/O port addresses.

Configuring IRQ Addresses

When you're configuring IRQ addresses, you should be aware of the following standard assignments for devices:

IRQ	Reserved For
0	System Timer (always)
1	Keyboard (always)

Chapter 12: Supporting Devices

IRQ	Reserved For
2	Cascade IRQ for handling signals from IRQs 8–15; can sometimes be used for devices, although generally it's a good idea to avoid using it
3	Serial ports (COM2 and COM4)
4	Serial ports (COM1 and COM3)
5	Printer port 2 (LPT2); can often be used for other devices like sound cards because few systems have two LPT ports installed
6	Floppy disk controller (always)
7	Printer port 1 (LPT1); older sound cards shared this IRQ with the printer under DOS, but that's not possible under Windows 98
8	System CMOS/Real-Time Clock (always)
9	Usually open
10	Cascade IRQ for passing IRQ signals from IRQs 8–15 to IRQ 2
11	Often occupied by installed SCSI controller; otherwise available
12	PS/2 Mouse Port (available for use if a serial mouse is being used instead)
13	Numeric data processor (always in 80486 and Pentium processors; was optional with 80386 family and not used for 80486sx family)
14	Usually open, unless system has two hard disk controllers, in which case one will be assigned IRQ 14
15	Usually used by hard disk controller

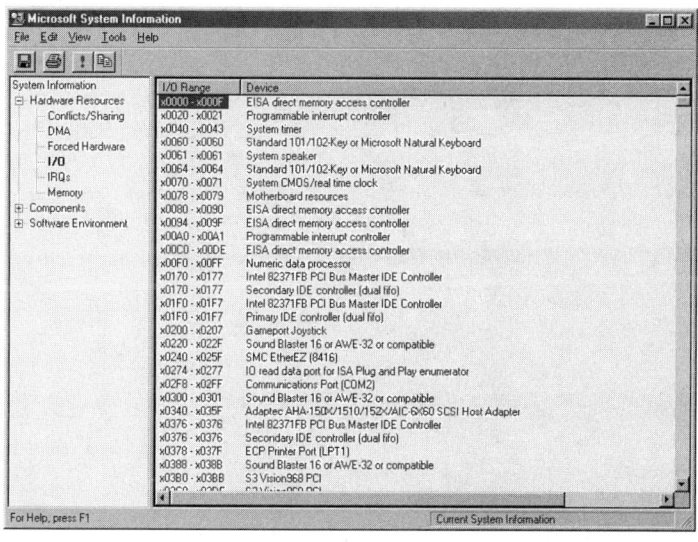

Figure 12.4
Typical I/O port address assignments.

Part III: Windows 98 Operations

There are two good ways to view the specific device assignments being used in any particular system. The first is to use the Microsoft System Information utility included with Windows 98 (MSINFO32.EXE). The second involves opening the System control panel, moving to the Device Manager tab, selecting Computer at the top of the tree, and clicking the P**r**operties button, which brings up the Computer Properties dialog box shown in Figure 12.5. Use the option buttons at the top of the dialog box to look at different types of reserved resources.

> **Note** For the remainder of the chapter, the Device Manager tab in the System control panel is referred to simply as "Device Manager."

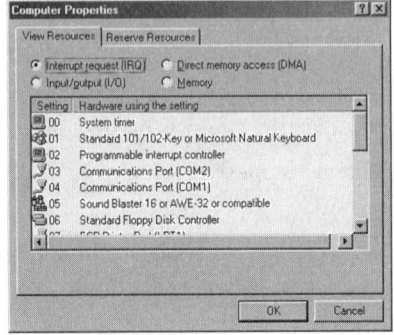

Figure 12.5
Using Device Manager to view resource assignments.

You can also view the specific resource assignments for a single device, if you need to. Using Device Manager, select the device you want to view and click the P**r**operties button. Then move to the Resources tab, which will show you the resources being used by that device, as in Figure 12.6.

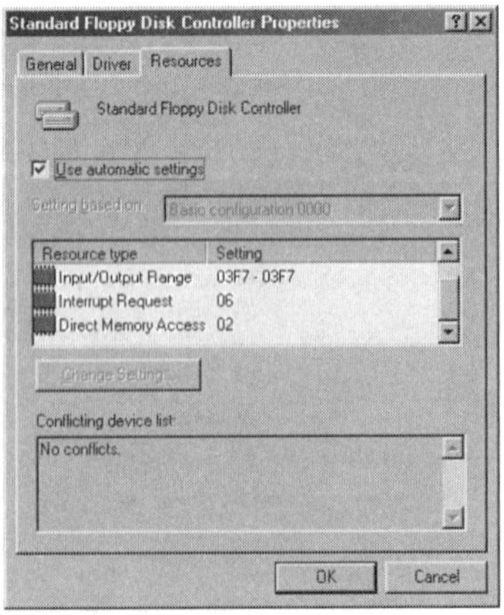

Figure 12.6
Viewing resources for a specific device.

Understanding Plug and Play

Plug and Play (PnP) is a collection of specifications that provide automatic configuration of devices supporting PnP. For full support of PnP functions, the system must have a PnP-capable Basic Input/Output System (BIOS). The goals for the PnP design are to do the following:

- Maximize compatibility with existing ISA devices
- Eliminate conflicts when the system carries out its Power-On Self Test (POST)
- Allow PnP configuration of motherboard resources
- Allow for system event notifications of PnP device state changes
- Provide Operating-System–independent support

PnP meets these original design goals. Using PnP, devices can be automatically configured quickly and easily so that a system avoids any resource conflicts.

PnP works differently for different data busses. Following are some of the key points for different busses you might encounter:

- **ISA.** Industry Standard Architecture (ISA) busses can support PnP, although BIOS support is also required to get the full benefit of PnP. When the system boots, the ISA bus enumerator identifies all bus-connected devices and reads their configuration requirements and current, default settings. This is done initially by assigning each card an I/O port and then using that port to carry out further configurations. As each card is isolated, it is assigned an ID and serial number, and then its detailed information is read and catalogued. The system then arbitrates the different resource requirements, arrives at a configuration that will permit all devices to work, and sets each card accordingly, as necessary. For non-PnP devices, configuration information is determined when Windows 98 is installed, and the information from that configuration is stored in the Registry.

> **Tip** Some newer systems support a Plug and Play setting in their CMOS setup program. Such settings must be turned on (to enable full PnP support) *prior* to installing Windows 98. If Windows 98 is mistakenly installed on such a system with the setting turned off, then some devices may not be fully recognized by the operating system, or may not function normally.
>
> When this happens, you can enable the setting and rerun the Windows 98 installation program to correct the installation.

- **EISA.** The Enhanced Industry Standard Architecture (EISA) supports software-based configuration of installed hardware; the features that support this can be read by Windows 98 and used to mediate contention with other devices. Windows 98 cannot configure EISA-based cards, however; instead, you must use the EISA configuration utility provided with the computer system.

- **PCI.** The peripheral component interconnect (PCI) bus is a sub-bus of a primary system bus (usually ISA). PCI only supports PnP when the primary bus supports PnP.

- **SCSI.** The Small Computer Standard Interface (SCSI) bus is a device bus that supports hard disks, CD-ROM drives, and other high-throughput devices such as scanners. PnP SCSI systems allow automatic configuration not only of the SCSI host adapter, but also of all the connected SCSI devices connected to the SCSI bus (generally seen only with SCSI-3). Note that an installed SCSI bus is controlled through one of the system busses, such as ISA, EISA, or PCI, even when SCSI support is built in to the motherboard.

- **PC Card.** The PC Card (formerly PCMCIA) specification supports small, credit-card–sized devices for use with desktop and portable computers. The PC Card specification fully supports PnP, as do all PC card devices.

Understanding Real-Mode versus Protected-Mode Drivers

Windows 98 supports two types of device drivers: real- and protected-mode. Real-mode drivers are generally designed for MS-DOS systems, but can still be used under Windows 98. They are loaded through the CONFIG.SYS file and not by Windows 98 itself. Because they are loaded before Windows 98 boots, they run in real-mode on the system, and can be accessed by any processes running under Windows 98, such as MS-DOS programs that can make use of them. Because they are running in real mode, however, they can be somewhat less stable than protected-mode drivers, and they do not receive the benefits of Windows 98's Plug and Play support. Still, when necessary, the ability to load them can help you access a device that you could not make use of in any other way.

Protected-mode drivers are loaded by Windows 98 through the Device Manager tree (stored in the system's Registry). They, too, can be accessed by any processes running on the system, including most MS-DOS programs, and Win16 and Win32 programs.

A number of real-mode device drivers are known to work under Windows 98 and are supported. They are listed in the IOS.INI file stored in the \Windows directory. You should check this file; some of these drivers have protected-mode versions available, a fact that is noted (usually with "PM driver exists") in this file.

Managing Devices

Knowing about device technology won't help you when it's time to manage the devices! In this section you learn how to work with devices and Windows 98. You'll find out about adding and removing devices, working with non-PnP devices, and resolving configuration problems. You'll also learn about working with certain specific device types.

Installing New Devices

There are two types of devices you install under Windows 98: bus-connected devices and peripheral devices (which usually connect to some sort of adapter on the bus or on the motherboard). Installing and configuring peripheral devices, such as modems, printers, and some multimedia devices, is covered elsewhere in this book. Here, you'll learn about bus-connected device management.

Installing PnP devices on PnP-capable systems is fairly easy. Generally, you simply install the device and then boot the system. The BIOS should recognize that a new device has been added, and should automatically install the necessary device drivers, or at least prompt you for the appropriate device drivers from a manufacturer-supplied floppy disk or the Windows 98 CD-ROM.

If the system isn't recognizing a PnP device that you've just installed, check the following:

- If the system has a CMOS setting that controls whether or not PnP is supported, make sure that it's enabled

- Use the Add New Hardware wizard to attempt to detect the device; sometimes devices will show up this way

- Ensure that the device is functioning properly. Many bus-connected devices have diagnostic programs that you can run from the DOS prompt, usually after booting a command-prompt–only session.

If these steps fail to recognize the device, contact either the computer manufacturer or the device manufacturer for additional assistance. In rare cases there may be some sort of incompatibility that they should know about, or they may be able to advise you on additional steps, given their particular hardware.

Tip | If a PnP device in a PnP system isn't being recognized, force-loading its driver (which you can do if Add New Hardware fails to detect it) usually won't resolve the problem.

Installing a non-PnP device may involve additional steps, depending on the device itself. Basically, installing such a device revolves around three key steps: configuring the device appropriately, installing the device, and then installing the driver in Windows 98. Depending on the device, you might perform the configuration step either before or after it's installed. For example, a device with dip switches or jumpers must be configured prior to installation. Other devices may be configurable from software supplied with the device. Check the documentation that came with the device.

> ### Dip Switches and Jumpers: An Idea Whose Time Has Passed
>
> Although it would be nice to fully eradicate dip switches and jumpers on devices, sometimes you still have to deal with them. The good news is that once they're set, you usually don't have to mess with them ever again.
>
> *Jumpers* are small, rectangular pieces of plastic (usually black, with a gold-plated sheet of metal inside) that are designed to fit over two or more pins on an interface card, or on the motherboard. They are usually a bit smaller than the diameter of a pencil eraser. *Dip switches* are made up of small switch blocks (often light blue or black, with white switches), in which each switch can be set to two or three positions.
>
> Dip switches almost always have two positions, with one direction representing on (or 1) and one representing off (or 0). Jumpers represent on (or 1) when they connect two pins, and off (or 0) when they are connected to only one pin.
>
> It's always best if you have the documentation that describes the available jumpers or dip switches, because every card uses them differently, and you often can't figure out how they should be set. On better-designed cards, however, printed clues next to the switches or jumper pins can often help you discern their purpose and use when no other avenues are available. For instance, SCSI devices sometimes have to have their SCSI address set to a number between 0 and 7, so if you see an eight-position dip switch and printing on the circuit card next to it that says "address," or "SCSIID," or something like that, you can usually guess that those switches set the address. Sometimes they're a bit harder to figure out, because you can also count to 7 with only three binary digits (001 = 1, 010 = 2, and so on up to 111, which equals 7 in binary), and some cards use this device.
>
> Trying to guess at dip switch settings and jumper settings is almost always a bad idea, although sometimes you simply have no choice. One thing to check first, however, is for a Web site for the manufacturer of the card or device. Most companies publish these settings for their cards and devices, even long after they're no longer being sold.

To configure a non-PnP device, you first have to find out what resources it requires so that you can set it appropriately. Open Device Manager, select Computer in the hardware tree, and then click the P<u>r</u>operties button. Using the dialog box shown in Figure 12.5, locate available resources that the device needs: IRQs, DMA channels, and Memory I/O Ports.

Chapter 12: Supporting Devices

After you have identified the resources, you may want to reserve them. This is important for devices that may not be installed all the time. Reserving the resources needed by a device ensures that other devices won't be assigned those resources in error. In the Computer Properties dialog box, move to the Reserve Resources tab shown in Figure 12.7. For each of the required resources, click the **A**dd button and reserve the resources needed by the device.

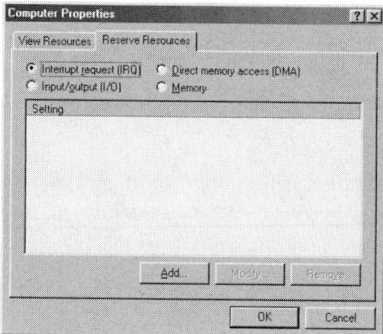

Figure 12.7
Use this dialog box to reserve resources for devices.

Next, configure and install the device. This may be done on the device itself before it's installed, or you may have to install it first and then use a software program (possibly DOS-based) to set the device to use the resources you identified in the previous step.

After the device is configured and installed, start the system. You should then run the Add New Hardware Wizard to let Windows 98 identify the device, if it can. If it is not identified by the wizard, you can specify the driver manually in the Add New Hardware dialog box shown in Figure 12.8. Select the appropriate category and click the Next button.

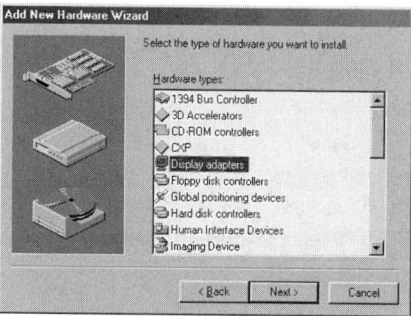

Figure 12.8
Manually selecting a hardware category.

Next you see a dialog box in which you choose both the manufacturer and the exact model of the device (see Figure 12.9). Select both settings, and click Next to install the driver. If the device you're installing is not listed, and you have a floppy disk or set of driver files from the manufacturer, click **H**ave Disk, and then select the driver files for installation.

Figure 12.9
Choosing a manufacturer and model.

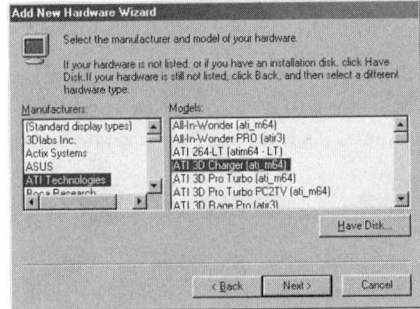

After you've installed the appropriate driver by using the preceding steps, shut down and restart the system (it's best to power-off the system). After you restart the system, the device should be active and available. You can check the device's status in Device Manager.

> **Tip** If a device doesn't function when the system boots, you may be able to garner some information as to what the problem is by performing a logged boot with the Windows Startup menu. See Chapter 36, "The Windows 98 Boot Process and Emergency Recovery," for more information on performing a logged boot. Information in Chapter 37, "Tools and Strategies for Troubleshooting Windows 98," may also be helpful.

If the device is not functioning, open Device Manager, select the device (it should have a trouble icon next to it), and click the P*r*operties button. Move to the Resources tab, which should show what conflicts exist. Figure 12.10 shows the Resources tab for a working device.

Figure 12.10
A device's Resources tab in Device Manager.

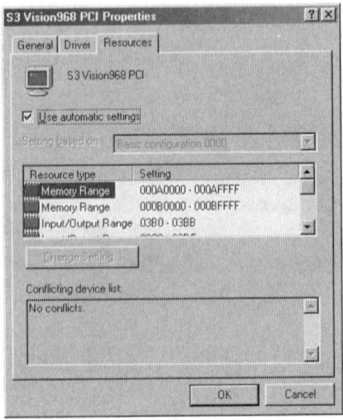

If there is a conflict, try deselecting the **U**se Automatic Settings check box, select the resource type that you need to change, and then click the **C**hange Setting button. You can select other resources for the device in this way, although you may need to reconfigure the device after you've done so, using whatever procedure the device requires.

Updating and Removing Device Drivers

Updating device drivers with newer versions is a simple procedure. First, of course, you need to obtain the newer drivers. With some devices, the manufacturer may specify an installation routine. Otherwise, open Device Manager and move to the Driver tab in the Properties dialog box for the device. Click the <u>U</u>pdate Driver button to load the new device driver. You will be prompted for the new driver files' location.

To remove a device from the system, open Device Manager, select the device, and then click the R<u>e</u>move button. If you are using Hardware Profiles, you see the Confirm Device Removal dialog box shown in Figure 12.11, which asks whether you want to remove the device generally, or only from the current Hardware Profile. Choose the appropriate response and click OK.

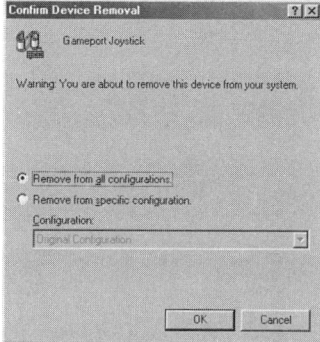

Figure 12.11
Confirm Device Removal dialog box.

> **Note** See Chapter 9, "Hardware Profiles" for details on managing Hardware Profiles under Windows 98.

Recovering from Windows 3.x Driver Installations

It is possible to install a 32-bit device driver intended for use under Windows 3.x into Windows 98, which can cause problems. To remove the driver, you have to remove any reference to it from the SYSTEM.INI file. If the system is booting, you can simply edit the SYSTEM.INI file with Notepad. If it is not booting, however, you first need to boot the system in Command Prompt Only mode (Safe Mode may also work), and then remove all references to the device from the SYSTEM.INI file in the \WINDOWS directory. (Settings in SYSTEM.INI override settings in the Registry.) Then, using Safe Mode, remove references to the device in Device Manager. Finally, restart the system and use the procedure discussed earlier in this chapter for installing device drivers in Windows 98.

Understanding Specific Devices

Many different devices have settings and features of which you may not be aware. This section discusses different device capabilities and tips, to help you manage such devices. Note that some device information may be found in other chapters that focus on different subjects, such as Multimedia devices or modems.

System Devices

A number of the default system devices listed in Device Manager have settings that control the way they behave. You control these settings through each device's Properties dialog box. Figure 12.12 shows Device Manager with a number of system devices from a standard ISA/PCI system displayed.

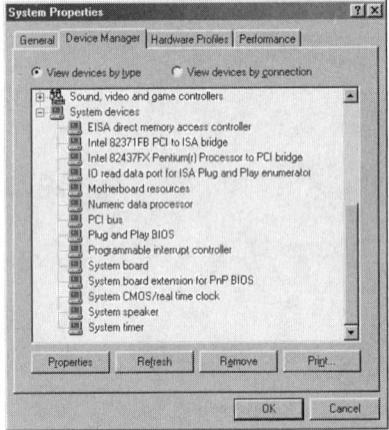

Figure 12.12
Device Manager with a standard set of system devices.

Table 12.1 shows you available settings for system devices that support such settings.

Table 12.1
System Device Settings

Device	Setting	Description
EISA Direct Memory Access Controller	Reserve DMA **B**uffer	Lets you reserve a certain amount of memory for the DMA buffer (by default, 16KB is set aside by the operating system).

Device	Setting	Description
	Restrict **D**MA Transfers	Lets you specify that DMA transfers must take place below either 16MB or 4GB (in the virtual memory space). Some SCSI hard disks on older systems can only support DMA transfers below 16MB.
Numeric Data Processor	Use numeric processor	This device's Settings tab reports on whether the system has the infamous Pentium floating point bug. If so, you can choose to force Windows to use internal floating-point emulation routines by choosing **N**ever Use the Numeric Data Processor.
PCI Bus	Device Enumeration	This setting lets you choose to use either the hardware or the system's BIOS to report on PCI devices connected to the bus. Generally, Use **H**ardware should be selected, although if a PCI-connected device isn't working properly, you can try the Use **B**IOS setting.
	Override Bridges	When selected, causes the system to ignore the system's BIOS settings for PCI devices.
	IRQ Steering	Windows 98 cannot assign IRQs to PCI devices. Normally, this is not a problem, as the bus itself resolves most such problems. For some devices, however, you may want to activate a feature called *IRQ steering*, in which Windows 98 can intercept IRQ configuration requests for PCI devices and "steer" them to an unused IRQ. Typically, this feature is used only with docking computers.
Plug and Play BIOS	Disable **N**VRAM/	Updates if Windows is not starting or shutting down ESCD. Select this setting properly. Sometimes there can be problems when Windows tries to update the system's Plug and Play BIOS settings.

Display Adapters

Display adapter drivers can be maintained in two ways: through Device Manager and through the Display control panel. To install and maintain display adapter drivers through the Display control panel, move to the Settings tab and click the Advanced button. Then move to the Adapter tab and click the Change button.

The Advanced button on the Settings tab displays the properties for the display adapter, divided up into multiple tabs. There are a number of useful settings on these tabs. Figure 12.13 shows the first such tab, General. On this tab you can choose the size of fonts that you want to use with the display, and you can specify how you should be prompted and how the system should react to different selected monitor resolutions and color depths. You can also choose to display the settings icon on the taskbar, so that you can quickly make most monitor changes "on the fly."

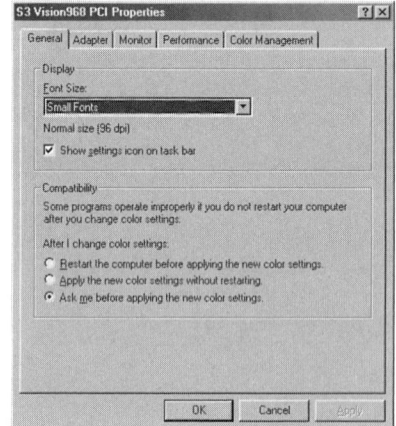

Figure 12.13
Display adapter properties, General tab.

The Adapter tab, shown in Figure 12.14, shows you detailed information about the display adapter, and also lets you choose the refresh rate at which to drive the monitor. Note that the monitor must support the combination of resolution, color depth, and refresh rate that you select, or your display may become unreadable (boot in Safe Mode and correct the setting, if necessary).

The Monitor tab lets you choose whether the monitor is Plug and Play-compliant, whether the system should automatically try to detect Plug and Play monitors, and whether the system should reset the display whenever the system's power management suspends and then resumes operations. You can also specify a different monitor by clicking the Change button on the Monitor tab. Note that it's important that you select a monitor on the Monitor tab that matches the actual, physical monitor, so that Windows can correctly set the refresh rate and other properties appropriately.

Chapter 12: Supporting Devices 279

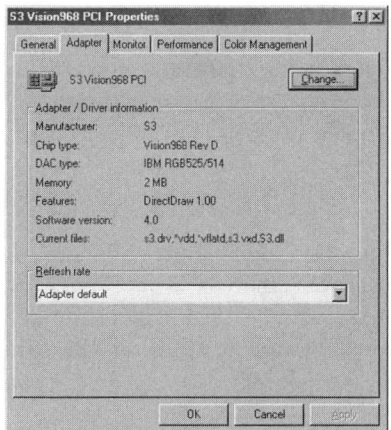

Figure 12.14
Display adapter properties, Adapter tab.

On the Performance tab you can drag a slider control to affect how much of the display adapter's acceleration feature should be used by Windows. If you are having strange display problems, such as clipped regions of the screen, or other problems when certain types of programs run, try reducing the acceleration setting on the Performance tab.

The final tab, Color Management, lets you choose an appropriate color management (*.ICM) file for your specific monitor. You may have to acquire such a file from your monitor's manufacturer. Using the Color Management tab, you can more closely approximate color standards for a given monitor.

Note   A display's *color depth*, the number of colors it can display, is controlled by the amount of memory available on the display adapter (as well as the capabilities of the monitor). For instance, a monochrome 640 × 480 display requires only 307,200 bits, or about 38KB. In this instance, only one bit of memory is required for each pixel. To display more colors you need more bits per displayed pixel. The following table shows the number of bits per pixel required for different color depths:

Color Depth	Bits per Pixel
Monochrome	1
16 Colors	4
256 Colors	8
32,768 Colors	15
65,536 Colors (High Color)	16
16.7 Million Colors (True Color)	32

Multiple Monitor Support

New to Windows 98 is the ability to support multiple monitors on multiple display adapters. If you have the right hardware, this can be a very useful feature. For example, you can program on one monitor and test your code on another. Or you can work on a document on one monitor, and keep your appointments and email open on another. The possibilities are limited only by your imagination.

To use Multiple Monitor support, you must be using PCI- or AGP-based display adapters, and of course you must have one display adapter for each monitor you want to drive. Install the second display adapter just as you would any other device: install it with the system off, turn on the system, and let PnP detect and install the appropriate drivers. Restart Windows 98, and you should be off and running. Note that the following display adapter chip sets are known to be supported at this time:

- ATI 3D Rage Pro
- ATI Mach64 GX
- ATI Rage 1 and 2
- Cirrus 5436, 7548, and 5446
- S3 764V+, 765, and Trio 64V2
- S3 Aurora
- S3 ViRGE
- Trident 9685, 9680, 9682, 9385, 9382, and 938-1

Other adapter types may also be supported. Check with the manufacturer of the adapter you want to use.

When you boot a system that is successfully using multiple monitors, the secondary monitor should display a message as the system initializes, indicating that the monitor is functioning. If you do not see such a message, verify that the display adapter uses a supported chip set (check the preceding list) and that the driver is properly installed (look in Device Manager).

Some programs may not function correctly with multiple monitors. For instance, programs that use Adobe Type Manager, as well as some remote control programs or programs that bypass the Windows graphical management services will not work correctly. If you suspect an application-specific problem (test and make sure that the built-in Windows applications work properly with both monitors), you should contact the application vendor for more information.

Serial Ports

Communications ports (also known as COM ports, serial ports, and RS-232C ports) are typically used to communicate with modems or to interface to certain other RS-232C devices. Generally, COM ports don't require much support, but supporting more than two COM ports can become problematic. Basic PCs support as many as four COM ports (COM1–COM4) but assign them standard IRQs in such a way that it is virtually impossible to use all four ports at once. By default, COM1 and COM3 use IRQ 4, while COM2 and COM4 use IRQ 3. Remember that you cannot generally share IRQ assignments between devices simultaneously. Therefore, a serial mouse connected to COM1 and a modem using COM3 will not work simultaneously unless one of them uses a different IRQ. For PnP-based computers, Windows 98 avoids such conflicts by remapping the IRQs. For non-PnP systems, you will have to do this yourself, using Device Manager. You can assign COM3 and COM4 to other available IRQs in the system.

Tip When you assign COM numbers to devices, such as an installed internal-modem, remember that you cannot have missing COM port numbers. For instance, if a system has COM1 and COM2 serial ports on its motherboard, you cannot set an internal modem to act as COM4 unless some other device is acting as COM3.

Windows 98 will support up to eight COM ports, provided there are sufficient IRQs available (not an easy task!). If you require more than four COM ports for some application, a better solution is to purchase and use a multi-port communications card (such as the excellent cards from Digi), which usually will support eight or more COM ports using a single IRQ on the system. Such devices are commonly used for modem pools, for instance.

Conclusion

One of the real benefits of Windows 95, and now of Windows 98, is its support for Plug and Play hardware. If you remember the nightmare of supporting devices in the pre-PnP world, you undoubtedly find PnP to be a welcome feature. Using current hardware, PnP makes managing the devices on the system almost completely painless.

In this chapter you learned about PnP and how it works. You also learned about automatically and manually managing device drivers on a Windows 98 system, and finally reviewed some information about some specific device types. For more detailed device information not discussed in this chapter, see appropriate topics elsewhere in this book. For instance, you might want to review the following chapters:

- Chapter 6, "Control Panel"

- Chapter 9, "Hardware Profiles"
- Chapter 13, "Printing"
- Chapter 14, "Multimedia"
- Chapter 17, "File Systems: File and Disk Resources"
- Chapter 26, "Windows 98 and Remote Communication"

CHAPTER 13

Printing

Printing is still an important function is most desktop environments, and Windows 98 provides an array of useful and convenient printing features.

Windows 98 Printing Subsystem

Windows 98's printing subsystem is similar to Windows 95's, as you can see from Figure 13.1. When a Win16 or Win32 application prints a document, the graphics device interface (GDI) creates an *enhanced metafile* (EMF), which contains data and instructions for the printer. The EMF is then passed to the print spooler, a 32-bit subsystem component that interprets the EMF data and translates it into a format that is discernible to the print driver. The spooler also temporarily stores the print data, if necessary, while the print document waits for an available printer. In Windows 98, the printer driver system consists of a universal driver, which performs driver functions common to all print drivers, and one of several minidrivers. A minidriver provides functions specific to a particular printer. Several minidrivers can be present on the system at once, each offering access to a different type of printer, as shown in Figure 13.1.

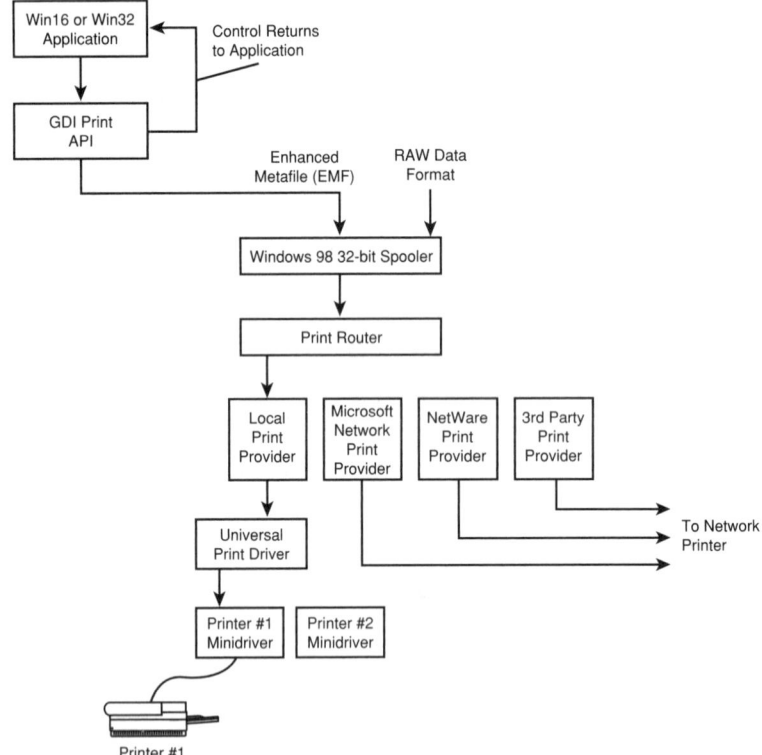

Figure 13.1
The Windows 98 printing process.

Depending on your system's configuration, Windows 98 can return control to the application while the EMF spools, or it can send the EMF to the spooler and then return control. (You'll learn more about configuring spool properties later in this chapter.)

Data bound for postscript printers spools as postscript RAW printer data (refer to Figure 13.1). The RAW data format is an alternative to the EMF format. According to Microsoft,

RAW print data takes longer to spool in Windows 98. Also, because RAW print data cannot spool in the background, control will not return to the application until all data has been spooled.

MS-DOS applications in Windows 98 print directly to the spooler from a virtual printer port in the virtual DOS machine, as shown in Figure 13.2. You can choose to disable spooling for MS-DOS print jobs, as described later in this chapter.

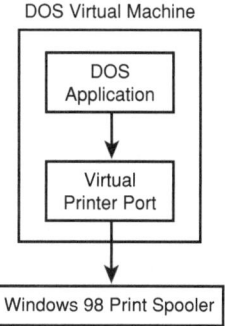

Figure 13.2
Printing from MS-DOS.

Local versus Network Printers

Windows 98 classifies printers into two types: local printers and network printers. When the print job leaves the spooler (refer to Figure 13.1), it passes to the print router. The print router routes the print job to either the local print provider (for processing and printing from the local machine) or to the network. A local printer is a printer that is physically connected to the Windows 98 computer and that is served by the local print provider within the Windows 98 printing subsystem, as shown in Figure 13.3. A network computer is physically attached to a different computer, as shown in Figure 13.4. Print jobs sent to a network printer pass from the print router to a network print provider and over the network to the print server machine (refer to Figure 13.1). A network printer is most often local to another Windows computer. As a matter of daily operations, the difference between a local and a network printer is largely hidden. Local and network printers coexist in the Printers folder, and the user can choose either a local or a network printer from a drop-down list in a Windows application.

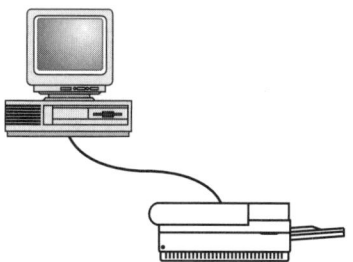

Figure 13.3
A local printer is attached to the local machine.

Figure 13.4
A network printer is attached to a different computer and accessed through the network.

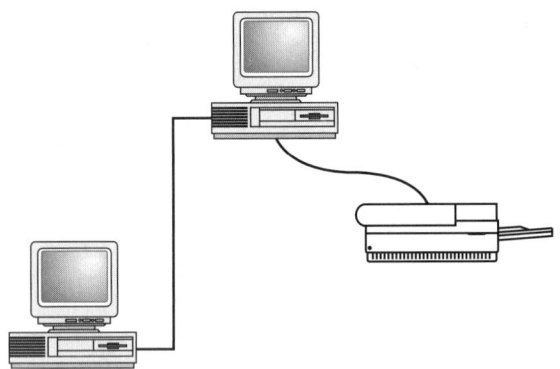

> **Note** The steps for installing a local printer and a network printer are, of course, different. To install a local printer you must create a new printer definition. To install a network printer you must locate an existing printer on the network. Windows 98's Add Printer Wizard takes care of most of the details—you just have to be prepared to choose whether the new printer will be a local printer or a network printer.

You'll learn more later in this chapter in the section on "Installing a Local Printer" and "Setting Up a Network Printer."

Using the Printers Folder

The Printers folder is the center for Windows 98 printer configuration. To access the Printers folder, click on the Start button, select **S**ettings and then choose **P**rinters. The Printers folder is shown in Figure 13.5.

You can use the Printers folder for tasks such as the following:

- To install a new printer: Click the Add Printer icon. The steps for installing a new printer are described later in this chapter.

- To access the printer window: The printer window displays current print activity for the printer—documents waiting to print, status, owner, progress—and lets you purge or pause a print job.

- To access the Printer Properties dialog box: The Printer Properties dialog box, discussed later in this chapter, enables you to view and modify printer configuration settings.

- To share a printer: You can share a local printer so that network users can install it as a network printer and print to it. You must install a File and Printer sharing service

(File and Printer Sharing for Microsoft Networks or File and Printer Sharing for NetWare Networks) before you can share a printer.

■ To set a new default printer.

■ To remove a printer.

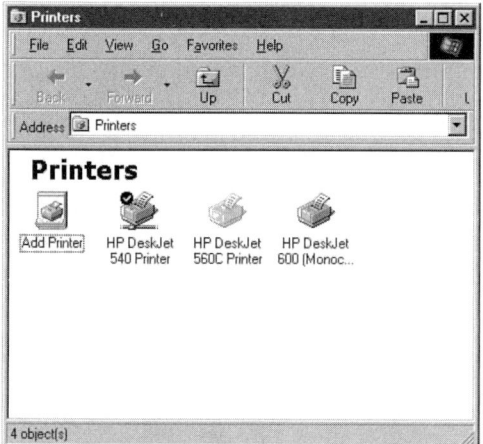

Figure 13.5
The Printers folder provides a central place from which to manage all your local and network printers.

The printers presently installed on the system appear as icons in the Printers folders. To pause or resume printing, set the default printer, take the printer offline, purge print documents, share the printer, or view the printer properties, right-click on a printer icon and choose the appropriate options from the context menu, shown in Figure 13.6.

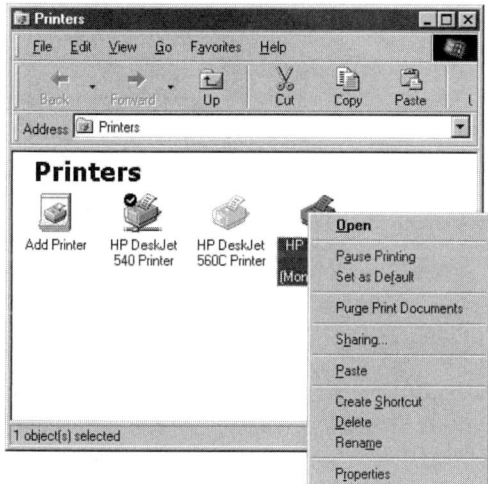

Figure 13.6
Right-click on a printer icon in the Printers folder to access the printer's context menu.

Default Printer

The default printer, as the name implies, is the printer selected by default when you print from an application. The default printer is also the printer used when you click on the printer icon in a Windows application toolbar. In the Printers folder, the icon for the default printer has a check mark beside it, as shown in Figure 13.5.

The first printer you install automatically becomes the default printer, and it remains the default printer until you change the default setting. To change the default printer, right-click on a printer in the Printers folder and select Set as default from the context menu.

Configuring Printers

To view or modify a printer's configuration settings, right-click on the printer in the Printer's folder and select Properties. The Printer Properties dialog box is shown in Figure 13.7.

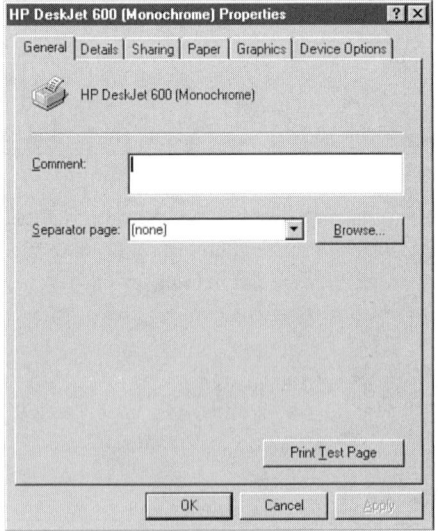

Figure 13.7
The Properties dialog box for a printer contains several tabs, each containing various options that you can set for the printer.

Because the Properties dialog box is directly related to the functions exposed through the printer's driver, the features and options vary somewhat from one printer to another. Figure 13.7 shows a typical Printer Properties dialog box. Your printer may not have some of these options, it may have additional options, or some of the options may appear in different places. Descriptions of the tabs in Figure 13.7 follow:

- **General**. The General tab lets you add a comment that identifies the printer, add or change the separator page, or print a test page. The separator page option is discussed in the next section. A test page will verify that you can access the printer correctly from Windows. The test page also provides some useful information about the printer configuration, such as the driver name, the port name, the data format, and the files used by the driver.

- **Details**. The Details tab, shown in Figure 13.8, lets you change the port or driver for the printer. You'll learn more about port and spool settings later in this chapter. The Capture Printer port button lets you map a virtual printer port to a network printer path. You may need to print from certain MS-DOS applications. (For information on how to do this, see the "Printing from MS-DOS Applications" section, later in this chapter.) The Timeout settings determine how long Windows 98 will attempt to print before reporting that an error has occurred. For example, if your printer is turned off and the timeout period is 15 seconds, after 15 seconds, Windows 98 will display an error message stating that it cannot print. Windows will then try to print again after the period of time specified in the Transmission retry box.

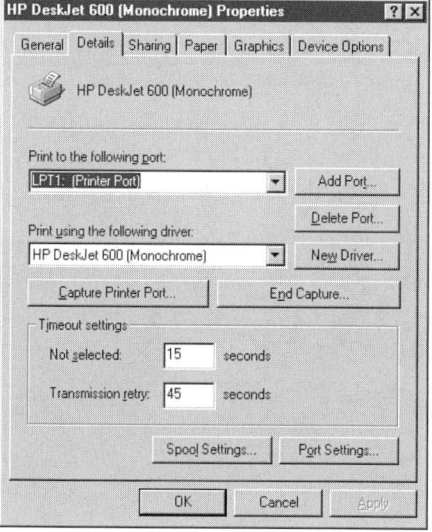

Figure 13.8
The Printer Properties Details tab for a typical printer.

- **Sharing**. The Sharing tab lets you share the printer on the network so that network users can access it. This is the same tab you'll see when you right-click on the printer icon and choose sharing (refer to Figure 13.6). You can specify a share name for the printer, and set security for accessing the share. (See Chapter 21, "Understanding Windows 98 Networking," for a discussion of share-level and user-level security.) The share name is the name that appears in network browse lists. Note that the printer name, which appears with the printer icon, is not the same as the printer's share name.

- **Paper**. Set paper size and orientation.

- **Graphics**. Use this tab to set dithering, resolution, and print intensity. (Settings vary depending on the printer.)

- **Device Options**. In the case of the printer whose dialog box is shown in Figure 13.7, the device option settings let you define a print quality mode.

Separator Page

A separator page is a page inserted after each printed document that helps keep one print job separate from the next. You can choose to use either a full page containing graphics supplied by Windows 98, a simple page that contains only text, or any custom page you select. The custom page can be any Windows metafile (a file with the .wmf extension).

Spool Settings

The Spool Settings button on the Details tab lets you define how the spooler will spool and print documents. In the Spool Settings dialog box, shown in Figure 13.9, you can configure the spooler to expect EMF or RAW printer data format for this printer. You can also determine whether to print directly to the printer or to use the print spooler. The Spool print jobs option almost always returns control to the application sooner than the Print directly to the printer option. If you elect to use the spooler, you have two options:

- Start printing after the last page is spooled

- Start printing after the first page is spooled

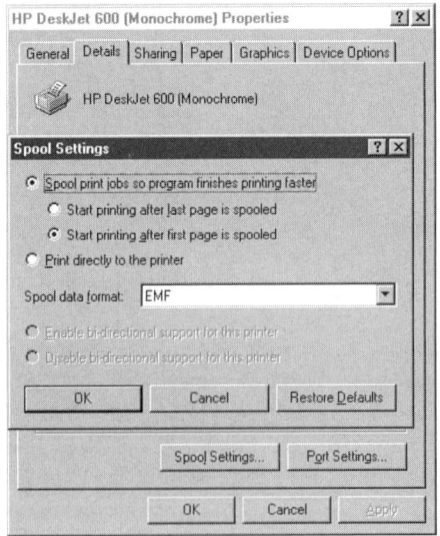

Figure 13.9
The Spool Settings dialog box.

You can also enable or disable bidirectional support if your printer is attached to an Enhanced Capabilities Port (ECP) and has a cable that supports ECP. (See this chapter's "Installing a Local Printer" section for more information about ECP.)

Printing from MS-DOS Applications

As described earlier in this chapter, by default, MS-DOS applications print to the spooler through a virtual printer port. Microsoft designed Windows 98's spooling feature to support the widest possible range of DOS applications. Because printing in DOS applications is implemented by the application itself, however, and because DOS applications sometimes implement printing in nonstandard ways, some DOS applications may not function properly in this default configuration. Windows 98 provides the following alternatives for MS-DOS printing support:

- You can choose not to spool MS-DOS print jobs—printing directly to the printer is a closer approximation to the native DOS environment.

- For network printers, you can map a network drive to an LPT port. When the DOS application prints to the local port, Windows 98 will then redirect the request to the network.

To disable spooling for MS-DOS print jobs, follow these steps:

1. Right-click on a printer icon in the Printers folder and choose Properties.

2. In the Printer Properties dialog box, select the Details tab.

3. Click on the Port Settings button.

4. In the Configure LPT port dialog box, clear the check box labeled Spool MS-DOS print jobs.

The preceding procedure will disable spooling for MS-DOS print jobs only. Other print jobs will continue to spool. To disable spooling on all print jobs, click on the Spool Settings button in the Printer Properties Details tab, and select Print directly to the printer (as described earlier in this chapter).

To map a local printer port to a network printer, follow these steps:

1. Right-click on a printer icon in the Printers folder and choose Properties.

2. In the Printer Properties dialog box, select the Details tab.

3. Click on the Capture Printer Port button.

4. In the Capture Printer Port dialog box, select a device name (LPT1, LPT2) and enter a path to the network printer. Click on OK. You can also choose whether you want to reconnect to the printer at logon.

Installing a Local Printer

Before you attempt to set up a local printer on your computer, you need to make sure that you can connect to that printer from your computer. Here are some of the things you need to check:

- Which port the printer must be plugged into

- Whether the printer is properly connected (physically) to the computer

- Whether the printer is turned on (if it isn't, Windows 98 won't be able to detect the printer)

- The exact make and model of that printer; for example, HP DeskJet 500

Assuming that your printer is Plug and Play–compliant, installing your printer is as easy as turning on your attached printer and booting into Windows 98. Plug and Play can install your printer either during the Windows 98 installation process or at any time thereafter when you want to add a printer. When Windows 98 loads it should automatically detect that the printer has been added to your computer. It will then display a dialog box that informs you of this fact. After Windows 98 has identified the printer, it will attempt to install the correct driver for that printer. At this point it may prompt you to insert the Windows 98 CD-ROM. After you have done that it will look for that driver on that disk. If the driver did not come with Windows 98, or if you have an updated driver that you want to install instead, simply insert the driver disk from your hardware manufacturer into a disk drive and direct Windows 98 to that drive.

For this process to work properly, you have to make sure that the printer you want to add complies with the Plug and Play standard.

If Windows 98 does not automatically recognize your printer you can still add the printer manually, using the Add Printer Wizard.

To access the Add Printer Wizard, open the Printers folder and double-click on the Add Printer icon. After the Add Printer Wizard window appears, click on the Next button to begin using the wizard.

Select the radio button for Local printer and click the Next button. You will be asked to choose the manufacturer and printer model for your printer, as shown in Figure 13.10. Scroll down to the name (or abbreviation) for your printer's manufacturer in the left window of this page of the wizard. When you select that name by clicking on it a list of all available printers from that manufacturer will appear in the window on the right. Select your printer's model by clicking on its name in this window.

Chapter 13: Printing

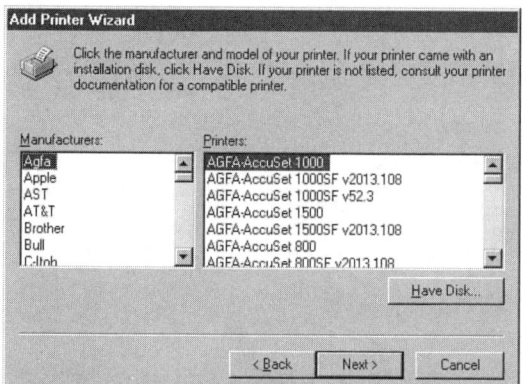

Figure 13.10

In the Add Printer Wizard, select the manufacturer and model for the printer you want to add.

Tip	When the Add Printer Wizard prompts you to choose a printer manufacturer and model, you can quickly skip to the list of your hardware manufacturer's printers by pressing the first letter of the manufacturer's name.

Unless your computer is a very recent model, it is very likely that Windows 98 already has a driver for your printer. Windows 98 includes drivers for more than 1,000 different printers. If your printer is not among those listed, however, you will have to click on the Have Disk button and insert a disk containing your printer's drivers into either the floppy disk drive or the CD-ROM drive. These drivers should have been supplied to you on disk when you bought your computer. After you indicate the drive on which Windows 98 should look, it will read the disk you have inserted and will list any available printer drivers found on that disk. Note that the driver might be in a subdirectory on the disk, so you should check the documentation that came with your printer if you are unable to locate the driver. In the event that you are still unable to locate the driver, you will need to contact the printer's manufacturer to obtain a Windows 98 driver for your printer (a Windows 95 driver should also work).

Note	If your printer's drivers did not come with Windows 98 and you cannot find your disk, you can always download the files from the manufacturer's web site.

After you have selected the correct manufacturer and printer model, click on the Next button. You will then be asked to choose the port on which you want to install the printer, as shown in Figure 13.11. This is the hardware port on your computer, to which you have attached the printer. In most cases the correct port is LPT1, although you may need to check with your computer's manufacturer or the documentation that came with your computer, to determine which port you should select.

Figure 13.11
The Add Printer Wizard asks you to select the port to which your printer is attached.

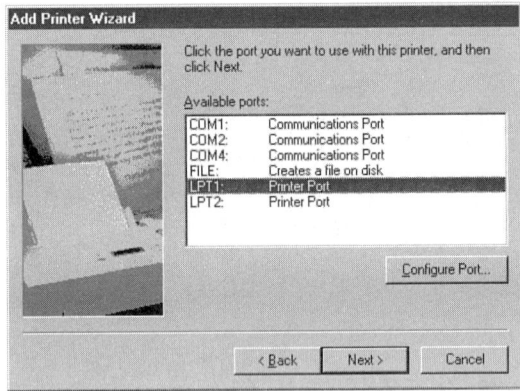

As part of the process of selecting a port, you can also configure the port, having Windows 98 always check the status of the port before it prints. If you want to change these settings, click on the Configure Port button found on this page of the Add Printer Wizard.

If your system contains an Enhanced Capability Port (ECP), you should install the printer to that port unless it is already being used by another device. ECP supports a higher bandwidth and allows bidirectional information to be passed between the computer and the printer.

After selecting a port for your printer you will be asked to choose a name for the printer. In most cases the default, which is usually the brand and model number, should suffice, but if you have multiple printers you may prefer to think of a name that reminds you of the printer's location. If you already have another printer installed on your computer, you will be asked whether you want the new printer to be the default Windows printer.

You will then come to the last page of the Add Printer Wizard, where you will be asked whether you want to print a test page. Microsoft recommends that you print a test page when you install a printer. This is a good opportunity to make sure everything is working correctly. Simply choose the Yes radio button, which is selected by default, and a test page will be printed as soon as your printer has been installed.

When you click on the Finish button, Windows 98 will install and configure the printer for your computer. Unless the drivers for this printer have previously been added to your computer, a dialog box will appear asking you to insert the Windows 98 CD-ROM. After you put the CD-ROM into the drive and click the OK button, the printer driver and any other necessary files will be copied to your computer. Then an icon for your printer will appear in the Printers folder. If this is the only printer installed on your computer it will automatically be selected as the default printer.

Setting Up a Network Printer

Setting up a network printer in Windows 98 can be as easy as connecting to a local printer. Windows 98's Point and Print feature will usually allow you to automatically install the correct network printer driver without requiring the Windows 98 CD-ROM or another disk containing the printer driver. Through Point and Print, when you use the Add Printer Wizard to add a network printer, Windows 98 will often be able to download the printer driver from the computer or server to which the printer is attached.

Before attempting to set up a network printer on your computer, you need to know how to connect to the printer. Here is some of the information you need to know:

- The name that the printer and its attached computer or server (if applicable), use on the network

- Whether the desired network printer is set up for sharing over the network—you can't install a network printer unless the printer it references is shared—and whether the permissions for the printer support network access from the account you're using

- The exact model of that printer, such as HP LaserJet 5

Open the Printers folder and double-click on the Add Printer icon. The Add Printer Wizard appears. Select the radio button for Network Printer and click the Next button.

You are asked to supply the location of the printer on the network. If you already know the share name of the printer and the computer name of the computer to which it is attached, you can simply type the path in the box labeled Network **p**ath or queue name, as shown in Figure 13.12. You need to supply the universal naming convention (UNC) path for the location of the printer, such as *computername**printername*, where *computername* is the name of the computer to which the printer is attached and *printername* is the share name of the printer.

If you are not sure of the exact name of the computer and printer on the network, click on the B**r**owse button.

> **Note** You can choose to install a single printer each time you run the Add Printer Wizard. If you want to install more than one printer on your computer you have to add them one at a time.

Before you move on to the next window in the Add Printer Wizard, check the correct radio button indicating whether you want to print from MS-DOS–based programs. If you select Yes and click on the Next button, the next window of the wizard will request that you capture a printer port for these MS-DOS programs. As described earlier in this chapter, MS-DOS programs often need to believe that they are printing to a local port. If you capture a port, when MS-DOS programs attempt to print to this port, Windows 98 will redirect the print job to the network printer automatically.

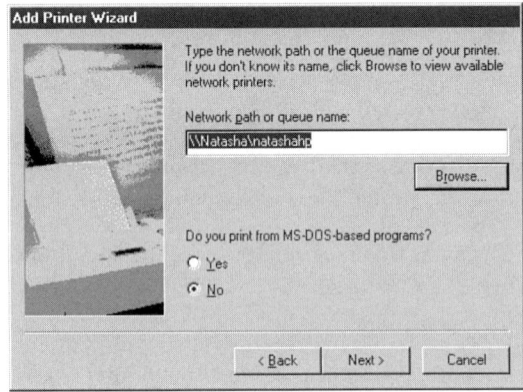

Figure 13.12
Enter the UNC path for the share name of the printer you want to install as a network printer.

> **Note** If the printer isn't configured for Point and Print, you may be asked to provide a manufacturer and model, as you would with a local printer.

As with local printers, the Add Printer Wizard will ask whether you want to print a test page. Select the Yes radio button if you want to see whether your connection to the network printer is working properly. After you have decided whether to print a test page, press the Finish button to install the printer on your computer.

After you have selected the network printer that you want to install and have finished with the Add Printer Wizard, Windows 98 will connect to that printer to determine its exact type. Having determined the make and model of the printer, Windows 98 will then see whether you already have a correct version of that printer's driver available on your computer. If you do, the printer should install correctly and you will be finished adding this printer to your Printers folder. In most cases, however, Windows 98 will either download the correct driver to your computer or you will be prompted to insert a disk containing the driver into one of your disk drives.

> **Tip** Although you can use the Add Printer Wizard to add a network printer to your computer, an easier way is to open Network Neighborhood and browse for the printer (you will probably first have to double-click on the icon for the computer to which the printer is attached). After you have found the printer, right-click on the printer's icon and choose Install. This will open the Add Printer Wizard but skip several windows, thus making it easier and quicker to add a network printer.

Point and Print

After you have finished with the Add Printer Wizard, Windows 98 will attempt to install the printer driver from the computer to which the printer is attached. In many cases, if the shared printer is set up correctly on the computer to which it is attached, Windows 98 will be able to download the printer driver from that computer and install it on your computer. This feature is known as Point and Print.

Assuming that this process works correctly on your computer, you should see a dialog box telling you that Windows 98 has found the proper driver on the remote computer and is installing the driver on your computer. After this process is finished, you can connect to and use that printer.

For the Point and Print feature to work properly, the computer to which the shared printer is attached must be running Windows 98, Windows NT Server, or Novell Netware. This feature does not always work properly, however, and you may still have to install the printer driver from either the Windows 98 CD-ROM or the printer driver disk supplied by your printer manufacturer.

If you are unable to install the driver for your printer through Point and Print, Windows 98 will attempt to install the driver from disk. If the driver was supplied on the Windows 98 CD-ROM, you will be prompted to insert that disk into your disk drive. If the driver is only available on a floppy disk or a different CD-ROM, however, you will need to direct Windows 98 to the location of that driver by browsing to its location on the disk.

Printing from Applications

In Windows 98, when you print from a Windows application, you can change a number of the printer's configurations within the application itself for the print job you are processing. These changes apply only to the application in which you are working; when you later open another application, the normal default settings will appear.

In most Windows applications you can print the document that you are working on by clicking a toolbar button or by selecting **P**rint from the **F**ile pull-down menu. After you tell the application to print the document, you will likely be presented with a window in which you can change any settings for that print job. Note that although you don't always see this window when you choose a Print button on a toolbar, you should always see a Print window if you use the pull-down menu.

Figure 13.13 shows the Print dialog box as it appears in the WordPad application that comes with Windows 98. This window shows the relevant information on the selected printer, such as the printer's name and its current status. To change from the default printer to a different printer, simply choose the other printer from the drop-down box.

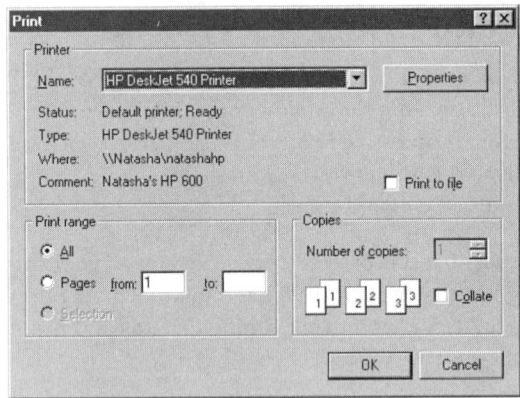

Figure 13.13
The WordPad printer dialog box.

If you click the Properties button a separate window appears that contains many of the same properties settings that are available for this printer in the Printers folder.

Note that the Print dialog box includes an option to print to a file rather than to the selected printer. If you choose this option, the printer output will be saved in a data file.

Managing Print Jobs

To view the status of a printer, you can open the printer window for that device. If you are in the process of printing a document from your computer, you can click on the printer icon in the system tray to bring up the window for that printer. You can also open that printer's window by double-clicking on its icon in the Printers folder.

When you open a printer window, all the currently pending documents for that printer are displayed. The pending print jobs are shown in order in the print queue, with the job at the top of the queue showing the document currently being printed. Any documents below that will be printed in descending order.

Other information presented in this queue window includes:

- **Status.** This tells you such things as whether the document is currently printing or is paused.

- **Owner.** The owner is the user who sent the document to the printer.

- **Progress.** This parameter displays the progress of the print job.

- **Started at.** As the name implies, this tells you the time at which the print job was started.

By right-clicking on any of your pending print jobs, you can choose to either pause or cancel that job. When you pause a print job, it will be skipped over when its place in the queue comes up. You can exercise control over your own documents, depending on the security configuration, but you may not be able to pause or cancel other people's print jobs unless you have administrative privileges on that printer.

In addition to pausing or canceling print jobs, you can elect to purge all pending documents by selecting that option from the **P**rinter pull-down menu, subject to the security restrictions discussed earlier regarding other user's documents. You can also change any of the properties for the selected printer by choosing P**r**operties from the **P**rinter pull-down menu.

Special Printing Considerations

Most of the main printing features found in Windows 98 have already been discussed, but a number of other areas are worth considering. This section looks at the following topics:

- Dragging and dropping a file onto a printer's icon
- Printing a file from any disk drive through the Windows Explorer
- Printing frames in HTML documents viewed in Internet Explorer
- Printing documents containing color graphics
- Printing when your printer is unavailable

Drag-and-Drop Printing

If you drag and drop a document icon onto a printer icon, Windows 98 will print the document. One strategy is to create a desktop shortcut for one or more of your installed printers. You can then drag documents from any window and drop them onto the printer shortcut.

To create a desktop shortcut for one of your printers, open the Printers folder. With either your left or right mouse button, select the printer's icon from the folder and drag it to the desktop. When you release the mouse button, a shortcut for the printer will be created.

> **Note** If you prefer not to create a desktop shortcut for the printer, you can drag and drop documents directly to the printer's icon in the Printers folder.

When you drag a document onto a printer icon, Windows 98 opens the related application, prints the document within the program, and then closes that application. Because Windows 98 looks for a program that has previously been associated with that type of file in order for it to open an application and print the document, you need to have previously installed a program on your computer that is registered for handling that file type. Thus, if you want to print a document created in Microsoft Excel, you need to have Excel loaded on your computer.

Printing Files from Disk

In addition to printing files by dragging and dropping them onto printer icons, you can print them directly from disk. In most cases this is the quickest way to print a document without having to open the application.

To print a file directly from disk, select the file from within Windows Explorer. The file can be located on any floppy, hard, or network drive to which you have access. Right-click on the file and choose **P**rint. Windows 98 will open the application associated with the file type extension, print the file in that application, and close the application automatically.

Printing Frames in Internet Explorer

The print window that appears when you are printing from an application will normally appear consistent from program to program, but one difference occurs when you print a document that contains multiple frames within Internet Explorer. When a web page contains multiple frames, although it appears to be a single page, it is actually made up of multiple pages which appear within a single frame set. All of these frames are separate documents that can be printed out through your computer.

When you print a page containing multiple frames, the print window will include additional options not found when you print from other applications. You can elect to print the selected frame (usually the main, or largest, frame), to print all of the frames individually, or to print the frame set as it appears on your screen. You can also select the option to print all linked documents, in which case Internet Explorer will print all pages for which hyperlinks appear on the page you are printing. Alternatively, you can print a table containing links for these documents.

For further information on printing within Internet Explorer see Chapter 27, "Internet Browsers in Windows 98."

Printing in Color

One possible problem when you print color graphics is that the color displayed on your monitor might not match the color generated by the printer. To help alleviate this problem, Microsoft has included support for Image Color Matching (ICM) in Windows 98. Windows 95 supported ICM 1.0; Windows 98 supports the newer ICM 2.0, which includes a number of technical improvements. The end result is a better correlation between the colors as they appear on your monitor and those that are generated by your color printer. Since ICM is supported on multiple platforms, the images you create in Windows 98 applications should appear virtually the same on computers that are running other ICM 2.0–compliant operating systems.

Offline Printing

As its name implies, offline printing enables you to generate print jobs when your computer is not connected to a printer, and to have them printed at a later time. Offline printing is useful for a laptop computer that may spend much of the time disconnected from the printer. Similarly, in a network environment, users may want to print to a printer that is temporarily offline for servicing.

> **Note** Offline printing only works for network printers, and requires the use of the print spooler.

To use offline printing, open the Printers folder and select the network printer you want to use offline. Right-click on the printer's icon and choose Use Printer Offline. Any print jobs you generate will be held in the queue until you instruct Windows 98 to actually print these jobs. When you want to print the stored jobs, right-click on the printer's icon and deselect the Use Printer Offline option.

If your laptop is configured to be used with a docking station, when you boot your computer, Windows 98 will automatically select offline printing if it detects that you are not connected to the docking station. If you later boot your laptop while it is attached to the network, the offline printing feature will be turned off and any stored print jobs will be sent to your printer.

Removing Printers

To remove a printer and its related drivers from your computer, open the Printers folder. Right-click on the printer's icon and choose **D**elete. Windows 98 will ask you to confirm that you want to remove that printer from your computer. Click on the Yes button, and the printer will then be removed from your computer.

During the process of removing the printer, a dialog box will appear asking whether you also want to remove the files used by that printer. The files to which Windows 98 is referring are the printer's driver and any other related files needed by that particular printer. If you think you might use that printer in the future, you can choose No to keep these files on your computer. By doing so you will not need to install the files from the Windows 98 CD-ROM the next time you add the printer to your computer. Otherwise, choose Yes to remove all the files associated with this printer from your computer.

Working with Fonts

When you install a printer on your computer several fonts specifically supported by that printer may also be installed. Additionally, Windows 98 supplies a number of fonts. You can also add fonts to your Windows 98 configuration. *Soft fonts* are fonts installed directly into Windows 98. You install and manage soft fonts through the Fonts folder in Control Panel.

The Printer Properties dialog box for your printer may include a Fonts tab, which lets you install and manage printer-resident or cartridge fonts for the printer.

> **Note** A printing administration utility such as HP JetAdmin also lets you install and manage printer-resident fonts.

Windows 98 supports the four types of fonts named here:

Name of Font Type	Font File Extension
TrueType	.TTF
OpenType	.OTF
Vector	.FON
Raster	.FON

To install a soft font, follow these steps:

1. Double-click the Fonts icon in the Control Panel.

2. In the Fonts folder, select Install New Font from the File pull-down menu.

3. In the Add Fonts dialog box, shown in Figure 13.14, navigate to the location of the fonts file for the font you want to install. Click on the Network button to map a network drive to the font file.

You can also use the Fonts folder to see what any installed font will look like in your applications and printed documents. If you double-click a font icon, a separate viewer window appears; it contains information about the font as well as a display of how characters (such as letters) will appear. You can also elect to print an example of this font from within this viewer window.

To delete a soft font from your system, right-click on the font icon in the Fonts folder and choose Delete. A dialog box will ask whether you want to delete this font from your system. If you select Yes, the font and any related files will be deleted.

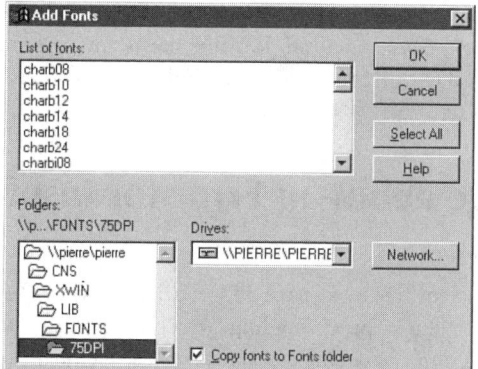

Figure 13.14
The Add Fonts dialog box.

Troubleshooting Printer Problems

Windows 98 includes a Print Troubleshooter, a wizard-like guide designed to help you solve common print errors. If you experience a printing problem in Windows 98 and are not able to fix it on your own, try the Print Troubleshooter before seeking technical support.

To start the Print Troubleshooter, click on the Start button and select **H**elp. When the Help window opens, double-click on the Troubleshooting book icon and then on the Windows 98 Troubleshooters icon. A list of Troubleshooters will appear. Click on Print in this list to open the Windows 98 Print Troubleshooter.

To use the Troubleshooter, select the radio button for the type of problem closest to the one you are experiencing. Then press the Next button and proceed through the steps, which are designed to help solve your problem. Although the Print Troubleshooter will help you isolate some of the most common problems, there are many types of problems the Printer Troubleshooter won't catch.

Some of these printer problems and their resolutions follow.

Your Printer Does Not Print

- Check to make sure that the printer is turned on and is not offline, and that it has paper.

- Make sure that the cables are attached properly. You might want to disconnect and reconnect the cables to ensure a good connection.

- Try turning the printer off, waiting a few seconds, and then turning it on again. This could clear any memory problems that it might be having.

- Check the printer on your computer queue for additional information as to why the job might not be printing. Purge all documents from the queue and try to print the document again.

- If you are printing to a network printer, try opening the printer from the Printers section of the Control Panel. If the printer is turned off, is offline, or is having problems, you might not be able to connect to the printer, which may indicate that a network problem exists.

You Receive a Message about an Error for Insufficient Memory or Disk Space

- Make sure that you have sufficient free disk space on the drive on which Windows 98 is installed. By default Windows 98 uses print spooling, which temporarily stores the print job on your hard drive. If you don't have sufficient hard disk space the print spooler will not function properly.

- Close all open applications except the one from which you are printing. Then try to print again. You may need to consider adding more memory (RAM) to your computer.

Your Print Spooler Might Not Be Functioning Properly, Causing an Error When You Try to Print

- If an unexplained error occurs when you try to print a document it may be because the print spooler is not working properly. The first thing you might try is deleting any old print spool files. These are files that might be left from occasions when a spooled document did not fully print or an error occurred. These files can conflict with current print spool files and should be removed if you are experiencing problems with printing. To remove these old files, delete all files with the .spl extension, which should be located in your Windows System/Spool/Printers directory.

- If this does not solve your problem you should try disabling print spooling. To disable print spooling, open the Printer Properties dialog box for the printer, select the Details tab, click on spool settings, and, in the Spool Settings dialog box, select Print directly to the printer.

Conclusion

This chapter described how to install, configure, and manage local and network printers. The chapter discussed the Windows 98 printer subsystem and described how to use the Printers folder and the Add Printer Wizard. The chapter also discussed some special Windows 98 printing features, such as point and print, drag and drop, offline printing, and HTML frame set printing.

Multimedia

Media are the electronic and mechanical means a computer uses to communicate with you. The monitor and video card combination provide you with something to see. Speakers and a sound device supply the sound. Force-feedback systems—joysticks that fight back and special computer chairs that rock and roll—take advantage of your sense of touch. These are the media discussed in this chapter.

The term multi *comes into play when Windows 98 synchronizes the activities of the various media. Given Windows 98's function as a multimedia mediator, this chapter spends more time on hardware concerns than many other chapters in this book. This multimedia discussion proceeds according to the following outline:*

- The PC 98 specification: anticipating hardware requirements
- Installation: preparing to upgrade
- Bus standards: moving data through the computer
- Software standards: looking beneath the surface
- Sight: taking a look at video
- Sound: giving audio a fair hearing
- Touch: getting in touch with input devices
- A simple example: putting WordPad to work
- Troubleshooting: crushing bugs

The PC 98 Specification

Microsoft and Intel created a "PC 98" specification for use in developing hardware for Windows 98 and Windows NT 5.0. It first specifies a "Basic PC 98" and goes on to outline three main PC categories that build on the Basic PC's foundation: the Consumer PC, the Office PC, and the Entertainment PC.

According to Microsoft and Intel, the Basic PC requires the following hardware (or their equivalents):

- A 200 MHz Pentium MMX processor
- 256 K Level 2 cache
- 32 M RAM (64 M recommended)

The Consumer PC targets the relatively non-networked home user who will balance the checkbook, connect to the Internet, and play the occasional game. The Office PC is designed for a networked office environment where the goal is to keep the total cost of ownership (TCO) low.

The Entertainment PC is the most technologically ambitious category. Because the reader of this chapter is (or will be) serious about not compromising his or her computer's multimedia performance, the Entertainment PC category should be considered the most reasonable Windows 98 baseline. Recommended components for Entertainment PC systems include the following:

- Two USB (Universal Serial Bus) ports
- Two IEEE 1394 (FireWire) ports

- No ISA (Industry Standard Architecture) expansion slots—ISA is no longer the industry standard!

- A DVD-ROM drive

- Audio support for 3D effects, music synthesis, and echo cancellation

- An AGP (Advanced Graphic Port) savvy graphics adapter

- Hardware acceleration for 2D and 3D graphics

- Support for analog video input and capture

- An analog television tuner

- Support for DTV (digital television) beginning in 1999

Now you know what Microsoft and Intel expect you to own if you intend to take full advantage of Windows 98's multimedia offerings.

An interesting item in the preceding Entertainment PC list is the "no ISA" requirement. In particular, 16-bit support is fading fast. This may cause you to grind your teeth a bit if you recently shelled out a chunk of change for a high-end ISA sound card.

A corollary to the "no ISA" law is "get lots of PCI slots" if you intend to take your multimedia explorations to the limit. To upgrade an older bare-bones motherboard, for example, you may be adding a DVD/MPEG decoder card, a video card, a network card (if you stick with old-fashioned Ethernet), a SCSI (Small Computer System Interface) card, a sound card, a TV tuner card, and other sundry slot fillers. As time passes, more and more of the card functionality will be built into the motherboard (such as DVD/MPEG decoding) or be rendered obsolete by new technologies (such as USB and IEEE 1394 usurping SCSI's traditional role). But if you have a motherboard you want to upgrade *right now*, take the time to plan how you want to allocate your precious PCI slot resources.

Installing Multimedia

Because Windows 98 differs from its older kin, you should rightly expect some software installation glitches. In the heat of battle, you may be tempted to delete old programs and drivers using brute force. Resist that temptation! Windows 98 is happiest when you use your original setup program to install or uninstall software. Ideally, a good installer provides an uninstall option that not only cleans out the program files and any associated DLLs but also tidies up the Windows Registry.

If your software's installer does not offer an uninstall option, the next place to go is to Windows' Add/Remove Programs Control Panel (see Figure 14.1).

Figure 14.1

The Windows 98 Add/Remove Programs Control Panel.

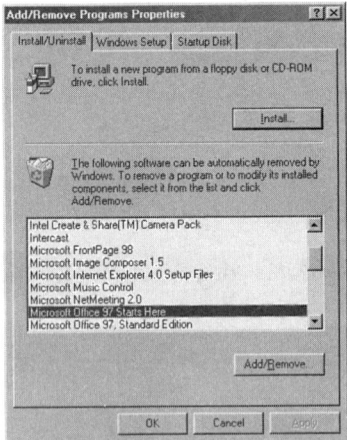

There may be cases in which neither of these installation or uninstallation options applies (with an old DOS-based game, for example). But it is important to let Windows do as much of the bookkeeping for you as possible. The last thing you want to do is to spend hours trying to figure out why the proper driver for your sound or video card won't load.

Note As you open up packages containing the new software and hardware you'll be purchasing, you may ask this question: Where is the paper documentation? The minimal amount of printed material can be ascribed to a number of factors:

- The wizards in Windows 98 (and in most modern software packages) are intelligent enough to handle the vast majority of installation situations.

- The emphasis on online documentation—particularly as it relates to grabbing late-breaking updates from the Web—allows manufacturers to provide interactive, up-to-date information for their products.

- Paper documentation is more expensive for the manufacturer to create and ship.

Don't be fooled by the absence of printed information. If you want to take full advantage of your new multimedia capabilities, inspect the electronic documentation. If you are one of those folks who has to have paper documentation, use the Custom option in your software's Setup program to install the documentation by itself before you install the main program. Also visit the company's web site and see whether there are fresh tips, warnings, or patches. Then you can print out everything you require before the new software has a chance to confuse your printer or crash your computer!

Understanding Bus Standards

Take a moment to familiarize yourself with this list of pertinent acronyms:

USB	Universal Serial Bus
IEEE 1394	Institute of Electrical and Electronic Engineers specification 1394 ("FireWire" is Apple's term)
PCI	Peripheral Component Interconnect
PC Card	PC Card (or PCMCIA—Personal Computer Memory Card International Association)
ISA	Industry Standard Architecture
SCSI	Small Computer System Interface

A *bus* is a collection of wires that connects the individual computer components—processor, memory, video, and audio chip sets. A *bus standard* is a set of rules that dictates how data is sent through a bus. Fast and efficient buses and bus standards are crucial elements in a multimedia computer because of the large amount of time-sensitive data that must be moved and processed.

Windows 98 emphasizes the use of three bus standards (USB, IEEE 1394, and PCI), discourages the use of ISA, and politely tolerates the use of SCSI. Portable computers use PC Cards—adapters that allow bus connections through miniaturized (3.3-mm to 10.5-mm thick) connectors. The following sections discuss the three bus types most commonly associated with multimedia: USB, IEEE 1394, and SCSI.

USB

If you've purchased a computer within the last year, it may already be equipped with USB. The name itself—Universal Serial Bus—expresses its goal: to provide all the functionality traditionally supplied by serial and parallel ports. USB intends to eliminate the headaches traditionally associated with adding PC peripherals (such as setting dip switches, jumpers, IRQs, DMA channels and I/O addresses). USB can do the following:

- Provide a data transfer rate of 12 Mbps
- Provide power to external devices
- Allow you to "hot swap" devices without requiring that you open the computer case or shut off the power
- Allow you to "daisy chain" up to 127 USB devices with cables up to 15 feet in length
- Support Plug and Play

USB's speed allows it to handle all but the most demanding I/O (input/output) chores. Keyboards, joysticks, modems, audio, and low-resolution video can all use USB. With USB, you don't have to open the computer's case to install a new peripheral. When you plug in a new USB device, Windows 98's Device Manager immediately gets to work, firing up the Add New Hardware Wizard and requesting any driver software the new device may require. Typically, you do not have to restart the computer. Multimedia mavens are arguably the prime benefactors in the move to USB.

USB-savvy keyboards, scanners, printers, CD-ROM drives, digital cameras, digital speakers, PC telephones, computer monitors, digital audio decoders, digital joysticks, and sophisticated game controllers promise to ease the pain of installation and setup.

You can view the latest USB lore at `http://www.usb.org`.

> **Tip**
>
> If you think something has gone wrong with the installation of your USB device, open the System Control Panel and click the Device Manager tab. Your new device should appear under the appropriate main device heading. In the example shown in Figure 14.2, the USB videoconferencing hardware appears under the Imaging Device heading.
>
> Check the driver properties to make sure that Windows 98 properly recognizes your hardware.

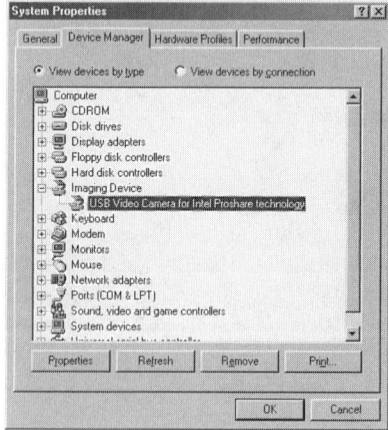

Figure 14.2
USB videoconferencing hardware in the System Control Panel's Device Manager.

IEEE 1394 (FireWire)

So you aren't satisfied with USB's 12 Mbps data transfer rate? You need to pipeline some high-resolution video and a bunch of high-quality audio tracks down the wire? Then step up to 100+ Mbps data transfer rates of IEEE 1394. According to IEEE gurus, 100 Mbps is just the beginning. The goal is to transfer at least 3.2 Gbps—gigabits per second—in the not-too-distant future. Like USB, IEEE 1394 supports hot swapping, daisy chaining of up to 63 devices, and Plug and Play operation.

Because IEEE 1394 is more expensive to implement, its rate of adoption may be slightly slower than that of USB. But with the Intel/Microsoft PC 98 calling for IEEE 1394 to replace Integrated Drive Electronics (IDE) and AT Attachment Packet Interface (ATAPI), you won't have to wait long.

If you don't want to wait at all, you can currently buy PCI-to-IEEE 1394 interface cards. Some of these cards provide both 1394 and SCSI standards. If you want to cover all your input/output bases without sacrificing too many PCI slots, this option is cheaper than buying a PCI expansion chassis.

More information can be found at http://developer.intel.com/solutions/tech/1394.htm.

SCSI

SCSI was the external bus speed king for a number of years. If you are coming to Windows 98 from the Macintosh multimedia world, you probably already have some SCSI devices at hand.

Over the years, SCSI chefs have been busy whipping up a variety of SCSI flavors:

- SCSI-1 (finalized in 1986) transfers data at 5 Mbps over an 8-bit ("narrow") bus. Up to seven SCSI devices can be daisy-chained to the SCSI controller card.

- SCSI-2 (finalized in 1990) added new features and paved the way for Fast and Wide SCSI options.

    - Fast SCSI transfers data at 10 Mbps over a narrow bus.

    - Wide SCSI transfers data at 10 Mbps over a 16-bit or 32-bit bus. Up to 15 devices can be daisy-chained to a Wide SCSI controller card.

    - Fast Wide SCSI transfers data at 20 Mbps.

- SCSI-3 (never finalized) is credited with introducing the "ultra" speed-doubling label to the SCSI family of terms.

    - Ultra SCSI transfers data at 20 Mbps over a narrow bus.

    - Ultra Wide SCSI (also known as SCSI-3) transfers data at 40 Mbps.

- Predictably, the "Ultra2" SCSI designation means that the transfer rate has been doubled again. Allowable cable lengths also increase from 10 feet to 30 feet.

    - Ultra2 Wide SCSI transfers data at 80 Mbps.

> **Tip** Although Wide Ultra SCSI is fast and sexy, consider your needs when shopping for a SCSI card. There is normally a considerable difference in cost between a plain-jane Fast SCSI-2 card and the Wide and Ultra SCSI card variations. If you just perform the occasional scan or are going to connect to an old, narrow SCSI hard drive, a top-of-the-line SCSI card is probably overkill.

Although rumor had it that SCSI devices were intended to be hot-swappable, it hasn't worked out that way in practice. Connecting or disconnecting a device from the SCSI chain while the power is on is not a good idea.

A chain of SCSI devices has to be "terminated" properly. SCSI terminators function as electronic shock absorbers, preventing data signals from being reflected back into the path of oncoming new data traffic. Most modern SCSI devices support "active" termination. If a device is actively terminated, it automatically senses its place in the SCSI chain and adjusts its behavior accordingly.

> **Tip** If you are shopping for a SCSI device (such as a scanner or hard drive), check to see whether it supports active termination. Active termination ensures that you don't have to worry about your whole SCSI configuration every time you rearrange your SCSI peripherals.

Understanding Software Standards

Windows 98's job is to coordinate the activity of all your new hardware and to translate information from one digital language into another. When you play a game, for example, the images on the screen must be synchronized with the sound coming out the speakers. Both video and audio, in turn, must respond quickly to new commands sent in from the joystick. If you consider manipulating high-resolution three-dimensional images, playing back sound sources that can be localized anywhere in the listener's field of hearing, and sending feedback to a joystick (telling it to fight back depending on the game's status), you can appreciate the magnitude of the multimedia coordination task. DirectX is the software that performs the coordination. Codecs (compressor/decompressor) provide the translations that convert specially encoded computer data into visual, audible, or tactile feedback. The following sections provide brief overviews of these processes.

DirectX

DirectX, originally intended to make Windows more game friendly, has extended its reach in Windows 98. DirectX now provides the infrastructure on which Windows 98's multimedia features depend. DirectX 5.0—the version included in the beta release of Windows 98—consists of six components:

- **DirectDraw**—originally Intel's Display Control Interface (DCI)—is the senior member of the DirectX family. DirectDraw's job is to speed up the 2D graphics response.

- **DirectSound** allows the sound (including 3D audio effects) to respond as quickly as the graphics. This DirectX component, for example, is in charge of WAV file playback.

- **Direct3D** speeds up and eases the pain of creating and manipulating a 3D graphics environment.

- **DirectInput** talks to your keyboard, mouse, joystick, graphics tablet, force-feedback device, or any other input device that Windows supports.

- **DirectSetup** makes it easy for DirectX to perform an installation.

- **AutoPlay** is the component that can automatically start a program from a compact disc or DVD as soon as it is inserted into the drive.

Additional DirectX components—DirectShow, DirectAnimation, DirectModel, VRML, DirectPlay, and Direct3D Retained Mode—are located at a higher-level "media layer," whose job is to further integrate the activity of the lower-level DirectX components. Taking the reins from the Windows 95's Media Control Interface (MCI), DirectShow is the component primarily responsible for communicating with DVD. Finally, more DirectX goodies are in the pipeline. DirectMusic, for example, will provide support for Musical Instrument Digital Interface (MIDI) and other interactive music applications.

The diagram in Figure 14.3 is taken from Microsoft's DirectX 5.0 Driver Development Kit.

The high-level software (usually an open software application) talks to DirectDraw. DirectDraw, in turn, talks to HAL and HEL—the Hardware Abstraction Layer and the Hardware Emulation Layer, respectively. HEL comes into play when the hardware vendor does not provide a DirectX driver. True to its name, the HEL provides an emulated DirectX driver that allows DirectX access to the hardware.

> **Note** Although the diagram in Figure 14.3 shows the configuration of DirectDraw, most of the other DirectX elements fit into the Windows picture in a similar fashion.

Unless you're a programmer, you probably have little reason to delve into DirectX's inner workings. But if your multimedia applications begin acting odd, you may want to do some DirectX troubleshooting. See the "Troubleshooting" section at the end of this chapter for some DirectX tips.

For the latest DirectX news, check http://www.microsoft.com/DirectX.

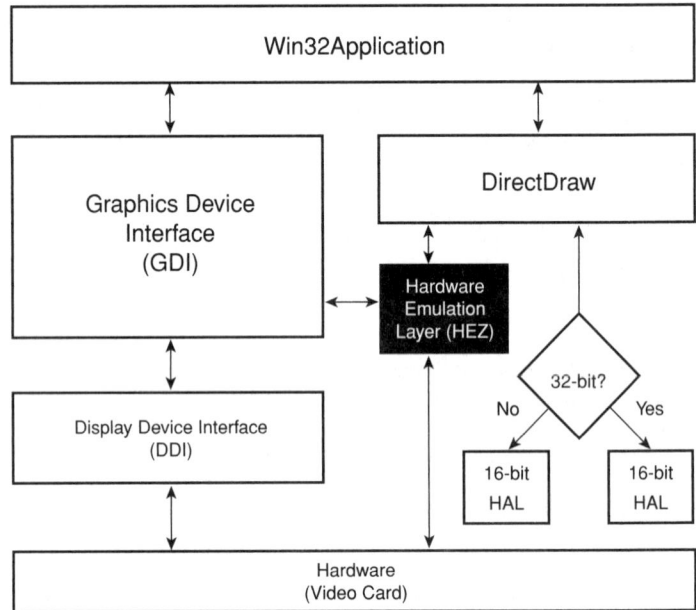

Figure 14.3
DirectDraw in relation to other system software elements.

Codecs

A *codec* (compressor/decompressor) performs the work of converting raw data either to or from an encoded state. Codecs are necessary because many languages are spoken in the digital realm, and many hurdles (such as low-bandwidth pipelines) may have to be negotiated. The choice of codec—along with bit rate, color depth, and key frames—determines the size and quality of your processed file. For example, Windows 98's Sound Recorder Format option offers to save your recorded sound at CD Quality, Radio Quality, or Telephone Quality. A CD-quality file sounds good but is very large in size. A telephone-quality file doesn't sound as good as a CD-quality file but is much smaller in size. Different codecs offer different trade-offs for file size and quality. Because the theory behind all codecs—video and audio—is the same, both types are discussed in this section.

You can check to see which codecs are installed in your system by opening the Multimedia Control Panel, clicking the Devices tab, and opening the Video or Audio Compression Codecs list (see Figure 14.4).

Because the list of specific codecs you encounter changes as time passes, the following text discusses codecs in a general way.

Codec Speeds and Sizes

If you look at the list of Windows 98 video and audio codecs, you'll notice that there are quite a number of them. The list is lengthy because choosing a codec isn't as simple a process as some users (or technical support people) might wish. At the simplest level, codecs typically give you a choice between required processor power and size: The less the file has to be processed, the larger the file will probably be. Raw video data, for example, is relatively easy for a Pentium-class computer to handle but it requires a very large pipeline and, if you want to record it, a very, very large hard drive. On the other hand, if you are constrained by a 56 K modem and only a few gigabytes of storage space, the data must be compressed before it is transmitted and decompressed when it is received, placing more demands on the CPU.

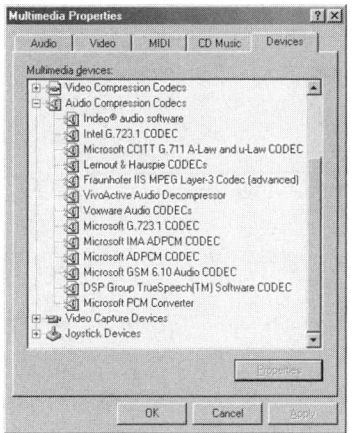

Figure 14.4
An example of Windows 98's Audio Compression Codecs list.

Once you face the inevitability of compression, you've begun the journey down the slippery slope of quality trade-offs. Do you require the unvarnished truth in your video and audio? If so, your compression schemes have to be "lossless"—every bit you encode on one end must come out in the decoding. Or can you live with a subtle diminution of quality? Can you even get by with a grainy, pixilated, color-challenged postage stamp of a picture? If so, you can choose a codec that employs a "lossy" encoding scheme—some of the less-important bits are thrown away by the encoder.

Which bits are the "less-important" ones? Different codecs embody different philosophies, but there are two broad categories: interframe and intraframe compression. Interframe, as its name suggests, determines the differences between two separate frames and throws away the common information. Intraframe compression looks at all the pixels in one frame and outputs a shorthand description.

Because one minute of uncompressed standard broadcast-quality video (at 30 frames per second) consumes over a gigabyte of memory, there is no such thing as a lossless video codec. But that's okay because uncompressed video typically contains a lot of redundant information when you analyze it on a frame-by-frame basis. Audio files, however, can use lossless compression schemes because the traditional upper limit of a 48 KHz sampling rate can easily be accommodated by Pentium-class computers.

Of course, you may not want to limit your audience to Windows owners. There are other operating systems: Mac OS, UNIX, BeOS, Windows 3.x, and even DOS! If you want your end product to be universally viewable, pick a format (AIFF audio, for example) that is available across the broadest variety of platforms.

The decoding of a file does not necessarily require as much number crunching as the encoding of a file. Asymmetrical encoding schemes, such as MPEG, perform a considerable amount of data massaging during the encoding process. When the MPEG file is played back, it doesn't demand as much of the CPU's attention. Asymmetrical encoding also lends itself to interframe analysis because the encoder usually has the leisure to look over a number of frames during the compression process. A symmetrical approach, such as Indeo video R3.2, is more evenhanded. If a computer can play back a file that was symmetrically encoded, chances are that computer can successfully record that same type of file.

Symmetry is relatively important for situations in which you anticipate having the same resources on both ends of the distribution pipeline. Internet communications devices, for example, usually use symmetrical codecs to encode and decode video and audio. Asymmetry is more desirable in one-way distribution, where the author has the time and money to preprocess the file. The MPEG files on a DVD-Video release are a prime example of an asymmetrical situation.

Window 98's Sound Recorder is the best place to see (or at least hear) codecs in action. Sound Recorder's File menu contains a Properties command that allows you to choose from a number of audio codecs. The "Sound Recorder" section, later in this chapter, contains an example that describes the codec selection process in more detail.

In general, your video/audio codec choices are as follows:

- How much (if any) of the original information can you stand to lose?
- If you have to lose information, how do you want to lose it?
- How big do you want the final, encoded file to be?
- Which operating systems will your audience use?
- How much computing power is available on the encoding computer?
- How much computing power is available on the decoding computer?
- Is the computer on the receiving end equipped with a codec that will allow your file to be decoded?

Because the world of codecs is still rapidly evolving, and because the video or audio editing package you buy will undoubtedly contain recommendations as to what format is best suited to a particular condition, we won't cover specific codec quirks. But there is one codec standard whose stock seems to rise daily: MPEG (Moving Picture Experts Group).

MPEG

MPEG is a family of formats that currently contains MPEG-1 (video and audio storage), MPEG-2 (digital television), MPEG-4 (multimedia), and MPEG-7 (content description). There is no MPEG-3. Originally intended to work with HDTV (high-definition television), MPEG-3 was dropped when the digital television movers and shakers decided to use MPEG-2 instead. MPEG-4 and MPEG-7 have not yet been generally implemented. This section touches on the most important aspects of MPEG-1 and MPEG-2.

> **Note** If you have spent much time on the Internet, you have probably heard people discuss MPEG-3, or MP3—particularly in reference to audio files. What they are really describing is the MPEG-1, Layer 3 format.

MPEG in all its manifestations uses lossy compression algorithms. For video, MPEG employs both interframe and intraframe techniques in sophisticated ways to achieve a very substantial reduction in file size. MPEG audio relies on psychoacoustic phenomenon (such as the "masking" effect)—also referred to as "perceptual coding"—to filter out data that the human ear cannot detect.

MPEG requires lots of horsepower, particularly for encoding. Until recently, additional MPEG hardware was usually necessary to manipulate MPEG images at anything approaching 30 frames per second, the broadcast video standard. But with the advent of Pentium II-class processors and higher-speed data buses, MPEG encoding and decoding can be performed in software.

The layers of MPEG-1 audio all share the same make-the-best-of-a-lossy-situation philosophy. MPEG audio layers are differentiated by how hard they have to work to keep the perceived audio information accurate. Layer 1 uses relatively simple psychoacoustic models, meaning that the processor doesn't have to work too hard to encode or decode MPEG Layer 1 audio files. Layer 2's codec incorporates more sophisticated models, the codec works harder, and the resultant files are smaller than Layer 1 files. Layer 3 applies the most complex formulas to the raw material, works the hardest, and produces the smallest output files. Using Layer 3, you can compress a 12 M audio file down to a 1 M Layer 3 file and still retain CD-quality audio. If your audience requires only FM-quality audio, that same 12 M file can be squeezed down to 500 K. If audio quality is far down on your list (as in simple voice communication), you can squeeze that 12 M file down to 125 K and still be able to understand what is being said. Likewise, MPEG video schemes provide compression ratios of up to 30:1.

For the latest in MPEG developments, visit http://www.mpeg.org.

Other Video and Audio File Formats

Here is a list of the most common video and audio formats, followed by their filename extensions:

- Audio-Video Interleaved (.AVI). Microsoft's video file format.
- QuickTime (.MOV). Apple's video file format.
- Wave (.WAV). Microsoft's audio file format.
- AU (.AU or .SND). The most popular UNIX audio file format.
- AIFF (.AIF or .AIFF). A high-quality audio format used on many platforms.

For audio formats, you get your pick of sampling sizes (8-bit or 16-bit), number of channels (stereo or mono), and sampling rates (from 8 KHz to 48 KHz).

Because all these formats use symmetrical codecs, you have to make a not-so-simple choice between size and quality when you decide to create a file. Given all the possible combinations of options, perhaps the best way to decide is to take a sample file (preferably one of high quality), save it in a number of formats, and play back the results. An even easier way to decide is to accept the default format in the multimedia application you are using and not worry about it!

A vast amount of information is available on the subject of file formats—and the information changes rapidly. The best way to ferret out the most up-to-date news is to go to Yahoo! (http://www.yahoo.com) and search on **data formats**. You'll find more than you bargained for.

Understanding Video Requirements

DVD and TV tuners are the high-profile video gadgets that have been grabbing most of the Windows 98 attention. But to take full advantage of these new media, a number of prerequisites must be satisfied. The following sections discuss video hardware considerations and then look at the software ramifications.

Video Card Memory

You should have distilled the essence of this chapter's message by now: *More!* You shouldn't be surprised to learn, then, that you should pack as much memory into your video card as you can afford. A DVD/MPEG decoder card will probably object to 256 colors and refuse to run, so consider 16-bit color to be the multimedia minimum. Combine the thousands-of-colors minimum with a bare-bones resolution of 800×600 (640×480 resolution is simply too low), and you end up with a minimum Video RAM requirement of 2 M. Because RAM is so cheap, you may as well install at least 4 M up front and not worry about running with a marginal amount of video RAM.

A less cut-and-dried decision is what kind of memory your video card should use. In very rough order from lowest to highest power (and cost), your options are DRAM (Dynamic Random Access Memory), EDO RAM (Extended Data Out RAM), SGRAM (Synchronous Graphic Random Access Memory), MDRAM (Multibank DRAM), VRAM (Video RAM), WRAM (Window RAM), and RDRAM (Rambus DRAM). If you are buying a new system from a reputable manufacturer, the amount and type of the memory you receive in the box is probably more than adequate. But if you are upgrading an older system and your old video card uses DRAM, you may want to consider buying a new video card that sports a faster variety of memory (VRAM, SGRAM, or MDRAM), particularly if you are adding a DVD-ROM drive.

Video Card Speed

You've undoubtedly seen ads touting video acceleration, be it 2D or 3D. *Acceleration* simply means that the video card has its own processor. Acceleration may have been a big deal a few years ago, but it is pretty standard fare today. The question is now how much acceleration is enough.

The RAMDAC (Random Access Memory Digital-to-Analog Converter) is the device that does the processing on the video card. It has to be fast enough to provide a steady stream of information to your monitor. Otherwise, your monitor will *flicker*—a phenomenon that sounds more innocuous than it really is. Remember the queasy feeling you develop in the pit of your stomach when you have to endure the presence of a failing fluorescent bulb? That's flicker.

On the other hand, if the *refresh rate* of your video system—the speed at which your video card and monitor agree to redraw the screen—is high enough to eliminate the perception of flicker, there is no reason to require a higher-performance video card. If your video system can supply a refresh rate of 85 Hz at a resolution of 1024×768, that should satisfy all but the most demanding user. A 72 Hz refresh rate is usually adequate.

Another technique to speed up video has recently lent its acronym—AGP (Accelerated Graphics Port)—to the legions of computer acronyms. The idea behind AGP is simple: Provide a dedicated path between the video processor and system memory. AGP gives the video processor the opportunity to get what it needs when it needs it without having to wait for any other device and without having to clog any of the other data buses with video information. AGP is essentially a carpool lane for video information.

Although the target audience for the initial wave of AGP-enhanced computers is professionals who require the power to render 3D video quickly, AGP will soon appear in mainstream consumer-level machines.

You can get more information from Intel's AGP web site at http://developer.intel.com/technology/agp/.

General Video/TV Tuner/MPEG Decoder Card Installation Tips

Keep the following tips in mind when you're installing multimedia hardware:

- Make sure that the computer, the monitor, and any peripherals attached to the computer are turned off before you begin yanking or fastening cards and connectors.

- If your card contains jumpers or any other suspicious-looking pins or switches, triple-check their settings against your card's and your computer's documentation. The older the card, the more important this step becomes.

- Once you have firmly pressed the cards into their slots, make sure that the brackets are screwed down. Inspect the cards carefully to ensure that one card does not touch another.

- If you have installed an MPEG decoder or a TV tuner card, remember to connect the internal audio cable(s) to your sound card, DVD drive, or CD drive. An internal audio cable is typically gray with either small black (or smaller white) connectors on the ends.

DVD (Digital Versatile Disc or Digital Video Disc)

Famous or infamous, DVD has at last arrived. Its storage capacity and format flexibility bring the fame. Its copy protection and horsepower requirements rate the infamy. But just about everyone agrees that DVD is the heir to the CD, VHS, and Laserdisc legacies. Let's review all the sections covered in this chapter so far and see how DVD fits in.

Although the absolute bare minimum that most DVD-equipped computers require is a true 133 MHz Pentium-compatible (OverDrive doesn't count), the farther upscale you can climb, the better. Most DVD-ROM drives require an MPEG decoder. That decoder occupies a PCI slot or an IEEE 1394 connection or a slot in the SCSI chain. No matter how it attaches, Windows 98's automatic configuration wizards kick in and guide you through the installation process. The codecs required—most notably MPEG—are installed and DirectX is engaged. If there are any problems, such as a DVD-hostile video configuration, alert boxes appear to describe the source of the problem.

Even though your DVD-ROM drive is probably not accompanied by a large, printed manual, it behooves you to peruse the online DVD documentation. This recommendation also applies to each and every DVD disc you buy. DVD's flexibility allows the creator of each disc to add a raft of features to their presentation that another disc may lack entirely. If you sense an open-ended quality in the DVD Player's help file, that's why.

Tip	Speaking of the DVD Player's help file, you should use it right away (but it may already be too late)!

> If you are concerned about using the parental control features of DVD Player, you must be the first to get to the DVD Logon dialog box (available from the Options menu). The first person to find the Logon dialog box determines the passwords that dictate who can and cannot watch a DVD.

Flavors of DVD

Now that we're in the DVD section, it's time to be a little more specific about the varieties of DVD.

The thing that resembles a high-tech cup holder is a DVD-ROM (DVD Read-Only Memory) drive. It can read DVD-ROM discs that can hold from 4.7 gigabytes (G) to 17 G of data. One subset of DVD-ROM is DVD-Video. DVD-Video is the motion-picture data format we've all heard so much about. A DVD-ROM, like a CD-ROM, can also hold other types of computer data. A stand-alone DVD-Video player can play a DVD-Video disc but cannot play a DVD-ROM disc because the computerless stand-alone player doesn't know what to do with the computer-oriented data files.

As time goes on, other products will appear with *DVD* in their names:

- DVD-R, a write-once recordable medium similar in function to CD-R.

- DVD+RW, a write-many medium similar in function to CD-RW.

- DVD-RAM, another write-many medium that requires the disc to be protected by a special cartridge.

- DVD-Audio, a format intended to replace CD-DA (Compact Disc Digital Audio) when DVDs replace CDs.

Divx is another format whose future is uncertain as of this writing. *Divx* is DVD-Video wedded to a pay-for-play mechanism. A Divx disc would have a low initial purchase price. For that low price, you receive the ability to watch the Divx movie for a certain period of time (perhaps for 48 hours after the initial viewing) or a certain number of times (perhaps three viewings). If you want to see the movie after the initial period expires, you'd have to buy and download an authorization code to unlock more time or viewings. Because the Divx debate is still in progress, it is doubtful that the first release of Windows 98's DVD Player will support any Divx functionality. But if a Divx standard is embraced, there will probably be an update that adds the Divx "feature."

Things You Can Do with DVD

The quantity of storage supplied by a DVD, combined with the sophisticated navigational architecture that DVD producers can use, allows more playback flexibility than any of DVD's predecessors, including CD, VHS, or film.

For example, a cinema purist can view his or her favorite flick in a variety of *aspect ratios* (the ratio of height to width). The aspect ratio of your computer monitor (and American TV) is 4:3; the aspect ratio at your favorite movie theater is 16:9 (featured in "letterboxed" editions on video tapes, for example). If you don't want to lose a portion of your DVD movie's visual content to the "pan-and-scan" cropping of the picture that television viewing has traditionally sanctioned, DVD Player allows you to choose your favorite format.

Dolby Audio Options

DVD can also bring theater-quality sound into your home. The audio features you hear the most about are Dolby Digital (or AC-3), Dolby Pro Logic, and Dolby Surround.

Dolby Digital, which first made its appearance in 1992, provides 5.1 channels of audio for your listening pleasure. 5.1 is not a typo; the ".1" channel is for subwoofer data. Because the frequency range of a subwoofer tops out at around 120 Hz, its reduced audio demands relegate it to "small" channel status. Dolby Digital consists of the following channels:

- Three full-range front channels: left, right, and center
- Two full-range surround channels, usually positioned at the sides of or behind the listener: left and right
- One (optional) low-frequency subwoofer channel

Dolby Surround Pro Logic, the predecessor of Dolby Digital, made its debut in 1987. It uses four full-range channels:

- Three front channels: left, right, and center
- One surround channel, usually reproduced through two speakers positioned at the sides of or behind the listener

Dolby Surround, released in 1982, is the oldest of these audio architectures. It consists of three full-range channels:

- Two front channels: left and right
- One surround channel, usually reproduced through two speakers positioned at the sides of or behind the listener

If you are interested in the audio side of the multimedia equation, you should keep these distinctions in mind. Just because your DVD setup can play back Dolby Digital does not mean that every DVD or CD you pop into the drive will be sonically rendered in 5.1-channel splendor. Check the fine print. A DVD must be encoded using Digital Dolby before it can play back Digital Dolby. When you purchase a DVD, check to make sure that the box says *Dolby Surround, Dolby Digital 5.1,* or something similar to ensure that your audio expectations are properly set.

On the other hand, don't panic if your sound system is an old-fashioned stereo. All DVDs have a built-in two-channel Dolby Digital decoder that takes the 5.1 channels and mixes them down to two.

Because the DVD arena is still rapidly evolving, DVD Player doesn't offer many audio features. The first two generations of DVD drive/MPEG decoder card packages didn't usually offer separate conventional audio outputs for the various channels. The full set of discrete channel information was usually available only through an S/PDIF (Sony/Philips Digital Interface) connector or an optical output on the DVD/MPEG decoder card. The S/PDIF or optical output was connected to an external surround processor. The surround processor was then hooked into the amplifiers and speakers, and off you went. But new DVD systems have built-in Dolby support, making the external surround processor unnecessary. As these changes make their way into the marketplace, DVD Player will be revised or supplemented by third-party DVD playback software.

> **A Little More DVD Player Advice**
>
> By default, DVD Player tries to begin playing a disc—the AutoPlay feature—as soon as one is placed in the drive. If you don't want DVD Player to start up immediately, press and hold the Shift key when you insert a DVD. You can permanently disable AutoPlay by going to the Device Manager and deselecting the Auto Insert Notification option.
>
> As mentioned earlier in this section, the DVD format presents many more multimedia opportunities than its predecessors. You can jump from one section of a movie to another, choose alternate views or scene takes, display subtitles, listen to alternate languages, and view additional information. The decision to implement any of these features and the design of the implementation is up to the DVD producer. This is another reason behind the simplicity of DVD Player. The best way to begin investigating the features offered on a particular DVD is to right-click the DVD Player's Play button.
>
> Speaking of languages, why not brush up on your foreign languages? You can display subtitles in one language and audio in another!

Things You *Can't* Do with DVD

The DVD acronym has been interpreted a number of different ways. If you are familiar with the historical struggles associated with DVD, another apt interpretation would be "Delayed Video Disc." Alas, the delays have not been caused by technical difficulties. The ongoing DVD saga is primarily a story of politics and high finance. In addition to taking advantage of DVD's loudly touted qualities, a number of interested parties saw in DVD the ability to correct some of the "mistakes" made in the Compact Disc specification. The CD's biggest flaw is that it (or the material on it) can be easily copied. So before you blame Windows 98 or your DVD drive for failing to respond to an old-fashioned drag-and-drop, consider the following three elements of DVD copy protection:

- Macrovision/APS (Analog Protection System)
- Serial Copy Generation Management System (CGMS)
- Content Scrambling System (CSS)

The Macrovision copy protection adds a signal to your DVD/MPEG decoder's composite and S-Video outputs that confuses most video recorders. This confusion manifests itself as random shifts in picture brightness and color. Because your video monitor is more forgiving than the typical VCR, plugging your DVD/MPEG decoder card's composite/S-Video output directly into your TV should result in a clear picture. Unfortunately, this can limit your ability to route your DVD signal through your VCR to your TV—even if you have no intention of copying the DVD onto tape. If you are not aware of the Macrovision/APS scheme, you may well tear your hair out troubleshooting hardware and software in an effort to "fix" components that are working flawlessly. The reason this is called an Analog Protection System is that the composite and S-Video outputs are analog, not digital.

The Serial Copy Generation Management System has been around for awhile, first surfacing in the DAT (Digital Audio Tape) world. It limits your ability to make digital copies of a file. For example, if you attempt to digitally transfer a file to a DAT deck, the copy management system may disable your DAT's record function.

The Content Scrambling System is a fancy way of saying that the data files on the DVD are encrypted. This encryption process is linked to a regional coding scheme. *Regional coding* allows a particular DVD to be displayed only on a DVD Player that was sold in a particular region. For example, if you tried to play a United States/Canada DVD in a Mexican DVD Player, regional coding would not decrypt the content and you'd be out of luck. Neither DVD Player nor Windows 98 can do anything about that!

TV Tuners

WebTV for Windows is the TV software bundled with Windows 98. WebTV consists of two main parts: the software that displays the output from your tuner/broadcast card and the Internet-savvy electronic program guide. One feature not included in the WebTV for Windows package is video capture. WebTV presents you with an abundance of information—whether you want it or not! The one thing to remember about WebTV is that pressing the Alt key displays the menu bar and the full set of WebTV's controls (see Figure 14.5).

You need a TV tuner card to use WebTV. TV tuner cards take an analog television signal from an antenna or cable source and digitize it. The series of digital snapshots the tuner card takes can be set to a certain rate (frames per second), a certain size, and a certain color depth. The American broadcast standard specifies 30 fps (frames per second). The typical full-screen capture size for a computer monitor is 640×480 pixels. Keep these numbers in mind when the time comes to make trade-offs in file size and image quality. As you would expect, the guidelines that apply to DVD—the more video memory and faster processor you have, the better—also apply to TV tuners.

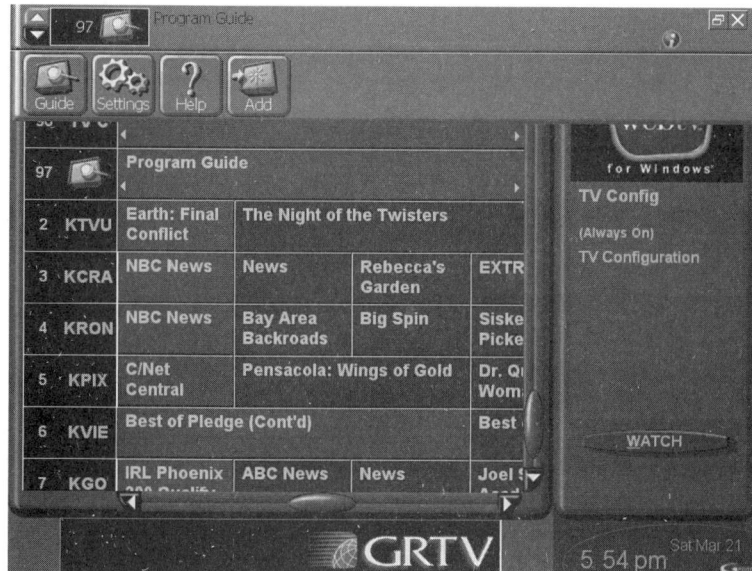

Figure 14.5
WebTV's controls display when you press the Alt key.

The TV tuner card provides audio output through either an internal audio connection to your sound card or through audio outputs on the back of the TV tuner card itself. Keep in mind that many cheaper, older TV tuner cards are monophonic. If you want stereo or surround sound TV audio, check carefully before you buy.

Installing a TV tuner card is like installing just about anything else in Windows 98. When the computer wakes up with a new card in a slot, the hardware installation wizard goes to work and prompts you for the necessary Windows 98 and TV tuner manufacturer disks. But if Windows 98 did not install WebTV on your computer by default, you have to go back to the Windows 98 CD, run Setup, and add WebTV to your system by using Setup's Custom option. Be prepared: WebTV takes up more than 20M of hard drive space.

Once WebTV is installed, it can dial into your Internet service provider and download a program guide for your viewing area. Then you can use your computer like a regular (albeit expensive) TV set. You can also begin to investigate the very new world of Internet television broadcasts.

Video Capture

Even though no video capture application is part of Windows 98, most TV tuner cards offer a video capture option. In addition, many inexpensive video cameras are available that allow you to record video on your computer. As mentioned earlier in this chapter, video data can quickly suck up all your computer's CPU and hard drive resources. The file size versus picture quality trade-offs discussed in the "Codecs" section, earlier in this chapter, will weigh heavily on your mind. Here are a few general video capture guidelines to keep in mind:

- The smaller the size of the video capture, the better. It make sense—a smaller video image requires less data to fill, making it easier for the processor and video card to keep up. Of course, you can reach the point of diminishing returns. If the video resembles a dancing postage stamp (as it might if its dimensions are reduced to 160×120 pixels), the size may be too small.

- The fewer bits used in the format—15 bits instead of 24 or 32 bits—the better.

- The lower the frame rate, the better. If you can live with capturing 15 fps instead of 30 fps, you'll cut your file size and your processor demands in half.

- If you can live without the audio, don't capture it. For example, if you are editing some home videos into a soon-to-be cult classic, and you intend to overdub a new soundtrack, don't capture the original audio.

- Close as many other applications and background processes as you can. Your computer has to devote most of its attention to processing the video. Don't distract it by running other applications in the background.

The documentation that comes with your TV tuner or video capture system undoubtedly offers more tips.

Cameras and Scanners

Windows 98 has a Scanners and Cameras Control Panel (see Figure 14.6). But you won't see it until you install a digital camera or a scanner that uses a COM or LPT port.

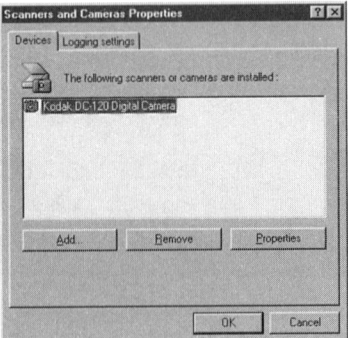

Figure 14.6
The Scanners and Cameras Control Panel.

Note Video devices connected to your computer through USB, IEEE 1394, or SCSI connections *do not* appear in the Cameras and Scanners Control Panel. To make sure that you aren't missing anything, look for configuration information in the System Control Panel's Device Manager page.

If you want to quickly test one of the devices listed in the Scanners and Cameras Control Panel, select the device, click the Properties button, and then click the Test Scanner or Camera button in the General tab of the device's Properties dialog box.

The other device-specific tab—Color Management—allows you to change the color profile associated with your scanner or camera. If you are experiencing color-matching problems between your scanner/camera and a display device (a monitor or printer), you may want to check your input device manufacturer's Web site for new color profiles to download and try.

Use the Logging Settings tab to change the way Windows 98 keeps track of the scanner and camera activity. The *STI* in STICLI and STIMON stands for Still Image (device). You will probably never have a reason to change these settings.

Other than having their own control panel, scanners and cameras have to abide by the same rules that apply to the other devices discussed in this chapter.

Media Player

The Media Player is the jack-of-all-multimedia-trades in Windows 98. It can play CD audio, MIDI, WAV, and AVI files. Media Player can even play DVD VOB (Video OBject) files— but it won't let you copy and paste images from DVD to some other application.

Figure 14.7 shows three copies of Media Player playing three different types of files.

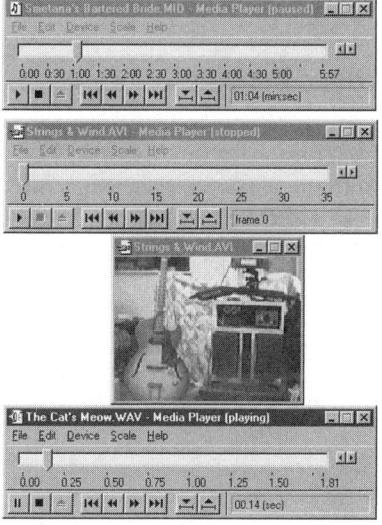

Figure 14.7
Media Players playing MID, AVI, and WAV files.

In the figure, the first Media Player has a MIDI file open. The second Media Player has an AVI file open and is displaying it in the window just below the Media Player's console. The third Media Player is playing a WAV file in a loop. Notice that the Media Player in charge of the AVI file indicates its progress in terms of frames; the first and third Media Players display a time scale in their progress indicators. If you are playing back a video file, you can choose to see the playback progress in either frames or time.

The Media Player shares its Properties dialog boxes (in the Device menu) with the Multimedia Control Panel. Put another way, the Multimedia Control Panel is a collection of all the properties you'd find if you opened different file types with the Media Player (see Figure 14.8). When you use the Media Player to view an AVI file, and you select Properties from the Device menu, you are looking at the Video playback properties for all of Windows 98.

Figure 14.8
The Video playback properties as opened from Media Player.

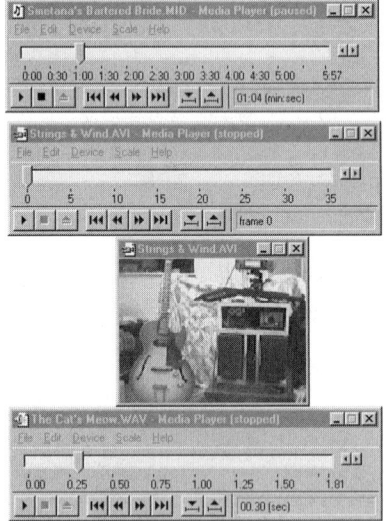

The global sharing of the Video properties means that if you are using Media Player to view an AVI file, and you change the Show Video In property, that change is reflected in all subsequent Media Player playbacks. Window size preferences are not saved with specific AVI files.

Media Player also globally shares the Volume Control. When you choose Volume Control from the Media Player's Device menu, you see your whole Volume Control mixing console spring to life (see Figure 14.9). Once again, that means if you pump up the volume for one WAV file, all subsequent WAV files are played back at that same volume. And if you turn up the master volume, be prepared for a surprisingly penetrating system beep!

ActiveMovie Control

The ActiveMovie Control (AMC) looks like a stripped-down Media Player. If you drag a video or audio file to an open ActiveMovie window, the file plays immediately. Perhaps the best way to differentiate Media Player from AMC is to remember that AMC is intended primarily to

Chapter 14: Multimedia   329

display streamed files (audio and video) from your network or from the Internet. The Media Player, on the other hand, is a self-contained application designed to play files found on one of your drives.

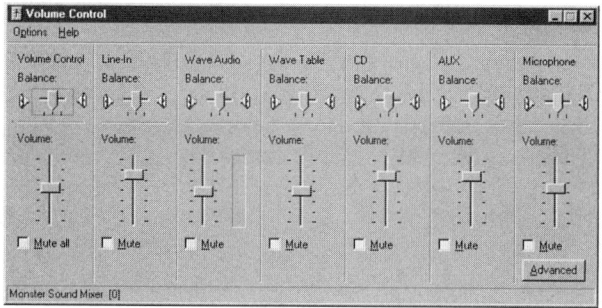

Figure 14.9

The Volume Control in action.

ActiveMovie Control shares the Multimedia Control Panel and Volume Control settings with the Media Player. But ActiveMovie Control can also tell you more than you may want to know about your audio and video configuration. To take a peek behind the scenes, right-click anywhere in an ActiveMovie Control window and select the Properties option from the drop-down list. (*Universal Windows 98 Snoop Tip:* Right-click everything!) You see four properties tabs: Playback, Movie Size, Controls, and Advanced (see Figure 14.10).

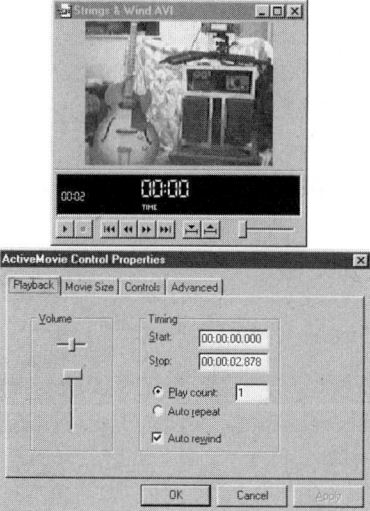

Figure 14.10

The ActiveMovie Control Properties dialog box in action.

The contents of these tabs change depending on what you are playing back. In Figure 14.10, ActiveMovie Control is playing an AVI file, so just about all the options are visible.

The first three tabs are familiar enough. The volume and stereo panning controls on the Playback tab allow you to adjust the sound *for this playback only*—the settings disappear as soon as you close the file. The Playback Timing options are similar to those available in Media Player. The Movie Size tab duplicates the Video tab in the Multimedia Control Panel and the Media Player's Properties command in its Device menu. The Controls tab allows you to tweak ActiveMovie Control's interface to your liking.

The fourth ActiveMovie Control Properties tab—Advanced—peels back Windows 98's thin veneer of civilization and exposes some of the innards (see Figure 14.11). If you didn't believe in DirectX before, you should by now. Figure 14.11 shows three Advanced tabs: Quality, DirectDraw, and Performance.

Figure 14.11
Advanced DirectDraw Properties for an ActiveMovie Control AVI playback session.

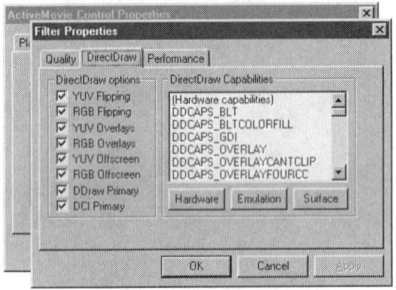

The Quality tab is handy if you suspect that your video (or audio) playback isn't up to snuff. This tab can tell you the number of frames played, the number of frames dropped, the average frame rate, and more. The DirectDraw tab allows you to go in and play with DirectDraw's options. It also tells you how much of your DirectDraw support is real and how much is emulated. (Refer to the DirectDraw diagram in Figure 14.3 for a quick review.) Finally, the Performance tab allows you to turn attributes on and off—which may come in handy while troubleshooting an esoteric bug.

WordPad and Cardfile

The Windows 98 WordPad and Cardfile applications may not be the first to come to mind when you consider a multimedia project, but both can store and present audio and video clips. The example at the end of this chapter uses WordPad as the framework into which WAV, MIDI, and AVI files are placed.

Understanding Sound Requirements

High-quality audio output is essential to the Entertainment PC. The following sections begin with a discussion of multimedia audio hardware and move on to Windows 98's audio applications.

Installing a Sound Card

As mentioned earlier in this chapter, Windows 98 strongly favors PCI cards and DirectX software drivers. These are two assets many legacy ISA sound cards don't possess. If you plan on using a cheap older ISA sound card with Windows 98, you may be in for some disappointment (and a bit of frustration). On the other hand, if you have big plans for all your PCI slots, you may want to stick with an ISA sound card just to keep a PCI slot open.

A number of ISA sound cards lived on the fringes of Windows 95's Plug and Play spectrum. Windows 98 may not cut fringe cards much slack and may not do to much to notify you of any problem. If your ISA card becomes mute after a Windows 98 installation, you may or may not receive an alert that one or more of your audio drivers did not load. A trip to the Device Manager will probably help you identify the troublemaker—it will be flagged in the Sound, Video and Games Controllers list by either a yellow exclamation point or a red *X*. At this point, your only hope probably rests with the Web site of your sound card manufacturer. If a new Windows 98-compatible driver has been posted, download it, update your driver(s), and keep your fingers crossed. If not, it's time to go shopping for a new sound card.

New audio cards no longer support FM synthesis or other low-fi audio techniques that were cobbled together in the DOS days. If you really want to keep those old sounds, you'll be motivated to find a way to keep your old card. One response to the need for legacy audio is the sound accelerator card. Sound accelerators are usually PCI cards that leverage the sounds from your old ISA card while adding new audio features to your computer. A cable is usually included with a sound accelerator that takes the audio output from the old card and runs it to the input of the new card. But if your old ISA card won't work at all (see the previous paragraph), a sound accelerator has no input to leverage.

Most new sound cards come with a cornucopia of connectors, but the set of connections is not at all standard from one card to the next. For example, some cards provide headphone outputs, but others offer only line-level outputs. If your card does not support built-in support for headphones, you'll have to use an external amplifier to hear your sound card. Some sound cards provide S/PDIF outputs (discussed in the "DVD" section, earlier in this chapter). Then there are internal connectors that allow you to attach audio cables to your CD, DVD, and TV tuner subsystems. Many sound cards also provide connectors that accommodate proprietary daughterboards to expand memory or add features. If you have a good idea how you intend to use your sound card, you'll have a better idea about which connections are most important to you.

In your sound card research, you may run across the terms full duplex and half duplex. *Full duplex* means that the card can record and play audio simultaneously. *Half duplex* means that the card can either play or record, but it can't do both at the same time. Virtually all modern sound cards support full-duplex operation, but you may as well check—particularly if you are thinking about purchasing a cheapie sound card.

> **Note** See Chapter 12, "Supporting Devices," for more information about installing devices in Windows 98.

Microphones

You can go down to the corner drugstore, buy a six-dollar microphone, and plug it into your sound card. Of course, you'll end up with audio fidelity equivalent to the drive-up intercom at McDonald's. Or, if you've chosen the wrong microphone, you'll end up with the sound of silence.

There are two types of microphones: dynamic and condenser. A *dynamic microphone* operates like a loudspeaker in reverse—it uses a magnet to transform audible input into electrical output. A dynamic microphone does not require a battery or any external source of power. A *condenser microphone*, on the other hand, changes a quality called *capacitance* in response to the sound it senses—by itself, it generates no electrical output. A condenser microphone requires a battery or some external power source in order to operate. Therefore, if you plug the wrong type of microphone into your sound card, your input quality will probably range from bad to nonexistent. If your sound card doesn't come with a microphone, check the box carefully to make sure that you end up purchasing a mike that matches your card.

Speakers

It's an old bromide but it's true: Speakers are the most important part of an audio system. If you have to make trade-offs when budgeting for your multimedia components, make sure that your speaker allotment doesn't get slashed because you spent too much on another bell or whistle.

Speaker advice could fill another long chapter, but there is one recent development in speakers that directly relates to Windows 98: USB speakers. USB speakers don't need a sound card if the other components, such as the CD drive, are capable of playing audio over the USB bus. You'll also need at least a 166 MHz Pentium-class computer with 32 M of RAM to do justice to your USB speaker setup. Like other USB components, just plug the USB speakers into the USB slot. As is the case whenever you are installing any new component, you should have the Windows 98 CD nearby just in case the installation wizard has to grab a driver it didn't get the first time around.

Chapter 14: Multimedia

3D and "Surround" Sound

In the "DVD" section of this chapter, the varieties of Dolby Surround sound were discussed. 3D and surround sound are not confined to Dolby, however. A number of games have used 3D and surround sound techniques for years. Although the meanings of both *3D* and *surround* have been stretched and confused as the audio hype increases, here is a quick definition of some buzzwords that you may encounter when looking to add an audio device to Windows 98.

Surround sound usually implies an expanded plane of sound—creating the electronic illusion of separating two speakers by an ever-increasing distance. Surround sound also implies that the surround processor adds subtle sonic elements to simulate the sound characteristics of a particular room or concert hall.

3D sound aims to locate sonic objects at precise points in the sphere around the listener. If an evil entity is breathing heavily to your left and a battle cruiser is coming up on you from the rear, you'll know where they are without seeing them.

If you install new audio software that adds either surround or 3D capabilities to Window 98, be sure that the new software works properly with Windows 98. For example, some third-party software may install its own volume control, causing confusion or conflicts. The lesson: Watch a third-party installer very carefully and make sure that you know which Windows pieces the new program has modified.

MIDI Capabilities

Musical Instrument Digital Interface (MIDI) is the descendant of the piano roll. A MIDI file does not contain any sound files. Instead, a MIDI file is a blueprint that a MIDI application uses to play sound synthesizers, either internally on the sound card or on an external MIDI tone module or keyboard. Because MIDI files are only blueprints, MIDI file sizes are typically very small. MIDI files larger than 200 K are very rare.

MIDI provides *channels*: independent pipelines through which the musical instructions can pass. In the beginning (1983), the maximum number of MIDI channels was 16. That meant 16 different MIDI instruments—pianos, drums, horns, strings, and so on—could be controlled simultaneously from a single MIDI file. Today, the number of MIDI channels you can use is limited only by the size of your bank account.

With hard drive capacities mushrooming into the gigabyte regions, MIDI's small file size isn't quite the boon it once was. Furthermore, MIDI output depends on the kindness of strangers—in this case, sound cards that may range in quality from sublime to ridiculous. If MIDI is important to you, make sure that you buy a card that features high-quality built-in sounds.

The most common variety of MIDI these days is General MIDI (GM). The intent behind GM was to create a standard among MIDI playback devices that allowed a file created on one

MIDI system to sound "right" on another system. But how does a manufacturer differentiate itself if its GM module sounds exactly like someone else's module? *Answer:* By not sounding *exactly* like anything else. So each manufacturer created a GM sound set with its own special sound. Unfortunately, it doesn't take much to screw up the orchestral mix that involves ten MIDI instruments. Take General MIDI claims with a grain of salt.

The MIDI-only card—so painfully common in the DOS days—has become virtually extinct. MIDI is now available as part of the feature set of all but the cheapest sound cards. Frequently, MIDI documentation refers to *MPU-401*—an ancient moniker provided by Roland Corp. *Beware:* Even though some card manufacturers provide a MIDI port (usually a DB-15 connector), they may not provide the MIDI cable itself. A MIDI cable typically costs around $30. If you are buying a sound card, check the box carefully to see whether or not a MIDI cable is included.

If you have MIDI-equipped external tone modules or keyboards, you don't have to live with your sound card's audio translation of MIDI files. You can connect external modules or keyboards to your MIDI port and have your computer control the external devices. Once you have your MIDI interface set up—a process that normally is handled by your sound card's installation setup wizard—you plug your MIDI-Out cable to the MIDI-In port on your tone module or keyboard. Windows 98's Media Player can play back MIDI files.

You can also connect your computer's MIDI-In cable to your tone module/keyboard MIDI-Out jack. Unfortunately, your computer's MIDI-In won't do you any good unless you buy an application that allows you to record MIDI data. No MIDI recorder is built into Windows 98. MIDI applications run the whole spectrum of prices and features, from $20 to $600 or more.

Use the MIDI page in the Multimedia Control Panel to switch back and forth between your internal sound card and your external MIDI setup (see Figure 14.12).

Figure 14.12

The Multimedia Control Panel's MIDI page.

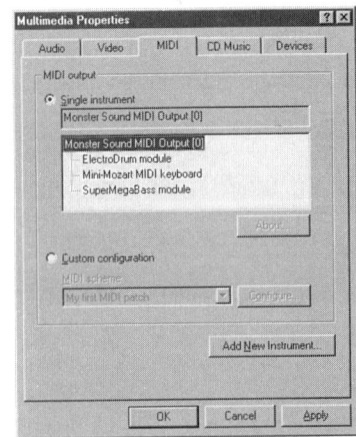

Chapter 14: Multimedia

The Multimedia Control Panel's MIDI page permits you to assign a given MIDI channel to a specific output device. For example, a MIDI musician has three external MIDI devices: An ElectroDrum module that, out of sheer spite, is set to receive information on MIDI channel 1. There is also a SuperMegaBass MIDI module dedicated to nothing but bass sounds. That module is set to receive information on MIDI channel 3. The SuperMegaBass module is monophonic—it can play only one note at a time. The ElectroDrum is polyphonic—it can play more than one note at a time, such as a bass drum and a snare drum. The Mini-Mozart MIDI keyboard is a keyboard that also contains a built-in synthesizer. It can play more than one note at a time (all the notes of a chord, for example) and it is multitimbral—it can play more than one "voice" or "patch" at a time. We've assigned multiple MIDI channels to the Mini-Mozart so that it can play the keyboard, guitar, saxophone, and kazoo parts while the SuperMegaBass plays the bass part and the ElectroDrum bangs away. To store this configuration in Windows 98, we created `My first MIDI patch` by clicking the Configure button in the MIDI page, which produces the MIDI Configuration dialog box (see Figure 14.13).

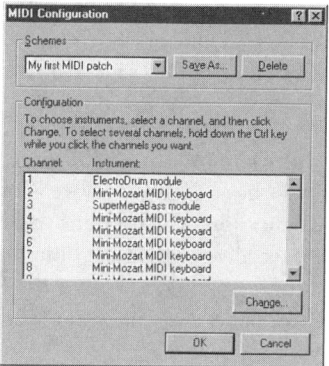

Figure 14.13
`My first MIDI patch` *in the MIDI Configuration dialog box.*

To change the configuration of a MIDI channel in the Configuration list, select the channel you want to redefine, click the Change button, and select the MIDI instrument you want to assign to that channel. To add a new MIDI instrument, back out to the main MIDI window, click Add New Instrument, and follow the MIDI Instrument Installation Wizard.

The Percussion on Channel 16 option in the MIDI Instrument Installation Wizard is an arcane reference to the fact that General MIDI plays the percussion (that is, drums) on MIDI channel 10. Other non-General MIDI instruments can put the percussion on any MIDI channel. Long ago, most MIDI musicians put the percussion track on MIDI channel 16 (the last MIDI channel in those dark, distant days).

Deleting a MIDI instrument isn't terribly intuitive. Go to the Multimedia Control Panel's Devices page and open up the MIDI Devices and Instruments hierarchy. In the example shown in Figure 14.14, the SuperMegaBass instrument is slated for deletion, so it is selected in the list.

Figure 14.14
Selecting a MIDI instrument for deletion.

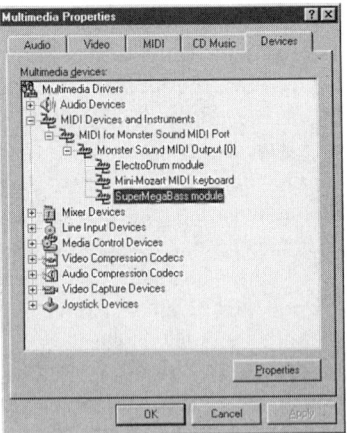

To finish the deletion process, click the Properties button and then click the Remove button in the General page. While you're in this neck of the Windows 98 woods, you can check the details of each MIDI device and instrument by clicking the General and Details tabs presented after you click the Properties button.

This example was designed to take you on a quick tour of the MIDI page. In actual practice, you'll spend very little time here. Even the most basic MIDI software allows you to assign instruments and channels from within the application, which means you're probably in luck: Basic MIDI recording and editing software is usually bundled with most sound cards. Still, if you have a complex MIDI setup geared to running 32, 64, 128, or more MIDI channels, you may want to stop in at the Multimedia Control Panel every once in a while to make sure that all your MIDI pipes are connected properly.

To find out more about MIDI, visit `http://www.midi.org`.

CD Player

The CD Player in Windows 98 remains pretty much unchanged from the version in Windows 95. It supplies all the functionality you expect from a full-featured CD player: Play, Pause, Stop, Previous Track, Rewind, Fast Forward, Next Track, and Eject. The Continuous Play and Random Play features are available on just about any CD player.

A task CD Player can perform that most stand-alone CD players cannot is keeping track of play lists. When you select Edit Play List from the Disc menu, the Disc Settings window opens, allowing you to enter or edit data in the play list (see Figure 14.15).

Every commercial audio CD is assigned a unique code. CD Player reads that code, associates that code with the title and track information you enter, and stores the result in the `CDPLAYER.INI` file. If you have spent a lot of time entering CD track information, you should back up your `CDPLAYER.INI` file from time to time.

Chapter 14: Multimedia **337**

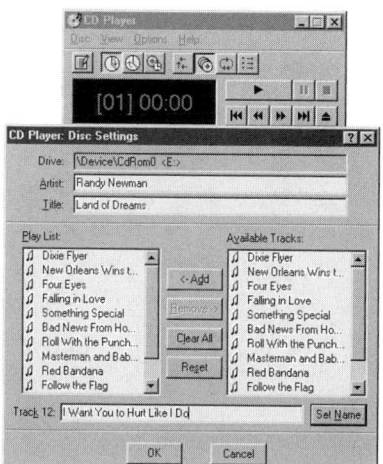

Figure 14.15
Entering track names into the CD Player's play list.

CD Player can also play CDs in a DVD drive. Just select the drive you want to listen to from the Artist drop-down list. Furthermore, if you have CD and DVD drives, you can use the Multi-disc Play option (in the Options menu) to create your own mini-jukebox (see Figure 14.16).

Figure 14.16
Using the CD and DVD drives as a two-CD jukebox.

The AutoPlay function described in the "DVD" section, earlier in this chapter, also applies to the CD. If you don't want a particular CD to start playing as soon as you insert it, hold down the Shift key. If you want to permanently disable the AutoPlay feature for the CD drive, open the CD drive's Properties dialog box in the System Control Panel's Device Manager and clear the Auto Insert Notification checkbox.

If you can't remember the name of a tune but you know that the tune you want is somewhere on a CD, you can select the Intro Play option from the Options menu to listen to only the beginning of each track. You can adjust the length of the Intro Play time by selecting Preferences from the Options menu and adjusting the Intro Play Length value in the Preferences window (see Figure 14.17).

Volume Control

The Volume Control will be familiar to Windows 95 users. Single-click the little speaker icon in the system tray and the master volume slider will appear (see Figure 14.18).

Figure 14.17
CD Player's Preferences window.

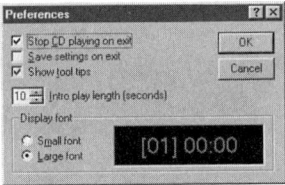

Figure 14.18
The basic volume control.

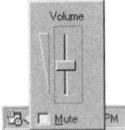

Lurking behind that one master volume slider is a whole nest of subordinate sliders. To view the whole Volume Control family, double-click the speaker icon (see Figure 14.19).

Figure 14.19
The whole Volume Control mixing panel.

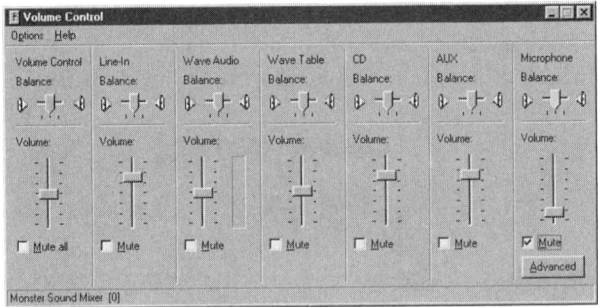

If more people knew about the existence of this more complete "mixing console," it would probably eliminate many desperate "no sound out" calls to tech support.

Instead of trying to explain the Volume Control all by itself, an example of the use of the Volume Control panel is combined with the Sound Recorder example in the following section.

Sound Recorder

The Sound Recorder is a simple Windows 98 application that should seem familiar to you from previous generations. But its simplicity can be deceiving if the elements on which the Sound Recorder depends are not adjusted properly. Instead of pointing out the obvious features of Sound Recorder, this section presents an example of the Sound Recorder in action. This example should provide you with a better understanding of how the Windows 98 audio components work together.

The following example requires a computer equipped with a sound card (preferably full duplex), a microphone, and at least one speaker (or a set of headphones).

1. Open Sound Recorder.

2. From the Sound Recorder's Edit menu, select Audio Properties.

3. In the Recording area of the Audio Properties dialog box, make sure that the sound input device you are going to use is selected. This example uses the microphone input from a Monster Sound card, so the Monster Sound Wave Input device is selected (see Figure 14.20).

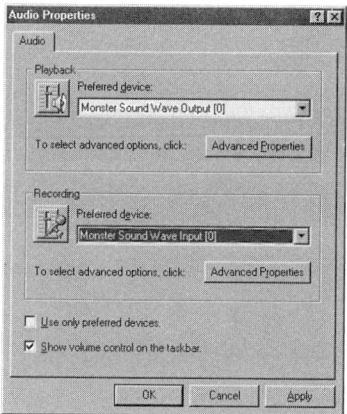

Figure 14.20
The Sound Recorder's Audio Properties dialog box.

4. Click the microphone/volume control icon in the Recording area of the Audio Properties dialog box. The Recording Control window opens, displaying your input volume and panning options (see Figure 14.21).

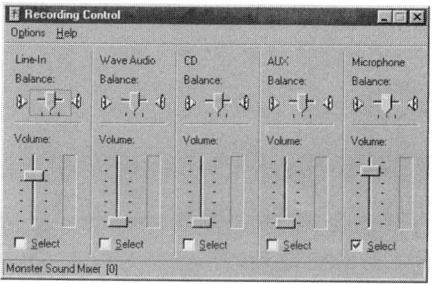

Figure 14.21
The Recording Control window.

5. Make sure that the Select checkbox is selected for the input device you want to use. You can select only one input device—microphone, CD, Line-In, and so on—at a time.

6. Adjust the input level and stereo balance to your needs. The output of the microphone used in this example is fairly weak, so the input level is rather high. If your signal source is strong, you may not have to turn up the input nearly this much. Unfortunately, there is

no sophisticated input-level testing option available, so you should count on a couple of trial-and-error run-throughs. But after all, this is free software!

7. Return to the Audio Properties dialog box and click OK to close it.

8. From the File menu, select the Properties command. The dialog box that appears allows you to specify the file format you want to use. The format you chose affects the recording quality of your end product and the recording time you have available.

9. In the Format Conversion area of the Properties dialog box, choose Recording Formats from the drop-down list and click Convert Now.

10. The Sound Selection dialog box appears, offering you a vast number of format and sample rate options. You can save combinations of file format and sample rate as presets. Windows 98 provides three default presets: CD Quality, Radio Quality, and Telephone Quality. Because the goal of this example is to produce a cheesy little system beep/document annotation using a cheap microphone, Telephone Quality is selected (see Figure 14.22). This low-quality option won't waste hard drive space and processor power on an undeserving audio sample.

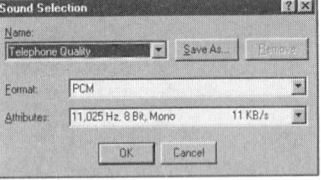

Figure 14.22
Audio choices offered by the Sound Selection dialog box.

> **Note**   To create your own Sound Selection presets, simply choose a Format/Attributes combination (such as MPEG Layer-3 and 32 KBit/s, 16,000 Hz, Stereo, 4 KB/s), click Save As, supply a name for your preset, and click OK. Your new preset appears as the new Sound Selection name.

11. After you choose your Format and Attributes options, click OK to close the Sound Selection dialog box.

12. Click OK to close the Properties dialog box.

13. Click the Record button and make noise. Notice that the Length indicator on the right side displays the maximum amount of recording time. This time is a function of the Format/Attributes choice you made in the Sound Selection dialog box and the amount of free space on your hard drive. If you don't have enough recording time available, consider another, lower-quality Format/Attributes option or free up some hard drive space.

Chapter 14: Multimedia

14. When you've finished making noise, click the Stop button. If you run out of hard drive space, Windows 98 clicks the Stop button for you (not recommended).

15. Right-click the speaker icon in Windows 98's status bar to open the Volume Control window. Now you can adjust your playback configuration. Make sure that the Mute checkbox is not selected for the device you want to listen to.

16. Click the Sound Recorder's Play button and listen to the output. Adjust the output level as necessary. In this example, the Wave Audio device has an LED-like level meter that visually indicates the audio level (see Figure 14.23).

Figure 14.23
The Volume Control window during Sound Recorder playback.

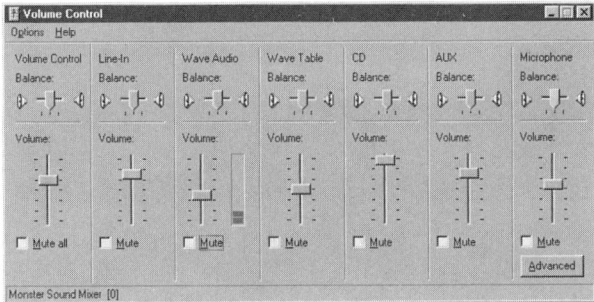

17. Edit your file using the various functions Sound Recorder has to offer—Mix with File, Increase/Decrease Volume, Increase/Decrease Speed, Add Echo, and Reverse. See the "Modifying Sound Files" section of Sound Recorder's online help for details.

18. If you want to save your file in a format different from the one in which you recorded, select Save As from the File menu and click the Change button in the Save As dialog box. The Sound Selection dialog box (discussed in step 10) appears, giving you a whole range of Format/Attributes options. Make your choices and close the Sound Selection dialog box.

19. Name your new audio file and save it.

Of course, after you have your volume and format settings defined, recording a sound will not be a 19-step process. But this little exercise can remind you of the number of options available through the uncluttered Sound Recorder and Volume Control interfaces.

Understanding Touch (Input/Output) Hardware

Force-feedback devices—joysticks, pedals, and even pneumatic bladders (to put in your gaming chair)—are on the way! Those items can be added to the legion of familiar input devices Windows 98 (specifically, DirectX) is designed to accommodate to provide new ways in which you can physically interact with your computer. Alas, the Windows 98 Game Controllers Control Panel isn't nearly as exciting or complex as the software and hardware it supports. That's okay; we want the setup part to be easy.

As it does with any other Plug and Play device, Windows 98 will install the appropriate driver software as soon as it detects a new game controller device (a joystick, game pad, steering wheel, and so on). Each device appears in the Game Controllers Control Panel list. If you have just installed a new controller, open the Game Controllers Control Panel, select the name of the new controller, click the Properties button, and click the Test tab in that controller's Properties window (see Figure 14.24).

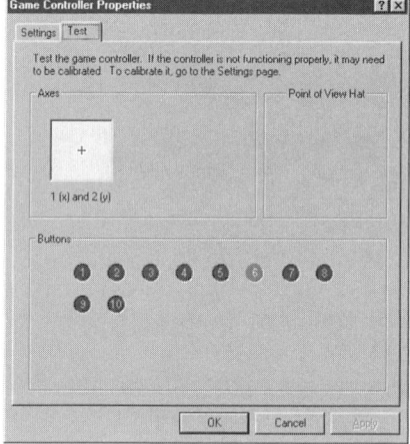

Figure 14.24
Testing a controller's button #6.

If your controller fails the test, you can back up to the Game Controller Properties' Settings tab, click Calibration, and follow a wizard through a calibration routine (see Figure 14.25).

If you want to assign a controller to a specific controller ID, back up to the main Game Controllers dialog box and click the Advanced tab. This page presents a list of controller IDs (see Figure 14.26). Choose an ID number, click Change, select a controller type from the list, and click OK to complete the controller ID assignment.

Chapter 14: Multimedia

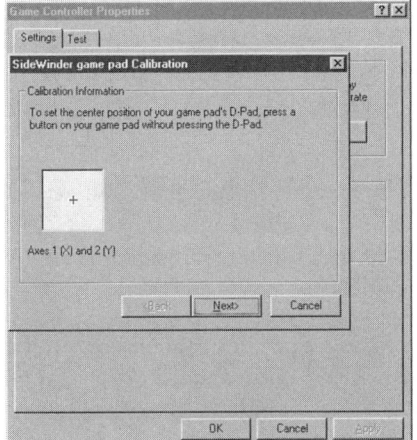

Figure 14.25
Calibrating a game pad.

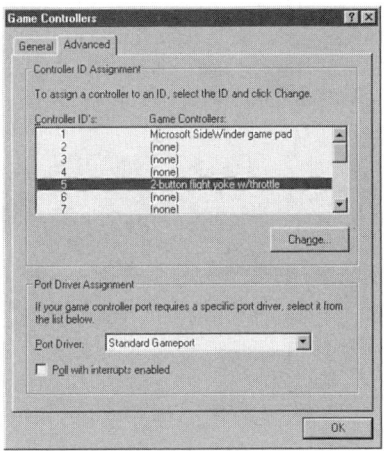

Figure 14.26
Assigning a new controller to ID #5.

A Simple Example

Let's look at an example that puts some of Windows 98's entertainment accessories to work. The end product is a WordPad document that contains a sound file (The Cat's Meow), a MIDI file (Smetana's Bartered Bride), and a movie (Strings and Wind). We'll use WordPad because it ships as part of Windows 98 and because WordPad, Sound Recorder, Media Player all support OLE—Object Linking and Embedding. Because the vast majority of modern Windows software supports OLE, you can transfer ideas contained in this example to your favorite Windows software.

The first step is to create the individual sound, MIDI, and movie files. Unfortunately, only one of these three files can be created with a basic Windows 98 application: The Cat's Meow was recorded using Sound Recorder. The MIDI file was created with a commercial MIDI music application (using an external MIDI keyboard, MIDI drum pad, and General MIDI tone module). The AVI file was created using the video capture function of a USB video-conferencing hardware and software package.

The Cat's Meow is the recording of a cat's meow—descriptive filenames are always helpful! The recording hardware consisted of an ISA sound card and the condenser microphone it required. Extravagantly, it was recorded in CD-quality stereo using the PCM 44,100 Hz, 16-bit stereo codec. The completed file was dragged and dropped into a new WordPad document.

Smetana's Bartered Bride—a MIDI file—was created in a commercial MIDI application and stored on the hard drive. The MIDI file was then opened in the Media Player and dragged into the WordPad document.

Strings and Wind is a short AVI movie file captured in 160×120 resolution at 15 frames per second with a pixel depth of 12 using the I420 codec. Sound for the AVI file was captured at 11,025 Hz in 8-bit mono. The file was saved to the hard disk. The file's icon was then dragged to the WordPad document. The completed WordPad document was then saved to the hard drive as `Multimedia Mania.doc`. Figure 14.27 shows a view of the end product.

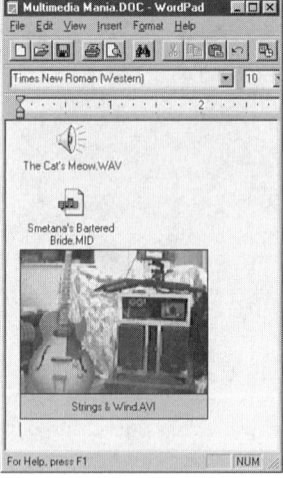

Figure 14.27
A multimedia-enhanced WordPad document.

To use `Multimedia Mania.doc`, the user simply opens the document and double-clicks the media element he or she wants to audition. You can also inspect the properties of the various elements by right-clicking their icons.

Your documents need not be as crude as `Multimedia Mania.doc`. Instead of a cat's meow, the audio file could be a voice annotation of some sort—perhaps a clip from an important speech. The MIDI file could be used to convey a musical idea without having to rely on a huge WAV file. (In this example, Smetana's Bartered Bride is a seven-minute orchestral piece that occupies only 200 K of disk space.) The movie could be a video capture of some blooper—America's Funniest AVI Files. Windows 98's mixed-media presentation options are limited only by your imagination and your pocketbook.

But don't get completely carried away. Embedding multimedia files in a document can soon cause the size of that document to balloon to unmanageable proportions. To keep the overall file size to a minimum, you have some options:

- Compress the file using a file compression program. The disadvantage of compression is that the recipient has to decompress the file before viewing it.

- Lower the quality of your files. For example, The Cat's Meow didn't really need to be recorded in CD-quality stereo. If the audio file is converted to MPEG Layer-3 at 8 KHz monophonic, the size of the audio file shrinks dramatically, and the eventual recipient of the file may not (in this example, at any rate) notice the lower quality.

- Instead of embedding the files in the document, link the files to the WordPad document. Doing so produces a very small file that won't work on anyone else's computer. If the document is created to be run on your computer and all its pieces are going to remain in the same locations, linking makes a lot of sense. But if you intend to email this document to someone else, you'll have to bundle up the linked files and send them as well.

This is indeed a simple example. If you are using Microsoft Office or any other application that supports OLE, your embedding and linking options are limited only by the size of your hard drive, the speed of your processor, and (if you try to distribute the files) the strength of your network.

Troubleshooting

Windows 98 installation and error-checking routines are clever but not omniscient. Sooner or later, you'll have to deal with a multimedia device that does not want to perform. The next section, "Dodging the Bullet," provides some tips on how to prevent failures before they occur. "Biting the Bullet" discusses what to do and where to look when you're faced with restoring your computer's multimedia health.

Dodging the Bullet

Here are two courses of preventative action you can take:

- Hit the Web and do all your detailed research up front. Know how the pieces fit together. For example, make sure that your DVD drive and MPEG decoder board will work with your video card and drivers. Check for the latest driver revisions—maybe your old card has a new driver revision that will work with Windows 98. This tip applies to anything you intend to add to your system—hard drives, video cameras, and so on.

- Don't buy everything at once, particularly if you are going the bargain route. Buy the cornerstone of your addition and read *all* the documentation. All the small but crucial little exceptions and caveats are *not* printed on the box! Before you disassemble your computer, find the pertinent web sites and download all the latest info and driver software.

Cheap Route Case Study

John Doe bought a no-name DVD-ROM kit in a plain white box. Mr. Doe knew enough about the history of DVD-ROM to know that, at that low, low price, the drive had to be a first-generation Toshiba model. He figured that at least he could use *Toshiba* and *DVD* as leverage in his web and Usenet searches. Not surprisingly, the DVD-ROM and its MPEG decoder card were not well documented—the drive/board combination was apparently originally intended to be sold to a large, famous computer manufacturer as an OEM (Original Equipment Manufacturer) kit. But the documentation did provide an URL, which is all a good detective needs these days!

The documentation also provided minimal clues about the compatibility of this DVD-ROM. If you're a pessimistic sort, suspicious gaps in the documentation can also be used as clues about what your hardware will *not* work with. In short, if your hardware or software isn't mentioned, expect the worst. In Mr. Doe's case, the video card—a first-generation oddball 3D accelerator—wasn't listed as compatible with this DVD-ROM drive. "Who knows," John thought. "Maybe the manufacturer of my old 3D accelerator has developed new drivers that work with my DVD." So he checked and, sure enough, new drivers were available.

Mr. Doe downloaded and installed the new 3D drivers, installed the DVD hardware and software—but disappointingly, the DVD didn't work too well. John was somewhat able to get video on his monitor, but the system as a whole didn't really function as it should. Even with the new driver, his 3D setup was just not up to the task. So he decided to replace the old 3D setup with a new video card—a cheap new video card.

Going back to the DVD documentation (both printed and from the Web site), Mr. Doe distilled a list of video chip sets that would satisfy the DVD and would also be compatible with the rest of his system. With this list in hand, John went back to the computer hardware store and began rifling through the video cards. The $200-plus options were enticing, but provided way more video power than he needed. A popular video card that fit his video chipset criteria was on sale for $100. John gave it a long, hard look. This card was manufactured by a reputable company that could provide potentially valuable technical support. But Mr. Doe wasn't ready to end his search quite yet.

As he thumbed through the dusty ranks of no-name video cards, John ran across a $20 model that used the same video chip set as the more expensive cards. It didn't include any bundled software, and promised very little documentation or technical support. For the savings, however, Mr. Doe was willing to make that sacrifice.

John plunked down two sawbucks for the cheapie video card and took it home. It didn't come loaded with lots of memory, but that was okay for the short term. Video RAM was very cheap and this gave Mr. Doe the option to add memory at his leisure. The documentation was predictably poor, but this company did have a web site. Windows 98 recognized the new hardware and installed its drivers without a fuss. It worked on the first try!

Biting the Bullet

Here are some tips to consider when your multimedia installation exercise has resulted in less than satisfying results:

- Suspicious of the installation? After an installation, restart at least one more time than you think necessary.

- Is your digital audio output distorted? Turn down the volume in the Volume Control Panel. Or there could be some sort of 3D audio enhancement software adding distortion to the signal path. Turn off 3D audio or readjust its parameters.

- Has a new volume control replaced the stock Windows 98 volume control? If so, remove one of the volume controls or read the documentation to see what workarounds are suggested.

- Are the USB devices not responding? Make sure that USB is enabled. If you get no USB response at all, go to the System Control Panel, click the Device Manager tab, and check the properties of all the Universal Serial Bus controllers. Make sure that the Disable in This Hardware Profile option is not checked.

Control Panels

There are two levels of problems: relatively minor configuration problems and relatively major functionality problems. The majority of multimedia configuration options can be found in the Multimedia Control Panel, the Scanners and Cameras Control Panel, and the Game Controllers Control Panel. Many of the options in these control panels have been discussed earlier in the chapter.

There are some key locations in Windows 98 from which you can attack the bigger functionality problems. The Multimedia Control Panel's Devices page is one such place (see Figure 14.28).

Figure 14.28
The Multimedia Control Panel's Devices page.

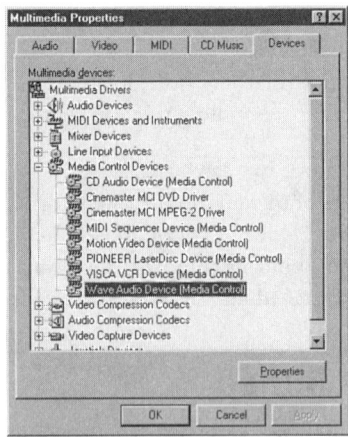

Using the Properties dialog boxes of the devices in this list, you can change some parameters associated with that device (the parameters available depend on the device chosen), turn the device driver on or off, or remove the device driver.

Another key troubleshooting location is the System Control Panel's Device Manager page (see Figure 14.29).

Figure 14.29
The System Control Panel's Device Manager page.

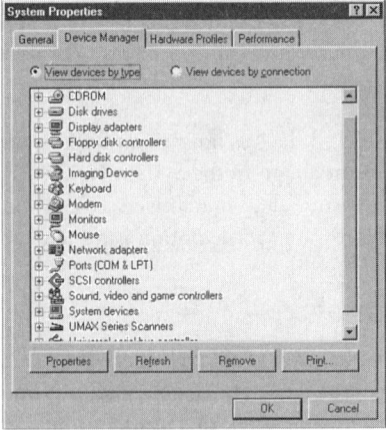

The Device Manager tells you which devices are properly loaded. For example, if you have just installed a new piece of hardware or updated a driver, and that device is not working, go to the Device Manager and find the name of the device in the list. If a device is marked with a yellow exclamation point or a red X, there's a problem. Double-click a device name to open its Properties dialog box. The pages in the Properties dialog box usually provide more information about any problems. You can also modify the device settings, check driver revision numbers, and update driver software from here as well. Figure 14.30 shows the Settings page for a DVD-ROM drive.

Chapter 14: Multimedia

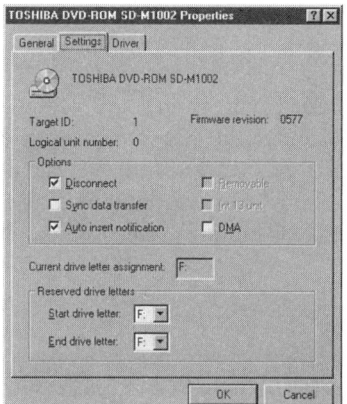

Figure 14.30
An example of a particular device's Device Manager Settings page.

This Settings page, for example, is the place to go to turn off Auto Insert Notification (the feature that starts a program on a CD or DVD automatically as soon as the disc is popped into the drive). This Settings page is also the place to go to assign a drive letter. Different devices feature various options on these pages.

If you're having a major problem, and all your reconfiguration and driver update efforts don't budge the yellow exclamation point or the red X, you can always select the device in the main Device Manager list and click Remove (see Figure 14.31).

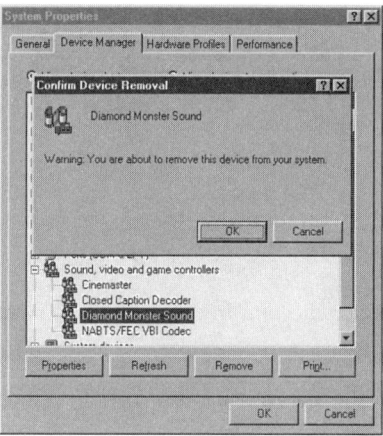

Figure 14.31
Using the Device Manager to remove a device.

Warning It is normally *not* a good idea to remove a device unless you have the Windows 98 CD and all applicable driver disks at hand. Chances are you'll need them when your computer restarts.

When the removal is complete, Windows 98 suggests that you restart the computer right away. Follow that recommendation.

If the problematic device is still physically installed in (or attached to) the computer, the Windows 98 Plug and Play elves go to work and do their best to correctly install the driver software this time around. If everything fails—new drivers (from the manufacturer's web site), configuration tweaks, and wholesale removals and reinstallations—it may be time to check with your vendor and inquire about deeper compatibility problems or hardware failures.

SCSI Concerns

Most SCSI problems have their roots in one of two main areas: termination and SCSI ID number. As mentioned earlier in this chapter, a chain of SCSI devices must be properly terminated. Most modern SCSI devices use active termination to keep the SCSI activity healthy. But if you've attached an older SCSI device, such as an old hard drive, you may have to add a terminator to the end of the SCSI line. Check the documentation that came with your hardware.

Each SCSI device requires a SCSI device ID number. This ID assignment is usually accomplished using a numbered switch on the back of the case. Some SCSI hardware (first-generation Zip drives, for example) allowed you to choose from only two of the possible eight ID numbers. As long as no two SCSI devices in the chain use the same ID number, you should be okay. Your SCSI adapter should be accompanied by diagnostic software that allows you to see who is claiming which ID in the SCSI chain (see Figure 14.32).

Figure 14.32
An example of SCSI diagnostic software.

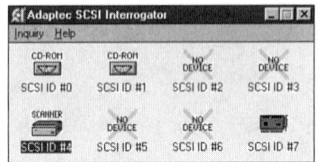

DirectX

Microsoft has provided a DirectX diagnostic checklist in the online help system. To use the DirectX Troubleshooter, follow these steps:

1. Select the Windows Help file from the Start menu.

2. Type **DirectX** in the Search box.

3. Click the List Topics button.

4. Select DirectX Troubleshooter from the Topics list.

5. Click the hyperlink to start the DirectX Troubleshooter.

You'll see the DirectX Troubleshooter in the Help window, as shown in Figure 14.33.

Chapter 14: Multimedia

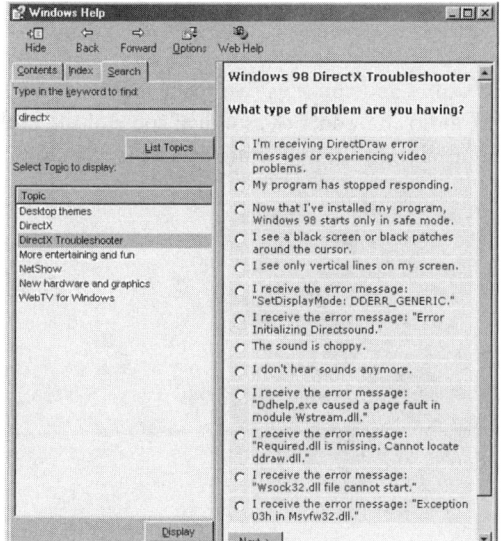

Figure 14.33
The DirectX Troubleshooter.

DVD Hiccups

If your DVD playback is occasionally interrupted, or if you hear pops in the audio, your computer may be too occupied with the Windows 98 background processes to devote adequate attention to its demanding video and audio decoding duties. *Background processes*—small programs that start and run invisibly—can interrupt the steady flow of data that video and audio require, particularly if your computer has a slower processor. Examples of software that runs in the background include screen-savers, network software, antivirus software, Microsoft's Office Shortcut bar, and fax/answering machine software. To see a list of Windows 98's background processes, press Ctrl+Alt+Delete. A list of currently active applications appears in a Close Program window. Click the Close Program's Cancel button to resume normal Windows 98 activity and then find and shut down any of the unnecessary programs.

Audio Problems

If you can't hear the audio from your CD or DVD drives through your sound card, first check the main volume control and the big volume control mixer. The volume sliders you want to use should be set at reasonable levels and should not be muted. If the software settings are okay, check the hardware. Make sure that you connected the audio outputs from the backs of the CD and DVD drives to the CD and AUX inputs of your sound card. Check your CD or DVD hardware installation documentation for details.

Windows 98's online help contains a good troubleshooting section. To view its recommendations, go to the Index and select the Sound Cards, Troubleshooting topic.

Conclusion

This chapter described some of the features and concepts that make up Windows 98 multimedia. The chapter discussed video and audio components, as well as some of the multimedia formats and standards. For more on installing and supporting devices in Windows 98, see Chapter 12.

OLE, COM, DCOM, and ActiveX

This chapter defines OLE, COM, DCOM, and ActiveX. It also addresses how to use these technologies in a Windows 98 environment.

The section "Understanding Client/Server Application Concepts" introduces and defines these four technologies. This section describes at a high level how Windows 98 works with programs, and how programs work with each other. The concepts introduced in this section will help you understand the section "Using the DCOMCNFG Utility" and the section "Using OLE."

The section "Sample Files Included on the CD" lists files referenced in the "Using OLE" section.

The section "Using OLE" shows you how to use Object Linking and Embedding to create and edit complex compound documents. The use of compound documents allows documents to present information to users in a more "document-centric" and therefore a less "application-centric" format. Many commonly used applications such as Microsoft Word, Excel, and PowerPoint, as well as many non–Microsoft applications, can be used to create compound documents. This section addresses the differences between linked documents and embedded documents and when each is most appropriate.

The section "Using the DCOMCNFG Utility" describes how to use the DCOMCNFG utility to change the Registry settings of server applications. Use this utility to specify which machine a client program should use to establish a session with a given server program. Also, you can make other changes relating to security, identity, and authentication.

Understanding Client/Server Application Concepts

The four technologies of OLE, COM, DCOM, and ActiveX are all related in that they provide some level of functionality when client and server programs need to communicate with each other. This section introduces each of these technologies and describes their purpose and use; it also provides an overview of how Windows 98 determines which server application to launch when a client program requests the services provided by a server application.

What is a Client/Server Application?

A *client/server program* is comprised of two programs that work together to provide some level of functionality to the user (see Figure 15.1).

Figure 15.1
A client program running on one machine and the server program running on another machine.

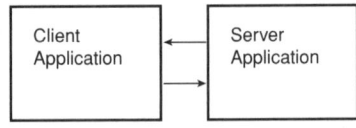

One or Two Machines

Many client and server programs are written as a pair, intended to work only together.

Other times, a shrink-wrapped server program such as Microsoft Word is used with a client program that is written at some later date by any programmer. For example, if a programmer wants to provide the ability to perform spell checking in his program, he could either write his own spell checker or use the CheckSpelling function exposed within Microsoft Word. Obviously, using a debugged program that provides the functionality you need can cut development time and costs.

Another scenario involves the combined use of two programs that were written in isolation, for instance, by two different manufacturers.

Both the client and the server programs can run on a single PC, or they can run on two different PCs that have some form of LAN, WAN, or Dial-Up Networking connection between them.

What Benefits Does Client/Server Provide?

The ability to segment a program and run the client portion on one machine and the server portion on another machine allows for a great deal of flexibility. One benefit is a reduction of hardware costs while maintaining throughput. Perhaps the server portion requires large amounts of RAM, or heavy utilization of the processor. The server portion of the program can be run on a machine with the necessary resources to handle the program, while the client portion can run on less substantial desktop machines. This reduces overall hardware costs by allowing the purchase of lower-end desktop machines.

Another benefit of client/server is the ability to place the server where the data resides; this can greatly reduce network traffic. Assume a program accesses very large data files, but needs to display only small amounts of data to the user. If the data files are stored on a file server and accessed by a traditional non–client/server program, the entire file usually must be pulled across the LAN or WAN by the user's program. However, by writing a client/server program and locating the server on the same machine as the data files, the client can send a small request to the server indicating the desired data. The server then reads the large data file, locates the desired data, and finally returns only the data requested to the client program via the LAN or WAN.

If both the client and server programs run on a single machine, the client program can still gain functionality provided by the server program. This can also make it easier for users to access data they need from a single document, rather than from multiple applications.

Another advantage is in the ability to reuse and leverage existing software, as in the earlier CheckSpelling example. This can reduce both development costs and timeframes.

What Are 3-Tier and N-Tier Applications?

A *3-Tier* application has three programs that could run on one, two, or three machines (see Figure 15.2). One program is strictly a client, the second is strictly a server, the third program sits in the middle and is written to be both client and server. This middle tier acts as a server to the client program and as a client to the server program.

Three-tier applications allow a great deal of flexibility regarding where software components run. A typical scenario for a three-tier application places the server program on a central corporate server. Regional office servers run the middle-tier program, while the client program runs on end-user desktop machines in the regional offices. This example is only one scenario. However, other alternatives might include placing the middle tier on the corporate server or on the end-user desktop computer, if it makes more sense.

Figure 15.2
A 3-Tier application running on three separate machines.

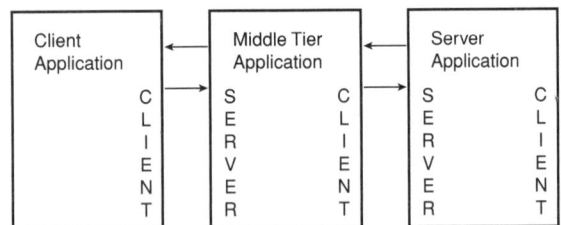

One or Two or Three Machines

N-Tier is a term that applies to three or more tiers in which there can be multiple (*N*) middle-tier programs between a client and a server. Each middle tier acts as both client and server. Many corporate applications are written as N-Tier applications. This approach allows for easy replacement of one portion such as a middle tier without requiring replacement of other tiers. This flexibility allows programmers to design code as modules, and simply replace one module with another when business rules or other functionality requires change.

Business rules are software checks run on newly entered data to ensure that incorrect or incomplete data is corrected prior to its being stored in databases or written to files. Business rules reside in almost every program and are often implemented within the middle tiers. Several examples of business rules might be a ZIP code that must contain only numeric characters, a required delivery address for shipments, or a maximum allowable discount for any product.

There is, however, an associated cost dependent on which tier holds the business rule(s). To illustrate this point, study the following example of a fictitious national retail chain store . This company has 100 stores with 50 Point of Sales stations per store, or a total of 5000 P.O.S. stations nationwide.

Suppose the client tier in the Point of Sales application has a rule that limits the maximum discount to 30%. The corporation makes a decision to allow up to a 40% discount. This business decision could require installing new programs on 5000 P.O.S. machines with many hours devoted to the installation. In this case, placing business rules on a client tier has disadvantages.

Equally difficult would be placing the business rules on the central corporate server. This placement incurs a great deal of WAN network traffic and burdens the corporate server with the mundane task of validating data.

If the business rules are instead placed on a middle-tier component located on a departmental (store) server, a balance between the two extremes is struck. If each store has 50 P.O.S.

machines and one departmental server, then only the 100 store servers would require the new program. The client program incurs LAN traffic to the store server to validate data, but does not incur WAN traffic for validation.

What are OLE, COM, DCOM, and ActiveX?

OLE stands for Object Linking and Embedding. This technology first appeared in Windows 3.1 as OLE 1.0. By using OLE, you can create what is known as a compound document. A *compound document* simply contains data from two or more applications. For instance, an employee performance appraisal document created with Word could include the cell range from an Excel spreadsheet that displays salary history for the employee. This "document-centric" approach allows a manager to view both the written appraisal and the salary information in a single document from a single application.

The data from one application can be either linked or embedded in the other. In the performance appraisal example, if the data is *linked,* then changes to the spreadsheet are visible when the performance appraisal Word document is next opened. If data is *embedded,* changes to the spreadsheet are not updated in the Word document—there is no link between these two files.

Both linked and embedded data can be edited by their native applications; Excel is used to edit the spreadsheet portion of the appraisal, whereas Word is used for word processing the remainder of the performance appraisal. In this example, Word is the client application and Excel is the server application.

OLE evolved into OLE 2.0, which allowed for *in-place editing*. This feature allows the menu and toolbars of the server program to temporarily replace those of the client program while the user edits linked or embedded objects. With in-place editing, the user can edit the entire document without leaving the host application.

Another twist of OLE is *OLE Automation*. By using OLE Automation, a client program can launch a server and then use the services and functionality of the server program. The server can run as a task hidden from the user or it can be made visible for user interaction or display of data.

Up to this point, both client and server applications resided on the same machines. With *Network OLE*, the server program resides on a different machine from the client program. This not only allows for client and server processes, but also enables these processes to reside on client and server machines.

Microsoft now refers to OLE 1.0, OLE 2.0, OLE Automation, and Network OLE as OLE for simplicity. These variations of OLE all rely on an architecture known as COM.

COM stands for Component Object Model (see Figure 15.3). COM is a specification developed by Microsoft that describes how Component Objects should interface (communicate) with each other. A *Component Object* is a generic term that applies to many different types of software: client programs, middle-tier programs, server programs, individual controls such as a calendar control, databases, and entire applications. The COM specification by design is open, flexible, and nonrestrictive. COM describes how Component Objects should interface with each other, but does not prescribe how the code that implements the interface is written. This flexibility allows programs to be developed using different languages from different vendors, such as C++, Visual Basic, J++, or MicroFocus Cobol. For example, the client-tier program can be written with Visual Basic, the middle-tier program using C++, and the server using J++. The beauty of COM is its provision for easy component replacement with a new version of a program, such as the middle-tier program, without requiring changes to the other components.

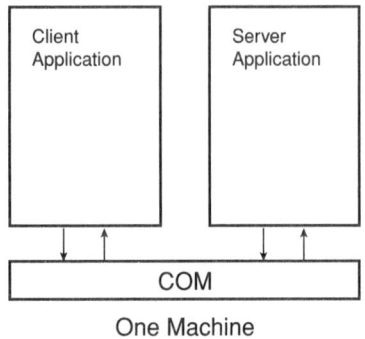

Figure 15.3
COM allows two programs to communicate on a single machine.

DCOM stands for Distributed COM. By using DCOM, COM components can be placed on different machines and seamlessly communicate with one another without requiring changes to any of the components. DCOM relies on the widely utilized DCE-RPC (RPC) for network communication. By using RPC, DCOM running on one machine can establish a connection with DCOM running on another machine. After they are connected, DCOM acts as a middleman between the COM layers on the two machines (see Figure 15.4). Another great feature of DCOM comes from its reliance on RPC. Windows 98, Windows NT, UNIX, Macintosh, and many mainframe systems support RPC and potentially can use DCOM. You can download or purchase DCOM for a growing number of UNIX and mainframe systems. By using DCOM, components can reside not only on different machines but also on different platforms and still easily communicate with each other.

ActiveX is a term that applies to both controls and servers (or code components). With the recent popularity of the Internet, web pages began to evolve from static displays of text and pictures to a more interactive format. One way to achieve this format is to place controls onto the web page. If the control is not currently installed on the user's machine, the web browser can download and install it for the user. It is important to remember that controls developed by using the full COM specification are relatively large and take a long time to download. ActiveX controls, on the other hand, use a subset of the complete COM specification; this allows for smaller file size and, therefore, quicker downloading.

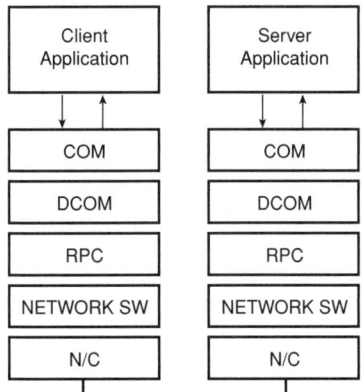

Figure 15.4
The software and hardware layers used when applications on different machines communicate using DCOM.

What Are Objects, Classes, and Instances?

Object is a generic term that applies to units of software. The intent is for an object to be self-sufficient and self-managing. An object should not depend on other software in order to run properly. This is not to say an object cannot communicate with other objects; however, one object does not depend on other objects in order to function.

Objects include both code and data. Some code and data are private to the object and not accessible from outside itself; other portions of code and data can be made available (or exposed) for use by other programs. For instance, Word exposes the CheckSpelling function, which is code made available for use by other programs.

Objects include many types of software, such as entire applications, individual controls, databases, and so on. Objects are composed of one or more classes; these classes contain software functions such as CheckSpelling. If these classes are marked as public, they are exposed by the compiler. The compiler generates a COM interface for the class and the functions within it, thereby allowing access from outside the object.

Before you can use an object, you must create an *instance* of the object. For example, if you want to build a new house, you need a set of plans or blueprints. You can't live in the plans; you must first create an instance of a house based on the plans. One fact about a plan is that from them you can build many instances, all of which are identical. In this example, a class correlates to the plans or blueprints. You must create an instance of a class before it can be used. To use another analogy, consider creating cookies using a cookie cutter. The cookie cutter is the class; it defines the shape of every instance created. From this one class, you can create many identical instances. Think of differently shaped cookie cutters (star, bell, tree, and so on) as different classes.

To see an example of how Windows 98 creates instances of class objects, do this little experiment:

1. Minimize all applications.

2. Point the mouse toward the middle of your desktop (not at any existing icon), then click the right mouse button. Choose New, then choose Briefcase.

3. Repeat step 2 several more times.

You have just created several instances of the Briefcase object. This implies there must be a Briefcase class. To verify this, do the following:

1. Launch the Registry Editor by choosing Start, Run. Type **REGEDIT** and click OK.

2. Open the HKEY_CLASSES_ROOT subtree. Scroll down past all the three character extensions; the registered classes appear next. Scroll until you locate the Briefcase class.

3. Open up the Briefcase object and notice the ClassID subkey (see Figure 15.5).

Figure 15.5
The Briefcase class within HKEY_CLASSES_ROOT.

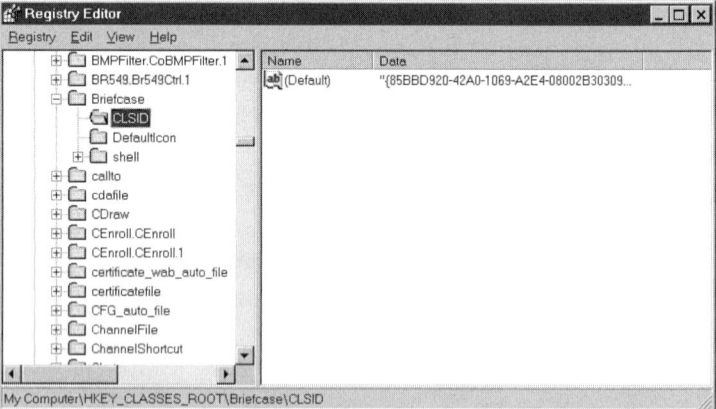

What are GUIDs and CLSIDs?

Microsoft decided to use GUIDs (Globally Unique Identifiers) to uniquely identify a variety of objects. *GUID* is a generic term used to describe other more specific identifiers such as CLSID (Class ID), Interface (Interface ID), and TypeLib (Type Library ID). All of these identifiers represent extremely large numbers; these identifiers are all 128-bit integers, which translates to $3.4e^*38$, or 340,000,000,000,000,000,000,000,000,000,000,000,000. These numbers are represented in hex and appear as 32-hex digits; this is an example of a GUID {85BBD920-42A0-1069-A2E4-08002B30309D}.

GUIDs are randomly generated by the compiler during compilation of .EXE, .DLL, and .OCX files then assigned to public classes, interfaces, and so on. After they are compiled, the GUIDs never change.

By following GUID references, Windows 98, COM, and DCOM can locate a specific class or interface on this or another machine.

Fortunately, GUID creation and usage happen automatically, reliably, and without any user intervention.

Understanding HKEY_CLASSES_ROOT

Object .EXE, .DLL., and .OCX files that contain public classes must be registered in order for Windows 98, COM, and DCOM to locate and use them. These items are registered within HKEY_CLASSES_ROOT. The registration process adds key and data values in several locations. Normally, this registration process is part of the installation process of applications, or occurs automatically during the download process of .OCX controls. However, if you copy files onto a machine, they are not automatically registered. Executable servers (with an .EXE extension) self-register the first time they run, and .DLL and .OCX files can be manually registered using the REGSVR32.EXE program. After they are registered, controls and code components are usable by other OLE-compatible clients.

As you install applications onto your Windows 98 machine, you should see additional entries within HKEY_CLASSES_ROOT. If you scroll through the entries in HKEY_CLASSES_ROOT, you should see a number of entries for Excel, Access, Word, and PowerPoint if these applications have been installed.

How Windows 98 Creates an Instance of an Object

When a user double-clicks on a file with a .doc extension, WordPad launches to display the document, or (if it is installed) Word launches instead to display the document. The system may have Word 2.0, Word 6.0, or Word 8.0 installed. This example is taken from a machine with Word 8.0 installed.

First, the .doc file extension is looked up in HKEY_CLASSES_ROOT (see Figure 15.6).

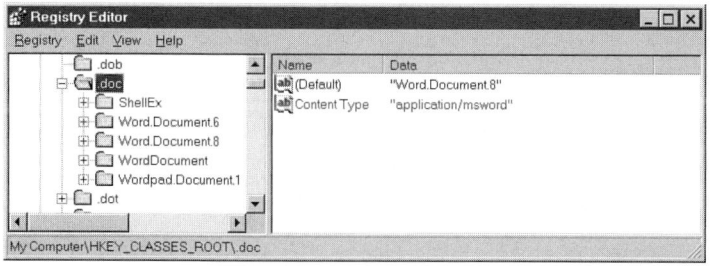

Figure 15.6
The Registry entry for .doc extensions.

The value named (Default) points to Word.Document.8 as the next location in the Registry to check.

Scroll down toward the bottom of HKEY_CLASSES_ROOT to find Word.Document.8 (see Figure 15.7). The entry Word.Document.8 is known as a *ProgID*. Often client programs use the ProgID to create an instance of an object. Notice the Subkey named CLSID and the (Default) value of {00020906-0000-0000-C000-000000000046}.

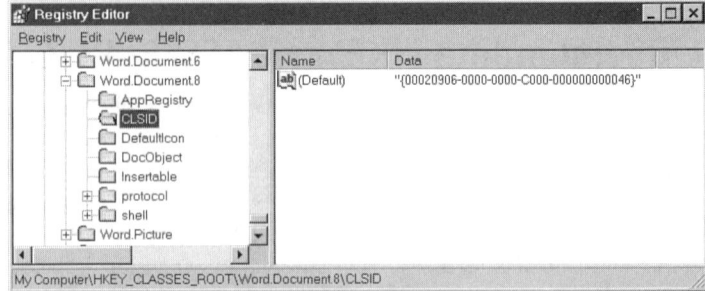

Figure 15.7
The Registry entry for Word.Document.8.

Scroll toward the top of the Registry to find the CLSID key. Open the CLSID key, then scroll to locate the {00020906-0000-0000-C000-000000000046} entry (see Figure 15.8). The LocalServer32 key points to D:\msoffice\Office\Winword.e XE as the location of the program. Windows 98 then launches Winword.e XE to display the file with the .doc extension.

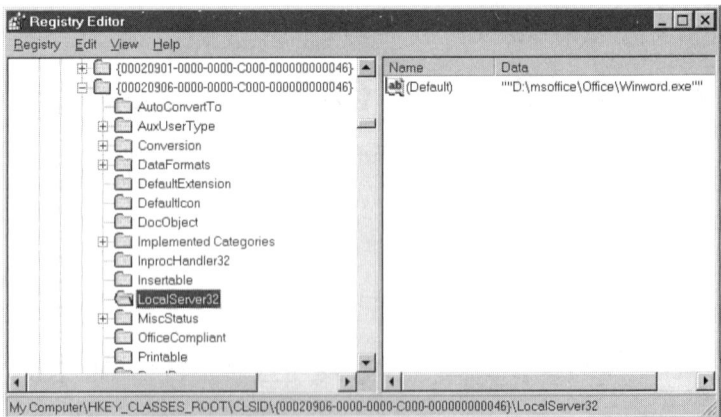

Figure 15.8
The Registry entry for CLSID {00020906-0000-0000-C000-000000000046}.

Windows 98 follows this or a similar process whenever a user double-clicks a file with an associated extension, a client program requests an instance of a server created, or a user double-clicks a linked or embedded object within a compound document.

What Are Compound Documents?

A *compound document* is simply a file such as a .doc, .xls, or .ppt file that is capable of holding data created by the object information of other programs. To the user, a compound document presents a unified interface to data best created and maintained by other programs. Data from the other program can be embedded within the compound document, and therefore, does not change in relation to external documents. Alternatively, data from other documents can be linked. In this case, changes to the externally linked document are seen when the compound document is displayed. Compound documents rely on the ability to create and use files in a Structured Storage format.

What Is Structured Storage?

Structured storage can be thought of as a mini-file system within a single file (see Figure 15.9). The storage file contains two types of objects: storage objects and stream objects. *Storage objects* are analogous to directories in a file system; *stream objects* are analogous to files. The storage file starts with a root storage object and a single stream object. This original stream object holds the data created from the host (or container) application.

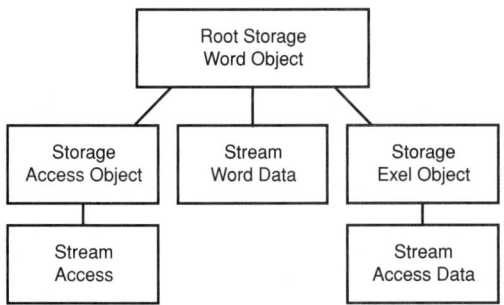

Figure 15.9
Storage and stream objects within a compound document File.

For instance, if you create a Word document, the text you type is stored in the original stream object. Later on, you link or embed an Excel spreadsheet. A new storage object is created below the root storage, and a new stream object is created below the storage object to hold spreadsheet data. This ability to nest storage in this manner allows for development of complex compound documents.

Sample Files Included on the CD

You can locate the following Word documents and Excel worksheets on the CD-ROM accompanying this book. These documents and worksheets can make it easy to follow the creation of Compound Documents described in the following "Using OLE" section.

Weekly Time and Expense Report.doc

Hours.xls

Expenses.xls

Salesperson of the Month.doc

Car Sales.xls

Using OLE

The following sections present how to create, use, and edit both linked and embedded Compound Documents. The examples shown use Word and Excel, but similar procedures can be used by many OLE-compliant applications.

Building Compound Documents

OLE makes building compound documents so easy that you may have created compound documents without even realizing what you have done.

The first step to creating a compound document is launching the container application; the examples in this chapter use Word as the container application. In OLE terms, the *container application* is the client program. At a later time, when data is linked or embedded, the application(s) used to create that other data are considered *server applications*.

When choosing a container application, consider starting with the application best suited to create and edit the majority of the data. For instance, if the majority of the data is textual, choose a word processor as the container application.

Creating Embedded Documents

One way to create an embedded document is to use an existing file created by another application. In this example, two Excel Spreadsheets, one to calculate the number of hours worked and the other to calculate expenses, are embedded into a Time and Expense Report document created with Word:

1. Create and save the two Excel spreadsheets. (Alternatively, use the files named Hours.xls and Expenses.xls included on the CD-ROM that accompanies this book.)

2. Launch Word and create a new document. (Alternatively, use the file named Weekly Time and Expense Report.doc included on the CD.)

3. Type the text that you want to appear in the Word document.

4. Place the insertion point at the location in the Word document at which you want to place the first spreadsheet.

Chapter 15: OLE, COM, DCOM, and ActiveX

5. On Word's menu choose **I**nsert, **O**bject. The Object dialog box appears.

6. Choose the Create from **F**ile tab. Next, type the name of the file, or use the **B**rowse button to locate the desired Excel spreadsheet (see Figure 15.10). Disregard the Lin**k** to File checkbox for this example, but if in the future you want to create a linked document, you would select this checkbox.

7. Finally, click OK to embed the document.

8. To embed the second spreadsheet, place the insertion point at the location in the Word document where you want the second spreadsheet. Repeat steps 4 through 7 to choose and embed the second spreadsheet.

9. Finish the Word document, and then save it.

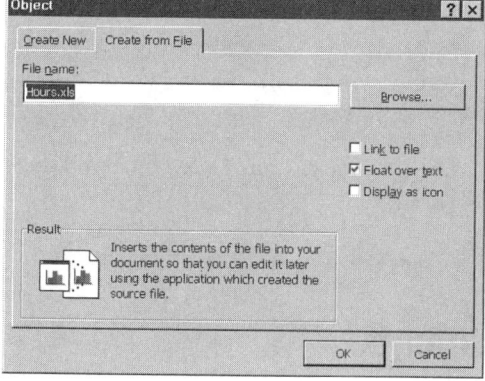

Figure 15.10
*The Create from **F**ile tab used to select an object for embedding.*

An alternate way to create embedded documents does not require first creating a file from the server application:

1. Launch Word and create a new document. (Alternatively, use the file named Weekly Time and Expense Report.doc included on this book's CD-ROM.)

2. Type the text that you want to appear in the Word document.

3. Place the insertion point at the location in the Word document at which you want to place a new spreadsheet.

4. On Word's menu choose **I**nsert, **O**bject. The Object dialog box appears.

5. Choose the Create **N**ew tab, then select one of the registered OLE Server applications listed in the **O**bject Type list. For this example, choose Microsoft Excel Worksheet. Click OK.

Excel (the server application) launches automatically and provides a worksheet window. Notice that the menus and toolbars from Excel have temporarily replaced Word's menus and toolbars. You can resize the worksheet, enter cell headings, create formulas, and so on. However, when you click the mouse outside of the delimited worksheet area, Excel terminates and the menus and toolbars for Word reappear.

6. Finish the Word document, and then save it.

Using In-place Editing

Editing a compound document is very easy. Servers that are OLE 2.0-compliant allow *in-place editing*. This simply means that the user can edit the embedded or linked data objects within the structure of the container document. To see how to accomplish this, follow these steps:

1. Launch Word and open one of the Word documents you created that contains an embedded document.

2. Double-click on an embedded worksheet object. Excel launches automatically. Now make whatever editing changes you want to the worksheet.

3. When you are done, simply click outside the delimited area of the worksheet. The edit window closes and Excel automatically quits.

4. To save the changes, choose **F**ile, **S**ave or click the disk icon.

Creating Linked Documents

There are several ways to create linked documents. You typically use a linked document when multiple users need to see and/or update information in real time. Linked documents always start by using an existing external file. Changes made to the external file are visible when viewed by the compound document.

The external file can be located locally or on a different machine in either a read-only or read-write share point. These share permissions can control whether users can only view the linked data, or if they have the ability to change the data. In either case, the data reflects the current contents of the file at the time the host document is opened.

In this example, a sales manager allows access to a spreadsheet on his machine. Salespersons use a Word document to view sales figures:

1. Create and save an Excel spreadsheet with monthly sales figures. (Alternatively, use the file named Car Sales.xls on the CD.)

2. Launch Word and create a new document, then type the text that you want to appear in the Word document. (Alternatively, use the file Salesperson of the Month.doc included on the CD.)

Chapter 15: OLE, COM, DCOM, and ActiveX

3. Place the insertion point at the location in the Word document at which you want to place the worksheet.

4. On Word's menu choose **I**nsert, **O**bject. The Object dialog box appears.

5. Choose the Create from **F**ile tab. Next, type the name of the file, or use the **B**rowse button to locate the desired Excel spreadsheet (refer to Figure 15.10). (Alternatively, use the file Car Sales.xls included on the CD.) Choose the checkbox labeled Lin**k** to File.

6. Finally, click OK to link the document.

7. Finish the Word document, and then save it.

Editing Linked Documents

Editing a linked compound document can be very simple. However, unlike embedded documents, edits to linked documents are not performed in-place. Edits to linked documents launch a separate visible instance of the application used to create the linked data. This separate application is considered a warning to the user that they are updating an external file and not merely updating an embedded document. To see how to accomplish this action, follow these steps:

1. Launch Word and open one of the Word documents you created that contains a linked document.

2. Double-click on a linked worksheet object. Excel launches automatically. Now make whatever editing changes you want to the worksheet.

3. When you are done, save the file; choose **F**ile, **S**ave. Choose **F**ile, E**x**it to return to the host document.

Drag-and-Drop Linking

Another way to create a link is to use drag-and-drop linking. By using this technique you can select a portion of the external document rather than the entire external document. For this example, use the same files as in the previous linking examples. Follow these steps:

1. Open Excel, then create and save an Excel spreadsheet with monthly sales figures. (Alternatively, use the file named Car Sales.xls on the CD.)

2. Launch Word and create a new document, and then type the text that you want to appear in the Word document. (Alternatively, use the file Salesperson of the Month.doc included on the CD.)

3. In Excel, highlight the cells you want to link into the Word document. If you have opened Car Sales.xls, drag the mouse to select D1 through D6. Right-click the mouse within the selected range, then choose **C**opy from the pop-up menu.

4. Return to Word and place the insertion point at the location where you want to insert the link. Then choose **E**dit Paste **S**pecial from Word's menu. The Paste Special dialog box appears.

5. In the Paste Special dialog box, choose Paste **L**ink, and then select Microsoft Excel Worksheet Object from the list of available objects.

6. Finally, click the OK button to link the document.

7. Finish the Word document, and then save it.

Using the DCOMCNFG Utility

As described earlier, DCOM allows you to place client and server components on different machines. Following installation of a client component, the client computer has no knowledge as to which other computer holds the server component to communicate with. Configuring the client computer with the proper name of the server computer that contains the server component is one of the configuration tasks performed by DCOMCNFG. Assume that a server component used in a bank has the capability to access your bank account. The server component should be configured with information restricting who is allowed to see your account balance, and further restricts who has the ability to perform transactions on your account. DCOMCNFG has the ability to configure software use on a user-by-user basis, and even on a function-by-function basis if needed. As an administrator, you use DCOMCNFG to configure both the client and the server computers to ensure both secure and reliable communication.

The default security mechanism used by Windows 98 is known as share-level security, but is considered to be a relatively weak form of security. Windows 98 can alternately be configured to use user-level security, which is a more robust security scheme; however, in order to provide user-level security on Windows 98 you also use an external security provider such as a Windows NT Domain Controller or a NetWare server. DCOM relies on user-level security to protect the data that it accesses. Whenever a user attempts to access a resource, his UserID is checked against the security provider to determine if he should be allowed access.

Windows 98 requires that you change to user-level security prior to configuring DCOM. In fact, if you attempt to run DCOMCNFG while using share-level security, you see a dialog box stating that you must change to user-level security prior to using DCOM or DCOMCNFG (see Figure 15.11).

Figure 15.11
The dialog box you see when you run DCOMCNFG using share-level security.

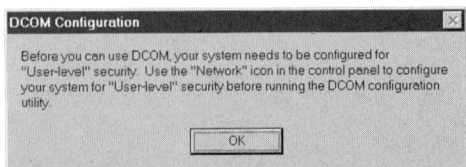

The DCOMCNFG utility displays information about server applications that are read from the Registry, and also makes changes to the Registry. The majority of the configuration takes place within the HKEY_CLASSES_ROOT subtree.

DCOM on Windows 98

If you have configured DCOM on Windows NT, you should be aware that there are several differences when configuring DCOM on Windows 98. On Windows NT, the DCOM server can be launched on demand by a DCOM request from a remote DCOM client program; Windows 98 does not automatically launch the server. Typically, DCOM server components are run on NT servers instead of Windows 98 computers. However, if you want to use Windows 98 as a DCOM server you should provide a means to launch the server application during system boot.

Second, DCOM servers typically remain loaded in memory only as long as there is a client using the server. When the last client program ends, the server removes itself from memory. If a DCOM server is intended for use on Windows 98, it can be written so that it remains in memory indefinitely and does not follow the default behavior of a DCOM server. (The server program included on the accompanying CD-ROM is written to run indefinitely.)

Note If both the client and server components reside on a single Windows 98 machine, the server does launch automatically when the client is run. This, however, is because COM is starting the server rather than DCOM.

Client/Server Program Included on the CD-ROM

The CD-ROM that accompanies this book includes a simple client/server program that you can install and use to test DCOM and configure DCOM using DCOMCNFG. Three setup programs are associated with this chapter: One installs only the server, one installs only the client, and another installs both the client and server on a single machine. Use the third setup if you want to test DCOM's ability to alternate where the client looks for the server (between the local machine and a remote machine). You can install the server-only setup on a remote machine, then alternate the client between the two server components.

The client program provides a user interface and accesses the server component. The server component includes two functions: One calculates mortgage payments and the other reverses a string of characters.

If you install the client/server program from the CD, you can use REGEDIT to see what DCOM has configured. The text refers to specific GUIDs and classes registered during the installation process.

If you would like, you can use REGEDIT to view HKEY_CLASSES_ROOT. After the installation you see the following:

A ProgID named DCOMDemo.Application

A CLSID of {FCB0026A-D7FA-11D1-8DE5-0020AF27BBB5}

These two entries are also repeated within the AppID section of HKEY_CLASSES_ROOT. DCOM places the name of the Remote Server in the RemoteServerName key of the CLSID.

Before you can do any configuration using DCOMCNFG, you first need a Windows NT Domain (or other security provider), and you must configure Windows 98 with user-level security. The steps to accomplish this are covered next.

Changing Windows 98 to User-level Security

To change Windows 98 from share-level to user-level security, follow the steps below. Chapter 21, "Understanding Windows 98 Networking," describes user-level security in greater detail. The following procedure is provided for your convenience:

1. Identify the security provider that you will use. Ensure that you have a valid account on the security provider by checking with the system administrator. Verify that your Windows 98 machine is running a transport protocol capable of communicating with the security provider.

2. Choose Start, Settings, Control Panel. Choose the Network icon. The Network dialog box opens.

3. Choose the Access Control tab (see Figure 15.12). Then choose User-level Access Control. In the Obtain List of Users and Groups From text box, type the name of an NT Domain. Click OK.

4. A dialog box appears warning you that all existing shares will be removed. Click Yes to continue.

5. You may be prompted for the Windows 98 CD to copy files to the hard drive. Following file copy, the System Settings Change dialog box appears, indicating that the computer must restart for the new settings to take effect. Click Yes to allow restart.

6. Following the restart, log on to Windows 98, then choose Start, Settings, Control Panel. Click the Network icon. The Network dialog box opens.

7. On the Configuration tab, select Client for Microsoft Networks, and then choose the Properties button. The Client for Microsoft Networks Properties dialog box appears (see Figure 15.13).

Chapter 15: OLE, COM, DCOM, and ActiveX 371

8. Choose the **L**og On to Windows NT Domain checkbox. In the Windows NT Domain text box, type the name of the NT Domain you want to use for authentication. Click the OK button.

9. The System Settings Change dialog box appears, indicating that the computer must restart for the new settings to take effect. Click **Y**es to allow the restart.

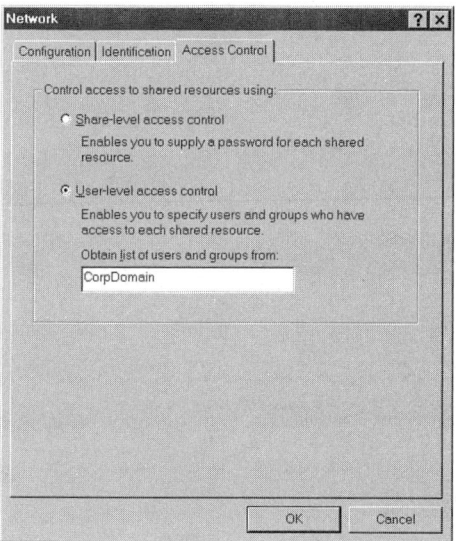

Figure 15.12
The Access Control property page from the Network applet.

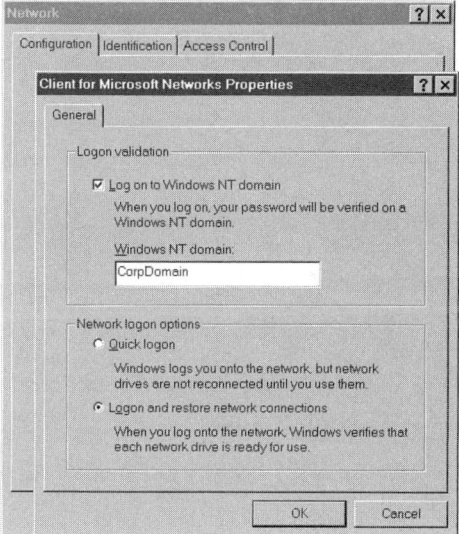

Figure 15.13
The Client for Microsoft Networks properties page.

Select a Location in Which to Run the Server

After logging on to Windows 98 and being validated by a security provider, you can run the DCOMCNFG program. By using this utility you can determine where clients running on your Windows 98 machine will look for the server. For server components located on the computer you are configuring, you can select who has the ability to access and use the server component.

To launch the DCOM Configuration Utility, follow these steps:

1. Choose Start, Run.

2. Type **DCOMCNFG** in the Open text box, then click OK.

The Distributed COM Configuration Properties dialog box appears. In the Applications list, you see the OLE servers that have been registered on your machine. Through this utility, you can set default configuration settings that apply to OLE servers, or you can establish settings for a specific server that override the default settings (see Figure 15.14).

Figure 15.14
The Distributed COM Configuration Properties dialog box.

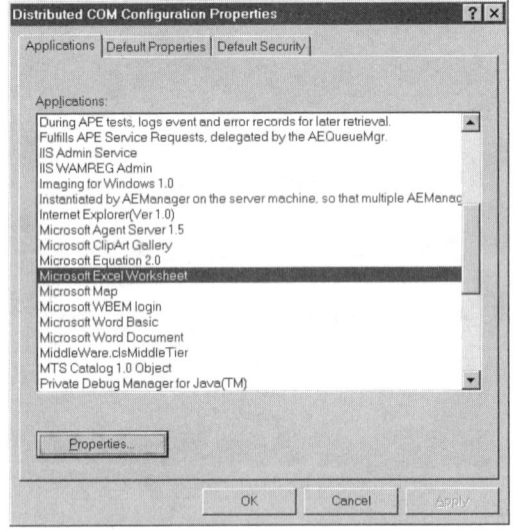

OLE servers (ActiveX servers) are typically registered by the setup program that installs the server; however, as an administrator, you can register and unregister server components manually. The process used to register a server component varies, depending on whether the component is an .EXE or a .DLL file.

All ActiveX/OLE server registrations occur within the HKEY_CLASSES_ROOT subtree.

Chapter 15: OLE, COM, DCOM, and ActiveX **373**

Server components compiled as .EXE files self-register the first time they are run. Locate the name of the .EXE server file and double-click it. The server runs momentarily, then ends. In the process, the server checks the Registry and if not already registered, it registers itself. To unregister a server, run the .EXE file with the **/unregserver** switch. Server components compiled as .DLL (and .OCX for ActiveX controls) are registered by using the REGSVR32.EXE program. For instance, to register a .DLL file named MiddleTier.DLL, you would enter **REGSVR32 MiddleTier.DLL** from the Run command or a Command Prompt. To unregister the same .DLL you would enter **REGSVR32 /u MiddleTier.DLL** from the Run command or the command prompt.

Alternately, many 32-bit servers are unregistered when you remove the server application by using the Add/Remove Programs icon in Control Panel.

To establish DCOM settings for an individual server, select the server from the Applications list, then choose the Properties button.

The General tab displays information about the server (see Figure 15.15). There are no configuration settings on this tab.

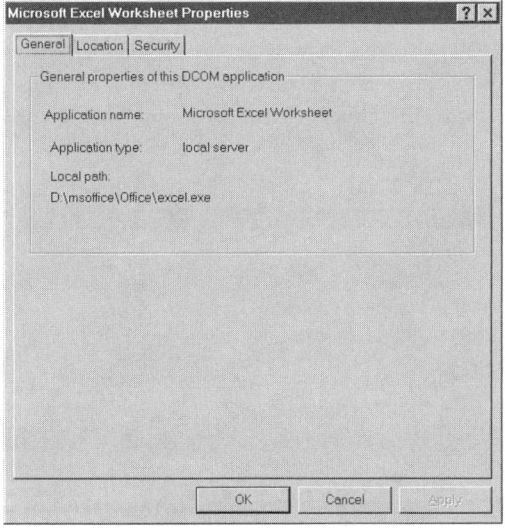

Figure 15.15
The General tab of the Microsoft Excel Worksheet Properties dialog box.

The Location tab (see Figure 15.16) allows you to determine where a client program will look to find the server. The default setting is set up to run the server on the local machine. You can choose to run the server on a specific remote machine by selecting Run Application on the Following Computer and typing the name of the machine where the remote server application is located. You can also choose to run the application on the server that contains the data. After you have made your selections, click the Apply or the OK button.

Figure 15.16
The Location tab of the Microsoft Excel Worksheet Properties dialog box.

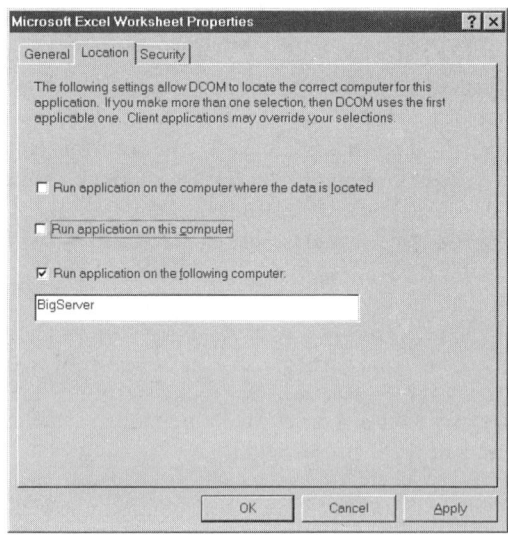

Use Appropriate Security Settings

The Security tab (see Figure 15.17) allows you to accept the default security settings, or to establish individual security settings for this server. To establish specific security settings, choose Use Custom Access Permissions, then choose the Edit button. The Access Permissions dialog box appears.

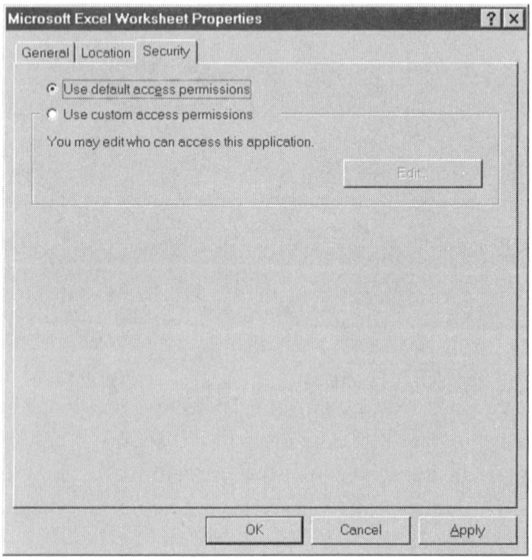

Figure 15.17
The Security tab of the Microsoft Excel Worksheet Properties dialog box.

Chapter 15: OLE, COM, DCOM, and ActiveX

The Access Permissions dialog box (see Figure 15.18) displays the users or groups that have been granted access to this server. To grant additional users or groups access to the server, choose the **A**dd button. The Access Permissions dialog box appears.

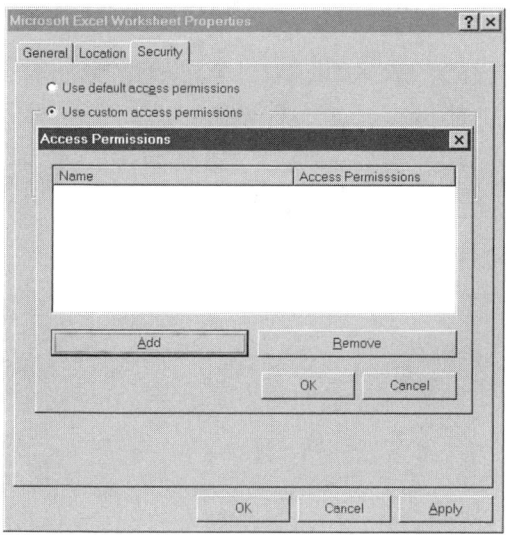

Figure 15.18
The Access Permissions dialog box.

The Add Access Permissions dialog box (see Figure 15.19) allows you to choose users or groups that can use DCOM server applications. Select the names of users or groups from the **N**ame list on the left, then choose either **G**rant Access or **D**eny Access. The names move to the corresponding window. When you have made your selections, click OK. The Registry is updated to reflect your new settings.

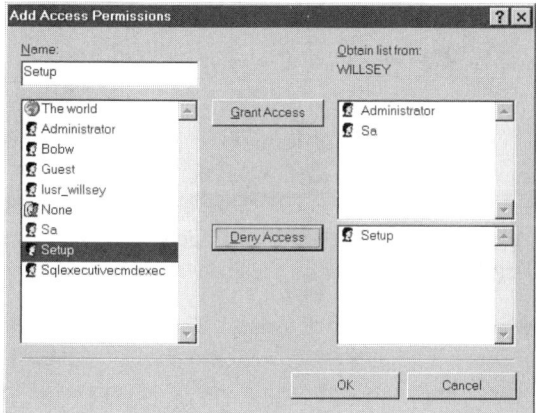

Figure 15.19
The Add Access Permissions dialog box.

Establish Default DCOM Settings

The Default Properties tab on the Distributed COM Configuration Properties dialog box (see Figure 15.20) allows you to establish default settings for server applications on this machine. Remember that individual settings can override the default settings you establish here.

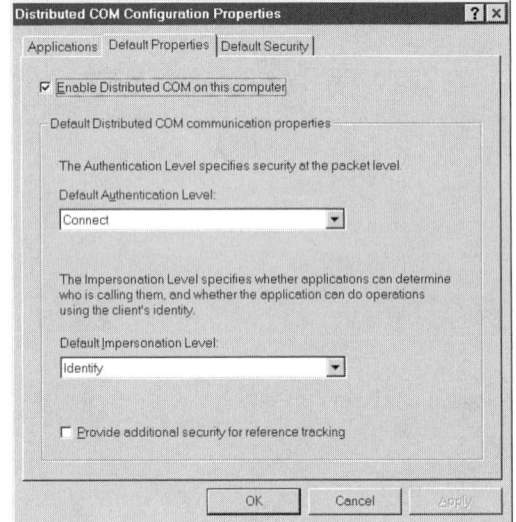

Figure 15.20
The Default Properties tab from the Distributed COM Configuration Properties dialog box.

The **E**nable Distributed COM on this Computer check box determines whether DCOM on this machine is allowed to communicate with DCOM on another machine.

The Default A**u**thentication Level list has two choices: None and Connect. This selection determines whether the security provider is checked by an inbound DCOM request. If you do not want to authenticate users, choose None. If you choose Connect, the security provider is checked for authentication when a DCOM connection request is received.

The Default **I**mpersonation Level selection determines whether the server application can temporarily impersonate the UserID and password of the user on the client computer. This is useful and often necessary in order to gain access to sensitive data. Remember, server components are used by many people; some people require access to secure data and others do not. Identify allows the server to identify the UserID of the client. Impersonate allows the server to temporarily assume the security attributes of the user on the client computer.

The Default Security tab (see Figure 15.21) allows you to establish users and groups who have default permission to access servers on this computer. To establish or change these settings, choose the Edit Default button. The Add Access Permissions dialog box appears.

Chapter 15: OLE, COM, DCOM, and ActiveX   **377**

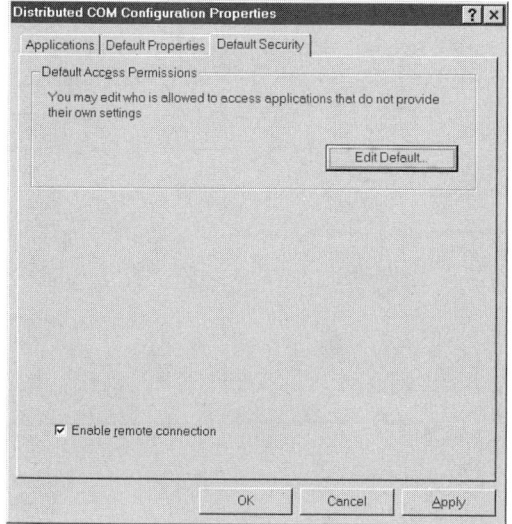

Figure 15.21
The Default Security tab from the Distributed COM Configuration Properties dialog box.

The Add Access Permissions dialog box (see Figure 15.22) is used to grant or deny access to the DCOM server application. Select the names of users or groups from the **N**ame list on the left, then choose either **G**rant Access or **D**eny Access. The names move to the corresponding window. When you have made your selections, click OK. The Registry is updated to reflect your new settings.

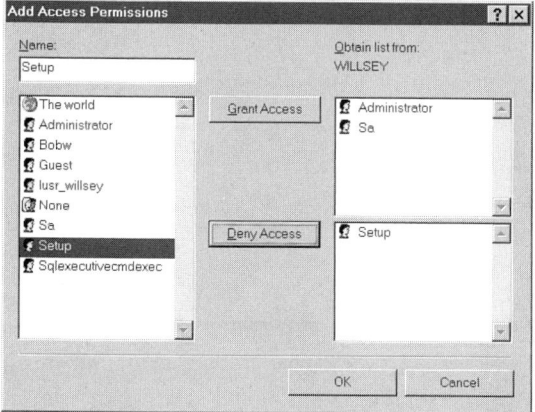

Figure 15.22
The Add Access Permissions dialog box.

Conclusion

This chapter introduced several key client/server technologies available today on Windows 98. These technologies are open and supported by Windows NT, and to some extent by Macintosh, UNIX, and some mainframe platforms.

In corporate environments you might expect to see a growing number of applications using client/server and N-Tier applications. As a system administrator, you should know how to install, configure, and test distributed applications to ensure both reliable and secure connectivity between components.

CHAPTER 16

Windows 98 ODBC Connectivity

This chapter addresses the use of ODBC (Open Database Connectivity) and the issues of successfully connecting a client program running on Windows 98 to a database server running on another machine. If you have never done this before, you may want to read the next few pages, which provide an overview of client/server database concepts, ODBC terminology, and the parameters used in an ODBC Connect String.

This chapter includes two examples of creating DSNs (Data Source Names). One example shows how to create a DSN that connects to a SQL Server; the second depicts a connection to an Access database. Both examples address how to create user, system, and file DSNs.

A program on the CD ROM allows you to experiment with various ODBC parameters to see what effect they have on the connection process.

Finally, this chapter includes sections that address how to install or upgrade ODBC, troubleshooting ODBC connection problems, and advanced ODBC tuning options.

Client/Server Database Concepts

You are probably reading this chapter because you need to connect an application program running on a Windows 98 client computer to a database located on some server, such as an NT Server, a UNIX box, or a mainframe system. This chapter concentrates on two-tier client/server architecture, but it is also applicable to N-tier (3 or more-layer) architecture. See Chapter 15, "OLE, COM, DCOM, and ActiveX," for more information on N-tier architecture.

Databases used by PC users fall into one of two categories: file type or client/server type databases.

File type databases such as Access and Paradox were designed primarily as single-user, relatively small databases in which the data, the user interface and, if required, the database engine all resided on a single end-user machine. Today, many file type databases are network capable and can support multiple users accessing data simultaneously either with or without ODBC. However, file type databases were not designed for this purpose and therefore suffer under heavy workloads. While there are ODBC drivers written to allow access to file type databases, this was not the primary intent of ODBC (see Figure 16.1).

Figure 16.1
This diagram shows the major components in a file type database.

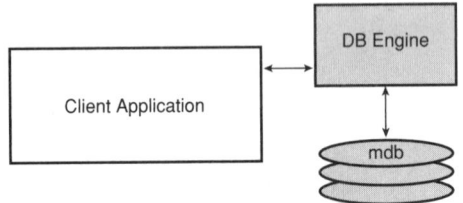

PC Running Windows 98

In contrast, client/server type databases (see Figure 16.2) such as SQL Server, ORACLE, and Informix were specifically designed to handle many users accessing large centralized databases over communication lines. The server runs an engine (a program) that accepts requests in the form of a SQL statement from the client machine, locates those records matching the SQL statement, and finally returns the data matching the request to the client via the communication lines. The engine is often written as a multithreaded program that can process requests from multiple users simultaneously. Database server machines often contain large amounts of

RAM, multiple processors and high-speed disk subsystems to handle the heavy workloads imposed by many users.

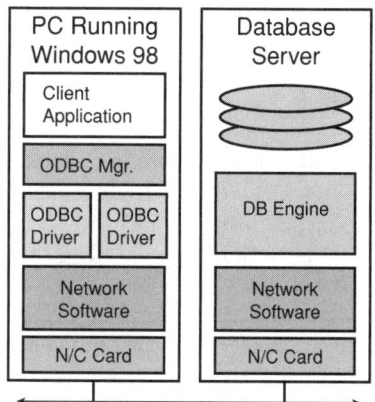

Figure 16.2
This diagram shows the major components found in a client/server database.

A single database engine running on a server platform usually services multiple databases. For example, a database engine might service requests from the Accounting department against the AP and AR databases, whereas the Sales department might need access to the ForecastSales and ClosedSales databases. ODBC's primary focus is to allow client programs to access these server type databases.

Now you have been introduced to the big picture and some terminology from the database server side. You might be wondering how Windows 98 fits in or, more importantly, what you as a system administrator need to do in order for Windows 98 to successfully communicate with a database on a database server.

When an application running on Windows 98 attempts to access a database engine located on a remote server, many layers of software and hardware must work together to establish the connection. In addition to the standard networking components that you must install and configure, you must also install and configure software that fits between your application program and the networking software.

On Windows 98, you must install and configure an ODBC Manager and at least one ODBC Driver. The application program talks to the ODBC Manager when it needs to access a database. Based on configuration settings, the ODBC Manager selects an ODBC driver that can talk to the database engine. After the database driver is selected and loaded in memory, data flows between the application and the networking software through the database driver.

In the Control Panel is a 32bit ODBC applet. This applet is used to configure parameters such as which ODBC Driver to use, what database server to connect to, and what database on the database engine to access. The same applet allows you to set configuration parameters for your application program to access local files on your Windows 98 computer, as well as set configuration for client/server databases. These configuration settings can be unique to a specific user, shared among multiple users of a Windows 98 computer, or copied as a file to many machines. (The procedures to install ODBC software and to configure it properly are covered later in this chapter.)

An Overview of ODBC

ODBC (Open Database Connectivity) is an Application Programming Interface (API) developed by Microsoft that has been widely adopted by many industry database manufacturers. ODBC allows programmers the ability to write application programs that universally access Relational Databases Management Systems (RDBMS) such as SQL Server, ORACLE, Informix, and others.

ODBC frees customers and application programmers from the requirements of a specific database implementation or manufacturer. Customers have the ability to port their data to another RDBMS for reasons such as increased performance, cost savings, or platform change while maintaining the ability of the application program to access the data.

However, the freedom of data portability comes with a cost. In order to provide portability, ODBC uses ANSI Standard SQL statements, which provide a generic method for programmers to access data. This generic approach allows for portability but precludes the ability of the application programmer to take advantage of special features and SQL extensions associated with a specific database engine. In other words, if an application programmer chooses to use the native database interface instead of ODBC, the speed of access may be faster and the functionality may be greater. But this comes at the cost of rewriting the application if it is necessary to port the data to another database engine.

ODBC Drivers

ODBC implementation relies on drivers that abstract differences in database implementation from the application program in a manner similar to how printer or NIC drivers abstract the implementation of specific printer devices or NIC cards. For example, to communicate with SQL Server you need an ODBC driver written specifically to talk to SQL Server.

Microsoft has written ODBC drivers for its own products and several competing products. Microsoft has also written drivers for SQL Server and a partial ORACLE driver for client/server database engines, as well as drivers for Fox Pro, Access, Paradox, and dBase file type databases. Microsoft also has drivers for non-database data sources such as Excel spreadsheets and comma-delimited text files. There are, however, many other database manufacturers and third-party companies that have written ODBC drivers for databases found on mainframe, UNIX, and other platforms.

Not all ODBC drivers are created equal. In Windows 98, 32-bit applications must use 32-bit ODBC drivers whereas 16-bit applications must use a 16-bit ODBC Manager and 16-bit

ODBC drivers. Additionally, the ODBC specification allows drivers to conform to various levels of the specification. The level of conformance the driver is written to meet determines the level of functionality provided. Lastly, differences in how the drivers are written may result in speed differences between otherwise similar drivers.

The ODBC Manager

In addition to the ODBC driver(s), you also use an ODBC Manager program (refer to Figure 16.2) that for the most part is transparent to the user. The ODBC Manager (ODBC32.DLL) and driver require several parameters in order to successfully connect to the desired database. The ODBC Manager handles loading the specified ODBC driver, querying the driver for its level of conformance, and passing connection parameters, read and write data, error information, and so on, between the application program and the ODBC driver.

Connecting to the Database

Before data can be read from or written to the database, a connection must be established. Often the source of the data is on another machine that must be accessed via a LAN or WAN connection. To successfully connect, ODBC uses the following parameters:

> **Note** The first five parameters are *required* to establish a connection.

- DRIVER   The ODBC Driver to use
- SERVER   The name of the server to connect
- DATABASE   The name of the database you want to access
- UID   The UserID that has been granted access to the database
- PWD   The password associated with the UserID parameter
- DSN   The DSN (Data Source Name), which provides some of the connection parameters (optional)
- WSID   The name of your Windows 98 computer (optional)
- APP   The name of the client program's executable file (optional)

The ODBC parameters required to establish a connection can be supplied from one source, or a combination of several sources. One source is from within the application program itself, in which case these parameters are supplied by the programmer. A second source is through a DSN; a DSN is usually created by the system administrator. A third is Windows 98, which can supply the UserID and password entered by the user during logon. Another source is the user himself, who, when prompted with a dialog box, can select a DSN and also enter a UserID and password.

If the program includes the required parameters, it should connect directly to the database when run. A problem with this is that it requires changes to the program if the database is ported to another server or RDBMS.

Usually, the program includes the DSN and possibly the DATABASE and UID parameters. This affords local administrators or management the flexibility to determine which server to place the database on, or which RDBMS to use. The ODBC Manager can also prompt the user with a dialog box (see Figure 16.3), in which the user can provide the missing PWD or both the UID and PWD parameters in order to promote security. If the UID and PWD parameters are missing, the Windows 98 logon UserID and password are used for these parameters.

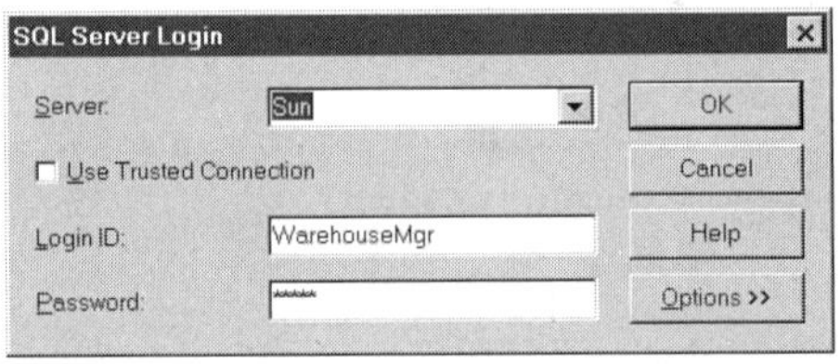

Figure 16.3
This dialog box allows users to enter a UserID and/or password, or choose a DSN.

Note By using the accompanying CD-ROM you can install a program that allows you to experiment with ODBC connectivity. This program was written with Visual Basic 5.0 and has been tested against the Pubs database included with SQL Server version 6.5 and the Northwind database included with Access 97. This program allows you to quickly change, include, or exclude various ODBC parameters, then attempt to establish a connection. After you're connected, you can query tables and views from the database.

The ODBC Connect String

As mentioned earlier, there are several sources that can supply ODBC parameters. Inside a program these parameters reside in what is known as an ODBC Connect String; outside the program these parameters are supplied by a DSN. The ODBC Connect String is compiled as part of the program and therefore does not change. The application program looks to itself first for the ODBC parameters. If some ODBC parameters are missing, the program then can use a DSN or can prompt the user for the missing parameters.

One way to supply the ODBC parameters is for the application program to include an ODBC Connect String. Programs often include an ODBC Connect String, which includes some or all of the ODBC parameters. ODBC connect strings should not include any extra spaces (although you must exactly match the DRIVER name, which often does include spaces), but must terminate each parameter with a semicolon.

The following examples show several connect strings and explain what happens when they are used. Assume that the client program is attempting to access the Inventory database on a SQL Server named Sun; the user account is WarehouseMgr and the password is 98765.

```
"UID=WarehouseMgr;PWD=98765;DRIVER=SQL Server;SERVER=Sun;DATABASE=Inventory;"
```

In the preceding ODBC Connect String, the required parameters are included and the client program can connect without any user intervention. The programmer can control whether a dialog box (refer to Figure 16.3) is displayed to the user during the connection sequence. In this case it is not necessary.

```
"DRIVER=SQL Server;SERVER=Sun;DATABASE=Inventory;"
```

In this ODBC Connect String, neither the UID nor the PWD parameter is included. In this case, the ODBC Manager uses the UserID and password from the Windows 98 logon process. If the programmer displays the dialog box, it is prefilled with the logon UserID and Password. If the dialog box is not displayed, a connection is attempted using the logon UserID and Password.

```
"UID=WarehouseMgr;DRIVER=SQL Server;SERVER=Sun;DATABASE=Inventory;"
```

In this ODBC Connect String, the PWD parameter is not included. The programmer can choose to display the dialog box with the UID prefilled. The user must then enter the proper password to connect successfully.

The three preceding examples all require client program recompilation if the database is not called Inventory on a SQL Server named Sun.

```
"UID=WarehouseMgr;DSN=InventoryDSN;"
```

Assume the DSN named InventoryDSN supplies the proper server, driver, and database parameters. This ODBC Connect String works the same as the previous example except that now you have freedom to move the database without recompiling the program by changing these parameters in the DSN.

```
"DSN=InventoryDSN;"
```

Assume the DSN named InventoryDSN supplies the proper server, driver, and database parameters. In this example, the ODBC Manager uses the UserID and password from the Windows 98 logon process. If the programmer displays the dialog box to the user, it is prefilled with the logon UserID and Password. If the dialog box is not displayed to the user, a connection is attempted using the current Windows 98 logon UserID and Password.

Creating a DSN

The last two ODBC Connect String examples in the previous section include a DSN parameter. The DSN parameter supplies a name, which is compared with the Data Source Names (DSNs) on the system. If the DSN name matches the name from the DSN parameter, contents of the DSN such as the server, driver, and database are used to establish the connection. Using DSNs provides greater flexibility over ODBC Connect Strings. In some cases this flexibility is desired. However, in other cases, the ease of use offered by the ODBC Connect String is preferred.

You create a DSN by using the Control Panel 32bit ODBC applet. A DSN cannot supply either the UID or PWD parameters but can supply other parameters, including several not found in the ODBC Connect String.

> **Note** If both a DSN and the ODBC Connect String provide the driver, database, or server parameters, the parameter(s) from the ODBC Connect String take precedence and are used.

By using the 32bit ODBC applet you can create three types of DSNs: User DSNs, System DSNs, and File DSNs.

A *User DSN* is stored in the User Profile of the currently logged-on user and is usable by that user account. A *System DSN* is available to any user on this machine and to system applications. Both of these DSN types are stored in the Registry and are typically created by an administrator on a machine-by-machine basis.

A *File DSN* can be built on one machine and then copied to other machines that have a need for similar DSNs. Remember that DSNs do not hold UID or PWD parameters, so copying DSNs should not impose a security risk.

Steps to Create a DSN

To create or update a DSN you must first open the ODBC Data Source Administrator. To do this, choose Start, **S**ettings, **C**ontrol Panel, 32bit ODBC. You should see the ODBC Data Source Administrator applet that appears in Figure 16.4.

> **Note** The Windows 98 installation process does not automatically install or update ODBC because the files are located outside the Windows 98 directory on the CD. Your system may have an old version of the 32bit ODBC applet left over from Windows 95 or the installation of an application such as Visual Basic or Access. Or, you may not have a 32bit ODBC applet at all in Control Panel.

Chapter 16: Windows 98 ODBC Connectivity

Therefore, you may need to manually force the ODBC installation process if any of the following three scenarios are true:

- The 32bit ODBC icon is not present within Control Panel.
- The ODBC Data Source Administrator window appears substantially different from the one shown in Figure 16.4.
- The screens or wizards you see do not substantially match the figures shown throughout the rest of this chapter.

If you determine that you need to install or upgrade ODBC, see the section "Install or Upgrade ODBC" later in this chapter.

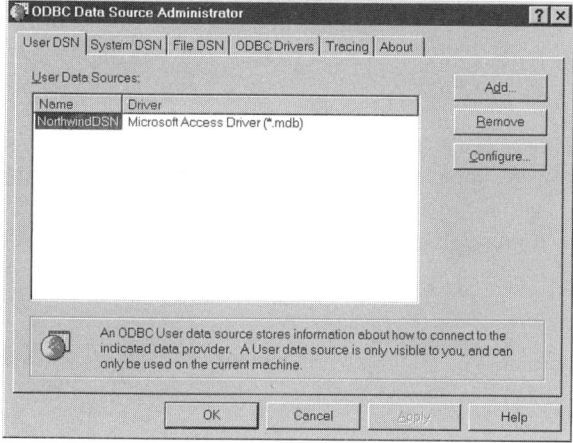

Figure 16.4
The ODBC Data Source Administrator applet is used to create and maintain DSNs.

Note The dialog-box names and choices you see as you create a DSN can change depending on which ODBC Driver you choose. The basic steps involved, however, are fairly similar. As you create either a User, System, or File DSN you can follow either of two samples. One sample creates a DSN for SQL Server as an example of a server type RDBMS. The second sample creates a DSN for a Microsoft Access database as an example of a file type database.

The next few sections describe how to create DSNs. As a system administrator you should decide which type of DSN best fits the current needs of your system.

If many machines require identical DSNs to access a central database, then a file type DSN is probably the best choice. You can create one File DSN for the database and then copy the file to all machines that need access to that database.

If several people use Windows 98 and it is configured to maintain separate user profiles, then User DSNs are a good choice. User DSNs can reduce user confusion and promote security by limiting available choices to only those required by a given user.

A System DSN is available to all users and also to services running on the computer. If multiple users of a system need access to the same database, creating one system DSN is less work than creating multiple identical User DSNs.

To learn how to create a DSN, proceed to any of the following sections, which describe the creation of all three types of DSNs.

Creating a User DSN

To create a new User Data Source Name choose the User DSN tab in the 32bit ODBC Control Panel, and, depending on the driver you're installing, proceed either to the "Common SQL Server Driver Steps" section, or to the "Common Microsoft Access (.mdb) Driver Steps" section, later in this chapter.

Creating a System DSN

To create a new System Data Source Name, choose the System DSN tab in the 32bit ODBC Control Panel. Then, proceed to either the "Common SQL Server Driver Steps" section, or the "Common Microsoft Access (.mdb) Driver Steps" section, later in this chapter.

Creating a File DSN

To create a new File DSN, choose the File DSN tab in the 32bit ODBC Control Panel. Then follow these steps:

1. Use the Look In folder selection window to browse for a specific directory holding File DSNs. The default folder location is \Program Files\Common Files\Odbc\Data Sources.

2. Click the Set Directory button to set the directory identified in the Look In window as the default directory for DSNs.

3. To continue creating a new File DSN, click the Add button. The Create New Data Source screen appears (see Figure 16.5).

4. Type an identifiable name (for example, Inventory File DSN), then choose the Next> button. A Create New Data Source confirmation screen appears (see Figure 16.6).

5. If you agree with the information displayed on the confirmation screen, click Finish.

6. At this point you must complete the creation of the File DSN. Depending on which ODBC driver you want to use, proceed to either the "Common SQL Server Driver Steps" section, or the "Common Microsoft Access (.mdb) Driver Steps" section, later in this chapter.

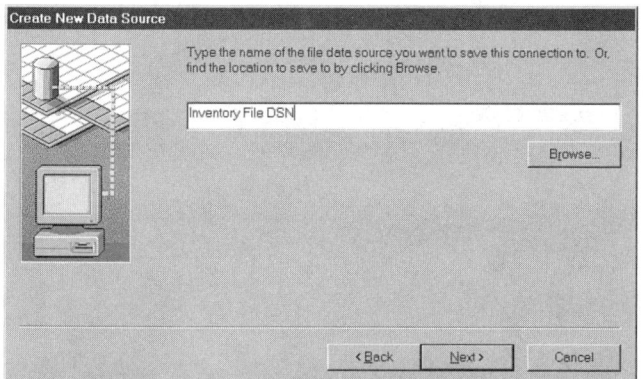

Figure 16.5
This Create New Data Source window allows you to type in the name of the file DSN you are creating.

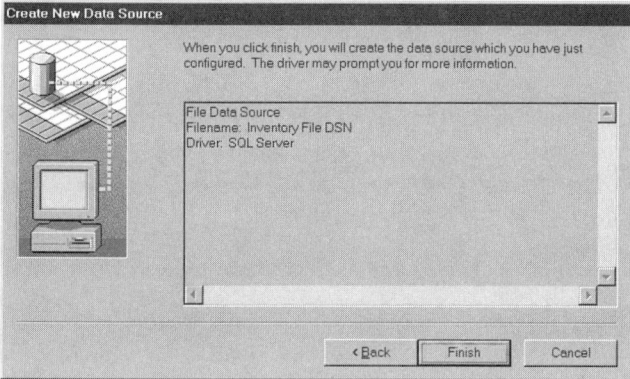

Figure 16.6
This Create New Data Source window displays confirmation information of the DSN you are about to create.

Common SQL Server Driver Steps

To add a new DSN, click the **A**dd button. You should see the Create New Data Source dialog box (see Figure 16.7). Select the desired ODBC driver (for example, SQL Server) from the list of installed ODBC Drivers. Then click Finish.

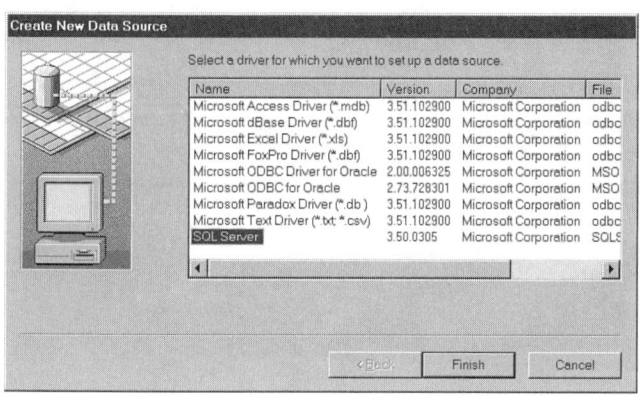

Figure 16.7
The Create New Data Source window allows you to select from the currently installed ODBC drivers.

The first screen of the Create a New Data Source to SQL Server Wizard appears (see Figure 16.8). This wizard steps you through the process of creating a new DSN for SQL Server.

Figure 16.8

The first screen of the Create a New Data Source to SQL Server Wizard allows you to name your DSN and Server.

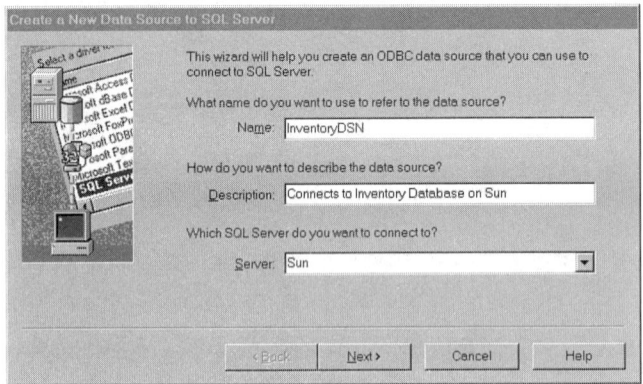

In the Na**m**e field, type in the name you want to use for this DSN. If the client program includes a DSN parameter in its ODBC Connect String, then you should type exactly the same name. Using the earlier example, enter InventoryDSN. If the ODBC Connect String does not include a DSN, create a name that is easily identified.

In the **D**escription field you may optionally type a short description to identify the usage of this DSN.

In the **S**erver field, type the name of the server. Do not use an UNC name (a double backslash). If the server is your Windows 98 machine you can choose Local from the drop-down list.

When you are finished, click **N**ext. The second screen of the wizard appears (see Figure 16.9).

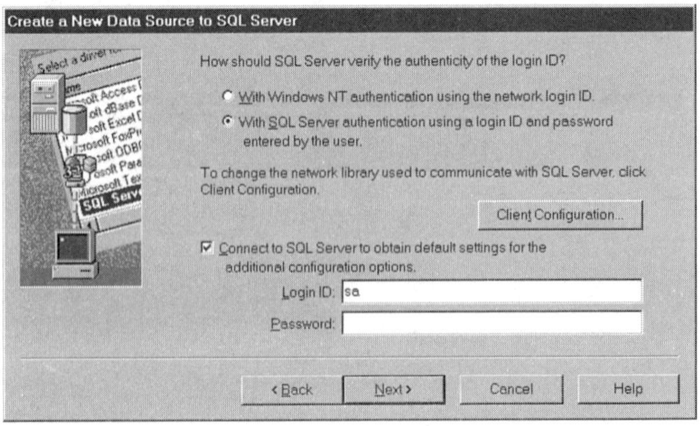

Figure 16.9

In Screen 2 of the Create a New Data Source to SQL Server Wizard you can choose how SQL Server will authenticate you.

Chapter 16: Windows 98 ODBC Connectivity

The DBA can set up the SQL Server to perform user authentication to use Windows NT user accounts, or to use accounts local to SQL Server. The DBA who administers the SQL Server can tell you which authentication method you should choose. Choose the appropriate option from the two choices based on the DBA's answer.

The Clien**t** Configuration button is used to locate and change DLLs used for ODBC to network protocol connectivity. Named Pipes is the default choice, but other choices can increase the speed of connection depending on how the SQL Server is configured. Options available under this button are addressed later in the section "Advanced ODBC Tuning Options."

You can complete the rest of the DSN by using the default values, or you can have the DSN Creation Wizard connect to the SQL Server at this time to query it for specific information such as the names of available databases. To gather the specific information, select the checkbox next to **C**onnects to SQL Server to Obtain. If you choose the **W**ith Windows NT Authentication option, your current logon UserID and password are used to connect. Otherwise, with the With **S**QL Server Authentication option you can type a valid UserID and password into the respective **L**ogin ID and **P**assword fields. If you don't select the **C**onnects to SQL Server to Obtain box, then default information is used on the following wizard screens.

> **Note** The Logon ID and Password do not pose a security concern because they are not retained in the DSN. They are used only to query the database for specifics during the creation of the DSN.

When you are finished, click the **N**ext button. The third screen of the wizard appears (see Figure 16.10).

If on the previous screen, you chose to let the wizard query the SQL Server for specifics, you can select Change the **D**efault Database To and also select which database you want to use as the default for this DSN. Choosing a specific database can speed the initial connection during user logon.

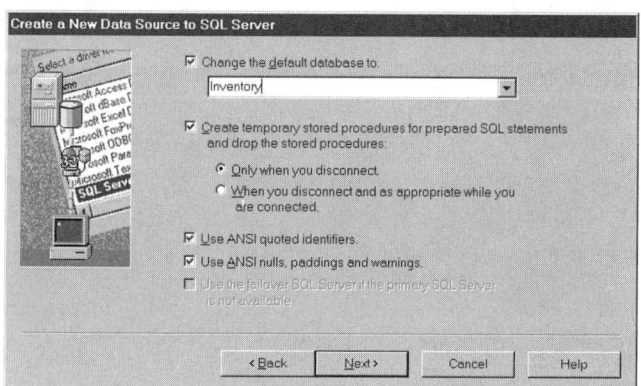

Figure 16.10
Screen 3 of the Create a New Data Source to SQL Server Wizard allows you to choose the default database for this DSN.

If the wizard did not obtain specifics, then (default) is used and cannot be changed. During user logon to SQL Server the database designated as default for that user account is used.

The second checkbox and two option buttons determine how long to retain temporary prepared SQL Statements on the SQL Server. These selections can influence the speed of application execution and the amount of memory (tempdb) used on the SQL Server. For example, when the checkbox is not selected you cannot create temporary prepared statements on the SQL Server, which causes additional, slower SQL processing but requires less memory utilization. When this option is selected, a prepared statement can be stored for future use, thus increasing access speed upon subsequent use. You may want to ask the application programmer which option works best for a given application.

ANSI syntax uses double quotes for table and column names, and single quotes for strings. SQL Statements generated from Access do not differentiate between single and double quotes. You should deselect the Use ANSI Quoted Identifiers option if Access generates the SQL Statements. You should select Use ANSI Nulls, Paddings and Warnings only if you want to use the ANSI handling for these items.

If on the previous screen you allowed the wizard to query the SQL Server and the SQL Server was set up for failover to an alternate server, you then have the ability to select or deselect the last checkbox; otherwise, this option is grayed out and cannot be changed. This selection determines whether to use the failover server in the event of a failure.

When you are finished, click the **N**ext button. The fourth screen of the wizard appears (see Figure 16.11).

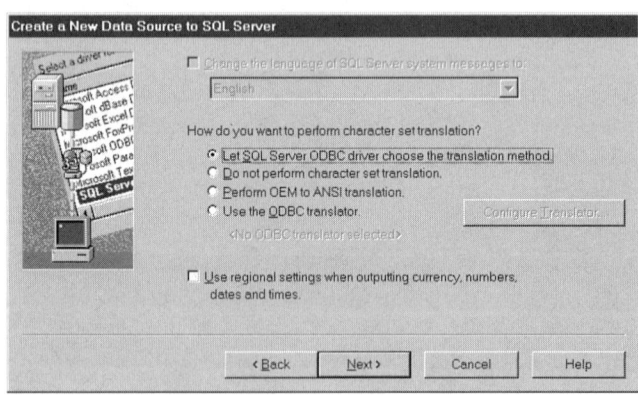

Figure 16.11

This screen allows you to make choices that affect character sets and local representations for Time, Dates, and Currency.

Choices that you make on this screen affect how data and messages are presented to the user. In many cases these options are left at their default values.

The first option allows SQL Server to display error messages and other dialog boxes in any of several languages, including English, French, German, and so on.

Chapter 16: Windows 98 ODBC Connectivity

The group of four options in the center of the screen allows you to select a specific character-translation set. You should check with the SQL Server DBA to determine if it is necessary to change from the default value.

- Choose the first option to allow SQL Server to determine the translation scheme it determines will work best.

- Choose the second option for no translation. By choosing this option, you could speed data transfer if both the SQL Server and the Client computers are using the same code page.

- Choose the third option if data stored on the SQL Server uses a non-ANSI standard character set. This causes extended characters to be translated to their ANSI equivalent.

- Choose this option and click the Configure **T**ranslator button to designate a specific translation library. For example, this option could be used to select a translator that translates characters into a mainframe-equivalent character set to ensure that reports generated on the PC sort the same as reports from the mainframe.

Select the **U**se Regional Settings check box if the SQL Server is located in one country and clients are located in other countries. This allows the display of dates, time, and currency using local formats. For example, October 11, 1998, is represented as 11/10/98 internationally and 10/11/98 domestically.

When you are finished, click the **N**ext button. The fifth screen of the wizard appears (see Figure 16.12).

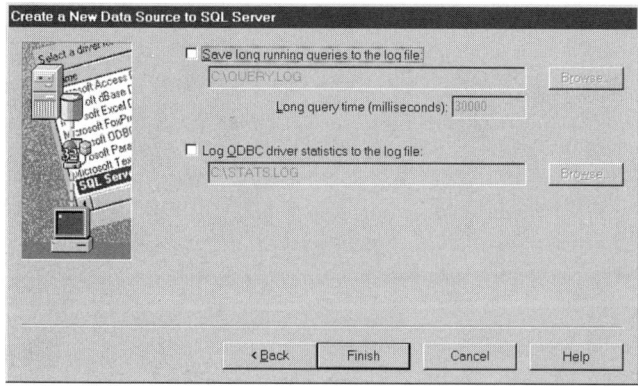

Figure 16.12
Screen 5 of the Create a New Data Source to SQL Server Wizard allows you to create log files of ODBC activity.

If you want to determine whether any query is taking an especially long time to complete, you can select Save Long Running Queries to the Log File. Enter the path and name of the log file you want created. Also set the time threshold in milliseconds. This log can identify long-running queries. You might consider running applications with long queries during non-peak processing periods.

394   Part III: Windows 98 Operations

If you want to keep statistics of ODBC operations, you can select the Log ODBC Driver Statistics to the Log File option. Enter the path and filename of the log file you want created. The file generated is tab delimited, and can be analyzed by Excel or any other program that uses this format.

When you are finished, click **F**inish. The confirmation screen of the wizard appears (see Figure 16.13).

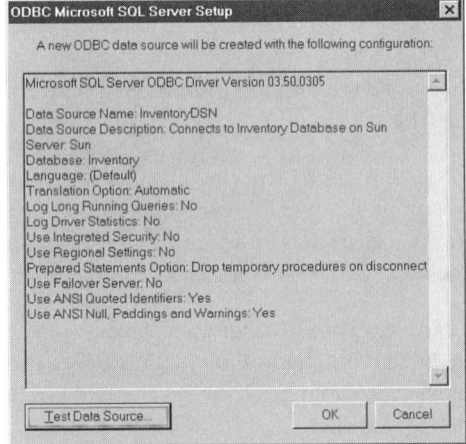

Figure 16.13
The ODBC Microsoft SQL Server Setup screen allows you to review a summary of the DSN you are about to create.

You will probably want to test the DSN before you save it to ensure that it works correctly. To do this, select **T**est Data Source. You should see a screen similar to Figure 16.14. If the tests completed successfully, click OK twice to complete and save the DSN you just created.

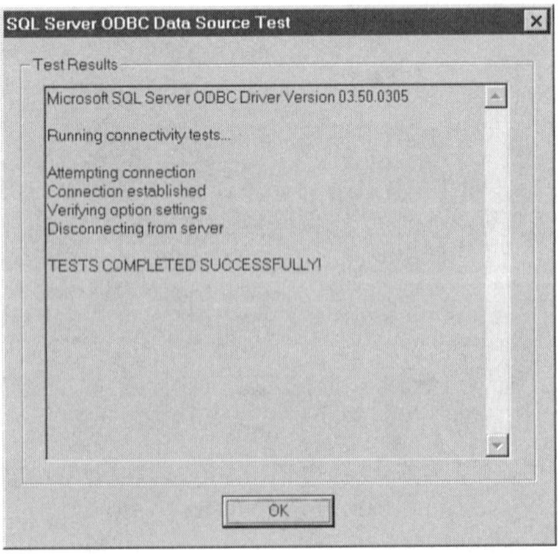

Figure 16.14
The SQL Server ODBC Data Source Test screen shows the results of an connection request using your DSN.

Common Steps for Microsoft Access Driver (.mdb)

Click A**d**d from the User DSN, System DSN, or File DSN tab (refer to Figure 16.4). You will see the Create New Data Source screen (see Figure 16.15).

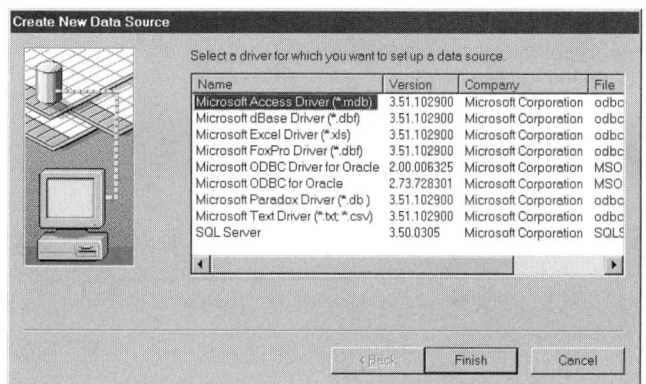

Figure 16.15
The Create New Data Source screen allows you to select an ODBC driver.

Select the desired ODBC driver (for example, Microsoft Access Driver (.mdb))from the list of installed ODBC Drivers. Then click Finish. The ODBC Microsoft Access 97 Setup screen appears (see Figure 16.16).

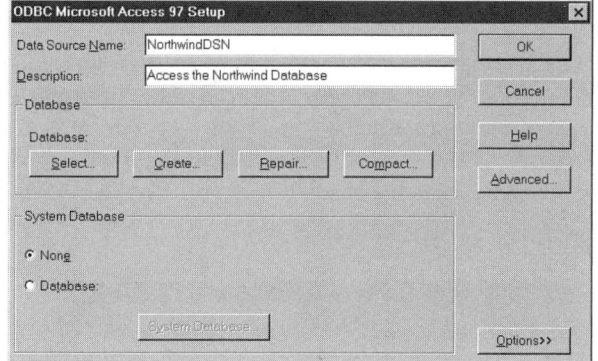

Figure 16.16
The ODBC Microsoft Access 97 Setup screen allows you to create a DSN for your Access database as well as to perform several maintenance functions.

A dialog box corresponding to the ODBC Driver you selected appears. In this example it is named ODBC Microsoft Access 97 Setup.

In the Data Source **N**ame field, type in the name you want to use for this DSN. If the client program includes a DSN parameter in its ODBC Connect String, type in exactly the same name. This example creates a DSN named NorthwindDSN. If the ODBC Connect String does not include a DSN, create a name that is easily identifiable.

In the **D**escription field, you may optionally type a description to help distinguish this DSN.

Click **S**elect. The Select Database screen appears (see Figure 16.17).

Figure 16.17
The Select Database dialog box allows you to select the path and filename of the file type database.

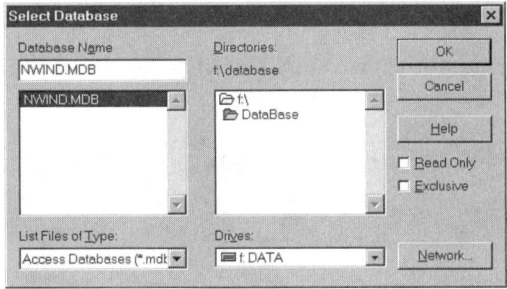

The Select Database dialog box allows you to search locally or on the network for the desire database file. Navigate until you locate the Access database for which you want to create DSN. Select the database name and click OK. You will return to ODBC Microsoft Access 9 Setup screen (refer to Figure 16.16). You should see the name of the database file you selected Click OK to complete the DSN creation

Installing or Upgrading ODB

Windows 98 does not automatically install or upgrade ODBC. Therefore, you may not see 32bit ODBC icon within Control Panel, or if the 32bit ODBC icon is present, it may no include File DSNs or the ODBC Wizards described earlier in this chapter

Installing or upgrading ODBC follows identical steps. Open the Add/Remove Programs apple in Control Panel by selecting Start, Settings, Control Panel, Add/Remove Programs. When th Add/Remove Programs Properties applet appears, select the Windows Setup tab and click th **H**ave Disk button. Insert the Windows 98 CD-ROM when the Install From Disk scree appears, choose the Browse button. The Open file dialog box appears next (see Figure 16.18) Select the iis.inf file from the \add-ons\pws directory on your Windows 98 CD-ROM

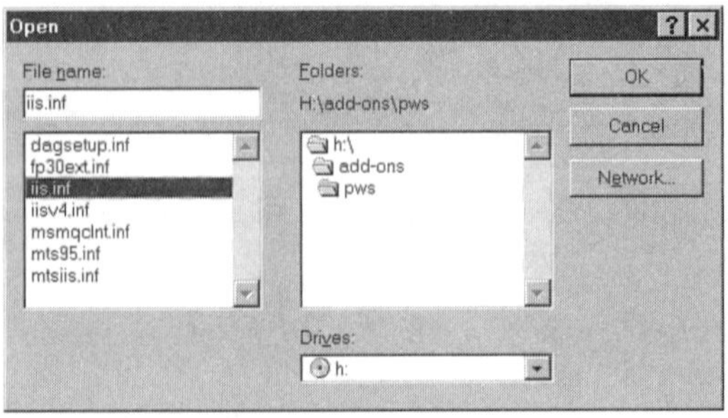

Figure 16.18
Use the Open dialog box to select the iis.inf file from your Windows 98 CD-ROM.

Chapter 16: Windows 98 ODBC Connectivity

Select OK in the Open dialog box and OK again from the Install From Disk dialog box.

The Have Disk screen appears again; choose Microsoft Data Access Components 1.5 and click the **D**etails button (see Figure 16.19). The Microsoft Data Access Components 1.5 screen appears (see Figure 16.20).

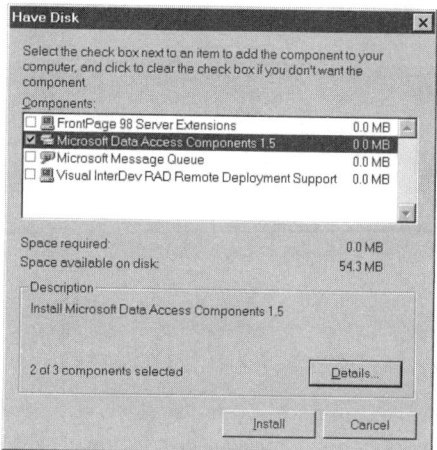

Figure 16.19
Use the Have Disk dialog box to select Microsoft Data Access Components 1.5.

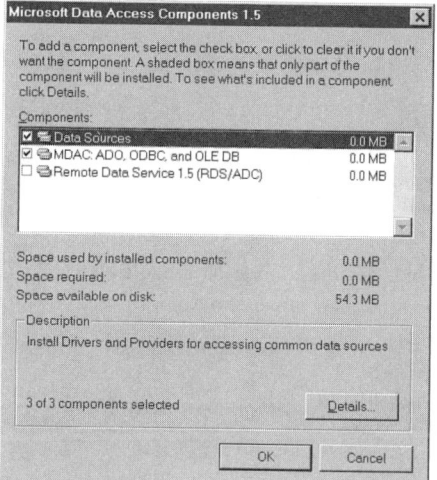

Figure 16.20
Use the Microsoft Data Access Components 1.5 dialog box to select Data Sources and ODBC.

Choose both the Data Sources and the MDAC, ADO, ODBC, and OLE DB selections, then click OK. This returns you to the Have Disk screen; click the **I**nstall button to install the files.

Troubleshooting ODBC Connection Problems

Problems in establishing an ODBC connection generally fall into one of five categories. These problems should be corrected or ruled out in the following order:

1. Network connectivity problems
2. Security problems
3. Basic ODBC parameter problems
4. Advanced ODBC parameter problems
5. Functionality problems

Correcting Network Connectivity Problems

In order for your Windows 98 machine to connect to a remote server, both machines and the intervening network routers typically must support the transport protocol that you choose to use. There are exceptions, however, such as when you use a tunneling protocol, or if there is mainframe access through an SNA gateway.

If both machines are using TCP/IP, you can use the Ping command to check for basic connectivity.

> **Note** Ping does not work through proxy servers.

If the server is located on a Windows NT or other Server Message Block (SMB)–based server you can use the NET VIEW \\<server-name> command to determine if any share points are visible on the server.

The driver and server ODBC parameters are both used at this time in order for ODBC to start the process of establishing a connection. If you have errors in the connection, be sure these parameters are correct.

Correcting Security Problems

Assuming that basic network connectivity is present, you must next present valid identification in the form of an acceptable UserID and Password to the operating system on the database server. Often this is where people run into the greatest difficulty. If you are connecting to an NT Server you must present the following identification:

- Be a member of an NT Domain of which the NT Server is a member.
- Be a member of a Domain the NT Server Domain trusts.
- Supply the proper UserID and Password of an account on the NT Server.

Sometimes supplying the proper account information still is not sufficient to establish a connection. Try to establish a persistent connection to a share point on the server that hosts the database that you want to connect to. Sometimes, simply having an existing connection allows the database connection to be made more readily. If the database server has no share points that you can connect to, try to establish a connection to another server in the same NT domain as the database server.

If you are able to successfully log on to the server that hosts your database you have eliminated many variables and unknowns.

Correcting Basic ODBC Parameter Problems

The UID, PWD, and database parameters come into play at this time. The UID and PWD are used to gain access to the database engine. On a SQL Server the UID and PWD can be used by either standard or integrated security. Standard security uses user accounts within SQL Server, while integrated security uses NT domain accounts. If you use incorrect UID or PWD parameters you typically receive a message such as `Login failed`. If the database server authenticates your account, the database parameter locates the database. If the database name is incorrect, you do not connect. Lastly, the supplied UserID and Password require permission to access the designated Database. Accounts are typically granted access only to those databases for which the user has a business need.

Correcting Advanced ODBC Parameter Problems

Changes made by choosing the Clien**t** Configuration… button (refer to Figure 16.9), can make or prevent a client connection to the database server. Basically the client computer and the database server must both be set up with choices that are compatible with each other. For instance, when SQL Server is installed, it defaults to Named Pipes as the IPC mechanism for network communication. Likewise, the default option when creating a DSN for SQL Server is also Named Pipes (see Figure 16.23, later in this chapter). As you can imagine, if either the server or the client is set up with nonmatching values, the mismatch can prevent ODBC communication even though previous checks of connectivity using Ping and the Net Use commands work successfully.

Therefore, if you have not yet been able to establish a connection you may want to check with the DBA for the database server to find out which IPC network choice(s) the database server supports. Then choose a matching option for the client.

Note For more information on IPC network choices see the section named "Advanced ODBC Tuning Options" later in this chapter.

If you are still having difficulty connecting, you can generate a trace of every ODBC command and response. The file output is a standard ASCII file viewable from WordPad. You will most likely need someone familiar with ODBC API programming to interpret the trace and determine where the problem lies.

To perform a trace, select the Tracing tab from the 32bit ODBC applet (see Figure 16.21), then choose Start Tracing Now. Leaving the ODBC Data Source Administrator window open, switch to your app and attempt to connect. Wait for the connection attempt to fail. Return to the Tracing tab of ODBC Data Source Administrator and press the same button, which should now display Stop Tracing Now, and close the ODBC Data Source administrator to release the log file. Use Explorer to locate and display the log file. (SQL.LOG is the default name of the log.)

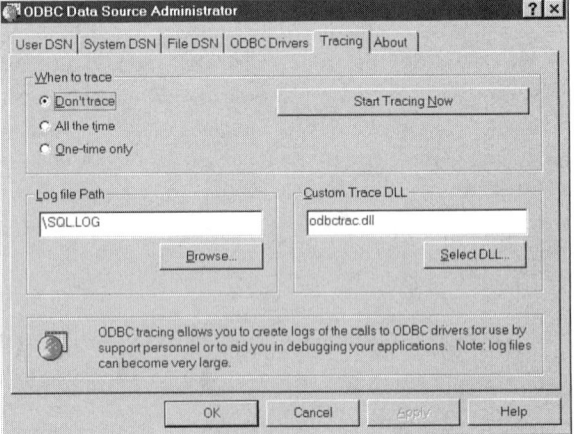

Figure 16.21
Use the Tracing tab of the 32bit ODBC applet to start and stop tracing ODBC Commands.

Note The logfile can quickly grow to a very large size; for example, opening a connection to the pubs database, reading the Authors table once, and closing the connection creates a logfile of about 117KB.

Correcting Functionality Problems

Sometimes, although an application program is able to establish a connection with a particular database server, the client program does not offer full functionality. Yet the same application is fully functional when connected to a different database server.

Chapter 16: Windows 98 ODBC Connectivity

This difference in functionality can be due to an ODBC driver that does not support the levels of ODBC conformance required by the application program. Check the version number and manufacturer of the ODBC driver in order to locate specifications as to the level of conformance offered. You can use the ODBC Drivers tab of the 32bit ODBC applet to display the version levels of installed ODBC drivers (see Figure 16.22).

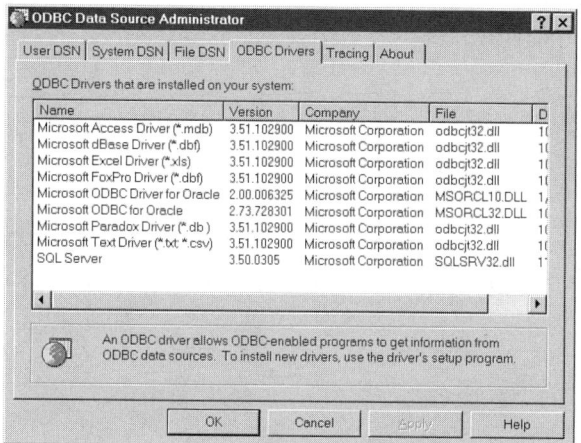

Figure 16.22
Use the ODBC Drivers tab of the 32bit ODBC applet to determine the manufacturer and version number of installed ODBC drivers.

You can also check with the programmer or company that developed the client application to determine the level of conformance required. If the program requires a level of conformance higher that what the ODBC driver provides, then you will need to install a newer version of the driver, or an ODBC driver from another manufacturer, that provides the level of conformance required by the application.

Advanced ODBC Tuning Options

Most options that you can control when creating a DSN have little effect on performance or speed of connection and operation. The performance of the application is much more in the programmer's hands. The programmer's use of SQL queries of varying degrees of efficiency can greatly affect the performance. The options and ODBC parameters under your control generally determine whether you connect at all, rather than how fast.

With that in mind, there are a few things you can do that affect performance. You can change the name of the default database to the name of the database you want to connect to. Refer to Figure 16.10 and the accompanying description for information about creating a SQL Server DSN.

If the database server supports multiple IPC mechanisms, you can also see an increase in speed by choosing a different network library. For instance, changing from Named Pipes to TCP/IP

Sockets can speed up the connection process. Be sure to check with the DBA for the database server to find out which IPC network choice(s) the database server supports.

> **Note** Changing the Network Library parameters could cause your client program to stop working, or to start working if it currently is not. Also be aware that integrated security on SQL Server uses only the Named Pipes network library.

To change the network library, click the Clien**t** Configuration button (refer to Figure 16.9) and choose the Net Library tab (see Figure 16.23). Choose the Default Network drop-down list to display a list of network IPC types. Select the desired IPC type from the list, then click the Done button. Complete the creation or update of the DSN as described earlier in this chapter.

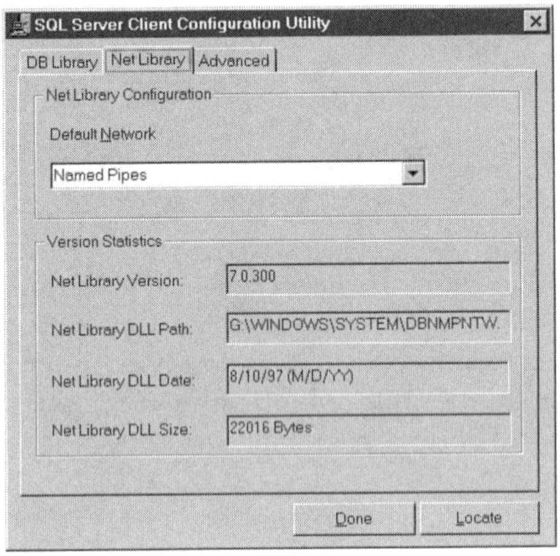

Figure 16.23
Use the Net Library tab of the 32bit ODBC applet to select a different IPC network type.

Conclusion

The need to configure client workstations for ODBC will increase as corporations in America and around the world migrate their applications to client/server and N-tier models. Fortunately, the wizards included with Windows 98 make it easier than ever before to create and test the DSN's ability to connect.

Because ODBC is so widely used, database customers have a great deal of freedom in selecting both platforms and database vendors. DSNs make it easy for system administrators to react to changes that inevitably occur in today's dynamically changing business environment.

File Systems: File and Disk Resources

When you think about it, you'll probably agree that the disk subsystem is one of the most important systems in any computer. Not only is it intimately involved in the operation of the system (although the same can be said of the processor, memory, and video adapter), it's the component responsible for storing all the work product generated on most systems. Its health is therefore vital to avoid data loss.

In this chapter, you learn all about Windows 98 disk and file systems. You learn about the underlying technology and design of disk and file systems and about how to use and maintain them.

Exploring Hard Disk Drives

Hard disk drives are hermetically-sealed devices that contain a number of *platters*, which spin rapidly when the drive is powered up. (It's been said that if you were to remove a platter while it was spinning and put it on its edge on the ground, it would go about 60 to 100 mph.) Different disks have different numbers of platters. All platters spin on a common *spindle*. Each platter has its own read/write *head*, which "floats" a small distance over the platter surface when the disk is operating. The distance the read/write head floats above the platter is about one-quarter the diameter of a human hair. Platters are rigid, usually made out of aluminum or glass, and coated with a magnetic material and other layers that give them the capability to store magnetically encoded bits of data.

Each platter has a number of *tracks*. Each track is divided into *sectors*, which are always equivalent to 512 bytes of data. An individual track (for example, track 23) on all the platters together is called a *cylinder*.

A specific area of the hard disk drive is addressed using a combination of three values: cylinder, head (platter), and sector. For example, cylinder 46, head 2, sector 231 refers to a single 512-byte sector within a hard disk drive.

Different hard disk drives have different *geometries*, which is the arrangement and number of platters (heads), cylinders, and sectors. The values for a particular hard disk drive are stored in the computer's CMOS.

> **Tip** To calculate the maximum theoretical capacity for a drive, simply multiply the number of heads by the number of cylinders by the number of sectors per track by 512 bytes per sector.

Understanding Partitions

Individual hard disk drives can be divided into *partitions*, which are logical subdivisions of the hard disk device. Each hard disk drive can have up to four partitions. A partition can be either *primary* or *extended*. A hard disk can have up to four primary partitions, although only one primary partition can be active at a time. Extended partitions are made up of *logical drives*, which are distinct hard disk letters that appear for the operating system. A hard disk can have only one extended partition. Typically, hard disks that result in multiple drive letters are configured with a single primary partition and a single extended partition, with the extended partition containing from one to many logical drive letters. (You can have any number of logical drives within an extended partition; in reality, you are limited to the number of available drive letters, up to the letter Z.)

Suppose that you are setting up a hard disk and want to divide it in such a way that you end up with four drive letters, from C to F. You create a single primary partition (Windows 98 can

Chapter 17: File Systems: File and Disk Resources

boot and run only from a primary partition) that is the size needed for the C drive. You also create a single extended partition, which has three logical drives created within it, each logical drive being the size needed for drive letters D, E, and F.

> **Note** For a secondary hard disk drive (one that does not have to boot an operating system), you can configure the hard disk to consist of a single extended partition made up of one or more logical drives.

Partitions under Windows 98 are set up and maintained using a program called FDISK (short for Fixed Disk Setup Program). FDISK lets you view your current partition arrangement and also delete and create partitions.

Partition data for a hard disk drive is stored as part of the Master Boot Record (MBR) located at cylinder 0, head 0, sector 1. A 64-byte section of the MBR contains the partition configuration for the hard disk. Each partition is defined by a 16-byte entry (which means that there can be no more than four partitions, because 16 bytes times four partitions is 64 bytes). Within the MBR sector, the partition data is stored starting at decimal offset 446 and uses up the remainder of the 512-byte MBR sector (the last 2 bytes are not related to the partition data, but are the end-of-sector marker, which is always 0x55AA).

Each 16-byte partition table entry is arranged as follows:

- Byte 00 stores the boot indicator, which is always either 0x00 or 0x80. 0x80 indicates that the partition is used for booting the system; 0x00 indicates that the partition is not used for booting.

- Byte 01 stores the starting head number of the partition.

- Bytes 02 and 03 store a combined entry locating the starting sector and cylinder of the partition. The first 6 bits store the starting sector; the remaining 10 bits store the starting cylinder number.

- Byte 04 stores the System ID. This ID indicates the file system being used on the partition and is set by the FORMAT command when the partition is formatted with a particular file system (such as FAT16, FAT32, or—on Windows NT—NTFS).

- Byte 05 stores the ending head number.

- Bytes 06 and 07 are another combined entry storing the ending sector and cylinder of the partition. Again, the first 6 bits store the ending sector; the remaining 10 bits store the ending cylinder number.

- Bytes 08 to 11 store the *relative sector*, which is the relative sector number at which the partition starts.

- Bytes 12 to 15 store the number of sectors within the partition.

Logical drives store their partition data somewhat differently than primary and extended partitions. What happens is this: An extended partition entry in the MBR partition table indicates the extended partition's first sector, which is the location of the first logical drive in the extended partition (an extended partition must contain at least one logical drive if it is to function). The first sector of the first logical drive stores *another* partition table. This logical drive partition table is stored in the last 64 bytes of that first sector (leaving 2 bytes for the end-of-sector marker) arranged just like the main partition table in the MBR. However, the logical drive's partition table contains only two entries: The first entry contains the configuration for that logical drive, and the second entry contains the configuration of the next logical drive. Entries three and four are empty and are not used. The second entry points to the next logical drive, which again contains its own logical drive partition table, and so forth. As you can see, logical drives within an extended partition are therefore defined by this linked list of partition tables, each one pointing to the next.

Understanding FAT

Any operating system relies on one or more *file systems*, which are the methods used to store files on storage devices. There are many different kinds of file systems, such as FAT, New Technology File System (NTFS), High Performance File System (HPFS), CD-ROM File System (CDFS), and so forth. Windows 98 can use four different file systems: FAT16, FAT32, CDFS, and Universal File System (UFS) for DVD-ROM drives. Most of the following discussion about FAT concerns FAT16—differences between FAT16 and FAT32 are discussed in the following section.

FAT stands for File Allocation Table, a method for storing files and file directories on a hard disk. FAT has a long history, being used first under MS-DOS. Through a variety of techniques, including the new FAT32 variant, FAT has been extended and improved over the years.

A FAT-formatted volume is arranged starting with a Partition Boot Sector, followed by two identical copies of the FAT (FAT1 and FAT2), the root directory listing, and then the remainder of the volume. Two copies of the FAT are stored in case one is damaged.

The Partition Boot Sector contains the information needed to boot an operating system (if the partition is a primary partition intended for that purpose). The data in the Partition Boot Sector is described in the following chart.

Bytes	Description
3	Jump instruction
8	OEM Operating System name in text format
25	BIOS Parameter Block
26	Extended BIOS Parameter Block
448	Bootstrap code

Chapter 17: File Systems: File and Disk Resources

The BIOS Parameter Blocks (both normal and extended) store additional configuration information about the volume, such as the number of bytes per sector, number of sectors per cluster, number of root directory entries, and so forth.

FAT volumes are divided into allocation units, called *clusters*. FAT16 can handle up to 16 bits worth of clusters (65,535). FAT32 can handle up to 32 bits worth of clusters (4,294,967,295). Depending on the size of the volume, clusters can be different sizes. The minimum cluster size is 512 bytes; larger clusters are always a power of 2 multiples of 512 bytes (for example, 1024 bytes, 2048 bytes, 4096 bytes, and so on). The maximum cluster size under FAT is 65,535 bytes, or 64 K.

Every file on a FAT volume consumes at least one cluster, regardless of the file's size or the size of the clusters. On a volume using 32 K clusters, a 1-byte file consumes 32 K of available disk space. If a file on the same volume was 32 K + 1 byte long, it would consume two clusters—32 K in the first cluster, plus 1 byte in the next cluster.

FAT16 volumes can be no longer than 4,095 M, because 65,535 maximum clusters times the maximum cluster size of 65,535 bytes yields 4,294,836,225 bytes, which is equivalent to 4,095 M, or 4 G. The following chart shows the maximum volume sizes and their corresponding cluster sizes.

Volume Size	Cluster Size
32 M	512 bytes
64 M	1 K
128 M	2 K
255 M	4 K
511 M	8 K
1023 M	16 K
2047 M	32 K
4095 M	64 K

The FAT table is a simple linked list. Each file's entry in the directory points to the first cluster used. Using the corresponding FAT table entry, the operating system can then work down the list of FAT entries for each cluster, locating each of the clusters occupied by a file. Consider the following example: A file is 70 K long, and the volume uses 32 K clusters. The file's entry in the directory says that the first cluster is number 2,345. The operating system then finds all the pieces of the file by first reading FAT entry 2,345 (for the first 32 K of the file). The FAT entry indicates that the next cluster is, say, number 4,123 (for the second 32 K of the file). Cluster 4,123 indicates that the next cluster is number 932 (the remaining 8 K of the file). The FAT entry for cluster 932 stores `0xFFFF` instead of a pointer to the next cluster, thereby indicating that the last cluster for the file has been reached.

Each FAT entry corresponds to a cluster, and contains relatively simple information:

- Whether or not the cluster is in use
- Whether or not the cluster is marked bad
- A pointer (a 16-bit entry on FAT16) for the next cluster in the chain, or a value (`0xFFFF`) indicating that the cluster is the last one occupied by a file

File information is stored within the volume's data area, except for the root directory, which is in a fixed position on a FAT16 volume. The root directory is limited to 512 entries on FAT16.

Each directory on a FAT volume is actually a file, but one that is marked as being a directory entry so that the operating system knows how to deal with it. (Unless you are editing the byte-by-byte information on a disk, you won't be aware that a directory is actually a file.) Within the directory "file" are entries for all the files and subdirectories in the directory. When you enter a DIR command at a command prompt, you are simply displaying the contents of the directory file, formatted so that it's easy to read. Directories consume clusters just as files do. Notice that directories are *not* the FAT; the FAT is simply a table that lets the operating system locate parts of the files and directories listed in a directory, starting with the root directory.

Each directory entry contains the following information:

- The name of the file or directory, stored as 11 bytes (in 8.3 format; the period is not stored)
- 8 bits indicating the attributes of the entry
- 24 bits indicating the time the file was created
- 16 bits indicating the date the file was created
- 16 bits indicating the date the file was last accessed
- 16 bits indicating the time the file was last modified
- 16 bits indicating the date the file was last modified
- 16 bits (on FAT16) indicating the first cluster number occupied by the entry
- 32 bits indicating the size of the entry

The attribute bits indicate whether an entry is for a file or another directory (a subdirectory), whether or not the entry is for a volume label, and the user-settable attributes (read-only, system, hidden, and archive).

Chapter 17: File Systems: File and Disk Resources

To tie all the parts of this discussion together, let's examine an extended example: A file called TEST.FIL is stored in the directory C:\Windows\System\, is 50 K long, and is being read into an application. The sample volume uses clusters that are 32 K long. (Some steps are simplified because they're not relevant to this discussion).

1. The application requests the file's data from the operating system. The application sends the operating system the file's name and directory, in the form of a fully qualified pathname: C:\Windows\System\TEST.FIL.

2. The operating system locates the file by first scanning the entries in the root directory of drive C for an entry called Windows that has the directory attribute set (indicating that it's a directory).

3. The Windows directory entry indicates that it starts at cluster 555. The FAT is then read; using the linked list in the FAT described earlier in this section, the operating system discovers that the Windows directory occupies clusters 1123, 2342, 523, and 4923. Using that information, the operating system reads the Windows directory and scans it for an entry called System.

4. An entry called System is found in the \Windows directory listing, and it has its directory attribute set. The System entry indicates that number 1154 is its first cluster.

5. The FAT is read again, starting at cluster 1154 and following the chain until all System directory clusters are known. Using that information, the operating system reads the System directory table into memory and scans it for an entry called TEST.FIL. The entry is found, and its directory attribute is clear, indicating that it's a file. By reading that entry, the operating system finds that the first cluster of TEST.FIL is number 2987.

6. The FAT is read again, starting at cluster 2987. Using the linked list, the operating system locates both of the clusters holding TEST.FIL and can then read both clusters' contents into memory.

7. The operating system then passes the cluster contents (the file's contents) to the application as a stream of bytes.

As you can see, retrieving a file is a lot of work! Fortunately, the system keeps most directory entries—as well as the entire FAT table—in RAM, so the necessity to read the directories and FAT entries doesn't require much disk activity. However, notice that writing changes to a file requires quite a few steps (all of which require disk writes), because all the following things must take place when a file is saved:

- Based on the size of the file, the operating system must scan the FAT for free clusters that can be assigned to the file.

- Both copies of the FAT must have the new linked list for the file written to them.

- The directory that contains the file must have its entry for the file created or modified.

- Finally, the file's contents are saved.

When you realize all the work that has to be done to open, read, and write files, it's a wonder that it doesn't take more time to do it all!

Understanding FAT32

Starting with Windows OEM Service Release 2 (OSR2) and continuing into Windows 98, Microsoft developed a modified version of FAT called FAT32. Because hard disk drives were growing in capacity so rapidly, the move to FAT32 was required to support larger drives without having to use unreasonably large cluster sizes.

FAT32 works substantially the same way as FAT16, and Microsoft worked to keep differences minimal to reduce compatibility problems. However, there are some key differences:

- Each FAT entry now consumes 4 bytes rather than 2 bytes (32 bits versus 16 bits). This change plus the fact that there may be many more FAT entries means that the FAT itself is much larger under FAT32.

- The MBR is expanded from one to two sectors to allow for a larger BIOS Parameter Block, as well as duplicate copies of the boot record (providing additional redundancy over FAT16).

- The root directory is no longer located in a fixed position immediately following the two copies of the FAT, as is the case with FAT16. Instead, the root directory is now treated the same as any other directory and can be placed anywhere on the volume. Because of this, the root directory is no longer limited to 512 entries.

- Directory entries themselves are unchanged, except that the 2 bytes unused under MS-DOS and Windows (all versions) that were set aside in the directory entry and intended for OS/2 Extended Attributes are now used to store the extra 16 bits required to index to a full 32-bit cluster number.

- The minimum cluster size under FAT32 is 4 K instead of the 512-byte clusters supported for very small FAT16 drives.

All these changes, as well as some other optimizations, offer these advantages over FAT16:

- Single partitions can now extend to 2 terabytes (1024 G).

- On larger partitions, such as those up to 8 G, cluster sizes of only 4 K can be used, instead of the 128 K theoretical cluster size that FAT16 would have to use—were it even possible for FAT16 to support 8 G partitions. Overall, because the clusters under FAT32 are generally smaller than those in FAT16, about 15 percent more disk space is available because of reduced slack space in the clusters.

- FAT32 is more reliable than FAT16, and the possible points of failure have been reduced, partly by keeping a redundant copy of the boot record on FAT32 drives.

- Because FAT32 partitions generally use 4 K clusters (which also happens to be the size of the pages of memory used by the virtual memory manager), paging activity is faster and requires less overhead.

- Applications launch faster from FAT32 drives.

There are also some drawbacks to consider when thinking about using FAT32:

- FAT32 is not yet supported by Windows NT (up to version 4), so you cannot convert the primary partition if you want to dual-boot Windows 98 and Windows NT. Logical drives formatted with FAT32 are ignored by Windows NT 4 (it is not yet clear whether Windows NT 5 will support FAT32 drives, although it seems unthinkable that it would not).

- You cannot reverse the Windows 98 conversion process that easily upgrades FAT16 drives to FAT32. Instead, to return a drive to FAT16 from FAT32, you must repartition and reformat the drive.

- All utilities that rely on the FAT16 file system do not work with FAT32, including disk sector editors, older defragmentation programs, and all (at the time of this writing) disk compression programs (including the DriveSpace program that comes with Windows 98). However, updated versions should be available shortly after Windows 98 is available.

- If you convert the primary partition to FAT32, you will be unable to access the drive by booting MS-DOS (such as from an MS-DOS bootable floppy disk).

Understanding Long Filenames on FAT

As is probably clear from the preceding discussions about FAT16 and FAT32, there is no room set aside in either file system to store more than the 8.3 filenames supported under DOS. And yet Windows 95 and Windows 98 (not to mention Windows NT) support long filenames on such FAT volumes. How is this possible?

Recall that individual directory entries have a number of attribute bits, one of which is set if the entry indicates a volume label. In earlier MS-DOS versions, there was usually only a single such entry, located in the root directory, that stored the volume label for the drive. MS-DOS ignores additional directory entries that have this attribute set, as do most utility programs.

Microsoft developed a scheme whereby long filenames could be supported on FAT volumes by using this volume label directory attribute. When you create a long filename under Windows 98, such as MYLONGFILE.TXT, multiple directory entries may be created, with the second and successive entries being flagged with the volume label attribute (so that MS-DOS and other utilities ignore those entries). Windows 98 stores pieces of each long filename in each of these entries, with up to 11 characters stored per entry. In the case of MYLONGFILE.TXT, there are two directory entries: the first is stored as MYLONG~1.TXT, while the second entry stores the remainder of the full filename and is not individually viewable, except with a disk sector editor.

Long filenames under Windows 98 must follow these rules:

- They can have multiple spaces and multiple periods.

- The short portion of the filename can use only the following special characters:
  $ % ' - _ @ ~ ` ! ( ) ^ # &

- Long filenames can additionally use these special characters:
  + , ; = [ ]

- Maximum long filename length is 254 characters, including the extension.

- The maximum length of a fully qualified pathname under Windows 98 is 260 characters. In other words, if you have a filename that is 254 characters long, it can have a directory name associated with it that is only 4 characters long.

- If you copy or move files with a utility that doesn't support long filenames, or copy or move files to a file server that doesn't support long filenames, the long filenames are lost.

- When using a long filename at the MS-DOS prompt, if the filename includes spaces, you must surround the filename with quotation marks (").

One problem of which you should be aware occurs at the MS-DOS command prompt. The command-line buffer at the command prompt is limited to 128 characters, by default. Because of that, you can't use MS-DOS commands for long filenames if the command plus the filename exceeds 128 characters. You can expand the MS-DOS command-line buffer to help address this problem by placing the command SHELL=C:\WINDOWS\COMMAND.COM /U:255 in the CONFIG.SYS file (255 is the absolute maximum value).

Understanding NTFS

Although NTFS is not supported under Windows 98 (nor does Microsoft plan to support it), a discussion about Windows file systems isn't complete without an overview of NTFS.

New Technology File System (NTFS) was designed to be an "industrial strength" file system, appropriate for use on file servers and other high-end systems. NTFS includes the following features:

- It is transaction oriented, and failures to complete a disk transaction can be reversed during a system CHKDSK, safely and easily.

Chapter 17: File Systems: File and Disk Resources

- It supports *hot-fixing*, in which data on marginal areas of the disk are automatically moved to another part of the disk, and the questionable part of the disk is marked so that it is not used again.

- It provides full support for long filenames in the file system.

- It retains the time of last file access (FAT simply stores the date of last access).

- Volumes and files under NTFS can occupy up to 2^{64} bytes (16 *exabytes*).

- It makes use of a binary tree-based file table, which can be searched much more quickly than a FAT.

- NTFS stores clusters more efficiently than does FAT; the file system works to avoid fragmentation much more effectively than FAT. Moreover, because of the B-tree search tree NTFS uses to find clusters, fragmentation causes less degradation with NTFS than with FAT.

Unlike High Performance File System (HPFS, designed for OS/2), NTFS uses clusters of varying sizes, similar to the FAT scheme. However, cluster sizes under NTFS are much smaller than FAT16 clusters, as follows:

Partition Size	Cluster Size
512 M	512 bytes
1024 M	1 K
2048 M	2 K
4096 M	4 K
8192 M	8 K
16384 M	16 K
32768 M	32 K
>32768 M	64 K

NTFS volumes are arranged into the following areas:

- Partition Boot Sector
- Master File Table
- NTFS System Files
- File Area

The Master File Table area and NTFS System Files are actually part of the same area on the disk, made up of 16 records (only 11 are used at this time), each one having a filename, as follows:

System File	Filename	Description
Master File Table	$Mft	Contains the contents of the NTFS volume
Master File Table #2	$MftMirr	Duplicate of the first three records of the Master File Table
Log File	$LogFile	Transaction log used to recover disk transactions in case of error (such as a power failure while writing a transaction)
Volume	$Volume	Volume information, such as name, NTFS version information, and so on
Attribute Definition Table	$AttrDef	A table listing attributes used on the volume
Root Filename Index	$.	The root directory contents
Cluster Bitmap	$Bitmap	A bitmap showing used and unused clusters on the volume; used for rapidly allocating clusters
Partition Boot Sector	$Boot	Bootstrap program for the volume
Bad Cluster File	$BadClus	List of bad clusters on the volume
Quota Table	$Quota	Stores disk quota information for volume users
Upcase Table	$Upcase	Table used to convert lowercase letters to uppercase letters, using Unicode

Each file on an NTFS system is seen as a set of *file attributes* (which are quite unlike the file attribute flags used under FAT). NTFS can have file attributes for data in the file, for security information, for *file metadata* (such as icons), and even for the name of the file. (These file attributes are similar to the OLE file format in which individual files can be made up of separate streams of data.)

Understanding DriveSpace

Windows 98 includes disk compression software called *DriveSpace*, which operates only on FAT16-based volumes. DriveSpace creates a single file on the volume, in which it stores all the files. The DriveSpace driver then "hides" the actual volume from the system and replaces it with a virtual volume, which is the contents of the compressed file system. DriveSpace is limited to being used on volumes with a size of 2 G or less. You learn more about DriveSpace disk compression later in this chapter.

DriveSpace can store files using three different compression levels: no compression, HiPack compression, and UltraPack compression. UltraPack compression is approximately 30 percent more efficient than HiPack compression, but requires a minimum of a Pentium-class computer and suffers from greater performance reduction.

Comparing File Systems

For hard disk drives, you have three file system choices under Windows 98:

- FAT16
- FAT16 with DriveSpace compression
- FAT32

Interestingly enough, the choice that offers the best overall performance is FAT16 with DriveSpace compression, but with the compression level set to perform *no compression*. Because DriveSpace volumes store data more efficiently than FAT (and use a single FAT chain on the real FAT16 drive), they can read and write data more quickly than equivalent FAT16 drives. Note that FAT16 with DriveSpace compression set to either HiPack or UltraPack performs more poorly than FAT16.

Generally, FAT16 performs better than FAT32, with about an overall 5 percent advantage in performance. However, this slight performance advantage may be offset by FAT32's other features, such as more efficient use of disk space. And these two factors are not the only things you have to consider when choosing which file system to run: You also have to think about compatibility, whether you require the use of any utility software that won't work with FAT32, or if you want to dual-boot Windows NT (which isn't able to access FAT32 volumes).

Understanding Storage Hardware

Disk subsystems are made up of three primary components: the hard disk itself, the interface between the hard disk controller and the hard disk, and the bus interface between the computer system and the disk controller. These three components work together and play a large part in disk performance.

Hard disk drive performance is measured using the following factors:

- **Average Seek Time.** Defines the average amount of time it takes the hard disk to locate a particular track on the disk.

- **Average Latency.** The average amount of time it takes the disk to spin so that the required sector is in place to be read by the heads. Average Latency is largely affected by the speed at which the internal platters spin.

- **Average Access Time.** The average amount of time it takes to start retrieving data from a particular sector. This value is the sum of the Average Seek Time and the Average Latency.

- **Data Transfer Rate.** The speed at which data is read from the drive once the heads start to read (or write) the data.

Depending on the application, Average Access Time and Data Transfer Rate may both play roles in the ultimate performance of an application.

Hard disk drive controllers are connected to the computer through one of the system buses, of which there are several different types. Ranging from slowest to fastest, they are ISA, EISA, VL-Bus, and PCI. Even with systems that integrate disk controllers on their motherboards, the disk controller still exists on one of these types of buses (usually PCI in today's PCs). Using a disk controller on a local bus, such as PCI, guarantees the best performance for transferring data from the hard disk to the system, all else being equal.

Hard disk controllers and hard disks also have to communicate, and there are a number of different methods in which this is accomplished. On most desktop systems, a drive interface called EIDE (Enhanced IDE), also known as Fast-ATA, is the most prevalent.

EIDE disk interfaces are not terribly intelligent; they rely on the computer's processor to perform much of their work (which is the reason they are less expensive than other disk interface alternatives). There are several methods through which an EIDE disk interface works with the computer system to perform these data transfers. The primary method is called Programmed Input/Output, or PIO. PIO Mode 3 and PIO Mode 4 are most commonly seen today; they transfer data at a peak rate of 11 MBps and 16.6 MBps, respectively.

The other major drive interface standard is called Small Computer Systems Interface (SCSI, pronounced "scuzzy"). SCSI comes in three flavors: SCSI-1, SCSI-2, and SCSI-3. Basically, the higher the SCSI number, the faster the drive interface operates. SCSI-2 supports transfer rates of 10 to 20 MBps; SCSI-3 (formerly called UltraSCSI) supports rates of 20 to 40 MBps. Different SCSI-2 systems may use techniques called *fast SCSI* and *wide SCSI* which defines how the data is transferred from the disk to the controller—fast SCSI uses a faster transmission frequency and wide SCSI transfers twice as much data at a time.

Generically, SCSI supports many features that make it the primary choice for network file servers and other high-end systems. These features include *scatter/gather*, *connect/disconnect*, *elevator seeking*, and *tag command queuing*.

Because Windows 98 does not make good use of the more advanced SCSI features, EIDE drive systems and SCSI drive systems under Windows 98 tend to operate at about the same speed, with EIDE systems sometimes having a slight performance edge. It's a different story under

Windows NT, however; SCSI systems almost always outperform their equivalent EIDE systems under that operating system. Therefore, if you plan on dual-booting both Windows 98 and Windows NT, you should prefer systems that have SCSI-based disk subsystems.

Configuring Disk Subsystems

When choosing and configuring a disk subsystem, you face many choices. What hard disk interface to use? How should hard disks and CD-ROMs be connected to the hard disk interfaces in different situations? Which file system should be used when the drives are formatted? How should the drives be partitioned? In this section, you learn about the factors that go into making these choices.

First, when selecting a disk subsystem for a computer running Windows 98, it helps to get the fastest and largest disks available within your budget. Because there is no performance benefit to SCSI under Windows 98, unless you plan on running Windows NT in the near future, you can save some money and purchase an EIDE-based disk system.

Deciding on file systems and partitioning schemes requires that you balance all your requirements in a way that makes sense to you. Most of these factors have already been discussed in this chapter, but are recapped here:

- Multiple volumes are more difficult to manage than a single volume.

- Single volumes store files less efficiently than several smaller volumes (use the cluster size charts earlier in the chapter to understand how this logic works).

- FAT32 is, overall, a little bit slower than FAT16 (about 2 to 5 percent slower).

- FAT32 stores files much more efficiently than FAT16 and allows greater volume sizes without sacrificing too much wasted space.

- FAT32 isn't compatible with Windows NT.

- When installing multiple hard disks, if possible, try to keep them on separate disk controllers.

- Try to keep any installed CD-ROM drives on their own disk controllers. If at all possible, do *not* locate them on the same EIDE controller as a hard disk drive because the CD-ROM will slow the performance of the hard disk.

- You cannot use DriveSpace compression on FAT32 volumes or on FAT16 volumes of more than 2 G.

- If you can avoid using DriveSpace, do so. Although it can offer performance improvements when used with its compression feature turned off, it complicates the system somewhat more than necessary. And, of course, using DriveSpace with compression slows the performance of the disk system—sometimes dramatically—and makes it harder to repair errors that may occur on the hard disk.

If you're a systems professional learning about how all these factors work together and how to implement them, consider using a good tape drive so that you can more easily reconfigure a system based on any changing requirements, and so that you can actually try different disk configurations with Windows 98.

Understanding Windows 98 Disk Operations

The first part of this chapter deals with how disks work, how file systems work, how they work under Windows 98, and so forth. In this remaining part of the chapter, you learn about actual disk operations under Windows 98: how to partition, format, defragment, compress, test, and repair your disk file systems.

Partitioning Hard Disks

Partitioning hard disks (review the rules for disk partitions earlier in this chapter) is accomplished using a program called FDISK, which runs from the command line. Generally, disk partitions are created before installing Windows 98, although strictly speaking, you have to create only a primary partition before installing Windows 98 and can then run FDISK in a Windows 98 MS-DOS window to create further partitions. Once you make changes in FDISK to change partitions, you must restart the system for the partition changes to take effect (and before the partition or logical drive can be formatted). FDISK's main screen is shown in Figure 17.1.

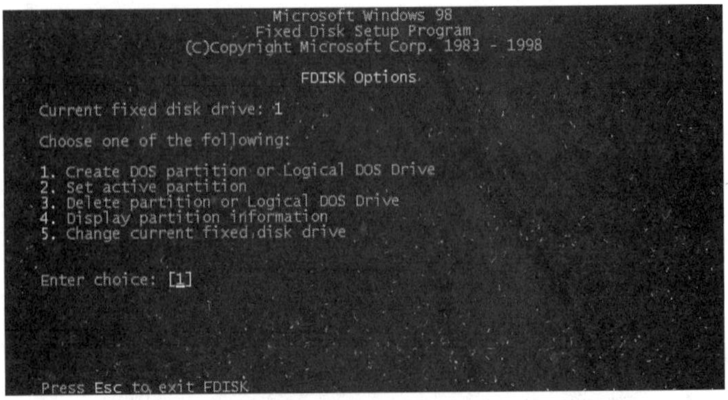

Figure 17.1
The main screen of the FDISK Fixed Disk Setup Program.

Chapter 17: File Systems: File and Disk Resources

FDISK is a straightforward program to use. Simply select the menu choices corresponding to what you want to do and follow the prompts. For dangerous tasks, such as removing existing partitions, FDISK warns you before carrying out the action.

> **Warning** Even though FDISK is simple to use, its capability to destroy data means that you should treat it with respect. Think carefully about removing existing partitions and about re-creating other partitions because data stored on the removed partitions is not accessible after the partitions are removed.

Formatting Disks

Once a volume is partitioned, you can format it. Formatting prepares a volume to receive data using the file system selected with FDISK. Volumes can be formatted in one of two ways: through a graphical utility accessed from My Computer or Windows Explorer, or through the FORMAT command used at the command line. Both methods provide the same result.

To format a volume from the Windows desktop, open My Computer, right-click the drive you want to format, and choose For**m**at from the shortcut menu. You then see the Format dialog box shown in Figure 17.2. Table 17.1 lists the options available in the Format dialog box.

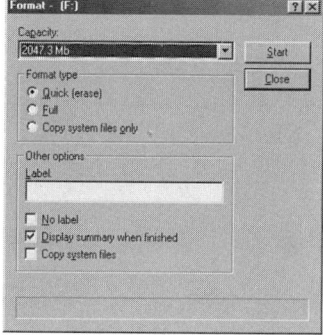

Figure 17.2
The Format dialog box.

Table 17.1
Options in the Format Dialog Box

Option	Description
Quick (erase)	Quick-formats an already-formatted volume, with the effect of simply erasing all the contents of the volume quickly.
Full	Formats an unformatted volume. This option causes each and every cluster on the volume to be formatted.

continues

Table 17.1, Continued
Options in the Format Dialog Box

Option	Description
Copy System Files **O**nly	Prepares a volume to be made bootable. Do not use this option for formatting hard disks under Windows 98.
Label	Allows you to enter a volume label in the field, which is used to identify the volume.
No Label	Select this checkbox to avoid creating a volume label.
Display Summary When Finished	Displays a summary screen after the format is complete showing you various statistics about the newly formatted volume.
Copy S**y**stem Files	Causes boot files to be placed on the formatted volume, making it bootable. Do not use this option when formatting hard disks under Windows 98.

You can also format volumes using the FORMAT command from a command prompt window. The syntax for the format command is as follows:

FORMAT *drive_letter:* [/V:*label*] [/Q] [/S]

In this syntax, the following parameters are used:

Parameter	Meaning
Drive_letter:	The letter of the drive to be formatted
/V:*label*	Specifies a volume label
/Q	Performs a quick format
/S	Makes the formatted drive bootable

You typically use the command-line version of FORMAT when booting the system with the EBD. For example, to start over with a system and reinstall Windows 98, you can boot the EBD and then use the command FORMAT C: /V:Win98 /S to format the primary partition and prepare for the Windows 98 installation program.

Defragmenting Hard Disks

As you learned earlier in this chapter, the files that occupy FAT hard disks become fragmented over time. Because FAT simply locates new file clusters in the first available space on the disk, as files are deleted and other files grow, the contents of files tend to spread over the disk, reducing performance when accessing those files. On a disk that has a fragmentation level of

Chapter 17: File Systems: File and Disk Resources   **421**

10 percent or more (that is, 10 percent of the files are fragmented), you will experience perceptible reductions in the performance of the system.

To defragment a hard drive, open My Computer or Windows Explorer and right-click the drive you want to defragment; choose P**r**operties from the shortcut menu. Click **D**efragment Now to begin the defragmentation process. Alternatively, you can start the Disk Defragmenter program from the Start Menu/Programs/Accessories/System Tools menu, and then choose a drive to defragment (you can also choose to defragment all hard drives if you start Disk Defragmenter in this way).

| Tip | Under Windows 98, you should schedule frequent disk defragmentation using the Task Scheduler (see Chapter 34, "Automating Tasks"). It's often a good idea to completely defragment busy systems once a week; Task Scheduler can be set to do this while you're not using the computer. |

After starting Disk Defragmenter, you see a status display while the drive is being defragmented. You can continue to use the computer while this process completes, but you should avoid any activity that involves writing data to the drive being defragmented (doing so causes the defragmenter to have to start over with the drive). While the Status window is displayed, you can click the Sho**w** Details button to view a graphical representation of the disk clusters as they are moved around on the disk (see Figure 17.3). Each box in the Show Details window represents one disk cluster.

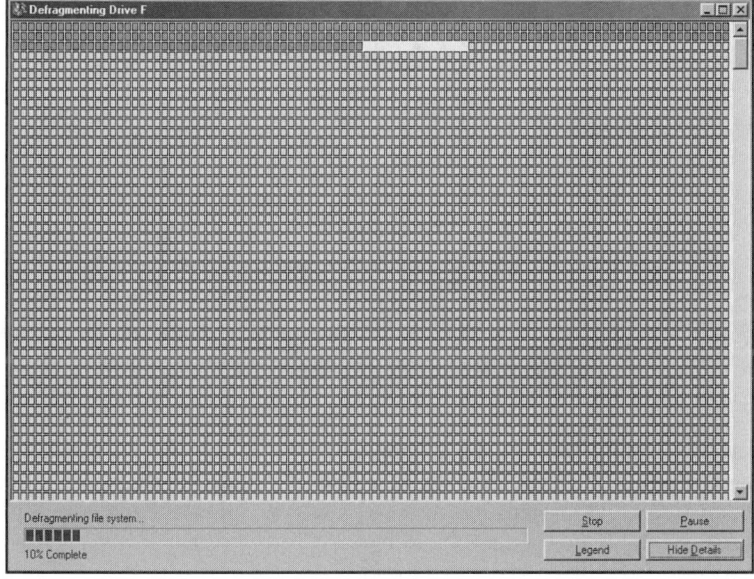

Figure 17.3
Watching Disk Defragmenter do its work.

Testing Hard Disk Drives

Hard disks can and do develop errors occasionally. Sometimes, these are file system errors (meaning that something in the directory or FAT is inconsistent with the contents of the disk); sometimes, the error is caused by bad spots developing on the disk (which happens occasionally and is not usually cause for concern). However, developing bad sectors is cause for great concern if it continues to happen or involves more than a couple of bad sectors; you should replace hard disks that exhibit these characteristics.

You can test for and repair most disk errors using a program called ScanDisk, which can be run from within Windows, from the command line, or from the EBD. ScanDisk can examine the directory and FAT structures on the disk and can also perform a surface scan, in which it tests each and every disk cluster on the disk to ensure that all are readable.

Note Under Windows 98, the command-prompt version of ScanDisk is run whenever the system starts without having been properly shut down. Directory problems can frequently develop when systems aren't properly shut down; running ScanDisk at startup after a bad shut down greatly reduces chances for subsequent disk problems.

Start ScanDisk in one of two ways: Open a drive's Properties dialog box, select the Tools tab, and click **C**heck Now; alternatively, start the program from the Start Menu/Programs/ Accessories/System Tools menu. In both cases, you see the main ScanDisk screen shown in Figure 17.4.

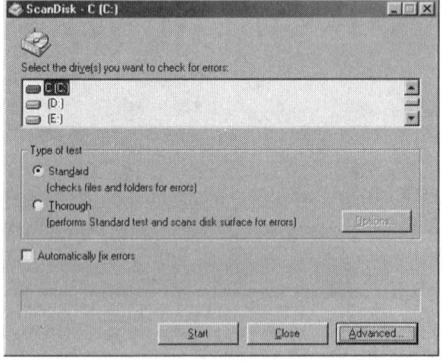

Figure 17.4
The main ScanDisk screen.

You have several options when using ScanDisk. First, choose whether to perform a Stan**d**ard or **T**horough test (the Standard test only checks directory and FAT structures). Then choose whether any errors encountered should be repaired automatically by ScanDisk; if you leave this checkbox blank, ScanDisk prompts you when it finds errors.

If you choose to perform a Thorough scan, click the **O**ptions button to display the Surface Scan Options dialog box shown in Figure 17.5. The possible settings are shown in Table 17.2.

Chapter 17: File Systems: File and Disk Resources

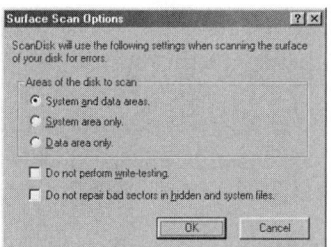

Figure 17.5
The ScanDisk Surface Scan Options dialog box.

Table 17.2
ScanDisk Surface Scan Options

Surface Scan Option	Description
Areas of the Disk to Scan	Controls which areas of the disk system are scanned. Choose System Area to check the FAT and other control structures for the partition.
Do Not Perform **W**rite-Testing	When this option is deselected, ScanDisk reads the contents of each cluster to ensure that all clusters can be read, and then writes the contents back to the same location to ensure that they can be written. Selecting this checkbox skips the write portion of the testing.
Do Not Repair Bad Sectors in Files **H**idden and System Files	When ScanDisk does a surface scan and finds bad sectors, it moves the file contents stored in that sector to another location on the disk and marks the sectors as bad so that they are not reused. Checking this box avoids this action for any files that have their hidden or system attributes set. Some software programs require that a file be stored in a particular location; moving such files may cause those programs to stop functioning.

From ScanDisk's main window, you can also click the **A**dvanced button to change how ScanDisk operates. Doing so displays the ScanDisk Advanced Options dialog box shown in Figure 17.6. Table 17.3 defines the options in this dialog box.

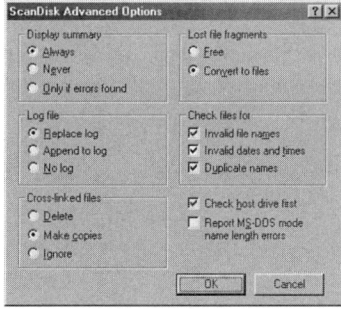

Figure 17.6
The ScanDisk Advanced Options dialog box.

Table 17.3
ScanDisk Advanced Options

ScanDisk Advanced Option	Description
Display Summary section	Controls whether the summary window is displayed when ScanDisk finishes.
Log File section	Controls how ScanDisk keeps log files of its actions. (The log file is called `C:\SCANDISK.LOG`.)
Cross-Linked Files section	Controls how ScanDisk should handle any cross-linked files, where two separate files both claim the same cluster on the disk.
Lost File Fragments section	Controls how ScanDisk should handle lost file fragments.
Check Files For section	Controls which directory integrity tests ScanDisk will perform.
Check **H**ost Drive First	Used only for compressed volumes. This option causes the host drive to be checked before the contents of the compressed drive are tested.
Report M**S**-DOS Mode Name Length Errors	Reports filenames that are not properly recognized by MS-DOS.

Using DriveSpace

Windows 98 includes a feature called DriveSpace, which can automatically compress the data stored on FAT16 drives. When a drive is compressed using DriveSpace, all files read from and written to the drive are automatically compressed using settings you define. Many application data files may consume as little as one-quarter their original size when they are compressed. (However, already compressed files such as `.ZIP` or `.JPG` files cannot be compressed further, and most `.EXE` files don't compress very much.)

Start DriveSpace by opening it from Start Menu/Programs/Accessories/System Tools. The main DriveSpace window is shown in Figure 17.7.

To compress a drive, first select it in the DriveSpace window and then choose the **C**ompress command from the **D**rive menu. You are shown a summary of the effect of compressing the drive (see Figure 17.8).

Click the Options button to control how the compressed drive is created. Figure 17.9 shows the Compression Options dialog box.

Chapter 17: File Systems: File and Disk Resources   **425**

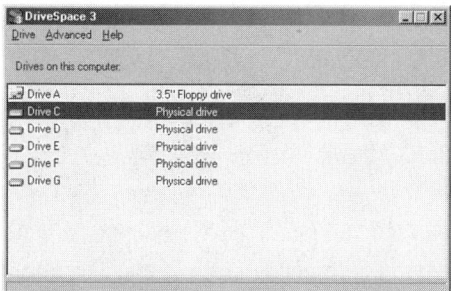

Figure 17.7
The main Windows 98 DriveSpace window.

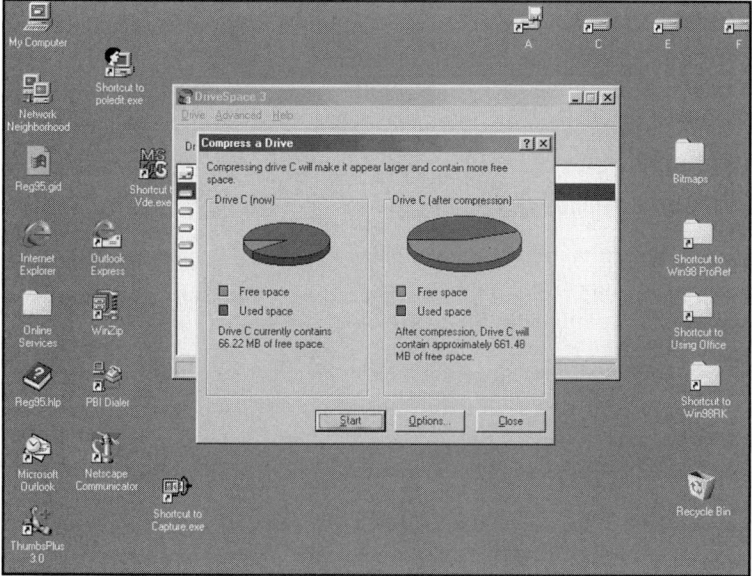

Figure 17.8
The DriveSpace compression estimate.

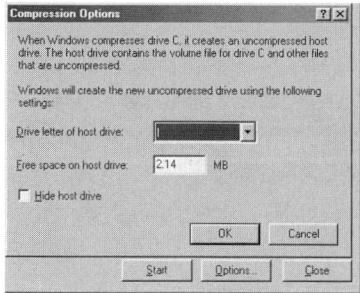

Figure 17.9
The DriveSpace Compression Options dialog box.

In the Compression Options dialog box, you can choose the drive letter to be reserved for the host drive as well as whether or not the host drive will be hidden from the system. You can also choose how much free space to keep open on the host drive.

> **What's a Host Drive?**
>
> When DriveSpace compresses a drive (for example, drive C), it changes the letter of the actual drive to something else (usually the next available drive letter in the system). On the actual drive partition, it creates a single file that contains the drive's contents, which are compressed within the file. The compressed file is *mounted* so that it appears as an actual drive, using the original drive letter of the host drive.
>
> However, if you were to boot an MS-DOS disk and examine drive C in this example, you would see the *actual* drive C (the host drive) and not the compressed contents. For the whole illusion to work, and for you to access the contents of the compressed drive, the DriveSpace driver (`DRVSPACE.BIN`) must be loaded into memory.

Compressing a drive can take a long time, often several hours. It's a good idea to start the compression process when the computer won't need to be used for a while.

Maintaining a Compressed Drive

Once a drive is compressed, you can use all the normal Windows 98 disk maintenance tools on it, such as ScanDisk or Disk Defragmenter. Those utilities automatically compensate for the compressed drive and carry out their functions on it normally.

You must do several additional things to maintain compressed drives, however. First, you may want to change the compression level used to store files. There are four compression levels: no compression, Normal Compression, HiPack Compression, and UltraPack Compression. Higher compression levels make available more space on the drive but at the cost of disk performance.

You adjust the compression level used to store new files using the DriveSpace utility. Access the **A**dvanced menu and choose **O**ptions to display the Disk Compression Settings dialog box shown in Figure 17.10. Choose from the available options to select a compression level for new files being stored on the compressed drive.

Figure 17.10
The Disk Compression Settings dialog box.

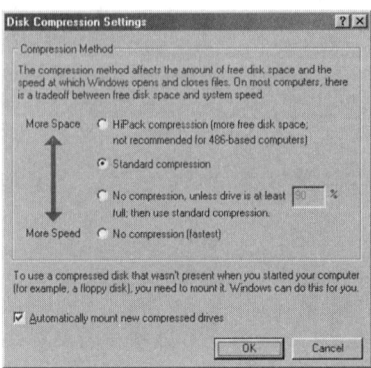

Notice that there is no setting for UltraPack Compression on the Disk Compression Settings dialog box. This is because UltraPack Compression is used only to compress files that haven't been used for a period of time; it is not used for normal file save operations. To adjust the compression level of files stored on the compressed drive, you use a program called the Compression Agent. The Compression Agent (accessed from the Start Menu/Programs/Accessories/System Tools menu) can change a file's compression level to the UltraPack level and can also adjust all the other file's compression levels based on settings you choose. You typically run Compression Agent on a regular basis to optimize how compressed files are stored on the disk; you normally run the Compression Agent through Task Scheduler. Figure 17.11 shows Compression Agent's main window.

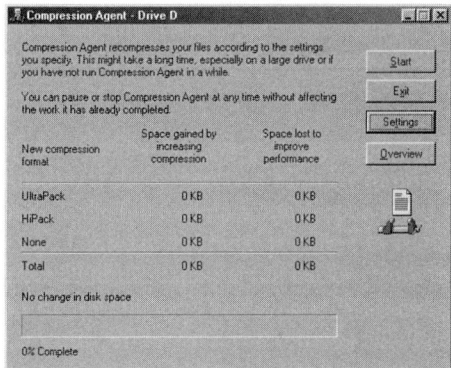

Figure 17.11
The main window of the Compression Agent.

To choose the settings for Compression Agent, click the Se**t**tings button to display the Compression Agent Settings dialog box (see Figure 17.12).

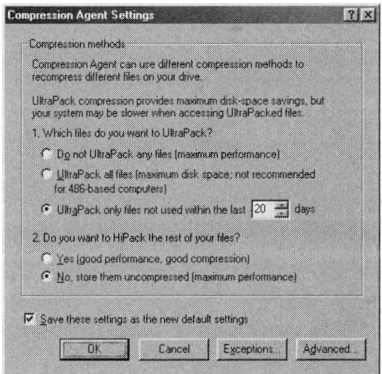

Figure 17.12
The Compression Agent Settings dialog box.

Use the settings in the Compression Agent Settings dialog box to strike your preferred balance between available disk space and performance. A good rule of thumb is to use UltraPack only for files that haven't been accessed in 20 to 30 days; leave the files you access frequently stored either with no compression or with HiPack compression.

For performance reasons, you may want Compression Agent to never compress files of a certain type. You can use the E**x**ceptions button to define specific files, entire folders, or all files that share a particular file extension, and you can define how such files will be compressed, exclusive of the default Compression Agent settings. The Add Exceptions dialog box is shown in Figure 17.13.

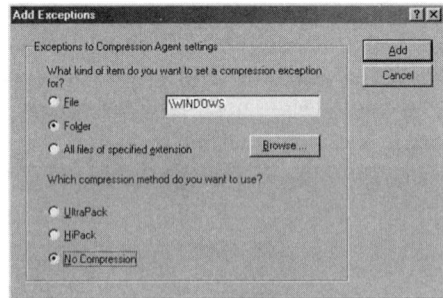

Figure 17.13
The Add Exceptions dialog box.

Disk Compression Notes

Compressing a disk using DriveSpace should be done only when there are no other good alternatives, such as adding more physical disk space or reducing the number of files that must be stored. Although compressed drives can extend the life of a disk drive significantly by making much more space available, there are problems you can encounter and should be aware of:

- Compressed drives are more complex for the operating system to support than uncompressed drives. Although DriveSpace is very reliable, it imposes additional complexity on the system, and complexity usually reduces overall system reliability, even if only by a small amount.

- It is harder to recover a system that uses compressed drives from a disk failure. Many tricks you can perform on pure FAT drives can't be used for compressed drives.

- If you take advantage of a compressed drive, you may not be able to easily uncompress it if you decide to reverse the process. To uncompress a drive, you must make sure that all the files stored on the compressed drive can still fit on the original drive without compression.

- If you take advantage of compression, you will experience reduced system performance. In addition, the author has noticed that the performance of compressed drives degrades much faster than FAT as fragmentation increases, so you have to defragment them more frequently.

Conclusion

In this chapter, you learned about hard disks and file systems under Windows 98. You also learned about the NTFS file system that Windows NT uses. You learned how long filenames are stored, how FAT16 and FAT32 compare, and how FAT16 and FAT32 are structured. You also learned how to perform common operations on hard disk drives, such as defragmenting them, repairing errors, and compressing them.

You can continue exploring the architecture of Windows 98 by examining Chapter 11, "Windows 98 Architecture and Application Support," or you can continue learning about devices in Windows 98 by reading Chapter 12, "Supporting Devices." Other chapters closely related to disk support include Chapter 20, "Backup and Restore"; Chapter 35, "Tools and Strategies for Optimizing Windows 98"; and Chapter 36, "The Windows 98 Boot Process and Emergency Recovery."

CHAPTER 18

Viruses in Windows 98

At 9:05 a.m. you get a call from a user: She just arrived at work and her computer won't boot and she's frustrated. You head off to her desk, but before getting there you're paged to call another extension. Stopping to use a phone in the hallway, you speak to another user, complaining of the same problem. "Well, that's weird," you think to yourself. Going to the first user's computer, you try another boot, only to discover that, although the hard disk seems to be working properly, it's acting as if the hard disk were wiped completely clean, without even a partition table or Master Boot Record (MBR). As you're looking the problem over, three other users from nearby see you, come over, and ask, "Is the network down? None of our computers will start up." Taking a quick look at one of their systems, you see the same symptoms as the first system. More users see you, and start heading over to talk to you, obvious concern on their faces. "Hey, what's going on with all the computers?" they ask.

With a sinking feeling in the pit of your stomach, you suddenly realize what's happening: A virus must have gotten into the system, spread throughout all of the computers, and "dropped its payload," wiping out every computer's partition table and boot sector, and probably destroying all the files stored locally. You start thinking about the job ahead of you: Every system must be booted from a clean floppy disk, repartitioned, and reformatted; Windows 98 and all user applications must be reinstalled; and any backups (which must first be assured of being virus-free) must be restored. Each computer will take several hours to complete, and there are *hundreds* of computers to take care of. There's no way, with the staffing you have, to get this all done by tomorrow, even by the end of the week, even working 24-hour days, even bringing in outside help (who won't understand all of the standards and conventions used in your company). The entire company is shut down for the week, *at best*.

Thinking about the not-yet-installed network virus protection software still sitting on your desk, you think about having to explain what has happened to your bosses, their bosses, and eventually the CEO and Chairman—not to mention all of the users.

"Is a good reference worth it, or should I just go clean out my desk before they realize what's going on and lynch me?" you muse to yourself.

You've just been hit by a computer virus.

Understanding Malicious Programs

A computer *virus* is simply a software program that replicates itself. Often, viruses (not "virii" as some would think) are designed to replicate themselves without being detected, until triggered by some event to carry out other instructions. These other instructions, called the *payload,* may do any number of things, depending on the intentions of the programmer who wrote the virus. A payload might simply display an amusing or political message on the screen, or it might erase all files it can, or even destroy the computer's boot sectors and partition tables. The extent of the damage can be severe and far-reaching.

Viruses are not the only types of malicious programs in existence, but sometimes these other types of programs are mistaken for viruses. Malicious programs come in many forms:

- **Viruses**, already discussed, replicate themselves as many times as possible, usually in such a way that there is a good chance of their being transmitted to another computer, where they can continue to spread.

- **Trojan Horses** are programs that appear to have an innocent purpose, but carry out some undesired action after they are started. For instance, you may download a game from the Internet, and while you're using it, it's secretly erasing files on your hard disk.

Chapter 18: Viruses in Windows 98

Trojan Horses are named for the mythical story in which Greek soldiers hid themselves in a giant horse placed outside the city of Troy. Mistaking it for a gift, the Trojans brought it into the city, and the Greeks emerged from the horse and attacked the city from within.

- **Logic Bombs** are pieces of code inserted into an otherwise useful program, and which carry out some action when triggered. For instance, a software program may have code that destroys itself unless the bomb's programmer disarms the logic bomb.

- **Worms** are programs that transmit themselves through a network, from one computer to another. They do not replicate themselves, generally. Worms may be designed to collect information about each system they visit and transmit the information (such as user lists) to another location, for example.

This chapter concerns itself primarily with viruses, because they pose the greatest threat and are relatively easy to protect against, provided you have the right information and take good precautions. The most important thing is to remember to take precautions *before* you have the lesson hammered into you, similar to the little scenario presented at the beginning of the chapter.

Another important thing to realize is that the threat from computer viruses is growing dramatically. Consider the growth rate of known viruses:

Year	Number of Known Viruses
1990	18
1991	1,075
1992	2,423
1993	3,587
1994	5,475
1995	7,669
1996	10,835
1997	16,215

A study done by the National Computer Security Association (NCSA) and various members of the antivirus community revealed the following data:

- 90% of all surveyed sites with 500 or more PCs experienced a virus incident, in which 25 or more PCs were simultaneously affected, *each month.*

- In larger organizations, the likelihood of encountering a virus infection is about one chance per 100 PCs, *per month*.

- 30% of sites reported server downtime of 5.8 hours (average) from a single virus infection.

- Over 46% of sites that experienced virus incidents took more than 19 days to completely recover.

- 37% reported that single incidents cost close to $1,999, sometimes more.

Clearly, viruses are a major threat and are not to be taken lightly.

Understanding Virus Types

Viruses come in different varieties. In many cases, there could also be a number of slight variants on a particular theme, where a programmer modifies an existing virus to suit a particular whim (it's easier to do this than to write a new virus from scratch). Here are the main classifications of viruses:

- **Boot Sector Viruses** occupy the boot sectors of hard and floppy disks. A boot sector virus transmits itself by infecting a formatted floppy disk. All formatted disks, whether or not they are bootable, contain a small boot sector program (this program is what displays the message "Non system disk or disk error," should you accidentally leave it in the drive and boot the system). When such a disk is booted up, the boot sector of the hard disk is then infected, and subsequent floppy disks are then infected.

- **Macro Viruses** infect the documents of popular applications, such as Microsoft Word or Excel, and are written in the macro language of those applications. The number of known macro viruses has increased dramatically in recent years, starting from the first known macro virus called WM/Concept (WM stands for Word Macro) discovered just two years ago, to over 1,500 known macro viruses today. Macro viruses now account for the vast majority of virus infections. They spread rapidly because documents tend to be exchanged between computers much more frequently these days than disks and program files. Moreover, although most people know that programs can contain viruses, not everyone has yet learned that documents can, too.

- **File Viruses** typically infect executable files, such as .COM or .EXE files. They transmit themselves to other .COM and .EXE files on the system when you run an infected program.

- **Polymorphic Viruses** try to escape detection by constantly changing their sequence of instructions, which is what some virus scanners use to detect viruses. Often, they self-encrypt themselves, using different keys, to accomplish this feat. Some of these can mutate into as many as two billion different forms.

- **Stealth Viruses** help escape detection by "spoofing" certain commands in the operating system. For instance, they may cause the DIR command to fail to show an infected file's increased size, or modification date. When they are running and consuming system memory, they often hide this loss of memory, too.

- **Multipartite Viruses** combine qualities of both file and boot sector viruses. They typically enter through an executable program, and then infect the computer's boot sector when run.

- **Companion Viruses** take advantage of a trick in MS-DOS whereby a program with a .COM file extension is executed in favor of a program with an .EXE extension that shares the same filename. For instance, if you have a program called EDIT.EXE under MS-DOS, a virus might create a copy of itself as EDIT.COM. Simply typing EDIT and pressing Enter at the command line will execute the virus code instead of the intended program (and if the virus is well-written, it will automatically start EDIT.EXE for you once it's loaded, so that you don't notice what's happening).

When Is a Virus Actually a Virus?

With the growing ubiquity of email, a new sort of pseudovirus has emerged, which you might call the warning virus. Taking the form of emailed dire warnings about avoiding messages that have certain words in their subject lines (like "Good Times" or "Join the Crew"), these messages are often convincingly written, at least well enough to fool most users.

The simple fact is this: There is no known bona fide email that has ever usefully informed people about a virus. Furthermore, your system cannot be infected by a virus just because you open an email message and read it. Although downloading an attached program could invite a virus, you won't contract it by reading the message.

Other forms of these warning viruses also concern other, nonvirus-related, frauds. There are some that promise to donate a few cents to cancer research (or whatever) for every person you forward the message to. Often, these are just schemes to harvest email addresses, which are useful for sending out advertisements later.

Basically, the rule is this: Don't ever rely on emailed warnings about *anything*. Instead, check with reputable sources or web sites for correct information.

As a personal note, I'd urge you, as a fellow computer professional, to take a few minutes to reply to people who forward these types of messages and explain to them that the warning is probably a fraud, and that they do more harm than good by forwarding these messages to lots of people. I've found it useful to refer them to good web sites that contain information about such scams. One such site is www.urbanlegends.com. Or, better yet, search www.yahoo.com with the words "Urban Legends" and visit one of the many sites that publish this information.

Understanding How Viruses Infect Files

You should already understand how most programs function at the machine level. Every program is a series of machine language instructions, some of which jump to other locations in the program. Most viruses insert themselves into programs by inserting an unconditional jump instruction at the beginning of the program, which jumps to the end of the program file where the virus has been added. The virus instructions then execute, and finally execute another jump instruction back to where the original program left off. Using this method, a virus can be activated by these jump instructions anywhere in a program, although usually it's done at the very beginning. Viruses using this method of execution are called *non-overwriters* or *appenders*.

There are some viruses called *overwriters* that simply overlay program instructions with virus instructions. These viruses are easily detected, because your own program typically no longer operates in their presence.

Understanding Virus Creation

If you came to this section hoping for a tutorial on how to create viruses, you're going to be disappointed. The intention of this section is to point out that anyone with an Internet connection using one of the popular search engines can find all sorts of virus resources on various hacker sites. Some of the sites examined by this author when researching the chapter contained examples of program code useful for creating viruses (including source code for complete viruses), discussions on how to escape detection from virus scanners, and even entire "virus construction sets" which enable you to create a virus by using building blocks contained in the kits. You should realize that it's easy to create viruses, even if someone isn't otherwise a good enough programmer to be able to do it himself. All you need is the desire to do it.

Understanding Viral Transmission

Viruses spread through a number of different means, but always by the exchange of some program file between computers. As already discussed, the viral program files can inhabit programs, documents that support a sufficiently powerful macro language, or boot sectors on disks. The most common routes of transmission include the following:

- Downloaded documents or programs from the Internet
- Programs or documents sent as attachments to email messages
- Programs or documents shared on a network
- Floppy disks used on different computers, or sent from one person to another

A good prevention strategy must anticipate and handle all these possibilities.

Viruses tend to be classified as either fast infectors or slow infectors. A *fast infector* infects all files it can access, as rapidly as possible. A *slow infector* is more choosy about how and when it infects files, with the idea being that you're less likely to notice it and take steps to remove it. Slow infectors tend to be more dangerous because they can often do a lot of damage before being detected. However, antivirus software should detect both types of viruses equally well.

Windows 98 contains some features that help stop viral transmission, such as detecting changes to the Master Boot Record on the computer, and preventing certain low-level disk access attempts (such as attempts to change the MBR while Windows 98 is running). Newer versions of Microsoft Office also offer features that help you notice viral infection, such as alerting you when you open a document that contains an auto-executing macro, which could indicate a possible virus. However, these features just slow down viruses, and newer viruses invariably emerge that can counteract such measures.

Recognizing Viruses

Here's the only good news in this whole subject area: Most viruses are poorly written, and cause perceptible impacts to the operation of most computers. For instance, a virus-infected system might operate much more slowly, access the disk in ways that you don't expect, cause some programs to work incorrectly, or show other signs that a virus is present, such as mysteriously missing disk or memory space on the system.

So, any time a system is behaving in unexpected ways, you should add "viral infection" to your list of candidate causes, in addition to the more mundane possibilities of buggy programs, corrupted files, and failed hardware.

Preventing Viruses

If you think about the different ways that a virus gets onto a computer, it all boils down to one of three possible routes: through a network connection, a modem connection, or a floppy disk. To adequately protect a Windows 98 workstation, you should run antivirus software, which protects against all of these transmission sources.

Antivirus software automatically scans both the memory in the computer and the files accessed by the computer, either on-demand or on-access. *On-demand* scanning is when you deliberately use the antivirus software to scan all of the files on a disk, whereas *on-access* scanning automatically scans all files that are accessed (read or written) by the computer. Most antivirus programs employ both methods.

There are a quite a few antivirus programs from which you can choose, including the following popular packages:

- Norton AntiVirus from Symantec
- McAfee VirusScan from Network Associates

- F-Protect from FRISK Software International

- IBM AntiVirus

- Dr. Solomon's Anti-Virus

Not all antivirus programs are created equal, but the preceding programs are all well-known and have been around long enough to be trusted choices. Most antivirus programs for individual workstations cost between $50 and $150, although volume discounts are usually available if you are seeking a site license to protect multiple machines. All the products listed will scan the computer's memory, files, and disks, using both on-demand and on-access techniques.

In addition to workstation-based antivirus software, you should also implement file server antivirus software. Programs intended to run on NetWare and Windows NT Servers automatically scan files stored on them, and may even examine data streams transmitted through their network interfaces for virus signatures. Implementing a server-based solution closes another possible door to viral transmission. Most of the antivirus programs for desktop computers also have server-side versions, and they often work in concert with their desktop-based brethren. Also, since updating virus definition files can be a chore, it's a good idea to choose a package that helps you automate this process, through either a push agent or some other mechanism.

In addition to running antivirus software, which should be considered a requirement, also consider implementing the following policies and practices within your organization:

- Implement a good backup program, which includes the ability to restore files backed up at various times in the past. This may enable you to find a particular file and restore it from before it was infected.

- Ensure that software entering the organization is from reputable sources. There have been well-publicized cases of viruses being transmitted through shrink-wrapped software, but they are very rare and the previous experience has made software vendors extremely conscious of this threat and they take careful measures to prevent infection through their products.

- Encourage people to write-protect their disks, particularly those that are used only to run programs (such as diagnostic programs or demonstration programs). A virus cannot infect a write-protected disk.

- Establish policies that discourage users from bringing in unapproved software, whether from commercial sources, emails from friends, or from their home collection.

- If your PCs support a feature where they will first try to boot from the hard disk before trying a floppy disk, enable this feature. This prevents accidental infection of boot sector viruses from floppy disks.

- Find out whether antivirus software exists for your email server, particularly if it is connected to Internet email. Viruses often enter through attachments, and antivirus scanners exist for some of the most popular email servers.

- Make sure you have original copies of all applications, rather than relying on restoration of applications for reinstallation.

- If you aren't running antivirus software on your workstations, you should implement a policy where all incoming disks are checked by the MIS department or by using a published procedure.

The way to handle viruses is to prevent them before they can get in.

Conclusion

In this chapter, you learned about viruses and other malicious programs that you could encounter under Windows 98, and more importantly you learned how to prevent viruses on individual workstations and network servers. Taking an active approach to preventing viruses is one of the smartest things you can do to avoid catastrophe.

Windows 98 for Portables

Windows 98 includes several features that make it an ideal platform for portable PCs. Some of these features actually began with Windows 95; others are more recent innovations. This chapter examines some Windows 98 features that serve the portable user.

A portable PC is like any other PC. It has a hard drive, a floppy drive, a screen, and a pointing device. Newer notebooks may also have CD-ROM drives, modems, or network adapters. The rules for networking, configuring, and managing Windows 98 on a portable computer are essentially the same as on a desktop computer. There are, however, some special considerations due to the special needs and functions of a portable PC. This chapter examines the following Windows 98 features in the context of their relevance to the portable environment:

- PC Card Devices
- Hardware Profiles
- Power Management
- Direct cable Networking
- Infrared Monitor
- Briefcase

If you travel with a laptop, your dial-up modem connection is an important component of your computer's configuration. See Chapter 26, "Windows 98 and Remote Communication," for a discussion of Windows 98's dialup features, including the Calling Locations feature, which lets laptop owners define separate dialing properties for different locations.

> **Note** Many of the special considerations for portable PCs are related to the somewhat-more-finicky portable hardware. For a complete discussion of hardware-related issues regarding your own PC, consult the vendor documentation.

PC Card Devices

Windows 98 provides enhanced support for PC Card devices. Although Windows 98 provides the most functionality with the new 32-bit CardBus PC Cards, the older 16-bit PC Cards (as well as the older PCMCIA cards) are also supported. Windows 98 has its own integrated card and socket services to support dynamically loadable 32-bit virtual device drivers that consume zero conventional memory.

Because Windows 98 supports Plug and Play, installing a new PC Card is as easy as plugging in the new card. Windows 98 automatically realizes that you have added a device. Windows 98 attempts to identify the device and then loads the appropriate drivers for it. After the device has been identified, the network drivers are also loaded so that network connectivity is readily available. When the PC Card is removed, the unnecessary drivers are removed from memory.

> **Note** Be aware that hot swapping and the dynamic loading and unloading of drivers is only supported for devices that have a 32-bit protected mode Windows 98 driver.

Chapter 19: Windows 98 for Portables

Some of the other new functions supported by Windows 98 are as follows:

- Improved battery performance for mobile PCs with PCMCIA cards.

- CardBus support. CardBus is a 32-bit implementation of the PC Card that is tied to the PCI bus in the mobile device for faster performance and Plug and Play capability.

- PC Cards that operate at the new lower voltage of 3.3V.

- Multifunction PC Cards. Even though it would not seem new for Windows 98 to support multifunction cards, the way in which Windows 98 supports them is new. In Windows 95, the multifunction cards were treated as one device that could not be configured separately. In Windows 98, a multifunction card is treated in such a way that each capability of the multifunction card is treated independently.

To observe the detected PC Cards and make minor changes such as stopping a card's function so that it can be removed, select PC Card (PCMCIA) from the Control Panel. The window should be similar to the one shown in Figure 19.1.

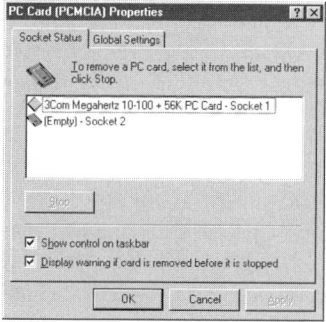

Figure 19.1
The PC Card (PCMCIA) Properties window.

Hardware Profiles

Although Hardware Profiles can be used on all Windows 98 computers, Microsoft created the Windows Hardware Profile feature for the portable user. A *Hardware Profile* is a predefined collection of hardware elements. At boot time, when you specify a Hardware Profile, you specify a set of hardware components that will be available to Windows 98. See Chapter 9, "Hardware Profiles," for a discussion of Hardware Profiles in Windows 98.

The principle purpose of Hardware Profiles is to support portable PCs that may be using a docking station. A *docking station* is a home-based (or office-based) connecting point through which the portable PC can connect to non-portable components.

By using Hardware Profiles, the user can define a different set of hardware components for the *docked* state as opposed to the *undocked* state. In the home environment, where it may be attached to non-portable peripherals, the computer can boot to a predefined Hardware Profile without having to reinstall all the temporary hardware. When the user travels with the computer, the computer can boot to the undocked profile without generating messages about missing devices.

You do not need an actual docking station in order to use Hardware Profiles. If, for instance, your laptop PC supports a desktop monitor or keyboard, you could use a Hardware Profile to define a temporary desktop environment.

If your Hardware Profiles are different enough, Windows 98 will automatically choose the profile that coincides with the hardware it detects on your system. If Windows 98 can't determine which profile to use, it displays the Hardware Profiles in a menu and lets you choose one.

See Chapter 9 for a complete discussion of how to configure and manage Hardware Profiles in Windows 98.

Windows 98 has built-in support for *hot docking* (where the docking or undocking takes place with the computer running at full power) and *cold docking* (where the state change occurs and the PC must be powered off and restarted). In addition, Windows 98 supports hot swapping of compatible components such as Windows 98-compliant PC Cards.

> **Note** Windows 98 provides full, protected-mode support for removable media often used in portable environments, such as JAZ, ZIP, LS-120, Floppy, Bernoulli, and others. Windows 98 also supports the ability to lock or unlock a device to block the media from being removed accidentally. In addition, Windows 98 also supports software-based ejection for supported media.

Power Management

One of the most common complaints mobile users have is the short length of time that their batteries power their portable platforms. Some of the new features in Windows 98 are designed to help conserve the power that a mobile machine uses. Windows 98 includes support for Advanced Configuration and Power Interface (ACPI), Advanced Power Management (APM) and the new Simply Interactive PC (SIPC) initiative. One of the characteristics of the SIPC initiative is the OnNow design. *OnNow* is a term used for a PC that is always on but appears to be off when not in active use.

Windows 98's OnNow feature effectively manages the power consumption of the PC in a dynamic fashion. OnNow keeps an unused PC in a ready state with minimal power draw and

Chapter 19: Windows 98 for Portables

then instantly switches to full power when a user accesses the PC. OnNow effectively minimizes battery usage for portable PCs that are left on, and it helps you avoid the long boot process in situations when you would otherwise need to turn your computer off.

OnNow directs power consumption for all of the system components and peripherals. (Previously, the computer's BIOS directed the management of power.) In addition to putting the computer in *sleep* mode, in which the computer appears off but can still respond to wakeup events, OnNow manages power to system devices, selectively reducing power consumption for unused components if necessary. OnNow also interacts with OnNow-aware desktop applications to reduce unnecessary activities in low-power situations.

OnNow uses the Advanced Configuration and Power Interface (ACPI) specification. The *ACPI* specification defines an abstract of the hardware interface necessary to implement a standard power management capability to control the power consumption of the PC. The most important characteristic required to implement ACPI is a BIOS that supports the ACPI specification. The BIOS must be able to provide the operating system with a description of the device configuration and the power control hardware interface.

> **Note** Power management in an older PC, in which the BIOS controls the power management, will still work with the Windows 98 power management features, but the BIOS will control the power consumption rather than the operating system. If the BIOS controls the power management, the PC could be using Advanced Power Management (APM) to conserve power. APM settings are managed through the BIOS Setup menu at system startup.

Windows 98 allows the user to monitor and configure the power settings using power schemes. A power scheme is a set of power management settings defining when OnNow should put the system on standby, and when it should put the monitor or hard disk in "hibernation." Windows 98 comes with the following predefined power schemes:

- Home/Office Desk—This is typically best for desktop machines.

- Portable/Laptop—The setting of choice for laptops. The settings are designed to conserve battery power.

- Always On—Used for a server.

You can activate or edit a power scheme (or create a new power scheme) by using the Power Management applet in the Control Panel. Figure 19.2 shows the Power Management Properties dialog box. In this figure you can see that this configuration is set for a Portable/Laptop. You can also see that the scheme can be customized and then saved by using the Save As button.

Part III: Windows 98 Operations

Figure 19.2
The Power Management Properties window.

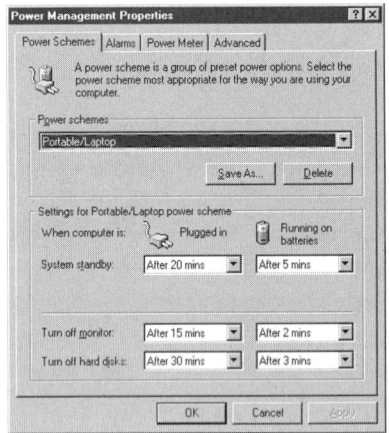

> **Note** It is important to note the Power Management Properties dialog box on your PC may differ from the Power Management Properties dialog box shown here or found on another PC. The available options vary according to your hardware.

You can see in Figure 19.2 that there are tabs for setting alarms, observing the power status, and configuring advanced properties. Figure 19.3 shows the Alarms tab on which you can configure alarm actions for both the low battery and critical battery states. Figure 19.4 shows the Power Meter tab. With the Power Meter tab, you can track two batteries. You can get more information about individual batteries by clicking the battery icon.

Figure 19.3
The Alarms tab for the Power Management Properties.

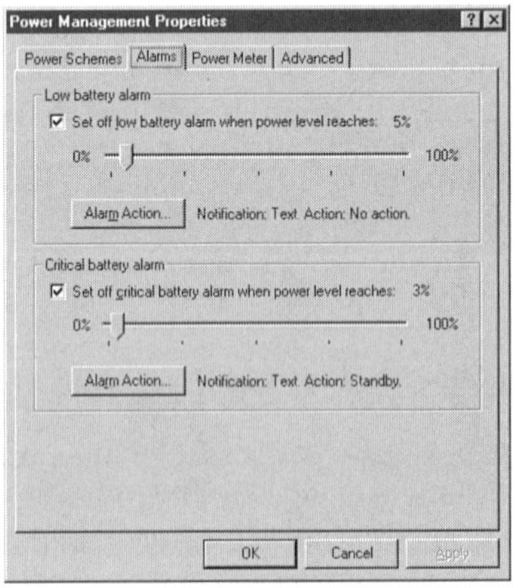

Chapter 19: Windows 98 for Portables

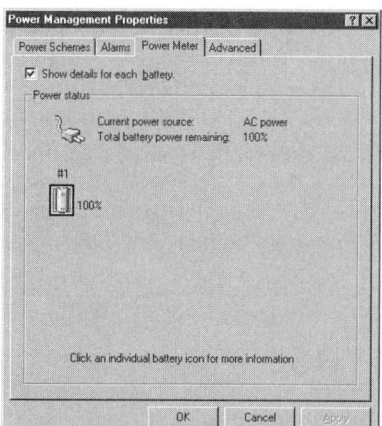

Figure 19.4
The Power Meter tab of the Power Management Properties.

Direct Cable Networking

Windows 98 borrows a feature from Windows 95 called Direct Cable Connection. *Direct Cable Connection* lets you network to another computer by using a parallel or serial cable. You do not need a network adapter card or Ethernet cabling to network PCs using Direct Cable networking. Chapter 22, "Peer-to-Peer Networking," describes Direct Cable networking in Windows 98.

Direct Cable networking means that you don't need specialized network hardware in order to connect your laptop to your home or office PC. You can connect directly and share files and printers with very little effort or expense.

See Chapter 22 for more information about Direct Cable networking.

Infrared Monitor

Windows 98 provides ample support for infrared wireless networking. Infrared networking is a common method for networking a portable PC. You must have the necessary infrared hardware in order to use Windows 98's infrared networking features.

Microsoft Infrared 3.0 (which is included with Windows 98) supports the Infrared Data Association standards IrDA 1.0 and IrDA 2.0.

If you have an infrared device installed on your system, you can use the Infrared Monitor application to manage and monitor your infrared network. Infrared Monitor tells you if any infrared devices are currently within range of your PC. Infrared Monitor also tracks the status of infrared connections and lets you enable and disable infrared services.

At setup, you can install Infrared Monitor by choosing Infrared as an optional component in the Communications group. If you didn't install Infrared Monitor at Setup, it becomes available if you add a new infrared device by using the Add New Hardware Wizard. If Infrared Monitor doesn't appear in the taskbar when you install an infrared device, you may need to open the Infrared Monitor Control Panel and choose the Display the Infrared Monitor icon on the taskbar in the Preferences menu.

See Windows 98 Online Help for more information about using Infrared Monitor.

Mastering the Briefcase

For users who have a desktop and a portable computer to travel with, keeping files synchronized between the two systems can be very difficult at times. Windows 95 provided users with a new way to keep disparate machines synchronized. Windows 98 keeps that same idea and provides some enhancements to it.

Windows 98 includes the My Briefcase feature introduced with Windows 95. Briefcase is essentially a container (*a briefcase*) that contains files that may need to pass from a home PC to a portable PC and back again. You can work on a particular spreadsheet at the office and take that spreadsheet home with you on weekends, and you can take that same spreadsheet on business trips. Allowing multiple versions of the same file to exist simultaneously can present a dangerous situation. You might forget which version is most current and save over the latest changes. Or, you might save over your master copy with a temporary version you didn't really want to save. Briefcase provides version management of documents and other application files.

The Windows 98 Briefcase is normally installed during a Portable installation or if you choose a Custom installation and select the Briefcase option. If for some reason it is not installed at that time, follow these instructions to install it:

1. Go to the Control Panel and select the Add/Remove Programs applet.

2. When the Add/Remove Programs window opens, select the Windows Setup tab as shown in Figure 19.5.

3. Click once on the Accessories category and then click the Details button.

4. Click the checkbox next to Briefcase in the Components list and then click OK.

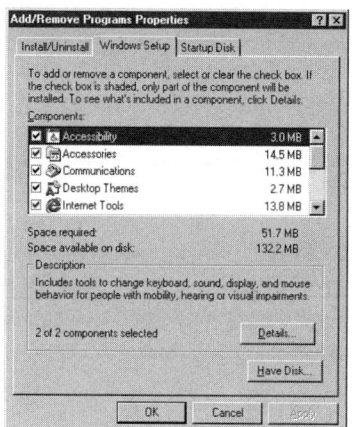

Figure 19.5
The Windows Setup tab of the Add/Remove Programs.

Once you have Briefcase installed, it will create a new folder called My Briefcase on your desktop.

The normal method for selecting files to keep synchronized would be to browse the primary machine from the secondary machine. In other words, use the laptop to browse the Network Neighborhood to find the other machine (the desktop). Once you have found the desktop machine, browse around for the file or files you would like to keep synchronized.

When you find the folder or file that you want to synchronize, simply click and drag that item out of the Network Neighborhood and on top of the My Briefcase folder.

> **Note** Although you can click and drag the items by using the left or primary mouse button, it is always better to click and drag with the right, or secondary, mouse button. Doing so results in a drop-down menu box from which to choose the appropriate option. It even gives you a chance to cancel—just in case.

When you open My Briefcase for the first time, you should get a helpful window like the one shown in Figure 19.6.

Once the My Briefcase folder is open, you can proceed to drag files into it from the other machine (which should be shown in Network Neighborhood). In Figure 19.7 you can see where a folder called IP Calc was just dragged from the folder of Subnetcalc on the Desktop to the My Briefcase on the portable machine. You can also see the drop-down menu box that is presented when the right or secondary mouse button is used. The choice of Make Sync Copy is highlighted.

Figure 19.6

Helping you use the Briefcase. Windows 98 is designed for the job.

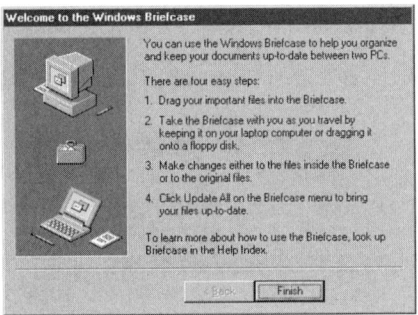

Figure 19.7

Dragging files from the desktop to the portable machine.

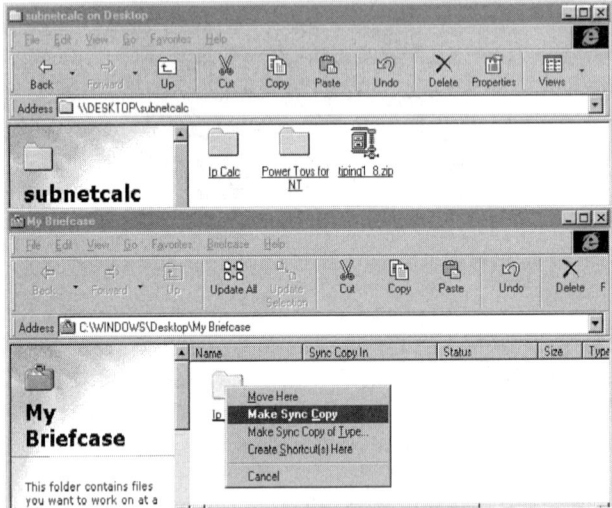

After you have dragged all of the files that need to be synchronized into the Briefcase, you can take your portable machine on the road and work with those files. When you return to the office and reconnect to the network, open Briefcase on the portable computer and check the status of the briefcased files (see Figure 19.8). Briefcase compares the briefcased files with the home copy. The Status column in the Briefcase window shows which files need updating. Click Update All to update all the files in the briefcase, or click Update Selection to update a selected file.

If you click on Update All in the Briefcase window, you will get a box that looks similar to the box in Figure 19.9. The Update My Briefcase dialog box shows the actions that must take place in order to synchronize the briefcased files. By default, Briefcase assumes you'll want to replace the older file with the newer file. To choose a different action, right-click on the file and select a different action from the context menu.

Click the Update button to start an update.

Chapter 19: Windows 98 for Portables   **451**

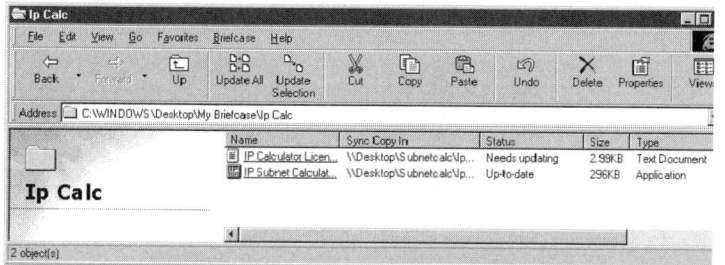

Figure 19.8
The Briefcase after being on the road. Notice that one of the files needs updating.

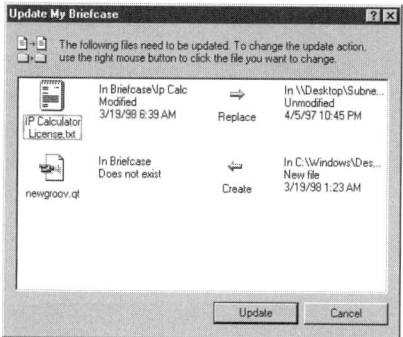

Figure 19.9
Using the Update All feature of the Briefcase.

One of the questions most often asked about this process is whether the briefcased file can change on both PCs or only on one PC. The answer depends on the document type and whether Windows 98 has a handler for the application type that the document or file in question is used by. If Windows 98 does have a handler for that file type, then Windows 98 will use the handler to alert the application to merge the two files. When you click the Update button, the files will be re-synchronized.

To create a new Briefcase folder, simply browse My Computer or use Explorer to locate the folder in which you would like to create the new Briefcase. Once you are located in the correct folder, you can right-click any unused area in the folder, and then click New, Briefcase (see Figure 19.10).

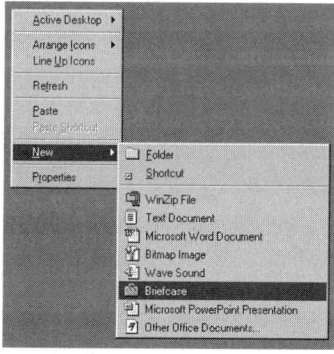

Figure 19.10
Creating a new Briefcase folder.

After the New Briefcase has been created, you can rename it if you want. On the other hand, if you need to remove a Briefcase folder, you can simply click and drag the Briefcase icon to the Recycle Bin or right-click the folder and select Delete.

You can also use My Briefcase through a floppy disk. If you wanted to use the floppy disk method of synchronizing files, simply copy the files you want to synchronize to the floppy disk from the desktop computer. Then take the floppy disk to the portable machine and copy the files from the floppy disk into the Briefcase. Then when you are ready to resynchronize, simply put the disk back in and then go to the Briefcase and click Update All. From that point you can copy the files on the disk back to the desktop if you want. (It is obviously much easier to do this with a network connection of some sort—remember you can use a network or dial-up connection or a Direct Cable Connection.)

Another alternative is to place the Briefcase folder on the floppy disk itself. The Briefcase then travels with you to the other PC where it will synchronize with the indigenous files. When you return, put the disk back in the desktop PC, access the Briefcase folder, and Briefcase will update the files on the desktop PC. This method allows you to have multiple briefcases. Some users create multiple briefcases, each on a different floppy disk and each dedicated to a different type of file.

Conclusion

Windows 98 includes several features that support mobile computing. From PC Card support to support for the latest in power management technologies, Windows 98 was built with the portable user in mind. This chapter explored some of the Windows 98 portable-computing features. For more information related to portables in Windows 98, see the following chapters:

- Chapter 12, "Supporting Devices," for more information on the types of devices that Windows 98 supports and how to implement them

- Chapter 22, "Peer-to-Peer Networking," for additional help in setting up a Direct Cable Connection

- Chapter 26, "Windows 98 and Remote Communication," to see how to set up a Dial-up Networking Connection so that you can use the Briefcase

Backup and Restore

If you're a systems professional, then you should already know about the importance of good backups of the system and of important data. If you don't know this, then it's probably the most important lesson you can take away from this book: Making regular backups is a requirement when using computers. Period.

Horror stories abound to teach this lesson, and you usually don't have to work with computers (particularly PCs) for very long before you get your own lesson in backups. There's nothing quite like getting a call from someone asking for help and discovering that their data is beyond repair, and then hearing that long silence on the telephone after you ask the question, "When did you make your last backup?" People sometimes lose months of work because of failures to perform regular backups using a good procedure, and sometimes they lose months of *other people's* work, too. The amount of dollars lost in such incidents can be staggering.

There are many reasons that backups fail, including the following:

- Reliance on users to make their own backups in some fashion. This is a recipe for disaster because in any group of users, the ones who will actually do this regularly probably don't exceed 5% of the total.

- Failure to periodically attempt restoration from backups. Situations can arise in which the backup software and hardware seem to be working fine, but in actuality don't contain data that can be restored.

- Failure to log or track backups, or to set up a system so that more than one person keeps an eye on things to ensure that the backups are being properly performed.

- Failure to use adequate tape rotation schemes. Tapes can and do go bad, and they'll inevitably go bad just when you actually need to restore from them, so it's important to have sufficient backup media so that a good rotation scheme can be put into place.

Windows 98 will not often be used to store files for many users, and so the subject of backups is necessarily more limited than it would be for, say, a network file server. However, there are situations in which data must be backed up from a Windows 98 system, and a solid grasp of the different techniques and software you can use with Windows 98 backups is an important topic.

Evaluating Backup Requirements

When evaluating specific backup requirements in a given situation, start by looking at the value of the information—or the cost to replace it—should it be lost. This should be known for different periods of time, as well. For instance, it may be a trivial matter to lose a single day's worth of data because very little data might be accumulated in a day and it might be easily re-entered. But it may be far more than ten times as expensive to lose ten days worth of data, because the source data may be more difficult to retrieve after a period of time, or the productivity impact from rebuilding that data may not be as easily borne. You should think about impacts resulting from losing a day's data, a week's data, a month's data, and three month's data. If it's not a linear curve, then you have to take that into account when you design the backup strategy.

Next, you need to know the amount of data that must be backed up, both infrequently and frequently. For instance, on a system that runs a simple, stable set of applications, it's probably required that you do a complete backup of the entire system (operating system, applications, and data) only every week or every month, whereas you may need to back up the actual data files on a daily basis. You'll need to know the amount of data required for both types of backups in this situation.

As part of calculating the backup size requirements, keep in mind that certain aspects of the system probably don't require backing up if you have the source media. Even in the case of a catastrophic hardware failure, you should have your original operating system and application installation media that you can use to quickly rebuild the system, and your backups may only need to store the actual data files. (However, even when this is the case, it's always a good idea to get a complete system backup at least once in a while as an added measure of security.)

> **Tip** For critical systems, it's a good idea to maintain a "rebuild kit" that contains all the information you would need to rebuild the system from scratch. This kit should be readily available and should be designed to speed the rebuilding of the system (because you invariably need it at 2:00 a.m. because the system is required when people come to work in a few hours). Rebuild kits should contain, at a minimum, an Emergency Boot Disk (EBD) for the system, all of the operating system and application CD-ROMs or disks, the hardware diagnostic and setup programs, and whatever instructions would be necessary to set the system up again should the hard disk or another key component need to be replaced. Additionally, you can keep information in the rebuild kit on service providers, the exact configuration of the system when it was built, the original invoice for any warranty disputes that may arise, and a log book in which all changes to the system are written.

The next thing to evaluate is how much time you have to perform the backup. Some systems may need to be available nearly 24 hours a day, so this can be an important thing to know. Most systems, however, can easily be taken down and made available for backups at night or over weekends. Often, backups can be started as the last person leaves, and let run overnight. Still, make sure you evaluate this.

Finally, evaluate whether there are existing backup systems in place on which you can "piggyback." For example, an individual system may be able to simply copy its data files up to a network file server every night, where it is then backed up by the same large-scale backup system that takes care of the file server itself. Alternately, if an organization is already using a large number of DAT backup devices, then it would be a good idea to stick with that standard unless there is a compelling reason to use a different type of system. Yet another alternative is to install special client software that works with a network backup system to back up individual workstations over a network.

All of the above factors (plus, of course, your budget) should help you to choose appropriate backup hardware, software, and a plan.

Choosing Backup Hardware

Assuming that you must purchase new backup hardware for a system, you will find a number of proven, good choices, depending on your actual needs. When choosing a backup technology, consider the following factors:

- Reliability of the hardware and the media
- Cost of the hardware and the media
- Storage capacity
- Likely frequency of restorations
- Importance of fitting entire backup onto a single piece of media

Table 20.1 reviews different types of backup technologies, their approximate costs, and the relative pros and cons of each. Note that prices of drives, media, and costs per MB in Table 20.1 are approximate.

Table 20.1
Backup Technologies

Name	Est. Cost of Drive	Est. Cost of Media	Media Capacity	Pros and Cons
ZIP	$149	$15	100MB	-Very Small Capacity; +Random Access; Drive: $1.49/MB; Media: $0.15/MB
JAZ	$600	$100	1GB	-Small Capacity; +Random Access; Drive: $0.60/MB; Media: $0.10/MB
Writable CD	$600	$7	600MB	-Small Capacity; -Media not reusable; (write-once); +Random Access; Drive: $0.9375/MB; Media: $0.0109/MB (but can only be used once)
QIC/Travan	$250	$20–40	2–8GB	-Slower than other tapes; +Very low drive cost/MB; Drive: $0.06/MB; Media: $0.075/MB

Name	Est. Cost of Drive	Est. Cost of Media	Media Capacity	Pros and Cons
DAT DDS-1	$600	$15–20	2–4GB	-Low tape capacity; -Higher drive cost/MB than QIC/Travan; +Lower media cost/MB than QIC/Travan; Drive: $0.20/MB; Media: $0.0058/MB
DAT DDS-2	$1000	$20–25	8GB	+Lower tape cost/MB than QIC/Travan or DAT DDS-1; Drive: $0.125/MB; Media: $0.0028/MB
8mm	$1500	$50	5–GB	+Proven technology; -No longer cost-competitive with newer DAT/QIC capacities; -Relatively slow tape seek times for restoration of individual files; Drive: $0.23/MB; Media: $0.007/MB
DLT	$5000–8000	$100	40–80GB	+Very reliable; +Very fast; +Highest per-tape capacities; +Extremely low media cost per MB; Drive: $0.10/MB; Media: $0.00125/MB

Choosing Backup Software

Windows 98 includes a vastly improved backup and restore application called Microsoft Backup (discussed in detail in the later section "Using Microsoft Backup"). Microsoft Backup was developed for Windows 98 by Seagate Software, makers of a more comprehensive backup product called Backup Exec. Obviously, because Microsoft Backup is included for free with Windows 98, you should consider it as a first alternative.

Microsoft Backup may not meet your needs, however. The main limitation is that it is not possible to set up scheduled backups with it that start at a specified time. You must start the backups manually. However, you can pre-select files or directories and load the backup settings from a file, easing this burden somewhat.

If Microsoft Backup doesn't meet your needs, there are many other alternatives, most of them reasonably priced. The first option is to upgrade to Backup Exec from Seagate Software. There are also many other third-party backup software solutions from numerous vendors, such as Norton Backup from Symantec. Most of these programs cost less than $100 and will work with virtually all tape drives. Also, the tape drive that you purchase may come with backup software included for Windows 95 or Windows 98.

Choosing a Backup Rotation Strategy

With all of the preceding information known, you can now plan a backup rotation strategy, which addresses how backup media is rotated. Backup rotations are designed to accomplish the following goals:

- Rebuild the system, with the most recent possible data, in case of a catastrophic failure.

- Restore files from older tapes that may have been accidentally erased or damaged and not quickly noticed.

- Protect against backup media failure.

- Protect the data from an environmental failure, such as a fire, that would destroy the original system and data.

Windows 98 maintains a special bit for each file on the system called the *archive bit*. The archive bit indicates the backup status of the file. When a file is modified, its archive bit is set to "on," indicating that the file should be backed up. When the backup is accomplished, the archive bit is cleared. By using this archive bit and the backup software (Microsoft Backup or others all work the same way in this regard), you can make the following types of backups:

- A *full backup*, where all selected directories and files are backed up, regardless of their archive bit state. Full backups clear the archive bit on all of the backed-up files when the backup is finished.

- An *incremental backup*, where only files with their archive bit set are backed up. This backs up all files changed since the last full or incremental backup. Incremental backups clear the archive bit of the backed-up files; those files will not be backed up during the next incremental backup unless they are modified again and their archive bits set back on.

- A *differential backup*, which is similar to the incremental backup in that it backs up only files with their archive bits set. The key difference in a differential backup is that the archive bits are left on. Subsequent differential backups will back up those same files again, plus any new ones that have been modified

In a perfect world, it would be nice to always perform full backups. If the system were to fail, you would need only the most recent backup tape to fully restore the system. However, there are a number of reasons why it may not be desirable to do a full backup all the time. For one thing, perhaps there is inadequate time to perform a full backup each day. Another reason is to extend the life of your media and tape drive by reducing the amount of work that they must do. This needs to be balanced against the increased time it takes to restore from a combination of full and incremental or differential backups, however, and the increased possibility of being unable to properly restore from a combination approach.

One common way that these types of backups are mixed is to perform a full backup of the system once a week, and only perform incremental or differential backups each day of the week. Examine the following examples:

- Perform a full backup every Friday night, and incremental backups on Monday through Thursday. If the system fails Monday morning before any data is entered, you only need to restore the full backup from the previous Friday night. If, however, the system fails on, say, Thursday morning, you have to sequentially restore four tapes in order to retrieve all of the data: the full backup from the previous Friday, then the incremental tapes from Monday, Tuesday, and Wednesday nights. Moreover, in order to guarantee the integrity of the data, you must be able to restore *all* of those tapes, and in their proper sequence. Otherwise, you run the risk of ending up with mismatched data files. In this scenario, you have four media-based points of failure, which might be more risk than you care for.

- Perform a full backup every Friday night, and differential backups Monday through Thursday. In this scenario, if the system fails Monday morning, you just restore the previous Friday night's tape. However, if the system fails on Thursday morning, you only have to restore two tapes: The last full backup from Friday night, plus the differential backup from Wednesday night. Because differential backups continually back up all changed files since the last full backup, you never need to restore more than two tapes, thereby reducing the number of possible points of media failure

The general rule of thumb is this: Incremental backups generally minimize the amount of time needed to perform each daily backup, but they take longer to restore and you have a greater risk of media failure. Differential backups take longer to make, but reduce the time required to restore and reduce the risk of media failure.

All of this needs to be balanced against the nature of the data, the amount of risk you're willing to take versus the cost of each back up, the capacity of the tapes, and the amount of time in which you must make each regular backup.

The most common backup rotation scheme is called *Grandfather-Father-Son (GFS)*. A common way to implement this scheme is to use at least eight tapes. Four of the tapes are labeled "Monday" through "Thursday." Four more tapes are labeled "Friday 1," "Friday 2," up to "Friday 4." Each day Monday through Thursday you use one of those labeled tapes, replacing the data stored the previous week. Each Friday tape corresponds to which Friday in the month you are on: On the first Friday you use Friday 1, and so forth. Finally, on the last day of each month you prepare a month-end tape, which is not reused, but is instead kept off-site in case an environmental failure destroys the system and all locally stored tapes.

There are three main variations of the GFS scheme. In the first, you simply make a full backup of the system, each and every time you perform a backup. This offers the greatest amount of media redundancy and the minimum amount of restoration time. In the second, you perform a full backup on each of the Friday tapes and the monthly tape, but only perform incremental backups during the week. In the third, you do much the same thing, but use differential backups instead of incremental backups.

> **Tip** If your data is super-critical and not easily reconstructed, you can often perform full backups every night, and also squeeze in a quick incremental backup at lunch time. This way you can't lose more than a half-day's worth of data instead of a full day.

You can also choose simpler rotation schemes instead of GFS. For instance, you may just use two or three tapes, and rotate them in sequence, overwriting the old data each time you do so. This lets you restore to any of the previous three day's data. The shortfall here is that sometimes you may need to go back further in time to restore data that had been erased or damaged without anyone immediately noticing it. You can combat this problem by using several weekend or month-end rotating tapes.

Why Would You Want to Limit the Number of Tapes You Keep?

In these litigious times, it can be advisable to limit the number of backup tapes you keep. If your company were sued, it's possible that all computer files relating to a particular matter could be required to be produced to satisfy a subpoena. If this happens, and you have hundreds of backup tapes going back several years, your company may well have to carefully examine all of the files on each and every backup tape in order to locate all of the required information. You can imagine the nightmare that would ensue! (And you can also bet that the brunt of it would fall onto your shoulders!) You should consult with your company's legal counsel about the advisability of putting into place an "electronic document retention policy" where you make a tradeoff between this risk and the risk of data loss and arrive at some happy compromise. For instance, perhaps you might set up a scheme where you implement GFS as described previously, but destroy all tapes older than one year (or reuse them—it doesn't really matter which). This would limit the number of backups that would need to be searched to 20 tapes (12 monthly tapes, four weekly tapes, and four daily tapes).

One factor to keep in mind when considering different tape rotation schemes is the *granularity* of your backups. Broadly speaking, this is the flexibility you retain to recover data from earlier tapes. In the standard GFS scheme in which full backups are made all the time, you can restore a file from any given day for a week's time, for any given week-ending (Friday) for a month's time, or for any given month for a year's time. You could not, however, restore a file that was created three months ago in the middle of the month and erased (or damaged) before the month was over, because a clean copy wouldn't exist on *any* of the backup tapes.

> **Granularity and Data Corruption: A Tricky Balance**
>
> One reason to carefully consider granularity is the possibility of data becoming corrupt and the situation not being noticed. For instance, this author once worked with a database file that had been corrupted several weeks earlier, but had been continuing to function and seemed normal. As problems developed, however, and we worked to solve the problem, the database vendor's technical support staff discovered that a portion of the database that wasn't regularly used had become lost and wasn't repairable. The only way to recover the database and ensure that it was clean was to restore backups, further and further back in time, until a copy of the database that didn't have the damage was restored, and then re-enter the data that was added since that time. Because of the increasing granularity of backups as we had to go further and further back into time, the amount of data that would need to be re-entered grew almost exponentially.

The best advice you can take for choosing a rotation scheme for important data is this: Unless there are reasons to do otherwise (as already discussed), use the GFS scheme with full backups every time, and destroy tapes older than one year. This maximizes the safety of your data, maximizes your restoration flexibility, minimizes the risk of media failure, and keeps any legal risk to a reasonable minimum. If other factors force you to choose a different scheme, use the discussions in this section to arrive at the best compromise for a given situation.

Tip After arriving at a proposed backup scheme, it's important to discuss the relative merits and capabilities with interested parties in your company's management structure. At a minimum, this will probably include the Controller, CFO, COO, and possible the CEO. There may be other members of upper management, too, who should understand the restoration capabilities you will have going forward. The last thing you want to have happen in case of data loss is having a bunch of people pointing fingers in your direction for having an "inadequate" backup scheme in place.

Using Microsoft Backup

As previously discussed, Windows 98 includes new backup software—an improvement over the backup software included with Windows 95. Called Microsoft Backup, the software is made by Seagate Software, makers of the popular product Backup Exec. Microsoft Backup sports the following features:

- Works with virtually all tape and removable media devices based on ATAPI/IDE and SCSI interfaces

- Can back up to other hard disks, floppy disks, and network shares

- Allows selection of specific files and directories, or entire hard disk partitions; also lets you ignore files based on file specifications

- Supports full, incremental, and differential backups

- Backs up Windows 98 long filenames

- Backs up the Windows Registry

- Can compress and verify backup data

The only real limitation to Microsoft Backup is that it does not support unattended scheduled backups. Instead, backups must be initiated manually.

> **Note** Microsoft Backup is not installed as part of a typical Windows 98 installation. Use the Add/Remove Programs Control Panel to add it to a Windows 98 system.

You start Microsoft Backup by opening the Start menu, Programs, Accessories, System Tools menu. When it begins, you see the screen shown in Figure 20.1.

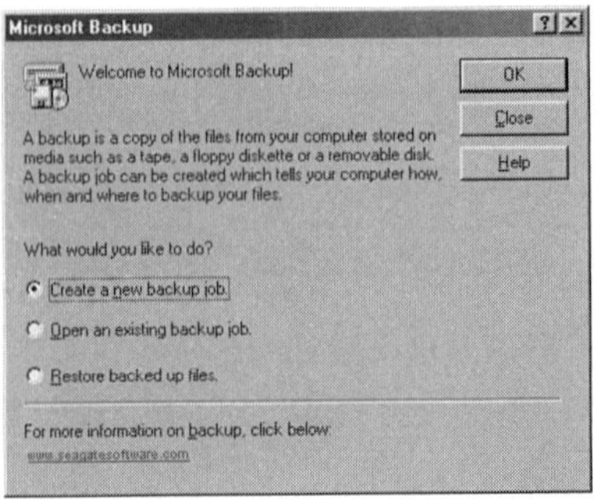

Figure 20.1
Starting Microsoft Backup.

From the opening screen, you can choose to create a new backup, open a previously saved backup, or restore files. Each of these choices starts a wizard that walks you through the requisite steps. Or, to access the entire Microsoft Backup program, you can click the **C**lose button, which brings up the full program from which you can perform any of these functions, shown in Figure 20.2.

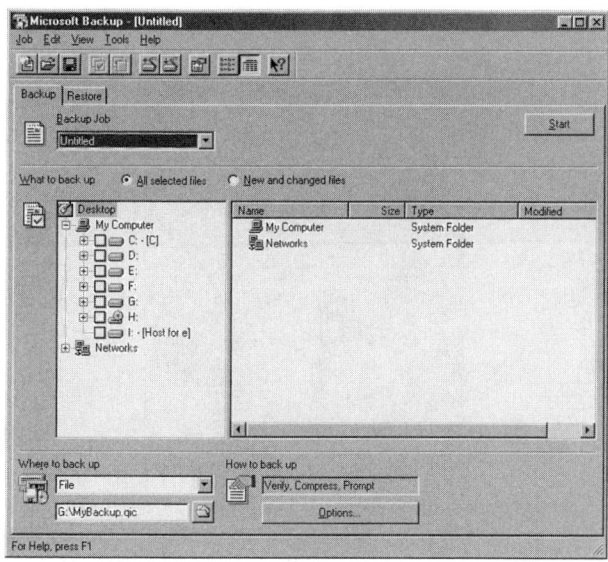

Figure 20.2
Microsoft Backup's main window with the Backup tab selected.

Select either the Backup or Restore tab to perform that respective function. Using the Backup tab, use the left pane to open and select drives and directories. Selected directories display their file contents in the right pane, where you can select individual files. Clicking on a checkbox selects or deselects a directory or file for backup.

You can choose from a variety of backup options with the **O**ptions button, which displays the Backup Job Options dialog box shown in Figure 20.3.

Using the Backup Job Options dialog box, you can choose from the following options:

- On the General tab, you can choose whether to perform a comparison of the backed-up data to the original to confirm that the tape contains valid data. You can also choose whether to compress the data on the backup device, which may increase the amount of data that can be stored, depending on the level of compression in the original files (you should not choose to compress data that is already compressed because this actually increases the amount of space needed in the backup). Finally, you can choose whether backups overwrite earlier data.

- The Password tab lets you establish a password for the backup. The data cannot be restored if the password is not known.

- The Type tab lets you choose between full, incremental, and differential backup types.

- The Exclude tab lets you skip files based on file specifications you can enter.

- The Report tab lets you choose what information is shown in the post-backup report.

- The Advanced tab lets you choose whether to include a copy of the Windows Registry in the backup.

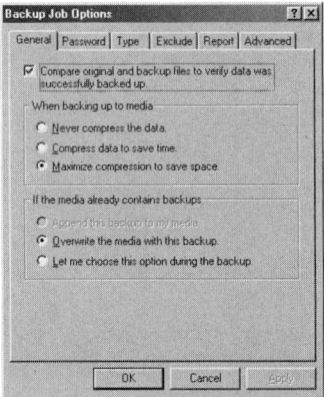

Figure 20.3
Backup Job Options dialog box.

After selecting a set of files and choosing your backup job options, you can estimate the amount of space required for the backup. Pull down the **V**iew menu and choose Selection **I**nformation to see the estimate.

Before running a backup, you should save the backup criteria if you expect to perform similar backups in the future. Use the Save **A**s command in the **F**ile menu to do this.

The Restore tab lets you choose restoration options. Microsoft Backup keeps a catalog of backups you've made. You use these catalogs to restore files or complete backup sets. Figure 20.4 shows the Restore tab.

To restore files, select them using the selection panes just as you do for selecting files to back up. Also, check the Restore Options dialog box by clicking the **O**ptions button, shown in Figure 20.5.

The Restore Options dialog box is simpler than the Backup Options dialog box, and lets you choose from the following options:

- The General tab lets you choose how files should be restored when the file exists in the restore destination.

- The Report tab lets you choose what information is reported after the restoration is complete.

- The Advanced tab lets you choose whether to restore the Windows Registry.

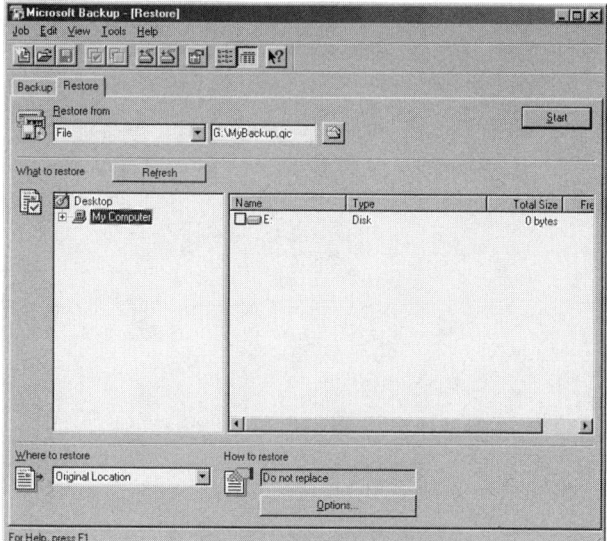

Figure 20.4
Microsoft Backup's Restore tab.

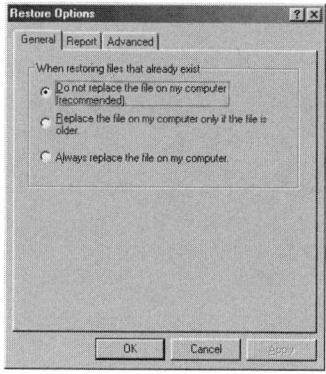

Figure 20.5
Restore Options dialog box.

As you can see, using Microsoft Backup is straightforward. It is a well-designed, reliable backup and restoration program that should meet most common backup software needs.

Conclusion

Performing regular system backups is an important responsibility. The reliability of today's computer hardware (particularly hard disks) often makes this seem like a thankless and useless chore, but having a good backup available will eventually save you many headaches, and possibly save your job if they're your responsibility. In this chapter, you learned about general backup technology, different backup hardware and media choices, different backup software choices, and how to design a good backup program given different needs. You also learned about Microsoft Backup, a good general-purpose backup program that is included with Windows 98.

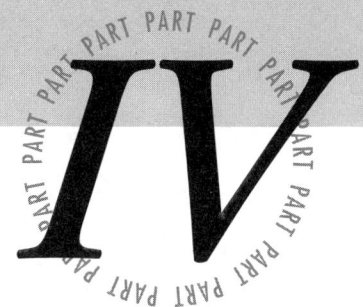

Networking Windows 98

21	Understanding Windows 98 Networking	469
22	Peer-to-Peer Networking	503
23	Windows 98 in Windows NT Domains	517
24	Windows 98 with NetWare/InternetWare Networks	529
25	Windows 98 with TCP/IP	539
26	Windows 98 and Remote Communication	563

Understanding Windows 98 Networking

*T*his chapter provides an in-depth look at the components involved in setting up Windows 98 to participate in a networked environment. To completely understand the concepts presented in this chapter, it is first necessary to look at the networking architecture around which Windows 98 is built. This chapter will discuss network adapters, services, protocols, clients, security, cabling, and other issues that relate to networking Windows 98.

The idea of networking is to enable users to share resources and information. The thought here is that the capability to share will promote the exchange of ideas more quickly and will conserve on the expense of providing costly dedicated resources to each user.

A *network* is probably best defined as two or more devices with the capability to share resources and information. No matter how large or how small the network is, there are certain rules (protocols and standards) that must be followed to ensure that the network works correctly and that it will work with other network components. The most basic of these rules is an outline for communication between two devices that was established by the International Organization for Standardization (ISO). The ISO developed a model called the seven-layer model that specifies seven distinct functions that must occur for a device to communicate with another device. This model is also referred to as the Open Systems Interconnection (OSI) model because it defines these seven layers with respect to the communication process. The OSI model does not follow any individual vendor's established protocols and standards.

The idea behind the OSI model is that any vendor can create a product that will work with a product from any other vendor as long as each vendor followed the guidelines established for each layer of the OSI model. As you can see in Figure 21.1, each of the seven OSI layers defines a distinct function that is separate from the other layers. Each layer is dependent upon the layer below it to provide a certain function and each layer is responsible to provide the layer above it with a certain function. You can also see in Figure 21.1 that the communication process involves using the OSI model from layer 7 down to layer 1 when sending a message, but it uses the OSI model from layer 1 up to layer 7 when receiving a message.

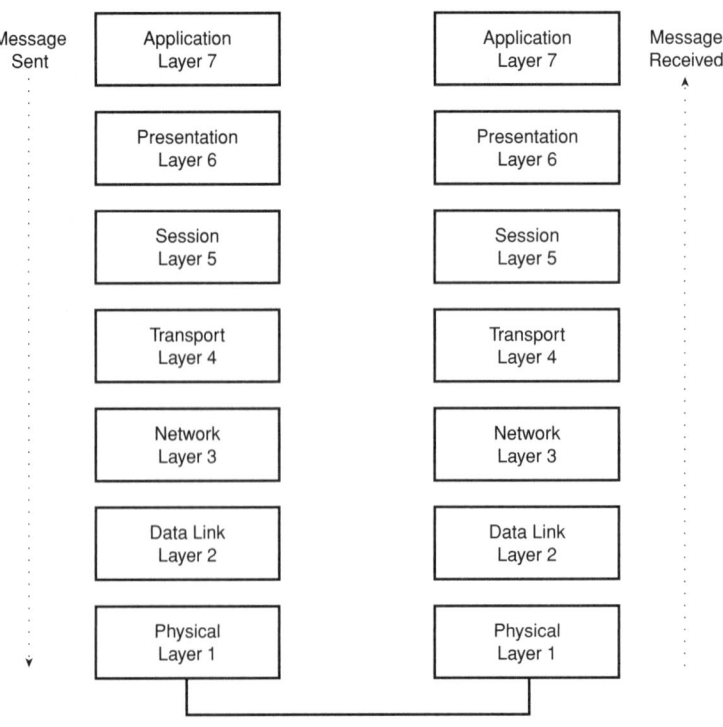

Figure 21.1
Using the ISO OSI Seven-Layer Model to communicate between systems.

Chapter 21: Understanding Windows 98 Networking

For Windows 98 to participate in a network, it must use and implement software and hardware components that follow the design of the OSI model. Windows 98 has an open, modular design called the Network Provider Interface (NPI) that allows support for multiple networks to exist simultaneously. The NPI consists of two components, the Application Program Interface (API) and the Network Provider (NP). The API requests network services, such as connecting to a server or queuing a print job. The NP takes care of providing those services for the API.

Windows 98 has three built-in Network Providers: WinNet16, NetWare, and Windows. The WinNet16 provider is used to provide services for 16-bit APIs. The NetWare provider makes services available to APIs requesting services from a NetWare network. The Windows provider is a 32-bit provider that makes services available for other Windows networks such as Windows NT and Windows 98. Figure 21.2 shows how the APIs and the NPs interface with the rest of the Windows 98 layered architecture.

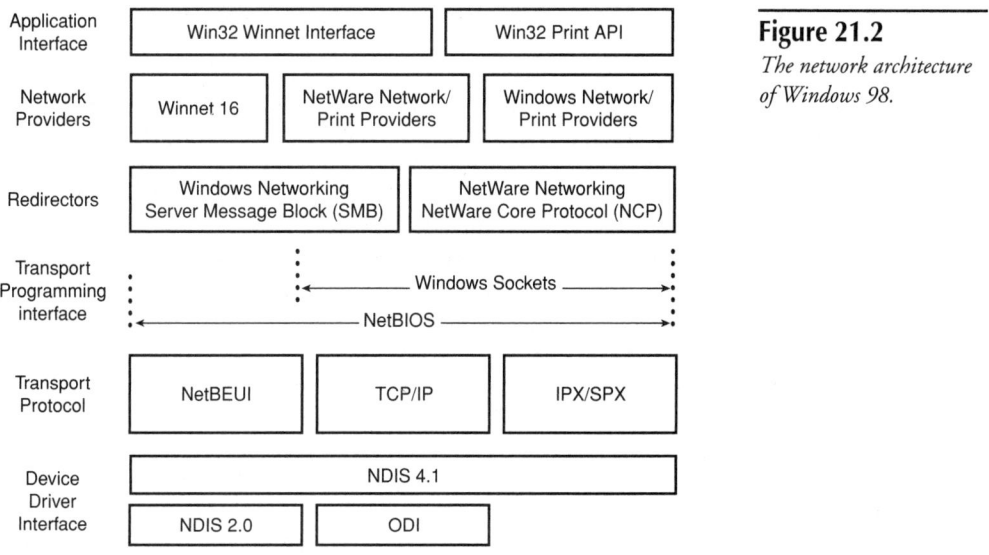

Figure 21.2
The network architecture of Windows 98.

Figure 21.2 also shows some of the additional components that make up the Windows 98 network architecture. Those additional components are the IFS Manager, the redirectors and the transport protocols. The Installable File System (IFS) Manager consists of two components, a set of file system APIs and loadable File System Drivers (FSD). Multiple FSDs can exist in the system at the same time. Using the FSDs, the IFS Manager can provide the capability for multiple types of network redirectors to locate, open, read, write and delete files and services. File systems such as FAT, FAT32, VFAT, and CDFS are all supported. The IFS interfaces have been documented so that different vendors of network services will have this information when designing and implementing their redirectors for Windows 98.

The redirectors included with Windows 98 are the Server Message Block (SMB) redirector and the NetWare Core Protocol (NCP) redirector. The SMB redirector component (VREDIR.VXD) that is included as a part of the Client for Microsoft Networks supports all of the networks based on Microsoft networking. It is a 32-bit virtual device driver with a zero conventional memory footprint that can be dynamically loaded by the system as needed. The NCP redirector component (NWREDIR.VXD) that is included as a part of the Client for NetWare Networks supports all of the networks based on NetWare networking. It is also a 32-bit virtual device driver. Windows 98 also supports redirectors from other vendors. In addition, Windows 98 can also support multiple 32-bit redirectors and one WinNet16 redirector simultaneously.

The most important transport protocols included with Windows 98 are NetBEUI, TCP/IP and IPX/SPX. These are examined in greater detail in the Network Protocols section later in this chapter, but a quick explanation of each of them is presented here. It should also be noted that while these three transport protocols are the primary ones included with Windows 98, also included are an ATM protocol, a Fast Infrared Protocol, a protocol for Banyan networks and DLC support for network printing.

While NetBEUI supports Microsoft networking and can be used with Windows NT, Windows for Workgroups, LAN Manager, and some other products. NetBEUI, which stands for NetBIOS Extended User Interface is a non-routable protocol. Simply stated, the NetBEUI protocol does not keep track of information that applies to layer 3 of the OSI model, the Network layer. Consequently, NetBEUI is intended for use only on internal networks that do not need to be routed because NetBEUI cannot determine which network it is on. Because NetBEUI does not have to keep track of this extra information, it tends to be a leaner protocol that can be used in fast, high-performance fashion. Some networks are set up to use NetBEUI as the default protocol so that communication on the internal network is very quick while having TCP/IP or IPX/SPX as the secondary protocol for communication outside of the network.

TCP/IP or Transmission Control Protocol/Internet Protocol is the protocol of choice for today's large, robust, interconnected networks. It is also the protocol required for communication across the Internet. The TCP/IP protocol consists of a suite of complementary protocols of which the primary two are the TCP and the IP. IP is a layer 3 protocol (the network layer of the OSI model) which keeps track of the network information. Each device using the TCP/IP protocol is assigned an IP address in the format of xxx.xxx.xxx.xxx where each series of xxx represents a binary number from 0 to 255. Some portion of that IP address is used to determine the network address and the remainder is used to identify the host address. See Chapter 25, "Windows 98 with TCP/IP," for more on TCP/IP addressing.

The TCP portion of TCP/IP is a layer 4 (the transport layer of the OSI model) protocol that is used to establish connections for applications. The TCP/IP suite contains two different transport layer protocols: the TCP (a connection-oriented, reliable protocol) and the User Datagram Protocol (UDP—a connectionless protocol typically used for messaging functions and other processes not requiring a connection). Above layer 4, the TCP/IP suite consists of a number of other protocols including File Transfer Protocol (FTP), Simple Network Management Protocol (SNMP) and Domain Name System (DNS). Although this description of the TCP/IP suite of protocols attempts to neatly map TCP/IP to the layers of the OSI model, TCP/IP predates the OSI model and does not strictly conform to the design of the OSI model.

Internetwork Packet eXchange/Sequential Packet eXchange (IPX/SPX) is the default protocol designed to be fully compatible with Novell's IPX/SPX implementation. IPX/SPX can be used to communicate directly with a Novell NetWare server or with other computers running IPX/SPX such as a Windows 98 or a Windows NT machine. IPX/SPX is a routable protocol that can be used across bridges and routers that support IPX/SPX. IPX/SPX is required when the Client for NetWare Networks is installed, and is installed automatically.

Note On Windows NT 4.0 machines, the IPX/SPX implementation is referred to as NWLink.

To successfully use Windows 98 on a network, you must have selected and installed the appropriate client software for the network you will be using. In addition, you will have to identify and install the appropriate transport protocol. As you can see from Figure 21.1, you will still need a component that operates at the physical layer for the communication process to work between your devices. One of the components that you will need at this physical layer is a network adapter.

Network Adapters

There are four items that can be installed from the Network Properties dialog box in Windows 98. They are Clients, Adapters, Protocols, and Services. This section will focus on the installation, use, and configuration of network adapters within Windows 98. A *network adapter card*, also referred to as a *Network Interface Card (NIC)*, is a physical component that is plugged into the motherboard of the computer. There are also some external NICs that can be connected via a parallel port and there are NICs that are PC Cards for use in portable computers, but most commonly they are used inside the PC. Once you have installed the network adapter, you will have to configure Windows 98 to use it.

If a network adapter is Plug-and-Play (PnP) compliant, Windows 98 will install it without much user intervention. Otherwise, you'll need to use the manual method, which can be tedious. To install a NIC using Plug and Play requires three things:

- A Plug-and-Play–compliant operating system. Windows 98 is fully Plug-and-Play compliant.

- A Plug-and-Play–compliant computer. Basically, the BIOS of the machine must be able to recognize and configure Plug-and-Play devices.

- A Plug-and-Play–compliant device. In this case, the Network Interface Card must be a Plug-and-Play–compliant adapter.

If your components meet the requirements, then you should be able to follow the onscreen instructions presented by Windows 98 to install your adapter. The steps involved usually follow this pattern:

1. Shut down Windows 98 and turn off the PC. Install the Plug-and-Play adapter in a spare slot in your PC according to the manufacturer's directions. Make sure you install the card into the correct type of slot if your PC has more than one type of slot.

2. Once you have installed the adapter in the PC per the manufacturer's instructions, put the PC back together and turn on the PC. When the PC boots up, the Plug-and-Play BIOS should see the new component and configure it automatically for your system with the settings that the new card requires.

3. When Windows 98 loads, it should also recognize the new component and prompt you to provide a driver for the new device. The Add New Hardware Wizard will prompt you through a series of dialog boxes that will ask you for the locations you would like to search for the most updated driver for the device. Figure 21.3 shows an example of one of the dialog boxes you may be presented with.

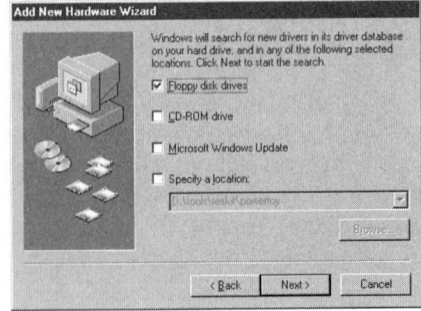

Figure 21.3
The Add New Hardware Wizard automatically runs when a new Plug-and-Play component is detected in the system. Here a new Network Adapter is being installed and configured.

4. Once Windows 98 has enough information to install the driver for the new adapter, files will be copied for the driver and other required networking components. You may need to have your Windows 98 files available for some of the information that is copied.

Note There are many operations that take place in configuring Windows 98 that require the use of the Windows 98 program files. Adding a network adapter is just one of those operations. You can make this operation easier and faster by

Chapter 21: Understanding Windows 98 Networking

> storing a copy of the Windows 98 cabinet files (files that have a .CAB extension) on the hard drive of your Windows 98 machine. When you need the files for a new component, as indicated in step 4, you will already have them available.

5. When Windows 98 has copied all the files it needs, it will finish setting up the device and you will be able to use it.

To install a non-PnP adapter in your system can be somewhat tedious because it involves manually configuring the adapter to work in your system. Non-PnP adapters (sometimes referred to as *legacy adapters*) require the installer to configure the adapter either through some type of jumper or dip switch on the card itself or through a proprietary software program that can configure the card. Depending upon the card, you may be required to configure the interrupt, I/O address, ROM address, DMA, or some other type of setting. To find out what settings are required and/or available, you will need to use the manufacturer's instructions for the card.

Once you have installed the card and configured the settings, Windows 98 may or may not recognize the card. If Windows 98 does recognize the card, you will be able to follow onscreen instructions similar to those for a PnP adapter. If Windows 98 is not able to recognize the card or automatically detect the card's resource requirements, you will have to manually install and/or configure the card using the Network Properties dialog box or the System Device Manager. To use the Network Properties dialog box to add and configure a network adapter:

1. If you have not already tried to add the card using the Add New Hardware option in Control Panel, you should do that first. If the Add New Hardware Wizard is not successful, proceed with step 2.

2. In the Control Panel, double-click Network.

3. Figure 21.4 shows an example of the Network properties dialog box. You will need to click the Add button to add an adapter.

4. From the new dialog box, double-click Adapter or single-click Adapter to highlight it and then click the Add button.

5. From the Select Network Adapters dialog box shown in Figure 21.5, you will need to select the manufacturer of the adapter in the left pane and the model of the Network Adapter in the right pane. If you have a disk provided by the manufacturer for the network adapter, click the Have Disk button and follow the instructions presented by Windows 98.

Figure 21.4

*The Network properties dialog box. Use the **A**dd button to add a new adapter, client, service, or protocol.*

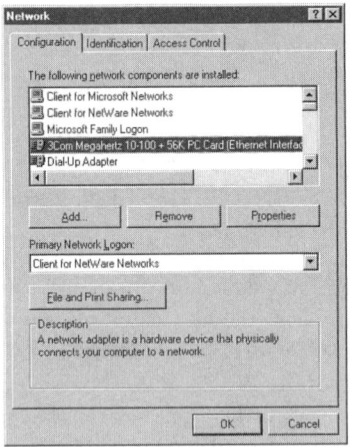

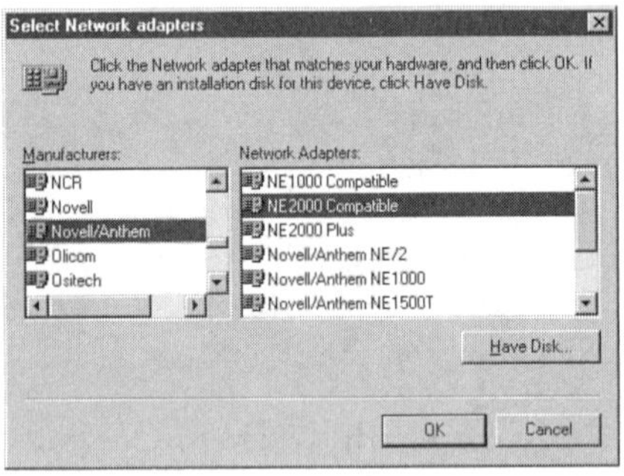

Figure 21.5

*Using the Select Network Adapters dialog box to identify the manufacturer and model of the new adapter. Click **H**ave Disk if the manufacturer has provided a driver disk.*

6. After you have selected the appropriate adapter, click OK and then Windows 98 will copy files to install and configure the adapter.

7. After the file copy is complete, you will be able to select the adapter in the Network properties dialog box and click the Properties button to examine the configuration of the adapter you have added. This should open a dialog box similar to the one shown in Figure 21.6.

8. If the properties dialog box for this new adapter does not show a Resources tab, then you will not be able to configure the adapter from here. You will have to use the System - Device Manager in the Control Panel. To make changes to the settings for this adapter, select the resources tab. The default resources for this adapter may or may not be in conflict with other components in the machine. Figure 21.6 shows an example of a newly installed adapter whose default resources are in conflict with another device in the PC.

9. Using the provided list boxes, set the parameters for your adapter to match the parameters you set the card to when you installed it. Then click the OK button.

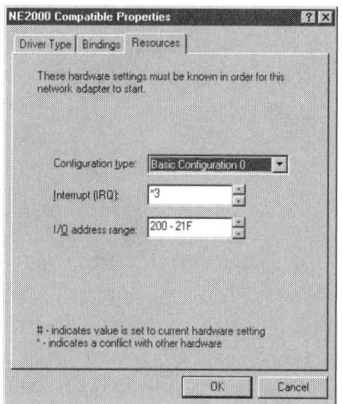

Figure 21.6
The Resources tab for a newly installed network adapter. Notice that one of the default settings is in conflict with another device in the PC.

10. Click the OK button on the Network properties dialog box and Windows 98 will copy any additional files if necessary and then prompt you to restart your PC. If you have configured everything correctly, your network adapter will be functioning correctly when Windows 98 restarts.

Once your network adapter has been installed, there are very few modifications, if any, that will need to be made to it. If you examine the properties of the adapter, you will notice that most adapters have a tab for Driver Type and a tab for Bindings. The Driver Type tab allows you to select either a 32-bit or 16-bit driver for the card. Most new cards will only allow you to select the 32-bit driver. The Bindings tab will give you the ability to determine which protocols will be bound to this adapter. Binding the protocol to the adapter allows the adapter to use that protocol. For example, if you want to use TCP/IP on your network adapter, then TCP/IP will have to be bound to the adapter by checking the box for TCP/IP on the Bindings tab. Figure 21.7 provides an example of some of the available protocols being bound to an adapter. In order to bind a protocol to the adapter, the protocol must have already been installed.

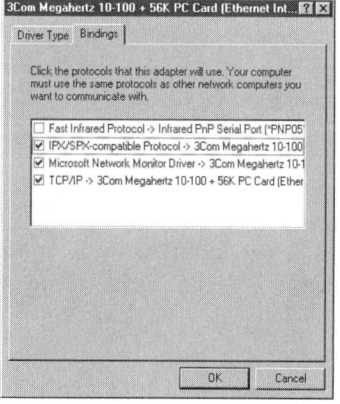

Figure 21.7
Binding protocols to an adapter. A checked box indicates that the protocol will be available for use by that adapter.

The network adapter is just one of the four network items that can be installed in Windows 98. Being able to share the resources over the network is also crucial to setting up Windows 98 networking. File and Printer sharing is just one of the network services available in Windows 98.

Network Services

One of the primary reasons to set up a network is to enable users to share resources and information. To enable this functionality within Windows 98, you must install a network service that provides the capability to share files and printers. The two primary network services available in Windows 98 are the File and Printer Sharing for Microsoft Networks service and the File and Printer Sharing for NetWare Networks service. One of the services that was not originally available with Windows 95 but has been added in Windows 98 is the Service for NetWare Directory Services.

To add a service to Windows 98 you will need to access the Network properties from the Control Panel or use the shortcut described earlier in this chapter. Then proceed as follows:

1. Click the Add button on the Network properties dialog box.

2. From the Select Network Component Type dialog box, select Service and then click Add. You can also just double-click Service.

3. From the Select Network Service window, you will need to select the Manufacturer in the left-hand pane and the Network Service in the right-hand pane. Figure 21.8 illustrates an example of selecting the File and Printer Sharing for Microsoft Networks.

Figure 21.8
Adding a Network Service to the Network Properties.

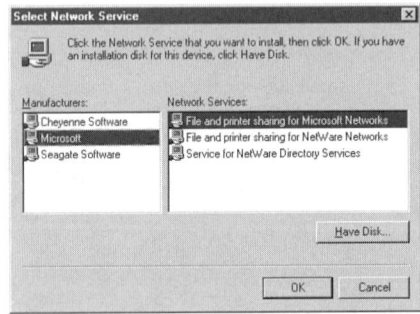

4. Click the OK button to add the service.

5. Once you are back at the Network properties dialog box, you can select the service in the Network Component list box and then click the Properties button to examine and configure any properties this service might have. Some services do not have any properties that are configurable from this dialog box.

Some of the other available services within Windows 98 include agents for Cheyenne Software's ARCserve, Seagate Software's Backup Exec and the Microsoft Network Monitor.

There is also a service that can be installed that allows Remote Registry Editing on Windows 98 machines. Some of these services must be installed using the Add/Remove Programs in the Control Panel.

> **Note** The File and Print sharing button in the Network Properties dialog box (refer to Figure 21.4) lets you enable or disable file sharing and printer sharing. Click on the File and Print sharing button and make sure the appropriate boxes are checked if you wish to share files or printers.

The only way that the adapters and services will be able to communicate on the network is if the Windows 98 machine has been configured with the appropriate transport protocol. The three primary transport protocols included were discussed very briefly in the first part of this chapter, but the closer look provided in the next section will give you a better understanding of how to install and configure them.

Network Protocols

Whether you choose to implement NetBEUI, TCP/IP or IPX/SPX, or a combination of them, this section will explain how to install them and configure the options available with each one. The installation process for each of these protocols is the same so it will be covered only once. The configuration options for each protocol differ greatly though so they will be covered separately. To install a network protocol:

1. As with the Network adapters and services mentioned earlier, you must get to the Network properties dialog box and click the Add button.

2. Select Protocol from the list of Network Component Types and then click the Add button.

3. From the next dialog box, select the manufacturer and the protocol you wish to install and then click the OK button.

4. Now you will be able to configure the protocol you have added from the Network properties dialog box by selecting the protocol and then clicking the Properties button.

Each of the installable protocols within Windows 98 has different configuration options. The first of these protocols in the NetBEUI protocol. As you can see in Figure 21.9 there may be more than one instance of the NetBEUI protocol depending upon the number of adapters you have installed and, more importantly, the number of adapters you have the protocol bound to. Here are the options available with the NetBEUI protocol.

The Properties for the NetBEUI protocol are relatively simple. There are two tabs, one for the Bindings and one for the Advanced options. The Bindings tab allows you to configure which Clients and Services will use this protocol as their transport protocol. To improve the speed of your Windows 98 machine, you should select only the Clients and Services that require the use of the NetBEUI protocol. See the example in Figure 21.10.

Figure 21.9
Multiple instances of the same protocol in the Windows 98 Network properties dialog box.

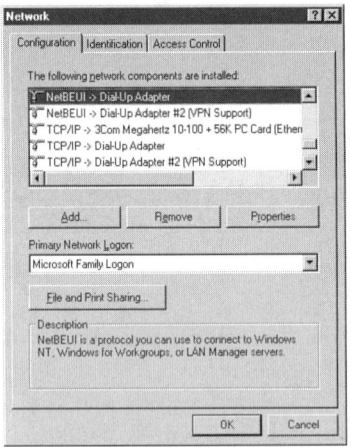

Figure 21.10
The Bindings tab of the NetBEUI protocol. Only select the clients and services that are necessary.

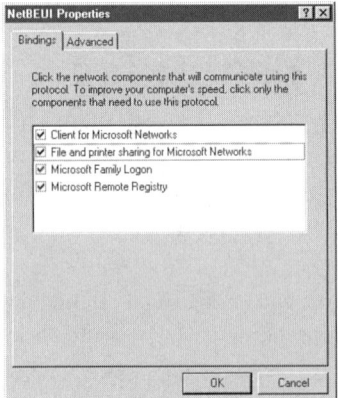

The Advanced tab of the NetBEUI protocol is used to modify the settings for Maximum Sessions and NCBS. Maximum Sessions specifies the number of connections to remote computers that can be made from this redirector. Network Control BlockS (NCBS) is used to identify the number of NetBIOS commands that can be used. These parameters do not normally need to be altered.

The TCP/IP Properties usually have seven tabs to configure. In addition to the Bindings and Advanced tabs that the NetBEUI protocol has, the TCP/IP properties will also have tabs for DNS Configuration, Gateway, WINS Configuration, IP Address, and NetBIOS. The NetBIOS tab will allow you to select the option to support NetBIOS applications on the TCP/IP protocol. NetBIOS is also required to resolve NetBEUI names over TCP/IP.

The IP Address tab and the Gateway tab are used to tell Windows 98 about your network configuration. The two options available on the IP Address tab are automatic configuration of the IP Address or manual configuration. If your network has a server running the Dynamic Host Configuration Protocol (DHCP), then you may not have to fill out anything on the IP

Chapter 21: Understanding Windows 98 Networking

Address tab other than selecting the radio button for obtaining an IP Address automatically. On the other hand, if you will be setting this information up manually, select the other radio button for specifying the IP Address and fill in the station's IP Address and Subnet mask. Remember that the IP Address must be a unique number for this station and you will also need to put in the IP address of the preferred router that will allow you access outside your network. That router address is referred to as the Gateway address and should be added on the Gateway tab. See Chapter 25 for more on configuring TCP/IP.

To configure the IPX/SPX protocol, you will normally have to evaluate the settings on the Bindings, Advanced and NetBIOS tabs. The Bindings tab for the IPX/SPX protocol is essentially the same as the Bindings tab for the other two protocols. You will need to choose which clients and services you would like to use this protocol. To improve performance, be sure to check only the ones you need. The Advanced tab may have several different parameters that you can set. Most of the default values will not need to be changed. Here are the common properties and values for the IPX/SPX Advanced tab:

- Force even-length IPX packets. Used only in monolithic implementations that cannot handle odd-length packets.

- Frame type. Allows you to force a particular frame type to be used. Windows 98 will, at boot time, send out a RIP request that allows it to evaluate the most commonly used frame type on the network. Windows 98 will make that frame type the default. If you should need to override this or force a particular frame type, you should set that here.

- Maximum connections. This is one of the values that Windows 98 configures dynamically. It determines the amount of connections that IPX will allow.

- Maximum sockets. Windows 98 also configures this value dynamically. This value specifies the number of IPX sockets that are assigned.

- Network address. Again, Windows 98 configures this value dynamically. This sets the IPX network address.

- Source routing. This value is used to specify a cache size when using source routing. This value is not needed unless you are using a token-ring network.

The last tab for the IPX/SPX protocol is the NetBIOS tab. If you want to allow NetBIOS to be used over IPX, then select the check box for I want to **e**nable NetBIOS over IPX/SPX. Doing so will allow applications that require this feature to be able to operate with this machine over the network. It is not uncommon to be running applications that require this feature; Lotus Notes is just one example of an application that does require it.

The fourth item that must be installed in the Network properties dialog box is a network client.

Network Clients

To be able to successfully use the network you must have your Windows 98 machine set up as a client of the network. When you are installing and setting up a network client, you will have to choose which client or clients you require and configure them appropriately. The most prevalent clients for Windows 98 are the Client for Microsoft Networks and the Client for NetWare Networks. A new client called the Microsoft Family Logon has been added in Windows 98.

To add a client to the Network properties dialog box, click the **A**dd button and then find Client in the list of components. You can either double-click Client or select Client and then click Add. From the Select Network Client dialog box you will need to select the Manufacturer and then the appropriate Network Client. Once you have selected the correct options, click the OK button to add the client to the list of installed components in the Network properties dialog box.

To modify a network client's properties, select the appropriate network client in the Network properties dialog box and then click P**r**operties. You can also double-click the client to edit its properties. If you are going to modify the properties of one of the primary clients included with Windows 98 then you will have different options to configure for each one. The Microsoft Family Logon does not have any editable properties. The Client for Microsoft Networks does have two options that you can set. You can see in Figure 21.11 that there are two sections to the Client for Microsoft Networks properties dialog box: the Logon Validation settings and the settings for Network Logon Options. Let's look at the Logon Validation settings first.

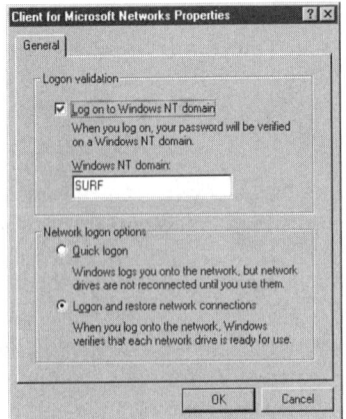

Figure 21.11
Editing the Client for Microsoft Networks properties.

The first item in the Logon Validation settings is the Log on to Windows NT Domain checkbox. If you decide to set this workstation up to log on to a Windows NT domain, you will have the capability to set additional security options for this workstation. A Windows NT domain provides a secure database of user accounts and security settings. If you have created or will be creating a user account in a Windows NT Domain and you want to take advantage of these additional security options, then you should click once inside the checkbox for Log on to Windows NT Domain. This will place a check in the box selecting that option and you will also need to fill in the Windows NT Domain box with the name of the domain in which the user accounts are stored. The Windows NT Domain box can contain the name of a Windows NT or a LAN Manager domain or the name of a Windows NT computer (version 3.1 or later) where the valid user account will exist.

The next area on the Client for Microsoft Network Properties box is the Network Logon Options (refer to Figure 21.11). There are only two possible settings in this area so selecting one of them will automatically deselect the other. The choice you will have to make depends on how quickly you want Windows 98 to start up. For the fastest startup, you should select the top option of Quick Logon. Quick Logon will not attempt to reconnect the network drive connections you have previously established. The drive letters for these network connections will still appear in your drive listings, but the connection to the resource will not be established until you attempt to use that drive.

On the other hand, if you want to make sure that all of your network drive connections are reestablished as Windows 98 starts, then you should select the lower option of Logon and Restore Network Connections.

One of the ways to make sure that commonly used resources are easily available is to set up a drive mapping to that resource. Drive mappings assign a drive letter to a network resource, such as a folder on another computer on the network. For example, drive J: might be mapped to a folder (directory) called DATA that is located on another computer. Another way to view this is to look at the J: drive mapping as though it were a pointer to a network resource. Instead of having to search for that resource every time you need it, you can click on drive J: and it will "point to" the resource. Now when you need the DATA you can open drive J: and have access to it rather than having to search the Network Neighborhood for it again. If you select the first option of Quick Logon, then when you start Windows 98, your network connections will not be reconnected. You will still have a drive letter J:, but the connection to the other machine will not have been established yet. When you go to select drive J: the connection will be established at that point and it may take a few seconds to set the connection up and have the window open that displays the contents of the resource that J: is pointing to.

If you select the other option, Logon and Restore Network Connections, then Windows 98 will try to establish all of your drive connections as the machine boots up. Depending upon the number of drive mappings you have established, this can slow down your startup time by anywhere from a few seconds to several seconds. The option you select will depend on your preferences.

The Client for NetWare Networks can also be configured with different options. To examine and configure the available options for the Client for NetWare Networks, make sure the network client is installed and then select the client and click the Properties button. Figure 21.12 shows an example of the Client for NetWare Networks properties.

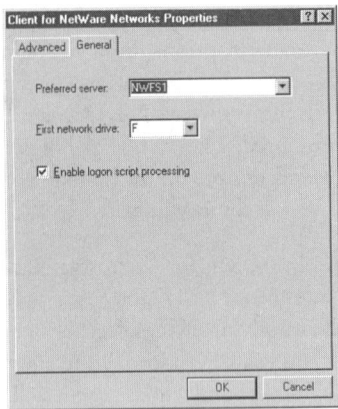

Figure 21.12
Configuring the Client for NetWare Networks properties dialog box.

As you can see from Figure 21.12, there will normally be at least two tabs of Properties to configure. The General tab has three configurable options that let you define the NetWare environment for this machine. The first option, Preferred Server, lets you decide with which NetWare server you will authenticate the logon name and password. The second option, First Network Drive, allows you to determine the drive letter to start with when setting up network drive connections. This normally defaults to drive F: for NetWare networks. The last option is a checkbox that you can select to enable NetWare login scripts to be processed as part of the login procedure. If you do not want the login scripts to be executed when you log in, then deselect the checkbox.

For you to be able to log in to the NetWare server of your choice and Windows 98 at the same time, you must also check to make sure that the Primary Network Logon has been configured to reflect Client for NetWare Networks. To check this, look at the Network Properties window in the section "Primary Network Logon."

You may also want to consider using the IntraNetWare Client for Windows 95 from Novell. The Novell client has been designed by Novell for access to Novell networks and servers and has some capabilities that the Microsoft client does not have. (Many believe, however, that Microsoft's Client for NetWare Networks is faster and more stable than Novell's equivalent—see Chapter 24, "Windows 98 with NetWare/InternetWare Networks".)

Here are some of the notable exceptions for each client:

- The Microsoft client will not allow you to run the Novell utilities, Novell Application Launcher, Novell IP Gateway and others. You should use the Novell client you will need to have access to these utilities.

- If you want to use the Microsoft network management tools to manage Windows 98, you should use the Microsoft client.

- If you want to use NetWare IP, you will need to use the Novell client. The Microsoft client does not support NetWare IP.

- There are many NLM (NetWare Loadable Module) products that require a native IPX/SPX protocol and will not work with the Microsoft "compatible" protocol.

- If you want to use the advanced security features available with the NetWare NCP packet signature then you will need to use the Novell client.

Figure 21.13 illustrates some of the available configuration options with the Novell client. Editing the properties for the Novell client is done in the same way as the Microsoft client. Simply select the client from the list in Network properties dialog box and then double-click it or click the Properties button.

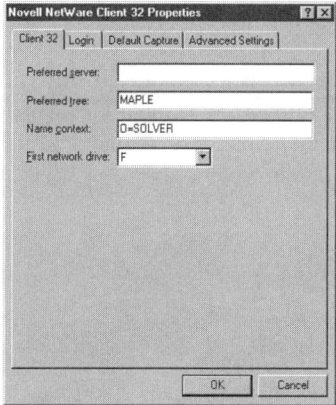

Figure 21.13

Configuring the Novell IntraNetWare Client for Windows 95.

One of the programs installed with the IntraNetWare Client is Novell Login. The Novell Login program can be run from the Start menu and allows you to configure your login for either a Novell 3.X server, a Novell 4.X NDS Tree, or a Novell 4.X server running bindery emulation.

The other client included with Windows 98 is the Microsoft Family Logon. If you have enabled user profiles on your Windows 98 system and configured the Microsoft Family Logon, then the Microsoft Family Logon will present a list of available users at boot time. This will allow users to select their name from the list and type in their password rather than having to type in their name and password.

Cabling

Using the previously mentioned network components, you will be able to configure your Windows 98 machine to participate on a network. However, there is still one component that must be set up correctly for the complete communication process to take place as is pictured back in Figure 21.1. That other component is the network cable or media.

There are many different types of network media that can be used and each one has advantages and disadvantages. Each type of media is typically associated with a particular standard. For example, if you intend to set up a 10Base-T network, you would be using Unshielded Twisted Pair (UTP) wiring. The two most common forms of media that are used in networks today are Unshielded Twisted Pair (UTP) cable and thin Coaxial cable (Coax). UTP, as previously mentioned, is normally used for a 10Base-T network whereas thin coaxial is normally used for a 10Base-2 network. Some other standards you might hear mentioned are 10Base-5, which is also referred to as Thick Ethernet (because it uses a thick coaxial cable) and Token Ring (which can be set up using coaxial or UTP cable). Some networks might be connected using other forms of media such as fiber-optic cables or a wireless media such as infrared or microwave. This section examines the pros and cons of UTP and thin Coax and describes some of the limitations and configuration requirements of each.

Unshielded Twisted Pair (UTP) cable is a four-pair wire that is usually made up of eight 24-gauge, individual copper strands coated with a thin, colored PVC coating. Each of the individual wires has a corresponding partner wire that it is twisted around and those two partner wires make up one pair. Figure 21.14 shows an example of UTP cable.

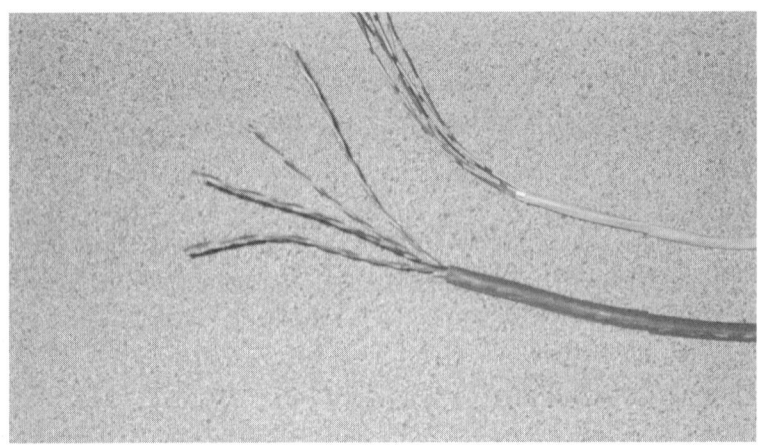

Figure 21.14
Category 3 Unshielded Twisted Pair (UTP) cable.

To set up a network using UTP as the cabling method requires only four individual wires (two pair) but the 4-pair wire is typically what is recommended and used. There are different categories of UTP wire depending upon the characteristics of the cable. For example, you can use Category 3 UTP cable to set up a network that transmits information at speeds of up to 10 million bits per second, but you would most likely want to use Category 5 UTP cable if you were going to set up a network capable of speeds up to 100 million bits per second. There are other Categories of UTP cable such as Categories 1, 2, 3, 4 and even 6, but the most common implementations for today's networks are Category 3 or 5. Typically, the higher the category number, the better the cable is at carrying the network signal and resisting outside interference.

Chapter 21: Understanding Windows 98 Networking

Once you have decided whether to use Category 3 or Category 5 cable, you will need to determine how many computers will need to be connected to the network. Each computer that will be connected to the network will have to have a cable that runs from the computer back to a central connecting point commonly called a hub. These cable runs are also known as home-runs because each computer has to be connected back to the home base or hub. These cable runs should not exceed 100 meters per the standards published by the Institute of Electrical and Electronics Engineers (IEEE). You will also need to have a hub with enough ports to connect all of your computers.

This design layout is often referred to as a star topology. A topology is the layout of the network. There are three distinct types of topologies that can be used: star, bus, and ring. Another form of topology, the hybrid, simply combines two or more of the standard types to form a hybrid topology. The most common are the star, which is normally implemented with UTP cable, and the bus, which is normally implemented with coaxial cable.

Each of these cable runs must have a connector on each end that allows the media to be connected to the device. With UTP cable, the most common connector is an eight-position modular plug sometimes referred to as a RJ-45 connector. Where each individual wire fits into the connector is determined by the wiring standard that you choose to follow. Some of the more commonly used wiring standards are 568A, 568B and 10BASE-T. The Electronics Industries Association (EIA) publishes the 568 standards and the 10BASE-T standard is highlighted in the IEEE standards. The cable that is used to connect the computer to the hub should use the same wiring standard on both ends of the cable.

The only other thing required to cable the computers together is to plug them in at each end. One end connects to the RJ-45 port on the Network Adapter and the other end plugs into one of the available ports on the hub. Make sure you do not plug one of the computers into a port on the hub labeled "uplink." Uplink ports are configured with the pairs reversed so that they can be used to connect to another hub rather than a computer. After ensuring that the hub has power and the computers are connected to it, you should be ready to share files and information over your new network.

While this is a very simplified overview of the steps necessary to establish a UTP network, it still provides a general idea of what must be accomplished. It is recommended that you review the manufacturer's instructions for the network adapters and the hub when setting up your network. You may also want to consider purchasing pre-made UTP cable if you are not experienced at making your own.

> **Note** Another good reference book for information about networks is *Networking Essentials Training Guide*, published by New Riders.

The other common type of cable used to create a local area network (LAN) is thin coaxial cable. Thin coaxial cable is often referred to as Thinnet, Cheapernet, and 10BASE-2. This is because it is thinner and cheaper than thick coaxial cable and because it is used to set up a network that complies with the 10BASE-2 standard published by the IEEE. Thinnet is usually marked with a stamp that identifies it as RG58/U which is just one of many grades of coaxial cable. It is important to use this grade so that the characteristics of the cable match the design of the adapters and devices that will connect to the cable. Figure 21.15 has an example of Thinnet cable.

Figure 21.15
RG58/U Thinnet coaxial cable.

To set up a network using Thinnet, you will have to have a splice in the cable at every point where a computer will attach. Unlike UTP, which has a separate cable run to each computer, Thinnet relies on one cable that connects to all of the computers. This connection layout is referred to as a bus topology. Everywhere there is a splice in the cable you will have to use a connector to attach the cable to the computer and then back to the other side of the cable run. The connectors that are used for coaxial cable are called BNC connectors, barrel connectors or, sometimes, British Naval Connectors. The connector that is used to splice the cable and add a connection for the computer is called a "T" connector. It is called that because it resembles the letter T in its shape with three connections that can be made to it. One of the female sides of a T-connector will be attached to one end of the coaxial cable run, the male side will be connected to the network adapter in the computer, and the other female side will be attached to the continuing cable run. A bus topology must be terminated at each end to prevent signals from bouncing and interfering with the network traffic. Thinnet segments must be terminated with a 50-ohm resisting terminator and this usually resembles a small cap that fits on the trailing end of a T-connector when there is no additional cable to run. Thinnet segments should also be grounded at one end using a grounding clip on the terminator. A Thinnet segment should not extend beyond 185 meters nor should it have more than 30 devices connected to a segment. There should be a minimum of 0.5 meters between T-connectors.

Once again, this is a very simplified overview of the steps involved in setting up your Windows 98 network using Thinnet cable. You will want to follow the manufacturer's instructions for the network adapters in addition to having some additional information about setting up a

Thinnet network. If you do not have the proper tools and experience with making your own Thinnet cables, it is highly recommended that you purchase pre-made cables. Now let's review some of the limitations:

- A UTP network requires more cable because each computer must have its own cable that runs back to the hub. These runs cannot be longer than 100 meters. A UTP network can end up costing more than a Thinnet network because it requires an additional device to connect all of the computers together (the hub).

- A Thinnet network cannot have more than 30 devices per segment. Segments can be connected together with repeaters, but there may be no more than five segments and only three of those segments can be populated with devices. There is a minimum of 0.5 meters between devices and each end of the segment must be terminated. An individual segment should not be more than 185 meters.

Now that you have the information you need to set up and use the network, let's examine the additional options you have for configuring the network.

Configuring Identification Properties

The Identification tab in the Network properties dialog box lets you specify a computer name and the workgroup that this machine will participate in. When choosing a computer name it is a good idea to use a scheme that can be easily followed and understood across the network. A computer name must be unique on the network. You could name the machines after the primary user but that could lead to potential confusion between logon names and computer names. You could name the machines by their serial numbers, but it would probably be very hard to figure out which machine you were browsing for without some type of translation table beside you.

The computer name is the NetBIOS name that is used to identify the computer on the network. Many applications and protocols require a valid NetBIOS name to function. The computer name must be 15 characters or less and it cannot contain any blank spaces. Figure 21.16 shows an example of the Identification tab in the Network properties dialog box.

The workgroup name does not have to be unique and you would normally not want it to be. Choosing a workgroup for the computer to belong to helps define what will exist in the local Network Neighborhood. For example, if you choose to put this Windows 98 computer in the SAND workgroup, then you would type SAND in the workgroup name box. When a user uses this computer to browse the network, they will select the Network Neighborhood. The first Network Neighborhood window that opens will show the resources available in the SAND workgroup. There may be additional resources listed if you have configured some of the options mentioned earlier in the chapter. If the machine is part of an NT domain, placing the domain name in the workgroup name field will also make domain browsing easier.

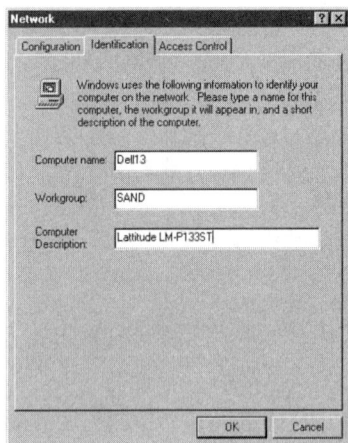

Figure 21.16
Using the Identification tab in the Network properties to establish the computer name, workgroup and description.

The Computer Description box allows you to put a comment that may be available to other users browsing the network. You could describe the location of the machine, its configuration or whatever information you feel would be appropriate. When you have finished making changes to the Identification tab, click OK to continue.

Windows 98 Security

A *share* is a resource that is made available to the network. You can share Windows 98 resources, such as folders, printers, and drives, so that network users can access them, and you can protect those shares by restricting access to the resource. Windows 98 provides two security schemes for protecting network resources:

- Share-level security. Password protection applied to network shares
- User-level security. User and group access permissions applied to network shares

These two security options are discussed in the following sections.

To make your Windows 98 resources available to other network users, you must first make sure that File and Printer Sharing is installed. Windows 98 includes a pair of file and printer sharing services: File and printer sharing for Microsoft networks and File and Printer sharing for NetWare networks. To make sure one of these services is installed, go to the Network properties dialog box and scroll down through the list of the installed network components; see if one of the file and printer sharing services is installed. If it is not listed, be sure to add it before attempting to follow the rest of the instructions presented here.

Once you have enabled the appropriate File and Printer Sharing service, you will be able to share folders and printers with other users. Sharing can be done using share-level security or user-level security. To check which type of security you have configured for your machine, look at the Access Control tab in the Network properties dialog box.

Share-level Security

Share-level security lets you share a resource on the network and then protect that shared resource with a password. To set up share-level security, make sure that the radio button for Share-level access control in the Network Properties Access Control tab is selected. Click OK to finish with the Network properties and you should now be able to share folders and printers and assign share-level access to them.

To give you an idea of the capabilities of share-level security, let's examine the procedures necessary to set up a share for a folder and give users access to it. In this example a folder named WORD will be shared so that network users will have access to it.

Note Until you share a folder, network users do not have access to it from the network. However, if you were to share a folder called ONE that contained another folder called TWO, users will be able to access the TWO folder by connecting to the ONE folder and then opening the TWO folder. For this reason, you should be very careful when determining what folder or folders to share. If you share the C: folder on your machine, users will have access to the entire C: drive.

1. Locate the folder you want to share and right-click the folder to open the drop-down box. From the drop-down box, select S**h**aring. Figure 21.17 shows the Sharing dialog box for a folder named WORD.

2. Click the radio button for Shared As to set up the share.

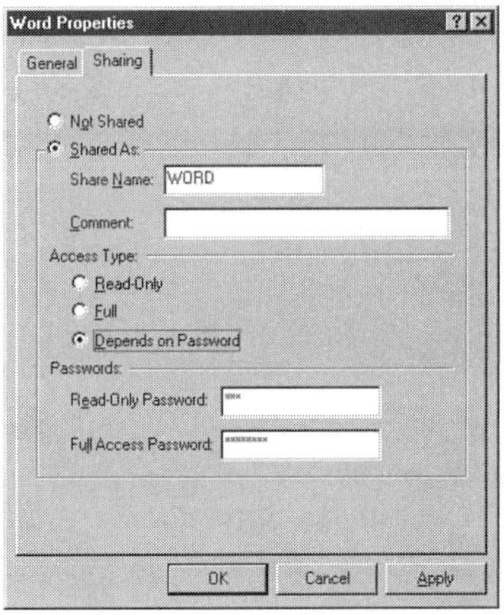

Figure 21.17
Sharing a folder named WORD with share-level security.

3. The Share Name box will default to the name of the resource you just selected (in this case, WORD). If you want to assign a different share name to this resource, you can type that in the box. If you will be sharing these resources with DOS users, it would be best to keep the share names to eight characters or less.

4. The Comment box allows you to put a description of the shared resource for users to examine when they are browsing the network.

5. The Access Type section of the dialog box lets you define whether users will have Read-Only access, Full access, or read or full access that Depends on Password. If you give users read-only access to the resource, they will not be able to modify or delete anything, but they will be able to open it, run it, look at it, and copy it to their machine where they will be able to make changes if they wish. Users with full access will be able to do all of those things plus add, delete, and modify.

6. In the Passwords section you can put in a password that will be required to gain the type of access you have authorized. For example, if you select read-only access for the users, you will be able to go to Read-Only Password and put in a password that will be required to gain read-only access to this resource. The Full-Access Password box will remain dim unless you have selected full-access or the depends on Password option. If you did select the depends on Password option, you will be able to put in one password for read-only access and a different password for full access. Windows 98 will make sure that you use different passwords for the two types of access.

7. Clicking the OK button will finish setting up the shared resource. If you have entered any passwords, you will be required to verify them at this time to make sure you did not type them in incorrectly.

When you have completed verifying the passwords, you will see that the icon for the resource now has a hand under it to indicate that it has been shared. Now that you have set up a resource with share-level security, you should be able to see that there is not really any way to assign various levels of access to various users. You have the capability to assign read-only access or full access but no way to determine who gets access unless you tell only certain people what the password is. You have to use the same password for each user who wants to access that resource. There is one other type of access level that you can assign with share-level access and that is no access. Of course, the only way to assign no access is to either not share the resource or make sure that users with no access do not find out the password.

If you want to create a much more effective security system with Windows 98, you will want to look into using user-level security for your computer.

| **Tip** | You can create hidden shares, which others cannot see in Network Neighborhood, but can still share if they know the exact name of the resource. Append a dollar sign ($) onto the name of the share to cause it to be hidden. |

User-level Security

The most secure way to set up security in Windows 98 is through user-level security. User-level security obtains some extra help in setting up Windows 98 security by having the users authenticated by a secure server such as a Windows NT machine or a NetWare server. User-level security cannot be set up using only Windows 98 machines. To configure Windows 98 for user-level security, go to the Access Control tab in the Network properties dialog box and click the radio button for User-level Access Control. Doing so will make available the lower box of Obtain List of Users and Groups From. See Figure 21.18 for an example.

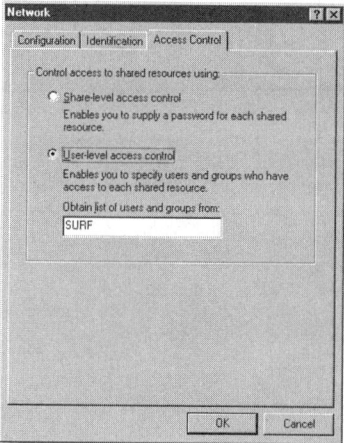

Figure 21.18
Setting up the Access Control tab in the Network properties to enforce user-level security.

Fill in the box labeled Obtain_List of Users and Groups From with the name of the secure server that will be used to authenticate the users. The secure server can be a Windows NT or a LAN Manager domain, a NetWare server or a Windows NT machine (Workstation or Server, version 3.1 or later). This machine or domain will be used to verify the correct login and passwords of all of the users that attempt to use resources on this Windows 98 machine. Once these settings have been made, you will be able to start sharing files and printers to specific users and groups with various levels of security.

To set up a shared folder and enable user-level access to it, find the folder you wish to share and right-click it. From the drop-down menu, select Sharing and you will be able to make changes to the sharing properties for that folder. As with share-level security, you will need to check the Shared As radio button and fill in a Share Name and a Comment if you wish. As you can see from Figure 21.19 this Sharing dialog box looks a little different from the one used for share-level access.

Now you can add users to the list by clicking the Add button and selecting the users to whom you would like to give Read Only, Full Access and Custom access. Figure 21.20 shows an example of pulling up the user list on a Windows NT domain named SURF to assign users and privileges.

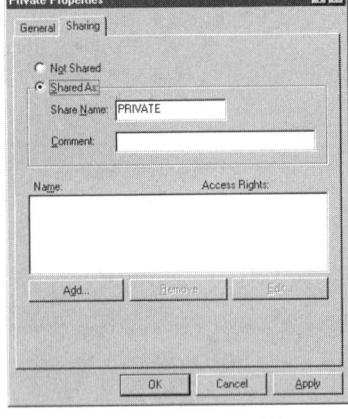

Figure 21.19
Setting up a shared folder using user-level security.

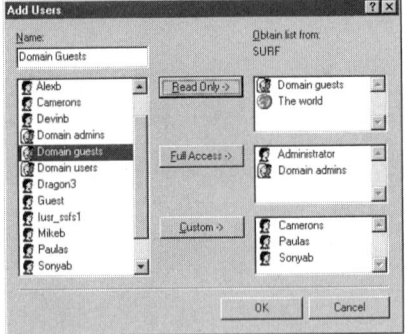

Figure 21.20
Adding users from the domain list to user list for the shared folder on the Windows 98 machine.

If you select to give some users custom access, then when you click OK, the Change Access Rights dialog box as seen in Figure 21.21 will pop up to let you configure the custom access for that user or users. Although you will initially be assigning the same custom access for all of the users that you put in the custom box, you can always go back and edit them individually.

Figure 21.21
Configuring custom access privileges for users.

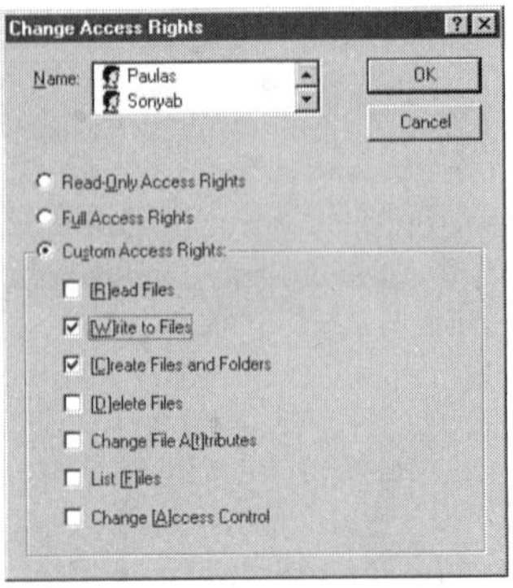

Chapter 21: Understanding Windows 98 Networking

> **Note** User-level access control lets you manage users and groups, and assign access, using the standard fileserver management tools, such as User Manager for Domains for Windows NT networks, or SysCon for NetWare networks.

Once you have set up the custom rights, clicking OK will bring you back to the sharing properties window. From this window you will now be able to select individual users or groups and modify their access privileges on a one-by-one basis if you like. The levels of access you can assign for these users and groups include the following:

- Read the Files. Includes the capability to run most executables and batch files.
- Write to Files. Gives users the capability to add to or modify existing files.
- Create Files and Folders. Gives users the capability to add new files and folders.
- Delete Files. Gives the users the capability to remove files and folders.
- Change File Attributes. Gives the users the capability to modify the DOS file attributes.
- List Files. Gives users the capability to see the files as if they did a DIR of the files.
- Change **A**ccess Control. Allows users to determine who has access and who does not.

With this capability, you can assign very detailed levels of access to individual users or groups of users based on the user information contained on the secure machine or domain from which you are pulling the user and group list. It is important to note that while Windows 98 can provide some security, the security provided is done on a per-share basis. With NetWare or Windows NT, an administrator can assign security on a directory or even individual files if necessary, but this is not possible with Windows 98. Windows 98 can assign security only to the shares that are created.

Windows 98 Logon

When a user logs on to a Windows 98 machine, the type of logon box he will have and the resources he will have access to are determined by how the logon parameters are configured for that machine. There are essentially two types of logons that can be accomplished with Windows 98.

- A user can log on to Windows 98 using a user name and password.
- A user can log on to a Windows NT domain, a NetWare network, or some other network for which Windows 98 has a 32-bit client.

Windows 98 can also be used to log the user on to Windows 98 and all available networks. When a user has logged on to Windows 98 and tries to access a network resource, the password he uses to connect to the resource is cached (stored) in a .PWL file. The next time the user needs to connect to that resource, he will not have to remember the password because Windows 98 will use the cached password for him automatically. The default parameters for Windows 98 are to cache passwords, but if a user deselects the "Save this password in your password list" option, the password will not be cached. Also, the administrator can use System Policies (see Chapter 7, "System Policies") to restrict a user's capability to cache passwords. Caching passwords could be a potential security issue on some networks. Although the passwords stored in the .PWL file are encrypted, logging on to Windows 98 unlocks the file so that Windows 98 can use it to perform automatic logons. This means that a cracker (hacker with evil intentions) who acquired a valid Windows 98 logon name and password would be able to use not only the Windows 98 workstation, but also any resources for which that user had cached passwords.

Because a user can cache passwords, Windows 98 has also provided a Control Panel applet that allows the user to manage his passwords. Selecting the Passwords applet from the Control Panel allows the user to change the passwords used for Windows 98 logon and any other resources he has cached a password for. All the user has to do is select the button for Change Windows Password or Change Other Passwords. If the user selects the Change Windows Password button, he will also be given an opportunity to select any of the other resources he has cached passwords for and force him to be changed to the same password as the new Windows 98 logon password if he desires.

To configure the Primary Network Logon, go to the Network properties dialog box and choose the appropriate Client in the Primary Network **L**ogon box. Depending upon the clients you have installed, you may have one or more of these choices:

- Client for Microsoft Networks
- Client for NetWare Networks
- Microsoft Family Logon
- Windows Logon

If you select the primary network logon to be the Client for Microsoft Networks, when you reboot the machine and prepare to log on, the logon dialog box you will see should look similar to the one in Figure 21.22. Notice that you have fields available for the **U**ser Name, **P**assword, and **D**omain. Clicking OK will attempt to validate you against the domain you specify in the logon dialog box.

If you specify the Client for NetWare Networks as your primary network logon, then upon rebooting you should have a login dialog box, similar to the one in Figure 21.23. Notice that just as with the Microsoft logon box you will need to put in your **U**ser Name and **P**assword but you will have to put in the Login **S**erver in the third box.

Chapter 21: Understanding Windows 98 Networking

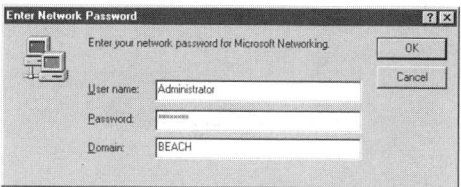

Figure 21.22

Logging on to Windows 98 with the Client for Microsoft Networks configured as the primary network logon.

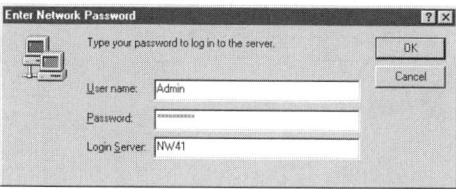

Figure 21.23

Logging on to Windows 98 with the Client for NetWare Networks configured as the primary network logon.

If you have installed and configured the Service for NetWare Directory Services, then the login box you will see will resemble the one shown in Figure 21.24. In this login box, the default tree and context have already been configured and you will just need to put in your **U**ser Name and **P**assword. If the default values will not work for this login then you can click the **A**dvanced button to change the login settings.

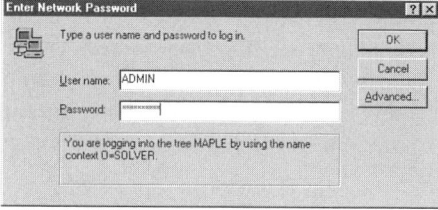

Figure 21.24

Logging in to Windows 98 with the Client for NetWare Networks configured as the primary network logon and with the Service for NetWare Directory Services installed and configured.

When you are logging on for the first time you will need to put in both your user name and password. However, during subsequent logins, Windows 98 will remember the name of the last user to log on and will place that last user name in the user name box. If this user is logging on again then he will have to put in only his password to log in. If another user is going to log in then he will have to change the name in the user name box and put in the correct password for his account.

The other type of logon that is supported is the Microsoft Family Logon. For this client to work correctly you will need to have already set up your Windows 98 machine to use user profiles. When you have user profiles enabled, and you select the Microsoft Family Logon as the primary network logon then you will have a logon screen that resembles the one shown in Figure 21.25 when you restart the computer. This login dialog box will allow you to select the user from the list of configured users (those who have user profiles on this machine) and then type in the appropriate password.

Figure 21.25

Logging in to Windows 98 with the Microsoft Family Logon configured as the primary network logon. User profiles must be enabled for this method to work properly.

Finding Network Resources

After all of the network components are installed and correctly configured, users will be able to use the network. If the user's desktop has already been predefined with shortcuts that point to the programs he will need access to, then the user will not have to spend a lot of time looking for network resources. If the user needs to find something on the network, there are a couple of different ways that he can accomplish that task.

If the user knows the name of the computer he is looking for on the network, then one of the easiest ways to find it is to let Windows 98 find it for him. To let Windows 98 find a computer for you, click the Start button on the taskbar and then select **F**ind. From the list of find items, select **C**omputer. On the Computer Name tab put the name of the computer you would like to find in the **N**amed box. Click F**i**nd Now and Windows 98 will begin searching for the computer. If Windows 98 finds the computer it will be displayed in a box that drops down below the find dialog box. Look at Figure 21.26 for an example of a computer that has been located. The name and location of the computer will be displayed as well as any comment for that machine.

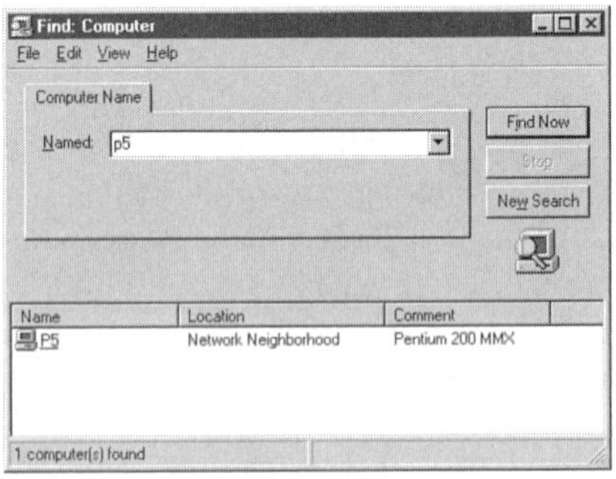

Figure 21.26

Using Find to locate a resource on the network.

The other way that users can locate available network resources is to browse the Network Neighborhood. Browsing the network is the same for all network providers whether your network is a Windows NT network, a NetWare network, or a Windows 98 peer network. If you do not want to maintain drive mappings for every resource you want to connect to then you can simply use Network Neighborhood to find the resource you wish to use and select it

Chapter 21: Understanding Windows 98 Networking

from within Network Neighborhood. Browsing for a resource and subsequently connecting to it is as simple as making a few mouse clicks.

To browse through the Network Neighborhood, select it and open it from the desktop. The first Network Neighborhood window should show you all of the devices in your current workgroup in addition to an icon for the Entire Network. Figure 21.27 gives you an example of what this window might look like. If you wish to browse for resources outside of your workgroup then you will need to select and open the Entire Network to gain access to other workgroups and domains. If the resource you are attempting to find is in your workgroup then select and open the icon for the computer where the resources resides. This will present you with a listing of the shared resources on that computer. Locate, select, and open the shared resource and continue drilling down to deeper layers if necessary until you get to the item you are looking for.

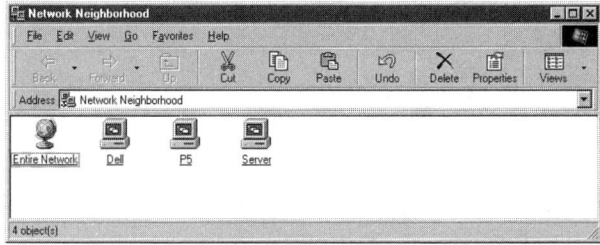

Figure 21.27
Looking through the Network Neighborhood for Network resources.

If this resource is something that you will need access to often, then here are a couple of suggestions for making the resource easier to get to:

- You can place a shortcut to the resource on your desktop. The easiest way to create this shortcut is to use Network Neighborhood to locate the resource. When you have located it in one of the Network Neighborhood windows, right-click the icon and (while keeping the right mouse button depressed) drag the icon to the desktop. When you get to the desktop, release the mouse button and select Create **S**hortcut(s) Here from the list. Then the next time you need to access that resource, you will be able to simply click the shortcut on your desktop and get to the resource very quickly.

- If you want to browse the resources available on a particular machine but do not want to set up a static drive mapping for the resource, you can get there using the Run command. Click the Start button on the taskbar and then select **R**un. In the **O**pen box, type in the Universal Naming Convention (UNC) path for the resource or device you wish to browse. UNC names follow the format of \\device\share. They start with two backslashes followed by the device name. Another backslash follows immediately and then the share name of the shared resource. The share name for the resource is whatever was typed in the Share Name box when the share was established.

If you do decide that you would like to have a drive letter mapped to a resource (some programs will require this) then you will need to right-click Network Neighborhood and select

Map **N**etwork Drive from the drop-down list. In the Map Network Drive dialog box, you will need to choose a **D**rive letter and put in a **P**ath. As you can see from the example in Figure 21.28, you will need to put the path in using the UNC name. There is also a checkbox to select whether or not you want this drive mapping to Reconne**c**t at logon.

Figure 21.28

Mapping a network drive to a resource.

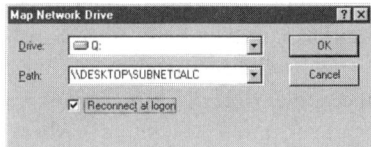

Locating and mapping network resources can also be done at the command prompt with the net commands. Here are a couple of net commands you might find useful at the command prompt:

- Typing in `net view /workgroup:workgroupname` where you substitute the *workgroupname* with the name of the workgroup you want to view the contents of will give you a list of the members of the workgroup.

- Once you have a list of the workgroup members, you can find out what resources are available on a particular machine by typing in net view \\computername where you replace computername with the name of the computer for which you would like to get a list of resources.

- You can also set up a drive mapping for a resource by typing in **net use** * *device**share* where you would replace the *device* and *share* with the appropriate names for the resource for which you are setting up the map. The asterisk is used to represent the next available drive letter. If you would like to use a specific drive letter such as R, you would type **net use R:** *device**share*.

To see what other net commands are available and how to use them, type in **net /? | more** at the command prompt.

Browsing in a Windows 98 environment involves many other steps.

To browse the network, a Windows 98 machine must obtain a browse list from either a Master Browse Server or a Backup Browse Server. When a Windows 98 machine is first started up, it checks to see if there are any other Master Browse Servers present for the current workgroup. If one is not present, then that Windows 98 workstation can become the Master Browse Server. If there is already a Master Browse Server, then the Windows 98 workstation checks to see how many computers are in the workgroup and how many Backup Browse Servers are present. If the ratio exceeds 15 to 1, then that workstation can become a Backup Browse Server. There is normally one Backup Browse Server for every 15 computers in the workgroup.

Chapter 21: Understanding Windows 98 Networking

By using the service File and Printer Sharing for Microsoft Networks the workstation browse server status can be changed. As you can see from Figure 21.29, one of the settings under the Advanced tab of this service's properties is the option for the Browse Master parameter. The three possible choices here are Automatic, Disabled, and Enabled.

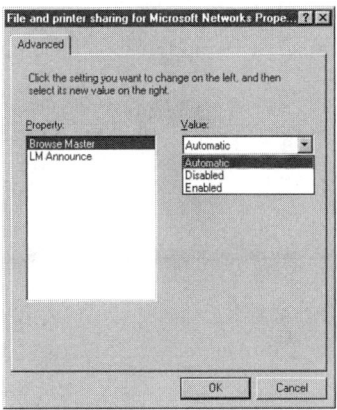

Figure 21.29

Using the File and Printer Sharing for Microsoft Networks service properties to change the Browse Server settings.

- Automatic is the default option, which allows Windows 98 to make the decision as to whether the computer will become a browse server.

- Disabled is the option to choose if you are positive that this machine should never be a browse server. Being a browse server on the network does use some of the workstation's resources to handle the browse requests. If you do not want this workstation to be tied up handling network browse requests, then you might choose this option. Just remember that at least one computer in the workgroup must have the Automatic or Enabled option turned on or users will not be able to browse the network.

- Enabled specifies that this computer should maintain the browse list for the workgroup.

Some other interesting notes about browsing with Windows 98:

- When a Windows 98 machine first connects to the network, it announces itself to the Master Browse Server so that it can be added to the browse list. The Master Browse Server notifies the Backup Browse Servers that a changed list is available but they have approximately 15 minutes to obtain the new list. Therefore, it can take a few minutes for computers to show up in the workgroup.

- If a user shuts off his Windows 98 machine without going through the Shut Down procedure, then it can take as long as 45 minutes for a computer name to be removed from the browse list. This is just one more reason to make sure users shut down their machines properly. Doing so allows the Master Browse Server to be notified and then remove the machine name from the browse list.

Mapping Network Shares

In the Windows environment, there are two ways to access files in a share: You can open Network Neighborhood and browse through the list, opening the share and using the files within it (you can do the same thing using Windows Explorer, of course). Or, you can map a network drive, which creates a simulated hard disk drive letter on the local computer, which is mapped to a remote network resource. Mapped drives appear in My Computer just as if they were local drives.

To map a network drive, right-click on Network Neighborhood (or on the share that you want to map), and choose Map **N**etwork Drive, which activates the dialog box shown in Figure 21.30.

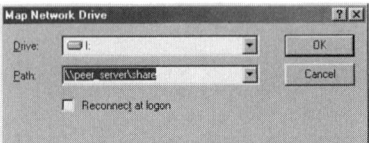

Figure 21.30
Map Network Drive dialog box.

You choose the drive letter that you want to use for the mapped drive, and then specify the UNC path of the network share you want to access. Select the Reconne**c**t at Logon checkbox to cause the mapped drive to be reconnected automatically the next time you log in. The Reconnect at Logon checkbox causes a persistent connection.

To disconnect a mapped drive, right-click on Network Neighborhood and choose **D**isconnect Network Drive from the pop-up menu. You then see a dialog box from which you can choose which mapped drive you want to discontinue.

Conclusion

Windows 98 continues to build on the capabilities of Microsoft Networking. With Windows 98 you can browse for, find, connect to, and use multiple types of network resources on multiple types of networks. Whether you are using coaxial cable or unshielded twisted pair, TCP/IP or NetBEUI, the Client for Microsoft Networks or the Client for NetWare Networks, using the network is made virtually seamless by Windows 98.

Windows 98 also provides for some security of the information contained both on the machine and on the network. By using the password-caching features and the user- and share-level security settings, Windows 98 can be set up to enhance security while making security easier for the users to work with.

In order for all of this to work, it is important that all of the settings, properties, and values be configured correctly. While Windows 98 provides all of these great networking features, proper installation, setup, and administration of the network settings will ensure success with Windows 98 networking.

Peer-to-Peer Networking

Windows 98 can serve as both a network client and as a network server (it's a floor wax and a dessert topping!). While you would never use the server capabilities of Windows 98 to host a large network on which you would instead use NetWare or Windows NT Server, the peer-to-peer networking capabilities in Windows 98 are sufficient for a number of uses, including:

- Sharing disk resources over a larger network
- Sharing a CD-ROM drive with another computer that either doesn't have one, or that needs to share access to a single CD-ROM
- Sharing printers over a larger network
- Setting up a small office or home office (SOHO) network
- Allowing a backup system to access local resources for backup

In this chapter, you learn about Windows 98 peer-to-peer networking capabilities: how to set them up, how to use them, and how to administer them. The information in this chapter can be used to fulfill any of the networking needs described in the preceding list.

> **Note** For basic networking information, be sure to first read Chapter 21, "Understanding Windows 98 Networking."

Understanding Windows 98 Peer Networking Capabilities

There are two main networking models in use: client-server and peer-to-peer. In a traditional client/server network, there is a dedicated server that has only the job of storing files for users (clients) in a central location, and also providing access to other network resources, such as printers and CD-ROM drives. In a peer-to-peer network, each computer is responsible for sharing files and printers with all of the other computers on the network.

Client/server networks, with a dedicated server, are best for larger groups of computers, particularly when there is someone with enough technical knowledge to manage the server and the network itself. Companies implement dedicated server networks when they grow to 10–25 computers, although there are exceptions (some smaller companies may implement a dedicated server if they have a specific need and if they have the technical know-how to manage one; other larger companies may maintain a peer network configuration up to as many as 50 computers). Smaller groups of computers are usually best served by a peer network.

Peer-to-peer networks have the following advantages and disadvantages:

Advantages of peer networks:

- Easier to set up
- Easier to maintain
- Much less expensive than dedicated server networks
- Spread the burden of providing services over many computers

Disadvantages of peer networks:

- Less secure
- More difficult to manage effectively

Chapter 22: Peer-to-Peer Networking

- Harder to back up all network resources

- Higher-end network applications may require a network operating system (such as NetWare or Windows NT Server) on which to run

- Clients that also provide services to others may perform more poorly

Windows 98 includes reliable peer networking capabilities that allow you to access resources on a Windows 98 system from other systems, be they other Windows 98 systems, Windows 95 systems, Windows NT systems, or even DOS systems. Using these capabilities, client computers can perform the following tasks:

> **Note** Although you're learning about peer-to-peer networking, in any network transaction there is still always a *server* (the one with the resource) and a *client* (the one using the resource). In a peer network, all of the computers tend to be both clients *and* servers.

- Browse all computers that are sharing resources

- Browse shared drives, folders, and files

- Open and work with shared files

- Map shared drives or folders to local drive letters

- Print to shared printers

- Remotely administer Windows 98 systems providing peer networking services

For a system to share its files and printers across a network, a number of things must be true:

- Both the server and client must be running the same network client software: Client for Microsoft Networks or Client for NetWare Networks (both can be run if necessary).

- The server must have the File and Printer Sharing service installed, either for NetWare or Microsoft networks (you can use only one or the other).

- Both the server and client must be using a compatible network protocol, such as NetBEUI, IPX/SPX, or TCP/IP.

- A compatible physical network connection must be in place between the server and client. Examples include Ethernet, Token Ring, and Dial-Up Networking over either a modem or a direct-cable serial connection (this supports only peer resource sharing between two computers, and is much slower than the other choices).

- Selected resources on the server must be designated as being shared.

- If user-level security is being used, the specified users must be created on the peer server, or taken from a NetWare server or a Windows NT system.

- The server and client must have defined computer and workgroup names (although the workgroup name does not need to match).

Choosing Microsoft or NetWare Peer Services and Protocols

Windows 98 can perform peer networking by using either the File and Printer Sharing service for NetWare or Microsoft networks. However, you can use only one of these peer networking services at a time. In other words, while you can run both clients simultaneously and access NetWare or Microsoft networks with them, you can perform peer networking using only one or the other services.

You should choose the peer networking service based on the most-used client service you need to run. If you need to access NetWare servers, then use File and Printer Sharing for NetWare networks. Otherwise, using File and Printer Sharing for Microsoft networks is usually the best choice, whether or not you're also accessing Windows NT Servers.

For small networks, the NetBEUI protocol is your best bet. The only drawback to NetBEUI is that it isn't routable, so if there's a router involved on your network (for example, in a larger corporate network), then TCP/IP will work better. If you're using the File and Printer Sharing service for NetWare networks, then you need to use the IPX/SPX protocol regardless.

Choosing Hardware for a Small Peer Network

If you need to network just a few computers together (up to about eight), and don't need any of the advanced security or networking features offered by Windows NT Server or NetWare, then Windows 98 provides a good platform for building such a network. With Windows 98, you can easily share files and printers across a network, which is what is needed most of the time, anyway; most small networks can still be very productive without the features of NetWare or Windows NT Server.

For setting up small home networks, or small office networks, it's best to go with some standard choices for these requirements, and it's easy and relatively inexpensive to do so. Consider the following items:

- You need to decide how you will wire the network (even if it's just wires snaked across a room). You'll need to know the location of each computer, and where you plan to locate the hub.

- You should purchase a simple 10Base-T Ethernet hub (one with four to eight ports) that will cost about $150. You should choose a hub from a reputable manufacturer, such as

Asante, SMC, 3Com, or HP. While these companies make high-end hubs costing close to $1,000, they also offer small office hubs in the price range described.

- For each computer, you will need a standard 10Base-T Ethernet card, costing between $60–$100. Again, stick with name brands for these cards. 3Com or SMC are both very good (and often can be ordered along with new computers, built into their motherboards) and there are many others, besides (the author and technical editor both prefer 3Com, by the way).

- You will need an appropriate number of 10Base-T cables to run from each computer to the hub location. No cable can be longer than about 300 feet (100 meters). If you plan to occupy the space for more than a year or so, then it may make sense to bring in a network wiring professional to do a professional job and run the cables through the walls.

10Base-T or 10Base-2?

There are two forms of Ethernet that are widely used these days: 10Base-T (also called *twisted-pair Ethernet*) and 10Base-2 (also called *thin Ethernet*). 10Base-T Ethernet uses a star configuration with a hub to which all the computers connect. Its main advantage is that if the wiring from the hub to any computer is disconnected or broken, everything else keeps working. 10Base-2, on the other hand, uses a bus configuration where each computer is connected to the cable, one right after the other; if there's a break in the cable, the whole thing stops working. The main advantage to 10Base-2 is that it's often the cheapest way to connect several computers together that are in the same room, because there's no hub or extra wiring to have to purchase.

Most companies are phasing out 10Base-2, but if you are setting up a small peer network, where all of the computers are close together, then you may want to consider it.

If you decide to implement a 10Base-2 network, follow these rules:

- The maximum length of the total network cable cannot exceed 185 meters, unless you extend it with a repeater every 185 meters (up to three segments, total, are allowed).

- There should be no less than one meter of cable between each computer.

- You must use RG/58 cable; mixing cable types can cause problems.

- Each end of the cable must have a 50-ohm resistor connected, or the network won't operate.

- You cannot connect more than 30 network devices to the network, unless you extend the network with either a repeater or router.

Once you have the hardware installed and connected, you can then set up each workstation so that it has the requisite software. The following section describes this process.

Setting Up Windows 98 for Peer Networks

There are four components that must be installed into Windows 98 before you can try to connect to other computers over the network (and these steps must be carried out for each system, of course). Chapter 21 describes the Windows 98 network components in greater detail. This section gives you a quick look at how to set up peer-to-peer networking.

First, you need to load the drivers for the network card that has been installed. For newer Plug and Play systems, this should have been easily accomplished when you started the system after installing the network interface card (NIC). If not, see Chapter 12, "Supporting Devices," for instructions on manually setting up the NIC driver.

Next, you need to install the network client software that you will use. As previously discussed, you have two choices: Client for Microsoft Networks and Client for NetWare Networks. If you need to connect to both peer resources and to a Windows NT Server, or if you will be doing only Windows 98 peer networking, then choose Client for Microsoft Networks. If you need to connect to a NetWare server, choose Client for NetWare Networks. To install either client, follow these steps:

1. Open the Network control panel. On the Configuration tab, click the **A**dd button.

2. On the Select Network Component Type dialog box, choose Client and click OK (see Figure 22.1).

Figure 22.1
Choosing a network component to install.

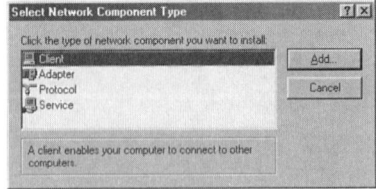

3. You now see the Select Network Client dialog box, shown in Figure 22.2. Choose Microsoft as the manufacturer, and then choose either Client for Microsoft Networks or Client for NetWare Networks (this example assumes Client for Microsoft Networks). After clicking OK, you may be prompted for your Windows 98 CD-ROM.

4. After returning to the Network control panel's Configuration tab, click **A**dd again. This time, choose Protocol on the Select Network Component Type dialog box.

Chapter 22: Peer-to-Peer Networking   **509**

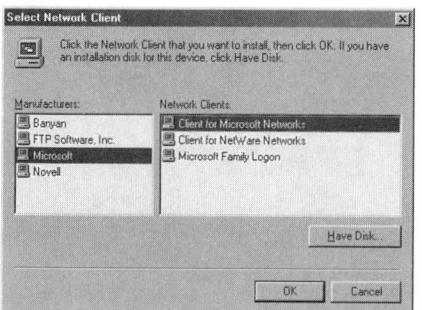

Figure 22.2
Choosing a network client type.

5. In the Select Network Protocol dialog box (see Figure 22.3), choose Microsoft, and then choose NetBEUI, TCP/IP, or IPX/SPX-Compatible depending on whether you chose Microsoft or NetWare client in step 3.

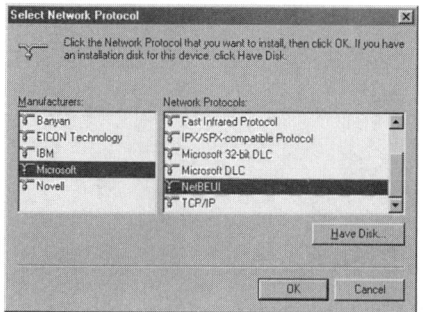

Figure 22.3
Choosing a network protocol.

6. Click **A**dd again on the Network control panel's Configuration dialog. This time, choose Service in the Select Network Component Type dialog box.

7. In the Select Network Service dialog box (see Figure 22.4), choose either File and Printer Sharing for Microsoft Networks or File and Printer Sharing for NetWare Networks and click OK.

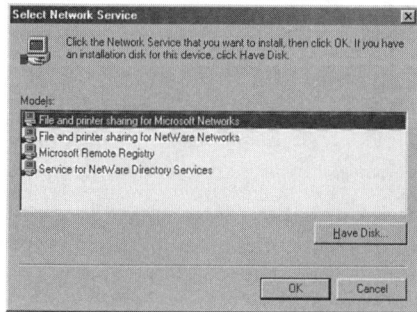

Figure 22.4
Choosing a File and Printer Sharing service.

8. Back again on the Network control panel's Configuration tab, click the **F**ile and Print Sharing button, which shows you the File and Print Sharing dialog box shown in Figure 22.5. Enable either or both types of resource sharing and click OK.

Figure 22.5
Enabling File and Print sharing.

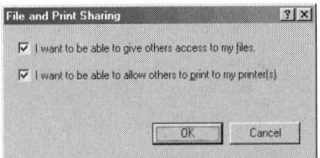

9. Next, use the Identification tab of the Network control panel to designate a workgroup and computer name for the system. This is discussed in more detail in the next section.

10. Click OK to close the Network control panel. You may be prompted again for your Windows 98 CD-ROM, and you will need to restart the computer when prompted to do so.

Tip At any time up until you click OK on the Network control panel's dialog box, you can cancel all changes with the Cancel button.

Direct Cable Peer Networking

For simple, low-bandwidth connections between two computers, such as a connection between a laptop and a desktop PC, a network adapter card and network cabling is not necessary. Instead, you can network the computers directly by using a serial or parallel cable. Windows 98 provides two methods for setting up a direct cable networking connection, as follows:

- The Direct Cable Connection accessory (in the Accessories/Communication group) launches a wizard that sets up a direct-cable connection.

- The Control Panel Modems application lets you configure a serial or parallel connection as a modem connection. You can access the other computer through this modem-cable connection by using Dial-Up Networking.

The following sections discuss these alternatives.

Direct Cable Connection

The Direct Cable Connection accessory sets up a direct serial or parallel connection between two PCs. Direct Cable Connection is in the Accessories/Communications group. If this applet is not present on your system, install it through the Add Programs Control Panel.

Chapter 22: Peer-to-Peer Networking

A direct cable network connection is much like any other network connection—the two computers must use compatible protocols, and you can establish security using the user-level or share-level security models (as described in Chapter 21). To install a direct-cable network connection:

1. Double-click the Direct Cable Connection icon in the Accessories/Communications group to launch the Direct Cable Connection wizard (see Figure 22.6).

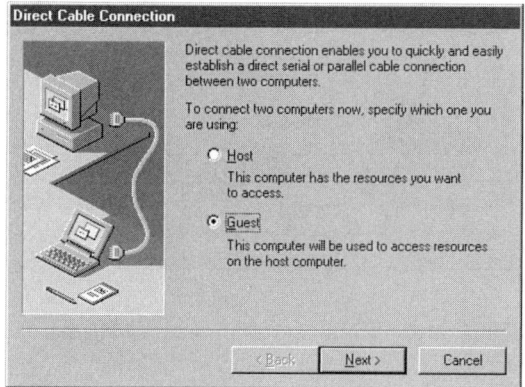

Figure 22.6

The Direct Cable Connection Wizard.

2. The wizard will ask if you want the computer to act as a *guest* (to access shared files on another PC) or a *host* (refer to Figure 22.6). The host option lets the PC act as either a host or a guest—you can either share files or access shared files on another computer. If a host PC is connected to a network, the guest can reach the network through the host. Click Next.

3. Choose which port you'd like to use for the direct cable connection (see Figure 22.7). Plug the cable into the port. Click Next.

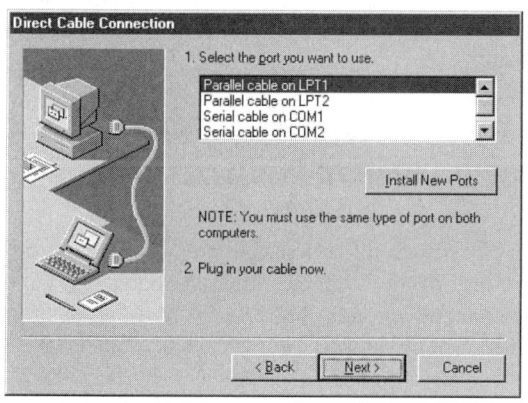

Figure 22.7

Choose a port and cable type in the Direct Cable Connection wizard.

4. If you are configuring the computer as a host, and the computer isn't currently configured with shared resources, the wizard will prompt you to create some shared folders that the guest can access (see Figure 22.8). Follow the instructions and click Next.

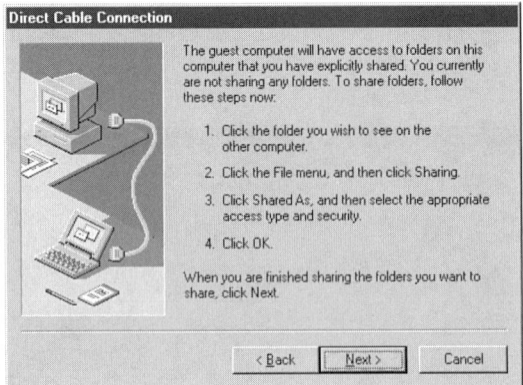

Figure 22.8
The Direct Cable Connection wizard prompts you to share folders on the host.

5. The wizard instructs you to plug the cable into both computers (if you haven't done so already) and to run the Direct Cable Connection wizard on the other PC. You are offered the option of setting password protection for the host PC. Check the Use Password Protection box to set up password protection, and click on Set Password to enter a password for the host.

6. Click Finish.

The direct cable connection can act as a NetBIOS gateway to a TCP/IP network. If you plan to use the host as a gateway to a TCP/IP network, use NetBEUI for the direct cable connection.

> **Note** You cannot use Direct Cable Connection and Dial-Up Networking at the same time. Shut down all Dial-Up Networking connections before you attempt to use Direct Cable Connection.

Direct Connection Through Dial-Up Networking

You can also connect two PCs through a serial or parallel connection by using Dial-Up Networking (DUN). See Chapter 26 for a complete description of Windows 98's Dial-Up Networking feature. Once you set this up, you "dial" the other computer—just as you do with a remote Internet connection—over a modem cable. The Direct Cable "modem" is configured the same way as a real modem, with a bound network protocol, such as TCP/IP, on each end.

When you open the Modems control panel and choose to add a new modem, and then choose to manually select one from a list, you can choose (Standard Modem Types) in the Manufacturer list, and then either Dial-Up Networking Serial Cable Between 2 PCs or Dial-Up Networking Parallel Cable Between 2 PCs.

Once the modem cable is installed, set up a Dial-Up Networking connection through the modem (see Chapter 26).

> **Note** You can purchase the special cables required to connect two computers by using DUN from most computer stores. If you are setting up a serial connection, you purchase a null-modem cable that has a female RS-232C connector (9- or 25-pin, as appropriate for the computers) on each end. If you are setting up a parallel connection, ask for a parallel-to-parallel cable, such as the one used by LapLink or other direct-connect programs (it should have a male DB25 connector on each end, with all wires supported).

Understanding Workgroups and Identification

For peer networking, Windows 98 supports a Workgroup model that lets you divide up the resources (computers) on the peer network into groupings of computers. These groups do not have any function other than to help users browse the computers available and more easily find the one that they're looking for. Workgroups do not deny access to users in different workgroups, nor do they have to be created and maintained. All that must be done is to identify each computer as being in a particular workgroup.

For example, in a larger organization using peer networking, you might create workgroups for each department: one for finance, operations, marketing, sales, and so forth. When a user goes to locate a particular computer, they can more easily find it by opening one of the workgroups shown inside Network Neighborhood.

> ### File and Printer Sharing for Microsoft Networks: Browse Masters
>
> If you use File and Printer Sharing for Microsoft Networks, the peer network uses some of the computers within each workgroup as *master browse servers,* or *browse masters.* These computers, which are "elected" from among all the computers in the workgroup, maintain the list of all computers and resources within the workgroup. Depending on the number of computers in the workgroup, there may be more than one Browse Master, and there may also be Backup Browse Masters. Generally, there is one Browse Master for each 15 computers in a workgroup. There will also be at least one Browse Master for each protocol used in each workgroup, so if you are using both NetBEUI and TCP/IP, there will be at least two Browse Masters, one per protocol.
>
> *continues*

> *continued*
>
> It is the Browse Master's job to respond to peer network browse requests from other computers wishing to view the resources, usually through Network Neighborhood. If a Browse Master leaves the network (is turned off or shut down), a new one will automatically be elected. The use of Browse Masters significantly reduces network traffic, because it eliminates the need for a peer workstation to have to query every computer within the workgroup in order to find out what resources are available. Instead, it can request a single list from the Browser Master, using a single network transaction.
>
> There is a slight memory cost for a computer acting as a Browse Master, and on some systems you may want to control whether or not they can be used for this purpose. You do this by opening the Network control panel, and then on the Configuration tab, you open the properties for File and Printer Sharing for Microsoft Networks. In the dialog box that appears, you can choose from three possible settings for the Browse Master setting: Automatic, Disable, and Enable. Automatic means that the computer may be elected to be the Browse Master, Disable means that it never will be, and Enable means that it will always be a Browse Master whenever it is turned on and participating in the workgroup.

Each computer is also identified to the network for this same purpose with a computer name. You can assign whatever name you like to each computer, which is then shown as the peer network is browsed. Most people use the user's name to identify their computer, but you can use any name that makes sense.

Both the workgroup and the computer name are set by using the Identification tab of the Network control panel, shown in Figure 22.9.

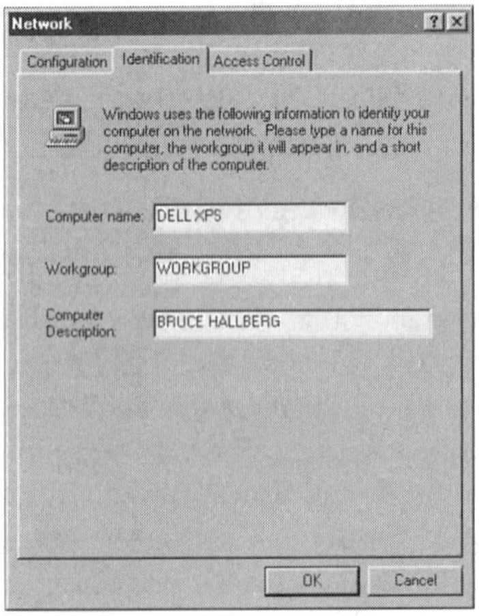

Figure 22.9
Specifying a workgroup and computer name.

Troubleshooting Peer Networking Problems

Peer networks are fairly straightforward, but there are always problems that can crop up with any network. There are many possible points of failure, particularly when you're just setting one up. If you're having trouble with a peer network, consider the following items:

- Ensure that the network interface card is functioning. For instance, does Device Manager report a problem with the network interface card? Also, some NICs have their own diagnostic programs that can help identify a bad card.

- If you're using a 10Base-T network, is the hub functioning? It should include lights that indicate when it "sees" data on the network (traffic lights), and you should see these lights illuminate as you power a computer up that is properly connected.

- Many 10Base-T Ethernet cards also support 100Mbps speeds (100Base-T). If this is the case, make sure that all of the cards on the network are set the same way, and if you're using the 100Mbps setting, make sure the hub supports that speed. Also, the network cards and hubs must also have the same setting for whether they are operating at full or half-duplex operation.

- If you're using a thin-Ethernet (10Base-2) network, make sure that you're using the right type of cable (RG-58) and that you have the correct terminators installed at each end of the network (they must be 50-ohm terminators). Also, ensure that the T-connectors are properly connected to the NIC cards, and that any barrel connectors are firmly connected.

- Make sure that all the computers have the same network settings in the Network control panel; they should all be using the same client, protocol, and File and Printer Sharing service.

- If the problem is that no computers can see any others, particularly when there are more than two computers, suspect the wiring or the network hub. If you're setting up a two-computer peer network, and can borrow a third computer, this can be very useful in helping you to determine if the problem is with either of the computers, or with the wiring or hub.

- Sometimes a computer won't appear in the Network Neighborhood list when it is turned on because the Browse Master hasn't updated its list yet. You can still access such computers by using the Start Menu/Find/Computer command and then specifying the name of the computer you are trying to access.

- If a computer listed in the workgroup isn't responding and you can't open its shares, it may be because it was improperly shut down or lost power. It can take between 10-45 minutes for the Browse Master to realize that a computer is missing from the Workgroup if it didn't go through a normal shutdown process. Even when it is normally shut down, it still takes a while for the list of available computers to be updated, particularly if the computers on the network are busy (updating the browse list is a low-priority job).

- TCP/IP settings can often be tricky to get right. You should check and make sure that all of the TCP/IP settings are correct for each computer. See Chapter 25, "Windows 98 with TCP/IP," for more information.

Conclusion

Peer networks can be useful in certain circumstances, such as when setting up a small network that needs only peer capabilities, or when you need to share a resource across a corporate network on occasion. However, they are much more difficult to centrally manage than a network based on Windows NT Server or NetWare. Moreover, in a larger environment, it can be wise to disable peer networking from the clients, because users will invariably share resources inappropriately, and your company may have security requirements that will be unintentionally violated.

In this chapter, you learned about peer networking features in Windows 98, how to install them, and how to use them. You should use this chapter in concert with Chapter 21, "Understanding Windows 98 Networking." Also, if you want to perform peer networking within a traditional network environment, make sure to read Chapter 23, "Windows 98 in Windows NT Domains" and Chapter 24, "Windows 98 with NetWare/InternetWare Networks."

Windows 98 in Windows NT Domains

Windows 98 machines can coexist comfortably in a Windows 98-only workgroup, sharing files and printers without the need for oversight from a server-based system. For bigger networks, however (say, larger than eight or nine PCs), and for more complicated networking situations, involving routers, roving users, shared workstations, and the like, the workgroup model has some limitations. One of the biggest limitations of a workgroup, other than its limited size, is that there is no common security database. The decentralized logon and resource security of a peer-to-peer network can become confusing, unmanageable, and, often, unreliable as users struggle to unravel who shared what with whom and from where.

The Windows NT domain model provides for more systematic and reliable management of network resources. In a Windows NT domain, a single computer (or a group of computers) called domain controllers maintain the security database for the whole network. When a user logs on from a client machine—in this case, a Windows 98 machine—the user's logon request passes from the client to the domain controller, where it is approved or disapproved depending on whether the user's credentials match the settings stored in the domain account database. Domain user accounts are independent of any particular client machine—a domain user named MATTIE can log on as MATTIE from any machine in the domain and still gain access to the same domain-based account.

The domain networking model is really the standard networking model for all but the simplest Microsoft networks. If you have 10 or more computers, or if you want a mo ' versatile and systematic approach to security and resource management, you'd better think about a Windows NT domain.

A domain requires at least one Windows NT Server system acting as a primary domain controller (PDC). The rest of the computers could, theoretically, all be some form of client machines, including Windows 98 clients. Depending on your network's size and level of traffic, you may want to add one or more additional Windows NT domain controllers (called Backup Domain Controllers—BDCs). A BDC is a good idea no matter how small your network is: When one domain controller is down, the other can continue to provide authentication. When you establish a domain, Windows 98 clients can use the domain accounts database (located on the domain controllers) for logon and resource security.

Windows NT Server is a more sophisticated operating system than Windows 98, and it comes with mor êsophisticated tools that expand and enhance the Microsoft networking environment. In addition to a common security, a Windows NT server network can provide enhanced services that aren't available in Windows 98. You'll learn about some of those services in the next section.

Configuring a Windows NT Server machine is, of course, the subject for a Windows NT Server book and not a Windows 98 book. This chapter won't attempt to fathom the intricacies of configuring a Windows NT Server system but will focus on setting up and using Windows 98 as a domain client.

What You Get with Windows NT Server

A Windows NT Server system provides the network with several important features that aren't available in Windows 98. You can configure Windows 98 to make use of these networking features. Some of the advanced networking features available to Windows 98 clients through Windows NT Server are as follows:

- **DHCP Services.** A Windows 98 client can obtain dynamic IP address from a Windows NT Server system acting as a DHCP server. (See Chapter 25, "Windows 98 with TCP/IP.")

- **DNS Server.** A Windows NT Server can provide TCP/IP hostname name resolution through the DNS Server service. (See Chapter 25.)

- **WINS.** A Windows NT Server system can provide NetBIOS name resolution through the WINS service (see Chapter 25).

- **Centralized Security.** Windows NT Server can provide the network with a centralized security system (see the preceding section).

- **Secure File Storage.** Windows NT's NTFS file system provides the network with local file-level security. You can apply permission directly to folders and files.

- **Roving and mandatory user profiles.** A Windows NT Server acting as a domain controller can pass the user's personal desktop environment—shortcuts, wallpaper, favorite Web links, to whatever client machine the user happens to be using. (See Chapter 8, "User Profiles.") A mandatory profile is a roving profile that the user can't alter. You can preconfigure a mandatory desktop environment by using mandatory profiles.

These features are discussed throughout this book. The domain client role is so important to Windows 98 that it spills into many aspects of configuration and management.

Configuring Windows 98 as a Domain Client

Chapter 21 discussed the steps for configuring networking in Windows 98. A Windows 98 domain client requires the same basic networking components as any other Windows 98 system. You must configure services, adapters, protocols, and protocol bindings. In particular, if you want your Windows 98 system to function as part of a domain, attend to the following steps:

1. In the Configuration tab of the Network Control Panel (see Figure 23.1), choose Client for Microsoft Networks as the Primary Network Logon.

    Make sure Client for Microsoft Networks is installed as a network client. If it is not installed, click the Add button, choose Client from the component list and click Add. Then choose Microsoft from the Manufacturers list, select Client for Microsoft Networks, and click OK.

Figure 23.1
The Network Control Panel Configuration tab.

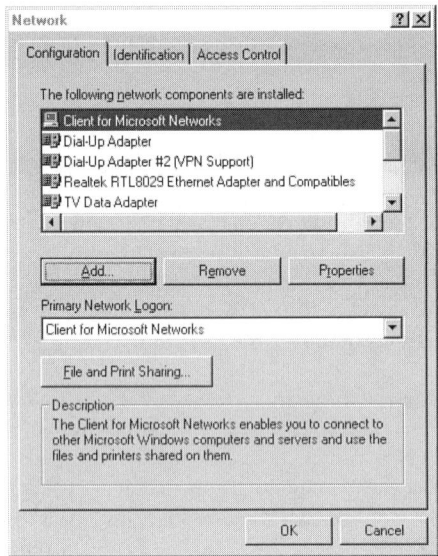

2. Once Client for Microsoft Networks is installed, double-click on it in the configuration tab (see Figure 23.1). You'll see the Client for Microsoft Networks Properties dialog box (see Figure 23.2).

3. In the Client for Microsoft Networks Properties dialog box (see Figure 23.2), check the box labeled Log on to Windows NT domain and enter the domain name in the space provided. Configure a logon option and click OK.

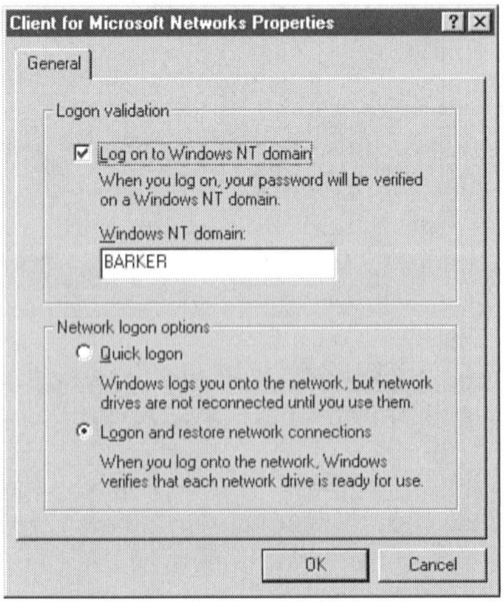

Figure 23.2
The Client for Microsoft Networks Properties dialog box.

Chapter 23: Windows 98 in Windows NT Domains **521**

4. If you want the Windows 98 client to share resources on the domain, click the button labeled File and Print Sharing (in the Configuration tab of the Network Control Panel) and choose to share files and/or printers.

5. Make sure the adapter that will access the Windows NT domain is properly installed and configured (see Chapter 21).

6. Click the Access Control tab in the Network dialog box (see Figure 23.3). If you want to use the domain user and group lists to control access to shared resources on the Windows 98 machine, select the button labeled User-level access control and enter the name of the domain in the box labeled Obtain list of users and groups from. Click OK.

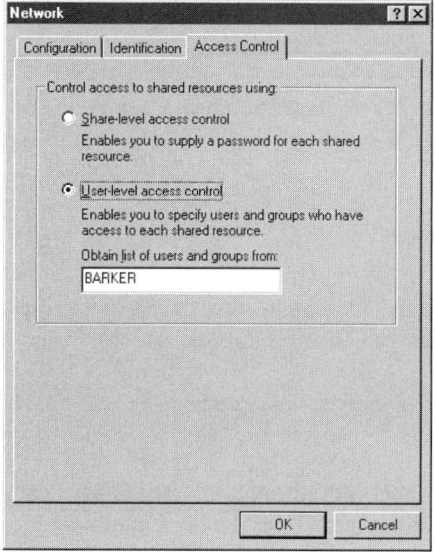

Figure 23.3
The Network Control Panel Access Control tab.

7. Restart your computer if necessary.

Note As you learned in Chapter 21, you can enable user-level access control in the Access Control tab (refer to Figure 23.3) without configuring Windows 98 as a domain client. In that case, the Windows 98 machine would obtain a user list from a Windows NT or NetWare system but would not log on through the domain. You'll learn more about domain logon in the next section.

Once you log on to the Windows NT domain, you'll have access to domain resources through your domain user account and the group accounts associated with your user account. You'll be able to share drives, directories, and printers on the network and assign permissions to domain users and groups for those shared resources (see Chapter 21).

Windows 98 in Windows NT Domains

In a Windows NT domain, the domain controller(s) becomes a central point for managing user accounts. Through Windows NT Server's User Manager for Domains utility, you can configure any of the following features for a user account:

- Home directories
- User profiles
- Group memberships
- Logon Hours
- Logon workstations

Although a full discussion of Windows NT configuration belongs in another book, the preceding items are important facets of Windows 98 domain configuration and deserve mention here.

Home Directories

Each user in a Windows NT domain can have a home directory. A home directory is a central default location for users' files and user configuration information (see Figure 23.4). In the case of a Windows 98 machine, the home directory is also the home for a roaming or mandatory user profile that will be accessible to users no matter where they log on. (See Chapter 8 for more on user profiles.)

The user's home directory becomes the default starting point for File Open and Save As commands, and it also appears as a starting point from the command prompt. The home directory can be a local directory on the user's PC, but it can also reside on a network share, such as on the domain controller or another network server. If the home directory resides on a network share, it can *follow* the user, much as a roaming user profile follows the user. A user who moves to a different workstation can still have easy, convenient access to any files stored on the home directory (see Figure 23.5).

A home directory scheme also provides a convenient and simple method for performing backups and providing fault tolerance for user files. A series of home directories—each bearing the name of the user—can be stored together on a fault tolerant drive or on a drive that is subject to a rigid and regular backup regimen.

To specify a home directory in Windows NT Server's User Manager for Domains, follow these steps:

1. Double-click a user account in the User Manager for Domains main window to open the User Properties dialog box.

Chapter 23: Windows 98 in Windows NT Domains   **523**

2. In the User Properties dialog box, click the Profiles button.

3. In the User Environment Profiles dialog box (see Figure 23.6), specify a home directory for the user account.

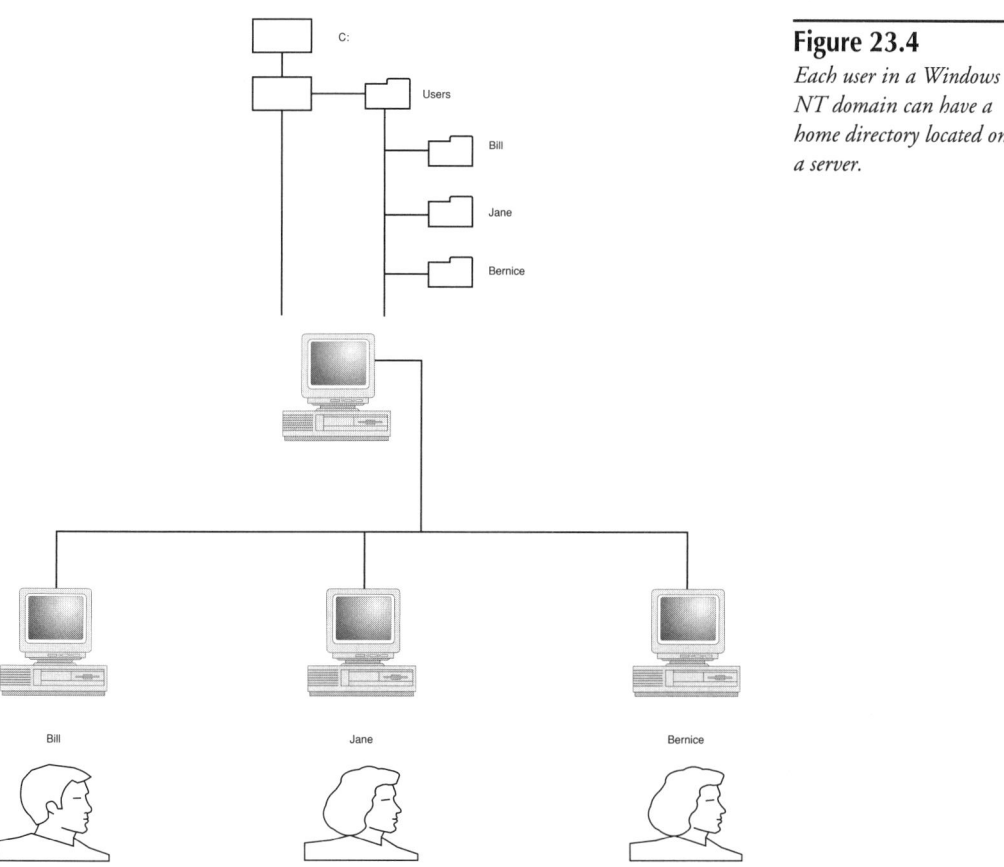

Figure 23.4
Each user in a Windows NT domain can have a home directory located on a server.

Note Note that a Windows 95/98 client cannot use the User Profile path setting in the User Environment Profiles dialog box. For Windows 98 clients, a mandatory or roaming user profile should be located in the home directory. See Chapter 8.

User Profiles

A user profile is a bundle of user-specific configuration information. See Chapter 8 for a complete discussion of user profiles in Windows 98. In a domain environment, the user's domain user account can include a reference to a network-based user profile that will follow the user to whatever workstation she uses to log on. A user in the engineering department, for instance, can log on to a machine in the accounting department and still see the desktop settings and user preferences she sees from her home workstation.

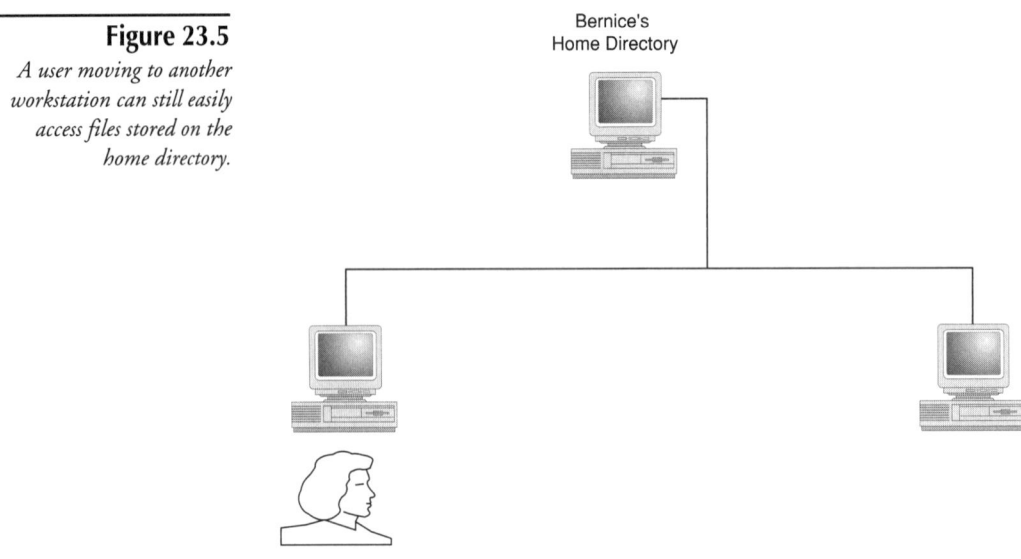

Figure 23.5
A user moving to another workstation can still easily access files stored on the home directory.

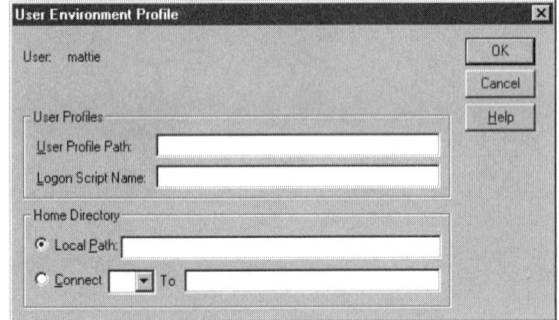

Figure 23.6
Windows NT's User Manager for Domains User Environment Profile dialog box.

Group Memberships

In a domain-based security environment, resource permissions are typically assigned to user accounts through group memberships. Windows 98 (as you learned in Chapter 21) does not provide native support for user and group permissions, but it can acquire a user-level permissions list from a domain or from a Windows NT Workstation or NetWare server machine.

A group is a collection of users with common rights and permissions. The concept of a group greatly simplifies the assignment of resource permissions. For instance, all users in the Accounting department may need access to the same spreadsheets and the same printer. Rather than individually configuring access to each of these resources for every user, the network administrator can simply assign access to a group called the Accounting group and make sure that each user who needs these resources is a member of the Accounting group.

When a Windows 98 user logs on to the domain, she gains access to all network resources that have been assigned to the user's account either explicitly or through group memberships.

Logon Hours

In Windows NT Server's User Manager for Domains, you can define the exact times during which you'll allow a user to log on to the network. You can specify the times of the day and the days of the week in which you'll allow a particular user to access the network (see Figure 23.7).

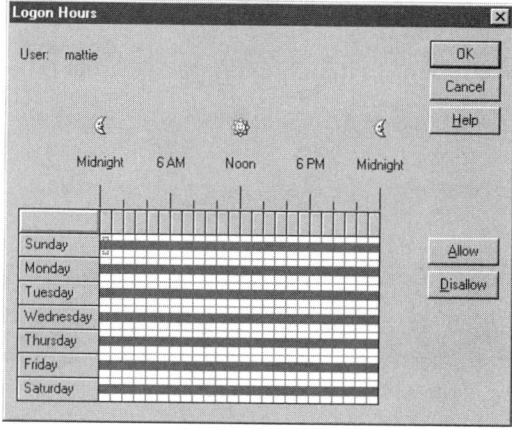

Figure 23.7
Windows NT's User Manager for Domains lets you schedule the user's access to the network.

Logon Workstations

In the User Manager for Domains Logon Workstations dialog box (see Figure 23.8), you can designate specific workstations to which you'll allow a particular user to log on.

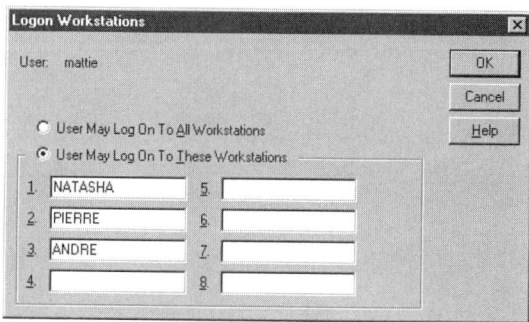

Figure 23.8
Windows NT's User Manager for Domains lets you designate a Logon Workstation.

A major feature of NT domain security is that it is designed to be independent of a particular client machine. (Typically, a user can log on from any workstation that participates in domain security.) The Logon Workstations feature lets you restrict that freedom.

Managing Windows 98 from the Domain

On larger networks, system management becomes more of a problem and efficient system management becomes more of a priority. The best strategy is for the network administrator to do as much as possible from a single desktop, rather than wandering around the office troubleshooting each troubled workstation locally.

A tool provided with Windows 98, Net Watcher, lets you manage shares on a remote Windows 98 machine. To use Net Watcher, you must enable remote adminstration on the computer you want to administer.

Microsoft provides several other tools that make it easier to manage and troubleshoot Windows NT domains. These tools include:

- System Policy Editor
- Registry Editor
- SMS System Monitor

You can remotely administer a Windows 98 machine from a Windows NT Server system using any of these tools. To administer a Windows 98 system using these tools, you must enable remote administration and also install the Microsoft Remote Registry service.

When you configure Windows 98 for user-level access control (described earlier in this chapter), Windows 98 automatically enables remote administration for members of the Domain Administrators group. Domain administrators can, therefore, manage connections and shares on a Windows 98 machine configured for user-level security. To manually enable remote administration, or to add other users to the list of those who can perform remote administration tasks, start the Passwords control panel and select the Remote Administration tab (see Figure 23.9) Check the checkbox to enable or disable remote administration for this PC. To add another user or group to the remote access permission list, click on the Add button.

To use tools such as Registry Editor, System Policy Editor, or SMS Network Monitor for remote administration, you must install the Microsoft Remote Registry Service. To install the Remote Registry Service:

1. Start the Network Control.

2. In the Configuration tab, click the Add button.

Chapter 23: Windows 98 in Windows NT Domains

3. In the Select Component Type dialog box, choose Service.

4. In the Select Network Service dialog box, click the Have Disk button.

5. Insert the Windows 98 CD in the CD-ROM drive and browse to the Admin\Nettools\remotreg directory. Windows 98 will select the file regsrv.inf. If the Admin\Nettools\remotreg directory isn't present on the disk, search for the remotreg directory or the regsrv.inf file.

Once the Remote Registry service is installed, remote users will be able to manage the Windows 98 machine.

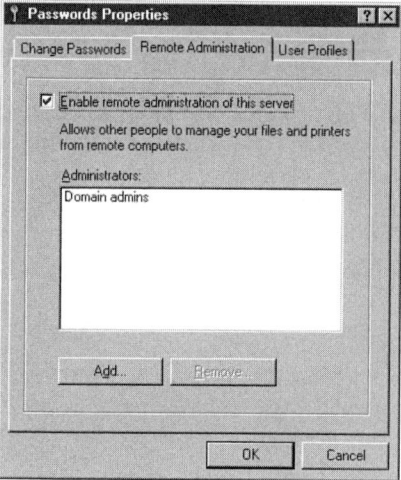

Figure 23.9
The Passwords Control Panel Remote Administration tab.

Managing the Domain from Windows 98

Microsoft also makes some of Windows NT's domain management tools available for Windows 98 machines. If these server tools are installed on the Windows 98 machine, a network administrator can perform a large amount of the domain management from Windows 98.

This package of domain management tools is available through Windows NT Server's Network Client Administrator tool. Through Network Client Administrator, you can make these tools available for a Windows 98 machine to download and install. This package of Server tools includes the following:

- Event Viewer
- File Security tab
- Print Security tab

- Server Manager
- User Manager for Domains
- User Manager Extensions for Services for NetWare
- File and Print Services for NetWare

To install the server tools, start Windows NT's Network Client Administrator, select Copy Client-based Network Administration Tools, and then follow the instructions. See Windows NT Server help.

Conclusion

This chapter describes how to configure Windows 98 as a Windows NT domain client. The chapter also summarizes some of the features that make a domain different from a small Windows 98 workgroup and described some tools for managing Windows 98 from the network and managing the network from Windows 98.

Windows 98 with NetWare/ InternetWare Networks

*M*any Windows 98 computers do their work connected to networks, and most installed networks use a version of Novell NetWare (called InternetWare in some versions, although this chapter uses the generic NetWare name). Windows 98 includes software that lets it act as a client to NetWare servers, enabling users to easily and seamlessly access shared resources, such as files and printers, on NetWare servers.

In this chapter, you learn about Windows 98 NetWare support: how it works, how to install it, and how to make changes that enable Windows 98 to operate more easily with NetWare file and print servers.

Understanding NetWare

The NetWare product line from Novell is one of the oldest and best established in the networking world. In its latest version, NetWare 4.11, it provides fast, efficient, and stable file and print services to small, medium, and large networks. NetWare's strengths are the following:

- It performs file and print networking services faster than other alternatives, such as Windows NT Server 4, on equivalent hardware.

- It is very secure; NetWare is one of the hardest Network Operating Systems (NOS) to crack.

- It is well supported; Novell has been supporting NetWare for a long time, and the company understands the various needs that professional network managers have for different support functions. For example, listings of discovered bugs in NetWare are readily available so that managers can plan around them or apply patches to correct them. Moreover, because NetWare is so widely used, more vendors and networking professionals know NetWare than any other file and print server system.

- It provides a set of directory services (on NetWare 4.*x*) that let larger organizations tie together all their NetWare services and resources into a single NetWare Directory Services (NDS) tree, making management much easier than it would be otherwise.

- It is the most flexible file and print services server on the market, through a combination of included features and third-party add-ons that extend NetWare's feature set.

Although Windows NT has been installed in place of some NetWare file servers, NetWare still owns most of the installed file and print server market and continues to be an excellent choice for most organizations.

Understanding NetWare Support in Windows 98

For Windows 98 to connect to any network server, a number of components must be installed:

- A driver must exist for the network hardware, typically in the form of a network adapter card, also known as a Network Interface Card (NIC) driver.

- The appropriate networking protocol support must be installed.

- Client software that supports the target file server type must be loaded and configured.

- Any optional networking service software should be installed.

Chapter 24: Windows 98 with NetWare/InternetWare Networks

Windows 98 can connect to NetWare networks that use NetWare 2.15, 3.*x*, and 4.*x* with software included with Windows 98. The networking software is installed through the Network Control Panel and uses the following configurations:

- For the networking hardware, the appropriate networking hardware driver must be loaded. This driver may be for an ethernet NIC, a token ring NIC, or any other type of network interface supported by the target NetWare servers and the cabling type installed. Also supported are connections to NetWare servers through Dial-Up Networking connections that use modems.

- The IPX/SPX protocol must be installed; NetWare connectivity requires this protocol. The Microsoft-supplied and written IPX/SPX-Compatible Protocol works nicely with NetWare servers, although some applications that rely on certain Novell APIs may require the Novell client.

- Microsoft has included the Microsoft Client for NetWare Networks with Windows 98. This small, fast client layer translates NetWare services for Windows 98 so that NetWare services act like locally connected devices in My Computer or the Printers folder (although with different settings needed to define the NetWare settings for those resources).

- Microsoft also supplies a networking service called Service for NetWare Directory Services, which gives the Windows 98 client full access to NDS services on NetWare 4.*x* servers.

Note Novell also supplies client software for Windows 98; it can be obtained from the Novell web site at www.novell.com. However, we recommend that you use the software included with Windows 98; our experience has shown it to be more stable and to consume much less memory than the Novell versions, although at the expense of some additional functionality provided by the Novell client software. Using the Microsoft software, you can run all Novell utilities, including NDS-based utilities such as NWAdmin.

It is possible to configure Windows 98 to use Novell-supplied real-mode software to connect and work with NetWare networks, but it is not advisable. Such configurations, using Novell's ODI drivers or VLM drivers, are far more complex and are easily outperformed by the 32-bit protected-mode drivers from Microsoft or from Novell. Unless you're running applications that rely on features in those drivers (which isn't terribly likely), you're better off avoiding them.

Microsoft Client for NetWare Networks

The Microsoft-supplied client software for connecting to NetWare networks is a fast, stable, small implementation that achieves excellent performance and is very reliable and simple to set up and use. Some benefits to using Microsoft Client for NetWare Networks follow.

- Has a fully 32-bit, protected-mode client that detracts no conventional memory from the MS-DOS command prompt under Windows 98

- Includes features to enable client computers to perform peer networking of files and printers in a NetWare environment

- Supports MS-DOS and most NetWare Application Programming Interfaces (APIs) for support of NetWare features

- Automatically reconnects dropped server connections

- Supports packet burst for enhanced performance over wide area network (WAN) links

- Supports NetWare logon scripts and NDS tree settings

In some instances you may want to choose a different client, such as Novell's version for the following reasons::

- Microsoft Client for NetWare Networks does not support NetWare NCP Packet Signature, which can provide better security for servers and clients.

- NetWare IP is not supported (although of course Windows 98 supports standard TCP/IP).

- Some applications may rely on Novell's client.

Installing Microsoft Client for NetWare Networks

You install all network-specific software under Windows 98 using the Network Control Panel object, shown already configured in Figure 24.1. You can use this dialog box to select the appropriate client, network protocol, NIC support, and needed networking services.

To add support for NetWare networks, follow these steps. (Make sure to have your Windows 98 CD-ROM or other installation media available.)

1. Click the **A**dd button on the Configuration tab of the Network Control Panel to open the Select Network Component Type dialog box shown in Figure 24.2.

2. Select Client and then click the **A**dd button to open the Select Network Client dialog box shown in Figure 24.3.

Chapter 24: Windows 98 with NetWare/InternetWare Networks

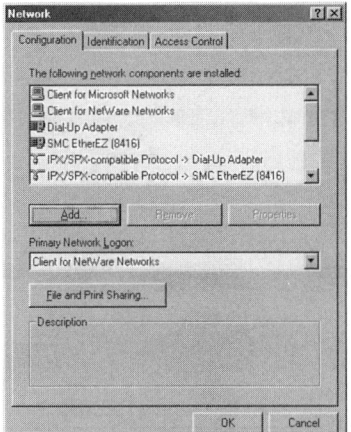

Figure 24.1
Network Control Panel already configured for NetWare support.

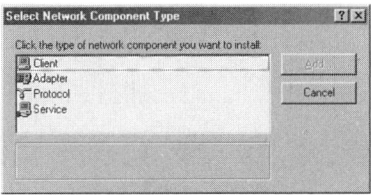

Figure 24.2
Select Network Component Type dialog box.

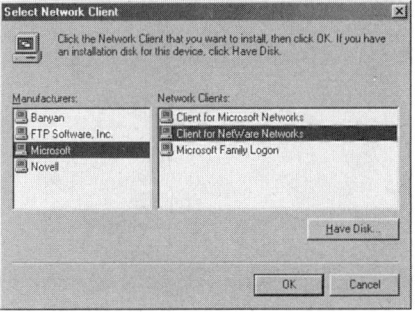

Figure 24.3
Select Network Client dialog box.

3. Choose Microsoft in the **M**anufacturers pane and then Client for NetWare Networks in the Network Clients pane; then click OK.

4. The NetWare client will be installed, as well as the IPX/SPX compatible protocol. Insert the Windows 98 CD-ROM if you are prompted to do so.

5. If you will be connecting to NetWare 4.*x* servers and you want to access the NDS tree, you also need to install the Service for NetWare Directory Services. From the Network Control Panel, click **A**dd again and then choose Service in the Select Network Component Type dialog box (refer to Figure 24.2).

6. In the Select Network Service dialog box, shown in Figure 24.4, choose Service for NetWare Directory Services and click OK.

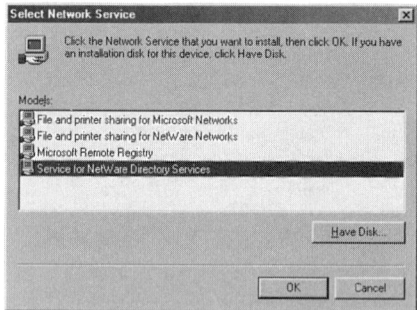

Figure 24.4
The Select Network Service dialog box.

7. If you want to make file and print services on the workstation available to other clients using peer-to-peer networking in the NetWare environment, enter the Select Network Service dialog box again and choose File and Print Sharing for NetWare Networks.

After installing the necessary components, you then should configure them before restarting the computer and connecting to the network. From the Configuration tab of the Network Control Panel, select the Client for NetWare Networks and access its Properties dialog box, shown in Figure 24.5. Define both the preferred logon server as well as the first drive letter available for network mapping on the client (usually F: drive). Also, if you want the client computer to process NetWare logon scripts, make sure the logon script check box is selected.

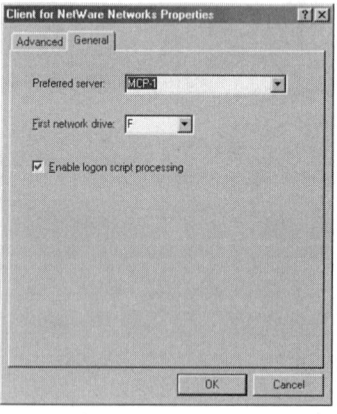

Figure 24.5
Configuring the Client for NetWare Networks.

If you are using the Service for NetWare Directory Services, open its Properties dialog box, shown in Figure 24.6. Make sure to set the preferred tree and workstation context in the provided fields.

Chapter 24: Windows 98 with NetWare/InternetWare Networks

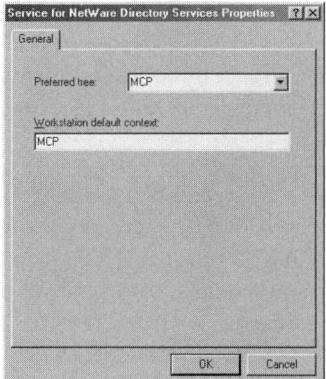

Figure 24.6
Configuring Service for NetWare Directory Services.

Finally, on the Configuration tab of the Network Control Panel, select the desired Primary Network Logon. This option does not have to be set to Client for NetWare Networks if you instead want to primarily log on to another network, but if you are connected only to a NetWare network, then you should choose that setting.

You can now click the OK button to save the Network Control Panel changes. You may be prompted for your Windows 98 CD-ROM at this point, and you will need to restart the computer for the new networking software to be functional.

Long Filename Support on NetWare Volumes

Windows 98 can store and access long filenames stored on NetWare 3.x and 4.x volumes, provided the appropriate name space is loaded and enabled for the NetWare volume. On NetWare 3.x (up to 3.11) servers, this name space is the OS/2 name space, loaded as OS2.NAM on the NetWare server. For NetWare 3.12 and above servers (including 4.x), this name space was renamed to LONGNAME.NAM, which provides the same services.

To add long filename support to a NetWare volume, you use the file server console, and one of the following commands:

```
ADD NAME SPACE OS2 TO VOLUME volume_name
ADD NAME SPACE LONGNAME TO VOLUME volume_name
```

where *volume_name* is the name of the volume to which you are adding support. Adding a new name space to a NetWare volume requires some consideration, and you should consult your NetWare documentation for full details. However, pay attention to the increased memory requirements on servers supporting additional name spaces. Also, you should add name spaces only when the server is idle, and you should plan on rebooting the server after the name space is added to the volume (you can do all volumes at one time and then reboot once). Note that rebooting the server is not strictly required under NetWare for this operation, but doing so may avoid problems.

Before rebooting the server, you should add the command LOAD OS2.NAM or LOAD LONGNAME.NAM to the system's STARTUP.NCF file. However, NetWare is intelligent enough to automatically load the appropriate support files when it mounts volumes that contain added name spaces, so this step isn't strictly required; it's just good practice to manually add the appropriate entry.

Long filename support changed somewhat as it evolved in NetWare 3.*x* and 4.*x* versions, and Windows 98 can be set to support these different long filename versions. By default, Windows 98 includes the appropriate command in the Registry to enable long filename support on all NetWare volumes that include it. However, you should know where this is accomplished. The Registry key `HKEY_LOCAL_MACHINE\System\CurrentControlSet\Services\VxD\Nwredir` should contain a *binary* value named `SupportLFN` with its value set to `0x02`. Other possible values are `0x00`, which disables support for long filenames, and `0x01`, which supports long filenames only on NetWare 3.12 and greater servers (those using LONGNAME.NAM rather than OS2.NAM). The value `0x02` supports long filenames on all NetWare servers that support the OS/2 or LONGFILE name spaces.

You can also enforce the long filename setting in the Registry through a System Policy setting. You can use the Policy Editor (with WINDOWS.ADM as an applied template) to open a Computer Policy and navigate to the policy setting Windows 98 Network/Microsoft Client for NetWare Networks/Support Long Filenames. Set the value to either `All NetWare Servers That Support LFNs` or `NetWare 3.12 and Above` (corresponding to values `0x02` and `0x01` for the SupportLFN Registry setting, respectively).

Common Problems and Solutions

As you have seen, setting up and configuring client support for NetWare networks is relatively straightforward and painless. However, some common problems do occur, and a little preparation can help you rapidly overcome these issues.

The Windows Logon Appears Instead of the NetWare Logon

This condition indicates that either the Microsoft Client for NetWare Networks wasn't selected in the Network Control Panel (double-check this setting) or that something is making the network unavailable, which causes Windows to fall back and use the Windows logon screen. The following are possible causes:

- The preferred server is down or not responding, or the preferred server setting in the Microsoft Client for NetWare Networks properties dialog box is incorrectly set.

- A hardware failure, such as a failed NIC or network cable, is affecting the workstation.

- Some key component required for the NetWare client has been removed or incorrectly configured (check to ensure that all required components are available).

Standard troubleshooting techniques are required here; the basic problem is that the workstation is unable to communicate with the file server. You should first examine other workstations to see whether they are experiencing similar problems. Then, examine the network cabling and the network hubs (for 10BASE-T) for reported problems. Make sure to look at Device Manager in the System Control Panel to ensure that the NIC is functioning normally. Finally, check all of the components required for NetWare connectivity to ensure that they are present and configured properly. You may have to remove and re-install NetWare support if a key file has become damaged.

Another possible cause of this problem is an incorrect frame type setting. NetWare networks using ethernet can use any of several frame types, including 802.2, 802.3, and Ethernet II. Open the Network Control Panel and access the properties for the IPX/SPX Compatible Protocol. Move to the Advanced tab and check the Frame Type setting, which is normally set to Auto. Try setting it to the known frame type being used on the NetWare servers.

Logon to NetWare Servers Is Rejected

If you are able to log into your preferred server, but not to other servers, the cause of the problem is probably unsynchronized passwords on each server. The Client for NetWare Networks uses a single set of credentials that you type when you log in. Use the Novell SETPASS command to ensure that your passwords on all desired servers are synchronized.

Another possible reason for the logon to be rejected is that the account has been locked out from the server for some reason. Often, this situation is due to an Intruder Lockout, which occurs when an incorrect password is provided too many times to attempt to log in to the server. Work with the Network Administrator to clear the lockout and resolve the incorrect password problem.

Another possible cause is that the NDS tree or context is set incorrectly. Open the properties for Service for NetWare Directory Services and check these two settings. If necessary, compare them with another client computer that is known to be working.

Logon Script Does Not Run

This usual cause of this problem is that the appropriate check box is not selected in the Client for NetWare Networks properties dialog box. Make sure that the **E**nable Logon Script Processing check box is enabled.

Conclusion

In this chapter, you learned how to set up Windows 98 with its included software for accessing NetWare networks with servers running from NetWare 2.15 to the most current version of NetWare. You learned about the software needed to access NetWare resources and about installing and configuring long filename support, both for the Windows 98 client and for the NetWare server.

Use the information in this chapter with the other chapters that discuss Windows 98 networking:

- Chapter 21, "Understanding Windows 98 Networking"
- Chapter 22, "Peer-to-Peer Networking"
- Chapter 23, "Windows 98 in Windows NT Domains"
- Chapter 26, "Windows 98 and Remote Communication"

Windows 98 with TCP/IP

The rise of the Internet and the recent emphasis on interoperability have only increased the stature of TCP/IP. The TCP/IP protocol suite, which grew up around UNIX, is quickly becoming the universal network protocol, and Microsoft provides some new and innovative features with Windows 98's TCP/IP. If you're accessing the Internet, you'll need to use TCP/IP. If your Windows 98 computer will be part of a routed, non-Novell LAN or WAN, the chances are you'll need TCP/IP. Windows 98's new Automatic Private IP Addressing feature (APIPA) makes it easier than ever for even small workgroups and single-subnet local networks to use TCP/IP.

This chapter discusses some basic TCP/IP configuration issues and shows how you can configure Windows 98 to operate on a TCP/IP network.

TCP/IP Concepts

TCP/IP, like any other networking protocol, is a system of rules that facilitates communication among computers. An implementation of TCP/IP, such as Windows 98's TCP/IP implementation, is a software component that carries out the tasks associated with communication through the TCP/IP protocol. Chapter 21, "Understanding Windows 98 Networking," discussed the basics of protocols and protocol bindings in Windows 98 and described how to configure network protocols using the Control Panel Network application. TCP/IP generally requires more configuration than other protocols, and this chapter will help you understand some of those configuration options.

TCP/IP is often referred to as a "protocol suite" or a "protocol stack" because it is a collection of related protocols and applications that provide Wide Area Networking (WAN) and Local Area Networking (LAN) functionality.

The TCP/IP suite includes protocols used to communicate at the network level, protocols used to manage the transfer at the internet level, and the application programming interfaces provided at the application level of the network model shown in Figure 25.1 below.

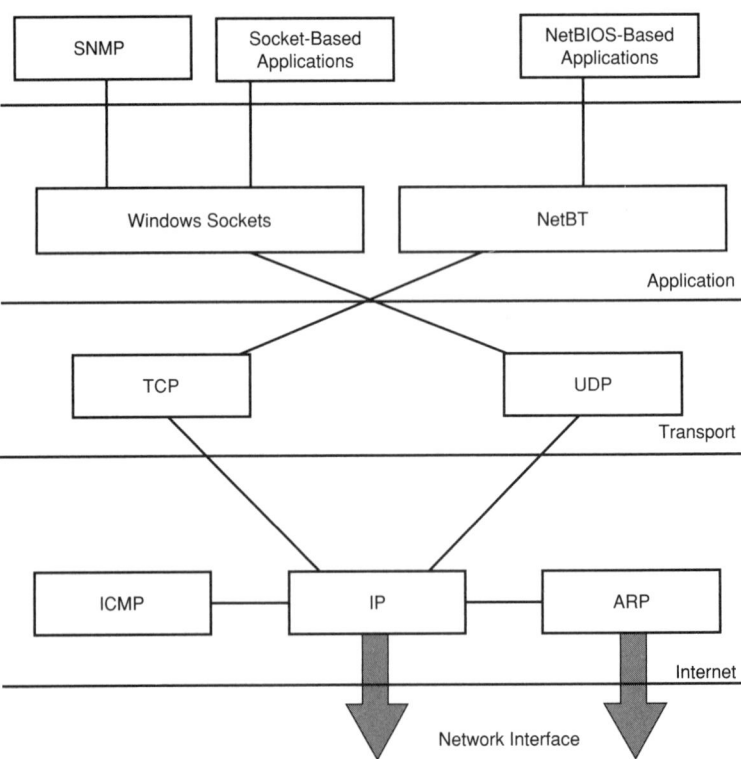

Figure 25.1
The TCP/IP network model - broken down by layers.

Chapter 25: Windows 98 with TCP/IP

Every computer in a TCP/IP network has a unique IP address. An IP address is a logical address identifying the computer on the network. The IP address is a 32-bit binary number. To make the IP address more memorable and less intimidating, the 32 bits are subdivided into 4 sets of 8 bits, known as octets. The IP address almost always appears in decimal form. In decimal form, each octet is represented with a number less than or equal to 255 (which is 2^8-1). The four octets are separated by periods, producing an address such as:

12.234.5.67   (read as twelve dot two thirty-four dot five dot sixty-seven)

Note The ARP protocol translates IP addresses to Ethernet or Token Ring physical addresses for the subnet. The physical address is a permanent address associated with each network adapter. For more on ARP, see the discussion of the ARP utility, later in this chapter.

The IP address consists of two parts: a network ID and a host ID. All computers on any given network segment will have the same network ID. You'll learn more about IP addressing later in this chapter.

Windows 98 supports three methods for aquiring an IP address. Choosing a method to use will depend on your network and your needs. The IP address configuration methods as follows:

Manual. You can directly define an IP address and subnet mask for your Windows 98 machine in the Network Control Panel.

Dynamic. Windows 98 supports Dynamic Host Configuration Protocol (DHCP). A DHCP server on your network can dynamically assign a temporary IP address (and other settings) to the Windows 98 machine. The advantage of dynamic IP address assignment is that a large group of occasional users can share a smaller number of IP addresses. This is especially useful on the Internet, where the number of available addresses is limited. An Internet provider can lease an IP address to a connecting user, and at the end of the session, lease the same address to another user. Dynamic IP address assignment can also save administration time for large networks because client machines don't have to be manually configured.

Automatic. Windows 98 includes a new feature called Automatic Private IP Addressing (APIPA), which automatically creates an IP address for the Windows 98 machine if no IP address is specified. APIPA has some limitations and is only practical for very small networks (see the section on APIPA later in this chapter). For very small networks, APIPA lets you use TCP/IP without ever having to learn anything about IP addressing and subnet masks. APIPA can also provide connectivity on a DHCP-based network when the DHCP server is not available to assign an address.

These three address configuration methods are each discussed in later sections. You must assign a legal and appropriate IP address to your computer if you want it to operate on a TCP/IP network.

Referring to computers in the form of binary 32-bit octets is convenient for computers, but it is less convenient for flesh-based devices such as humans. Computers on a TCP/IP network typically are referenced by a human-friendly name that is then resolved to an IP address by the computers on the network. Windows 98 supports two schemes for assigning names to computers, as follows:

- **Hostnames.** Hostnames are assigned and resolved using the Domain Naming System (DNS). DNS, which has long been part of TCP/IP, is the vast name-resolution scheme used on the Internet. DNS is what allows you to access an Internet node by its domain name (e.g., www.microsoft.com). Private TCP/IP networks can also use DNS to locate computers using user-friendly names. You can configure Windows 98 to access a DNS server for DNS name-resolution queries, or you can create a Hosts file, which contains DNS-name-to-IP-address mappings.

- **NetBIOS names.** Every computer on a Microsoft network has a NetBIOS computer name, a name used to identify the computer for purposes of browsing and locating resources. (See Chapter 21 for more on computer names in Windows 98.) A WINS server (Windows Internet Name Service) can associate NetBIOS computer names with IP addresses. Windows 98 can access a WINS server for NetBIOS to IP address name resolution queries. Windows 98 can also use a static file called the LMHOSTS file for NetBIOS name resolution, or, on the local subnet, Windows 98 can resolve NetBIOS computer name queries through local broadcast.

These name-resolution schemes are discussed later in the chapter.

Another important concept you'll need in order to understand TCP/IP networking is a gateway. The term gateway has many definitions within the world of networking, and recently has come to mean a device that performs some form of protocol translation. Within TCP/IP, however, a gateway is simply a router that acts as a conduit from the subnet to the greater network. The default gateway (which you can specify through Windows 98's TCP/IP settings) is the default location where Windows 98 will send packets addressed to destinations beyond the subnet.

TCP/IP is designed to serve very large networks. Indeed, the Internet (the largest TCP/IP network) covers the entire planet and is many times larger than anyone ever imagined a network could be even a few years ago. To help manage and troubleshoot traffic over the great spaces of the network, TCP/IP comes with a number of useful utilities. Some of these utilities are also useful on small networks. A later section of this chapter discusses their TCP/IP utilities.

Configuring TCP/IP

As mentioned earlier, there are three methods for assigning a TCP/IP address to a Windows 98 machine, as follows:

- **Manual.** You can directly configure an IP address and subnet mask.

- **Dynamic.** You can let a DHCP server assign an IP address and other TCP/IP settings to the Windows 98 machine.

- **Automatic.** Your Windows 98 machine can create its own IP address using Automatic Private IP Addressing (APIPA).

As is so often the case, the manual method is the easiest to understand conceptually, but the most time-consuming to implement (especially on a network) because it requires you to directly configure an IP address and subnet mask for each network node. The manual method (and the dynamic method, if you're using an onsite DHCP server) require you to have some conception of what you'd like the IP address to be. The IP address for a given computer must fit into a coordinated addressing scheme for the complete network (see "Understanding IP Addressing," later in this chapter). The automatic method, which uses Windows 98's new APIPA feature, does not require any knowledge of IP addressing techniques and is thus ideal for small networks with little or no on-site technical administration.

Configure TCP/IP properties through the Network Control Panel. You must first make sure TCP/IP is installed and bound to the network adapter through which you wish to connect to the network. (See Chapter 21 for more on installing and binding network protocols.) To access the TCP/IP Properties dialog box (see Figure 25.2), open the Network Control Panel and double-click on the icon showing TCP/IP bound to the relevant network adapter.

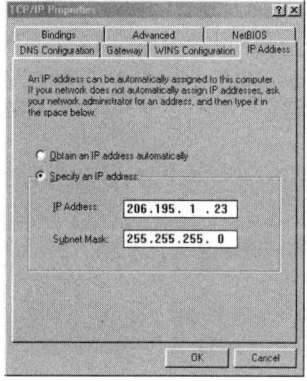

Figure 25.2
The TCP/IP Properties dialog box.

The TCP/IP Properties dialog box includes seven tabs, as follows:

- **IP Address.** The IP Address tab lets you specify whether the Windows 98 machine will receive a dynamic IP address (from a DHCP server) or whether the address will be configured manually. Choose Obtain an IP address automatically if the computer will receive an IP address from a DHCP server (see Figure 25.2). Choose Specify an IP Address to manually configure an IP address and subnet mask. Enter the IP address and subnet mask in the space provided.

- **WINS Configuration.** The WINS Configuration tab lets you configure the PC to access a WINS server for NetBIOS-to-IP-address name resolution (discussed later in this chapter).

- **Gateway.** The Gateway tab lets you enter the addresses of one or more gateways. A gateway is a router—a device through which the Windows 98 machine will access remote parts of the network. The first gateway in the list becomes the default gateway.

- **DNS Configuration.** The DNS Configuration tab lets you enable DNS and configure Windows 98 to function as part of a DNS domain (see the section on configuring DNS, later in this chapter).

- **NetBIOS.** The NetBIOS tab allows you to select the option to support NetBIOS applications on the TCP/IP protocol. NetBIOS provides an upper-layer interface for TCP/IP. Certain native Windows services, such as the browser service, require NetBIOS.

- **Advanced.** The Advanced tab lets you set TCP/IP as the default network protocol.

- **Bindings.** The Bindings tab lets you specify whether you wish to bind the TCP/IP protocol to the services Client for Microsoft Networks and/or File and Print Sharing for Microsoft Networks. See Chapter 21 for more on network bindings.

If you're connecting to the network through a dial-up adapter, as would be the case if you're configuring dial-up access to an Internet provider, Microsoft recommends that you configure TCP/IP settings through the Dial-Up Networking connection rather than through the Network Control Panel. (See Chapter 26, "Windows 98 and Remote Communication," for more on Dial-Up Networking.)

Dynamic IP Address Assignment with DHCP

The *Dynamic Host Configuration Protocol* (DHCP) is a centralized method for providing IP addresses and all or most of the associated other IP setup information for a client. When the client is first booted, a Discovery packet is sent on the local network. DHCP servers listen for these Discovery packets and send an Offer packet back to the requesting host. The host then responds with a yes to the first offer, no to all other current offers. The DHCP server then sends a final Acknowledge packet to the host. After this point in the process, the client will have a valid IP address and all associated options, like WINS server(s), DNS server(s), Node Type, Scope ID and or Router IP, will also be configured.

If a certain machine needs to have a permanent IP address, then the DHCP service can be configured to always provide the same IP address for that machine based on its Media Access Control (MAC) address.

To set up Windows 98 for DHCP, select the radio button labeled Obtain an IP Address Automatically, in the IP Address tab of the TCP/IP Properties dialog box (as described earlier in this chapter).

Automatic IP Address Assignment with APIPA

Windows 98's Automatic Private IP Addressing (APIPA) feature is designed to ensure that your computer will still be able to connect to the network if an IP address isn't available. APIPA has two primary functions, as follows:

- To let users on very small networks use TCP/IP even if they don't know anything about IP addressing.

- To provide a means for DHCP client to get on the network when a DHCP server isn't available.

At startup, if your Windows 98 computer isn't manually configured with an IP address, it looks for a DHCP server. If it can't find a DHCP Server, it does one of the following:

- If Windows 98 finds a default gateway, it keeps the previous IP address.

- If it can't find a default gateway, it assigns itself a Class B IP address using a random-like algorithm based on the network adapter address.

The Windows 98 computer then communicates using the Net 10 (10.X.X.X) address format. APIPA machine will not be able to use WINS or DNS, and they will not be able to communicate with nodes that are inaccessible through Net 10 addressing.

If A DHCP server comes back online, the APIPA computer accepts a new leased IP address and discontinues the APIPA address.

APIPA is a viable option for small, simple networks (fewer than 10 nodes, according to Microsoft), but for larger networks or for subnetted networks, APIPA is not a permanent solution.

Name Resolution

Windows 98 can employ several different methods for resolving host names and computer names into IP addresses (and resolving IP addresses into names). If Windows 98 encounters a name where it might have expected an IP address, it checks the following:

Local Host Name. Is the name requested the same as the current host name?

HOSTS file. Look through the HOSTS file, which provides IP-to-DNS-name mappings

DNS. Send a request to a DNS server if one is configured

WINS. Send a request to a WINS server if one is configured

Broadcast. Send a broadcast on the local network to resolve IP-to-computer-name queries

LMHOSTS file. Look through the LMHOSTS file, which provides a static table of IP-to-computer-name mappings

A summary of these name-resolution techniques is as follows:

- To resolve DNS host names to IP addresses, you can either provide the Windows 98 machine with a HOSTS file that tabulates IP-to-host-name mappings for the network, or you can specify the address of a DNS server, to which the Windows 98 machine will direct DNS name resolution requests.

- To resolve NetBIOS computer names to IP addresses, you can either specify the address of a WINS server, to which the Windows 98 machine will direct name resolution requests, or you can provide an LMHOSTS file, which tabulates IP-to-computer-name mappings. Even without an LMHOSTS file or a WINS server, Windows 98 can resolve computer names to IP addresses for the local subnet using B-node broadcasts.

Native Windows networking features, such as Network Neighborhood, use Windows computer names to support network browsing. If your network is using TCP/IP, you must provide some form of IP-to-computer-name resolution if you wish to support browsing across routers.

Note A Windows NT Server system can act as a DNS Server or a WINS server.

The following sections describe how to configure Windows 98 to use a DNS server, a HOSTS file, a WINS server, or an LMOSTS file.

Setting Up Windows 98 for a DNS Server

To set up a Windows 98 machine to use DNS, select the DNS Configuration tab in the TCP/IP Properties dialog box and make the following entries:

1. Select the radio button to **E**nable DNS.

2. Although the **H**ost field may be any legal name, the default host name would normally be the computer name. You can put in another name here to use as the host name without affecting the computer name. The host name is used together with the domain name to create what is known as a Fully Qualified Domain Name (FQDN) for the machine. When the machine does a DNS query, the local domain name is appended to the short name (host name) to create a FQDN.

> **Note** The DNS domain name is unrelated to the Windows NT domain name. You'll configure a DNS domain name when you set up a DNS server. If you want your network to be available by host name over the Internet, you'll need to register a domain name with InterNIC: http://rs.internic.net.

3. Put the domain name in the D**o**main name box. This is the name of the Internet domain and is not the same as a Windows NT or LAN Manager domain. NT and LAN Manager domains are logical groupings of computers for administrative purposes. This would be a domain name such as mcp.com. As stated in step 2, this information will be appended to the host name to generate FQDNs for query resolutions. The domain name field is optional, but the more information you provide, the fewer problems you are likely to encounter.

4. In the DNS Server Search Order box, type in the IP address of up to three DNS servers that you want to use for name resolution. The order in which these servers will be searched will depend on the order in which you type them. The first one in the list will be the first one searched and so on (see Figure 25.3 for an example). Once you have typed in the IP address of the DNS server, click the A**d**d button to add it to the list. If you need to rearrange the order in which the severs are searched, you will need to manually reconfigure them by removing and adding them until the list is in the order you desire.

5. If you would like to have additional domain suffixes appended to the host name and searched in queries, type in the names of those additional domain suffixes to the Domain Suffix Search Order box and click A**d**d to add them to the list. You may enter up to five additional suffixes to search.

If you plan on using WINS in Windows 98, then you will also need to configure the WINS configuration tab. WINS reduces the amount of local broadcast traffic done for name resolution. WINS can be used alone or in conjunction with DNS. WINS also enables the users on the network to browse across the routers without having to have a special configuration file for each machine.

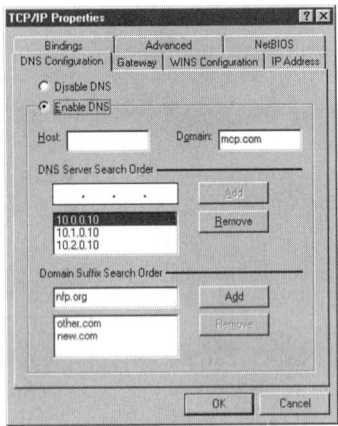

Figure 25.3
Configuring the DNS Configuration tab for the TCP/IP protocol.

Setting Up Windows 98 for a HOSTS File

HOSTS Files

In the early days of TCP/IP, the HOSTS file was used to translate known DNS host names into their equivalent IP address. The HOSTS file is a simple text file with one line for each record. A record consisted of one IP address followed by one or more host names to be used for that IP address. For example, a sample of a host file may look like the following:

Table 25.1
Sample HOST File

199.72.26.10	callen	CALLEN	callen.mis	# Win 98
199.72.26.11	rakesh	RAKESH	rakesh.fin	# P200 NT
199.72.26.12	cindy	CINDY	cindy.fin	# Alpha VMS
199.72.26.13	sarah	SARAH	sarah.accts	# P200 Linux

In Table 25.1, above, the host names cindy, CINDY, and cindy.fin all refer to the IP address 199.72.26.12. The other names can be used to indicate groupings, computer types, locations, or anything else you desire.

See the sample HOSTS file HOSTS.SAM in the \Windows directory for a discussion of HOSTS file format. You can edit the HOSTS file using any text editor, such as Notepad.

Because the HOSTS file must be manually configured, you'll need to continually update the file whenever there is a change to an address. The HOSTS file goes in the \Windows directory; it has no extention.

> **Note** You must select the Enable DNS option in the DNS Configuration tab of the TCP/IP Properties dialog box in order to use a HOSTS or LMHOSTS file.

Setting Up Windows 98 for a WINS Server

To set up WINS, select the WINS configuration tab and make the following entries:

1. Click the radio button to **E**nable WINS Resolution.

2. In the **W**INS Server Search Order box, type the IP addresses of the Primary and Secondary WINS servers. Click the **A**dd button to add them to the list.

3. You can enter a scope identifier in the S**c**ope ID box if you will be using NetBIOS over TCP/IP and require it on your network for a group of computers to communicate with each other and not outside their group.

4. If you will be using DHCP and have configured the IP Address tab to automatically assign the IP address, then the radio button for Use D**H**CP for WINS Resolution will be available to select. If you select this option, then you may leave the rest of the fields blank and have the DHCP server provide your Windows 98 machine with the information it needs.

> **Note** Don't forget that if you have more than one adapter in your Windows 98 machine, you may have to configure these items more than once or possibly with different settings for different adapters.

Setting Up Windows 98 for an LMHOSTS File

The LMHOSTS provides static mapping of computer names to IP addresses. Like the HOSTS file, LMHOSTS must be updated manually. Using LMHOSTS is therefore less convenient and not as versatile as using a WINS server for name resolution, but in some situations, an LMHOSTS file is still a viable option.

See the sample LMHOSTS file LMHOSTS.SAM in the \Windows directory for a discussion of LMHOSTS file format. You can edit the LMHOSTS file using any text editor, such as Notepad. The LMHOSTS file goes in the \Windows directory; it has no extension.

TCP/IP Tools

The TCP/IP suite is full of useful user and administrative tools. Most of the tools are run from the command line. This means you must run them from the command prompt or, in some cases where there is a GUI display, the RUN command in the Start menu, or double-click the executable in Explorer or My Computer.

WINIPCFG

The Windows 95/98 IP Configuration Display utility provides a basic view of the IP configuration. If the More Info >> button is clicked, then a complete listing of options appears as in Figure 25.4 below. This figure shows a basic configuration of a host with IP and Mask. This display also displays the MAC address of the network interface card. This host has been set as Broadcast Node Type since no other methods of host name resolution are configured, like DNS or WINS.

Figure 25.4
WINIPCFG Utility - Basic Host Configuration of IP and Mask value.

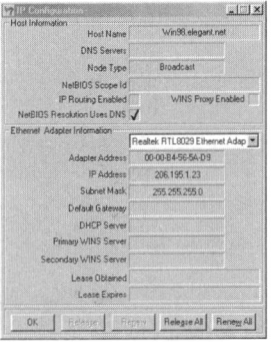

Telnet

Windows 98 provides a TELNET client application. This is a basic terminal emulation package providing connectivity to any terminal based operating system like UNIX and VMS. A terminal emulation provides interpretation of standard escape sequences that indicate cursor movement, cursor position, screen color, screen reverse, screen flashing, and terminal beep operations to name a few.

The client can be used to connect to any host. If you are connected to the Internet or have an internal DNS service, you can use a fully qualified domain name, FQDN, to access the host. If you have WINS, you can use the NetBIOS name. If you have neither WINS nor DNS, you may need an LMHOSTS file or a HOSTS file with host name information in it for every host you want to access by name. If all else fails, you can use the IP address of the host, no matter what, assuming, of course, you know it.

To use TELNET (see Figure 25.5), at the command prompt, enter the command with the host name or IP address as an argument such as:

    TELNET   HOSTNAME.DOMAIN.ORG

    TELNET   NetBIOSName

    TELNET   XX.YY.AA.BB

You can also create a shortcut to TELNET on your desktop or in your Start menu settings, per Windows 98 standard methods. With a shortcut, you can include the IP address of a specific host if desired, otherwise it will ask for the host or IP address to connect to. Remember the host names must have some resolution method available, otherwise only the IP address will work.

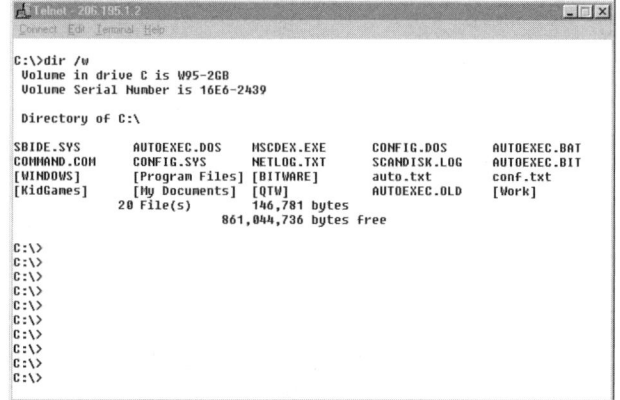

Figure 25.5
The TELNET Application; Connecting to the world, connected to a TELNET Daemon running on NT, at an NT CMD.EXE prompt.

FTP

Another standard utility supplied with TCP/IP is the client application FTP, or File Transfer Protocol. This is similar to a TELNET session except that it has some specific commands for retrieving, (GET, a file) and uploading, (PUT, a file). You can also do multiple file transfers with MGET and MPUT commands within FTP.

Like a TELNET session, an FTP session is terminal based and requires validation at the server host. You need to know an account name and password at the FTP server to gain access.

The FTP protocol was one of the building blocks of the Internet. To allow anyone access to an FTP site on the Internet, a special login name was used called anonymous. You need to supply your email address as the password for anonymous access.

To use the FTP utility at the command prompt, like TELNET (see Figure 25.6), enter the command with the host, FQDN, or IP address of the FTP site to visit. For example:

FTP   FTP.CLASSIC.COM

FTP   206.195.1.2

This would connect you to the CLASSIC.COM FTP server host, assuming the name can be translated to a valid IP address by some service, HOST file, LMHOST file, or DNS service.

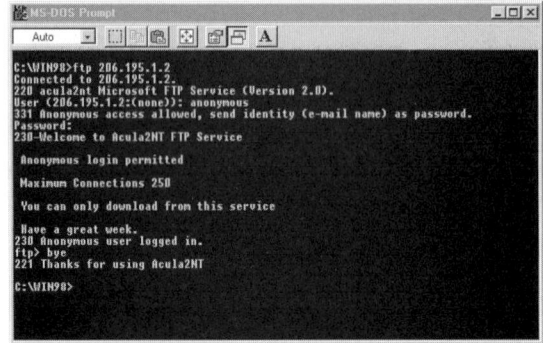

Figure 25.6
The FTP Client—Sample connection (to NT IIS).

PING

The first tool of TCP/IP is the connectivity tool known as PING (see Figure 25.7). PING sends packets from one host asking for a return of the same information. A successful PING of another host provides delivery timing information and proves all software and hardware on both machines is functioning properly.

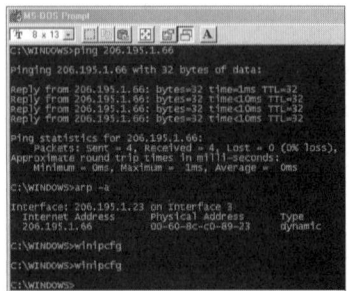

Figure 25.7
PING Utility from the DOS Command Prompt— defaults to 4 test packets.

ROUTE

The ROUTE command can be used to display the current routing table, as well as add, modify or delete any routes in the table. You only need to add a route if you have multiple network interfaces.

Windows 98 has been upgraded to provide basic routing functionality. This requires two network interfaces on a single host. The concept of routing is that the software at one interface receives a packet destined for the other interface. The software then transfers the packet to the other interface with all required IP packet header changes for the new network. This is called IP Forwarding.

To enable the actual routing service, you would need to click the Enable Routing check box in the WINIPCFG utility as shown in Figure 25.8.

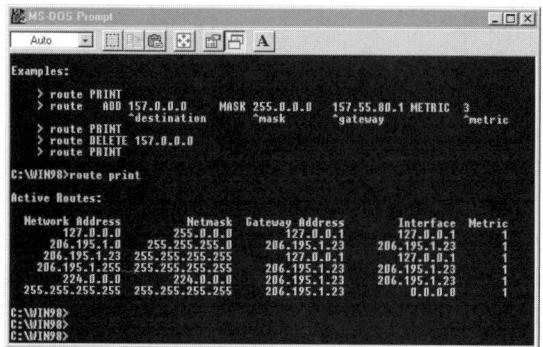

Figure 25.8
ROUTE Command Sample Output after last part of help output.

TRACERT

To test your wide area network connectivity, you can use TRACERT at the command prompt. This command actually sends out PING commands with incrementing by 1 Time-To-Live (TTL) values starting with 1. This forces the first router to send an Internet Communication Message Protocol, ICMP, error message back. TRACERT displays the IP and possibly the name of each target along the path to the remote host by incrementally forcing the next host after each error response until the actual destination host responds.

You will only need this on the rare occasion that the network response is slow or dead. You can see at which point along the path the congestion is occurring. The average user will never need to use this utility.

Other Utilities

The NetBIOS Over TCP/IP statistics are available using NBTSTAT at the DOS command prompt. The information is time specific in that the entries only last between 2 and 10 minutes after their last use. When a NetBIOS request is made and the destination machine name is unknown, your system broadcasts a request for the name on the local network. If a machine answers, with its MAC address, then this MAC address is stored in the NetBIOS cache for use by the protocol to transfer data between the source and destination. NBTSTAT displays the names and their MAC addresses in this table.

The only reason you might use this utility is to troubleshoot a connection that is not correct or not working. You would check the NBTSTAT entries with NBTSTAT -N and compare the results with the MAC hardware address of the correct machine. The average user will not need to use this utility.

Understanding IP Addressing

Every computer on a network must be uniquely identified so that network applications will know where to send data. On a TCP/IP network, this unique identification comes in the form of an IP address. In TCP/IP, every connection to the network must have a valid IP address. While it's tempting to think that a network device (such as a computer, router, or printer) has the network address, this is not the case. It is actually the device's connection to the network that has the address. Some devices (routers, for example) will have more than one connection to a network and will need more than one IP address. In this section, we'll look briefly at how IP addressing works.

The IP Address Format

If you've used a TCP/IP-based network (and the Internet qualifies), you've probably seen IP addresses. They typically take a dotted decimal form, such as 192.102.11.103—four numbers ranging from 0 to 255, separated by decimal points. What you may not know, however, is that this dotted decimal notation is really just a human-friendly way of representing the address's true form, which is as a 32-bit binary number. This 32-bit number is broken down into four 8-bit segments called octets. Each of these octets ranges from 00000000 (0 in decimal) to 11111111 (255 in decimal). Written out in binary format, the IP address example I gave earlier (192.102.11.103) looks like this (I added the spaces to make it easier to look at):

11000000 1100110 00001011 1100111.

Network and Host IDs

Every IP address contains two parts: a Network ID and a Host ID. The Network ID defines the network segment on which a particular connection exists. The Host ID identifies that connection on that network. Think of it this way. Your house has a street address, something like 123 Main Street. That street address is like an IP address and can also be broken down into two parts. The street name, Main Street, is like the Network ID in an IP address. The street number, 123, is like the Host ID in an IP address and identifies the house on that street.

In an IP address, however, things are the opposite way around from a street address. The Network ID is on the left and the Host ID is on the right. Take the IP address we used earlier, 192.102.11.103. The left two octets (192.102) might be the Network ID and the right two octets (11.103) might be the Host ID. You probably noticed I used the word *might*. That's because where the split occurs in the IP address can change. This leaves room for flexibility in assigning IP addresses.

Address Classes

The Network Information Center (NIC) is responsible for assigning IP addresses. They have three classes of address that they can assign: A, B, and C. Class A networks are assigned to big companies, Class B to medium sized-companies, and Class C to smaller companies. Class A and B addresses are no longer available. They have all been given out. The way that these classes are determined is where that split between network ID and Host ID occurs. Take a look at table 25.2.

Note Note that the terms Network Information Center and Network Interface Card have the same abbreviation (NIC).

Table 25.2
NIC Network Classes

Class	Format	First Octet	Networks	Hosts
A	N.H.H.H	1-127	127	16 million
B	N.N.H.H	128-191	16,384	65,534
C	N.N.N.H	192-223	2 million	254

The first column in Table 25.2 shows the class of the network. The second shows how many octets of the IP address are assigned to be the Network ID and the Host ID. The class defines a default subnet mask, and the subnet mask defines how the IP address is divided between the Network ID and the Host ID. You can also customize the subnet mask, as described later in this chapter. In a Class A network the first octet is the Network ID and the last three octets are the host ID. This means that there are a relatively small number of class A networks (127), but that each can have a large number of hosts (over 16 million). Finally, the table shows what the decimal range of the first octet is for that class. Class A networks range from 1-127. In a class B network, you can see that the first *two* octets are used as the Network ID and the last two as the Host ID. This means more networks (16 thousand), but fewer hosts per network (only 65,000).

> **Note** Addresses beginning with 127 are actually reserved for internal use and cannot be used for IP network addresses. This address is referred to as the local host and is commonly numbered 127.0.0.1 although any valid octal numbers after the 127 are considered the same in most cases.
>
> The first octet range from 224-239 is used for multicast addresses, allowing hosts to broadcast to multiple destinations. The range from 240-255 is used for experimental purposes.

Subnets

Often, your network will be divided into smaller networks called subnets. This division can be useful for many reasons, including the reduction of network traffic and the simplification of network management. But, what do you do if you need to subnet your network and you've only been given one network address? TCP/IP allows for a nice solution to this problem, called *subnetting*. Subnetting allows an IP address to be broken down into smaller, logical subnets. Basically, what happens is you take the original Host ID of the IP address and break it down into a subnet address and host address. Referring back to our example of the street address, this would be akin to breaking down a street number into apartments or suites.

Subnetting works something like this. Assume that your company has been assigned a Class B address by the NIC. This address is 131.107.x.x. Remember that a class B address typically uses the first two octets as the Network ID. In this example, therefore, the Network ID would be 131.107. As is, we have one network which can have just over 65,000 hosts on it, each host identified on the network by the second two octets of the IP address. That's fine if we want a network that large. We have another option, though. We can take the Host ID (the third and fourth octet) and make one the subnet ID and one the Host ID. Now we have one big network (represented by 131.107.x.x), which is divided into 254 subnetworks (131.107.1-254.x), each of which can have 254 hosts (131.107.x.1-254).

Subnet Masking

The idea of subnetting is pretty simple, but how do we actually do it? Subnetting is accomplished using something called a subnet mask. A subnet mask is another 32-bit binary number that identifies which part of an IP address is the network ID and which part is the Host ID. In binary, the subnet mask will always be a string of ones followed by a string of zeros, like this:

11111111 11111111 00000000 00000000

The shift between one and zero indicates where the network ID of the IP address the subnet mask defines ends and where the Host ID begins. Like the IP address, the subnet mask is often represented in dotted decimal notation. Thus, the example above would be 255.255.0.0.

Let's take a look at an example. Assume that I have a standard Class B address, like 131.107.34.123. The default subnet mask for a Class B address is 255.255.0.0. When I give a host the address 131.107.34.123 and the subnet mask 255.255.0.0, the first two octets (131.107) are used as the network ID and the last two (34.123) are used as the host ID. If I decide to subnet my network, as in the example we discussed earlier, I might use the subnet mask 255.255.255.0. Now, the first three octets (131.107.34) are used as the network ID and only the last (123) is the host ID.

So far, we've looked at subnet masks in which each octet is either 255 (11111111 in binary) or 0 (00000000 in binary). You can actually make the division at any point *after* the default division used for your network class. This allows you to customize the number of subnets and hosts per subnet to more precisely meet your situation. Using the previous example again, you might decide that instead of having 254 subnets and 254 hosts per subnet, you may need more hosts on each subnet. You could create a custom subnet mask which would allow just that. It's easiest to understand this if we look at it in binary. To get 254 subnets and 254 hosts, we used the following subnet mask:

11111111 11111111 11111111 00000000 (255.255.255.0)

To create a situation where we have more hosts per subnet, we would simply increase the size of the Host ID by moving the subnet mask to the left. We might, for example, use a subnet mask like this one:

11111111 11111111 11110000 00000000 (255.255.240.0)

Developing Your Network

To develop addresses for your own TCP/IP network, first, figure out how many clients you will need to accommodate at an absolute maximum for any one area and then start with the network class that supports at least that many hosts. For example, if there is less than 254 hosts in any network, use all class C network numbers, just make them up like 222.1.1.0 is the first network all the way up to 222.1.254.0 is the 254th network. That is a total of almost 64,000 possible IP addresses, 254 networks each with 254 hosts, to choose from. This should be enough in most cases. Use the default mask of 255.255.255.0 for each network.

If you need more than 254 in any one site and no more than 65,000 then use a class B network address of your choice. For example, you could use 134.1.0.0 for the first network and 134.254.0.0 for the last network, providing 254 networks of 64,000 clients per network, whether you use them all or need them. Use the default mask of 255.255.0.0 for each network. In this case your client numbers for any one given network range from x.y.0.254 to x.y.255.254.

Hopefully, this has given you a little understanding of how IP addressing works. Obviously, there's more to it than I can cover in a section like this one.

SNMP and Windows 98

The Simple Network Management Protocol, or SNMP, is another specialized protocol used to monitor and manage hosts remotely. Windows 98 comes with an agent. An agent is a service that accepts specific requests for information about various parameters on this host. The agent allows a controlling SNMP management utility, like Tivoli, CA Unicenter, Openview, Netview and many more, to 'watch' over each SNMP client on the network. The manager can set counters to specific values or reset them to zero, set threshold values that will cause the local agent to send an alert or trap back to the management software in the case of an error. The SNMP agent provides a simple method of watching and tracking all nodes on the network that have SNMP agents. Almost every network device built within the last few years will be SNMP agent equipped.

To install a local SNMP agent for Windows 98, you need to install it from the Add Services in the Services panel of Network Icon from Control Panel. The software is located on your installation CD-ROM in:

E:\TOOLS\NETTOOLS\SNMP   (assuming E: is your CD-ROM)

Once installed, any SNMP Manager will be able to set traps and get information, based on the SNMP version 1 specification.

Accessing UNIX Hosts with Windows 98

As noted above with the TELNET utility, accessing a UNIX host is made easy from Windows 98. Run the command line TELNET to start the GUI interface, or create a shortcut on your desktop to it (right-click desktop/New/Shortcut, enter TELNET, press Enter twice), then click the shortcut. If you know the address or the name of the host you can start the TELNET program with this host name as the only argument on the line (or update your shortcut with this host name) as in:

```
TELNET UNIXHOST
```

Once you are connected to the UNIXHOST machine, you will be prompted to log in. This login is requesting you to enter a valid login name from the UNIXHOST passwd file, nothing to do with the Windows login names although they may match. You will also be prompted for a password for that login name if one is needed. After a successful login, your process will be started and you will be in some program, usually a program called a shell that is similar to a DOS command line, although, again, you could be starting a program designated by the UNIXHOST administrator for that particular login. To exit the command line shell you would type in EXIT and press return. This would end your login session on the UNIXHOST machine and return you to a blank TELNET program on your Windows 98 machine.

Chapter 25: Windows 98 with TCP/IP

Table 25.3
Basic DOS and UNIX Command Comparison with Examples

DOS	UNIX
DIR D:\wfw\system	ls /c/wfw/system
COPY C:\config.sys c:\bck	cp /c/config.sys /bck
REN C:\config.old config.new	mv /c/config.old /c/config.new
DEL C:\config.001	rm /c/config.001
DELTREE \app1 \app2	rm -r /app1 /app2
TYPE config.sys	cat /c/config.sys
CD \wfw\system	cd /c/wfw/system
A:	(N/A)

Note that UNIX uses the forward slash whereas DOS uses the backslash. There is a UNIX equivalent for almost every DOS command. Consult a UNIX reference for more on UNIX commmands.

Personal Web Server Service

An optional package contained on the installation CD, within the \ADD-ONS\PWS directory is the Personal Web Server installation package; use PWSSETUP.EXE to install.

```
E:\ADD-ONS\PWS\PWSSETUP.EXE   (if E: is your CD-ROM)
```

This service makes your Windows 98 system into a "mini" web page server. This is designed for light usage and is not intended as a full Web server service, this is a weak cousin of Internet Information Server, IIS, for NT.

You should install the Personal Web Server service only if you want others to access your web published documents from your machine directly instead of from some central server. If no central server exists, this is an easy way to provide basic local web services. Access to your machine will be via Internet Explorer or any other web browser.

Note that you must create the actual web pages with any text editor or any advanced web publishing tool like FrontPage 98 from Microsoft. You'll learn more about Web publsihing and Personal Web Server in Chapter 29, "Windows 98 as an Internet/Intranet Server."

Common Problems and Solutions

Some of the most common problems come from bad configuration or incomplete configuration of your IP information. Minimally you need at least a unique IP address and a network mask. Optionally you need a Default Gateway IP address if there are other networks to reach. Other useful options are DNS and/or WINS server IP addresses for host name resolution and improved browsing functionality (from WINS only). If you are still having some problems, check below for some common solutions.

`No network:`

> Network card is not functioning properly, incorrect setup parameter. Go back to the diagnostics that came with the NIC and test it. Most NIC's provide a diagnostic and setup utility. You need two machines with the same type of NIC to run the network test. One machine must be set to send packets, the other is set to receive. If you have many NIC's to set up and test, you can use the same host to send packets to all other hosts as receivers. This will provide standard connection and diagnostic tests.

`Cannot see any other machines in network neighborhood:`

> Wrong subnet or incorrect IP address for this network, check your settings.

> Wrong mask for this network or subnet, check your settings in Network applet of Control Panel, click on the TCP/IP protocol, and then click Properties.

> NIC not functioning correctly, see `No Network:` above.

> Cabling not correctly installed or connected for network. Always check your cabling to ensure it works with at least one host. Test all cables against this one host to ensure they work.

`Cannot Locate Another Host (with PING, TELNET, FTP, etc)`

> Wrong subnet or incorrect IP address for this network or

> Wrong mask for this network or subnet, see notes above.

> NIC not functioning correctly, see `No Network:` above.

> Cabling not correctly installed or connected for network.

> Try pinging your software, then your address or another host, first host may be down.

`Duplicate IP`

> You have configured the same IP as another machine OR DHCP is leasing out an IP that another machine has already taken (Service Pack 3 on NT updates the DHCP server so

that it PINGS the next available lease address three times by default on the network before allowing lease, thus ensuring no duplicate addresses are used). Just try another one or go talk to someone who sets the IP addresses. You can always PING the host from another running machine to see what IP it is then check with WINS or DNS for who should have it. The PING will return a MAC address, so you can always track that down as well by actually going to every machine on the network and checking the MAC address on each NIC.

`Cannot Browse the rest of the network`

Wrong IP address or network mask, check your settings against network settings.

WINS may not be configured properly or at all, need WINS to browse past your LAN.

Wrong Default Mask used, not getting to the remote network.

Wrong Gateway address used, not getting to the remote network, check settings in all cases.

`Slow Response to PING, TELNET requests to other hosts`

WINS and/or DNS services incorrectly set up, requests must time out first before you can continue. Check whether the IP addresses are correct for either or both of these services.

`Telnet or FTP session very slow to start or never completes connection`

Host name is not resolving back to you correctly. The remote host may need an entry in a host file for them to resolve back to you. Press Control+C to stop the program at the command prompt. You may have to wait up to 2 minutes for the GUI interface to respond when there is a network error but it should eventually time-out, be patient or do something else in another window.

`Cannot 'See' This Machine with SNMP`

Intall or re-install service, check if service is running correctly in Control Panel Services.

Check that your network is set up correctly as indicated above, see `No Network`.

`Cannot Run X Windows from UNIX`

You need to install a third-party X Server product to run an X session on Windows 98. There are many available like www.Hummingbird.com and www.Intergraph.com.

Conclusion

This chapter described the TCP/IP protocol and you can configure and manage in Windows 98. You learned about IP addressing and name resolution and about some of the TCP/IP utilities, such as TELNET, FTP, PING, WINIPCFG, and more. This chapter also discussed SNMP and described some of the pitfalls you may encounter when setting up or using TCP/IP in Windows 98.

Windows 98 and Remote Communication

One of the most powerful and flexible features in Windows 98's arsenal of networking and communications tools is its remote communications features. The most common use of the remote communications features is accessing the Internet, but there's a wealth of other possibilities: setting up the machine as a dial-in server, creating virtual private networks, and so on.

Windows 3.x was originally shipped with little more than the ability to contact a host computer through a dial-up with a dumb terminal interface. Later, the Internet became a public phenomenon instead of a private resource, and dial-up connections to the Internet became commonplace. Dialing directly into a host was no longer the only way to connect, and far from the most efficient. At this point, Windows 95 was introduced, and because of Windows 95's open-ended networking and telephony architecture, it was relatively easy to give Windows 95 dial-up connectivity that could use every available network protocol, including and especially TCP/IP.

All of these features have been carried over into Windows 98 and enhanced considerably. Windows 98 also contains support for the new protocol named Point-to-Point Tunneling Protocol (PPTP), which lets people use dial-up connections to create virtual private networks (VPN) using public networks, such as the Internet. VPNs make it possible to safely connect to private resources, such as a shared network drive, without fear of someone intercepting the communication.

Windows 98 includes features that make it possible to fully exploit TCP/IP's capabilities. One such feature is Multilink, which enables you to bond together several dial-up or ISDN connections and treat them as a single TCP/IP link with a single address. This increases throughput and bandwidth dramatically.

Another new feature to Windows 98 is the Dial-Up Server, which was originally provided as part of Plus! for Windows 95. The Dial-Up Server enables users to dial directly into your computer and use it either as a gateway to other systems (such as the Internet) or simply as a repository for files or resources. Previously, the only way to do this was with a third-party program (such as Symantec's pcANYWHERE), or with Windows NT. You'll learn more about Windows 98's Dial-Up Server in Chapter 29, "Windows 98 as an Internet/Intranet Server."

In this chapter, you'll learn how to do the following:

- Understand basic Dial-Up Networking protocols and capabilities
- Set up Windows 98's Dial-Up Networking features
- Edit the properties for a Dial-Up Networking connection
- Write scripts to support DUN connections
- Use Multilink on DUN connections to enhance bandwidth

Understanding Dial-Up Networking Capabilities

Dial-Up Networking is the catch-all description for any Windows 98 services that allow a modem, ISDN line or other dial-up device to serve as a connection to a network. When using Dial-Up Networking, any software that requires a network connection operates seamlessly with a modem, albeit with slower throughput than a full-fledged network link.

Note The term dial-up device is used to refer to hardware that uses a phone line or other non-dedicated network cable to make a connection to a network server. Dial-up devices can include modems, ISDN adapters, cable modems, and ADSL adapters. It does not refer to network hardware such as network interface cards, switchers, routers, or hubs.

Dial-Up Networking is not, by default, installed with Windows 98 unless you have also installed a modem and the appropriate network protocols, such as TCP/IP.

Generally, Dial-Up Networking is used to make three kinds of connections in Windows 98: Internet connections, connections to virtual private networks (VPNs), and direct connections to host computers (for BBSes, gateways, or remote-control software).

Internet Connectivity

Connecting to the Internet is probably the single most common use for Dial-Up Networking in Windows 98 because much of Windows 98's feature set is enhanced and enriched by having an Internet connection.

Connecting to the Internet through Dial-Up Networking requires that you know the name and server addresses of your Internet provider and that you have the TCP/IP protocol installed in your network stack and bound to the Dial-Up Adapter. Most ISPs provide client software that performs the configuration and dialing for you, but it's best to learn how to perform the needed configurations yourself. This is described in detail later in the chapter.

VPN (Virtual Private Network) Connectivity

A virtual private network, or VPN, is a new and extremely useful technology that makes it possible to use the Internet as a secure backbone for a private network.

One of the VPN protocols, PPTP, is Microsoft's variant of TCP/IP, which is used to establish a private communications channel with a specific computer. It can be used over either a direct-dial or third-party (for example, general Internet) TCP/IP connection. Other protocols used to establish VPN connections include IPsec and SOCKS, but this chapter focuses on using PPTP.

As mentioned before, with PPTP you use the Internet as the backbone for your communications, rather than setting up a dedicated dial-up connection. PPTP also affords much greater security than conventional Internet protocols, which prevents transmissions across the Internet from being intercepted and keeps unauthorized users out of the network you want to share. Finally, PPTP lets you make use of high-speed dial-ups and uses less hardware than a direct-dial setup.

Direct-Dial Connectivity

One of the most secure ways to establish communication between two computers is to have one dial directly into the other. Direct-dial connectivity was the basis for nearly every computer BBS until the explosion of the Internet.

There are many third-party products and protocols that support direct-dialing, such as Symantec's pcANYWHERE 32.

The big drawback to using direct-dial is that for each individual connection to the server, there must be a separate telephone line. Bigger organizations can better afford to implement direct-dial, but unless the number of dial-ups is limited to one or two, this can be a costly scheme to implement for smaller organizations (such as homes or businesses).

Protocols Used in Remote Communications

There is no real way to forge a data connection between two computers without both of them using a common protocol. This section looks at the most common protocols used in Windows' remote communications components.

TCP/IP

Right now, TCP/IP is *the* protocol. The Internet is built on it, and many computers and operating systems (including Windows) use it as the main communication standard between computers in local area networks. It's flexible and universal; it can be adapted to serve a great number of needs, and there's almost no operating system or computer that can't make use of it.

When TCP/IP is used with remote communications to connect to an Internet dial-up, there are two basic ways TCP/IP can be implemented: SLIP and PPP.

- SLIP stands for *Single Line Protocol*. Older Internet providers use SLIP as their dial-up methodology, which was designed specifically to carry TCP/IP and nothing else. SLIP requires the user to hard-code the connection addresses, and for that reason, it has fallen into disfavor. SLIP does not support features like PPTP and Multilink, either.

- PPP is an abbreviation of *Point-to-Point Protocol*. PPP has more or less eclipsed SLIP as the standard way for dial-up connections to use TCP/IP. Because it's more versatile in its design, it can also be used to encapsulate other protocols such as IPX/SPX or NetBEUI. It is easier to work with than SLIP because it automatically detects and assigns the proper server and client addresses. PPP can also be used to perform Multilink connections and carry PPTP packets.

IPX/SPX

IPX/SPX (an abbreviation of Internetwork Packet Exchange/Sequenced Packet Exchange) is the protocol on which the Novell Netware operating system is based. Like TCP/IP, it's routable, meaning it can be used on wide-area networks as well as LANs.

IPX/SPX is generally not used in Windows 98 (or Windows-to-Windows) connectivity, unless you are dialing into a Novell-based server that has resources that can only be accessed through IPX/SPX, such as a print server or a network drive. However, some LANs do use IPX/SPX without having Novell resources simply because it's a convenient and routable protocol that requires far less setup than TCP/IP. However, non-Novell IPX/SPX LANs are becoming less common because of TCP/IP's omnipresence.

NetBEUI

NetBEUI is the least flexible of the most commonly used network protocols. Because it's not routable, it is designed to work only in LAN environments of 50 nodes or fewer. Windows 98's remote communications support NetBEUI, but it should only be enabled when dialing into a network that explicitly requires it, such as a private LAN.

PPTP

Point-to-Point Tunneling Protocol, as mentioned before, is a Microsoft protocol for creating virtual private networks across the Internet. It is not the only protocol for creating VPNs, but because it comes as part of the available Windows 98 networking components, it is the only one covered in this chapter. Other protocols, such as SOCKS or IPsec, require third-party implementations.

Servers Used in Remote Communications

Every remote communications setup needs a server. Sometimes the term server can be misleading because a server doesn't have to be a powerful computer. The server is just the generic name for whichever computer is hosting the connections. When you set up remote communications in Windows 98, it's important that you know what type of server is hosting your connection. With this knowledge you'll be able to correctly configure your networking settings and get the best possible throughput and feature set.

UNIX or Generic Internet

If you are using Windows 98 to connect to the Internet, chances are you are dialing into a UNIX system of some sort. Most ISPs use a variety of UNIX to provide connectivity both within their network and to the outside world. Most of these providers use PPP (rather than SLIP) in their TCP/IP connections and do not support IPX/SPX or NetBEUI because there is no need for it.

Windows NT 4.0 or Higher

Windows NT servers can carry a great variety of services, from conventional Internet and PPP connectivity to IPX/SPX and NetBEUI. If you are using an Internet provider that uses NT servers, you generally don't need to know this; your connection will be a generic PPP dialup. You need to configure explicitly for a Windows NT 4.0 server only when you are accessing shared resources, such as network drives or printers.

Windows NT 3.5/3.1 and Windows 3.*x*

If you are making connections with older versions of Windows or Windows NT, you need to be explicit about this in your Dial-Up Networking settings. Older editions of Windows NT (those prior to 4.0) had their own proprietary Microsoft protocols, and these have been included in Dial-Up Networking for the sake of backwards compatibility. Generally, these older proprietary protocols are not used unless you know that you will be dialing into or making contact with an older server.

Windows 98/95

Connecting between Windows 98 machines (or from Windows 98 to Windows 95 machines) on a LAN was simple enough before. However, the provisions for dialing directly from one machine to another—or accessing another machine securely through the Internet—were limited and only possible through third-party products. The addition of the Dial-Up Server and PPTP in Windows 98 fixes both of those shortcomings and makes Windows 98 a viable platform for hosting a low-cost dial-up or PPTP server.

Installing Dial-Up Networking

When Windows 98 is first installed, it installs the Dial-Up Networking components as a matter of course if a modem is present. Dial-Up Networking cannot be installed without a modem or ISDN device present.

If you have a modem present, you should see a Dial-Up Networking icon when you open My Computer (see Figure 26.1).

Chapter 26: Windows 98 and Remote Communication

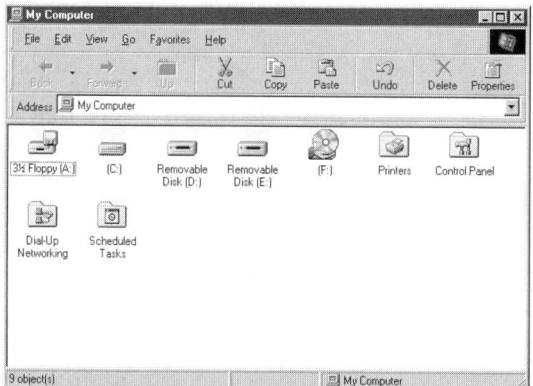

Figure 26.1
The Dial-Up Networking icon, as it appears in My Computer.

Installing Dial-Up Networking Manually

If you have a modem installed, but no Dial-Up Networking icon is present, then you need to install Dial-Up Networking manually as follows.

1. Go to the Control Panel and open the Add/Remove Programs icon. Click the Windows Setup tab and select Communications.

2. Click **D**etails to bring up the list of components under Communications (see Figure 26.2).

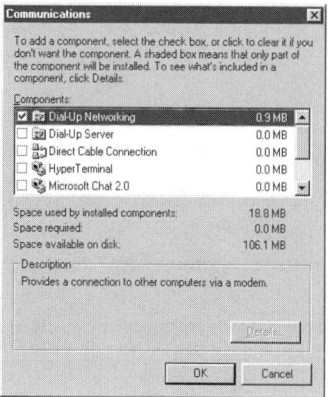

Figure 26.2
The Dial-Up Networking component as listed in Add/Remove Programs.

3. Check the box for Dial-Up Networking and click OK. Click OK on the Add/Remove Programs Properties sheet. The computer prompts you to insert the Windows 98 CD-ROM or to specify a path to the needed files.

4. Reboot when the computer has finished copying files.

The main component of Dial-Up Networking is the Dial-Up Adapter, which can be seen in the Network Configuration sheet (see Figure 26.3). This driver enables the network stack to look at the modem as though it were another network adapter and to treat the data being pumped through it in that fashion.

Figure 26.3
The Dial-Up Adapter in the Network Configuration sheet.

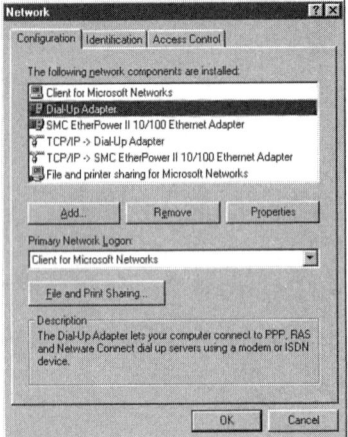

Note America Online, or AOL, installs a dial-up adapter of its own into the network stack. If you are not using Windows 98's own Dial-Up Networking, AOL's adapter assumes the same function. If you *are* using DUN and AOL, delete the AOL dial-up adapter to avoid conflicts.

Installing Commonly Needed Network Protocols

Not every network protocol is needed for Dial-Up Networking. In fact, having superfluous protocols installed can degrade the performance of the network link even if you're not operating on a dial-up connection. Here is a list of the common types of dial-up connections and the necessary protocols.

- For dialing into an ISP or other Internet access node, install TCP/IP.

- For dialing into a Novell-based server to access shared resources, install IPX/SPX.

- For accessing a small, nonrouted LAN that uses the NetBeui protocol, install NetBEUI. (Some smaller networks also use IPX/SPX for future expandability; check with the network administrator.)

- For private networks, install the Microsoft Virtual Private Networking Adapter.

Checking Protocol Bindings

If you are using Dial-Up Networking in conjunction with other *kinds* of networking—for example, if you also have a LAN through which files and printers are shared—then you should change the *bindings* of the needed protocols and not delete them entirely. For example, if you have an Internet connection through a dial-up line and a LAN, you will probably be using TCP/IP for the Internet and either NetBEUI or IPX/SPX for the LAN. If you open the Network Properties sheet (available through the Network icon in Control Panel), you can see the arrangements of the bindings. In Figure 26.4, NetBEUI is bound only to the LAN interface (the SMC EtherPower adapter), whereas TCP/IP is bound exclusively to the Dial-Up Adapter. There are two main advantages to doing this:

- Fewer bindings mean less memory devoted to the network stack, and consequently, faster network operations.

- If you use different protocols to access your LAN as opposed to the Internet, it's much harder for someone to stumble across (or break into) your LAN and perhaps exploit what's there. You can safely use TCP/IP for both LAN and WAN connections if you have a firewall. However, conventional users who have both LAN and direct-to-Internet setups should consider configuring their bindings so that Internet TCP/IP users can't access the LAN.

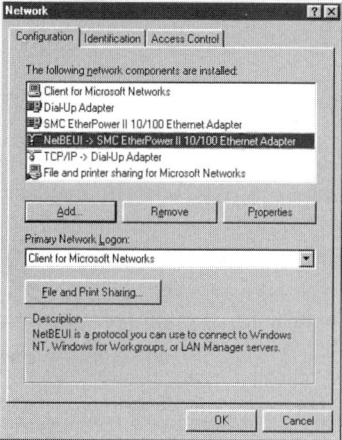

Figure 26.4
Two protocols bound to two different adapters.

If you're just using TCP/IP for everything—Internet and LAN connections—then you need to have TCP/IP bound to both the Dial-Up Adapter and the LAN adapter. By default, whenever you install any new protocol, it is bound to each adapter in the system, so you might not have to change anything if you've installed TCP/IP already. Figure 26.5 has an example of how this is represented in the Network Properties sheet.

For a more complete discussion of network protocols and network bindings, read Chapter 21, "Understanding Windows 98 Networking."

Figure 26.5
One protocol bound to all adapters.

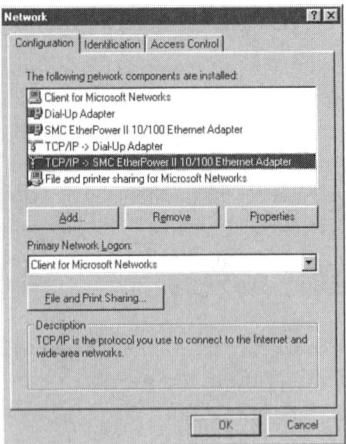

Configuring Hardware for Dial-Up Networking

It's wrong to assume that the default configuration for a modem produces the best results. The majority of the time, you'll need to tune your modem's settings to get the fastest possible connection and the best possible throughput.

On-Board Hardware Settings

Actually, the best place to start is with the computer itself. If you are running Windows 98 on a pre-1995 computer, check to see what kind of UART the computer is using. A UART is the controller chip that governs a serial port and comes in two basic varieties: 8250 (old and slow, not capable of anything above 9600 baud) and 16500 and higher. Older computers that use an 8250 or original—version 16550 (as opposed to a 16550A or higher)—will not be able to get the highest possible throughput from modems that run at 33.6 Kbaud or faster.

To determine what kind of UART is being used with your modem, open the Control Panel, then Modems. Click the Diagnostics tab; then select the modem whose UART you want to poll from the list and click **M**ore Info. The computer polls the modem for a few seconds and then produces a report like the one in Figure 26.6. The type of UART you have installed is described there.

In the Figure 26.6, the UART is listed as an NS 16550AN. This is a revised version of the original 16550 UART that has the capacity to handle high-speed throughput, the variety needed for modems that perform at better than 33.6 Kbaud. If you are using an internal modem, you should still receive a report about which UART is being used in the modem. Many internal modems don't use the most recent variety of UART either and should not be relied upon for heavy use.

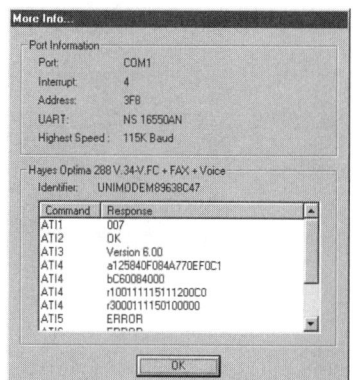

Figure 26.6
The Modems Diagnostics report, with the type of UART installed.

Tip If you discover that your external modem is connected to an on-board port that uses an older UART, don't panic. It's possible to buy a COM: port with a state-of-the-art UART chip for less than $20 from most computer suppliers. The port is mounted on a 16-bit ISA adapter and can be set to use any of the four common COM: port addresses. Also remember to disable the on-board COM: port that uses the same address if you're planning on replacing an existing COM: port with it.

Software and Hardware Compression Settings

Most of the protocols that are used over dial-up connections employ compression of some kind. TCP/IP, for instance, can be compressed through settings in Dial-Up Networking. However, this software-level compression often causes performance and throughput degradation when it's coupled with the hardware-level compression that is present in most modems.

Modem hardware compression is not designed to compress binary data, but rather to accelerate ASCII or 7-bit transfers. When this compression is coupled with the binary-level packet compression used in Windows' TCP/IP stack, throughput can actually be slower, and there's the additional overhead of compression in the modem itself. I have personally seen throughput on a 56K modem be degraded down to nearly half because of this problem.

The solution, at least where TCP/IP is involved, is to disable *all* hardware-level compression and use TCP/IP packet and header compression. Start by disabling modem compression.

1. Open the Modems window from Control Panel, and select the modem that you plan to use to perform Dial-Up Networking; click P**r**operties.

2. Click the Connection tab of the Properties sheet. Click the Ad**v**anced Settings button.

3. In the Advanced Connections Settings window, uncheck the **C**ompress Data check box. If it's already unchecked, leave it alone. (The Use **E**rror Control and **R**equired to Connect

check boxes should be enabled, however.) See Figure 26.7 for an example of how this should look.

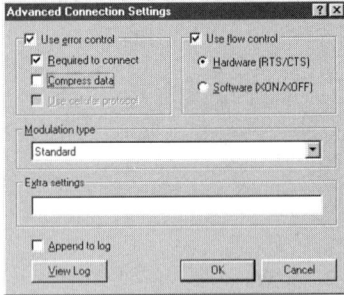

Figure 26.7
Turning off hardware compression for a Dial-Up Networking modem.

4. Click OK to return to the Connection tab; then click OK again to return to the Modems Properties sheet. Click Close. You should reboot to make sure the settings take effect.

The next step is to enable software-level compression, which is discussed during the actual configuration of Dial-Up Networking settings.

Hardware Buffering

Recent-model UART controllers support a data-flow buffering scheme called FIFO, or First In/First Out, which maximizes throughput in both directions. Some modems do not have this feature enabled by default, but it's relatively easy to activate.

1. Open the Modems window from Control Panel; select the modem that you plan to use to perform Dial-Up Networking, and click P**r**operties.

2. Click the Connection tab of the Properties sheet. Click the P**o**rt Settings button, which brings up the Advanced Port Settings window (see Figure 26.8).

3. Click the Use **F**IFO Buffers check box to turn it on. Remember that you need at least a 16550 UART to exploit this feature.

4. Move both the **R**eceive and **T**ransmit Buffer sliders all the way to the right. This maximizes the use of the FIFO buffer for both sent and received data.

5. Click OK on the open windows to close them down.

Tip | If you experience a lot of data errors or even a dropped connection, especially if you're using a slower computer (such as a 486/50) while using Dial-Up Networking, try decreasing the FIFO buffering a notch. A slower computer might have trouble keeping up with buffered high-speed communications.

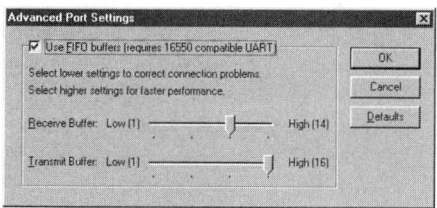

Figure 26.8
The Advanced Port Settings/Hardware Buffering window.

Other Settings and Configurations

There are a host of other minor settings and choices that can affect the quality of your Dial-Up Networking connection.

- Use the proper dial-up for your modem's capacities. If you have a V.90 or 56K-compatible modem, don't waste it on a dial-up that doesn't support them. If you know your ISP supports V.90 or 56K, for instance, get in touch with your ISP and find out which dial-ups to use for high-speed connections.

- Use the maximum speed settings possible for your modem port. To change the speed settings for a modem port, open Modems from Control Panel, select the modem in question, and click Properties. The M̲aximum Speed drop-down list contains all the possible speeds that modem's port can operate at. You might need to experiment with different settings to see which ones work.

Configuring Dial-Up Properties

This section covers how to create and edit a Dial-Up Networking connection. A connection is stored as an icon in the Dial-Up Networking folder. Each connection can be set to contact a different host through a different phone number and use different network properties and connectivity settings.

When a connection is activated, it prompts the user for a password (unless one has already been supplied in a previous DUN session). It then dials out and makes the connection.

To create and edit DUN connections, open My Computer, and then Dial-Up Networking. For an example of what the DUN folder looks like with a connection already in it, see Figure 26.9.

Generally, the DUN folder is empty save for the Make New Connection icon.

Deleting an existing connection is done in the same fashion as deleting a file: drag the icon for the connection to the Recycle Bin, or select it and hit the Delete key.

Figure 26.9
The Dial-Up Networking folder with a connection already in it.

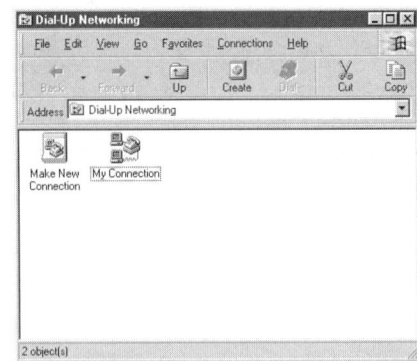

The Make New Connection Wizard

When you activate Make New Connection, this brings up the Make New Connection Wizard, which is covered here step-by-step.

1. The first screen of the Make New Connection Wizard (see Figure 26.10) prompts you for a name for the computer you are dialing and the device you will use to make the connection. The name is arbitrary and is only for your own identification. For example, if you dial into an ISP, you could call this one Internet.

Figure 26.10
The first screen of the Make New Connection Wizard, where you enter the name of the connection and the device used to make it.

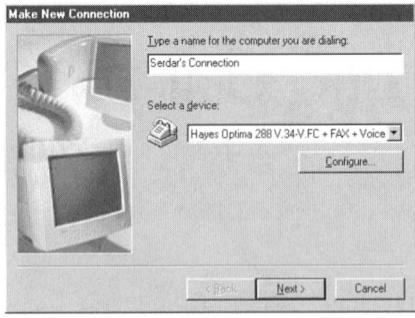

2. The Device Selection drop-down lists all the DUN devices available in your system—all modems, all ISDN devices, and so on. Select the appropriate device from the list. (If you click the **C**onfigure button, the properties sheet for the selected device appears.) Click **N**ext to continue.

3. The next screen (see Figure 26.11) prompts you for the area code and phone number of the computer you are contacting. Enter the appropriate number and area code. If you are calling a computer in another country, select the country code as well. Click **N**ext to continue.

Chapter 26: Windows 98 and Remote Communication

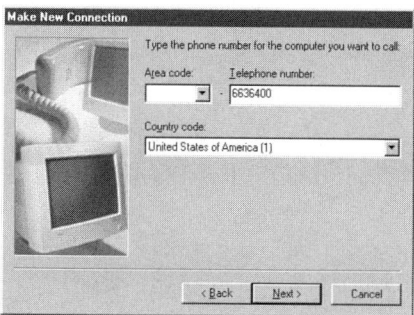

Figure 26.11
Entering the phone number and area code for the remote computer.

4. The final screen of the wizard confirms that you've created a connection. Click Finish to save the results, or **B**ack to return to earlier screens and make changes.

After the connection is saved, you can edit more of the properties in it by right-clicking the icon for the connection in the Dial-Up Networking folder and selecting Properties.

Connection Properties

The Properties sheet for a Dial-Up Networking connection is divided into four tabs: General, Server Types, Scripting, and Multilink.

General

The General tab of the Connection Properties sheet, as shown in Figure 26.12, deals with the most basic properties of the connection: the phone number and the connection device.

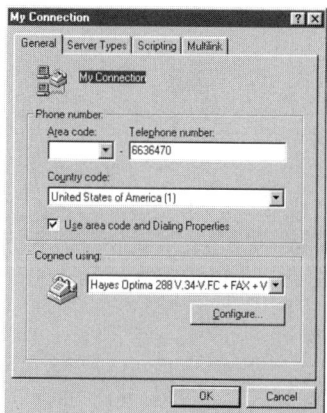

Figure 26.12
The General tab of the Connection Properties sheet.

The A**r**ea Code, Tele**p**hone Number and Co**u**ntry Code fields are identical in form and function to the ones featured in the DUN Wizard. The only new field is the U**s**e Area Code and Dialing Properties check box, which should be checked to take advantage of the area code and location information already entered into the system.

The Connect Using drop-down list is also identical to the one featured in the DUN Wizard. If you want to change which dial-up device is used with this connection, you can select one from the list. The Configure button, as with the DUN Wizard, brings up the modem's Properties sheet.

Server Types

The Server Types tab (see Figure 26.13) contains some of the most important settings that you will need to make Dial-Up Networking work properly. Know what kind of connection you'll be making and to what kind of server before you change these settings.

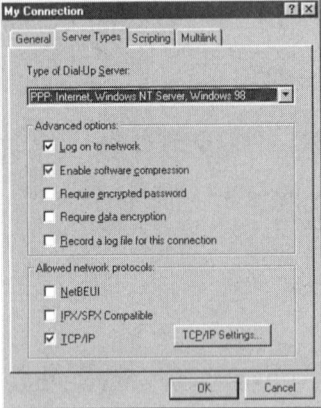

Figure 26.13
The Server Types tab.

Type of Dial-Up Server

This drop-down list contains all the types of dial-up servers that can be accessed through Windows 98's Dial-Up Networking.

- **CSLIP:** UNIX Connection with IP Header Compression: This is a specialized type of TCP/IP connection that should only be used with providers that explicitly require it. Usually you will only use PPP for an Internet connection.

- **NRN:** NetWare Connect Version 1.0 and 1.1: This lets you dial into a Novell NetWare server that uses the NetWare Connect protocol for dial-up connections.

- **PPP:** Internet, Windows NT Server, Windows 98: This is the most commonly used type of server; the vast majority of ISPs use PPP. Also, connecting to a Windows NT Server or another Windows 98 host machine usually involves PPP.

- **SLIP:** UNIX Connection: This type of connection is generally only used with older UNIX machines that support shell accounts.

Chapter 26: Windows 98 and Remote Communication

- **Windows for Workgroups and Windows NT 3.1:** Another proprietary server type, this is to be used exclusively in conjunction with dialing into older Windows networks. It is provided here mostly for the sake of backwards compatibility.

Advanced Options

The Advanced Options subsection of the Server Types tab has several check-box options that need to be examined carefully because using the wrong settings can prevent you from logging in correctly.

- **Log on to Network:** This option is used only when you are dialing into a system where you are accessing shared resources, such as network drives. The username and password you provide are passed to the host and used in an attempt to log you on remotely and attach you as a user to that system. If you are merely using the host computer as a gateway to the Internet, this option should not be checked.

- **Enable Software Compression:** This option, when checked, performs packet-level compression on the data stream to and from the host. *This option should be used in place of the hardware-level compression option that can be found on most modems because it produces far better results than the hardware compression.*

- **Require Encrypted Password:** Some providers or systems require the password to the encrypted using a simple one-way hash function. Usually this will not be the case, but if it is, enable this option. Any attempt to connect to a system that doesn't support password encryption when this is checked will not work.

- **Require Data Encryption:** Enabling this option will require that the data stream be encrypted in both directions. Not all providers or hosts support this function, so it should only be enabled if it's explicitly required.

- **Record a Log File for This Connection:** Checking this option enables logging for a DUN connection and is useful if you're trying to troubleshoot a cantankerous connection. The resulting log is stored in a file with the .LOG extension in the \Windows directory. The name of the file is the same as the name of the device for this DUN connection.

Allowed Network Protocols

With each connection, you need to explicitly state which network protocols will be used. Dial-Up Networking only allows three at this time: NetBEUI, IPX/SPX, and TCP/IP. Depending on the kind of resources you're connecting to, check the appropriate boxes. For instance, an Internet-only connection needs TCP/IP and nothing else. Someone dialing into their remote NetWare server to access both shared resources on the server and the Internet would check IPX/SPX and TCP/IP.

If TCP/IP is checked, then you must click the TCP/IP Settings button and fill in the needed information, as detailed in the following section.

TCP/IP Settings

When dialing into a TCP/IP-based server, you need to provide the IP address information for both your computer and the host. Your network administrator or ISP can provide you with these numbers. The TCP/IP Settings window is shown in Figure 26.14.

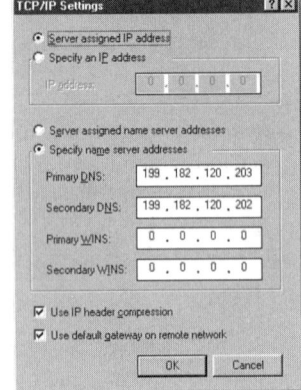

Figure 26.14
The TCP/IP Settings window.

- **Server Assigned IP Address:** Checking this button enables the server to assign your machine a dynamic IP address for the session. This is usually the case with ISPs that rely on pools of dynamic IP addresses for their clients.

- **Specify an IP Address:** Checking this button enables you to type in a 32-bit decimal-dotted IP address for your machine. You should only use this option if you are using a hard-assigned IP number from your provider or server.

- **Server Assigned Name Server Addresses:** Selecting this button enables the server to provide your machine with the addresses of the name server used in TCP/IP host lookups. If your provider or server has given you an IP address for the DNS server, however, look to the next option.

- **Specify Name Server Addresses:** Selecting this button lets you type in 32-bit decimal-dotted addresses for both the primary and secondary DNS servers in your provider or server network. If you're using an NT-based TCP/IP server, you can also provide primary and secondary WINS addresses, but generally, this is not required for generic Internet connections.

- **Use IP Header Compression:** Turning on this option forces the network stack to compress the headers for all TCP/IP packets. It should be enabled, unless your server does not support it.

- **Use Default Gateway on Remote Network:** If you are dialed into a wide-area network, such as an ISP, this option should be enabled. If you're dialed into a server that has

TCP/IP as one service among man — or if TCP/IP is also used as the protocol for access to shared resources, like network drives— then disable this option. Otherwise *all* TCP/IP traffic will be routed to the outside world!

Scripting

The Scripting tab (see Figure 26.15) lets you associate a script with a Dial-Up Networking connection. A script contains a set of instructions on how to perform the login and user- and password verification phase of the connection. Scripts use an .SCP extension and are plain-text files. Details on how to write a script are given later in the chapter.

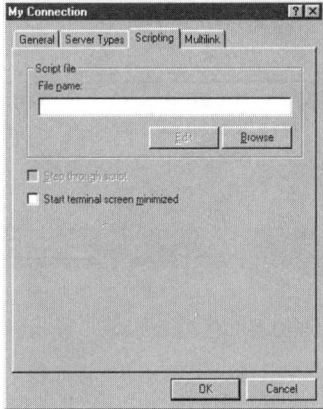

Figure 26.15
The Scripting tab.

Windows 98 includes three prewritten scripts that can be modified or used as-is to perform DUN connections.

- CIS.SCP lets you connect to the CompuServe Information Service.

- PPPMENU.SCP establishes a connection with a host that uses PPP and a menu system. The menu choices can be edited.

- SLIP.SCP/SLIPMENU.SCP establishes a connection with a SLIP-based service, both with and without menus.

All of these scripts can be accessed by hitting the **B**rowse button and choosing the appropriate filename. If you know the name of the script you want to use, you can enter its file and pathname in the File **N**ame text box, or you can punch **B**rowse and hunt for it manually.

The **S**tep Through Script option, when checked, lets you go step-by-step through a script when it's running and determine if the script is running correctly. Start Terminal Screen **M**inimized turns off the terminal screen display entirely when the script is running in the event that you don't need visual confirmation of what's happening.

Multilink

The Multilink tab (see Figure 26.16) lets you enable the Multilink feature in Dial-Up Networking, which allows more than one modem to be treated as a single device. Two 56K modems on separate lines could be channel-bonded in this fashion to act like a single 128K device.

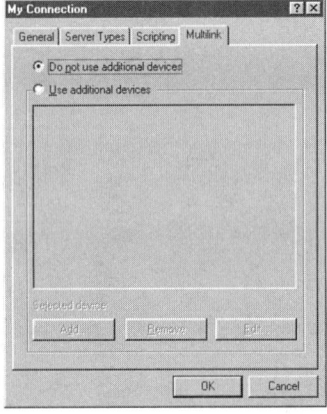

Figure 26.16
The Multilink tab with no additional devices installed.

If you don't have more than one modem installed, Multilink is not available, and the only option available is Do **N**ot Use Additional Devices.

If you do have extra modems and want to bond them together for this connection, click the **U**se Additional Devices button. This enables the options in the lower part of the window:

- **A**dd: Clicking the Add button brings up the Edit Extra Device window (see Figure 26.17), where you can select another dial-up device to use as well as the phone number that device dials out to. After you have selected another device and entered the appropriate phone number, click OK to return to the Multilink tab. The newly added device appears in the Device Name list box.

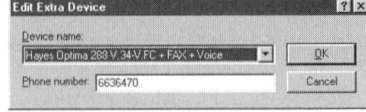

Figure 26.17
The Edit Extra Device window.

- **Remove:** Click this button to remove the currently selected device. To select a device, click its name in the Device Name list box.

- **E**dit: This brings up the Edit Extra Device Window for the selected device.

Dial-Up Scripting

A fair amount of the time, you will be using Dial-Up Networking to access a network that has a fairly rigid login procedure. Dial-Up Networking can intelligently detect and respond properly to standard Login and Password prompts, but it can't deal with the elaborate logins that CompuServe or many smaller ISPs might use. To that end, Dial-Up Networking has a scripting engine, called Dial-Up Scripting. With it, you can write a simple script to handle oddball prompts, wait for instructions, send commands and, to a degree, change line settings.

To create a script for a Dial-Up Networking connection, open the connection's Properties sheet, go to the Scripting tab, and type the name for a script (remember to use the .SCP extension) in the File **N**ame text box. Click Edit. You'll be prompted to create a new file; when you answer Yes, Notepad appears with a blank document.

Listing 26.1 shows a sample script. If you are already familiar with scripting or programming, a good deal of this is familiar territory.

Listing 26.1 Sample Script

```
proc main
    transmit "^M"
    waitfor "Login:"
    transmit $USERID
    transmit "^M"
    waitfor "Password:"
    transmit $PASSWORD
    transmit "^M"
endproc
```

The first line in the script has the command `proc main`. `Proc` is an abbreviation for procedure, or a set of commands to be executed. `Main` is the label used to describe the procedure where all execution in the script starts. The `endproc` statement tells the script processor where that procedure ends.

| Tip | All DUN scripts need to have a `main` procedure or they won't work correctly. |

The two most commonly used commands are repeated several times throughout this script: `transmit` and `waitfor`. There are several other commands:

- `transmit` sends an alphanumeric string—the text enclosed in quotes—to the host. The `transmit "^m"` statement at the top of the script sends a carriage return to the host to get the attention of your ISP's server. Some ISPs do not require this, but it's a good idea to send an attention-getting signal of some kind regardless.

    `transmit` can also send two variables: `$USERNAME` and `$PASSWORD` (refer to Listing 26.2). These are the username and password that were passed to DUN when it is activated (more on that follows).

- `waitfor` forces the computer to wait for a string from the host that matches the quoted text. In this case, we know that at some point the host will respond with the text Login:. Note that `waitfor` waits for any text, no matter what it contains inside. Even if the computer sent Host 651 Login: it would still only see the Login: at the end of the line.

> **Note** Some ISPs force you to provide your name with a symbol in front of it, which denotes a PPP or SLIP connection. For example, for PPP connections, Netcom requires you to put a hash symbol, or #, in front of your username.

- `delay x`: Wait X number of seconds. This could be to give a server time to respond. Generally, the `waitfor` command is preferable because you can use it to watch for a number of different prompts.

- `set port`: This enables you to make changes to your COM port settings. For example, in the CIS.SCP file, there are the commands `set port databits 7` and `set port parity even`. These change the number of data bits and the parity setting on the port so that the initial connection to CIS (which uses seven data bits and even parity) won't come out garbled.

When the script terminates, the computer attempts to negotiate a connection with the host and begin the session proper.

After you've customized the script to your Internet provider, you need to bind it to your connection. Highlight your connection in Connections check box, and hit Browse to locate the script you just wrote. You can also check the box to step through the script one line at a time or uncheck the box to start the terminal screen minimized, which enables you to see your script in action.

> **Warning** Make sure that your Dial-Up Networking connection does not bring up a terminal window after dialing because it would interfere with the script. To check this, right-click your connection; choose Properties, press the Configure button, and finally click the Options tab. There, you can turn off the Bring Up Terminal Window Before/After Dialing options.

Multilink

Multilink, previously only available in Windows NT, is a simple way to cheaply expand the bandwidth available to Windows 98 and Dial-Up Networking. If you have more than one modem installed in your computer, you can bond the two together to create a virtual connection that has the bandwidth of both devices combined. For example, if you had two 56K modems, together they could be treated as a single 128K device.

Multilink has its limitations. It requires a server or an ISP that explicitly supports it. Some ISPs are aware of Multilink and do not allow it on their servers to prevent the obvious bandwidth-hogging that this would enable. Also, it cannot be used on two separate ISPs. Finally, it requires a separate modem and a separate phone line for each discrete connection; two modems obviously can't be used on the same line!

To enable Multilink, right-click your connection, choose Properties, click the Multilink tab, and add a Multilink device as described previously. The next time you dial out with this connection, both devices dial simultaneously and use the same login script and server parameters to connect.

Here are some of the most common problems with Multilink and their solutions.

- The connection does not stay up, or the computer reports that it could not establish a connection with the host. This is generally due to the server or ISP not supporting Multilink connections. When this is the case, the connection might appear to be established and then dropped for no apparent reason.

    Another possible reason for this is a noisy connection. Make sure both lines are relatively noise-free.

- The connection is never made. Make sure each modem *on its own* can make a successful connection to the host. Configure a DUN connection for each modem separately, and try them out independent of each other. Then create a Multilink connection and try them out together. In this fashion, you can often determine if there are problems with the individual lines before trying to forge them together.

- Throughput is slow. Despite the added bandwidth, you may get slow throughput if your port or modem settings are not maximized. Test each modem separately, as described previously, and make sure both of them can connect at the highest possible speeds. Make sure ports and FIFO buffers are set to the maximum supportable settings.

Using Dial-Up Networking

Now that you've learned how to create and edit Dial-Up Networking connections, let's put it to use. In this example, you're going to make a connection to a local ISP node. Assume that the DUN connections settings are already set up properly. You'll be using a PPP connection with a server that can work automatically with DUN's login/password protocols, so no scripting is needed.

Dialing Out and Logging In

To use a DUN connection, click (or double-click, depending on how Explorer is configured) the icon for it in the Dial-Up Networking folder to activate it. When activated, you get the Connect To window (see Figure 26.18).

Figure 26.18
The Connect To window.

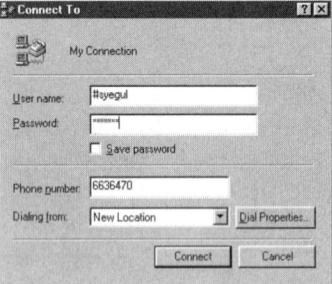

Click the **U**ser Name and **P**assword fields and fill them in with the appropriate settings for your ISP or server. Note that passwords are only echoed as asterisks. (In this case, the hash symbol in front of the user account name is required by Netcom to identify a user with a PPP account. Your own ISP might work differently.)

The **S**ave Password check box, when checked, preserves the password field for future sessions. Leave this unchecked if you are concerned about security; then the machine will prompt you for the password each time you fire up the connection. Checking the box leaves the password in the field the next time you bring up the connection.

The Phone **N**umber field contains the phone number of the ISP or server you are dialing into. If you change this here, the changes aren't permanent unless you make a successful connection.

The Dialing **F**rom field lists all the possible machine locations configured into Windows 98. Because each location uses a different area code, the dialing information might change if you change this. Clicking the Dial Properties button brings you to the My Locations tab (see Chapter 6, "Control Panel.")

When everything is ready, click the Connect button. The computer then attempts to dial out and contact the host system. You see a Connecting To… dialog box, as shown in Figure 26.19.

Figure 26.19
The Connecting To… dialog box, while dialing out to a server.

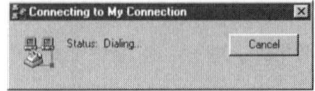

After the computer finishes dialing, the Connecting To… dialog box shows you prompts to indicate how far along it is in the login process.

Chapter 26: Windows 98 and Remote Communication   **587**

- Verifying User Name and Password...: During this prompt, DUN is attempting to respond to Login and Password prompts with the user-provided information. If this part of the login seems to be taking a long time, there's a chance that the server is overloaded, or that the username and password are incorrect.

- Logging Onto Network...: At this point DUN has passed the login phase and is now attempting to contact the remote host's network.

If the connection is successful, the Connection Established dialog box appears (see Figure 26.20). You also will see the DUN Monitor icon in the System Tray (see Figure 26.21).

At this point, you should have access to the network resources available from the server. If you are using DUN to access an ISP, then all Internet-related applications should be working. If you are dialing into a remote server to access remote drives or printers, your Network Neighborhood should update to reflect the newly available resources.

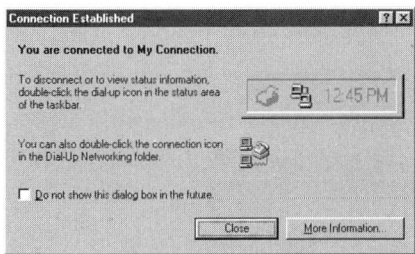

Figure 26.20
The Connection Established dialog box.

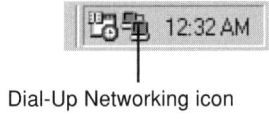
Dial-Up Networking icon

Figure 26.21
The Dial-Up Networking Monitor in the System Tray. The green lights indicate data transfer.

If you double-click the DUN Monitor icon, you get more details about the connection (see Figure 26.22).

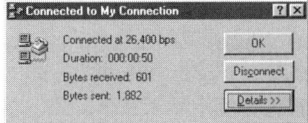

Figure 26.22
The Dial-Up Networking monitor, expanded.

Configuring PPTP

Making a PPTP connection between two computers requires that you have PPTP installed on both of them. PPTP is installed as an adapter driver in the Network Control Panel.

To install PPTP, open the Network icon of the Control Panel and click **A**dd to add a new driver. Choose a new Adapter, and then click on Microsoft for the manufacturer and Microsoft Virtual Private Networking Adapter for the adapter itself. When you click OK and begin the actual install, Windows 98 installs both the adapter driver and the NDISWAN protocol, which is needed for wide area communications. You need to reboot the computer to make the changes take hold.

After you have PPTP's adapter and protocol set up, you also need to configure a Dial-Up Networking connection to use PPTP. This is done *separately* from the DUN connection you use to connect to the Internet because the Internet is used only as the transport. Here's how to configure a new DUN connection to use with PPTP:

1. In the Dial-Up Networking folder, click Make New Connection to start creating a new DUN connection.

2. When asked for a device to use for the connection, select Microsoft VPN Adapter instead of a Modem. Click Ne**x**t.

3. Type in the host name or 32-bit IP address of the computer you are connecting to. Click Ne**x**t. The new connection is saved.

To make use of the PPTP connection, simply launch it the same way you would a conventional DUN connection. For example, if you're on a LAN and you use PPTP to talk privately to another computer, launch the PPTP DUN connection.

If you need to use a DUN connection to access the Internet, launch that first, and then launch the PPTP connection after you're logged in and connected to the Internet.

Troubleshooting Dial-Up Connections

When a Dial-Up Networking connection fails, most people are inclined to grow frustrated because of the number of possible variables. Being systematic and checking the most obvious things first can help you cut down enormously on the amount of troubleshooting needed.

Here is a list of problems and recommended solutions for troubleshooting Dial-Up Networking:

- **I've dialed into my server to get access to shared resources, and I know my password is correct, but I still can't see anything.** There are two common reasons for this. One, you don't have the correct network protocols installed (such as IPX/SPX or NetBEUI). Double-check the installed protocols in the computer *as well as the protocols enabled in that Dial-Up connection.*

    The other common reason is that you have not properly set the computer's workgroup or domain-name credentials. Check to make sure you have the correct workgroup or domain name specified.

- **The modem won't respond to any commands.** First, if the modem is external, make sure the cable is plugged in securely at both ends and is the correct type. (Don't use null-modem cables to connect a modem to a PC because the wiring is different from a conventional communications cable.) If it's an internal modem, make sure it shows up as a functioning device in the Device Manager.

  Additionally, if the modem is external check the settings for the port it's plugged into through Device Manager, and make sure the port itself is not conflicting with hardware or deactivated in BIOS.

  Third, check the COM port speed settings (described earlier in the chapter). Too high a setting will not allow the computer to communicate with the modem.

  Sometimes an external modem will get stuck and not respond to commands. In this case, try turning the modem off and then on again to bring its settings back.

- **When I dial into my server for both shared resources and TCP/IP connectivity, I get one but not the other.** Generally, a problem like this is due to the TCP/IP stack being misconfigured. For instance, you might need to specify a DNS server address if your server doesn't automatically provide those numbers.

- **My modem supports 56K, but when I dial into my ISP's 56K node, I only get 33.6K or 48K.** First, 56K modems are widely known not to be able to achieve speeds better than 53K because of current FCC standards regarding phone lines. That said, the quality of the phone lines you use to connect to a 56K-enabled server have a tremendous impact on your connection speeds and throughput. Most rural phone exchanges, for instance, cannot go above 33.6.

Dial-Up Server

Dial-Up Server is a new add-on component for Windows 98 that enables you to use a Windows 98 machine as a dial-up server. All network resources that are available through the system—shared drives, TCP/IP access—are made available to a user who dials in.

Installing Dial-Up Server

Dial-Up Server is not installed by default. To install it, open the Control Panel, and then click the Add/Remove Programs icon. Select the Windows Setup tab; then click Communications and **D**etails. Check the Dial-Up Server check box to install the Dial-Up Server program and then click OK. You'll be prompted to provide the Windows 98 CD-ROM or a path to the needed files. You must also reboot the computer for the changes to take effect.

Configuring Dial-Up Server

After you have Dial-Up Server installed, you'll need to configure it for the modem(s) you plan to enable caller access on. To edit Dial-Up Server settings, open the Dial-Up Networking window and select the **C**onnections menu item and then select **D**ial-Up Server. The Dial-Up Server window appears (see Figure 26.23).

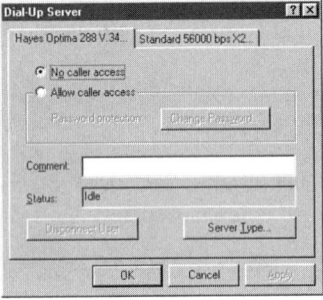

Figure 26.23
The Dial-Up Server window.

Each modem available to the system is listed as a separate tab in the Dial-Up Server window. Configuring Dial-Up Server works on a modem-by-modem basis, with all modems set by default not to accept incoming calls. Choose the modem you want to set up to accept incoming calls and select A**l**low Caller Access to enable that modem.

The Password Protection: Change Pass**w**ord button lets you set a password to be used by all users who dial in. When you click it, you get the Dial-Up Networking Password window (see Figure 26.24).

Figure 26.24
The Dial-Up Networking Password window.

If you've already been using a password and want to change it, enter it into the **O**ld Password text box. Type the new password in both the **N**ew Password and the **C**onfirm New Password text boxes; then click OK to return to the Dial-Up Server window.

The Co**m**ment text box lets you provide a simple line of text to describe the modem. You can leave this blank if you want.

The **S**tatus text box, which is not editable, shows the current state of the modem:

- **Idle:** The modem is not available for dialing in.
- **Monitoring:** The modem is waiting for a call.

If a user is currently connected, you can disconnect them manually by clicking the Disconnect User button.

The Server Type button lets you configure what kind of dial-up server you want your computer to behave like. Click it, and the Server Types window appears (see Figure 26.25).

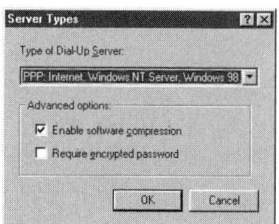

Figure 26.25
The Server Types window.

The Types of Dial-Up Server drop-down list lists two basic types of dial-up server behavior that you can have Dial-Up Server emulate:

- **PPP:** This allows users to dial in and use PPP to make a connection. This is the most common type of connection to use and will probably yield the best results.

- **Windows for Workgroups and Windows NT 3.1:** This options forces compatibility with older versions of Windows that do not use PPP connectivity. Use this only if you are providing connectivity for people using those operating systems.

The Enable Software Compression check box enables users dialing in to use software compression in their network stack (usually for TCP/IP connections). It should be checked, unless you do not want to enable compression for some reason.

The Require Encrypted Password forces the clients to submit a password that is encrypted. (You can enable encrypted passwords in the Server Types tab of the properties for a DUN Connection.)

Dial-Up Server in Operation

When at least one modem is enabled for dial-in in Dial-Up Server, an icon appears in the System Tray that indicates Dial-Up Server is working (see Figure 26.26). You can access the Dial-Up Server Properties window by double-clicking the icon. To shut off the icon, you must disable all caller access on all modems.

Dial-up Server Icon

Figure 26.26
The Dial-Up Server icon.

Conclusion

This chapter discussed how you can connect to the Internet using Dial-Up Networking and how you can create Virtual Private Networks and Dial-Up Server connections hosted through Windows 98. The power of Windows 98's remote communication features is immense. If you have a phone line, the whole of the Internet can be as close to you as your desktop.

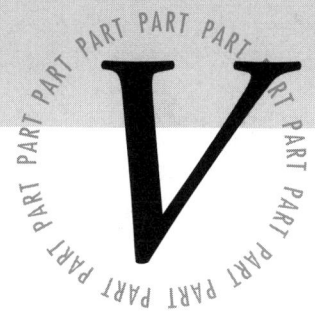

Windows 98 and the Internet

27	Internet Browsers in Windows 98 595
28	Setting Up Windows 98 for the Internet..................................... 651
29	Windows 98 as an Internet/Intranet Server 667
30	Internet Security 689
31	Mail Management in Windows 98 709

Internet Browsers in Windows 98

If you paid any attention at all to technology news during the winter of 1997-1998, you heard about the debate between the Department of Justice and Microsoft as to the role of the browser in Windows. How important is it, and why is it worth such a hassle?

Well, it's pretty important because browsing is an integral part of Windows 98. Even the Help Engine would lose features if browsing were disabled. This chapter examines the role that Microsoft planned for the browser in Windows 98 and shows how to configure and operate the two most popular browsers—Internet

Explorer and Netscape Navigator—in the Windows 98 environment. For additional information about configuring Windows 98 for the Internet, see the following chapters:

- Chapter 28, "Setting Up Windows 98 for the Internet," describes some additional aspects of Internet configuration. Chapter 28 is closely related to the material in this chapter.

- Chapter 29, "Windows 98 as an Internet/Intranet Server," discusses how to provide Web content through Windows 98.

- Chapter 30, "Internet Security" takes a closer look at some of the security issues you have to consider when implementing Internet browsing under Windows 98.

You may also want to refer to Chapter 25, "Windows 98 with TCP/IP" for a discussion of how to set up your computer to use TCP/IP (the Internet protocol suite).

Overview of Browsing in Windows 98

Recently, Microsoft has been incorporating Web-based features into more and more of its products—even apart from the brouhaha over Internet Explorer's integration into Windows. For example, Office 97's word processor allows you to format hyperlinks so that you can create a connection between documents stored on the local computer and documents on the Web. With Windows 98, the connection has become even tighter, as instant Web access becomes possible from anywhere in the operating system.

How Windows 98 Integrates Browsing with the Desktop

In addition to making Internet Explorer immediately available from the toolbar, Windows 98 integrates browsing into the desktop.

If you upgraded from Windows 95, you'll notice that the desktop has some new features in it. By default, it looks similar to the old Windows 95 desktop—the expected array of desktop icons and the toolbar. If you upgraded from a working copy of Windows 95, you'll even find all your documents in the Documents folder, but as you can see in Figure 27.1, there are a few other changes.

The differences in the appearance of the desktop are related to the concept of the *active desktop*, a place with content that can be dynamically updated. For example, you can place on your desktop a link to the *New York Times* channel site, and update the information there as the page is updated at intervals during the day. Although this may not appear immediately different from what you can already do with a separate browser, there *is* a difference: You don't have to open a browser to get to the site because the link is stored on your desktop.

Chapter 27: Internet Browsers in Windows 98 — **597**

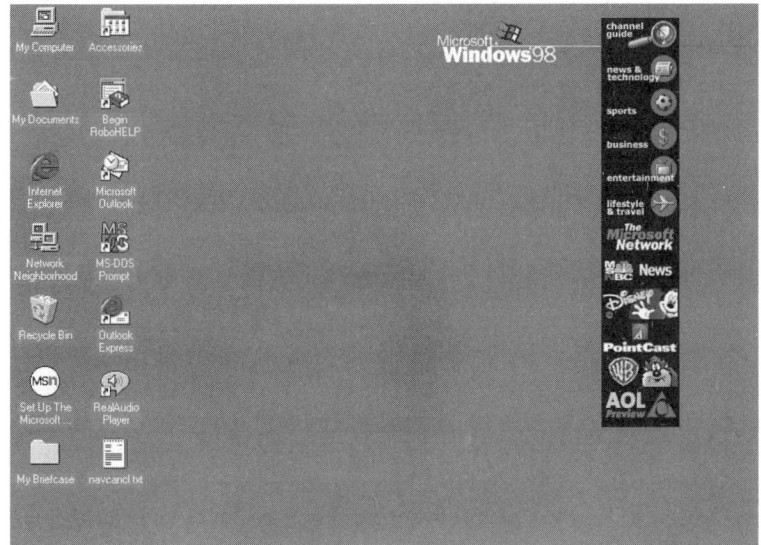

Figure 27.1
The integration of the Web into the Windows 98 desktop.

In addition to *site links*, you can also have *information links*, with periodically updated content. These links can follow the "ticker" format or the minibrowser format (see Figure 27.2). Either way, information links provide you with a quick way of reviewing regularly changing content, such as news or stock quotes.

Figure 27.2
Get regularly updated headlines delivered right to your desktop through information links.

The point is that the desktop can include shortcuts not only to local and network-accessible data and applications, but to Web content as well. By default, the Windows 98 desktop *is* a Web browser. And its live content makes it a very addictive one. (News junkies are going to *love* the *New York Times* ticker.)

> **Tip** If you don't want to use the Desktop's browsing capabilities, you can disable its Web page functionality. Right-click anywhere in the open area of the desktop. A pop-up menu appears. Deselect the View as **W**eb Page option.

How does the active desktop work? As Chapter 1 describes, the active desktop is built in two layers: A transparent icon layer that displays all your shortcuts (including those already there if you upgraded from Windows 95) and a base HTML layer that supports any HTML content, including documents and ActiveX and Java scripts—even downloading new drivers for you from Microsoft's Web site if you choose.

You can think of it as an overlay of the familiar Windows 95 desktop on top of a new desktop engine: It looks like the old desktop (or it can—you have that option) but it doesn't work like it. Instead, it's integrated with IE4. This design is intended to make file location transparent and unimportant to the user. More than ever, you don't have to know where something is or how to get to it; you just have to set up the link. With the new browser interface, that capability is extended from the company network to the Web.

Linking to documents isn't the only new capability of the new interface, however. The desktop is a complete browser; these days, browsing means not just reading linked documents but a host of other functions. Table 27.1 explains the IE4 features now integrated into the Windows 98 desktop.

Table 27.1
Additional Browsing Features Integrated into Windows 98

Feature	Description
Subscriptions	When you add a site to your Favorites folder, you also have the option of subscribing to it at one of two levels: one to alert you of changes to the site, and one to download those changes to your desktop.
Channels	Some sites called *channels* give you the option of putting links to the content right on your desktop so that you can see what's available without opening a browser. These desktop channels may take the form of a ticker or a small browser window, and are updated when your channels are updated.
Security	Setting security options may be nothing new, but these security options are detailed and comprehensive, permitting you to determine what kinds of applets can be downloaded and run to your computer, and what kind of content people using the computer may view. You can also use these settings to secure your online shopping information, including credit card and shipping address.

Chapter 27: Internet Browsers in Windows 98

Feature	Description
Outlook Express	Windows 98 is integrated with email, so you can send messages or post to newsgroups no matter where you are or what you're doing. As you can with channels, you can use Outlook Express to download newsgroup content to be read while offline.
NetMeeting	This online conferencing tool allows you to contact people using online voice and video.
Microsoft Chat	From your user interface, you can open an online chat program to connect to other members of the network. You can talk to people publicly or privately. You can also save the results of the chat.
FrontPage Express	This simpler version of FrontPage allows you to create your own Web content using templates.

We'll discuss the mechanics of how to use and set up these features in "Internet Explorer 4," later in this chapter.

Note The active desktop is available not only with Windows 98, but with Windows NT 4.0 or Windows 95 if you install IE4 with either the Standard or Full option.

Several Windows 98 applets already include the IE4 interface. For example, when you open My Computer in Windows 98, you can see not only the local drives and network access, but from the Favorites menu, you can view connections to Web sites (see Figure 27.3).

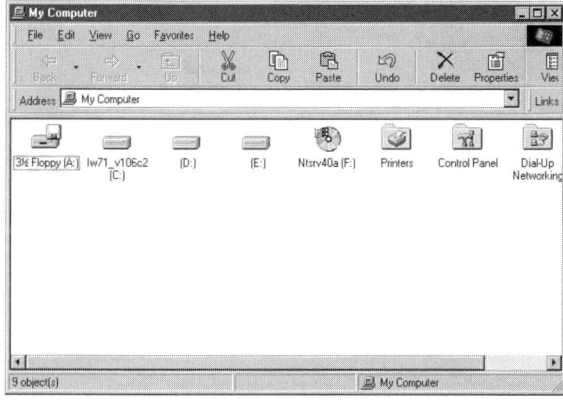

Figure 27.3
My Computer now has some of the tools associated with a browser.

Part V: Windows 98 and the Internet

> **Tip** Use the Back and Forward buttons to move between the folder you were just looking at and the one you are looking at now. You don't have to flip through a plethora of open windows any more.

As shown in Figure 27.4, Explorer not only maintains a record of current connections and files, it also provides access to the Web sites in your Favorites folder without requiring you to open IE4 first.

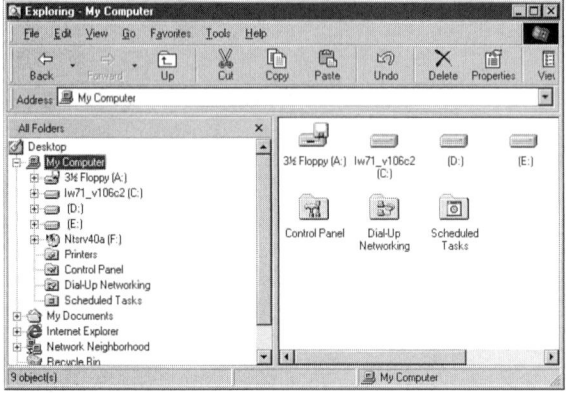

Figure 27.4
Browse not only the network but your favorite Web sites with Explorer.

Help not only maintains a list of local Help files, it can also provide access to Microsoft's online support without your having to take an extra step (see Figure 27.5).

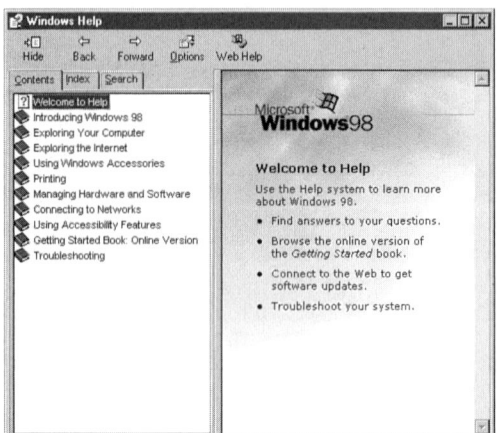

Figure 27.5
You can connect to Microsoft's online product support straight from the Windows 98 Help engine.

Chapter 27: Internet Browsers in Windows 98

Those folders are already part of the IE4 interface, but almost any folder can be integrated with IE4. You can even edit a folder's appearance with the Customize This Folder Wizard, available in the **V**iew menu of most folders. When you start the wizard, you see a dialog box like the one in Figure 27.6. The option you're looking for in this case is the first one, to create an HTML document. Read the instructions in the following page, then make any changes you like in your HTML editor (for example, Notepad). When you close the editor, the changes you made are saved and applied to the folder.

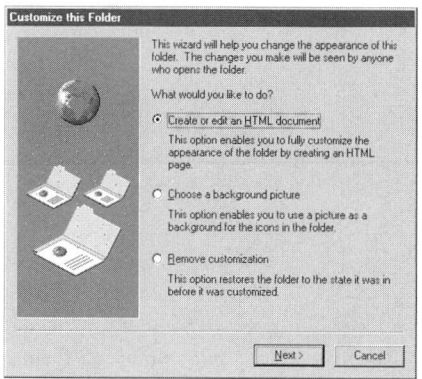

Figure 27.6
Turn any folder into a Web page.

Note You cannot create a Web view for every folder, but most folders support this feature.

The Role of the Default Browser

Even with the integration of the browser into the desktop, the role of the default browser has not changed significantly—it's still the browser used to open HTML and HTM documents. This chapter discusses both IE4 and Netscape Communicator; the user interface isn't affected whether you use IE4 or Netscape as your default browser. All the windows retain the look and feel of IE4; when you access some part of the active desktop—for example, a link to an online document accessible through Help—then IE4 is the browser used. The default browser affects only documents saved to the local machine, links in email messages, and the Favorites menu accessible from the Start menu.

Configuring and Using Browsers

You can use the browser as-is, with almost no personalizing or tuning. But IE4 and Netscape Communicator offer you such a host of options that it's a shame not to examine them.

Note Both IE4 and Netscape Communicator include not only browsing capabilities but applications that support email, newsgroups, and page authoring. This chapter focuses on their capabilities as browsers; other features are discussed in this book in the appropriate chapters.

Internet Explorer 4

IE4 is the browser currently included with Windows 98 (unless the Department of Justice makes Microsoft offer versions of Windows 98 with and without the browser) and is available for download from Microsoft's Web site at www.microsoft.com. Before you can use the browser, however, there's the matter of setup.

Setting Up IE4

To customize the content sent to you and how your browser interacts with it, you must choose Internet Options from the View menu. When you do, you should see a dialog box like the one shown in Figure 27.7, with tabs for the various configuration options.

Figure 27.7
Setting up general Internet options.

Most of these Internet options are fairly straightforward, but some require a little explanation. The following sections explain how to accomplish various configuration tasks. Table 27.2 is a quick reference of configuration tasks and where you set them up in IE4's Internet Settings dialog box. More details about each of these tasks is provided in the following sections.

Chapter 27: Internet Browsers in Windows 98 **603**

Table 27.2
Internet Configuration Tasks and their Internet Settings Dialog Box Tabs

Configuration Task	Tab
Create a new dial-up networking connection	Connection
Define the appearance of IE4 output	General
Delete the contents of the cache	General
Set the amount of disk space that can be used for cached files	General
Set up applications to cooperate with IE4	Programs
Set up content filters for your browser	Content
Set up your computer for use with a proxy server	Connection
Set up your computer for use with the Internet	Connection
Specify a new home page for IE4	General
Specify how many days IE should remember URLs	General
Specify where IE should store cached pages	General
Tell IE how often to update cached versions of previously visited sites	General

Note Security settings (including certificates and profiles) are not discussed here, but are explained in detail in Chapter 30, "Internet Security."

Create a New Dial-Up Networking Connection

You can run the Connection Wizard from within IE4. To do so, click the Connection tab of the Internet Settings dialog box and click the Connect button in the Connection section. To set up the connection, follow the instructions in the wizard (see Figure 27.8).

Set Up Your Computer for Use with a Proxy Server

If you're connecting to the Internet with a proxy server, be sure to check that box in the Proxy Server section of Connection page of the Internet Settings dialog box. Fill in the fully qualified domain name or IP address of the server and the port to which you'll be connecting. If your network uses more than one proxy server for different protocols, click the Advanced button to finish configuring the proxy server connection in the dialog box shown in Figure 27.9. See Chapter 28, "Setting Up Windows 98 for the Internet," for more information about connecting to the Internet through a proxy server.

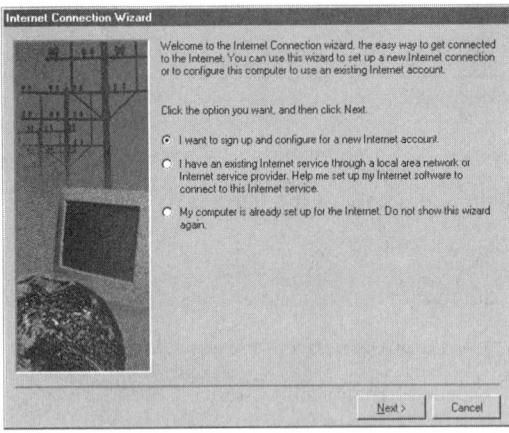

Figure 27.8
You can configure all Internet settings from within IE4.

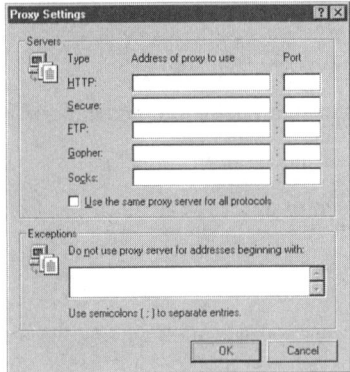

Figure 27.9
Identify the proxy server to use for a variety of protocols.

If you want to connect directly to a server without going through the proxy, enter the domain name (such as `microsoft.com`) in the Exceptions box.

Add a Dial-Up Networking Connection

After the Internet connection is set up, you can click the Settings button on the Connection page to configure settings for the connection: telephone number to dial in to, device to use (if you have more than one modem installed), modem settings, and logon settings. To set up a new connection from within IE4, click the Settings button on the Connection page to open the dialog box shown in Figure 27.10, and then click the Next button to create a new connection.

Let a Remote Server Configure Your IE4 Settings

Some people may have to read no further because their network administrator has installed the Internet Explorer Admin Kit, and a server on the network will download IE4 settings to their

Chapter 27: Internet Browsers in Windows 98   **605**

computers. If your network is set up in this way, click the Configure button on the Connection page and enter the URL of the server. By default, changes to the setting are downloaded each time you start the browser (and have a live connection to the server). If you want, you can also click the Refresh button shown in Figure 27.11 to immediately download the current settings.

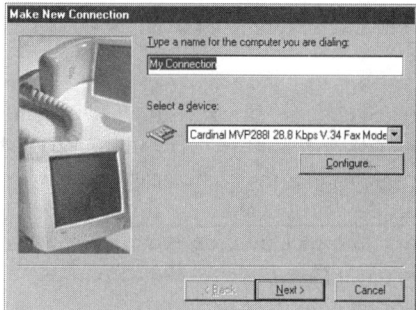

Figure 27.10
Create a new modem connection.

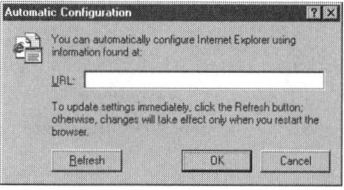

Figure 27.11
Click the Refresh button to update IE4 settings downloaded from a server.

Note The Internet Explorer Admin Kit is Microsoft's tool for administering setup of IE4 for Windows 95, Windows NT 3.5x and 4.0, Macintosh, and UNIX Solaris. With this tool, network administrators can define sets of options (up to ten distinct sets) and download those sets to user desktops. For more information on the Internet Explorer Admin Kit—and to download the free software—go to http://ieak.microsoft.com/.

Specify a New Home Page for IE4

The *home page* is the page that loads whenever you start your browser. You can return to this page at any time by clicking the Home button, so the page you pick should be something you refer to a great deal.

Type the new URL (Uniform Resource Locator) in the Address text box. If the browser is already displaying the page you want to make the home page, just click Use Current. If you want to revert to the default home page (www.microsoft.com/msoffice), choose Use Default. To load no page when you start up IE, choose Use Blank.

Tip If you plan to open IE4 while offline, you can choose Use Blank or specify a local document for a home page so that you don't waste time waiting for IE to try to load a page it can't get to.

Tell IE How Often to Update Cached Versions of Previously Visited Sites

By default, when you start IE and open a Web page, IE caches the page's contents and uses the cached copy for the remainder of the session. If you move on to another page, then change your mind and return to the previous page, IE uses the cached copy so that it doesn't have to reload the page, thus speeding up the display. These copies are stored in the \Temporary Internet Files folder of your Windows 98 installation (or, if user profiles are enabled, the pages are stored in the Temporary Internet Files folder of the current user's profile directory). The cached pages are not deleted when you close IE4.

The only catch to using the cached files is that any updates to the page are not reflected because IE isn't pulling the page from the Web server again, but is using its own copy. This isn't a problem with many pages, but pages with content that changes regularly may benefit from being updated more often. Thus, if you have a fast connection and reference a lot of pages with fast-changing content, you may want to instruct IE to update pages every time it visits a page.

To do so, click the Settings button in the Temporary Internet Files section. You'll see a dialog box like the one shown in Figure 27.12.

Figure 27.12
Determining how often cached pages are updated.

The particulars of the three options are described in Table 27.3.

Table 27.3
Page Caching Options

Update Frequency	Description	Ramifications	Recommended Use
Every visit to the page	Reloads the page every time you return to it.	Reflects all changes to the page, but slows down browsing because the page must be reloaded every time.	Best for those who frequently visit pages that change often (especially if they have a high-speed Net connection), or for those people who leave their browser open for days on end.
Every time you start Internet Explorer	Caches pages when they're accessed for the first time during an Internet Explorer session. IE checks for new content only when you start Explorer.	Does not reflect changes to the page when reloaded again during the same session, unless the Reload button is used.	Suitable for most purposes. This is the default option.
Never	Always uses the page in the cache.	Does not reflect changes to the page (unless the Reload button is used), but loads quickly.	Best for those who visit pages with static content and who are interested in viewing pages as quickly as possible.

Specify Where IE Should Store Cached Pages

By default, cached pages are stored in a subdirectory of your Windows 98 installation. You can choose to move the temporary storage to another folder on the same disk or on another hard disk.

> **Tip** Move the IE cache to another disk if you have another disk that is much faster than the one on which Windows 98 is installed, or if space on that drive is at a premium.

In the Settings dialog box displayed in Figure 27.12, click the Move Folder button to specify a new location for the cached files. You can choose any drive to which you have current access. After you make your selection, the change does not take effect until you restart your computer.

> **Warning** If you think you're going to want to move the cache file, move it before you've done much with IE. Moving the cache file deletes all the settings related to your Web subscriptions.

Although the buttons for viewing the contents of the cache and the buttons for viewing downloaded files are next to each other, moving the cache does not affect the location of the ActiveX controls downloaded to your computer (the \Downloaded Program Files folder in your Windows 98 installation). To see these files, click the View Files button.

Set the Amount of Disk Space That Can Be Used for Cached Files

By default, IE uses 3 percent of whatever disk the cache is on to store files. You can increase or decrease this amount from the Settings dialog box. The more disk space you allot to caching, the more pages you can cache. To change the proportion of disk space, move the Amount of Disk Space to Use slider bar up or down.

Changing the cache size does not immediately affect the amount of free space on the drive; it only tells the system how much room it can have for caching. When configuring the proportion of space you allocate to the cache, keep in mind that 3 percent of a modern drive is a *lot* of space—on a 2G drive, that's 60M. If you are caching to a large hard drive, you can probably reduce the amount of space reserved for your cache without any ill effects.

Delete the Contents of the Cache

To empty the cache without closing IE, click the Delete Files button in the Temporary Internet Files section of the General tab (see Figure 27.13).

When you do, you are asked to confirm the exercise and also whether you want to delete all locally stored subscription information (see Figure 27.14).

When you've done so, all files in the cache (and, optionally, all local subscription information) are deleted.

Specify How Many Days IE Should Remember URLs

IE remembers the URLs of pages you've visited recently—by default, over the past 20 days. To return to one of those pages, click it in the History list.

Chapter 27: Internet Browsers in Windows 98

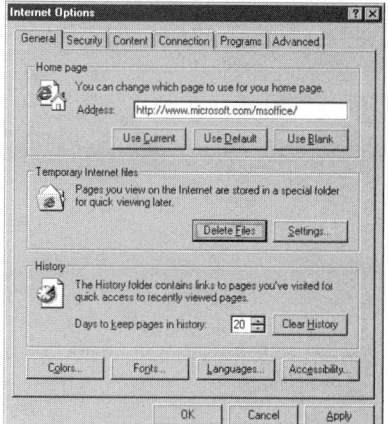

Figure 27.13
Removing all files from the cache.

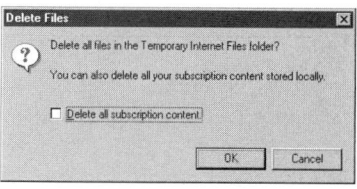

Figure 27.14
Confirm deletion of the contents of the cache.

If you decide that the default of 20 days is more or less than you need, you can set a different time by typing a new number in the History section of the General page of the IE4 options. To clear the contents of the History list entirely (for example, if you don't want anyone to know where you've been online for the past 20 days), click the Clear History button. You are asked to confirm the deletion; do so, and the list is emptied.

> **Warning** The History list may tell you that URLs take up 0 to 1K of disk space. Although technically accurate, this number doesn't tell the whole story. The FAT32 file system used by Windows 98 has clusters with a minimum size of 4K—and up to 16K or 32K I size. Therefore, each of those 1K URLs takes up at least 4K on your hard disk, and sometimes far more.

Define the Appearance of Your Browser Output

Some Web pages are set up to have a certain appearance in terms of fonts and colors. Some pages, however, use whatever font and color selections the user defines.

Click the Colors button at the bottom of the General page to display the dialog box shown in Figure 27.15.

Figure 27.15
Editing color options.

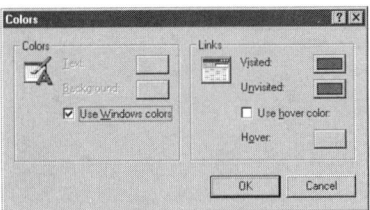

Click the color boxes to change their color.

- If you select Use Windows Colors (it is selected by default), your color display settings are used for your browser views. Deselect this option if you want to choose colors for the text and background from the Windows palette.

- Edit the appearance of links you have followed and those you have not yet followed. The defaults are blue for unfollowed links and purple for links already viewed.

- If you want, you can highlight links when the cursor is positioned over them (an action called *hovering*); this can make it easier to tell when the cursor is positioned over a link. When you enable this option, you can select a color for links over which the cursor is hovering. The default is red.

- Click the Fonts button at the bottom of the General page to open a dialog box like the one shown in Figure 27.16. Select options from the lists to change the font settings. By default, these settings apply only to text that has not been directly formatted by the page's author.

Figure 27.16
The Fonts dialog box.

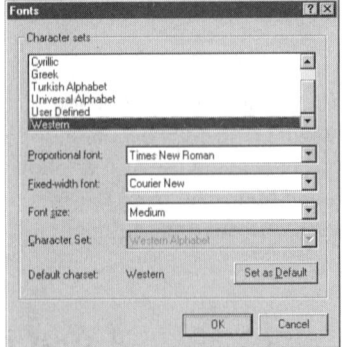

> **Tip**   If you want to use the fonts specified by the Web author, but just want to change their relative size or their alphabet, select View|Fonts and choose the size (Smallest to Largest; the default is Medium) and the language to use.

Chapter 27: Internet Browsers in Windows 98

- The default character set does not change the language in which Web documents appear (it's a pity that translation can't take place so easily). The default character set determines the characters that can be displayed. The default is Western.

- The proportional font is used to display standard text in a page. If the book you are reading were a Web page, this text would be displayed in the selected proportional font. You can choose a proportional font from all fonts currently installed on the computer.

- The fixed-width font is used to display the program font or other standard-sized text. If this book were a Web page, any program code would be displayed in the selected fixed-width font. Only Courier and Lucida Console are available for fixed-width fonts, and only Lucida Console is available for most character sets.

- The font size determines how proportionally big the font is. Medium is the default; make it bigger or smaller to make it easier to read or to make more text visible onscreen.

- The default character set is the one used when no other character set is specified. By default, it's the Western character set. To change it, select another character set and click the Set as **D**efault button.

Note *Character sets* are sets of code and character mappings that tell Windows 98 how to display a given code. For example, code `063` in one character set might be the letter A, but code `063` in another character set might be the dollar sign.

Character sets are important if you want to view Web pages written in a language other than English, as you can if you click the Languages button at the bottom of the General page (see Figure 27.17). Once again, installing another language does not translate documents for you, but it does make it possible for you to read documents written in more than one language.

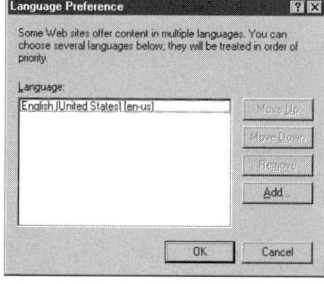

Figure 27.17
You must install a character set to support the language you choose.

If you want to customize the color and font settings for *all* pages, including those formatted by the Web author, click the Accessibility... button on the bottom of the General page and specify the options you want to control (see Figure 27.18).

Figure 27.18

Overriding a Web author's formatting.

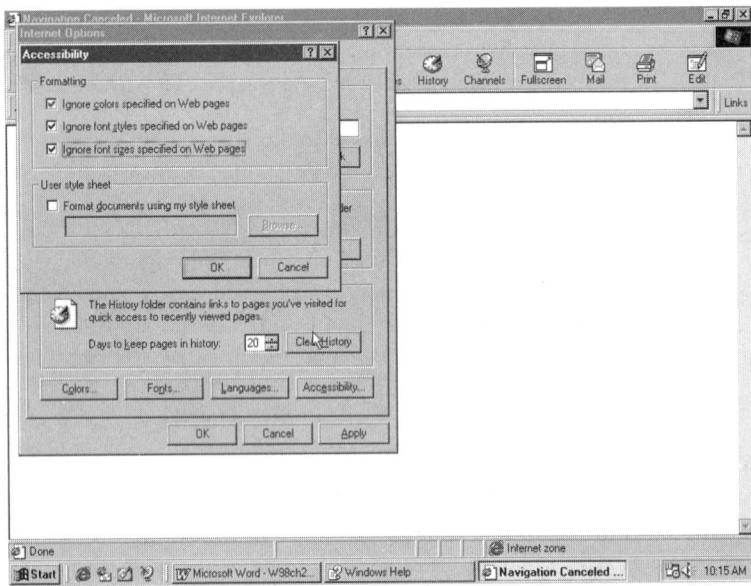

If you select all these settings, you override not only font and color, but any wallpaper the Web page's author used—essentially, the page will look like a text page with whatever graphics the author used. (Frankly, I find this capability a godsend for those pages with terrifically vivid wallpaper.)

Set Up Content Filters for Your Browser

You can set up filtering so that access to sex-based or violence-based pages is restricted. (Then again, you might not want to. Don't interpret this section as any kind of recommendation of what you *should* do about enabling access controls.)

Assuming that you want some control over what people using the browser are viewing, choose Internet Options from the View menu and click Content tab (see Figure 27.19).

Ratings are not enabled by default. To enable them, click the Enable button. You are asked to provide a password and then to confirm it. When you've provided and verified a password, you'll see a dialog box like the one in Figure 27.20.

| Note | Remember this password: You'll need it if you ever want to adjust your ratings settings. |

Chapter 27: Internet Browsers in Windows 98

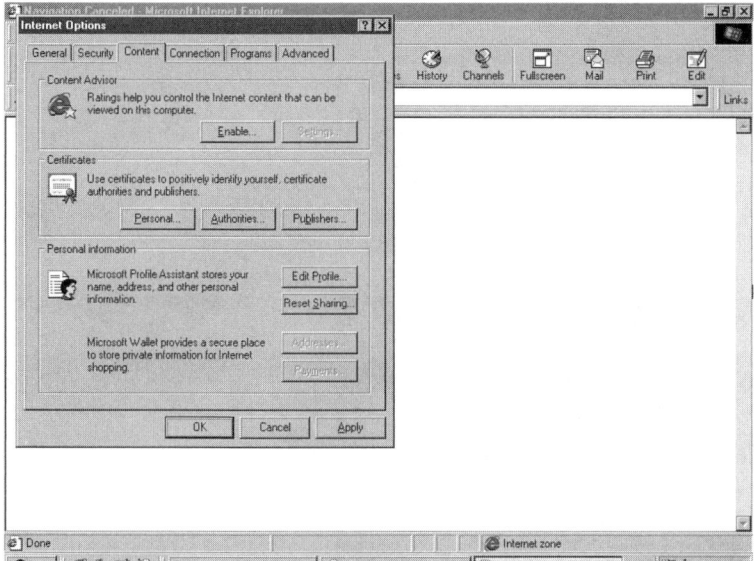

Figure 27.19
Preparing to censor user content.

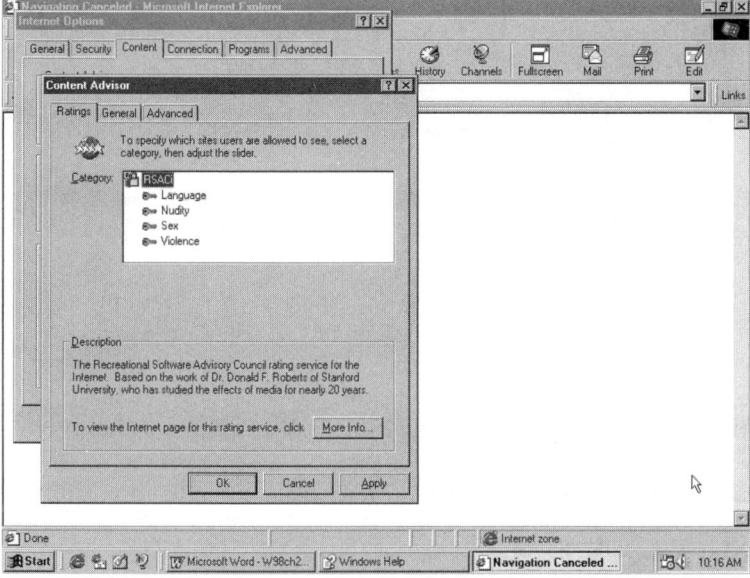

Figure 27.20
Click a topic to adjust its rating.

The default settings are most restrictive, permitting you to download only sites with the following characteristics:

- No profanity; slang only

- No nudity whatsoever

- No sexual activity portrayed

- No violence (aggressive, natural, or accidental)

Highlight a topic in the list to adjust its rating as shown in Figure 27.21.

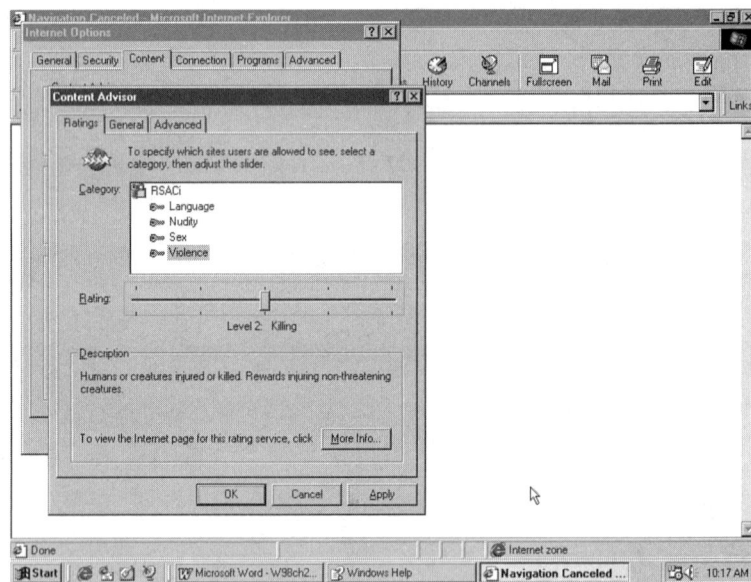

Figure 27.21

Setting ratings for violence content.

A site must participate in the rating scheme to be filtered for explicit reasons. Unsurprisingly, many sites with content that the Recreational Software Advisory Council (the group that designed the ratings used by IE4) would find objectionable have declined to be rated. Even some sites with unobjectionable content may be unrated—the *New York Times* Online Edition, for example. If you enable ratings, by default you're declined access to unrated sites—although you can provide the supervisor's password to get to the site. Each time you access another page within that site, you have to provide the password again.

When you've made your choices, close the Internet Settings dialog box. The ratings take effect immediately, although pages already in the cache are not affected.

If you try to access a page that contains restricted content, the page does not load and you see a dialog box informing you that you can't access the page and listing the reasons why (for example, `RSACi Nudity-Level 3: Frontal Nudity Level`).

Chapter 27: Internet Browsers in Windows 98   **615**

As previously mentioned, IE4 comes with one ratings system. You can download other systems to use and load them into the `System` folder of your Windows 98 installation. To use a new rating system, click the Advanced tab of the Content Advisor dialog box.

> **Note** In addition to providing access to rating criteria, the Content page also contains settings for security certificates, as discussed in Chapter 30, "Internet Security," for the Microsoft Wallet (a storage place for purchasing information, so that you don't have to look it up each time you buy something online), and for the Microsoft Profile Assistant (a place in which you can enter personal information for those Web sites that request it).

Set Up Applications to Cooperate with IE4

IE4 can work in cooperation with other applications to support mail, news, Internet telephoning, calendars, and contact lists. Defaults exist for all these settings (with the exception of an Internet calendar option), but you can also choose any other installed applications from the drop-down list shown in Figure 27.22.

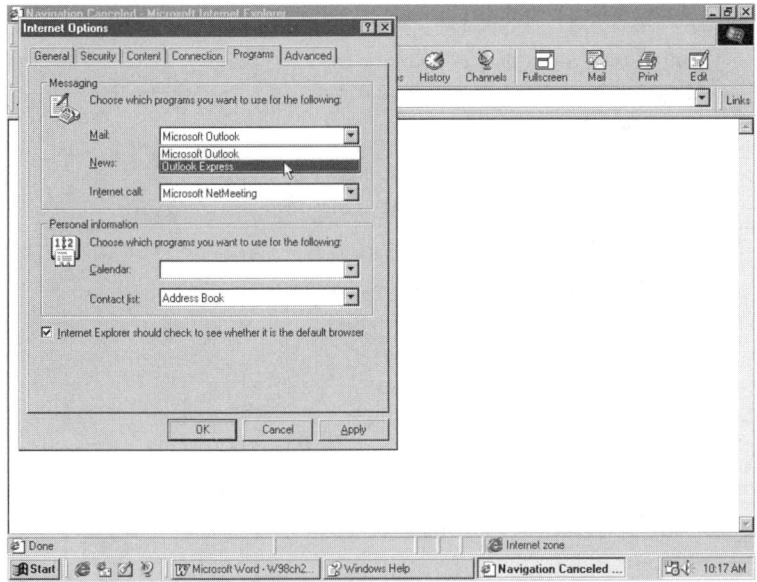

Figure 27.22
Choosing a new email program to use with IE4.

Fine-Tuning Internet Explorer 4

The Advanced tab of the Internet Options dialog box contains all the settings that don't fit anywhere else. Some options you may never have to touch, but some options bear examination. Table 27.4 lists these options, tells you what they mean, and specifies whether they're enabled by default.

Table 27.4
Advanced IE4 Browsing Options

Option	Description	Enabled by Default?
Autoscan Common Root Domains	Tells IE4 to check the common domains (`.mil`, `.org`, `.com`, `.edu`, and so on) if it can't find a match with the URL you typed. For example, `microsoft.edu` would be resolved if Autoscan was on, because it would check in the `.com` domain for a Microsoft entry.	Yes
Browse in a New Process	Opens a new instance of IE4 every time you open a new browser-compatible file. Requires more memory, but increases system stability because buggy programs affect only the new process.	No
Disable Script Debugging	Turns off a script debugger so that you no longer see error messages if a page's Java or ActiveX script contains errors.	No
Enable Page Hit Counting	Permits authors of the sites you visit to track your Web usage, even if you are viewing pages offline.	Yes
Enable Page Transitions	As you're leaving one page for another, the first page fades out as the next page fades in.	Yes
Enable Scheduled Subscription Updates	Tells IE4 to update subscriptions automatically. For this to work, you must also enable automatic connectivity.	Yes
Launch Browser in Full-Screen Window	Self-explanatory.	No
Launch Channels in Full-Screen Window	Self-explanatory.	Yes
Show Channel Bar at Startup (If Active Desktop Is Off)	Normally, the channel bar appears only if Active Desktop is on.	No
Show Friendly URLs	Displays the full URL of sites on the status bar.	No
Show IE4 on the Desktop	Puts an IE4 logo on the Desktop.	Yes

Chapter 27: Internet Browsers in Windows 98

Option	Description	Enabled by Default?
Show Welcome Message Each Time I Log On	Shows the Welcome to Active Desktop message at logon.	Yes
Use AutoComplete	As you're typing in URLs, will complete them for you if it's a site that you've visited before.	Yes
Use Smooth Scrolling	Scrolls output at a predetermined rate to even it out.	Yes

In addition to the browsing options, you can also configure settings from the Advanced tab related to the following topics:

- User accessibility
- Multimedia display (sounds, images, animations, and video)
- Link display
- Java settings
- HTTP settings

Tip You can click a button on the Advanced tab to restore all settings to their default value.

Using Internet Explorer 4

You've set up the options you want. Now you're prepared to use the browser's many capabilities. Table 27.5 is a quick reference to IE4's browsing capabilities and where you access them.

Table 27.5
Common IE4 Tasks and How to Execute Them

Task	Menu Location
Copy objects from a Web page	Select the objects, then select **E**dit,**C**opy
Exit IE4	**F**ile,Close
Find a channel and subscribe to it	Go,Channel Guide

continues

Table 27.5, Continued
Common IE4 Tasks and How to Execute Them

Task	Menu Location
Find a word on a page	Edit,Find
Make a shortcut to a page on your desktop	File,Send,Shortcut to Desktop
Move quickly to a frequently referenced site	Choose the site from the Favorites menu
Open a link to a folder or file	File,Open
Open a new browser window	File,New,Window
Organize and manage subscriptions	Favorites,Manage Subscriptions
Organize your saved links	Favorites,Organize Favorites
Print hard copy of a Web page	File,Print
Save a Web page to your computer	File,Save As
Save links for future reference	Favorites,Add Favorites
See an editable copy of a document's source code	View,Source
Show someone else a Web page	File,Send,Page/Link by Email
Stop loading a page	View,Stop
Update a page's information	View,Refresh
Update all channels and subscriptions at once	Go,Manage Subscriptions,Update All
Update all channels and subscriptions at once	Favorites,Manage Subscriptions,Update All
View the properties of the current Web page	File,Properties
Work offline	File,Work Offline

The following sections explain these tasks in more detail.

> **Tip** To select from the toolbars available to you in your browser, open the View menu and enable the tools you want. To remove the menu bar entirely, choose View|Full Screen or click the Full Screen button on your toolbar.

Open a New Browser Window

Choose File,New,Window to open a new instance of the browser. You cannot use the Back and Forward buttons to navigate between the two screens.

Open a Link

To open a link to a folder or document, choose **O**pen from the **F**ile menu; in the Open dialog box, type the path or URL as appropriate. As shown in Figure 27.23, the dialog box remembers paths you've taken recently, so you can choose an entry from the drop-down list.

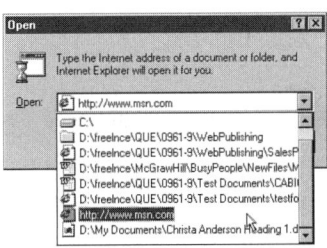

Figure 27.23
Click a previously accessed link to open it.

After you've chosen the link, IE4 shows the contents of the folder or file you selected. If you've selected a folder instead of an online document, the IE4 display changes to My Computer—the differences are not immediately obvious (for example, the options in the **F**ile|New menu are different) but present.

If you have Office 97 installed, files associated with the suite's programs appear in the drop-down list of recently accessed files. Otherwise, you can open only browser-compatible files such as HTML documents, JPG images, and text files, among others.

> **Note** You can use the Back button in the toolbar to return to the previous window only if you opened an online document.

Save a Web Page to Your Computer

You can save a page locally (or on the network), perhaps to use its source code as a template for something you want to do or as a sample document. To do so, choose **F**ile, Save **A**s. You can save the document either as an .HTM document (the default) or as text (not the source code, but as the words displayed onscreen).

Print Hard Copy of a Web Page

To print a page, first check the print settings (**F**ile,Page Set**u**p) to make sure that the page is oriented properly and that the header and footer coding prints the information you want. By default, the window's name and the page count (centered) appear in the header, and the URL and the current date are in the footer. Table 27.6 describes the codes available to you.

Table 27.6
Print Codes for Headers and Footers of Web Pages

Code	Information It Prints
&&	An ampersand
&b	Centers the text immediately following the code
&b&b	Centers the text immediately following the code and right-justifies the next text
&d	Date in short format (as defined by the settings in Regional Settings)
&D	Date in long format (as defined by the settings in Regional Settings)
&p	Current page number
&P	Total number of pages in the document
&t	Local system time, in the format specified in Regional Settings
&T	Local system time using a 24-hour clock
&u	Page URL
&w	Window title (as defined in the HTML source)

> **Tip** You can also write your own static text to appear in the header or footer, such as `Printed by Joanne`.

These settings apply to all future print jobs until you adjust them.

When you have set up the page properly, click OK to set the changes and then choose **P**rint from the **F**ile menu (see Figure 27.24).

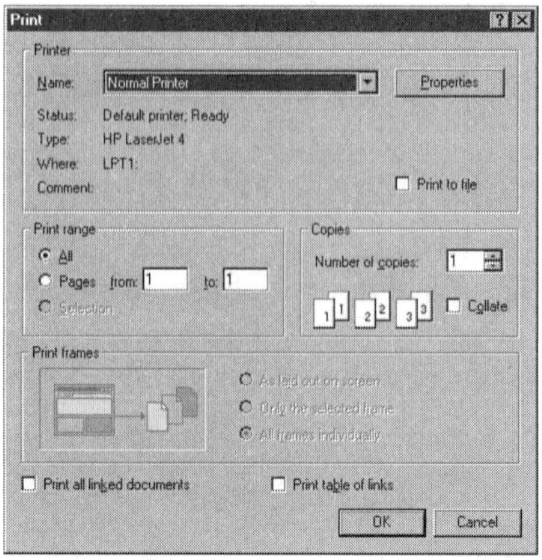

Figure 27.24
Setting final printing options.

Chapter 27: Internet Browsers in Windows 98   621

> **Tip** You can also right-click a page to open the Print dialog box.

Most of the information in this dialog box should look familiar: Choose the printer to which you want to send the job (the options in the figure are the boringly named Normal Printer and Color Printer), make sure that the printer is ready to go, print to a file if you want, and choose a range of pages and the number of copies to produce. The only information specific to printing Web pages is that related to the appearance of frames and to printing links.

If the page you're printing contains *frames* (sections visually divided from other sections), you have the option of printing all information as displayed onscreen, only the contents of the selected frame, or the contents of all frames, but separately. The option you choose depends on the page you're printing. For example, if a frame off to the left displays a table of contents for the entire site for easy navigation between documents, you may want to print only the frame with the active document; but if a table appears in a frame, you may want to print the whole thing.

By default, only the current document is printed, but the current document can contain links to related documents. You can choose either to print all linked documents in addition to the active one, or to print a table of linked documents at the bottom of the screen (a reference of sorts for people reading the printed document who may want to know where to get more information).

When the printing options are set properly, click OK; the print job is sent to the spooler.

Make a Shortcut to a Page

To quickly access a page, you don't have to add it to your Favorites folder; instead, you can add it to your desktop. To do so, choose File,Send,Shortcut to Desktop. When you click this shortcut (and you have an active Net connection), the browser opens and moves to the linked URL.

Show Someone Else a Web Page

If you want someone else to see the page you're looking at, you can send them either the page as an attachment or the link to it. To do so, choose File,Send,Page by Email (or Link by Email), fill in the email address of the recipient, and send the message.

View the Properties of a Web Page

To get basic information about a Web page (its URL, title, size, and modification dates) choose Properties from the File menu. From the Properties sheet that appears, you can also view any security certificates for the page (if any) and check it for errors.

Set Up IE4 to Work Offline

When you're not connected to the Internet and don't need to be, letting IE4 try to find online documents can waste time. If you're going to be viewing previously downloaded content, you can choose to work offline by choosing **F**ile, Work Offline.

> **Note** If you try to access a document that is only available online, you are prompted to indicate whether you want to connect to the Internet to get the document or to forget it and keep working offline.

Exit IE4

Choose **C**lose from the **F**ile menu.

Copy Objects from a Web Page

Select the text or image you want to copy and choose **E**dit, **C**opy. Alternatively, right-click the selected text and choose **C**opy from the pop-up menu that appears.

> **Tip** To select all text in a document, choose **E**dit, Select All.

Find a Word on a Page

If you've performed a Web search for documents on a certain topic and chosen one to open, you may not immediately see the topic you were looking for. To find a word within a page, choose **E**dit, Find (on this Page) or press Ctrl+F.

> **Note** Word searches are page specific, not site specific. To find a word within a given site, use the site's search engine, if it has one.

Stop Loading a Page

Sometimes, after you've clicked a link or typed an URL, you realize that wasn't where you wanted to go after all. To stop loading a page, choose Stop from the **V**iew menu, or click the Stop button on the standard toolbar.

Reload a Page

IE4 does not automatically update pages that have changed, but uses the copy downloaded for local access. If you have reason to believe that a page's content has changed (for example,

Chapter 27: Internet Browsers in Windows 98   **623**

you've had your browser open all day and your browser was open to a newspaper's site), you can get the newest data at the site by choosing **V**iew,Refresh or clicking the Refresh button on the standard toolbar.

See a Document's Source Code

HTML documents are not created "as is" but are composed of code that a browser interprets to have a certain appearance. To view the source code for a page, choose **V**iew, Source. The coding appears in the window of an HTML editor, such as Notepad.

You can edit the source code and save the changes locally, if you want to create your own version of the Web page. The changes do not affect the original document on the Web server or the document in your cache.

Move Quickly to a Frequently Referenced Site

IE4 offers some convenient methods of getting to sites you go to frequently—either those you selected yourself or those Microsoft thought you would like. Table 27.7 outlines these shortcuts.

> **Note**   The Favorites menu is accessible from both IE4 and My Computer.

Table 27.7
Navigation Shortcuts

To Get Here…	Do This…
A list of recently accessed documents, organized by the day on which you accessed them. By default, this list shows the last 20 days.	Click the History button on the standard toolbar. A frame on the left side of your browser opens, showing folders for each of the last 20 days.
A page from which you can search the Web using any of several search engines.	Click the Search button on the standard toolbar to open a frame in your browser that offers access to the Pick of the Day search engine or several others. Alternatively, navigate to Microsoft's search site by choosing Go,**S**earch the Web.
A page you've added to your Favorites folder.	Click the Favorites button on the toolbar, or open the Favorites menu and choose the link from the menu.

continues

Table 27.7, Continued
Navigation Shortcuts

To Get Here...	Do This...
A page you just looked at.	Navigate with the Back and Forward buttons to move between recently viewed pages. Both these buttons have drop-down menus to let you choose a site to leap to.
My Computer.	Choose Go, My Computer to close IE4 and open My Computer, you cannot use the Back button to return to the previous page.
My Documents.	Choose Go, My Documents to close IE4 and open My Computer, you cannot use the Back button to return to the previous page.
One of the sites Microsoft has created for IE4 users.	Choose the link or Microsoft folder from the Favorites menu.
The channel guide.	Choose Go, Channel Guide.
Your home page.	Click the Home button on the standard toolbar, or choose Go, Home Page.

> **Tip** If you click the Search button, you can keep a menu of search engines in a frame on the left side of your browser.

Save Links for Future Reference

When you find a page or site that you like, you can save its URL in a folder so you can return to it easily. Just choose Favorites, Add to Favorites and the page will be saved, listed according to its title.

When you add a link to the Favorites folder, you have three options:

- Adding the link to your Favorites folder
- Adding the link, and also subscribing to the page so you get email notification of updates to the site
- Adding the link, and also subscribing to the page so IE4 downloads the page automatically for offline viewing

If you don't expect a page's content to change or you don't care whether it does, choose the first option. Choose the second for pages that you expect to change, but don't expect to change very often—I subscribed to MSDN's online library like this. Choose the third option for pages that you expect to change often, such as news or weather sites. Pages to which you subscribe are stored in your subscriptions folder.

> **Note** IE4 will automatically import any bookmarks you had created in another, previously installed, browser. These are stored in an Imported Bookmarks folder accessible from the Favorites menu.

Organize Your Saved Links

Once you've added more than a few entries to your Favorites folder, or if you're sharing a browser with someone else who's also adding links, it may become difficult to find the link you want at a glance. To facilitate the organization of your link list, you can create folders and store your links in them. When you create a new entry in the Favorites folder, you have the option of creating it in the main menu, in a previously created folder, or in a new folder you create at the time you are making the link.

To organize marked links, choose **F**ile, Organize Favorites (see Figure 27.25).

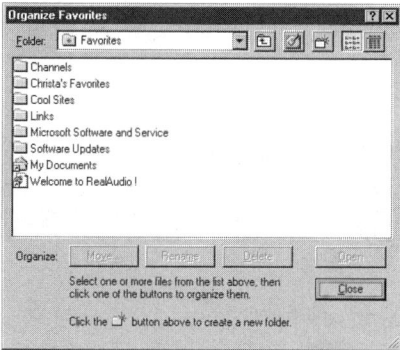

Figure 27.25
Move links to existing folders or create new ones.

Folders can contain subfolders; for example, you can create a folder called `Joe's Links`, and then a folder within that one called `Windows NT Links` so that Joe can store all his Windows NT–related links there.

Find a Channel and Subscribe to It

At its IE4 site, Microsoft maintains a source of channels to which you can subscribe. To find channels that meet your needs, go to this site (choose **G**o, Channel Guide) and either choose a topic (see Figure 27.26) or click the Find button at the top of the screen to search for a topic.

Figure 27.26
Finding a channel based on topic.

If you click the Find button to search for channels about a certain topic (for example, if you are searching for `football`), you are presented with a list of channels that meet the requirements (see Figure 27.27).

Figure 27.27
Search results for `football`.

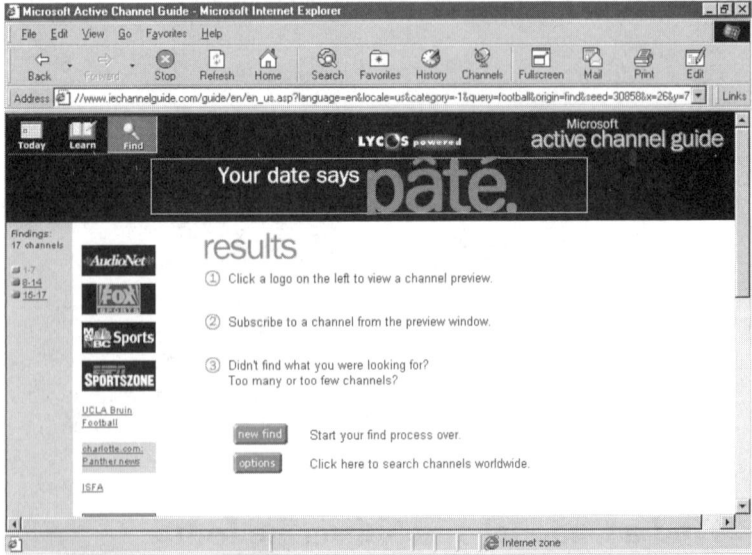

If you choose instead to search the Web for channels, you have two options:

- Search the Web for channels in a certain language (the default is English, and you're warned that it may be hard to find channels in any other language), from a certain country, and according to a specified topic.

- Search the Web for channels from certain page types: home pages, images, and so forth.

Thus far, I've had better luck with the Find tool to locate channels on the Microsoft Web site. I found *fewer* hits for `football` with a Web-wide search than with a Microsoft one.

Manage Channel Subscriptions

You can right-click channels and subscriptions (channels are always stored in the channel bar located on the right side of the desktop) to update them or manage their subscription properties. However, if you want to manage more than one channel, it may be simpler to open a window that lets you do it all at once. Choose **G**o,Manage Subscriptions to display a dialog box like the one in Figure 27.28, showing all your current subscriptions, their URLs, their last and scheduled updates, how much information was last downloaded, and so on.

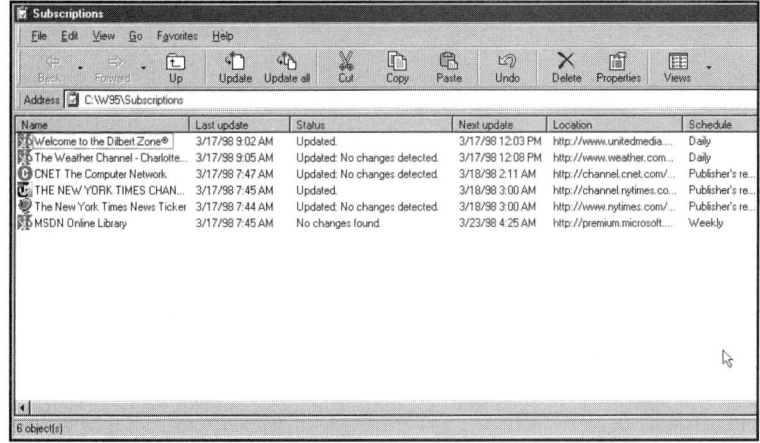

Figure 27.28
Manage several subscriptions at once.

Update All Channels and Subscriptions at Once

Choose **G**o, Update All to make all channel and subscription data current.

Netscape Communicator

Netscape is the other popular browser on Windows-based systems. The Communicator version, available for download from `http://www.netscape.com/download/index.html?cp=hmp03sdow` (as are some other Netscape products) has many features in common with IE4. Once you know how to set up and configure one of these browsers, you can manage the other (allowing for some differences in setup and features).

Setting Up Netscape

Communicator stores its user settings under <u>E</u>dit, Preferences. Select this menu item to display a dialog box like the one in Figure 27.29.

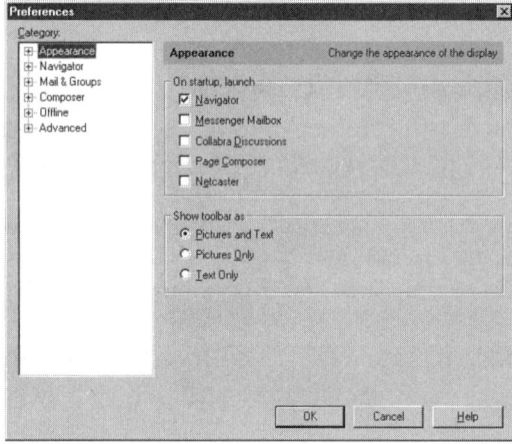

Figure 27.29
Setting up Netscape options.

Table 27.8 is a quick reference to the configuration options offered in the Properties dialog box and where you can set them. The options are explained in more detail in the following sections.

Table 27.8
Netscape Communicator Tasks and Where to Set Them

Task	Section
Change the colors used to display pages	Appearances, Colors
Change the fonts used to display pages	Appearances, Fonts
Change the toolbar options	Appearances
Choose a Communicator application to launch on startup	Appearances
Choose language alternatives for Netscape to use	Navigator, Languages
Choose new encoding for all documents viewed	Appearance, Fonts
Configure cookie acceptance	Advanced
Create and edit file associations	Navigator, Applications

Chapter 27: Internet Browsers in Windows 98

Task	Section
Pick a new home page	Navigator
Set other Communicator options	Advanced
Specify a start page	Navigator
Tell Communicator how long to remember recently visited URLs	Navigator
Tell Communicator to forget all recently visited sites	Navigator
Work offline	Offline

Change the Toolbar Options

Turn to the Appearances section of the Preferences dialog box and choose the option you want in the Set Toolbar As section.

Choose a Communicator Application to Launch on Startup

Netscape Navigator, the browser, is only one of the applications incorporated into Communicator. By default, it's the only one you see because Communicator automatically starts only the browser. To change the startup application, or to start up more than one application, click the Appearances tab of the Preferences dialog box and select the applications you want to launch with Navigator.

> **Note** As does IE4, Communicator supports channels, but you must start the Netcaster application to set them up.

Specify a Start Page

By default, the browser navigates to the home page you've specified. Alternatively, you can tell Communicator to begin with a blank page or the last page you visited before closing the browser. To do so, click the Navigator tab of the Properties dialog box (refer to Figure 27.29) and choose the page you want to begin with.

> **Tip** If you plan to work offline, tell Communicator to start with either a blank page or a locally stored page so that it doesn't waste time trying to load a page it can't get to.

Pick a New Home Page

Most users have a home page they'd rather use than the default Netscape home page (`netscape.com`). To set up a new home page, click the Navigator tab of the Preferences dialog box and either type the new URL or, if you're at the page you want to use as the home page, click the Use Current Page button.

If you have a locally stored HTML document you want to make your home page, either type the path or click the Browse button to search for the document. The default directory is the `Program` directory in your Netscape installation.

> **Tip** Make a local page your home page. Communicator starts more quickly if it doesn't have to try to load a page across the net.

Tell Communicator How Long to Remember Recently Visited URLs

By default, Netscape remembers all URLs visited for the past nine days and stores them in a file called *the History*. As the links become more than nine days old, they're removed from the file. To edit the time URLs spend in the History, click the Navigator tab of the Preferences dialog box and type a new number in the box provided.

Tell Communicator to Forget All Recently Visited Sites

You can delete the contents of the History and begin afresh. To do so, click the Navigator tab of the Preferences dialog box and click the Clear History button.

Choose Language Alternatives for Netscape to Use

Some servers offer pages in more than one language (for example, in English and Japanese). By default, Netscape always requests the English version, but you can also tell it to use another language if one is available. To do so, turn to the Languages section of the Navigator tab in the Preferences dialog box and click the Add button to display a list of supported languages (see Figure 27.30).

Once you have more than one language installed, you can adjust their relative priority by selecting a language in the list and clicking the up and down arrows (see Figure 27.31). The order in which you place the languages determines which version of a page you'll see if multiple versions exist.

> **Note** The language settings have no effect on the character set used. Even if you delete English from the list and retain only Japanese, it will have no effect if you visit a site available only in English; the site still appears in English.

Chapter 27: Internet Browsers in Windows 98

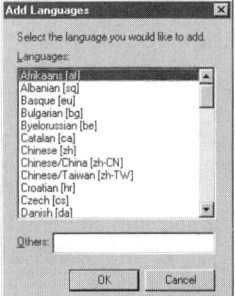

Figure 27.30
Adding support for another language.

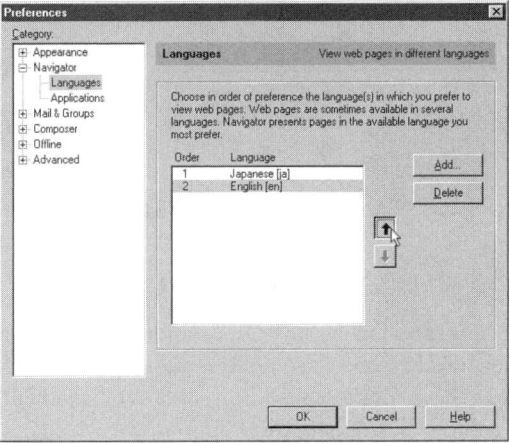

Figure 27.31
Adjusting language preferences.

Choose New Encoding for All Documents Viewed

A *character set* determines how unencoded text is displayed. The Netscape default character set is Western. To change it for all documents, turn to the Fonts section of the Appearances tab in the Preferences dialog box and choose a new language from the drop-down list. This choice does not affect the words in the documents you view, but it may affect the way the document looks. For example, using the Turkish encoding makes the text in a document big and blocky, whereas using the Japanese encoding makes the font smaller. In neither case, however, does the text become unreadable in English.

> **Tip**　To change the encoding for the current document, choose View, Encoding and choose from the submenu of encoding formats.

Change the Fonts Used to Display Pages

Look at the Fonts subsection of the Appearances tab in the Preferences dialog box (see Figure 27.32). The variable-width font is used for most text on a page; the fixed-width font is used for text the Web author has defined to be static in its arrangement on the page (such as code lines). You can set any locally installed font to be the variable-width font, but only fixed width fonts (such as Courier New or Lucida Console) are available for the fixed-width font.

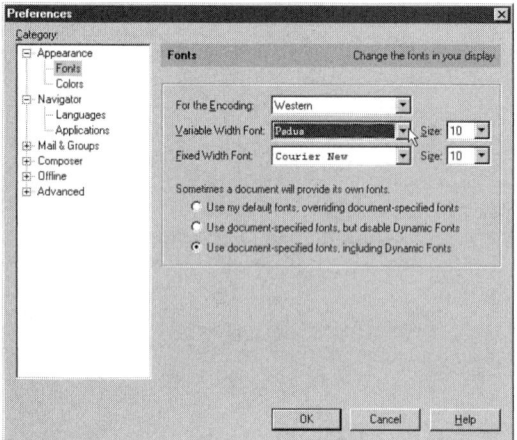

Figure 27.32

Choosing new fonts to use with Communicator.

Specify the font size to the right of the font type: just type the size you want to use.

Many pages use *dynamic fonts,* or fonts specified by the page's author. Dynamic fonts take time to display because they must be downloaded to your computer, but they have the advantage of letting you see the content exactly as the author intended it, regardless of whether the fonts the author used are available on your computer. You have three options when it comes to choosing the fonts to use:

- Always download the author's fonts (the default).
- Download the author's fonts only if the fonts are not available locally.
- Use only the user-specified default fonts.

Tip If you have a wide variety of fonts loaded locally, you can reduce the time it takes to load pages by choosing to download fonts only when they're not available on your computer, while still seeing the page as the author intended.

If you don't want to manually set a font size, but find the current font size too big or too small, choose **V**iew, In**c**rease Font or **V**iew, **D**ecrease Font.

Change the Colors Used to Display Pages

Browsers display links with different colors to help you determine whether you've already followed them. In the Colors section of the Appearances page, you can set the colors used to signify followed and unfollowed links. (If you've visited the site pointed to in a link, Netscape assumes that you've followed the link; whether you got to that page from the page with the link on it or in another way isn't the issue.) To change the colors used to mark followed and unfollowed links, click the colored boxes to open a palette of other colors. Just make sure that you do not pick the same color for both, or you won't be able to tell where you've been.

You can also change the colors used to display page text when no background color or wallpaper has been set by the Web author. You can choose colors individually by clicking them and choosing from a palette, or you can click the check box to use the colors you chose for your Windows color scheme.

If the page's author *has* defined a background color or wallpaper, you can override it by selecting the Always Use My Colors, Overriding Document box. Although this means that you'll miss out on some of the author's creativity, it can be easier on the eyes if you spend a lot of time online and have visited one too many sites with obnoxious wallpaper. Even those bright-white backgrounds used by many sites can contribute to the "reading print on a light bulb" effect.

Create and Edit File Associations

Netscape uses helper applications for files it can't support by itself. The helper application in question is determined by file associations set in Explorer or My Computer, but the associations are also editable from within Netscape. (Those changes apply to the rest of Windows.) Turn to the Applications subsection of the Navigator page to manage file associations within Netscape (see Figure 27.33).

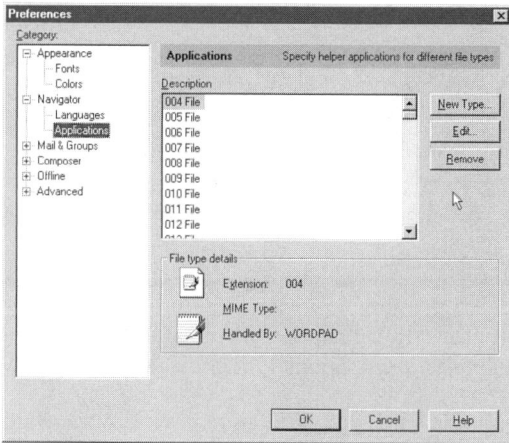

Figure 27.33
Specifying helper applications.

To create a new file association (for example, when you've got a file with an extension you haven't yet registered), click the New Type button and provide the information requested (see Figure 27.34).

Figure 27.34
Creating a new file association.

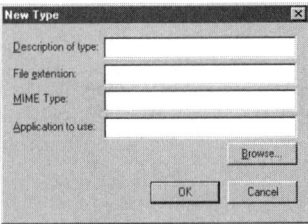

Most of these fields are self-explanatory: Describe the file type as you see fit, enter its application, and provide the path to the helper application you want to use to support it.

The only field name that may need some explanation is the MIME Type field. *MIME types* allow files not supported by a browser to be opened by "helper applications." Not all file associations require MIME types to be specified (any application that's part of Windows 98 won't require it), but you have to specify a MIME type for any application that isn't part of the OS. MIME types are divided into two parts: their type and subtype, like this: `type/subtype`. The *type* is its type of executable and *subtype* is its name. Thus, if you associated an extension with Word, its MIME type would look like this: `application/msword`.

Editing a file association allows you to specify its MIME type, define its associated application, and determine what should be done with it (see Figure 27.35).

Figure 27.35
Editing file associations.

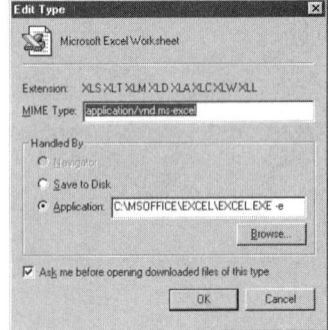

By default, files are associated with their helper applications when they are downloaded, but you're asked before the file is run. This precaution protects you from virus attacks because a virus program can't hurt you until it runs. If you're positive that your download sources are safe, you can choose to run helper applications as soon as the file is downloaded.

If you know you're not going to be using a file type, you can remove it by selecting it and clicking the Remove button.

Warning If you remove a file type from the list, you cannot open any files with that extension until you re-create another file association for it.

Work Offline

By default, Communicator begins in online work mode, expecting a live Internet connection. If you're not always connected to the Internet when you open your browser, you may get tired of pounding the Stop button to abort a loading action. Instead, turn to the Offline page of the Properties dialog box (see Figure 27.36) and choose either O**ff**line Work Mode or **A**sk Me (to be asked whether Communicator should start in online or offline mode). You can still point your browser to online URLs when in offline mode; you just have to start up your net connection before you can access those sites.

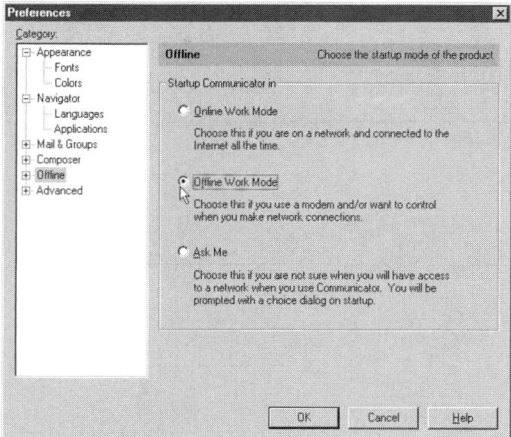

Figure 27.36
Choosing to work in offline mode.

Configure Cookie Acceptance

Cookies are small text files downloaded to your computer that permit a Web site to determine whether you've visited their site. Shopping sites use them to let you browse pages and pick out merchandise, so that the contents of your "shopping cart" remain consistent; other sites (such as Microsoft's) use cookies to identify users of services you have to register for, such as reading premium content. If you delete your cookies (they're just text files), those Web sites can no longer tell that you've been there. Deleting cookies also removes any record of your having been at the site, empties your shopping cart, and forces you to register to read premium content.

Cookies are text files—they can't be used to download viruses to your computer, or anything like that. However, you may want to disable them for reasons of privacy. In the Advanced page of the Properties dialog box, Communicator lets you disable some or all cookies, and lets you decide whether or not you want to accept each cookie as it is offered (see Figure 27.37).

I *don't* recommend clicking the button to have Communicator warn you before accepting all cookies because some sites (GeoCities is famous for this) have a *lot* of cookies and you may have to click half a dozen times to get to a page. Disabling cookies altogether prevents anyone from knowing that you have been to their site, but it also makes it hard or impossible for you to use some features of Web sites that depend on them. If you don't want to accept all cookies, accepting only cookies that go back to the server that originated them, so that the server knows you're there, seems to be the best compromise.

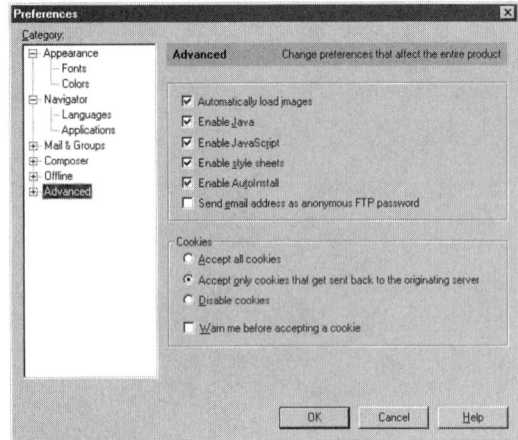

Figure 27.37
Configure cookie acceptance to protect your privacy.

> **Note** By default, your browser is set up to accept all cookies.

Configuring Other Options

In addition to cookie configuration, Communicator stores some other settings in the Advanced page of the Properties page, as described in Table 27.9.

Table 27.9
Advanced Communicator Options

Option	Description	Enabled by Default?
Automatically load images	Displays inline images onscreen without prompting. If deselected to speed download time, you can show images for a page by choosing View, Show Images.	Yes
Enable Java	Allows Java applets to run.	Yes
Enable JavaScript	Allows JavaScript embedded in a Web page to execute.	Yes
Enable style sheets	Allows formatting to take place as specified by style sheets.	Yes

Option	Description	Enabled by Default?
Enable AutoInstall	Allows automatic updates of Communicator across the network.	Yes
Send email address as anonymous FTP password	Public FTP servers normally let you log in with user name anonymous and a password of your email address.	No

Using Communicator

Communicator has many of the same features as IE4, but they are arranged differently. Table 27.10 lists some common browsing actions and how you can do them. The following sections explain these actions in more detail.

Table 27.10
Common Communicator Browsing Functions

Task	Location
Copy selected text from a Web page	Edit, Copy
Examine a page's source code	View, Page Source
Find an instance of a word within a page	Edit, Find in Page
Mark links for future reference	Communicator, Bookmarks, Add Bookmark
Navigate quickly between marked pages	Communicator, Bookmarks
Open a new instance of Navigator from within Communicator	File, New, Navigator Window
Open a page available either locally or on the network	File, Open Page
Organize marked links	Communicator, Bookmarks, Edit Bookmarks
Prepare to work offline	File, Go Offline
Print a Web page	File, Print
Reload a page from its source	View, Reload
Search the Internet for people	Edit, Search Directory
Search the Internet for topics	Edit, Search Internet
Send someone a page using email	File, Send Page
Stop a page from loading	View, Stop Page

Open a New Instance of Navigator from Communicator

To open a new instance of Navigator from Communicator, choose File, New, Navigator Window.

Open a Page Available Either Locally or on the Network

Choose File, Open Page and enter the path or URL of the file you want to open (see Figure 27.38).

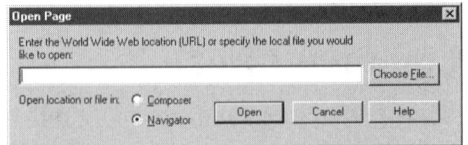

Figure 27.38
Opening a new HTML page.

If the page to open is local, you can click the Choose File button to browse for it (the default path is to the Program folder in your Netscape installation). If the page is online, you have to supply the URL. Make sure that you've chosen to open the file in Navigator (the default) and click Open.

Send Someone a Page Using Email

You can show someone a Web page by sending them a copy of the page (and a link to the real thing) using email. To do so, choose File, Send Page (see Figure 27.39) and supply the email address of the person to send it to. Click the Send button, and the page is sent. The recipient receives an email message containing the text of the page and, if his or her email program supports it, links both to the URL you sent and to links within the page.

Figure 27.39
Sending a copy of the National Marrow Donors Program main page.

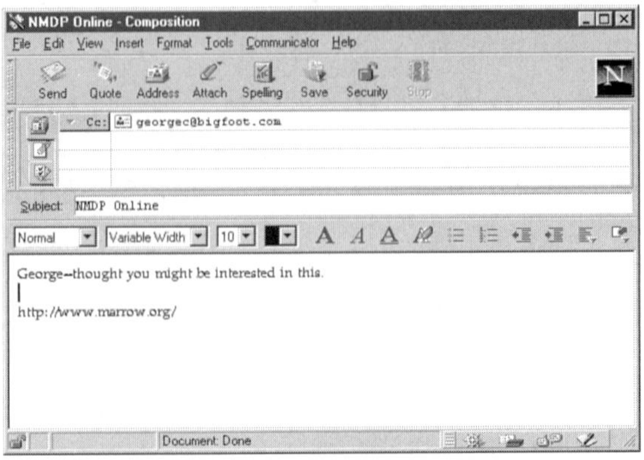

Prepare to Work Offline

If you're preparing to log off the Internet but want to have the most recent online data available, don't just log off, choose File, Go Offline. As shown in Figure 27.40, you are asked whether you want to send and receive all mail and download any waiting messages in newsgroups. (Unfortunately, this option offers no interface for updating all channels and subscriptions before logging off.)

Figure 27.40
Downloading mail and newsgroup postings in preparation to work offline.

Note If you're subscribed to more than one newsgroup, click the Select Items for Download button to choose which newsgroups you want to download, if not all of them.

After you select the options you want, click Go Offline, and your connection will be severed.

Print a Web Page

Before you print a Web page, first choose File|Page Setup to make sure that the proper settings are selected (see Figure 27.41).

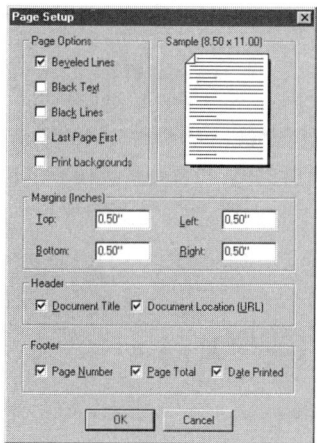

Figure 27.41
Setting up a page's print options.

Most of these options are pretty obvious—you choose the items to print, configure a header and footer, and pick the margins. Most of these options can be left alone, but if you're trying for a particular effect, you can experiment with the Page Options in the upper-left corner of the dialog box.

Click OK, and the page options are set for all future print jobs until you edit them again.

Once you have set up the page, you don't have to print a test page to make sure that everything worked out as planned. Instead, choose File, Print Preview to render a sample of the page, complete with header and footer information (see Figure 27.42).

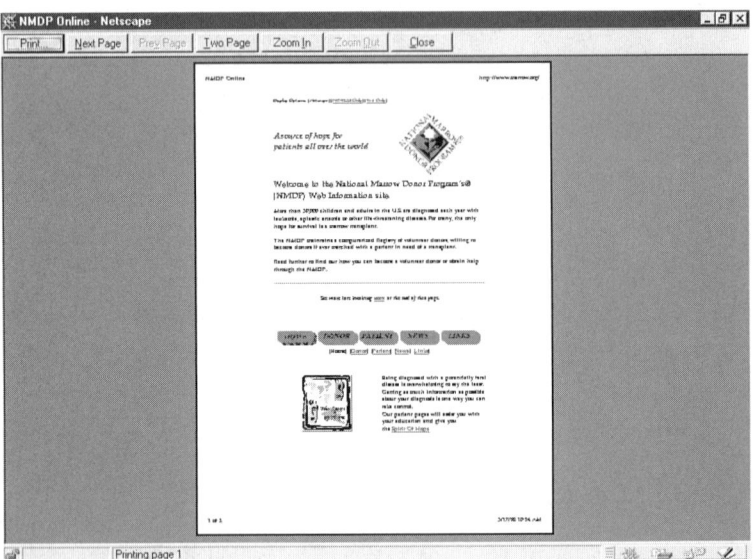

Figure 27.42
Previewing a page before printing.

Zoom in on part of the page to make sure that it looks as you think it should, or move to the next page (if there is one) to make sure that your options work as well there as they did on the first page.

> **Tip** Print Preview can help you avoid cutting off text with margins, something some Web pages have a problem with because they were not formatted to be printed.

When you've checked it out, either click the Print button to start the print job or click Close to exit the previewer and check print settings.

The Print dialog box that appears when you choose File, Print is pretty much the same as any Print dialog box. Make sure that you're printing to the correct printer, specify the correct page range and number of pages, and you're ready to go. Communicator does not allow for special printing of links, so links are printed only as underlined text. You can't create a table of links or automatically print all linked documents.

Copy Text from a Web Page

You can highlight text and choose Edit, Copy to place a copy of it in the Clipboard, or you can copy a whole page's text by first choosing Edit, Select All and then copying the text. Only the text itself is copied, not the formatting.

Find an Instance of a Word in a Page

Even after you've used a search engine to find a page that contains the text you're looking for, it's not always immediately apparent where that word appears in the document—or in what context. To quickly find a word within a page, choose Edit, Find in Page. You see a dialog box like the one in Figure 27.43.

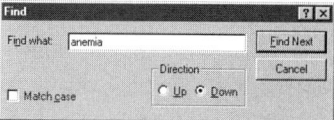

Figure 27.43
Searching for a word within a page.

Type the word you want to look for (and specify whether or not you want the search to be case sensitive) and click Find Next. Communicator jumps to the next instance of that word in the document and highlights it. If that's not the instance you're looking for, you can either click Cancel or try again by clicking Find Next. When you've found the word you're looking for, click Cancel to close the dialog box.

> **Tip** Search in both directions—up and down—before giving up. It's easy to accidentally click within a page so that you're no longer at the top of the page. Find has no "search all" setting.

To find the same word in another document, you can just choose Edit, Find Again.

Search the Internet

Netscape maintains a page of links to various search engines. To access it, choose Edit, Search Internet. Either choose the featured search engine (which varies with the day) or click one of the many other links available to get to that search engine.

> **Tip** Be sure to check out the Search Engines link. Some popular search engines are displayed there instead of on the main page.

Search a Name Directory

The content of many, if not most, U.S. telephone books is online and stored in one of several directories: Four11, InfoSpace, WhoWhere, and so forth. To search for someone's contact information, choose Edit,Search Directory.

You can search for someone based on one or more of the following criteria:

- Name
- Email address
- Phone number
- Organization (the organization providing the email services, not necessarily the organization he or she works for)
- City
- Street

Define a text string for each criterion you choose, specifying text that must be included in the criteria, that the criteria do not include, are or are not, or begin with.

To select additional options to search by, click the More button; to use fewer options, click the Fewer button. The more options you choose, the more likely it is that your search will return options that match what you're looking for. A sample return might look like the one shown in Figure 27.44.

Figure 27.44
Searching the Internet for a person.

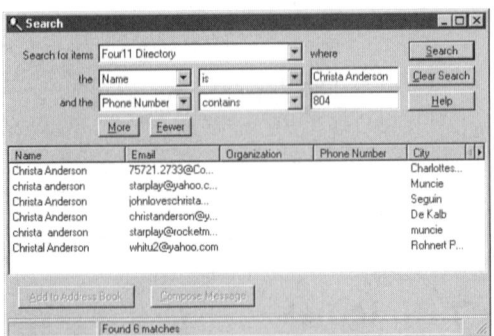

From the results screen, you can select one of the individuals returned by the search and send him or her email, or you can add that email address to your address book.

Some searches are more complete than others, but the information in them is not always fully accurate. After searching for myself in three directories, I found only one entry using my proper email address (or one of them) and one using my proper address—and those two entries weren't identical.

Chapter 27: Internet Browsers in Windows 98   643

> **Tip**   Some directory search engines are more accurate than others. If your number is unlisted, you should not appear in any directory at all. If you are unlisted and show up in one, or are not unlisted but do not want people to be able to look up your home address online, visit the home page for the search engine and ask to be removed. People with unlisted numbers should have to do this only once, but people with listed numbers will have to go back every few months and request to be removed again, because the lists are updated regularly from the telephone book.

Other directory search engines are available when you click the Lookup button on the personal toolbar. Links grouped by topic are available when you click the Internet button next to it.

Navigate Quickly Between Pages

Typing URLs all the time is no fun at all, so Communicator includes some navigation tools to help you get around while keeping the typing to a minimum:

- Links to search engines, directory search engines, and software updates
- Lists of recently accessed sites
- Lists of bookmarked links

The search and directory engines are discussed elsewhere, in "Search the Internet." Communicator has bookmarked the software updates page so that it is accessible from **H**elp, **S**oftware Updates.

Recently accessed sites are available in a few areas:

- If the site you want to see is the one you were just looking at, you can click the Back and Forward buttons on the toolbar. Alternatively, you can click the drop-down arrows on these buttons to see a list of URLs accessed during this Communicator session.

- The Netsite list in the top center of the screen not only shows the present URL, but also lists the last 16 URLs directly navigated to—not just during this session, but with Communicator since it was installed. (Not all links you have accessed are shown, just those you navigated to directly.)

- Links you have bookmarked are available in the Bookmarks file. To access it, choose **C**ommunicator|**B**ookmarks and select from the list. When you select a link in the list, you navigate immediately to it.

- The History (**C**ommunicator, **H**istory) contains all the links accessed for the past few days (nine days by default). These links are contained in a folder you can sort by name, location, dates first and last visited, when the link expires, or how many visits you've made there in the past nine days (see Figure 27.45).

Notice that URLs and locally stored HTML documents are both recorded in the History.

Figure 27.45

Contents of the History.

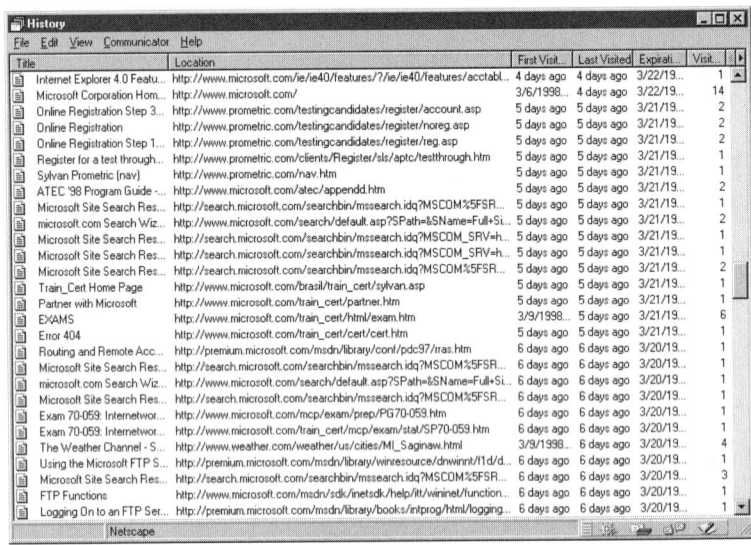

Tip	If you notice you're visiting a particular page frequently, you can bookmark it directly from the History folder: Choose **F**ile, Add to Boo**k**marks.

Table 27.11 lists some navigation goals and how to accomplish them.

Table 27.11
Moving Among Pages with Communicator

To Get Here...	Do This...
A list of recently accessed documents	Choose **C**ommunicator, **H**istory to open the History folder.
A page from which you can search the Web using any one of several search engines	Click the Search button on the standard toolbar, the Lookup button on the personal toolbar, or choose **E**dit, Search Internet.
A page that you've bookmarked	Choose **C**ommunicator, **B**ookmarks.
A page you just looked at	Navigate with the Back and Forward buttons to move between recently viewed pages. Both buttons have drop-down menus to let you choose a site to leap to.
Your home page	Click the Home button on the standard toolbar.

Mark Links for Future Reference

It's anyone's guess how many sites and pages are on the Web. Even if there were an accurate count today, by the time you have read these words the number would be out of date. If you're reading a page and realize that you're likely to need it again, you don't have to depend on being able to find it in Communicator History or in the Location drop-down list. Instead, while still on the page, choose **C**ommunicator, **B**ookmarks, Add Bookmar**k**.

If you've previously organized your bookmarks into folders (see the next section, "Organize Marked Links"), you can create the bookmark in a particular folder by choosing **F**ile Bookmark instead of Add Bookmar**k** (the latter option creates the bookmark in the main bookmark directory).

Organize Marked Links

After you create more than a few bookmarks, or if more than one person is using the same browser, you may have a tough time finding the bookmark you want with only a quick glance. If you have lots of bookmarks, it may be time to organize the links. Choose **C**ommunicator, **B**ookmarks, Edit **B**ookmarks to open the folder of marked links (see Figure 27.46).

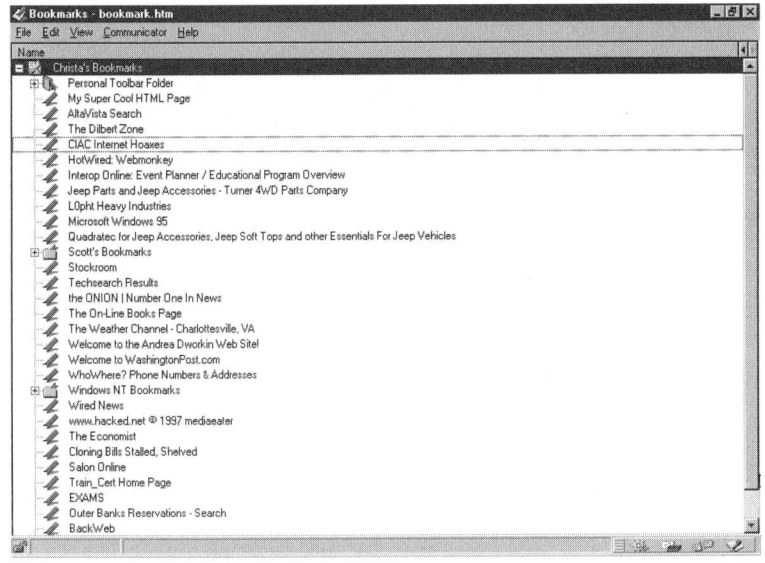

Figure 27.46
Organize bookmarks so that you can find your favorite links more easily.

I've previously created a couple of different folders for bookmarks: one for Scott and one for my Windows NT information. To create a folder, position the cursor in the folder in which you want to create the folder (folders can contain other folders) and choose **F**ile, New **F**older. A dialog box like the one shown in Figure 27.47 appears.

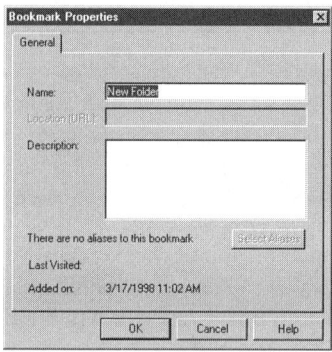

Figure 27.47
Creating a new bookmark folder.

Describe the folder if you want (you don't have to) and click OK.

You can now add new bookmarks to that folder directly. But what about bookmarks already made? Move bookmarks to that folder by clicking and dragging them into the folder.

| Tip | You can organize bookmarks within folders by dragging them to change their order, or by sorting them according to the criteria in the **V**iew menu: name, location, creation date, or date last visited. |

When you're done organizing bookmarks, exit the Bookmark folder as you would any other Windows folder. All changes are saved automatically.

Examine a Page's Source Code

Get an idea of how that well-executed page was put together by choosing **V**iew, Page **S**ource. This option opens an instance of an HTML editor (such as Notepad) in which you can see the coding used for a page—and can even make changes to that code. Changes made can be saved locally but do not affect the original file.

Reload a Page from its Source

To make sure that a page is working from current information instead of a cached copy of the page, choose **V**iew, **R**eload or click the Reload button on the toolbar.

Stop a Page from Loading

If you click a link and realize that you don't want to go there after all, you don't have to wait for the page to load and then click the Back button. Instead, choose **V**iew, **S**top Page Loading or click the Stop button on the toolbar. The loading process ceases and you remain at the original page.

Chapter 27: Internet Browsers in Windows 98

Get Information About the Current Page

Find out what structures are in a document, how large it is, where it's stored in the cache, and what kind of security is attached to it by selecting <u>V</u>iew, Page <u>I</u>nfo (see Figure 27.48).

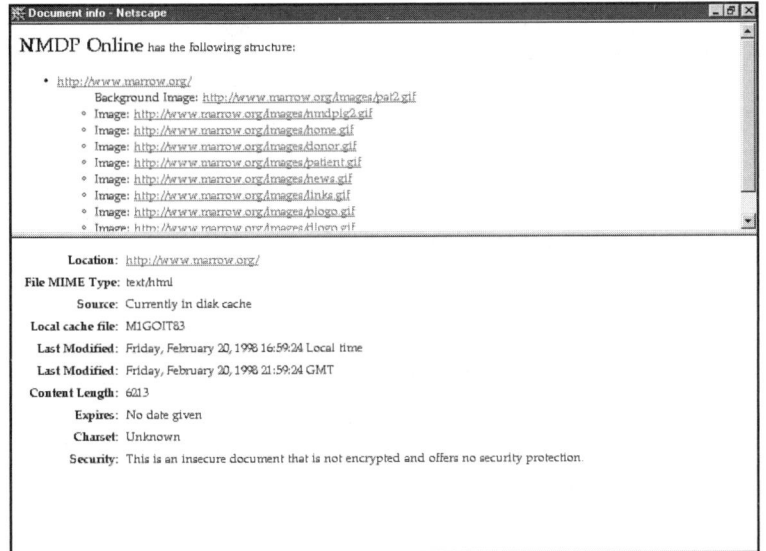

Figure 27.48
Getting information about the current page.

Tip	Follow a link in the Page Info window to display the file described at the bottom of the screen.

Using Netcaster

Netscape doesn't incorporate channel connectivity into its browser as IE4 does. Instead, the channel tool is a separate part of the Communicator suite that can be loaded from the Communicator menu. Like the channel function in IE4, Netcaster provides access to *channels* (Web sites that deliver their content automatically to your desktop). Netcaster offers access to channels and Web sites in two places: in a ready-made list of channels, accessible from the Channel Finder bar, or in My Channels, a collection of channels to which you have personally subscribed. You can even set your favorite channel as the background for your desktop (Netscape calls this a *webtop*) so that you can view new information as it comes in without first activating the channel.

> **Note** The problem with a webtop is that it covers up all the icons on your desktop. You have to close the webtop to access anything stored on the desktop.

Netcaster isn't a great implementation of channel surfing. Its separation from the browser for browser-like functions makes it difficult to use because it makes viewing and subscribing to channels separate actions. But the real problem with the tool is that it's slow. Let's face it: Not every machine running Windows 98 is a power engine; many of them are personal desktop systems. I tested Netcaster on a 486 with 16M of RAM installed. IE4 worked fine under these conditions. Netcaster, on the other hand, flunked. Running on its own, it's slow—but running with other applications minimized onscreen, it's pretty much unusable. Until its performance is boosted, it's outclassed by the IE4 channel capabilities.

IE4 Versus Netscape: Which Is Better?

The obvious answer to the question of whether Netscape or Internet Explorer is better is the consultant's reply: "It depends." It depends on both what you're trying to accomplish and personal prejudice: Some people really like using the browser that comes with Windows, and some people really don't.

The two browsers have many of the same features, but often organize them differently or offer different supersets of the same features. For example, both offer the Work Offline option, but when you choose to work offline with Communicator, you're asked whether you want to download mail and newsgroup postings first (IE4 doesn't do that). On the other hand, IE4 offers some printing options that Communicator does not have (such as more elaborate header and footer settings and the ability to automatically print linked files). Both browsers also have access to channels, but whereas IE4 incorporates Internet channel browsing into its browser interface, Communicator implements another application, Netcaster, for channel browsing.

The biggest difference between the two browsers, unsurprisingly, is the way they're incorporated into the operating system. IE4, of course, is perfectly incorporated: Using the browser, you can merrily navigate between online documents and local folders without skipping a beat. Sometimes you have to look twice to realize what part of Windows 98 you're in—you may have started out in IE4 but are now in My Computer because you needed a local file instead of an online document. Communicator is not well incorporated into the operating system. It's a browser that can cooperate well with Windows 98, but it is a separate application nonetheless. This doesn't mean that IE4 is necessarily superior to Communicator, only that IE4 was designed to be the basis of a specific operating system and Communicator was not.

Table 27.12 lists the more advanced options available to the browsers (we'll assume that both can open a new instance of the browser) and a comparison of which browser has it and which does not.

Chapter 27: Internet Browsers in Windows 98   **649**

Table 27.12
Comparing and Contrasting IE4 and Communicator

Feature	Present in IE4?	Present in Communicator?
Access to channels	Yes	No, unless you open Netcaster
Access to email	Yes	Yes
Access to instant messaging software	No	Yes
Access to newsgroups	Yes	Yes
Built-in content filters	Yes	No
Customize headers and footers of printed pages.	Yes	Yes, but with fewer options
Detailed document properties sheets	No	Yes
Easy access to cache	Yes	No
Email a page or link to a page	Yes	Yes (although it mails the page and the link; you can't separate the two)
Open dialog box has drop-down list of recently accessed local and online documents	Yes	No
Preview documents before printing	No	Yes
Print linked documents or add a table of links	Yes	No
Sort contents of history list	Yes (organized by date)	Yes (organized by user's choice of criteria)
Work offline with previously downloaded data	Yes, but does not prompt for one last download	Yes

The race looks pretty close, doesn't it? The feature lists match up pretty well, but the final response to the question of which browser is better seems to depend on two issues: stability and speed. When Netscape Communicator version 4.05 came out in April 1998, CNet published a review of the IE4 and Netscape Communicator (http://www.cnet.com/Content/Reviews/Compare/Browsers4/ss01.html). In this poll, Netscape 4.05 won out because of its wider cross-platform availability: Netscape is available for every version of Windows 3.x and later, for the Macintosh, and for numerous flavors of UNIX. IE4 is available only for Windows, Macintosh, and Solaris, and it is fully implemented only on Windows. Regarding the issue of stability, a crash in Netscape means that the browser has died, not that an integral part of the operating system has died, as a crash means with IE4. IE4 comes out ahead in terms of performance and integration, however; the browser is faster, and all its features are available from within the browser, instead of requiring you to choose from a suite of miniapplications.

My personal experience in using both browsers extensively leads me to agree with CNet's review—but not completely. Netscape is slow to start (it takes time to load all those plug-ins), and it takes longer to load pages than does IE4. I have had more problems with Netscape crashing than with IE4 (Netscape seems to have an uneasy relationship with Eudora Light 3.05, which supports hyperlinks, but now and then when you click on one, Communicator crashes). When IE4 has had problems, I've been able to reset the desktop by clicking the recovery screen's link to restore desktop settings. I prefer the integrated interface of IE4 to the more modular one of Communicator, especially IE4's capability to display channels, marked links, search engines, and the History folder to one side of the browser display. However, Netscape Communicator has a couple features I wish IE4 had—particularly the capability to disable cookies selectively and the communication suite's independence of the Windows interface. CNet's right—it's easier to configure the entire browser from a single cascaded dialog box than by flipping through tabs with some odd organizational quirks. Netscape also fully supports Java; as of the spring of 1998, IE4 has become decaffeinated.

Netscape Communicator has one serious disadvantage when it comes to user profiles (the Windows method of providing a custom user interface to each user of a particular machine). User profiles store all user interface data (anything loaded in USER.DAT and stored in the Registry key HKEY_CURRENT_USER)—so you can save application settings to the user profile. IE4 stores all user-specified browser configuration settings in this Registry key, as does Netscape Navigator 3.0, but Communicator also stores some settings in HKEY_LOCAL_MACHINE to improve browser performance. Sadly, this arrangement means that you can't set Communicator preferences to be part of custom user profiles.

In short, if you're working in a cross-platform environment and want a browser that will work pretty well across all platforms, Communicator is the better choice. If you're working in a Windows 98 environment and want to take advantage of all the features of that operating system, you may be better off with IE4.

Conclusion

This chapter has presented browsing with Windows 98 in a nutshell. The two most popular PC-based Web browsers these days are IE4 and Netscape Communicator. With IE4, you can access integrated browsing in a way new to the browsing world because the Web and your computer become increasingly intermingled. Netscape Communicator doesn't offer the same degree of integration, but it has some nice features that IE4 lacks and is less likely to bring down your operating system in flames if it crashes. From the information in this chapter, you should be able to figure out which browser will work better for you and how to get the most out of the browser you select.

Setting Up Windows 98 for the Internet

With its closely integrated browser, Windows 98 is made for the Internet—if you don't plan to get online, you miss out on a lot of the new features of the operating system. This chapter discusses the following:

- How to set up Windows 98 to use an Internet connection
- The function of Internet Service Providers
- How and when to use Internet proxies
- The distinctions between Java and ActiveX, and their implications for working online

The Connection Tab

Setting up an Internet connection can be done from a single location with Windows 98: the Connection tab on the Internet Properties dialog box (see Figure 28.1) You can access this dialog box from IE4's View menu, or by clicking the Internet applet in the Control Panel.

Figure 28.1
Set up and edit Internet connections from the Connection Manager.

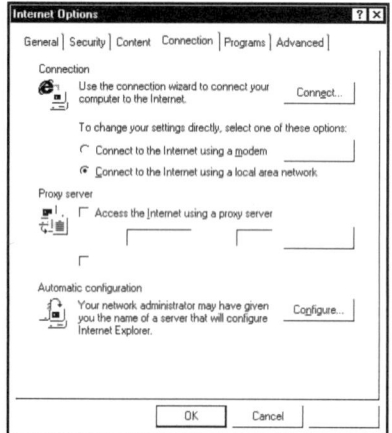

Setting Up an Internet Connection

Windows 98 offers two methods of connecting to the Internet. If you use the Internet Connection Wizard, it attempts to find a dial-up service for you, choosing from a list of locally available services. If you want to set up the connection manually, click the Settings button to add a new connection.

Using the Connection Wizard

To create a new connection, click the Connect button on the top of the Connection tab in the Internet Control Panel applet to begin the Internet Connection Wizard, as shown in Figure 28.2.

Choose the option for setting up a new Internet connection and click Next. In the next stage, Windows 98 attempts to connect to a referral service (it's at an 800 number) to find the ISPs in your area.

> **Tip** Insert your Windows 98 installation CD in the drive—you'll need it for this stage.

When you've got your installation CD near at hand, click OK to continue.

Chapter 28: Setting Up Windows 98 for the Internet

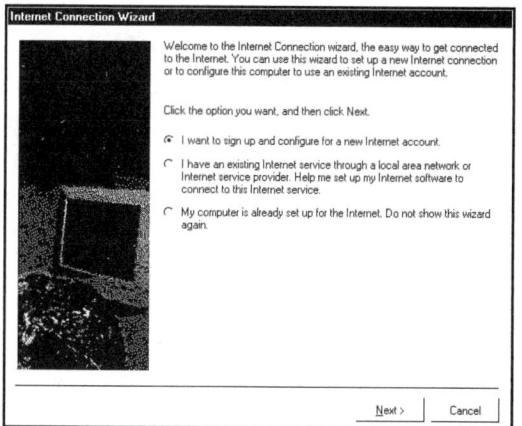

Figure 28.2
Create new connections with the Internet Connection Wizard.

Manual Connection Setup

To set up a new connection, click on the Settings button in the Connection Manager to open the Dial-Up Settings dialog box (see Figure 28.3).

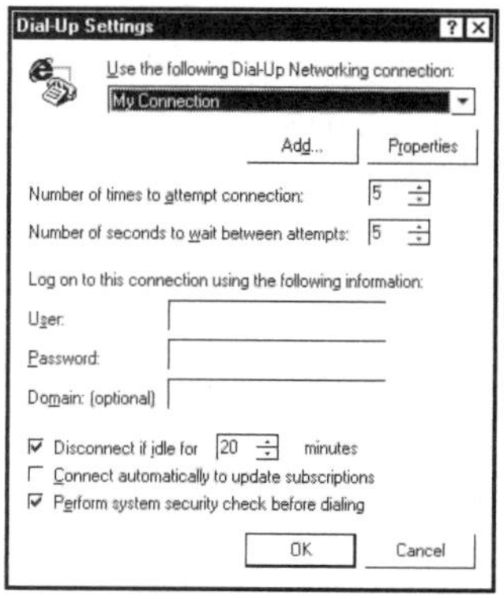

Figure 28.3
Edit an existing account's properties or create a new one.

Click the Add button to open the Make New Connection Wizard and create a new account. You'll need to provide the following information:

- The name of the connection, perhaps something that identifies it by type or purpose

- The make of modem, if you don't want to use the one that the Make New Connection Wizard detects

- The area code and telephone number of the computer to call (in this case, your ISP, although this will work for any dial-up connection) and its country code

Part V: Windows 98 and the Internet

> **Tip** You can also access the Make New Connection Wizard by clicking the Make New Connection applet in the Dial-Up Networking folder.

When you've provided all this information and clicked Finish, the connection will be added to your Dial-Up Networking folder, accessible from within My Computer. Before you exit, you'll have the chance to add further information to your new connection (see Figure 28.4).

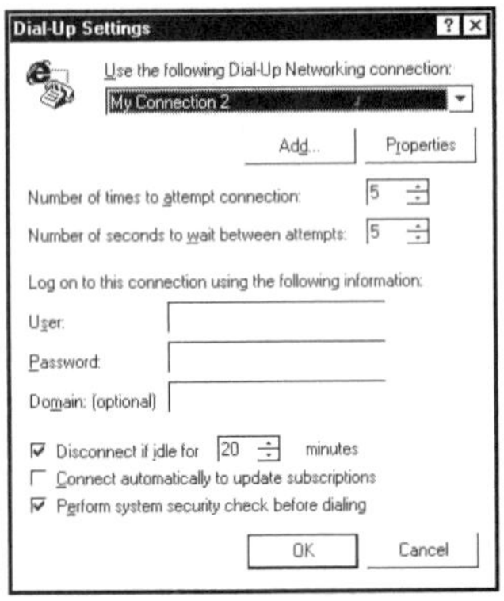

Figure 28.4
Providing logon information for a new connection.

The number of attempts to make and the time to wait between attempts are fairly self-explanatory: If the first attempt to dial in fails (perhaps because of a busy signal), then the number is retried until the dial-in succeeds or the number of times to retry has been exceeded. The user name, password, and domain all refer not to your local network but to the settings for your Internet account.

The connection settings are intended to help you budget your online time. By default, if you don't use your Internet connection (that is, there are no keystrokes or mouse clicks passed to Internet applications) for twenty minutes, then the connection will be disconnected. Channel and link subscriptions, discussed in Chapter 27, "Internet Browsers in Windows 98," are not automatically updated at the specified times unless you're already logged on.

> **Note** You can choose to automatically log on to update subscriptions only if you're using Dial-Up Networking (DUN) to connect to the Internet. For example, I have cable modem access that has its own connection program, so telling DUN to log on doesn't permit me to connect with the cable modem.

The final option, asking IE4 to prompt you for password information before dialing, is useful when other people have access to your computer and you want to be sure that they can't use your account without your permission.

Chapter 28: Setting Up Windows 98 for the Internet

The Properties... button in the Dial-Up Settings dialog box (see Figure 28.5) provides access to other options that you may not need to change, but should be familiar with (see Table 28.1).

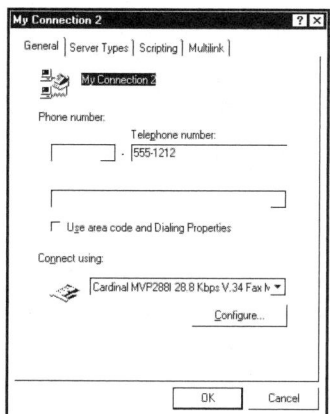

Figure 28.5
Connection Properties.

Table 28.1
Advanced Dial-Up Networking Settings

Property	Name	Location in Connection Properties
Change the telephone number and area code to call	Area code, telephone number, country code	General tab
Choose a script to run at logon (sometimes necessary for a SLIP connection)	Scripting	Scripting tab
Choose network protocols allowed access to the connection	Allowed Network Protocols	Server Types tab
Combine physical data channels to increase bandwidth	Use additional devices	Multilink tab
Force the user of that connection to use the specified telephone number	Use area code and dial-up properties (disable this feature)	General tab
Pick a transport protocol (SLIP or PPP)	Type of Dial-Up Server	Server Types tab

continues

Table 28.1, Continued
Advanced Dial-Up Networking Settings

Property	Name	Location in Connection Properties
Set connection parameters (software compression, session logging)	Advanced Options	Server Types tab
Set connection security information (data encryption, software encryption, and userlogon)	Advanced Options	Server Types tab
Set options for running a logon script	Step through script; start terminal screen minimized	Scripting tab
Specify a new modem to use for that connection	Specify button	General tab

Tip The General tab in the Properties dialog box also provides access to modem settings and protocol information.

Internet Service Providers

Connecting to the Internet is technically simpler than it used to be, but the dazzling array of service providers and types of access can make it difficult to choose one. Although space in this chapter prevents us from doing an exhaustive analysis of every type of Internet access available, this section describes some of the features of the Internet Service Providers (ISPs) from which most single users will choose.

Basic Internet Access

In most of the United States, you have access to some kind of generic dial-in service, whether from a national name such as AT&T or a local operation such as Jeff and Akbar's Internet Connections and Tofu Hut. Whatever the size, the essential structure is much the same: You dial in to the Internet server(s) and those servers are connected to a backbone of the Internet.

For a monthly fee, you'll pay for a telephone number and passworded account that gives you access to the Internet, an email account, and sometimes a few megabytes of storage space on a web server so you can have your own web page if you want it. Rates vary, as do line charges—some carriers offer a flat-rate unlimited service, and others charge by the hour.

The speed of these providers varies with their hardware (in some areas, 56Kbps modem connections are available, but other areas still offer only 28.8Kbps or even less—33.6 access is common), but you can't ever get faster service than your provider has modems.

Today, online services such as America Online, CompuServe, Prodigy, and The Microsoft Network function in much the same manner as the national general Internet Providers. Their email services are no longer limited to their networks (as once used to be the case, leading people to accumulate long lists of email addresses with different providers so that they could communicate with each other). These services do have some extra features that add value to the Internet connection; for example, CompuServe maintains forums similar to newsgroups in content and level of variety, but moderated so that spamming—offtopic advertisements on the group and unsolicited mailings—are not a problem for those who care to join in the conversation.

ISDN

Analog modems have reached some pretty stellar speeds these days, but even as recently as the mid-'90s they were about half as fast as they are today. In the mid-1990s, some telephone companies began offering a digital service called ISDN, which offered a service called Basic Rate ISDN—two 64Kbps lines that could be used either singly to provide simultaneous upstream and downstream access to the network, or in combination to provide a 128Kbps pipe that could only transmit data one way at a time.

ISDN isn't as simple a procedure as getting an analog connection, and the startup costs were higher. Instead of going to the local computer store, buying a modem, and getting an account with the local provider, you had to call the telephone company, make sure that ISDN was available in the area, get access to a digital line, and have people come out to set up the hardware (a network card and ISDN bridge) and software. Not a cheap proposition—costs varied across the United States—and not always a simple one, particularly when the service was first offered. When the Washington DC-area consulting company I worked for at that time decided to get ISDN access, the ISDN expert from the company took the shrink-wrap off the toolkit required to install the hardware, and it took the better part of two days to get it set up properly.

After it was set up, however, ISDN definitely had its place: It was much faster than the available analog modems, and made some data-heavy uses for the Internet—such as browsing the Web—much more approachable. These days, however, it seems possible that the niche occupied by ISDN might be filled by a fairly new technology: cable modems.

Cable Modems

Cable modem access is now available from cable television providers in many parts of the United States. The name is a bit of a misnomer—it's not exactly a modem, but an RG-58 Ethernet connection to the cable company that offers you LAN-speed access to the Internet.

> **Note** That's the theory, anyway. For example, actual line speeds for my cable modem provider are closer to 100Kbps, not the 10Mbps physically possible with the cable type. As with any Internet access, access speed is partially determined by the size of the pipeline your cable provider has.

The cable company installs an additional Ethernet card in your computer and attaches it to your existing cable hookup (or a new hookup, if necessary), with the network connection leading out of the building.

The speed of the connection varies, depending on whether you're uploading information or downloading it. If you have the same line speed for both types of communications, it's called a *two-way connection*. If you're using your existing modem for sending information to the Net and only using the cable connection to download, then that's a *one-way connection*. For most people's purposes, the one-way connection is adequate because the bulk of connect time is spent downloading information to your computer, as in reading web pages or visiting FTP sites. Few individual users upload much more data than email or web page additions. And because the technology uses an existing physical infrastructure, in the places where the cabling is already available the connection is not that much more expensive than access through an ordinary ISP.

ISP Tips

No matter what type of access you're shopping for, call around and compare services before signing up with an ISP. Get details about the following:

- User-to-modem ratios (if it's much higher than 10:1, you're likely to encounter busy signals)

- Whether the ISP maintains redundant access to the Net so that if one line goes down the link is still maintained

- Whether any start-up fees or installation fees apply

- What the access speed is

- How much the service costs per hour, or whether an unlimited access plan is available

- What technical support is available and what hours it keeps

Using Internet Proxies

One of the troubles with accessing the Internet is that in doing so you're joining a network, and network membership means that other people have access to your computer—and your data. Because Windows 98 does not offer any local access protection, it's a little more vulnerable to attack than more secure operating systems such as Windows NT, which can set permissions as far down as the file level even on unshared files.

To increase security, therefore, particularly for those working on a LAN, you can connect to the Internet with an intermediary called a *proxy server*. People on the Internet will still be able to get to the proxy server (although the nature of this access will be limited) but they won't be able to connect to the rest of the network without explicit permission.

To set up IE4 to use a proxy server, turn to the Connection Manager tab in the Internet Options dialog box (see Figure 28.6) and check the Access the Internet using a proxy server box.

- If you plan to use the same proxy server for all connections, fill in its address (either by name or by IP address) and the port to use to connect to the Internet.

- If you plan to use a different proxy server for different kinds of connections or want to specify certain addresses for which a proxy is not required, click the Advanced button to access the Proxy Settings dialog box (see Figure 28.7).

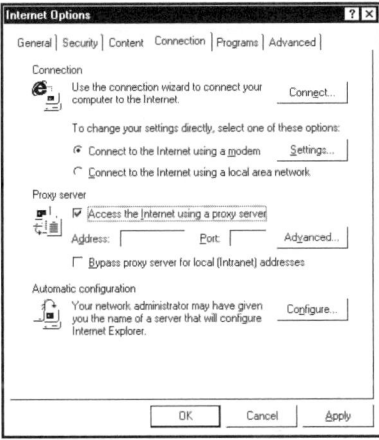

Figure 28.6
The Internet Options dialog box.

If you supplied an address in the Connection Manager's main dialog box, it will be entered here in all the options (except for Sockets) and the option to use the same proxy server for all addresses will be enabled. Deselect the option and fill in the addresses for the proxies you want to use with the following syntax:

```
http://<address>:<port>
```

In this syntax, *address* is the fully qualified domain name of the server and *port* is the port number to use.

> **Note** You can use either the fully qualified domain name of the server or its IP address, but if you use the latter be sure not to include leading zeroes.

In the Connection tab, you have the option of specifying whether to use proxy servers for local intranet content. The Advanced settings let you carry this further, supplying the names of servers you can connect to without using a proxy. Type the names of these servers (for example, server.com) into the Exceptions box, separating all entries with a semicolon.

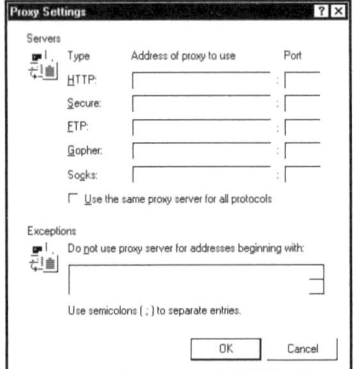

Figure 28.7
Advanced Proxy Settings.

Understanding Java and ActiveX

Accessing web content is a largely static affair. You log on, you point your browser to an URL, and you see the content of the current page on your screen. The page is downloaded to a local cache so that you can return to it quickly if you want, but nothing actually *happens* on your computer other than rendering of the images that make up the page.

Unless Java or ActiveX applets are included in the page, that is.

Simply put, Java and ActiveX are simple programming languages. *Java* is an object-oriented language originally developed by Sun Microsystems, intended to run on any platform. Most programming languages are platform-specific, meaning that if you want to run the same application on more than one platform you must compile one version of the application for each platform. When selling software, this isn't a problem—you just note the supported platform on the box. But when making an application available to all comers, it's inconvenient to have to tell people, "Click here if you're running Windows, here if you're running Berkeley UNIX, here if you're running Mac System 7," and so on, to lead them to the proper version of the application. Instead, Java applets bring with them a virtual machine that supplies an environment in which they can run without regard to the operating system of the computer to which they're downloaded.

> **Note** Java is indeed supposed to be fully platform independent, but not all Java applications are. Microsoft's new Java controls in J++ enable some extra functionality not found in the ordinary Java language, but which depend on functions found in Windows. That is, applications written with the extra features will not provide those extra features unless the user is running Windows.

ActiveX is similar in concept to Java, but not identical. Rather than being a platform-independent language that can run on a variety of different machines, ActiveX is a set of controls that make applications written in a variety of languages—C++, Delphi, J++, and Visual Basic—network accessible. Essentially, ActiveX provides a means of enabling disparate objects to communicate with each other.

In a network computing environment, users with ActiveX support would be able to access information on a server database or run applications on that server via their browser. The only limitation to this is that ActiveX is Windows-specific—you can access ActiveX functionality only when using Windows. (Microsoft has stated its commitment to port ActiveX to the Macintosh and UNIX, but this hasn't yet happened.)

Implications for Browsing

Not all Java and ActiveX applications are downloaded to the system to be run separately. Some applications are part of a web page and can be used to display multimedia content without downloading .WAV files to the user's machine, make some kinds of forms, or generally provide dynamic content on web pages. Without access to Java and ActiveX controls, your web content is apt to be more static. Some of these applets are necessary for running certain browser applications, as well—for example, to access the channel functionality of Netscape, you need to run a Java applet.

Implications for Internet Security

Any time you let an unknown application run on your computer, you're exposing yourself to malicious programming, and Java and ActiveX programs are no exception. Java applications typically run in their virtual machine, independent of the rest of the computer (this is known as a *sandbox*) but when ActiveX applications are downloaded to the machine, they're run like any other .EXE file.

Breaches of Internet security can conceivably be broken down into four categories:

- System modification (changing or deleting disk contents)
- Invasion of privacy (stealing passwords or other information from your disk)
- Denial of service (crashing the browser)
- Antagonism (displaying annoying messages or pictures)

Java's virtual machine design is secure against the first two problems, but not as well defended against the latter two. A bug in Java can make it possible for a malicious application to crash the Java virtual machine, and there's little that can be done to prevent an application from doing what it's supposed to be doing, and if that includes printing obscene messages, that's the end of it. Another problem is that Java is not implemented in precisely the same way on all browsers. A hole discovered in February 1997 allowed malicious Java applets running under Netscape to report a server's IP address even if running behind a firewall, but could supply more complete information when running under Internet Explorer.

> **Note** In March 1998, IE4 was made officially "decaffeinated" by its lack of officially recognized support of Java.

The open nature of ActiveX controls makes them far less secure than Java applets; because they run as ordinary executable files, they're open to pretty much any of these four security concerns. Plug-ins exist to let someone remotely shut down your computer via ActiveX controls, or edit data on your hard disk.

> **Note** Viruses, you will recall, are just .EXE files. You can't tell the function of an executable file from its name.

ActiveX security is handled from a few different angles. First, Microsoft provides a code-signing program called *Authenticode*, which programmers can use to identify themselves (name, email address, and other information). Based on this information, users can choose to run or cancel the ActiveX control. This isn't exactly a secure option, however; all this program can tell you is that someone signed the code. Whether that signature is valid, or whether the signature will do you any good after the damage from a malicious application has been done, is another question entirely. That is, after your hard disk has been maliciously formatted, you can write a nasty email to the putative author of the control to complain about it, but that's about it.

So what *can* you do about Java and ActiveX security? Security experts tend to agree that the best defense against malicious applications is to deny them access. This limits the functionality of some web pages, but will make your system more secure. To set up this security, turn to the Security tab of the Internet Properties dialog box, accessible from IE4's View menu. Choose the Custom option, and then click Settings to hand-tune the security settings for Java and ActiveX controls (see Figure 28.8).

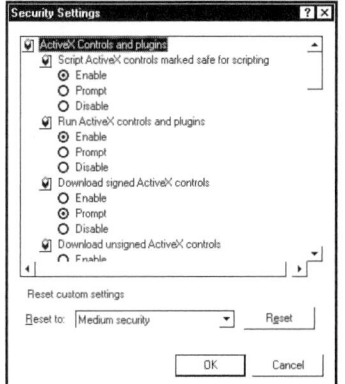

Figure 28.8
Security settings for Java and ActiveX browser functionality.

The level of security that you choose is the baseline for operations on the computer. If you specify a certain level of access to your system and a Java or ActiveX applet needs more access, then the applet will have to ask before gaining the increased access.

The details of the security settings and their implications are discussed in Chapter 30, "Internet Security," but the basic message here is that by default, Internet security with IE4 is at the user's discretion—you're prompted to confirm downloading applets to your system, but they're not disabled. To keep functionality, you may want to do this, but in terms of security it's better to disable Java and especially ActiveX support.

Problems and Solutions

Connecting to the Internet is not always a trouble-free process. The following sections identify some common problems, possible diagnoses, and how you can resolve the problems.

Cannot Connect to ISP

If the connection you've set up for your ISP doesn't work, start by isolating the problem. Is the line busy? Hang up and wait a few minutes before trying again. (Weekends, especially Sunday nights, seem to be prime busy-signal times for overloaded ISPs.) If the provider can't connect you, then check the following:

- Is the telephone number accurate?

- Are your username and password entered accurately?

- Are you supplying any scripts needed to connect to this provider?

If you're supplying all necessary information and are sure that it's accurate, try rebooting and reattempting the connection. If that doesn't work, contact technical support for the ISP and ask if there's a physical problem in the area.

Summer storms, for example, can lead to connection problems. Your computers might be protected from power surges caused by electrical storms, but your telephone lines probably aren't. Also, heavy rain can adversely affect telephone lines, causing excessive noise on them and preventing a reliable connection from being made (even if your voice service still works; data is more persnickety about noise than voice is). Sometimes, you can get help from the telephone company if that's the case, but in extreme cases all you can do is wait out the storm.

A final problem with logging on can be due to a downed logon server, which you should find out about when you're told that the system is not responding. (Give the connection a couple of tries before assuming that this is the problem—connection glitches can result in the same message.) Technical support should be able to tell you whether the logon server is malfunctioning.

Cannot Connect to Email or Web

If you can log on to the Internet but can't access email or the Web, the problem likely lies in your connection to the relevant server. Make sure that you've specified the right IP address for email servers (more on this in Chapter 31, "Mail Management in Windows 98"). If the connection seems to hang, try disconnecting from the Internet altogether, rebooting, and attempting the connection again.

If you attempt to log on to your POP-3 server at the same time that mail is being deposited in your mailbox, you may get an error message telling you that your mailbox is locked by another application. If this happens, you'll have to manually supply your email password (which may not be the same as your Internet connection password) to log on. Until the other server has released your mailbox, however, you won't be able to log on to the mail server and download your messages.

HTML Documents Are Not Opening with Desired Browser

Some of us have more than one browser installed. If you attempt to connect to a link in an email message or open a web page saved to disk and the wrong browser opens, all that means is that you need to make sure that you've got the proper default browser selected and the file associations are set for the proper browser.

> **Note** You can't always tell what application is associated with a file by the icon used to display the file. It's possible to have a file associated with one application (say, Netscape) and using the icon of another (say, IE4).

Chapter 28: Setting Up Windows 98 for the Internet   **665**

To edit file associations for HTML and other web-related files, open Explorer (not IE4, but Explorer) and choose Folder Options from the View menu. The Folder Options dialog box will open; click on the File Types tab (see Figure 28.9).

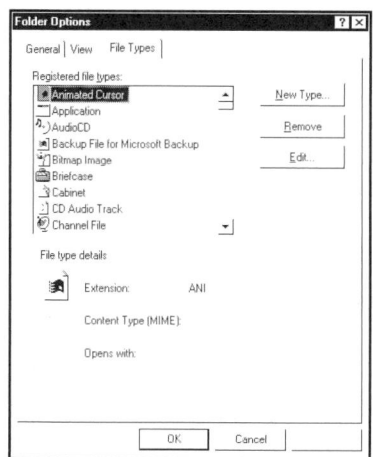

Figure 28.9
Editing file associations.

As you can see from the dialog box, file types are based on file extension: Change a file's extension to associate it with a new application. In this case, however, you'll need to change the application association with a certain extension. Scroll down in the list until you find the registered file type that you want to edit. For example, to use IE4 instead of Netscape to open Netscape Hypertext documents, select that option in the list. When you've found the file type whose association you want to change, highlight it in the list and click the Edit button shown in Figure 28.10.

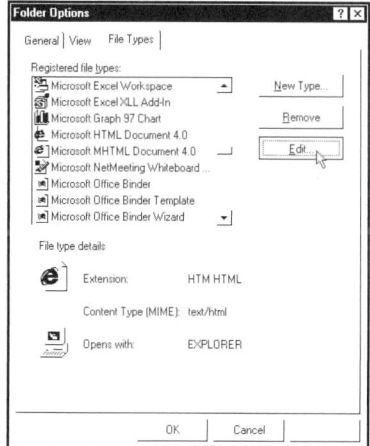

Figure 28.10
Editing file types.

Some files, such as HTML files, allow you to associate different applications with different actions—for example, you might use the browser to view a file, but Notepad to open it for editing. In the Actions box, highlight the action for which you want to change the association and click the Edit button. In the Editing Action for Type dialog box that appears (see Figure 28.11), browse for the application that you want to use to perform that action. When you've got it, click OK.

Figure 28.11
The Editing Action for Type dialog box.

Conclusion

Setting up a connection to the Internet from Windows 98 isn't difficult, but it takes a little care and some planning. Know the speed of connection you want, how much you're willing to pay for it, and how often you want access to it, and your job is mostly done. After a connection is established, it tends to keep working; in my experience, Internet connections go down because of physical problems that interrupt access, not because of any arcane protocol errors.

Windows 98 as an Internet/Intranet Server

Windows 98 provides the tools you need to host and develop content for a web server from your computer. The Windows 98 Personal Web Server enables your computer to serve as a web server for an intranet site running on a closed network or an Internet site open to the public. With the Home Page Wizard and FrontPage Express, web development tools also come as part of the Windows 98 operating system. Whether you want to host an Internet or intranet site or just be able to test web pages on your computer before transferring them to another server, Windows 98 includes the web site tools you need to create a site and keep it running.

This chapter is designed to help you set up an Internet or intranet site using Windows 98. It also covers some of the things that you need to consider when setting up a site, such as determining what sort of content you will be providing. Finally, the chapter looks at how to create content for your site using FrontPage Express and other tools and how to implement such content as Dynamic HTML and Active Server Pages.

Some Initial Considerations

Before digging into the specifics of setting up an Internet or intranet site, it is important to first examine some basics, such as (1) the differences between these types of sites and (2) what sort of hardware you need.

This chapter defines an *Internet site* as one that is connected continuously, or at least periodically, to the Internet through a direct connection (such as through a leased line or a local area network connection) or a dial-up connection through an Internet service provider. It is generally not behind a firewall or other filtering device and can be accessed by anyone on the Internet. Conversely, an *intranet site* is accessible only by other computers that have access to your local or wide area network. Both Internet and intranet sites are usually referred to collectively as *web sites* in this chapter unless specified otherwise.

In general, you would use Windows 98 as a web server only if you expect to receive a small amount of traffic, such as less than a few hundred total site hits per day. Windows 98 is not really designed to handle a large volume of traffic, and it also lacks some of the more advanced features found in Windows NT. Thus your best bet is to use Windows 98 as a web server for intranet sites only because both traffic and security concerns are usually going to be lower on a local network.

For an intranet site, you will need to be connected to a network through a network interface card. In most cases (unless you are using some special third-party software), the TCP/IP networking protocol must be used by your computer as well as by everyone on the network who will be accessing the site.

If you want to set up an Internet site, you need to have a connection to the Internet. If you want people on the Internet to have continuous access to your site, you need an Internet connection through a local area network (with no firewall between your computer and the Internet to prohibit access to your computer) or some type of continuous modem connection, such as a leased line or a cable modem. Because a dial-up connection doesn't offer a continuous connection to the Internet, you can't use a dial-up connection unless you merely want to experiment with setting up a site or the site is available only during certain hours. Just as with an intranet site, you must configure your computer to use the TCP/IP networking protocol because TCP/IP is the central protocol used to transmit data over the Internet.

Even if you don't use Windows 98 to host an Internet or intranet site, you may want to install the web server if you maintain a web site on another computer. For example, if you create web pages for use on a personal web site or your company's web site that is hosted on another computer, you can use your computer to create and test the pages before transferring those files to the host computer. Indeed, this situation is probably the most common use for the web server that comes with Windows 98.

What's Included with Personal Web Server

The Windows 98 Personal Web Server contains advanced server components previously found only in expensive web server programs designed to run on operating systems such as Windows NT and UNIX. Considering the fact that this software is provided free of charge, you are really getting a bargain by purchasing Windows 98 and installing this web server software.

The Windows 98 web server software components, all of which are installed through the Personal Web Server installation program, include the following:

- **Personal Web Server 4.0.** Based on Internet Information Server 4.0, this component actually provides the web server functionality. You can use Personal Web Server to host Internet or intranet sites or to test web pages that you develop before transferring them to another web server. This web server also includes the capability to use Active Server Pages (ASP) to run server-side scripting for advanced web site application design.

- **FrontPage 98 Server Extensions.** You can install these additional components on your web server to allow the use of WebBots and other proprietary features found in Microsoft's FrontPage, FrontPage Express, and Visual InterDev HTML authoring tools.

- **Data Access Components 1.5.** If you plan to use Active Server Pages or any other means by which your web server can interact with databases on your computer or your network, you should install these components. They include Open Database Connectivity (ODBC), ActiveX Data Objects (ADO), and other data access devices.

- **Transaction Server 2.0.** Web applications, as well as Personal Web Server, use this server component.

- **Microsoft Message Queue Server 1.0.** This option is not installed by default, but you may want to install it if you are developing web applications that need to quickly and reliably communicate with other applications located either on your computer or network.

- **Visual InterDev Remote Deployment Support.** If you select the Custom installation of Personal Web Server, you can install this option to enable other people on your network to use Microsoft's Visual InterDev tool to remotely deploy applications on your web server.

Due to the complexity of many of the components listed here, this chapter limits its discussion to those that reside within the Personal Web Server software.

Installing Personal Web Server

Personal Web Server is a version of Internet Information Server (which runs on Windows NT) that has been tailored for use on a Windows 98 computer. Although it lacks some of the load handling and security additions found in Internet Information Server, Personal Web Server is a well-designed web server, which should suit your needs on a site with relatively little traffic.

Although this web server is included with Windows 98, it is not automatically installed as part of the Windows 98 installation. If you check in the Internet Explorer program group located off of the Start button, you will find an icon for Personal Web Server. However, if you click on this icon, Internet Explorer will open a web page on your computer that merely tells you how to install that tool from the Windows 98 CD-ROM.

To install the Personal Web Server:

1. Insert the Windows 98 disk into your CD-ROM disk drive.

2. Click the Start button and choose **R**un.

3. Type the following (substituting the actual drive letter of your CD-ROM for the letter D): **D:\add-ons\pws\setup.exe**.

4. Click the OK button or press the Enter key.

After you perform these steps, the Personal Web Server Setup program will run. On the main screen, press the **N**ext button to advance to the screen where you select what type of installation you want to perform. The choices are Minimum, Typical, and Custom. If you are not sure which options to choose, then you should probably select the Typical installation. In most cases, you will find that the Typical installation contains everything you need to run your site.

Select the Custom installation if you want to see all available options. When you click this button, the Custom setup screen appears, as shown in Figure 29.1. Scroll through the various components to see the default selections. If you make no changes, you will be installing the same components as those selected in the Typical installation.

To see any available subcomponents that are available for the components shown on this screen, simply select the component and click on the **S**how Subcomponents button. For example, if you show the available subcomponents of the PWS component and then display the Documentation subcomponents, you can see that the Active Server Pages documentation is not installed by default. If you plan to use Active Server Pages, VBScript, or JScript on your site, you should probably select this option because the documentation that comes with Personal Web Server is actually quite good.

Chapter 29: Windows 98 as an Internet/Intranet Server

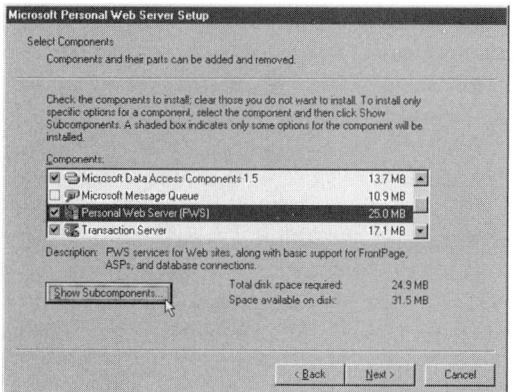

Figure 29.1
By choosing the Custom installation option, you can specify which elements to install with Personal Web Server.

After you have selected the custom components and subcomponents that you want to install, when you click on the Next button, you are asked to specify the home directory for your web site. If you choose the default, Personal Web Server creates your web site in the InetPub/ wwwroot directory on the drive where Windows 98 is installed. Finally, you may be asked where you want to install the program files for Transaction Server. Again, unless you want to install these files in a different drive or directory, just accept the default.

The Personal Web Server Setup program will then install all selected components and subcomponents. After the installation is complete, you may be prompted to restart your computer.

When the installation settings are finalized, you will notice two new icons. One is the Publish icon, located on your Windows desktop. The other is an icon in your system tray that continuously indicates whether the web server is running. Double-clicking on either of these icons opens the Personal Web Manager window from which you can further customize and administer your web site, as discussed in the next section of this chapter.

Configuring Personal Web Server

After you install the Personal Web Server software on your computer, you may need to configure the site before using it. Microsoft has included the Personal Web Manager utility in Windows 98 to help you configure and maintain your web site. This section examines the functionality provided with that utility. However, before you begin setting up your web server and filling it with content, you should do some planning to help ensure that your site is organized, which will make it easier to use and maintain.

Planning Your Web Site

Before you actually start creating directories and content for your web site, you first need to spend some time planning the structure that you will be using for your site. In setting up your web site, try to plan its structure in a logical way. Because web sites use a directory structure (they are, after all, made up of directories located on a web server), set up your directories and subdirectories in a way that makes sense.

For example, if you are running a fairly small site, keep all your images in one folder so that you always know where to find them (preferably in a directory called "images" or something clear and simple) and keep related sets of web pages within the same directory. Don't wait until a directory starts getting too full to move files around, because your users might lose track of these changes. The reason is that users may have made bookmarks (also known as Favorites in Internet Explorer) for these pages, and when you move them, they will end up as broken links for those users. The best way to accommodate future growth is to try to plan ahead before you build a new page or set of pages and make sure that you put it in a sensible place when you first publish the page to your web site.

You should also keep at least one copy of everything that is on your web server on a detached computer or on a backup disk or tape for two reasons. The first reason is that you always want an extra copy in case your computer goes down and you need to transfer the information to another web server in a hurry. The second reason is that you need to edit and test your content properly to make sure it works before transferring it to the web server, and you want to work with a copy rather than the version that is on the web server. Even if you decide to edit the material in a separate directory on the same computer that functions as your web server, be sure to keep a copy of that material on another computer. The second computer can then either serve as an alternative web server or can be used to transfer the files to an alternative web server if the main web server computer goes down.

Security Issues

If you set up Personal Web Server correctly (as described in this chapter), it will make available to other users only the content of your root web directory and any other virtual directory that you add to your site. Unless you specifically convert a directory or its parent directory to a virtual directory—that is, by enabling web sharing for that directory—other users will not be able to see it. Further, unless you specifically enable directory browsing for your web site, users who do not know the file's name and location within your web server directory structure will not be able to view the file.

Some of the things that you can do to protect your computer from an attack are

- **Don't enable directory browsing.** As discussed in more detail later in this chapter, if you enable directory browsing, users can see every file contained within the directories for which you have enabled web sharing. To help prevent security breaches, including giving users the ability to see any confidential files within your web server, you normally should not use directory browsing.

- **Limit users to viewing and running scripts.** When you set up a virtual directory, only select the View and Script options, which enable users to view content and run any server-side scripts found in your web pages. Don't give users the ability to execute files on the server.

- **Enable the Activity Log.** Personal Web Server comes with the capability to log all users. This feature keeps a list of each user's IP address and the pages that he or she accessed. If you suspect that someone is trying to break into your site, you can review this log to find that person's identity by tracking down his or her IP address.

- **Use ASP to authenticate users.** Personal Web Server includes support for ASP through which you can write server-side scripting that requires each user to be authenticated before he or she can access your site. The web server can require each user to log on, and it can compare the username and password the user enters against authentication information in your database. If the information doesn't match, the user won't be authenticated and can't see any content on your site.

For additional information on Internet security issues, be sure to read Chapter 30, "Internet Security."

Using Personal Web Manager

To help you administer your web site, Windows 98 includes a utility called Personal Web Manager. To access this utility at any time, double-click either the Publish icon on your Windows Desktop or the Personal Web Server icon located in the system tray. The Main page for Personal Web Publisher is shown in Figure 29.2.

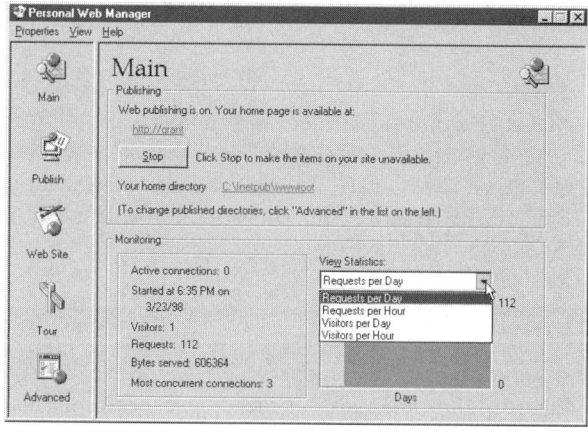

Figure 29.2
Personal Web Manager provides an easy interface through which you can administer your web site.

The Main Page

The Main page contains a button to stop and start the web server (which is a service running on your computer), as well as a reporting area where you can view statistics about your web site. You might want to stop the web server if you aren't using it because your computer runs marginally slower while the server is running. You might also want to stop this service if you experience errors or other problems with the web server. Stopping and restarting the service can sometimes fix any problem you are experiencing.

If you prefer, you can also pause the web service by choosing Pa**u**se Service from the Properties pull-down menu. By pausing the service, you can stop it without fully unloading it, which means that you can restart it more quickly.

The Main page also displays the statistics for your site, such as how many site hits you have had. The types of reports that you can view are Requests by Day, Requests by Hour, Visitors by Day, and Visitors by Hour. Requests refer to total requests, not just total page requests. Thus if a page consists of HTML plus three images on that page, a request for this page usually registers as four requests: one for the HTML found on the page and one request for each image. (The images on the web page are stored in different locations.) Similarly, the number of visitors might not be correct because of the way that web sessions are opened and closed. If a person visits your site more than once within a few minutes, the web server may count that person as more than one visitor. Thus the reports that you get from the Personal Web Manager might not always be accurate.

From the Main page, you can access any other Personal Web Manager page by either selecting that page's icon from the left pane of this window or choosing the page from the View pull-down menu. We look at each of those pages next except for the Publishing Wizard and the Home Page Wizard, both of which are covered in the section on creating content for your web site. Before you go any further in the Personal Web Manager, however, you might want to take the Personal Web Server Tour by clicking on the Tour icon in the left pane.

Taking the Tour

When you open the Tour page, the large right pane changes and an interactive tour becomes available. This tour provides an overview of the Personal Web Server and offers a few hints and tips along the way. If you have never used a web server, you may find the information especially helpful. Even if you have used other web servers, this quick tour provides a few useful tips for using the Personal Web Server.

Setting Advanced Options

You can view the Advanced settings page by clicking on that page's icon in the left pane. This page enables you to view and add virtual directories to your site, determine the default document for your site, allow directory browsing, and save an activity log (see Figure 29.3).

Using Virtual Directories

Virtual directories enable you to add directories to your web site even if they are not physically located in the root directory for your web server, which by default is your Inetpub\wwwroot

Chapter 29: Windows 98 as an Internet/Intranet Server

directory. Any directory located on your computer or on any network drive to which you have access can be defined as a virtual directory. Although you can add directories by using the Add button located on this page, another example of how easy it is to make a directory into a virtual directory on your web server is to select any directory within Windows Explorer.

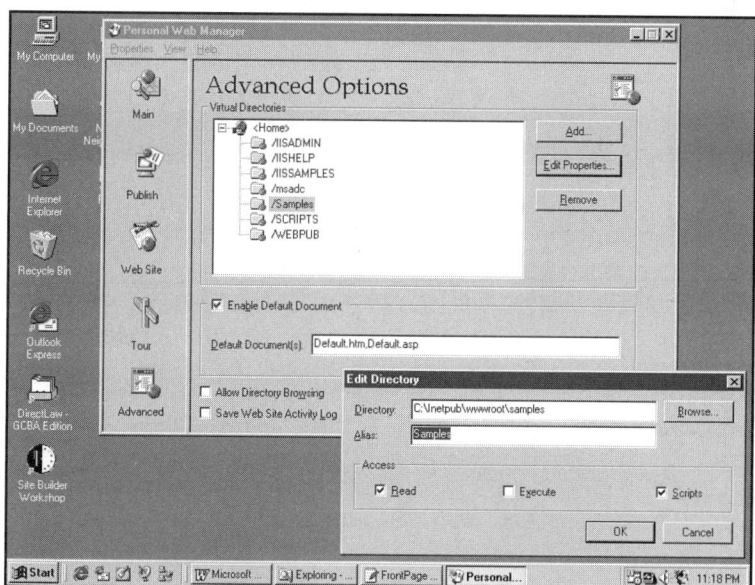

Figure 29.3
You can use the Advanced Options page in Personal Web Manager to perform tasks such as adding virtual directories and enabling directory browsing.

From Windows Explorer, right-click on a directory and select P**r**operties. Click on the Web Sharing tab on the properties sheet and choose the Share This Folder option. Another window pop ups. In the Alias box, enter the name of the virtual directory on your web server for which this directory will be known (see Figure 29.4). For example, if you want people to access this directory on your web server by typing http://*yourservername*/downloads, then give this directory an alias of downloads. When you click on the OK button, a virtual directory named download will be created on your web server.

In addition to creating virtual directories, you can determine which rights viewers will have to that directory. If you select a virtual directory from the Advanced page of the Personal Web Manager and click on the E**d**it Properties button, a window will appear with three separate access options: Read, Execute, and Scripts. In most cases, the read and scripts options are selected by default, and they are the options that you would normally want to select. The read option enables viewers to view pages in this virtual directory. The scripts option allows the web server to process any scripts contained on those pages. If you expect to use ASP in this directory, then you must enable the scripts option; otherwise, the server will not process the server-side scripting on those pages. Finally, the execute option enables viewers to run any executable programs or commands that are found in the virtual directory on the web server. Due to obvious security concerns that may arise from allowing viewers to execute programs on the server, you will almost always want to disable this form of access, particularly on an Internet site.

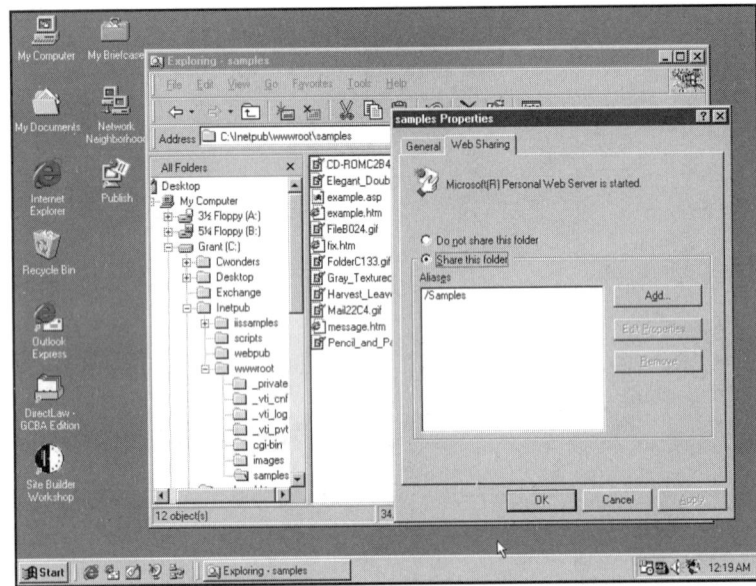

Figure 29.4
You can convert any directory into a virtual directory on your web server.

Determining the Default Document

The default document name for your web site is the HTML or ASP document that your web server looks for when a user requests information from your home address or from a directory without naming a particular page. By default, these document names are Default.htm and Default.asp. Thus if a viewer enters the URL http://www.*yoursite*.com, where *yoursite* is a link to your web site, the web server would look for a document named Default.htm or Default.asp in the root directory of your web site (normally InetPub/wwwroot). The server would then process that page and pass the HTML back to the viewer's browser.

If you want to change the default document names, you can do so from the Advanced page in Personal Web Manager. In many cases, it is a good idea to add an HTML page that uses one of these default names into each directory on your web site. Doing so ensures that users who do not request a specific page will see a page that indicates the directory's contents. Those users can then view other pages by clicking on links from that HTML page. A good practice is to name the home page in each directory by one of your default document names. Then name the server so that it can automatically select that home page when the user enters a root or directory site without requesting a specific page.

Directory Browsing

As discussed in the previous section on default documents, if a user enters a directory name in the URL for your web server, but does not specify any page within that directory (for example, http://www.yoursite.com/directory), the web server will display the default document for that directory. However, if no default document exists in that directory, an error will usually be returned to the user's browser, indicating that he or she does not have the right to browse the directory. In other words, directory browsing is not enabled by default in the Personal Web Server.

What is directory browsing? As the name indicates, the *directory browsing* feature enables you to view the entire contents of a web server directory from which you can select any page that you want to view. If you have ever seen the contents of an FTP site directory displayed within your browser, then you have seen what directory browsing looks like to a viewer.

In some cases, you might not care whether viewers can see the entire listing of every directory. However, it is usually best not to enable directory browsing because it can open up a large security hole by allowing other people to see the entire structure of your site. This information might help an unscrupulous viewer hack into your site. Nevertheless, if you want to enable directory browsing, then you can do so by selecting that option on the Advanced page. Note that the directory browsing option applies to your entire site, and Personal Web Server has no way to limit directory browsing on individual virtual directories.

Activity Log

One form of security that you can implement on your site is to use the activity log option found on the Advanced page. This feature maintains a log of every user who connects to your site and tracks every page that users request. The log file is maintained in an Internet standard format and should be automatically stored in the Log File/W3SPC1 folder found in your Windows System directory. This file can be viewed by any text editor. The filenames will likely begin with the letters *nc* and are followed by a date designation. Thus a file generated in December 1998 will begin with nc9812. The log file indicates the IP address of the user accessing your site, the exact page accessed at your site, and each specific file requested.

Activity log files can get very long and can cause some level of system degradation if you have a lot of traffic on your site. Therefore, you might want to disable activity logging unless you are experiencing security problems, such as people trying to break into your site.

Creating Content for Your Site

After you install Personal Web Server and set up your web site, you will need to either create new content for that site or import existing content, for example, from another web server that you previously set up. To import content, you can copy files to your web site directories in the same manner that you copy other files to your computer. This content can be copied to your computer either from a disk or from a network or Internet connection (such as by using FTP to transport files from another web server).

This section explains how to create content for your site by using the tools supplied with Windows 98. However, equally important to exploring the tools used to create this content is the planning that should precede this task. Just as you need to organize the structure of your web site, it is also important to determine what type of content you will be providing and what limitations might prevent you from effectively reaching your target audience. This section begins by briefly addressing some of these basic considerations; then you learn how to create this content and take a quick look at two relatively new types of Internet content: Dynamic HTML and Active Server Pages.

General Considerations

Windows 98 contains the tools you need to build content for and run a web server. When you are developing content for a web site and deciding how to build the site, you need to consider who your audience is and what type of content you are trying to provide.

Know Your Audience

To properly plan for and implement a web site on your Windows 98 computer, you need to determine who will be viewing your site. Will it be employees from within your company accessing an intranet site? Will it be clients coming in from the outside and accessing an Internet site? Both? Who your audience is and where they are coming from have a lot to do with what sort of content you provide, as well as the manner in which it is supplied.

For example, how will your audience connect to your site? If it is an intranet site and if everyone uses the same web browser on a Windows 95, Windows 98, or Windows NT computer, then determining how you will provide content to your viewers is easier. On an intranet site where every viewer is connected to your web server over a local area network, you don't have to concern yourself as much with connection speeds and how long it will take the user to download graphics from your pages to their browsers. However, you still have to consider network congestion issues that may arise if your content requires lots of trips back and forth to the web server.

If you are running an intranet with Windows 95, 98, and NT clients, you can also use ActiveX controls, VBScript, and other Microsoft-centric web elements without being concerned about whether these programming components will work properly on the users' computers. Additionally, if everyone on your intranet uses a single web browser such as Internet Explorer, it is much easier for you to know that your web pages will appear virtually identical on every computer.

Unfortunately, even if your site does run on an intranet, you probably won't have all 32-bit Windows clients because you may have computers running Windows 3.1, MS-DOS,

Macintosh, or UNIX as their operating system. Thus depending on your network configuration, you may have to make at least some modifications in the type of content you present to ensure that everyone has the capability of viewing and interacting with material on your site. Similarly, if you have Internet traffic on your site, you will have a broad range of compatibility issues to consider, some of which are discussed in more detail later in the chapter.

Know the Content Your Audience Wants or Needs

For a site to be a success, it must be visually easy to understand and must provide something of worth to the viewer. If people browsing your site can't find their way around, or if there is nothing of particular interest for them, they probably won't be visiting your site again anytime soon, if ever. Thus once you determine who your audience is, you need to decide what content you can place on your site to keep them coming back again and again.

For example, if you are designing a company intranet, think about what sort of information the employees would want to see. For example, your home page might have some content that changes regularly, such as headlines for company news that link to the entire story. Although many companies put such items as their office manual and employee directory on their intranet, there are much more interesting things you can provide. If your company is publicly traded and many of the employees own stock in the company, you can set up a page where users can enter the total number of shares that they own. They can then click a button that tells the web server to obtain the latest share pricing information and multiply that by the number of shares to return a web page showing the total current value of their investment. Alternatively, you could use an ActiveX control in the form of a stock ticker to enable employees to keep up-to-date on the latest price. If the employees are running Internet Explorer 4.0 with the Active Desktop option enabled, they could even place this stock ticker on their desktop where they can see it even if their web browser isn't running.

Other possible interesting uses for an intranet site include publishing weekly newsletters, displaying today's lunch menu from the cafeteria, providing electronic versions of company forms that can be processed on-line, and giving users the ability to check the current value of their company-managed retirement holdings. The breadth of the type of content that you can provide is limited only by your imagination. Even if a site is used only for internal purposes, there are still a lot of ways to make it interesting, keep the users happy and coming back for more, and ensure that your organization is getting a meaningful return on its investment.

For an Internet site, the goal is to provide content that will keep your audience coming back on a regular basis so that they can see new product announcements and other information. If you work for a software development company, providing trial versions of your software, free bug fixes, and updated technical support information are good ways to keep your customers happy and interested. Again, the type of information that you can provide is virtually unlimited, and your goal should be to try to provide the type of content that you think your viewers might want. Be sure to provide links on your home page and elsewhere that make it easy for viewers to feedback on your site via email so that you can find out what they like and hate about your site.

Handling Compatibility Issues

If most or all of your viewers are coming from the Internet or if many types of computers are used on your local or wide area network to access an intranet, the decision of how to program your site becomes much more complicated because of potential compatibility issues. Rather than using ActiveX controls or VBScript, you might consider sticking to elements such as Java applets and Java Script, both of which are supported by a variety of browsers, if you need to use anything other than standard HTML to format your pages. You will also have to test your site fairly extensively with a variety of browsers and screen resolutions. Each browser displays HTML differently, and even though Java is supposed to run equally well on all platforms, different browsers handle Java through various compilers and virtual machines with the result that what works fine on one browser causes problems on another. Even if you limit yourself to testing your pages in Microsoft Internet Explorer and Netscape Navigator, your viewers will be using several different versions (including interim versions) of these browsers to visit your site.

Some web authors handle these problems by preparing multiple versions of pages on their sites. Their web server detects which browser is being used by a viewer and directs the browser to the most compatible page. This approach causes a lot of extra work on the part of the web author, but many people view this solution as a necessary evil. Other authors handle these compatibility issues by either writing primarily to one browser (presumably the one that most of their viewers use) or else simply giving up some web site functionality in lieu of compatibility.

Although various opinions exist as to how to handle these compatibility issues, the best and most time-efficient solution may be to maintain a single set of web pages and write them in such a way that every browser can see and interact with the most important aspects of your site. You can then program additional "bonus" content that is visible with one or more browsers that a significant portion of your viewers use.

For example, if your viewer uses Internet Explorer 3.0 or later, you can place an ActiveX control on a page that displays an activation button. Pressing that button activates VBScript on the page and causes the browser to perform some action, such as loading a different web page or downloading a file.

However, viewers with browsers that don't recognize ActiveX controls still need to have access to that capability. Therefore, you must place something such as a standard hyperlink on the page to enable those users to access the same information without pressing the button. Viewers with browsers having the capability of seeing this button (see Figure 29.5) may think "hey, what a neat button," whereas those without the capability won't even realize that they are missing anything. This small example demonstrates one way to provide content that is useful to everyone while providing additional appeal to those using a browser for which you are writing a particular feature.

In addressing compatibility issues, one factor that works in your favor is that browsers do not display content that they do not recognize. Thus in the preceding example, browsers that do not recognize ActiveX controls simply skip over that code. Although Microsoft and Netscape, the two principal software development companies that make web browsers, have pledged to adhere more strictly to HTML standards in the future, the browsers do handle some technologies (such as Dynamic HTML and channels) in different ways. A way to work around this problem is to supply the code necessary for both browsers on the same page. The Netscape and Microsoft browsers process only the code they recognize (they ignore the other code), thus giving you the result you want in a single web page.

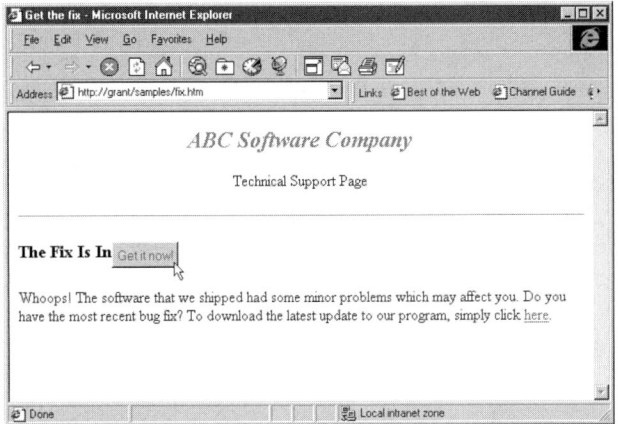

Figure 29.5
The button on this web page is visible to some browsers; for others, this web page provides backward compatibility in the form of hyperlinks and standard HTML.

Using the Home Page Wizard

Windows 98 provides two main tools designed to create web site content: the Home Page Wizard and FrontPage Express. The Home Page Wizard (see Figure 29.6) is launched by clicking on the web Site icon in Personal Web Manager. Similar to wizards in other Microsoft products, Home Page Wizard walks you through the steps needed to create a default home page for your web site.

As you step through the wizard, it asks you to choose from among several templates that can be used to determine how your web page will look. Unfortunately, the wizard does not give you a very good idea of how this template will look until later in the process of creating your site. You will have to use the trial-and-error method of using a template and then choosing a different one later if it doesn't suit you.

You will be given the option to include a guest book and to add a drop box on your site to make it easy for people to send you email. The guest book enables both you and other users to view comments left by viewers, and the drop box enables users to send you messages through the web server. You can view these messages by clicking on the Web Site icon in the Personal Web Manager anytime after you set up your home page using the Home Page Wizard. You can also click on the Web Site icon to use the Home Page Wizard to make additional changes to your home page. To create pages other than your main (home) page, however, you will have to move on to FrontPage Express.

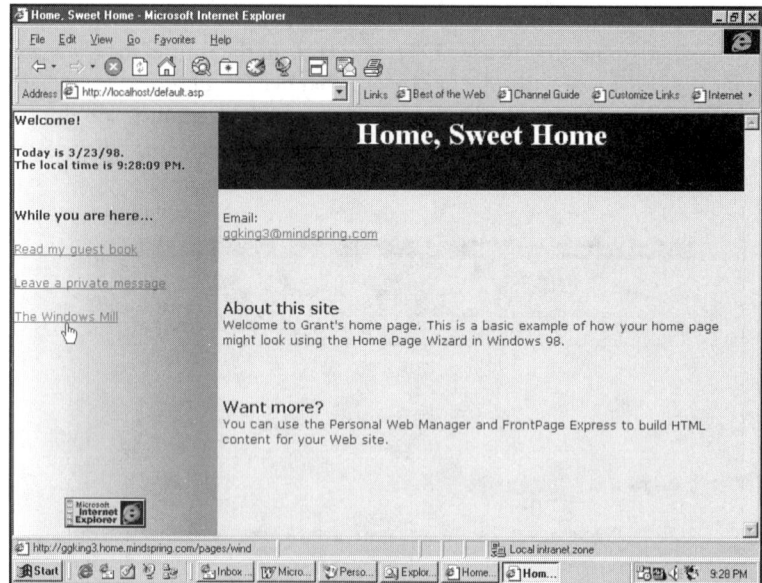

Figure 29.6
The Home Page Wizard makes it easy to assemble a basic page for your web site, such as the one shown here.

Using FrontPage Express

FrontPage Express is the HTML editor that comes with Windows 98. Although it has many of the HTML editing features that come with the full Microsoft FrontPage editor, it lacks most wizards and the site management tools that come with FrontPage.

> **Tip**
> When you install Windows 98, FrontPage should automatically be registered as the default editor for any HTML files located on your computer. If it isn't or if you want to change the default editor to something other than FrontPage Express, then you will need to change the file registration information for HTML files to use FrontPage Express as your HTML editor. To do so, open Windows Explorer and choose Options from the View pull-down menu. Select the File Types tab and scroll down until you see a file type such as Microsoft HTML Document 4.0 that will be associated with files that have the extension of HTM and HTML. Select that file type and click on the Edit button. In the Actions window, select the New button. In the next window that pops up, type **Edit** into the Action textbox. Click the Browse button to locate and select the executable file for FrontPage Express or any other HTML editor that you want to use (the default location for FrontPage Express is C:\Program Files\Frontpage Express\bin\Fpxpress.exe). Then click OK to close this window and click OK again to register your selected editor. From now on, anytime you right-click on an HTML file and choose Edit, the new default editor you selected will launch and display the selected file.

Chapter 29: Windows 98 as an Internet/Intranet Server

When you open FrontPage Express, it contains a blank page. If you start typing text, it will appear on the open HTML page just as if you were typing in a work processing program such as WordPad. If you have not used an HTML Editor before, try using the pull-down menus and toolbar buttons to insert horizontal lines (to break up sections of your page), insert images and animation, place a timestamp on your page through the WebBot feature, and include background music that can play while someone is looking at the page. You can also insert ActiveX controls and set their properties on your page. With a small amount of tinkering, you might end up with a page that looks like the one in Figure 29.7.

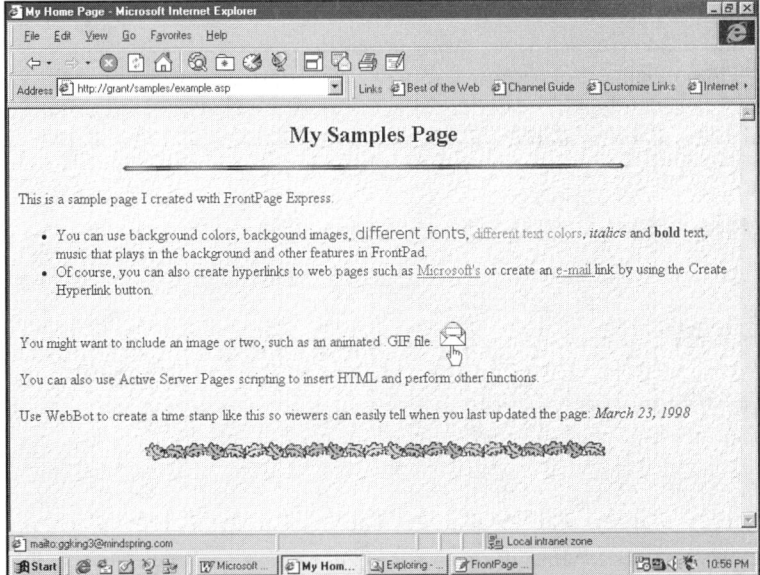

Figure 29.7

FrontPage Express is a simple HTML editor that supports the basic features you need to create a web page.

Although FrontPage Express does not include all of the features found in the full FrontPage product, many users find that it is all they need for editing HTML documents. In fact, many web site developers use simple text editors (such as the NotePad application that comes with Windows 98) to create their web pages. FrontPage Express is an effective tool that allows the average person who doesn't need site management tools and who doesn't plan on using frames or other advanced elements to create web pages without having to know any HTML.

Note that FrontPage Express does contain some basic predefined pages for creating forms or surveys to which users can respond. To access these predefined pages, choose New from the File pull-down menu and then select the type of page that you want to create. You can also create and change tables in your web pages by using the available options in the Table pull-down menu. Tables are commonly used on web sites to layout and display text, graphics, and other content in a way that is not possible with plain HTML.

To use other advanced HTML features, you can add them directly into the source code by either choosing HTML Markup from the Insert pull-down menu or by choosing HTML from the View pull-down menu. The latter method opens a separate window in which you can directly edit all the HTML for the page. One disadvantage of using FrontPage Express is its anemic help documentation. For the most part you are on your own if you have any questions about how to use FrontPage Express' features. Fortunately, any book written about the most recent version of FrontPage should be able to answer any questions you might have about FrontPage Express.

Using the Publishing Wizard

After you create your web site content and test it with one or more web browsers, you may want to transfer these files to another web server. Most people develop and test content on their local web server before moving it to another web server, such as one provided by their Internet Service Provider, where it will be viewed by other people. In such a case, you can use the Publishing Wizard to transfer your web site files to any other web server.

Developing with New Content Types

Since the release of Windows 95, Microsoft Internet Explorer 3.0 and 4.0 have brought a host of new content possibilities to Windows 98–based web sites, such as the use of ActiveX controls, scripting based on Visual Basic and Java, and cascading style sheets. With Internet Explorer 4.0 comes new content that can be implemented on your Windows 98 web site and viewed on computers running Internet Explorer 4.0. This section explains how to add some of the newest content types to your Windows 98 web site.

Dynamic HTML

Windows 98 and Internet Explorer 4.0 introduce a new level of interactivity in web pages with Dynamic HTML. Originally code-named Trident and planned for inclusion in Internet Explorer 5.0, Dynamic HTML enables you to create web pages with which your viewers can easily interact to dynamically change the content of the page without requiring repeated trips back to the web server for the requested material. You can place graphics on your web site that change and move about the page either on their own or due to actions of the viewer. Client-side scripting, ActiveX controls, and other features enable you to use Dynamic HTML to make your web pages much more interesting.

Rather than serve as an overall discussion of Dynamic HTML, this section provides a sample of what the code used for this new content actually looks like and explains how it works in a web page.

Internet Explorer 4.0 introduces a new Dynamic HTML Document Object Model to replace the one found in Internet Explorer 3.0. One of the features of the new object model is the use of scripting (VBScript in the following example) to trigger certain events when a user interacts with a page, such as when the user's mouse passes over an image or area of text.

Chapter 29: Windows 98 as an Internet/Intranet Server

In Listing 29.1, Visual Basic scripting defines three different ways in which the browser can respond to the viewer's interaction with the page (see Chapter 33, "Windows Scripting with Windows 98 Scripting Host," for more on VBScript). In the first two subroutines, if the viewer moves a mouse over the wrong image, a dialog box tells the user to try again. This behavior is accomplished through the `onmouseover` event, although you can also use events such as `onclick` and `onkeypress` to provide different ways for the code to execute. Note that the code in the first two subroutines references the wrong images (`wrong1` and `wrong2`), and the third subroutine displays the message of the day when the viewer moves the mouse over the correct image (`right1`) will appear. The images themselves are coded with an `id` tag so that VBScript can identify them and respond properly when the viewer moves his or her mouse over a selected image.

Listing 29.1 This Example Shows Some Basic Dynamic HTML Scripting

```
<html>
<SCRIPT LANGUAGE="VBSCRIPT">
SUB wrong1_onmouseover
    Msg = "Sorry, wrong image.  Try again."
        Style = vbOKOnly + vbInformation
        Title = "Sorry"
        Response = MsgBox(Msg, Style, Title)
END SUB

SUB wrong2_onmouseover
    Msg = "Sorry, wrong image.  Try again."
        Style = vbOKOnly + vbInformation
        Title = "Sorry"
        Response = MsgBox(Msg, Style, Title)
END SUB

SUB right1_onmouseover
    Msg = "Today's message: Have a great day!"
        Style = vbOKOnly + vbInformation
        Title = "You got it!"
        Response = MsgBox(Msg, Style, Title)
END SUB

</SCRIPT>

<head>
<title>The Message Game</title>
</head>

<body bgcolor="#FFFFFF">

<h2 align="center">The Message Game</h2>

<p>Can you find the hidden message? <img id=wrong1 src="FolderC133.gif"
width="24" height="19"></p>
```

continues

Listing 29.1 Continued

```
<p>By moving your mouse over the correct image you will get
today's message.<img id=right1 src="CD-ROMC2B4.gif" width="20" height="17"></p>

<p>Good luck. <img id=wrong2 src="Pencil_and_PaperD1F1.gif" width="20"
height="18"></p>
</body>
</html>
```

When this page is loaded into an Internet Explorer 4.0 browser window, the viewer sees what appears to be a standard HTML page containing some text and a few images. However, as provided by the preceding code, when the viewer moves a mouse over an image, a dialog box automatically pops up and tells the viewer whether he or she has chosen the correct image, as shown in Figure 29.8.

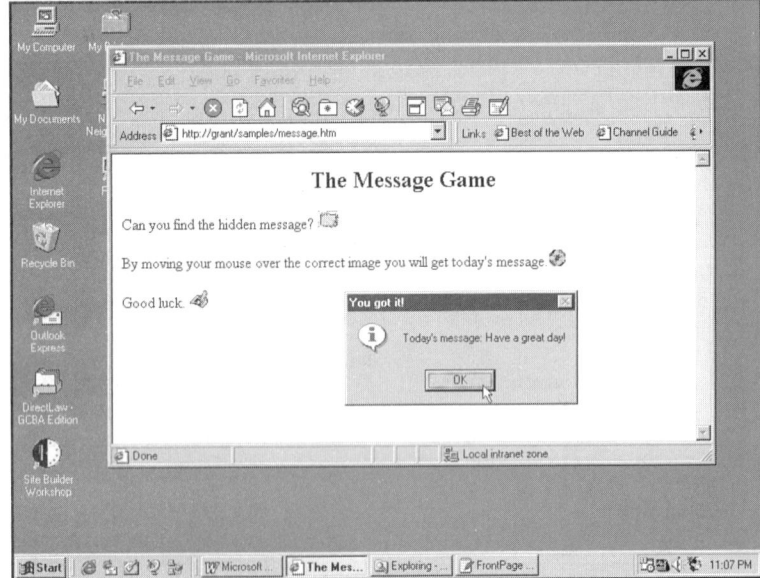

Figure 29.8
This screen shows how the preceding HTML code appears when the viewer passes a mouse over the correct image.

This fairly basic example of Dynamic HTML should give you an idea of the ways in which you can take advantage of this new capability on your web site. To get more information on Dynamic HTML, you can download the Internet Client Software Development Kit (SDK) from Microsoft's web site at http://www.microsoft.com/msdn/sdk/inetsdk/asetup/default.htm.

Using Active Server Pages

One of the most interesting features found in Personal Web Server is its support for ASP. Introduced first in Internet Information Server 3.0, ASP is a way to use server-side scripting to create dynamic web sites while shielding the script from the eyes of users who visit your site, thus protecting your scripting work.

What is *server-side scripting?* Simply put, it is scripting that runs on the web server and performs various tasks just as a server might do in any other client/server application that you design. This type of scripting should be contrasted against client-side scripting, in which script is downloaded to, and processed by, the user's web browser as part of HTML. The preceding section on Dynamic HTML contained an example of client-side scripting. Although a site that uses ASP might also use client-side scripting, ASP provides capabilities far beyond those of a browser. There are a lot of advanced things that you can do with ASP, such as allow your users to view and change information on databases located on your web server or on another computer on your network. You can also create session variables that are maintained from page to page and that are unique to a particular user as long as they are connected to any of your web pages. Another use of ASP is to redirect a web browser to a different page—for example, if the page has moved to a new location.

When the Personal Web Server processes server-side scripting and renders HTML, the resulting source code appears no different to the web browser than if ASP was not involved at all. For example, ASP scripting generated the second to last sentence on the web page in Figure 29.7. While it appears within the browser and the source code sent to the browser as standard HTML, a simple ASP script renders this HTML and writes it to the source code delivered to the user's browser.

For detailed information and several tutorials on using ASP in your web pages, be sure to see the online documentation provided with Personal Web Server. ASP documentation is not installed by default, so refer to the previous section on installing Personal Web Server for information on installing this documentation as part of a custom setup.

Conclusion

Microsoft has provided a simple yet powerful web server with Windows 98. You can use Personal Web Server to set up a web site for limited intranet or Internet use. Several tools are also provided to create and maintain content on your web site. Through support for client and server-side scripting, Personal Web Server also supports the latest functionality for developing dynamic web sites that will attract users to your site. Then it is up to you to use the content and site organizational guidelines outlined in this chapter to keep your viewers coming back for more. With a little effort, even a novice can create interesting web sites with Windows 98.

Internet Security

This chapter identifies the most significant security concerns that you should be aware of as you access the Internet from Windows 98. In addition to knowing how to identify these threats, you also need to learn ways to minimize or eliminate them.

Among other things, this chapter examines the following topics:

- How you can enable file sharing while protecting that data from Internet users
- The security risks associated with ActiveX controls, Java applets, and Active Scripting
- How the specific software that you are running can open up your computer to use by other people

- Security zones and how to customize them for your environment
- Conducting secure transactions such as online purchases and banking

The Problem of Internet Security

Security concerns often prevent users from fully exploiting the Internet's vast resources. Although these security risks are real, they are often not as threatening as people believe. With the proper understanding of the risks and the proper configuration of your system, you can minimize and often eliminate these risks.

As a practical matter, the likelihood that a user would encounter problems in any of these areas when dealing with a trusted web site is rather small. Due to the use of encryption by web sites and browsers that support it, using your credit card to buy something over the Internet is at least as safe as, if not safer than, giving someone your credit card number over the phone or in person. However, you have to use common sense anytime you give out such information, whether it be over the Internet or in your nearby restaurant.

In 1996 and 1997, there were an increasing number of incidents where someone would find a new hole in the security of Internet Explorer. Some of these holes were rather insignificant, but others had a greater possibility of actually opening up your computer to malicious activity. This led Microsoft to post several updates to Internet Explorer that fixed these problems as they became known. Several critics maintained that, due to its support for ActiveX controls and its closer link to the operating system, Internet Explorer contained inherent security problems that could not be solved without substantial changes. It was against this background that Microsoft continued its efforts to make one the securest and most versatile web browsers available. Although no browser can ever be 100 percent effective against all forms of security risks, Microsoft's efforts to address these security issues led to the new features found in Windows 98 and Internet Explorer 4.0.

Internet Explorer 4.0 includes a number of security advancements, such as support for Secure Sockets Layer 3.0, Transport Layer Security (a new secure channel protocol), CryptoAPI (a way to handle elements such as encryption, decryption, and digital signatures through the use of a standard application programming interface), and Microsoft Wallet. However, some of the most innovative and helpful security advances relate to the ability to assign different levels of trust to web sites, ActiveX controls, Java applets, and other web content, and these are some of the topics in this chapter.

Chapter 30: Internet Security

Possible Threats (Ways to Break In)

When it comes to security on the Internet, there are two real types of security situations:

- Your system will be susceptible to malicious code (such as a Java applet or ActiveX control) that someone else has created and distributed.

- Your system will be susceptible to unauthorized access.

This section alerts you to the most likely ways in which someone else could cause problems on your computer; the section "Setting Up Internet Security" later in the chapter provides the details on protecting yourself from each type of vulnerability. Although Windows 98 is configured by default to protect you against many of these security risks, you need to fully understand them to effectively protect yourself against such security breaches.

File and Printer Sharing

One of the most obvious and problematic ways to open up your computer to possible security problems is to enable file and printer sharing. If you open the Control Panel and double-click the Network icon, the next window contains networking information, such as the various network protocols that are installed on your system, as well as a button for File and Print Sharing. If you click this button, a smaller window enables you to share your files and printer with other people, as shown in Figure 30.1.

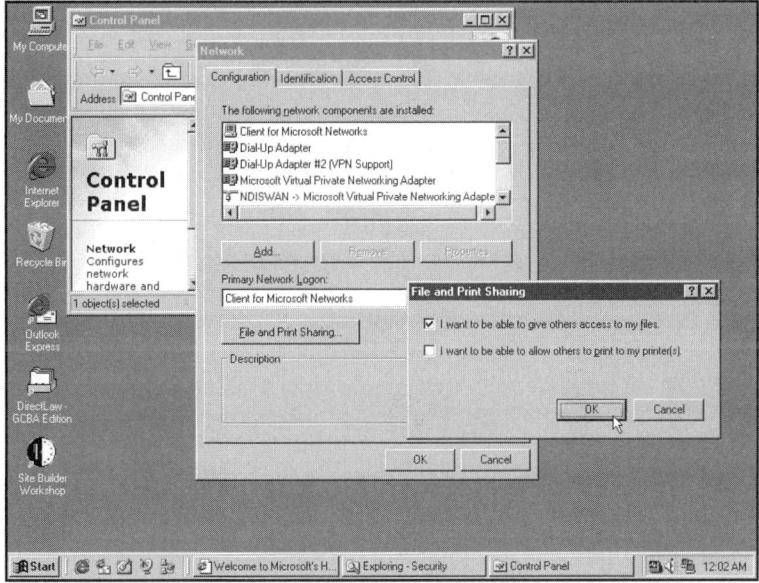

Figure 30.1
If you permit file sharing on your computer, you could unknowingly allow other people to access your system while you are connected to the Internet.

Normally you would select either of these options only if you were connected to a local or wide area network where you wanted to share these things with other users on that closed network. However, by enabling these options, you open up the possibility that other users on the Internet may be able to access your computer as well. Although the possibility of this happening is probably remote at best if you use a dial-up connection, you should strongly consider disabling this feature in the TCP/IP settings for your dial-up adapter, particularly if you often remain connected to the Internet for very long periods of time. Similarly, if you have a direct connection to the Internet, such as on a local area network, you should probably not enable this capability unless you also use a firewall to prevent users outside of the network from accessing your computer.

> **Note** A *firewall* is a system designed to prevent unauthorized access to or from a network. Firewalls can be implemented as software or hardware and frequently are used as both. All messages passing to or from the network must go through the firewall. The firewall examines every message and blocks any that do not match specified criteria. This criteria can take several forms, allowing the blocking of messages to or from certain IP addresses and/or messages of a certain type or from a certain application.
>
> Firewalls can be useful in several situations. First, they can prevent unauthorized access by users on the Internet to a local network. Second, firewalls can prevent certain types of access by users on the local network to the Internet; for example, you can use firewalls to discourage employees from browsing certain web sites or newsgroups.

Windows 98 alerts you if you attempt to enable file sharing on the same TCP/IP connection that you use to connect to the Internet, such as over a dial-up adapter. Microsoft highly recommends that you disable file sharing on the connection used for the Internet. For additional information on enabling file sharing on your computer while still protecting yourself from Internet-based attacks, see the section "Setting Up Internet Security," later in the chapter.

ActiveX Controls

ActiveX controls are programming components that can be added to a web page to give it functionality previously available only in stand-alone Windows applications. You can use ActiveX controls for thousands of applications, such as easily providing database access within a web page or providing a viewer for streaming video and other content. Most ActiveX controls can be used either within a browser that supports such controls, such as Internet Explorer, or in a software application. Although a large variety of different ActiveX controls can be purchased or, in some cases, downloaded for free from software vendors such as Microsoft, you can also use languages such as Visual Basic and C++ to create your own ActiveX controls

One of the greatest advantages of ActiveX controls is that they can interact directly with the Windows operating system; for example, ActiveX controls can make Application Programming Interface (API) calls and perform other system-level functions. Although this functionality makes it a lot easier to create applications that run on the Internet, it also creates a large security hole. An ActiveX control can be designed to shut down your computer, erase your hard drive, and perform just about any other task that can be done with other Windows programs. As such, ActiveX controls can be much more dangerous than computer viruses and other such problems that you may have tried to protect yourself against in the past. Thus you should exercise a degree of caution in allowing the use of ActiveX controls on your system.

The main way to protect yourself against malicious ActiveX controls is to monitor which controls you allow to be installed and executed on your computer. You can restrict the use of ActiveX controls by using the security zone settings provided through Internet Explorer 4.0 and discussed fully in the section "Security Zones." The Windows 98 Authenticode 2.0 technology, also discussed later in the chapter, can determine whether the control has been signed. Then you can decide whether to use the control based on the information supplied by that signature. In the end, unless you elect to block all ActiveX controls, you will need to exercise some common discretion before allowing controls to be installed on your computer. Thus, although you might allow controls signed by Microsoft to be installed, you should be wary about allowing the use of controls on sites that you do not fully trust. This vigilance offers virtually the same level of protection that you would obtain from a retail software product. You can elect to enable ActiveX controls only from companies or services that you trust.

Java Applets

An important change in Java support in Internet Explorer 4.0 is the capability of Java applets to work outside the "sandbox." Originally designed to address security concerns about Java applets, the sandbox model ensures that Java applets downloaded to a browser over a network (including the Internet) can work only within the browser itself and cannot access the disk drives or other parts of the system. In Internet Explorer 4.0, users also have the option of allowing Java applets to work outside the sandbox and have access to all parts of the computer, including the capability to write to the hard drive and access the operating system itself.

This feature opens security issues that are similar to concerns about ActiveX controls. To assure protection from malicious code, the capability of working outside the sandbox should be used only with the new security features in Internet Explorer 4.0. For more information on using Java applets with the related security options, see the "Security Zones" section of this chapter.

Active Scripting

A related area that presents security issues is Active Scripting. Just like ActiveX controls and Java applets, scripts are downloaded from web sites and executed within the browser. The two types of Active Scripting supported natively in Internet Explorer 4.0 are VBScript and JScript. Both of these are subsets of established programming languages.

VBScript is based on Microsoft's Visual Basic language that is used to develop software for Windows operating systems. Many of the advanced features in Visual Basic are also found in VBScript. Although you can't directly access the operating system in the same depth as with ActiveX controls, allowing the use of VBScript raises security concerns not found in straight HTML, because the script executes one or more procedures from within your browser.

Similarly, JScript, which is based on the Java language, also executes within the browser to perform tasks designated by the script. Although VBScript and JScript don't have the same degree of system-level contact available to ActiveX controls and Java applets someone with malicious intent may be able to use these scripting languages to damage to your system.

Just as with other programming elements, you can either limit or completely disable Active Scripting within Internet Explorer 4.0. These security precautions are discussed more fully in the section "Setting Up Internet Security."

Other Threats

In addition to the major security risks that might arise when you connect to the Internet, many other security risks are associated with the specific software in use on your computer. Some programs allow you to enable different, proprietary forms of file sharing and remote computer control over the Internet. The use of any such program would raise security concerns because it allows people to connect to your computer, and as such you need to exercise discretion in the degree and frequency with which you use this type of software. Similarly, some Internet Chat programs enable you to transfer files from your computer to other users on the Internet. Again, anytime you open a door to your computer, you create a possible means by which an unscrupulous user might attempt to copy or delete files from your computer without your knowledge and consent. Although any such software can have great uses and make your computer a better tool, you should always take extra precautions and make sure that you fully understand the related security mechanisms and risks before using such software.

Another potential security risk associated with the Internet involves sending personal data to a web server over an unsecured connection. Any time you visit a web site; fill out a form with your name, address, and other information; and press the Submit button, the data usually travels in an unsecured form across the Internet to its destination on the web server to which you are connected. As such it could be intercepted along the way. Interception is a particular concern regarding the transmission of credit card numbers and other sensitive data. Although in most cases it is unlikely that anyone would attempt to intercept this data, you should attempt to protect this information as much as possible by using secure web sites.

Secure web sites use encryption to set up a secure connection between your web browser and the web server to which you are connecting. Data is encrypted on your computer, sent over the Internet, and decrypted on the web server. This added security mechanism makes it nearly impossible for anyone to effectively intercept and misuse your sensitive information. For additional information about encryption and secure transaction on the Internet, see the sections "128-Bit Encryption" and "Secure Transactions" later in this chapter.

Setting Up Internet Security

Having examined the major security risks associated with browsing the Internet, this discussion now turns to methods and procedures that you can take to protect yourself from these risks. By properly configuring file and printer sharing, and through the effective use of the security zones included with Internet Explorer 4.0, you can enjoy safe browsing with little real risk. Features such as Certificate Management enable you to predetermine which software is trusted and can be installed without any intervention on your part.

Configuring File and Printer Sharing

As mentioned previously, the security risk in using file and printer sharing is relatively small if your connections to the Internet are for short periods and you use a dial-up connection. The risk is low in this environment because anyone trying to access your computer would need to know (1) how to locate your computer, such as by its IP address, and (2) that you were online at the time that he or she wanted to gain access. Most Internet Service Providers assign a different IP address to your computer each time that you connect, which makes it relatively difficult for someone to locate your IP address and attempt to connect to your computer. Further, unless you had just hit that person's web site (some sites log the IP addresses of all viewers) or unless you had given someone your IP address while your were online, such as exchanging information in a Chat session, most people would have a difficult time determining when you were online. Because few users could determine both your IP address and your online status, the likelihood of anyone connecting to your computer is relatively low.

> **Note** If you're online permanently, through a cable modem or a direct Internet connection, the file and printer sharing poses a much more significant risk.

Note that if you want to enable file sharing (see Figure 30.2) over the TCP/IP protocol for some reason, for example, you use TCP/IP over your local network and you also use that same connection (as opposed to a modem) to connect to the Internet, then you can further protect your computer from this type of attack by requiring passwords to access data and by making all access read-only. Merely enabling file sharing on your computer opens up few real security problems unless you actually select files, directories, or disk drives to share. This is done in the Windows Explorer. By right-clicking on any of these and choosing the S<u>h</u>aring option, a window will open that allows you to set the level of access for other users.

Figure 30.2

If you decide to enable file sharing on your computer, be sure to use some form of additional protection such as requiring the use of a password to access the data.

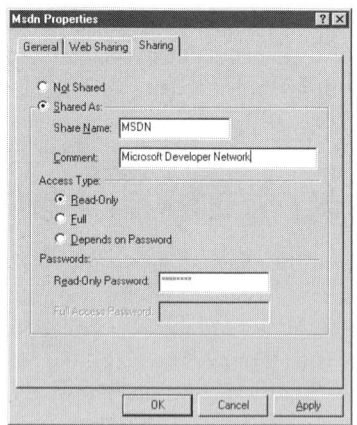

By selecting the **S**hared As option, you can specify a password that a user has to know before he or she can access any shared data. The best option would be to make all access read-only and to require a password for that capability.

In most cases, however, the best solution to protect your files from access by other Internet users is to disable file and printer sharing for the TCP/IP protocol that is bound to your dial-up adapter. If you have configured your computer to access the Internet through a modem, you can disable file and print sharing for that dial-up adapter while retaining sharing on a separate TCP/IP connection to a local network through a network interface card. To do so, open the Control Panel and then double-click on the Network icon. The list of network components on the Configuration tab should include one that says TCP/IP->Dial-Up Adapter, as shown in Figure 30.3.

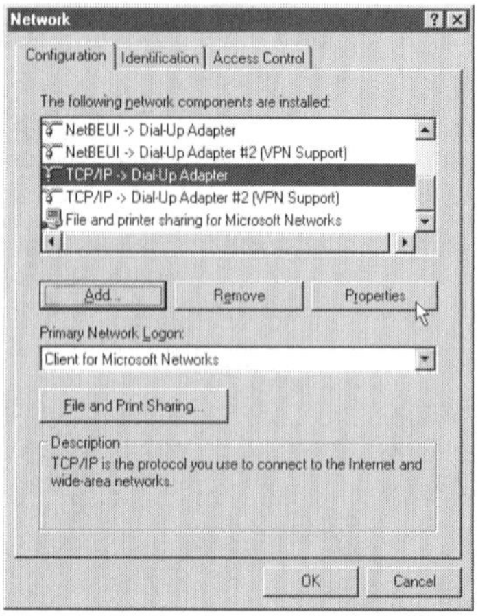

Figure 30.3

Through the Network component in the Control Panel, you can select the TCP/IP connection for which you wish to disable file and print sharing.

Chapter 30: Internet Security

Select that network component by clicking on it; then click on the P**r**operties button to display a Properties window containing information specific to that TCP/IP connection (see Figure 30.4). Before that second window opens, an informational dialog box may tell you that most TCP/IP changes should be made to the Dial-UP Networking connection information for your specific Internet Service Provider. However, you have to change your global TCP/IP Dial-UP Adapter settings to disable file and print sharing, so click on the OK button in this dialog box to proceed to the Properties sheet.

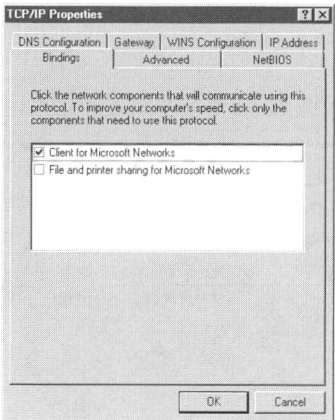

Figure 30.4
The TCP/IP Properties sheet for your Dial-Up Adapter contains the global settings that need to be changed to disable file and printer sharing for that connection.

In the TCP/IP Properties sheet, select the Bindings tab. Assuming that you have previously enabled file or print sharing as discussed earlier in this section, at least two selections should be available; one of these selections is File and Printer Sharing for Microsoft Networks. If this selection is enabled (if its checkbox is checked), then disable it by removing the check from the check box, as shown in Figure 30.4. Click the OK button to close this window and click the OK button on the Network window to enable these settings. You may be prompted to restart your computer, after which file and printer sharing is no longer be enabled for that dial-up adapter. If you have multiple dial-up adapters, then you need to reconfigure each of them in this same manner.

Note If you enable file and printer sharing on a computer that is also configured with a dial-up adapter, the next time you start that computer, Windows 98 should display a System Security Check warning about sharing files and printers over an Internet connection. It will then ask whether you want to disable sharing over the TCP/IP connection on your dial-up adapter, which Microsoft highly recommends. If you choose to disable it, then Windows 98 should automatically make the changes described for your dial-up adapter.

Protocol Isolation

If you are connected to both a local network and to the Internet, you may be able to use an option known as protocol isolation to increase security. *Protocol isolation* is the process of isolating different networks from one another by using separate protocols on them. For example, assume you have a computer that is connected to the Internet and to a local network. For the connection to the Internet, you must use the TCP/IP protocol. However, you can use a different protocol, such as IPX/SPX, to connect to your local network. This approach prevents anyone who gains access to your system through the Internet from going beyond that point to access the local network.

Security Zones

One way that Windows 98 and Internet Explorer 4.0 address ongoing security issues is with *security zones*. Every zone has a different level of security, and you can assign these zones to individual web sites, effectively allowing you do designate the security that should be applied to any site you visit. By default, all web sites belong in the Internet zone. This section starts by examining the zones and then explains how to add sites to other zones.

Types of Security Zones

Each security zone has its own security settings. This section looks at the default security settings, but you can also customize the settings for any zone. Internet Explorer 4.0 contains the following four zones:

- **Internet.** The Internet zone has a high level of security and prompts the user before allowing ActiveX controls or Java applets to install within Internet Explorer.

- **Local/Intranet.** The local intranet zone has the lowest level of security, allowing any trusted ActiveX control or Java applet to run on the browser and even have access to the disk drive and other parts of the operating system without prompting you about potential security risks.

- **Trusted Sites.** Trusted sites have a medium level of security by default that would allow trusted ActiveX controls and Java applets to run within the browser, but not have access to anything on the computer outside of the browser itself.

- **Restricted Sites.** Restricted sites are known to exploit security weaknesses or contain malicious code. These sites are set to the highest level of security to prevent any scripting or other programming elements from executing or even loading.

These four security configurations can either be selected by the user or be designated by a system administrator using the Internet Explorer Administration Kit (IEAK). The administrator can use the IEAK to determine which levels of security to assign to each zone and to prevent the user from making any changes to those classifications. The administrator can also assign certain web sites to each zone. For the intranet zone, all IP addresses located behind a corporate firewall might be included, or the list may include just the IP address for the intranet web server(s) to which the user may need to connect. Through the Automatic Configuration and Proxy Server capabilities in Internet Explorer 4.0 and the IEAK, the browser can be set to check for updated security information, including changes to security zone configurations, each time the browser loads.

Adding Sites to Security Zones

When you visit a site in Internet Explorer, the default setting for that site is usually the Internet zone unless you are viewing a site on your local network, in which case the intranet zone will normally be enabled by default. By adding a site to a different zone, each time that you visit that site your security level automatically changes to reflect the level of the zone to which you have assigned that site. Your browser's security level remains at that level until you switch to another site.

To add a site to a zone, select Internet Options from the View menu of Internet Explorer 4.0. On the property sheet that opens, click the Security tab. Use the drop-down menu to select the zone to which you want to add a site and click Add Site. In the Trusted Sites Zone dialog box, you can enter the URL for the site you wish to add.

The two zones to which you should particularly consider adding sites are the trusted sites and restricted sites zones. As the name implies, trusted sites are Internet sites that you trust to contain content that is not harmful to your computer. For example, it is not likely that Microsoft would place any ActiveX controls on its site that would erase your hard drive without your consent. Therefore, you can probably add Microsoft's site to your list of trusted sites. One of the main advantages of adding a site to your trusted sites list is that you won't be prevented from downloading and installing ActiveX controls and other components through your web browser, which can happen if you have placed your security settings at the highest level.

The restricted sites zone is a good place to enter sites that you know might cause harm to your computer. For example, if you just read about a web site devoted to computer hacking and you want to go view it, it might not be a bad idea to place the site into your restricted sites zone. You would still be able to view the site, but anything on that site that could cause problems on your computer, such as malicious Java applets or ActiveX controls, would be prevented from running or even being installed on your computer. Similarly, if you occasionally visit a site that uses a lot of scripting and ActiveX controls that you don't want to view, you can prevent those items from loading on your computer by entering the site as a restricted site.

If you select the local intranet zone and choose to add one or more sites, a new pop-up window replaces the window that appears on the trusted and restricted sites zones. By default, this new window includes three types of sites that are unique to intranets:

- **Local sites not included in other security zones.** This type of site represents any site on your local network (including your own computer) that you have not specifically added to any other zone, such as to the restricted sites zone.

- **Sites that bypass your proxy server.** You would normally set up Internet Explorer not to use a proxy server to connect to sites on your network because you might have to go through a firewall before or after going through the proxy server. Thus, sites that bypass your proxy server are usually assumed to be local (intranet) sites.

- **All network paths (including those using the Universal Naming Convention, or UNC).** Because you can enter directory and UNC path names into the address bar of Internet Explorer to browse these directories, all such network paths will normally be within your local network.

Note that regardless of whether you choose to leave these options enabled, you can also manually add sites to the local intranet zone in the same manner that you do with the trusted and restricted sites zones. To do so, click on the Advanced button within the Local Intranet Zone configuration window shown in Figure 30.5. Then you can add any sites that you want to include in this zone.

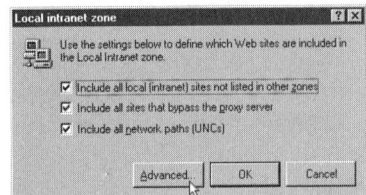

Figure 30.5
The local intranet zone contains additional settings to determine which sites should be included within that zone.

Customizing Security Zones

Although you can choose to use the default security setting for each zone or change the setting to one of the other default settings (high, medium, or low security), you can also exercise fine grain control over your settings by choosing the Custom security level. Viewing the Custom settings also enables you see exactly what the default settings are for the three default security levels.

To customize the settings for a particular security zone, first select that zone then select the Custom option, and click on the Settings button. A Security Settings window appears from which you can designate your custom settings for that zone (as shown in Figure 30.6).

The drop-down box near the bottom of this window enables you to select the default level of security you want to restore. If you select one of these default levels and click on the Reset button, the security settings will be reset according to that default. You can then scroll through the many security settings in this window and see how each one is set for any given default. This information should help you choose a default if you don't want to customize your settings in this window.

Chapter 30: Internet Security

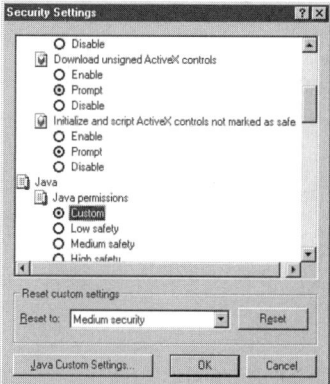

Figure 30.6
You can customize the settings for any security zone.

Among the security settings that you can customize, the following settings give you the option of choosing Enable, Prompt, or Disable. The Enable option means that you will not be prompted before downloading or running the component in question. The settings available with these options include

- **Script ActiveX Controls Marked Safe for Scripting.** This option determines whether script, such as VBScript and JScript, will be allowed to interact with ActiveX controls that you have previously designated as safe.

- **Run ActiveX Controls and Plugins.** This option determines whether ActiveX controls and plugins (such as viewers for proprietary content like streaming video) that you have previously downloaded and installed will be run within your browser.

- **Download Signed ActiveX Controls.** ActiveX Controls that are signed using Authenticode technology enable you to determine who created the control. Note that this option merely determines whether the controls can be downloaded automatically within Internet Explorer, not whether they will be installed.

- **Download Unsigned ActiveX Controls.** Not all ActiveX controls are signed by their creators. If you choose Disable, you will not be able to download any of these.

- **Initialize and Script ActiveX Controls Not Marked as Safe.** By selecting Prompt or Enable, you can use controls and related scripting even if you have not yet marked them as safe following their download.

- **Active Scripting.** This option determines whether any client-side script (VBScript and JScript) will be run within your browser.

- **Scripting of Java Applets.** Active Scripting that interacts with Java applets can be disabled through this setting.

- **File Downloads.** The only choices here are Enable or Disable. In most cases, you would have no reason to disable this setting unless you are a network administrator and you want to prevent users from downloading software to their computers.

- **Font Download.** Internet Explorer 4.0 permits web site authors to use custom fonts on their pages and to configure those pages to prompt your browser to automatically download and install those fonts for the limited purpose of viewing those pages.

- **Submit Non-Encrypted Form Data.** In most cases, you have no need to encrypt form data that you enter on web pages (for example, a form requesting your name and e-mail address).

- **Launching Applications and Files in an IFRAME.** This option refers to an HTML tag that is supported in Internet Explorer 4.0 for inline floating frames. This option should probably be set no higher or lower than other such settings (such as for ActiveX controls).

- **Installation of Desktop Items.** These are desktop components and other such items that can be installed on your Active Desktop (assuming that you have enabled the Active Desktop). These items can include HTML, ActiveX controls, Java applets, and just about anything else that can run within Internet Explorer but that have been designated to run on your desktop.

- **Drag and Drop or Copy and Paste Files.** This option supports common Windows functionality for files within Internet Explorer. Thus if Microsoft Word is installed on your computer, you could drag a Word document from Windows Explorer and drop it into Internet Explorer, which would then display that page within the browser window.

You can also choose security settings for the following options:

- **Java Permissions.** You can either select from among the default security levels provided here (low, medium, or high), disable Java completely, or select your own custom settings. If you select Custom, you can click the Java Custom Settings button to choose from a number of different security settings. For more information see "Customizing Java Settings."

- **User Authentication.** This option determines whether your logon information is cached for future use when you visit a web page that requires you to log on.

- **Software Channel Permissions.** Similar to other channels in Internet Explorer 4.0, these special channels help you connect to an Internet or intranet site from which you can download software, such as for updates to Internet Explorer. In most cases, the only channels you would visit are for products that are installed on your computer, some of which may automatically install channels in your Favorites pull-down menu in Internet Explorer.

Customizing Java Settings

Java applets in Internet Explorer 4.0 obtain new capabilities, but also can be limited by security features. As previously discussed in the Java section of this chapter, Java applets can run outside the sandbox in Internet Explorer 4.0. However, because allowing such applets to write to disk drives and access the operating system is highly risky, particularly when the code is downloaded from an unknown source, Windows 98 provides new security safeguards to help protect your computer. One way of adding a level of trust to downloaded Java applets is through Microsoft's Authenticode technology, which asks you to decide whether to run an applet before the applet is loaded onto your computer. The information presented can include the capabilities of the applet, such as the fact that it may be designed to transfer information back over the network or to write to the disk drives. Based on these signed capabilities, you can decide whether to load the applet on your machine.

You can customize the security settings for Java if you don't want to use the default settings provided in Internet Explorer.

As indicated in the "Customizing Security Zones" section, you can fine-tune the security settings for Java components on your system. To do so, choose Internet Options from the View pull-down menu in Internet Explorer and then click on the Security tab. Choose a zone for which you wish to customize the Java settings, select Custom, and then click on the Settings button. In the Security settings window, select Custom under Java permissions and click on the Java Custom Settings buttons. If you are familiar with Java, you might want to customize some of the many different security options available here according to the exact level of protection that you want.

Authenticode

Security in Internet Explorer 4.0 is also enhanced through the use of Authenticode 2.0, an updated version of the authenticating technology designed to identify ActiveX controls, executables, and Java applets that have been digitally signed using this product. Software developers use this process to obtain a digital certificate from a third-party certificate authority; this certificate enables developers to apply a unique digital signature and time stamp to the code being distributed. Because the certificates use a high level of encryption to protect the digital signature, all certificates have a limited lifetime that is set to expire prior to any date by which the encryption used for the certificate could be cracked. This technology makes it very difficult for someone to impersonate another software publisher. When you download a file that has been digitally signed using Authenticode, Internet Explorer tells you who the author of the software is and asks whether you want to install it.

A new feature in Authenticode 2.0 allows Internet Explorer 4.0 to automatically check the authority who issued the certificate to determine whether the certificate has been revoked since the time it was issued. Thus if a software developer distributes malicious code and if this fact comes to the attention of the certificate vendor, the vendor will revoke the certificate. In such an event, you may get a warning of this revocation at the time that you are asked whether to install the software.

Certificate Management

Administrators can also ensure a minimum level of safety on their networks though the use of Certificate Management. By using the Internet Explorer Administration Kit, network administrators can preselect which digital certificates from software vendors a user is allowed to accept to receive trusted code. The administrator can also designate which certificates the user cannot accept. Thus if an ActiveX control or Java applet being downloaded presents a certificate that is predesignated as being either trusted or not to the browser, the browser can automatically accept or reject the code without the user's intervention. If a certificate server is set up on your network, you can preconfigure users' browsers to automatically accept software signed with certificates issued by that server. Thus software signed by internal software developers could be installed and run without any intervention by the user.

Like other security-related features, the user's web browser can be set to automatically check each time it is loaded to see whether the centrally maintained list of authorized certificates has changed since the last time the user ran the browser. Consequently, the administrator can be assured that every copy of Internet Explorer 4.0 running on the network has the latest security information.

128-Bit Encryption

One of the ways that you can protect your private information, such as when you are purchasing goods over the Internet, is to use the highest level of encryption that is available for your browser. Both Microsoft and Netscape provide 128-bit encryption for their browsers, which is substantially stronger than the 40-bit encryption algorithm supported in the standard version of their browsers. The 128-bit version is currently only available to users in the United States and Canada.

In many cases, you will find that you have the 40-bit version of Internet Explorer even if you purchased your copy of Windows 98 in the United States or Canada. You can determine the encryption strength of your version of Internet Explorer by one of two means:

- **View the About option.** The About option from the Help pull-down menu in Internet Explorer tells you whether you are using 40- or 128-bit encryption.

- **Check your schannel.dll properties.** Open your Windows System folder in Windows Explorer and find the file schannel.dll. Right-click on the file and choose Properties. Click on the Version tab where you can see whether the file is the export (40-bit) or the U.S. and Canada (128-bit) version.

If you determine that you are using the 40-bit version, you can download the files needed to convert Internet Explorer to 128-bit from Microsoft's web site. Go to http://www.

microsoft.com/ie and navigate to the Download section where you can get these files. The web server will verify that you are connecting to the Internet from a location within the United States or Canada, after which you will have to fill out a form verifying that you are legally able to possess this higher strength form of encryption.

Other Security Features in Internet Explorer

To access even more security features in Internet Explorer, choose Internet Options from the View pull-down menu and then select the Advanced tab. One set of options on this tab is labeled Security (see Figure 30.7). With these settings, you can disable Secure Sockets Layer connections (more fully discussed in the Secure Transaction section below), warn you if a site's security certificate appears to be invalid, and warn you when you are moving from a secure page to an unsecured page.

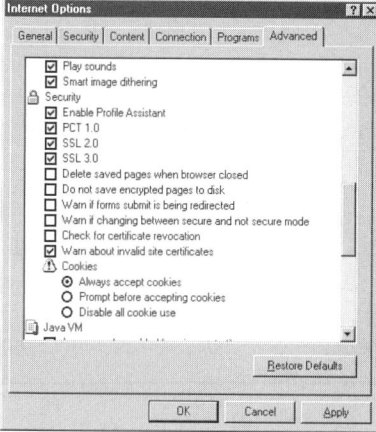

Figure 30.7

In addition to security zones, you can use the Advanced tab within the Internet Options tab in Internet Explorer to set various other security options.

One of the options provided here is to refuse to accept cookies sent to your browser by web sites. Cookies are one of the most misunderstood elements on the Internet. Cookies are generally used by web servers for functions such as keeping track of you as you move about a site. Cookies can store your site preferences and hold data about your session while you are connected to that server. You should be aware that many sites that require user authentication to access that site use cookies to identify you as you move from page to page after being authenticated. If you set the cookies settings in Internet Explorer to refuse all cookies, then you will probably not be able to access such sites. Because cookies are benign by nature, in most cases you should allow them unless you have strong privacy concerns; even then, you might have to enable cookies occasionally to access sites that require their use.

Secure Transactions

As discussed earlier in this chapter, some people are very sensitive about the possible security risks involved in transmitting personal information over the Internet. Regardless of whether this concern is justified or not, Microsoft, Netscape, IBM, and other corporations that are trying to promote commerce on the Internet have continued to increase security on the Internet on both the client and server side. One of the longest standing forms of protecting personal data on the Internet is the use of encryption to secure transactions. Microsoft has taken additional steps to provide other proprietary forms of protection in the form of Microsoft Wallet. This section briefly addresses the use of these technologies in the continuing effort to promote secure transactions in which consumers will feel more comfortable buying goods and services on the Internet.

Encryption

Although you should not generally be concerned about transmitting basic information such as your name and address over the Internet, you should not transmit your credit card number or conduct online banking over the Internet unless you have a secure, encrypted connection to the web server to which you are sending the information. This is really a matter of common sense. Just as you would not give your credit card information to someone on the phone unless you trusted that party, such as a company from which you routinely purchase goods, you should try to protect your credit card information as it travels across the Internet.

Most web sites that take credit cards for goods and services purchased over the Internet use a secure web page to obtain this information from you. Similarly, banks and stock trading services that allow you to make transactions over the Internet need to provide a secure way to exchange information with you. You can tell when you are connecting to a secure web site if a gold lock icon appears in the status bar at the bottom of Internet Explorer's window. Most secure sites use a URL prefix of https:// rather than http://, so this prefix is another indicator that you are probably connecting to a secure site.

However, if you want to be sure that the site is using a secure connection that you can trust, you may want to check the properties for that page. To do so, choose P**r**operties from the **F**ile pull-down menu in Internet Explorer. In the properties window, click on the Certificates button. The next window should display information about the owner of the certificate as well as the certificate authority that granted the certificate. The level of encryption employed by that site and other such information is also available by clicking on the various properties listed in this window.

Microsoft's Internet Explorer browser supports several Internet protocols for using encryption to establish secure connections. The most common protocol currently employed by web sites is Secure Sockets Layer versions 2.0 and 3.0. This protocol uses a public/private key for encryption that, when combined with 128-bit encryption, makes it almost impossible for your data to be decrypted by any entity except the web server that established the secure connection with your web browser. Other security protocols that are either directly supported by Internet Explorer or that are being jointly developed by Microsoft and other organizations include Personal Communications Technology, Secure Electronics Transactions, and Transport Layer Security. The main things that you should be concerned about, however, are (1) that the version of Internet Explorer 4.0 supplied with Windows 98 supports all standards-based web sites that use secure communications and (2) that Microsoft is continuing to work with other organizations to improve security and increase your comfort level in conducting secure transactions over the Internet.

Microsoft Wallet

One of the technologies that Microsoft is promoting in its quest to increase Internet security is its own proprietary mechanism for securely transmitting personal and financial information from your computer to a web server. Microsoft Wallet, also known as Microsoft Payment Selector, enables you to store your credit card, address, and other information securely on your computer and then pass this information on to merchants from whom you purchase goods and services over the Internet. Note that information entered into Microsoft Wallet can be transferred to a third party only if that party's web site is set up to receive such information.

To enter information into Microsoft Wallet, choose Internet Options from the View pull-down menu in Internet Explorer and then click on the Content tab. If Microsoft Wallet is installed on your system, then the Addresses and Payments buttons will be enabled. Microsoft Wallet is an ActiveX control that might not be installed on your system by default. If it is not installed, you can add it by using Add/Remove Programs in the Control Panel and then selecting the Windows Setup tab. Microsoft Wallet is one of the Internet Tools subcomponents.

Conclusion

This chapter discussed Windows 98 Internet security features and described some strategies for securing your Windows 98 PC from malicious code and unauthorized access. For more on configuring Windows 98 for the Internet, see Chapter 28 "Setting Up Windows 98 for the Internet." You may also wish to see Chapter 25, "Windows 98 with TCP/IP," which discusses how to install and configure the Internet protocol TCP/IP.

Mail Management in Windows 98

*E*mail has gone from being a mild curiosity and a mere convenience to being an absolute necessity. Whether you're getting office emails or running a business, it's just about impossible to function in today's computing world without some access to email. In this chapter, we'll discuss both the low-level details of how email works and the upper-level details of how to set it up to work with Windows 98.

Email and How it Works

Sending email is like sending any other data across a network. First, a connection is made and the packet with appropriate routing and data information is assembled. Then the packet is sent to its destination, sometimes with receipt information returned to the user to let him or her know whether the packet was successfully transmitted. Read on to learn more about the details of SMTP, the protocol used to transmit email, and the contents of the packets themselves.

The Simple Mail Transfer Protocol (SMTP)

The basis of email transfer on the Internet is the Simple Mail Transfer Protocol (SMTP). SMTP is designed to reliably transfer mail between an SMTP client and an SMTP server. It's not a transport protocol itself, but runs on top of one (most often TCP, but it doesn't have to be the same transport protocol on both ends) that can give it a reliable connection. The relaying of SMTP-based data is invisible to the user.

Follow these steps to send an email message via SMTP:

1. A transmission channel is established.

2. The SMTP client sends the message to the SMTP server, which may be either the final destination (if the source and destination are using the same transport service) or a relay point on the way to the final destination. If the latter, as with a POP-3 server, then the SMTP server establishes a connection—from here on, it becomes an SMTP client itself. In case the mail is relayed, the SMTP server receives from the client not only the mailbox name of the message's recipient, but the name of the destination host.

   Note Internet Service Providers typically provide an SMTP server to be the relay between the client and the message's final destination.

3. The SMTP client initiates a mail transaction (a series of commands that identify the sender and recipient) and transmits the email message itself. If the same message is being sent to more than one recipient, only one copy of the message is transmitted to the destination (or relay) host.

4. The SMTP server responds, indicating that the command was successful, that more data is needed to complete the transmission, or that a temporary or permanent error condition exists that prevents the message from being transmitted at this time.

5. After the mail message has been transmitted, the client can either shut down the connection or send another message.

> **Note** An SMTP client can use its server not just for sending mail, but for other functions such as verifying email addresses and retrieving mailing-list subscribers' addresses.

Elements of an Email Message

An email message consists of two main elements: an envelope and its content. The envelope includes the following:

- The originator's address (to which error reports should be sent)
- A delivery mode indicating where the message should be delivered
- One or more recipient addresses
- Any protocol extensions

The content is the part you see when you open an email message and includes the following:

- The headers
- The body

Headers are always ASCII-based, but the body can be either ASCII-based (as it is for an ordinary text message) or can use extensions such as MIME or UUencode to make binary attachments.

Attachments

SMTP's fundamental design allows it to transmit only data based on the ASCII character set, so, beginning in about 1990, extensions to SMTP's design were made to allow it to include binary attachments (and some other changes). These extensions are included in a Registry of possibilities. For attachments, SMTP supports MIME, discussed in the following section.

Encoding Formats

SMTP was not originally designed for use with binary attachments, and in fact not every email system uses SMTP—others use MAPI (Message Application Programming Interface) or MHS (Message Handling System) instead. Even getting the disparate email systems to talk to each other for ASCII documents was impossible at one time, let alone getting them to read each other's attachments.

The safest way to ensure that an email message travels through various mail servers on its way to its destination is to treat the whole thing as an ASCII file, ignoring anything that is not in ASCII text format. This includes most data files (word processing documents, spreadsheets, and databases), any kind of image file, any kind of executable application, any compressed files, and probably anything else that isn't readable in a text editor such as NotePad or EDIT.COM. In other words, if you can't paste data into the body of a simple emailer (forget the ones that support HTML for the moment) then any self-respecting mail protocol will discard it.

Thus, encoding formats to turn those binary attachments into ASCII format had to be developed to work with email. You've got three options to choose from:

- BinHex
- UUencode/Decode
- MIME

Note Both the email sender and recipient must use the same encoding format for the binary file in question. You cannot uudecode a MIME file, even if both sender and recipient support both encoding schemes.

Modern email programs often do the encoding and decoding automatically for you, so you never see it. Some older ones, however, would include the "ASCII-fied" binary file in the body of the message (looking like lines and lines of gibberish), with a note telling the recipient which decoder he or she needed to use to translate the file back into its binary format. In such a case, you'd need to cut the encoded data from the email message, paste it into a text editor such as Notepad, save the file, then run a decoder on it. If done properly and with the proper decoder, at the end you'd have the binary file back.

Let's take a look at how each works.

BinHex

BinHex (Binary to Hexadecimal Converter) was originally developed for the Macintosh but is now also supported on the PC—Eudora Light, for example, supports BinHex as one of its standard encoding schemes. If your email program doesn't support BinHex automatic decoding, you can identify a BinHex file by the starting line of the ASCII "garbage" that will appear in the body of the email message:

```
this file must be converted with BinHex 4.0
```

To convert this file, cut the garbage and paste it into a text file, saving it with an extension of .HQX and run it through a BinHex converter.

UUencode

UUencode (UNIX-to-UNIX Encode) was the first binary-to-ASCII converter used on the Internet. Since its presentation in 1980, it has been a standard part of UNIX, and versions for PCs and Macintoshes are also available. You can identify the "garbage" text of UUencoded files by the way they begin— with the following line:

```
begin 0755 filename
```

To decode the file, cut all the text from the begin keyword to the end keyword, and paste it into a text editor. Save the file, then run UUdecode on the file like this:

```
uudecode filename
```

If your emailer supports automatic UUdecoding, you won't have to do this extra step—the binary file will be automatically converted to its original state.

MIME

BinHex and UUencode permit you to attach binary files to ASCII messages. MIME goes one step beyond that, allowing you to transform the messages themselves.

MIME (Multipurpose Internet Mail Extensions) is a set of specifications that permits you to send email messages in a format other than 128-character ASCII. MIME supports the following:

- Character sets other than ASCII, permitting languages to be sent in languages other than English

- Unlimited line length and message length (although some email programs will refuse messages greater than a preset size)

> **Note** Prior to the introduction of MIME, lines in an email message could be no longer than 1000 characters before a line break was required.

- Formatted text
- Images
- Sounds
- Other encapsulated messages
- Attachments
- Pointers to other files

These features were not all exclusive to MIME when this specification was developed. They were special, however, in that they were not proprietary: If one MIME user sent another an email message, the recipient would receive what the sender intended. This scenario ignores the question of whether all of the file formats were readable by the recipient, but that's another matter, and not related to the question of what is possible to reliably send and receive, as long as the implementations of MIME follow the standards.

Rather than treating all encoded information the same, the MIME standard defines seven content types, described in Table 31.1.

Table 31.1
MIME Data Types

Type	Description	Further Information
Applications	Indicates data that does not fit into any other category. Binary data and data to be processed by a mail-based application are included in this category.	The subtypes of this type include the suggested filename, the general category of data type (for user information), and the padding used to make the number of bits divisible by eight (by bytes).
Audio	Includes all audio data.	Requires a speaker or telephone to "display" this data.
Image	Includes .GIF and .JPG files.	Requires a display device (printer, monitor, fax machine) to display data.
Message	Indicates that this is an encapsulated message.	Encapsulated messages may be forwarded messages, messages split into several pieces because they're too long to be sent in one piece (in which case they'll be referenced as "Part X of Y") or external references to messages not downloaded but available.
Multipart	Indicates data consisting of multiple parts, each with its own data type.	Each part will be defined in its own section. Multipart data may be supplied either as content to all be read, or for the email program to pick the best format for that reader (for example, if an ASCII and an HTML version of the same text were both available).

Chapter 31: Mail Management in Windows 98

Type	Description	Further Information
Text	Indicates text content (not necessarily ASCII).	This text may be either ASCII-compatible (plaintext) or Rich Text, which may be formatted.
Video	Indicates that the content includes a time-varying image.	This standard is used very loosely. MPEG is the supported format.

In addition to these named types, MIME also supports application-specific types that email programs can use by common consent. Any type name that begins with X is a private type that can be used by other mail systems supporting the same MIME type.

These content types are part of the MIME headers, following this syntax:

```
Mime version 1.0
Content-Type: multipart/mixed; boundary"="
```

In this example, *multipart* is the content type and *mixed* is the subtype to that content type. All content types have subtypes, even if it's only one (as for content type Video).

The encoding used for MIME depends on the type of data being transferred. If the data is mostly binary, then Base64 is used, producing a text file that looks quite a bit like a UUencoded file. If the data is largely text with some additional formatting, then the encoding scheme may be Quoted-Printable, which allows the user not only to read the text portion of the document in its ASCII form, but also to decode the file into an exact duplicate of the original.

Note MIME is a complicated and still-developing standard. For further detail, look up RFC1521 on the Web.

Configuring an Email Client

There are three main server types:

- POP (for receiving email)
- SMTP (for sending email)
- LDAP (directory services)

These server types are described in more detail in the following sections.

POP (Post Office Protocol) Server

It was mentioned earlier how mail gets *to* the Internet, but how do you retrieve it? A standard for doing so, called the Post Office Protocol (POP) is now in its third version and widely implemented. Heard of accessing a POP3 server? That's what you're connecting to.

The function of a POP3 server is similar to that of SMTP, only in reverse. POP3 servers listen on port 110 for incoming requests from POP clients. A client running TCP establishes a connection with the POP3 server and logs on. If the logon is successful (that is, the user name and password match an account in the mail database) then the server passes the client—allows it to request transactions. At that point, the server figures out how many email messages are waiting for the client, tells the client to expect that number, and downloads them to the client. When the email has all been transferred, the client quits the TCP connection to the server and the mail session is completed.

> **Tip** If you're concerned about others getting access to your email, you can opt to log on to the POP server manually, rather than caching your password.

Specifying a POP3 server is simply a matter of filling in the server's fully qualified domain name in the email settings dialog box, perhaps in the Hosts section if there is one. If the POP server and the SMTP server are on the same machine, then you may have to supply only a single server name.

If you're logging on to your POP account from a computer other than the one you normally use, you may not want to download your messages permanently, deleting them from the server. In that case, you can opt to leave your messages on the server so that each time you connect, they're all still there.

SMTP (Simple Mail Transfer Protocol) Server

The fundamentals of SMTP performance were discussed earlier in this chapter in the section on how email works. Essentially, SMTP is the protocol used to upload mail messages to the Internet for delivery.

To send mail, therefore, you must identify the SMTP server to upload mail to. Somewhere in your email program's settings you'll have a place to enter the name of your SMTP server. In some cases, this server may have the same fully qualified domain name as your POP server; if so, then either fill in the same name or (if permitted) leave the space blank, as shown in the Eudora Light settings shown in Figure 31.1.

Chapter 31: Mail Management in Windows 98

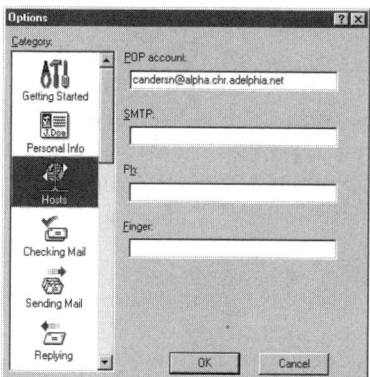

Figure 31.1
POP and SNMP server addresses.

LDAP (Lightweight Directory Access Protocol) Server

It's pretty simple to see why you'd want access to servers that let you send and receive email. Why do you need one with access to directory services (and what *are* directory services, anyway?) Well you don't have to have such access, and not all email programs can provide it, but directory services and LDAP have their place. Here's a little background on what it is that you're configuring access to.

One of the biggest issues surrounding the Internet is the question of how to *find* everybody attached to it. If you think about it, it's a daunting prospect: Millions of users around the globe are attached to the Internet by one means or another, and you can send email to any of them. This is accomplished with a general set of services called Directory Services, which supply the following services:

- White and yellow pages directories
- Resource location
- Mail address lookup

In short, just about any activity that involves finding something or someone is supported by directory services.

The obvious problem with such a huge directory is updating it regularly, as resource and human content and location on the Net is so dynamic. Telephone books get out of date, but their contents are generally fairly static. A dynamic community such as that of the Internet changes almost daily. Additionally, the number of people involved is enormous. To return to the telephone book analogy, most communities maintain a single book for a city or metropolitan area. How much time would it take to retrieve data from a country-wide telephone book or a single global one? Further, what happens if you want to look up someone in Africa but the Australia part of the directory is down? As they're in the same place, you can't get to any of the data if a centralized location is inaccessible.

X.500 is a directory service standard intended to work around both of these problems by distributing the global directory services among a number of sites. Each site running X.500 is responsible only for its section of the directory, so maintenance and updates can be done quickly. Even so, X.500 appears to users as a single global namespace, so users don't have to connect to several servers to get all the data they want. This directory service provides powerful searching techniques and support for image formats (specifically .JPG), which enable photographs to be included in the directory services.

> **Note** Like other directory services such as Whois and DNS, X.500 isn't without its problems. Its distributed nature slows down searches and the habit of some implementations of caching all responses before returning any to the user can take additional time. For security reasons, users may not even get all hits returned to them at once, but may have to make several searches to retrieve all the data. This type of directory services is still under development, however, and its designers are attempting to increase its responsiveness.

That's one implementation of the directory services end. How to get to it? Originally, X.500 directory services were readable with DAP, the Directory Access Protocol. For large machines, this TCP-dependent protocol was acceptable, but it didn't work well on smaller clients that may not have access to the full TCP/IP stack. So in 1993 the University of Michigan designed and developed a simpler version of DAP that would run on Macintosh computers and Windows with the existing TCP/IP stack. This more streamlined version is known as the Light Directory Access Protocol (LDAP).

LDAP defines the following components:

- A data model, which defines the syntax of the data in the directory
- An organizational model, which defines how that data is organized
- A security model, which defines how data is accessed in a secure manner
- A functional model, which defines how the directory can be queried and modified
- A topological model, which defines how the directory service integrates with other directory services to form a global namespace on the Internet

What this means in practical terms is that if your email program supports LDAP then you've got access to a global search directory. In Outlook Express, for example, you've already got several LDAP servers (as can be seen in the Internet Accounts dialog box shown in Figure 31.2), and the option of adding more to the list.

Chapter 31: Mail Management in Windows 98

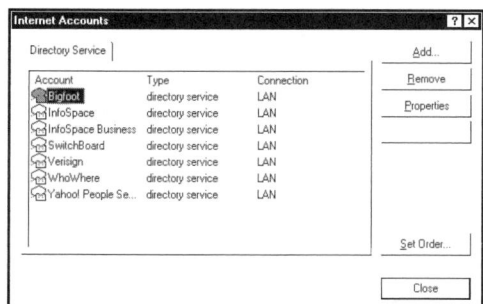

Figure 31.2
Installed LDAP servers.

Working with Specific Email Clients

So far in this chapter, a lot of the theory behind how email works has been covered. To round off, let's take a look at how several popular retail and freeware email programs work.

> **Note** This is *not* an exhaustive guide to using every email client in the world, but is simply intended as a basic reference for some of the more common programs. For further details, check your email program's documentation or online Help.

Begin by examining what all email programs have in common in terms of organization and functions.

Anatomy of an Emailer

The basic structure of a modern email program is a system of messages and folders similar to the file and directory structure used in Windows 98. As messages come in, they're moved to the folder representing the In box, and as the user reads them she has the option of moving those messages to either a predefined folder or a custom one made for the user's purposes. Even when messages are deleted, they're put into a folder—even if it's called Trash. In some email programs, folders contain other folders, for further organization. The method by which this is done varies with the email program; for one example, look at Figure 31.3, taken from Eudora Light 3.0.

This is one implementation of the folder/subfolder paradigm. In Eudora, there are three entities: folders, mailboxes, and messages. Folders must contain at least one mailbox, and may contain other folders. Mailboxes can only contain messages, not folders or other mailboxes.

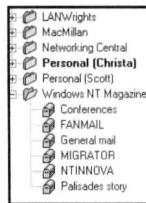

Figure 31.3
Folders and mailboxes in Eudora Light.

Email Functionality

Email programs have functional similarity in addition to their structural one. The following sections describe the features included in most or all of the sample email programs outlined here, discuss how you might use these, and explain how to *perform* these actions.

Create or Open a Text File

Some email programs let you write not only in email but in a separate text attachment. This can be useful not only for writing emails that you want to think about before sending (have you ever written a message, queued it to save it, but then accidentally sent it?) but also for opening text attachments without having to open another program. These text editors may not contain any advanced options, but they can be a handy way to view and create ASCII content without dragging out Notepad.

Save an Email Message As a File

If you want to keep an email message but access it from Explorer, rather than from the hard disk (perhaps to import it into a word processing program), you can save it as a file. You can save just the text or the whole thing including the headers, and it is saved as a text document.

Print a Message

To create a hard copy of a message, choose the Print option. This creates a replica of the email message in its entirety, including headers, so if you want only the text, save the text as a file first, or copy it to the email-based text editor and save that.

Undo an Action

Whether you regret deleting that paragraph, transferring a file to a new mailbox, or queuing a message for delivery, you can often reverse the action with the Undo switch. This function does *not*, however, act on any mail that's already left your mailbox—that is, after a message is sent, you can't change your mind about sending it.

Cut, Copy, and Paste Text

Modern email programs offer the common word-processing tools of cut, copy, and paste so you can perform the following actions:

- Move or copy text from one message to another.

- Insert text from another document, such as a word processor.

- With the Paste as Quotation feature, paste text with leading brackets or lines so that it's clear that the text is being quoted from the original message.

> **Tip** You can select the text to manipulate by dragging the mouse over it to highlight it or by using the Select All feature to copy all message text.

Delete Messages

To remove a message from its storage folder and prepare it for permanent deletion, you can delete it or transfer it to the Trash folder (if one exists) or the program's equivalent. It's roughly equivalent to the function of the Recycle Bin in Windows, in that you have a place to store files when you're pretty sure that you're not going to need them again, but want to have a chance to transfer them back to an active folder if it becomes necessary. To delete the "trashed" messages permanently, empty the Trash folder.

> **Warning** Not all email programs maintain a folder for deleted messages from which they can be retrieved. Particularly in older email programs, a message, once deleted, is gone forever.

Organize Mail

As discussed earlier, most modern mail programs maintain some kind of folder system so you can organize mail by subject, recipient, or whatever criteria you find useful. Messages are typically placed in the In box when downloaded from the mail server, but you can drag or transfer them to a new folder, whether a previously existing one or one you create. To view the contents of that mailbox, click on its icon or choose it from the email program's menu.

You can organize mail within folders by a variety of criteria, the exact nature of which depends on the particular email program. Sorting your messages by sender, date received, or subject can make it much easier to find a particular message that you might need.

Although mail is typically delivered to the In box when delivered, some email programs support a means to route messages to different mailboxes as they come in. To do this, specify filters to use, based on information in the header fields (such as who the message is from, or its subject header) or text in the body of the message. These filters can be applied not only upon receipt of mail but afterwards, so you can sort through the contents of your In box in one motion.

> **Note** Some email programs permit you to not only transfer mail, but automatically route mail to a specified user upon the mail's receipt.

Find Message Content

If you get a lot of mail, or don't recall which of the twelve messages from a single person included that person's telephone number, even a folder system can't always help you find the message you need. In that case, you'll need some mechanism by which you can search content without opening each and every message. Many modern email programs include a Find tool for this purpose.

Create Mail

When creating a mail message, you have several options, outlined in Table 31.2.

Table 31.2
New Message Options

Option	Description	Information Required
New Message	A new message, with no automatic references to existing ones.	Message text, recipient's name, and a subject header.
Reply	Copies the text of the original message to a new message (with some kind of formatting to indicate that it's quoted) and retains the same subject header with some kind of text to indicate that it's in reference to a previous message. Replies go to the sender.	Message text. Subject header may be edited.
Reply to All	Like a reply, except that the reply text is sent to all recipients of the original message.	Message text. Subject header may be edited. Typically, to reply to all original recipients, you must do something special—hold down the Shift key while replying, or choose the option from a menu.

Option	Description	Information Required
Forward	Copies the text of a message to a new message (with some kind of formatting to indicate that it's quoted) and retains the same subject header, sometimes with some additional text to indicate that this is a forwarded message. No recipient is automatically designated. The sender is the person doing the forwarding.	Any additional message text. Subject header may be edited.
Redirect	Like forwarding, except that the message is formatted to come from the original sender, not the person passing the message along (although the message may be said to be sent "by way of" the intermediary, and text is not printed as a quote. Basically, the message retains the appearance of the original.	Any additional message text, and a recipient. Subject header may be edited.

Change Message Status or Priority

An email program can code a message based on its status, whether that be read, unread, replied to, forwarded, or some other criteria. Some mail programs permit you to change the status of a message so that it looks as though something else was done to it—a read message now unread, or a forwarding notice removed.

A message can also be coded on the basis of a priority. By default, messages are generally sent with a normal priority, but some email programs support means to send them as urgent, or unimportant, allowing you to rank incoming messages based on their importance. For your own purposes, you might also be able to adjust the priority of your received messages so you know which ones to reply to first. Note that marking an email message you're sending as urgent won't have any effect on how quickly it gets to its destination; the Internet cares not for your personal concerns. All that changing a message's priority will do is perhaps get the attention of the recipient so that he or she opens it quickly—although you can't be sure of *that*, either.

Create Recipient Aliases

Email addresses are easier to remember than IP addresses, but complicated ones aren't always at your fingertips when you need them. To get around this problem, modern email programs often include an *alias* function that allows you to assign names to email addresses, so that all you need to type, for example, is **Fred** to send email to **fred_stanivlasky@navydept.us.ship.org**. The email program will automatically translate your alias into an email address that your SMTP server can understand.

> **Note** Email programs use a variety of terminology to describe this assigning of easy-to-remember names to email addresses, but in the SMTP standard this is known as creating an alias.

Aliases can also be a handy way of grouping email recipients. Create an alias that includes all the email addresses of your working group, and when you address email to that alias all those people will be included in the To:, Cc:, or Bcc: fields.

Change Your Email Password

If you're concerned about email security and have elected to log on to your POP3 server manually to pick up mail, you may want to change your password from time to time. Most email programs have some capability for letting you change or delete your current password, contingent on knowing the original.

Look Up an Email Address

If you know the name of the person you want to write but not their email address, you can sometimes use your email program to retrieve it from the global directory services described in the earlier section on LDAP. Look for an option that directs you to Directory Services, and enter the name of the person you're looking for.

> **Tip** Directory services in which you can find out anyone's email address are a great idea, but some bugs are still being worked out of them. Entries are often inaccurate or outdated, or simply refer to someone else. Before sending confidential information to someone whose address you retrieved from a global directory service, it's wise to send them a preliminary email making sure that they are who you think they are. I've received several letters from people who clearly believed that there could be only one "Christa Anderson."

Create a Signature

Customized signatures can be a handy way of always including any or all of the following at the end of your emails:

- Contact information
- Business advertisements

- Web page URLs
- Poetry or quotes that are meaningful to you

Modern email programs let you create a signature file so that the text you want is appended to the end of all outgoing mail, The rule of thumb is that if it can be written in ASCII text, it can be included in a signature file. Some programs even let you supply a regular signature file and an alternate, perhaps to use for business and personal email.

> **Note** Signature files more than four lines long are generally considered a netiquette no-no.

Attach Binary Files

If you want to send something other than ASCII text files across the Internet, you'll need to create an attachment and choose an encoding scheme. MIME seems to be in use for most people using PCs, but you may have to use another encoding scheme for some people.

Edit User Preferences

All email programs offer some interface for editing mailing preferences. The options depend on the mailer, but you can generally choose from among most of the following:

- Your user name, which controls the name that people see when they get your emails
- The addresses of your mail and directory service servers
- Options for checking mail, such as frequency, type of authentication to provide, and mail retrieval
- Options for sending mail
- Options for replying to messages
- Options for attaching and downloading binary and text files
- Display and print fonts to use
- The appearance of the interface, including toolbars and menus to display
- Font formatting information to process in received mail
- Advanced emailing options tuning protocol use and alerts

Conclusion

That's a quick roundup of email capabilities in Windows 98 and in general. At this point, you should have a basic understanding of what's going on when you send and receive email, how attachments work (and why they sometimes *don't* work) and some of the services available to you with modern email clients.

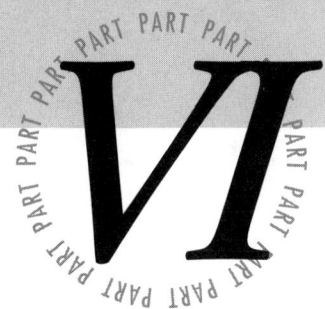

Customizing Windows 98

32 Windows 98 Configuration Files 729

33 Windows Scripting with Windows 98 Scripting Host 741

34 Automating Tasks 777

CHAPTER 32

Windows 98 Configuration Files

Windows 98 relies on certain key files when it starts. These files affect the configuration and operating behavior of Windows 98, and you can make changes that directly change these values. Under Windows 98, the following are key startup configuration files:

- MSDOS.SYS
- IO.SYS
- CONFIG.SYS
- AUTOEXEC.BAT
- WIN.INI
- SYSTEM.INI

You can edit all of these files except for IO.SYS, which is included in the list because it plays a key role in startup configuration (as you will see). In this chapter, you learn about how these files work, when they are accessed, and what changes you can make to them. Any of the editable files can be edited with any text editor, such as Windows Notepad or the MS-DOS EDIT command.

IO.SYS and MSDOS.SYS

The IO.SYS and MSDOS.SYS files are the first files processed as Windows 98 boots. IO.SYS is a binary file that is not editable, but which sets certain parameters for the system. You can override the settings made by IO.SYS with countermanding settings in CONFIG.SYS. (These commands were set by CONFIG.SYS prior to Windows 95.) You may want to change the commands set by IO.SYS when running Windows 98 in command-prompt mode (via the Windows Startup menu) or the configuration of the DOS virtual machines within Windows 98.

The commands set by IO.SYS (some of them changeable by countermanding commands in CONFIG.SYS) are as follows:

- **BUFFERS=*x*.** This command sets aside a number of file buffers for improving disk access times for applications running from the command line environment that use MS-DOS calls for file access. The default value set in IO.SYS is 30; you can set a higher value in CONFIG.SYS.

- **DOS=HIGH.** By default IO.SYS executes this command. If you need DOS=LOW, set the command in CONFIG.SYS. By default, when DOS=HIGH the UMB value is automatically included if EMM386.EXE is also being loaded by CONFIG.SYS.

- **FCBS=*x*.** Creates File Control Blocks (FCBs) for older MS-DOS applications. The default value set by IO.SYS is 4; you can increase it in CONFIG.SYS if needed by an older application.

- **FILES=*x*.** By default IO.SYS sets this value to 60. This command sets aside a quantity of file buffers to use for opening files with MS-DOS system calls, and is not used by Win16 or Win32 applications. You can set a different value in CONFIG.SYS, but it must be greater than the default set by IO.SYS.

- **HIMEM.SYS.** This file initializes the High Memory Area (HMA) for DOS virtual machines. It is loaded by default in IO.SYS.

- **IFSHLP.SYS.** The Installable File System Helper program loads file system device drivers. Until IFSHLP.SYS is loaded by IO.SYS, only a minimal file system is available to the system.

Chapter 32: Windows 98 Configuration Files

- **LASTDRIVE=x.** Set by default to the letter z, this command sets aside space to be used for drive letter assignments.

- **SHELL=COMMAND.COM.** Set by default in IO.SYS, you can use different SHELL parameters within CONFIG.SYS if needed by some application.

- **STACKS=x.** Sets aside a number and size of stack frames for use with older applications. The default value is 9,256, which creates nine stack frames of 256 bytes each. You can set a higher value with an entry in CONFIG.SYS.

For more detail on setting CONFIG.SYS commands such as the preceding, see the following section, "CONFIG.SYS."

The MSDOS.SYS file is an editable text file that contains commands that control how Windows 98 starts. Table 32.1 details the possible MSDOS.SYS settings and their affects.

Table 32.1
Possible Settings for MSDOS.SYS

Setting	Description
HostWinBootDrv=x	Specifies the drive letter of the root directory from which Windows 98 boots.
WinBootDir=x	Specifies the directory in which Windows 98 is installed. It is usually set to C:\WINDOWS.
WinDir=x	Specifies the directory in which Windows 98 is installed. It is usually set to be the same as WinBootDir.
BootDelay=x	No longer needed in Windows 98, this caused a brief delay when the message "Loading Windows 95" was displayed so that the user could press the F8 key to access the Windows Startup menu.
BootFailSafe=x	When set to 1, causes the system to start in Safe Mode. Set to 0, the system starts normally.
BootGUI=x	Set to 1 (the default), initializes the Windows 98 graphical user interface during startup. Setting it to 0 causes a command prompt version of Windows 98 to be started instead.
BootKeys=x	No longer needed in Windows 98, this setting set to 1 enabled the startup keys (F5, F6, and F8) under Windows 95.
BootMenu=x	When set to 1, automatically displays the Windows Startup menu. Set to 0 the system boots normally.

continues

Table 32.1, Continued
Possible Settings for MSDOS.SYS

Setting	Description
BootMenuDefault=x	Sets the default Windows Startup menu selection if no action is taken by the user for the number of seconds specified in BootMenuDelay.
BootMenuDelay=x	Sets the number of seconds (default is 30) to display the Windows Startup menu before the default startup action is taken.
BootMulti=x	Set to 1, this enables dual-booting with MS-DOS or Windows NT.
BootWarn=x	Set to 1 (the default), this causes the Safe Mode startup warning to appear.
BootWin=x	Set to 1 (the default), this causes Windows 98 to be the primary OS on the machine; setting it to 0 causes MS-DOS (if installed) to be the default.
DblSpace=x	Set to 1 (the default), causes DoubleSpace support to be automatically loaded during startup.
DoubleBuffer=x	Set to 1, this enables double-buffering for any connected SCSI devices. The default is 0.
DrvSpace=x	Set to 1 (the default), this enables the automatic loading of DriveSpace support during startup.
LoadTop=x	Set to 1 (default is 0), causes COMMAND.COM and DRVSPACE.BIN to load at the top of the 640-KB real-mode memory space; this can be required for compatibility with some real-mode network drivers.
Logo=x	Set to 1 (the default), causes the Windows 98 animated splash screen to display while system startup is carried out.
Network=x	If set to 1, enables a Windows Startup menu choice of Safe Mode with Networking. If networking is installed, the default is 1, otherwise it is 0.

CONFIG.SYS

Windows 98 uses a file called IO.SYS for the purpose originally served by CONFIG.SYS, which is to load key device drivers and initialize the most basic parts of the operating system

Chapter 32: Windows 98 Configuration Files

before the command environment is created. CONFIG.SYS still exists in Windows 98, however, for compatibility purposes with older applications. In fact, some older MS-DOS applications could refuse to run if they don't find a particular command present in the CONFIG.SYS file, regardless of whether or not the settings in IO.SYS would satisfy their needs. For most Windows 98 systems, no commands are needed in CONFIG.SYS; all its former purposes should be served by IO.SYS and drivers loaded directly by Windows 98.

When Windows 98 is installed on top of an MS-DOS/Windows 3.x system, the following lines in CONFIG.SYS are automatically deleted, if found:

- IFSHLP.SYS
- FASTOPEN.EXE
- SHARE.EXE or SHARE.COM
- SMARTDRV.SYS or SMARTDRV.EXE

In addition to the preceding, many other lines may be deleted if found, such as those required to support other operating systems, or those used by older applications that might conflict with the smooth operation of Windows 98.

Commands listed in CONFIG.SYS are loaded in the order in which they appear in the file. Table 32.2 details the commands possible in Windows 98's CONFIG.SYS file.

Table 32.2
Possible CONFIG.SYS Commands in Windows 98

Command	Description
BREAK=ON/OFF	Enables or disables extended Ctrl+C or Ctrl+Break checking in MS-DOS virtual machines.
BUFFERS=x	Specifies a number of disk buffers to use for caching file reads and writes for older MS-DOS programs. The Windows 98 default is 30; setting lower values in CONFIG.SYS is ignored.
COUNTRY=x	Used for specifying different country conventions (display of dates, currency symbols, etc.).
DEVICE=x	Loads the real-mode device driver specified by x.
DEVICEHIGH=x	Loads the real-mode device driver specified by x into upper memory.

continues

Table 32.2, Continued
Possible CONFIG.SYS Commands in Windows 98

Command	Description
DOS=HIGH/LOW,UMB	Loads part of MS-DOS into the Upper Memory Area (HMA) if DOS=HIGH is specified. Adding, UMB causes MS-DOS to manage the Upper Memory Blocks (UMBs).
DRIVPARM=x	Sets device driver parameters for drives on the system.
FCBS=x	Creates File Control Blocks for access by some older MS-DOS applications. By default this is set to 4; you must specify a greater number in CONFIG.SYS or this line will be ignored.
FILES=x	Creates file handles for older MS-DOS applications. By default this value is set to 60; you must specify a greater number in CONFIG.SYS or this line will be ignored.
LASTDRIVE=x	Sets the number of drive letters available to MS-DOS programs. By default this value is set to the letter z.
REM	Causes text on the remainder of the line to be ignored; used for including remarks in the file.
SHELL=x	Used to specify the command processor, which is COMMAND.COM by default.
STACKS=x,x	Specifies a quantity and size of stack frames to be created in the MS-DOS virtual machines. The default setting is 9,256.

By using the DEVICE= statement, you can choose to load the following device drivers in CONFIG.SYS if needed; they are still included with Windows 98 for compatibility purposes:

- DISPLAY.SYS
- EMM386.EXE
- HIMEM.SYS
- KEYBOARD.SYS
- CDROMDRV.SYS

You can also choose to load other device drivers that may be required and that you may have from other sources; the preceding list merely represents the CONFIG.SYS drivers included with Windows 98 for compatibility purposes.

AUTOEXEC.BAT

AUTOEXEC.BAT is an MS-DOS batch file executed automatically as Windows 98 boots. Included for compatibility with MS-DOS programs, it is not needed for most Windows 98 systems.

Under previous versions of MS-DOS and Windows 3.x, certain commands were commonly placed in AUTOEXEC.BAT for the startup environment. These settings are now made in IO.SYS and are not needed in AUTOEXEC.BAT, even for MS-DOS virtual machines; however, you can specify changes to modify most of these settings in AUTOEXEC.BAT if needed. The default settings provided by IO.SYS now include the following:

- SET PATH=C:\WINDOWS;C:\WINDOWS\COMMAND
- PROMPT=pg
- SET TMP=C:\WINDOWS\TEMP
- SET TEMP=C:\WINDOWS\TEMP
- SET COMPSPEC=C:\WINDOWS\COMMAND\COMMAND.COM

If you edit AUTOEXEC.BAT under Windows 98, you'll have to observe some precautions to avoid problems:

- Do not load any disk-caching software with the AUTOEXEC.BAT file, including SMARTDRV. This software will conflict with the built-in caching in Windows 98.

- Do not load any mouse drivers in AUTOEXEC.BAT because Windows 98 provides such support.

- If previous versions of Windows are in different directories on the system, make sure to avoid including them in any PATH commands.

- Make sure that C:\WINDOWS and C:\WINDOWS\COMMAND are included in any PATH commands you set.

- The networking drivers and devices are not yet initialized when AUTOEXEC.BAT processes, and so any commands dependent on the network will not work properly. Instead, if you need to execute commands at startup that are network dependent, create a separate batch file and place it in the Windows 98 Startup folder.

WIN.INI and SYSTEM.INI

WIN.INI is an initialization file originally used in the Windows 3.x family of products. Some Win16 applications may still rely on settings in this file, and may still make changes to this file to create the desired behavior under Windows 98. Because of this, WIN.INI is still included with Windows 98 and still functions, although some of the lines used under Windows 98 are removed during installation and instead now exist purely in the Registry.

When you make changes to Windows 98's configuration, those changes are automatically updated into the appropriate INI files (if they're supposed to be listed there). For instance, when you make desktop configuration changes, WIN.INI is updated by Windows 98.

Some common WIN.INI section headings are shown in Table 32.3.

Table 32.3
Common WIN.INI Section Headings

Section Heading	Description
[windows]	Settings load and run programs when Windows starts.
[Desktop]	Settings define graphical configuration of the desktop.
[Intl]	Settings define country-specific configuration information.
[Fonts]	Incremental fonts loaded in the system.
[FontSubstitutes]	TrueType font substitutions for common font families.
[Compatibility]	Configuration changes for compatibility of Win16 applications.
[Compatibility32]	Configuration changes for compatibility of certain Win32 applications.
[mci extensions]	Drivers needed to process multimedia files.
[MCICompatibility]	Compatibility settings for certain multimedia types.
[ModuleCompatibility]	Compatibility settings for certain software modules.
[Extensions]	Settings define which Win16 applications are associated with which file extensions.
[Ports]	Ports and their default settings.
[embedding]	OLE information.
[Devices]	Additional device drivers.
[PrinterPorts]	Printer ports.
[Colors]	System color settings.

Chapter 32: Windows 98 Configuration Files

In addition to WIN.INI, there also exists a file called SYSTEM.INI that behaves similarly, but is oriented toward operating system settings rather than application and desktop settings under Windows. You will generally not need to make manual changes to SYSTEM.INI unless instructed by a support person from Microsoft or an applications vendor. However, a sample SYSTEM.INI is shown in Listing 32.1.

Listing 32.1 A Sample SYSTEM.INI

```
subtype=
type=4
keyboard.dll=
oemansi.bin=

[boot.description]
keyboard.typ=Standard 101/102-Key or Microsoft Natural Keyboard
aspect=100,96,96
display.drv=S3 Vision968 PCI
mouse.drv=Standard mouse
system.drv=Standard PC

[386Enh]
ebios=*ebios
device=*vshare
device=*dynapage
device=*vcd
device=*vpd
device=*int13
mouse=*vmouse, msmouse.vxd
woafont=dosapp.fon
PagingDrive=G:
device=*enable
keyboard=*vkd

[power.drv]

[drivers]
wavemapper=*.drv
MSACM.imaadpcm=*.acm
MSACM.msadpcm=*.acm
wave=mmsystem.dll
midi=mmsystem.dll

[iccvid.drv]

[mciseq.drv]

[mci]
cdaudio=mcicda.drv
sequencer=mciseq.drv
waveaudio=mciwave.drv
```

continues

Listing 32.1 Continued

```
avivideo=mciavi.drv
videodisc=mcipionr.drv
vcr=mcivisca.drv
QTWVideo=C:\WIN95\SYSTEM\MCIQTW.DRV
MPEGVideo=mciqtz.drv

[NonWindowsApp]
TTInitialSizes=4 5 6 7 8 9 10 11 12 13 14 15 16 18 20 22

[vcache]

[NWNP32]

[MSNP32]

[display]

[drivers32]
msacm.msg711=msg711.acm
vidc.CVID=iccvid.dll
VIDC.IV31=ir32_32.dll
VIDC.IV32=ir32_32.dll
vidc.MSVC=msvidc32.dll
VIDC.MRLE=msrle32.dll
MSACM.MSNAUDIO=msnaudio.acm
VIDC.IV50=ir50_32.dll
msacm.lhacm=lhacm.acm
msacm.msg723=msg723.acm
vidc.M263=msh263.drv
vidc.M261=msh261.drv
msacm.l3acm=l3codeca.acm
VIDC.VDOM=vdowave.drv
VIDC.MPG4=msscmc32.dll
vidc.vivo=ivvideo.dll
msacm.vivog723=vivog723.acm
msacm.voxacm119=vdk32119.acm
VIDC.TR20=tr2032.dll
VIDC.UCOD=clrviddd.dll
msacm.l3codec
msacm.iac2=C:\WIN95\SYSTEM\IAC25_32.AX
VIDC.IV41=ir41_32.dll
VIDC.YVU9=iyvu9_32.dll
MSACM.imaadpcm=imaadp32.acm
MSACM.msadpcm=msadp32.acm
MSACM.msgsm610=msgsm32.acm
MSACM.trspch=tssoft32.acm

[Password Lists]
BRUCEH=C:\WIN95\BRUCEH.PWL
BRUCE=C:\WIN95\BRUCE.PWL
```

```
[boot]
system.drv=system.drv
drivers=mmsystem.dll
user.exe=user.exe
gdi.exe=gdi.exe
sound.drv=mmsound.drv
dibeng.drv=dibeng.dll
comm.drv=comm.drv
shell=Explorer.exe
keyboard.drv=keyboard.drv
fonts.fon=vgasys.fon
fixedfon.fon=vgafix.fon
oemfonts.fon=vgaoem.fon
386Grabber=vgafull.3gr
display.drv=pnpdrvr.drv
mouse.drv=mouse.drv
*DisplayFallback=0

[TTFontDimenCache]
0 4=2 4
0 5=3 5
0 6=4 6
0 7=4 7
0 8=5 8
0 9=5 9
0 10=6 10
0 11=7 11
0 12=7 12
0 13=8 13
0 14=8 14
0 15=9 15
0 16=10 16
0 18=11 18
0 20=12 20
0 22=13 22
```

Conclusion

This chapter described the key Windows 98 startup files MSDOS.SYS, IO.SYS, CONFIG.SYS, AUTOEXEC.BAT, WIN.INI, and SYSTEM.INI. These files still play a role in Windows 98, although most of Windows 98's configuration information resides in the Registry files USER.DAT and SYSTEM.DAT. (See Chapter 10, "Mastering the Windows 98 Registry," for a discussion of the Windows 98 Registry.)

For more information on the role of the Registry and the startup files in the boot process, see Chapter 36, "The Windows 98 Boot Process and Emergency Recovery."

Windows Scripting with Windows 98 Scripting Host

This chapter shows you how to use VBScript and the Windows Scripting Host (WSH) to automate administrative and production tasks. Administrative tasks are the little, frequently repeated, but critical configuration or maintenance tasks that are necessary to keep your system healthy. These include tasks such as the following:

- "Patching" the Windows Registry
- Mounting or unmounting network resources
- Performing frequent backups of selected files and directories

- Monitoring boot logs and other tracking information for unexpected changes
- Configuring more efficient desktops for inexperienced users

Production tasks are those operations that are always a part of completing one's work product. These are often trivial, but are repeated so often that they become frustrating time sinks. Alternatively, they can be error-prone, complex sequences of operations. Production tasks include tasks such as the following:

- "Closing the books" and printing financial reports
- Exporting names and addresses from an order-entry system to a word-processing program and performing a mail-merge to prepare pieces for a direct mail promotion
- Zipping a directory, FTPing the contents to a server, and sending email to notify the recipient
- Rearranging your desktop when you switch from one kind of project to another

This chapter shows how you can use WSH and VBScript to automate both administrative and production tasks. I'll introduce WSH scripting through a series of example scripts. Each of these scripts is chosen to illustrate an important scripting technique or an important WSH object. Before attacking the examples, though, I'll give you some background information about VBScript and COM and describe the WSH object model. The background information will help you understand the context in which WSH fits. The WSH object model is the technical foundation you'll need to understand the examples. To help you develop your own scripts, I'll also introduce you to the VBScript Debugger and other tools that make WSH scripting easier. Throughout, though, I'll assume you have some familiarity with VBA or some other dialect of VB. To teach programming (or even Visual Basic) from scratch is far beyond the scope of this chapter.

Background

In part because of the emphasis on user-driven interfaces, prior editions of Windows have not been well suited for production work. Until now, Windows has supplied only one user-oriented tool for automating tasks—the DOS command language. Unfortunately, few applications provide a command-line interface rich enough to allow them to be well controlled from a DOS batch script. While some applications supply a macro language that can support external automation using only the command interface, that solution imposes a heavy learning curve for the average administrator or power user. Stooping to a macro-based implementation for every automation task forces the administrator or user to become expert in every application's user interface and macro syntax. In any but the simplest production environments, that's just not realistic.

Recently Microsoft has pushed two technologies that, combined, address this need. First is the *Common Object Model* (*COM*, formerly known as OLE and sometimes as OLE Automation or just Automation). The COM standard specifies how programs can expose their internal objects to other programs. The second technology is Visual Basic; both standard Visual Basic (VB) and Visual Basic for Applications (VBA). VB is a simple-to-learn language that can manipulate COM objects as if they were an intrinsic part of the language. During the last few years, Microsoft has revised their core applications to expose virtually all their functionality through some COM object and to use VBA as the application's internal macro language. Thus, a programmer can now incorporate an Excel spreadsheet, a Word document, or an Access database and all its functionality directly into a new application, just by referencing the appropriate COM object. Obviously, this is very attractive technology—so attractive that there are now hundreds of thousands of programmers conversant in Visual Basic and the use of various COM objects.

While VB and COM are powerful enough to "script" production and administrative tasks, for several reasons, VB isn't quite the right tool for the job. First, VB programs can't be modified outside the VB development environment. That makes VB impractical for scripting because administrative scripts often need to be modified ad hoc" on the station on which they are being used. It's just not cost effective to put a complete VB development environment on every workstation just so the administrator can make a quick adjustment to some script. For the same reasons, VB is not the right tool for production scripting. Production scripts are most effective when users can make changes. Users should be able to adjust scripts for small changes (like different directory names) without calling on the administrator. Finally, VB isn't the right language because it's too big. VB is geared for producing visual user interfaces. That means the runtime library is laden with large, complex visual objects. It's a waste of overhead to load such a library just to connect a network printer or execute a Word mail merge.

Enter *VBScript*, a VB dialect originally developed for use in web pages. Programs in VBScript are simple text files, so they can be written and modified by anyone with a text editor. Unfortunately, until recently, VBScript could only be executed as part of a web document. Because nearly everyone has a web browser, that wouldn't be a great limitation, but the security needs of a browser and the system-manipulation needs of a scripting language are directly at odds. For a browser to be secure, it should prevent a web page from modifying the file system or launching arbitrary tasks. For a scripting language to be useful, it must allow the script to do just those things and more.

Microsoft has now addressed these VBScript limitations by creating *WSH*, a stand-alone host that can execute VBScript programs directly. Because WSH occupies a minimal footprint and is being distributed free, it is ideal for production and administrative automation. Sites can easily afford to place a copy of WSH on every machine. (WSH is included as part of Windows 98.) Scripting in VBScript is a natural for Windows administrators because most are already familiar with the language features in VBScript, either from writing application macros in VBA or through using VBScript to create web pages. (The following sidebar, "The VBScript Language Model," explains how VBScript differs from VBA.)

The VBScript hosted by WSH is the same language as that used to control the server in Active Server Pages and to control the browser in active web pages. (In fact, WSH, Internet Explorer, and Internet Information Server all use the same language engine—implemented as a separate OLE component—to interpret VBScript programs.) Even so, because WSH supplies a completely different execution environment (a different object model), using VBScript with WSH is substantially different than using it in web pages. Web scripts must manipulate the browser, various document components, and various server-side services. Automation scripts, on the other hand, must be able to manipulate file systems, execute programs, and configure system parameters. The following sidebar introduces the WSH Object Model.

The VBScript Language Model

VBScript is mostly a proper subset of VBA. (VBScript does include a suite of string manipulation and formatting functions that are not in VBA.) VBScript omits those VBA features that involve significant translation overhead (such as strong type checking facilities) or that comprise a security risk (such as file I/O). VBScript does not support the following:

- Types other than variant (in particular, there is no support for user-defined types)
- Many of the more advanced control statements
- Traditional Basic I/O features
- Conditional compilation features

While there are several other small differences (for example, you can't base arrays), these four categories encompass the most significant differences. As you can see from the following discussion, a lot is left out of VBScript; but then, it needs to be small and quick to fit its intended role.

Types and Type Checking

VBScript is almost type ignorant. While you can still declare variables using Dim, you can specify only one type: variant. Everything—variables, object references, arguments—is represented as a variant. VBScript, however, is not a typeless language. Although everything is represented as a variant, VBS is aware of the underlying type and still warns you if a parameter doesn't match the type requirements of a COM interface. Unfortunately, that's about the only time you'll get warned about type mismatches. Oddly enough, even though everything is represented as a variant, type conversions are not automatic. You must still convert strings to integers before you can perform arithmetic on them.

Besides outlawing the intrinsic types, VBScript also outlaws user-defined types. This is not a language for creating complex data structures! In fact, you can't even use TypeOf to determine the type of existing objects. With only one all-purpose data type, it might seem reasonable to construct all data structures from an all-purpose aggregation, such as a collection. Don't count on it. VBScript also omits virtually all the collection manipulation features of VBA. Add, Count, Item, Remove, and ! are all missing. The only operations supported on collections are For Each .... Next, ordinal selection, and selection using a key. (The keys themselves, though, are inaccessible.)

Although it's easy to say that all the type mechanism is gone, it's hard to get used to the implications. If you've been writing large, object-oriented programs, you'll be pretty uncomfortable when you realize that along with Type ... End Type you've also lost New, ParamArray, Property Get, Property Let, and Property Set.

Control Statements

Several VBA control structures have been omitted, but most won't be missed. The most inconvenient changes are the omission of With ... End With and the restriction of Select Case to single-valued cases. Other omissions include Do Events, GoSub ... Return, GoTo, On Error GoTo, On Error ... Resume, Resume, Resume Next, On ... GoSub, On ... GoTo, line numbers, and line labels.

Although this list includes many error-handling structures, the basic error handler, On Error Resume Next, is still present. The Error Method is gone, but the Err object and all of its properties are still available. Thus, you can still write capable error handlers, but you just have to work a little harder to craft the right expression.

Basic File I/O

What can I say? It's gone. All gone. So is the Debug object. Remember, VBScript was designed to use in web documents. Web documents aren't supposed to do file I/O.

A new runtime library for WSH does, however, include objects that allow you to do file I/O. I'll discuss these in more detail in the section on the WSH Object Model.

Conditional Compilation

Again, VBScript just doesn't have any—but then again, why would an interpreted language have support for conditional compilation? All the same, it would be nice to have a manifest constant and a file include capability.

Other Differences

The other differences are relatively few and innocuous (at least for most scripting users). For example, all financial functions have been omitted; as have the Lset and Rset string functions. You can get a complete language specification by downloading vbsdoc.exe from **www.microsoft.com/scripting/vbscript/download/vbsdown.htm**. Despite these omissions, VBScript is still a powerful, highly usable language. If you're wondering what's left, just scan the lists of keywords and functions in the language specification referenced previously. Even with all the omissions, VBScript is still a rich and versatile language.

The WSH Object Model

The *Windows Scripting Host* supplies objects to support parameterized execution, system configuration, network configuration, simple user interactions, and file system operations. The objects that supply these services, however, aren't all independent COM components. Many classes are only accessible through the methods or properties of some larger class. Table 33.1 lists the objects and details their access, methods, and properties.

Table 33.1
WSH/VBScript Objects

Class Name	Access	Methods	Properties
Supplied by Wscript.exe or Cscript.Exe			
Err	Err	Description HelpContext HelpFile Number Source	Clear Raise
Wscript	Wscript	CreateObject Disconnect Object Echo GetObject Quit	Application Arguments FullName Name Path ScriptFullName ScriptName Version
WshArguments	Wscript.Arguments		Item, Count, Length
Supplied by WSHom.Ocx			
WshShell	Wscript. CreateObject ("WshShell")	Environment SpecialFolders	CreateShortcut Expand- Environment- Strings Popup RegDelete RegRead RegWrite Run

Chapter 33: Windows Scripting with Windows 98 Scripting Host

Class Name	Access	Methods	Properties
Supplied by WSHom.Ocx			
WshNetwork	Wscript.CreateObject ("Wscript.Network")	ComputerName UserDomain UserName	AddPrinterConnection EnumNetworkDrives EnumPrinterConnections MapNetworkDrive RemoveNetworkDrive RemovePrinterConnection SetDefaultPrinter
WshCollection	Returned from methods WshNetwork.EnumNetworkDrives or WshNetwork.EnumPrinterConnections	Item Count Length	
WshEnvironment	Returned as property WshShell.Environment	Item Count Length	Remove
WshShortcut	Returned from method WshShell.CreateShortcut	Arguments Description Hotkey IconLocation TargetPath WindowStyle WorkingDirectory	Save
WshSpecialFolders	Returned as property WshShell.SpecialFolders	Item Count Length	
WshURLShortcut	Returned from method WshShell.CreateShortcut	FullName TargetPath	Save

continues

Table 33.1, Continued
WSH/VBScript Objects

Class Name	Access	Methods	Properties
Supplied by SCRRUN.DLL			
Dictionary	Wscript.CreateObject ("Scripting.Dictionary")	CompareMode Count Item Key	Add Exists Items Keys Remove RemoveAll
Drive	Select from Drives collection or as return from method FileSystemObject.GetDrive(drivespec)	AvailableSpace DriveLetter DriveType FileSystem FreeSpace IsReady Path RootFolder SerialNumber ShareName TotalSize VolumeName	
Drives	Collection, available as property FillesystemObject.Drives	Count Item	
File	Select from Files collection or returned from method FileSystemObject.Drive	Attributes DateCreated DateLastAccessed DateLastModified TextStream Name ParentFolder Path ShortName ShortPath Size Type	Copy Delete Move OpenAs- GetFile- (filespec)

Chapter 33: Windows Scripting with Windows 98 Scripting Host

Class Name	Access	Methods	Properties
Supplied by SCRRUN.DLL			
Files	Collection, returned from method FileSystemObject.GetFolder(folderspec)	Count Item	
FileSystemObject	Wscript.CreateObject ("Scripting.FileSystemObject")	Drives	BuildPath CopyFile CopyFolder CreateFolder CreateTextFile DeleteFile DeleteFolder DriveExists FileExists FolderExists GetAbsolutePathName GetBaseName GetDrive GetDriveName GetExtensionName GetFile GetFileName GetFolder GetParentFolderName GetSpecialFolder GetTempName MoveFile MoveFolder OpenTextFile
Folder		Attributes DateCreated DateLastAccessed DateLastModified Drive	Copy Delete Move CreateTextFile

continues

Table 33.1, Continued
WSH/VBScript Objects

Class Name	Access	Methods	Properties

Supplied by SCRRUN.DLL

Class Name	Access	Methods	Properties
		IsRootFolder	
		Name	
		ParentFolder	
		Path	
		ShortName	
		ShortPath	
		Size	
		SubFolders	
Folders		Count	AddFolders
		Item	
TextStream		AtEndOfLine	Close
		AtEndOfStream	Read
		Column	ReadAll
		Line	ReadLine
			Skip
			SkipLine
			Write
			WriteLine
			WriteBlank-Lines

The services provided by WSH objects are partitioned into six top-level objects: Wscript, WshShell, WshNetwork, Err, Scripting.Dictionary, and Scripting.FileSystemObject.

Wscript is the executive module. It supplies the methods to create and release other objects (including all COM components), to identify the running script and access its arguments, and to generate output messages (the Echo method).

WshShell provides primitive user interface capabilities and access to the local system. Through WshShell, you can manipulate environment variables, the desktop, and the Registry. You can get limited input from the user through the WshShell.Popup method.

WshNetwork supplies access to network resources and configuration. Through this object you can manage network drives and printers.

Err is the same object as available in VBA. By testing Err and querying its properties, you can collect information about program errors.

The *Dictionary* object implements an associative array. By using CreateObject, you can create as many dictionary instances as you might need. In most scripting applications, the flexibility and convenience of this object more than compensates for the loss of language support for user-defined types.

Similarly, the *FileSystemObject* compensates for the absence of intrinsic I/O functions. This object provides a rich set of methods and properties to support file and folder manipulation. One of its methods will create a TextStream object—a text file that acts much like traditional DOS or UNIX streams.

The Execution Environment

Microsoft actually supplies two implementations of the scripting host, Wscript and Cscript. *Wscript* is the native windows version of the host. All of the examples in this chapter were developed and tested under Wscript. To launch a script by using Wscript (assuming it has been selected as the default application for .vbs files) you merely double-click on some visual representation of the script file.

Cscript is a command-line-oriented implementation of the scripting host. You could think of Cscript as the native DOS version of the host. To launch a script with Cscript, you must either use Run on the Start menu or execute a command line in a DOS window.

When scripts execute under Cscript, all output generated by Wscript.Echo is redirected to the DOS standard output channel. Under Cscript, using the OpenTextFile method of the file system object, you can even open the console device (CON:) and read from standard input.

Thus, in addition to the WSH object model, a script executing under Cscript has limited access to standard input and standard output. Scripts executing under Wscript do not.

Another minor difference between the two hosts is the ease with which you can specify command-line arguments. Under Cscript, the arguments are simply part of the invoking command. If the script is to execute under Wscript, you have three alternatives:

- Launch the script by typing the command (with arguments) in the Start menu's Run dialog box
- Launch the script from a shortcut that includes the command-line arguments
- Create a .wsh file to specify the execution parameters

The .wsh file is a control file that specifies the execution parameters using an .ini-like format. Using a .wsh file enables you to override (on a script-by-script basis) the default options for the scripting host. The .wsh file also allows you to specify the command line and arguments for the script.

These minor differences make Cscript a more natural fit for scripts that are to communicate with other DOS applications.

Writing Scripts

This section introduces you to some of the basics of scripting in the WSH environment. It isn't meant to be an introduction to Visual Basic. In fact, this section will be most meaningful to those who have already done some VB programming. This section isn't even meant to be a complete reference to the WSH environment, though in some instances I do give the syntax for specific WSH methods.

The goal in the following is to present a sampler—a collection of scripts and script fragments that will give you a feel for what can be accomplished in WSH/VBScript and what's involved in writing working scripts. To make the material accessible to as many as possible, I begin with some very basic topics, like generating output, and proceed to more complex topics. Except for the last program, I have attempted to keep the listings short, straightforward, and limited to a subset of the language—again, to help those who are not experts in Visual Basic get a feel for what's involved.

For full details about the language syntax and semantics and about the public interfaces to the WSH objects, you should see the reference materials listed in the "Scripting Resources" section near the end of this chapter.

Basic I/O

The simplest WSH script is probably the following one-liner:

```
MsgBox "Hello World"
```

This script generates the vbOK-style dialog box in Figure 33.1. As the Visual Basic title bar suggests this program doesn't really use anything special from WSH. In particular, it doesn't use any WSH objects. But, it's important to remember that most of the VBA commands are still available in VBScript.

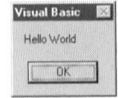

Figure 33.1
This dialog box is generated by the MsgBox command. Note the contents of the title bar.

Although MsgBox is still available, administrative scripts should probably generate their output using the WSH Echo method. An Echo-based version of the Hello World program looks like this:

```
Wscript.Echo "Hello World"
```

Chapter 33: Windows Scripting with Windows 98 Scripting Host

This version uses the Echo method of the WScript object to generate the dialog box shown in Figure 33.2. Note that the Wscript object doesn't need to be instantiated—it's always available to a WSH script.

Figure 33.2
The Echo-based Hello-World script produces this dialog box. Note that the title bar says Windows Scripting Host instead of Visual Basic.

The Echo method also generates a simple vbOK-style dialog box, but the box's title bar reads Windows Scripting Host instead of Visual Basic.

Wscript's Echo method takes any number of arguments, but doesn't really support any variations; you always get a vanilla vbOK-style dialog box that contains a concatenated list of the arguments. Even so, Echo does have advantages over MsgBox. The Echo method aims to be the Windows equivalent of the DOS ECHO command. Microsoft supplies the WSH executive in two different forms: Cscript, the command-line oriented version; and Wscript, the windows version. All output generated by the Echo method is directed to DOS's standard output channel when run under Cscript and to a vbOK dialog box when run under Wscript. Thus, using Wscript.Echo for simple output allows you to interactively test a script in the Windows environment, but then use the production version of the script in a traditional batch environment.

For greater control over the dialog box and for simple input you can use WshShell's Popup method. The Popup method understands most of the standard Visual Basic dialog box styles and returns a value indicating which button the user clicked to close the box. The calling syntax is as follows:

```
WshShell.Popup strText, [natSecondsToWait], [strTitle],[natType])
```

Popup returns an integer indicating which button the user clicked.

Because Popup is a member of the Shell object, programs must instantiate the Shell object by calling Wscript.CreateObject before calling Popup. The following program creates an instance of WshShell and then uses PopUp to collect some information about the user:

```
Option Explicit
Dim objWsh
Dim natIsOld
Set objWsh = Wscript.CreateObject("Wscript.Shell")
natIsMale = objWsh.Popup( "Are you Male?",, _
                 "User Information",vbYesNo)
```

Note the use of Set to save a reference to the object created by the call to CreateObject. If you omit the Set keyword, the following line will generate an Object Doesn't Support this Property or Method error.

The call to Popup creates a dialog box complete with custom title bar (see Figure 33.3). The Popup function then returns either vbYES or vbNO, much like any similar call to VB's MsgBox function.

Figure 33.3

This Popup-generated dialog box has a custom title bar and returns the user's selection as an integer.

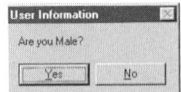

Enumerating the Environment

In addition to Basic I/O, the shell object supplies information about the script and its environment. The program in Listing 33.1 uses the Environment property of the Shell to generate a listing of all current environment strings. The report shown in Figure 33.4 illustrates one of the fundamental differences between Windows 98 and Windows NT. Windows NT partitions its variable space—Windows 98 does not. If this script were run on an NT machine, each section would include some output. This WSH Script reports the contents of all current environment variables.

Listing 33.1   Envex.vbs

```
Option Explicit

Dim strMsg
Dim CRLF
Dim TAB
Dim wshShell
Dim strVar

CRLF = Chr(13) & Chr(10)
TAB = Chr(09)

'Uncomment the following line before debugging
'with the script debugger
'WScript.Echo "Envex waiting for Debugger"


Set wshShell = WScript.CreateObject("WScript.Shell")


StrMsg = "Current Environment Variables (Default):"
For Each strVar in wshShell.Environment
```

Chapter 33: Windows Scripting with Windows 98 Scripting Host

```
            strMsg = strMsg & CRLF & TAB & strVar
Next

StrMsg = StrMsg & CRLF & CRLF & "Current Environment Variables (System):"
For Each strVar in wshShell.Environment("System")
        strMsg = strMsg & CRLF & TAB & strVar
Next

StrMsg = StrMsg & CRLF & CRLF & "Current Environment Variables (User):"
For Each strVar in wshShell.Environment("User")
        strMsg = strMsg & CRLF & TAB & strVar
Next

StrMsg = StrMsg & CRLF & CRLF & "Current Environment Variables (Volatile):"
For Each strVar in wshShell.Environment("Volatile")
        strMsg = strMsg & CRLF & TAB & strVar
Next

StrMsg = StrMsg & CRLF & CRLF & "Current Environment Variables (Process):"
For Each strVar in wshShell.Environment("Process")
        strMsg = strMsg & CRLF & TAB & strVar
Next

WScript.Echo strMsg

WScript.DisconnectObject(wshShell)
WScript.Quit
```

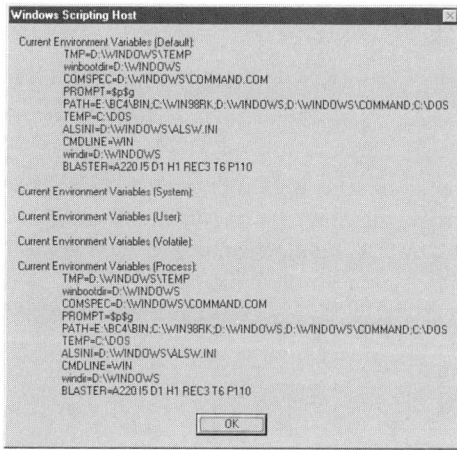

Figure 33.4

The script in Listing 33.1 will always generate a report similar to this when run under Windows 98.

The following loop iterates over each of the strings in the Environment collection—available only as a property of the WSH Shell object:

```
For Each strVar in wshShell.Environment
        strMsg = strMsg & CRLF & TAB & strVar
Next
```

Listing 33.1 was written to report on the environment variables of an NT host, which are partitioned into four separate access spaces. Figure 33.4, however, was generated by running the script on Windows 98, in which the environment variables are all contained in a single name space.

You can use similar code and the Wscript.Arguments collection to generate a list of the command-line arguments passed to a script. Scripts can report singular environment characteristics just by echoing the property. For example, the following will report the filename of the script in which it appears:

```
Wscript.Echo Wscript.ScriptName
```

The following are the last two lines in Listing 33.1, which release the Script's instance of the WSH shell object, and then quit the WSH executive:

```
WScript.DisconnectObject(wshShell)
WScript.Quit
```

These lines aren't required. WSH automatically reduces the reference count to the Shell object and exits after it reaches the end of the script. Windows then frees the resources associated with the Shell object. I've included these lines because I believe it's good programming practice to clean up after yourself.

Using the Network Object

The network object, class WshNetwork, includes properties and methods that allow you to identify and manage network resources. Scripts can acquire their host's network name, the current user's name, and the current domain name by retrieving the appropriate properties from the network object.

Enumerating Resources

The network object also includes methods that return a collection of strings describing current network file and printer resources. These collections are of class WshCollection (an all-purpose container class) and are only accessible by walking the members of the collection.

The following two lines create a network object and use it to instantiate a collection of strings describing the network drives:

```
Set wshNet = WScript.CreateObject("WScript.Network")
set drives = wshNet.EnumNetworkDrives
```

The resulting drives collection is a set of paired strings. The first string in a pair describes the local mapping for the network resource. The second string in a pair is the network path to the same resource. When a network resource has no local mapping, the first string in the pair is a zero-length string. The same convention is used to represent printer resources.

To process these pairs properly, a script must walk the strings in order, keeping track of whether the current string is a drive designator or a path. Listing 33.2 shows how to access

Chapter 33: Windows Scripting with Windows 98 Scripting Host

these collections to produce a report (see Figure 33.5) of currently connected network file and printer resources. Inside of the For Each loop, a Boolean (blnPath) is used to keep track of whether the current string represents a local mapping or a network path. This WSH Script reports all currently connected network resources.

Listing 33.2   Netex.vbs

```
Option Explicit

Dim strMsg
Dim CRLF
Dim TAB
Dim wshNet

CRLF = Chr(13) & Chr(10)
TAB = Chr(09)

Set wshNet = WScript.CreateObject("WScript.Network")

strMsg = "Network Properties:"

strMsg = strMsg & CRLF & "Computer Name " & TAB & wshNet.ComputerName
strMsg = strMsg & CRLF & "User Domain "   & TAB & wshNet.UserDomain
strMsg = strMsg & CRLF & "User Name "     & TAB & wshNet.UserName

strMsg = strMsg & CRLF & "Network Drives"

Dim drives
Dim blnPath
set drives = wshNet.EnumNetworkDrives

blnPath = False
For each id in drives
   if blnPath then
       strMsg = strMsg & id
   else
       strMSG = strMsg & CRLF & TAB &  id & " = "
   end if
   blnPath = NOT blnPath
next

Dim printers, id
set printers = wshNet.EnumPrinterConnections
strMsg = strMsg & CRLF & "Network Printers"

blnPath = False
For each id in printers
   if blnPath then
       strMsg = strMsg & id
   else
       strMSG = strMsg & CRLF & TAB &  id & " = "
   end if
```

continues

Listing 33.2 Continued

```
    blnPath = NOT blnPath
next


WScript.Echo strMsg

WScript.DisconnectObject wshNet
WScript.Quit
```

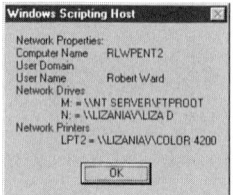

Figure 33.5
The script in Listing 33.2 produces this report of network resources.

While it's useful to know what network resources are connected, it's even more useful to be able to modify those from a script. The next two examples show how to remove and connect network resources from a script.

Disconnecting Resources

Listing 33.3 shows how to use the RemoveNetworkDrive and RemovePrinterConnection methods to drop all network connections. The script produces a dialog box that lists the disconnected resources (see Figure 33.6). The Remove methods have this syntax:

```
WshNetwork.RemoveNetworkDrive strName, [bForce], [bUpdateProfile]
WshNetwork.RemovePrinterConnection strName, [bForce],
                                   [bUpdateProfile]
```

Setting bForce to True will cause the resource to be disconnected even if it is currently in use by someone else. Setting bUpdateProfile to True will cause this mapping to be saved in the user's profile. This WSH Script disconnects all network resources.

Listing 33.3 Netex2.vbs

```
Option Explicit

Dim strMsg
Dim CRLF
Dim TAB
Dim wshNet

CRLF = Chr(13) & Chr(10)
TAB = Chr(09)

Set wshNet = WScript.CreateObject("WScript.Network")
```

Chapter 33: Windows Scripting with Windows 98 Scripting Host

```
Dim drives
Dim count, i
set drives = wshNet.EnumNetworkDrives
count = drives.count

strMsg = "Removing " & count/2 & " Drive Connections"

do while drives.count > 0
   if drives.item(i) <> "" then
      strMsg = strMsg & CRLF & TAB & drives.item(i) & " = " & drives.item(i+1)
      wshNet.RemoveNetworkDrive drives.item(i),1
   else
      if drives.item(i+1) <> "" then
         strMsg = strMsg & CRLF & TAB & " = " & drives.item(i+1)
         wshNet.RemoveNetworkDrive drives.item(i+1),1
      end if
   end if
   set drives = wshNet.EnumNetworkDrives
loop

Dim printers
set printers = wshNet.EnumPrinterConnections
count = printers.count

StrMsg = StrMsg & CRLF & CRLF & "Removing " & count/2 & " Printer Connections"

do while printers.count > 0

   if printers.item(i) <> "" then
      strMsg = strMsg & CRLF & TAB & printers.item(i) & " = " & printers.item(i+1)
      wshNet.RemovePrinterConnection printers.item(i),1
   else
      if printers.item(i+1) <> "" then
         strMsg = strMsg & CRLF & TAB & " = " & printers.item(i+1)
         wshNet.RemovePrinterConnection printers.item(i+1)
      end if
   end if
   set printers = wshNet.EnumPrinterConnections

loop


WScript.Echo strMsg
WScript.DisconnectObject wshNet
WScript.Quit
```

The Remove methods behave differently depending on whether they are called with a local resource designator or with a network path. When called with a local resource identifier, the Remove method will remove the entire resource. That is, the result of the call will be the removal of both local identifier and network path strings from the WshCollection. On the other hand, if called with a network path, both strings will be removed only if there is no local mapping for the resource.

Figure 33.6
The script in Listing 33.3 produces this report before disconnecting all network resources.

Thus the loop in Listing 33.3 invokes the Remove method on the local designator, if there is one, and invokes the Remove method on the network path otherwise. After removing a resource, the loop reinstantiates the network object. I found that if I didn't rebuild the network object, subsequent Removes wouldn't properly index the target string.

Connecting Resources

As promised, Listing 33.4 shows how to connect network resources from a script. This example assumes that the network resources are supplied by two different hosts that each require a different password from the user at the beginning of each session. Some users find such situations very confusing. This script simplifies the logon process by asking the user for each password and then using those passwords to connect to the appropriate resources. This WSH Script prompts the user for two passwords and then connects to resources on two different UNIX hosts.

Listing 33.4 Netex3b.vbs

```
Option Explicit

Dim strMsg
Dim CRLF, TAB
Dim wshNet
Dim strPword, strPword2

CRLF = Chr(13) & Chr(10)
TAB = Chr(09)

Set wshNet = WScript.CreateObject("WScript.Network")

strPword = inputbox("Enter your Department password.", "Department Login")
strPword2 = inputbox("Enter your WebMaster password.", "Web Master Login")
call wshNet.MapNetworkDrive ("M:", "\\DeptHost\Deptdir", ,,strPword)
call wshNet.MapNetworkDrive ("N:", "\\Gateway\WebRoot", ,,strPword2)
call wshNet.AddPrinterConnection ( "LPT2" ,"\\DeptHost\color 4200",,,strPword)

WScript.DisconnectObject wshNet
WScript.Quit
```

This example uses the InputBox function from Visual Basic to retrieve the two passwords (see Figure 33.7). Although InputBox is a convenient tool for getting textual input, it's not ideal

Chapter 33: Windows Scripting with Windows 98 Scripting Host 761

for a password application because it echoes the password to the screen where others can see it. In a production environment, you would use a COM object for this task.

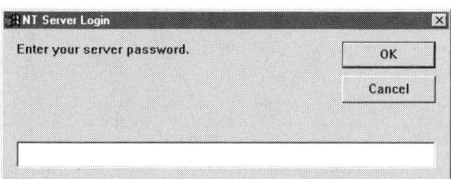

Figure 33.7
The script in Listing 33.4 generates two password dialog boxes similar to this one.

After the password is available, the script calls AddPrinterConnection and MapNetworkDrive to connect the resources. The syntax for these methods is as follows:

```
WshNetwork.AddPrinterConnection strLocalName, _
    strRemoteName, [bUpdateProfile], [strUser], [strPassword]
WshNetwork.MapNetworkDrive strLocalName, _
    strRemoteName, [bUpdateProfile], [strUser], [strPassword]
```

When the bUpdateProfile flag is True, the mapping will be stored in the user's profile.

Sequencing Jobs

Scripting for production tasks is primarily a matter of sequencing tasks or jobs. To handle this task well in the Windows environment, the scripting language must be able to manipulate not only traditional command-line–oriented applications, but also modern, complex COM objects. VBScript is well suited to this challenge.

Invoking Scripts or Programs

Listing 33.5 shows how to use the Shell's Run method to sequence three other scripts. This example uses the network scripts developed earlier to report on currently connected resources, disconnect all resources, and collect reconnect to specific resources. An administrator might use a script such as this to configure someone's workstation at logon. Alternatively, a power user might create a similar script to quickly reconfigure her network resources as she shifts from one task to another. This WSH Script invokes the scripts in Listings 33.2, 33.3, and 33.4 to reconfigure a user's network connections.

Listing 33.5   runex.vbs

```
Option Explicit

Dim strDTopPath
Dim wshShell

Set wshShell = WScript.CreateObject("WScript.Shell")

strDTopPath = wshShell.SpecialFolders("Desktop")
```

continues

Listing 33.5 Continued

```
Call wshShell.Run(strDTopPath & "\netex2.vbs",,True)
Call wshShell.Run(strDTopPath & "\netex3b.vbs",,True)
Call wshShell.Run(strDTopPath & "\netex.vbs",,True)

WScript.DisconnectObject(wshShell)
WScript.Quit
```

This example assumes that the three network scripts reside directly on the desktop. The network scripts can be invoked directly (just as if someone had double-clicked their icons), because the WSH executive can exploit the file associations known to Windows.

The syntax for the Run method is as follows:

```
WshShell.Run strCommand, [intWindowStyle], [bWaitOnReturn]
```

By default, the Run method will spawn the task and return immediately to the script. In this example bWaitOnReturn is set to 1 to force the script to wait for each command to complete before launching the next command.

Manipulating COM Objects

The script in Listing 33.6 illustrates how easily VBScript can manipulate COM objects. This example uses Word to open a file, perform a mail merge, and print the result. You can do the same by using VB or VBA, but with WSH installed, any user can create or modify such a script without needing a full development environment. This Script opens an instance of Word, opens a file, performs a mail merge, and then prints the result.

Listing 33.6 wordex.vbs

```
Option Explicit

Dim objWrd
Dim wrdDoc
Dim objMerge

Set objWrd = WScript.CreateObject("Word.Application")
'objWrd.Visible = True
Set wrdDoc = objWrd.Documents.Open ("d:\My Documents\labels.doc")
set objMerge = objWrd.ActiveDocument.MailMerge
objMerge.Execute
wrdDoc.PrintOut
objWrd.Quit 0
WScript.DisconnectObject objWrd
WScript.Quit
```

As you can see, VBScript makes the connection to the COM object nearly invisible. The challenging part becomes identifying the object, method, or property to perform the desired task. Microsoft's Office components help by recording their macros in VBA. If you need to automate some task involving an Office application, follow this procedure:

1. Open the Microsoft Office application.

2. Choose Macro from the Tools menu and start the macro recorder.

3. Using only keystrokes, perform the operation.

4. Stop the macro recorder.

5. Open the new macro for editing.

When you open the macro for editing, you'll be viewing the VBA code necessary to perform the task without the intervention of a user. This code seldom works directly—it depends too much on decisions made by the user as they position the cursor. The macro code does, however, show you what objects, methods, and properties you need to understand to write the script. Note also that the method and property references in the macro are all relative to the unnamed Office application (for example, the Word.Application object if the macro was recorded in Word). In the WSH/VBScript environment, you must create an explicit reference to the application object and then invoke the appropriate methods as members of that reference. Thus a Word macro might include only the following (or worse, only MailMerge, since the ActiveDocument is the default document):

```
ActiveDocument.MailMerge
```

The VBScript version, however, should look like this:

```
objWrd.ActiveDocument.MailMerge
```

After you have identified the key objects and methods by reviewing the macro, you can find the appropriate syntax in the online Visual Basic reference for that Office component. Word Help is not very friendly here—it doesn't index any of the VBA documentation.

If you have Visual Basic available (which sort of defeats the purpose of using VBScript), you can use VB's object browser to get similar information. Open a project (even an empty new project will do), select the References item from the Project menu, and check the Office component you plan to use. For example, checking the Microsoft Word entry makes the type library for Word.Application available. When the appropriate type library is available you can search quickly and conveniently for all the syntax information about any object, method, property, or intrinsic constant.

An Extended Example

As a final example, I've created a script that swaps different sets of shortcuts to and from the user's desktop. With this utility, when I switch from working on graphics projects to working on financial analyses, I can quickly remove all the graphics-related shortcuts from my desktop and replace them with shortcuts appropriate to financial work. When I'm ready to do some programming, I can remove all the financial clutter and replace it with programming shortcuts.

(Note that the Toolbars in Windows 98 implement virtually the same functionality—the shortcuts are just displayed as buttons or icons in the toolbars rather than as icons on the desktop.)

In addition to being a useful tool, this example demonstrates several WSH features. The script uses the Filesystem object to manipulate folders and files and various WshShell methods to create shortcuts. It reads arguments from its command line and manipulates Excel through the application's COM interface. Finally, unlike the other examples in this chapter, it is large enough to be structured as a collection of subroutines.

Overview

This utility uses an Excel Workbook as a database. Each distinct set of shortcuts (I call these sets "worksets") is stored on a separate sheet of the Excel Workbook. Each worksheet lists the information needed to create the related shortcuts with columns for the shortcut name, the program directory, the program name, and any command-line arguments (see Figure 33.8). The utility uses a special worksheet named XCLEANUPX to keep track of which shortcuts it last wrote to the desktop so that the script can reliably remove only its own postings each time it posts a new set.

The script expects to be called either with a single argument corresponding to the name of a worksheet in the Excel workbook, or with no arguments.

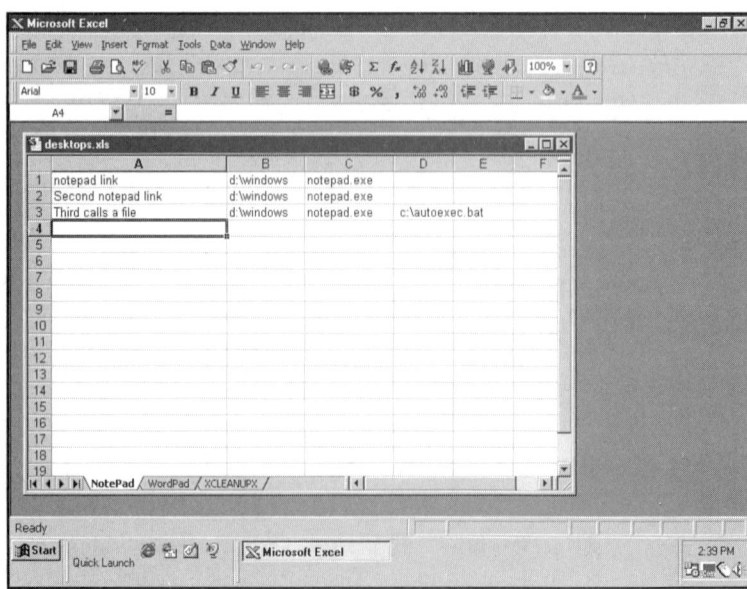

Figure 33.8
This screen capture shows one of the worksheets in the Excel shortcut database. Notice that each sheet tab has been renamed to reflect the workset's name.

Chapter 33: Windows Scripting with Windows 98 Scripting Host

If called with no arguments, the script self-installs by creating a workset folder in the Start menu, creating submenu items for each of the labeled tabs in the Excel workbook, and adding desktop shortcuts for each of the shortcuts listed in the first worksheet (see Figure 33.9). Before creating the new folder, the script checks for an existing folder. It then creates one shortcut in that folder for each of the labeled worksheets in the Excel workbook. Finally, it finds the first worksheet and creates shortcuts (on the desktop) for each line in the worksheet.

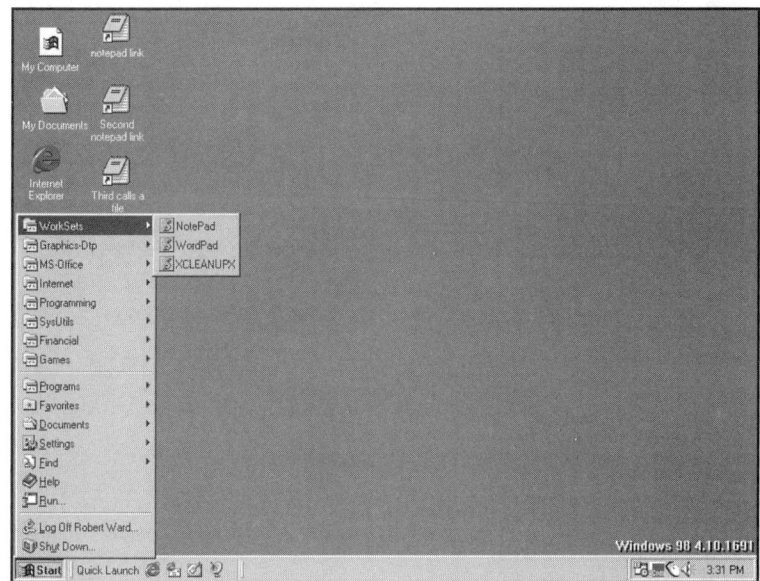

Figure 33.9
The desktop utility installs itself in the Start menu. Note that the shortcuts corresponding to the Notebook worksheet have also been added to the desktop.

Each of these shortcuts invokes the desktop script, passing an argument that specifies which workset is to be installed. (A special argument XCLEANUPX causes Desktop to delete all the shortcuts on the XCLEANUPX page without posting any new shortcuts.)

When invoked with an argument corresponding to the name of a regular worksheet, the Desktop script does the following:

- Deletes all shortcuts listed on the XCLEANUPX sheet
- Clears all entries from the XCLEANUPX sheet
- Adds the list of shortcuts from the worksheet named in the input argument to the desktop
- Copies the named worksheet to the XCLEANUPX sheet (for use during the next swap)

Figure 33.10 shows the results of calling Desktop with the argument wordpad. Note that the three Notepad shortcuts present in Figure 33.9 have been removed and replaced by a single Wordpad shortcut.

Figure 33.10
This screen capture shows how the desktop looks after the Wordpad workset is installed.

The Code

This example makes extensive use of the WshShortcut, the filesystem, and the Excell.Application objects. I'll limit my comments here to the two WSH specific objects.

Creating a Shortcut

The MakeLink subroutine (at the end of Listing 33.7) shows all of the steps necessary to create a shortcut. First, the code creates a shortcut object using the WshShell.CreateShortcut method. Because this method returns an object reference, its return value must be assigned using the Set keyword. This is the code for the Desktop utility.

Listing 33.7   desktop.vbs

```
Option Explicit

Dim strScriptName
Dim strScriptDir
Dim strXlsName
Dim strRemoveName

strScriptName = "desktop.vbs"
strScriptDir = "d:\windows\desktop"
strXlsName = "desktops.xls"
strRemoveName = "OldLinks"
Dim wshShell
```

Chapter 33: Windows Scripting with Windows 98 Scripting Host

```
' Initialize shell and retreive path to desktop
Set wshShell = WScript.CreateObject("WScript.Shell")
'wshShell.Popup "Wait for debug"

Dim DesktopPath
DesktopPath=WshShell.SpecialFolders("Desktop")

' Start an invisible instance of EXCEL
' and open the shortcuts file
Dim objXL
Set objXl = WScript.CreateObject("EXCEL.application")
objXL.Workbooks.Open DesktopPath & "\Desktops"
'objXL.Visible = True

'Initialize an instance of the file system object
Dim fs
Set fs= WScript.CreateObject("Scripting.FileSystemObject")

'If called with no arguments, re-install the virtual desktop
'links in the start menu
'Otherwise, install the set requested by the input argument

Dim wshArgs
Set wshArgs=wscript.arguments

If wshArgs.Count = 0 Then
   Call InstallStartLinks(objXL)
    ' and install the first sheet links as the default
   Call InstallNewLinks(objXL, objXl.Worksheets(1).Name)
Else
   If wshArgs.item(0) = strRemoveName Then
     Call RemoveOldLinks(objXL)
   Else
      If blnArgInSheet(wshArgs.item(0)) Then
        ' this is driven by the OldLinks sheet
        Call RemoveOldLinks(objXL)
        ' this writes a new OldLinks sheet
        Call InstallNewLinks(objXL, wshArgs.item(0))
      End If
   End If
End If

'Done, either because work is done, or because args are wrong
' either way, clean up and quit

objXL.activeWorkbook.Save
objXL.application.quit

' InstallStartLinks creates the Desktops folder, if necessary
' and inserts appropriate shortcuts to this script
```

continues

Listing 33.7 Continued

```
Sub InstallStartLinks(objXL)

   'check for WorkSets folder in Startup Directory
   Dim strStartPath, strWorkPath
   strStartPath = wshShell.SpecialFolders("StartMenu")
   strWorkPath = strStartPath & "\WorkSets"
   if NOT(fs.FolderExists(strWorkPath)) Then
      fs.CreateFolder(strWorkPath)
   end if
   Dim objWs
   Dim strSheetName, strFilePath
   For each objWs in objXL.Worksheets
      objWs.activate
      strSheetName = objWs.Name
      strFilePath=strWorkPath & "\" & strSheetname & ".vbs"
      if NOT (fs.FileExists(strFilePath)) then
         ' build an appropriately named shortcut to this script
         Call MakeLink(strSheetName, strWorkPath, strScriptDir, strScriptName,
➥strSheetName)
      end if
   Next
End Sub

' blnArgInSheet makes certain that a sheet exits with
' a name that matches the requested argument ... just
' in case the script gets called with a bad argument

Function blnArgInSheet(strArgument)
   Dim objWs
   Dim strSheetName
   For each objWs in objXL.Worksheets
      objWs.activate
      strSheetName = objWs.Name
      if strSheetName = strArgument then
         blnArgInSheet = True
         exit function
      end if
   Next
   blnArgInSheet = False
End Function

Sub InstallNewLinks(objXL, strSheetName)

   ' Activate the sheet with the requested set of links
   objXL.Worksheets(strSheetName).Activate
   ' Select the first cell
   objXL.ActiveSheet.Range("A1").Activate

   ' Now loop through the rows until you find a blank
   Dim strShortCutName
```

Chapter 33: Windows Scripting with Windows 98 Scripting Host

```
    Dim strDirectory
    Dim strShortCutPgm
    Dim strShortCutArgs
    Dim NumRows
    NumRows = 0
    Do While objXL.ActiveCell.Value <> ""
       strShortCutName = objXL.ActiveCell.Value
       'reference the next column
       strDirectory =objXL.ActiveCell.Offset(0,1).Value
       'and the next
       strShortCutPgm =objXL.ActiveCell.Offset(0,2).Value
       'and now get arguments if any
       strShortCutArgs = objXL.ActiveCell.Offset(0,3).Value
       Call MakeLink(strShortCutName, DeskTopPath, strDirectory, strShortCutPgm,
➥strShortCutArgs)
       'now step to the next row
       objXL.ActiveCell.Offset(1,0).Activate
       NumRows = NumRows + 1
    Loop
    'Now copy the range to the OldLinks Sheet
    objXL.ActiveSheet.Range("A1:A10").Copy
    objXL.Worksheets(strRemoveName).Activate
    objXL.ActiveSheet.Range("A1").Select
    objXL.ActiveSheet.Paste

End Sub

' RemoveOldLinks deletes the shortcuts most recently
' installed by this script and clears the sheet
' named OldLinks as a side-effect

Sub RemoveOldLinks(objXL)

    ' Activate the sheet with the requested set of links
    objXL.Worksheets(strRemoveName).Activate

    ' Select the first cell
    objXL.ActiveSheet.Range("A1").Activate

    ' Now loop through the rows until you find a blank
    Dim strShortCutName
    Dim strFullPath
    Do While objXL.ActiveCell.Value <> ""
       strShortCutName = objXL.ActiveCell.Value
       objXL.ActiveCell.Value = ""
       strFullPath = DesktopPath & "\" & strShortCutName & ".lnk"
       fs.DeleteFile(strFullPath)
       'now step to the next row
       objXL.ActiveCell.Offset(1,0).Activate
    Loop
End Sub
```

continues

Listing 33.7 Continued

```
Sub MakeLink(strFriendlyName, strLinkPath, strDirectory, strProgram, strArgs)

    Dim Shortcut

    ' Create the link file on the desktop
    Set Shortcut = WSHShell.CreateShortcut(strLinkPath & "\" & strFriendlyName &
➥".lnk")

    ' Set shortcut object properties
    Shortcut.TargetPath = strDirectory & "\" & strProgram
    Shortcut.WorkingDirectory = strDirectory
    Shortcut.WindowStyle = 4
    Shortcut.IconLocation = strDirectory & "\" & strProgram
    If strArgs <> "" Then
        ShortCut.Arguments=strArgs
    End If
    ' Save it
    Shortcut.Save

End Sub
```

After it is instantiated, the shortcut object is initialized by a series of assignments to its various properties. In this instance, the code assumes that the target path and working directory are always the same. In other applications, those paths might be different.

Finally, after the object is initialized, it is saved. The .lnk file is not created until the object is saved.

Using the Filesystem Object

The filesystem object is used to remove shortcut (.lnk) files and to find and create folders. A new filesystem object is instantiated with the following:

```
Set fs=Wscript.CreateObject("Scripting.FileSystemObject")
```

The same filesystem object is used for all references to the file system, so it only needs to be instantiated one time.

The InstallStartLinks subroutine uses the FolderExists method of the file system to check whether a Worksets folder exists in the Start menu. If not, the subroutine immediately creates the Worksets folder using the filesystem object's CreateFolder method. Later in the same routine, the script uses the FileExists method to determine if new links should be installed in the Worksets directory.

The RemoveOldLinks subroutine uses the filesystem object's DeleteFile method to remove shortcut files.

The syntax for these four methods is as follows:

```
ObjFs.FolderExists( folderspec )
ObjFs.CreateFolder( foldername )
ObjFs.FileExists( filespec )
ObjFs.DeleteFile filespec [, force]
```

As you saw from inspecting Table 33.1, these four methods are only a fraction of the methods supported by the filesystem object. This object also supplies all the methods you need to read and write from text files (represented as TextStream objects). For more information about the filesystem object and specifically about using the TextStream object, see the *Microsoft Visual Basic Scripting Edition Language Reference*, available online at **http://www.microsoft.com/scripting/vbscript/download/vbsdown.htm**.

Using the Script Debugger

You can get Microsoft's Script Debugger v. 1.0 free from the Microsoft Scripting site, **http://www.microsoft.com/scripting**. This simple debugger was originally designed to support breakpoint tracing of web-hosted scripts—whether executing in the browser or on the server. It can also be used to trace execution of scripts executing in the WSH environment, although starting a session isn't quite as easy as in the web environment. (More on that later.)

The Script Debugger is very functional despite its simplicity. After it is attached to your running script, the debugger allows you to control execution using the familiar step, step over, and step into commands. An evaluation window (called the *command window*) allows you to probe variables and interactively experiment with troublesome expressions.

If you are accustomed to working with a type-smart debugger and browser such as the one in Visual Studio, you may be a little disappointed with Script Debugger. The Script Debugger is most useful when applied to the logic of your own script. It doesn't have enough type information or formatting flexibility to help in diagnosing interface problems between your script and a COM object, for example. Don't expect to examine pointer values or other low-level structures in the command window. This debugger doesn't understand much beyond VB strings and integers.

Starting a Session

Unlike the debuggers in an integrated development environment, the Script Debugger doesn't automatically have access to the executing source; you must manually attach the debugging process to the script process you want to examine. To attach the debugger you must perform these steps:

   1. Modify the script so that it will pause and wait for user input as soon as it opens.

2. Launch the script.

3. Launch the debugger.

4. If the Running Documents window isn't visible, open it using the View menu.

5. Open the various branches of the Running Documents tree view until you find your script.

6. Double-click on your script. The debugger should load the script file into the source window at this point.

7. From the Debug menu select Break at Next Statement.

8. Click on the dialog (or do whatever else it takes) to make your script resume execution.

The debugger should now take control and halt execution on the first line following the line where your script was waiting.

I like to use the following line to pause the script while I attach the debugger:

```
WScript.Echo "Envex waiting for Debugger"
```

You can comment this line out (as in Listing 33.1) when you aren't debugging and then remove the comment apostrophe when you need to start a debugging session. Figures 33.11 and 33.12 show the debugger being attached to a debug version of Listing 33.1. Figure 33.13 shows the easiest way to examine a variable.

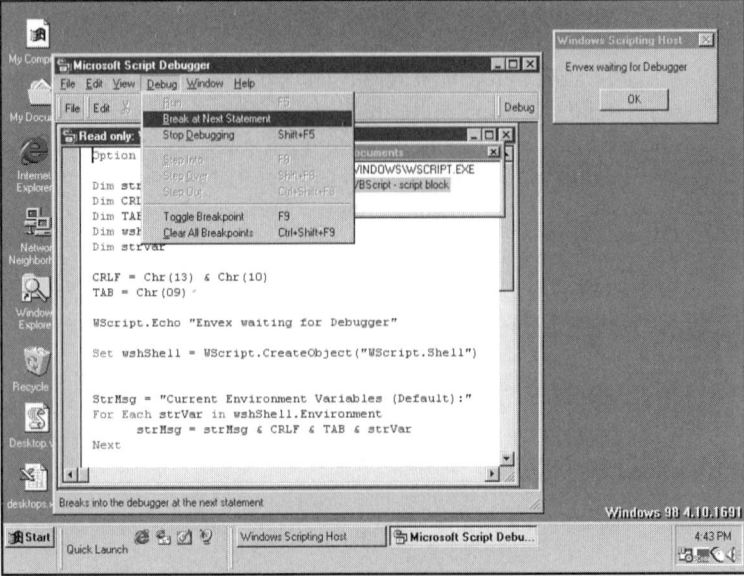

Figure 33.11
In this screen capture, the script under test is waiting for user input, and the debugger is active and configured to break at the next statement.

Chapter 33: Windows Scripting with Windows 98 Scripting Host

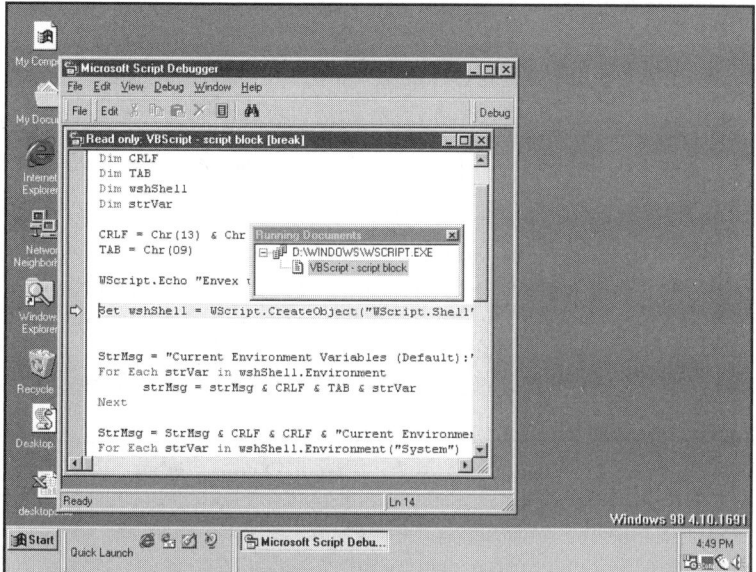

Figure 33.12
At this point, the debugger has full control. The initial dialog box has been dismissed and the debugger has halted the script on the line following the initial call to Echo.

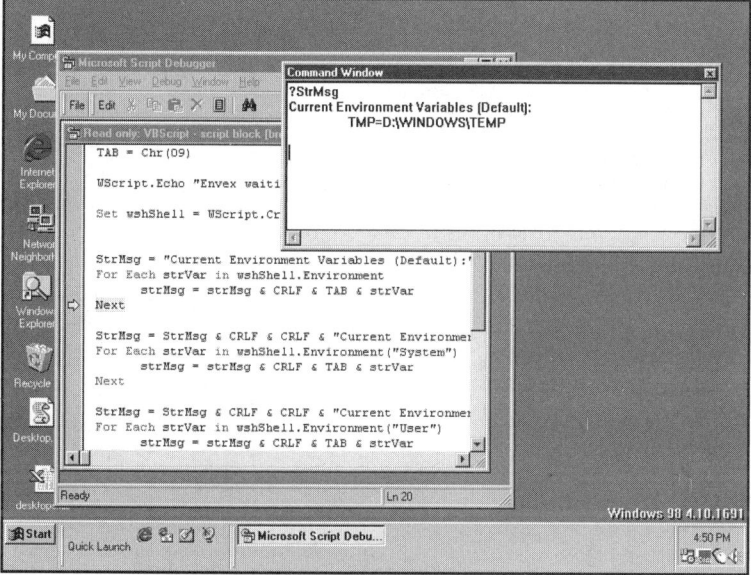

Figure 33.13
Here I have used the debugger to step through the first iteration of the top loop and then printed the current contents of strMsg in the command window.

An Open Architecture

Earlier I mentioned that the VBScript engine was separate from the Windows Scripting Host. This reflects a design decision to separate knowledge about the scripting language from knowledge about how to manipulate the environment. When VBScript is used for client-side web scripting, the environment consists of the resources available in the browser, and the browser is connected directly to the scripting engine (the browser "hosts" the script). When VBScript is used in server-side web scripting, the http server functions as the scripting host.

It is this separation that allows the same language engine to be used in different environments. WSH is just another "container" that knows how to interface with the language engine and that provides certain general services.

One consequence of this design decision is that different language engines can be used with each of the scripting hosts. Microsoft supplies both a Jscript (Java) and VBScript engine with their browsers and with WSH. You can expect to see other language engines available in the future because Microsoft has made public the full specification of the language engine/scripting host interface.

A second consequence is that developers are free to use the language engine and components of the scripting host in their own applications. Thus if you've written an editor, you could add VBScript as your editor's scripting (macro) language by simply embedding Microsoft's scripting control in the application. You must license this technology if you choose to use it, but as of this writing the license "fee" is simply an acknowledgment added to your application's About box.

For more information about this technology, see the ActiveX scripting links on the "Related Links" page at Microsoft's scripting site, described in the next section.

Scripting Resources

The main source for information about VBScript is Microsoft's scripting site at **http://www.microsoft.com/scripting**. Although most of the information at this site assumes you are doing web scripting, it does have links to WSH resources. In particular, you can download the following executable components from this site:

- The Windows Scripting Host (Wscript and Cscript) and runtime library.
- The VBScript Scripting Engine.
- The Script Debugger.
- ACLIST, a handy utility for exploring the ActiveX controls available on your machine. This little utility also makes it much easier to reference ActiveX controls in web pages.

You can also view and download the latest version of these documents:

- A technical paper that describes the WSH object model

- The *Visual Basic Scripting Edition Language and Run-Time Reference*
- Script Debugger documentation

There are several discussion groups devoted to scripting:

- **microsoft.public.scripting.vbscript** covers web-based scripting.
- **microsoft.public.scripting.remote** covers remote scripting.
- **microsoft.public.scripting.debugger** covers use of the Script Debugger.
- **microsoft.public.scripting.hosting** covers issues related to writing your own scripting engine.
- **microsoft.public.scripting.wsh** covers WSH scripting.

Conclusion

The Windows Scripting Host opens a whole new realm of applications to Visual Basic programmers and plugs a significant hole in the Windows environment. Now administrators have a lightweight tool that is powerful enough to address the many configuration and monitoring issues present at any large site. Similarly, users and programmers have a convenient Windows-based tool for creating the little "productivity" scripts that make such a huge difference in the efficiency of any computing-intense work activity.

Because Microsoft has made it easy and inexpensive for other developers to add VBScript to their own applications, one can reasonably expect to see growing support for VBScript as a standard application scripting language.

While this chapter is certainly not the definitive reference for either VBScript or WSH, I hope it has convinced you that WSH/VBScript offers a well-chosen alternative for administrative and production scripting. With these examples and the resources named previously, you should have all you need to begin writing scripts for your own use.

Automating Tasks

Windows 98 provides some important automation features that weren't available in off-the-shelf versions of Windows 95. Scheduling with Task Scheduler means you can run jobs routinely—they are never forgotten or ignored. The Maintenance Wizard helps you configure utilities to keep your computer running smoothly. Also new to Windows 98 is Windows Scripting Host, a robust mechanism designed to help you automate basic desktop functions (see Chapter 33, "Windows Scripting with Windows 98 Scripting Host").

Understanding Task Scheduler

Task Scheduler is a background application that loads each time you start Windows 98. You use Task Scheduler to schedule routine disk-maintenance operations or to schedule any other tasks that you need to run on a recurring basis.

You can access Task Scheduler in the following ways:

- Double-click the Task Scheduler icon in the Notification Area of the taskbar.
- Open My Computer. Choose the Scheduled Tasks folder.
- Click the Start button, and then click **P**rograms, Accessories, System Tools, Scheduled Tasks.

During installation, Windows 98 creates three scheduled tasks for you, as shown in Figure 34.1.

Figure 34.1
Windows 98 automatically sets up ScanDisk, Defragmenter, and Disk Cleanup scheduled tasks.

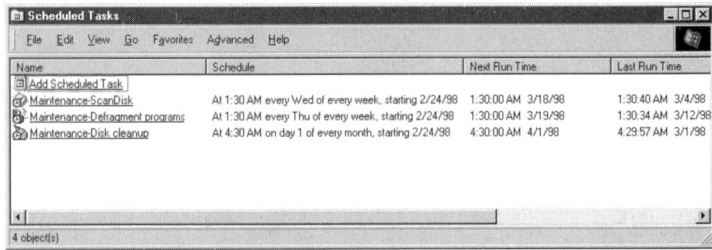

Before you set up your own scheduled tasks, it is important to understand the concept behind Task Scheduler. Task Scheduler can launch only program files, data files from registered application programs, or script programs. Think of Task Scheduler as an automatic way of using the Windows Run Command dialog box at a prearranged time. Table 34.1 is a list of the supported files types.

Table 34.1
Task Scheduler File Types

File Type Description	General Description
Executable files	File extensions .com and .exe. Command line switches are allowed.
DOS batch files	File extension .bat.
Windows application files	Any Windows program data file with a registered file type extension.
Windows Scripting Host	File extensions .js and .vbs.

Scheduled tasks are inserted into the Task Scheduler application where you carry out all scheduling and task-modification functions. From the Task Scheduler, you will be able to:

- Check the status of a running task
- Modify runtime properties of a task
- Check the log file of a task
- End a running task
- Add new tasks
- Delete tasks

Automating Tasks with the Task Scheduler

By scheduling tasks to run on a regular basis, your productivity will improve. Think about the routines you perform manually in Windows. Is there an icon you click regularly to generate a report? Do you open a spreadsheet at the same time every day? Maybe you use a zip disk to back up files on your hard disk every day. Here are some examples of the types of tasks you can schedule:

- Open documents or spreadsheets on certain days of the week, or every month.
- Run applications off-hours that use macros or print reports.
- Run batch files.
- Map a network drive during nonpeak periods to copy a file to your computer.

Note Task Scheduler is an updated version of the Microsoft Plus! System Agent. All System Agent scheduled events present on your system were automatically converted to Task Scheduler during the Windows 98 installation routine.

Using the Scheduled Task Wizard

You add all tasks and set all basic properties of a task through the Scheduled Task Wizard. The Scheduled Task Wizard uses a step-by-step approach to walk you through scheduling tasks and setting all the runtime properties necessary for tasks to execute.

To add a new task to Task Scheduler, double-click the Task Scheduler icon in the Notification Area of the taskbar. Click the Add Scheduled Task icon to launch the Scheduled Task Wizard program, as shown in Figure 34.2.

Figure 34.2
Add a scheduled task with the Scheduled Task Wizard.

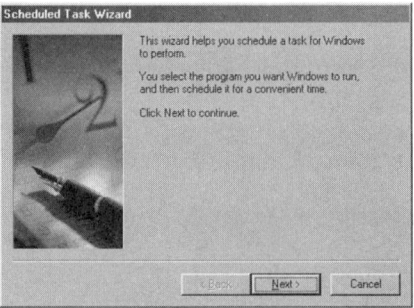

Click **N**ext to continue. The Wizard presents a list of registered Windows application programs found on your PC, as shown in Figure 34.3. By default, all registered applications appear in the program selection box. Select the program you want to schedule. Click the B**r**owse button to search your hard disk for other applications not found in the program selection box, such as DOS programs or batch files.

Figure 34.3
Select the program you want to schedule.

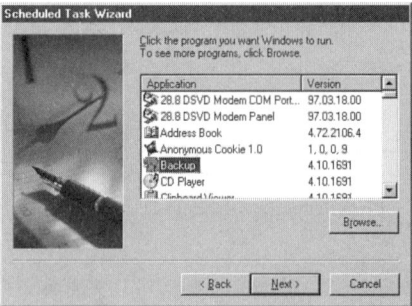

Click **N**ext. Accept the default task name or replace the name of the task with a more friendly name that describes the program to be used or the task to be scheduled, if you want to. From the Perform this task list, choose an interval (frequency) or event from which to trigger the execution of the task, as shown in Figure 34.4.

Figure 34.4
Name the scheduled task and specify an interval or event.

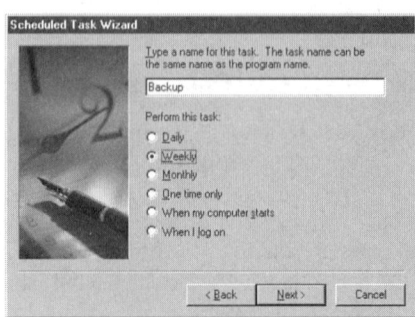

Depending on the interval or event you have chosen for your task, you will be presented with a different dialog box for each setting. The available choices are shown in Table 34.2.

Table 34.2
Scheduled Task Intervals and Events

Task Interval	Interval Options	Values	Start Options
Daily	Every day	Date	
	Weekdays Only		
		Number of days between runs	1–365
Weekly	Every number of weeks		1–52
	Days of the week	Mon.–Sun.	
Monthly	Day of the month		1–31
	1st, 2nd, 3rd, 4th, or last day	Mon.–Sun.	
One Time			None
System Startup			None
Logon			None

Choose an interval or event. Click **N**ext. The Scheduled Task Wizard tells you that your task has been successfully scheduled, as shown in Figure 34.5.

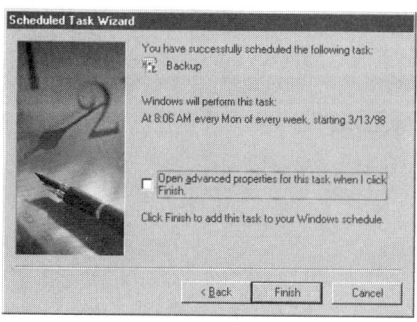

Figure 34.5

The scheduled task is ready to be entered in your Windows schedule.

Enable the **A**dvanced properties check box if you want to further customize settings at the conclusion of the Wizard. These advanced properties are optional. To view the advanced properties later, right-click a Scheduled Task, and then choose P**r**operties.

Click Finish to end the Scheduled Task Wizard. Your new scheduled task now appears in the Scheduled Tasks window, as shown in Figure 34.6.

Figure 34.6
The Scheduled Task Wizard has added the new task to your Windows schedule.

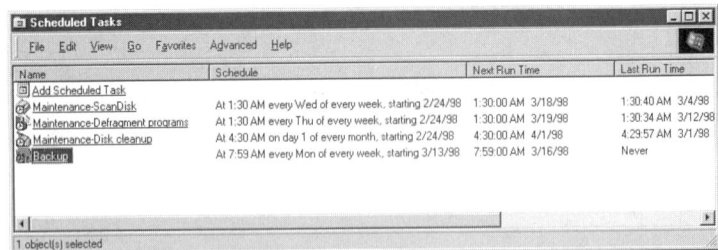

Deleting and Modifying Tasks

Each task in Task Scheduler can be modified or deleted. Right-click a task and choose P**r**operties to modify its settings, or choose **D**elete to remove the task from the Scheduled Tasks window.

You can easily modify the settings or properties of a scheduled task.

| Tip | To run a task immediately, right-click the task and choose Run. |

Task Scheduler Advanced Options

The Task Wizard enables you to set job intervals to run as frequently as every day. As shown in Table 34.3, you can use the Task Scheduler Advanced properties to schedule down to the minute. The Optional settings enable you to configure Task Scheduler to perform a post-task deletion, run a task only when the computer is idle, or enable power-management options.

Table 34.3
Task Scheduler Advanced and Optional Settings

Advanced Schedule Options	Optional Settings
Start and End Date	Task Completed Options
Repeat Task Options	Idle Time Settings
Stop Time	Power Management Options

Advanced schedule properties are not set through the Task Wizard. Rather, you right-click a scheduled task, choose P**r**operties, and then select the Schedule tab. Then click the Ad**v**anced button. Using the Advanced Schedule Options dialog box, tailor the options to meet your task's requirements, as shown in Figure 34.7.

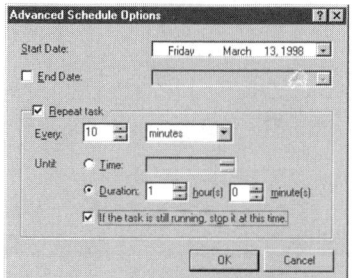

Figure 34.7

Set advanced schedule options to meet your requirements.

Tip Tasks are stored on your hard disk in the `C:\Windows\Tasks` folder. This is a special Windows system folder. To view the contents of this folder, use Windows Explorer or navigate to the folder from the MS-DOS command prompt. A task is assigned a .job file extension. To edit a task from Windows Explorer, right-click the task and then choose P**r**operties.

From the Advanced Properties tab, you can specify the following optional settings:

- Start date
- End date
- Repeat interval (minutes or hours)
- Repeat Task duration (hours and minutes)
- Running Task Stop Time

You can set the Scheduler to repeat a task by the minute or by the hour for any duration. Or you can repeat a task until a specified time. After the end time is reached, you can elect to terminate the task.

Advanced Options are used to set the scheduler to stop a job before a particularly resource-intensive task starts. For example, you can make sure that ScanDisk or Defragmenter stops before you start Disk Cleanup.

Click on a scheduled task's P**r**operties Settings tab to control task completion and idle time, and to enable power-management features as follows:

- **Scheduled Task Completed.** Choose to delete the task after it runs. You can also tell the scheduler to shut down the task after a certain number of hours. This is useful if you've scheduled a job to run over a weekend and the job becomes idle for some reason.

- **Idle Time.** Tell the Scheduler to run the task only after your computer has been idle a certain number of minutes. Another option is to stop the task if the computer is in use. This is a good option for maintenance utilities such as ScanDisk and Defragment.

- **Power Management.** You can prohibit tasks from running if you are on battery, or stop them if battery mode begins. Also, you can tell Scheduler to wake the computer to run the task.

Task Scheduler Limitations

You will undoubtedly find ways to schedule multiple jobs to suit your needs. In that regard, Task Scheduler helps you become more efficient and more productive. Task Scheduler only runs programs, however; it does not interact with them. After Task Scheduler launches your application, its job is finished.

If, for example, your application must display a dialog box because user intervention is required (a choice or selection must be made), the program will halt. Task Scheduler is not a macro-like program designed to supply keystrokes or enter other information.

It might be possible to use a third-party batch or macro language program to create the necessary steps to activate a program, and then step through the required commands, or you might be able to use the new Windows Scripting Host feature to execute a custom script (see Chapter 33). This macro or batch program could then be entered as a scheduled task.

> **Note** An application waiting for a response will sit indefinitely unless you set the scheduler option to terminate the job after a specified period of time.

Scheduling Tune-Ups with the Maintenance Wizard

Think of the Maintenance Wizard as an office manager. Someone who must schedule and coordinate clerks to organize the files, make sure the custodial service empties the trash, and periodically send someone to inspect the building's foundation for any sign of weakness. The Maintenance Wizard consists of the three components shown in Table 34.4.

Chapter 34: Automating Tasks

Table 34.4
Maintenance Wizard Utilities Programs

Name	Description
Disk Defragmenter	Logically organizes files and folders on your hard disk for faster access
Scandisk	Checks your hard disk for file system problems
Disk Cleanup	Deletes unnecessary files on your hard disk

These maintenance utilities have already been set up in your Scheduler Tasks folder as part of the Windows 98 installation routine. You can start the Maintenance Wizard at any time, however, to collectively run the maintenance programs or to modify program settings. To start the Maintenance Wizard, use either of the following methods:

- Click Start, and then choose **R**un. In the Open text box, type **tuneup**, and then press Enter.

- Click Start, and then choose **P**rograms, Accessories, System Tools, Maintenance Wizard.

The Maintenance Wizard dialog box opens, as shown in Figure 34.8.

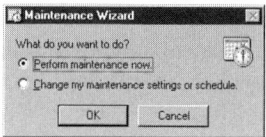

Figure 34.8
Perform maintenance now or change the settings or schedule.

Tip You can edit each maintenance task manually from the Task Scheduler folder.

You are presented with two options—either perform maintenance now or change your settings or schedule. To tune your system now, enable the **P**erform Maintenance Now radio button and then click OK. To customize the way the Maintenance Wizard functions, or to change settings and schedules, enable the Change My Maintenance Settings or Schedule radio button and then click OK.

The most complete way to schedule maintenance is to select the Custom option. If you choose this route, you will have to make a number of choices about the way your computer will be optimized. The following choices are available:

- When do you want Windows to run maintenance?

- Which programs, if any, do you want to eliminate from Windows Startup? Windows will start up faster if no programs load from the Windows Startup folder.

- Do you want to enable Disk Defragmenter?

- Do you run a Standard or Thorough ScanDisk test?

- Should ScanDisk automatically fix errors?

- Which types of unnecessary files should be deleted during Disk Cleanup?

Now that the jobs are scheduled on a regular basis, a certain amount of planning might be necessary. Depending on the size and number of hard disks and the other jobs you have running, if you were to run a thorough ScanDisk every night, you should probably make sure that it doesn't conflict with other tasks. You also wouldn't want it to interrupt you when you are working at your computer.

Maintenance Wizard and Improved System Performance

Any solid disk-management program for your computer should include backing up files regularly, running ScanDisk to check the integrity of your disk(s), and using Defrag to keep the files on disk in order. The key is to run these tasks on a regular basis. Chances are, on most computers without scheduling, these tasks are not done as regularly as they should be. Another facet of good disk management is to be sure to delete temporary files and any leftover files from setup applications. With the exception of a backup, the Maintenance Wizard schedules all these system activities as regularly as you need.

See Chapter 35, "Tools and Strategies for Optimizing Windows 98," for more information about ScanDisk and Defrag. See Chapter 20, "Backup and Restore," for a discussion of Windows 98 Backup.

The Windows Scripting Host

Windows Scripting Host (WSH) is a language-independent scripting host for Microsoft 32-bit Windows platforms. Thanks to this powerful Windows scripting feature, Windows 98 can execute custom scripts that perform complex tasks within the Windows environment. Windows scripting greatly expands the range and complexity of automatable tasks. You create a script that executes a complex operation within Windows, and then configure the Task Scheduler to execute that script at some regular interval. See Chapter 33, "Windows Scripting with Windows 98 Scripting Host," for more information about the types of scripts you can automate by using Windows Scripting Host.

Note Windows 98 ships with 11 sample scripts. During installation these scripts are installed in the `C:\Windows\Samples\Wsh` folder.

Conclusion

Windows 98's Task Scheduler automatically launches applications and performs routine maintenance tasks. The Task Scheduler is somewhat limited in that it won't let you preconfigure responses to input requests. You can, however, perform complex operations through the Task Scheduler by using Windows scripts and batch files.

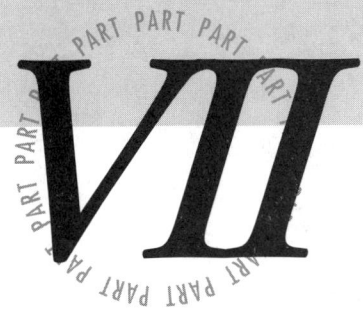

Troubleshooting and Optimizing Windows 98

35 Tools and Strategies for Optimizing Windows 98 791

36 The Windows 98 Boot Process and Emergency Recovery 819

37 Tools and Strategies for Troubleshooting Windows 98 835

CHAPTER 35

Tools and Strategies for Optimizing Windows 98

Solving thorny performance problems is one of the most rewarding—and sometimes frustrating—things you can do with computers. It's like solving a puzzle; sometimes you find an easy solution that makes the puzzle come together quickly, while other times it requires a lot more effort to solve. Performance problems are a lot like this. Improving the performance of a system or its applications requires patience, a keen understanding of how the system works, and a strong approach to problem solving. In this chapter, you learn how to identify and resolve performance problems under Windows 98. You'll learn about various types of performance problems, and you'll also learn about using all of the available performance-measuring and tuning features of Windows 98.

Tip — To get the most out of this chapter, start with a strong understanding of Windows 98's architecture. You should review Chapter 11, "Windows 98 Architecture and Application Support," before reading this chapter because this chapter assumes that the concepts and information in Chapter 11 are already well understood.

Understanding Performance Problems and Bottlenecks

What exactly is a performance problem? It's simple: Anytime you find that you want or need more performance from an application, you have a performance problem. Sometimes the application and system are already running as fast as they possibly can, in which case a faster computer may be required. Often, however, you can make significant improvements in performance through configuration changes to a computer or the operating system, or by upgrading a single component of the computer. Identifying the limiting factor in a performance problem is the first step to resolving it.

A *bottleneck* occurs when there is a single point in the system that is restricting performance, much like a four-lane highway that narrows briefly down to two lanes; all the traffic up to the bottleneck is restricted to the speed of the bottleneck area. It's sort of like the old saying: A chain is only as strong as its weakest link. You fix bottlenecks by identifying them and removing or resolving them. First, however, you have to find them, and that's one area in which a lot of knowledge, testing work, and experimentation (plus some luck!) comes into play. Performance-tuning work is often called a "black art," because being successful at it seemingly requires deals with the devil. It can truly be a tricky area to master.

Understanding TOTE Methodology

Sometimes you can resolve a performance problem quickly and easily. Perhaps it's a problem you've seen before, or perhaps the solution falls readily to hand. More often, however, you need to proceed in a stepwise fashion, carefully working through the problem. The best approach to take involves a methodology called *TOTE*, which stands for Test-Operate-Test-Exit. You initially test the problem to characterize it and ensure that it's repeatable and measurable. You then make a single change to the system that you think may resolve the problem (Operate). After that, you test to see if the change solved the problem. If so, you're done (Exit). If you didn't solve the problem, you loop back to the Operate step to try again, and maybe reverse the last change you made if it didn't make any difference.

For all but the simplest performance problems, it's vital that you proceed carefully. There are a number of hazards that you need to avoid, including the following:

- If you make more than one change at a time in the Operate phase, you risk not knowing what change actually solved the problem (and some of the changes may have negative long-term consequences). And if you've worsened performance, you won't know which of the changes caused the additional slowdown. It's important to change one thing at a time, and then test the results of that change—otherwise, you won't learn very much about solving the problem in the future.

- You must be able to accurately and repeatedly test the condition you're trying to solve. If your testing method isn't accurate or repeatable enough, you run the risk of not knowing whether each change you make actually makes a difference, and you could lose the ability to see small improvements, thinking that they're simply random variations. It's crucial that you have an accurate and repeatable test for the Test phases.

- As the old saying goes, "If you don't know where you're going, you just may get there." The problem, of course, is that you won't know where "there" is. You need to know what your Exit criteria are—when is the problem solved? This requires assessing the situation, the costs resulting from the performance problem (and balancing them against the cost of the performance troubleshooting work you do), so that you can know when to invoke the Exit phase of the TOTE methodology. Like it or not, sometimes you have to throw in the towel when it becomes unprofitable to proceed further.

It's also important to look first for non-performance-related changes that you might be able to make that could solve the problem. Not every performance problem is solved by making a computer operate faster. Sometimes you can change the procedure that a user follows so that the performance problem no longer exists, in that it's not important anymore. When assessing a situation that seems to involve a performance problem, first ask yourself if there is a non-technical way to solve the problem. There often is, and sometimes nontechnical solutions yield much larger payoffs for everyone involved, and they're sometimes much easier and less expensive to implement.

General Performance Improvements for Windows 98

At some point, a user may come to you with what appears to be a thorny performance problem, and you undertake Herculean efforts to solve it, only to discover after spending a lot of time that the problem was something very simple, like a fragmented hard disk. Don't overlook the obvious! It's usually a good idea when doing performance work to first make all of the general performance improvements you know about; these efforts might solve the problem easily and quickly. Many of these tasks are things that you can do to any system, almost falling under the category of general maintenance. These tasks, however, can often reveal or solve seemingly huge performance problems. In the following sections, all of the general performance tests and optimizations you can perform under Windows 98 are discussed, along with specific tips for improving Windows 98 performance in a number of areas.

Memory Optimization

One of the first things to look at is how the physical RAM in the system is working. Extremely common performance problems arise from inadequate RAM for the demands being placed on the system. This is closely related to virtual memory optimization, discussed in the next section.

Memory problems can be caused by the following:

- There could be inadequate RAM for the demands being placed on the system.

- Crashed applications can still consume system RAM, causing inadequate RAM.

- Applications might not be freeing up memory resources appropriately (called *memory leaks*).

- Windows 98 maintains three key shared memory resources: System, User, and GDI. These resources can fall to dangerous levels, causing unpredictable behavior on the system.

- Some applications cause excessive memory fragmentation over time.

To determine if there's inadequate RAM, you can use Windows 98's System Monitor to look at available memory and swap file utilization. Compare Allocated Memory to the amount of RAM in the system. If the Allocated Memory counter in System Monitor is significantly higher than the amount of installed RAM (look for a 2:1 or 3:1 ratio of allocated:installed RAM), then you need to improve the RAM situation. You can run fewer programs, remove unneeded applications or system services, or add more RAM to the system. You generally don't want Allocated Memory to exceed double the amount of installed memory.

To examine shared memory resource utilization, run the Windows 98 Resource Meter, which displays a percentage utilization for each of the three key shared memory resources in Windows 98. If any of these fall below 15%, you can have problems with the system's behavior, including performance problems. When this happens, restart the system and immediately run Resource Meter, and refer to it as you perform the tasks leading up to the performance problem. Once you've identified which step or program is causing the resource levels to fall precipitously, you can look for alternatives that make fewer demands on the shared resources.

If you think the cause is a previously crashed application, restart the system and use System Monitor to see if the available memory levels are significantly improved when the steps leading up to the performance problem are duplicated.

> **Tip** Unfortunately, software bugs can cause unpredictable, seemingly random behavior on a system. Over time, these problems can accrue and can cause performance problems, even when the system otherwise appears to be running well. The first order of business when addressing any performance complaint is

> to do a complete restart of the computer in question. If nothing else, the restart ensures that you're working with a clean slate before you spend a lot of time working on a problem. Memory-related performance problems, in particular, often are resolved with a clean restart of a system.

Virtual Memory Optimization

The most common way that inadequate RAM expresses itself is through excessive use of the paging file. The performance danger is a condition known as *thrashing*, in which the running applications require more system memory than there is RAM, and so memory pages are furiously paged back and forth from the system paging file to try to meet all the demands. When this happens, virtually every memory access by an application requires that a memory page be brought back into RAM from the paging file (and some pages moved back to the paging file), which causes extreme performance problems. Thrashing is the biggest performance-killer you can have!

Sometimes a lot of disk access by an application can cause what appears to be thrashing, when it is really just a lot of normal disk reads and writes. Before concluding that a system is thrashing, you need to look at some performance information. Using System Monitor, examine the counters for Page-Ins and Page-Outs, which indicate the number of pages being paged in and out of the swap file. If these numbers are relatively low and are more "bursty" than steady, then the problem may not be thrashing. You can also compare Page-Ins and Page-Outs with Disk Reads and Disk Writes to see what percentage of disk activity is due to application file reads and writes versus page file activity.

Note The terms *page file* and *swap file* are synonymous in Windows 98, and you will often see these terms used interchangeably. This is technically incorrect: Windows 98 uses paging and a page file exclusively and does not perform *swapping* or use a swap file. The terms *swapping* and *swap file* are actually holdovers from Windows 3.1, which used swapping of 64KB pieces of memory for its virtual memory rather than the paging of 4KB pages of memory that Windows 98 actually uses.

There are only a few ways to deal with thrashing when it occurs:

- Increase the amount of RAM in the system to eliminate the cause of thrashing.

- Reduce the amount of RAM needed by reconfiguring the applications, removing unneeded system services (such as network protocols that aren't being used), or running fewer applications at a time.

- Try to optimize the paging file's activity.

To optimize a paging file's settings, use the Performance tab of the System Control Panel and click the **V**irtual Memory button. This activates the Virtual Memory dialog box shown in Figure 35.1.

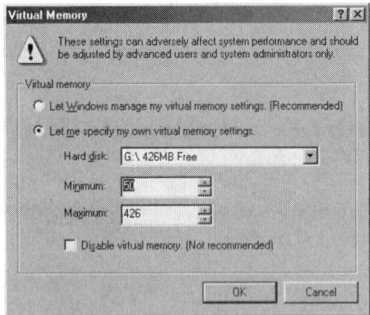

Figure 35.1
You can optimize the system's virtual memory settings with the Virtual Memory dialog box.

To optimize the settings for virtual memory, use these tips:

- Relocate the virtual memory file to the *most active* partition of the *least active* physical disk. You choose the least active physical disk to ensure that the disk heads on the disk are free to work with the paging file, and you choose the most active partition on that disk to ensure that the disk heads are most often in the general vicinity (partition) of the physical location of the swap file.

- Make sure that the swap file location isn't conflicting with the location where an application is reading and writing files. To optimize a system for a particular application, the ideal situation is to have Windows itself on its own disk drive, the application and its data files on their own disk drive, and the paging file on its own disk drive. If you have only two disks, locate Windows and the paging file on one disk, and the application and its data on the second disk. If you have one hard disk partitioned into many partitions, you'll probably have the best luck with Windows, its paging file, and the application and its data files all on a single partition.

- Periodically check System Monitor to see how large the Swap File In Use counter reads. Set the Mi**n**imum setting on the Virtual Memory dialog box to be equal to or greater than the largest Swap File In Use size you've seen. This ensures that the system never has to waste time increasing the size of the paging file as system demands increase.

- While not a performance-improving setting, make absolutely sure that the Ma**x**imum setting in the Virtual Memory dialog box leaves adequate room for the heaviest-possible virtual memory needs.

- If you relocate the paging file to another disk, make sure you completely defragment the disk before relocating the paging file; this ensures that the resulting paging file is as defragmented as possible when it is created.

File System Optimization

Windows 98 can use one of two file systems: FAT16 or FAT32. In certain situations, FAT32 performs better than FAT16, depending on the partitioning of the hard disks and their performance characteristics. Included in Windows 98 is a tool that lets you easily upgrade a FAT16 file system to FAT32. However, keep in mind that as of the time of this writing, Windows NT does not support the FAT32 file system, and so a computer dual-booting both Windows NT and Windows 98 is not able to see or work with FAT32 partitions when running Windows NT. Also for this reason, you cannot upgrade the primary boot partition to FAT32 if you want to dual-boot Windows NT.

Because of the way that FAT (both FAT16 and FAT32) allocates space on hard disks, over time files may become fragmented, where a single file will have its contents spread over many different, noncontiguous areas of the physical disk. You can perform a defragmentation to periodically relocate all of the files on a disk so that they are contiguous, which improves performance.

To defragment a disk, right-click on the disk in Explorer or My Computer and choose Properties. Move to the Tools tab and click the **D**efragment Now button. Defragmentation proceeds immediately. On large disks with many discontiguous files, defragmentation may take 20 minutes or more to complete. It's a good idea to train your users how to do this, so that they can periodically run this process. You can also use the Scheduled Tasks feature of Windows 98 to schedule automatic periodic defragmentations.

File system performance problems are sometimes caused by errors in the file system. Cross-linked files, lost clusters, and even marginal areas of the disk can cause the system to operate more slowly than expected. It's a good idea to do a full test of the disk before proceeding with detailed performance work. From the Tools tab of the disk properties dialog box, click **C**heck Now to start ScanDisk, and make sure you click the **T**horough button to perform a complete surface test with ScanDisk.

Generally, compressing a hard disk drive with DriveSpace causes reduced system speed, because the system must compress and decompress data written to and read from the disk for every disk read and write. However, some applications may actually perform faster on a compressed drive. If you consider a disk-bound application (meaning disk performance is the bottleneck) that uses very large, very compressible files, then the added overhead of the disk compression may be more than offset by having to read and write fewer actual bytes to the disk. For example, consider an application that reads and writes to a 50MB file that largely has repeated data in it. If the application reads 1MB of data at a time, and with compression that 1MB of data actually takes only 100KB on the compressed drive, then the system has to transfer only the smaller amount from and to the disk. On computers that have very fast processors but very slow disk drives, disk compression can help the applications to run faster because of the reduced need to transfer data to and from the drive. Unfortunately, you simply have to test this if you suspect it might help. You can always uncompress a drive if compressing it didn't help, or if it hinders performance.

Hard Disk Optimization

How you configure the hard disks of a system has a lot to do with how well they perform. On Windows 98 systems, EIDE and SCSI hard disks perform comparably if the hard disk speed is the same. However, if you can configure the disks in the system so that they spread their activity across multiple controllers, this can make the system perform better. For example, many newer systems have two EIDE controllers on their motherboards. If you have two hard disks in the system, consider connecting each disk to its own EIDE controller rather than having both of them on a single controller. This reduces contention on the EIDE bus. Also consider any impact from using the CD-ROM drive, which may also use an EIDE connection to the system. If the performance problem exists when the CD-ROM is being constantly accessed by an application, consider moving the CD-ROM to its own EIDE controller, or consider upgrading to a SCSI-based CD-ROM that doesn't contend with the hard disks at all.

> **Note** Under Windows 98, most EIDE disk systems perform on par with most SCSI disk systems. Windows NT is a different story, however, where SCSI disk systems almost always outperform EIDE disk systems. This difference in performance occurs because Windows NT takes much better advantage of certain SCSI features such as Scatter/Gather and Connect/Disconnect.

If your system is using an EIDE or SCSI controller on an add-on card that is connected to an ISA or EISA bus, consider upgrading to a PCI or VESA controller. The improved performance of the PCI or VESA buses pays off nicely in terms of disk performance.

Graphics Optimization

There are unfortunately not many tuning steps you can take to improve graphics performance. First, you need to identify whether you're experiencing a graphics-based performance problem or something else. You generally know that a performance problem is graphics based when you experience inadequate performance when heavy screen updating is taking place, when images are "jerky" as they update, or when there is little else happening on the system (such as CD-ROM reads or hard disk reads and writes).

> **Note** There are many downloadable utilities that can help you test the graphics performance of a system. One of the best is the WinBench program from Ziff-Davis. Go to the site **www.zdbop.com** to download the latest version of WinBench.

Graphics performance on a system is mostly a function of the display adapter installed into the system and the bus type into which it is installed. Because so much data is written to a graphics controller, install one that uses the fastest bus in a system, such as the PCI bus. Other tips for improving graphics performance include the following:

- Check with the vendor for updated display adapter drivers. Often, newer drivers include performance improvements that the vendor has discovered and implemented.

- On systems with very slow graphics subsystems, use the lowest resolution and color depth needed for the application. This can drastically reduce the amount of data that needs to be written to the graphics adapter, often by as much as several orders of magnitude when complex bitmaps are rendered on the display.

- Fortunately, graphics adapters aren't terribly expensive. You may be able to upgrade to a much faster, more optimized adapter for as little as $200.

- On the Performance tab of the System Control Panel, click the **G**raphics button to open the Advanced Graphics Settings dialog box shown in Figure 35.2. Make sure the slider is set to Full. You should set this slider to a lower value only if you are experiencing functional problems with the display output.

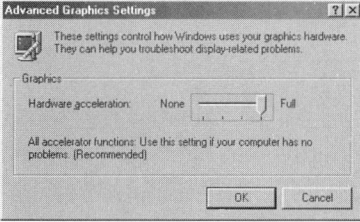

Figure 35.2
Make sure the slider in the Advanced Graphics Settings dialog box is set to Full.

Optimizing Printing

Printing performance problems can have a lot of impact to users' productivity. If a user needs to wait for 30 minutes for a report to finish printing, and the printer is taking an inordinate amount of time to print each page, then you probably have a printing performance problem that you can address.

> **Note** For network-based printers, the information in this section along with information in the later section "Optimizing Network Performance" will address improving printer performance.

Before looking at the printing subsystem for a suspected printing performance problem, first ensure that the problem does not originate elsewhere. For instance, some applications may be experiencing a performance problem in their ability to collect and output data, and the printing subsystem itself may be running just fine. You should carefully analyze the application's behavior while printing to determine if the printing subsystem is the bottleneck, or if it's something else limiting the collection and organization of data for the printout. The best way to do this is to measure printing performance with similar applications that create similar types of output. If the other application prints fine, then you should suspect the application that's experiencing the problem first.

There are three main areas that affect printing performance:

- The rendering of the printed pages on the system before they are sent to the printer
- The transmission of the printed data to the printer
- The speed of the printer to render printed output and to move the pages through the print process

You measure printing performance in Windows 98 by using two measurements. The first is called *Return to Application (RTA) speed*; it is the speed at which the application becomes responsive again once the print command has been issued. The other measurement is called *printer page drop speed*; it is the speed at which the print job is completed after the print command is issued. Before proceeding, determine if your problem is with the RTA speed or the printer page drop speed.

Printer Rendering and Spooling

Before output is sent to the printer, it is typically spooled to a file on the local hard disk, and certain operations may take place on the printed output at this stage. This area is a common source for printing performance slowdowns. If, when the print command is issued, it seems that there is excessive disk activity before the printer starts outputting pages, then you want to examine this area for improvements.

Start by opening the printer's Properties dialog box. Open My Computer, then Printers, and then right-click on the printer and choose Properties. Move to the Details tab and click on the Spoo**l** Settings button, which reveals the dialog box shown in Figure 35.3.

Figure 35.3
The Spool Settings dialog box.

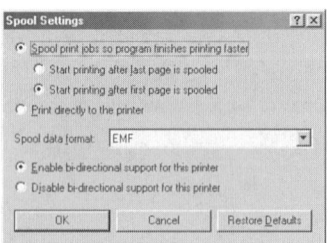

To maximize the RTA speed, choose **S**pool Print Jobs so Program Finishes Printing Faster and then choose Start Printing **A**fter First Page Is Spooled. On slower computers, you night achieve better print performance by choosing Start Printing After **L**ast Page Is Spooled.

To maximize the printer page drop speed, choose **P**rint Directly to the Printer. The application will stay busy until the printout is complete (or at least until it's fully sent to the printer's memory) but the system will be free to devote all of the processor time to composing the print pages, and so the printer page drop speed will be best with this setting.

By default, Windows spools printer output to the disk by using the Enhanced MetaFile (EMF) format. This spooler format offers the best performance. The alternate spooler format, RAW, may solve printing problems but is also slower than EMF.

Printer Transmission Speed

The speed at which the computer can send data to the printer can play a major role in printing performance. To maximize transmission speed performance, follow these guidelines:

- If you have a choice, use a parallel printer connection rather than a serial connection. Parallel ports transmit data much faster than serial ports.

- Always use a high quality printer cable. Cables that allow electrical noise or that have poor connections can slow printer output, and can also cause quality problems in the printouts.

- If the computer lets you configure a parallel printer port for ECP mode, and the printer supports it, choose it. ECP-configured ports operate much faster than standard parallel interfaces.

Printer Rendering Speed

Most print jobs are composed of both text and graphics mixed on each page. Complex instructions are sent to the printer to render this information into the printed result. On complex jobs, a lot of processing is required by the printer. For instance, PostScript printers require quite a bit of processing in order to compose most pages.

> **Note** Some of the properties tabs discussed here may be different (or nonexistent) for your printer because the tabs are dependent on the printer driver installed. The options discussed in this chapter are common for HP LaserJet printers; your printer could have different options.

You can make some adjustments and choices that might improve the rendering speed for printouts. Using the printer's Properties dialog box, move to the Fonts tab as shown in Figure 35.4.

On the Fonts tab, experiment with different settings for how fonts are downloaded to the printer. Downloading TrueType fonts as either bitmap or outline soft fonts will generally print the fastest, while printing TrueType fonts as graphics often improves their appearance and can be faster for pages that are largely graphic with little text.

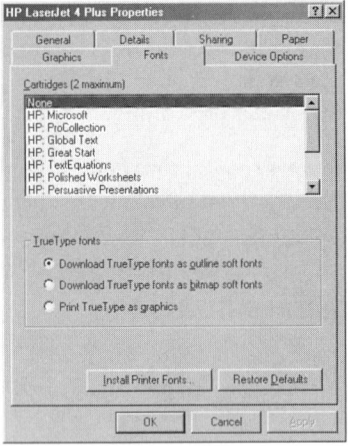

Figure 35.4
The printer's Properties dialog box showing the Fonts tab.

Another setting that changes how the printer renders pages can be found in the Graphics tab, shown in Figure 35.5. Use the **R**esolution setting to change how many dots per inch are printed. If the printout contains few, simple graphics and speed is important, a lower resolution may help. Also, select Use **V**ector Graphics whenever possible, as they are often much faster than raster graphics for the printer.

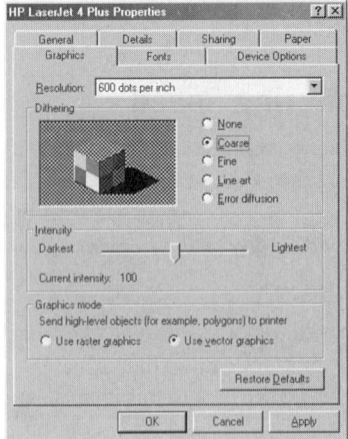

Figure 35.5
The printer's Properites dialog box showing the Graphics tab.

The job of rendering graphical pages is incredibly complex, and often requires a speedy processor in the printer itself, along with a lot of memory. If printer rendering speed is slowing you down, you might be forced to get a faster printer. Generally, more expensive printers include much faster processors and render pages much more quickly.

If you have a choice, PostScript printers almost always render graphical pages more slowly than other technologies, such as HP's Printer Control Language (PCL). Many PostScript printers also support PCL, so use them in the faster PCL mode as long as your print jobs render correctly in that mode.

Network Optimization

Optimizing the performance of networks requires a book all its own, but there are some common things you can do that can have a large impact on any network-connected computer. The first order of business is to isolate the network as the source of the performance slowdown. Believe it or not, applications running over a network, with their files stored on a remote file server, often perform better than applications running purely on a local computer. With a network that isn't very busy and that has adequate hardware for its servers, this is often the case. So the first thing to do is find out whether or not the network is actually causing problems. Things to look for here include comparing the speed of one computer to others that run the same application over the network, to see if just the one computer is having a network-specific problem, and trying to run the application purely from local hard disks to eliminate the network from the problem temporarily. Doing both things will start to give you a feeling for how the network is impacting an application's performance.

Network performance problems fall into two broad categories: performance problems due to the design of the network, and performance problems that involve the network interface on a particular computer. Following are some tips for optimizing network performance in both of these categories:

- Try running client/server applications with TCP/IP instead of IPX/SPX if you have a choice. TCP/IP generally supports larger packet sizes than IPX/SPX, and so performance is sometimes better depending on the application and the bottleneck. IPX/SPX is also the more "chatty" protocol and sends and receives a lot more status information than TCP/IP, so an IPX/SPX-based network tends to be busier than a TCP/IP network.

- It sounds simple, but it's easy to overlook this one: A bad network cable can often play a large role in poor network performance. Even on 10Base-T networks, you may want to try swapping the cables from the wall to the network computer and from the patch panel to the hub to isolate the network cabling. If all else fails, you can also move the computer to a different node (one that is known to operate normally) on the network to make sure in-wall wiring isn't to blame. This author once saw a workstation that performed at about 10% of its speed because of a 10Base-T patch cable from the wall to the computer. Swapping it fixed the problem. The insidious thing was that the computer basically worked on the network. The trouble was due to excessive retries required when large amounts of data needed to be transmitted to the workstation. The same thing can happen with 10Base-2 (Thin Ethernet) networks, too.

- Make sure to remove any protocols and other network service software that isn't needed for a computer because unneeded protocols and services sap performance, even when not being used. Use the Network Control Panel to remove any unneeded network service software from the unit.

- If you have manageable hubs, check the port statistics for the computer in question. These statistics may give you a clue as to what's happening. You'll want to compare the port statistics with the overall hub and network statistics, too. Check for statistics indicating short packets (*runt packet*) and long events. Also, take a very close look at the collision statistics on Ethernet networks. The number of dropped packets due to collisions shouldn't exceed 5% of the total number of packets transmitted; if it does, consider breaking the network up into smaller networks.

- Network interface cards (NICs) sometimes go bad. Try replacing the NIC for a computer experiencing network performance problems.

- If you have a 100Mbps backbone for the network and the client computer has a 10/100-Mbps NIC, you can try moving the workstation directly onto the backbone to see if the problem is bandwidth-related. Some applications do move enormous amounts of data across a network, and may require the higher bandwidth connection to their server. (Of course, the server in question must also be on the backbone for the workstation to benefit from this test.)

Solving network performance problems can be difficult, even at best. Just remember to work through all the possible bottlenecks between the workstation and server in a methodical fashion, and you're sure to find the bottleneck and can then work to resolve it.

Optimizing Application Performance

Up until now you've learned only about performance tips for different areas of the computer and its support mechanisms. However, performance complaints are often related to a specific application's speed. Sometimes you can make changes in the application itself that solve its performance problems. Consider the following ideas when thinking about application performance:

- Are you using the latest update of the application, and have you discussed the performance problem with the application vendor? Vendors often know about common sources of poor performance with their applications, and can usually give you very good advice for tuning their application or configuring a computer to optimally support their application. Turning to the vendor of the application for help can often save you a lot of time when solving a performance problem.

- Try locating the application and its data files on a different partition. You may get markedly better performance on different drives, particularly if they use a different file system. Don't forget that network shares are also drives that you can use to test this; sometimes applications run faster on a network share than they do locally.

- Make sure no other applications are running when you test the application. Contention for the system may impact one application even when it appears that others are running fine.

Chapter 35: Tools and Strategies for Optimizing Windows 98

- Installed utility programs can sap a computer's performance. Remove any unnecessary utilities from the system's Startup folder. Common sources of trouble include third-party screen savers, Microsoft Fast Find, and sometimes Office Startup.

- A subsequently installed DLL may slow an application. You should try reinstalling any applications that are performing poorly. Similarly, sometimes a key application file is damaged on the system's disk, and this may not cause an actual error that you can diagnose and solve, but it may cause performance problems. Completely remove the application and reinstall it if you suspect this might be the case. Use Windows 98's Version Conflict Manager and System File Checker to examine these possibilities.

- For DOS applications, tweak the settings in the program's Properties dialog box, particularly these:

    - Set to run in a full screen rather than a window

    - Avoid using the Protected checkbox on the Memory tab

    - Turn off any memory support types not needed by the application

    - Set the idle sensitivity to low

    - Turn off Mouse Quick Edit, and turn on mouse exclusive mode

    - Turn off Allow Sc**r**een Saver

    - On the Screen tab, turn off Dynamic **M**emory Allocation

    - Turn on Fast ROM **E**mulation

    All of these DOS program settings can improve performance, sometimes dramatically.

- For Win16-based applications, make sure that no other Win16 applications are running at the same time. This avoids problems arising from poor cooperative multitasking within the Win16 virtual machine.

- For Win32 applications, there is nothing in Windows 98 itself to tune their performance (you can tune the system, but you can't do much to change how the application runs). However, you can try running the application under Windows NT, if possible. A specific application may perform much better under Windows NT Workstation than Windows 98. This isn't often the case, but sometimes it is, especially if the application can benefit from any NTFS-formatted partitions on the Windows NT system. For example, a client/server client application that this author recently tested generally performed much better under Windows NT. Not only did it perform better, but many copies of the application could be run simultaneously under Windows NT, whereas it was really possible to run only one copy under Windows 98. This benefit is very application-specific, however; some applications may run faster under Windows 98. When in doubt, test it!

- Applications sometimes don't relinquish memory objects properly over time. You can identify such problems with System Monitor (discussed later in the section "System Monitor") and can restart the application periodically to automatically free up all the resources initialized by the application.

Using Windows 98 Performance Tools

There are several tools included with Windows 98 that play a key role in optimizing the performance of the system. In this section, you learn about these tools. Other tools that are more directed to troubleshooting are discussed in Chapter 37, "Tools and Strategies for Troubleshooting Windows 98." These other troubleshooting tools, however, can also play a role in solving a performance problem, particularly when the performance problem is due to actual trouble in the system rather than a bottleneck of some sort. When working with a thorny performance problem, don't overlook the troubleshooting tools discussed in Chapter 37.

Windows Tune-Up

Windows Tune-Up is a program that leads the user through a series of performance optimizations on a Windows 98 computer. New to Windows 98, Windows Tune-Up makes it easy for the average user to do some of the things that used to require the skills of a person with more training.

Windows Tune-Up walks the user through the following tasks, step by step:

- Disk Cleanup is run to remove any unnecessary files from the system's hard disks.
- ScanDisk is run to check for errors on the hard disks.
- Disk Defragmenter is run to defragment the contents of the hard disks on the system.

Although you can perform all of these optimizations manually, you can instruct users to run Windows Tune-Up, an easy program that will painlessly lead them through all these steps.

Resource Meter

Resource Meter is a small application that monitors the amount of shared resource memory available on a Windows 98 system. You can find it in the System Tools folder (Start menu, Programs, Accessories, System Tools). Running this application displays a small meter on the TaskBar. You can keep an eye on it when working through the steps of a performance problem to see if inadequate system resources are related to the problem. Hovering the mouse pointer over the meter will display the percentages free for each of the three main shared memory resources in Windows 98: User, System, and GDI. You can also double-click on the meter to display the dialog box version of the display, shown in Figure 35.6.

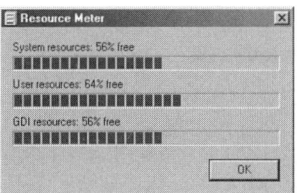

Figure 35.6
Resource Meter can show you if inadequate shared resources are causing a performance problem.

System Monitor

Windows 98 includes a system monitoring tool that is extremely helpful when diagnosing performance problems. System Monitor, shown in Figure 35.7, offers you a wealth of information about what is happening on a system and should be a core tool in your performance-tuning toolbox.

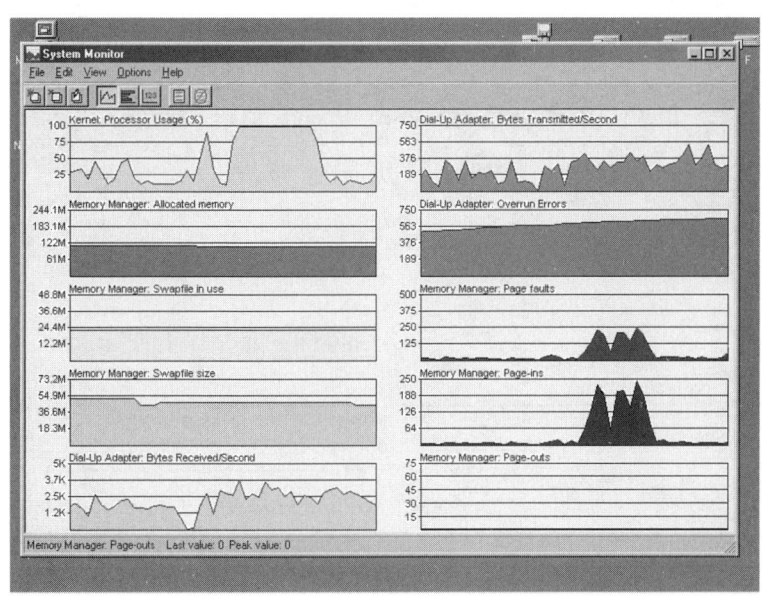

Figure 35.7
System Monitor displaying line charts.

Within System Monitor, you can select from a number of different performance counters available in Windows 98. You add and remove them as needed. System Monitor also supports three different ways of displaying performance counters: line charts, bar charts, and numeric charts. You can see a sample line chart in Figure 35.7, while Figures 36.8 and 36.9 show examples of bar and numeric charts.

To add a new counter to System Monitor's display, access the **E**dit menu and choose **A**dd Item. You see the Add Item dialog box shown in Figure 35.10.

Figure 35.8
System Monitor displaying bar charts.

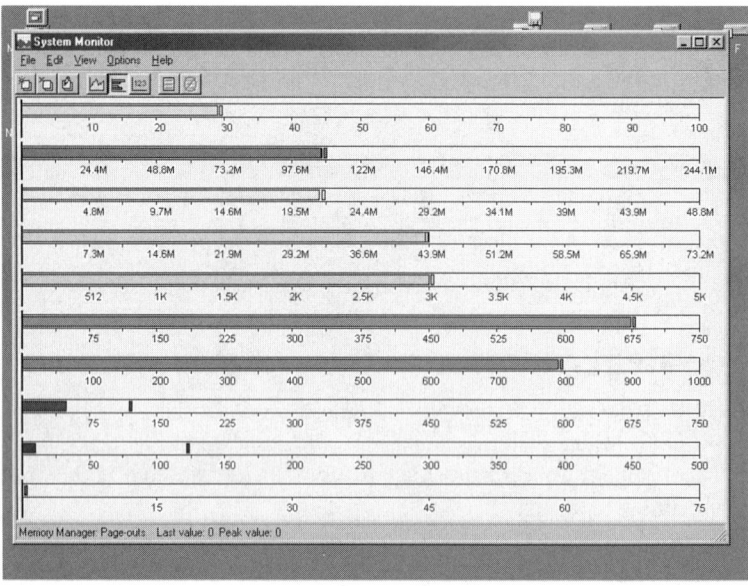

Figure 35.9
System Monitor displaying numeric charts.

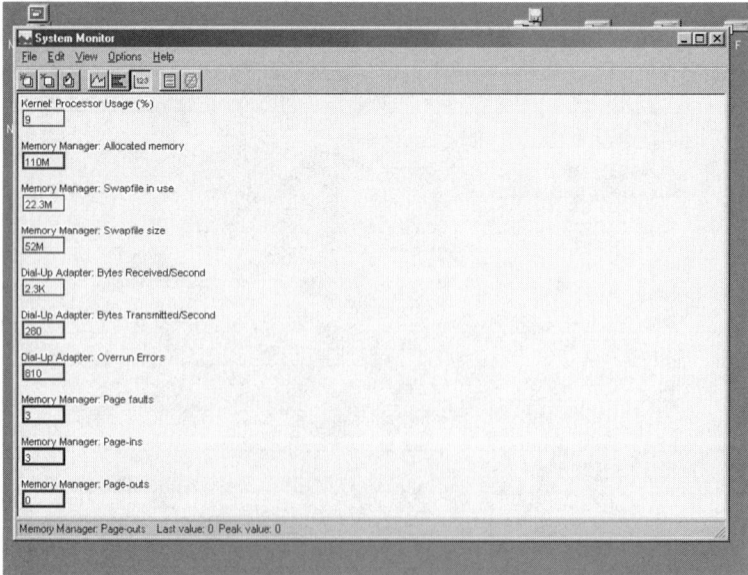

Each performance counter category is listed in the **C**ategory listing; selecting one reveals the actual performance counters available in that category in the **I**tem list. You can select multiple counters to add by holding down the Ctrl key while you click on each one, then click OK to add them to System Monitor's display. Consider the following tips for performance counters to watch as you duplicate a performance problem:

- You will always want to monitor Kernel: Processor Usage to see the approximate percentage of time that the processor is busy. Some performance problems are due to the speed of the processor. Also, check this value when the computer appears idle; a background process may be consuming more processor time than you realize.

- Watch the activity in Memory Manager: Page Faults, Page-Ins, and Page-Outs to see if the system is thrashing.

- You can get a sense of how disk-bound an application is by looking at File System: Bytes Read/Second and Bytes Written/Second. You may also want to watch File System: Reads/Second and Writes/Second to approximate the efficiency of the reads and writes (you generally want the most bytes per read and write, although you can't often control this within an application).

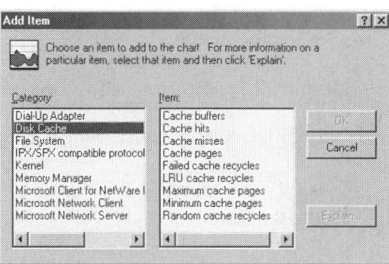

Figure 35.10
System Monitor's Add Item dialog box.

Table 35.1 lists the performance counters available along with descriptions of what they monitor. Note that Windows 98 offers many additional performance counters compared to Windows 95.

Table 35.1
System Monitor Performance Counters

Category	Counter	Notes
Dial-Up Adapter	Alignment Errors	Number of serial port alignment errors; may indicate a bad port or cable.
	Buffer Overruns	Number of times the serial buffer was overrun; check the error control and handshaking settings to improve this.
	Bytes Received/ Second	Number of bytes received per second through the dial-up adapter.
	Bytes Transmitted/ Second	Number of bytes transmitted per second through the dial-up adapter.

continues

Table 35.1, Continued
System Monitor Performance Counters

Category	Counter	Notes
	Connection Speed	Reported connection speed in bits per second.
	CRC Errors	Number of Cyclic Redundancy Check (CRC) errors.
	Frames Received/Second	Number of frames received by the dial-up adapter per second.
	Frames Transmitted/Second	Number of frames sent through the dial-up adapter per second.
	Framing Errors	Number of framing errors within the serial port of the dial-up adapter.
	Incomplete Frames	Number of incomplete frames received.
	Overrun Errors	Number of overrun errors within the serial port.
	Total Bytes Received	Total number of bytes received since System Monitor was started.
	Total Bytes Transmitted	Total number of bytes transmitted since System Monitor was started.
Disk Cache	Cache Buffers	Number of current buffers in the cache.
	Cache Hits	Number of times a request for data was satisfied with data in the cache. You want this number to be as high as possible; if it seems too low, reducing memory load may let the cache grow larger, possibly increasing the likelihood of finding needed data in the cache.
	Cache Misses	Number of times data was not found in the cache and had to be read from the disk. Optimally, this number should be as low as possible; reducing memory load may help reduce this value.
	Cache Pages	Number of pages stored in the cache.
	Failed Cache Recycles	Number of times a cache recycle request failed; generally indicates that the cache is full and there is little available memory in the system.
	LRU Cache Recycles	Number of times the cache is searched, from oldest data to newest, to find buffers that can be freed up. This happens when new data needs to be

Category	Counter	Notes
		added to an already full cache, and when the system needs to reduce the cache size and use its memory for other purposes. You should see only very occasional cache recycles, optimally.
	Maximum Cache Pages	The maximum number of cache pages stored since System Monitor was started.
	Minimum Cache Pages	The minimum number of cache pages stored since System Monitor was started.
	Random Cache Recycles	Number of times the cache was randomly searched for buffers that could be freed up.
File System	Bytes Read/Second	Number of bytes being read from all file systems per second.
	Bytes Written/Second	Number of bytes being written to all file systems per second.
	Dirty Data	Number of bytes in the cache waiting to be written to a disk. Note that dirty data is stored in blocks, so the bytes reported here may be larger than the actual bytes to be written; it is a count of the total bytes in the waiting blocks rather than the bytes within the blocks.
	Reads/Second	Number of read operations per second for all file systems.
	Writes/Second	Number of write operations per second for all file systems.
IPX/SPX–Compatible Protocol	IPX Packets Lost/Second	Number of IPX packets that were ignored for some reason, often because they were incorrectly formed.
	IPX Packets Received/Second	Number of IPX packets received and accepted per second.
	IPX Packets Sent/Second	Number of IPX packets sent by the computer per second.
	Open Sockets	Number of currently open IPX sockets.
	Routing Table Entries	Number of IPX network routes listed in the system's routing table.

continues

Table 35.1, Continued
System Monitor Performance Counters

Category	Counter	Notes
	SAP Table Entries	Number of received service advertisement packets (SAP).
	SPX Packets Received/Second	Number of SPX packets received per second.
	SPX Packets Sent/Second	Number of SPX packets sent per second.
Kernel	Processor Usage	Percentage utilization of the processor at any given second.
	Threads	Number of threads running in the system at any given time.
	Virtual Machines	Number of virtual machines running in the system at any given time.
Memory Manager	Allocated Memory	Total amount of memory in use by the system and applications.
	Discards	Number of pages that have been removed from memory because they're no longer needed in RAM.
	Disk Cache Size	The current size of the disk cache; Windows 98 adjusts the cache size aggressively based on the needs of the system, so this value may change rapidly when memory load changes.
	Instance Faults	Number of instance faults per second.
	Locked Memory	Amount of allocated memory that is locked (and is therefore unswappable).
	Locked Non-cache Pages	Number of locked memory pages that are not part of the cache.
	Maximum Disk Cache Size	Largest possible size of the disk cache based on system configuration.
	Mid Disk Cache Size	The mid disk cache size based on a moving average.
	Minimum Disk Cache Size	Smallest possible disk cache size based on system configuration.

Chapter 35: Tools and Strategies for Optimizing Windows 98

Category	Counter	Notes
	Other Memory	Amount of non-pageable allocated memory.
	Page Faults	Number of page faults per second. A *page fault* occurs when memory is requested that is not present in RAM but is instead in the swap file.
	Page-ins	Number of pages moved into RAM from the paging file per second.
	Page-outs	Number of pages moved into the paging file from RAM per second.
	Pages Mapped from Cache	Number of memory pages mapped from the cache; used with memory-mapped files.
	Swapfile Defective	Number of defective bytes in the swap file, in increments equal to the page size (4KB). A defective swap file page can be caused by disk read and write errors.
	Swapfile in Use	Number of in-use bytes stored in the paging file.
	Swapfile Size	The current size of the paging file.
	Swappable Memory	Number of bytes that can be stored in the paging file at any given time.
Microsoft Client for NetWare Networks	Burst Packets Dropped	Number of IPX/SPX burst packets that were received damaged and dropped.
	Burst Receive Gap Time	Microseconds of gap between burst packets.
	Burst Send Gap Time	Microseconds of gap between outgoing burst packets.
	Bytes in Cache	Number of network bytes being cached by the network client.
	Bytes Read per Second	Number of bytes read through the client per second.
	Bytes Written per Second	Number of bytes written through the client per second.
	Dirty Bytes in Cache	Number of bytes of write-behind data in the client's cache waiting to be sent over the network.

continues

Table 35.1, Continued
System Monitor Performance Counters

Category	Counter	Notes
	NCP Packets Dropped	Number of NCP packets received damaged and dropped.
	Requests Pending	Number of server requests waiting for a response from the server.
Microsoft Network Client	Bytes Read/Second	Number of bytes read per second through the client.
	Bytes Written/Second	Number of bytes written per second through the client.
	Number of Nets	Number of networks known to the client.
	Open Files	Number of files open through the network client.
	Resources	Number of resources being used by the client.
	Sessions	Number of network sessions open by the client.
	Transactions/Second	Number of transactions being processed per second.
Microsoft Network Server	Buffers	Number of buffers allocated by the server.
	Bytes Read/Sec	Number of bytes read by the server per second.
	Bytes Written/Sec	Number of bytes written by the server per second.
	Bytes/Sec	Number of bytes read or written by the server per second.
	Memory	Amount of memory being used by the server.
	NBs	Number of network buffers maintained by the server.
	Server Threads	Number of threads being used by the server.

System Monitor does exact a small performance penalty through its monitoring activities. However, the impact will be relatively small and should be balanced in terms of not causing radical changes in how single aspects of the system are performing.

Other Performance Tools

If all the tools discussed in this chapter fail to resolve or characterize a performance problem for you, you'll need to turn to third-party tools for additional assistance. These other tools fall into two broad categories: system performance-measuring tools and application-measurement tools.

There are many third-party programs that can measure the performance of a system in different ways and report on the results. You can run an initial test to measure the base case, and then make configuration changes and rerun the tests. It is important when doing this to ensure that the system's performance is causing the performance complaint, and not specific application behavior. You can find an excellent set of tools to measure system performance from Ziff-Davis at the **www.zdbop.com** Web site. There are many others as well, available at any site that carries shareware and freeware software. Utilities exist to measure disk speed, graphic speed, and memory speed.

Application-measurement tools are less powerful, but are important for testing an application's performance. Key to this effort is the ability to script a set of application commands that demonstrate the performance problem. Depending on the application, you may then be able to build a batch file that causes the application to start and the script to execute, or you may be able to find tools that will duplicate user involvement precisely for the application and wrap the results within a timer. Once you can do this, you can start making changes and retesting. Or, you may be able to build a program in an application's programming language that times a set of operations and displays the results, which you can then use for benchmarking the performance problem.

Windows 98 Configuration Recommendations

You can have the most perfectly tuned system in the world, but if it is fundamentally unable to offer the performance needed, you won't be able to find magical ways to solve its performance problems. You need to start with a system that is adequately sized to meet the demands you need to place on the system.

For general desktop application work, a computer with a Pentium 133 is perfectly adequate. It is more important that the system have enough RAM to meet the needs of the applications. For a busy desktop computer running Windows 98 and, for example, Microsoft Office, at least 24MB of RAM will yield good performance, but 36MB of RAM is preferred (and you may still see improvements up to 48 or 64MB of RAM). Most performance problems are due to inadequate RAM, so be sure to use the information in this chapter to look carefully at memory load before deciding that a system needs more RAM.

For heavy application development work or heavy database application work, a more powerful computer is called for. You should try to use a system with at least a Pentium 200 or faster processor, and, more important, the system should have 64MB or more of RAM. While this may seem like a lot, RAM prices have fallen to incredibly low levels, and you can purchase and install this much RAM inexpensively relative to the performance benefit realized.

It is best to use systems with Enhanced Data-Out (EDO) RAM when possible. EDO RAM performs much faster than traditional RAM. Also, depending on your need for reliability, you should think about using a computer that uses parity RAM or ECC RAM, both of which can detect memory errors if they occur. Many inexpensive computers lower their price by avoiding parity or ECC RAM, but such systems can produce erroneous results when a memory chip isn't working properly.

Many applications rely on speedy disk subsystems. Always purchase the fastest hard disks you can find; they don't cost a lot more than their less-expensive brethren, but the performance boost can be significant. It's also important to get the fastest disk controller you can, and it should be made for the fastest bus in the system (usually the PCI bus). If the system has more than one disk controller and you are using more than one disk, spread the load of the disk drives across the different controllers whenever possible.

Note As Robert Heinlein was fond of saying, "There ain't no such thing as a free lunch" (TANSTAAFL). As a rule, more expensive component choices will perform better than less expensive components. While there are always exceptions to the rule, the rule is true much more often than not. It's easy to find inexpensive computers that actually perform much more poorly than other computers, even when the other computers use slower processors! This is because the other components of the computer don't perform well, and moreover don't work together well. Be sure to buy system components wisely, but don't be penny-wise and pound-foolish.

With regard to the other components of the system, purchase the best ones you can find that meet the needs of the applications that will be run. It's important to know the exact demands that will be placed on the system, as some components make tradeoffs in performance because they are targeted to different types of application loads. For example, some graphics adapters are wonderfully fast when rendering 3-D images for game software, but may perform below average when handling standard Windows desktop rendering chores.

Conclusion

Improving the performance of a system is one of the most fun, most rewarding, most educational activities you can pursue in your systems work. Finding small changes that result in large improvements increases your knowledge of systems and Windows 98, and can pay off handsomely in user productivity.

In this chapter, you learned about the key performance areas of Windows 98 and also learned suggestions for improving Windows 98's performance in a number of key areas. You also learned about two tools that are valuable in performance-tuning a system: Windows Tune-Up (which runs other performance-enhancing tools: Disk Cleanup, ScanDisk, and Disk Defragmenter) and System Monitor. Finally, some recommendations for system selection were given that may help you to choose appropriate systems for the needs of the systems.

The next chapter, "The Windows 98 Boot Process and Emergency Recovery," shows you how to prepare for and handle emergency system recovery for a Windows 98 system. You also may want to continue in the same vein as this chapter by jumping to Chapter 37, "Tools and Strategies for Troubleshooting Windows 98," which is often a subject that goes hand-in-hand with performance tuning.

The Windows 98 Boot Process and Emergency Recovery

Sometimes you find yourself in a jam—a real jam, where your system won't start. What's the problem? What to do? How to handle it? That's part of the subject of this chapter: Emergency Recovery. Chapter 37, "Tools and Strategies for Troubleshooting Windows 98" covers dealing with individual hardware devices, software that isn't working correctly, or other aberrant behavior on your system. But Chapter 37 assumes that your system is starting (more or less). Not here, though: This chapter will get you on the road to recovery when you can't even get the darn thing booted. And because emergency recovery is closely related to how Windows 98 boots, you'll also learn about the Windows 98 boot process in this chapter.

In this chapter you learn about the following:

- How Windows 98 boots
- Different kinds of startup problems
- How to deal with the different types of startup problems
- How to use the Windows 98 Startup menu to attempt recovery
- Understanding, preparing, and using a Windows 98 Emergency Boot Disk (EBD)

Startup problems can be among the most frustrating because you have so little information with which to work. There are no friendly little trouble icons in Device Manager to show you where the trouble is, usually. As you will see, however, solving startup problems is more a matter of working through the different possibilities, one by one.

Understanding the Windows 98 Boot Process

Windows 98 goes through a series of steps as it boots the computer. If everything's working well, you won't care about the details about how Windows 98 gets the computer from an off state to when it displays the opening desktop. However, when troubleshooting boot problems, it's helpful to understand how booting works.

When a computer is powered up, the first thing that happens is that a program built into the computer's Basic Input/Output System (BIOS) runs and performs a *Power-On Self Test (POST)*. The POST tests all the key system components to make sure that they're all there and that they're minimally functioning. Also, the RAM in the computer is briefly tested during the POST.

After the POST completes, the BIOS automatically loads a small program from the primary hard disk on the system (or from a disk drive, or in rare cases a CD-ROM). This small program is called a *bootstrap* because it helps the computer "pull itself up by its bootstraps." The bootstrap loads the operating system's own bootstrap program from special startup sectors on the hard disk and transfers control to the operating system. The operating system programs then proceed to initialize the hard disk's file system, and control is transferred to other programs, on down the line until the system is completely booted.

The first phase of Windows 98's startup process involves scanning the installed hardware in the system and selecting the appropriate Hardware Profile from the Registry. After the Hardware Profile is activated, Windows 98 processes any commands found first in the CONFIG.SYS

Chapter 36: The Windows 98 Boot Process and Emergency Recovery

file, and then the AUTOEXEC.BAT file, both located in the root directory of the primary boot device. Note that although CONFIG.SYS and AUTOEXEC.BAT are not required for Windows 98, they are still processed in case they are needed for compatibility with older software or hardware on the system. Any drivers loaded by CONFIG.SYS and AUTOEXEC.BAT are real-mode drivers; the operating system has not yet switched the system into protected mode.

Windows 98 then proceeds to load WIN.COM and any VxD device drivers needed for the system. There are both *static* VxDs that are loaded during each boot and *dynamically loaded* VxDs that may or may not be loaded, depending on the selected Hardware Profile. The individual VxD device drivers are all contained in a file called VMM32.VXD.

The VxDs that are part of VMM32.VXD are loaded based on entries found in the Registry at HKEY_LOCAL_MACHINE\System\CurrentControlSet\Services\VxD. If there are conflicting entries in the SYSTEM.INI file, the entries in SYSTEM.INI will take precedence over the Registry entries.

After the VxDs are loaded, Windows 98 switches the computer into protected mode to proceed. The first thing that happens during this phase is that the Configuration Manager is loaded and started, which then queries all Plug and Play devices in the system; if the system's BIOS doesn't support Plug and Play, then the various buses in the system are scanned for installed devices. Based on the information gleaned from the Plug and Play queries or the bus scanning, dynamic protected-mode drivers are loaded for the installed devices. After the device drivers are loaded, any resource conflicts between the devices (such as IRQ assignments) are resolved by the Configuration Manager.

Next, a variety of files are loaded: KERNEL32.DLL and KRNL386.EXE (contain the basic components of Windows and the Windows device drivers, respectively), GDI.EXE and GDI32.EXE (handle the graphical interface duties for the operating system), and USER.EXE and USER32.EXE (provide the user-interface programming for Windows 98). Any related resources, such as icons, images, and fonts, are then loaded. Next, WIN.INI is processed and the desktop software is loaded and started. When User Profiles are active on the system, a logon prompt for the system then displays. After the user logs on, any settings specified for the User Profile are processed. Finally, any programs listed in the Startup folder are loaded for the user while the desktop initializes.

Windows 98 Startup Files

There are seven key files that form the base of Windows 98's startup behavior. They are all (except for WIN.INI and SYSTEM.INI) located in the root directory of the primary boot device, usually C:.

- IO.SYS—This is the bootstrap program for Windows 98.

- MSDOS.SYS—This file is actually an ASCII text file that can be edited and contains a few startup settings for the system. Table 36.1 describes all the settings you can use in MSDOS.SYS.

- CONFIG.SYS and AUTOEXEC.BAT—These files contain any device drivers and commands required for backward compatibility.

- SYSTEM.INI and WIN.INI—These files are for compatibility for older Windows 3.x programs.

- BOOTLOG.TXT—This is a detailed account of the system's most recent logged startup.

Understanding Startup Problems

If a Windows 98 computer won't boot, the trouble is most likely due to one of the following reasons:

- Something has caused the boot partition on the primary hard disk to stop functioning properly.

- Some other hardware device has failed and is keeping Windows 98 from completing its boot process.

- One or more key files that Windows 98 depends on has become corrupted and no longer works.

You'll take different paths for resolving each of these errors. The following sections discuss each type of problem in more detail.

Warning This author can't count the number of times he's worked through a failure with someone, only to determine that the failure required a restoration of data from a backup, and then discovering from a panicked user that there are no backups—or only very old backups—available. The very best emergency recovery tool anyone can ever have is a current, reliable backup of the system. Computers can and do fail, and sometimes spectacularly. A good backup system in place will prevent you from losing thousands of hours of accumulated work that is irreplaceable. If you're in an environment that relies on users to perform their own backups, you owe it to them to hammer this point home as forcefully as you can. Even better, find a way to take backups out of their hands and set up a reliable system to take care of this necessary chore.

Resolving Hard Disk Problems

Hard disk drives are much more reliable than in years past. It used to be that they had a Mean Time Between Failure (MTBF) of about five to seven years. Now, most drives quote MTBFs of 20 years or more. Still, even with this increased reliability (or more optimistic marketing—we're not sure), hard drives can still fail. Sometimes they fail slowly, accumulating bad sectors at a gradual rate, which then accelerate over time, and sometimes fail suddenly, going dead for no apparent reason. The first order of business is to ascertain whether the hard disk has failed. Afterward, if you determine that the primary boot drive has indeed failed, you can take these steps to replace it and rebuild your system:

- When the computer boots, you should see the hard disk drive light (the actual light on the drive itself, if possible, rather than the "echoed" light on most cases) illuminate as the system goes through its Power On Self Test (POST) and the drive receives power from the system. If this isn't happening, check the drive's data and power cables to ensure that they haven't become loose.

- If the drive still isn't showing even rudimentary signs of life (no spin-up noises, no drive lights, and so on), try disconnecting any other hard drives in the system, particularly those on the same EIDE or SCSI bus; sometimes a drive (hard drive or CD-ROM) further down the chain can fail and can keep the primary drive from operating. You may have to reconfigure the drive to make this work; for instance, on EIDE drives you might have to reset jumpers on the primary drive to indicate that there are no longer any slave drives connected. Also, don't forget to reseat the drive controller board, if the system uses one. You can also relocate the drive controller board to another slot; sometimes slots go bad.

- If the drive in question is a SCSI drive, check the drive's SCSI address and the termination settings, as well as the terminator itself if there is one.

- If you're still not getting normal POST lights (and maybe not even startup noises) try replacing the disk controller with an identical model set with the same settings and try to boot again. Some failed drives will spin up, emit some loud "clicking" noises, and then stop spinning. If this happens, recovering the drive is a lost cause and it should be replaced.

- Don't forget to double-check the computer's CMOS settings to ensure they haven't been cleared or changed; if the CMOS doesn't show the drives properly, you'll have to re-detect them using whatever procedure is appropriate for the system.

- Boot the system with its Emergency Boot Disk (discussed in detail later in this chapter). See if you can find the drive with FDISK, or even with the DIR command.

- Sometimes hard disks, particularly when they get old, experience problems starting when they're cold. What happens is that the lubricant has a higher viscosity when cold, and some of the metals in the drive shrink as a result of the colder temperature; the result is increased friction and sometimes the drive motor can't overcome it until the drive or the ambient temperature in the case warms up. If all the preceding has failed and the drive still isn't starting or responding, try these last-ditch attempts:

1. Leave the system powered on for an extended period (at least an hour) and then try to restart the system with a warm boot. If you can do this in a warm environment, it may help.

2. If the drive still isn't starting after going through this warm-up phase, try a cool-down phase and leave the system powered off overnight, and try it again first thing in the morning.

3. This is really a desperate move, but the author has seen it work before: Warm up the system for an hour by leaving it on, and then give the hard drive a couple of sturdy whacks with the heel of your hand, then do a warm boot. (Make sure you've tried everything else first, because this can damage the drive!)

- These last-ditch attempts might at least get the drive to spin up and let you recover any valuable data that you might otherwise lose. If you're lucky and recover some data, immediately replace the drive because any drive that requires these extreme measures shouldn't be trusted!

If all the preceding steps fail, you've most likely got a failed primary drive on your hands. You'll need to replace it, reinstall Windows 98, reinstall all of your applications, and then restore your data from backup.

> **Tip** Most hard disk drives have at least a one-year warranty. If the drive has failed, you might be able to get a free replacement from the drive's manufacturer or your computer's manufacturer.

Assuming you are getting normal POST behavior from the drive (the hard disk lights flash normally during startup and normal sounds emanate from the drive), then you start to get into other configuration problem possibilities. Check the following:

- Do you see the message `Loading Windows 98` or the Windows 98 splash screen when the computer boots? If so, then the drive itself is working (although it may contain a lot of bad sectors); jump to the later section "Resolving System File Problems" for instructions on dealing with your problem.

- Can you start Windows 98 in Safe Mode? If so, you probably don't have a hard drive problem at all; continue troubleshooting the problem first according to the later section "Resolving System File Problems" and then to Chapter 37, "Tools and Strategies for Troubleshooting Windows 98."

- If the drive seems to be succeeding at POST, but the system never displays `Loading Windows 98`, your hard disk configuration may have been changed, or your boot sector on the drive may have become damaged. There are two things to check here:

  1. Start the system with the EBD and see if you can do a DIR of your C: drive. If so, perform a SCANDISK on the C: drive, and then use the SYS command that is part of the EBD to reinstall the system files on the drive. Continue with the "Resolving System File Problems" section.

  2. Start the system with the EBD and use FDISK to see if the disk partition data has been lost for some reason. You *may* be able to repartition the disk and have it start functioning again, with your data mostly intact. However, this requires that the partition be created *exactly* as it was when the system was last working, and this is a chancy proposition at best. Chances are you'll have to repartition the drive and reinstall Windows 98 and your applications.

Resolving Other Hardware Problems

Sometimes a system won't boot and the problem isn't due to the hard disk drive. It might be due to another device in the system that's failing in some way and preventing a startup, or it may be a number of different possible file problems. This section deals with the former possibility, while the next two deal with the latter.

If the system starts to boot, displays the message `Loading Windows 98` and possibly the Windows 98 splash screen, but then stops booting, try these steps to find out if there's other hardware in the system preventing startup:

- Try to start the system in Safe Mode. Hold down the left Ctrl key while the system starts. This should display the Windows Startup menu, from which you can choose Safe Mode. Safe Mode starts Windows 98 and loads as few drivers as possible. If you can get into Safe Mode, use the Device Manager tab in the System Control Panel to search for any reported hardware errors.

- If the startup fails when the Windows 98 splash screen is displayed, press the Esc key. This should display the DOS startup screen and show you the status of any non-Windows drivers that the system is loading. When diagnosing boot problems, you should press Esc as soon as the splash screen appears, and once again when it reappears, and then watch the messages as the drivers load; you might see one that's causing the system to fail its boot. It's also possible that some command or driver was added to the system's CONFIG.SYS or AUTOEXEC.BAT file and is preventing startup. If this is the case, restart the system using the Windows Startup menu (hold down the left Ctrl key while the system starts) and then choose Command Prompt Only from the menu. Edit (the EDIT program is in C:\Windows\Command) the CONFIG.SYS and

AUTOEXEC.BAT files to remove any unneeded commands. You might want to remove all of the commands in those files temporarily to isolate the trouble—just put the keyword REM in front of all of the lines. Later, you can remove the REMs one by one to determine which line was the culprit.

- Using the Windows 98 Startup Menu, choose Option 2: Logged. This creates a file called BOOTLOG.TXT in the root of the startup drive. When the boot fails, you can restart in Command Prompt Mode (Option 5) or from the EBD to view the contents of the file, which may show you what the problem is; each device driver and system service loaded gets logged to the file, and you can easily see any failures that occurred.

- If you suspect a particular hardware device, perhaps one that has been acting peculiar leading up the boot failure, you should disconnect it from the system and try to boot.

If the above ideas and the previous section fail to get Windows 98 started for you, then you're most likely suffering from a problem with one or more system files that are corrupt or missing. Proceed to the next section to deal with those problems.

Resolving System File Problems

Windows 98 processes many files in order to boot properly and display the desktop. If one or more of the critical files are damaged or missing, the system may not be able to boot or recover from the problem. Follow these steps to diagnose and resolve these problems:

- Try to start the system in Safe Mode. This loads a minimal set of drivers. If you can get Safe Mode running, and then determine that there are no hardware failures in the system, you can run one of several tools to try to resolve any Windows 98 file problems, in this order:

    1. SCANREG checks the system Registry for problems. Type SCANREG /? for different command-line options for fixing the Registry and restoring a previous backup of the Registry.

    2. SCANDISK checks the system drive for errors, both in the directory structure and throughout the surface of the disk.

    3. Run System Information (from the Start menu, Programs, Accessories, System Tools menu). Scan its information tree for clues indicating a problem, and run additional tools from its **T**ools menu as indicated in the following steps.

    4. Run System File Checker from System Information, which examines all the Windows 98 files and automatically reloads any corrupt or incorrect files from the Windows 98 CD-ROM.

5. Run Dr. Watson from System Information, which causes the Dr. Watson icon to appear on the TaskBar. Click the icon and then choose Dr. Watson from the pop-up menu. The Dr. Watson program scans the system and reports any errors it finds.

6. Run System Configuration Utility (described in the next section) to enable special startup features that may let you isolate a specific startup troublespot.

- If you cannot start the system in Safe Mode, try Option 2 (Logged) from the Windows Startup menu. Let the startup fail, and then access the C:\BOOTLOG.TXT file to see if you can discover which file or driver is bad (you may have to boot the system with the EBD or to a command prompt to view BOOTLOG.TXT). Using the information in BOOTLOG.TXT, replace the driver or device that is indicating a problem.

- Start the system with the EBD, which now lets you boot from a disk with CD-ROM support. Run Windows' SETUP.EXE from the Windows 98 CD-ROM and reinstall Windows. Your Windows 98 settings should be preserved, and any corrupt files should be replaced.

- If the system is failing to boot, but you've eliminated hardware or disk configuration as possible causes, it's possible that the system boot files have been removed or have become corrupt. Start the system with the EBD and then use the SYS command from the EBD directory to reload the boot files. Then try to restart the system.

Basically, if you've eliminated hardware as a boot failure cause, and you've eliminated other hardware or disk configuration as a cause, your primary goal is to boot the system in either Safe Mode or with the EBD, and then replace any known bad files or simply reinstall Windows 98 from your CD-ROM. After working through this section and the previous two sections, you should have a system that boots, and can then proceed to more detailed troubleshooting if necessary, as discussed in Chapter 37.

Troubleshooting Startup Problems with System Configuration Utility

Windows 98 includes a tool called *System Configuration Utility* that lets you selectively enable and disable certain startup parameters. System Configuration Utility replaces SYSEDIT.EXE, and is a much more powerful utility for controlling the Windows 98 startup files. You can start it by using the Run command from the Startup menu and then typing MSCONFIG. You can also access it from the **T**ools menu of the System Information Utility.

To use System Configuration Utility, you must be able to start the system in some fashion, even if only in Safe Mode. You can then use the settings in System Configuration Utility to try to isolate the problem. System Configuration Utility is shown in Figure 36.1.

Figure 36.1
System Configuration Utility's General tab.

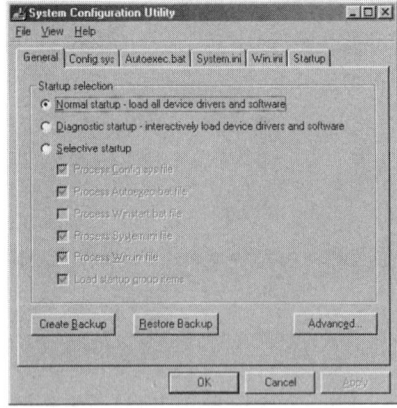

The General tab lets you choose how Windows 98 will boot next. You can choose from the following three choices:

- **N**ormal Startup
- **D**iagnostic Startup, where you are prompted for each startup step, just as if you had chosen Step-By-Step Confirmation in the Windows Startup menu
- **S**elective Startup, where you can choose different startup files to process or not process

If the system boots in Safe Mode but not normally, use the **S**elective Startup option to disable elements that you think may be related to the startup problem, such as CONFIG.SYS, AUTOEXEC.BAT, WIN.INI, or SYSTEM.INI. If this fails to resolve the problem, choosing **D**iagnostic Startup gives you a few more choices during the startup.

Click the Advanc**e**d button in the General tab to bring up the Advanced Troubleshooting Settings dialog box shown in Figure 36.2. Here you can choose even more settings that may help you diagnose and solve the startup problem, as described in Table 36.1.

Figure 36.2
Advanced Troubleshooting Settings dialog box.

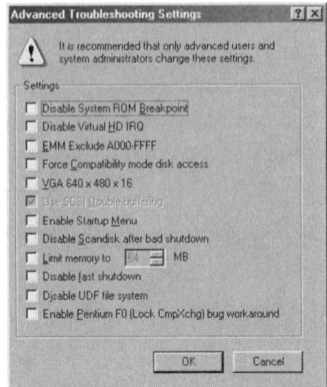

Table 36.1
Advanced Troubleshooting Settings

Setting	Description
Disable System ROM **B**reakpoint	Forces Windows to avoid using the first 1 MB of memory for the system ROM breakpoint
Disable Virtual **HD** IRQ	Disables the Windows code that handles IRQ signals for the hard disk and instead forces the system to use the ROM BIOS routines for handling hard disk IRQ signals
EMM Exclude A000-FFFF	Forces Windows to avoid using the area traditionally set aside for EMM memory
Force **C**ompatibility Mode Disk Access	Bypasses protected mode support for disk access and instead routes disk access through real mode
VGA 640×480×16	Forces the system to start in basic VGA display mode
Use SCSI **D**ouble-buffering	Causes the system to use SCSI double-buffering, which may resolve SCSI I/O problems; setting can also be forced through MSDOS.SYS
Enable Startup **M**enu	Forces the Windows Startup menu to appear without having to hold down the Ctrl key during boot
Disable **S**candisk After Bad Shutdown	Bypasses the automatic SCANDISK after the system was not shut down gracefully
Limit Memory To	Limits the addressable system RAM to the amount specified, which can be useful for diagnosing suspected RAM problems
Disable **F**ast Shutdown	Disables the shutdown performance enhancements; for use if Windows 98 is having trouble shutting down properly
D**i**sable UDF File System	Disables support for Universal Disk Format; for use only when troubleshooting DVD players
Enable **P**entium F0 Bug Workaround	For Pentiums at the F0 revision level, turns off alternate code that attempts to handle a bug on the processor

The remaining tabs in the System Configuration Utility all work the same way: They display the various settings associated with the tab's file, and let you selectively activate or deactivate those settings. Figure 36.3 shows the CONFIG.SYS tab; the others also offer listings with checkboxes for enabling or disabling specific settings.

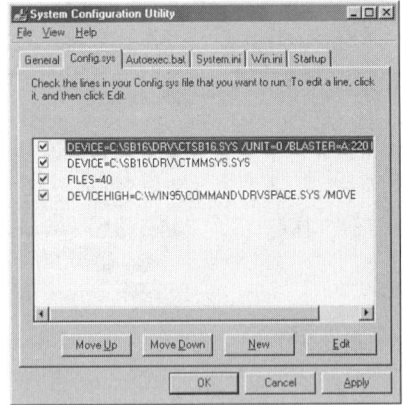

Figure 36.3
System Configuration Utility's config.sys tab.

Understanding the Windows Startup Menu

Windows 98 lets you access a Windows Startup menu that enables you to try to start the system in various ways from the primary boot partition. Under Windows 95 you accessed the startup menu by pressing the F8 key when the message `Loading Windows 95` appeared. Under Windows 98 you instead hold down the left Ctrl key while the system starts. You then see the Windows Startup menu, which lets you choose from the following options:

- Normal— Choose Option 1 to cause the system to attempt to boot normally.

- Logged (BOOTLOG.TXT)— Boots the system normally, but logs all startup activity to a file called BOOTLOG.TXT located in the root directory of the startup drive. This file may contain valuable clues indicating various startup problems or driver failures.

- Safe Mode— Safe Mode starts the Windows 98 desktop with the minimal set of drivers running in standard VGA mode. The purpose of Safe Mode is to give you access to the graphical configuration tools in Windows 98, such as the Control Panel objects, to resolve any problems with the system.

- Step-by-Step Confirmation— This startup choice prompts you for each key startup area, which you can choose to process or not process. You are prompted with each of the following questions:

    - Load DoubleSpace Driver?

    - Process the System Registry?

    - Create a Startup Log File (BOOTLOG.TXT)?

Chapter 36: The Windows 98 Boot Process and Emergency Recovery   **831**

- Process your startup device drivers (CONFIG.SYS)? Answering Yes then prompts you for each line in the CONFIG.SYS file.

- Process your startup command file (AUTOEXEC.BAT)? Answering Yes then prompts you for each line in the AUTOEXEC.BAT file.

- Run WIN?

- Load all Windows Device Drivers? Answering Yes then prompts you for the main drivers, one-by-one.

■ Command Prompt Only— This option loads enough of Windows 98 to start an MS-DOS command prompt, from which you can then access the system files and make necessary changes and run necessary character-mode utilities.

■ Safe Mode Command Prompt Only— This option loads a minimal set of drivers in order to start an MS-DOS command prompt.

If a system is having trouble starting, first try to start the system in Safe Mode. If that fails to start the system, try both Command Prompt Only and Safe Mode Command Prompt Only to try to get to a command prompt. If you cannot get to a command prompt using these methods, you'll have to use the EBD, discussed in the next section.

Understanding, Preparing, and Using an Emergency Boot Disk

When you install Windows 98, and whenever you make major configuration changes to the system, you should prepare a Windows 98 Emergency Boot Disk (EBD). The EBD is a boot disk that starts the system without accessing any files stored on the hard drives, and gives you a command prompt along with the most common utilities needed to resolve emergency boot problems. The EBD has been significantly enhanced in Windows 98 over the one used with Windows 95.

> **Warning** Do not attempt to use a Windows 95 EBD to recover a Windows 98 system. You must use a Windows 98 EBD.

The EBD boots the system and creates a 2MB RAM disk, onto which it places the key utilities you may need to repair a system. When you boot a system with its EBD, you see a menu with three choices:

- Start the Computer with CD-ROM Support
- Start the Computer without CD-ROM Support
- View the Help File

Generally you will choose to start the system with CD-ROM support. There are general-purpose CD-ROM drivers on the EBD that can initialize most IDE- and SCSI-based CD-ROM drives. If you cannot access your CD-ROM drive after starting the EBD in this mode, you'll have to modify the EBD's CONFIG.SYS and AUTOEXEC.BAT file to use the appropriate drivers for your system's CD-ROM (see Chapter 2, "Installing Windows 98"). You want CD-ROM support so that you can replace corrupted Windows system files or reinstall Windows 98 from the CD-ROM.

Preparing the EBD

To prepare the EBD, you'll need a 1.44MB disk that contains no bad sectors. Start by opening the Add/Remove Programs Control Panel, and then move to the Startup Disk tab shown in Figure 36.4. Click the Create Disk button to build the EBD disk.

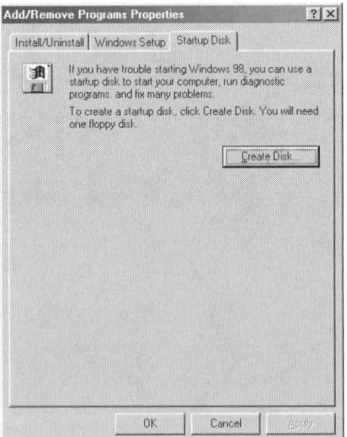

Figure 36.4
Add/Remove Program's Startup Disk tab.

Tip It's a good idea to test the EBD by trying to boot the system with it after you've prepared it. Waiting until the system fails to boot is no time to find that your EBD doesn't work for some reason!

You should update the EBD whenever you make major configuration changes to the system, such as adding or removing hard disk drives or CD-ROM drives. However, the EBD has been designed to be as general as possible, and you can often use another computer's EBD to boot a similar system (as long as the EBD you use was created from a Windows 98 system).

Understanding the EBD

The EBD boots the Windows 98 version of MS-DOS, and then creates a 2MB RAM drive to hold the EBD utilities. The utilities are automatically copied to the RAM drive. The RAM drive is created using the first drive letter that follows any hard drives defined in the system, but before the CD-ROM drive letter. Your CD-ROM drive letter will therefore be moved up one letter when booting from the EBD.

The EBD utilities are stored in a file called EBD.CAB on the EBD disk. EBD.CAB is a compressed file that is automatically decompressed to the created RAM drive as the EBD boots. Table 36.2 details the EBD utilities contained in the EBD.CAB file.

Table 36.2
EBD Utilities

Utility Name	Purpose
ATTRIB.EXE	Utility that lets you set file attributes; you may use this to remove a file's hidden or read-only attributes prior to replacement, for instance.
CHKDSK.EXE	Abbreviated version of SCANDISK that checks a drive's directory structure for errors.
DEBUG.EXE	MS-DOS debugger, which lets you perform byte-level patching of files.
EDIT.EXE	Simple text editing program for making changes to system text files, such as CONFIG.SYS or AUTOEXEC.BAT.
EXT.EXE	New file extraction utility that makes it easy to search the Windows 98 .CAB files on the CD-ROM for individual files and extract those files to a destination of your choice.
FORMAT.COM	Utility to format disks.
MSCDEX.EXE	CD-ROM extensions for MS-DOS.
SCANDISK.EXE	Comprehensive disk testing tool; checks both directory structures and can perform surface analyses.
SCANDISK.INI	Configuration file for SCANDISK.EXE.
SYS.COM	Utility that places system boot files onto a disk.
UNINSTAL.EXE	Utility that uninstalls Windows 98.

Using the EBD

After you have booted a system with the EBD, you'll want to follow certain steps to resolve most startup problems. First, you should run SCANDISK on the boot drive, drive C:. Any errors in the directory structure that are keeping the system from starting should be resolved by SCANDISK. Take careful note of any files that SCANDISK indicates are damaged (contain bad sectors, are cross-linked, or have other problems); you should replace them from the Windows 98 CD-ROM after SCANDISK repairs the problems on the disk.

If a few damaged files were indicated by SCANDISK, then use the EXT utility to extract fresh copies of those files from the Windows 98 CD-ROM. Simply type EXT from the RAM disk command prompt, and then indicate what file you want to replace, where the Windows 98 .CAB files are located (usually *x:*\WIN98 where *x:* is your CD-ROM drive letter), and where you want the extracted file to be placed (usually either C:\WINDOWS, C:\WINDOWS\SYSTEM, or C:\WINDOWS\SYSTEM32 as appropriate for the file).

If there appear to be many damaged files, and you think that any bad sectors on the hard disk were fully repaired by SCANDISK, you should run Windows Setup from the Windows 98 CD-ROM to reinstall all the Windows 98 files. Also, if all else fails, go ahead and try to reinstall Windows 98 using this method; many problems will be automatically resolved by reinstalling the operating system. You shouldn't lose your Windows settings by doing this.

If none of the preceding suggestions work and Windows 98 still won't boot, you're certain that the hard disks in the system are fine, and that there aren't other hardware problems causing Windows to fail to boot, try this last resort: Use the UNINSTAL utility in the EBD to remove Windows 98, and then reinstall Windows 98 from scratch. You will lose your Windows 98 settings, and will have to reinstall your applications.

Conclusion

Solving startup problems can be frustrating and challenging. Fortunately, there are some powerful tools that let you access a Windows 98 computer without needing Windows 98 itself, such as various Windows Startup menu options and the Windows EBD. By using such tools, along with other emergency troubleshooting tools discussed in this chapter, you should be able to recover from any such emergency.

The next chapter, "Tools and Strategies for Troubleshooting Windows 98" continues the troubleshooting topic with specific advice on troubleshooting various possible problems, along with coverage for the troubleshooting tools included in Windows 98.

CHAPTER 37

Tools and Strategies for Troubleshooting Windows 98

Performance tuning, discussed in Chapter 35, "Tools and Strategies for Optimizing Windows 98," is one of the most interesting and rewarding kinds of advanced work you can do with Windows 98. Troubleshooting, on the other hand, can sometimes be rewarding and interesting, but it also offers vast potential for frustration. This is particularly true when you're unable to resolve a problem and conclude that it's better to throw in the towel and reinstall all the software on the computer, replace the computer, or whatever else you might have to do.

The good news is that Windows 98 includes a number of powerful new tools to add to your troubleshooting toolbox. With these new tools, you'll find that trouble-shooting Windows 98 is much more productive than troubleshooting Windows 95. In this chapter, you learn about the tools included with Windows 98 that can help your troubleshooting efforts, along with strategies for their use.

Troubleshooting Overview

System trouble comes in all shapes and sizes. You might have erratic behavior from a device, seemingly random application or system crashes, or bizarre behavior from applications that don't do what they're supposed to do. There are common threads to solving all of these problems, though, and the following sections discuss good troubleshooting practices that will help you.

Communicating with Users

Usually, the problems that you'll be called on to solve aren't your own, but are problems of the users you're supporting. This adds an entirely new dimension to most troubleshooting endeavors and is an area where many systems people are sadly deficient. You'll find, however, that mastering this tricky area results in a number of payoffs, including

- Faster trouble identification and resolution
- Less wasted time from chasing improperly understood problems
- Happier (and more productive) users

The most successful troubleshooters have mastered the skill of communicating with users. In my experience, this skill is somewhat more valuable than top-notch technical skills. Although you obviously also need to know your stuff technically, you'll waste a lot of time and be less effective than otherwise unless you become good at working with users. The upshot is that it's sometimes just as enjoyable to troubleshoot users as it is to troubleshoot systems.

Doing a good job communicating with users boils down to several skills. The first one is calming the user. Often, users won't come to you for help until they've almost literally beat their heads against the wall trying to resolve the problem themselves. (Although some users will involve you for trivial problems without falling back on their own resources first, most users do try to do things on their own.) When they contact you, they're likely to be frustrated, and some people will be looking for someone (anyone!) to blame for their frustration. Moreover, you'll have a difficult time getting accurate information from them if they're in a frustrated state of mind.

The first skill, therefore, is to calm the user. When it becomes necessary to do this, you'll find that the most important things are the following:

- Don't take their frustration personally, even if it's temporarily directed at you. Remaining calm in such circumstances can be difficult, and some people have an amazing knack for bringing you immediately to their same level of frustration (although you'll be frustrated with *them*, rather than their computer problem). It's best to remain professional and keep your cool. Avoid letting little signs of annoyance creep into your voice or expression.

- Avoid making them look or feel foolish. This can also be difficult to do, because there will be times when people will come to you with problems that you find obvious and tiresome. ("Have you tried pressing the little key marked Caps Lock? It makes all the letters you type uppercase. Do you know what 'uppercase' means?" is not a productive thing to say). It's important to bite your tongue if you find yourself about to say something that is patronizing or condescending. Giving in to this temptation almost immediately destroys any chance you'll have of resolving the problem quickly and efficiently.

- Acknowledge and validate their problem. By saying something as simple as "Oh yes, that problem would certainly frustrate me!" establishes some rapport with them, and you'll find it has an immediate positive effect on your ability to work through the problem with them to completion.

It's worthwhile to establish some trust with the person and calm them down before moving on to tackling the actual problem. You'll solve problems much more quickly when you do.

The second skill is communicating accurately. The difficulty here is that often users have strange ways of referring to things on their computer or describing events. It's important that you get them to describe their problem in *sensory-specific language*. This means that you get them to offer you information about exactly what they did, saw, and heard when they experienced the problem. With some people, this is difficult, because they seem to want to interpret everything they do; it's almost as if they're incapable of simply telling you what keys they pressed, what commands they selected, and what happened. With these sorts of people, things are tricky because you'll have to feed them possibilities for confirmation, and it's really easy to let this sound condescending and make them defensive. About 20 percent of the population seems to have trouble describing things in a way that will be useful for you, so you're going to have to learn how to tease out the information you need from such people.

> ### "What's a Hard Drive?!?"
> One amusing thing that I experienced was an organization where the users kept persisting in calling their system units hard drives. Even when I explained the difference to them, this strange nomenclature kept cropping up. It was almost like there was some sort of weird rampant language virus running amok in the company.
>
> *continues*

> *continues*
>
> One day I realized what was going on. When support people worked with users and observed their systems, they looked at the hard disk indicator light on the system unit and said things like, "Wow, your hard drive seems awfully busy." The users, not realizing that the light indicated a device *within* the system unit, figured out (incorrectly) that the light indicated the activity of their entire system unit, and therefore the system unit must be called a hard drive.

Another barrier to accurate communication occurs when users have high opinions of their own computer skills, and want to offer you their diagnosis rather than the detailed information that you actually need. You should develop strategies for handling such people. The key is to avoid contradicting their opinion while gathering the information you need. You can say things like, "Yes, I had a similar thing happen the other day, but it actually turned out to be something else. What, exactly, are you doing and seeing?"

Part of accurate communication often involves having the user show you what's happening. Because there will be times when people won't be able to communicate their problem to you effectively, get them to demonstrate the problem for you. By watching them, you'll be able to see what's really happening. When doing troubleshooting over the phone, you can do much the same thing by having them go through each step, and report what you want to see, and then have them type or do exactly what you tell them.

The last skill involves something that will improve your troubleshooting over the long term. Build trust with your users. This means several things: Be honest when you don't know what's causing a problem. Follow up with them when you say you'll follow up with them even if it's only to tell them that you haven't yet solved their problem. Treat them the same way that you would like to be treated in similar circumstances. A helpful idea to keep in mind when you have trouble respecting a user's problem is this: What's important to people is what they *think* is important to them.

Identifying Problems

Before you can solve a problem, you have to know exactly what the problem is. This first means knowing if you can reproduce a problem. Unfortunately, you'll see many problems in your career that can't be reproduced. They're usually caused by possibilities such as bugs in software that cause seemingly random behavior, misreads or miswrites of data, power surges, or—for all you know—cosmic rays. It's been said that 90 percent of computer problems are easily solved by rebooting the system, and it's true. Unless a particular system is experiencing a high rate of such problems, it's not going to be worth your time to chase these troubleshooting ghosts. Instead, restart the system and move on. Sometimes you have to explain this to your users, too. You have to tell them that sometimes, weird things happen for no reason, but to let you know if they see any other odd behavior in the next few days.

After determining that a problem is repeatable, the next step in identification is *isolation*. Is the problem with a modem, or the telephone connection, or the serial port, or the cable from the serial port to the modem? Is the problem with an errant software application, or the RAM in the system? Isolation involves systematically eliminating possible sources for the problem. Isolating a problem might mean trying to reproduce it on an identical system, to provoke a similar problem with another application, or even systematically replacing components of a system until you find the cause. Isolating problems requires patience. Over time, however, you'll gain experience so that you can narrow down a set of possibilities based on similar problems you've seen and resolved.

Solving Problems Systematically

The final overall skill needed to become a strong troubleshooter involves approaching problems systematically. People who jump around a problem and try everything that pops into their heads simultaneously, invariably end up making the problem worse, or at best, solving the problem without knowing the cause or the actual resolution.

Instead, you need to work systematically, both when isolating a problem and when trying possible solutions to the problem. With complex problems, you might want to make a list of the steps to take, and then work through those steps one by one. Not only will you avoid frustration this way, but you'll learn more about the problem and its resolution than otherwise.

Knowing the Top Causes for System Problems

System problems can manifest in many different ways, and yet they all resolve down to one of several possibilities. Keep this in mind when identifying and isolating a problem, because one of the troubleshooting steps you can take involves eliminating these different possibilities and narrowing down your list of suspects.

- **Hardware conflicts**. Only seen when setting up a new system or making hardware changes, hardware conflicts are detected by Windows 98 and reported to you; often they are resolved without intervention. Additionally, Plug and Play helps resolve such problems most of the time. However, at times hardware conflicts might still occur. Hardware conflicts are caused by hardware sharing IRQs, using overlapping I/O ports, or using the same DMA channel. Hardware conflicts might only reveal themselves when two devices are used at the same time. For example, if a serial mouse and a modem are somehow sharing one of the system's IRQs, everything works fine until you try to use the modem attached to the conflicting serial port. Many of the troubleshooting tools in Windows 98 help you detect such problems.

- **Hardware incompatibilities**. Sometimes devices installed into a computer are simply incompatible with something in the system itself or other devices installed in the system. With modern PCI buses and Plug and Play, hardware incompatibilities are rare, but they do occur. Often, the only way to resolve them is to change the incompatible device with another device from a different manufacturer or a different model.

- **Software incompatibilities**. Sometimes software on a system is incompatible with other software on the same system. For example, two different applications might both rely on different versions of a key system .DLL file. Installing the second application might update that .DLL file to an older one included with the new application, thereby breaking the previously installed (and previously working) application. Reinstalling the earlier application might cause the second application to stop working or to start working oddly. Fortunately, a new tool in Windows 98, called Version Conflict Manager, can help you resolve such problems.

- **Corrupt files**. Sometimes files on a disk system are corrupted. For example, maybe the system locked up once when key files were open and the system's disk cache hadn't yet flushed, or maybe there's a bad sector or cylinder on the hard disk. Corrupt files can often be anticipated after ScanDisk finds and corrects problems on a hard disk. If a Windows file is corrupt, a new Windows 98 troubleshooting tool, called System File Checker, easily finds corrupted Windows files and helps you to restore them. Another tool, called Registry Checker, can test the Windows 98 Registry for problems.

- **User errors**. Sometimes users play with their system's settings and do not come clean when you have to try to resolve such problems. Detecting and correcting incorrect system settings can be difficult. Your best offense for problems like this is to understand all the possible system settings and what they do; restore a backed-up copy of the USER.DAT and SYSTEM.DAT files; remove and reinstall Windows 98 and its applications; or interrogate the user with a bright light and a rubber hose.

- **Hardware failures**. With all of the different hardware devices installed in a system, it's no wonder that sometimes one of them fails. Isolating such a problem is easy if the hardware simply fails outright but becomes difficult if the hardware acts up intermittently.

In addition to the previously listed problems, there are sometimes random, one-time problems that clear up when a system is restarted.

Windows 98 Troubleshooting Tools

The troubleshooting tools included in Windows 98 are substantially improved over those in Windows 95. Not only have some familiar tools been reworked and improved, but many new tools have been added to solve problems that occur regularly enough to warrant them. In the following sections, you learn how to use the troubleshooting tools that come with Windows 98 and solve common problems with them.

Microsoft System Information

You might remember a tool called MSD in Windows 95, which reported on hardware configuration, installed Windows-based drivers, and so on. It has been replaced in Windows 98 with an entirely new tool called Microsoft System Information (MSI). MSI is found in the Start/Programs/Accessories/System Tools folder, or by using the filename MSINFO32.EXE with the Run command of the Start menu. Figure 37.1 shows the main screen in MSI.

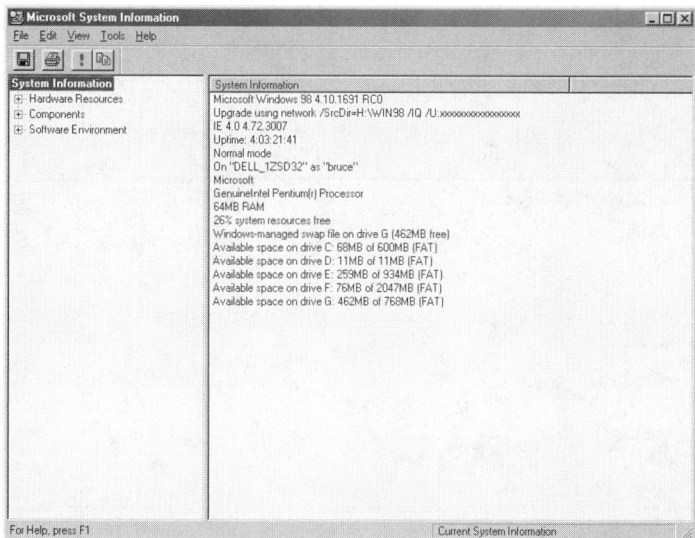

Figure 37.1

The Microsoft System Information tool is new for Windows 98.

MSI serves two valuable functions. First, it displays a plethora of information about the computer hardware and its configuration, about Windows 98 itself, and about the software configured on the system. Second, it serves as a launch pad for other troubleshooting tools, listed on its **T**ools menu. When accessing most of the tools discussed in this chapter, you'll find it's easiest to first start MSI and then run the other tools from MSI.

MSI displays three different classes of information, listed in the left pane. The Hardware Resources branch displays information about IRQs, DMAs, memory I/O port addresses, and so on. The Components branch lists information about different types of components in the system, such as its display, keyboard, multimedia devices, and so on. The Software Environment branch shows information about drivers and modules loaded and running in the system. Figure 37.2 shows MSI with all of its branches open and the Ports category of Components selected.

Many of the pages displayed in MSI let you select the information you want to see using option buttons at the top of the display page in the right pane. Typically, you can choose to display either Basic Information, Advanced Information, or History. Basic Information overviews the selected page's data; Advanced Information shows you much more detailed information. The History selection shows the configuration history of the selected information category. Table 37.1 lists the different information pages available in MSI.

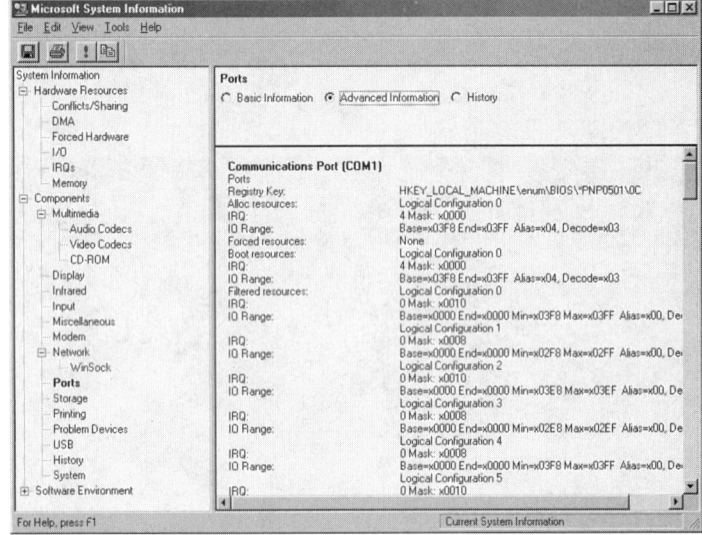

Figure 37.2
MSI with one of its information pages displayed.

Table 37.1
MSI Information Pages

Page	Describes
Hardware Resources Branch	
Conflicts/Sharing	All IRQs on the system that are being shared or are in conflict; this is an important page to view if a system is experiencing problems that might be due to hardware conflicts.
DMA	Displays assigned DMA channels.
Forced Hardware	Any hardware devices that have had their configuration forced through Device Manager settings.
I/O	All assigned I/O memory addresses in the system.
IRQs	All assigned IRQs in the system.
Memory	Hardware memory area assignments.
Components Branch	
Multimedia	Information about installed multimedia devices. Sub-branches include information on audio and video codecs and any installed CD-ROM devices.

Chapter 37: Tools and Strategies for Troubleshooting Windows 98 — 843

Page	Describes
Display	Information about video cards and attached monitors.
Infrared	Information about any installed infrared interface devices.
Input	Information about installed keyboards and pointing devices.
Miscellaneous	Information about printers and tape backup devices.
Modem	Information about installed modems.
Network	All installed networking software; network interface cards, protocols, clients, and file and print sharing drivers. A sub-branch shows information about Windows Sockets (WINSOCK).
Ports	Installed serial and parallel ports.
Storage	Installed storage interface cards (floppy, EIDE, and SCSI) and attached devices.
Printing	Overall printing configuration.
Problem Devices	A list of any devices reporting a problem state.
USB	Universal Serial Bus devices.
History	The history of all configuration changes to the system (hardware configuration and driver changes) since Windows 98 was initially installed. This is a valuable page when troubleshooting.
System	Motherboard devices and settings.
Software Environment Branch	
Drivers/kernel Drivers	Installed kernel-level drivers.
Drivers/MS-DOS Drivers	Installed MS-DOS device drivers.
Drivers/User Mode Drivers	Installed user-level drivers.
16-bit Modules Loaded	All 16-bit software modules running on the system.
32-bit Modules Loaded	All 32-bit software modules running on the system.
Running Tasks	All tasks running on the system.
Startup Programs	All programs that are started at various times in the system. Shows more detailed startup program information than that shown in the Startup menu.
System Hooks	Any running software that has hooked system resources.
OLE Registration	Registered OLE clients and servers loaded through .INI files and through the Registry.

When troubleshooting a system, start with MSI and examine the following key pages for information that might indicate the source of the trouble:

- Conflicts/Sharing—Check this page for information about which devices are sharing single IRQ lines. It can sometimes be acceptable for devices to share a single IRQ, provided that both devices do not run simultaneously. Note that some IRQ sharing entries you see might simply be subcomponents of a single device, which is fine.

- Problem Devices—This page shows any devices in the system that are reporting trouble. The listing is similar to what you see in Device Manager when devices display an information or trouble icon next to their listing.

- History—One of the most valuable sources of information in MSI, this page shows the complete history of all hardware configuration changes and device driver changes. Scan this page (it can be long) to look for changes that the user made to the system that are resulting in problems.

If one of the previous pages shows some kind of trouble, other detailed pages of MSI might yield additional information. For example, if you see in the History page that the driver for the hard disk subsystem has recently been changed, you can then examine the Storage page for additional details about those devices.

After examining the information pages in MSI, use the MSI **T**ools menu to launch any of the following troubleshooting tools:

- Signature Verification Tool
- Windows Report Tool
- Version Conflict Manager
- System File Checker
- Registry Checker
- Automatic Skip Driver Agent
- Dr. Watson
- System Configuration Utility
- ScanDisk

The following sections discuss most of these Windows 98 troubleshooting tools. (See Chapter 36, "The Windows 98 Boot Process and Emergency Recovery," for a description of System Configuration Utility.)

Signature Verification Tool

The Signature Verification Tool lets you search for files on the system that have been signed or not signed by their publishers. This can be useful when searching for Internet-downloaded modules that might be causing problems. The Signature Verification Tool is simply a modified version of the standard Find dialog box in Windows 98 used to search for filenames. Figure 37.3 shows the Signature Verification Tool.

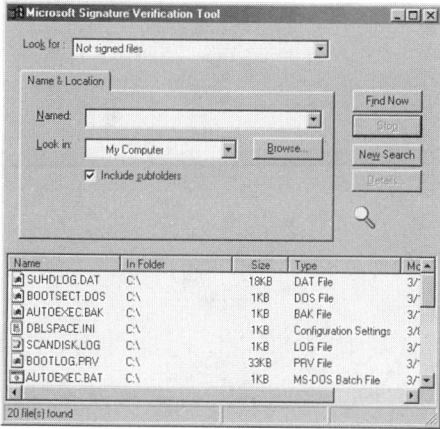

Figure 37.3
The Signature Verification Tool is new in Windows 98.

Windows Report Tool

The Windows Report Tool gathers information on a bug in Windows itself. It automatically includes copies of all key system configuration files, system settings, and descriptions of the problem that you describe. A Microsoft Support Engineer might request that you prepare a report file for examination when trying to debug a problem that you report. Figure 37.4 shows a sample report.

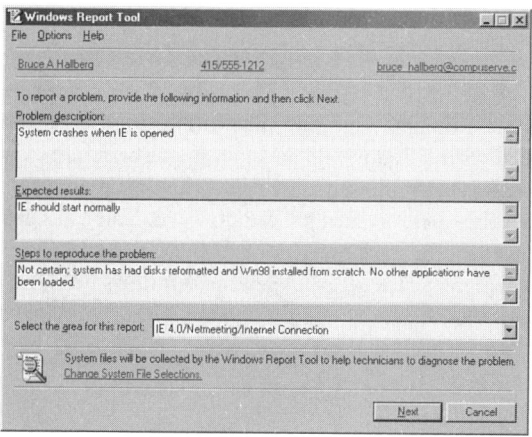

Figure 37.4
The Windows Report Tool is new in Windows 98.

You can customize the information included within the Windows Report file, and might be requested to do so by Microsoft. First, access the **C**ollected Information command in the **O**ptions menu, which displays the Collected Information dialog box shown in Figure 37.5. Select or deselect the files to be included with the check boxes shown. You can also include files not listed by clicking the **A**dd button and then selecting any files that should be included, such as application-specific .INI files.

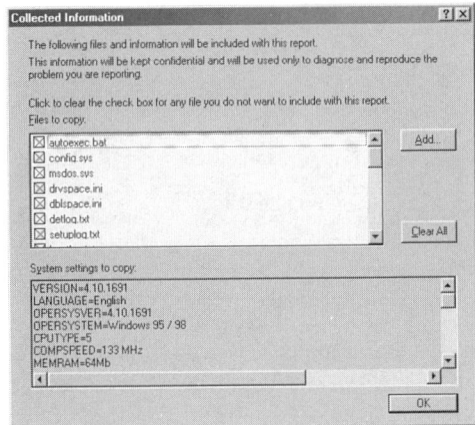

Figure 37.5
The Collected Information dialog box.

Before creating the report file and sending it, also access the **U**ser Information command in the **O**ptions menu. It lists your name, address, and telephone contact information. This information should be correct in case you need to be contacted further to resolve the problem.

After completing the information, use the **S**ave command on the **F**ile menu to prepare the report file. Report files are compressed into .CAB files, which are then extracted by the receiving engineer. You can then email the .CAB file as directed.

Version Conflict Manager

When Windows 98 is installed onto a functioning system, it backs up the key system .DLL files it finds before replacing them with its own versions. This might cause problems for some installed applications. Additionally, you might have had some installed .DLL files that were a later version than the ones included with Windows 98 and that might be required by your applications. The Version Conflict Manager shows you which .DLL files that were backed up have a higher version number than the ones installed by Windows 98. You can select .DLL files from the list and restore them from the backup, replacing the Windows 98 versions of those files. This should be done with great care because the non-Windows 98 .DLL files might cause other problems in the system. Figure 37.6 shows the Version Conflict Manager.

Chapter 37: Tools and Strategies for Troubleshooting Windows 98

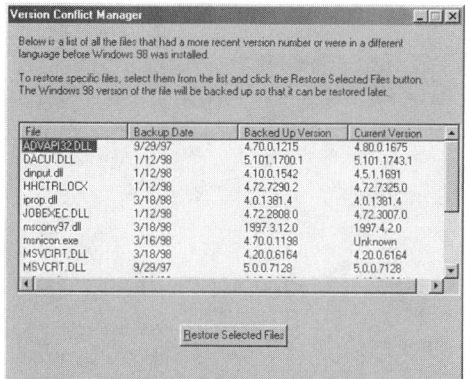

Figure 37.6
The Version Conflict Manager is new for Windows 98.

System File Checker

One of the biggest troubleshooting problems in previous versions of Windows was the inability to verify the integrity of the operating system's files. Their integrity could be damaged from several causes: bad sectors on the disk, an incorrect copy from the original CD-ROM during installation, or by being overwritten by subsequently installed applications. Corrupted system files can play havoc on a system, resulting in application or operating system crashes, or erratic behavior that is difficult to pin down. Now, with Windows 98's System File Checker, you can scan all of the Windows 98 files to ensure that they haven't become corrupted or replaced by incorrect versions. When you start System File Checker, you see the window shown in Figure 37.7.

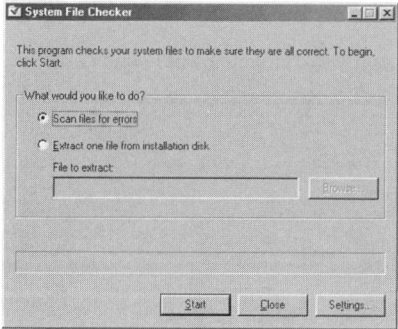

Figure 37.7
The System File Checker is new for Windows 98.

Generally, you can click the **S**tart button to start the scan of files. System File Checker compares the CRC values and version numbers of the installed Windows 98 files with a database of expected values. When it finds a problem, a dialog box appears asking you what action it should take with the file in question. Figure 37.8 shows such a dialog box.

Figure 37.8
The File Changed dialog box in System File Checker.

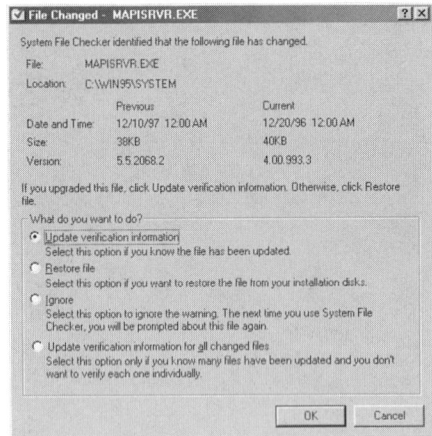

When System File Checker finds a questionable file, you can choose from among the following actions:

- Update Verification Information—This updates the Windows 98 file database with the new version information and CRC values for the file. Selecting this means that the next time you run System File Checker, the file will not be identified as being questionable.

- Restore File—This causes the file to be restored from the Windows 98 installation point (CD-ROM or network share).

- Ignore—Ignores the warning on the selected file. You will be prompted about the file the next time you run System File Checker.

- Update Verification Information for All Changed Files—The current file and all subsequent changed files will have their information updated in the verification database. There is generally no reason to choose this option unless you are building a new verification database.

Before running System File Checker, you can adjust its options. From the main window, click the Settings button to open the dialog box. Figure 37.9 shows the Settings tab of System File Checker Settings dialog box.

On the Settings tab, you can choose how flagged files are backed up. You can always back them up to a directory before restoring different versions from the installation media. You can be prompted on a case-by-case basis for whether they should be backed up, or you can choose to never back them up. You can also change the location to which the files will be backed up before System File Checker restores them. Additionally, on the Settings tab, you can control how the System File Checker log is maintained, and you can view the log file from previous uses of System File Checker. Finally, you can direct whether System File Checker looks for changed or deleted files with the appropriate check boxes.

Chapter 37: Tools and Strategies for Troubleshooting Windows 98 **849**

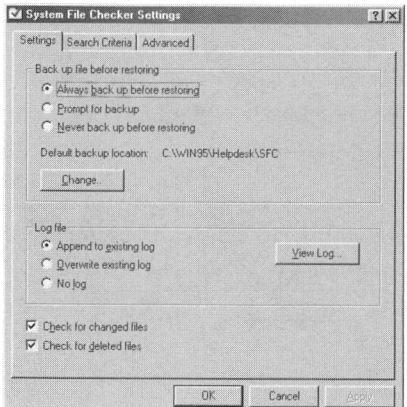

Figure 37.9
System File Checker Settings dialog box's Settings tab.

The Search Criteria tab (see Figure 37.10) defines which directories are checked by System File Checker. If you are creating a new verification database, you can define which directories are tracked and can include application directories if needed by using this tab. You can also define which file extensions are checked.

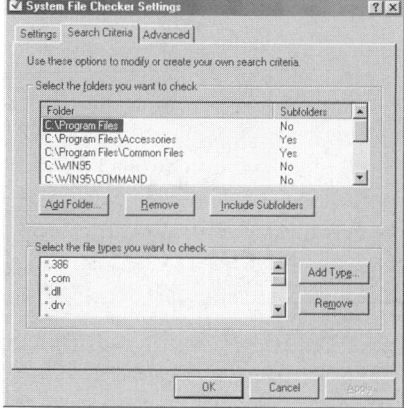

Figure 39.10
System File Checker Settings dialog box's Search Criteria tab.

The final tab, Advanced (see Figure 37.11), lets you choose which verification database is used by System File Checker; it also lets you create a new database. Should you require, you can also select the original verification database installed with Windows 98 by clicking the **R**estore Defaults button.

When installing Windows 98 workstations into an organization, it makes sense to run System File Checker as a final step (after all applications and services have been installed and configured). Additionally, you should create a new verification database, using the Search Criteria tab to select all the directories that contain files that make up the default system configuration. This gives you two benefits that can help future troubleshooting efforts: It gives you a baseline from which to measure changes to the system, and it also monitors application files and settings to ensure that they do not become damaged. After creating the database with the Advanced tab and selecting all the appropriate file types and directories with the Search Criteria tab, run System File Checker and choose Update Verification Information for **A**ll Changed Files at the first prompted file.

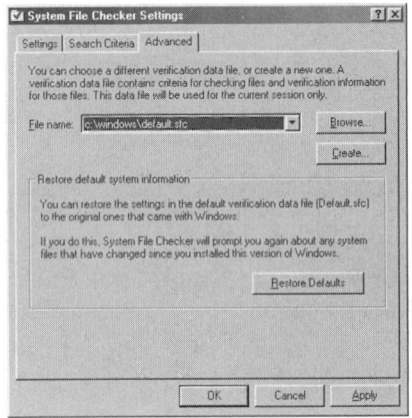

Figure 37.11
System File Checker Settings dialog box's Advanced tab.

Registry Checker

It's unfortunate, but sometimes a system's Registry becomes corrupted. Because the Registry contains so many vital system settings, corruption in either the SYSTEM.DAT or USER.DAT files can wreak havoc with a system. The trouble is, you don't often know whether or not the Registry's corrupted, and you might not know if the backups you have of the Registry are corrupted, either. Windows 98 includes a new tool called the Registry Checker, which quickly scans the Registry files for corrupted data. Note that Registry Checker cannot find incorrect settings within the Registry, just corrupted Registry files.

When you run Registry Checker, you see a simple bar chart showing its progress. It typically finishes checking the Registry within 15-30 seconds. If the Registry has not been backed up on the day on which you run Registry Checker, it prompts you with a message box asking if you would like it backed up immediately.

Automatic Skip Driver Agent

Some device failures cause Windows 98 to run improperly. When this type of failure is detected, you can use the Automatic Skip Driver Agent (ASD) to control whether that device will be started for future Windows 98 startups.

Starting ASD from MSI shows you any critical driver failures on the machine and allows you to designate their new startup status. If there are no driver failures recorded, you see a message to that effect.

Dr. Watson

Dr. Watson is a program that runs in the background and can detect system errors when they occur. When this happens, Dr. Watson creates a log file that contains the state of the system. Dr. Watson log files might be requested by Microsoft Technical Support to help diagnose a tricky problem in the operating system.

Dr. Watson has been reworked for Windows 98 and now includes a number of system state information tabs when it is run in its Advanced mode. Upon starting Dr. Watson, you see its Diagnosis page (see Figure 37.12). On this tab, any peculiarities about the state of the system detected by Dr. Watson are reported.

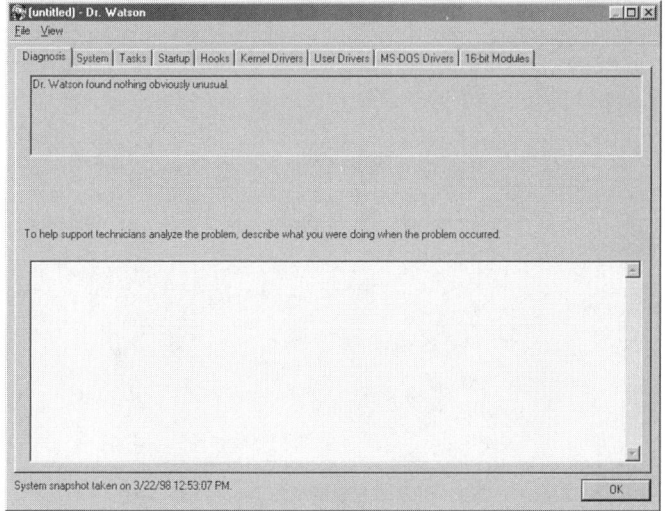

Figure 37.12

Dr. Watson is updated for Windows 98.

If the information tabs indicated in Figure 37.12 are not visible, access the **V**iew menu and choose **A**dvanced View to display them. Each of the remaining tabs shows information about various aspects of the system. These information tabs are similar to the information pages shown in MSI, although they are less extensive.

To control Dr. Watson's settings, access the **V**iew menu and choose **O**ptions. You see the Dr. Watson Options dialog box shown in Figure 37.13. You can control how many log entries are maintained by Dr. Watson, the directory in which they are stored, as well as the number of instructions and stack frames that will be disassembled in the Dr. Watson log files. You can also choose whether to open the Dr. Watson window in **S**tandard or **A**dvanced view. (The difference is the access to the additional information tabs.)

Figure 37.13
Dr. Watson Options dialog box.

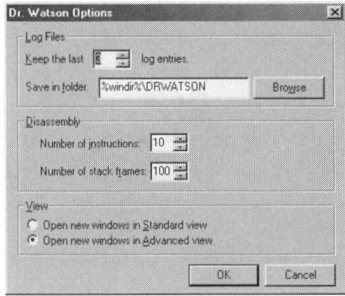

ScanDisk

The ScanDisk utility is unchanged from Windows 95. You use it to detect directory structure problems on a disk, and you can perform detailed disk surface analysis testing. Figure 37.14 shows the ScanDisk utility.

Figure 37.14
ScanDisk is the same as it was in Windows 95.

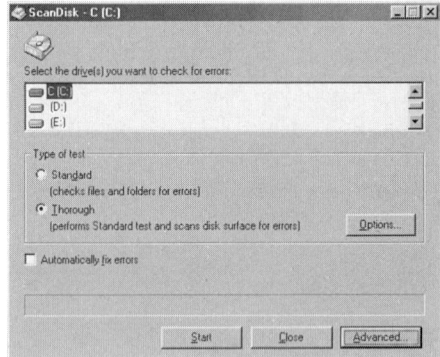

You should run ScanDisk prior to doing more detailed troubleshooting on Windows 98 systems. Many system problems are caused by lost clusters or other errors in the disk system that ScanDisk can detect and fix.

The ScanDisk Advanced Options dialog box lets you choose how ScanDisk operates, and is shown in Figure 37.15. You can control whether summary displays are shown after ScanDisk finishes, how ScanDisk maintains its log file (usually C:\SCANDISK.LOG), how ScanDisk handles cross-linked files, how it handles lost clusters, and what types of tests it performs on the directories it examines.

FileWise

Problems with Windows 98 systems or applications are often caused by inappropriate changes to files. Perhaps a file has become changed due to an error, from a virus, or from some other reason. A utility that is located on the Windows 98 CD-ROM can help you detect such problems.

Chapter 37: Tools and Strategies for Troubleshooting Windows 98

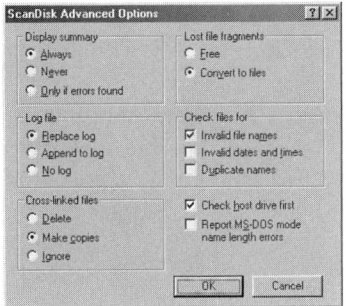

Figure 37.15
ScanDisk Advanced Options dialog box.

Located in the \Tools\Reskit\Diagnose directory, FileWise (FILEWISE.EXE) lets you select files or entire directory structures and then displays detailed information about all of the files it finds. It then can be made to calculate Cyclic Redundancy Check (CRC) values for all of the files, and the resulting information can be saved into a text file. You can then use FileWise to perform a similar test of a supposedly matching set of files, and then compare the two text files for differences that should not exist. For example, you might compare the files stored in the \Windows directory of two different machines, one of which is having strange problems, but both of which are configured the same. In this context, FileWise can help you identify files that don't match, and might help you find the source of the problem. Another way to use FileWise is to make a "snapshot" of a set of files prior to making some change to a system, and then using FileWise to make another "snapshot" after the change is complete. You can then compare the resulting saved text files in order to learn what was changed in the files as a result of the modification. FileWise is shown in Figure 37.16.

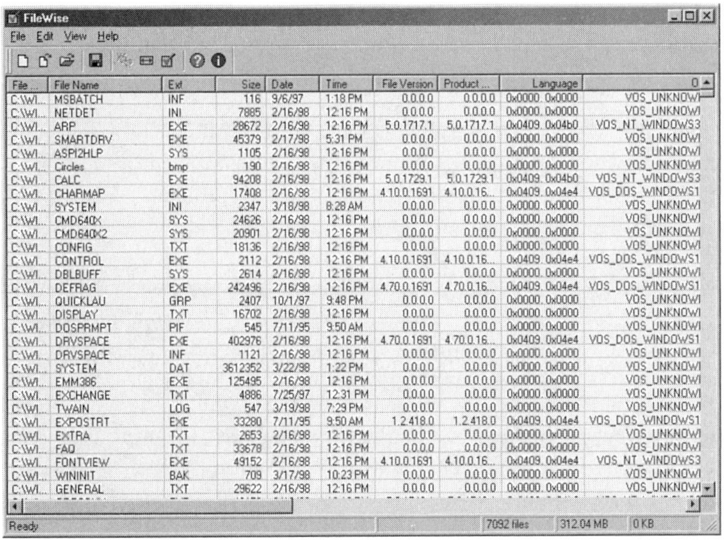

Figure 37.16
FileWise is on the Windows 98 CD-ROM.

After starting FileWise, open its **F**ile menu and choose **A**dd a File or Add a **D**irectory. Select the files or directories that you want FileWise to analyze. After it finishes loading all of the file information, click the Generate CRCs button on its toolbar. Calculating CRCs might take a while for very large sets of files. When finished, use the **S**ave command (in the **F**ile menu) to save a text file containing all of the file details. Follow the same steps with another machine, a copy of a directory on the same machine, or after some change that you want to analyze. You can then compare the two text files to learn which files were changed between the two FileWise analyses.

Troubleshooting Specific Problems

You've learned about general troubleshooting practice and about the troubleshooting tools included with Windows 98. Armed with this knowledge, you can start to work through most Windows 98 system problems. However, until you gain experience dealing with a variety of problems, you might spend unnecessary amounts of time looking for problems in areas not indicated by a problem. The following sections discuss a number of common types of problems that you might be called on to solve under Windows 98. It discusses their causes and shows you which tools to use (and in which order) to rapidly resolve the problem.

> **Note** Problems with system boot or startup are discussed in Chapter 36, "The Windows 98 Boot Process and Emergency Recovery."

Before pursuing any troubleshooting activity on a system, there are some steps that you should always take. Not only do these steps eliminate some common problems, but they are easily performed:

- Completely shut down the system, power it down, and restart it. Many problems disappear with a clean restart of the system, and most of those that do vanish do not reoccur. Make sure to test for the problem after doing this; if the problem remains, continue troubleshooting.

- Run ScanDisk against the drive that holds Windows 98, the drive that holds the Windows 98 paging file (if different), and any drives holding the affected application's program files or data files. This eliminates directory corruption and disk surface problems as possible causes.

- Run Registry Checker to test the integrity of the Registry databases. Running Registry Checker takes less than a minute, and can reveal Registry corruption, which can cause all sorts of strange behavior on a system.

- Open Device Manager (in the System Control Panel) and see if the system is reporting problems with any devices.

After performing these steps, if the problem has not been revealed or corrected, proceed with the following sections.

Application Crashes Regularly

Problems with applications crashing on a regular basis can be common. The first step is to determine if only one application is crashing, if a set of common applications are crashing, or if all applications are crashing.

Problems with a single application crashing are almost always related to one of several possible causes:

- A bug in the application might be causing the trouble; you'll have to check with the vendor for new or updated versions of the application, or discuss with them known incompatibilities for their applications that might apply. A bug should be suspected if the application crash is perfectly repeatable— for example, if every time you select a particular menu item or perform a set of actions, the application crashes.

- A file that is part of the application might be corrupted or bad for some reason. Solving this cause is typically as simple as removing the application and then reinstalling it. This cause might or might not be perfectly repeatable. If the application behaves normally when initially installed but then experiences the problem after a period of time, even after you remove and reinstall the application, consider creating a new System File Checker database that includes the application's directories in addition to the Windows 98 directories. Also, create the new database immediately after reinstallation of the application. Then, when the trouble appears, System File Checker might help you discover which file is being damaged.

- There might be a Windows support file that has been changed and is now incompatible or corrupted. Run System File Checker and Version Conflict Manager to look for reported files that are likely to be used by the application. For example, if the problem is with a communications program and System File Checker reports trouble with the file UNIMODEM.DRV, that file is probably involved in the problem. If this is the case, first try reinstalling the application, and then try using System File Checker to restore the affected files from the Windows 98 installation media.

- The data file or files used by the application might be corrupted. For example, it is possible to open Word or Excel files that initially work fine but then crash the application after performing some task such as scrolling to the bottom of the file. This sort of behavior is almost always due to a corrupt data file, particularly when the behavior does not occur when working with other files. You can try several things when this happens. Try to get a clean replacement of the data file; restore a clean copy from backup; use a tool appropriate to the application to recover any data in the file. Alternatively, you might be able to copy and paste some data from the bad file into a new one. (Just be careful not to cut and paste the troublesome area!)

When you have trouble with a group of applications, the trick is to find out what is common among the applications. There is almost always a common .DLL, system service, or device upon which all the applications depend. Use MSI to look for devices that are in conflict or are reporting trouble, and then use System File Checker to check the Windows 98 .DLL files and system services. Replace or repair any devices that aren't working properly or are in conflict. Reinstalling one of the crashing applications might resolve the problem for all of them. As a last resort, you can try reinstalling Windows 98 itself.

> **Warning** I hope that you think this goes without saying: All important data files on a system should be regularly backed up, *before* trouble strikes. You should also make an extra backup of the system before doing most troubleshooting work.

If all applications on the system are crashing regularly, then the problem is not with the applications, but with the operating system or the computer hardware. See the following section for information on resolving these problems.

System Crashes Regularly

Problems where the system is crashing regularly can be extremely difficult to resolve because there are many possible sources, and the trouble might be intermittent. Moreover, the system might report all sorts of different problems over time, none of which will tell you what's really causing the trouble. Chasing down these gremlins can be time-consuming and may become expensive if the cause seems rooted in hardware and you don't have spare parts with which to experiment. Proceed as follows:

- Run System File Checker to test the integrity of the Windows 98 system files; repair or reinstall damaged files as needed.

- Examine MSI or Device Manager for obvious device problems. Work to resolve any IRQ conflicts reported by MSI.

- Run ScanDisk and make sure to perform a detailed surface analysis of all hard disks in the system.

- Run the latest version of a virus-checking program such as VirusScan from Network Associates or Norton AntiVirus from Symantec. If either detects a virus, make sure to follow their instructions for dealing with it.

- Reinstall Windows 98 and its applications. If the problem reoccurs, suspect the following possible hardware sources: hard disk drive experiencing intermittent failures (usually detected over time by ScanDisk) or bad RAM on the system. If possible, replace those components with backup components. For RAM, you might be able to remove half of system RAM, see if the problem reoccurs, and then swap the remaining half of RAM with the half you removed. If the problem is still occurring, then bad RAM is not the issue and you can reinstall all RAM.

- The BIOS of some motherboards lets you choose the number of wait states and other memory management parameters for the system. If so, set all such parameters to their slowest, least-aggressive settings. If the problem goes away, then the settings in BIOS weren't appropriate for the system, or some component of the system (probably on the motherboard, including RAM) has probably degraded. The motherboard and RAM might need to be replaced.

- Because Windows 98 and its applications are very video-intensive, problems with the display adapter or its drivers can cause frequent system crashes. To test them, you should first try to install a newer version of the video drivers, and then try to replace the display adapter.

- Some problem in the system's BIOS can cause system crashes. Check with the computer manufacturer for an updated BIOS; often you can download files over the Internet and update the BIOS without having to replace any actual chips on the motherboard.

- Some of the weirdest, least-explicable problems are caused by bad drive cables in the system. If possible and if nothing else seems to be working, replace the floppy disk drive cable, the hard disk data cable, and the CD-ROM data cables with new ones.

Hard Disk Trouble

Hard disks usually fail in one of two ways: Either they go completely dead and never work again, or they start to develop bad sectors, often at an increasing rate. There's not much you can do about the former except to replace the drive and start over, restoring your data from backup. In the latter case, you should regularly run ScanDisk; if errors keep cropping up on the surface scan, then make a fresh backup of your data and replace the drive as soon as possible. Cases where hard drives are failing by sectors going bad over time do not usually stabilize, so it's not a matter of fixing the bad sectors and continuing.

Modem/Serial Port Trouble

Problems with modem connections can be very tricky to resolve because although you will usually know that something is wrong with the dial-up connection, there are many possible sources of failure, mirrored on both sides of the connection. Check the following to see if the problem is on a particular side:

- Make sure that the telephone lines are functioning normally by plugging a telephone into cable coming from the wall that plugs into the modem. You should be able to hear a dial tone, and should be able to call a number without hearing excessive noise.

- Make sure that the modem is functioning. Using a terminal program, like HyperTerminal, send standard AT commands to the modem to see if it responds normally. Try ATZ to reset the modem and ATH1 and ATH0 to pick up the line, and then hang it back up again. Also, open the Modem Properties dialog box, move to the Diagnostics tab, and click the **M**ore Info button to have the modem driver test the modem.

- If the problem occurs only when connecting to one remote number, then the problem is likely on their end. Try to contact the administrator of the remote system to report the trouble.

- Use MSI to make sure that the serial port IRQ isn't being shared with another device or serial port. By default, COM1 and COM3 use IRQ 4; COM2 and COM4 use IRQ 3. You can't have two COM ports using a single IRQ at the same time. Some older Ethernet network cards often came set to IRQ 3 by default; if you're using such a card, make sure it's set to a free IRQ line.

- Sometimes modems start to act strangely, for a variety of unrepeatable reasons. You should try resetting the modem completely by powering it off and on if it's an external modem, or by performing a cold boot of the system if it's an internal modem. (Internal modems don't reset with warm boots, nor do serial ports.)

Conclusion

As pointed out in the chapter introduction, troubleshooting tricky problems can be very frustrating and rewarding. In this chapter, you learned about general troubleshooting practice (including how to gather troubleshooting information from users), about the troubleshooting tools included with Windows 98, and about some specific advice for troubleshooting common problems on Windows 98 systems.

Although this chapter should serve to help you solve a problem, don't forget other resources that are available to you. Sometimes people spend inordinate amounts of time troubleshooting some problem, when they could have solved the problem in one-tenth the time if they had used a different resource. Application vendors and hardware manufacturers are invaluable sources of assistance when troubleshooting, and most maintain Web pages that contain troubleshooting information. For Windows 98 problems, don't forget to consult the Microsoft Knowledge Base, which lists problems encountered and solved by Microsoft Software Engineers.

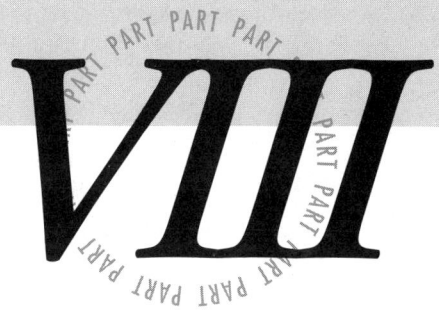

Appendixes

A Windows 98 Accessories 861

B Windows 95/98 Device Manager Error Codes 865

C Command-Line Reference 873

D Installation Script 905

Windows 98 Accessories

The Accessories are a collection of useful utilities and applications included with Windows 98. Many of these Accessories fall into a few distinct groups: Communications, Entertainment, System Tools, and so on. Overall, the only thing these Accessories have in common is that they are found in the same place because there is no other place to put them. Most of the Accessories are optional components that you can include during Setup or add later using the Windows 98 tab of the Add/Remove Programs Control Panel. However, not all the optional components are Accessories. The Windows 98 Setup options (Typical, Custom, Portable, Compact) each include a collection of Accessories (refer to Table 1.2).

Table A.1 provides a brief summary of Windows 98 Accessories with references to chapters in which the Accessories are discussed in detail. You might not see all these Accessories on your PC when you select Start Menu/Programs/Accessories. If you're looking for an Accessory and can't find it through the Start menu, try the Add/Remove Programs Control Panel.

Table A.1
Windows 98 Accessories

Group	Name	Description	Chapter
Accessibility	Accessibility Wizard	Wizard that installs and configures accessibility features	
	Magnifier	Desktop magnifying glass: follows the cursor with a magnified view	
Communications	Dial-up Networking	Folder that lets you create and manage dial-up connections; also accessible from My Computer	26
	Direct Cable Connection	Folder that lets you network two PCs through a serial or parallel connection—without additional networking hardware	19, 22
	Hyperterminal	Terminal emulation; emulates various terminal types, including VT100, Minitel, and so on; includes autodetect option	25
	Phone Dialer	Simple telephone dialer program; initiates modem connections	26
Entertainment	ActiveMovie Control	Displays streamed files; provides other multimedia features	14
	CD Player	Allows you to play audio CDs on your PC	14
	Interactive CD Sampler		
	Media Player	Plays various media files	14
	Sound Recorder	Records audio input	14
	Trial Programs		
	Volume Control	Volume settings for various audio formats	14
	WebTV for Windows	Lets you use your computer as a $2,000 television; requires additional hardware	14

Appendix A: Windows 98 Accessories **863**

Group	Name	Description	Chapter
Games	Free Cell		
	Hearts		
	Minesweeper		
	Solitaire		
System Tools	Backup	Backs up files for permanent storage	20
	Character Map	Lets you insert special characters in documents	
	Clipboard Viewer	Displays the current contents of the virtual clipboard; clipboard is the temporary place where the data goes when you perform a cut or copy operation	
	Compression Agent	Provides enhanced configuration and management for compressed drives	17
	Disk Cleanup	Looks for unnecessary files; helps free disk space	17
	Disk Defragmenter	Defragments disks	17
	Drive Converter (FAT32)	Converts FAT16 partitions to FAT32	17
	DriveSpace	Compresses drives for more efficient storage	17
	Maintenance Wizard	Performs routine system maintenance at regular intervals; defragments, checks for disk errors, deletes unnecessary files	35
	Net Watcher	Provides network management functions; lets you view network connections, shares, open files, and so on	21
	Resource Meter	Displays current resource usage	36
	ScanDisk	Scans disks for disk errors	17
	Scheduled Tasks	Lets you automate and schedule system tasks and other executable operations	35

continues

Table A.1, Continued
Windows 98 Accessories

Group	Name	Description	Chapter
	System Information	Provides system information about hardware, Windows components, and software environment. The Tools menu provides access to several other troubleshooting tools, such as System File Checker and System Configuration Utility	38
	System Monitor	Tracks and displays information on several performance parameters; helps you optimize system performance	36
	Welcome to Windows	Invokes a guided tour of Windows 98 features	
	Calculator	An onscreen calculator; includes standard and scientific modes	
	Imaging	Provides quick viewing of various image formats	
	Notepad	The venerable Windows text editor	
	Paint	Basic painting/graphics application	
	WordPad	Scaled-down word processor ("Word Light")	

Windows 95/98 Device Manager Error Codes

The following summary of Device Manager Error codes is from the Microsoft TechNet CD-ROM. TechNet is a vast reference of technical tips, articles, and information on all Microsoft software products and is a useful resource for any network professional. TechNet is, in fact, one of Microsoft's best products.

To obtain a subscription to TechNet, contact Microsoft:

Microsoft TechNet
One Microsoft Way
Redmond WA 98052

technet@microsoft.com

1-800-344-2121

PSS ID number: Q125174

Article last modified on 05-21-1996

PSS database name: WIN95X

Summary

This article lists error codes that may be reported by Device Manager and describes how to resolve the errors. To view error codes, follow these steps:

1. In Control Panel, double-click System.
2. Click the Device Manager tab.
3. Double-click a device type (for example, double-click Mouse) to see the devices in that category.
4. Double-click a device to view its properties. If an error code has been generated, the code appears in the Device Status box on the General tab.

More Information

Code 1

This code means the system has not had a chance to configure the device.

To resolve this error code, use Device Manager to remove the device and then run the Add New Hardware tool in Control Panel.

Appendix B: Windows 95/98 Device Manager Error Codes **867**

Code 2

This code means the device loader (DevLoader) failed to load a device.

To resolve this error code, use Device Manager to remove the device and then run the Add New Hardware tool in Control Panel.

Code 3

This code means the system has run out of memory.

To resolve this error code, use Device Manager to remove the device and then run the Add New Hardware tool in Control Panel.

Code 4

This code means the .inf file for this device is incorrect. For example, the .inf file specifies a field that should be text but is binary instead.

To resolve this error code, use Device Manager to remove the device and then run the Add New Hardware tool in Control Panel. If you continue to receive this error code, contact the hardware's manufacturer for an updated .inf file.

Code 5

This code means there was a device failure due to the lack of an arbitrator. If a device requests a resource type for which there is no arbitrator, you receive this error code.

To resolve this error code, use Device Manager to remove the device and then run the Add New Hardware tool in Control Panel.

Code 6

This code means there is a conflict between this device and another device.

To resolve this error code, see the "Troubleshooting Conflicting Hardware" topic in Windows 95 Help or see the following article in the Microsoft Knowledge Base:

    ARTICLE ID: Q133240

    TITLE: Troubleshooting Device Conflicts with Device Manager

Code 7

This code means that no configuration can be performed on the device.

If the device works correctly, you do need not to perform any steps to correct the code. If the device does not work correctly, use Device Manager to remove the device and then run the Add New Hardware tool in Control Panel. If you continue to receive this error code and the device does not function properly, check with the hardware's manufacturer or the Microsoft Software Library for an updated driver.

Code 8

This code means the device loader (DevLoader) for a device could not be found. For example, the .inf file for the device may refer to a missing or invalid file.

To resolve this error code, use Device Manager to remove the device and then run the Add New Hardware tool in Control Panel. If you continue to receive this error code, contact the hardware's manufacturer about an updated .inf file.

Code 9

This code means that the information in the Registry for this device is invalid.

To resolve this error code, use Device Manager to remove the device and then run the Add New Hardware tool in Control Panel. If you continue to receive this error code, contact the hardware's manufacturer for the proper Registry settings.

Code 10

This code means that the device failed to start (for example, it is missing or is not working properly).

To resolve this error code, make sure the device is attached to the computer correctly. For example, make sure all cables are plugged in fully and that all adapter cards are plugged into their slots fully.

Code 11

This code means that the device failed.

To resolve this error code, use Device Manager to remove the device and then run the Add New Hardware tool in Control Panel.

Code 12

This code means one of the resource arbitrators failed. This can occur if the device is software-configurable and it does not currently have a resource, if the system is out of resources (for example, all the interrupts are in use), or if the device requests a resource and that resource is currently in use by another device that will not release the resource.

To resolve this error code, see the "Troubleshooting Conflicting Hardware" topic in Windows 95 Help or see the following article in the Microsoft Knowledge Base:

ARTICLE ID: Q133240

TITLE: Troubleshooting Device Conflicts with Device Manager

Code 13

This code means the device failed due to a problem in the device driver.

To resolve this error code, use Device Manager to remove the device and then run the Add New Hardware tool in Control Panel.

Code 14

This code means the device has a problem that may be resolved by restarting your computer.

To resolve this error code, shut down Windows 95, turn off your computer, and then turn it back on.

Code 15

This code means the device's resources are conflicting with another device's resources.

To resolve this error code, see the "Troubleshooting Conflicting Hardware" topic in Windows 95 Help or see the following article in the Microsoft Knowledge Base:

ARTICLE ID: Q133240

TITLE: Troubleshooting Device Conflicts with Device Manager

Code 16

This code means the device was not fully detected. When a device is not fully detected, all of its resources may not be recorded.

To resolve this error code, click the Resources tab in the device's properties to manually enter the settings.

Code 17

This code means the device is a multiple-function device and the .inf file for the device is providing invalid information on how to split the device's resources to the child devices.

To resolve this error code, use Device Manager to remove the device and then run the Add New Hardware tool in Control Panel. If you continue to receive this error code, contact the hardware's manufacturer about an updated .inf file.

Code 18

This code means that an error has occurred and the device needs to be reinstalled.

To resolve this error code, use Device Manager to remove the device and then run the Add New Hardware tool in Control Panel.

Code 19

This code means the Registry returned an unknown result.

To resolve this error code, use Device Manager to remove the device and then run the Add New Hardware tool in Control Panel.

Code 20

This code means VxD Loader (Vxdldr) returned an unknown result. For example, there could a version mismatch between the device driver and the operating system.

To resolve this error code, use Device Manager to remove the device and then run the Add New Hardware tool in Control Panel.

Code 21

This code means the device has a problem that may be resolved by restarting your computer.

To resolve this error code, shut down Windows 95, turn off your computer, and then turn it back on.

Code 22

This code means the device is disabled.

To resolve this error code, enable the device. To do so, follow these steps:

1. In Control Panel, double-click System.

Appendix B: Windows 95/98 Device Manager Error Codes

2. Click the Device Manager tab.

3. Double-click the category for the device you want to enable and then double-click the device.

4. In the Device Usage box, click the check box for the configuration in which you want to enable the device. For example, click the Original Configuration (Current) check box to select it.

5. Click OK and then click Close.

6. Shut down and restart your computer.

Code 23

This code means the device loader delayed the start of a device and then failed to inform Windows 95 when it was ready to start the device.

To resolve this error code, use Device Manager to remove the device and then run the Add New Hardware tool in Control Panel.

Code 24

This code means that the device was not found (for example, it is missing or is not working properly).

To resolve this error code, make sure the device is attached to your computer correctly. For example, make sure all cables are plugged in fully and that all adapter cards are plugged into their slots fully.

Code 25

This code occurs only during the first reboot in Windows 95 Setup and is not visible.

No resolution is necessary.

Code 26

This code means a device failed to load or that there may be a problem in the device driver (for example, the file may be damaged).

To resolve this error code, use Device Manager to remove the device and then run the Add New Hardware tool in Control Panel. If you continue to receive this error code, check with the hardware's manufacturer or the Microsoft Software Library for an updated driver.

Code 27

This code means the portion of the Registry describing possible resources for a device does not contain valid entries. For example, the device is marked as configurable, but the configuration information in the .inf file is set to hardwired.

To resolve this error code, use Device Manager to remove the device and then run the Add New Hardware tool in Control Panel.

Code 28

This code means the device was not installed completely.

To resolve this error code, click the Driver tab in the device's properties and then click Change Driver to update the driver.

Code 29

This code means the device has been disabled because it does not work properly and cannot be made to work properly with Windows 95.

You may be able to resolve this error code by enabling or disabling the device in the computer's CMOS settings. Windows 95 cannot override this setting. Please contact the computer's manufacturer for assistance with using the computer's CMOS setup program.

Code 30

This code means that an IRQ cannot be shared. This problem may occur when a PCI/EISA SCSI controller is sharing an IRQ that is also in use by a real-mode device driver that Windows 95 does not take over.

To resolve this error code, remove the real-mode driver that is using the same IRQ as this device. The real-mode driver may be loading in the Config.sys or Autoexec.bat file.

Command-Line Reference

This appendix is structured in the following manner:

- *"Command-Line Structure"* describes the basic structure of all commands.
- *"Internal Commands"* describes the basic commands that are part of COMMAND.COM.
- *"System Commands"* covers commands that change system-level properties.
- *"Disk and File Commands"* describes commands that manipulate disk and file structures.
- *"Network Commands"* describes commands that check and adjust network parameters.

Command-Line Structure

The command-line structure of Windows 98 is the same as MS-DOS and Windows 95 commands. An executable file ends in the extension .EXE, .COM, or .BAT. The typical command structure is as follows:

`C:\command.exe parameter /switch`

Example:

`C:\copy.exe C:\myfile.txt A:\ /V`

In this example, the command is FORMAT.EXE with a parameter of `C:` and a switch of `/s`. This command tells Windows 98 to format the C: drive and place the system files on it after the format is complete. This command structure is consistent throughout Windows 98. Some commands may not have switches or parameters, but those that do use this structure.

> **Note** Depending on the command, the dash (-) may be substituted for the front slash (/) before a switch.

Internal Commands

Several basic Windows 98 commands are loaded into memory at all times. These commands are actually part of the file COMMAND.COM that defines the command-line environment. In fact, when you run a command prompt in Windows 98, you are actually executing the file COMMAND.COM. These commands are called internal commands because they do not exist on the disk. In contrast, external commands are actually executable files on the hard drive. The following list shows all the internal commands included with Windows 98.

BREAK

Activates extended CTRL+C checking

CD (CHDIR)

Changes the active directory

CHCP

Changes the current Code Page number

CLS
Clears the screen

COPY
Copies files from one location to another

CTTY
Changes the control terminal of the system

DATE
Modifies the system date

DEL (ERASE)
Deletes unwanted files from a disk

DIR
Displays a list of files in the current directory

EXIT
Exits the current command prompt

LH
Loads a program into upper memory

MD (MKDIR)
Creates a directory on a disk

PATH
Sets the PATH system environment variable

PROMPT
Sets the command prompt

RD (RMDIR)
Removes an empty directory from a disk

REN (RENAME)
Renames a file on a disk

SET
Sets and displays environment variable

TIME
Sets and displays the system time

TYPE
Displays the contents of ASCII files

VER
Displays the current version of Windows on the system

VERIFY
Sets an environment variable that instructs Windows 98 to verify that files are written correctly

VOL
Displays the volume label and serial number for a specified disk

System Commands

You can use system commands to display and modify the environment settings of the system. The following system commands are included with Windows 98.

ACCWIZ

`C:\Windows\System\ACCWIZ.EXE`

This command starts the Windows Accessibility Settings Wizard. This wizard allows you to change the various accessibility settings that are available in the Accessibility icon under the Control Panel. This application gives you the same control as the Accessibility properties page but in a wizard format.

DEBUG

`C:\Windows\Command\DEBUG.EXE`

Debug is an interactive program to test and edit any type of file on the system. To load a program into debug, type the following command:

`DEBUG filename`

Debug loads the file and displays a Debug prompt. The Debug prompt is a dash (-). To display the commands you can use in Debug, type **?** and press Enter. Debug displays the contents of the file in hexadecimal and allows you to change the values. Debug is intended for programmers with a knowledge of Assembler and hexadecimal. Debug is a complicated tool that this book does not cover in detail.

> **Warning** Debug enables you to modify any file on your disk, including Windows system files. Do not make any modifications using Debug unless you are absolutely sure you know what you are doing. You can easily destroy your system files beyond repair using this utility.

DOSKEY

`C:\Windows\Command\DOSKEY.COM`

DOSKEY is a program that enables you to create a command buffer in memory. This buffer holds the last several commands that you typed. You can recall these commands by pressing the up-arrow key on the keyboard. You can scroll forward in the list of commands with the down-arrow key. This command is handy when you need to type the same several commands repeatedly.

DOSKEY Parameters and Switches

- /BUFSIZE

    Changes the size of the command buffer

- /ECHO

    Displays or suppresses display of macros

- /FILE

    Points to a file containing multiple macros

- /HISTORY

    Shows a list of the commands in the buffer

- /INSERT

    Inserts new characters while typing

- /KEYSIZE

    Adjusts keyboard buffer size

- /LINE

    Adjusts size of line buffer

- /MACROS

    Displays all macros in use

- /OVERSTRIKE

    Overwrites any characters on the current line

- REINSTALL

    Starts a new copy of DOSKEY

EDIT

C:\Windows\Command\EDIT.COM

Edit is a simple text editor that can be used at the command prompt. It is nearly identical to the editor included with Windows 95 and previous versions of MS-DOS. You can use EDIT to create and modify any ASCII file.

EDIT Parameters and Switches

- /B

    Forces EDIT to display in monochrome

- /H

    Displays the maximum number of lines that will fit on the screen

- /R

    Loads files as read-only

- /S

    Restricts the use of long filenames when saving

- /<nnn>

    Forces word wrapping at <nnn> characters

- filename

    The file to load into EDIT

KEYB

`C:\Windows\Command\KEYB.COM`

The KEYB command configures your keyboard for a specific language. To use a keyboard definition file to remap your keyboard, type the following command:

`C;\KEYB filename`

The filename parameter is the name of the keyboard map file. This file instructs Windows 98 to load the custom keyboard map into memory. KEYB is a handy way to customize functional keys for a specific application.

KEYB Parameters and Switches

- xx

    Specifies a two-letter keyboard code

- yyy

    Specifies the code-page used for the character set

- /E

    Informs Windows that an enhanced keyboard is in use

- /ID:nnn

    Specifies the ID of the keyboard currently in use

MEM

C:\Windows\Command\MEM.EXE

The MEM command displays the amount of memory in your system. It breaks the output into conventional, upper, reserved, extended, total, and free memory.

MEM Parameters and Switches

- /C

    Lists all programs currently running classified by memory usage

- /D

    Displays the status of each memory register along with driver information

- /F

    Displays detailed information on the amount of free memory in the system

- /M program

    Displays memory information for a specific program in memory; must be followed by the name of the program

- /P

    Pauses after each screen

MODE

C:\Windows\Command\MODE.COM

This command configures system-level devices such as COM and LPT ports. The command syntax depends on the task you are trying to complete. You can use this command to set baud and parity rates for your COM ports, for example. This command is rarely used, as these settings can be made from the GUI.

MORE

C:\Windows\Command\MORE.COM

MORE is a program that Displays output from other commands one page at a time. This command is usually piped onto another command. For example, you can use the following command to force the TYPE command to display a large file one page at a time:

C:\TYPE longfile.txt ¦ MORE

This command prevents the text from scrolling to the end. The MORE command is handy when another command does not contain a switch that pauses output after each screen is

Appendix C: Command-Line Reference   **881**

displayed. If MORE is used as the primary command, it will display the contents of the file as if you used the TYPE command. The following command produces the same syntax as the preceding command:

`C:\MORE longfile.txt`

NLSFUNC

`C:\Windows\Command\NLSFUNC.EXE`

The NLSFUNC command loads country-specific information into the system. You usually use this command with other country-specific commands, such as KEYB, to convert your system for use in a specific country. This command requires a file containing the country-specific information. The following command loads the information from the spain.nfo file:

`C;\NLSFUNC spain.nfo`

PROGMAN

`C:\Windows\PROGMAN.EXE`

PROGMAN launches the classic Windows Program Manager. Although the Explorer interface included with Windows 95 and Windows 98 provides more functionality and ease of use, some people prefer the classic Program Manager interface from Windows 3.1. Running PROGMAN launches this interface.

REGEDIT

`C:\Winodws\REGEDIT.EXE`

This command launches the Windows 98 Registry Editor. You can use the Registry Editor to modify system settings; its use is covered extensively in other sections of this book. It is important to mention here, as it is not displayed as an icon by default in the Windows GUI.

> **Warning** It is possible to cripple your system by making the wrong changes in Registry Editor. Be sure you understand the ramifications of your changes before you make them.

SETVER

`C:\Windows\SETVER.EXE`

This command sets the version number that Windows 98 reports to a program. This information is important when running certain applications that run only under a previous version of Windows. The following command sets the reported version of WIN.COM to 3.11:

`C:\SETVER WIN.COM 3.11`

Now when an application requests the version number for this file, it receives 3.11 instead of 4.1. This setting fools the application into thinking it is running under Windows for Workgroups.

SETVER Parameters and Switches

- FILENAME

    The file whose version is to be altered

- n.nn

    The parameter that specifies the new version number to be assigned

- /D

    The switch that deletes the version table information for the specified file

- /Q

    Suppresses the warning message displayed when the /D switch is used

START

`C:\Windows\Command\START.EXE`

You can use this command to run a Windows or DOS program. The reason you would use this command rather than just typing the filename of the program is that it enables you to specify how the program initially runs. To run the GO.BAT file in the background you would use the following command:

`C:\START /m GO.BAT`

START Parameters and Switches

- /M

    Starts the program minimized in the background.

- /MAX

    Starts the program maximized in the foreground.

- /R

    Runs the program restored (foreground).

- /W

    The command prompt does not return until the other program exits.

WINFILE

`C:\Windows\WINFILE.EXE`

This command starts the classic Windows File Manager. This program was replaced by Windows Explorer in Windows 95, but some users prefer to use the File Manager from Windows 3.1. This command was included to give you both options.

WINVER

`C:\Windows\WINVER.EXE`

This command displays the version of Windows currently running on the system.

Disk and File Commands

Disk and file commands enable you to manipulate files on your system. This section covers the disk and file commands included with Windows 98.

ATTRIB

`C:\Windows\Command\ATTRIB.EXE`

This command changes file attributes from the command line. Each file on the system contains an attribute that Windows 98 uses to protect important files. The attributes are as follows:

- `Archive (A)`

  This attribute means the file is an all-purpose file that has no modification restrictions placed on it.

- `System (S)`

  The system attribute tells Windows that the file is part of the operating system and should not be directly modified by the user.

- `Read-Only (R)`

  The read-only attribute protects the file from being modified or deleted. A user can execute and view the file, but Windows will not allow you to make any changes to it.

- `Hidden (H)`

  The hidden attribute tells Windows that the file should not be listed using a DIR command. The logic behind this attribute is that a file cannot be corrupted if it is not seen.

To change the attributes of your files with the ATTRIB command, you would use the following syntax:

```
ATTRIB [+R ¦ -R] [+A ¦ -A] [+S ¦ -S] [+H ¦ -H] filename
```

The plus- and minus-sign parameters add or remove the specified attribute. For example, to add the hidden and read-only attributes to a file called testdata.dat, use the following command:

```
C:\ATTRIB +H +R testdata.dat
```

You can verify that the attributes have been changed by using the following command:

```
C:\ATTRIB testdata.day
```

Using the ATTRIB command with just the filename displays the list of attributes associated with that file.

If you want to change the attribute for all files in a specified path, you can use the /s switch with the command.

```
C;\ATTRIB +r C:\DATA /s
```

This command adds the read-only attribute to all files in the C:\DATA directory.

CHKDSK

```
C:\Windows\Command\CHKDSK.EXE
```

The CHKDSK command runs a quick check of your disk drive and displays a report showing the allocation of space on the disk. CHKDSK can fix minor problems on a disk such as file fragmentation. The following command checks a disk and repairs any errors:

```
C:\CHKDSK C: /F
```

CHKDSK Parameters and Switches

- /F

    Tells CHKDSK to fix any errors found on the disk

- /V

    Displays the name and path of every file on a disk

DELTREE

```
C:\Windows\Command\DELTREE.EXE
```

The DELTREE command deletes every file in a specified directory and then deletes the folder. This utility is useful for removing unwanted file structures from your drive. For example, to

Appendix C: Command-Line Reference

remove a directory called olddata that contains multiple subdirectories use the following command:

`C:\DELTREE D:\olddata`

> **Warning** This command-line utility deletes the specified directory structure without using the Recycle Bin. Be very careful when using this command.

DELTREE Parameters and Switches

- /Y

    Tells DELTREE to delete the structure without prompting you for confirmation

- path

    Supplies the directory you want to delete

DISKCOPY

`C:\Windows\Command\DISKCOPY.COM`

This command copies the contents of one disk to another and offers an easy way to duplicate floppy disks. The disadvantage of DISKCOPY is that both disks must be the same type. Because DISKCOPY copies files by tracks, both types of media must have the same number of tracks. For example, you cannot use DISKCOPY to copy the contents of a 5.25" floppy to a 3.5" floppy. To copy the contents of one disk to another using only one disk drive, use the following syntax:

`C:\DISKCOPY a: a:`

DISKCOPY Parameters and Switches

- /1

    Forces DISKCOPY to copy only one side of the disk

- /V

    Verifies the information during transfer

- /M

    Forces multipass copy in memory

EXTRACT

C:\Windows\Command\EXTRACT.EXE

The EXTRACT command extracts individual files from the cabinet files in which Microsoft stores files on distribution media. CAB files can be found on almost every CD or disk that Microsoft distributes. The syntax of the EXTRACT command is as follows:

C:\EXTRACT cabfile.cab desiredfile.xxx

EXTRACT Parameters and Switches

- /A

    Processes all cabinets starting with the one specified

- /C

    Copies source file to destination

- /D

    Displays directory of specified cabinet

- /E

    Extracts all files

- /L

    Specifies where to place files after extraction

- /Y

    Suppresses the confirmation prompt to overwrite existing files

FC

C:\Windows\Command\FC.EXE

The FC command compares two files and shows the differences between them. To compare the files file1.dat and file2.dat, use the following command:

C:\FC file1.dat file2.dat

FC Parameters and Switches

- /A

    Displays first and last lines of differences only

Appendix C: Command-Line Reference

- /B

    Forces a binary comparison

- /C

    Ignores case in letters

- /L

    Forces ASCII comparison

- /LBn

    Sets maximum number of mismatches

- /N

    Displays line number when using an ASCII comparison

- /T

    Does not treat tabs as spaces

- /W

    Removes tabs and spaces before comparing the files

- /nn

    Specifies the number of consecutive matching lines required after a mismatch is detected

FDISK

`C:\Windows\Command\FDISK.EXE`

The FDISK utility creates and deletes partitions on a hard drive. To view partition information from the command line, use the following command:

`C:\FDISK /STATUS`

FIND

`C:\Windows\Command\FIND.EXE`

The FIND command locates a text string in a specified file. For example, to find the word service in the file dept.dat, use the following command:

`C:\FIND "service" dept.dat`

FIND Parameters and Switches

- /V

  Displays every line in the specified file that does not contain the specified text string

- /C

  Displays only the number of lines containing the string, as opposed to displaying the lines themselves

- /N

  Displays line numbers with the lines

- /I

  Ignores case

FORMAT

`C:\Windows\Command\FORMAT.COM`

The format command is used to format a disk. For example, to format a floppy disk in the A: drive, use the following command:

`C:\FORMAT A:`

FORMAT Parameters and Switches

- /V

  Specifies the volume label for the disk

- /Q

  Forces a quick (erase only) format

- /F:size

  Specifies the size of the disk to be formatted

- /B

  Allocates space on the disk for system files

- /S

  Copies the system files to the disk after formatting

- /T:tracks

    Specifies the number of tracks on each side of the disk

- /N:sectors

    Specifies the number of sectors on the track

- /1

    Formats only one side of a floppy disk

- /4

    Allows the format of a 360 K floppy in a 720 K drive

- /8

    Forces eight sectors per track

- /C

    Performs a test on any clusters that have been marked as bad

LABEL

`C:\Windows\Command\LABEL.EXE`

The label command enables you to add a volume label to a disk. To add the label HDD1 to your C: drive, use the following command:

`C:\LABEL C: HDD1`

To view the label on your disk, type **LABEL** or **DIR**.

MOVE

`C:\Windows\Command\MOVE.EXE`

The MOVE command moves files from one location to another. It accomplishes this job by copying the file to the new location and then deleting the old file. The effect is similar to dragging a file to a new location in Windows Explorer while holding down the Shift key. To move the file exam.dat from C:\data to C:\archive, use the following command:

`C:\MOVE C:\data\exam.dat C:\archive\exam.dat`

If you want to rename the file to exam.arc while you move it, modify the command as follows:

`C:\MOVE C:\data\exam.dat C:\archive\exam.arc`

You can also use the MOVE command to rename a directory without actually moving anything. To rename the data directory to examdata without altering any of the files contained in it, use the following command:

```
C:\MOVE C:\data C:\examdata
```

SORT

```
C:\Windows\Command\SORT.EXE
```

The SORT command sorts input and displays the results. For example, to sort the names in the file names.txt and write them to the file sortname.txt, use the following command:

```
C:\SORT names.txt sortname.txt
```

You can also pipe other commands through the SORT command to sort the output of the primary command. For example, you can type the contents of the autoexec.bat file and display each line in alphabetical order with this command:

```
C:\TYPE autoexec.bat | SORT
```

SORT Parameters and Switches

- /R

    Sorts the input in descending order

- /+n

    Sorts the input by the character in column n

SUBST

```
C:\Windows\Command\SUBST.EXE
```

The SUBST command associates a path with a drive letter. For example, the following command associates the path C:\WINDOWS\SYSTEM with the drive letter F.

```
C:\SUBST F: C:\WINDOWS\SYSTEM
```

This command enables you to quickly access your system directory without having to type the path repeatedly. Windows 98 also displays a new drive in My Computer and Windows Explorer that corresponds to the specified path. The drive mapping remains in effect until the system is rebooted or until you use the following command to remove the association:

```
C:\SUBST F: /D
```

Appendix C: Command-Line Reference   **891**

XCOPY

C:\Windows\Command\XCOPY.EXE

The XCOPY command copies files and directories from one disk to another. This command is similar to the DISKCOPY command except that XCOPY does not require both disks to be of the same type. Therefore, you can use XCOPY to copy files from a 2 GB hard drive to a 6 GB hard drive. The reason is that XCOPY does a bit-for-bit transfer rather than copying by tracks. To copy the contents of C: drive to D: drive, use the following command:

C:\XCOPY C: D:

XCOPY Parameters and Switches

- /A

    Copies files without changing file attributes

- /M

    Turns off the Archive attribute when copying files

- /D:date

    Copies only the files that have been modified after a certain date

- /P

    Prompts before creating each file

- /S

    Instructs XCOPY not to copy empty directories

- /E

    Instructs XCOPY to copy empty directories

- /W

    Prompts for confirmation before copying

- /C

    Continues copying even if an error occurs

- /I

    Assumes destination is a directory if it does not exist and multiple files are being copied

- /Q

  Copies without displaying filenames

- /F

  Displays full filename while copying

- /L

  Displays files that will be copied

- /H

  Copies hidden and system files also

- /R

  Overwrites read-only files

- /T

  Creates directory structure without copying the files

- /U

  Overwrites files that already exist in destination

- /K

  Copies attributes with files

- /Y

  Does not prompt to overwrite existing files

- /-Y

  Prompts before overwriting existing files

- /N

  Copies using the short filenames

Network Commands

Network commands display and modify network settings. This section covers the command-line network commands included with Windows 98.

ARP

C:\Windows\ARP.EXE

The ARP command enables you to display and modify the ARP tables used by Address Resolution Protocol to resolve IP addresses to MAC addresses. To display the current ARP tables, type the following command:

C:\ARP -a

To add a static entry to the ARP table that associates IP address 172.221.138.14 to MAC address 00-aa-0b-21-c4-02, you would type the following command:

C:\ARP -s 172.221.138.14 00-aa-0b-21-c4-02

Putting this entry in your ARP table effectively ties an IP address to a specific NIC card. Whenever your machine tries to communicate with 172.221.138.14, it will tie the specified MAC address into the packet header. You can delete this static ARP table entry with the following command:

C:\ARP -d 172.221.138.14

ARP Parameters and Switches

> **Note** Notice that the switches for this command use the dash (-) instead of the front slash (/).

- -A

    Displays the current ARP table entries.

- -N xxx.xxx.xxx.xxx

    Displays the ARP table of the NIC specified by IP address. This feature is handy if you have a multihomed machine and you need the ARP entries for a specific NIC.

- -D

    Deletes the entry for the specified IP address.

- -S

    Adds an entry to the ARP table.

FTP

C:\Windows\FTP.EXE

The FTP command starts the command-line File Transfer Protocol utility. This program is used to transfer files with an FTP server. To connect with the FTP server ftp.microsoft.com, type the following command:

C:\FTP ftp.microsoft.com

You will be prompted for a username and password. After entering this information, you are returned to the FTP prompt. Several commands in the FTP program enable you to navigate through an FTP server. For example, to change to the public directory and download a file called filelist.txt on an FTP server, type the following command:

```
FTP> cd public
FTP> get filelist.txt
```

> **Note** Most FTP servers are case sensitive. The reason is that most FTP servers are running on UNIX systems and UNIX differentiates between case. If a filename is Filelist.TXT, you must type the name exactly, including case. Typing **GET FILELIST.TXT** results in a File Not Found error.

FTP Command Reference

- !

    Drops you to a command prompt without exiting FTP. To return to FTP from the command shell, you must use the EXIT command.

- ?

    Displays a list of commands.

- APPEND

    Appends a file to the end of another file.

- ASCII

    Sets the transfer mode to ASCII.

- BELL

    Causes the system to beep when a command is completed.

- BINARY

    Sets the transfer mode to binary.

- BYE

    Disconnects from the remote system and exits FTP.

- CD

    Changes the active directory on the remote system.

- CLOSE

    Disconnects from the remote system.

- DELETE

    Deletes a file on the remote machine.

- DEBUG

    Activates debug mode.

- DIR

    Displays a list of files in the active directory on the remote system.

- DISCONNECT

    Disconnects from the remote system.

- GET

    Transfers a file from the remote system to the local system.

- GLOB

    Expands local filenames.

- HASH

    Prints a # for each buffer transferred. Used to monitor file transfer progress.

- HELP

    Displays a list of available commands.

- LCD

    Changes the active directory on the local machine.

- **LITERAL**

  Sends an arbitrary command.

- **LS**

  Displays the contents of the active directory on the remote machine.

- **MDELETE**

  Deletes multiple files.

- **MDIR**

  Displays the contents of multiple directories on the remote machine.

- **MGET**

  Transfers multiple files from the remote machine to the local machine.

- **MKDIR**

  Create a directory on the remote machine.

- **MLS**

  Displays the contents of multiple directories on the remote machine.

- **MPUT**

  Transfers multiple files from the local machine to the remote machine.

- **OPEN**

  Establishes a connection to an FTP server.

- **PROMPT**

  Forces interactive prompts on any of the multiple-file commands.

- **PUT**

  Transfers files from the local machine to the remote machine.

- **PWD**

  Shows the contents of the active directory on the local machine.

- **QUIT**

  Exits FTP.

- QUOTE

    Sends an arbitrary FTP command.

- RECV

    Transfers a file from the remote machine to the local machine.

- REMOTEHELP

    Requests help from the remote server.

- RENAME

    Renames a file.

- RMDIR

    Removes a directory on the remote system.

- SEND

    Transfers a file from the local machine to the remote machine.

- STATUS

    Shows the current environment settings.

- TRACE

    Activates tracing of packets.

- TYPE

    Changes file transfer type.

- USER

    Changes logon credentials without disconnecting from the FTP server.

- VERBOSE

    Activates detailed responses.

IPCONFIG

`C:\Windows\IPCONFIG.EXE`

The IPCONFIG command displays a listing of the IP configuration. To display this information, type the following command:

`C:\IPCONFIG`

If you are using DHCP, you can use the IPCONFIG command to release and renew your IP address.

IPCONFIG Parameters and Switches

- /ALL

  Displays detailed information

- /BATCH filename

  Writes the information to a specified filename

- RENEW_ALL (DHCP only)

  Renews the IP address for all adapters on the system

- RELEASE_ALL (DHCP only)

  Releases all IP addresses on all adapters

- RENEW n

  Renews IP address for the specified adapter

- RELEASE n

  Releases IP address for the specified adapter

> **Note** The n in the last two switches refers to the LANA number of the card. You can see these numbers by running the IPCONFIG command with no switches.

NBTSTAT

```
C:\Windows\NBTSTAT.EXE
```

You can use the NBTSTAT command to view current IP connections that are using NetBIOS over TCP/IP. To view the remote machine name table for a machine with an IP address of 169.254.36.201, use the following command:

```
C:\NBTSTAT -A 169.254.36.201
```

NBTSTAT Parameters and Switches

- -a

  Displays the remote machine's name table given its name

Appendix C: Command-Line Reference

- -A

    Displays the remote machine's name table given its IP address

- -c

    Displays the remote name cache

- -n

    Displays local NetBIOS names

- -r

    Lists names resolved by broadcast and WINS

- -R

    Reloads the remote name table

- -S

    Lists sessions table using IP addresses

- -s

    Lists sessions table, but resolves IP addresses using the HOSTS file

Note Notice that the switches for this command use the dash (-) instead of the front slash (/) and that they are case sensitive.

NET

C:\Windows\NET.EXE

The NET command displays and manages NetBIOS connections to other machines. For example, you can view any network drive mappings with the following command:

C:\NET USE

The NET command is broken into sections depending on the first parameter in the command. The following commands are available using the NET command.

NET CONFIG

The NET CONFIG command displays your current computer name, workgroup name, username, and software versions.

NET DIAG

The NET DIAG command enables you to test the connection between two machines on a network. When you run NET DIAG on the first machine, it becomes a network diagnostics server. Subsequent machines connect to this server when they run NET DIAG.

NET HELP

The NET HELP command provides detailed help on each NET command. You can also use NET HELP to decipher an error number that you receive from a NET command.

NET INIT

The NET INIT command initializes the network. NET INIT loads the NIC drivers and the protocols, but doesn't bind them to the Protocol Manager. This command is rarely used anymore as most networking will be handled by protected mode drivers in Windows 98.

NET LOGOFF

This command removes the network bindings from your NIC, which breaks all network connections. This command prevents any network traffic from reaching your system.

NET LOGON

This command enables you to connect to other machines by identifying you as a member of a workgroup. This command is rarely used, as you are given the option to log on when you start Windows 98.

NET PASSWORD

This command changes your network password, that is, the password stored in the username.PWL file on your system. Changing your password affects all subsequent logons including logon from the GUI at system startup.

NET PRINT

This command enables you to view the printer queues on any network printers you have configured. This command is also rarely used, as it is much easier to use the Printers window in the GUI to view print jobs.

NET START

The NET START command enables you to start network services. The downside is that you cannot start network services from a command prompt. To use this command, you need to run Windows 98 in MS-DOS mode. This command enables you to connect to the network in a fully DOS-compatible environment.

NET STOP

This command stops all network services. Like the NET START command, you cannot stop network services from a command prompt. This command is of value only if you are running in MS-DOS mode.

NET TIME

The NET TIME command synchronizes your system clock with another machine on this network. To synchronize your clock with a computer named TIMESERVER, use the following command:

```
C:\NET TIME \\TIMESERVER
```

NET USE

The NET USE command maps local drives to network shares. To view a listing of drive mappings on your system, type the NET USE command with no parameters. To map your M: drive to the Public share on a computer named HAL9000 from the command prompt, use the following command:

```
C:\NET USE M: \\HAL9000\PUBLIC
```

To remove this drive mapping, use the following command:

```
C:\NET USE M: /DELETE
```

NET VER

This command displays the type and version of the current redirector.

NET VIEW

The NET VIEW command requests a list of machines that are on the network from the system designated as the master browser. This list is often more up-to-date than what you see in Network Neighborhood. The reason is that the machine list displayed in Network Neighborhood comes from a backup browser that may not have the latest update from the master browser yet.

NETSTAT

```
C:\Windows\NETSTAT.EXE
```

The NETSTAT command displays a list of current IP connections as well as protocol statistics. This information is useful in troubleshooting connection problems. The NETSTAT command uses the following switches to modify its output:

- -A

    Displays all connections

- -E

    Displays ethernet statistics

- -N

    Displays IP addresses and ports numerically

- -P protocol

    Displays connections for only the specified protocol

- -R

    Displays the routing table

- -S

    Displays statistics separated by protocol

PING

`C:\Windows\PING.EXE`

PING measures the stability of a connection by sending ICMP requests to a remote host and measuring the amount of time it takes to receive a response. You can send a ping to either a machine name or an IP address. To ping the IP address 134.16.27.218, use the following command:

`C:\PING 134.16.27.218`

ROUTE

`C:\Windows\ROUTE.EXE`

You can use the ROUTE command to view and manage the routing table. The *routing table* is a table of static routes that direct traffic across the network. Four subcommands used with the ROUTE command enable you to perform various functions on your routing tables. They are as follows:

- PRINT

    Displays information in the routing table

- ADD

    Adds a route to the routing table

- CHANGE

    Modifies a route in the routing table

- DELETE

    Deletes a route from the routing table

To view the current routing table, use the following:

`C:\ROUTE PRINT`

To add a static route to the routing table that directs all traffic headed to the 234.0.0.0 subnet through the router 186.124.18.1, you would use the following syntax:

`C:\ROUTE ADD 234.0.0.0 255.255.255.0 186.124.18.1`

To change this route to point to the router 186.124.18.2, you would use the following command:

`C:\ROUTE CHANGE 234.0.0.0 255.255.255.0 186.124.18.2`

Finally, to delete this route from the routing table, use the following command:

`C:\ROUTE DELETE 234.0.0.0`

TRACERT

`C:\Windows\TRACERT.EXE`

TRACERT traces the route to a remote machine. For example, you may want to see how many routers you go through when you connect to www.microsoft.com. You could then use this information to help troubleshoot where connection problems may exist. To trace a route to www.microsoft.com, use the following command:

`C:\TRACERT www.microsoft.com`

The following switches are available for the TRACERT command:

- -D

    Suppresses name resolution

- -H nn

    Maximum number of hops TRACERT will allow before failure

- -W nn

    Specifies the amount of time to wait for each hop before timeout

Installation Script

A Windows 98 installation script file is a Windows INF file. INF files typically provide instructions for installing devices or applications in Windows. An installation script is a special kind of INF file that provides instructions for installing Windows 98.

Generally, the best way to create an installation script is to use Batch98 (described in Chapter 2, "Installing Windows 98"). You may, however, occasionally need to modify an existing script or study a script for troubleshooting purposes. Your installation plan, for instance, may lend itself to a solution in which you create multiple scripts by modifying a template script directly rather than by using the Batch98 script-generating feature described in Chapter 2. This appendix provides some basic information on what you'll find in a

Windows 98 installation script. It is worth noting that, although Microsoft provides sample installation scripts and provides information on installation scripts through the Resource Kit and TechNet, officially, Microsoft "...does not encourage or support changes to INF files."

> **Note** You can gain insights on installation scripts by generating your own script by using Batch98 and then viewing or editing it with a standard text editor such as Notepad.

Just as an INI file does, an INF file groups configuration and installation information into predefined sections. Section titles are enclosed in square brackets. Installation script section titles and descriptions are shown in Table D.1. You'll learn more about each of these installation file sections later in this chapter.

Table D.1
Installation Script Section Titles

Section	Description
[Setup]	Settings relating to the actual setup process.
[System]	System and device settings (e.g., monitor, mouse, language support).
[NameandOrg]	Name and Organization settings for the PC; appear in the System Application General tab.
[Network] and network-related sections	Settings describing protocols, clients, and network services.
[Optional Components]	Settings describing which Windows 98 components to install.
[Printers]	Settings defining the printer configuration for the PC.
[InstallLocationsMRU]	UNC paths; lets you predefine a list of path options that you can choose during Setup.
[Strings]	String key definitions—Setup expands a string enclosed in percent signs (%) to the value defined in this section. Strings keys can make the script easier to read and modify.
[Install] and related file-installation sections	Settings that let you copy additional files to the new PC along with the installation.

Each section of the installation script contains several options settings. You do not need to use all the possible settings in your installation script. The following sections describe some of the settings and show you how to use installation script settings to configure certain important features, as follows:

Appendix D: Installation Script

- Automated installation
- Optional-default installation
- Regional settings
- Network settings
- Optional components
- Registry file
- User profiles
- Remote administration

Automated Installation

If you are looking for the simplest possible automated setup, and you do not care about achieving a specialized configuration, your installation script can be very short. You need only tell Setup not to issue any prompts and provide settings for the few values for which Setup may not have a default. In the case of an upgrade, Setup can use the existing settings for almost all values. Microsoft provides the following script (minbatch.inf) as a minimal script for upgrades from previous versions of Windows:

```
[Setup]
Express=1
EBD=0
uninstall=0
vrc=1
[NameAndOrg]
Display=0
[Network]
Display=0
```

The [Setup] parameters are as follows:

- *Express.* Tells Setup whether to stop for user setup information. 0=do not stop for user input. 1=stop for user input.

- *EBD (Emergency Boot Disk).* 0=do not create a boot disk. 1=create a boot disk.

- *Uninstall.* 0=do not let the user choose uninstall and do not back up the previous Windows installation. 1=let the user choose an uninstall option. 5=create the backup files necessary for uninstalling Windows 98 automatically. If you choose to create the uninstall backup files, specify a backup directory by adding the following parameter to the [Setup] section: *BackupDir=OldWin*, where *OldWin* is the name of the uninstall directory.

- *vrc.* A setting that tells Setup whether to ask for confirmation before overwriting a more recent version of a file. 0=prompt for confirmation. 1=overwrite without prompting for confirmation.

The setting Display=0 in the [NameAndOrg] section tells Setup to use default name and organization information. In the case of an upgrade, the default would be the name and organization settings from the last installation. A value of Display=1 would cause Setup to prompt for the name and organization. Alternatively, you can enter the Name and Organization (Org) settings directly. The following example defines name and organization settings and tells Setup not to prompt:

```
[NameAndOrg]
Name="Zesty Higgins"
Org="NASA Spacefood Consortium"
Display=0
```

If you enter Display=1 along with specific Name and Org settings, Setup will prompt the user for a value and use the predefined settings as defaults.

The value Display=0 in the [Network] section tells Setup not to display network configuration dialog boxes during setup.

You'll learn more about the [Network] section later in this chapter. The [Setup] section in the following example is expanded to include some other useful parameters:

```
[Setup]
Express=1
EBD=0
unistall=0
vrc=1
InstallDir="c:\Win_dest"
InstallType=3
TimeZone="Central"
DevicePath=1
```

The additional [Setup] settings are as follows:

- *InstallDir.* The destination directory name for the Windows files. (The default is "C:\Windows.")

- *InstallType.* A value representing the installation type option (also called the Setup option). The installation type defines a collection of components that will be installed on your system. 0=Compact; 1=Typical; 2=Portable; 3=Custom. See Chapter 1, "Deploying Windows 98," and Chapter 2 for more on Windows 98 installation types.

- *TimeZone.* A string defining the time zone. (Manual installations prompt you to enter a time zone setting. This parameter lets you automate time zone selection.)

- *DevicePath.* Tells Setup whether to configure the Windows 98 system to check a network path for INF files when installing devices. This enables the network to have one central location for INF files. 1=use an INF source path to find INFs. 0=don't use a source path (just check the C:\Windows\Inf directory).

The [System] section provides some basic system settings. A [System] section is not required for automated setup (because Setup is capable of configuring system settings using autodetection and defaults); however, you may want to use a [System] section to configure the display resolution or a specific device for which autodetection is unreliable. The [System] section is also used to configure regional settings.

A typical [System] section might be as follows:

```
[System]
Displchar=16,640,480
Locale=L0409
SelectedKeyboard=KEYBOARD_00000409
```

The Locale and SelectKeyboard parameters are related to the regional settings, which are discussed in the following section. Displchar describes the display characteristics for the system. On a Windows 98 computer, you can find the display characteristic settings in the Settings tab of Control Panel's Display application. The Displchar format is as follows:

```
Displchar=color_depth,horiz_res,vert_res
color_depth: bits per pixel: 4 (for 16-color); 8 (for 256-color); 16 (for 16-bit
➥High Color); 24 (for 24-bit True color).
Horiz_res: horizontal (x) resolution.
Vert_res: vertical (y) resolution.
```

You can use the [System] section to specify other items such as display driver, monitor, mouse, and power management settings. (Typically, this isn't necessary; wherever possible, it is preferable to let Setup detect the hardware.)

Windows 98 maintains an INF directory (in the Windows directory) with an INF file for each type of device (KEYBOARD.INF, MONITOR.INF, MSMOUSE.INF, and so on). The setting for each device in the [System] section should reference the appropriate item in the INF file for the device (see Table D.2). Depending on the type of device, the [System] setting should refer to an INF section name or INF description.

Table D.2
INF Directory

Parameter	Value Should Match	INF File
Display	INF description	MSDISP.INF
Keyboard	INF description	KEYBOARD.INF
Locale	INF section name	LOCALE.INF
Machine	INF section name	MACHINE.INF

continues

Table D.2, Continued
INF Directory

Parameter	Value Should Match	INF File
Monitor	INF section name	MONITOR.INF
Mouse	INF section name	MSMOUSE.INF
PenWindows	INF section name	PENWIN.INF
Power	INF section name	MACHINE.INF
SelectedKeyboard	INF section name	MULTILNG.INF
Tablet	INF section name	PENDRV.INF

If you find it necessary to specify the devices in the [System] section, you might want to consult the device vendor to determine the correct installation script settings. If you decide to go spelunking for a setting in the device INF (refer to Table D.2), note that, typically, the actual model names are listed in the [Strings] section and a string parameter then substitutes for the applicable section name or description. Typical devices callouts, for instance, may appear as follows:

```
[System]
Mouse="Standard Serial Mouse"
Monitor= "Panosonic C1381"
```

The term "Standard Serial Mouse" appears in long a list of mouse devices in the [Strings] section of the MSMOUSE.INF. An associated string is then used for the actual device description elsewhere in the file.

Regional Settings

The installation script's regional settings enable you to localize your Windows 98 installation for a particular language, time zone, and keyboard format. Sample regional settings are as follows:

```
[Setup]
TimeZone="Central"
[System]
Multilanguage=english
locale=L0409
SelectedKeyboard=KEYBOARD_00000409
```

The [System] settings refer to entries in the applicable INF files (refer to the preceding section). The easiest way to add regional settings to your installation script is to edit the script template regional.inf, included on the CD-ROM that comes with this book. Regional.inf lists the various options for time zone, keyboard, and locale settings.

Note If you're performing an upgrade, Setup will carry over regional settings from the old installation.

Network Settings

You can use the installation script to define a complete network configuration. To specify a network configuration, you'll need a [Network] section, which defines general network settings, and one or more other network-related sections with values for specific protocol and service components specified in the [Network] section. Table D.3 describes some of the installation script's network-related sections. For information on configuring other Windows 98 clients, protocols, and services through the installation script, see the Windows 95 or Windows 98 Resource Kit.

Note You don't have to provide a networking section with the installation script. For upgrades, Setup will retain the existing networking configuration if you don't supply networking information with the installation script. (Just make sure you run Setup from Windows 4 if you're performing a network installation without information in the script. If you run Setup from MS-DOS, Setup will install the default networking configuration, which could make the network inaccessible—including the network installation share.)

Table D.3
Network-related Installation Script Sections

Section	Description
[Network]	General networking information—computer name, security parameters, and so on
[MSTCP]	TCP/IP parameters
[NWLink]	Parameters relating to Windows 98's IPX/SPX-compatible protocol
[NWRedir]	Client for NetWare Networks settings
[NWServer]	File and Print Sharing for NetWare Networks settings
[Vredir]	Client for Microsoft Networks settings
[Vserver]	File and Print Sharing for Microsoft Networks settings

Listing D.1 is an example of a typical [Network] section with related sections. Many of the entries are self-explanatory if you have a basic understanding of Microsoft networking. See the comments in the listing for additional information. Table D.4 describes some additional settings that aren't included in the listing.

In general, settings that aren't required in Windows 98 aren't required in the installation script. For instance, because you aren't required to use DNS, you aren't required to provide the address for a DNS server. Note, however, that if you don't provide a DNS server, you should set the DNS parameter to 0 to disable DNS.

Listing D.1 Installation Script Network Section

```
[Network]
ComputerName="sonya"
Workgroup="BARKER"
Description="200 MHz Pentium"
Display=0                ;Do not prompt
PrimaryLogon=VREDIR      ;Microsoft Network is primary logon
Clients=VREDIR, NWREDIR  ;Install Client for Microsoft
                         ;Networks and also Client for
                         ;NetWare Networks
Protocols=NETBEUI, NWLINK, NWNBLINK, MSTCP
                         ;Install NetBeui,
                   ;IPX/SPX-compatible (NWLink)
                   ;IPX/SPX NetBios support (NWNBLINK)
                 ;MSTCP (Microsoft TCP/IP)
                 ;
DefaultProtocol=MSTCP    ;TCP/IP is default
Services=VSERVER, NWSERVER  ;Install File and Print Sharing
                         ; Microsoft Networks and also
                         ;File and Print Sharing for
                         ; NetWare Networks
                         ;
Security=DOMAIN    ;Use user-level security validated through
                   ;NT domain. Other options: Security=
                   ;SHARE: share-level security;
                 ;NWSERVER: user-level; use NetWare server;
                 ;MSSERVER: user-level; use NT workstation.
                 ;
PassThroughAgent="BARKER"   ;Domain name or name of server
                            ;providing security.

[NWLINK]
Frame_Type=4             ;Frame type.
NetBIOS=1                  ;Specifies NetBIOS/NWLink

[MSTCP]
LMHOSTS=1                       ;Use LMHOSTS; 0=do not use
LMHOSTPath="C:\WINDOWS\LMHOSTS" ;LMHOSTS path
DHCP=0                          ;Don't use DHCP; 1=use
DNS=1                           ;Use DNS; 1=don't use
WINS=Y                          ;Enable WINS resolution
DNSServers=160.99.89.17          ;DNS server(s)
```

```
Domain=barker                    ;DNS domain
Hostname=sonya
Gateways=145.122.99.109
IPAddress=145.122.131.145
IPMask=255.255.0.0
WINSServer1=145.122.16.150

[VREDIR]               ;Client for Microsoft Network settings
ValidatedLogon=1       ;Validate logon on domain(0=don't)
LogonDomain="BARKER"   ;Name of logon domain

[VSERVER]              ;File and Print Sharing for Microsoft
                       ; Networks settings
                       ;
LMAnnounce=0           ; PC will not announce its presence to LAN
                       ; MAN network. (1=will announce)
MaintainServerList=2   ;Browse master status
                       ;0=disabled (can't be browse master)
                       ;1=enabled  (is the browse master)
                       ;2=auto (can become browse master)

[NWREDIR]              ;Client for NetWare networks settings
FirstNetDrive=G
PreferredServer="NWServer"
ProcessLoginScript=1   ;Enables login script processing
                       ;under Client for NW Networks

[NWSERVER]             ;File and Print Sharing for NetWare
                       ;Networks settings
                       ;
BrowseMaster=0         ;Browse master status:
                       ;0=can't be a browse master
                       ;1=can be a browse master
                       ;2=preferred browse master
                       ;
Use_SAP                ;Enables/Disables SAP browsing
                       ;0=disable SAP browsing
                       ;1=enable SAP browsing
```

Table D.4
Other [Network] and Network-related Settings

Section	Entry	Description
[Network]	RemoveBinding	Removes binding between two components (provides comma-separated list of component INF device IDs)
[MSTCP]	DomainOrder	Specifies search order for DNS domains (provides comma-separated list of DNS domains)

continues

Table D.4, Continued
Other [Network] and Network-related Settings

Section	Entry	Description
	ScopeID	Specifies scope ID; used for NetBIOS over TCP/IP (see Chapter 25, "Windows 98 with TCP/IP")
	SecondaryWINS	Address of secondary WINS server
[NWRedir]	SearchMode	Specifies NetWare search mode (default is 0)

Refer to Listing D.1 for basic network settings.

Note that, if you're performing a network installation, you must ensure that Setup has enough networking information to log on and connect to the installation share during the final installation phase. If you're upgrading and running Setup from within Windows 3.1 or Windows 95, Setup will retain the existing configuration. If you're performing a new install or running Setup from MS-DOS, or if you are changing the network configuration, you must provide Setup with the necessary logon information. If the installation share resides on an NT domain, specify a ComputerName and PassThroughAgent in the [Network] section and make sure the ValidatedLogon and LogonDomain settings in the [Vredir] section are correct. If the installation files are on a NetWare server, ensure that the NetWare-related settings in the [Network] and [NWRedir] sections (such as the PreferredServer) are correct.

If you are performing multiple network installations, it is a very good idea to start with a test installation to make sure the installation script and all other features of Setup function properly in your environment.

> **Note** If you have more than one network adapter (for example, both a network card and a dial-up adapter) and if you generated the installation script using Batch98, be wary of Batch98's multiple-adapter limitation (described in Chapter 2). Batch98's registry-scan Gather Now function bases its network settings on one of the two adapters, and it doesn't always choose the adapter you need to log on to the domain. (You can correct this problem within Batch98 by manually configuring Network Options.) Make sure the network settings in the installation script enable you to log on to a domain or server that will validate your access to the installation share.

You can use the [Network] section to specify a network adapter or disable the detection of network adapters. Microsoft, however, does not recommend overriding Setup's native detection by calling out an adapter configuration in the installation script. In most cases, it is better to leave network adapters out of the script and let Setup find and configure them automatically.

To specify a network adapter, provide the adapter's device ID (found in the adapter INF file) as a value for the NetCards entry in the [Network] section. You must then include a section with the adapter's device ID and include in that section any parameters from the [net_card.NDI] section of the adapter's INF file for which you do not want to use the specified default. Additional adapter-related settings include the following:

- *IgnoreDetectedNetCards.* Tells Setup whether to ignore all detected adapters. 0=install detected adapters; 1=ignore detected adapters (use only adapters defined with the NetCards parameter).

- *ValidateNetCardResources.* Specifies whether Setup should display a dialog box to resolve adapter resource conflicts. 0=do not display dialog box; 1=display dialog box.

The adapter card settings may look something like this:

```
[Network]
Netcards=your_card        ;your_card=Device ID for your
                          ; network card as
                          ;specified in the INF file for the
                          ;adapter. Multiple entries should be
                          ;separated with commas.
IgnoreDetectedNetCards=1  ;ignore cards detected by Setup.

ValidateNetCardResources=1 ;Do not display wizard to resolve
                           ; resource conflicts

[your_card]
...
```

Settings will vary depending on adapter. See the [*your_card*.NDI] section of the adapter's INF file.

Optional Components

The [OptionalComponents] section of the installation script tells Setup which optional Windows 98 components to install on the system. For a discussion of Windows 98 optional components, see Chapter 1.

The [OptionalComponents] section is not required. You can assign a standard package of components using the InstallType setting in the [Setup] section (described earlier in this chapter). The default InstallType value is 1 (Typical).

The format for the [OptionalComponents] section is as follows:

```
[OptionalComponents]
"Accessibility Options"=0
"Briefcase"=0
"Calculator"=1
```

A value of 1 tells Setup to install the optional component. A value of 0 tells Setup not to install the component. If you don't include an entry for the optional component (and if the component isn't part of the active InstallType package), Setup will not install the component.

Batch98 provides entries for all optional components and sets the value for disabled components to 0.

Printers

The [Printers] section lets Setup configure printers while it performs the installation. You can specify either local printers or network printers. The format for an entry in the [Printers] section is as follows:

```
"printer_name"="driver",port
```

- *printer_name*. A name for the printer. The name must follow all rules for Printer names (see Chapter 13, "Printing").

- *driver*. The exact driver name for the printer driver. See the list labeled Printers in the Add Printers Wizard for a list of printer driver names.

- *port*. For a local printer, the port associated with the printer (such as LPT1; see the Add Printer Wizard). For a network printer, the UNC path to the printer.

Following is an example of a [Printers] section:

```
[Printers]
"downstairs_print"="HP DeskJet600",LPT1
"upstatirs_print"="HP DeskJet500",\\natasha\natprint
```

Setup's MRU List

The *MRU (Most Recently Used)* list is a prominent feature of the Windows environment. The MRU list is the list you get when you click on the arrow to the right of a text box: It displays the most recent entries that have been typed into the box. You can use the installation script to preconfigure an MRU list that will provide UNC path options during Setup.

The MRU list option is useful if you are setting up several machines that are mostly identical but that, for some reason, require you to reference different network locations during Setup. For instance, you may need to configure two otherwise identical machines to receive user-level security from different NT Workstation machines. Or, the two machines may need to access different printers. In these cases, you may want to run the same installation script on both machines (for the sake of simplicity) and let the various network path options appear in the MRU list so that you can easily select them during the installation.

Of course, if you choose to perform a totally automated installation (by disabling all user prompts), it won't matter what you choose to put in the MRU list—you still won't have the chance to answer any screen prompts. This option is only for cases in which you expect to perform at least part of the installation interactively.

> **Note** An earlier section, "Automated Installation," describes how you can limit the interactive input by separately disabling setup-related prompts, name/organization prompts, and network-related prompts.

If you have slightly different configurations for two machines and you want to perform a fully automated installation, an alternative to this MRU-list option is to manually make the necessary modifications to the installation script and save the script under two different names to run on the different machines.

The format for the [InstallLocationsMRU] section is as follows:

```
[InstallLocationsMRU]
\\Pierre\Install
\\Natasha\CDRom
\\PrinceAndre\Printer1
```

Installing New Files, Changing Configuration Files, and Modifying the Registry

The [Install] section provides some important advanced features that extend the capabilities of an installation script. Specifically, the [Install] section enables you to perform the following tasks:

- *Copy files to the new PC.* You can designate additional files that Setup will copy along with the installation. You can use this option to copy shortcuts, corporate logos, Help files, or even programs that you want to add to the new configuration.

- *Update configuration files.* You can automatically make changes to autoexec.bat, config.sys, and existing ini files.

- *Modify the Registry.* You can add, remove, or modify Registry keys directly.

The ability to modify the Registry directly is at the heart of the [Install] section's subtlety and power. Like any other feature that lets you operate freely within the Registry, this feature requires deliberation and care. Microsoft offers some templates and guidelines for how to use the [Install] section to accomplish specific tasks—you'll learn more about those tasks later in this section.

Each entry in the [Install] section takes as a value a comma-delimited list of section headings referring to other sections that contain pertinent instructions. You'll see an example of the [Install] and install-related sections later in this chapter. The parameters of the [Install] section are as follows:

- *Addreg.* Points to section(s) that contain additions or modifications to the Registry
- *Delreg.* Points to section(s) that contain values you want to delete from the Registry
- *UpdateInis.* Points to section(s) that contain new settings for Windows ini files
- *UpdateAutoBat.* Points to section(s) that contain updates to Autoexec.bat
- *UpdateCfgsys.* Points to section(s) that contain updates to Config.sys
- *Copyfiles.* A predefined list of files to the new installation

> **Note** Remember that the role of the Windows configuration files (autoexec.bat, config.sys, and the inis) has narrowed considerably with Windows 95 and 98. The primary use of these files is to support legacy applications. See Chapter 32, "Windows 98 Configuration Files," for more information about Windows configuration files.

The number of possible scenarios for employing the features of the [Install] section is as limitless as the Registry itself, but, for practical matters, the principal reasons for adding this complexity to the installation script are as follows:

- To include a Registry file that will import Registry settings directly to the new installation
- To enable System Policies, User Profiles, Remote Registry Administration, or other features on the new machine
- To coax Setup into installing applications along with the Windows installation
- To import files, shortcuts, or icons, and so forth, to the new machine

Batch98, described earlier in this chapter, lets you add a Registry file and/or a System Policy file and automatically updates the [Install] section of the installation script accordingly. If possible, it is always easier to use a Batch98 script or a template script rather than trying to configure Registry settings yourself.

Microsoft's INF template userprof.inf shows how to enable Group Policies, User Profiles, and Remote Registry Administration. Listing D.2 is a composite of userprof.inf's [Install], a Batch98 [Install], and other Microsoft [Install] sample information. The code in Listing D.2 performs the following tasks:

Appendix D: Installation Script

- Enable user profiles
- Enable group policies
- Import the Registry file reg1.reg
- Copy a group of files (spacefood.inc) related to the computer's corporate environment

> **Note** A .reg Registry file does not have to contain a complete copy of the Registry. You can export a single tree or subtree to a Registry file (see Chapter 10, "Mastering the Windows 98 Registry"). You can thus selectively copy only part of the Registry and handle the rest of the configuration through auto-detection, script settings, and defaults.

Listing D.2 Sample [Install] and Install-related Sections

```
; You must also make sure that the related support files
; (REGSERV.EXE, WINREG.DLL, GROUPPOL.INF, GROUPPOL.DLL) have been
; copied from the Windows 95 compact disc to the server that contains
; the Windows 95 Source files.

; If you use INF Installer to set up the source files for group policies
; with the Windows 95 source files on the network, you can
; install group policies by just adding Services=grouppol in the [Network]
➥section.


[NETWORK]

Services=remotereg


; The following entries enable user profiles,
; remote administration of the Registry, and group policies




[INSTALL]
Addreg=User.Profiles.Reg, Group.Policies.Reg, Remote.Admin, RegistrySettings
Copyfiles=Group.Policies.Copy, Spacefood.Inc

[USER.PROFILES.REG]
HKLM,Network\Logon,UserProfiles,1,1


; In the following example, %Server_Username% must be defined in a [Strings]
➥section.
```

continues

Listing D.2 Continued

```
;   The Registry location is defined by the value
➥HKLM,"Security\Access\Admin\Remote".
[REMOTE.ADMIN]
HKLM,"Security\Access\Admin\Remote",%Server_Username%,1,ff,00

[GROUP.POLICIES.REG]
HKLM,Network\Logon,PolicyHandler,,"GROUPPOL.DLL,ProcessPolicies"
HKLM,System\CurrentControlSet\Services\MSNP32\NetworkProvider,GroupFcn,,
➥"GROUPPOL.DLL,NTGetUserGroups"
HKLM,System\CurrentControlSet\Services\NWNP32\NetworkProvider,GroupFcn,,
➥"GROUPPOL.DLL,NWGetUserGroups"

[GROUP.POLICIES.COPY]
grouppol.dll

[DESTINATIONDIRS]
Group.Policies.Copy=11      ; LDID_SYS

[RegistrySettings]
HKLM,%KEY_RUNONCE%,BatchReg1,,"%25%\regedit.exe /s %1%\reg1.reg"

;   Notice that under the [Strings] section, the percentage sign is NOT used.
;   Remove ";" and type the name for the server or domain containing group policies.

[Sapcefood.inc]
\\Pierre\pierreC\c:\spacefood\logo.bmp
\\Pierre\pierreC\c:\spacefood\info.hlp
\\Pierre\pierreC\c:\spacefood\expenses.xls
\\Pierre\pierreC\c:\spacefood\jokes.ha

;[STRINGS]
;Server_Username = "Server\Name"
KEY_RUNONCE="SOFTWARE\Microsoft\Windows\CurrentVersion\RunOnce"
```

Index

Symbols

.INI files, 107
10Base-2 Ethernet hub, 507
10Base-T Ethernet hub, 507
32bit ODBC applet
   Control Panel, 126, 381
   DSNs, creating, 386-388
3D sound, 333

A

acceleration (video), 319
Access databases
   DSNs, 395-396
   file type, 380
Access Control tab, Batch98, 68
access rights and permissions
   network logons, 18
   user-level security, 495
   Web site directories, 675
Access Permissions dialog box, 374
Accessibility options
   Control Panel, 128-129
   importing default Registry settings, 119
   Internet Explorer, 617
Accessibility Wizard, 862
Accessories, 861
accounts
   Internet, 653
   Upgrade, push Win98 installs, 85
   Users Control Panel options, 151
ACCWIZ command, 877
ACLIST utility, 774
activating new hardware profiles, 193
Active Channels, 34
Active Desktop, 32-33
   Active Desktop Gallery, 33
   browse features, 598-600
   customizing folders, 34
   information links, 597
   overviews, 598
   security zone options, 702
   site links, 596
   starting, 33
   wallpaper, 33
Active Scripting, Internet security, 693
Active Server Pages, Personal Web Server, 669
ActiveMovie control, 328-330, 862
ActiveX, 358
ActiveX controls, Internet security, 661-662, 692, 701
activity logs, Web sites, 677

Adapter tab, Display adapter properties, 278
adapters, network, 473
   Driver Type and Bindings tabs, 478
   installing, 474-475
   [Network] section, minbatch.inf script, 914
   see also network adapters
Add Access Permissions dialog box, 375-377
Add Exceptions dialog box, Compression Agent, 428
Add New Hardware Wizard, 273
   checking hardware support, 39
   Control Panel, 130
   network adapters, installing, 474
Add Printer Wizard, installing local/network printers, 292, 295
Add/Remove Programs Control Panel, 130, 307
adding
   actions to menus, Registry Editor, 221
   applications, 130
   Favorites menu items, 624
   hardware, 130
   modems, 139
   network clients, 482
   Web sites to security zones, 699-700
Additional Clients tab, Batch98, 68
Addreg parameter, minbatch.inf script, 918
Address toolbar, 27
addresses
   email
      finding via directory services, 724
      Netscape Communicator searches, 643
   IP, 541, 557
   IRQ, configuring, 266-268
administration
   scripts
      automating tasks, 741
      VB limitations, 743
   Web sites, 673
   Zero Administration Windows tools, 97

Advanced Configuration and Power Interface (ACPI), 444-445
advanced options
   Internet Explorer, 615-616
   Netscape Communicator, 636
   ODBC, 399-401
   Troubleshooting settings, System Configuration utility, 829
Advanced Options button, Batch98, 63, 69
Advanced Options dialog box, ScanDisk, 423
Advanced Power Management (APM), 444-445
advantages
   Internet Explorer, 648-649
   Netscape Communicator, 648-649
   Registry over system files, 200
   Windows 98, 11-12
   Windows NT, 12
   WSH scripts, 743
agents, SNMP, 558
AGP (Accelerated Graphics Port), 319
alias branches, Registry, 201-202
aliases, email recipients, 723
America On-Line (AOL)
   dial-up adapter, 570
   Internet connections, 657
animation menu option, 134
anonymous FTP access, 551
ANSI handling, DSNs, 392
anti-aliasing, screen display, 134
anti-virus utilities, 437-439
   closing prior to Windows install, 40
   Setup failures, 75
APIPA (Automatic Private IP Addressing), 539-541, 545
APIs (Application Programming Interfaces)
   ODBC, 382
   types, 247-248
APP parameter, ODBC, 383
Appearance tab, Display Control Panel, 133

appenders (viruses), 436
applets
   Internet, 652
   Java, 660
      security, 693
   ODBC Data Source Administrator, 386
   Power Management, 445
applications, 232
   adding, 130
   Backup Exec, 458
   backups, 457
   closing prior to Windows install, 40
   crashes, troubleshooting, 855-856
   Intrared Monitor, 447-448
   Microsoft Backup, 457
   MS-DOS program properties, 250-258
   Norton Backup, 458
   operating systems
      APIs, 247-248
      installing and removing MS-DOS applications, 250
      MS-DOS, 249
      OLE, 248
   optimizing performance, 804
   performance tools, 815
   printing, 297
   removing, 130
   running under Win98, 47
   see also programs
Applications Programming Interface, *See* APIs
AppStation mode, Zero Administration Kit, 99
AppUser group, policy settings, 100-101
archive bits, backups, 458
ARP command, 893
art, *see* graphics
ASCII text format, email attachments, 712
ASP (Active Server Pages), 669, 686
aspect ratios, DVD, 322
assigning IP addresses, 543

associations for files
   HTML, 665
   Netscape Communicator, 633
attachments, email, 725
   encoding/decoding, 711-712
   MIME format, 713-715
   UUencode format, 713
ATTRIB command, 883-884
audience considerations, Web sites, 678-679
audio
   Dolby options and DVD, 322-323
   file formats, 317
   multimedia requirements, 331
      CD Player, 336-337
      Control Panel options, 142
      microphones, 332
      MIDI, 333-335
      Sound Recorder, 338-341
      speakers, 332
      Volume Control, 337
   sound cards, installing, 331
   troubleshooting multimedia installation, 351
   see also sound
authentication, SQL Server DSNs, 391
Authenticode
   ActiveX security, 662
   Internet security, 703
AUTOEXEC.BAT file, 107, 735, 822
   editing, 735
   MS-DOS customization, 252-253
Autohide option, taskbar, 28
AUTOMATE.INF script, 61
automated installs
   Batch98 prompt options, 66
   network installs, 84
   scripts, 907
   tasks, 741-743
automatic
   hardware detection, 263
   IP addresses, APIPA, 545

Automatic Skip Driver Agent, 844, 850
automating tasks via scripts, 742
   Task Scheduler, 779
   WSH, 786
AutoPlay function, CD Player, 337

B

background of Microsoft scripting, 742
background processes (DVD), 351
Background tab, Display Control Panel, 133
backgrounds, folders, 34
Backup Exec, 458
Backup tab, Microsoft Backup, 463
Backup utility, 863
backups, 453
   archive bits, 458
   compression, 463
   costs of data restoration, 454
   data comparison, 463
   differential, 458
   directories, 463
   estimating space needs, 464
   evaluating requirements, 454
   excluding files, 464
   files, 463
   full, 458
   Grandfather-Father-Son, 459
   granularity, 461
   hard drives, 463
   hardware choices, 456
   hardware profiles, 197
   incremental, 458
   legal issues, 460
   Microsoft Backup, 462
   mixing types, 459
   overwriting data, 463
   passwords, 463
   piggybacking, 455
   post-backup report, 464
   quantity of data, 454
   reasons for failure, 454
   rebuild kits for critical systems, 455
   Registry, 464
   restoration options, 464
   reviewing strategies, 461
   rotation strategies, 458
   software choices, 457
   system files, Windows install, 42
   time constraints, 455
base priority classes, scheduling threads, 236
Basic I/O script, 752
Basic Input/Output System, *see* BIOS
batch files, Windows 98 installs, 87
Batch98 utility
   Access Control tab, 68
   Additional Clients tab, 68
   Advanced Options button, 63, 69
   automated installs, Setup prompt options, 66
   Clients tab, 68
   configuring networks, 66-68
   Desktop tab, 65
   Display Settings tab, 66
   File Save feature, named install scripts, 85
   General Setup button, 64
   General Setup options button, 63
   Install Info tab, 64
   install scripts, 62
      multiples, 70-71
      system settings, 64
   MRU Locations tab, 66
   Multiple Machine-Name Save feature, 70
   Network Options tab, 66-68
   Optional Components button, 63, 69
   predefined install scripts, 84
   Printers tab, 65
   Protocols tab, 67
   Registry, exporting to file, 70
   Services tab, 68
   starting, 63
   system policies, 69
benefits of upgrades, 13
binary files, email attachments, 725

Binary values, 109
BinHex encoding, email attachments, 712
BIOS (Basic Input/Output System), 820
bitmaps, viewing contents as icons, 226
body, email messages, 711
bookmarks
   Internet Explorer, 625
   Netscape Communicator, 643-645
boosting
   priority levels, threads, 237
   program priority in scheduling, 235
boot disks
   EBD, 831
   network installs, 88-93
boot partitions
   problems, 822
   rebuilding, 823
   Setup problems, 77
boot process, 820
   compatibility checking, 821
   device drivers, 821
   EBD, 833
   hangups, 825
   hardware
      problems, 822
      profiles, 192, 820
   reloading boot files, 827
   Setup log files, 73
   troubleshooting, 822
      System Configuration tool, 827
   user profiles, 821
   VxD drivers, 821
boot sector
   problems, 825
   viruses, 434
BOOTLOG.TXT file, 74, 822, 826
bootstrap program, 820
bottlenecks, 792-793
   file system, 797
   graphics, 798
   hard disks, 798

networks, 803-804
   printing, 799
   RAM, 794
   virtual memory, 795
BREAK command, 874
Briefcase, 29, 448-452
browse masters, Microsoft Networks, 513
browsers
   ActiveX controls, 661
   Active Desktop features, 598-600
   budgeting online time, 654
   comparing, 648-649
   configuring, 601-602
   defaults, 601
   dynamic HTML, 684
   Internet Explorer
      opening window, 618
      security, 690
      settings options, 137
   Java applets, 661
   Netscape Communicator, 627-629
   networks, finding resources, 500-501
   security
      ActiveX issues, 662
      Java issues, 662
   site compatibility issues, 680
   Web site directories, 677
   see also Internet Explorer; Netscape Communicator
budgeting Internet time, 654
BUFFERS=x command, IO.SYS file, 730
bugs
   programs, 794, 855
   Windows system, describing via Report tool, 846
building compound documents with OLE, 364
busses, 309
   enumerators, 244
   standards, 309-312

business rules, 356
button clicked script, 753
button options for mouse, 141

C

cabinet files, storing, 474, 479
cable modems, Internet connections, 658
cables, network performance, 803
caching
    passwords, network logons, 495
    pages, Internet Explorer, 607-608
calculating backup requirements, 455
Calculator, 864
cameras (digital), 326
capacity, hard disk drives, 404
CardBus support, 443
Cardfile multimedia features, 330
cascading Control Panel, 122
CATEGORY keyword, 170
CD with book
    client/server program, 369
    sample files included, 363
CD command, 874
CD music
    CD Player, 336-337, 862
    Multimedia Control Panel options, 142
CD-ROM boot disks, 58
censoring viewable content, Web pages, 612
Certificate Management, digital certificates, 704
certificates, Web script security, 703
channels
    Internet Explorer
        Channel Guide, 624
        subscriptions, 625-627
        updates, 627
    MIDI, 333
    Netcaster, 647
chapter reference table for Control Panel, 126
Character Map accessory, 863

character sets
    Internet Explorer, 611
    Netscape Communicator, 631
character translation sets, DSNs, 393
Chat programs, security issues, 694
CHAT.ADM policy template, 163
CHCP command, 874
CHDIR command, 874
Cheapernet, *see* Thinnet networks
checking files for problems, FileWise tool, 852-854
child restrictions for Web viewing, 614
CHKDSK command, 884
class definition subkeys, file type icons, 219-221
CLASS keyword, 170
classes, 359
    IP addresses, 555
    priority levels, 236
    public, registering, 361
    WshCollection, 756
click speed of mouse, 141
Client for Microsoft Networks, 17, 482-483, 496
Client for NetWare Networks, 483, 496
client-side scripting, 687
client/server
    applications, 356
    databases, 380
    networking, 14-15, 504-505
    testing and configuring DCOM, 369
clients
    Client for Microsoft Networks, 17
    email
        LDAP servers, 717
        passwords, 724
        POP servers, 716
        recipient aliases, 723
        SMTP servers, 716
    NetWare networks, 17, 83

network
  adding, 482
  Microsoft Family Logon, 485
  modifying properties, 482-484
SMTP, 710
Telnet, 550
thin, 95-96
Windows NT, Windows 98 network installs, 82
Clipboard Viewer, 863
CLS command, 875
CLSIDs, desktop icons, 223
clusters (FAT), 407
CMOS settings
  drive detection problems, 823
  Plug and Play setup, 269
codecs
  MPEG, 317
  speeds and sizes, 314-315
  Sound Recorder, 316
  video and audio file formats, 317
cold docking, 444
cold hard drive problems, 823
collection operations, VBScript, 745
collision rates and network performance, 804
color depth of displays, controlling, 279
color options
  configuring for Internet Explorer, 609-611
  monitors, 132
  Netscape Communicator, 632
  printing, 300
color schemes, 133
COM (Common Object Model)
  manipulation scripts, 762
  objects, 743
command line
  arguments
    script, 756
    Wscript, 751
  Cscript host, 751
  launching Control Panel objects, 121
  structural overview, 874
command subkeys, 219
command switches, Setup, 46
commands
  ACCWIZ, 877
  adding to menus, 24, 221
  ARP, 893
  ATTRIB, 883-884
  BREAK, 874
  CD, 874
  changing hotkeys, 222
  CHCP, 874
  CHDIR, 874
  CHKDSK, 884
  CLS, 875
  CONFIG.SYS file, 733
  COPY, 875
  CTTY, 875
  DATE, 875
  DEBUG, 877
  DEL, 875
  DELTREE, 884
  DEVICE=, 734
  Dial-Up Scripting, 583
  DIR, 875
  DISKCOPY, 885
  DOSKEY, 877
  EDIT, 878
  ERASE, 875
  EXIT, 875
  EXTRACT, 886
  FC, 886
  FDISK, 887
  FIND, 887
  FORMAT, 888
  FTP, 894-897
  internal system, 874
  IPCONFIG, 897-898
  KEYB, 879
  LABEL, 889

LH, 875
MD, 875
MEM, 880
MKDIR, 875
MODE, 880
MORE, 880
MOVE, 889
NBTSTAT, 898
NET parameters, 899-901
NET VIEW, 398
NETSTAT, 901
network, 893
NLSFUNC, 881
PATH, 875
PING, 902
PROGMAN, 881
PROMPT, 876
RD, 876
REGEDIT, 881
REN, 876
RENAME, 876
RMDIR, 876
ROUTE, 552, 902
SET, 876
SETVER, 881
SORT, 890
START, 882
SUBST, 890
TIME, 876
TRACERT, 553, 903
tracing ODBC problems, 400
TYPE, 876
VER, 876
VERIFY, 876
VOL, 876
WINFILE, 883
WINVER, 883
XCOPY, 891
common problems and solutions, 560, 839
common Setup failure causes, 75
COMMON.ADM policy template, 163

communications ports, 281
Communicator, *see* Netscape Communicator
Compact install option, 19
companion viruses, 435
comparing
    backup data, 463
    file systems for hard disk drives, 415
    Internet Explorer to Netscape, 648-649
compatibility checking, boot process, 821
compatibility issues, Web sites, 680
Component Object Model, *see* COM
components
    installing, 19
    LDAP, 718
    network architecture, 471
    networks, 16
    optional, 19-20
components of operating systems
    Configuration Manager, 245
    core components, 246
    device drivers, 243-244
    Installable File System Manager, 249
    overview, 247
    the shell, 246
    Virtual Machine Manager, 245, 249
compound documents, 357, 362
    editing with in-place editing, 366
    OLE, 248, 364
compressed drives
    error messages, 76
    maintaining, 426-427
    system performance, 797
compressing drives
    DriveSpace, 424-425
    problems, 428
compression, backups, 463
Compression Agent, 863
    compression levels, 427
    settings options, 427
compressor/decompressor, *see* codecs
CompuServe Internet connections, 657

computers
  install scripts, 84
  names, specifying for networks, 489-490, 542
  passwords, 143
  personal, 441-442
    Briefcase, 448-452
    dial-up modem connections, 442
    Direct Cable Connection, 447
    Hardware Profiles, 443-444
    Infrared Monitor application, 447-448
    PC Card device support, 442-443
    power management, 444-447
  power saving options, 145
  regional settings, 145
  time and date settings, 131
  Windows 98 install needs, 39
Computer Policies, 165-167, 176-178
condenser microphones, 332
CONF.ADM policy template, 163
CONFIG parameter, NET command, 899
CONFIG.POL file, 160, 200
CONFIG.SYS file, 107, 732, 822
  commands, 733-734
  lines deleted by Windows 98, 733
  MS-DOS, customizing, 252-253
configuration files, 729
Configuration Manager, 244
configuring
  Active Channels, 34
  Dial-Up Networking, 572-575, 587
  Dial-Up Server, 590-591
  hard drives, 825
  hardware, DOS/NT/Windows 3.0 installs, 55
  HOSTS files, 548
  Internet Explorer, 607-614
  Internet security, file/print sharing, 695-697
  IP addresses, 541
  LMHOSTS files, 549
  Netscape Communicator, 628
  network adapters, 68
  network protocols, 479-481
  networks, 66
  Personal Web Server, 671-672
  Primary Network Logon, 496-497
  printers, 288-289
  Recycle Bin, 31
  system, 106-113
  taskbar, 28
  TCP/IP, 543
  troubleshooting, 824
  Web browsers, 601-602
  Windows 98
    DHCP, 544
    DNS servers, 547
    domain client, 519-521
    hardware needs, 815
    INI file updates, 736
    WINS, 547-549
conflicts with hardware, 839
connect strings, ODBC, 384-386
connection script for network, 760
Connection tab
  Internet Properties dialog box, 652
Connection Wizard
  Internet connections, 603
connections
  Dial-Up Networking, troubleshooting, 588-589
  Internet, 651
    cable modems, 658
    Dial-Up Networking advanced settings, 655-656
    ISDN, 657
    ISPs, 656-657, 663
    logon data, 654
    manual method, 653
    online services, 657
    passwords, 654
    proxy servers, 659

security, 690-691, 703
Wizard method, 652
network installs, problems, 93
ODBC
   databases, 383
   troubleshooting, 398
   TCP/IP, 539
   UNIX hosts, 558
   WWW, 656-657
Consumer PC hardware requirements, 306-307
container applications, 364
content creation for Web sites, 677-679
content filters, Internet Explorer, 612-614
content types, MIME, 714
Context menu, Explorer, 26
Control Panel, 116
   32-bit ODBC applet, 126, 386
   Accessibility options, 128-129
   Add New Hardware Wizard, 130
   Add/Remove Programs option, 130
   cascading, 122
   chapter reference table, 126
   CPL files, 117
   Date/Time option, 131
   devices, 263
   direct access via Start menu, 122
   Display option, 132-133
   exporting default settings to users, 119
   Fonts option, 136
   Game Controllers option, 137
   Internet applet, 652
   Internet option, 137
   Keyboard option, 137
   launching objects directly, 121
   Mail option, 139
   Modems option, 139
   Mouse option, 141
   Multimedia option, 141
   Network option, 143
   object settings, 123-125
   ODBC applet, 381
   Passwords option, 143
   Power Management option, 145
   Printers option, 145
   Regional settings, 145
   Registry settings, 118
   Sounds option, 147
   starting hardware profiles, 193
   System option, 147-148
control statements, VBScript, 745
CONTROL.EXE file, opening Control Panel window, 122
controllers
   games, 137
   hard disk drives, 416
controls
   ActiveMovie, 862
   ActiveX, 661-662, 692
   Volume, 862
conventional memory Setup problems, 76
conversion of types, VBScript, 744
converting email attachments, 712-713
cookies
   Internet security, 705
   Netscape Communicator, 635
cooperative multitasking, 233-234
COPY command, 875
Copyfiles parameter, minbatch.inf script, 918
copying
   email text, 721
   files, Explorer, 25
   hardware profiles to create new profiles, 192
   text from pages, Netscape Communicator, 641
   Web page items, Internet Explorer, 622
core components of operating systems, 246
corrupt files, System File Checker options, 847
corruption and backup granularity, 461

costs of backup data restoration, 454
counters for system performance, 807
country-specific system settings, 145
CPL file extension, 116-117
crashes
    common Setup failure causes, 75
    troubleshooting, 856
CreateFolder method, WSH, 770
CreateObject, 751
creating
    Dial-Up Networking connections, 575
    embedded documents with OLE, 364-365
    linked documents with OLE, 366-367
critical sections, 239
critical system rebuild kits, 455
Cscript host, 751
CSLIP server (Dial-Up Networking), 578
CTTY command, 875
currency symbol options, 145
Custom install, Personal Web Server, 670
Customize This Folder Wizard, 601
customizing
    Control Panel objects, 116
    desktop, 18
    folders, Active Desktop, 34
    Maintenance Wizard operation, 785
    security zones, 700
    Setup via install scripts, 59
    Start menu, 24
    user profiles, 185
cutting email text, 721
cylinders, hard disk drives, 404

D

DAP (Directory Access Protocol), 718
Data Access Components, 669
data comparison, backups, 463
data corruption and backup granularity, 461
data types, MIME, 714
databases
    Access
        DSNs, 391, 396
        file type, 380
    client/server, 380
    engines, 381
    Informix client/server, 380
    ODBC connections, 383
    ORACLE, 380
    Paradox, 380
    SQL Server, 380
date, setting for system, 131
DATE command, 875
Date/Time option, Control Panel, 131
DCOM, 358
    configuring, 369
    default settings, establishing, 376
DCOMCNFG utility
    overview, 368
    server locations, 372-373
DEBUG command, 877
debugging scripts, 771-772
decoding email attachments, 712
decreasing submenu opening delay, Registry Editor, 225
DEFAULT.INF script, 61
DefaultIcon subkey, 219
    changing desktop icons, 223
    file type icons, 221
defaults
    Control Panel, exporting to users, 119
    DCOM, 376
    default document, Web sites, 676
    folder locations, changing via Registry Editor, 224
    Internet Explorer home page, 605
    printers, 288
    Web browsers, 601
defragmenting hard disks, 41, 420, 797, 806
DEL command, 875
DeleteFile method, WSH, 770

deleting
    email messages, 721
    file associations, 634
    History file contents, 630
    modems, 139
    printers from system, 301
    Recycle Bin items, 31
    Start menu items, 25
    tasks from Task Scheduler, 782
    Windows 98, 71-72
Delreg parameter, minbatch.inf script, 918
DELTREE command, 884
demand paging, 240
deploying Windows 98, planning process, 35-36
design layout, network media topologies, 487
designing Web sites, 671-672
    audience considerations, 678-679
    compatibility issues, 680
    content needs, 679
desktop, 21
    Active Desktop, 32-33
    Briefcase, 29
    customizing, 18
    Explorer, 25
    icons
        changing via Registry, 223
        CLSIDs, 223
        display options, 134
    Inbox, removing, 226
    Internet Explorer integration, 596
    My Computer, 28
    Network Neighborhood, 29
    network resources, finding, 498
    Recycling Bin, 31
    shortcuts, 29, 499
        shortcut script, 765, 768-770
    Start menu, 22-23
    taskbar, 26
    toolbar, 27
    tracking settings, Passwords Control Panel, 144
    utility script, 766, 768-770
    wallpaper, HTML-based, 33
    Web-based options, 33
Desktop tab, Batch98, 65
DETCRASH.LOG file, hardware detect failure log, 73
detecting
    hardware, Windows install, 43-44
    system errors via Dr. Watson, 851
determining active hardware profile, 194
DETLOG.TXT file, Setup log file, 45
device drivers, 270
    boot hangups, 825
    functions, 243
    loading at startup, 821
    PC Card for portable computers, 442-443
    printers, installing, 293
    removing Windows 3.x versions, 275
    Unified Device Driver model, 243
    updating, 275
    virtual device drivers, 244
Device Manager, 268
    display adapter drivers, 278-279
    error codes, 865-872
    hardware profiles, 192
        laptops, 194
    system devices, 276
    USB, installing, 310
    viewing resource assignments, 268
Device Manager tab, System Control Panel, 147
DEVICE= command, CONFIG.SYS file, 734
DevicePath parameter, minbatch.inf script, 908
devices
    automatic hardware detection, 263
    control panels, 263
    Direct Memory Access (DMA), 265
    EISA busses, 270

hardware
  configuration wizards, 263
  device tree, 263
  profiles, 192
hot-pluggable, 263
I/O port addresses, 266
installing, 271-274
IRQs, 264
  configuring addresses, 266
  viewing device assignments, 268
ISA busses, 269
key features, 262
managing, Registry options, 263
memory assignments, 266
minidrivers/universal drivers, 263
multiple monitor support, 280
PCI busses, 270
Plug and Play, 262
  PC card, 270
  resource mediation, 262
  SCSI busses, 270
removing from profiles, 194
serial ports, 281
virtual device drivers, 263
DHCP (Dynamic Host Configuration Protocol)
  MAC addresses, 545
  servers, 541
    dynamic IP addresses, 544
    locating, 545
DIAG parameter, NET command, 900
diagnosing boot problems, 825
Diagnostic Startup option, Sys Config utility, 828
Diagnostics tab, Modem Control Panel, 139
Dial-Up Adapter, 570
dial-up devices, 565
Dial-Up Networking
  Dial-Up Scripting, 583-584
  Dial-Up Server
    configuring, 590-591
    icon, 591
    installing, 589
  dialing out and logging in, 586-587
  direct-dial connectivity, 566
  hardware
    buffering, 574
    compression settings, 573
    configuring, 572, 575
    on-board settings, 572
  installing, 568
    manually, 569-570
    protocols, 570-571
  Internet connectivity, 565
  Multilink, 584-585
  overview, 564
  peer networks, 512
  PPTP, configuring, 587
  troubleshooting
    connections, 588-589
    data errors, 574
  virtual private networks, 565
Dial-Up Scripting, Dial-Up Networking, 583-584
Dial-Up Server, 564
dialing settings for modems, Telephony Control Panel, 151
dialog box script example, 753
Dictionary object, 751
differential backups, 458
digital certificates, Web script security, 703
Digital Versatile/Video Disc, *see* DVD
dip switches, installing devices, 272
DIR command, 875
Direct Cable Connection, peer networks, 447, 510-512, 862
direct Control Panel access via Start menu, 122
direct-dial connectivity, Dial-Up Networking, 566
DirectDraw, 313

directories
  backups, 463
  name, Netscape Communicator searches, 642
  sharing, 18
  structure repair, SCANDISK, 833
  user profiles, 183-184
  viewing via Explorer, 25
  Web sites
    access rights, 675
    browsing, 677
    virtual, 674-675
  Windows
    DOS/NT/Windows 3.0 installs, 52
    dual-boot option, 56
directory services, 717
  finding email addresses, 724
  X.500, 718
DirectX
  components, 312-313
  troubleshooting multimedia installation, 350
  Web site, 313
disability access options, Control Panel, 128
disabling
  file/print shares, Internet security, 692, 697
  print spooling for DOS, 291
  timeout feature, Windows install, 40
  TSRs, Windows install, 40
disconnecting
  Internet options, 654
  network resources, 758-759
discussion groups, WSH scripting, 775
Disk Cleanup, 863
  deleting unneeded files, 806
  Maintenance Wizard, 785
disk commands, 883
disk compression, problems, 428
Disk Defragmenter, 421, 785, 806, 863
disk subsystems, selecting and configuring, 417

DISKCOPY command, 885
display adapters
  maintaining drivers, 278-279
  optimizing, 799
Display option
  Control Panel, 132
  system icon options, 133
Display Settings tab, Batch98, 66
displaying routing tables, Route command, 552
displays
  anti-aliasing, 134
  color
    depth, 135
    Internet Explorer, 609-611
  fonts, Internet Explorer, 610-611
  resolution, 135
  settings options, 132
Distributed COM, *see* DCOM
Divx, 321
DLLs, 243
  ODBC to network connections, DSNs, 391
  ODBC32.DLL, 383
DNS (Domain Naming System), 542
  host name resolution, 546
  servers
    configuring, 547
    hostnames, 542, 547
    IP addresses, name resolution, 547
docking stations, 443
document-centric approach, 357
documents
  HTML, *see* Web pages
  WordPad, multi-media enhanced example, 343-344
Documents command (Start menu), 23
Dolby audio options and DVD, 322-323
domain client, configuring Windows 98, 519-521

domain model of networking, 518
domains
   Internet, DNS name resolution, 547
   managing from Windows 98, 526-527
   Windows 98 installs, 82
   Windows NT, installing Windows 98, 81-82
DOS
   boot partitions, Setup problems, 77
   dual-boot option, Windows 98, 56
   printing, 285, 291
   programs, troubleshooting, 805
   starting, dual-boot option, 56
   UNIX command comparison, 558
   upgrading to Windows 98, 53-55
DOS=HIGH command, IO.SYS file, 730
DOSKEY command, 877
double click
   hot zones, 227
   mouse speed, 141
down ISP logon servers, 664
downloading for offline viewing, *see* offline options
DR-DOS, Windows upgrades, 51
Dr. Solomon's Anti-Virus, 438
Dr. Watson, 844
   detecting system errors, 851
   system error checking, 827
drag-and-drop
   creating links, 367
   printing, 299-300
Drive Converter, 863
drive interfaces, hard disk drives, 416
drive mappings, 483
Drive menu commands, 424
DRIVER parameter, ODBC, 383
drivers
   Access, DSNs, 395
   boot hangups, 825
   display adapters, optimizing, 799
   loading at startup, 821

   modems, 151
   ODBC, 127, 382
      problems, 401
   printers
      installing, 293
      removing, 301
   real-mode CD-ROM, 59
   SQL Server, DSNs, 389
drives
   backups, 463
   compressing, 424-427
   DVD-ROM, 321
   hard disk, 404
      controllers, 416
      drive interfaces, 416
      DriveSpace, 414
      FAT, 406-412
      FAT32, 410-411
      file systems, comparing, 415
      NTFS, 412-414
      partitions, 404-406
      performance, measuring, 415
      testing, 422-423
   host, DriveSpace, 426
   tape, 418
DriveSpace, 863
   compression levels, 426
      problems, 428
   hard disk drives, 414
   host drives, 426
   initiating, 424-425
DSN parameters, ODBC connect strings, 386
DSNs (Data Source Names), 379
   32-bit ODBC Control Panel, 126
   Access
      databases, 396
      drivers, 395
      naming, 395
   advanced tuning options, 401
   ANSI handling, 392

character translation sets, 393
creating, ODBC Data Source
   Administrator, 386
databases, selecting, 391
DLLs, ODBC to network connections, 391
error message language options, 392
File DSNs, 386-388
logging options, 393
logons, 391
regional settings, 393
selecting type, 387
SQL Server
   authentication, 391
   drivers, 389
   naming DSN, 390
   server names, 390
statistic tracking, 394
System DSNs, 386-388
temporary prepared SQL Statements, 392
updating, 386
user DSNs, 386-388
dual-boot option
   Windows 98, 56
   Windows NT, 57
DUN, *see* Dial-Up Networking
duplicates, IP addresses, 560
DVD
   Content Scrambling System, 324
   Dolby audio options, 322-323
   drives, 321
   DVD Player, AutoPlay setting, 323
   features, 320
   Macrovision copy protection, 324
   Serial Copy Generation Management System, 324
   troubleshooting multimedia installation, 351
   types, 321
DVORAK keyboard option, 137
DWORD values, 109

dynamic
   fonts, Netscape Communicator, 632
   HTML, Web sites, 684
   IP addresses, DHCP servers, 544
   microphones, 332
   priority levels, scheduling threads, 237

E

EBD (Emergency Boot Disk), 831
   boot process, 833
   EXT utility file repair, 834
   preparing, 832
   reinstalling Windows 98, 834
   startup options, 831
   system file repair, 827
   system recovery, RAM drives, 833
   testing, 832
   Uninstall utility system repair, 834
   updating, 832
   utilities, 833
EBD parameter, minbatch.inf script, 907
EBD.CAB file, 833
Echo method, 750-752
ECP (Enhanced Capability Port), installing printers, 294
edge sensitivity, IRQs, 264
EDIT command, 878
editing
   AUTOEXEC.BAT file, 735
   compound documents, in-place editing, 366
   Dial-Up Networking connections, 575
   file associations, NetscapeComm, 634
   hardware profiles, 192
   linked documents with OLE, 367
   network clients, properties, 482-484
   Task Scheduler tasks, 782
Effects tab, Display Control Panel, system icon options, 133
EIA wiring standards, 487

EIDE, 416
  controllers, optimizing, 798
  hard drives, problems, 823
EISA busses, Plug and Play options, 270
EISA DMA controller, system device settings, 276
email, 710
  address searches, Netscape Communicator, 643
  attachments, 711-713, 725
  body, 711
  clients, 716-717
  contents, 711
  creating text files, 720
  cut/copy/paste options, 721
  directory services, finding addresses, 724
  envelopes, 711
  Eudora Light program, 719
  folders, 719-721
  headers, 711, 715
  in-box, 719
  logon problems, 664
  Mail Control Panel options, 139
  mailboxes, 719
  mailing preferences, 725
  messages, 719
    deleting, 721
    Find option, 722
    new message options, 722
    organizing, 721
    printing, 720
    priorities, 723
    saving as files, 720
    status, 723
  MIME content types, 714
  opening text files, 720
  passwords, 724
  recipient aliases, 723
  sending Web pages, Netscape Communicator, 638
  servers, 715-718
  signatures, 724
  SMTP transfer process, 710
  structure overview, 719
  text files, 720
  undo option, 720
embedding
  multimedia files in documents, 345
  OLE documents, 364-365
Emergency Boot Disk, 831
EMFs (Enhanced MetaFiles), printer instruction data, 284
enabling user profiles, 185
encoding formats, email attachments, 711
encryption, secure Internet transactions, 704-706
end-user operations, Total Cost of Operations, 96
Energy Star monitor options, 133
Enhanced MetaFile (EMF) format, print spooling, 801
Entertainment PC hardware requirements, 306
envelopes, email, 711
Environment script, 754
environment settings for users, 17
ERASE command, 875
Err object, 745, 750
error codes, Device Manager, 865-872
error handlers, VBScript, 745
error messages
  compressed drives, 76
  DSN language options, 392
estimating backup space needs, 464
Ethernet, 507
Eudora Light email program, 719
evaluating backup requirements, 454
event names for Windows 98, 223
Excel shortcut swapping script, 764-765, 768-770
excluding files from backups, 464
execution parameters, scripts, 751
EXIT command, 875
expanding Explorer icon cache, 225

Explorer, 25
    Context menu, 26
    copying files, 25
    defragmenting hard disks, 420
    File Types tab, 26
    Find command, 26
    Folder Options command, 26
    icon cache, expanding via Registry, 225
    Map Network Drive command, 26
    moving files, 25
    Network Neighborhood, 26
    properties, 25
    Properties dialog box, opening, 25
    viewing directories, 25
exporting
    default Control Panel settings to users, 119
    Registry, Batch98 option, 70
Express parameter, minbatch.inf script, 907
EXT utility, file repair via EBD, 834
extensions for files, 116, 665
EXTRACT command, 886

F

F-Protect (FRISK Software International), 438
failure of system, *see* crashes
FAT, hard disk drives
    clusters, 407
    directory entries, 408
    example of, 409
    functions of, 406
    long filenames, 411-412
    volume and cluster size, 407
FAT32, hard disk drives, 410-411
Favorites command (Start menu), 23
Favorites menu, Internet Explorer, 623
    adding items, 624
    organizing, 625
FC command, 886
FCBS=X command, IO.SYS file, 730

FDISK, partitioning hard disks, 405, 418, 887
File Allocation Table, *see* FAT
File and Print Sharing dialog box, 510
file associations
    Netscape Communicator, 633
    Registry, 217-219
file attributes, NTFS, 414
file commands, 883
File DSNs, 386-388
file formats, video and audio, 317
File Manager, *see* Explorer
file metadata, NTFS, 414
File Save feature, Batch98, 85
file servers, 15
file sharing, Internet security, 691, 695-697
file systems
    comparing, 415
    disk subsystems, selecting, 417
    DriveSpace, 414
    FAT, 409
        clusters, 407
        directory entries, 408
        long filenames, 411-412
        volume and cluster size, 407
    FAT32, 410-411
    NTFS
        clusters, 413
        features, 412
        file attributes, 414
    performance tuning, 797
    types, 406
file types
    changing icons, 221
    databases, 380
    Task Scheduler support, 778
    unknown, 227
file viruses, 434
FileExists method, WSH, 770
filenames
    long, 411-412
    removing tilde, 226

files
   AUTOEXEC.BAT, 107
      editing, 735
   backups, 463
   bitmaps, viewing contents as icons, 226
   BOOTLOG.TXT, 74
   Briefcase, 448-452
   CD, samples included on, 363
   checking for problems, FileWise tool, 852-854
   CONFIG.POL, 160
      Registry data, 200
   CONFIG.SYS, 107, 732-733
   configuration, 729
   CONTROL.EXE, opening Control Panel window, 122
   copying, Explorer, 25
   DETCRASH.LOG, hardware detect failure log, 73
   DETLOG.TXT, Setup log file, 45
   EBD.CAB, 833
   excluding from backups, 464
   extensions, 116
   HOSTS
      configuring, 548
      hostname resolution, 546
   HTML associations, 665
   .INI, 107
   IO.SYS, system parameters, 730
   LMHOSTS, 549
   MESSAGE.HTM, 685-686
   moving, Explorer, 25
   MSDOS.SYS, 731-732
   multimedia, embedding in documents, 345
   NETLOG.TXT, 74
   NetWare long file name support, 535-536
   policy template, 162-163, 168-169, 173-175
      keywords, 170-171
      strings and comments, 173
      WINDOWS.ADM, 176-180
   POLICY.POL, 107, 111-112, 200
   printing, 300
   REG, exporting Registry settings, 119
   SETUPLOG.TXT, install event log, 73
   shares, 502
   system policy, 157-162
   SYSTEM.DAT, 107-110
      Registry data, 200
   SYSTEM.INI, 737-739
   user profiles, 183
   USER.DAT, 107-110, 200
   WIN.INI section headings, 736
   WINDOWS.ADM, 176
      Computer Policies, 176-178
      User and Group Policies, 179-180
FILES=x command, IO.SYS file, 730
Filesystem object, 751, 764-766, 770
FileWise tool, checking file problems, 852-854
filtering, configuring for Internet Explorer, 612-614
FilterKeys feature, 128
Find options, 887
   email messages, 722
   Explorer, 26
   locating network computers, 498
   Start menu, 23
finding
   Control Panel settings, 123
   email addresses, directory services, 724
   hardware profile Registry keys, 196
   search items on pages, 641
   search topics on pages, 622
firewalls, 692
FireWire, *see* IEEE
flags (semaphores), 238
flat memory model, 239
flicker (video), 319
floppy disks, print options, 300
Folder Options command (View menu), 26

folders
  backgrounds, 34
  Briefcase, 448-452
  changing default locations, 224
  Control Panel, customizing properties, 116
  customizing Active Desktop, 34
  Dial-Up Networking, 862
  Direct Cable Connection, 862
  email, 719-721
  Printers, 286-288
  Start Menu, 24
  Web views, 601
fonts
  configuring for Internet Explorer, 610-611
  installing, 302
  listing by similarity, 136
  Netscape Communicator display options, 631-632
  printing, 302
    problems, 801
Fonts option, Control Panel, 136
footers, printing Web pages, 619
force-feedback devices, installing, 342
FORMAT command, formatting hard disks, 420, 888
formats, video and audio files, 317
formatting
  email messages, 725
  hard disks, 419-420
  IP addresses, 554
FQDNs (Fully Qualified Domain Names), 547
frames, Web pages, 300, 621
FrontPage 98 Server Extensions, 669
FrontPage Express, Web site content, 682-684
FTP (File Transfer Protocol), 551, 561, 894-897
full backups, 458
full duplex (sound cards), 332
functionality problems, ODBC, 400

G

game controller devices, installing, 342
games, 863
gateways, 542
GDI (graphics device interface)
  core component, 246
  print process, 284
geographic settings, DSNs, 393
geometries, hard disk drives, 404
Globally Unique Identifiers, *see* GUIDs
Grandfather-Father-Son backups, 459
granularity, backups, 461
graphics
  adapter problems, 799
  copying, Internet Explorer, 622
  performance options, 150, 798
  vector, printing, 802
  viewing content as icons, 226
group memberships, Windows NT Server domains, 524
Group Policies, 156-157, 167-168, 179-180
groupware programs, Time Zone tab issues, 131
GUIDs (Globally Unique Identifiers), 360

H

half duplex (sound cards), 332
handicapped accessibility, Control Panel, 128
hangups, boot process, 825
hard disk drives, 404
  backups, 463
  CMOS settings, detection problems, 823
  configuring, problems, 825
  controllers, 416
  defragmenting, 41, 420, 797
  drive interfaces, 416
  DriveSpace, 414
  FAT, 406-407, 411-412
  FAT32, 410-411

file systems, comparing, 415
formatting, 419-420
NTFS
   clusters, 413
   file attributes, 414
partitions, 404-406, 418
performance
   measuring, 415
   tuning, 798
problems, 823
replacing primary boot partition, 823
secondary, 405
testing via ScanDisk, 422-423
troubleshooting, 857
hardware
   backups, 456
   boot failure, 822
   configuration
      wizards, 263
      DOS/NT/Windows 3.0 installs, 55
   conflicts, 839
   detection
      failures, 75
      Windows install, 43
   device tree, 263
   Dial-Up Networking
      buffering, 574
      compression settings, 573
      configuring, 572, 575
      on-board settings, 572
   failures, 840
   incompatibilities, 839
   installing, 130
   legacy, Setup problems, 77
   modems, settings options, 139
   mouse settings, 141
   multimedia, installing, 320
   networking requirements, 530
   PC 98 specification requirements, 306-307
   peer networks, selecting for, 506-508
   problems, 825

   Registry settings, 107
   removing from profiles, 194
   touch (input/output), 342
   video
      cameras and scanners, 326
      DVD, 320-321
      DVD limitations, 323-324
      video card memory, 318
      video card speed, 319
   Windows 98 recommendations, 39-40, 815
Hardware Compatibility list, 40
hardware profiles, 18, 107, 112-113, 191-194
   activating, 193
   backups, 197
   boot process, 192, 820
   determining active, 194
   laptops, 194-195
   naming, 193
   portable computers, 443-444
   problems and solutions, 197
   Registry keys, 196
   repairing bad, 195
   unknown monitor errors, 197
Hardware Resources branch, MSI, 841-842
headers
   email, 711
   MIME, 715
   printing Web pages, 619
heads, hard disk drives, 404
hearing impairment accessibility, 128
Hello World (WHS Echo method example), 752
Help command (Start menu), 23
HELP parameter, NET command, 900
helper apps, Netscape Communicator, 633
hiding shares, 492
HighContrast feature, 129
HIMEM.SYS file, IO.SYS file, 730
History file, Netscape Communicator, 630, 643

History list, Internet Explorer, 608, 623
History page, MSI, 844
hits on Web sites, tracking, 674
HKEY_CLASSES_ROOT key, 107, 201, 217-219, 361
HKEY_CURRENT_CONFIG key, 108, 196, 201
HKEY_CURRENT_USER key, 108
HKEY_CURRENT_USER key, 202
HKEY_DYN_DATA key, 108, 201
HKEY_LOCAL_MACHINE key, 107-109, 201
HKEY_USERS key, 107, 201
home directories
 Web sites, 671
 Windows NT Server domains, 522
Home Page Wizard, Web site content, 681
home pages
 configuring for Internet Explorer, 605
 Netscape Communicator, 630
host drives, DriveSpace, 426
host IDs, IP addresses, 541, 554
hostnames
 DNS servers, 547
 IP addresses, 542
 networks, 542
 resolution, IP addresses, 546
hosts
 problems locating, 560
 scripting, 751
 UNIX connections, 558
HOSTS files
 configuring, 548
 hostname resolution, 546
hot docking, 444
hot-fixing (NTFS), 413
hot-pluggable devices, 263
hotkeys, changing for commands, 222
HTML
 dynamic, 684
 file associations, 665

wallpaper, 33
Web pages, viewing, 623, 646
see also Web pages
HTML editors, 682
Hydra system, 97
hyperlinks
 opening, 619
see also links
Hyperterminal, 862

I

I/O port addresses, supporting devices, 266
I/O script, 752
IBM AntiVirus, 438
icon cache, Explorer, expanding via Registry, 225
icons
 changing file type icons, 221
 desktop
  changing via Registry, 223
  CLSIDs, 223
  display options, 134
 Dial-Up Server, 591
 system display options, 133
identifying system problems, 838
idle time options, Task Scheduler, 784
IEEE
 cable run standards, 487
 Web site, 311
IFRAMEs, security zone options, 702
IFSHLP.SYS file, IO.SYS file, 730
images, *see* graphics
Imaging feature, 864
implicit yields, 234
importing Web site content, 677
In box, 721
 email, 719
 removing from desktop, 226
in-place editing
 compound documents, 366
 OLE 2.0, 357

incremental backups, 458
INETRES.ADM policy template, 163
INF template, userprof.inf, 918
information links, Active Desktop, 597
information pages, MSI, 841
Informix databases, 380
Infrared Monitor application, 447-448
INIPREP.INF script, 61
INIT parameter, NET command, 900
initiating ScanDisk, 422
InputBox function, using in WSH scripts, 760
Insert menu commands (Word), 365
inspecting Setup log files, 74
Install Info tab, Batch98, 64
install scripts, 61, 905
   automated installs, 907
   Batch98
      multiples, 70-71
      setup options, 62-63
   computer-specific, 84
   customizing Setup, 59
   minbatch.inf upgrade script, 907
   network installs, 81-84
   [Network] section, 912-914
   running Setup, 60
   section titles, 906
   system settings, 64
   templates, 60
   usage tips, 60
Install section, install script example, 917-920
Installable File System Manager, 245
installing
   devices, 271-274
   Dial-Up Networking, 568-571
   Dial-Up Server, 589
   fonts, 302
   hardware, 130
   Microsoft Client for NetWare Networks, 532

MS-DOS applications, 249
multimedia, 307, 320
   troubleshooting, 347-351
network adapters, 475
   Driver Type and Bindings tabs, 478
   legacy, 475
   Plug-and-Play, 474
network printers, 295-296
network protocols, 479
network services, 478
ODBC, 387, 396-397
peer network components, 508-510
Personal Web Server, 670
printers, 292-293
programs, 130
Remote Registry Service, 526
SNMP agent, 558
sound cards, 331
System Policy Editor, 158
Transaction Server, 671
Windows 98, 37
   batch files, 87
   components, 19
   compressed drive errors, 76
   copying files, 50
   defragmenting hard drives, 41
   disabling TSRs, 40
   DOS upgrades, 53-55
   dual-boot option, 56
   emergency boot disks, 49
   hardware configuring, 50
   hardware detection, 43
   hardware support, 39-40
   install scripts, 81-84
   install shares, networks, 55
   Internet channel sets, 49
   keyboard layouts, 48
   language options, 48
   network adapters, 91
   network boot disks, 88-93
   network configuring, 42
   network installs, 79-80

on NetWare networks, 83
on Windows NT domains, 81-82
optional components, 19-20
OS/2 upgrades, 51
planning process, 35-36
preparation, 38
process overview, 43-45
push method, 85-86
regional settings, 48
requirements, 13
safe detection, 44
saving prior system files, 48
saving system files, 49
Setup program, 45
system files backups, 42
system needs, 39
system time, 55
time zone, 55
troubleshooting network installs, 93
Windows version upgrades, 49-55
Windows scripts, 87
InstallLocationsMRU section, minbatch.inf script, 917
InstallStartLinks subroutine, WSH, 770
InstallType parameter, minbatch.inf script, 908
instances of objects, 359-362
Intel
  memory model, 239
  paging feature, 240
  PC 98 specifications, 306-307
  protected memory, privilege rings, 241
  Web sites, 319
Interactive CD Sampler, 862
interframe compression, 315
internal system commands, 874
Internet
  accounts, 653
  ActiveMovie Control, 328-330
  browsing, 596
  budgeting online time, 654

  connections, 651
    advanced DUN settings, 655-656
    advanced proxy settings, 659
    cable modems, 658
    ISDN, 657
    ISPs, 656-657, 663
    logon data, 654
    manual method, 653
    online services, 657
    passwords, 654
    proxy servers, 659
    TCP/IP, 539
    Wizard method, 652
  Dial-Up Networking, 565
  directory services, 717
  disconnect options, 654
  domains, DNS name resolution, 547
  down ISP logon servers, 664
  encryption, 706
  searches, 641
  secure transactions, 706
  security, 661, 690
    Active Scripting, 693
    ActiveX controls, 662, 692
    adding sites to zones, 699-700
    advanced proxy settings, 659
    Authenticode options, 703
    cookies, 705
    customizing security zones, 700
    encryption, 704
    file sharing, 695-697
    file/print sharing, 691
    firewalls, 692
    Java applets, 693
    Java issues, 662
    other potential threats, 694
    personal data, 694
    possible threats, 691
    print sharing, 695-697
    protocol isolation, 698
    proxy servers, 659
    security zones, 698

TCP/IP, 539
   transaction security, Microsoft Wallet, 707
   Web browsers, default options, 664
   Web sites, connections, 668
Internet applet, Control Panel, 652
Internet Chat, security issues, 694
Internet Connection Wizard, 652
Internet Control Panel, 137
Internet Explorer
   accessibility options, 617
   advanced options, 615-616
   advantages, 648-649
   bookmarks, 625
   browsing options, 617
   Channel Guide, 624
   channels
      subscriptions, 625-627
      updates, 627
   comparing to Netscape, 648-649
   configuring, 602
      cached page storage, 607-608
      character sets, 611
      color options, 609-611
      content filters, 612-614
      dial-up connections, 603-604
      fonts, 610-611
      History list URLs, 608
      home pages, 605
      program support, 615
      proxy servers, 603
      site updates, 606
   copying items from pages, 622
   desktop integration, 596
   dynamic HTML, 684
   Favorites menu, 623-625
   finding search topics on pages, 622
   History list, viewing, 623
   Java applet options, 703
   opening
      browser windows, 618
      links, 619
   page caching, 607
   printing Web pages
      frames, 300, 621
      header/footer codes, 619
   reloading pages, 622
   saving Web pages, 619
   security, 690, 694
      ActiveX controls, 692-693
      cookies, 705
      Java applets, 693
      scripts, 694
      zones, 698
   sending pages to others, 621
   settings options, 137
   shortcuts to pages, 621
   stopping page loading, 622
   viewing
      HTML code, 623
      Web page properties, 621
   working offline, 622
Internet Explorer Administration Kit, 698
Internet Options command (View menu), 602
Internet Service Providers, *see* ISPs
interprocess communication, 236
intraframe compression, 315
intranet sites, network connections, 668
IntraNetWare Client for Windows 95,
   configuring, 484
invocation script, 761
IO.SYS file, 821
   AUTOEXEC.BAT settings, 735
   BUFFERS=x command, 730
   DOS=HIGH command, 730
   FCBS=x command, 730
   FILES=x command, 730
   HIMEM.SYS file, 730
   IFSHLP.SYS file, 730
   LASTDRIVE=x command, 731
   SHELL=COMMAND.COM command,
     731

STACKS=x command, 731
system parameters, 730
IP addresses, 541
   automatic, APIPA feature, 541, 545
   classes, 555
   configuring, 541
      WINIPCFG options, 550
   DHCP servers, 541
   DNS servers, name resolution, 547
   duplicates, 560
   dynamic, DHCP servers, 544
   format, 554
   host IDs, 541, 554
   hostnames, 542
      resolution, HOSTS files, 548
   local hosts, 556
   manual, 543
   multicast addresses, 556
   name resolution, 546
   NetBIOS names, 542
   network IDs, 541, 554
   networks, 557
   octets, 541, 554
   static mapping, LMHOSTS files, 549
   subnet masks, 556-557
   subnetting, 556
IPC network choices, ODBC, 401
IPCONFIG command, 897-898
IPX/SPX networking, 473
   protocols, configuring, 481
   remote communications, 567
IRQs
   configuring addresses, 266
   devices, 264
   viewing device assignments, 268
ISA busses, Plug and Play options, 269
ISDN Internet connections, 657
ISO (International Standards Organization)
   network rules, 471
isolating problems, 839

ISPs (Internet Service Providers), 652, 656-657
   comparing services offered, 658
   connection problems, 663

J

Java
   applets, 660
      Internet Explorer options, 703
      security zone settings, 701
   sandbox, 661
   security, 662, 693
job automation, Task Scheduler, 778
joysticks, settings options, 137
JScript, Internet security, 694
jumpers for devices, installing, 272

K

Kernel core component, 246
KEYB command, 879
keyboard combinations, shortcuts, 30
keyboard layouts, Windows 98 install, 48
Keyboard option, Control Panel, 137
keys, Registry, 108
   Control Panel settings, 118
   exporting Control Panel defaults to users, 119-120
   file associations, 217-219
   hardware profiles, 196-197
   HKEY_CLASSES_ROOT, 201
   HKEY_CURRENT_CONFIG, 201
   HKEY_CURRENT_USER, 202
   HKEY_DYN_DATA, 201
   HKEY_LOCAL_MACHINE, 201
   HKEY_USERS root, 201
keywords
   CATEGORY, 170
   CLASS, 170
   PART, 171-173
   POLICY, 170-171

L

LABEL command, 889
language engines, scripts, 774
language options
    DSN error messages, 392
    Netscape Communicator, 630
    Windows 98 install, 48
Language tab, Keyboard Control Panel, 137
laptops, 442
    hardware profiles, 194-195
    see also portable computers
LASTDRIVE=x command, IO.SYS file, 731
launching
    Control Panel objects directly, 121
    see also starting
LDAP (Lightweight Directory Access Protocol)
    components, 718
    servers, 717-718
legacy
    adapters, installing, 475
    hardware, Setup problems, 77
legal issues and backups, 460
level sensitivity, IRQs, 264
LH command, 875
limitations of Task Scheduler, 784
limited operating modes for users, 99
linked documents, creating or editing with OLE, 366-367
links
    Bookmarks, Netscape Communicator, 643-645
    Favorites menu, organizing, 625
    opening, Internet Explorer, 619
    shortcuts, 30
Links toolbar, 27
listing fonts by similarity, 136
listings
    29.1 MESSAGE.HTM, dynamic HTML, 685-686
    34.1 Environment variable script, 754
    34.2 network drive info script, 757
    34.4 network connect script, 760
    34.5 reconfigure script, 761-762
    34.6 mail merge print script, 762
    34.7 Desktop utility script, 766-770
    D.1 install script [Network] section, 912
    D.2 [Install] section example, 920
    sample script, 583
LMHOSTS files
    configuring, 549
    NetBIOS names, 542
loading Web pages, Netscape Communicator, 646
local
    hosts, IP addresses, 556
    printers, 285
        installing, 292-293
        mapping to network printers, 291
    rebooting, 259
    user profiles, 17, 182
locating
    Control Panel settings, 123
    DHCP servers, 545
    hardware profile Registry keys, 196
location options for Windows folders, 224
locations for servers, selecting with DCOMCNFG utility, 372-373
lockups during Setup, 73
log files
    boot hangup problems, 826
    Setup, 45, 73
        inspecting, 74
        problem entries, 75
Log Off... command (Start menu), 23
Logged command (Startup menu), 830
logging site visits, Personal Web Server, 673
Logic Bombs, 432-433
logical drives, 404-406
LOGOFF parameter, NET command, 900
logon hours, Windows NT Server domains, 525

LOGON parameter, NET command, 900
logon scripts, push installs, 85-86
logons
    Dial-Up Networking, 586-587
    DSNs, 391-393
    email problems, 664
    Internet connections, 654
    NetWare, 536-537
    networks, access permissions, 18
    POP3 servers, problems, 664
    Primary Network Logon, configuring, 496-497
    types, 495
long filenames, FAT, 411-412

M

MAC addresses (Media Access Control), DHCP, 545
macro viruses, 434
macros, WSH script options, 763
mail merge print script, 762
Mail option, Control Panel, 139
mailboxes, 719
mailing preferences for email, 725
Main page, Personal Web Manager, 673
maintaining
    compressed drives, 426-427
    display adapter drivers, 278-279
Maintenance Wizard, 863
    customizing operation, 785
    starting, 785
    system performance tuning, 784-786
Make New Connection Wizard, Dial-Up Networking, 576, 654
MakeLink subroutine, WSH, 766
managing
    domains from Windows 98, 526-527
    print jobs, 298
    scheduling, 235
mandatory user profiles, 182-183, 187

manual download location for System Policies, 161-162
manual IP addresses, 543
Map Network Drive command (Tools menu), 26
mapping
    local printers to network printers, 291
    network drives
        accessing files in shares, 502
        network resources, finding, 499
McAfee VirusScan, 437
MD command, 875
measuring performance, hard disk drives, 415
media, network types, 305, 485-488
Media Player, 327-328, 862
MEM command, 880
memory
    address space layout, 242
    assignments, supporting devices, 266
    errors
        printing, 304
        ScanDisk, 76
    memory model, operating systems, 239-242
    monitoring shared resources, 794, 806
    optimizing, 794-795
    Setup conventional memory problems, 76
    video card requirements, 318
    virtual memory options, 150
menus
    adding actions, 221
    animation option, 134
Message Queue Server, 669
MESSAGE.HTM file, dynamic HTML, 685-686
messages, email, 246, 719
    cut/copy/paste options, 721
    deleting, 721
    Find option, 722
    new message options, 722
    organizing, 721

printing, 720
priorities, 723
saving as files, 720
status, 723
methods, WSH
  CreateFolder, 770
  DeleteFile, 770
  Echo, 750
  Echo (Hello World example), 752
  FileExists, 770
  OpenTextFile, 751
  Popup, 753
  Run, 762
  WshShell.CreateShortcut, 766
  WshShell.Popup, 750
microphones, 332
microprocessors, *see* processors
Microsoft
  Access, *see* Access databases
  Active Channel Web site, 34
  Backup, 457, 462-464
  browse masters, 513
  Client for NetWare Networks, 532-535
  Message Queue Server, 669
  Microsoft Family Logon, 485, 497
  Microsoft Script Debugger, 771-772
  NT Hydra system, 97
  ODBC drivers, 382
  Outlook, *see* Outlook
  PC 98 specifications, 306-307
  peer networks, NetWare comparison, 506
  TechNet CD-ROM, 865
MIDI, 333-334
  assigning channels to devices, 335
  deleting an instrument, 335
  Multimedia Control Panel options, 142
  Web site, 336
MIME (Multipurpose Internet Mail Extensions)
  content types, 714
  email attachments and headers, 713-715
  Netscape Communicator types, 634

minbatch.inf script, 62
  [Install] section, 917-919
  MRU list, 916
  [NameAndOrg] section, 908
  [Network] section, 908-911, 914
  network settings, 911
  [OptionalComponents] section, 915
  parameters, 908, 918
  [Printers] section, 916
  [Setup] section, 907-908
  [System] section, 909
  upgrade script, 907
minidriver architecture, supporting devices, 263
mixing backup types, 459
MKDIR command, 875
MODE command, 880
modems
  adding, 139
  cable modem Internet connections, 658
  Dial-Up Networking, peer networks, 512
  dialing settings, Telephony Control Panel, 151
  drivers, 151
  Internet Explorer connections, 604
  problems, 139, 857
  removing, 139
  troubleshooter tool, 139
Modems option, Control Panel, 139
modifying
  hardware profiles, 192
  see also editing
monitoring
  processors, performance tuning, 809
  shared resource memory, 806
monitors
  anti-aliasing, 134
  color depth, 135
  multiple monitor support, 280
  resolution, 135
  settings options, 132
  Windows install needs, 39

MORE command, 880
mouse speed and click options, 141
MouseKeys feature, 129
MOVE command, 889
movement impairment accessibility, 128
moving
   between pages, Netscape Communicator, 643-644
   email text, 721
   files, Explorer, 25
MPEG (Moving Picture Experts Group), 317
MRN server (Dial-Up Networking), 578
MRU (most recently used) list, 916
MS-DOS
   application support, 249
      installing and removing applications, 250
      setting program properties, 250-258
   commands and long filenames, 412
   dual-boot option, Windows 98, 56
   printing, 285, 291
   push installs, Win98 logon scripts, 86
MSDOS.SYS file, 731-732, 822
MSI (Microsoft System Information)
   Components branch, 841-842
   Conflicts/Sharing page, 844
   Hardware Resources branch, 841-842
   History page, 844
   information pages, 841
   Problem Devices page, 844
   Software Environment branch, 841-843
   troubleshooting tool, 841
MSN (Microsoft Network), Internet connections, 657
MSNET.INF script, 62
MTBF (Mean Time Between Failure), 823
multicast addresses, IP addresses, 556
Multilink, Dial-Up Networking, 584-585
multimedia, 305
   codecs, 314
   DirectX, 312, 313
   hardware, 320
      PC 98 specifications, 306-307
   installing, 307
   MPEG features, 317
   software
      Media Player requirements, 327-328
      standards, 312
   sound requirements, 331
      CD Player, 336-337
      microphones, 332
      MIDI, 333-335
      Sound Recorder, 338-341
      speakers, 332
      Volume Control, 337
   touch hardware, 342
   troubleshooting installation, 347
      audio, 351
      DirectX, 350
      DVD, 351
      SCSI, 350
Multimedia option, Control Panel, 141
Multimedia Sound Schemes option, 147
multipartite viruses, 435
multiple
   install scripts, Batch98 utility, 70-71
   monitor support, 280
   user profiles, 182
Multiple Machine-Name Save feature, Batch98, 70
Multipurpose Internet Mail Extensions, *see* MIME, 713
multitasking, 232-235, 244
mutex objects (semaphores), 239
MWNET.INF script, 62
My Channels, Netcaster, 647
My Computer
   defragmenting hard disks, 420
   formatting hard disks, 419
   Windows 98, 28

N

N-tier applications, 356
name directories, Netscape Communicator searches, 642
name resolution
   DNS servers, 547
   HOSTS files, 548
   IP addresses, 546
[NameAndOrg] section, minbatch.inf script, 908
naming
   Access DSNs, 395
   computers for networks, 489-490
   File DSNs, 388
   hardware profiles, 193
   printers, 288
nation-specific system settings, 145
National Computer Security Association, virus studies, 433
nationality settings, DSNs, 393
navigation options
   Internet Explorer, 617
   Netscape Communicator, 637, 643-644
Navigator, opening, 638
   see also Netscape Communicator
NBTSTAT command, 898
NBTSTAT utility, 553
NDS (NetWare Directory Services), 15
Net 10 IP addresses, 545
NET command parameters, 899-901
   checking ODBC connections, 398
   finding network resources, 500
Net Watcher, remote share management, 526, 863
NetBEUI
   networking, 472
   protocols, configuring, 479
   remote communications, 567

NetBIOS names
   IP addresses, 542
   LMHOSTS file, 542
   naming computers for networks, 489-490
   resolution, 546
Netcaster, 647
NETLOG.TXT file, 74
Netscape Communicator
   advanced options, 636
   advantages, 648-649
   Bookmarks, 643-645
   browsing options, 637
   character sets, 631
   comparing to Internet Explorer, 648
   configuring, 628
   cookies, 635
   display color options, 632
   file associations, 633
   font display options, 631-632
   helper apps, 633
   History file, 630, 643
   home pages, 630
   language options, 630
   MIME types, 634
   moving between pages, 643-644
   navigation options, 637
   Netcaster channels, 647
   Netsite list, 643
   offline work, 635, 639
   opening Navigator, 638
   reloading pages, 646
   searches
      Internet, 641
      name directories, 642
   sorting Bookmarks, 645
   start pages, 629
   startup program options, 629
   stopping page loading, 646
   toolbar settings, 629

Web pages
  copying text, 641
  finding items, 641
  opening, 638
  printing, 639-640
  viewing HTML code, 646-647
  webtops, 647
Netsite list, Netscape Communicator, 643
NETSTAT command, 901
NetWare
  hardware requirements, 530
  IPX/SPX protocol, 567
  long filename support, 536
  Microsoft Client for NetWare Networks, 532-535
  networks, 16
    CONFIG.POL file, 161
    Group Policies, 157
    installing Windows 98, 83
  overview, 530
  peer networks, 506
  software configurations, 531
  troubleshooting, 536-537
NetWare Core Protocol (NCP), 472
network adapters
  configuring, 68
  minbatch.inf script, 915
  Windows 98 install, 91
network boot disks, 88-93
Network Client Administrator, 88
network clients
  adding, 482
  properties
    Client for Microsoft Networks, 482
    Client for NetWare Networks, 483
    IntraNetWare Client for Windows 95, 484
    Microsoft Family Logon, 485
network commands, 893
network connect script, 760
Network Control Panel, 143
network drive info script, 756

network IDs, IP addresses, 541, 554
Network Interface Cards (NICs), 473
network libraries, ODBC, 402
network media, 485-488
Network Neighborhood, 26, 29
  network resources, finding, 498
  no other computers showing, 560
Network OLE, 357
network printers, 285, 295-296
  mapping local printers, 291
  sharing, 289
  UNC paths, 295
network services, installing, 478
network settings, minbatch.inf script, 911
[Network] section
  install scripts, 912-914
  minbatch.inf script, 908, 911, 914
networking
  adapters, 473
    Driver Type and Bindings tabs, 478
    installing, 474-475
  component requirements, 530
  managing domains from Windows 98, 527
  Microsoft Client for NetWare Networks, 532-535
  models, 517-518
  NetWare long filename support, 535-536
  overview, 469
  passwords, 143
  peer networks
    direct cable, 510-512
    setting up, 508-510
    troubleshooting, 515
    Workgroup model, 513-514
  redirectors, 472
  roving user profiles, 185
  settings options, 143
  software, 531-532
  transport protocols, 472-473
  user profiles, 182
  Windows 98 overview, 14-15
  Windows NT Server, 518

networks, 470
  adapters, 475
  browsing problems, 561
  client-server, 14-16
  components, 16, 471
  computer names, 542
  configuring
    Batch98 options, 66
    Internet Explorer, 604
  DHCP servers, locating, 545
  DNS hostnames, 542
  gateways, 542
  Group Policies, 156-157
  hostnames, 542
  intranet sites, 668
  IP addresses, 541, 557
    automatic, APIPA feature, 545
    classes, 555
    DHCP, 544
  logons
    access permissions, 18
    Primary Network Logon, 496
    types, 495
  NetBIOS names, 542
  NetWare, 16
    installing Windows 98, 83
  Network Providers Interface (NPI), 471
  peer-to-peer, 14
  performance tuning, 803-804
  portable computers, 447-448
  protecting resources, 490
  protocols, 17, 479-481
  resources
    disconnecting, 758-759
    finding, 498-501
    share-level security, 491
  runt packets, 804
  SNMP protocol, 558
  subnet masks, 543, 556-557
  System Policies, 160-162
  TCP/IP, IP addresses, 541
  UNIX, 16
  user-level security, 493-495
  UTP wiring, 487
  Windows 98 installs, 79
    automated, 84
    install scripts, 81-84
    install shares, 55
    NetWare networks, 83
    process overview, 80
    troubleshooting, 93
    Windows NT domains, 81-82
new features of Windows 98, 10-11
new message options, email, 722
New Technology File System, *see* NTFS
NIC (Network Information Center), assigning IP addresses, 555
NICs (Network Interface Cards)
  intranet site connections, 668
  network problems, 804
  problems, 560
NLSFUNC command, 881
non-overwriters (viruses), 436
non-PnP devices, installing, 273-274
Normal option (Startup menu), 830
Normal Startup option, Sys Config utility, 828
Norton AntiVirus, 437
Norton Backup, 458
notebook computers, *see* laptops
Notepad, 864
Novell
  DR-DOS, Windows 98 upgrades, 51
  IntraNetWare Client for Windows 95, configuring, 484
  Web site, 531
  see also NetWare
NT Hydra system, 97
NTFS (New Technology File System), 412-414
Numeric Data Processor, system device settings, 277
numerical representation, 145

O

Object Linking and Embedding, *see* OLE
objects, 359
   COM, 743, 762
   Control Panel, 117, 121-125
      properties dialog boxes, 116
   instances, 359-362
   storage and stream, 363
   VBScript, 746, 749
   WSH, 746, 749
      CreateObject, 751
      Dictionary, 751
      Err, 750
      filesystem, 764, 766, 770
      FileSystemObject, 751
      TextStream, 751, 771
      Wscript, 750
      WshNetwork, 750, 756
      Wshshell, 750, 753
      WshShortcut, 766
octets, IP addresses, 541, 554
ODBC (Open Database Connectivity), 379
   advanced tuning options, 401
   applet, 126, 381, 386-388
   APP parameter, 383
   client/server databases, 380
   connect strings, 384-386
   database connections, 383
   DRIVER parameter, 383
   drivers, 127, 382
   DSNs (Data Source Names), 126, 379
   installing, 387, 396-397
   IPC network choices, 401
   logging options, 393
   network libraries, 402
   overview, 382
   statistic tracking, 394
   tracing connections, 127
   troubleshooting, 398
      advanced parameters, 399
      functionality, 400
      network connections, 398
      parameters, 399
      security, 398
      tracing commands, 400
   upgrading, 396-397
   WSID parameter, 383
ODBC Data Source Administrator, DSNs, 386
ODBC Managers, 383
ODBC32.DLL, 383
OE.ADM policy template, 163
Office scripts, 763
offline options
   Internet Explorer, 622
   Netscape Communicator, 635, 639
   printing, 301
OLE
   application support, 248
   compound documents
      building, 364
      editing, 366
   embedded documents, 364-365
   linked documents, 366-367
OLE Automation, 357
on-access scanning for viruses, 437
one-way Internet connections, 658
online services, Internet connections, 657
OnNow design of Simply Interactive PC (SIPC), 444-445
opening
   browser windows, Internet Explorer, 618
   Control Panel objects directly, 121
   decreasing delay for submenu, Registry Editor, 225
   links, Internet Explorer, 619
   Maintenance Wizard, 785
   Microsoft Backup, 462
   Navigator, 638
   Properties dialog box, 25

Task Scheduler, 778
Taskbar Properties dialog box, 28
text files, email, 720
Web pages, Netscape Communicator, 638
OpenTextFile method, Cscript host, 751
OpenType fonts, 302
operating modes, limited, 99
operating systems
   application support, 247
      APIs, 247-248
      MS-DOS, 249-258
      OLE, 248
   components
      Configuration Manager, 244
      device drivers, 243-244
      Installable File System Manager, 249
      overview, 247
      shell, 246
      Virtual Machine Manager, 245
   file systems, 406
   local rebooting, 259
   memory model, 239-242
   multitasking, 232-234
   Plug and Play devices, 262
   processes and threads, 235
   scheduling, time slicing versus managed, 235-237
   semaphores, waits, and critical sections, 239, 244
   threads, scheduling in Windows 98, 238
   Windows NT Server, 518
optimizing
   file system, 797
   graphics, 798
   hard disks, 798
   memory, 794
   networks, 803-804
   page file, 796
   printing, 799
   programs, 804
   swap file, 796

   virtual memory, 795-796
   Windows 98, 791
optional components, Setup, 19-20
Optional Components button, Batch98, 63, 69
[OptionalComponents] section, minbatch.inf script, 915
ORACLE databases, client/server, 380
organizing
   Bookmarks, Netscape Communicator, 645
   email messages, 721
   Favorites menu, Internet Explorer, 625
orientation, printing, 289
Original Configuration hardware profile, backups, 197
orphaned shortcuts, 30
OS/2, upgrading to Windows 98, 51
Outlook Time Zone tab issues, 131
overviews
   Active Desktop, 598
   client/server databases, 380
   email structure, 719
   Internet browsing, 596
   networking, 14-15
   ODBC, 382
   Personal Web Server, 674
   Registry, 200
   TCP/IP, 540
   user profiles, 183-184
   Windows 98 install, 43-45, 80
overwriting
   backup data, 463
   viruses, 436

P

page caching, Internet Explorer, 607-608
pages, Web, *see* Web pages
paging feature and virtual memory, 240-241
paging file
   optimizing, 796
   performance problems, 795

Paint program, 864
paper sizes, printers, 289
Paradox file type databases, 380
parallel connections, direct, 510-512
parameters
    ARP command, 893
    CHKDSK command, 884
    DELTREE command, 885
    DISKCOPY command, 885
    DOSKEY command, 877
    EDIT command, 878
    EXTRACT command, 886
    FC command, 886
    FIND command, 888
    FORMAT command, 888
    FTP command, 894-897
    IPCONFIG command, 898
    KEYB command, 879
    MEM command, 880
    NBTSTAT command, 898
    ODBC
        connect strings, 385
        database connections, 383
        problems, 399
    SORT command, 890
    START command, 882
    XCOPY command, 891
PART keyword, 171-173
partitions, hard drives, 404-406, 418
PASSWORD parameter, NET command, 900
passwords
    backup data, 463
    Dial-Up Server, 590
    DVD Logon dialog box, 320
    email, 724
    Internet connections, 654
    networks
        logons, 495
        share-level security, 492
Passwords Control Panel, 110-111, 143, 156, 185

Paste Special dialog box, Word, 368
pasting email text, 721
PATH command, 875
pausing
    scripts for debugging, 772
    Web services, 674
payloads, 432
PC 98 specification hardware requirements, 306-307
PC Cards
    Plug and Play, 270
    portable computers, 442-443
PCI busses
    multimedia slot requirements, 307
    Plug and Play options, 270
    system device settings, 277
PCMCIA cards, *see* PC Cards
PCs
    Windows 98 install needs, 39
    see also computers
pedals for games, settings options, 137
peer networking, 14
    advantages and disadvantages, 504
    direct cable, 510-512
    Microsoft or NetWare, selecting, 506
    performing tasks, 505
    setting up, 508-510
    small peer networks, 506-508
    troubleshooting, 515
    Workgroup model, 513-514
performance
    file system data, 149
    graphics, 150
    hard disk drives, 415
    problems, 792-793
        file system, 797
        graphics, 798
        hard disks, 798
        networks, 803-804
        print spooling, 800
        printer rendering/transmission speed, 801

printing, 799
programs, 804
RAM, 794
virtual memory, 795
System Monitor counters, 807-814
tools, 806, 815
tuning, 791
   Maintenance Wizard, 784-786
   processor monitoring, 809
   System Monitor options, 807
   Win16 applications, 805
   Win32 applications, 805
Performance tab
   Display adapter properties, 279
   System Control Panel, 149
permissions
   network logons, 18
   Web site directories, 675
personal data, Internet security issues, 694
Personal Web Manager
   Main page, 673
   pausing Web services, 674
   tracking site hits, 674
   Web site management, 673
Personal Web Server, 559, 667
   Active Server Pages, 669, 686
   activity logs, 677
   audience considerations, 678-679
   compatibility issues, 680
   configuring, 671-672
   content needs, 679
   contents, 669
   Custom install, 670
   Data Access Components, 669
   directory browsing, 677
   Home Page Wizard, 681
   HTML editor options, 682
   installing, 670
   logging visits, 673
   Message Queue Server, 669
   planning Web sites, 678
   security, 672

   site content, 677
   Tour page, 674
   tracking site visits, 677
   Transaction Server, 669
   Typical install, 670
   Web sites
      default document, 676
      directory rights, 675
      home directories, 671
Phone Dialer, 862
phone lines, Internet connection problems, 664
photographs, *see* graphics
physical impairment accessibility, 128
pictures, *see* graphics
piggybacking backups, 455
Ping, 552, 902
   checking ODBC connections, 398
   problems, 561
planning
   Web sites, 671-672, 678
      audience considerations, 678-679
      compatibility issues, 680
      content needs, 679
   Windows 98 install process, 9, 35-36
platters, hard disk drives, 404
Plug and Play, 262
   BIOS, system device settings, 277
   checking during startup, 821
   design goals, 269
   device resource mediation, 262
   EISA busses, 270
   installing devices, 271
      network adapters, 474
      printers, 292
   ISA busses, 269
   PC Cards, 270
   PCI busses, 270
   SCSI busses, 270
Point and Print, 297
Point-to-Point Protocol, 566

Point-to-Point Tunneling Protocol, *see* PPTP
pointer options for mouse, 141
POLEDIT.EXE program, 157-158, 162
Policy Editor (System Policy Editor), 111-112
POLICY keyword, 170-171
policy templates, 157, 162-163, 168-169, 173-175
   Computer Policies, 176-178
   keywords, 170-171
   strings and comments, 173
   User and Group Policies, 179-180
POLICY.POL file, 107, 111-112, 200
polymorphic viruses, 434
POP (Post Office Protocol)
   logon problems, 664
   servers, 716
Popup method, WshShell object, 753
portable computers, 441-442
   Briefcase, 448-452
   dial-up modem connections, 442
   Direct Cable Connection, 447
   Hardware Profiles, 443-444
   Infrared Monitor application, 447-448
   PC Card device support, 442-443
   power management, 444-447
portable computers, 194
Portable install option, 19
ports, virtual printer, 289
POST (Power-On Self Test), 820
post-backup reports, 464
postscript printing, 284
power management/power saving, 133, 145
   applet, 445
   Control Panel option, 145
   portable computers, 444-447
   Task Scheduler, 784
Power-On Self Test, *see* POST
PPP server (Dial-Up Networking), 578

PPTP
   Dial-Up Networking, 565, 587
   remote communications, 567
predefined install scripts, Batch98, 84
preemptive multitasking, 234
preferences for email, 725
preparation
   Emergency Boot Disk, 832
   installation, 38
      disabling TSRs, 40
      hardware support, 39-40
      system needs, 39
preventative maintenance, 345-347
primary boot partition
   problems, 822
   rebuilding, 823
   startup troubleshooting, 830
Primary Network Logon, configuring, 496-497
Print dialog box, overview of buttons, 297
print mail merge script, 762
PRINT parameter, NET command, 900
printers
   configuring, 288-289
   default, 288
   installing, 292-293
   local, 285
   mapping local to network printers, 291
   naming, 288
   network, 285, 295-296
   page drop speed, 800
   paper sizes, 289
   removing, 301
   routers, 285
   sharing, 289
      Internet security, 691, 695-697
   virtual ports, 289
Printers Control Panel, 145
Printers folder, 288
[Printers] section, minbatch.inf script, 916
Printers tab, Batch98, 65

printing, 284
  color options, 300
  disabling spooling for DOS, 291
  DOS, 291
  drag-and-drop, 299-300
  email messages, 720
  EMFs, 284
  fonts, 302
    installing, 302
    problems, 801
  frames on Web pages, 300
  from disk, 300
  from programs, 297
  GDI process, 284
  managing jobs, 298
  memory errors, 304
  offline, 301
  orientation, 289
  performance tuning, 799
  Point and Print feature, 297
  postscript process, 284
  print queues, 298
  purging print jobs, 299
  resolution, 802
  RTA (Return to Application) speed, 800
  separator pages, 290
  spooling options, 290
  system reports, 148
  troubleshooting, 303-304
  vector graphics, 802
  viewing job status, 299
  Web pages
    Internet Explorer, 619-621
    Netscape Communicator, 639-640
priorities
  boosts in scheduling, 235
  email messages, 723
  scheduling thread inversions, 238
  Win32 program classes, 236
privilege rings, protected memory, 241
Problem Devices page, MSI, 844

problems
  Automatic Skip Driver Agent, 850
  boot process, 822
  boot sector, 825
  common causes, problems and solutions, 560, 839
  configuration, 824
  corrupt files, 840
  Dr. Watson, detecting system errors, 851
  EIDE hard drives, 823
  FileWise tool, 852-854
  FTP, 561
  hard drives, 823, 857
    configuration, 825
  hardware, 825
    conflicts, 839
    failures, 840
    incompatibilities, 839
    profiles, 197
    unknown monitor errors, 197
  Internet connections, 663
  IP address duplicates, 560
  isolating, 839
  locating hosts, 560
  modems, 139, 857
  network browsing, 561
  NICs, 560
  ODBC, 398
    advanced parameters, 399
    connections, 398
    functionality, 400
    parameters, 399
    security, 398
    tracing commands, 400
  performance, 792-793
    file system, 797
    graphics, 798
    hard disks, 798
    networks, 803-804
    print spooling, 800
    printers, 799-801

   programs, 804
   RAM, 794
   virtual memory, 795
Ping, 561
primary boot partition, 822
printing, 303-304
program crashes, 855-856
Registry Checker Tool, 850
ScanDisk, 852
SCSI drives, 823
serial ports, 857
Setup, 73
Setup log file entries, 75
Signature Verification Tool, 845
software incompatibilities, 840
solving systematically, 839
startup process, 827
subnetting, 560
system crashes regularly, 856
System File Checker, 847-849
system files, 826
Telnet, 561
user profiles, 187-188
user system settings errors, 840
users
   identifying, 838
   troubleshooting, 836-838
Version Conflict Manager, 846
Windows Report Tool, 845
see also troubleshooting
process overview
   operating systems, 235
   semaphores, waits, and critical sections, 239, 244
   Windows 98 install, 43-45
processors
   monitoring, performance tuning, 809
   Windows 98 needs, 13
   Windows install needs, 39
Prodigy Internet connections, 657
product ID code, Windows 98, 147

production scripts, 761
   automating tasks, 742
   VB limitations, 743
profiles
   boot process, 820
   hardware, 18, 191
   users, 17, 181
PROGMAN command, 881
program invocation script, 761
programs
   adding, 130
   Backup Exec, 458
   backups, 457
   closing prior to Windows install, 40
   configuring Internet Explorer support, 615
   CONTROL.EXE, opening Control Panel window, 122
   crashes, troubleshooting, 855-856
   Microsoft Backup, 457
   Norton Backup, 458
   performance tuning, 804
   POLEDIT.EXE, 157-158, 162
   printing, 297
   running under Win98, 47
   scheduling, Time Zone tab issues, 131
   WinBench, testing graphics performance, 798
Programs command (Start menu), 23
PROMPT command, 876
properties
   Explorer items, 25
   Internet Explorer, 137
   shortcuts, 30
   TCP/IP, 543
   Web pages, viewing in Internet Explorer, 621
Properties sheet, Dial-Up Networking, 577, 581-582
protected memory, privilege rings, 241-242
protected-mode device drivers, 270

protocols
   Dial-Up Networking
      checking bindings, 571
      installing, 570
   FTP, 551
   isolation, Internet security, 698
   network, installing and configuring, 479-481
   remote communications, 566-567
   SNMP, 558
   TCP/IP, 540, 543
   transport, 472-473
Protocols tab, Batch98, 67
proxy servers
   advanced settings, 659
   configuring for Internet Explorer, 603
   Internet connections, 659
public classes, registering, 361
purging print jobs, 299
push installs, 80
   logon scripts, 86
   Windows for Workgroups, 86-87
push method, Windows 98 installs, 85-86
PWD parameter, ODBC, 383, 399
PWS.ADM policy template, 163

Q-R

quantity of backup data, 454
quantum, 233
queue window, print jobs, 298
Quick Launch toolbar, 27

RAM
   drives, EBD system recovery, 833
   performance tuning, 794
   Windows 98 requirements, 13
   Windows install needs, 39
raster fonts, 302
RAW data format, postscript printing, 284
RD command, 876
RDBMS (Relational Databases Management Systems), 382

real-mode
   CD-ROM drivers, CD-ROM boot disks, 59
   device drivers, 270
reasons for backup failure, 454
rebooting, local, 259
rebuild kits for critical systems, 455
recipient aliases, email, 723
reconfiguration script, 761
recovering system via EBD, 831-833
Recycle Bin options, 31
redirectors, 472
refresh rate (video), 319
REG files, exporting Registry settings, 119
REGEDIT.EXE utility, 107, 881
regional coding, DVDs, 324
regional settings
   DSNs, 393
   minbatch.inf script, 910
   Windows 98 install, 48
Regional Settings Control Panel, 145
REGIONAL.INF script, 62
registering
   public classes, 361
   Windows 98, 45
Registration Wizard, 45
Registry, 106-107, 199
   alias branches, 201-202
   backups, 464
      Windows install, 42
   Batch98 options, 69
   changing file type icons, 221
   class definition subkeys, 219-221
   command subkeys, 219
   CONFIG.POL file, 200
   Control Panel settings, 118
   corrupt files, System File Checker options, 847
   DefaultIcon subkey, 219-221
   double-click hot zones, 227
   expanding Explorer icon cache, 225

exporting
    Batch98 option, 70
    Control Panel defaults to users, 119-120
file associations, 217-219
hardware profiles, 112-113
    backups, 197
    locating, 196
keys, 108
    HKEY_CLASSES_ROOT key, 201, 217
    HKEY_CURRENT_CONFIG key, 201
    HKEY_CURRENT_USER key, 202
    HKEY_DYN_DATA key, 201
    HKEY_LOCAL_MACHINE root key, 201
    HKEY_USERS root key, 201
management features, 109-110
POLICY.POL file, 200
removing
    Inbox from desktop, 226
    tilde from short filenames, 226
shell subkey, 219
ShellNew subkey, 220
System Policies, 111-112, 155-156, 162-168
    applying to networks, 160-162
    creating system policy file, 157-159
    enabling Group Policies, 156-157
    enabling User Policies, 156
    policy templates, 168-180
structure, 107-109, 200
SYSTEM.DAT file, 200
tips and tricks, 217
txtfilesubkey, 221
unknown file types, viewers, 227
User Profiles, 110-111
USER.DAT file, 200
viewing graphics contents as icons, 226
Registry Checker, 844, 850
Registry Editor, 107-108
    adding actions to menus, 221
    changing desktop icons, 223

changing hotkeys for commands, 222
changing Windows folder locations, 224
exporting settings to users, 119-120
hardware profiles, backups, 197
sounds for system events, 222
submenu opening delay, 225
reinstalling
    programs, crash repair, 856
    Windows 98 via EBD, 834
reloading pages
    Internet Explorer, 622
    Netscape Communicator, 646
relocating Windows folders, 224
remote communications, 563
    Dial-Up Networking, 564, 585
    protocols, 566-567
    servers, 567-568
remote connections, roving user profiles, 185
Remote Procedure Calls, 109
Remote Registry Service, installing, 526
remote servers, configuring Internet Explorer, 604
removing
    applications, 130
    device drivers, 275
    file associations, Netscape Communicator, 634
    Inbox from desktop, 226
    modems, 139
    MS-DOS applications, 249
    printers, 301
    Start menu items, 25
    tilde from short filenames, 226
    Windows 98, 71-72
    see also deleting
REN command, 876
RENAME command, 876
repairing
    bad hardware profiles, 195
    directories, SCANDISK, 833
    replacing primary boot partition, 823

requirements
   backups, 454
   Windows 98 installs, 13
resolution
   monitors, 135
   printing, 802
resolving hostnames to IP addresses, 546
Resource Meter, 863, checking shared memory resources, 794, 806
resources
   connect script, 760
   network, disconnecting, 758-759
responsiveness of double-clicking, 227
Restore tab, Microsoft Backup, 463
restoring
   backups, 464
   hardware profiles, 197
restrictions
   network access, 18
   Web sites, 698
reviewing backup strategies, 461
rights
   Web site directories, 675
   see also permissions
RMDIR command, 876
roaming user profiles, 17, 182
rollout planning, 35-36
root keys, Registry, 201
rotation strategies for backups, 458
Route command, displaying routing tables, 552, 902
routers, print, 285
routine job and task automation, Task Scheduler, 778
routing tables, displaying, 552
roving user profiles, 182-186
RTA (Return to Application) speed, printing, 800
Run command
   finding network resources, 499
   opening Control Panel objects, 121
   Start menu, 23

Run method, WSH, 762
running Setup via install scripts, 60
runt packets, 804

S

safe detection, Windows install, 44
Safe Mode
   boot hangups, 825
   Startup menu, 830
   troubleshooting system files, 826
Safe Recovery option, 73-74
sample script listing, 583
sandbox
   Java applets, Internet security, 693
   Java virtual machine, 661
saving
   email messages, 720
   Web pages, Internet Explorer, 619
ScanDisk, 844, 852, 863
   checking hard disks for errors, 806, 826
   directory structure repair, 833
   disk error checking, Windows install, 41
   hard disk optimizing, 797
   initiating, 422
   Maintenance Wizard, 785
   memory errors, 76
   running prior to upgrades, 51
   testing hard disk drives, 422-423
scanners (digital), 326
Scanners and Cameras Control Panel, 326
SCANREG, checking system Registry, 826
Schedule+, Time Zone tab issues, 131
Scheduled Task Wizard, 779-782, 863
scheduling
   operating systems, 232-233, 236-238
   programs, Time Zone tab issues, 131
   routine tasks and jobs, 778
   threads, 236-238
schemes
   settings options, 133
   sounds, 147

screen
- anti-aliasing, 134
- color depth, 135
- resolution, 135
- settings options, 132

Screen Saver tab, Display Control Panel, 133

Script Debugger, 771-772

scripting engine, Dial-Up Networking, 583-584

scripts, 741
- administrative tasks, 741
- background of Microsoft options, 742
- Basic I/O, 752
- button clicked, 753
- client-side, 687
- command line arguments, 756
- Cscript host, 751
- debugging, 771-772
- Desktop utility, 766-770
- dialog box example, 753
- Environment, 754
- execution parameters, wsh files, 751
- install, 61, 81-84, 905
- Internet security, 694
- invocation, 761
- language engines, 774
- mail merge print, 762
- minbatch.inf, 907
- network connect, 760
- network drive info, 756
- Office operations, 763
- pausing for debugging, 772
- production tasks, 742, 761
- reconfiguration, 761
- security zone options, 701
- server-side, 687
- shortcut swapping, 763-765, 768-770
- simple input, 753
- task automation, VB limitations, 743
- title bar dialog, 754
- UNIX connection, 760
- user info, 753
- Web site resources, 774
- writing, 752
- Wscript host, 751
- WSH
  - *advantages, 743*
  - *InputBox function usage, 760*
  - *Word macro options, 763*

SCSI, 311-312, 416
- busses, Plug and Play options, 270
- drive problems, 823
- troubleshooting multimedia installation, 350

searches
- finding items on pages, 641
- Internet, 641
- name directories, 642

secondary hard disk drives, 405

section headings, WIN.INI file, 736

section titles, install scripts, 906

secure transactions, Microsoft Wallet, 707

security
- ActiveX controls, 662
- Authenticode options, 662
- DCOMCNFG utility, 368
- domain model of networking, 518
- electronic transactions, 706
- Internet, 661, 690
  - *Active Scripting, 693*
  - *ActiveX controls, 692*
  - *adding sites to zones, 699-700*
  - *Authenticode options, 703*
  - *cookies, 705*
  - *customizing security zones, 700*
  - *encryption, 704*
  - *file sharing, 695-697*
  - *firewalls, 692*
  - *Java applets, 693*
  - *other potential threats, 694*
  - *personal data, 694*
  - *possible threats, 691*

    print sharing, 691, 695-697
    protocol isolation, 698
    proxy servers, 659
    security zones, 698
  Java, 662
  network resources, 491-493
  ODBC, 398
  Personal Web Server, 672
  servers, 374
  user-level security, 370
  Web sites, 672
  workgroup model of networking, 517
security zones
  Active Desktop options, 702
  ActiveX options, 701
  download options, 702
  IFRAME options, 702
  Internet Explorer, 698
  Java applet settings, 701
segments (memory), 239
selecting disk or file systems, 417
Selective Startup option, 828
semaphores, mutex objects, 238-239
sending Web pages to others, Internet Explorer, 621
sensitivity of double-clicking, 227
separator pages, printing, 290
serial connections, direct, 510-512
serial ports, 281, 857
SerialKey Device feature, 129
server applications, 364, 376
Server Message Blocks (SMBs), 472
server-based networks, 15
server-side scripting, 687
servers
  DHCP, 541
  Dial-Up Networking, 578
  DNS
    configuring, 547
    hostnames, 542
  email, 715-718
  file servers, 15
  LDAP, 717-718
  locations to run, selecting with DCOMCNFG utility, 372-373
  POP, 716
  remote communications, 567-568
  security issues, 374
  SMTP, 710, 716
  WINS, 542, 549
Services tab, Batch98, 68
SET command, 876
Settings command (Start menu), 23
settings options
  Control Panel objects, 123-125
  displays, 132
  hardware profiles, 192
  Internet Explorer, 137
Settings tab, Display Control Panel, 132
Setup
  Batch98 install script options, 63
  boot partition problems, 77
  command switches, 46
  common failure causes, 75
  conventional memory problems, 76
  dual-boot option, 56
  install process
    hardware detection, 43
    overview, 43
    safe detection, 44
  keyboard layouts, 48
  language options, 48
  legacy hardware problems, 77
  log files, 45, 73
    inspecting, 74
    problem entries, 75
  network connection failures, 75
  network installs, 83
  optional components, 19-20
  regional settings, 48
  running via install scripts, 60
  Safe Recovery option, 73-74

saving prior system files, 48
starting, 45
troubleshooting, 73
upgrades, 47
Windows directory name, 48
Setup Prompts tab, Batch98, 65-66
[Setup] section, minbatch.inf script, 907-908
SETUPLOG.TXT file, install event log, 73
SETVER command, 881
seven-layer model for networks, 470
share-level security, 491-492
shares, 490
   accessing files, 502
   directories, 18
   files, Internet security, 691
   hiding, 492
   memory resources, checking via Resource Meter, 794, 806
   printers, 289
     Internet security, 691
Sharing dialog box, network security, 491
shell
   functions, 246
   subkey, 219
SHELL.ADM policy template, 163
SHELL=COMMAND.COM command, IO.SYS file, 731
ShellNew subkey, 220
short filenames, removing tilde, 226
shortcut swapping script, 763-765, 768-770
shortcuts, 29
   keyboard combinations, 30
   network resources, finding, 499
   properties, 30
   Telnet, 551
   Web pages, Internet Explorer, 621
ShowSounds feature, 129
Signature Verification Tool, 844-845
signatures, email, 724
simple input script, 753
Simple Mail Transfer Protocol, *see* SMTP

Simply Interactive PC (SIPC), 444
Single Line Protocol (TCP/IP), 566
site links, Active Desktop, 596
site updates, configuring for Internet Explorer, 606
sites (Web), *see* Web sites
size options, Recycle Bin, 31
SLIP server (Dial-Up Networking), 578
Small Computer System Interface, *see* SCSI
SMS (System Management Server), Windows 98 installs, 87
SMTP (Simple Mail Transfer Protocol), 710
   clients, 710
   email transfer process, 710
   servers, 710, 716
SNMP (Simple Network Management Protocol) agents, 558
soft fonts, 302
software
   applications, tasks, or processes, 234
   backups, 457
   bugs, 794
   business rules, 356
   crashes, troubleshooting, 855-856
   Dial-Up Networking compression settings, 573
   incompatibilities, 840
   Media Player requirements, 327, 328
   networking
     configurations, 531
     Microsoft Client for NetWare Networks, 532-535
   objects, 359
   peer networks, installing, 508
   tasks, processes, 232
   video requirements, 324-325
   see also applications; programs
Software Environment branch, MSI, 841-843
solutions for common problems, 560
solving hardware profile problems, 197
SORT command, 890

sorting Bookmarks, Netscape
    Communicator, 645
sound
    associating with system events, 147
    multimedia requirements, 331
        CD Player, 336-337
        microphones, 332
        MIDI, 333-335
        Sound Recorder, 338-341
        speakers, 332
        Volume Control, 337
    schemes, 147
    system events, 222
sound cards
    full and half duplex, 332
    installing, 331
Sound Recorder, 862
    codec overview, 316
    features, 338-341
Sounds Control Panel, 147
SoundSentry feature, 129
source code of Web pages, viewing (Internet
    Explorer), 623
speakers, 332
speed, video card requirements, 319
Speed tab, Keyboard Control Panel, 137
spooling options
    disabling for DOS, 291
    printing, 290
    problems, 304
SQL Server
    databases, client/server, 380
    DSNs
        authentication, 391
        drivers, 390
STACKS=x command, IO.SYS file, 731
standalone systems, 15
START command, 882
Start menu, 22-23
    adding commands, 24
    customizing, 24

deleting items, 25
direct Control Panel access, 122
Find command, locating network
    computers, 498
Run command, opening Control Panel
    objects, 121
start pages, Netscape Communicator, 629
START parameter, NET command, 900
starting
    Active Desktop, 33
    Batch98 utility, 63
    Control Panel objects directly, 121
    DOS dual-boot option, 56
    Maintenance Wizard, 785
    Microsoft Backup, 462
    Navigator, 638
    new hardware profiles, 193
    Properties dialog box, 25
    Script Debugger sessions, 771
    Setup, 45
    System File Checker, 847
    Task Scheduler, 778
    Taskbar Properties dialog box, 28
    Web servers, 673
startup files, Windows 98, 821
Startup menu options, 830
startup process, 820
    compatibility checking, 821
    device drivers, 821
    EBD, 831
    hangups, 825
    hardware
        problems, 822
        profiles, 820
    reloading boot files, 827
    Setup log files, 73
    System Configuration tool, 827
    troubleshooting, 822
    user profiles, 821
    VxD drivers, 821
statements, VBScript, 745

static mapping, names to IP addresses, 549
statistics
   ODBC tracking, 394
   viewing for Web sites, 674
status option, email messages, 723
stealth viruses, 435
steering wheels for games, 137
Step-by-Step Confirmation (Startup menu), 830
StickyKeys feature, 128
STOP parameter, NET command, 901
stopping
   page loading
      Internet Explorer, 622
      Netscape Communicator, 646
   Web servers, 673
storage objects, 363
strategies
   backup rotation, 458
   problem solving, 835
stream objects, 363
String values, 109
structural overview of email, 719
structured storage, 363
subkeys
   class definition, 219-221
   command, 219
   DefaultIcon, 219
      changing desktop icons, 223
      file type icons, 221
   shell, 219
   ShellNew, 220
   txtfile, 221
submenus, decreasing opening delay, 225
subnet masks, network nodes, 543, 556-557, 560
subroutines, WSH, 766, 770
SUBS.ADM policy template, 163
subscriptions
   channels, 34, 625-627
   TechNet, 865

SUBST command, 890
suggestions for troubleshooting, 854
summary system performance data, 149
supporting devices
   automatic hardware detection, 263
   control panels, 263
   device drivers, 270
   DMA (Direct Memory Access), 265
   hardware configuration wizards, 263
   hardware device tree, 263
   hot-pluggable, 263
   I/O port addresses, 266
   installing, 271-274
   IRQs (Interrupt Requests), 264
   memory assignments, 266
   multiple monitor support, 280
   Plug and Play, 262
      ISA busses, 269
      PC cards, 270
      PCI busses, 270
   serial ports, 281
   virtual device drivers, 263
surround sound, 333
swap file, optimizing, 794-796
switches
   ARP command, 893
   CHKDSK command, 884
   DELTREE command, 885
   DISKCOPY command, 885
   DOSKEY command, 877
   EDIT command, 878
   EXTRACT command, 886
   FC command, 886
   FIND command, 888
   FORMAT command, 888
   FTP command, 894-897
   IPCONFIG command, 898
   KEYB command, 879
   MEM command, 880
   NBTSTAT command, 898
   Setup, 46

SORT command, 890
START command, 882
XCOPY command, 891
switching language options, 139
system
    commands, 874-876
    components, installing, 19
    configuring, 106-113
    errors, detecting via Dr. Watson, 851
    events, associating sounds, 147, 222-223
    icon options, 133
    install script settings, 64
    parameters, IO.SYS file, 730
    passwords, 143
    performance tuning
        Maintenance Wizard, 784-786
        Windows Tune-Up, 806
    power saving options, 145
    regional settings, 145
    regular crashes, 856
    reports, printing, 148
    time and date settings, 131
    ZAW tools, 97
System Configuration Utility, 844
    Advanced Troubleshooting settings, 829
    checking boot problems, 827
    startup problems, 827
System Control Panel, 147-149
system devices, Device Manager, 276
System DSNs, 386-388
System File Checker, 844, 847-849
    system file problems, 826
    troubleshooting programs, 805
system files
    backups, Windows install, 42
    saving for DOS/NT/Windows 3.0 installs, 53
    troubleshooting, 826
System Information tool, system file problems, 826, 864

System Monitor, 864
    checking page file, 795
    memory optimizing, 794
    performance counters, 807-814
    performance tuning, 807
System option, Control Panel, 193
System Policies, 28, 107-112, 154-155
    Batch98, 69
    limited operating modes, 99
    mandatory user profile differences, 183
System Policy Editor
    Computer Policies, 165-167
    Group Policies, 156-157, 167-168
    keywords, 170-171
    limited operating mode policies, 99
    policies
        applying to networks, 160-162
        creating, 162-166
        policy file creation, 157-159
        template files, 168-169, 173-180
    User Policies, 165-167
SYSTEM.DAT files, 107-110, 200
SYSTEM.INI file, 737-739, 822
[System] section, minbatch.inf script, 909
systematic problem solving, 839

T

tape drives, 418
task automation
    adding tasks to Task Scheduler, 779
    via scripts, 741-743
    WSH, 786
Task Scheduler
    defragmenting hard disks, 421
    deleting tasks, 782
    file type support, 778
    idle time options, 784
    limitations, 784
    power management options, 784
    repeat options, 782
    routine job and task automation, 778

start and end dates, 782
starting, 778
stop times, 782
task automation, 779
viewing folder contents, 783
taskbar, 26
   Autohide option, 28
   configuring, 28
   toolbars, 27
tasks, Task Scheduler, 232, 782
TaskStation mode, Zero Administration Kit, 98
TCO (Total Cost of Operations), 95-96
TCP/IP, 540
   configuring, 543
   gateways, 542
   hostnames, 542
   IP addresses, 554-556
   networks, 472
      IP addresses, 541, 557
      performance, 803
      protocols, 480
   properties, 543
   remote communications, 566
   subnet masks, 543, 556-557
   subnetting, 556
   utilities, 550
   Web site connections, 668
TechNet CD-ROM, 865
technologies for backups, 456-457
telephone lines, Internet connection problems, 664
Telephony Control Panel, modem dialing settings, 151
Telnet
   client, 550
   troubleshooting, 561
   UNIX host connections, 558
templates
   install scripts, 60
   userprof.inf, 918
   Web sites, 681

temporary prepared SQL Statements, DSNs, 392
terminal emulation, *see* Telnet
testing
   EBD, 832
   hard disk drives, ScanDisk, 422-423
   WAN connections, TRACERT command, 553
text
   copying
      Internet Explorer, 622
      Netscape Communicator, 641
   editors, 864
   email, cut/copy/paste options, 721
   files, 720
Text Stream objects, WSH, 751, 771
The Microsoft Network, Internet connections, 657
thin clients, 95-96
thin Ethernet, 507
Thinnet networks, 487-488
third-party performance tools, 815
thirty-two bit ODBC applet, Control Panel, 381
thrashing
   performance problems, 795
   virtual memory systems, 241
threads, operating systems, 235-238
tilde, removing from short filenames, 226
time, setting for system, 131
TIME command, 876
TIME parameter, NET command, 901
time slices, 233-234
time zones, Windows 98 install, 55
timeout feature, disabling for Windows install, 40
TimeZone parameter, minbatch.inf script, 908
tips
   application performance, 804
   optimizing network performance, 803

troubleshooting

Registry, 217
  troubleshooting, 854
title bar dialog script, 754
ToggleKeys feature, 129
toolbars
  Address, 27
  Desktop, 27
  Links, 27
  Netscape Communicator, 629
  Quick Launch, 27
Tools menu commands, 26
topologies, network media, 487
TOTE (Test-Operate-Test-Exit) problem solving method, 792
touch (input/output) hardware, multimedia, 342
Tour page, Personal Web Server, 674
TRACERT command, testing WAN connections, 553, 903
tracing commands, ODBC problems, 127, 400
trackballs, settings options, 141
tracking
  desktop settings, Passwords Control Panel, 144
  site hits, Personal Web Manager, 674
  ODBC statistics, 394
  Web site visits, 677
transaction security
  encryption, 704
  Microsoft Wallet, 707
  on the Web, 706
Transaction Server, 669-671
transfer process, SMTP email, 710
translation sets, DSNs, 393
transport protocols, 472
  IPX/SPX, 473
  NetBEUI, 472
  TCP/IP, 472
tricks for Registry, 217
Trojan Horses, 432

troubleshooting
  applications, 804
  Automatic Skip Driver Agent, 850
  boot sector, 825
  common problem causes, 839
  common problems and solutions, 560
  configuration, 824
  corrupt files, 840
  devices not functioning, 274
  Dial-Up Networking, 574, 588-589
  disk compression, 428
  DOS programs, 805
  Dr. Watson, detecting system errors, 851
  EIDE hard drives, 823
  file system problems, 797
  FileWise tool, 852-854
  FTP, 561
  hard disks, 798
  hard drives, 823, 857
    configuration, 825
  hardware, 825
    conflicts, 839
    failures, 840
    incompatibilities, 839
    profiles, 197
    unknown monitor errors, 197
  identifying problems, 838
  Internet connections, 663
  IP address duplicates, 560
  isolating problems, 839
  locating hosts, 560
  memory, 794
  Microsoft System Information, 841
  modems, 139, 857
  monitors, 798
  MultiLink, 585
  multimedia installation, 347, 350-351
  NetWare, 536-537
  networks
    browsing, 561
    installs, 93
    problems, 803-804

NICs, 560
ODBC, 398
   advanced parameters, 399
   functionality, 400
   network connections, 398
   parameters, 399
   security, 398
   tracing commands, 400
peer networks, 515
Ping, 561
Plug and Play devices, 271
preventative action, 345-347
primary boot partition, 822
printing, 303-304, 799-801
programs, 804
ScanDisk, 852
SCSI drives, 823
serial ports, 857
Setup, 73
Setup log file entries, 75
Signature Verification Tool, 845
software incompatibilities, 840
solving problems systematically, 839
startup process, 822
   System Configuration tool, 827
subnetting, 560
suggestions and tips, 854
system crashes regularly, 856
System File Checker, 847-849
system files, 826
Telnet, 561
tools, 840
USB install, 310
users
   problems, 836-838
   profiles, 187
   system settings errors, 840
Version Conflict Manager, 846
virtual memory, 795
Windows 98, 836
Windows Report Tool, 845

TrueType fonts, 302
trusted sites, 698
TSRs, disabling for Windows install, 40
tuning options, ODBC, 401
TV tuner cards
   video capture option, 325
   WebTV, 324
twisted-pair Ethernet, 507
two-tier client/server architecture, 380
two-way Internet connections, 658
txtfilesubkey, 221
TYPE command, 876
type conversion, VBScript, 744
types
   files, HTML documents, 666
   type checking, VBScript, 744
Typical install, Personal Web Server, 670
Typical install option, 19

U

UARTs, 572
UID parameter, ODBC problems, 399
UNC (universal naming convention), network printer paths, 295
undo option, email, 720
Unified Device Driver model, 243
Uninstall parameter, minbatch.inf script, 907
Uninstall utility, Windows 98 removal for system repair, 834
uninstalling
   programs, 130
   Windows 98, 71-72
universal driver architecture, supporting devices, 263
Universal Serial Bus, *see* USB
UNIX
   DOS command comparison, 558
   host connections, 558
      script, 760
   networks, 16
   servers, remote communications, 568

unknown file types, viewers, 227
unknown monitor errors, hardware profiles, 197
UpdateAutoBat parameter, minbatch.inf script, 918
UpdateCfgsys parameter, minbatch.inf script, 918
UpdateInis parameter, minbatch.inf script, 918
updates
   channels, Internet Explorer, 627
   device drivers, 275
   DSNs, ODBC Data Source Administrator, 386
   EBD, 832
   Web sites, configuring, Internet Explorer, 606
Upgrade account, push Win98 installs, 85
upgrading
   DOS, 53-55
   minbatch.inf script, 907
   ODBC, 396-397
   OS/2, 51
   Windows 3.x, 50-55
   Windows 95, 13
      copying files, 50
      emergency boot disks, 49
      hardware configuring, 50
      Internet channel sets, 49
      saving system files, 49
   Windows for Workgroups, 51
   Windows NT, 53-55
uplink ports, 487
URLs
   History list, Internet Explorer, 608, 624
   retaining in Netscape History file, 630
   scripting resource Web sites, 774
   VBScript info Web site, 745
   Visual Basic info Web site, 771
   WSH scripting discussion groups, 775
usage tips, install scripts, 60

USB
   features, 309
   Web site, 310
USE parameter, NET command, 901
User core component, 246
User DSNs, 386-388
user info script, 753
User Info tab, Batch98, 65
User Manager for Domains, logon scripts, push installs, 85
User Policies, 165-167
   enabling for SP, 156
   WINDOWS.ADM, 179-180
user profiles, 17, 107, 110-111, 181
   boot process, 821
   customizing, 185
   directories, 183-184
   enabling, 185
   file structure, 183
   local, 182
   mandatory, 182, 187
   multiple, 182
   problems, 187-188
   roaming, 182
   roving, 182-186
User Profiles tab
   Batch98, 66
   Passwords Control Panel, 144
user-defined types, VBScript, 744
user-level security, 370
   assigning access, 495
   setting up, 493
USER.DAT file, Registry data, 107-110, 200
USERPROF.INF script, 62
userprof.inf template, 918
users
   accessibility options, Internet Explorer, 617
   environment settings, 17
   exporting default Control Panel settings, 119

identifying problems, 838
limited operating modes, 99
Registry settings, Control Panel, 118
system account options, Users Control Panel, 151
system policies, 18
system settings errors, 840
troubleshooting problems, 836-838
Users Control Panel, user system account options, 151
utilities
   anti-virus, 437-439
   Automatic Skip Driver Agent, 850
   Backup, 863
   Batch98, 62-63
   Disk Cleanup, 785
   Disk Defragmenter, 785
   Dr. Watson, 827, 851
   EBD, 833
   EXT, file repair via EBD, 834
   FileWise tool, 852-854
   FTP, 551
   NBTSTAT, 553
   Ping, 552
   REGEDIT.EXE, 107
   Registry Checker Tool, 850
   ScanDisk, 785, 852
      checking system drive, 826
      running prior to upgrades, 51
   SCANREG, checking system Registry, 826
   Signature Verification tool, 845
   System Configuration
      Advanced Troubleshooting settings, 829
      checking boot problems, 827
      startup problems, 827
   System File Checker, 847-849
   System Information, 864
   TCP/IP, 550
   Telnet, 550
   TRACERT, testing WAN connections, 553
   troubleshooting tools, 840
   Uninstall, 834
   Version Conflict Manager, 846
   Windows Report tool, 845
   WINIPCFG, IP address configuration, 550
UTP wiring, networks, 486
UUencode format, email attachments, 713

V

value of backup data, 454
variables in scripts, debugging, 772
variant types, VBScript, 744
VB (Visual Basic), limitations for automated tasks, 743
VBA (Visual Basic for Applications), 743
VBScript, 741
   collection operations, 745
   control statements, 745
   error handlers, 745
   informational Web site, 745
   Internet security, 694
   language model, 744
   objects, 745-746, 749
   task automation, 743
   type conversion/type checking, 744
   user-defined types, 744
   variant types, 744
VBScript Scripting Engine, 774
vector
   fonts, 302
   graphics, printing, 802
VER command, 876
VER parameter, NET command, 901
VERIFY command, 876
Version Conflict Manager, troubleshooting programs, 805, 844-846
video
   compression, 315
   hardware requirements
      cameras, 326
      DVD, 320-324

scanners, 326
video cards, 318-319
Multimedia Control Panel options, 142
settings options, 132
software requirements
video capture, 325
WebTV for Windows, 324-325
View menu
Folder Options command, 26
Internet Options command, 602
VIEW parameter, NET command, 901
viewers for unknown file types, 227
viewing
cached pages, Internet Explorer, 608
directories, Explorer, 25
graphics, contents as icons, 226
History list, Internet Explorer, 623
HTML code, Netscape Communicator, 646
Internet Explorer
character sets, 611
color options, 609-611
content filters, 612-614
fonts, 610-611
page info, Netscape Communicator, 647
print job status, 299
statistics for Web sites, 674
Task Scheduler folder, 783
Web pages
content filters, 612
properties, Internet Explorer, 621
source code, Internet Explorer, 623
virtual device drivers, 244, 263
virtual directories, Web sites, 674-675
Virtual Machine Manager, 244-245
virtual memory, 240
optimizing, 795-796
settings options, 150
thrashing, 241
Virtual Machine Manager, 245
virtual printer ports, 289

virtual private networks, 564-565
viruses, 432-434
closing programs prior to Windows install, 40
executing, 436
origins, 436
preventing, 437-439
recognizing, 437
transmission procedure, 436-437
types, 434-435
Web sites with scam information, 435
Visual Basic, Web site info, 771
visual impairment accessibility, 128
Visual InterDev, remote support, 669
VOL command, 876
Volume Control, 337, 862
VPNs, *see* virtual private networks
vrc parameter, minbatch.inf script, 908

W

wait functions, 239
wallpaper, HTML, 33
WANs, testing connections, 553
Web browsers
ActiveX controls, 661
budgeting online time, 654
comparing, 648-649
configuring, 601-602
default options, 664
defaults, 601
dynamic HTML, 684
Internet Explorer
security, 690
settings options, 137
Java applets, 661
Netscape Communicator, 627-628
opening windows, Internet Explorer, 618
security, 662, 692
site compatibility issues, 680
see also Internet Explorer; Netscape Communicator; Netscape Navigator

Web pages
- default browser options, 664
- downloading for offline viewing, 639
- frames, printing, 300
- Internet Explorer options
  - *adding to Favorites menu, 624*
  - *color options, 609-611*
  - *content filters, 612-614*
  - *copying items, 622*
  - *default home page, 605*
  - *finding search topics, 622*
  - *fonts, 610-611*
  - *printing, 619-621*
  - *reloading, 622*
  - *saving, 619*
  - *sending to others, 621*
  - *shortcuts, 621*
  - *stopping loading, 622*
  - *viewing properties, 621*
  - *viewing source code, 623*
- Netscape Communicator options
  - *Bookmarks, 643-645*
  - *cookies, 635*
  - *copying text, 641*
  - *display color options, 632*
  - *file associations, 633*
  - *finding items on pages, 641*
  - *font options, 631-632*
  - *helper apps, 633*
  - *moving between, 643, 644*
  - *opening, 638-640*
  - *reloading, 646*
  - *sending via e-mail, 638*
  - *stopping loading, 646*
  - *viewing HTML, 646-647*

Web servers
- Personal Web Server, 667
- starting or stopping, 673

Web sites
- Active Channel, 34
- Active Server Pages, 686
- activity logs, 677
- adding to security zones, 699-700
- administration, 673
- audience considerations, 678-679
- Bookmarks, Netscape Communicator, 643
- color options, Internet Explorer, 609-611
- compatibility issues, 680
- content
  - *filters, Internet Explorer, 612-614*
  - *FrontPage Express, 682-684*
  - *Home Page Wizard, 681*
- customizing security zones, 700
- default document, 676
- directories
  - *access rights, 675*
  - *browsing, 677*
- DirectX, 313
- dynamic HTML, 684
- fonts, Internet Explorer, 610-611
- home directories, 671
- HTML editor options, 682
- IEEE 1394, 311
- importing content, 677
- Intel AGP, 319
- logging visits, Personal Web Server, 673
- marking with Bookmarks, Netscape Communicator, 645
- MIDI, 336
- Novell, 531
- Personal Web Manager, 673
- planning and design, 671-672, 678
- restricted, 698
- security, 672, 706
- TCP/IP connections, 668
- templates, 681
- tracking hits, 674, 677
- transaction security, 704, 707
- trusted, 698
- scripting resources, 774
- updates, configuring, 606
- USB, 310

VBScript information, 745
virtual directories, 674-675
Visual Basic info, 771
Windows 98 options, 668
WSH scripting discussion groups, 775
Yahoo!, 318
Web tab, Display Control Panel, 135
Web views, folders, 601
Web-based desktop options, 33
webtops, Netscape Communicator, 647
WebTV for Windows, 324, 862
Welcome to Windows feature, 864
Win 32 API, 247, 805
WIN.INI file, 736, 822
Win16 API, 248, 805
WinBench program, testing graphics performance, 798
Windows 3.x
   dual-boot option, 56
   network installs, 84
   push installs, 86
   servers, remote communications, 568
   upgrades, 47, 50, 53-55
Windows 95
   network installs, 84
   push installs, 86
   upgrades, 47-50
   Zero Administration Kit, 98
Windows 98
   Accessories, 861
   Active Channels, 34
   Active Desktop, 32-33
     browse features, 598-600
     overview, 598
     wallpaper, 33
   AUTOEXEC.BAT file, 735, 822
   backups, 453-455
   benefits of upgrades, 13
   boot process
     compatibility checking, 821
     device drivers, 821
     hardware profiles, 820
     troubleshooting, 822
     user profiles, 821
     VxD drivers, 821
   BOOTLOG.TXT file, 822
   Briefcase, 29
   bugs, describing via Report tool, 846
   CD-ROM boot disks, 58
   changing folder locations, Registry Editor, 224
   color schemes, 133
   CONFIG.SYS file, 732, 822
   configuration files, 729
   configuring
     DHCP, 544
     DNS servers, 547
     hardware needs, 815
     HOSTS files, 548
     INI file updates, 736
     LMHOSTS files, 549
     WINS, 547-549
   Control Panel, 115
   corrupt files, 840
   customizing Setup via install scripts, 59
   deployment planning, 9
   desktop, 21
   Device Manager error codes, 865-872
   dual-boot options, 56-57
   email, 710
   event names, 223
   Explorer, 25
   FrontPage Express, 682-684
   Hardware Compatibility list, 40
   hardware
     conflicts, 839
     failures, 840
     incompatibilities, 839
     profiles, 192
   installing, 37
     batch files, 87
     components, 19

compressed drive errors, 76
copying files, 50
defragmenting hard drives, 41
disabling TSRs, 40
DOS upgrades, 53-55
emergency boot disks, 49
fonts, 302
hardware configuring, 50
hardware detection, 43
hardware support, 39-40
install scripts, 81-84
install shares, networks, 55
Internet channel sets, 49
keyboard layouts, 48
language options, 48
local printers, 292-293
network adapters, 91
network boot disks, 88-93
network configuring, 42
network installs, 79-80
network printers, 295-296
on NetWare networks, 83
on Windows NT domains, 81-82
optional components, 19-20
OS/2 upgrades, 51
planning process, 35-36
preparation, 38
process overview, 43-45
push method, 85-86
regional settings, 48
requirements, 13
safe detection, 44
saving prior system files, 48
saving system files, 49
Setup program, 45
system files backups, 42
system needs, 39
system time, 55
time zone, 55
Windows directory name, 48
Windows scripts, 87

Internet connections, 651
   logon data, 654
   manual method, 653
   Wizard method, 652
IO.SYS file, 821
IP addresses, configuring, 541
limited operating modes, 99
local printers, 285
MSDOS.SYS file, 822
My Computer, 28
networks
   client systems, 16
   components, 16
   installs, troubleshooting, 93-94
   network printers, 285
Network Neighborhood, 29
new features, 10-11
ODBC, 387, 396
optimizing, 791
passwords, 143
performance tools, 806
Personal Web Server, 667-669
Point and Print feature, 297
printers, 284
   color options, 300
   drag-and-drop, 299-300
   fonts, 302
   offline, 301
   print queues, 298
   problems, 303-304
   removing printers, 301
product ID code, 147
RAM requirements, 13
Recycling Bin, 31
registration, 45
Registry, 199
reinstalling via EBD, 834
requirements, processor, 13
ScanDisk, running prior to upgrades, 51
Setup, Safe Recovery option, 73-74
shortcuts, 29

SNMP protocol, 558
software incompatibilities, 840
Start menu, 22-24
startup files, 821
Startup menu, 830
system files, troubleshooting, 826
SYSTEM.INI file, 737-739, 822
taskbar, 26-28
TCO (Total Cost of Operations), 95-96
TCP/IP, 540
troubleshooting, 836
    common problem causes, 839
    identifying problems, 838
    solving problems systematically, 839
    user problems, 836-838
uninstalling, 71-72
UNIX hosts, 558
upgrades, 51
user profiles, 17, 181
users
    environment settings, 17
    system settings errors, 840
virtual memory settings, 150
WIN.INI file, 736, 822
ZAW, 97
Windows directory, DOS/NT/Windows 3.0 installs, 52
Windows Explorer, *see* Explorer
Windows for Workgroups
    network boot disks, 91-93
    push installs, 86-87
    upgrading to 98, 51
Windows NT
    advantages over 98, 12
    DCOM, 369
    domains, 16, 81-82, 518
    dual-boot option, 57
    Network Client Administrator, 88
    networks, CONFIG.POL file, 160
    upgrading to 98, 53-55
Windows Report Tool, 844-846

Windows Tune-Up, system performance tuning, 806
Windows Update command (Start menu), 23
WINDOWS.ADM file, 163, 176-180
WINFILE command, 883
WINIPCFG utility, IP configuration data, 550
WINS
    configuring, 547-549
    servers, 542
WINVER command, 883
Wizards
    Accessibility, 862
    Add New Hardware, 130
        checking hardware support, 39
        network adapters, 474
    Add Printer, installing printers
        local, 292
        network, 295
    Connection, Internet connections, 603
    Customize This Folder, 601
    Direct Cable Connection, 510-512
    Home Page, Web site content, 681
    Internet Connection, 652
    Maintenance, 863
        system performance tuning, 784-786
    Make New Connection, 654
    Registration, 45
    Scheduled Task, 779-781
Word macros, WSH script options, 763
WordPad, multimedia features, 330, 343-344, 864
workgroups
    peer network model, 513-514, 517
    specifying for networks, 489-490
    Windows 98 installs, 82
working offline, 622, 639
workstations, limited operating modes, 99
Worms, 433
writing scripts, 752-754
Wscript, 750-751

WSH (Windows Scripting Host), 741
   advantages for scripts, 743
   classes, 756
   methods, 750-752, 762, 766, 770
   objects, 744-751, 764-766, 770-771
   scripts, 751-754, 760, 763
   subroutines, 766, 770, 786
   task automation, 786
WshCollection, 756
WshNetwork object, 750, 756
WshShell object, Popup method, 753
WshShell.CreateShortcut method, 766
WshShell.Popup method, 750
WshShortcut object, 766
WSID parameter, ODBC, 383
WWW (World Wide Web)
   connections, 656-657
   logon problems, 664

X-Y-Z

X Window, 561
X.500 directory services, 718
XCOPY command, 891

Yahoo! Web site, 318
yields, 233

ZAW (Zero Administration Windows), 97-98
   AppStation mode, 99
   AppUser group policies, 100
   TaskStation mode, 98
zones of security, Internet Explorer, 698